U.S.News & WORLD REPORT

2021 EDITION

BEST COLLEGES

Move-in day in August at the University of Colorado–Boulder

MARK MAKELA – GETTY IMAGES

ONTENTS

1 STUDY THE SCHOOLS

14 An Altered Path: Applying During the Pandemic
Learn how schools are adapting their admissions processes this year

18 A Case for the Liberal Arts
By boosting career prep, schools are making the degree more valuable

24 Spotlight on Public Health
COVID-19 promises to intensify the appeal of the undergraduate major

28 Learning the Language of Data
Demand is rising for grads with a knack for crunching numbers

32 Programs That Help Students Thrive
These institutions excel in offerings that help undergrads succeed

34 Girding for the Stresses of College
Experts share tips for parents and freshmen getting set for the first year

34

2 VISIT CAMPUS: TAKE A ROAD TRIP TO BOSTON

39 Northeastern University
Boston

45 Boston College
Chestnut Hill

51 Bentley University
Waltham

41 Boston University
Boston

48 Wellesley College
Wellesley

54 Tufts University
Medford

45

LIBRARY SERVICES

FROM TOP: ILLUSTRATION BY ANNA GODEASSI FOR USN&WR; BRETT ZIEGLER FOR USN&WR

CONTENTS

3 The U.S. News Rankings

58   How We Rank Colleges

62   Best National Universities

72   Best National Liberal Arts Colleges

78   Best Regional Universities

92   Best Regional Colleges

98   Best Historically Black Colleges

100   Best Business Programs

102   Best Engineering Programs

104   Best Computer Science Programs

106   Best Online Degree Programs

110   Best Colleges for Social Mobility

GETTY IMAGES

Build *your* future at Queens College.

- In top five whose students graduate with the least debt by *U.S. News & World Report* – Regional Universities – North

- Ranks fourth among all colleges for offering the best return on investment by *Business Insider*

- Offers over 100 areas of study with a world-class faculty of top researchers and master teachers

- Generous financial aid, over 100 student organizations and clubs, and affordable on-campus housing in Summit Apartments

www.qc.cuny.edu

CONTENTS

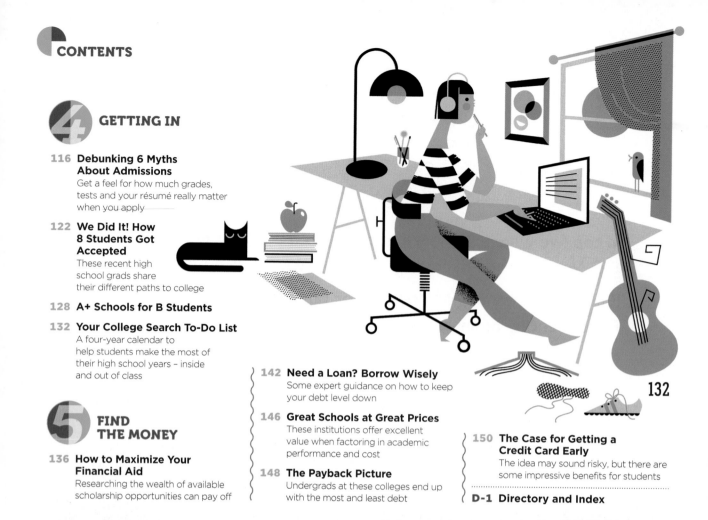

4 GETTING IN

116 Debunking 6 Myths About Admissions
Get a feel for how much grades, tests and your résumé really matter when you apply

122 We Did It! How 8 Students Got Accepted
These recent high school grads share their different paths to college

128 A+ Schools for B Students

132 Your College Search To-Do List
A four-year calendar to help students make the most of their high school years – inside and out of class

5 FIND THE MONEY

136 How to Maximize Your Financial Aid
Researching the wealth of available scholarship opportunities can pay off

142 Need a Loan? Borrow Wisely
Some expert guidance on how to keep your debt level down

146 Great Schools at Great Prices
These institutions offer excellent value when factoring in academic performance and cost

148 The Payback Picture
Undergrads at these colleges end up with the most and least debt

150 The Case for Getting a Credit Card Early
The idea may sound risky, but there are some impressive benefits for students

D-1 Directory and Index

132

142

FROM TOP: ILLUSTRATION BY KIRSTEN ULVE FOR USN&WR; RACHEL MUMMEY FOR USN&WR

BEST COLLEGES
2021 EDITION

YOUR COLLEGE GAME PLAN

Insider Advice

If you're looking for college advice, you've come to the right place. We provide expert tips to help families research, apply to and pay for college. Our articles and slideshows feature college admissions and financial aid officers, counselors, current students, graduates, parents and more, who all share their insights to help demystify the process.
usnews.com/collegeadvice

GETTING IN

College Admissions Playbook

Get tips from Varsity Tutors, an academic tutoring and test-prep provider and advertiser with U.S. News. This blog offers advice on mastering the SAT and ACT as well as the college application process.
usnews.com/collegeplaybook

COLLEGE VISITS

Take a Road Trip

We've gone on numerous trips to visit campuses in case you can't. Check out our compendium of more than 30 different trips to 100-plus schools.
usnews.com/roadtrips

RANKINGS INSIGHT

Morse Code Blog

Get the inside scoop on the rankings – and the commentary and controversy surrounding them – from U.S. News' Bob Morse, the mastermind behind our education rankings projects.
usnews.com/morsecode

IN-DEPTH DATA

College Compass

Gain access to the U.S. News College Compass, which offers comprehensive searchable data and tools for high school students starting down the path to campus. To get a 25% discount, subscribe at
usnews.com/compassoffer

PAYING FOR COLLEGE

Researching Aid

Visit our guide to all your possible sources of college funds. Learn about your savings options and financial aid, including which schools meet students' full need.
usnews.com/payforcollege

The Student Loan Ranger

If you're borrowing to finance your degree, don't fall into the trap of taking on too much debt. Experts provide guidance on this blog for those who must turn to student loans to pay for college.
usnews.com/studentloanranger

DISTANCE LEARNING

Online Education

Are you grappling with how to balance school with work or other obligations? Consult our rankings of the best online degree programs for leads on how to get your diploma without having to leave your home.
usnews.com/online

FOR SCHOOLS ONLY

Academic Insights

U.S. News Academic Insights is a peer benchmarking and performance assessment tool designed for colleges and universities. Gain exclusive access to 20-plus years of previously unpublished historical rankings data for undergraduate, graduate and online programs.
ai.usnews.com

This Spider is *a biologist.*

AT THE UNIVERSITY OF RICHMOND, you won't have to choose between your passions. We'll work closely with you to combine, expand, and ignite your interests through our rigorous curriculum: the hallmark of a Richmond education. When your ambition meets our journey-defining opportunities for real-world experience, you'll join a web of fellow Spiders who bring all they've got to all there is.

It starts within you. See how we help you bring it together.
ADMISSION.RICHMOND.EDU

LOOK DEEPER

Come for the views

no one else can see.

Peel back the surf, the sand

and the beautiful campus

we call home, and you'll

see a whole other world.

One equally stunning.

Because here, world-renowned

professors, Nobel laureates and

students reimagine what's

possible. Their collaboration

has transformed oil rigs into reefs

and reshaped international law.

Over half a century of invention — and

reinvention — has allowed our students

to achieve the unimaginable.

Picture what you might discover at

the No. 1 public university in the nation.

UC San Diego

Study the Schools

14 An Altered Path: Applying During the Pandemic

18 A Case for the Liberal Arts

24 Spotlight on Public Health

28 Learning the Language of Data

32 Programs That Help Students Thrive

34 Prepping for New Stresses

Northeastern University
BRETT ZIEGLER FOR USN&WR

An
Altered
Path
Ahead

Students applying to college
during the pandemic will find
some of the guidance changed

by **Margaret Loftus**

MONTHS OF REMOTE LEARNING. Standardized tests canceled. Campus visits post-
poned indefinitely. And who knows what
lies ahead? Being a sophomore or junior
in high school through the upheaval that
the COVID-19 pandemic wrought last
spring was hard, but negotiating the
college application process as the uncertainty continues may seem downright impossible.

The good news is that college admissions deans get it.
Little wonder, given that higher educators, too, are struggling to operate in a vastly changed landscape. Schools that
have opted not to stick entirely with online instruction
this fall are offering drastically different experiences than
in pre-pandemic times (and some have had to back away
from those plans again). Daily temperature checks, regular
testing, staggered class schedules, and half-full classrooms

– all are part of the new normal for those heading back to campus. And with football tailgates and big parties verboten, social life has been diminished.

In a statement released over the summer, more than 360 deans – from Ivy League schools, liberal arts colleges, and public research universities – sought to reassure this year's seniors that their applications won't be docked because of any setbacks due to the outbreak, whether that be missing an Advanced Placement or International Baccalaureate test or not being able to visit campus. They pledged to assess students in the context of the curriculum, academic resources, and support available to them.

"It's not just scary gatekeepers on the other side [of the admissions process]," says Hannah Serota, founder and CEO of Creative College Connections in Leesburg, Virginia. "Colleges do care about the students." Nonetheless, candidates wanting both a spot and financial aid will have a better shot if their applications reflect the full scope of their experience during the pandemic. To that end, the Common and Coalition for College applications have added special optional sections for students to explain how COVID-19 has affected them and their families.

TO TEST OR NOT? Perhaps no aspect of this forgiving admissions approach has been more touted than that of testing policy. Since several sittings of the SAT and ACT were canceled in the spring and summer, hundreds of schools have announced that they've dropped their testing requirement for fall 2021 admission. In all, more than half of the country's four-year colleges and universities have gone at least temporarily test-optional. And this year, the California Institute of Technology added its name at least temporarily to the growing list of schools that are now test-blind, meaning they don't consider test scores as they evaluate an application.

That doesn't mean students who apply to test-optional schools should automatically consider themselves off the hook, however. It still may be in your best interest to sit for the SAT and ACT, especially if you're in the market for state scholarship funds, which may still rely on test scores. Moreover, a solid "superscore" – your combined highest score from each section of the SAT or ACT – may give your application a leg up regardless of whether or not it's required. "When you don't submit test scores, it doesn't make it easier to assess your application," says Sam Bigelow, director of college counseling at Middlesex School in Concord, Massachusetts. "It's just that the other factors weigh more." And many students will benefit by presenting their test scores, Bigelow says.

Colleges also claim that they'll regard last spring's

The University of North Carolina reversed its decision to bring students to Chapel Hill this fall.

grades with compassion. Many high schools resorted to pass/fail or credit/no credit in place of letter grades during remote learning. If that was the case, offer as much context as possible on your application, advises Adam Miller, director of admission at Whitman College in Washington. "Make sure we understand what policies were in effect." The same goes for any part of your application that may have been negatively impacted. "If you have a significant issue that impacted your performance, I assure you that colleges will notice," says Moses Murphy, senior associate director of admissions at the University of Vermont. "It's strategic to address it." That can happen through teacher recommendations, your essay, or supplemental information you provide with your application.

Another casualty of COVID-19 – campus visits – largely migrated online in the spring. Colleges have now embraced virtual engagement for those who don't have the resources to travel to campus. Recruiting visits and college fairs alike have gone virtual. Most of these new options are nonevalua-

Early decision could offer more of an advantage than usual for students who already have their heart set on one college (and don't need to compare aid packages). Chances are that fewer students will choose to apply and commit early, especially when visits are impossible. But Bigelow cautions his students to carefully consider the stakes of making such a decision. "I tell them, 'You might be making a great strategic move but are you really ready to commit to a place for four years?'"

To be sure, most applicants can't settle on a school without considering financial aid. Many institutions are staring down serious budget shortfalls, between lost revenue and reductions in donations amid the economic uncertainty. And shrinking state budgets could mean less money for state schools in years to come. Still, admissions counselors predict, applicants might find some schools on their shortlist to be quite generous with merit aid as they compete to attract more of the shrinking pool of applicants. "There's going to be an awful lot of merit aid" given out by some schools, says Serota.

"Early decision could offer more of an advantage than usual."

tive, such as Instagram chats and online tours, but some schools do track applicants' "demonstrated interest." While some campuses may reopen for restricted outdoor-only visits, the virtual options may be the only way to get a feel for a school for now.

As for the competitiveness of getting in and getting financial aid at many schools, the outlook is unclear. Early on, counselors fielded concerns from parents that deferrals by this year's incoming freshman class would result in fewer spots in fall 2021. But any uptick in the number of students coming back from a year off may well be countered by enrollment declines among those who face economic challenges. "[Colleges] will likely increase the number they admit the following year to balance it out," predicts Jeff Allen, vice president for admissions and financial aid at Macalester College in Saint Paul, Minnesota.

CLOSER TO HOME. It's also possible that schools that draw nationally may have fewer high-powered applicants from afar to choose from, some experts say. "I'm hearing 'I want to stay close to home' more than in the past," says Serota. "I have some students who have shifted from looking away to looking closer and are hesitant about an airplane ride," she says. "There may be opportunities if you're willing to travel."

Meanwhile, getting your fair share of need-based aid might require some extra work. Since eligibility and the size of your "expected family contribution" are based on tax returns from two years ago, it will be up to families who've lost income in the economic downturn to relay their current financial picture to aid offices. "Rather than being an exception, it's going to be the rule that many families will have to revisit their financial profile this year," says Amanda Murrell, director of college counseling at Ashley Hall in Charleston, South Carolina. And if a package doesn't meet your needs, don't hesitate to appeal, urges Allen. "If there's an extenuating circumstance, that could lead to a substantial difference in the aid offered."

To hedge bets against further fallout from the pandemic, counselors suggest casting a wider net of applications this year, especially if you're applying for aid. "There's no magic number, but broadening your search will keep your options open," says Bigelow. In the meantime, try not to stress out as you embark on this journey, says Ethan Sawyer, author of "College Admission Essentials" and "College Essay Essentials." He tells his students to remember what he calls the college admission serenity prayer, "Focus on what you can control. Stay informed about the rest." ●

University of New Hampshire

A top-tier research institution

R1 CARNEGIE CLASSIFICATION

The University of New Hampshire, the state's flagship public research university, is one of the nation's highest-performing research universities and a leader in converting research into economic and societal impact. True to our land-grant mission, UNH is committed to research and scholarship that improves lives and addresses urgent challenges here in the Granite State and across the globe.

100+ PARTNERSHIPS ON NASA MISSIONS

TOP-TEN SCHOOL IN FUNDING FOR MARINE-RELATED RESEARCH

50+ RESEARCH CENTERS & INSTITUTES ON CAMPUS

Marcus Williams,
taking part in
Bowdoin's bootcamp

Liberal Arts &

Small colleges are stepping up their game to give grads more career-oriented skills training

by **Arlene Weintraub**

WHEN MARCUS WILLIAMS was a sophomore at Bowdoin College in Brunswick, Maine, he knew he needed help figuring out what he wanted to do with his life. Then the college offered him a chance to attend a winter break Career Bootcamp, a brand new, one-week program for second-years, during which he would take self-assessments to determine his skills and interests, learn to write a résumé and cover letter, network with alumni, and pursue internships in his chosen field.

"I was, like, 'Sign me up!'" says Williams, who is a double major in government and legal studies and sociology. "I was super-confused about what industries were out there, so we spent a good amount of time figuring out my skill set and what industries matched that. I ended up with a better sense of what I wanted to do. I started looking into law, consulting and diversity and inclusion." Shortly after he had finished

Practice, Too

the bootcamp, Williams sent his résumé to WEX, a financial technology company in nearby Portland. He ended up nabbing a paid internship for the summer at the company, where he worked in human resources, creating reports on corporate social responsibility and developing resources on diversity and inclusion. Now Williams is volunteering as a mentor for Career Bootcamp as he continues to explore career options in diversity and inclusion.

Bowdoin is among the growing group of colleges exploring new ways to boost the appeal of their liberal arts degrees. The value of the critical thinking, spirit of inquiry, teamwork and creative problem-solving such study fosters has been growing increasingly apparent to employers – and is only underscored during periods of crisis and uncertainty like the country has experienced in 2020, advocates argue. The initiatives these schools are undertaking include making their career services offerings more practical, expanding project-based curricula and pre-professional programs, and partnering with employers actively seeking liberal arts majors.

"We view the value of a liberal arts education as important and enduring," says Kristin Brennan, executive director of career exploration and development at Bowdoin. "But we have a practical bridge to build, which is to help students describe to employers the skills they've acquired from their liberal arts education, and to fill in the gaps by giving them skills associated with being on the job." To that end, Bowdoin offers workshops in topics like Excel and negotiation tactics, and holds networking events on campus and in cities around the country – and, this past spring and as is necessary, virtually – to connect students with alumni in a variety of industries.

The push by schools to prove their value comes amid parental concern that a hugely expensive education might not lead to a job – undoubtedly made more acute by the economic costs of the coronavirus pandemic – as well as a number of closings of small liberal arts colleges. In the past couple years, Mount Ida College and Newbury College in Massachusetts both shut their doors, as did Green Mountain College in Vermont.

LONG-TERM VALUE. Research has shown that a liberal arts preparation can offer tremendous value to employers – and consequently a great return on investment for grads. A study released earlier this year from the Georgetown University Center on Education and the Workforce found that the median ROI 40 years after enrollment in liberal arts colleges – mean-

ing one's lifetime earnings minus the cost of attending college – is 26% higher than the median return for all colleges. Bowdoin, which charges tuition and fees of $56,000-plus a year, is among the 10 liberal arts institutions with the highest ROI, according to the study.

"There is extraordinary pressure on institutions to make themselves relevant to an economic mission," says Anthony Carnevale, director of CEW at Georgetown and lead author of the study. "They still serve the intrinsic value of learning, but the market is demanding that they make their programs more relevant to students, who not only want a good education but also a job."

Toward that end, many colleges are putting new emphasis on work experience and are providing funding so students can complete unpaid internships. Connecticut College, for example, gives every student up to $3,000 to pursue internships and other experiential learning opportunities..

DEDICATED FUNDING. Carnegie Mellon University has launched a similar program for its humanities and social sciences students, offering a stipend to students who put in 30 hours per week at internships lasting eight to 10 weeks. In its first year, 2018, 24 students interned at 12 organizations. In 2020, 56 students were working – albeit remotely, thanks to the pandemic – at 36 diverse organizations, including the Pittsburgh mayor's office and the startup company Lifeware Labs.

CMU student Teresa Dietrich-O'Donnell spent one summer working for the Pittsburgh nonprofit Connecting Champions, which matches up pediatric cancer patients with mentors from the community who work in jobs they'd like to have when they grow up. Dietrich-O'Donnell, a double major in psychology and creative writing, says her time on the job, which entailed writing grant proposals and helping compose social media postings, solidified her interest in nonprofits – and the compensation from CMU was vital. "It was money the organization wouldn't have been able to provide themselves, but it was something I really needed to be able to stay in the city," says Dietrich-O'Donnell, who is originally from La Grange, Kentucky.

Some colleges are forming alliances with companies looking to tap a liberal-arts-focused talent pool, including Trinity College in Hartford, which partnered with Infosys in 2018. Infosys president Ravi Kumar says he became interested in hiring liberal arts majors a couple of years ago, after realizing a shift that was occurring in technology services. "We figured out that the world of digital services needs problem-finders as much as problem-solvers," Kumar says. In other words, Infosys needed talent who could help improve product design for clients, find new places for technology to be deployed and identify gaps in the services it was already providing. "To be at the frontier of problem-finding, you need skills like critical thinking, empa-

> ## "The lifetime return on investment for liberal arts schools is 26% higher than the return for all colleges."

thy and the ability to grasp different concepts. That's why the liberal arts will play a critical role in building digital services," Kumar says. Infosys typically hires about 500 design grads annually, plus another 500 people who completed other liberal arts degrees, although the economy will likely pause those plans temporarily. He predicts the numbers will grow based on the initial success of the program with Trinity.

POWERFUL PARTNERSHIPS. Infosys and the college worked together to create a training program for new employees who have liberal arts degrees. Trinity provides five weeks of training in business analysis, focusing on teaching new hires to apply skills learned in college to the job. That's followed by three weeks of training at Infosys. "We might have a philosophy professor that comes in and teaches deep listening, and then another professor will come in and teach writing or leadership," says Sonia Cardenas, vice president for strategic initiatives and innovation at Trinity. The Infosys training "focuses more on technology."

Trinity and Infosys also introduced Tech-Edge, a virtual program which ran for 2 1/2 weeks this past summer, for undergrads and recent graduates who are thinking about career possibilities in tech and business innovation. In daily Zoom sessions, participants

At Bucknell, where a new management school offers a foundation in the liberal arts

learned coding and other tech skills and heard from alumni with backgrounds spanning the liberal arts and in business and technology.

At DePauw University in Greencastle, Indiana, students aren't just trained in career skills, they're guaranteed jobs straight out of college. Under the Gold Commitment program, rolled out for the class entering in 2018, students who don't secure jobs or admission to graduate school within six months of earning their bachelor's degrees will either get hired by the university or can take an additional semester of classes at no charge. To be eligible for the guarantee, students must participate in 12 workshops in life planning and communication and collaboration. They're also expected to complete one applied-learning activity, such as a research project, an internship or an off-campus educational program.

DePauw also has opened a satellite office in an Indianapolis innovation center, where students can attend networking events with alumni working in different industries. Several local companies are pitching in to provide learning experiences and internships, including Eli Lilly, Cummins and KeyBank. "Liberal arts students tend to score high marks on critical thinking, creative writing, persuasion and debate, which are valuable tools for entering the world of business. But oftentimes they need training on a specific industry," says Steven Fouty, director of DePauw's McDermond Center for Management and Entrepreneurship. "We're connecting them to real-world businesses" to help them gain those skills, he adds.

BOOSTING BUSINESS. Employers' appreciation for liberal arts training is having an effect on business education. Bucknell University in Lewisburg, Pennsylvania, has been offering management courses for over 100 years, and, with demand for business train-

ing growing so intense in the last few years, the faculty decided to form a new school, the Freeman College of Management, offering seven management majors. Unlike at traditional business schools, however, the Freeman curriculum is built on a foundation of liberal arts. Accounting and finance majors, for example, are required to take a class called The Stakeholder Organization, which covers moral and ethical decisionmaking. For entrepreneurial-minded students, the school offers a major called Markets, Innovation and

Finding the Best Fit

Consider how schools match up with your academic, social and financial preferences

by **Katherine Hobson**

CHASE DUSEK TOOK his college search seriously. He started his research the summer after his sophomore year, turned to an outside counselor for help, went on a whopping 26 college tours and – most importantly – took time to soulsearch about exactly what he wanted in a school. He really enjoyed the small humanities program in his public high school, and realized he wanted to find that kind of experience in college. "I learned I loved interaction and engagement with the teacher and classmates," he says. That impetus – as well as prioritizing an academically challenging environment and the opportunity to participate in Greek life – ultimately led him to Ohio Wesleyan University, where he's a junior.

There are plenty of obvious factors in a college search: large or small, urban or rural, public or private. But at the end of the day, schools need to be a fit academically, socially and financially, says Maria Furtado, executive director of the nonprofit Colleges That Change Lives. A good academic fit includes strength in the major that you are considering, interesting classes and programs within that major, and an appropriate level of challenge, she says. Jayne Caflin Fonash, an independent education consultant

in Potomac Falls, Virginia, and the president of the National Association for College Admission Counseling, agrees that it's important to find a place where you have a good chance of thriving academically: "You want to be challenged and to grow, but you don't want to be overwhelmed." She also advises making sure there are opportunities beyond your chosen major in case you end up changing focus.

HOW YOU LEARN BEST. Consider what kind of learning environment you want, and not only in terms of class size or format. Experiential educa-

Design, including training in consumer behavior and techniques for transforming ideas into prototypes.

Halie Mariano, who graduated from Bucknell in 2020, double-majored in Managing for Sustainability at the Freeman College and anthropology at the College of Arts & Sciences. Career counselors at Bucknell helped Mariano secure internships at payroll-services provider Paychex, the community food bank of Rochester, New York, and Bucknell's Coal Region Field Station. She also worked with two sociology profes-

sors to study health care in Pennsylvania's coal region. Mariano hopes to work in public affairs before heading to law school.

"I was able to combine a management foundation with my passion for arts and sciences," Mariano says. "I've been able to push myself, taking history, environment studies, and more." She's confident that the "super well-rounded" combination of a traditional liberal arts education and plentiful career training has set her up for success. ●

vice president for enrollment and communications at Ohio Wesleyan. And dig deep into what really matters to you. To see how seriously schools took research opportunities, Dusek looked up academic publications by professors, then checked to see if any undergrads were co-authors.

Social and personal fit is another key component. "Will you find your people? Will you find your next set of really good friends?" says Furtado. Again, campus visits can be extremely helpful, but don't just stop with the tour, suggests Shannon Carr, interim vice president for enrollment at University of Puget Sound. She advises prospective students to eat in the dining hall, go to an event, read bulletin boards for information on student activities and check out the residence halls. You can also explore the town by walking around and by checking the local chamber of commerce or visitor's website to see if it's a place you want to live. Other virtual sources of information: the school's community events calendar and alumni magazine, which can give you a peek into what people do after they graduate, says Carr.

CRUNCH THE NUMBERS. Financial fit is the third key component. "Families need to spend more time talking candidly together about cost," says Emmi Harward, executive director of the Association of College Counselors in Independent Schools. That means using online calculators to figure out exactly what your financing options are and how much debt your family is willing to take on, she says. Fonash suggests checking out data for average salaries in your possible post-collegiate career field to get a reality check about what you can afford to borrow. Find out if merit-based aid – grant money keyed to academic achievements or special talents – is an option.

Experts advise figuring out the factors that are most important to you, and then keeping an open mind. If your priorities point you toward schools that you didn't expect or whose names you don't recognize, investigate them anyway, suggests Harward. And don't rely entirely on your first impression. Dusek's first visit to Ohio Wesleyan didn't wow him, but he was sold by his second visit, when he sat in on a macroeconomics class and was "blown away" by the professor. Now Dusek works as an Ohio Wesleyan lobby host, checking in prospective students and hoping they, too, will find a great fit.

tion, in the form of outside internships or co-ops (work experience integrated into the curriculum) or on-campus research with professors, can be just as important. "Ask yourself: Why am I doing this? What do I expect?" says Tamara Byland, assistant vice provost of admissions at the University of Cincinnati, whose co-op programs are a primary draw. On a campus visit, sit in on some classes in your areas of interest; seeing how faculty members engage students and how students interact with each other can tell you a lot, says Stefanie Niles,

The Spotlight on Public Health

COVID-19 promises to intensify the appeal of this hot field and its growing array of undergrad programs

*by **Elizabeth Gardner***

LEAH TROTMAN'S high school counselor noticed her strong interest in working for social change in communities of color in the Caribbean and suggested that Trotman consider pursuing public health. So the U.S. Virgin Islands native is now studying international relations and public health at Agnes Scott College in Georgia and spent the summer of 2019 interning at the Centers for Disease Control and Prevention in Atlanta. After she graduates in 2021, Trotman plans to devote some time to a fellowship in international health and government and then go on for a master's focused on disaster relief and emergency preparedness response. "I found context and practicality in public health," she says. "The field has so many different opportunities that I'm still learning about."

The COVID-19 pandemic has put public health in the limelight like never before, with epidemiological modeling and infection control in the news every day. But it was already booming. Amy Patterson, chair of Agnes Scott's public health department, says the discipline is one of the most popular majors at the college, teaching students core subjects like biostatistics, epidemiology, global health and medical anthropology while allowing them a broad range of electives in 16 other departments, including economics, biology, anthropology, psychology and history. "They can craft a major that speaks to their particular interests," she says.

While master's-level programs remain the most common form of public health study, a growing number of schools offer it as an undergraduate major or minor. Some schools take a broad liberal arts approach – allowing students to sign up for classes in anthropology, political science or sociology, say, in addition to core public health courses – while others are tightly focused in a specific field like environmental health or microbiology. A list is maintained by the Association of Schools and Programs of Public Health, which says applications to undergraduate programs at member schools have more than doubled in the past five years and numbered more than 23,000 in 2019. About 64% of public health majors go straight into a job upon graduation, while 26% pursue graduate education, according to ASPPH surveys.

DIVERSE PATHS. Students who aspire to leadership and management positions generally earn a master's degree in public health eventually, if not immediately

COURTESY OF MALLORY MANFREDINI

Agnes Scott College senior Leah Trotman, during her time studying abroad in Argentina

reshape communities to make everyone healthier. BU allows students to do a five-year joint-study program and graduate with either a Bachelor of Arts or a Bachelor of Science in public health and an MPH.

This past spring, COVID-19 gave Godley's undergraduates a real-time field experience as they returned to their communities to finish the school year and encountered a wide range of knowledge and attitudes about the pandemic. "They loved that they were able to use their knowledge of how epidemics work" to explain the situation and persuade people to treat the disease with the caution it deserves, she said. "I feel like I have dispersed 100 ambassadors for social distancing."

HANDS-ON LEARNING. The University of Washington, home of the Institute for Health Metrics and Evaluation that has produced widely quoted COVID-19 projections for mortality rates and where and when health care system resources would be most strained, has seen exponential growth in its undergraduate public health-global health majors since they were formally established in 2012. Students must apply to the program after they've completed their first two years of undergraduate study, and admission is limited to a cohort of 300 per year. "It would be way bigger if we didn't restrict it," says Sara Mackenzie, director of UW Public Health-Global Health Majors in the School of Public Health.

The program emphasizes hands-on learning: Each student must complete a senior capstone project that combines a 50-hour field placement with related academic work. For example, a student might work at a financial counseling center for impoverished families, helping them complete tax returns and connecting them with government benefit programs, and also make class presentations on the center's operations and the demographics and economic challenges of the population it serves.

after college, but many entry-level job paths are available for bachelor's-level candidates. Graduates of Boston University work in advocacy organizations, at state and local health departments, on legislators' staffs researching health policy, and as health educators, just to name a few of the avenues students have taken with a major or minor in the field, says Sophie Godley, director of undergraduate education for BU's School of Public Health. Some go on to medical or nursing school, armed with tools to understand how economics and the environment affect their patients' health, and to

Students graduate prepared to enter careers ranging from research to law, medicine, government and even health journalism. About one-fifth go on to graduate school and another fifth go directly into the public health workforce. "We design our degree as liberal education," Mackenzie says. "Our students learn about the real drivers of health, globally and locally, and then go into the broad array of career pathways that influence health."

While students from schools like BU and UW may pursue research careers, some undergraduate public health programs aim specifically to get students into the trenches, working to improve health in the community. "We focus on translating research into practice," says Joseph Robare, associate professor in the department of Public Health and Social Work at Slippery Rock University in Pennsylvania. "Once there's a vaccine for COVID-19, our graduates would focus on how to get individuals vaccinated." Students complete an internship, and coursework emphasizes practical matters like designing programs and getting grant funding.

About half of Slippery Rock's public health students are the first generation in their families to attend college. "They have to get out of school and make money, so they're looking for a degree that can do that," Robare says. One option is an accelerated undergraduate/graduate program allowing grads to emerge in five or six years with an advanced degree in occupational

"Internships are seen as a cornerstone of many public health curricula."

therapy, physical therapy or physician assistant studies. "It saves money and gets them into the field sooner," Robare says.

East Tennessee State University has one of the largest and oldest undergraduate public health programs in the country, established in 1955 and currently enrolling 550 students. Many ETSU undergrads come from central Appalachia, and Dean Randy Wykoff says 70% of the program's graduates go directly into the workforce, many in the Appalachia region. The College of Public Health offers five undergraduate degrees: public health, microbiology, human health, health administration and environmental health. ETSU student cohorts study together throughout the program and "get very close very quickly and lift each other up through crises," Wykoff says. "They become their own family."

EMPHASIZING INTERNSHIPS. The school owns a 140-acre farm where it operates a hands-on learning lab called "Project EARTH." Public health students learn how to use basic materials to build shelters, purify water, and create safe sanitation systems. They can apply these specific skills to work in low-resource areas in the U.S. and abroad – for example, several ETSU students have worked in South Africa establishing small family and community gardens – and they also learn more generally how to solve problems with whatever tools and resources happen to be available, Wykoff says.

William Haulbrook of Johnson City, Tennessee, came to ETSU intending to prepare for graduate work as a physical therapist and chose to major in public health because he believes it offers him both context for his planned PT studies and a broad array of career options if he decides to change his path later. "I'm not sure public health has ever been more at the forefront of the national and global consciousness than it is right now," he says.

Internships are seen as a cornerstone of many public health curricula. At ETSU all students must complete a two-to-three month internship, and they have plenty of choices. The school can arrange internships with more than 270 organizations around the world, including local, regional and state health systems; public health departments; not-for-profit organizations; federal agencies and international organizations as far-flung as the Philippines and China. Wykoff says many ETSU students end up with post-graduation job offers from their internship sites.

Agnes Scott College's program doesn't require an internship, but three out of four students do at least one and most do more than one – at the CDC, state and county health departments, and community organizations. Slippery Rock requires a 480-hour summer internship, and uses its internship agreements to match students with opportunities in the field they want to pursue after graduation, with government agencies, not-for-profit organizations, private corporations and research facilities.

Boston University doesn't require fieldwork until students start the master's degree program, but Godley says many do it as undergrads. Field placements can be local, national or international: For example, the school's internship program in Geneva, Switzerland, includes six weeks of coursework followed by eight weeks working full time at one of the many international organizations headquartered there. "By junior or senior year, they're ready to start testing their knowledge out in the community, and then when they come back, their classwork is more real because of their field experiences," she says.

Olivia Ancrum of Savannah, Georgia, entered Agnes Scott as an aspiring playwright, but switched to public health and graduated in the spring of 2020. She's now pursuing an MPH at the University of Washington. Many students don't realize just how vast the field is, she says. "If you're worried whether you can find a job after graduation, choosing public health gives you knowledge of medicine, history, epidemiology, health communication, policy, advocacy and global immersion. You can market yourself as adaptable, as a leader and as a critical learner." ●

AEROSOL SCIENTIST

CLAIM YOUR ROLE

Testing materials to solve shortages of personal equipment for medical workers, renowned aerosol scientist Linsey Marr has made public health safety her priority.

That's her role. Claim yours... vt.edu

1 STUDY THE SCHOOLS

Learning the **Language** of **Data**

Across disciplines, there's a demand for people with an aptitude for crunching numbers

by **Zackary Bennett**

MADDY MATURA TOOK AN EARLY interest in biology at Denison University in Ohio and over time discovered she had an affinity for a specific scientific approach to understanding human life: digging deep into data. The Chicago native ended up majoring in data analytics because she saw how valuable number-crunching has become in just about every field. Hospitals are using in-depth statistics to do predictive modeling of disease outcomes and to identify opportunities to intervene early and head off trouble, for example. Education officials analyze test results and grade trends to improve student performance. Credit card companies and financial institutions ferret out risks and fraud.

There are "a lot of cool applications in health care, especially in global health," says Matura, who had the opportunity to gain exposure to hospitals and health systems in Europe while studying abroad in Copenhagen, Denmark. The 2020 graduate is planning to put her data analytics degree to immediate use as a business consultant at Deloitte in New York City.

The basic notion of data science is to analyze information to improve performance or productivity, and the applications are "just endless," says Phil Bourne, a data science and biomedical engineering professor and dean of the new school of data science at the University of Virginia. UVA founded its data science school in 2019, and while the school currently only enrolls students pursuing master's degrees, Bourne says the admissions office's most frequently asked question from aspiring undergrads is when they will be able to take classes there.

An undergraduate minor has been approved and is on track to launch in 2021, with a bachelor's degree program to be offered soon after. UVA's master's curriculum includes classes like Data Min-

ing, Machine Learning and Ethics of Big Data, with a nod to "creating a culture of responsible data science," Bourne says. Ohio State University, the University of San Francisco, New York University and Drexel University in Philadelphia are among those schools with undergraduate programs in data science or analytics. Such programs typically involve a hearty dose of math, statistics and computer science or programming, with opportunities to apply those foundations to fields like health, business or the social sciences.

At Willamette University in Oregon, data science is offered as an undergraduate minor and major, and this fall, the university will launch a 3+1 undergraduate and master's joint degree in the field that can be completed in four years.

School officials expect that the major will become one of the larger ones at the liberal arts college in a few years.

A LIBERAL ARTS LENS. The inclusion of data science is a striking sign of how the liberal arts are being renovated for the 21st century, says Kelley Strawn, faculty associate dean for curriculum and undergraduate program coordinator for data science at Willamette. "We want to be relevant." The university's program is cross-disciplinary, relying on instructors from management, sociology, psychology, physics and biology in addition to the more traditional data-related areas like mathematics, economics and computer science. At Denison, students can take classes like Demography of Africa (in the fields of anthropology and sociology), Logic (in philosophy) and Analyzing Politics (in political science) to count toward the data analytics major.

"Pairing data science with just about anything else, I believe, is going to be a really, really successful and common strategy for students," says Strawn. In the Willamette Valley region of the Pacific Northwest, Strawn notes, the wine industry is booming, and "a data scientist who is well-trained could go to work for a winery and help them understand patterns, soil nutrition degradation and how they could use that

Master's students in UVA's new data science school, which opens to undergrads in 2021

A study session in math at Willamette University

information." (Willamette's program has no graduates yet, but recent management school grads have gone on to work as data analysts at Intel and for the Seattle Seahawks football team.)

The data mapping and tracking that have emerged from the coronavirus pandemic demonstrate the clear and vital applications in public health and health care. For years, many universities have been digging into the uses of data analytics in medicine, in some cases collaborating with their affiliated medical schools, hospitals or industry partners. Duke University School of Medicine in North Carolina houses the Duke Forge, a center where data science students can get hands-on experience working on health data projects. "There's a ton of potential there to be generated in health care," says Erich S. Huang, director of the Forge and chief data officer for quality at the Duke University Health System.

REAL-WORLD EXPERIENCE. For example, undergrads at Duke might analyze data to investigate potential bias affecting seniors on Medicare or work with clinicians in the Duke health system on applying state-of-the-art machine-learning tools to improve diagnosing and delivery of care. One undergrad student working with Huang used tools like Google Maps satellite data to estimate the prevalence of chronic diseases in specific communities.

Jobs in data science and advanced analytics were projected to grow by 28% over the last five years, with advertised average salaries of $80,200, more than $8,700 higher than the figure for other bachelor's- and graduate-level jobs, according to a 2017 report from IBM, the Business-Higher Education Forum and Burning Glass Technologies, a job market analytics firm. And the field of computer and information research scientists alone is expected to grow "much faster than average," according to the U.S. Bureau of Labor Statistics: by 16% between 2018 and 2028.

"There are literally hundreds of thousands of open jobs in this space that go unfilled," says Ana Echeverri, AI skills growth and strategy lead at IBM. Many new undergraduate and master's programs have been created, she says, as schools are recognizing the demand and are aiming to graduate individuals armed with analytical skills. IBM partnered with the University of Pennsylvania and the Linux Foundation to create an open-source project to help universities worldwide build data science programs from scratch faster.

Amanda Konet, a 2020 graduate of Ohio State University from Broadview Heights, Ohio, majored in data analytics with a minor in women's, gender and sexuality studies. "Working with nonprofits is a really big passion of mine," says Konet, who plans to pursue a master's degree in data science and perhaps a doctorate in a social science discipline. Her undergraduate minor helped expose her to the social applications of data, she says, and has inspired her to look into how she might apply analytics to help nonprofits, such as using data science to do better targeted – and more effective – outreach to donors. ⬤

Programs That Promote Student Success

SOME COLLEGES AND UNIVERSITIES are much more determined than others to provide undergrads with the best possible educational experience, recognizing that certain enriched offerings, from learning communities and internships to senior capstone projects, are linked to success. Here, U.S. News highlights schools with outstanding examples of eight programs that education experts, including staff members of the Association of American Colleges and Universities, agree are key. Excellence in such programs isn't directly measured in the Best Colleges overall rankings.

U.S. News surveyed college presidents, chief academic officers and deans of admissions in the spring and early summer of 2020, asking them to nominate up to 15 institutions with stellar examples of each program. The colleges ranked here received the most nominations for having especially strong programs.

(*Public)

▶ First-Year Experience

Orientation can go only so far in making freshmen feel connected. Many schools now build into the curriculum first-year seminars or other academic programs that bring small groups of students together with faculty or staff on a regular basis.

1 **Agnes Scott College** (GA)
2 **Elon University** (NC)
3 **Univ. of South Carolina***
4 **Berea College** (KY)
5 **Georgia State University***
6 **Appalachian State University** (NC)*
7 **Amherst College** (MA)
8 **Bayl or University** (TX)
9 **Abilene Christian University** (TX)
9 **Arizona State University-Tempe***
11 **Alverno College** (WI)
12 **Brown University** (RI)
13 **Butler University** (IN)
14 **Adrian College** (MI)
14 **Belmont University** (TN)
14 **William & Mary** (VA)*
14 **University of Texas-Austin***
14 **Yale University** (CT)

▶ Senior Capstone

Whether they're called a senior capstone or go by some other name, these culminating experiences ask students nearing the end of their college years to create a project that integrates and synthesizes what they've learned. The project might be a thesis, a performance or an exhibit of artwork.

1 **Princeton University** (NJ)
2 **College of Wooster** (OH)

3 **Yale University** (CT)
4 **Duke University** (NC)
5 **Elon University** (NC)
6 **Massachusetts Institute of Technology**
7 **Agnes Scott College** (GA)
7 **Stanford University** (CA)
9 **Brown University** (RI)
10 **Harvard University** (MA)
11 **Amherst College** (MA)
12 **Carleton College** (MN)
12 **Georgia Institute of Technology***
14 **Bates College** (ME)
14 **Northeastern University** (MA)
14 **University of Michigan-Ann Arbor***
14 **Worcester Polytechnic Inst.** (MA)
18 **Bard College** (NY)
18 **Butler University** (IN)"

▶ Co-ops/Internships

Schools nominated in this category require or encourage students to apply what they're learning in the classroom to work in the real world through closely supervised internships or practicums, or through cooperative education, in which one period of study typically alternates with one of work.

1 **Northeastern University** (MA)
2 **Drexel University** (PA)
3 **University of Cincinnati***
4 **Elon University** (NC)
5 **Georgia Institute of Technology***
6 **Berea College** (KY)
7 **Massachusetts Institute of Technology**
8 **Duke University** (NC)

9 **Endicott College** (MA)
9 **Stanford University** (CA)
11 **Northwestern University** (IL)
11 **Purdue University-West Lafayette** (IN)*
13 **Rochester Inst. of Technology** (NY)
14 **Agnes Scott College** (GA)
14 **Clemson University** (SC)*
16 **George Washington University** (DC)
17 **Claremont McKenna College** (CA)
18 **Cornell University** (NY)
19 **Carnegie Mellon University** (PA)
19 **Worcester Polytechnic Inst.** (MA)

▶ Learning Communities

In these communities, students typically take two or more linked courses as a group and get to know one another and their professors well. Some learning communities are also residential.

1 **Elon University** (NC)
2 **Yale University** (CT)
3 **Agnes Scott College** (GA)
3 **Amherst College** (MA)
5 **Appalachian State University** (NC)*
5 **Georgia State University***
7 **Belmont University** (TN)
7 **Evergreen State College** (WA)*
7 **Princeton University** (NJ)
10 **Michigan State University***

Elon University

16 **Duke University** (NC)
16 **Northeastern University** (MA)
19 **Butler University** (IN)
19 **Georgetown University** (DC)

▶ Undergraduate Research/Creative Projects

Independently or in small teams, and mentored by a faculty member, students do intensive and self-directed research or creative work that results in an original scholarly paper or product that can be formally presented on or off campus.

1 **Massachusetts Institute of Technology**
2 **Princeton University** (NJ)
3 **California Institute of Technology**
4 **Elon University** (NC)
5 **College of Wooster** (OH)
6 **Stanford University** (CA)
7 **University of Michigan-Ann Arbor***
8 **Georgia Institute of Technology***
9 **Davidson College** (NC)
9 **Duke University** (NC)
9 **Johns Hopkins University** (MD)
12 **Carnegie Mellon University** (PA)
13 **William & Mary** (VA)*
14 **Amherst College** (MA)
14 **Harvard University** (MA)
16 **University of Texas-Austin***
16 **Yale University** (CT)
18 **Carleton College** (MN)
18 **Harvey Mudd College** (CA)
20 **Brown University** (RI)

▶ Writing in the Disciplines

These colleges typically make writing a priority at all levels of instruction and across the curriculum. Students are encouraged to produce and refine various forms of writing for a range of audiences in different disciplines.

1 **Brown University** (RI)
2 **Duke University** (NC)
3 **Princeton University** (NJ)
4 **Cornell University** (NY)
5 **Harvard University** (MA)
5 **Yale University** (CT)
7 **Stanford University** (CA)
8 **Carleton College** (MN)
8 **Hamilton College** (NY)
10 **Columbia University** (NY)
10 **Elon University** (NC)
10 **Middlebury College** (VT)
13 **Massachusetts Institute of Technology**
13 **Williams College** (MA)
15 **Agnes Scott College** (GA)
15 **University of Iowa***
17 **Amherst College** (MA)

11 **Abilene Christian University** (TX)
11 **University of Michigan-Ann Arbor***
13 **Rice University** (TX)
13 **Univ. of Maryland-College Park***
15 **Clemson University** (SC)*
16 **Vanderbilt University** (TN)
17 **Dartmouth College** (NH)
17 **Davidson College** (NC)
17 **Duke University** (NC)

▶ Service Learning

Required (or for-credit) volunteer work in the community is an instructional strategy in these programs. What's learned in the field bolsters what happens in class, and vice versa.

1 **Berea College** (KY)
2 **Elon University** (NC)
3 **Tulane University** (LA)
4 **Abilene Christian University** (TX)
5 **Duke University** (NC)
5 **Seattle University**
5 **Stanford University** (CA)
8 **Boston College**
9 **Fairfield University** (CT)
9 **Michigan State University***
9 **Portland State University** (OR)*
9 **University of Notre Dame** (IN)
9 **Warren Wilson College** (NC)

14 **Appalachian State University** (NC)*
14 **Creighton University** (NE)
16 **Brown University** (RI)
16 **College of the Ozarks** (MO)
16 **Vanderbilt University** (TN)

▶ Study Abroad

Programs at these schools involve substantial academic work abroad for credit – a year, a semester or an intensive experience equal to a course – and considerable interaction with the local culture.

1 **Elon University** (NC)
2 **Arcadia University** (PA)
3 **Kalamazoo College** (MI)
4 **New York University**
5 **Goucher College** (MD)
6 **Middlebury College** (VT)
7 **American University** (DC)
7 **Dickinson College** (PA)
9 **Michigan State University***
10 **Agnes Scott College** (GA)
11 **Pepperdine University** (CA)
11 **Syracuse University** (NY)
13 **University of Evansville** (IN)
14 **Carleton College** (MN)
14 **St. Olaf College** (MN)
16 **Dartmouth College** (NH)

STUDY THE SCHOOLS

Girding for the Stresses of College

Two experts offer guidance to students and parents getting set for freshman year

IN RECENT YEARS, COLLEGES have seen a concerning increase in mental health issues such as anxiety and depression among students – and that was before the coronavirus pandemic disrupted campus life and threw the future into doubt. In "The Stressed Years of Their Lives," family psychologist **B. Janet Hibbs** and University of Pennsylvania psychiatrist **Anthony L. Rostain,** (both parents of college graduates) examine the challenges many students, parents and schools are facing and offer insights about what kinds of counseling and other services to look for when considering colleges. This interview has been edited for length and clarity.

Is there a mental health crisis on college campuses?

ALR: There is strong evidence of a legitimate and significant rise in levels of stress, distress and mental health disorders in college students over the last two decades. In part that's a reflection of the success we've had in identifying kids with issues, treating them and helping them adjust and adapt to the transition from high school to college. While college campus resources are being stretched, there are really good new programs that colleges are developing to expand students' capacity to be resilient in the face of stress. I'm not here to say the sky is falling; I'm here to say, yes, there's a crisis, but I think that everyone's eyes are now open to this, and people are talking about it and trying to handle it.

What can families do early on to help students prepare for changes to come?

BJH: Parents tend to be overinvolved, and they're anxious. They'll do everything they can to kind of catch their kids before they fall, so kids don't

have enough practice in some of the social-emotional maturity development. Instead of promoting childhood autonomy (which is really a parent's job), they're exerting more parental control because they're scared.

ALR: We talk in the book about social and emotional readiness. I think that practicing these skills is key: being able to take responsibility, practice self-management, handle social relationships and learn to exercise self-control. Developing the ability to cope with frustration, handling risk and at the same time being open and accepting, and also seeking help when you need it.

For parents, what are some warning signs of problems?

ALR: Differences in mood where the individual may be developing depression – they withdraw from their usual activities, they start to not sleep well, they are less engaged in their normal pursuits, they stop socializing as much. There's also concern about excessive alcohol or substance use.

BJH: About one-quarter of kids who arrive on college campus today have already been treated for or diagnosed with a mental health

search on connection suggests that having an adult mentor or adviser who actually knows what you're doing and is invested in you is also a key to helping young people succeed.

Can you give an example of an action to take in the face of a challenge?

BJH: Destructive perfectionism is something that very high-achieving kids often experience in college because they haven't had that much practice with failure. And by "failure," we can mean a lower grade than they thought they'd get. In our book, we talk about how a student's anxiety – constant pressure, constant striving – turned into a suicidal intent one evening after she'd been drinking. She came to see me in therapy, and after that we gradually involved her family in terms of the things she felt like she couldn't tell them before and things that made her feel like "I'm disappointing people." Through this process, she became more self-accepting, which is a key component of social-emotional maturity. She was able to tolerate her faults and mistakes while dealing with setbacks without feeling too ashamed.

What can colleges do to improve mental health on campus?

BJH: We'd recommend that mental health on campus begins with the acceptance letter. Parents want to understand the available resources, but even more so, they look to colleges and universities for direction about how to stay connected as they guide their child's

problem. The most common is anxiety, followed by depression. One of the good things about Gen Z is they are more open to seeking help, and they show a reduced negative stigma about mental health problems, with greater willingness to get treatment. Mental health literacy helps parents and kids be more alert and aware that this is treatable.

So how should parents respond if their child reports being anxious or depressed?

BJH: Listen. Don't judge them for telling you.

ALR: Normalize to the best extent possible – sometimes life is difficult. Make it clear to kids that these things are not untreatable.

What role can friends and peer support play? Do peer counselors or advisers help?

BJH: Basically, if social life fails, college fails. A key role of friends is to help individuals stay motivated and to encourage them to devote time and effort to learning. It's actually been shown that kids who graduate on time usually graduate in a friend group, and kids who don't graduate on time have somehow lost social connection or they drop out – literally or figuratively. The other re-

transition to college. As we discuss in our book, beyond emergency numbers and campus offices, we advocate for parents as partners with colleges through important discussions with their teens focusing on the importance of [privacy] waivers, risk management, mental health literacy and family mental health histories. These ongoing parent-teen discussions can promote social-emotional maturity and resilience. This guidance can lead to the crucial takeaway: Seek help when needed.

Once on campus, students may be more open to seeking help when student-led groups such as Active Minds and JED are represented. Beyond peer-led support, when a college counseling office triages a student's needs as beyond its availability or scope, we'd suggest that both parents and students ascertain that the college can provide a trusted referral network of nearby mental health practitioners.

What parting advice would you give students and parents preparing for that first year of college?

ALR: Take time to make friends, but also spend time getting to know your teachers and getting connected to clubs. Whatever you're excited about, give yourself a chance to explore those things.

BJH: [A parent] can try to reassure them that I'm not going to call you every week, asking "How's this class going? How's that class going?" They don't need a checkup all the time. Have a conversation. ●

Interviews with Alison Murtagh

A ROAD TRIP TO
BOSTON

39 Northeastern University
BOSTON

41 Boston University
BOSTON

45 Boston College
CHESTNUT HILL

48 Wellesley College
WELLESLEY

51 Bentley University
WALTHAM

54 Tufts University
MEDFORD

Visit Ca

mpus

A College Road Trip:
Boston

Tufts University
Medford

Bentley University
Waltham

Boston University
Boston

Boston College
Chestnut Hill

Northeastern University
Boston

Wellesley College
Wellesley

Greater Metro Area

by **Lindsay Cates**

The City's Many Attractions

In normal times, Boston has much to offer visitors – and students

Boston Common
139 Tremont St.
A 44-acre park and green space near the heart of downtown.

Boston Public Library
700 Boylston St.
Founded in 1848, Boston's library is the third largest collection in the United States.

Bunker Hill Monument
Monument Square, Charlestown
A memorial to the Battle of Bunker Hill, fought on June 17, 1775, one of the first major battles of the American Revolution.

Faneuil Hall
4 South Market St.
An indoor marketplace and shopping center. The hall opened in 1743 and has hosted many gatherings of revolutionaries, abolitionists and other historical figures.

Fenway Park
4 Jersey St.
Home to the Boston Red Sox, this stadium is the oldest Major League Baseball park in the U.S., built in 1912.

Franklin Park Zoo
1 Franklin Park Rd.
The city's largest zoo has been in operation for more than 100 years and is home to 1,000-plus animals.

John F. Kennedy Presidential Library and Museum
Columbia Point
A facility that honors the former Massachusetts senator and 35th president.

Museum of Fine Arts, Boston
465 Huntington Ave.
One of the largest museums in the country, it contains over 450,000 pieces of art. The museum has an affiliation with Tufts University.

New England Aquarium
1 Central Wharf
A public aquarium that draws more than 1.3 million visitors each year.

Old South Meeting House
310 Washington St.
A historic church notable for being where the Boston Tea Party was organized.

Old State House
206 Washington St.
Another building steeped in Revolutionary War-era history, the Old State House was once the seat of the Massachusetts General Court and is one of the oldest public buildings in the United States. The Boston Massacre occurred just outside the building on March 5, 1770.

Paul Revere House
19 North Square
The former home of the well-known American patriot is now a museum.

USS Constitution Museum
Charlestown Navy Yard
A museum about "Old Ironsides" in a restored shipyard building; the famous naval ship is open to the public as well.

The Boston area is a hub of higher ed, home to schools with rich histories that are also leaders in innovation. Before the pandemic, U.S. News visited several of them, bypassing Harvard and the Massachusetts Institute of Technology, where the acceptance rate is under 10%. In case you can't visit yourself in the months ahead, here's an inside look at a handful of New England institutions.

Northeastern University • BOSTON

DANIEL SNEYERS knew from the get-go that he wanted his college experience to combine his interests in business and engineering. Not only did Northeastern's curriculum allow the industrial engineering major to take classes in both fields, but also the university's emphasis on experiential learning armed Sneyers with two on-the-job experiences. During his sophomore year, he worked in strategy consulting at Bain & Company in Brazil, where he grew up;

he also spent a term junior year working as an iPhone operations program manager at Apple in California, where he applied his knowledge of finance, engineering and optimization on the capital expenditures team.

"I've been able to work in places that I could not have imagined possible," says Sneyers, who will graduate in 2021 with a bachelor's

Sketching out ideas on a handy whiteboard at Northeastern

in industrial engineering and a master's in operations research from the university's Galante Engineering Business Program. He landed the positions as part of Northeastern's co-op program (short for cooperative education), through which students alternate periods of full-time work with academic semesters in the classroom. About 99% of the private university's undergraduates participate in a co-op. Some spend time in Boston-based companies like Wayfair or General Electric – and some, like

Sneyers, opt to travel to one of more than 3,000 co-op employers around the world. Undergrads typically complete three co-ops during a five-year stint in college, or two over the course of four years, and during terms where they work, they don't pay tuition. In fact, most earn salaries. Just over half receive a full-time job offer from one of their co-op employers after they graduate.

The co-op experience is integrated with academics; students bring their classroom knowledge to their co-ops and then bring industry know-how back to campus.

CONNECTIONS. Students say that professors tend to be well-connected and helpful when it comes to tapping into professional networks. "You're able to build that relationship," says Kritika Singh, a recent bioengineering grad from McLean, Virginia, who completed one co-op in a chemical biology lab at Massachusetts General Hospital. The student-faculty ratio is 14:1, and classes average fewer than 20 undergrads.

Community service is also heavily emphasized, and more than 100 classes across eight colleges have built service learning with Boston-area nonprofits and government agencies into their coursework. During an Economics of Crime course, for example, Nathan Hostert, a fifth-year political science major from Wichita, Kansas, worked with the Fenway Community Center researching how to reduce neighborhood crime rates. And for those who want to venture further from campus, Northeastern's Global Experience Office works to make sure every student has the opportunity to go abroad.

DIGGING DEEP. For Singh, a 2020 Rhodes Scholar, research and mentorship defined her time at Northeastern. She wanted to "hit the ground running," so she linked up with the Office of Undergraduate Research and Fellowships freshman year to attend workshops, connect with mentors and write grant proposals. The move earned her a total of $13,500 in funding for an independent chemical biology research project.

Above, Northeastern's Interdisciplinary Science and Engineering Complex. Right, students between classes

Northeastern offers more than 280 majors, including 195 combined majors that allow students to complete co-ops in both fields. Among the examples are civil engineering and architectural studies, physics and music, and data science and journalism.

The frequent comings and goings for co-ops can take some getting used to, undergrads say, but the 480-plus clubs and activities on campus are a unifying force. The Huskies compete in 16 Division I sports, and students can get involved in more than 70 club and intramural teams. Fitness classes, mindfulness programs and mental health resources are also abundant.

Northeastern's tree-lined paths and outdoor study spots give the campus, located in the heart of Boston, a healthy dose of nature. All students live there their first two years; freshmen reside in Living Learning Communities based on common interests. Examples include Travel and Adventure, Social Change and Empowerment, and Technical Innovation and Creativity. Tunnels connecting key buildings help students avoid winter weather, and when temperatures climb, some of Boston's most popular attractions are within walking distance, including the Museum of Fine Arts, Newbury Street's shops, Fenway Park and the Charles River. ●

UNDERGRADUATES
Full-time: 14,156

TOTAL COST*
$72,862

U.S. NEWS RANKING
National Universities: #49

*Tuition, fees and room & board for 2020-21

Boston University

BOSTON

S **PANNING A TWO-MILE** stretch of Commonwealth Avenue along the south shore of the Charles River, BU is its own distinct neighborhood – and it mirrors the globe, says Kelly A. Walter, associate vice president for enrollment and dean of admissions. About a quarter of the undergrads typically are international students (from 130-plus countries) and 40% represent a race or ethnicity other than white.

Most students share a motivated mindset, observes Tyler Ross, a junior speech, language and hearing sciences major from Somers, New York. "Everyone really takes advantage of what BU has to offer," Ross notes. Those offerings include 10 undergraduate schools and colleges offering 250 majors, more than 450 student organizations, plentiful research opportunities and 24 Division I varsity sports teams. Popular majors include biology and health sciences; students can participate in professional training programs and conduct research at local hospitals.

Tatyana Da Rosa, a 2020 biology grad in the pre-med and veterinary medicine track from Brockton, Massachusetts, chose BU for the opportunities STEM majors get to study abroad. Her sophomore year she spent a semester in Madrid taking classes including cellular biology and organic chemistry; junior year, she knocked out her required biology courses during a tropical ecology program in Ecuador. "It just seamlessly worked into my schedule," says Da Rosa. Programs geared for students in music and drama, engineering, health and more make study abroad doable in just about any major.

Beyond the arts and sciences, BU

UNDERGRADUATES Full-time: 16,978
TOTAL COST* $74,712
U.S. NEWS RANKING National Universities: #42
*Tuition, fees and room & board for 2020-21

schools and programs include education and human development, business, hospitality administration and fine arts, which hosts more than 500 performances and exhibitions each year. About 150 first-years join the Kilachand Honors College, a smaller community in which students often participate in experiential learning opportunities like traveling to settlements of displaced Syrians and offering solutions to challenges they face.

FLEXIBILITY. Applicants to BU need to apply to a specific school, but switching from one to another is common. "It was easy to transfer, and so many people helped me along the way," says Ross, who started off in elementary education before moving to speech, language and hearing sciences in the College of Health & Rehabilitation Sciences: Sargent College.

A general education program that promotes cross-college teaching and research helps ensure that credits from one school can count in another. All students are required to take 10 to 12 HUB courses to master such "essential capacities" as quantitative reasoning; diversity, citizenship and global engagement; and communication. To address the philosophical inquiry capacity, say, students can choose from an array of classes in different majors, including Puzzles and Paradoxes (Philosophy) and Modern Political Theory (Political Science).

BU boasts a 10:1 student-faculty ratio, and professors are generally very approachable, though large lectures and labs often have teaching assistants who can be an easier first go-to, students say. More than two-thirds of classes enroll 30 or fewer students.

ABUNDANT RESOURCES. "It's a big school, but that only works to your advantage," says Da Rosa. Resources abound, including the Educational Resource Center for peer tutoring, language practice groups, and advising. The Center for Career Development offers help with résumé writing, networking, interviews and internships. At the Howard Thurman Center for Common Ground, students participate

An indoor training session for Boston University's Division I women's rowing team

Journalism students get hands-on experience in the TV studio. Left, a BU class

gram, professors live alongside students, serving as advocates and often planning bonding activities like French crepe-making or open tutoring hours.

For a break from the campus hustle and bustle, the nearby Charles River Esplanade offers jogging trails and kayaking. There's also BU Beach, a green space on campus (no sand, but cars passing on a major road nearby are said to sound like waves). About 13% of students join one of BU's 20 fraternities and sororities.

The T runs right through campus, giving students easy access to other Boston neighborhoods. However, students say there's plenty to do without leaving BU, from theater performances to cheering on the men's hockey team, which boasts 37 conference titles, has produced dozens of Olympic and NHL athletes, and has won The Beanpot – an annual tournament against local rivals Boston College, Northeastern and Harvard – 30 of the last 60-plus years. ●

in classes and programs like The Common Thread Podcast, art exhibits, book clubs, board games and events to share ideas, learn about differences and engage in discussions centered on community and culture.

Some 75% of BU students live on campus all four years in more than 140 residence halls, including a renovated 1920s luxury hotel, modern high-rises and charming brownstones overlooking the Charles River; many housing options boast sweeping city views. Through a faculty-in-residence pro-

Boston College • CHESTNUT HILL

FOUNDED BY THE JESUITS in 1863, Boston College wears its religious affiliation and mission of serving others and promoting social justice with pride, immersing students in the Catholic intellectual tradition through service programs, retreats and interdisciplinary classes.

"Wherever you come from, you're going to be challenged in some way, whether that be academically, spiritually or emotionally," says Armani Mitchell, a junior applied psychology and human development major from the Bronx, New York, who as a sophomore spent 12 hours a week mentoring middle school students from low-income backgrounds. The experience was part of a popular two-semester joint philosophy and theology program called PULSE in which students combat social injustice by working with marginalized populations.

While about 70% of BC's undergrads identify as Catholic, students say professors don't care what you believe, but they will expect you to think about why you believe what you do. More than 80% of students participate in service, and some classes include a service component.

The combination of a "do-good" mission, about 60 undergraduate majors and academic programs, and the opportunity to cheer on Division I sports teams creates a well-balanced place to spend four years, students say. BC's medium size ensures you'll see plenty of familiar faces, while it's

A student at work in Boston College's state-of-the-art Center for Isotope Geochemistry

UNDERGRADUATES
Full-time: 9,370

TOTAL COST*
$75,422

U.S. NEWS RANKING
National Universities:
#35

*Tuition, fees and room & board for 2020-21

still possible to "be anonymous" when you want to be, says Helen Fagan, a senior applied psychology and human development major from Wilmette, Illinois. She joined the McGillycuddy-Logue Fellows Program to pursue an interest in international social justice.

Plus, you get a best-of-both-worlds location. BC's campus is self-contained, full of green space and Gothic-style architecture, but it sits just 6 miles from the city center. Students often Uber or take the subway downtown for food, concerts or service work.

Everyone across all four undergraduate schools (arts and sciences, management, education and human development, and nursing) takes the same core curriculum, which re-

quires two classes each in theology and philosophy along with courses in writing, natural and social sciences, history, cultural diversity, literature, arts and math. A handful of popular team-taught classes offer first-years the chance to fulfill two core classes at once while exploring complex contemporary issues. Mitchell took a course on the rise of both the Black Lives Matter and #MeToo movements.

DOING GOOD. Distinctive interdisciplinary programs like Managing for Social Impact and the Public Good illustrate the school's focus on teaching students to make the world a better place – an aspect that sold senior Nicole Kearney on pursuing business at BC. "I needed somewhere that was going to broaden my horizons," says the Redding, Connecticut, native, who is pursuing majors in both marketing and the social impact option.

A variety of programs and grants offer undergraduates the opportunity to pursue research with faculty. Jian Zabalerio, a 2020 operations management grad from Morristown, New Jersey, participated in research into operational efficiency at Boston Children's Hospital. She also held two summer internships at GE Healthcare. Nearly 90% of BC students complete an internship during school.

BC has no Greek life, but students tend to get involved in clubs that they're really passionate about, says Fagan. All told, there are about 300 clubs and organizations on campus, including pre-professional groups and just-for-fun options like the slam poetry club.

Sports are a big draw. The Eagles compete in 31 Division I sports, and on football game days, "the campus comes alive," says Kearney. Hockey games are popular, too. One favorite tradition: "packing the T," where BC students fill the train cars en route to The Beanpot, an annual ice hockey tournament at TD Garden (about 45 minutes from campus by train) so that fans from BU and Northeastern further down the line can't get on. ●

BC's Bapst Library supports art, architecture, photography and related studies at the school.

Wellesley College

WELLESLEY

AFTER ATTENDING an all-girl's high school in Philadelphia, Auden Bunn wanted a college with the same supportive and welcoming feel. Bunn "fell in love" on a visit to Wellesley, one of just a few dozen women's colleges in the U.S. "I really love the community here, even though I identify as nonbinary," says the sophomore, who is considering a media arts and sciences major.

Wellesley's 8:1 student-faculty ratio creates an environment where "people care about your thoughts," says Paige Calvert, a 2020 English graduate from Madison, Connecticut. A so-called shadow grading policy allows first-year students to ease into a challenging curriculum and explore classes outside their comfort zone; all first-semester courses are graded pass-fail. Wellesley's roughly 2,500 undergraduates take a first-year writing seminar, fulfill a language requirement (10 choices are offered, including Swahili and Hebrew) and earn a range of other credits including in the natural sciences, quantitative reasoning, literature, art, history and multicultural studies.

Juniors and seniors can take one of the Calderwood Seminars in Public Writing, which teach the art of writing about topics in their academic field for the general public. Lauren Luo, a 2020 computer science and American studies grad from Hong Kong, practiced

UNDERGRADUATES
Full-time: **2,399**

TOTAL COST*
$76,220

U.S. NEWS RANKING
National Liberal Arts:
#4

*Tuition, fees and room & board
for 2020-21

Students rehearsing for the popular ascenDance Fall Showcase at Wellesley College

writing about technology for a lay audience, for example. In one assignment, she discussed the role of artificial intelligence in spreading mis- and disinformation that could impact the 2020 elections.

The Wellesley in Washington Summer Internship Program gives stipends to 20 students from any major to intern in the nation's capital, attending weekly seminars and receiving mentorship from Wellesley alums. Avery Restrepo, a 2020 international relations, political science and Spanish grad from Fairfield, Connecticut, spent the summer before senior year interning with the House Democratic Caucus. The Albright Institute, named for Wellesley alum and former Secretary of State Madeleine Albright, funds 40 fellows every year to participate in a global internship and discussion of global issues during Wintersession, a three-week period in January when it's possible to take a class, work on a thesis or study abroad.

Each fall, classes shut down for one day for the Tanner Conference, and students present their experiences with internships, civic engagement and study abroad. A similar event in the spring is dedicated to undergraduate research – something many students participate in at Wellesley or at several nearby schools such as Olin College of Engineering, Babson College and MIT.

TIGHTKNIT COMMUNITY. A strong sense of community makes it easy to get to know professors, students say. Faculty members frequently take part in student-run events; for example, in her role as college government committee chair for political and legislative awareness, Restrepo put together a panel of political science instructors to discuss presidential impeachment hearings.

Wellesley's picturesque campus surrounding Lake Waban is a pleasant retreat from the city, students observe, although it can feel isolating. A bus runs to Boston and Cambridge, while a Saturday-only

In class at Wellesley, where the 8:1 student-faculty ratio allows for plenty of discussion

Wellesley creates a warm and supportive environment, undergrads say.

shuttle takes students to Natick for movies, shopping and dining out.

There are no first-year-only dorms, and students say they enjoy getting to know the upperclasswomen in their residence halls.

Other popular activities include supporting Wellesley's 13 Division III sports teams, participating in club and intramural sports including Ultimate Frisbee and Quidditch, and joining cultural organizations. There is no Greek life, but six societies centered around topics like art, history, politics and Shakespeare occupy houses throughout campus.

Favorite traditions include cheering on runners in the Boston Marathon (the campus sits at the halfway point) and "hooprolling," when seniors compete to roll large hoops down Tupelo Lane on campus. Hoops are often decorated and passed down from so-called big sisters to little sisters. (First-year "littles" are paired with upperclass students who act as their "big" during a fall ceremony.)

Wellesley's alumni network is a draw for many, and includes Hillary Clinton and journalist Diane Sawyer. The Lulu Chow Wang Campus Center, named for an alumna who is a Wall Street pioneer and philanthropist, is a central gathering spot. The building was supposedly designed with no right angles to represent the notion that Wellesley women can't be put in boxes. ●

Bentley University

WALTHAM

DURING A SUMMER tax internship at PwC, Dominique Balzora-Rivert was surprised to find that many of her fellow interns had never heard of South Dakota v. Wayfair, Inc., a 2018 Supreme Court decision that affected state sales taxes. It was a case her professors at Bentley University had brought up many times. "That's when I realized Bentley was really preparing me for the world," says the recent grad in accounting and health and industry studies from Templeton, Massachusetts.

Bentley was founded a little more than a century ago to educate students in accounting and finance, and distinguishes itself with its business-focused curriculum that also integrates tech and the arts and sciences. Half of the school's 25 undergraduate majors are business-related, and there's a heavy focus on career preparation. During freshman year, nearly all students take Career Development 101.

"As soon as you come here, they teach you how to network," says Brandon Samba, a 2020 finance grad from San Diego with a global management minor. He put those skills to use as the founder of Captains of Capital, a club that teaches financial literacy to local kids from underserved backgrounds.

Bentley's 163-acre campus of brick buildings and picturesque green spaces is located in Waltham, a suburb with its own shops and restaurants about 10 miles from downtown Boston that is also home to Brandeis University. About 92% of undergrads complete at least one internship, often in the city, and 98% of students are in jobs or pursuing grad school by six months after

UNDERGRADUATES
Full-time: 4,177

TOTAL COST*
$71,410

U.S. NEWS RANKING
Regional University
(North): #1

*Tuition, fees and room & board for 2020-21

graduation. Popular employers include Dunkin' Brands, JPMorgan Chase, the Boston Red Sox and Aetna.

While most of Bentley's undergrads pursue business disciplines, many credit the school with seamlessly blending business with other subjects. Pursuing one of eight Liberal Studies majors (such as diversity and society, health and industry, or quantitative perspectives) is a popular route. Some 42% of students study abroad, and many get involved in service learning at more than 60 community partner sites.

FUSING DISCIPLINES. "No matter what, you're going to have some fusion of business and liberal arts and sciences," says senior Emily Miga of East Greenwich, Rhode Island, who wanted to blend her passions in business and creative writing and settled on a degree in marketing.

Students note that professors often bring real-world experience and a business perspective into discussions, enhancing classes like Disabilities in Society and Managing a Diverse Workplace. Miga recalls a history class on World War II that focused on how the war affected businesses. Bentley also offers an honors program providing students with research funding and small, seminar-style classes, as well as a Women's Leadership Program that grants $10,000 in tuition for all four years to all women accepted to it. (About 40% of students are women.)

Among the other real-world learning elements: a trading room with real-time stock market data and the CIS Sandbox, where tech-savvy undergrads build mobile apps, design video games and collaborate on projects. A user-experience lab

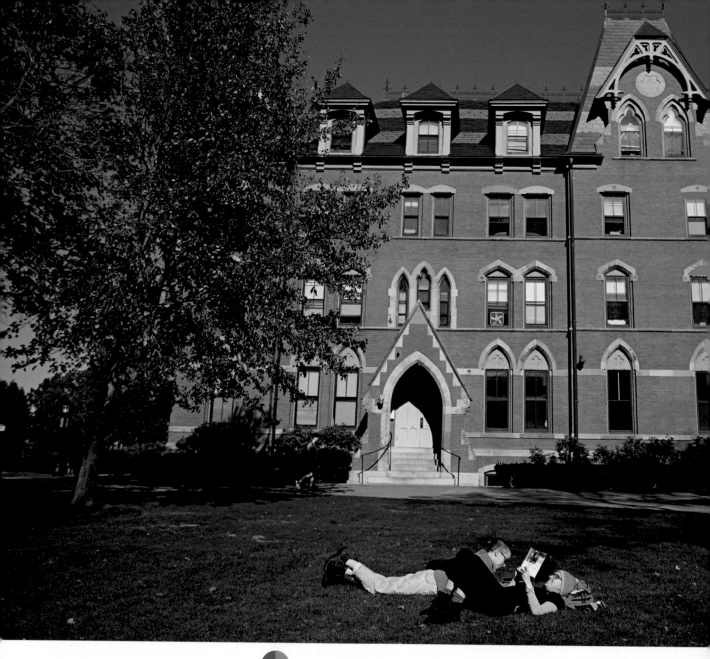

enables groups to improve the usability of tech products.

Students can choose from over 100 organizations, and they look forward to Spring Day, the Saturday before finals when instead of studying, everyone gathers to enjoy food trucks, activities and a concert. Recent performers: Jason Derulo, T-Pain and Ludacris. The Falcons compete in 20 Division II sports (hockey is Division I), and several club and intramural sports are offered. About 1 in 10 undergrads participate in Greek life.

The vibe at Bentley is collaborative rather than competitive, students say. "It's an environment where you can find your passion," says Balzora-Rivert, who plans on returning to PwC after graduation. ●

VISIT CAMPUS

Tufts University

MEDFORD

WITH NEARLY 6,000 undergrads, Tufts is a medium-sized university, but its 80-plus majors, opportunities for research and global study options give students the resources of a much larger school. Its ethos, an emphasis on civic engagement and hands-on learning, encourages undergrads to "think out-

wardly," says James M. Glaser, dean of the school of arts and sciences.

Senior Lily Campbell had her own such experience during a six-week program in France, where Tufts has a satellite campus. She made visits to the International Environment House (affiliated with the U.N.) and World Wildlife Fund, and discovered the field of environmental economics – the perfect combination of two chief

On campus at Tufts University; above, students at the well-regarded engineering school

UNDERGRADUATES
Full-time: 5,742

TOTAL COST*
$76,492

U.S. NEWS RANKING
National Universities:
#30

*Tuition, fees and room & board for 2020-21

interests. On campus and off, professors "show you how to take your hard skills and your passions and combine them together," says Campbell, a senior quantitative economics major from Bethesda, Maryland, who is completing a thesis examining the effects of climate change on global economies.

The Civic Semester has students taking classes on campus in August, then traveling for a semester of language immersion and part-time work at a community organization. Another program combines coursework and fieldwork in the local community.

The school of engineering is a big draw, with about 1 in 6 incoming students choosing one of its 16 majors. The curriculum puts an emphasis on collaborative and experiential learning, and every engineering student completes a final project, says Carter Silvey, a 2020 mechanical engineering and math graduate from Basking Ridge, New Jersey, who designed a device for warehouse workers to wear on their arms to more easily lift heavy loads.

Tufts also has its School of the Museum of Fine Arts, which has its own campus at the Museum of Fine Arts in Boston. Students can pursue a bachelor's in fine arts, exploring freely across mediums from ceramics and metalworking to photography.

Although students must apply to one of the three schools, they are free to take classes in the others. The average class size is 22, and relationships with faculty are a real part of the Tufts experience, students say. "They're willing to invest in you both personally and academically," says Vaishnavi Enaganti, a junior biopsychology major from Columbus, Ohio. After expressing interest in research, Enaganti was soon linked up with a professor to work about 20 hours a week in her genetics lab. The university offers several programs for funding undergraduate research, plus an international program that has student-faculty teams conducting research abroad.

On the whole, Tufts is full of people who are driven but also down-to-earth, undergrads say. More than 300 student organizations contribute to a fun, playful vibe. That's especially evident in Tufts Dance Collective, a competition for students who cannot dance – a much-anticipated event. "It's something that the whole school can really get behind," says Campbell.

PLENTY TO DO. The Jumbos compete in 30 Division III varsity sports. Nearly 1 in 8 students join one of 10 fraternities and sororities. Other options for student involvement include mock trial, public health club, and many competitive dance groups and cultural organizations. The largest student group is the Leonard Carmichael Society, an umbrella group for 32 service organizations that address community issues like literacy, homelessness and food security.

First- and second-year students are required to live on campus, located on a hill in Medford about 5 miles from the city. Tufts has striking views of the skyline, and shuttles connect the main campus with the school of the Museum of Fine Arts. Davis Square, located about a 15-minute walk from campus, is a hub for restaurants and shopping, as well as the closest T rail station for those wanting to venture into downtown Boston. ●

58   How We Rank Colleges

62   Best National Universities

72   Best National Liberal Arts Colleges

78   Best Regional Universities

92   Best Regional Colleges

98   Best Historically Black Colleges

100   Best Business Programs

102   Best Engineering Programs

104   Best Computer Science Programs

106   Best Online Degree Programs

110   Best Colleges for Social Mobility

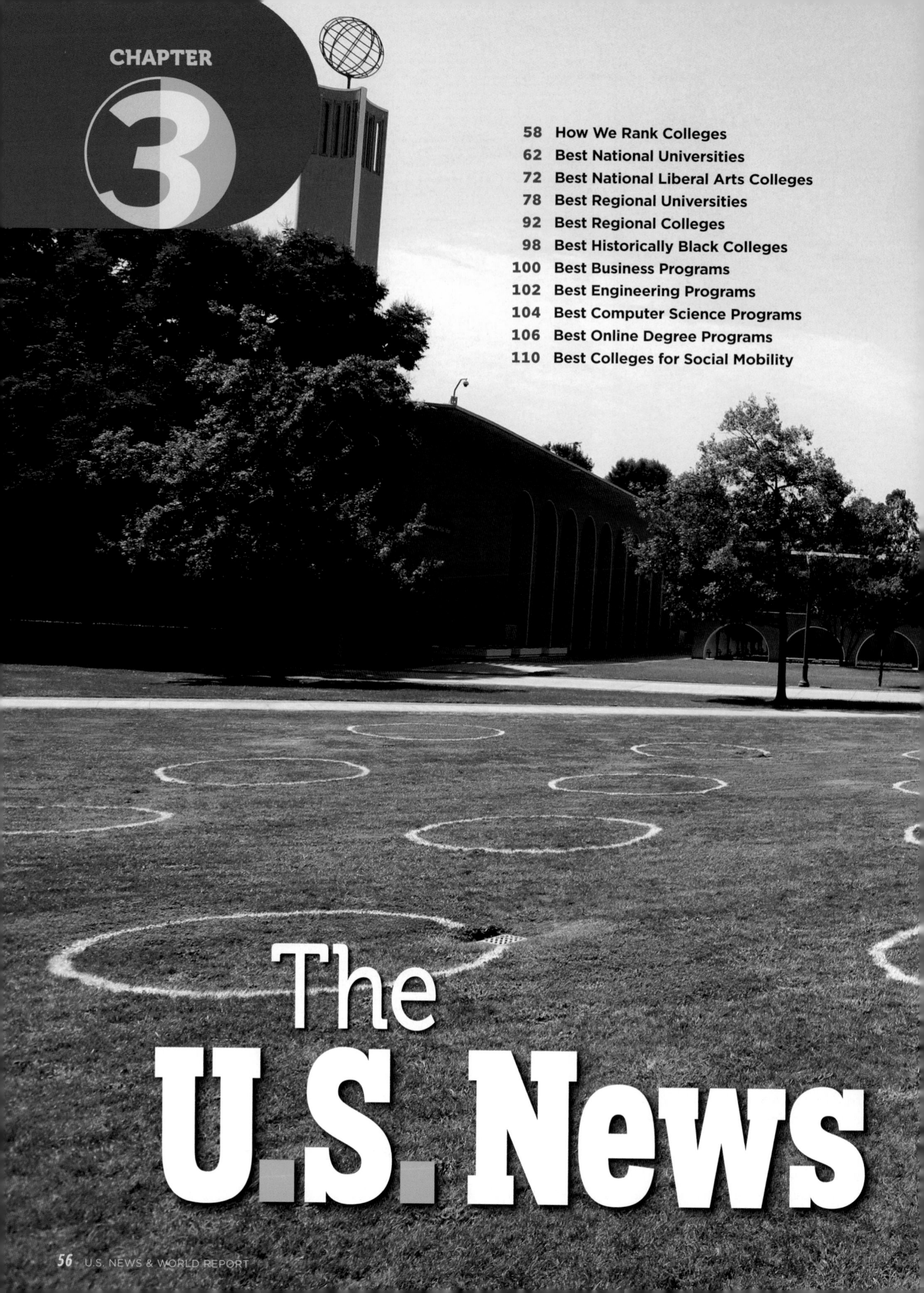

The U.S. News

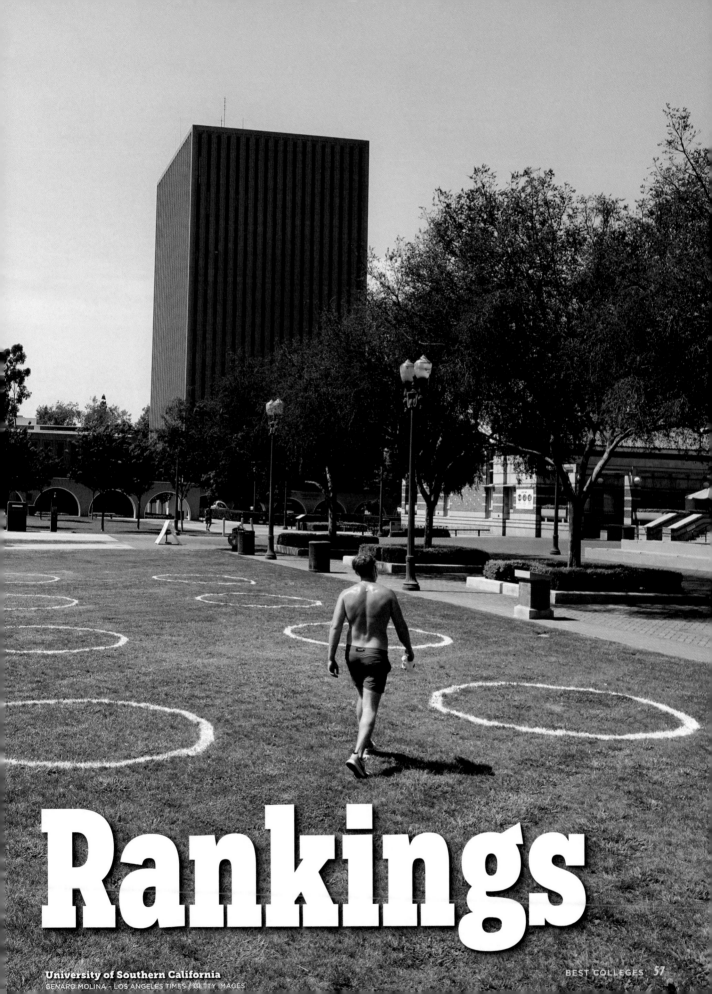

Rankings

How We Rank Colleges

How to make use of our statistics as you search for a good fit

by **Robert J. Morse** *and* **Eric M. Brooks**

DECIDING WHERE TO APPLY IS TOUGH. But the U.S. News Best Colleges rankings, now in their 36th year, are an excellent resource to tap as you begin your search. They can help you compare the academic quality of institutions you're considering based on such widely accepted indicators of excellence as graduation rates and the strength of the faculty. As you learn about colleges already on your shortlist, you may narrow your choices even further or discover unfamiliar new options. Yes, many factors other than those spotlighted here will figure in your decision, including location and the feel of campus life; the range of academic offerings and activities; and the cost. But combined with attention to such factors and to your own intuition, our rankings can be a powerful tool in your quest for the best fit.

How does the methodology work? The U.S. News ranking system rests on two pillars. The formula uses quantitative and qualitative statistical measures that education experts have proposed as reliable indicators of academic quality, and it is based on our researched view of what matters in education.

First, we categorize regionally accredited institutions by their mission, to establish valid comparisons: National Universities, National Liberal Arts Colleges, Regional Universities and Regional Colleges. The national universities offer a full range of undergraduate majors, plus master's and Ph.D. programs or professional practice doctorates, and emphasize faculty research (Page 62). The national liberal arts colleges focus almost exclusively on undergraduate education (Page 72). They award at least 50% of their degrees in the arts and sciences.

The regional universities (Page 78) offer a broad scope of undergraduate degrees and some master's degree programs but few, if any, doctoral programs. The regional colleges (Page 92) focus on undergraduate education but grant fewer than 50% of their degrees in liberal arts disciplines; this category also includes schools that have small bachelor's programs but primarily grant two-year associate degrees. The regional universities and regional colleges are further divided and ranked in four geographical groups: North, South, Midwest and West.

The framework used to group schools is derived from the 2018 update of the Carnegie Classification of Institutions of Higher Education's Basic Classification. The Carnegie classification is used extensively by higher education researchers; the U.S. Department of Education and many higher education associations use the system to organize their data and to determine colleges' eligibility for grant money, for example.

Next, we gather data from each college on 17 indicators of academic excellence. Each ranking factor is assigned a weight that reflects our research about how much a measure matters. Finally, the schools in each category are ranked against their peers using their overall scores, which are calculated from the sum of their indicators. The data used in these rankings pertain to fall 2019 and earlier. Consequently, the coronavirus pandemic did not impact the information colleges submitted to U.S. News. Nonetheless, to account for the huge disruption to higher education, we made a few changes this year. We placed reduced emphasis on admissions selectivity data and alumni giving, described below. And for the first time since the 2007 edition, schools that reported not using ACT and SAT scores for any admissions decisions were eligible to be ranked.

Still, some schools are not ranked (and do not appear in the tables) for other reasons. This occurred, for example, when they received too few ratings in their peer assessment survey or had a total enrollment of fewer than 200 students or when U.S. News could not obtain a six-year graduation rate. We also only assessed schools that enroll first-year students and offered some face-to-face instruction in 2018. As a result of these standards, many for-profit and upper division institutions are not included. We also did not rank highly specialized schools such as those in arts, health, business and engineering.

Colleges report most of the data themselves, via the annual U.S. News statistical survey. This year, 85% of the 1,452 ranked colleges and universities returned their statistical information. To ensure the highest possible quality of data, U.S. News compared schools' survey responses to their earlier cohorts' statistics, third-party data, and data reported by other schools. Schools were instructed to review, revise and verify the accuracy of their data, particularly any flagged by U.S. News as requiring a second look. They were also instructed to have a top academic official sign off on the accuracy of the data. Schools that declined to do so could still submit and be ranked but are footnoted.

For eligible colleges that declined to complete our survey (identified as nonresponders), we made extensive use of data they reported to the National Center for Education Statistics. Estimates were used in the calculations when schools failed to report data not available from other sources, although missing data are reported in the tables as N/A.

The indicators we use to capture academic quality, described below, include input measures that reflect schools' student bodies, faculties and resources, as well as outcome measures that signal how well institutions are engaging and educating their students. Outcome measures account for 40% of the overall score, up from 35% last year. A more detailed explanation of the methodology can be found at usnews.com/collegemeth.

OUTCOMES (weighted at 40%): The higher the proportion of first-year students who return to campus for sophomore year

and eventually graduate, the better a school most likely is at offering the classes and services needed to succeed. More than one-third of a school's rank reflects its success at retaining and graduating students within six years.

This measure has several components: six-year graduation and first-year retention rates (together accounting for 22% of the score); graduation rate performance, or how well a school performs at graduating students compared to a predicted graduation rate based on student and school characteristics (8%); a school's record on promoting social mobility by graduating students from low-income backgrounds (5%); and, new this year, two measures of the indebtedness of bachelor's degree graduates (5% total).

The average six-year graduation rate (of students entering in fall 2010 through fall 2013) was weighted at 17.6% of the score. Average first-year retention rate (of fall 2015 through fall 2018 entrants) was weighted at 4.4%.

A school's graduation rate performance shows the effect of programs and policies on the graduation rate when controlling for other factors that might influence it. These include spending per student, admissions selectivity, the proportion of undergraduates receiving Pell Grants, the proportion of federal financial aid recipients who were first-generation students, and – for national universities only – the proportion of undergrad degrees awarded in science, technology, engineering and mathematics disciplines. We compare a school's six-year graduation rate to the graduation rate we predicted for that class. If the actual graduation rate is higher than the predicted rate, then the college is enhancing achievement.

The social mobility measure assesses a school's performance at supporting students from underserved backgrounds relative to all students. It considers both a school's six-year graduation rate among students who received Pell Grants and how that performance compares with the graduation rate of all other students. Scores were then adjusted by the proportion of the entering class that was awarded Pell Grants, because achieving a higher graduation rate among students from low-income backgrounds is more challenging when a school has a larger proportion of such students.

The two new measures of graduate indebtedness were added in recognition of the burgeoning amount of outstanding student debt – now estimated at more than $1.5 trillion – and the long-lasting negative impact such borrowing can have on graduates' financial well-being. The two indicators are: average accumulated federal loan debt of students who borrowed (including co-signed loans but excluding parent loans) among

Weighing What's Important

The U.S. News rankings are based on several categories of quality indicators, listed below. Scores for each group are weighted as shown to arrive at a final overall score.

The Scoring Breakdown

Outcomes*	40%
Faculty Resources	20%
Expert Opinion	20%
Financial Resources	10%
Student Excellence	7%
Alumni Giving	3%

*Graduation, retention, graduation rate performance, graduate indebtedness, social mobility

2019 grads earning bachelor's degrees (3%), and the percentage of the class of 2019 that took out federal loans (2%).

FACULTY RESOURCES (20%): Research shows that the greater access students have to quality instructors, the more engaged they will be in class, the more they will learn, and the more likely they are to graduate. U.S. News uses five factors from the 2019-2020 academic year to assess commitment to instruction: class size, faculty salary, faculty with the highest degree in their field, student-faculty ratio, and proportion of faculty who are full time.

Class size is the most heavily weighted, at 8% of the score. The larger the proportion of fall 2019 classes a school reported as being of a smaller size, the more credit the school receives.

Faculty salary (7%) reflects the average pay of assistant, associate and full professors during the 2019-2020 academic year. The faculty salary figures were adjusted for regional price differences. The other factors are weighted as follows: proportion of full-time professors with the highest degree in their field (3%), student-faculty ratio (1%), and proportion of faculty who are full time (1%).

EXPERT OPINION (20%): We survey presidents, provosts and deans of admissions, asking them to rate the academic quality of peer institutions with which they are familiar on a scale of 1 (marginal) to 5 (distinguished). An institution known for having innovative approaches to teaching may perform especially well on this indicator, for example, whereas a school struggling to keep its accreditation will likely perform poorly. The peer assessment score is derived from averaging survey results from 2019 and 2020. Of the 4,816 academics who were sent questionnaires in 2020, 36.4% responded.

FINANCIAL RESOURCES (10%): Generous per-student spending indicates that a college can offer a variety of programs and services. U.S. News measures financial resources using average spending per student on instruction, research, student services and related educational expenditures in the 2018 and 2019 fiscal years.

STUDENT EXCELLENCE (7%, previously 10%): A school's academic atmosphere is influenced by the selectivity of its admissions. Simply put, students who achieved strong grades and test scores during high school have the highest probability of succeeding at college-level coursework, enabling instructors to design classes that have great rigor. Excellence is based on two ranking indicators, standardized tests and high school class standing. The test scores for the fall 2019 entering class

Footnotes
to the
Rankings Tables

1. This school declined to fill out the U.S. News & World Report main statistical survey. Data that appear are from either what the school reported in previous years or from another source, such as the National Center for Education Statistics.

2. SAT and/or ACT not required by school for some or all applicants.

3. In reporting SAT/ACT scores, the school did not include all students for whom it had scores or refused to tell U.S. News whether all students with scores had been included.

4. Data reported to U.S. News in previous years.

5. Data based on fewer than 20% of enrolled freshmen.

6. Some or all data reported to the National Center for Education Statistics.

7. School declined to have a school official verify the accuracy of the information contained in the U.S. News main statistical survey.

8. This rate, normally based on four years of data, is given here for fewer than four years because school didn't report rate for the most recent year or years to U.S. News.

9. SAT and/or ACT may not be required by school for some or all applicants, and in reporting SAT/ACT scores, the school did not include all students for whom it had scores or refused to tell U.S. News whether all students with scores had been included.

N/A means not available.

used in this year's rankings were weighted at 5%, down from 7.75%. High school class standing for the fall 2019 entering class was weighted at 2% (previously 2.25%). Schools sometimes fail to report SAT and ACT scores for athletes, international students, minority students, legacies, those admitted by special arrangement and those who started in the summer. For any school that did not report all scores (or declined to say whether all scores were reported), U.S. News discounted its test-score value by 15%. Additionally, if test scores reported represented less than 75% of students entering, the value was discounted by 15%.

As for high school class standing, U.S. News incorporates the proportion of first-year students at national universities and national liberal arts colleges who graduated in the top 10% of their high school classes. For regional universities and regional colleges, we used the proportion of those who graduated in the top quarter of their high school classes.

ALUMNI GIVING (3%, previously 5%): This is the average percentage of living alumni with bachelor's degrees who gave to their school during 2017-2018 and 2018-2019. Giving measures student satisfaction and postgraduate engagement.

TO ARRIVE AT A SCHOOL'S RANK, we calculated the weighted sum of its standardized scores. The scores were rescaled so the top college or university in each category received a value of 100 and the other schools' weighted scores were calculated as a proportion of the top score. Final scores were rounded to the nearest whole number and ranked in descending order. Tied schools appear in alphabetical order.

As you mine the tables that follow for insights (a sense of which schools might be impressed enough by your ACT or SAT scores to offer some merit aid, for example, or where you will be apt to get the most attention from professors), keep in mind that the rankings provide a launching pad for more research, not an easy answer. ●

USNEWS.COM/BESTCOLLEGES

▶ Visit **usnews.com** regularly while conducting your research, as U.S. News frequently adds content aimed at helping collegebound students find the best fit and get in. We also occasionally make updates when new data become available or new information changes the data.

Make your dream possible with

Crimson Education

Who We Are

Crimson Education is an education consulting company that helps students around the world get into their best-fit universities by creating personalized teams comprised of the top tutors, mentors, and admissions experts.

Our one-on-one sessions ensure that Crimson students get the support they need to stand out in today's highly competitive college admissions race.

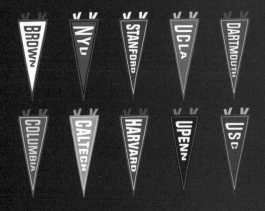

Our students have received offers from a wide range of top universities including:

BROWN · NYU · STANFORD · UCLA · DARTMOUTH

COLUMBIA · CALTECH · HARVARD · UPENN · USC

Our Services

Crimson's bespoke services help you to achieve your educational aims.

Admissions Consulting

Career Mentoring

Standardized Test Tutoring

 Extracurricular and Leadership

 Merit & Need Based Scholarships

Sports Recruitment

Our Results

267
Offers to the Ivy league

99
Offers to Oxford and Cambridge

1,400+
Offers to US Top 50 universities

600+
Offers to the UK Top 10 universities

Get in touch to learn more about our services:

+1 (888) 504-4424 | USA@CRIMSONEDUCATION.ORG | PAGES.CRIMSONEDUCATION.ORG/USNEWS

Best National Univer

Rank School (State) (*Public)	Overall score	Peer assessment score (5.0=highest)	Graduation and retention rank	Average first-year student retention rate	2019 graduation rate Predicted	2019 graduation rate Actual	Over-performance (+) Under-performance (-)	Pell recipient grad rate	Social mobility rank
1. Princeton University (NJ)	100	4.9	2	98%	93%	98%	+5	98%	203
2. Harvard University (MA)	98	4.9	2	97%	94%	97%	+3	95%	224
3. Columbia University (NY)	97	4.7	4	99%	93%	96%	+3	94%	119
4. Massachusetts Institute of Technology	96	4.9	10	99%	94%	95%	+1	91%	209
4. Yale University (CT)	96	4.8	1	99%	96%	97%	+1	95%	291
6. Stanford University (CA)	95	4.9	10	99%	95%	94%	-1	91%	251
6. University of Chicago	95	4.6	10	99%	98%	95%	-3	94%	334
8. University of Pennsylvania	94	4.6	4	98%	96%	96%	None	92%	265
9. California Institute of Technology	93	4.6	21	98%	97%	94%	-3	100%	340
9. Johns Hopkins University (MD)	93	4.7	18	98%	93%	94%	+1	92%	251
9. Northwestern University (IL)	93	4.5	10	98%	94%	94%	None	91%	243
12. Duke University (NC)	92	4.5	4	98%	95%	95%	None	90%	291
13. Dartmouth College (NH)	91	4.4	4	97%	95%	95%	None	93%	284
14. Brown University (RI)	88	4.5	4	98%	95%	96%	+1	92%	203
14. Vanderbilt University (TN)	88	4.3	18	97%	94%	93%	-1	90%	291
16. Rice University (TX)	87	4.2	18	97%	92%	93%	+1	89%	224
16. Washington University in St. Louis	87	4.2	10	97%	98%	95%	-3	95%	381
18. Cornell University (NY)	86	4.6	10	97%	93%	95%	+2	92%	251
19. University of Notre Dame (IN)	85	4.2	4	98%	96%	96%	None	92%	334
20. University of California–Los Angeles*	84	4.3	26	97%	83%	91%	+8	89%	13
21. Emory University (GA)	83	4.1	28	94%	89%	90%	+1	91%	135
22. University of California–Berkeley*	82	4.7	21	97%	87%	93%	+6	88%	76
23. Georgetown University (DC)	81	4.2	10	96%	96%	95%	-1	90%	284
24. University of Michigan–Ann Arbor*	80	4.5	21	97%	84%	93%	+9	88%	303
24. University of Southern California	80	3.9	26	96%	89%	91%	+2	90%	161
26. Carnegie Mellon University (PA)	79	4.3	28	97%	92%	90%	-2	91%	303
26. University of Virginia*	79	4.3	10	97%	94%	95%	+1	93%	318
28. U. of North Carolina–Chapel Hill*	78	4.2	28	97%	87%	91%	+4	89%	135
28. Wake Forest University (NC)	78	3.6	35	95%	95%	88%	-7	86%	357
30. New York University	77	4.0	47	94%	83%	85%	+2	80%	135
30. Tufts University (MA)	77	3.8	21	96%	96%	94%	-2	95%	318
30. University of California–Santa Barbara*	77	3.6	62	93%	80%	88%	+8	84%	13
30. University of Florida*	77	3.8	34	97%	81%	88%	+7	86%	48
34. University of Rochester (NY)	76	3.5	43	96%	88%	87%	-1	86%	209
35. Boston College	75	3.8	21	95%	92%	94%	+2	96%	259
35. Georgia Institute of Technology*	75	4.3	35	97%	89%	90%	+1	84%	259
35. University of California–Irvine*	75	3.8	52	93%	81%	84%	+3	84%	2
35. University of California–San Diego*	75	3.9	43	94%	82%	87%	+5	85%	33
39. University of California–Davis*	74	3.9	47	93%	80%	87%	+7	83%	15
39. William & Mary (VA)*	74	3.9	28	95%	93%	90%	-3	92%	340
41. Tulane University (LA)	73	3.6	52	93%	86%	86%	None	80%	377
42. Boston University	72	3.7	41	94%	84%	88%	+4	90%	237
42. Brandeis University (MA)	72	3.7	35	93%	87%	87%	None	83%	191
42. Case Western Reserve Univ. (OH)	72	3.7	62	93%	83%	84%	+1	82%	203
42. University of Texas at Austin*	72	4.2	52	95%	82%	86%	+4	79%	135
42. Univ. of Wisconsin–Madison*	72	4.1	41	95%	80%	88%	+8	79%	340
47. University of Georgia*	71	3.7	43	96%	77%	87%	+10	81%	191
47. University of Illinois–Urbana-Champaign*	71	3.9	52	93%	77%	85%	+8	80%	161
49. Lehigh University (PA)	70	3.4	35	95%	84%	90%	+6	83%	278
49. Northeastern University (MA)	70	3.5	35	97%	84%	89%	+5	87%	278
49. Pepperdine University (CA)	70	3.5	52	91%	78%	86%	+8	89%	113
49. University of Miami (FL)	70	3.5	64	92%	86%	83%	-3	80%	251

Note: Key to footnotes, Page 60

sities

Faculty resources rank	% of classes under 20 ('19)	% of classes of 50 or more ('19)	Student/ faculty ratio ('19)	Selectivity rank	SAT/ACT 25th-75th percentile ('19)	Freshmen in top 10% of HS class ('19)	Acceptance rate ('19)	Financial resources rank	Average alumni giving rate
5	75%	9%	5/1	12	1460-1570	91%	6%	12	55%
5	74%	11%	6/1	5	1460-1570	93%	5%	7	30%
2	82%	9%	6/1	5	1450-1570	96%	5%	10	31%
11	71%	11%	3/1	3	1510-1570	95%	7%	2	32%
8	73%	9%	6/1	5	1460-1570	92%	6%	1	26%
12	69%	11%	5/1	5	1440-1570	98%	4%	5	27%
1	79%	6%	5/1	1	1500-1570[2]	99%	6%	9	39%
3	71%	9%	6/1	5	1450-1560	94%	8%	14	38%
8	69%	8%	3/1	1	1530-1560	99%	6%	3	27%
15	77%	9%	6/1	3	1470-1570	98%	10%	3	35%
5	77%	5%	6/1	12	1440-1550	92%	9%	7	31%
4	70%	7%	6/1	5	33-35	95%	8%	15	32%
8	64%	7%	7/1	12	1440-1560	95%	8%	16	44%
17	69%	11%	6/1	16	1440-1570	91%	7%	24	30%
16	61%	8%	7/1	12	33-35	90%	9%	12	29%
13	69%	8%	6/1	5	1470-1570	93%	9%	23	30%
13	66%	10%	7/1	19	33-35[2]	84%	14%	6	24%
26	56%	18%	9/1	23	1400-1560	83%	11%	18	24%
19	62%	9%	9/1	16	32-35	90%	16%	25	42%
32	50%	22%	18/1	26	1280-1530	97%	12%	20	7%
20	62%	13%	9/1	23	1360-1530	84%	16%	16	20%
64	53%	19%	19/1	19	1310-1530	97%	17%	48	8%
31	60%	6%	11/1	19	1380-1550	85%	14%	33	29%
42	55%	18%	15/1	41	1340-1530[2]	78%[5]	23%	41	17%
42	61%	12%	8/1	32	1360-1530	90%[4]	11%	22	39%
20	66%	12%	7/1	16	1460-1560	88%	15%	33	15%
38	53%	15%	14/1	23	1340-1520	90%	24%	44	19%
84	41%	13%	14/1	32	27-33	78%	23%	33	18%
20	60%	2%	10/1	32	30-33[2]	75%	30%	10	23%
25	60%	10%	9/1	28	1350-1530[2]	79%	16%	28	11%
32	68%	8%	9/1	26	1390-1540	80%	15%	31	22%
23	51%	19%	17/1	28	1240-1490	100%	30%	64	17%
56	53%	10%	17/1	32	1310-1470	81%	37%	46	16%
17	77%	8%	10/1	79	1310-1500[9]	69%	30%	21	22%
42	49%	6%	11/1	41	1340-1500	82%[5]	27%	64	23%
84	44%	22%	19/1	19	1370-1530	90%	21%	59	17%
64	52%	23%	18/1	46	1160-1440	99%	27%	68	7%
93	47%	27%	19/1	30	1230-1490	100%	32%	25	4%
166	36%	30%	20/1	45	1150-1420	100%	39%	33	7%
42	53%	6%	11/1	32	1320-1510	75%	38%	108	28%
24	66%	6%	8/1	32	31-33	64%	13%	27	18%
26	62%	12%	10/1	51	1340-1510[2]	64%[5]	19%	48	10%
53	58%	11%	10/1	46	1350-1520[2]	56%	30%	48	19%
48	50%	14%	11/1	32	1340-1510	70%	27%	37	18%
116	37%	24%	18/1	32	1230-1480	87%	32%	76	9%
123	44%	22%	17/1	54	27-32	57%	54%	59	13%
67	48%	11%	17/1	54	1240-1420	60%	46%	119	13%
104	38%	21%	20/1	59	1220-1480	55%	59%	64	6%
38	51%	10%	9/1	51	1280-1450	58%	32%	52	15%
36	68%	6%	14/1	41	1390-1540	75%[5]	18%	72	12%
38	69%	2%	13/1	72	1230-1450	46%	32%	56	9%
56	51%	9%	12/1	54	1270-1440	59%	27%	28	10%

What Is a National University?

TO ASSESS MORE than 1,800 of the country's four-year colleges and universities, U.S. News first assigns each to a group of its peers, based on the categories of higher education institutions developed by the Carnegie Foundation for the Advancement of Teaching. The National Universities category consists of 389 institutions (209 public, 176 private and 4 for-profit) that offer a wide range of undergraduate majors as well as master's and doctoral degrees or professional practice doctorates; some institutions emphasize research. A list of the top 30 public national universities appears on Page 71.

Data on 17 indicators of academic quality are gathered from each institution. Schools are ranked by total weighted score; those tied are listed alphabetically. For a description of the methodology, see Page 58. For more on a college, turn to the directory at the back of the book.

Rank School (State) (*Public)	Overall score	Peer assessment score (5.0=highest)	Average first-year student retention rate	2019 graduation rate		Pell recipient grad rate	% of classes under 20 ('19)	% of classes of 50 or more ('19)	SAT/ACT 25th-75th percentile ('19)	Freshmen in top 10% of HS class ('19)	Accept-ance rate ('19)	Average alumni giving rate
				Predicted	Actual							
53. Ohio State University–Columbus*	69	3.8	94%	76%	86%	79%	32%	22%	28-32[2]	60%	54%	14%
53. Purdue University–West Lafayette (IN)*	69	3.8	92%	74%	82%	73%	39%	19%	1190-1440	49%	60%	17%
53. Rensselaer Polytechnic Inst. (NY)	69	3.6	93%	85%	85%	81%	54%	10%	1330-1510	63%	47%	10%
53. Santa Clara University (CA)	69	3.2	95%	82%	91%	88%	45%	0.4%	1280-1440	52%[5]	49%	19%
53. Villanova University (PA)	69	3.4	96%	86%	90%	88%	44%	3%	1320-1470	72%	28%	29%
58. Florida State University*	68	3.3	93%	70%	83%	81%	60%	11%	1200-1340	47%	36%	18%
58. Syracuse University (NY)	68	3.5	91%	76%	83%	81%	59%	10%	1180-1380[2]	33%	44%	11%
58. Univ. of Maryland–College Park*	68	3.8	95%	85%	87%	84%	45%	17%	1280-1480	69%	44%	6%
58. University of Pittsburgh*	68	3.6	93%	77%	83%	75%	45%	18%	1260-1440	53%	57%	7%
58. University of Washington*	68	3.9	94%	87%	84%	79%	29%	25%	1220-1470	59%	52%	11%
63. Pennsylvania State U.–Univ. Park*	67	3.7	93%	72%	86%	77%	29%	17%	1160-1370	43%[4]	49%	11%
63. Rutgers University–New Brunswick (NJ)*	67	3.4	93%	68%	84%	80%	42%	20%	1210-1430	38%	61%	7%
63. University of Connecticut*	67	3.4	93%	75%	85%	80%	53%	16%	1190-1390	55%	49%	8%
66. Fordham University (NY)	66	3.3	91%	77%	83%	80%	52%	1%	1240-1450	46%	46%	17%
66. George Washington University (DC)	66	3.6	92%	83%	82%	76%	52%	10%	1280-1470[2]	53%	41%	7%
66. Loyola Marymount University (CA)	66	3.1	90%	74%	80%	77%	55%	1%	1230-1410	47%[5]	44%	17%
66. Southern Methodist University (TX)	66	3.3	91%	81%	81%	73%	57%	10%	29-33	49%	47%	14%
66. Texas A&M University*	66	3.7	92%	75%	82%	76%	25%	28%	1160-1390	70%	58%	16%
66. Univ. of Massachusetts–Amherst*	66	3.5	91%	70%	82%	78%	50%	18%	1190-1390	31%	64%	9%
66. University of Minnesota–Twin Cities*	66	3.7	93%	76%	83%	77%	38%	19%	26-31	50%	57%	7%
66. Worcester Polytechnic Inst. (MA)	66	3.0	95%	84%	89%	85%	63%	11%	1310-1470[2]	63%	49%	9%
74. Clemson University (SC)*	65	3.4	93%	81%	84%	72%	53%	14%	1230-1400	56%	51%	23%
74. Virginia Tech*	65	3.7	93%	77%	86%	83%	29%	23%	1180-1390[2]	29%[5]	70%	13%
76. American University (DC)	64	3.3	89%	81%	79%	78%	55%	2%	1210-1390[2]	32%	36%	6%
76. Baylor University (TX)	64	3.3	89%	75%	78%	66%	53%	9%	26-32	44%	45%	14%
76. Indiana University–Bloomington*	64	3.7	91%	71%	79%	69%	39%	16%	1150-1360	35%	78%	12%
76. Yeshiva University (NY)	64	2.9	91%	83%	82%	79%	65%	1%	24-30	N/A	55%	14%
80. Brigham Young Univ.–Provo (UT)	63	3.2	90%	83%	78%	72%	46%	12%	26-31	56%	67%	12%
80. Gonzaga University (WA)	63	3.1	94%	77%	85%	85%	38%	1%	1200-1360	40%	62%	12%
80. Howard University (DC)	63	3.3	88%	58%	65%	60%	52%	6%	1130-1280	28%	36%	11%
80. Michigan State University*	63	3.6	92%	69%	81%	71%	24%	24%	1100-1320	28%	71%	6%
80. North Carolina State U.*	63	3.2	94%	76%	83%	78%	35%	16%	1250-1420[2]	50%	45%	11%
80. Stevens Institute of Technology (NJ)	63	2.9	95%	81%	85%	77%	44%	10%	1340-1500[2]	74%	40%	16%
80. Texas Christian University	63	3.1	91%	79%	83%	84%	40%	4%	25-31[2]	47%	47%	16%
80. University of Denver	63	3.1	87%	78%	77%	74%	61%	6%	26-31[2]	39%	59%	10%
88. Binghamton University–SUNY*	62	3.0	91%	74%	81%	81%	48%	13%	1280-1440	55%	41%	6%
88. Colorado School of Mines*	62	3.5	92%	81%	83%	78%	29%	21%	1260-1460	50%	53%	9%
88. Elon University (NC)	62	3.0	90%	79%	85%	88%	52%	0%	1160-1320[2]	25%	78%	25%
88. Marquette University (WI)	62	3.2	89%	74%	82%	77%	46%	9%	24-29	33%	83%	15%
88. Stony Brook–SUNY*	62	3.3	90%	67%	76%	80%	34%	25%	1230-1440	51%	44%	5%
88. University at Buffalo–SUNY*	62	3.2	87%	64%	75%	71%	30%	22%	1160-1340	30%	61%	11%
88. University of California–Riverside*	62	3.2	90%	72%	76%	75%	21%	32%	1110-1340[2]	94%	57%	2%
88. University of Iowa*	62	3.6	86%	69%	72%	60%	52%	13%	22-29	32%	83%	7%
88. University of San Diego	62	3.1	90%	77%	81%	79%	39%	0.1%	1190-1370[2]	33%	49%	11%
97. Auburn University (AL)*	61	3.3	91%	73%	79%	68%	36%	16%	25-31	33%	81%	14%
97. University of Arizona*	61	3.6	82%	66%	65%	59%	45%	16%	1110-1360[2]	36%	85%	9%
97. University of California–Merced*	61	2.8	83%	47%	69%	68%	29%	29%	980-1180	N/A	72%	10%
97. University of California–Santa Cruz*	61	3.2	90%	81%	77%	74%	20%	28%	1190-1390	96%	52%	3%
97. University of Delaware*	61	3.3	91%	76%	81%	72%	32%	17%	1170-1360[2]	30%	68%	9%
97. University of Utah*	61	3.3	90%	67%	70%	55%	39%	18%	22-29	N/A	62%	12%
103. Arizona State University–Tempe*	60	3.4	87%	64%	71%	63%	35%	18%	22-28[2]	31%	86%	9%
103. Clark University (MA)	60	2.8	87%	75%	79%	72%	54%	5%	1180-1370[2]	27%	53%	14%
103. Miami University–Oxford (OH)*	60	3.2	91%	74%	82%	75%	31%	12%	26-31	32%	80%	17%
103. Saint Louis University	60	3.1	91%	76%	80%	67%	39%	9%	25-30	38%	58%	10%
103. Temple University (PA)*	60	3.1	90%	61%	74%	65%	41%	8%	1120-1320[2]	36%	60%	5%
103. University of Colorado Boulder*	60	3.7	88%	73%	69%	61%	44%	17%	1140-1360	26%	78%	6%

Note: Key to footnotes, Page 60

Northwestern
University

Rank	School (State) (*Public)	Overall score	Peer assessment score (5.0=highest)	Average first-year student retention rate	2019 graduation rate Predicted	Actual	Pell recipient grad rate	% of classes under 20 ('19)	% of classes of 50 or more ('19)	SAT/ACT 25th-75th percentile ('19)	Freshmen in top 10% of HS class ('19)	Acceptance rate ('19)	Average alumni giving rate
103.	University of Oregon*	60	3.5	86%	67%	74%	67%	38%	21%	1100-1310[2]	26%[5]	82%	7%
103.	University of San Francisco	60	3.0	85%	69%	75%	76%	42%	2%	1130-1330[2]	32%	64%	6%
103.	University of South Florida*	60	2.8	91%	62%	75%	72%	44%	13%	1170-1330	34%	48%	12%
112.	Creighton University (NE)	59	3.0	89%	77%	78%	75%	46%	5%	23-29[2]	35%	74%	14%
112.	Loyola University Chicago	59	3.3	84%	70%	74%	67%	35%	6%	25-30	35%	67%	5%
112.	Rochester Inst. of Technology (NY)	59	3.5	89%	66%	69%	66%	48%	5%	1220-1410[2]	39%	70%	5%
112.	University of Illinois–Chicago*	59	3.1	80%	51%	61%	59%	35%	18%	1030-1260	28%	73%	2%
112.	University of La Verne (CA)	59	2.1	83%	49%	73%	71%	66%	0%	1040-1190[2]	21%	55%	4%
112.	University of Tennessee*	59	3.3	87%	72%	72%	62%	31%	15%	24-30	35%	79%	11%
118.	Iowa State University*	58	3.3	88%	69%	74%	65%	32%	20%	22-28	28%	92%	11%
118.	New Jersey Inst. of Technology*	58	2.8	88%	59%	67%	63%	37%	3%	1190-1390	31%	73%	9%
118.	Rutgers University–Newark (NJ)*	58	2.8	85%	54%	69%	71%	27%	16%	1020-1200	22%	72%	5%
118.	SUNY Col. of Envir. Sci. and Forestry*	58	2.7	80%	68%	75%	73%	51%	10%	1120-1300	31%	70%	15%
118.	Univ. of South Carolina*	58	3.2	88%	71%	77%	67%	38%	16%	1180-1370	28%	69%	11%
118.	University of Vermont*	58	3.1	87%	76%	76%	68%	49%	14%	1180-1360	34%	67%	8%
124.	Chapman University (CA)	57	2.6	90%	74%	81%	77%	44%	4%	1190-1380[2]	36%	56%	8%
124.	Clarkson University (NY)	57	2.7	89%	72%	81%	77%	53%	17%	1160-1350[2]	37%	75%	15%
124.	DePaul University (IL)	57	3.0	85%	62%	74%	68%	39%	1%	1070-1290[2]	N/A	68%	6%
124.	Drake University (IA)	57	2.8	87%	76%	82%	68%	49%	8%	24-31[2]	41%	68%	10%
124.	Gallaudet University (DC)	57	3.0	73%	54%	51%	49%	97%	0%	14-19	N/A	61%	10%
124.	Illinois Institute of Technology	57	2.9	91%	69%	70%	66%	44%	11%	1190-1400	47%	60%	6%
124.	Seattle University	57	2.7	86%	69%	73%	67%	62%	1%	1150-1330	28%	78%	6%
124.	University of Kansas*	57	3.4	84%	69%	66%	52%	47%	13%	22-29	29%	93%	12%
124.	Univ. of Missouri*	57	3.3	87%	70%	71%	59%	41%	15%	23-29	33%	81%	12%
133.	Drexel University (PA)	56	3.1	89%	69%	69%	62%	52%	10%	1190-1390	35%	75%	6%
133.	The New School (NY)	56	2.9	82%	67%	69%	63%	92%	1%	1150-1380[9]	20%[5]	57%	1%
133.	Seton Hall University (NJ)	56	3.0	84%	67%	73%	67%	49%	2%	1150-1330	34%	74%	11%
133.	Simmons University (MA)	56	2.4	83%	66%	81%	80%	66%	2%	1110-1290	28%	73%	12%
133.	University of Dayton (OH)	56	2.7	90%	74%	82%	75%	38%	4%	23-29[3]	27%	72%	12%[4]
133.	University of Kentucky*	56	3.2	84%	67%	66%	54%	34%	16%	22-29	33%	96%	11%
133.	Univ. of Nebraska–Lincoln*	56	3.3	83%	67%	65%	54%	36%	18%	22-28	28%	78%	17%
133.	University of Oklahoma*	56	3.2	90%	68%	70%	59%	45%	11%	23-29	33%	80%	8%
133.	University of St. Thomas (MN)	56	2.6	87%	71%	76%	71%	34%	1%	24-29	21%	83%	11%
133.	University of the Pacific (CA)	56	2.6	83%	65%	67%	63%	47%	7%	1120-1360	37%	66%	5%
143.	The Catholic University of America (DC)	55	2.9	86%	75%	72%	62%	60%	4%	1130-1330[2]	N/A	85%	10%
143.	Duquesne University (PA)	55	2.8	86%	69%	80%	72%	40%	9%	1130-1300[2]	25%	74%	6%
143.	George Mason University (VA)*	55	3.2	87%	64%	71%	67%	31%	14%	1110-1320[2]	15%	87%	2%
143.	Samford University (AL)	55	2.6	89%	77%	76%	65%	60%	3%	23-29	33%	83%	7%
143.	San Diego State University*	55	3.0	89%	61%	74%	70%	28%	25%	1110-1320	33%	34%	4%
143.	University of Alabama*	55	3.2	87%	73%	71%	56%	34%	21%	23-31	40%	83%	21%
143.	University of Cincinnati*	55	2.9	87%	62%	71%	60%	37%	17%	23-29	24%	77%	9%
143.	University of New Hampshire*	55	3.0	86%	67%	77%	73%	35%	16%	1070-1270[2]	22%	84%	7%
143.	University of Texas at Dallas*	55	2.9	88%	67%	71%	67%	20%	23%	1240-1460	39%	79%	3%
143.	University of Tulsa (OK)	55	2.7	89%	84%	72%	56%	58%	4%	24-31	56%	36%	15%
153.	Colorado State University*	54	3.1	85%	66%	70%	62%	29%	24%	1070-1290	21%	81%	10%
153.	Louisiana State University–Baton Rouge*	54	3.0	83%	66%	68%	57%	41%	17%	23-29	24%	75%	13%
153.	Michigan Technological University*	54	2.8	84%	66%	70%	59%	49%	14%	1170-1370	31%	74%	8%
153.	Oregon State University*	54	3.1	84%	63%	67%	56%	33%	21%	1080-1320	27%	84%	7%
153.	Quinnipiac University[1] (CT)	54	2.7	87%[8]	71%	77%[6]	73%[4]	45%[4]	2%[4]	1090-1260[4]	20%[4]	72%[4]	4%[4]
153.	Rutgers University–Camden (NJ)*	54	2.7	87%	53%	65%	64%	42%	8%	980-1170	19%	79%	4%
153.	University of Alabama at Birmingham*	54	2.9	83%	61%	63%	54%	44%	17%	22-29	29%	74%	6%
160.	Belmont University (TN)	53	2.7	83%	74%	72%	63%	46%	0.1%	24-29	32%	84%	9%
160.	Hofstra University (NY)	53	2.9	82%	67%	65%	58%	47%	2%	1160-1340[2]	32%	68%	12%
160.	Mercer University (GA)	53	2.6	87%	67%	66%	57%	55%	5%	1170-1340	36%	74%	10%
160.	University at Albany–SUNY*	53	2.9	82%	59%	63%	63%	30%	18%	1090-1250	18%	54%	6%
160.	University of Arkansas*	53	3.0	83%	67%	66%	49%	48%	17%	23-30	25%	77%	18%

Note: Key to footnotes, Page 60

Rank, School (State) (*Public)	Overall score	Peer assessment score (5.0=highest)	Average first-year student retention rate	2019 graduation rate		Pell recipient grad rate	% of classes under 20 ('19)	% of classes of 50 or more ('19)	SAT/ACT 25th-75th percentile ('19)	Freshmen in top 10% of HS class ('19)	Acceptance rate ('19)	Average alumni giving rate
				Predicted	Actual							
160. University of Central Florida*	53	2.9	90%	63%	72%	70%	27%	24%	1170-1340	36%	44%	4%
160. Univ. of Maryland–Baltimore County*	53	3.0	87%	66%	71%	70%	39%	14%	1180-1360	21%	61%	4%
160. University of Mississippi*	53	3.0	86%	66%	66%	51%	54%	12%	21-29[2]	25%	88%	9%
160. Valparaiso University (IN)	53	2.8	83%	69%	71%	66%	55%	5%	1070-1290	36%	86%	12%
160. Virginia Commonwealth University*	53	3.0	84%	62%	68%	63%	47%	16%	1070-1260[2]	18%	87%	5%
170. Adelphi University (NY)	52	2.3	81%	61%	73%	65%	48%	1%	1090-1270[9]	28%[5]	74%	7%
170. Kansas State University*	52	3.0	85%	66%	65%	52%	47%	12%	22-28	28%	96%	18%
170. St. John's University (NY)	52	2.8	84%	54%	63%	57%	33%	4%	1080-1300[2]	21%	72%	4%
170. University of Hawaii–Manoa*	52	2.8	79%	64%	61%	57%	51%	12%	1070-1270[3]	24%	58%	4%
170. University of Idaho*	52	2.8	79%	55%	56%	49%	57%	9%	1010-1240	18%	78%	9%
170. University of Rhode Island*	52	2.9	84%	63%	69%	62%	43%	11%	1080-1260[3]	18%	75%	5%
176. CUNY–City College[1]*	51	2.9	86%[8]	48%	51%[6]	44%[4]	33%[4]	3%[4]	950-1190[4]	N/A	38%[4]	9%[4]
176. Missouri U. of Science and Technology*	51	2.8	82%	67%	66%	56%	39%	18%	26-32	41%	79%	11%
176. Montclair State University (NJ)*	51	2.3	81%	48%	67%	66%	38%	3%	990-1180[2]	12%	76%	3%
176. Ohio University*	51	3.0	81%	59%	65%	54%	34%	16%	21-26	20%	82%	4%
176. St. John Fisher College (NY)	51	2.2	86%	65%	75%	74%	37%	2%	1070-1260	21%	64%	7%
176. Thomas Jefferson University (PA)	51	2.4	83%	67%	70%	59%	63%	4%	1070-1270	23%	66%	2%
176. University of Houston*	51	2.9	85%	59%	61%	58%	26%	24%	1140-1310	32%	65%	11%
176. University of Louisville (KY)*	51	2.9	80%	59%	59%	48%	42%	8%	22-29[3]	27%	70%	10%
176. Univ. of Massachusetts–Lowell*	51	2.6	85%	61%	66%	59%	47%	7%	1150-1320[2]	25%	73%	10%
176. University of St. Joseph (CT)	51	2.2	79%	48%	55%	48%	69%	0%	1030-1210[2]	17%	77%	9%
176. Washington State University*	51	3.1	80%	64%	60%	50%	33%	21%	1020-1240	N/A	76%	11%
187. Biola University (CA)	50	2.1	85%	69%	74%	66%	49%	5%	1080-1310	45%	71%	7%

Rank	School (State) (*Public)	Overall score	Peer assessment score (5.0=highest)	Average first-year student retention rate	2019 graduation rate		Pell recipient grad rate	% of classes under 20 ('19)	% of classes of 50 or more ('19)	SAT/ACT 25th-75th percentile ('19)	Freshmen in top 10% of HS class ('19)	Acceptance rate ('19)	Average alumni giving rate
					Predicted	Actual							
187.	Chatham University (PA)	50	2.3	81%	62%	70%	62%	61%	1%	1050-1270[2]	24%	62%	12%
187.	Florida International University*	50	2.6	89%	53%	61%	64%	30%	18%	1110-1280	35%[5]	58%	4%
187.	Oklahoma State University*	50	2.9	82%	64%	65%	49%	39%	16%	21-28	27%	70%	9%
187.	Pacific University (OR)	50	2.5	80%	63%	69%	61%	59%	2%	1060-1260	N/A	87%	7%
187.	Rowan University (NJ)*	50	2.4	84%	63%	72%	63%	33%	1%	990-1200	N/A	74%	3%
187.	University of Detroit Mercy	50	2.2	84%	61%	67%	60%	44%	3%	1060-1250	26%	77%	7%
187.	University of New Mexico*	50	2.9	77%	58%	53%	46%	58%	8%	19-25	N/A	49%	N/A
187.	University of North Carolina–Wilmington*	50	2.6	85%	68%	72%	67%	35%	8%	22-27	24%	65%	5%
196.	Bethel University (MN)	49	2.1	85%	70%	73%	66%	60%	1%	21-27	24%	79%	7%
196.	California State University–Fresno*	49	2.6	81%	39%	56%	53%	18%	8%	940-1130	15%	58%	3%
196.	Indiana University-Purdue U.–Indianapolis*	49	3.0	74%	51%	51%	41%	47%	8%	1000-1200	14%	81%	7%
196.	Loyola University New Orleans	49	2.8	81%	63%	62%	53%	43%	2%	22-28[2]	N/A[5]	75%	5%
196.	Maryville Univ. of St. Louis	49	2.0	85%	62%	71%	64%	67%	0.3%	20-25[2]	25%	83%	5%
196.	Robert Morris University (PA)	49	2.2	81%	55%	65%	55%	42%	3%	1020-1210	16%	84%	7%
196.	Seattle Pacific University	49	2.5	80%	68%	68%	60%	57%	2%	1020-1250	1%[4]	91%	4%
196.	Towson University (MD)*	49	2.5	85%	61%	71%	68%	30%	3%	1060-1220	15%	76%	4%
196.	University of Puerto Rico–Rio Piedras[1]*	49	2.5	77%[8]	55%	57%[8]	60%[4]	49%[4]	1%[4]	N/A[2]	N/A	43%[4]	N/A
196.	University of Wyoming*	49	2.8	77%	66%	60%	44%	38%	12%	22-28	24%	96%	7%
206.	Bellarmine University (KY)	48	2.2	78%	62%	66%	59%	54%	1%	22-28	N/A	84%	11%
206.	Florida Institute of Technology	48	2.5	81%	66%	59%	51%	47%	5%	1150-1360	26%	66%	7%
206.	Georgia State University*	48	3.0	82%	52%	55%	55%	23%	16%	990-1190[3]	N/A	57%	3%
206.	Illinois State University*	48	2.5	80%	59%	70%	59%	37%	10%	1020-1220	N/A	82%	6%
206.	Lipscomb University (TN)	48	2.2	82%	70%	68%	58%	60%	5%	23-29	27%	63%	12%
206.	Misericordia University (PA)	48	2.0	82%	60%	68%	56%	53%	0%	1050-1220	18%	86%	9%
206.	Mississippi State University*	48	2.8	80%	62%	61%	45%	40%	15%	22-30	30%	66%	17%
206.	Russell Sage College (NY)	48	2.1	77%	45%	71%	69%	54%	0%	900-1100[2]	15%	85%	7%
206.	Union University (TN)	48	2.0	86%	65%	68%	58%	73%	0%	22-30	36%	53%	3%
206.	University of Maine*	48	2.9	76%	59%	57%	48%	38%	16%	1050-1260	20%	90%	7%
206.	Widener University (PA)	48	2.3	81%	56%	65%	54%	56%	2%	1040-1210	N/A	72%	3%
217.	East Carolina University (NC)*	47	2.5	82%	57%	66%	62%	32%	17%	1030-1190	13%	79%	2%
217.	Hampton University (VA)	47	2.4	77%	59%	57%	50%	71%	9%	20-25[2]	12%	36%	17%
217.	Kent State University[7] (OH)*	47	2.6	81%	53%	60%	52%	53%	8%	20-26	17%	86%	3%
217.	Pace University (NY)	47	2.5	79%	57%	57%	48%	51%	3%	1050-1230[2]	18%	79%	4%
217.	Regis University (CO)	47	2.2	81%	61%	64%	66%	61%	1%	1030-1240	28%	71%	4%
217.	Sacred Heart University (CT)	47	2.4	83%	66%	73%	69%	39%	2%	1120-1260[2]	10%	64%	10%
217.	Texas Tech University*	47	3.0	85%	64%	61%	52%	26%	23%	1070-1260	19%	69%	11%
217.	University of Hartford (CT)	47	2.6	75%	58%	60%	48%	69%	0.1%	1030-1230[2]	N/A	76%	4%
217.	Univ. of Massachusetts–Dartmouth*	47	2.7	72%	55%	59%	54%	51%	10%	990-1190[2]	14%	75%	2%
217.	Wilkes University (PA)	47	2.0	77%	55%	63%	51%	62%	3%	1020-1218	20%	79%	13%
227.	Azusa Pacific University[1] (CA)	46	2.2	84%[8]	64%	67%[6]	65%[4]	57%[4]	2%[4]	1020-1240[4]	N/A	69%[4]	N/A
227.	Clarke University (IA)	46	2.1	72%	55%	63%	65%	77%	0.4%	18-23	17%	94%	14%
227.	Edgewood College (WI)	46	1.8	78%	58%	64%	55%	82%	0.3%	20-25	16%	72%	6%
227.	Gannon University (PA)	46	2.0	82%	59%	68%	56%	50%	0.3%	1030-1240	31%[5]	76%	6%
227.	George Fox University (OR)	46	2.1	83%	64%	68%	63%	53%	4%	1030-1270	32%	82%	5%
227.	Lincoln Memorial University (TN)	46	1.9	74%	46%	56%	54%	60%	3%	19-25[9]	22%	49%	4%
227.	Nova Southeastern University (FL)	46	2.0	79%	58%	57%	51%	74%	1%	1020-1250	34%	80%	3%
227.	University of Colorado Denver*	46	2.9	70%	58%	52%	50%	37%	9%	1000-1220	20%	67%	3%
227.	University of Indianapolis	46	2.4	75%	55%	59%	51%	59%	0.2%	980-1190	17%	83%	11%
227.	Univ. of Massachusetts–Boston*	46	2.7	77%	51%	49%	48%	37%	7%	1010-1220[2]	15%	76%	4%
227.	University of Nevada–Reno*	46	2.5	81%	60%	61%	54%	42%	21%	21-26	28%	88%	6%
227.	U. of North Carolina–Charlotte*	46	2.9	83%	60%	64%	63%	27%	25%	1120-1290	17%	65%	3%
227.	University of St. Francis (IL)	46	2.0	81%	53%	62%	53%	59%	1%	1030-1220[2]	N/A	46%	6%
227.	Western New England University (MA)	46	2.0	77%	60%	65%	61%	56%	1%	1080-1242[2]	22%	85%	4%
241.	Florida A&M University*	45	2.5	82%	44%	53%	52%	38%	11%	1030-1160	12%	36%	3%
241.	Immaculata University (PA)	45	1.9	80%	51%	67%	55%	80%	0%	980-1198[2]	7%	81%	7%

Note: Key to footnotes, Page 60

Rank. School (State) (*Public)	Overall score	Peer assessment score (5.0=highest)	Average first-year student retention rate	2019 graduation rate Predicted	2019 graduation rate Actual	Pell recipient grad rate	% of classes under 20 ('19)	% of classes of 50 or more ('19)	SAT/ACT 25th-75th percentile ('19)	Freshmen in top 10% of HS class ('19)	Acceptance rate ('19)	Average alumni giving rate
241. New Mexico State University*	45	2.6	74%	50%	48%	41%	46%	10%	18-23	22%	55%	6%
241. Oklahoma City University[1]	45	2.1	82%	70%	65%	57%	71%[4]	1%[4]	23-29[4]	31%[4]	76%[4]	4%
241. Shenandoah University (VA)	45	2.1	82%	58%	60%	52%	67%	1%	1000-1200	11%	76%	5%
241. University of Findlay (OH)	45	1.9	80%	62%	65%	78%	68%	1%	21-26	22%	77%	9%
241. Utah State University*	45	2.7	72%	62%	54%	45%	47%	12%	21-28	23%	91%	5%
241. West Virginia University[1]*	45	2.9	78%[8]	61%	58%[6]	47%[4]	35%[4]	20%[4]	21-27[4]	23%[4]	82%[4]	10%[4]
249. Central Michigan University*	44	2.4	76%	55%	61%	52%	35%	6%	990-1200	18%	70%	7%
249. Harding University (AR)	44	2.0	84%	69%	69%	56%	55%	7%	21-29	28%	61%	9%
249. Lesley University (MA)	44	2.2	80%	61%	59%[6]	N/A	70%	0%	1000-1210	5%	75%	N/A
249. Montana State University*	44	2.7	77%	63%	56%	49%	45%	13%	21-27	21%	82%	8%
249. St. Catherine University (MN)	44	2.1	80%	57%	63%	53%	67%	2%	19-25[3]	27%	67%	N/A
249. University of New England (ME)	44	2.2	79%	64%	68%	61%	55%	6%	1040-1220[2]	N/A	84%	6%
249. University of North Texas*	44	2.6	79%	56%	57%	55%	26%	20%	1060-1260	23%	74%	5%
249. University of South Dakota*	44	2.7	76%	61%	59%	48%	45%	7%	19-25	12%	86%	4%
249. Wayne State University (MI)*	44	2.6	80%	52%	48%	42%	30%	12%	1010-1230	18%[4]	73%	5%
258. Baker University (KS)	43	1.8	76%	56%	64%	56%	73%	0.3%	20-25	21%	88%	7%
258. Bowling Green State University (OH)*	43	2.7	77%	55%	60%	46%	42%	9%	20-25	16%	72%	5%
258. Campbell University (NC)	43	2.2	74%	58%	55%	48%	60%	4%	1030-1230	27%	78%	5%
258. College of St. Scholastica (MN)	43	1.9	81%	63%	69%	66%	54%	2%	22-26[9]	23%	75%	5%
258. Concordia University Wisconsin	43	2.1	78%	59%	64%	56%	59%	2%	21-26	32%	64%	3%
258. Old Dominion University (VA)*	43	2.6	79%	51%	53%	47%	37%	10%	980-1180[2]	10%	89%	4%
258. Southern Illinois University–Carbondale*	43	2.4	70%	50%	48%	36%	64%	4%	1070-1420	20%	66%	3%
258. University of Memphis*	43	2.6	74%	49%	53%	45%	48%	8%	19-26	16%	85%	5%
258. Univ. of Missouri–St. Louis*	43	2.5	76%	57%	52%	45%	55%	7%	21-27	32%	73%	4%
258. University of Montana*	43	2.8	69%	58%	49%	36%	57%	9%	20-26	16%	94%	8%
258. University of Nevada–Las Vegas*	43	2.7	77%	54%	45%	40%	36%	13%	19-25	23%	81%	4%
258. U. of North Carolina–Greensboro*	43	2.7	76%	54%	59%	57%	25%	20%	1000-1160	13%	82%	6%
258. University of North Dakota*	43	2.7	80%	68%	61%	48%	37%	11%	20-26	19%	81%	7%
258. Western Michigan University*	43	2.5	79%	56%	57%	49%	40%	10%	1000-1210	12%	80%	4%
272. Dallas Baptist University	42	2.1	74%	61%	58%	51%	66%	3%	21-26	24%	90%	1%
272. Florida Atlantic University*	42	2.5	80%	52%	50%	52%	25%	17%	1080-1240	16%	63%	3%
272. Long Island University (NY)	42	2.2	78%[8]	52%	46%	41%	66%	2%	1080-1290	19%	80%	3%
272. North Carolina A&T State Univ.*	42	2.3	78%	42%	51%	47%	25%	7%	960-1130	12%	58%	9%
272. Sam Houston State University (TX)*	42	2.3	76%	47%	55%	50%	29%	11%	990-1140	N/A	83%	7%
272. Tennessee Technological Univ.*	42	2.3	78%	54%	54%	46%	46%	10%	21-27[2]	28%	79%	6%
272. University of Akron (OH)*	42	2.3	73%	49%	52%	41%	43%	7%	19-25	16%	73%	3%
272. University of Alabama–Huntsville*	42	2.5	83%	64%	58%	41%	28%	22%	25-31	38%[5]	81%	2%
272. Univ. of Missouri–Kansas City*	42	2.6	75%	60%	50%	38%	49%	13%	21-28	30%	61%	5%
272. University of North Florida*	42	2.4	81%	62%	61%	60%	27%	11%	1090-1260	15%	72%	3%
272. University of the Incarnate Word (TX)	42	2.0	75%	48%	52%	48%	63%	2%	950-1160	18%	94%	4%
272. William Carey University (MS)	42	1.8	80%	47%	47%	48%	78%	1%	20-28	26%	55%	4%
284. Ball State University[1] (IN)*	41	2.6	79%[8]	56%	62%[6]	N/A	N/A	N/A	N/A[2]	N/A	65%[4]	N/A
284. Delaware State University*	41	2.3	72%	41%	42%	42%	46%	3%	820-1020	11%	53%	11%
284. D'Youville College (NY)	41	1.7	80%	60%	63%	53%	63%	1%	1080-1200	N/A	88%	12%
284. Gardner-Webb University (NC)	41	2.1	74%	54%	59%	49%	73%	0%	970-1180	13%	67%	2%
284. Indiana Univ. of Pennsylvania*	41	2.2	72%	47%	56%	43%	38%	9%	910-1120[3]	9%	93%	5%
284. Keiser University (FL)	41	1.6	81%	35%	60%	61%	45%	30%	N/A[2]	N/A	85%	1%[4]
284. Marshall University (WV)*	41	2.5	73%	49%	49%	40%	50%	4%	19-25	N/A	87%	4%
284. North Dakota State University*	41	2.5	79%	67%	60%	47%	36%	24%	21-26[3]	16%	94%	5%
284. Northern Arizona University*	41	2.6	76%	57%	57%	48%	31%	16%	19-25[2]	21%	85%	3%
284. Portland State University (OR)*	41	2.6	73%	53%	46%	45%	39%	11%	1000-1220[2]	15%	96%	1%
284. South Dakota State University*	41	2.6	78%	62%	56%	42%	29%	19%	19-26	16%	90%	8%
284. Touro College (NY)	41	1.8	75%	52%	62%	44%	87%	1%	22-29[2]	N/A	69%	N/A
284. University of Nebraska–Omaha*	41	2.6	76%	56%	51%	47%	44%	6%	19-26	16%	83%	5%
284. University of Texas–Rio Grande Valley*	41	2.2	75%[8]	34%	44%[6]	N/A	25%	14%	17-22	23%	80%	0.3%

School (State) (*Public)	Peer assessment score (5.0=highest)	Average first-year student retention rate	2019 graduation rate		Pell recipient grad rate	% of classes under 20 ('19)	% of classes of 50 or more ('19)	SAT/ACT 25th-75th percentile ('19)	Freshmen in top 10% of HS class ('19)	Acceptance rate ('19)	Average alumni giving rate
			Predicted	Actual							
SCHOOLS RANKED 298 THROUGH 389 ARE LISTED HERE ALPHABETICALLY											
Alliant International University[1] (CA)	1.4	67%[8]	40%	16%	N/A	73%[4]	1%[4]	N/A[2]	N/A	N/A	N/A
Andrews University (MI)	1.9	86%	65%	59%	47%	68%	3%	21-29	17%	67%	4%
Arkansas State University*	2.2	75%	50%	50%	38%	46%	6%	21-27[2]	23%	80%	9%
Augusta University (GA)*	2.1	73%	57%	40%	37%	N/A	N/A	19-26[3]	N/A	76%	3%
Aurora University[1] (IL)	1.9	72%[8]	46%	55%[6]	N/A	N/A	N/A	970-1150[4]	N/A	81%[4]	N/A
Barry University (FL)	2.1	63%	42%	35%	32%	69%	0%	930-1080	N/A	51%	1%[4]
Benedictine University (IL)	2.2	71%	55%	46%	40%	60%	0.2%	19-25	13%	42%	4%
Boise State University (ID)*	2.7	80%	56%	50%	41%	33%	11%	1030-1230[2]	15%	77%	6%
Cardinal Stritch University (WI)	1.9	71%	48%	50%	38%	72%	0.4%	18-23[2]	22%	81%	2%
Carson-Newman University (TN)	2.1	68%	54%	57%	48%	53%	0%	19-29	N/A	69%	8%
Clark Atlanta University	2.3	70%	40%	44%	42%	37%	5%	940-1080	10%	55%	10%
Cleveland State University*	2.3	72%	48%	46%	37%	36%	9%	18-24[3]	14%	94%	3%
Colorado Technical University[1]	2.2	43%[8]	33%	19%[6]	N/A	N/A	N/A	N/A[2]	N/A	N/A	N/A
Daemen College (NY)	1.7	78%	53%	62%	46%	66%	0.3%	1040-1240[2]	22%	62%	5%
Eastern Michigan University*	2.4	72%	51%	46%	39%	42%	3%	970-1190	13%	74%	2%
East Tennessee State University*	2.2	73%[8]	51%	50%	39%	58%	6%	20-27	32%	86%	N/A
Ferris State University (MI)*	2.1	77%	49%	53%	43%	53%	3%	930-1170[9]	N/A	87%	2%
Georgia Southern University*	2.5	79%	58%	50%	46%	33%	9%	1050-1200	17%[5]	54%	N/A
Grand Canyon University[1] (AZ)	1.8	65%[8]	47%	40%[6]	N/A	N/A	N/A	N/A[2]	N/A	73%[4]	N/A
Husson University (ME)	1.8	75%	51%	58%	50%	48%	0%	960-1140	12%	85%	3%
Idaho State University[1]*	2.5	66%[8]	53%	30%[6]	N/A	N/A	N/A	N/A[2]	N/A	N/A	N/A
Indiana State University*	2.5	65%	41%	41%	32%	35%	7%	910-1140[2]	13%	90%	6%
Jackson State University[1] (MS)*	2.1	62%[8]	42%	38%[6]	N/A	N/A	N/A	17-22[4]	N/A	69%[4]	N/A
Kennesaw State University (GA)*	2.4	79%	57%	46%	41%	25%	16%	1050-1230	15%	75%	2%
Lamar University (TX)*	2.0	65%	47%	34%	24%	39%	9%	960-1140	15%	84%	1%
Liberty University (VA)	1.7	83%	56%	52%	35%	33%	4%	1040-1260	N/A	51%	1%
Lindenwood University (MO)	1.9	70%	55%	50%	43%	69%	0.4%	20-25[2]	N/A	88%	3%
Louisiana Tech University*	2.5	80%	59%	60%	50%	37%	11%	22-28	25%	64%	9%
Mary Baldwin University (VA)	2.0	67%	45%	48%	46%	65%	0%	950-1130	10%	100%	7%
Metropolitan State University[1] (MN)*	1.8	70%[8]	37%	36%[6]	N/A	N/A	N/A	N/A[2]	N/A	54%[4]	N/A
Middle Tennessee State Univ.*	2.3	76%	49%	47%	41%	46%	7%	20-26	N/A	94%	3%
Mississippi College[1]	2.0	79%[8]	63%	57%[8]	33%[4]	59%[4]	3%[4]	21-28[4]	33%[4]	38%[4]	6%[4]
Missouri State University[1]*	2.4	78%[8]	58%	55%[8]	45%[4]	26%[4]	13%[4]	21-26[4]	22%[4]	85%[4]	5%[4]
Morgan State University (MD)*	2.3	73%	40%	43%	38%	48%	2%	920-1070	8%	68%	16%
National Louis University (IL)	1.9	62%[8]	32%	34%[6]	N/A	70%	0%	15-18[4]	N/A	98%	N/A
Northern Illinois University*	2.4	73%	49%	49%	39%	50%	7%	940-1180	14%	48%	4%
Northern Kentucky University*	2.2	71%	50%	48%	37%	41%	3%	20-26	N/A	90%	3%[4]
Oakland University (MI)*	2.2	76%	56%	57%	47%	38%	12%	1020-1230	22%	83%	3%
Our Lady of the Lake University (TX)	1.9	62%	35%	42%	41%	64%	0%	910-1070[2]	14%	68%	10%
Palm Beach Atlantic University (FL)	1.8	76%	59%	59%	54%	67%	0.3%	980-1200	N/A	95%	2%
Pontifical Catholic U. of Puerto Rico–Ponce[1]	2.2	81%[8]	27%	40%[8]	39%[4]	42%[4]	0%[4]	N/A[2]	N/A	92%[4]	N/A
Regent University (VA)	1.8	78%	50%	58%	52%	59%	1%	990-1220	10%	86%	1%
Roosevelt University (IL)	2.1	69%	47%	41%	37%	61%	1%	1010-1230	N/A[5]	67%	4%
Southern Illinois University Edwardsville*	2.2	75%	55%	49%	37%	50%	7%	20-26[3]	20%	86%	3%
Spalding University[1] (KY)	1.8	71%[8]	45%	43%[6]	N/A	N/A	N/A	18-23[4]	N/A	96%[4]	N/A
Stephen F. Austin State University[1] (TX)*	2.4	71%[8]	51%	45%[6]	N/A	N/A	N/A	990-1180[4]	N/A	68%[4]	N/A
Tennessee State University[7]*	2.2	55%	38%	35%	30%	60%[4]	2%[4]	17-21[3]	N/A	66%	N/A
Texas A&M University–Commerce*	2.3	66%	45%	48%	43%	36%	5%	950-1150	16%	36%	3%
Texas A&M University–Corpus Christi*	2.3	58%	46%	37%	29%	31%	16%	1010-1200	17%	83%	3%
Texas A&M Univ.–Kingsville*	2.2	68%	37%	39%	34%	36%	5%	940-1120	16%	77%	1%
Texas Southern University*	2.1	54%	30%	23%	22%	33%	9%	840-1000	5%	91%	4%
Texas State University*	2.2	77%	54%	54%	47%	30%	15%	1010-1180	12%	81%	3%
Texas Wesleyan University	2.2	51%	47%	29%	45%	69%	0.2%	975-1090[3]	10%[4]	19%	6%
Texas Woman's University*	2.4	76%	45%	43%	36%	49%	8%	930-1150[2]	18%	93%	2%

Note: Key to footnotes, Page 60

School (State) (*Public)	Peer assessment score (5.0=highest)	Average first-year student retention rate	2019 graduation rate Predicted	2019 graduation rate Actual	Pell recipient grad rate	% of classes under 20 ('19)	% of classes of 50 or more ('19)	SAT/ACT 25th-75th percentile ('19)	Freshmen in top 10% of HS class ('19)	Acceptance rate ('19)	Average alumni giving rate
CONTINUED (SCHOOLS RANKED 298 THROUGH 389 ARE LISTED HERE ALPHABETICALLY)											
Trevecca Nazarene University (TN)	1.8	78%[8]	54%	54%	42%	58%	6%	20-26	22%[4]	62%	3%
Trinity International University[1] (IL)	1.9	62%[8]	53%	52%[6]	43%[4]	83%[4]	0%[4]	20-25[4]	N/A	N/A	N/A
Union Institute and University[1] (OH)	1.9	32%[8]	23%	7%[8]	N/A	N/A	N/A	N/A[2]	N/A	N/A	N/A
Universidad Ana G. Mendez–Gurabo Campus[1] (PR)	2.0	75%[8]	23%	28%[6]	N/A	N/A	N/A	N/A[2]	N/A	N/A	N/A
University of Alaska–Fairbanks[1]*	2.6	75%[8]	58%	40%[6]	N/A	N/A	N/A	18-25[4]	N/A	76%[4]	N/A
University of Arkansas at Little Rock*	2.4	68%	48%	40%	32%	N/A	N/A	19-25	N/A	64%	N/A
University of Bridgeport[1] (CT)	1.9	67%[8]	39%	38%[8]	36%[4]	71%[4]	1%[4]	900-1090[4]	6%[4]	57%[4]	3%[4]
University of Central Arkansas*	2.1	74%	51%	43%	33%	53%	1%	21-27	22%	90%	7%
University of Charleston (WV)	2.3	64%	54%	38%	29%	58%	0%	19-24[2]	N/A	50%	5%
University of Colorado–Colorado Springs*	2.7	69%	58%	45%	38%	43%	7%	1020-1230	15%	89%	4%
University of Hawaii–Hilo*	2.5	70%[8]	50%	44%	42%	49%	2%	17-23[3]	16%	52%	N/A
University of Louisiana at Lafayette*	2.3	75%	51%	51%	42%	34%	9%	21-26	17%	68%	5%
University of Louisiana–Monroe*	2.1	73%	51%	47%	41%	46%	11%	20-25	22%	79%	3%
University of Mary (ND)	1.9	81%[8]	58%	54%	46%	68%	3%	21-26	N/A	98%	N/A
Univ. of Maryland Eastern Shore*	2.2	62%	42%	41%	42%	68%	2%	850-1030[2]	N/A	65%	1%
University of Michigan–Flint*	2.3	73%	48%	40%	35%	55%	2%	970-1220	19%	66%	1%
University of New Orleans*	2.3	66%	49%	42%	42%	38%	10%	20-25	14%	56%	4%
University of Northern Colorado*	2.4	71%	56%	52%	47%	36%	11%	970-1200	13%	91%	3%
University of Phoenix[1] (AZ)	1.3	33%[8]	42%	10%	N/A	N/A	N/A	N/A[2]	N/A	N/A	N/A
University of South Alabama*	2.2	75%	54%	46%	39%	52%	6%	20-27[2]	N/A	78%	N/A
Univ. of Southern Mississippi*	2.3	72%	49%	49%	36%	42%	11%	19-26	N/A	92%	7%
University of Tennessee–Chattanooga*	2.5	73%	53%	48%	40%	39%	10%	21-26	N/A	82%	4%
University of Texas at Arlington*	2.7	72%	56%	51%	50%	26%	32%	1040-1250	25%	83%	2%
University of Texas at San Antonio*	2.6	73%	52%	42%	44%	17%	31%	1030-1220	19%	77%	6%
University of Texas at Tyler*	2.2	64%	55%	42%	39%	41%	10%	1070-1240	14%	83%	1%
University of Texas–El Paso*	2.5	74%	39%	37%	34%	30%	17%	900-1110[2]	19%	100%	3%
University of the Cumberlands[1] (KY)	1.9	63%[8]	44%	39%[6]	N/A	N/A	N/A	20-26[4]	N/A	73%[4]	N/A
University of Toledo (OH)*	2.4	75%	54%	51%	37%	41%	14%	20-26	21%	95%	5%
University of West Georgia*	2.2	71%	43%	45%	43%	43%	7%	19-24[2]	9%	95%	3%
Univ. of Wisconsin–Milwaukee*	2.8	74%	52%	44%	37%	46%	10%	990-1140	N/A	57%	1%
Valdosta State University (GA)*	2.2	69%	48%	40%	35%	55%	3%	18-24	14%	93%	8%
Washburn University (KS)*	2.2	71%	52%	28%	18%	53%	2%	19-27	22%	97%	6%
Western Kentucky University*	2.3	72%	52%	52%	38%	47%	6%	20-27[2]	19%	56%	7%
Wichita State University (KS)*	2.5	72%	57%	50%	38%	46%	10%	19-25[4]	6%[4]	64%[4]	2%[4]
William Woods University[1] (MO)	1.9	74%[8]	56%	58%[6]	53%[4]	83%[4]	0%[4]	N/A[2]	N/A	100%	N/A
Wilmington University (DE)	2.1	61%	43%	22%	12%	96%	0%	N/A[2]	N/A	100%	N/A
Wingate University (NC)	2.1	71%	57%	50%	46%	41%	1%	930-1130	13%	90%	9%
Wright State University (OH)*	2.3	64%	51%	45%	31%	N/A	N/A	18-25	19%	95%	N/A

▶ The Top 30 Public National Universities

Rank School (State)

1. University of California–Los Angeles
2. University of California–Berkeley
3. University of Michigan–Ann Arbor
4. University of Virginia
5. U. of North Carolina–Chapel Hill
6. University of California–Santa Barbara
6. University of Florida

Rank School (State)

8. Georgia Institute of Technology
8. University of California–Irvine
8. University of California–San Diego
11. University of California–Davis
11. William & Mary (VA)
13. University of Texas at Austin
13. U. of Wisconsin–Madison
15. University of Georgia

Rank School (State)

15. University of Illinois–Urbana-Champaign
17. Ohio State University–Columbus
17. Purdue U.–West Lafayette (IN)
19. Florida State University
19. Univ. of Maryland–College Park
19. University of Pittsburgh
19. University of Washington

Rank School (State)

23. Pennsylvania State U.–Univ. Park
23. Rutgers U.–New Brunswick (NJ)
23. University of Connecticut
26. Texas A&M University
26. Univ. of Massachusetts–Amherst
26. University of Minnesota–Twin Cities
29. Clemson University (SC)
29. Virginia Tech

Best
National Liberal

Rank School (State) (*Public)	Overall score	Peer assessment score (5.0=highest)	Graduation and retention rank	Average first-year student retention rate	2019 graduation rate			Pell recipient grad rate	Social mobility rank
					Predicted	Actual	Over-performance (+) Under-performance (−)		
1. Williams College (MA)	100	4.6	1	98%	91%	95%	+4	94%	87
2. Amherst College (MA)	98	4.6	5	96%	90%	95%	+5	95%	63
3. Swarthmore College (PA)	95	4.6	1	98%	93%	94%	+1	95%	141
4. Pomona College (CA)	94	4.4	1	97%	90%	93%	+3	91%	103
4. Wellesley College (MA)	94	4.5	14	96%	90%	91%	+1	90%	63
6. Bowdoin College (ME)	93	4.5	1	97%	91%	95%	+4	94%	145
6. Claremont McKenna College (CA)	93	4.3	10	95%	89%	91%	+2	85%	178
6. United States Naval Academy (MD)*	93	4.4	18	97%	86%	92%	+6	N/A	N/A
9. Carleton College (MN)	91	4.3	7	96%	89%	92%	+3	92%	177
9. Hamilton College (NY)	91	4.0	10	95%	88%	93%	+5	95%	111
9. Middlebury College (VT)	91	4.3	7	95%	90%	93%	+3	92%	152
9. Washington and Lee University (VA)	91	4.0	7	96%	92%	94%	+2	91%	199
13. Grinnell College (IA)	89	4.2	33	94%	84%	89%	+5	91%	49
13. Vassar College (NY)	89	4.2	14	96%	85%	91%	+6	91%	19
15. Colby College (ME)	88	4.1	23	94%	89%	89%	None	92%	178
15. Davidson College (NC)	88	4.2	14	95%	90%	91%	+1	94%	173
15. Haverford College (PA)	88	4.2	10	97%	93%	90%	−3	91%	111
15. Smith College (MA)	88	4.3	24	94%	85%	89%	+4	90%	94
15. United States Military Academy (NY)*	88	4.3	33	96%	80%	85%	+5	N/A	N/A
20. Colgate University (NY)	87	4.1	18	94%	89%	91%	+2	88%	193
20. Wesleyan University (CT)	87	4.1	18	96%	85%	92%	+7	93%	120
22. Barnard College (NY)	86	4.0	10	95%	86%	92%	+6	92%	81
22. Bates College (ME)	86	4.1	18	95%	85%	91%	+6	91%	173
22. University of Richmond (VA)	86	4.0	30	94%	84%	89%	+5	89%	133
25. Colorado College	84	4.0	30	96%	87%	83%	−4	88%	188
25. Harvey Mudd College (CA)	84	4.4	5	98%	95%	92%	−3	100%	133
27. Macalester College (MN)	82	4.0	24	94%	85%	91%	+6	91%	126
28. Bryn Mawr College (PA)	81	4.1	43	92%	87%	84%	−3	86%	145
28. Kenyon College (OH)	81	3.9	24	91%	89%	89%	None	83%	211
28. Scripps College (CA)	81	3.9	33	92%	90%	90%	None	87%	178
28. Soka University of America (CA)	81	2.7	18	94%	83%	89%	+6	92%	26
28. United States Air Force Academy (CO)*	81	4.2	46	95%	86%	85%	−1	N/A	N/A
33. Berea College (KY)	80	3.6	130	83%	45%	68%	+23	67%	9
34. Bucknell University (PA)	79	4.0	24	93%	86%	90%	+4	89%	199
34. Mount Holyoke College (MA)	79	3.9	43	92%	82%	83%	+1	86%	157
36. College of the Holy Cross (MA)	78	3.7	14	95%	83%	90%	+7	88%	133
36. Oberlin College (OH)	78	3.9	40	90%	88%	86%	−2	83%	212
36. Pitzer College (CA)	78	3.8	40	93%	80%	85%	+5	84%	167
36. Skidmore College (NY)	78	3.7	33	92%	81%	88%	+7	90%	152
40. Lafayette College (PA)	76	3.6	24	94%	86%	88%	+2	89%	193
40. Occidental College (CA)	76	3.8	43	91%	79%	86%	+7	91%	73
40. Thomas Aquinas College (CA)	76	2.9	46	92%	69%	84%	+15	89%	3
43. Franklin & Marshall College (PA)	75	3.6	40	91%	82%	85%	+3	84%	123
44. Denison University (OH)	74	3.6	46	90%	77%	85%	+8	78%	133
44. Trinity College (CT)	74	3.6	46	90%	83%	83%	None	91%	193
44. Union College (NY)	74	3.4	38	93%	85%	82%	−3	88%	108
47. DePauw University (IN)	73	3.4	46	90%	78%	84%	+6	80%	108
47. Dickinson College (PA)	73	3.5	46	90%	81%	83%	+2	84%	178
47. The University of the South (TN)	73	3.6	64	88%	79%	79%	None	76%	94
47. Whitman College[1] (WA)	73	3.5	30	93%[8]	85%	88%[8]	+3	87%[4]	208

Note: Key to footnotes, Page 60.

Arts Colleges

Faculty resources rank	% of classes under 20 ('19)	% of classes of 50 or more ('19)	Student/ faculty ratio ('19)	Selectivity rank	SAT/ACT 25th-75th percentile ('19)	Freshmen in top 10% of HS class ('19)	Acceptance rate ('19)	Financial resources rank	Average alumni giving rate
7	75%	3%	7/1	5	1410-1550[2]	85%	13%	2	50%
16	71%	2%	7/1	4	1410-1550	88%	11%	4	45%
22	73%	3%	8/1	5	1380-1540[2]	87%	9%	6	34%
22	70%	0.2%	8/1	1	1390-1540[2]	93%	7%	9	24%
31	66%	0.4%	8/1	11	1360-1530	79%	22%	6	44%
44	68%	2%	9/1	8	1330-1520[2]	85%	9%	12	47%
2	83%	2%	8/1	19	1360-1510	83%[5]	10%	12	36%
14	64%	0%	8/1	38	1240-1460	54%	8%	3	16%
5	69%	0%	9/1	15	1360-1540	71%	19%	31	45%
3	78%	0.2%	9/1	5	1370-1520	83%	16%	26	39%
19	66%	2%	8/1	19	1360-1530	79%[5]	15%	4	37%
1	77%	0%	8/1	10	1360-1500	82%	19%	27	42%
9	64%	0%	9/1	19	1370-1530	62%	23%	17	32%
69	67%	0.2%	8/1	12	1370-1530	73%	24%	15	26%
7	73%	2%	9/1	16	1380-1520[2]	68%	10%	17	39%
16	70%	0.3%	9/1	17	1310-1485[2]	72%	18%	31	41%
44	73%	1%	9/1	2	1380-1540	92%	16%	25	36%
22	69%	4%	9/1	12	1330-1520[2]	75%	32%	17	30%
51	100%	0%	7/1	54	1160-1380	48%	10%	10	35%
9	70%	1%	9/1	17	1330-1500	69%	23%	27	37%
19	75%	3%	8/1	19	1320-1510[2]	67%	16%	38	30%
22	79%	6%	9/1	8	1340-1520	84%	11%	42	21%
31	69%	1%	10/1	23	1270-1480[2]	71%	12%	42	38%
5	73%	0.1%	8/1	28	1290-1460	59%	28%	17	23%
9	75%	0%	10/1	12	1300-1480[2]	82%	14%	17	20%
106	57%	5%	8/1	2	1490-1570	87%[4]	14%	17	21%
48	70%	1%	10/1	23	1320-1510	64%	32%	49	33%
48	72%	0.3%	9/1	23	1290-1510[2]	67%	33%	27	31%
26	75%	1%	9/1	28	1270-1460	57%	34%	34	30%
38	75%	0%	10/1	26	1333-1490	78%[5]	32%	33	20%
4	94%	0%	7/1	46	1240-1430	62%[5]	40%	1	22%
118	74%	0.2%	7/1	38	28-33	54%	11%	6	13%
63	75%	0%	10/1	92	23-27	25%	30%	24	15%
63	55%	1%	9/1	34	1255-1430[2]	58%	34%	34	26%
29	75%	1%	9/1	28	1270-1490[2]	52%	38%	38	31%
69	59%	1%	10/1	62	1260-1430[2]	53%	34%	49	44%
9	78%	1%	9/1	32	1280-1480	54%	36%	38	25%
51	72%	0%	10/1	62	1348-1480[2]	59%[5]	14%	34	22%
41	75%	0.1%	8/1	59	1220-1400[2]	32%[5]	30%	48	21%
69	59%	2%	10/1	41	1250-1440	54%	31%	42	29%
90	63%	0.2%	10/1	34	1300-1480	53%	37%	49	18%
31	100%	0%	11/1	72	1150-1390	29%[5]	79%	69	45%
51	65%	1%	9/1	26	1250-1460[2]	71%	30%	42	20%
51	65%	0.2%	9/1	28	27-31[2]	70%	29%	61	16%
38	72%	0.4%	9/1	68	1298-1450[2]	46%	33%	27	25%
41	68%	1%	10/1	32	1220-1420[2]	63%	43%	57	25%
29	76%	0%	8/1	62	1130-1360	43%	64%	61	20%
26	80%	0%	8/1	46	1240-1410[2]	42%	40%	64	24%
81	60%	1%	10/1	62	25-30[2]	32%	67%	49	31%
86	68%[4]	0%[4]	9/1[4]	34	29-32[4]	52%[4]	50%[4]	49	28%[4]

What Is a National Liberal Arts College?

THE COUNTRY'S 223 liberal arts colleges emphasize undergraduate education and award at least half of their degrees in the arts and sciences, which include such disciplines as English, the biological and physical sciences, history, foreign languages, and the visual and performing arts but exclude professional disciplines such as business, education and nursing. There are 200 private and 23 public liberal arts colleges; none are for-profit. The top public colleges appear below.

The Top 10 Public Colleges

Rank School (State)

1. **United States Naval Academy** (MD)
2. **United States Military Academy** (NY)
3. **United States Air Force Academy** (CO)
4. **Virginia Military Institute**
5. **St. Mary's College of Maryland**
6. **New College of Florida**
7. **University of Minnesota Morris**
7. **U. of North Carolina Asheville**
9. **Massachusetts Col. of Liberal Arts**
10. **Purchase College–SUNY**

Rank	School (State) (*Public)	Overall score	Peer assessment score (5.0=highest)	Average first-year student retention rate	2019 graduation rate Predicted	2019 graduation rate Actual	Pell recipient grad rate	% of classes under 20 ('19)	% of classes of 50 or more ('19)	SAT/ACT 25th-75th percentile ('19)	Freshmen in top 10% of HS class ('19)	Acceptance rate ('19)	Average alumni giving rate
51.	Connecticut College	72	3.5	90%	82%	84%	93%	75%	1%	1310-1450[2]	45%[5]	37%	26%
52.	Centre College (KY)	71	3.5	91%	79%	84%	87%	66%	0%	26-32	52%	76%	40%
52.	Furman University (SC)	71	3.6	91%	81%	83%	78%	66%	0%	28-32[2]	55%	57%	22%
54.	Bard College (NY)	70	3.5	85%	82%	77%	72%	80%	0.2%	1244-1413[2]	40%	65%	19%
54.	Gettysburg College (PA)	70	3.5	91%	85%	81%	78%	70%	1%	1280-1410	60%	48%	23%
54.	Hillsdale College (MI)	70	2.6	93%	83%	86%	N/A	78%	0%	29-33	N/A	48%	15%
54.	Rhodes College (TN)	70	3.6	92%	80%	80%	67%	71%	0%	27-32	52%	45%	26%
54.	Spelman College (GA)	70	3.7	90%	60%	75%	67%	62%	1%	1080-1230	24%	43%	28%
54.	St. Lawrence University (NY)	70	3.3	90%	75%	84%	80%	63%	1%	1160-1350[2]	42%	42%	22%
54.	Wabash College (IN)	70	3.4	89%	70%	74%	73%	74%	1%	1120-1320	25%	64%	40%
61.	Agnes Scott College (GA)	69	3.4	84%	69%	73%	73%	70%	0%	1130-1340[2]	32%	65%	26%
61.	Wheaton College (IL)	69	3.2	93%	82%	89%	86%	70%	2%	1220-1440	49%	85%	18%
63.	Lawrence University (WI)	68	3.3	88%	76%	79%	68%	79%	2%	25-32[2]	39%	62%	30%
63.	Reed College[1] (OR)	68	3.8	88%[8]	80%	80%[6]	N/A	N/A	N/A	1310-1520[4]	N/A	35%[4]	N/A
63.	Sarah Lawrence College (NY)	68	3.5	84%	76%	78%	74%	93%	0.3%	1240-1422[2]	36%	53%	18%
63.	St. John's College (MD)	68	3.4	87%	73%	69%	70%	89%	1%	1200-1420[2]	29%	60%	22%
67.	Kalamazoo College (MI)	67	3.4	89%	73%	86%	85%	62%	1%	1170-1370[2]	52%	76%	24%
67.	St. Olaf College (MN)	67	3.6	92%	81%	86%	86%	49%	3%	26-32[2]	46%	48%	19%
69.	College of Wooster (OH)	66	3.3	87%	76%	77%	72%	73%	1%	1150-1380	46%	55%	17%
69.	Virginia Military Institute*	66	3.2	86%	69%	79%	78%	81%	0.1%	1090-1270[3]	10%	60%	25%
69.	Wofford College (SC)	66	3.2	89%	75%	85%	84%	61%	0%	1190-1350[2]	39%	60%	20%
72.	Hobart & William Smith Colleges (NY)	64	3.3	86%	76%	77%	76%	68%	0%	1180-1360[2]	33%	66%	19%
72.	Knox College (IL)	64	3.1	84%	67%	74%	76%	76%	0%	1090-1350[2]	35%	68%	27%
72.	Muhlenberg College (PA)	64	3.1	90%	78%	85%	91%	74%	1%	1150-1340[2]	35%	66%	18%
72.	Willamette University (OR)	64	3.2	85%	73%	69%	67%	74%	0.2%	1140-1340[2]	48%	78%	11%
76.	Bennington College (VT)	63	2.9	79%	76%	76%	86%	90%	0.4%	1250-1440[2]	29%	61%	17%
76.	Cornell College (IA)	63	3.2	79%	70%	69%	65%	78%	0%	23-29[2]	17%	62%	16%
76.	Lewis & Clark College (OR)	63	3.4	84%	76%	77%	63%	67%	1%	1210-1400[2]	37%	72%	16%
76.	St. John's College (NM)	63	3.3	76%	70%	63%	50%	100%	0%	1270-1460[2]	42%	66%	16%
80.	Allegheny College (PA)	62	3.1	83%	70%	74%	66%	71%	1%	1170-1360[2]	40%	62%	20%
80.	Beloit College (WI)	62	3.1	82%	72%	75%	74%	66%	0%	1080-1380[2]	29%	62%	14%
80.	Illinois Wesleyan University	62	3.1	89%	76%	77%	76%	69%	2%	24-29	38%	61%	17%
80.	St. Mary's College of Maryland*	62	3.0	85%	70%	77%	69%	71%	0.3%	1060-1290[2]	26%	84%	11%
84.	Earlham College (IN)	61	3.2	82%	71%	64%	50%	75%	2%	1100-1370[2]	42%	63%	24%
84.	Gustavus Adolphus College (MN)	61	3.3	88%	72%	78%	75%	59%	0.2%	25-30[2]	31%	69%	19%
84.	Juniata College (PA)	61	2.8	84%	67%	80%	73%	73%	1%	1118-1320[2]	30%	71%	22%
84.	Lake Forest College (IL)	61	3.0	86%	65%	77%	81%	61%	0.3%	1080-1280[2]	40%	55%	22%
84.	New College of Florida*	61	3.1	81%	72%	64%	62%	86%	0%	1180-1360	22%	73%	16%
84.	Transylvania University (KY)	61	3.0	83%	72%	70%	65%	73%	0%	23-30[2]	28%	90%	28%
84.	University of Puget Sound (WA)	61	3.3	84%	73%	76%	65%	64%	1%	1150-1370[2]	30%	84%	11%
84.	Ursinus College (PA)	61	3.0	86%	70%	81%	75%	69%	1%	1150-1350[2]	21%	79%	16%
84.	Wheaton College (MA)	61	3.4	86%	75%	75%	77%	59%	1%	1150-1340[2]	23%	74%	17%
93.	Hendrix College (AR)	60	3.2	86%	74%	73%	63%	76%	0%	25-31[2]	36%	70%	21%
93.	Ohio Wesleyan University	60	3.1	79%	68%	65%	60%	73%	0%	22-28[2]	32%	67%	20%
93.	Principia College (IL)	60	2.1	90%	66%	80%	N/A	99%	0%	1010-1218	29%[5]	91%	22%
96.	Augustana College (IL)	59	3.1	87%	65%	71%	66%	69%	0.2%	1090-1320[2]	31%	57%	23%
96.	College of St. Benedict (MN)	59	3.0	86%	70%	80%	72%	54%	1%	22-28	28%	80%	15%
96.	Saint Mary's College (IN)	59	2.9	84%	67%	79%	73%	55%	1%	1060-1250[2]	39%	81%	30%
96.	Washington and Jefferson Col. (PA)	59	3.1	81%	69%	75%	63%	77%	0%	1090-1280[9]	24%	85%	14%
96.	Washington College (MD)	59	2.9	84%	72%	73%	72%	78%	0.3%	1090-1300	28%	92%	16%
101.	College of the Atlantic (ME)	58	2.8	80%	60%	52%	47%	91%	0%	1170-1340[2]	22%	72%	31%
102.	Austin College (TX)	57	3.1	81%	68%	72%	67%	62%	0.3%	1110-1310[2]	29%	51%	15%
102.	Hampden-Sydney College (VA)	57	3.0	82%	69%	68%	62%	75%	0%	1060-1320	7%	57%	23%
102.	Hanover College (IN)	57	2.8	79%	64%	69%	64%	72%	1%	1030-1240[2]	26%	65%	18%
102.	Hollins University (VA)	57	2.8	75%	63%	66%	60%	87%	0%	1070-1300[3]	29%	71%	24%
102.	Luther College (IA)	57	3.0	84%	72%	75%	65%	63%	1%	22-28	26%	62%	24%
102.	Randolph-Macon College (VA)	57	3.1	85%	64%	68%	63%	65%	0%	1050-1240	22%	71%	35%
102.	Saint Anselm College (NH)	57	2.7	89%	70%	78%	80%	75%	2%	1140-1300[2]	28%	75%	17%
102.	Southwestern University (TX)	57	3.1	85%	71%	69%	57%	56%	1%	1140-1320[2]	35%	49%	27%
102.	St. John's University (MN)	57	3.1	87%	71%	75%	66%	54%	1%	22-27	15%	78%	23%

Note: Key to footnotes, Page 60.

Middlebury
College

Rank School (State) (*Public)	Overall score	Peer assessment score (5.0=highest)	Average first-year student retention rate	2019 graduation rate Predicted	Actual	Pell recipient grad rate	% of classes under 20 ('19)	% of classes of 50 or more ('19)	SAT/ACT 25th-75th percentile ('19)	Freshmen in top 10% of HS class ('19)	Acceptance rate ('19)	Average alumni giving rate
102. Whittier College (CA)	57	3.1	77%	58%	72%	81%	51%	1%	1038-1220[2]	20%	57%	19%
112. Hope College (MI)	56	3.0	90%	72%	81%	69%	59%	3%	1130-1330	37%	86%	16%
113. Drew University (NJ)	55	2.9	85%	68%	69%	74%	69%	0.2%	1105-1300[2]	23%	71%	15%
113. Elizabethtown College (PA)	55	2.6	88%	68%	69%	61%	70%	0%	1080-1290	29%	81%	14%
113. Grove City College[1] (PA)	55	2.5	90%[8]	70%	82%[8]	N/A	55%[4]	3%[4]	1085-1275[4]	33%[4]	79%[4]	18%[4]
113. Millsaps College (MS)	55	3.0	78%	70%	70%	67%	73%	0%	21-26[3]	N/A	69%	16%
113. Stonehill College (MA)	55	2.8	87%	72%	82%	72%	52%	0.1%	1120-1290[2]	19%	68%	14%
113. Susquehanna University (PA)	55	2.9	85%	66%	72%	67%	58%	1%	1100-1290[2]	25%	85%	13%
113. Westmont College (CA)	55	2.7	81%	73%	79%	81%	61%	2%	1100-1330	33%	65%	11%
120. College of Idaho	54	2.7	76%	62%	65%	62%	60%	3%	1020-1240[2]	N/A	57%	28%[4]
120. Goucher College (MD)	54	3.1	77%	71%	66%	61%	71%	0.3%	1030-1260[2]	12%	81%	15%
120. Linfield University (OR)	54	2.7	82%	68%	74%	69%	79%	0%	1020-1220[2]	N/A	82%	11%
120. Lycoming College (PA)	54	2.6	78%	56%	67%	65%	66%	1%	1040-1220[2]	25%	62%	18%
120. Ripon College (WI)	54	2.7	77%	60%	67%	57%	65%	2%	19-25[2]	14%	70%	29%
120. Saint Michael's College (VT)	54	2.7	85%	71%	83%	77%	58%	1%	1155-1310[2]	21%	83%	19%
120. Westminster College (PA)	54	2.7	79%	57%	70%	66%	65%	0%	970-1180[2]	16%	67%	15%
127. Houghton College (NY)	52	2.4	83%	62%	76%	67%	71%	1%	1060-1320[2]	24%	93%	16%
127. Monmouth College (IL)	52	2.7	74%	56%	61%	51%	83%	0%	990-1220	13%	67%	16%
127. Presbyterian College (SC)	52	2.7	79%	68%	71%	69%	67%	0%	1000-1230[2]	24%	75%	15%
130. Albion College (MI)	51	2.8	79%	64%	70%	63%	64%	0%	990-1200[2]	N/A	69%	11%
130. Birmingham-Southern College (AL)	51	2.7	79%	68%	69%	50%	71%	0%	22-29[2]	24%	54%	15%
130. Coe College (IA)	51	2.9	78%	64%	65%	61%	68%	1%	21-27	26%	63%	14%
130. Concordia College–Moorhead (MN)	51	2.6	83%	70%	72%	67%	59%	0.2%	21-27	19%	68%	15%
130. Roanoke College (VA)	51	3.0	81%	65%	70%	57%	53%	0%	1050-1260[2]	17%	75%	16%
130. St. Norbert College (WI)	51	2.7	84%	67%	74%	76%	48%	0%	21-27	23%	80%	15%
136. Eckerd College (FL)	50	2.9	81%	70%	66%	60%	54%	0%	1090-1280[2]	N/A	67%	N/A
136. Franklin College (IN)	50	2.7	75%	54%	65%	58%	71%	0%	970-1180	17%	81%	16%
136. Meredith College (NC)	50	2.7	80%	60%	66%	60%	69%	0%	1020-1220	17%	65%	18%
136. Wells College[7] (NY)	50	2.6	73%	57%	55%	51%	84%	0%	950-1240[9]	19%	83%	24%[4]
140. Central College (IA)	49	2.6	81%	64%	67%	54%	69%	0%	19-25	18%	65%	9%
140. Covenant College (GA)	49	2.3	86%	65%	65%	69%	62%	1%	23-29	33%	98%	9%
140. Illinois College	49	2.5	78%	56%	63%	55%	57%	0%	960-1180[2]	21%	78%	19%
140. Moravian College (PA)	49	2.5	81%	59%	69%	63%	59%	1%	1040-1210[3]	15%	75%	16%
140. Randolph College (VA)	49	2.6	68%	59%	51%	42%	90%	0%	970-1180[2]	15%	90%	20%
140. Saint Vincent College (PA)	49	2.2	83%	59%	69%	63%	56%	0%	1030-1240	20%	68%	13%
140. Salem College (NC)	49	2.3	77%[8]	58%	59%	52%	90%	0%	17-23	14%	80%	16%
140. University of Minnesota Morris*	49	2.6	79%	62%	58%	52%	74%	2%	21-28	26%	57%	9%
140. U. of North Carolina Asheville*	49	3.2	75%	63%	59%	59%	52%	1%	1090-1270	14%	84%	4%
149. Hartwick College (NY)	48	2.6	72%	59%	64%	59%	70%	0.3%	1030-1210[2]	N/A	80%	12%
149. Massachusetts Col. of Liberal Arts*	48	2.5	74%	54%	61%	52%	69%	0%	960-1170	11%	82%	5%
149. Simpson College (IA)	48	2.5	78%	64%	72%	67%	77%	0.3%	19-25[2]	21%	81%	11%
149. Wesleyan College (GA)	48	3.0	71%	50%	48%	36%	74%	0%	940-1120	19%[4]	44%	21%
153. Wittenberg University (OH)	47	2.8	73%	63%	63%	48%	69%	1%	20-27[2]	14%	91%	14%
154. Emory and Henry College (VA)	46	2.7	74%	54%	54%	45%	69%	0.2%	960-1170	22%	73%	19%
155. Centenary College	45	2.3	74%	65%	59%	50%	72%	1%	19-26[2]	25%	60%	10%
155. Gordon College (MA)	45	2.4	84%	69%	69%	63%	65%	3%	1060-1310	25%	74%	10%
155. Guilford College (NC)	45	3.0	69%	53%	56%	52%	73%	0%	933-1180[2]	13%	75%	7%[4]
155. Marlboro College[1] (VT)	45	2.2	65%[8]	68%	60%[6]	N/A	100%[4]	0%[4]	1060-1360[4]	N/A	92%[4]	8%[4]
155. Morehouse College (GA)	45	3.5	80%	55%	54%	49%	45%	1%	995-1180[3]	2%[4]	51%	12%
155. Purchase College–SUNY*	45	2.7	82%	58%	61%	60%	65%	4%	1060-1260[2]	N/A	52%	3%
155. Westminster College[1] (MO)	45	2.5	75%[8]	62%	62%[6]	48%[4]	78%[4]	0%[4]	20-25[4]	20%[4]	94%[4]	16%[4]
162. Bryn Athyn Col. of New Church (PA)	44	1.8	67%[8]	53%	51%[6]	50%[4]	88%[4]	0%[4]	996-1203[4]	N/A	89%[4]	N/A
162. Sweet Briar College[7] (VA)	44	2.3	65%	70%	34%	31%	87%	0%	1010-1210[2]	22%[4]	96%	33%
162. Warren Wilson College (NC)	44	2.7	62%	65%	43%	48%	84%	0%	1040-1315[2]	8%	85%	14%
162. Wartburg College (IA)	44	2.7	79%	64%	62%	49%	53%	2%	21-26[3]	21%	75%	21%
166. Doane University (NE)	43	2.2	73%	59%	54%	42%	83%	1%	20-25[9]	13%	71%	14%
166. Lyon College (AR)	43	2.5	67%	60%	55%	66%	73%	1%	21-26	20%	44%	7%
166. Oglethorpe University (GA)	43	3.0	78%	57%	48%	41%	58%	0%	1110-1280	23%	68%	8%
166. University of Puerto Rico–Cayey[1]*	43	2.2	87%[8]	38%	48%[6]	N/A	N/A	N/A	998-1215[4]	N/A	72%[4]	N/A
166. University of Virginia–Wise*	43	2.5	66%	44%	45%[6]	50%[4]	77%	1%	970-1160	14%	77%	6%

Note: Key to footnotes, Page 60.

School (State) (*Public)	Peer assessment score (5.0=highest)	Average first-year student retention rate	Predicted	Actual	Pell recipient grad rate	% of classes under 20 ('19)	% of classes of 50 or more ('19)	SAT/ACT 25th-75th percentile ('19)	Freshmen in top 10% of HS class ('19)	Accept-ance rate ('19)	Average alumni giving rate
SCHOOLS RANKED 171 THROUGH 221 ARE LISTED HERE ALPHABETICALLY											
Albright College[1] (PA)	2.5	69%[8]	49%	53%[8]	46%[4]	59%[4]	1%[4]	1023-1200[4]	14%[4]	62%[4]	8%[4]
Allen University[1] (SC)	2.0	40%[8]	24%	24%[6]	N/A	N/A	N/A	N/A[2]	N/A	N/A	N/A
Aquinas College (MI)	2.3	77%	59%	61%	55%	75%	0.2%	1000-1200	N/A	69%	9%
Ave Maria University (FL)	2.2	70%	66%	58%	45%	55%	0.4%	1040-1230	N/A	85%	2%
Bennett College[1] (NC)	2.2	47%[8]	35%	37%[8]	32%[4]	66%[4]	1%[4]	800-1000[4]	3%[4]	96%[4]	17%[4]
Bethany College (WV)	2.3	66%	48%	46%	40%	87%	1%	890-1120	5%	95%	13%
Bethany Lutheran College (MN)	2.1	79%	61%	55%	51%	72%	1%	20-26	24%	73%	14%
Bethune-Cookman University (FL)	2.4	63%	27%	33%	34%	55%	3%	840-1010	13%	84%	4%
Blackburn College (IL)	2.1	62%	45%	41%	44%	83%	0%	910-1110	7%	57%	11%
Bloomfield College[1] (NJ)	2.1	63%[8]	28%	32%[6]	N/A	N/A	N/A	860-1060[4]	N/A	61%[4]	N/A
Brewton-Parker College (GA)	1.9	39%[8]	31%	20%	17%	76%	0%	880-1050	4%	96%	N/A
Bridgewater College (VA)	2.4	73%	56%	59%	51%	54%	0.2%	960-1180	14%	67%	12%
Cheyney U. of Pennsylvania[1]*	1.9	52%[8]	28%	19%[6]	N/A	N/A	N/A	N/A	N/A	N/A	N/A
Chowan University (NC)	2.0	51%	24%	27%	25%	51%	1%	790-970	3%	68%	6%
Dillard University[1] (LA)	2.6	70%[8]	38%	40%[6]	N/A	N/A	N/A	N/A	N/A	61%[4]	N/A
East-West University[1] (IL)	1.7	39%[8]	22%	10%[6]	N/A	N/A	N/A	N/A	N/A	N/A	N/A
Emmanuel College (MA)	2.4	79%	62%	66%	62%	40%	0%	1090-1250[2]	15%	78%	18%
Fisk University (TN)	2.9	80%	50%	50%	42%	64%	2%	18-24	20%	93%	31%
Fort Lewis College (CO)*	2.6	62%	52%	41%	35%	52%	2%	17-23	13%	91%	2%
Georgetown College (KY)	2.5	68%	57%	45%	40%	81%	0%	21-27	22%	63%	16%
Hampshire College[1] (MA)	2.5	79%[8]	68%	64%[6]	N/A	N/A	N/A	N/A[2]	N/A	63%[4]	N/A
Johnson C. Smith University[1] (NC)	2.3	68%[8]	34%	44%[6]	N/A	70%[4]	0%[4]	803-960	N/A	47%	N/A
Judson College (AL)	2.1	62%[8]	46%	37%	15%	97%	0%	17-21[9]	N/A	37%	N/A
The King's College (NY)	2.3	75%	62%	53%	30%	54%	4%	1100-1310	N/A	42%	N/A
Lane College (TN)	2.2	55%	18%	22%	21%	43%	0.3%	14-17[2]	N/A	61%	N/A
Louisiana State University–Alexandria*	2.0	56%	38%	32%	28%	59%	2%	17-21	15%	67%	3%
Mansfield University of Pennsylvania*	2.0	72%	45%	54%	47%	49%	3%	920-1120[2]	9%	94%	N/A
Marymount California University	3.0	61%	56%	33%	51%	54%	0%	920-1090[2]	N/A	86%	0.5%[4]
Marymount Manhattan College (NY)	2.5	72%	59%	53%	46%	84%	0%	980-1200	N/A	80%	4%
Pine Manor College (MA)	2.0	58%	30%	38%	40%	86%	0%	740-915[4]	N/A	45%	N/A
Providence Christian College[1] (CA)	2.0	66%[8]	60%	45%[6]	N/A	N/A	N/A	19-25[4]	N/A	88%[4]	N/A
Rust College[1] (MS)	2.1	71%[8]	22%	34%[6]	31%[4]	55%[4]	0%[4]	14-15[4]	N/A	53%[4]	N/A
Shepherd University (WV)*	2.3	66%	44%	49%	37%	65%	0%	970-1170	N/A	69%[4]	N/A
Southern Virginia University[1]	2.0	77%[8]	54%	30%[6]	N/A	N/A	N/A	20-26[4]	N/A	50%	14%
Spring Hill College (AL)	2.3	74%	60%	56%	48%	61%	0.3%	N/A[2]	N/A	93%[4]	N/A
Sterling College[1] (VT)	2.2	54%[8]	53%	57%[6]	N/A	N/A	N/A	N/A	N/A	33%	9%
Stillman College (AL)	2.6	66%[8]	33%	27%	33%	N/A	N/A	20-24	N/A	63%	9%
Talladega College (AL)	2.1	64%	27%	34%	39%	48%	6%	20-24	N/A	63%	9%
Tougaloo College[1] (MS)	2.3	72%[8]	41%	42%[8]	37%[4]	75%[4]	0.4%[4]	16-23[4]	28%[4]	91%[4]	28%[4]
University of Maine–Machias*	2.1	56%[8]	38%	31%	30%	79%	0%	850-1080[2]	4%	99%	N/A
University of Pikeville (KY)	2.2	59%	37%	28%	23%	61%	3%	18-24	17%	100%	3%
University of Puerto Rico–Ponce[1]*	2.3	85%[8]	26%	52%[8]	50%[4]	3%[4]	0%[4]	N/A	N/A	35%[4]	3%[4]
Univ. of Science and Arts of Okla.*	2.3	67%[8]	51%	39%	33%	75%	3%	19-24[4]	N/A	64%	N/A
University of South Carolina–Beaufort*	2.4	58%[8]	42%	31%	27%	56%	2%	930-1100	11%	63%	N/A
University of the West[1] (CA)	2.0	52%[8]	45%	49%[6]	N/A	N/A	N/A	N/A[2]	N/A	N/A	N/A
Univ. of Wisconsin–Parkside*	2.0	72%	47%	45%	40%	43%	6%	17-23[2]	11%	89%	1%
University of Wisconsin–Superior*	2.1	69%	56%	48%	45%	60%	2%	18-23	8%	78%	4%
Virginia Union University	2.1	63%	28%	29%	33%	69%	1%	770-929[2]	3%	63%	7%
Virginia Wesleyan University	2.5	61%	49%	48%	44%	57%	1%	950-1180	20%	77%	6%
Williams Baptist University (AR)	1.7	56%	42%	37%	33%	51%	1%	18-23	11%	59%	3%
Young Harris College (GA)	2.4	66%	50%	47%	27%	76%	0.4%	950-1130[2]	4%	65%	7%

Best Regional Universities

What Is a Regional University?

LIKE THE NATIONAL UNIVERSITIES, the institutions that appear here provide a full range of undergraduate majors and master's programs; the difference is that they offer few, if any, doctoral programs. The 594 universities in this category are not ranked nationally but rather against their peer group in one of four regions – North, South, Midwest and West – because in general they tend to draw students most heavily from surrounding states.

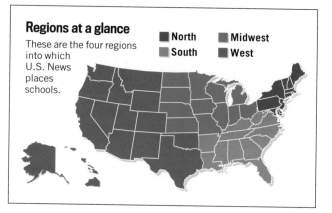

Regions at a glance
These are the four regions into which U.S. News places schools.
■ North ■ Midwest
■ South ■ West

NORTH ►

Rank	School (State) (*Public)	Overall score	Peer assessment score (5.0=highest)	Average first-year student retention rate	2019 graduation rate Predicted	2019 graduation rate Actual	% of classes under 20 ('19)	% of classes of 50 or more ('19)	Student/ faculty ratio ('19)	SAT/ACT 25th-75th percentile ('19)	Freshmen in top 25% of HS class ('19)	Accept-ance rate ('19)	Average alumni giving rate
1.	Bentley University (MA)	100	3.7	93%	85%	90%	27%	0%	11/1	1230-1410	73%	47%	6%
1.	Providence College (RI)	100	3.9	92%	83%	87%	53%	3%	11/1	1210-1350[2]	75%	47%	14%
3.	Fairfield University (CT)	94	3.7	90%	83%	83%	39%	2%	12/1	1210-1350[2]	73%	57%	19%
4.	Loyola University Maryland	92	3.8	87%	83%	83%	48%	1%	12/1	1143-1320[2]	60%[5]	80%	11%
5.	College of New Jersey*	91	3.6	94%	84%	86%	43%	0.2%	13/1	1160-1360	71%	49%	6%
6.	University of Scranton (PA)	89	3.5	87%	74%	83%	53%	0.1%	13/1	1120-1310	68%	76%	11%
7.	Bryant University (RI)	88	3.3	89%	76%	81%	27%	0%	13/1	1130-1300[2]	48%	71%	8%
8.	Saint Joseph's University (PA)	85	3.5	90%	77%	81%	44%	1%	10/1	1120-1300[2]	52%	75%	11%
9.	Emerson College (MA)	84	3.4	88%	82%	82%	70%	1%	13/1	1200-1410[2]	65%	33%	3%
9.	Ithaca College (NY)	84	3.7	85%	78%	74%	62%	2%	10/1	1160-1350[2]	57%	73%	7%
11.	Marist College (NY)	83	3.5	89%	79%	84%	44%	0%	16/1	1150-1330[2]	57%	49%	9%
12.	SUNY Polytechnic Inst.–Albany/Utica*	82	2.7	78%	72%	58%	61%	2%	13/1	1000-1360[3]	70%	69%	1%
13.	Manhattan College (NY)	76	3.1	84%	66%	71%	49%	0.2%	12/1	1060-1280[3]	52%	74%	14%
13.	SUNY–Geneseo*	76	3.5	86%	78%	80%	34%	8%	17/1	1120-1310	63%	65%	8%
15.	Siena College (NY)	75	3.0	87%	72%	80%	36%	0%	12/1	1070-1280[2]	51%	81%	14%
16.	CUNY–Baruch College*	74	3.2	90%	56%	70%	16%	17%	19/1	1130-1330	74%	43%	3%
17.	CUNY–Hunter College*	73	3.3	85%	53%	57%	35%	7%	13/1	1150-1350	57%[4]	35%	12%
17.	Le Moyne College (NY)	73	3.0	85%	67%	74%	48%	1%	12/1	1073-1280[2]	53%	74%	15%
[†]19.	Canisius College (NY)	69	2.8	84%	65%	73%	54%	0.2%	11/1	1030-1270	45%	83%	12%
19.	Messiah University (PA)	69	2.7	87%	78%	79%	54%	2%	12/1	1090-1310[2]	64%	76%	8%
19.	St. Bonaventure University (NY)	69	3.1	84%	67%	74%	44%	0.4%	12/1	1030-1240[2]	39%	75%	18%
23.	Endicott College (MA)	68	2.9	85%	68%	74%	68%	0%	13/1	1090-1240[2]	45%	69%	13%
23.	Monmouth University (NJ)	68	3.1	80%	65%	73%	42%	0.1%	12/1	1030-1210	42%	77%	4%
23.	Niagara University (NY)	68	2.9	84%	61%	73%	61%	1%	11/1	1020-1230[2]	40%	89%	10%
26.	La Salle University (PA)	67	2.9	74%	56%	66%	55%	0.4%	12/1	990-1190[2]	34%	78%	9%[4]
26.	Molloy College (NY)	67	2.5	87%	66%	74%	67%	3%	10/1	1020-1220	56%	78%	8%
26.	Springfield College (MA)	67	2.9	85%	61%	74%	48%	3%	11/1	1020-1220	33%	68%	12%
26.	St. Francis University (PA)	67	2.7	87%	63%	74%	66%	0%	16/1	1030-1250	52%	75%	14%
26.	Wagner College (NY)	67	2.9	82%	77%	73%	71%	2%	11/1	1070-1270[2]	51%	71%	6%
31.	Roger Williams University (RI)	66	3.0	82%	72%	67%	46%	0.4%	14/1	1065-1240[2]	37%	85%	4%
31.	Salve Regina University (RI)	66	2.9	84%	68%	78%	43%	0%	13/1	1100-1260[2]	43%	74%	15%
31.	Suffolk University (MA)	66	3.0	77%	66%	58%	44%	1%	15/1	1020-1210	43%	84%	6%
34.	McDaniel College (MD)	65	2.9	79%	67%	68%	68%	0%	12/1	988-1190[2]	44%	92%	12%
34.	New York Inst. of Technology	65	3.1	76%	61%	53%	63%	1%	11/1	1070-1295	N/A	68%	2%
34.	Ramapo College of New Jersey*	65	2.9	86%	66%	72%	36%	0%	16/1	1030-1220	41%	66%	3%
34.	Stockton University (NJ)*	65	2.8	86%	63%	77%	28%	2%	17/1	1020-1210[2]	41%	76%	1%
38.	Lebanon Valley College[1] (PA)	64	2.7	82%[8]	74%	74%[8]	62%[4]	2%[4]	10/1[4]	1068-1280[4]	48%[4]	78%[4]	13%[4]

[†]A university formerly tied at No. 19 has been unranked because of a data reporting error.

Note: Key to footnotes Page 60.

Rank School (State) (*Public)	Overall score	Peer assessment score (5.0=highest)	Average first-year student retention rate	2019 graduation rate		% of classes under 20 ('19)	% of classes of 50 or more ('19)	Student/ faculty ratio ('19)	SAT/ACT 25th-75th percentile ('19)	Freshmen in top 25% of HS class ('19)	Accept- ance rate ('19)	Average alumni giving rate
				Predicted	Actual							
38. Mercyhurst University (PA)	64	2.8	79%	59%	68%	68%	0.2%	14/1	1030-1220[2]	N/A	87%	11%
38. Mount St. Mary's University (MD)	64	3.1	76%	66%	69%	61%	0%	12/1	990-1200[2]	35%	75%	15%
38. Rider University (NJ)	64	2.8	78%	62%	67%	54%	1%	10/1	1020-1210[2]	35%	71%	6%
38. Wentworth Inst. of Technology (MA)	64	3.1	84%	64%	73%	40%	2%	18/1	1060-1270[2]	41%	69%	5%
43. Assumption University (MA)	63	2.8	83%	69%	70%	45%	0.2%	12/1	1090-1238[2]	41%	81%	12%
43. Seton Hill University (PA)	63	2.8	81%	60%	65%	69%	0.3%	14/1	1000-1220[2]	44%	77%	14%
45. Alfred University (NY)	62	2.9	73%	60%	57%	66%	3%	12/1	940-1180	33%	66%	10%
45. Arcadia University (PA)	62	2.7	78%	65%	66%	75%	0.2%	12/1	1030-1260[2]	47%	66%	7%
45. Merrimack College (MA)	62	3.0	83%	67%	75%	34%	1%	15/1	1033-1200[2]	24%	82%	8%
45. Nazareth College (NY)	62	2.7	83%	73%	71%	59%	0%	10/1	1100-1290[2]	59%	64%	10%
45. SUNY–New Paltz*	62	3.0	86%	68%	76%	28%	4%	16/1	1090-1200[3]	N/A[5]	45%	2%
50. CUNY–Queens College*	61	3.0	84%	55%	56%	35%	8%	16/1	1040-1200	N/A	49%	14%
50. Fairleigh Dickinson University (NJ)	61	3.2	79%	55%	56%	77%	1%	12/1	1000-1180[2]	42%	93%	3%
50. Iona College (NY)	61	2.9	75%	57%	64%	34%	0.2%	14/1	990-1170[2]	35%	84%	7%
50. St. Joseph's College–Brooklyn	61	2.5	81%	54%	62%	79%	1%	10/1	990-1190	N/A	71%	7%
50. SUNY–Oswego*	61	2.9	78%	61%	67%	54%	6%	17/1	1040-1220	53%	54%	5%
50. West Chester Univ. of Pennsylvania*	61	3.1	86%	62%	77%	25%	6%	19/1	1040-1210	34%	75%	4%
56. CUNY–Lehman College*	60	2.8	83%	38%	53%	46%	1%	18/1	950-1110	N/A	38%	14%
56. Hood College (MD)	60	2.9	76%	60%	65%	72%	0%	10/1	1000-1210[2]	37%	65%	12%
56. SUNY Maritime College*	60	3.0	84%	69%	75%	34%	2%	15/1	1090-1260	N/A[5]	74%	5%
59. Marywood University (PA)	59	2.6	85%	63%	67%	59%	0.2%	11/1	1000-1190	49%	78%	10%
59. Notre Dame of Maryland University	59	2.8	74%	58%	63%	87%	1%	7/1	920-1140[2]	42%	62%	11%
59. University of New Haven (CT)	59	2.8	78%	62%	61%	57%	2%	16/1	1030-1220[2]	42%	83%	6%
62. CUNY–Brooklyn College*	58	2.9	82%	48%	54%	33%	4%	18/1	1040-1220[3]	N/A	45%	5%
62. King's College (PA)	58	2.6	74%	60%	64%	56%	0.2%	13/1	990-1220[2]	35%	81%	12%
62. Monroe College (NY)	58	1.9	79%	30%	71%	55%	0.1%	15/1	960-1100[2]	N/A	48%	1%
62. Norwich University (VT)	58	2.8	79%	62%	61%	55%	1%	15/1	1040-1230[2]	34%	75%	15%
62. Waynesburg University (PA)	58	2.3	77%	59%	66%	69%	1%	12/1	950-1150	38%	93%	8%
67. Caldwell University (NJ)	57	2.5	80%	46%	69%	61%	1%	13/1	940-1150	27%	93%	9%
67. CUNY–John Jay Col. of Crim. Justice*	57	3.2	79%	43%	46%[6]	28%	1%	18/1	960-1130	N/A	41%	N/A
67. Salisbury University (MD)*	57	2.9	83%	68%	70%	38%	4%	15/1	1120-1280[2]	45%	74%	7%
67. SUNY–Fredonia*	57	2.6	75%	58%	64%	58%	3%	14/1	990-1200	41%	71%	4%
71. Carlow University (PA)	56	2.3	78%	47%	57%	80%	0.3%	11/1	980-1153	50%[4]	92%	8%
71. St. Joseph's College–Long Island (NY)	56	2.4	82%	57%	72%	62%	0%	15/1	1090-1230[9]	45%	46%	5%
71. SUNY College–Cortland*	56	2.9	79%	68%	71%	32%	6%	15/1	1030-1245[2]	N/A[5]	68%	6%
71. SUNY College–Potsdam*	56	2.6	75%	50%	61%	70%	2%	11/1	1110-1320[2]	39%	85%	2%
75. Champlain College (VT)	55	2.5	81%	65%	65%	70%	0%	12/1	1030-1260[9]	N/A	79%	7%
75. DeSales University (PA)	55	2.5	81%	65%	69%	50%	2%	13/1	930-1100[2]	38%	81%	9%
75. Saint Peter's University (NJ)	55	2.6	82%	43%	60%	61%	0%	14/1	N/A[2]	28%	86%	1%[4]
75. Southern New Hampshire University	55	2.9	71%	43%	67%	67%	0.1%	12/1	910-1180[4]	N/A	51%[4]	N/A
75. SUNY College–Oneonta[1]*	55	2.9	84%[8]	66%	73%[6]	N/A	N/A	18/1[4]	980-1180	36%	57%	6%
75. SUNY–Plattsburgh*	55	2.6	79%	59%	68%	42%	4%	15/1	980-1170[2]	19%	90%	9%
81. Manhattanville College (NY)	54	2.6	73%	61%	60%	75%	0%	11/1	1010-1190	44%	81%	3%
81. Stevenson University (MD)	54	2.8	79%	58%	60%	62%	0%	15/1	1030-1230[2]	58%	61%	5%
83. Eastern University (PA)	53	2.4	77%	60%	62%	84%	0.2%	10/1	980-1190	34%	73%	2%
83. Point Park University[1] (PA)	53	2.5	77%	54%	57%[6]	78%	0.3%	11/1	1020-1270[2]	47%	67%	8%
83. Roberts Wesleyan College (NY)	53	2.4	79%	62%	63%	77%	1%	11/1	1000-1170	36%	70%	4%
83. Slippery Rock U. of Pennsylvania*	53	2.8	82%	55%	68%	21%	9%	19/1	1010-1190[2]	32%	55%	3%
83. SUNY Brockport*	53	2.7	77%	56%	64%	39%	5%	17/1	850-1080[2]	N/A	75%	7%
88. Albertus Magnus College (CT)	52	2.4	69%	43%	61%	84%	0%	14/1	930-1150	26%	91%	8%
88. Shippensburg U. of Pennsylvania*	52	2.8	73%	53%	58%	44%	2%	17/1	1010-1190[2]	35%	64%	3%
90. Eastern Connecticut State University*	51	2.6	78%	59%	57%	38%	0%	15/1	980-1150	25%	87%	3%
90. Westfield State University (MA)*	51	2.5	76%	53%	61%	44%	1%	15/1	890-1090[4]	N/A	92%	3%
90. William Paterson Univ. of N.J.*	51	2.6	73%	50%	55%	50%	1%	14/1	970-1130	38%	75%	11%
93. Elms College (MA)	50	2.1	82%	52%	73%	77%	0.3%	12/1	1020-1240	51%	53%	9%
93. Geneva College (PA)	50	2.2	78%	58%	72%	72%	3%	15/1	1000-1210	33%	69%	7%
93. York College of Pennsylvania	50	2.5	79%	60%	63%	52%	0.1%	13/1	943-1130	N/A	64%	7%
96. Alvernia University (PA)	49	2.5	76%	53%	63%	59%	1%	9/1	963-1180	42%	61%	10%
96. Cedar Crest College (PA)	49	2.3	79%	52%	51%	81%	2%	12/1	938-1148[2]	N/A	75%	3%
96. Centenary University (NJ)	49	2.2	76%[8]	50%	54%	78%	0%					

NORTH ▶

Rank School (State) (*Public)	Overall score	Peer assessment score (5.0=highest)	Average first-year student retention rate	2019 graduation rate Predicted	2019 graduation rate Actual	% of classes under 20 ('19)	% of classes of 50 or more ('19)	Student/ faculty ratio ('19)	SAT/ACT 25th-75th percentile ('19)	Freshmen in top 25% of HS class ('19)	Accept- ance rate ('19)	Average alumni giving rate
96. College of Saint Rose (NY)	49	2.3	74%	58%	61%	69%	0.4%	14/1	990-1210[9]	37%	87%	11%[4]
96. Fitchburg State University (MA)*	49	2.5	75%	52%	58%	51%	0.3%	13/1	990-1150[2]	N/A	88%	3%
96. Johnson & Wales University (RI)	49	2.9	75%	58%	63%	46%	0%	19/1	1000-1190[2]	30%	93%	1%
96. Millersville U. of Pennsylvania*	49	2.7	77%	57%	57%	31%	5%	19/1	980-1170	29%	76%	3%
96. Utica College (NY)	49	2.6	73%	50%	54%	65%	0%	11/1	1010-1210[2]	31%	87%	6%
96. Worcester State University (MA)*	49	2.6	80%	56%	58%	46%	0.1%	17/1	950-1160[2]	N/A	81%	6%
105. Bay Path University (MA)	48	2.2	74%[8]	51%	54%	88%	0%	10/1	960-1170[2]	51%	72%	2%[4]
105. Bridgewater State University (MA)*	48	2.6	78%	53%	61%	45%	0.1%	18/1	970-1150[2]	N/A	88%	3%
105. Central Connecticut State University*	48	2.5	75%	53%	57%	44%	3%	14/1	970-1160[2]	28%	66%	3%
105. Framingham State University (MA)*	48	2.7	74%	53%	61%	50%	0.2%	13/1	960-1130	N/A	74%	4%
105. Mount St. Mary College (NY)	48	2.4	80%	57%	63%	63%	1%	13/1	970-1160	28%	94%	5%
105. SUNY Buffalo State*	48	2.9	63%	46%	46%	54%	3%	14/1	880-1070[3]	N/A	67%	2%
111. Lock Haven U. of Pennsylvania*	47	2.4	69%	49%	54%	51%	4%	14/1	920-1130	29%	95%	3%
111. University of Baltimore*	47	2.6	76%	48%	41%	58%	0%	12/1	970-1135	N/A	78%	3%
113. Chestnut Hill College (PA)	45	2.3	74%	51%	56%	83%	0%	9/1	918-1100	22%	65%	12%
113. Clarion U. of Pennsylvania*	45	2.3	74%	44%	54%	38%	5%	16/1	940-1130	36%	95%	3%
113. College of Mount St. Vincent (NY)	45	2.3	77%	46%	50%	50%	1%	12/1	910-1110	29%[4]	92%	12%
113. Frostburg State University[1] (MD)*	45	2.7	76%[8]	51%	49%[6]	50%[4]	3%[4]	16/1[4]	930-1120[4]	29%[4]	78%[4]	4%[4]
113. Georgian Court University (NJ)	45	2.2	78%	51%	54%	76%	0%	12/1	958-1160	33%	71%	6%
113. Gwynedd Mercy University (PA)	45	2.4	82%	48%	62%	61%	6%	10/1	930-1100	22%	95%	4%
113. Rhode Island College*	45	2.6	74%	52%	49%	55%	1%	13/1	880-1080	37%	78%	2%
113. St. Thomas Aquinas College (NY)	45	2.5	75%	54%	58%	67%	0%	18/1	890-1160[3]	27%[5]	81%	4%
121. Bloomsburg U. of Pennsylvania*	44	2.6	74%	52%	60%	27%	5%	17/1	950-1150	27%	84%	4%
121. Keuka College (NY)	44	2.4	72%	49%	55%	57%	1%	10/1	970-1178[2]	N/A	86%	10%
121. Plymouth State University (NH)*	44	2.6	69%	55%	54%	59%	1%	15/1	824-1174[2]	16%	85%	3%
121. Southern Connecticut State U.*	44	2.6	75%	52%	52%	45%	1%	13/1	910-1090	28%	69%	3%
125. Delaware Valley University (PA)	43	2.4	70%	60%	61%	61%	1%	13/1	970-1170[2]	35%	93%	5%
125. Kutztown Univ. of Pennsylvania*	43	2.6	74%	51%	54%	26%	7%	17/1	970-1140	27%	89%	5%
125. Lasell University (MA)	43	2.3	74%	58%	59%	63%	1%	14/1	980-1170[2]	32%	84%	6%
125. Salem State University (MA)*	43	2.5	76%	51%	57%	46%	0.4%	13/1	970-1150[2]	N/A	86%	3%
125. Wilson College (PA)	43	2.1	71%	59%	64%	79%	0.3%	12/1	910-1190[2]	41%	93%	14%
130. Western Connecticut State U.*	42	2.5	74%	56%	52%	36%	2%	12/1	1020-1220[2]	28%	76%	1%
131. Edinboro Univ. of Pennsylvania*	41	2.3	70%	47%	49%	48%	5%	15/1	970-1160	30%	83%	3%
132. CUNY–College of Staten Island*	40	2.5	78%	42%	47%	24%	6%	19/1	1010-1190	N/A	93%	1%
132. Kean University (NJ)*	40	2.6	74%	46%	47%	39%	1%	17/1	920-1100	N/A	69%	2%
132. La Roche University (PA)	40	2.1	70%	54%	55%	69%	1%	12/1	870-1140	26%	99%	6%
132. Neumann University (PA)	40	2.4	73%	49%	52%	61%	3%	14/1	920-1090	N/A	62%	6%

School (State) (*Public)	Peer assessment score (5.0=highest)	Average first-year student retention rate	2019 graduation rate Predicted	2019 graduation rate Actual	% of classes under 20 ('19)	% of classes of 50 or more ('19)	Student/ faculty ratio ('19)	SAT/ACT 25th-75th percentile ('19)	Freshmen in top 25% of HS class ('19)	Accept- ance rate ('19)	Average alumni giving rate
SCHOOLS RANKED 136 THROUGH 176 ARE LISTED HERE ALPHABETICALLY											
American International College (MA)	2.0	66%[8]	46%	44%	N/A	N/A	17/1	920-1100[4]	N/A	N/A	N/A
Anna Maria College[1] (MA)	1.9	69%[8]	52%	42%[6]	N/A	N/A	12/1[4]	903-1080[4]	21%[4]	75%[4]	6%
Bowie State University (MD)*	2.5	71%	43%	43%	46%	2%	15/1	860-1030	N/A	80%	5%
Cabrini University[1] (PA)	2.4	70%[8]	52%	58%[6]	N/A	N/A	11/1[4]	990-1170[4]	N/A	72%[4]	N/A
Cairn University[1] (PA)	2.1	77%[8]	60%	58%[6]	N/A	N/A	11/1[4]	890-1130[4]	N/A	89%[4]	6%[4]
California U. of Pennsylvania*	2.3	72%	48%	50%	37%	7%	17/1	910-1100[2]	25%	97%	2%
Cambridge College[1] (MA)	2.0	41%[8]	N/A	8%	N/A	N/A	11/1[4]	N/A	N/A	N/A	N/A
Concordia College–New York[1] (NY)	2.1	77%[8]	48%	48%[8]	71%[4]	1%[4]	10/1[4]	950-1118[4]	N/A	81%[4]	6%[4]
Coppin State University[1] (MD)*	2.3	64%[8]	39%	22%[6]	60%[4]	0.3%[4]	13/1[4]	880-1030[4]	N/A	38%[4]	N/A
Curry College (MA)	2.2	66%	57%	52%	62%	0%	12/1	943-1108[2]	23%[5]	91%	2%
Dominican College (NY)	2.2	72%	47%	47%	68%	0%	15/1	900-1110[2]	N/A	78%	2%
East Stroudsburg University (PA)*	2.6	70%	46%	52%	52%	7%	19/1	910-1100[2]	20%	76%	N/A
Felician University (NJ)	2.2	79%	42%	47%	61%	0.2%	14/1	900-1080	31%	86%	1%
Franklin Pierce University[1] (NH)	2.4	64%[8]	54%	47%[8]	62%[4]	2%[4]	12/1[4]	970-1160[4]	19%[4]	78%[4]	2%[4]
Goddard College[1] (VT)	2.1	59%[8]	53%	57%[6]	N/A	N/A	13/1[4]	N/A	N/A	100%[4]	N/A
Granite State College (NH)*	2.0	54%	36%	21%	88%	0%	11/1	N/A[2]	N/A	100%	9%
Harrisburg Univ. of Science and Tech. (PA)	2.2	64%[8]	29%	26%	56%	0%	29/1	N/A[2]	39%	84%	1%

Note: Key to footnotes Page 60.

CONTINUED (SCHOOLS RANKED 136 THROUGH 176 ARE LISTED HERE ALPHABETICALLY)

School (State) (*Public)	Peer assessment score (5.0=highest)	Average first-year student retention rate	2019 graduation rate Predicted	Actual	% of classes under 20 ('19)	% of classes of 50 or more ('19)	Student/faculty ratio ('19)	SAT/ACT 25th-75th percentile ('19)	Freshmen in top 25% of HS class ('19)	Acceptance rate ('19)	Average alumni giving rate
Holy Family University[1] (PA)	2.2	78%[8]	47%	59%[6]	N/A	N/A	12/1[4]	935-1090[4]	N/A	72%[4]	N/A
Lancaster Bible College (PA)	1.9	78%	55%	59%	80%[4]	0.3%[4]	14/1[4]	1000-1200[4]	N/A	96%	4%[4]
Lincoln University (PA)*	2.1	73%	42%	47%	53%	0.4%	15/1	870-1010	16%	83%	15%
Medaille College[1] (NY)	2.0	63%[8]	41%	43%[6]	N/A	N/A	12/1[4]	850-1100[4]	N/A	63%[4]	N/A
Mercy College (NY)	2.2	74%	37%	44%	55%	1%	17/1	890-1080[2]	N/A	82%	2%
Metropolitan College of New York[1]	2.0	39%[8]	35%	24%[6]	N/A	N/A	10/1[4]	N/A[2]	34%[4]	100%	6%
New England College (NH)	2.2	57%	40%	39%	87%	0%	15/1	920-940[2]	N/A	95%	2%
New Jersey City University*	2.3	75%	38%	41%	45%	1%	14/1	860-1080[3]	25%[4]	84%[4]	N/A
Northern Vermont University[1] (VT)*	2.1	66%[8]	51%	37%[6]	N/A	N/A	12/1	820-1070[2]	24%	98%	3%
Nyack College (NY)	2.0	67%	44%	38%	81%	0.4%	21/1	900-900[2]	N/A	64%	0%[4]
Post University (CT)	2.2	45%	40%	21%	46%	0%	12/1[4]	N/A[2]	N/A	73%[4]	N/A
Rivier University[1] (NH)	2.2	74%[8]	53%	54%[6]	N/A	N/A	12/1	920-1130[2]	N/A	66%	N/A
Rosemont College (PA)	2.2	66%	48%	58%	85%	0%	9/1	890-1096[2]	N/A	73%	9%
Saint Elizabeth University (NJ)	2.3	64%	36%	53%	77%	0%	13/1[4]	970-1170[4]	N/A	84%[4]	N/A
St. Joseph's College[1] (ME)	2.4	82%[8]	59%	59%[6]	N/A	N/A	13/1[4]	N/A[2]	N/A	N/A	N/A
Strayer University[1] (DC)	1.6	N/A	53%	40%[6]	N/A	N/A	29/1[4]	N/A[2]	N/A	N/A	N/A
SUNY College–Old Westbury*	2.5	78%	47%	46%[6]	21%[4]	0%[4]	24/1	910-1090[3]	N/A	78%	N/A
SUNY Empire State College*	2.3	51%[8]	33%	20%[6]	N/A	N/A	15/1	N/A[2]	N/A	63%	N/A
Thomas College[1] (ME)	2.1	66%[8]	47%	47%[6]	N/A	N/A	23/1[4]	N/A[2]	N/A	N/A	N/A
Trinity Washington University[1] (DC)	2.8	63%[8]	32%	35%[6]	N/A	N/A	12/1[4]	N/A[2]	N/A	95%[4]	N/A
University of Maryland Global Campus*	3.3	53%[8]	46%	11%[6]	88%	0%	19/1	N/A[2]	N/A	100%	N/A
University of Southern Maine*	2.6	68%	55%	40%	57%	3%	13/1	950-1160[2]	36%	81%	2%
Univ. of the District of Columbia*	2.1	64%	44%	24%	70%	0%	9/1	N/A	N/A	74%	N/A
Washington Adventist University[1] (MD)	1.9	77%[8]	54%	37%[8]	85%[4]	0%[4]	10/1[4]	860-1070[4]	N/A	52%[4]	1%[4]

SOUTH ▶

Rank	School (State) (*Public)	Overall score	Peer assessment score (5.0=highest)	Average first-year student retention rate	2019 graduation rate Predicted	Actual	% of classes under 20 ('19)	% of classes of 50 or more ('19)	Student/faculty ratio ('19)	SAT/ACT 25th-75th percentile ('19)	Freshmen in top 25% of HS class ('19)	Acceptance rate ('19)	Average alumni giving rate
1.	Rollins College (FL)	100	4.0	85%	78%	74%	65%	0%	11/1	1160-1340[2]	59%	58%	6%
2.	The Citadel, Military Coll. of SC*	94	4.1	85%	67%	74%	39%	0.1%	12/1	1050-1230	31%	75%	26%
3.	James Madison University (VA)*	91	4.1	90%	70%	84%	34%	12%	16/1	1120-1290[2]	33%	77%	7%
4.	Berry College (GA)	88	3.4	83%	70%	69%	59%	0.4%	11/1	1090-1320	61%	71%	17%
4.	Stetson University (FL)	88	3.7	78%	68%	65%	62%	1%	13/1	1110-1300[2]	56%	72%	7%
6.	Appalachian State University (NC)*	84	3.8	88%	66%	73%	36%	8%	16/1	21-26	52%	77%	6%
7.	Christopher Newport Univ. (VA)*	83	3.3	86%	70%	78%	61%	3%	14/1	1110-1280[2]	48%	72%	19%
8.	College of Charleston (SC)*	78	3.7	79%	72%	66%	41%	4%	14/1	1080-1260	52%	78%	4%
9.	Asbury University (KY)	77	3.1	83%	66%	68%	72%	0%	13/1	21-28[2]	48%	73%	16%
9.	Embry-Riddle Aeronautical U. (FL)	77	3.8	80%	68%	62%	20%	3%	17/1	1120-1360[2]	52%	61%	3%
9.	Florida Southern College	77	3.1	81%	66%	68%	61%	0%	14/1	1120-1265	58%	50%	11%
12.	John Brown University (AR)	75	2.9	82%	67%	72%	58%	0%	13/1	23-29[2]	70%	76%	9%
13.	Queens University of Charlotte (NC)	74	3.2	78%	66%	59%	71%	2%	10/1	1040-1240[2]	41%	65%	21%
13.	University of Tampa (FL)	74	3.5	77%	65%	58%	37%	3%	17/1	1100-1250	47%	45%	18%
13.	Winthrop University (SC)*	74	3.6	74%	57%	64%	53%	1%	13/1	950-1160	41%	69%	4%
16.	Longwood University (VA)*	73	3.1	78%	59%	66%	59%	1%	13/1	960-1150	33%	90%	9%
16.	Xavier University of Louisiana	73	3.4	72%	57%	51%	53%	3%	15/1	20-26	59%	60%	17%
18.	Milligan University (TN)	72	2.8	75%	69%	63%	77%	0.3%	9/1	22-28	N/A	99%	11%
18.	Univ. of Mary Washington (VA)*	72	3.3	82%	70%	64%	54%	5%	13/1	1080-1280[2]	41%	75%	24%
20.	Tuskegee University (AL)	71	3.2	71%	61%	50%	54%	6%	10/1	18-23	N/A	80%	3%
21.	Georgia College & State University*	69	3.4	85%	66%	64%	39%	3%	17/1	1110-1260	59%	50%	5%
22.	Christian Brothers University (TN)	68	2.8	78%	58%	60%	83%[4]	0.3%[4]	13/1[4]	20-25[4]	45%[4]	59%[4]	11%[4]
22.	Converse College[1] (SC)	68	2.7	71%[8]	56%	61%[8]	64%	0.3%	11/1	970-1170	22%	91%	10%
22.	University of Lynchburg (VA)	68	2.9	78%	61%	58%	27%	4%	17/1	20-25	39%	43%	5%
25.	Western Carolina University (NC)*	67	3.2	79%	53%	58%	63%	3%	15/1	21-28[2]	51%	83%	5%
26.	Murray State University (KY)*	66	3.2	77%	55%	55%	42%	0%	18/1	1040-1190[2]	27%	72%	4%
26.	Saint Leo University (FL)	66	3.0	71%	44%	47%	48%[4]	1%[4]	13/1	20-25	N/A	53%	8%
26.	University of Montevallo (AL)*	66	3.0	75%	60%	55%	71%	1%	11/1	18-25[2]	44%	92%	4%
29.	Jacksonville University (FL)	65	3.0	72%	58%	52%	61%	3%	11/1	18-25[2]	44%	64%	6%
30.	University of Tennessee–Martin*	64	3.0	75%	53%	47%	61%	3%	15/1	21-26	43%	64%	6%

SOUTH ▶

Rank	School (State) (*Public)	Overall score	Peer assessment score (5.0=highest)	Average first-year student retention rate	2019 graduation rate Predicted	2019 graduation rate Actual	% of classes under 20 ('19)	% of classes of 50 or more ('19)	Student/faculty ratio ('19)	SAT/ACT 25th-75th percentile ('19)	Freshmen in top 25% of HS class ('19)	Acceptance rate ('19)	Average alumni giving rate
31.	Eastern Mennonite University (VA)	63	2.6	77%	60%	58%	71%	1%	10/1	980-1210	N/A	65%	19%
31.	Marymount University (VA)	63	3.0	75%	65%	58%	57%	0.2%	12/1	940-1190[2]	30%	81%	5%[4]
33.	Bob Jones University (SC)	62	2.1	82%	57%	70%	65%	8%	14/1	20-28	35%	82%	9%
33.	Lee University (TN)	62	2.9	79%	57%	59%	57%	7%	15/1	21-28	49%	82%	6%
33.	Radford University (VA)*	62	3.1	73%	52%	55%	46%	6%	15/1	940-1110[2]	21%	75%	3%
36.	Brenau University (GA)	61	2.8	61%	47%	47%	84%	1%	9/1	900-1110[2]	37%	64%	5%
36.	Freed-Hardeman University (TN)	61	2.6	81%	64%	58%	59%	3%	13/1	21-28	56%	88%	8%
36.	University of North Georgia*	61	3.1	80%	59%	58%	37%	3%	19/1	1070-1230	48%	76%	7%
36.	University of West Florida*	61	3.1	79%	56%	46%	32%	7%	20/1	22-27	42%	31%	3%
40.	Morehead State University (KY)*	60	3.0	73%	46%	46%	57%	3%	16/1	20-26	49%	78%	9%
40.	University of North Alabama*	60	3.0	75%	50%	49%	53%	3%	19/1	20-26	46%	67%	6%
42.	Anderson University (SC)	59	2.9	78%	66%	66%	44%	8%	15/1	1060-1250	62%	69%	5%
42.	Columbia International Univ. (SC)	59	2.3	76%	56%	53%	58%	7%	14/1	930-1140	26%	48%	6%
42.	Lenoir-Rhyne University (NC)	59	2.8	71%	56%	52%	51%	0%	12/1	18-24	N/A	78%	12%
45.	Coastal Carolina University (SC)*	58	3.1	68%	55%	47%	38%	1%	16/1	1010-1170	35%	69%	10%
45.	U. of Puerto Rico–Mayaguez[1]*	58	2.5	88%[8]	44%	47%[6]	N/A	N/A	22/1[4]	N/A[2]	N/A	64%[4]	N/A
47.	Columbia College (SC)	56	2.6	70%	58%	60%	68%	0%	11/1	840-1040[2]	15%	97%	8%
47.	King University (TN)	56	2.6	68%	51%	58%	80%	0.4%	13/1	20-25[2]	41%	62%	5%
47.	Mississippi Univ. for Women*	56	3.0	64%	53%	40%	67%	6%	14/1	18-25	51%	97%	10%
47.	North Carolina Central Univ.*	56	2.6	79%	37%	49%	41%	5%	16/1	890-1050	24%	68%	8%
51.	Eastern Kentucky University*	55	2.9	74%	50%	50%	42%	5%	15/1	20-26	42%	94%	4%
51.	Troy University (AL)*	55	3.1	73%	55%	48%	60%	5%	17/1	18-24	N/A	88%	6%
53.	Austin Peay State University (TN)*	54	3.1	66%	43%	41%	47%	4%	17/1	19-24[2]	34%	95%	3%
53.	Belhaven University (MS)	54	2.9	66%	41%	50%	80%	2%	10/1	22-26[3]	41%[4]	49%	3%
53.	Lynn University (FL)	54	2.8	70%	59%	51%	44%	0.4%	18/1	970-1170[2]	N/A	74%	3%
53.	North Greenville University (SC)	54	2.5	71%	52%	59%	59%	3%	13/1	19-28	35%	61%	N/A
53.	Piedmont College (GA)	54	2.5	66%	55%	45%	77%	1%	11/1	960-1160[3]	36%	54%	4%
53.	Shorter University (GA)	54	2.4	59%[8]	46%	72%	68%	0%	12/1	930-1130	N/A	60%	1%
59.	Coker College[1] (SC)	53	2.6	57%[8]	43%	43%[8]	71%[4]	0%[4]	12/1[4]	17-22[4]	42%[4]	63%[4]	N/A
59.	Wheeling University (WV)	53	2.2	68%	60%	63%	57%[4]	0%[4]	16/1	19-24	32%[4]	69%	5%
59.	Winston-Salem State Univ.[1] (NC)*	53	2.7	77%[8]	41%	48%[6]	N/A	N/A	14/1[4]	890-1030[4]	N/A	65%[4]	N/A
62.	Charleston Southern University (SC)	52	2.9	67%	52%	41%	58%	1%	13/1	1020-1200	50%	50%	12%
62.	Jacksonville State University[1] (AL)*	52	2.9	76%[8]	51%	38%[8]	46%[4]	4%[4]	18/1[4]	19-26[4]	51%[4]	54%[4]	5%[4]
62.	West Virginia Wesleyan College	52	2.6	73%	62%	54%	54%	0.4%	14/1	940-1120	43%	64%	14%
65.	Bryan College (TN)	51	2.4	72%	55%	46%	67%	3%	13/1	21-26[2]	55%	51%	6%
65.	Thomas More University (KY)	51	2.4	65%	46%	54%	68%	0%	15/1	19-25	32%	91%	7%
65.	University of Mount Olive (NC)	51	2.3	64%[8]	43%	53%	59%	0%	15/1	16-22[2]	N/A	58%	N/A
68.	Florida Gulf Coast University*	50	2.9	79%	55%	50%	21%	12%	21/1	1060-1210[3]	43%	67%	2%
68.	Francis Marion University (SC)*	50	2.8	67%	46%	43%	55%	3%	14/1	16-21[3]	36%	69%	9%
68.	Southern Adventist University[1] (TN)	50	2.4	76%[8]	61%	46%[6]	64%[4]	5%[4]	13/1[4]	19-26[4]	N/A	93%[4]	10%[4]
68.	West Liberty University (WV)*	50	2.5	72%	44%	46%[6]	69%	0.4%	13/1	17-24	38%	71%	1%[4]
72.	Pfeiffer University[1] (NC)	49	2.3	61%[8]	52%	41%[6]	80%[4]	0%[4]	12/1[4]	900-1130[4]	31%[4]	65%[4]	10%[4]
73.	Auburn U. at Montgomery (AL)*	48	3.2	67%	47%	34%	45%	2%	16/1	19-23	46%	90%	3%
73.	Columbus State University (GA)*	48	2.8	74%	48%	40%	54%	4%	16/1	860-1100	42%	79%	3%
73.	Methodist University[1] (NC)	48	2.6	62%[8]	52%	38%[6]	68%[4]	0.1%[4]	9/1[4]	18-23[4]	37%[4]	55%[4]	8%[4]
73.	U. of North Carolina–Pembroke*	48	2.7	71%	44%	41%	47%	1%	18/1	17-21	37%	85%	2%
77.	Delta State University (MS)*	47	2.6	68%	50%	39%	63%	1%	13/1	18-24	41%	94%	2%
77.	EDP U. of Puerto Rico Inc–San Juan[1] (PR)	47	2.0	57%[8]	23%	43%[6]	N/A	N/A	16/1[4]	N/A[2]	N/A	86%[4]	N/A
77.	Southern Wesleyan University[1] (SC)	47	2.3	72%[8]	42%	52%[6]	N/A	N/A	14/1[4]	970-1150[4]	N/A	54%[4]	N/A
80.	Arkansas Tech University*	46	2.7	70%	36%	41%	47%	3%	18/1	18-25	36%	95%	3%
80.	Nicholls State University (LA)*	46	2.7	72%	45%	48%	42%	9%	20/1	20-25	43%	88%	6%
80.	Norfolk State University (VA)*	46	2.6	73%	41%	36%	57%	2%	16/1	860-1040	20%	90%	N/A
80.	Virginia State University[1]*	46	2.6	70%[8]	41%	42%[6]	N/A	N/A	13/1[4]	840-1010[4]	17%[4]	91%[4]	N/A
84.	Alcorn State University (MS)*	45	2.5	75%	37%	40%	N/A	N/A	17/1	17-24	24%	58%	8%
84.	South Carolina State University*	45	2.4	68%	38%	35%	58%	1%	15/1	15-17	25%	66%	6%
86.	Cumberland University (TN)	44	2.7	65%	45%	43%	47%	0.2%	16/1	19-23	N/A	61%	2%
86.	Henderson State University[1] (AR)*	44	2.5	63%[8]	48%	33%[6]	65%[4]	1%[4]	14/1[4]	19-25[4]	22%[4]	91%[4]	4%[4]
86.	Tusculum University (TN)	44	2.5	65%[8]	39%	41%	57%	0.3%	16/1	18-23	N/A	72%	2%
89.	Fayetteville State University (NC)*	43	2.4	72%	34%	34%	39%	1%	18/1	870-1010	27%	69%	2%
89.	Lindsey Wilson College (KY)	43	2.4	61%	36%	39%	57%	0%	16/1	18-24	35%	95%[4]	10%[4]
89.	Midway University (KY)	43	2.2	77%	45%	37%	57%	2%	17/1	19-23	30%	60%	1%

Note: Key to footnotes Page 60.

SMALL CAMPUS & BIG CITY

When everything New York City holds lies just outside a quintessential college campus, the opportunities are endless.

 MANHATTAN COLLEGE

EXPERIENCE THE UNCOMMON
MANHATTAN.EDU

SOUTH ▶

Rank School (State) (*Public)	Overall score	Peer assessment score (5.0=highest)	Average first-year student retention rate	2019 graduation rate Predicted	2019 graduation rate Actual	% of classes under 20 ('19)	% of classes of 50 or more ('19)	Student/ faculty ratio ('19)	SAT/ACT 25th-75th percentile ('19)	Freshmen in top 25% of HS class ('19)	Accept-ance rate ('19)	Average alumni giving rate
89. Northwestern State U. of Louisiana*	43	2.6	72%	44%	45%	50%	8%	20/1	19-24	42%	64%	N/A
89. Reinhardt University (GA)	43	2.5	60%	51%	41%	73%	0%	12/1	970-1180	30%	92%	3%
94. Alabama State University*	42	2.5	60%	31%	33%	60%	0.3%	15/1	15-20	N/A[5]	97%	6%
94. Campbellsville University (KY)	42	2.5	65%	42%	37%	73%	0.1%	14/1	18-23[2]	19%	70%	8%
94. Concord University (WV)*	42	2.4	63%	45%	40%	75%	0%	14/1	900-1110	36%	82%	3%
94. McNeese State University (LA)*	42	2.6	69%	46%	45%	41%	7%	20/1	20-24	46%	81%	5%
94. St. Thomas University (FL)	42	2.5	71%	40%	43%	28%	4%	12/1	890-1090	N/A	55%	9%
99. Fairmont State University (WV)*	41	2.5	66%	45%	43%	69%	2%	15/1	910-1110	36%	85%	1%
99. Southeastern Louisiana University*	41	2.6	66%	41%	39%	33%	6%	19/1	20-25	36%	91%	3%
99. Southern Arkansas University*	41	2.4	66%	39%	42%	50%	4%	17/1	18-24	37%	65%	3%
99. University of Holy Cross[1] (LA)	41	2.6	73%[8]	46%	44%[6]	N/A	N/A	10/1[4]	N/A[2]	N/A	35%[4]	N/A

School (State) (*Public)	Peer assessment score (5.0=highest)	Average first-year student retention rate	2019 graduation rate Predicted	2019 graduation rate Actual	% of classes under 20 ('19)	% of classes of 50 or more ('19)	Student/ faculty ratio ('19)	SAT/ACT 25th-75th percentile ('19)	Freshmen in top 25% of HS class ('19)	Accept-ance rate ('19)	Average alumni giving rate
SCHOOLS RANKED 103 THROUGH 133 ARE LISTED HERE ALPHABETICALLY											
Alabama Agricultural and Mechanical University*	2.4	58%	38%	30%	36%	5%	20/1	15-18	N/A	92%	14%
Albany State University[1] (GA)*	2.4	62%[8]	36%	33%[6]	46%[4]	1%[4]	18/1[4]	750-900[4]	21%[4]	89%[4]	0.4%[4]
Bayamon Central University[1] (PR)	2.1	48%[8]	17%	10%[6]	N/A	N/A	14/1[4]	N/A[2]	N/A	71%[4]	N/A
Bethel University (TN)	2.3	57%	33%	28%	66%	3%	15/1	16-20[2]	18%	90%	N/A
Caribbean University[1] (PR)	2.0	70%[8]	26%	32%[6]	N/A	N/A	14/1[4]	N/A[2]	N/A	N/A	N/A
Clayton State University (GA)*	2.4	70%	40%	31%	38%	4%	19/1	880-1020	N/A	51%	2%
ECPI University (VA)	1.7	50%[8]	35%	34%	88%	0.3%	11/1	N/A[2]	N/A	74%	N/A
Everglades University (FL)	1.9	62%[8]	37%	54%[6]	N/A	N/A	18/1	N/A[2]	N/A	75%	N/A
Faulkner University[1] (AL)	2.6	55%[8]	40%	29%[6]	68%[4]	2%[4]	12/1[4]	18-23[4]	N/A	52%[4]	1%[4]
Fort Valley State University (GA)*	2.4	75%	36%	35%	50%	2%	27/1	850-960	14%	55%	9%
Georgia Southwestern State University*	2.6	67%	48%	38%	56%	1%	17/1	940-1120	37%	58%	2%
Grambling State University[1] (LA)*	2.6	67%[8]	26%	34%[6]	33%[4]	9%[4]	25/1[4]	16-19[4]	14%[4]	96%[4]	N/A
Hodges University[1] (FL)	1.8	40%[8]	36%	18%[6]	N/A	N/A	12/1[4]	N/A[2]	N/A	77%[4]	N/A
Louisiana College[7]	2.3	58%	47%	37%	71%	0.3%	10/1	18-23	N/A	60%	N/A
Louisiana State University–Shreveport*	2.6	64%[8]	43%	31%	55%	3%	27/1	20-24	N/A	96%	5%[4]
Mississippi Valley State Univ.*	2.4	61%[8]	33%	32%	65%	1%	15/1	16-21	N/A	65%	N/A
Montreat College (NC)	2.3	60%[8]	53%	32%	78%[4]	0.4%[4]	11/1[4]	920-1140[4]	N/A	55%[4]	3%[4]
Pontifical Catholic U. of Puerto Rico–Arecibo[1]	2.3	74%[8]	30%	36%[6]	N/A	N/A	16/1[4]	N/A[2]	N/A	99%[4]	N/A
Salem University[1] (WV)	2.1	46%[8]	34%	10%[6]	N/A	N/A	22/1[4]	N/A[2]	N/A	N/A	N/A
Savannah State University[7] (GA)*	2.5	60%	33%	28%[8]	44%	1%	16/1	900-1030[3]	N/A	33%	5%[4]
Southeastern Baptist Theological Seminary[1] (NC)	2.5	79%[8]	41%	39%[6]	N/A	N/A	22/1[4]	N/A[2]	N/A	90%[4]	N/A
Southeastern University (FL)	2.4	68%	45%	40%	56%	5%	23/1	960-1180[3]	27%	48%	N/A
Southern Univ. and A&M College (LA)*	2.5	64%	33%	31%	38%	5%	21/1	17-20	14%	35%	15%
Southern University–New Orleans*	2.2	50%[8]	30%	21%	47%	0.3%	21/1	15-18	27%	60%	N/A
Thomas University[1] (GA)	2.1	51%[8]	37%	31%[6]	N/A	N/A	10/1[4]	N/A[2]	N/A	48%[4]	N/A
Union College[1] (KY)	2.4	62%[8]	41%	29%[6]	N/A	N/A	14/1[4]	18-23[4]	N/A	56%[4]	N/A
Universidad Ana G. Mendez–Carolina Campus[1] (PR)	1.9	72%[8]	18%	28%[6]	N/A	N/A	23/1[4]	N/A[2]	N/A	N/A	N/A
Universidad Ana G. Mendez–Cupey Campus[1] (PR)	1.9	71%[8]	20%	30%[6]	N/A	N/A	24/1[4]	N/A[2]	N/A	N/A	N/A
University of Arkansas–Monticello[1]*	2.3	57%[8]	29%	20%[6]	N/A	N/A	14/1[4]	N/A[2]	N/A	N/A	N/A
University of the Sacred Heart[1] (PR)	2.4	73%[8]	33%	39%[6]	N/A	N/A	20/1[4]	N/A[2]	N/A	N/A	N/A
University of West Alabama*	2.7	65%	40%	34%	66%	1%	14/1	18-22	N/A	35%	3%

MIDWEST ▶

Rank School (State) (*Public)	Overall score	Peer assessment score (5.0=highest)	Average first-year student retention rate	2019 graduation rate Predicted	2019 graduation rate Actual	% of classes under 20 ('19)	% of classes of 50 or more ('19)	Student/ faculty ratio ('19)	SAT/ACT 25th-75th percentile ('19)	Freshmen in top 25% of HS class ('19)	Accept-ance rate ('19)	Average alumni giving rate
1. Butler University (IN)	100	4.1	90%	84%	82%	50%	2%	11/1	1150-1330	77%	73%	21%
2. John Carroll University (OH)	90	3.7	86%	70%	76%	46%	0.1%	13/1	22-28	49%	86%	14%
3. Calvin University (MI)	89	3.6	86%	74%	76%	31%	1%	13/1	1130-1350[2]	62%	77%	18%
4. University of Evansville (IN)	88	3.6	86%	72%	68%	73%	0.4%	11/1	1090-1288[2]	75%	71%	12%
5. Bradley University (IL)	87	3.6	85%	71%	77%	59%	3%	12/1	1070-1270[2]	60%	70%	8%
5. Xavier University (OH)	87	4.0	85%	73%	73%	41%	1%	11/1	22-28[9]	52%	76%	15%

Note: Key to footnotes Page 60.

INTERNSHIPS

JUNIOR JOURNEY

4-YEAR GRADUATION

OUR GUARANTEES

Florida Southern College goes beyond the conventional college experience, guaranteeing each student an internship, a travel-study experience, and graduation in four years. These signature opportunities, combined with our devoted faculty and stunning historic campus, create a college experience unlike any other.

flsouthern.edu/**guarantees**

MIDWEST ▶

Rank	School (State) (*Public)	Overall score	Peer assessment score (5.0=highest)	Average first-year student retention rate	2019 graduation rate Predicted	2019 graduation rate Actual	% of classes under 20 ('19)	% of classes of 50 or more ('19)	Student/ faculty ratio ('19)	SAT/ACT 25th-75th percentile ('19)	Freshmen in top 25% of HS class ('19)	Accept- ance rate ('19)	Average alumni giving rate
7.	Truman State University (MO)*	82	3.8	85%	73%	75%	45%	1%	15/1	24-31	82%	63%	8%
8.	Milwaukee School of Engineering	81	3.6	85%	72%	65%	49%	0.2%	13/1	25-30	N/A	62%	7%
9.	Kettering University (MI)	76	3.2	92%	74%	63%	54%	0.4%	14/1	1190-1360	76%	73%	6%
10.	Baldwin Wallace University (OH)	75	3.3	80%	61%	65%	58%	1%	11/1	21-27[2]	48%	73%	7%
10.	Dominican University (IL)	75	3.1	78%	51%	64%	58%	1%	10/1	1000-1200	58%	64%	12%
10.	North Central College (IL)	75	3.3	79%	67%	69%	53%	0%	13/1	1030-1260	55%	54%	16%
13.	Augustana University (SD)	74	3.4	84%	75%	58%	51%	1%	11/1	23-29[2]	64%	67%	11%
13.	Rockhurst University (MO)	74	3.3	85%	67%	76%	31%	2%	14/1	21-27	59%	64%	12%
15.	Elmhurst University (IL)	73	3.2	80%	58%	70%	56%	0.1%	13/1	990-1210	52%	68%	7%
15.	Franciscan Univ. of Steubenville (OH)	73	2.7	86%	69%	77%	54%	1%	13/1	1090-1300	74%[5]	71%	10%
15.	Hamline University (MN)	73	3.4	79%	62%	70%	49%	1%	13/1	19-26	44%	68%	9%
15.	Indiana Wesleyan University–Marion	73	3.1	80%	59%	71%	67%	1%	14/1	1020-1220	60%	67%	9%
15.	Nebraska Wesleyan University	73	3.2	80%	66%	65%	71%	0.2%	10/1	22-28[2]	53%	68%	13%
15.	Webster University (MO)	73	3.0	78%	58%	58%	88%	0.2%	8/1[4]	21-28	47%[4]	57%	2%
21.	Augsburg University (MN)	72	3.3	75%	56%	57%	65%	0%	12/1	18-23[2]	N/A	59%	10%
21.	Cedarville University (OH)	72	2.9	85%	73%	75%	59%	6%	16/1	23-29	62%	79%	8%
21.	Otterbein University (OH)	72	3.4	83%	67%	66%	59%	2%	12/1	20-27	56%	81%	8%
24.	Lewis University (IL)	71	3.0	81%	58%	67%	61%	0%	13/1	1010-1200	46%	64%	5%
24.	University of Northern Iowa*	71	3.4	84%	65%	67%	31%	8%	17/1	20-26	45%	79%	8%
26.	Drury University (MO)	70	3.1	82%	57%	57%	57%	1%	11/1	22-28	60%	64%	10%
27.	St. Ambrose University (IA)	69	3.2	78%	60%	62%	65%	1%	11/1	20-25[3]	56%	64%	6%
28.	Grand Valley State University (MI)*	68	3.2	84%	61%	67%	24%	6%	16/1	1040-1250	46%	83%	4%
28.	Marian University (IN)	68	3.2	79%	58%	62%	69%	0.2%	13/1	970-1180[2]	51%	62%	10%
30.	Capital University (OH)	67	3.0	77%	59%	62%	65%	1%	12/1	20-26[3]	47%	72%	7%
31.	Univ. of Illinois–Springfield*	66	2.9	77%	56%	54%	55%	1%	13/1	995-1220	45%	77%	4%
31.	University of Michigan–Dearborn*	66	2.9	81%	57%	56%	45%	9%	16/1	1070-1300	N/A	62%	7%
33.	Bethel University (IN)	65	2.7	72%	56%	68%	67%	4%	11/1	950-1170	39%	94%	7%
33.	St. Mary's Univ. of Minnesota	65	3.0	78%	57%	64%	70%	0%	18/1	20-26	N/A	92%	8%
33.	Univ. of Nebraska–Kearney*	65	2.9	80%	55%	51%	57%	2%	13/1	20-26	45%	85%	7%
33.	Univ. of Wisconsin–La Crosse*	65	3.2	85%	70%	69%	27%	12%	19/1	23-27	57%	80%	4%
37.	Concordia University (NE)	64	2.8	76%	61%	65%	60%	1%	14/1	20-26	46%	78%	19%
37.	Lawrence Technological Univ. (MI)	64	3.0	79%[8]	67%	58%	75%	1%	11/1	1020-1270	N/A[5]	79%	5%
39.	Carroll University[1] (WI)	63	3.0	80%[8]	65%	64%[8]	55%[4]	2%[4]	14/1[4]	21-26[4]	N/A	69%[4]	8%[4]
39.	North Park University (IL)	63	3.0	75%	57%	62%	67%	1%	10/1	970-1180	N/A	48%	N/A
39.	University of Minnesota–Duluth*	63	3.1	79%	64%	62%	41%	14%	17/1	21-26	48%	76%	5%
39.	Univ. of Wisconsin–Eau Claire*	63	3.2	83%	64%	67%	21%	14%	22/1	21-26	48%	89%	6%
39.	Walsh University (OH)	63	2.8	77%	56%	62%	72%	0.3%	13/1	19-26[2]	N/A	76%	7%
44.	Buena Vista University (IA)	62	2.8	70%	56%	60%	79%	0.4%	8/1	19-25	43%	57%	5%
44.	Huntington University (IN)	62	2.6	82%	63%	70%	72%	1%	11/1	960-1140	37%	78%	16%
46.	Muskingum University (OH)	60	2.8	72%	51%	53%	75%	1%	13/1	18-23	40%	81%	10%
46.	Saint Mary-of-the-Woods College (IN)	60	2.6	69%	47%	56%	90%	0%	10/1	930-1120[2]	N/A	67%	22%
46.	Stephens College[1] (MO)	60	2.7	65%[8]	50%	53%[6]	85%[4]	2%[4]	7/1[4]	20-26[4]	37%[4]	N/A	7%[4]
46.	Ursuline College (OH)	60	2.7	72%	52%	53%	83%	0%	7/1	17-23	51%	85%	12%
46.	Winona State University (MN)*	60	2.9	77%	57%	59%	34%	8%	19/1	19-24	32%	68%	4%
51.	Anderson University (IN)	59	2.9	71%[8]	64%	60%	82%	1%	11/1	1000-1160	38%	62%	10%
51.	Ashland University (OH)	59	2.6	78%	56%	65%	52%	0.4%	13/1	19-24	43%	71%	6%
51.	Eastern Illinois University*	59	2.7	72%	52%	53%	50%	2%	14/1	18-23	37%	53%	3%
51.	Fontbonne University (MO)	59	2.6	76%	62%	54%	83%	0%	10/1	18-23	N/A	79%	5%
51.	McKendree University (IL)	59	2.7	76%	54%	60%	71%	0%	14/1	859-1268[2]	35%	63%	6%
51.	Mount Mercy University (IA)	59	2.6	72%	56%	64%	65%	1%	14/1	18-24	41%	66%	10%
51.	Spring Arbor University (MI)	59	2.7	79%	54%	59%	71%	0%	13/1	980-1220	50%	66%	6%
58.	Mount Mary University (WI)	58	2.6	73%	47%	65%	91%	0%	11/1	16-20	46%	58%	N/A
58.	Univ. of Wisconsin–Whitewater*	58	2.9	80%	52%	62%	34%	3%	19/1	19-24	31%	93%	5%
60.	Madonna University (MI)	57	2.6	77%	55%	59%	68%	1%	13/1	920-1140	31%	88%	1%
60.	Olivet Nazarene University (IL)	57	2.7	77%	60%	64%	52%	7%	17/1	960-1180[2]	41%	58%	11%
60.	Saint Xavier University (IL)	57	2.9	74%	50%	56%	43%	0%	16/1	960-1140	49%	73%	4%
60.	Trine University[1] (IN)	57	2.7	77%[8]	58%	59%[6]	50%[4]	1%[4]	15/1[4]	1010-1230[4]	46%[4]	73%[4]	N/A
60.	Western Illinois University*	57	2.6	68%	48%	51%	60%	2%	13/1	950-1150[2]	35%	57%	3%
65.	Alverno College (WI)	56	3.0	71%	43%	49%	91%	0%	9/1	18-21	N/A	69%	8%
65.	Morningside College (IA)	56	2.6	70%	59%	62%	63%	0%	13/1	19-25	40%	63%	20%

Note: Key to footnotes Page 60.

Rank	School (State) (*Public)	Overall score	Peer assessment score (5.0=highest)	Average first-year student retention rate	2019 graduation rate Predicted	Actual	% of classes under 20 ('19)	% of classes of 50 or more ('19)	Student/ faculty ratio ('19)	SAT/ACT 25th-75th percentile ('19)	Freshmen in top 25% of HS class ('19)	Accept- ance rate ('19)	Average alumni giving rate
65.	Univ. of Northwestern–St. Paul (MN)	56	2.6	83%[8]	64%	68%	54%	5%	17/1	21-28[2]	46%	92%	4%[4]
65.	University of Saint Francis (IN)	56	2.9	72%	53%	53%	64%	1%	11/1	948-1170	46%	96%	2%
65.	Univ. of Wisconsin–Stevens Point*	56	2.9	74%	57%	60%	35%	9%	18/1	19-25[9]	33%	84%	4%
65.	Viterbo University (WI)	56	2.9	80%[8]	58%	54%	61%	4%	11/1	21-25[2]	47%	77%	7%
71.	Malone University (OH)	55	2.6	71%	53%	54%	63%	1%	12/1	19-26	35%[4]	71%	7%
71.	Mount Vernon Nazarene U. (OH)	55	2.5	79%	53%	68%	65%	2%	16/1	20-25	48%	73%	N/A
71.	University of Wisconsin–Stout*	55	2.8	71%	55%	60%	42%	1%	18/1	20-25[4]	28%	89%	2%
74.	College of Saint Mary (NE)	54	2.7	76%	61%	52%	71%	0.3%	10/1	19-23[3]	42%	49%	11%
74.	Concordia University Chicago	54	2.7	67%	46%	47%	80%	0%	12/1	1010-1180	N/A	83%	6%
76.	Cornerstone University (MI)	53	2.5	80%	58%	61%	59%	1%	13/1	950-1190	47%	78%	3%
76.	Northern Michigan University*	53	3.0	76%	51%	53%	36%	8%	20/1	970-1190[3]	N/A	66%	3%
76.	Southeast Missouri State Univ.*	53	2.8	75%	51%	50%	49%	3%	19/1	19-25[2]	42%	86%	4%
76.	University of Central Missouri*	53	2.9	71%	51%	51%	51%	4%	17/1	19-25[2]	34%	65%	2%
80.	Concordia University–St. Paul (MN)	52	3.0	69%	47%	53%	65%	0%	18/1	17-24[9]	N/A	98%	4%
80.	Judson University (IL)	52	2.5	74%	59%	57%	77%	1%	13/1	890-1100	21%	37%	3%
80.	Minnesota State Univ.–Mankato*	52	2.9	74%	53%	50%	36%	8%	22/1	19-24	27%	63%	3%
80.	Mount St. Joseph University (OH)	52	2.5	73%	51%	51%	67%	0.3%	10/1	20-25	31%	61%	6%
80.	Northern State University (SD)*	52	2.6	75%	51%	52%	58%	3%	19/1	19-25	30%	85%	9%
85.	Emporia State University (KS)*	51	2.8	74%	51%	50%	52%	5%	17/1	19-25[2]	38%	85%	7%
86.	Bemidji State University (MN)*	50	2.7	70%[8]	53%	45%[6]	45%	7%	21/1	19-24[4]	36%	66%	6%
86.	Pittsburg State University (KS)*	50	2.7	74%	51%	52%	56%	5%	16/1	19-24[2]	39%	96%	5%
86.	St. Cloud State University (MN)*	50	2.8	69%	50%	47%	49%	3%	17/1	18-24	16%	90%	3%
86.	University of Sioux Falls (SD)	50	2.7	73%	60%	62%	53%	2%	17/1	20-25	39%	91%	4%
86.	Univ. of Wisconsin–River Falls*	50	2.7	75%	54%	58%	34%	8%	20/1	20-25[3]	31%	79%	6%[4]
91.	Dakota State University (SD)*	49	2.7	69%	50%	43%	51%	1%	19/1	19-25	23%	77%	5%
91.	Davenport University (MI)	49	2.4	72%	49%	51%	67%	0%	15/1	970-1160[2]	N/A	82%	1%
91.	Grace College and Seminary[1] (IN)	49	2.3	82%[8]	61%	60%[6]	N/A	N/A	19/1[4]	1020-1250[4]	N/A	82%[4]	N/A
91.	Greenville University (IL)	49	2.3	68%	54%	56%	59%	6%	13/1	960-1180	N/A	57%	14%[4]
91.	MidAmerica Nazarene University[1] (KS)	49	2.6	66%[8]	52%	49%[6]	69%[4]	4%[4]	9/1[4]	18-26[4]	42%[4]	59%[4]	N/A
91.	Siena Heights University[7] (MI)	49	2.7	71%[8]	49%	44%[6]	86%[4]	0%[4]	11/1[4]	870-1090[4]	29%[4]	69%[4]	2%[4]
91.	Wayne State College (NE)*	49	2.6	70%	49%	51%	43%	2%	21/1	18-25[2]	32%	100%	10%
98.	Friends University (KS)	48	2.6	71%	51%	48%	73%	2%	11/1	19-25	43%	46%	6%
98.	Minnesota State Univ.–Moorhead*	48	2.7	75%	57%	53%	44%	7%	19/1	19-24	31%	65%	3%
98.	University of Dubuque (IA)	48	2.6	63%	44%	43%	75%	0.2%	13/1	17-22[3]	19%	73%	7%
98.	University of Southern Indiana*	48	2.7	70%	50%	50%	45%	3%	17/1	980-1170	38%	93%	3%
98.	Univ. of Wisconsin–Platteville[1]*	48	2.7	78%[8]	57%	54%[6]	N/A	N/A	21/1[4]	20-26[4]	N/A	82%[4]	N/A
103.	Columbia College Chicago	47	2.6	69%	61%	50%	62%	2%	14/1	960-1200[2]	38%	90%	0.4%
103.	Northwest Missouri State Univ.*	47	2.8	75%	53%	51%	44%	6%	21/1	19-24	40%	84%	4%
103.	Ohio Dominican University	47	2.7	64%	54%	45%	56%	0%	13/1	19-25[2]	38%	71%	4%
103.	University of Saint Mary (KS)	47	2.7	65%	45%	51%	56%	0%	11/1	18-23	26%	84%	9%
103.	Univ. of Wisconsin–Green Bay[1]*	47	2.9	73%[8]	57%	51%[6]	N/A	N/A	23/1[4]	19-25[4]	N/A	79%[4]	N/A
108.	Mount Marty University (SD)	46	2.4	72%	56%	56%	74%	1%	12/1	18-24	N/A	72%	6%
108.	Univ. of Wisconsin–Oshkosh[1]*	46	2.8	77%[8]	54%	53%[6]	42%[4]	7%[4]	22/1[4]	20-24[4]	33%[4]	69%[4]	0.3%[4]
110.	Marian University (WI)	45	2.5	69%[8]	48%	56%	67%	1%	12/1	17-21[3]	24%	65%	3%
110.	Minot State University (ND)*	45	2.7	70%	56%	45%	69%	1%	11/1	18-23	31%	74%	4%[4]
112.	Fort Hays State University (KS)*	44	2.7	73%[8]	46%	44%	51%	3%	18/1	17-29[2]	35%	91%	11%[4]
112.	Indiana Tech	44	2.4	64%	31%	39%	56%	0%	11/1	930-1150	N/A	60%	2%
112.	Purdue University–Fort Wayne*	44	2.9	59%	49%	37%	51%	4%	16/1	970-1190	31%	81%	3%
112.	Southwest Baptist University (MO)	44	2.3	68%[8]	48%	47%	79%	1%	12/1	19-25	47%	71%	3%
112.	Youngstown State University (OH)*	44	2.7	76%	38%	41%	36%	6%	18/1	18-24	35%	68%	4%
117.	Newman University (KS)	43	2.6	76%	54%	44%	66%	1%	12/1	18-25[2]	50%	67%	3%
117.	Southwest Minnesota State U.[1]*	43	2.5	64%[8]	49%	47%[6]	54%[4]	2%[4]	14/1[4]	17-23[4]	21%[4]	60%[4]	N/A

MIDWEST ▶

School (State) (*Public)	Peer assessment score (5.0=highest)	Average first-year student retention rate	2019 graduation rate Predicted	2019 graduation rate Actual	% of classes under 20 ('19)	% of classes of 50 or more ('19)	Student/ faculty ratio ('19)	SAT/ACT 25th-75th percentile ('19)	Freshmen in top 25% of HS class ('19)	Accept-ance rate ('19)	Average alumni giving rate
SCHOOLS RANKED 119 THROUGH 156 ARE LISTED HERE ALPHABETICALLY											
Avila University[1] (MO)	2.6	67%[8]	50%	46%[6]	N/A	N/A	12/1[4]	19-23[4]	N/A	55%[4]	N/A
Baker College of Flint[1] (MI)	1.8	49%[8]	34%	15%[6]	N/A	N/A	8/1[4]	N/A[2]	N/A	53%[4]	N/A
Bellevue University[1] (NE)	2.3	66%[8]	44%	13%[6]	N/A	N/A	27/1[4]	N/A[2]	N/A	N/A	N/A
Black Hills State University (SD)*	2.6	64%	52%	34%[6]	N/A	N/A	18/1[4]	18-24	N/A	99%	N/A
Calumet College of St. Joseph (IN)	2.2	51%	40%	30%	70%	1%	11/1	810-1000[2]	14%	41%	1%
Chadron State College[1] (NE)*	2.3	61%[8]	53%	43%[6]	N/A	N/A	17/1[4]	N/A[2]	N/A	N/A	N/A
Chicago State University[1]*	1.8	61%[8]	42%	15%[6]	N/A	N/A	7/1[4]	16-20[4]	N/A	33%[4]	N/A
Columbia College[1] (MO)	2.6	63%[8]	36%	28%[6]	N/A	N/A	25/1[4]	N/A[2]	N/A	N/A	N/A
Crown College[1] (MN)	2.1	71%[8]	50%	55%[6]	N/A	N/A	18/1[4]	18-24[4]	N/A	55%[4]	N/A
DeVry University[1] (IL)	1.5	49%[8]	26%	24%[6]	N/A	N/A	20/1[4]	N/A[2]	N/A	94%[4]	N/A
Evangel University[7] (MO)	2.4	79%	55%	51%[6]	N/A	N/A	15/1[4]	N/A[2]	N/A	74%	N/A
Graceland University (IA)	2.2	63%	46%	45%	69%	1%	14/1	18-24	34%	58%	15%
Herzing University[1] (WI)	1.7	38%[8]	30%	28%[6]	61%	0%	17/1[4]	N/A[2]	N/A	100%[4]	N/A
Indiana University East*	2.3	65%	39%	40%	62%	2%	15/1	930-1140[2]	35%	63%	5%
Indiana University Northwest*	2.4	66%	46%	34%	52%	5%	14/1	910-1100	37%	75%	5%
Indiana University–South Bend*	2.6	65%	43%	38%	49%	3%	13/1	950-1130	30%	78%	5%
Indiana University Southeast*	2.4	61%	46%	36%	64%	0.4%	13/1	17-23	30%	82%	6%
Lake Erie College[1] (OH)	2.4	66%[8]	50%	47%[6]	N/A	N/A	14/1[4]	17-23[4]	N/A	65%[4]	N/A
Lakeland University[1] (WI)	2.1	66%[8]	47%	53%[6]	N/A	N/A	13/1[4]	16-22[4]	N/A	52%[4]	N/A
Lourdes University[1] (OH)	2.5	69%[8]	46%	32%[8]	53%[4]	0%[4]	14/1[4]	18-24[4]	40%[4]	90%[4]	N/A
Maharishi University of Management[1] (IA)	1.6	62%[8]	43%	64%[6]	N/A	N/A	10/1[4]	N/A[2]	N/A	100%[4]	N/A
Midland University[1] (NE)	2.4	62%[8]	50%	46%[6]	N/A	N/A	16/1[4]	18-23[4]	N/A	52%[4]	N/A
Missouri Baptist University[1]	2.3	62%[8]	46%	38%[6]	N/A	N/A	19/1[4]	19-23[4]	N/A	52%[4]	N/A
Missouri Western State University[1]*	2.2	65%[8]	42%	31%[6]	N/A	N/A	17/1[4]	N/A[2]	N/A	N/A	N/A
Northeastern Illinois University*	2.6	52%	43%	21%	67%	0%	13/1	830-1020	11%	58%	2%
Notre Dame College of Ohio[1]	2.4	63%[8]	42%	38%[6]	N/A	N/A	13/1[4]	17-21[4]	N/A	90%[4]	N/A
Ohio Christian University	2.0	63%[8]	31%	75%	N/A	N/A	11/1	N/A[2]	N/A	N/A	N/A
Park University (MO)	2.6	55%	42%	31%	76%	0%	15/1	17-23[2]	N/A	N/A	1%
Peru State College[1] (NE)*	2.3	63%[8]	44%	35%[6]	N/A	N/A	19/1[4]	N/A[2]	N/A	N/A	N/A
Purdue University–Northwest (IN)*	2.7	67%	54%	39%	51%	3%	12/1	980-1160	38%	98%	N/A
Rockford University (IL)	2.5	66%	50%	41%	73%	0%	10/1	960-1140	34%	54%	6%
Saginaw Valley State Univ. (MI)*	2.6	73%	51%	44%	31%	2%	17/1	980-1190	44%	73%	N/A
Shawnee State University (OH)*	2.2	72%	43%	31%	58%	2%	15/1	18-24[2]	37%	99%	1%
Silver Lake College[1] (WI)	1.9	63%[8]	44%	47%[6]	N/A	N/A	9/1[4]	15-19[4]	N/A	50%[4]	N/A
Southwestern College (KS)	2.1	61%	59%	42%	70%	2%	10/1	18-23	32%	51%	4%
Tiffin University (OH)	2.6	65%	45%	39%	44%	0%	15/1	17-22[2]	N/A	69%	4%
Upper Iowa University[1]	2.1	64%[8]	46%	43%[6]	85%[4]	0%[4]	10/1[4]	18-23[4]	15%[4]	81%[4]	4%[4]
Waldorf University[1] (IA)	1.9	55%[8]	44%	26%[6]	N/A	N/A	23/1[4]	17-22[4]	N/A	75%[4]	N/A

WEST ▶

Rank	School (State) (*Public)	Overall score	Peer assessment score (5.0=highest)	Average first-year student retention rate	2019 graduation rate Predicted	2019 graduation rate Actual	% of classes under 20 ('19)	% of classes of 50 or more ('19)	Student/ faculty ratio ('19)	SAT/ACT 25th-75th percentile ('19)	Freshmen in top 25% of HS class ('19)	Accept-ance rate ('19)	Average alumni giving rate
1.	Trinity University (TX)	100	4.1	90%	88%	76%	64%	1%	9/1	1290-1450	82%	29%	15%
2.	University of Portland[1] (OR)	86	3.9	90%	79%	81%	38%	1%	11/1	1150-1350	72%[4]	61%	11%[4]
3.	Cal. Polytech. State U.–San Luis Obispo*	81	4.2	95%	81%	83%	16%	12%	18/1	1240-1440[3]	85%	28%	4%
4.	Whitworth University (WA)	80	3.9	84%	72%	75%	60%	2%	12/1	1050-1290[2]	64%	91%	11%
5.	University of Redlands (CA)	75	3.3	85%[8]	70%	76%	64%	2%	12/1	1080-1270	73%	76%	11%
6.	St. Mary's College of California	74	3.5	85%	75%	76%	63%	0.1%	10/1	1060-1250[3]	N/A	81%	6%
6.	University of Dallas	74	3.6	83%	78%	71%	60%	3%	11/1	1130-1360[2]	66%	45%	16%
8.	St. Edward's University (TX)	72	3.6	80%	63%	64%	52%	0.2%	14/1	1060-1245	51%	88%	8%
8.	St. Mary's Univ. of San Antonio	72	3.4	75%	57%	60%	52%	0%	11/1	1040-1220	61%	79%	10%
10.	California Lutheran University	71	3.3	84%	72%	68%	55%	0.3%	15/1	1070-1250	65%	71%	12%
10.	California State Polytechnic U.–Pomona*	71	4.0	88%	46%	69%	17%	13%	24/1	1010-1270[3]	N/A	55%	3%
12.	Mills College (CA)	70	3.4	76%	71%	56%	84%	0.4%	10/1	1008-1240[4]	52%	77%	14%
13.	Point Loma Nazarene University (CA)	69	3.3	87%	75%	75%	40%	1%	14/1	1140-1310	78%	74%	6%
14.	California State U.–Long Beach*	68	3.6	88%	46%	74%	21%	8%	26/1	1040-1250	N/A	39%	3%
15.	Abilene Christian University (TX)	67	3.6	77%	70%	61%	46%	6%	14/1	21-28[2]	56%	61%	11%
16.	California State University–Fullerton*	66	3.5	88%	54%	70%	20%	9%	25/1	1030-1200	63%	53%	3%

Note: Key to footnotes Page 60.

WEST ▶

Rank School (State) (*Public)	Overall score	Peer assessment score (5.0=highest)	Average first-year student retention rate	2019 graduation rate Predicted	Actual	% of classes under 20 ('19)	% of classes of 50 or more ('19)	Student/faculty ratio ('19)	SAT/ACT 25th-75th percentile ('19)	Freshmen in top 25% of HS class ('19)	Accept-ance rate ('19)	Average alumni giving rate
16. Mount Saint Mary's University (CA)	66	3.2	76%	49%	66%	68%	1%	10/1	920-1170[2]	49%	90%	8%
18. N.M. Inst. of Mining and Tech.*	65	3.2	76%	75%	50%	66%	5%	11/1	23-29	68%	80%	N/A
18. University of St. Thomas (TX)	65	3.3	83%	62%	68%	51%	1%	12/1	1057-1242	48%	87%	8%
18. Western Washington University*	65	3.5	82%	65%	68%	42%	13%	19/1	1060-1280	51%	90%	4%
18. Westminster College (UT)	65	3.3	80%	68%	58%	76%	0%	9/1	19-29	51%	92%	10%
22. Pacific Lutheran University (WA)	64	3.5	82%	73%	69%	48%	3%	13/1	1080-1290[9]	N/A	86%	8%
22. San Jose State University (CA)*	64	3.7	86%	49%	64%	24%	10%	27/1	1030-1260[3]	N/A	64%	1%
24. Dominican University of California	61	2.9	87%	72%	70%	56%	0%	9/1	1030-1220[2]	54%	91%	6%
25. California State U.–Monterey Bay*	59	3.3	81%	54%	63%	24%	4%	25/1	960-1170	44%	75%	1%
26. California State University–Chico*	57	3.2	85%	62%	66%	29%	12%	23/1	990-1180	N/A	72%	4%
26. California State U.–Los Angeles*	57	3.3	81%	23%	52%	25%	7%	23/1	890-1080	N/A	48%	3%
26. LeTourneau University (TX)	57	3.0	79%	66%	63%	68%	1%	13/1	1090-1310[2]	53%	45%	4%
29. California State U.–Stanislaus*	56	3.1	83%	37%	59%	21%	6%	22/1	890-1070[2]	N/A	89%	1%
29. Chaminade University of Honolulu	56	3.0	79%	46%	59%	64%	0.4%	11/1	980-1150	41%	94%	3%
29. San Francisco State University*	56	3.4	79%	47%	57%	28%	12%	22/1	940-1150	N/A	67%	1%
29. University of Washington–Bothell[1]*	56	3.2	87%[8]	58%	62%[6]	N/A	N/A	20/1[4]	1030-1250[4]	N/A	79%[4]	N/A
33. Saint Martin's University (WA)	53	2.9	78%	63%	67%	70%	0%	12/1	970-1170[2]	57%[5]	96%	4%
33. Sonoma State University (CA)*	53	3.3	79%	56%	66%	24%[4]	19%[4]	23/1[4]	980-1170[4]	N/A	91%	N/A
35. Montana Technological University*	52	3.0	76%	66%	52%	64%	7%	13/1	21-26	55%	92%	14%
35. University of Washington–Tacoma[1]*	52	3.1	81%[8]	53%	58%[6]	N/A	N/A	16/1[4]	980-1190[4]	N/A	86%[4]	N/A
37. Fresno Pacific University (CA)	51	2.7	74%	58%	68%	72%	1%	13/1	870-980	55%	65%	N/A
37. Hardin-Simmons University (TX)	51	3.1	70%	64%	51%	61%	2%	14/1	18-23[2]	39%	84%	18%
37. Humboldt State University (CA)*	51	3.1	71%	50%	49%	31%	10%	19/1	970-1200[2]	31%	91%	3%
40. California Baptist University	50	2.8	76%	56%	63%	51%	5%	14/1	990-1210	40%	78%	1%
40. California State U.–Northridge*	50	3.4	79%	38%	55%	10%	14%	27/1	910-1130	N/A	57%	4%
40. California State U.–San Bernardino*	50	3.0	85%	34%	55%	23%	18%	28/1	910-1090[2]	N/A	69%	3%[4]
43. California State U.–Channel Islands[1]*	49	3.1	79%[8]	48%	57%[6]	N/A	N/A	22/1[4]	N/A[2]	N/A	78%[4]	N/A
43. California State U.–Sacramento*	49	3.3	82%	42%	55%	15%	16%	24/1	940-1140[2]	N/A	82%	1%
43. Evergreen State College (WA)*	49	3.3	66%	51%	50%	43%	9%	21/1	960-1210[2]	26%[5]	98%	2%
46. Univ. of Mary Hardin-Baylor (TX)	48	3.2	71%	58%	51%	50%	3%	17/1	1000-1190[3]	47%	87%	4%
47. Central Washington University*	47	3.0	72%	53%	58%	42%	3%	22/1	940-1130[9]	N/A	87%	2%
47. Oklahoma Christian U.	47	3.0	76%	67%	53%	63%	6%	13/1	21-27	51%	67%	12%
49. Concordia University (CA)	46	2.8	76%	60%	63%	55%	0%	16/1	990-1210	44%	71%	5%
50. Northwest Nazarene University (ID)	45	2.9	78%[8]	64%	63%	61%	3%	17/1	990-1190	48%[4]	86%	N/A
50. Woodbury University (CA)	45	2.4	78%	56%	54%	81%	0.3%	9/1	940-1220[2]	N/A	66%	2%
52. California State Univ.–Bakersfield*	44	3.1	74%	34%	42%[6]	35%	9%	21/1	880-1080[2]	N/A	79%	N/A
52. Eastern Washington University*	44	3.0	74%	51%	53%	42%	8%	18/1	880-1100	N/A	96%	2%[4]
52. The Master's U. and Seminary (CA)	44	2.3	85%	68%	69%	67%	7%	12/1	990-1320	61%	67%	6%
52. Northwest University (WA)	44	2.6	79%	58%	55%	70%	3%	8/1	1010-1215	N/A	93%	1%
52. Vanguard U. of Southern California	44	2.4	75%	54%	59%	52%	6%	15/1	980-1170	46%	49%	5%
57. Rocky Mountain College (MT)	43	2.8	68%	59%	49%	71%	0.4%	10/1	19-24	36%	59%	5%
58. California State U.–Dominguez Hills*	42	3.0	79%	32%	45%	23%	6%	26/1	850-1030[2]	N/A	79%	1%
58. Texas A&M International University*	42	2.9	78%	45%	48%	31%	16%	24/1	910-1090	55%	62%	5%
60. California State Univ.–San Marcos*	41	3.1	80%[8]	46%	54%	14%	8%	26/1	930-1130	N/A	62%	N/A
60. University of North Texas–Dallas[1]*	41	3.5	72%[8]	33%	30%[6]	52%[4]	0%[4]	17/1[4]	920-1080[4]	38%[4]	83%[4]	N/A
62. Hawaii Pacific University[1]	40	2.9	63%[8]	63%	44%[8]	56%[4]	1%[4]	15/1[4]	1020-1220[4]	46%[4]	75%[4]	1%[4]
62. Southern Utah University*	40	2.9	72%	58%	44%	37%	8%	20/1	20-27	45%	78%	4%
64. Holy Names University (CA)	39	2.5	72%	53%	48%	66%	0%	8/1	720-880	19%	63%	5%[4]
64. Houston Baptist University	39	2.9	70%	54%	44%	47%	6%	14/1	1020-1180	57%	70%	2%
64. Notre Dame de Namur University[1] (CA)	39	2.4	71%[8]	52%	49%[6]	72%[4]	0%[4]	11/1[4]	870-1060[4]	38%[4]	82%[4]	4%[4]
64. Tarleton State University (TX)*	39	3.0	68%	47%	49%	33%	9%	22/1	18-23	35%	56%	2%
68. Colorado Christian University	38	2.6	79%	61%	54%	56%	2%	13/1	22-28[2]	N/A	63%	1%
68. La Sierra University (CA)	38	2.4	81%[8]	57%	47%	67%	3%	12/1	910-1160	34%	55%	1%
68. Lubbock Christian University (TX)	38	2.8	69%	57%	50%	71%	1%	14/1	960-1170[3]	42%	91%	5%
68. Southern Nazarene University (OK)	38	2.7	75%[8]	56%	56%	72%	2%	13/1	18-24	N/A	82%	4%
68. University of Central Oklahoma*	38	3.1	63%	50%	36%	48%	1%	17/1	19-24	40%	77%	1%
68. U. of Texas of the Permian Basin*	38	2.7	62%	60%	40%	45%	6%	19/1	940-1132	48%	78%	1%
68. Western Oregon University*	38	2.9	72%	50%	41%	55%	3%	13/1	960-1170[2]	20%	85%	2%
75. Midwestern State University (TX)*	37	2.7	68%	51%	46%	41%	10%	17/1	17-22[2]	39%	79%	3%
75. Southern Oregon University*	37	3.0	69%	54%	46%	51%	4%	24/1	980-1200	N/A	78%	1%
75. University of Alaska–Anchorage*	37	3.2	68%	59%	32%	58%	3%	11/1	1020-1220[2]	35%	83%	2%

WEST ▶

Rank School (State) (*Public)	Overall score	Peer assessment score (5.0=highest)	Average first-year student retention rate	2019 graduation rate Predicted	2019 graduation rate Actual	% of classes under 20 ('19)	% of classes of 50 or more ('19)	Student/ faculty ratio ('19)	SAT/ACT 25th-75th percentile ('19)	Freshmen in top 25% of HS class ('19)	Accept- ance rate ('19)	Average alumni giving rate
75. Walla Walla University[1] (WA)	37	2.9	84%[8]	65%	57%[6]	N/A	N/A	14/1[4]	920-1210[4]	N/A	51%[4]	N/A
75. Western Colorado University*	37	2.6	67%	56%	51%	63%	0.4%	18/1	1000-1200	17%	84%	N/A
80. California State University–East Bay*	36	3.0	76%	43%	49%	11%	21%	23/1	900-1100[2]	N/A	76%	N/A
80. Texas A&M University–Texarkana*	36	2.7	58%[8]	51%	34%	67%	0.4%	12/1	19-23[2]	36%	94%	N/A
82. Bushnell University[7] (OR)	35	2.5	70%[8]	53%	52%	65%[4]	2%[4]	15/1[4]	935-1170[4]	42%[4]	62%[4]	4%[4]
83. West Texas A&M University*	34	3.0	66%	53%	46%	31%	9%	18/1	18-23	42%	69%	2%
84. Hope International University (CA)	33	2.3	68%	44%	54%	70%	0%	13/1	910-1070	27%	37%	6%
84. Southwestern Oklahoma State U.*	33	2.8	67%	49%	36%	54%	3%	18/1	18-24[2]	49%	91%	N/A
84. University of Guam*	33	2.5	75%[8]	47%	38%	59%	2%	16/1	N/A[2]	44%	90%	N/A
84. Weber State University (UT)*	33	3.3	65%	51%	34%	48%	6%	21/1	18-24[2]	30%	89%	2%
88. Alaska Pacific University	32	2.4	65%[8]	59%	52%[6]	N/A	N/A	7/1	N/A[2]	N/A	89%	1%
88. Eastern Oregon University*	32	2.9	70%	50%	27%	66%	3%	17/1	930-1145	40%	98%	N/A
88. University of Alaska–Southeast[7]*	32	2.6	62%[8]	63%	37%	87%	0%	9/1	N/A[2]	N/A	61%	N/A
91. Angelo State University (TX)*	31	2.9	68%	47%	40%	29%	8%	20/1	17-23	38%	77%	2%
92. Simpson University[1] (CA)	30	2.3	71%[8]	58%	55%[6]	N/A	N/A	11/1[4]	966-1160[4]	N/A	50%[4]	N/A
93. Colorado State University–Pueblo*	29	2.9	65%	43%	36%	48%	7%	15/1	940-1130	34%	93%	2%
93. Northeastern State University (OK)*	29	2.7	63%	45%	32%	48%	2%	19/1	18-24	52%	99%	1%

School (State) (*Public)	Peer assessment score (5.0=highest)	Average first-year student retention rate	2019 graduation rate Predicted	2019 graduation rate Actual	% of classes under 20 ('19)	% of classes of 50 or more ('19)	Student/ faculty ratio ('19)	SAT/ACT 25th-75th percentile ('19)	Freshmen in top 25% of HS class ('19)	Accept- ance rate ('19)	Average alumni giving rate
SCHOOLS RANKED 95 THROUGH 124 ARE LISTED HERE ALPHABETICALLY											
Academy of Art University (CA)	2.3	74%	64%	42%	93%	0%	14/1	N/A[2]	N/A	100%	N/A
Adams State University[1] (CO)*	2.4	59%[8]	45%	30%[6]	N/A	N/A	12/1[4]	870-1080[4]	N/A	99%[4]	N/A
Cameron University (OK)*	2.5	64%	36%	26%	49%	0.4%	19/1	16-21[2]	13%	100%	1%
City University of Seattle[1]	2.5	75%[8]	56%	24%[6]	N/A	N/A	6/1[4]	N/A[2]	N/A	N/A	N/A
Colorado Mesa University*	2.7	74%	42%	43%	48%	9%	20/1	930-1170	29%	78%	2%
Concordia University Texas[1]	2.7	61%[8]	56%	35%[6]	N/A	N/A	12/1[4]	940-1170[4]	N/A	91%[4]	N/A
East Central University (OK)*	2.4	55%	43%	37%	45%	3%	16/1	17-23	44%[4]	59%	N/A
Eastern New Mexico University[1]*	2.8	61%[8]	41%	32%[6]	67%[4]	2%[4]	17/1[4]	17-22[4]	32%[4]	60%[4]	3%[4]
Heritage University[1] (WA)	2.3	68%[8]	32%	22%[6]	N/A	N/A	7/1[4]	N/A[2]	N/A	N/A	N/A
Langston University[1] (OK)*	2.2	57%[8]	40%	20%[6]	51%[4]	7%[4]	16/1[4]	17-26[4]	N/A	55%[4]	N/A
Metropolitan State University of Denver[7]*	3.2	65%	44%	28%	42%	1%	18/1	880-1110[3]	14%	61%	N/A
Mid-America Christian University[1] (OK)	2.3	58%[8]	40%	38%[6]	N/A	N/A	7/1[4]	N/A[2]	N/A	N/A	N/A
Montana State Univ.–Billings*	3.1	57%	49%	24%	50%	2%	14/1	17-23[2]	31%	100%	3%
Naropa University (CO)	2.2	61%[8]	61%	34%	89%	1%	8/1	N/A[2]	N/A	99%	N/A
National University (CA)	2.2	58%[8]	56%	28%	74%	0%	16/1	N/A[2]	N/A	89%	N/A
New Mexico Highlands University*	2.5	52%[8]	37%	22%	74%[4]	1%[4]	14/1[4]	15-20[2]	30%	65%	N/A
Northwestern Oklahoma State U.*	2.5	56%	47%	31%	61%[4]	2%[4]	15/1	17-22	9%	68%	4%
Oklahoma Wesleyan University[1]	2.6	51%[8]	52%	41%[6]	N/A	N/A	13/1[4]	16-21[4]	N/A	68%[4]	N/A
Prairie View A&M University (TX)*	2.8	70%	37%	36%	18%	8%	17/1	870-1040	25%	80%	N/A
Prescott College[1] (AZ)	2.7	72%[8]	53%	38%[6]	N/A	N/A	9/1[4]	N/A[2]	N/A	95%[4]	N/A
Sierra Nevada University[1] (NV)	2.4	62%[8]	55%	41%[6]	N/A	N/A	10/1[4]	18-23[4]	N/A	64%[4]	N/A
Southeastern Oklahoma State U.[1]*	2.5	61%[8]	42%	28%[6]	N/A	N/A	20/1[4]	18-23[4]	N/A	75%[4]	N/A
Southwestern Assemblies of God University[1] (TX)	2.2	72%[8]	47%	46%[6]	N/A	N/A	15/1[4]	17-23[4]	N/A	91%[4]	N/A
Sul Ross State University (TX)*	2.5	57%[8]	39%	25%	76%	0.4%	13/1	15-19[2]	18%	81%	N/A
University of Houston–Downtown*	3.1	71%	39%	29%	26%	2%	19/1	920-1080	30%	89%	1%
University of Houston–Victoria[1]*	2.6	51%[8]	37%	18%[6]	N/A	N/A	15/1[4]	N/A[2]	N/A	54%[4]	N/A
University of the Southwest[1] (NM)	2.4	51%[8]	37%	19%[6]	N/A	N/A	14/1[4]	N/A	N/A	45%[4]	N/A
Utah Valley University[7]*	2.7	65%	47%	29%	40%	6%	24/1	18-25[2]	27%	100%	N/A
Wayland Baptist University (TX)	2.3	46%	46%	23%	84%	0.1%	6/1	16-22	22%	97%	1%
Western New Mexico University[1]*	2.5	57%[8]	36%	22%[6]	N/A	N/A	15/1[4]	N/A[2]	N/A	N/A	N/A

Note: Key to footnotes Page 60.

James Madison University

The Top Public Regional Universities ▶

NORTH
Rank School (State)

1. College of New Jersey
2. SUNY Polytechnic Institute– Albany/Utica
3. SUNY–Geneseo
4. CUNY–Baruch College
5. CUNY–Hunter College
†7. Ramapo College of New Jersey
7. Stockton University (NJ)
9. SUNY–New Paltz
10. CUNY–Queens College
10. SUNY–Oswego
10. West Chester University of Pennsylvania
13. CUNY–Lehman College
13. SUNY Maritime College
15. CUNY–Brooklyn College

SOUTH
Rank School (State)

1. The Citadel, Military College of SC
2. James Madison University (VA)
3. Appalachian State University (NC)
4. Christopher Newport U. (VA)
5. College of Charleston (SC)
6. Winthrop University (SC)
7. Longwood University (VA)
8. U. of Mary Washington (VA)
9. Georgia College & State University
10. Western Carolina University (NC)
11. Murray State University (KY)
11. University of Montevallo (AL)
13. University of Tennessee–Martin
14. Radford University (VA)
15. University of North Georgia
15. University of West Florida

MIDWEST
Rank School (State)

1. Truman State University (MO)
2. University of Northern Iowa
3. Grand Valley State University (MI)
4. University of Illinois–Springfield
4. University of Michigan–Dearborn
6. University of Nebraska–Kearney
6. University of Wisconsin– La Crosse
8. University of Minnesota–Duluth
8. U. of Wisconsin–Eau Claire
10. Winona State University (MN)
11. Eastern Illinois University
12. University of Wisconsin– Whitewater
13. Western Illinois University
14. U. of Wisconsin–Stevens Point
15. University of Wisconsin–Stout

WEST
Rank School (State)

1. California Polytechnic State U.– San Luis Obispo
2. Calif. State Polytechnic U.–Pomona
3. California State U.–Long Beach
4. California State U.–Fullerton
5. N.M. Inst. of Mining and Tech.
5. Western Washington University
7. San Jose State University (CA)
8. California State U.–Monterey Bay
9. California State University–Chico
9. California State U.–Los Angeles
11. California State U.–Stanislaus
11. San Francisco State University
11. University of Washington–Bothell
14. Sonoma State University (CA)
15. Montana Technological University
15. University of Washington–Tacoma

†A university previously ranked at No. 6 in the North has been unranked because of a data reporting error.

Best Regional Colleges

What Is a Regional College?

THESE SCHOOLS FOCUS almost entirely on the undergraduate experience and offer a broad range of programs in the liberal arts (which account for fewer than half of bachelor's degrees granted) and in fields such as business, nursing and education. They grant few graduate degrees. Because most of the 366 colleges in the category draw heavily from nearby states, they are ranked by region: North, South, Midwest, West.

Regions at a glance

These are the four regions into which U.S. News places schools.

■ North ■ Midwest
■ South ■ West

NORTH ▶

Rank	School (State) (*Public)	Overall score	Peer assessment score (5.0=highest)	Average first-year student retention rate	2019 graduation rate		% of classes under 20 ('19)	% of classes of 50 or more ('19)	Student/ faculty ratio ('19)	SAT/ACT 25th-75th percentile ('19)	Freshmen in top 25% of HS class ('19)	Accept- ance rate ('19)	Average alumni giving rate
					Predicted	Actual							
1.	U.S. Coast Guard Academy (CT)*	100	4.2	95%	77%	88%	55%	0.3%	7/1	1212-1400	84%	20%	N/A
2.	Cooper Union for Adv. of Sci. & Art (NY)	93	4.0	94%	89%	91%	74%	1%	8/1	1305-1530[2]	N/A	16%	20%
3.	U.S. Merchant Marine Acad.[1] (NY)*	72	3.8	94%[8]	83%	80%[6]	N/A	N/A	9/1[4]	1190-1330[4]	66%[4]	15%[4]	N/A
4.	Maine Maritime Academy*	67	3.8	82%	60%	71%	50%	0%	11/1	1010-1200	40%	45%	17%
5.	Massachusetts Maritime Academy*	57	3.7	87%	66%	76%	35%	1%	15/1	1020-1180	N/A	91%	9%
6.	Elmira College[1] (NY)	47	3.0	73%[8]	62%	63%[8]	81%[4]	0.4%[4]	10/1[4]	1070-1210[4]	N/A	84%[4]	13%[4]
6.	University of Maine–Farmington*	47	3.3	72%	49%	58%	72%	1%	11/1	940-1160[2]	37%	91%	4%
8.	Colby-Sawyer College (NH)	44	3.1	74%	60%	63%	60%	1%	13/1	1030-1230[2]	N/A	90%	10%
9.	Keene State College (NH)*	43	3.1	74%	50%	63%	54%	1%	13/1	960-1140[2]	20%	88%	3%
9.	SUNY College of Technology at Alfred*	43	3.2	70%	36%	68%	50%	1%	18/1	940-1170[2]	N/A	67%	2%
11.	Unity College[1] (ME)	40	2.9	69%[8]	49%	63%[6]	48%[4]	0%[4]	15/1[4]	1000-1260[4]	38%[4]	94%[4]	2%[4]
12.	Cazenovia College (NY)	39	3.0	71%	48%	58%	82%	0%	12/1	989-1239[2]	10%	94%	5%
13.	St. Francis College (NY)	38	2.9	77%	43%	58%	53%	1%	16/1	920-1130[2]	N/A	78%	7%
14.	SUNY College of Technology–Delhi*	37	3.2	72%	35%	54%	58%	1%	16/1	920-1120[2]	18%	72%	3%
15.	Bard College at Simon's Rock[7] (MA)	35	3.2	77%[8]	72%	34%[8]	97%	0%	6/1	N/A[2]	72%	92%	N/A
15.	New England Inst. of Technology (RI)	35	2.7	N/A	43%	53%	91%	0%	9/1	970-1147[2]	N/A	64%	N/A
15.	Pennsylvania College of Technology*	35	2.9	78%	48%	52%	67%	0%	14/1	970-1170[2]	22%	78%	1%
18.	SUNY Cobleskill*	34	2.9	72%	40%	54%	58%	4%	11/1	890-1100[2]	18%	93%	2%
19.	SUNY College of Technology–Canton*	33	3.2	74%	34%	53%	40%	2%	18/1	920-1110[2]	17%	85%	2%
19.	Univ. of Pittsburgh at Bradford*	33	3.2	68%[8]	46%	43%	66%	2%	15/1	970-1160	39%	58%	4%
21.	Farmingdale State College–SUNY*	31	3.1	82%	49%	57%	26%	1%	19/1	990-1150	28%	55%	0.3%
21.	Vermont Technical College*	31	2.8	78%	47%	46%	82%	0%	8/1	980-1170[2]	26%[4]	68%	1%
23.	Castleton University[1] (VT)*	30	3.0	72%[8]	46%	51%[6]	N/A	N/A	17/1[4]	930-1170[4]	27%[4]	87%[4]	4%[4]
24.	Vaughn Col. of Aeron. and Tech. (NY)	29	2.9	77%	40%	34%	60%	0%	16/1	963-1165	N/A	82%	5%[4]
25.	Pittsburgh Technical College	28	2.6	62%[8]	30%	57%	70%	0.4%	17/1	N/A[2]	N/A	77%	N/A
25.	SUNY Morrisville (NY)*	28	3.0	65%	38%	48%	60%	1%	14/1	930-1100[2]	16%	75%	3%
27.	Paul Smith's College (NY)	27	2.9	71%	48%	51%	58%	2%	12/1	N/A[2]	N/A	70%	8%
28.	Peirce College (PA)	26	2.3	67%[8]	27%	50%[8]	87%	0%	13/1	N/A[2]	N/A	N/A	N/A
28.	University of Maine–Presque Isle*	26	3.2	61%	38%	37%	78%	0%	13/1	870-1080[9]	23%	99%	0.3%
30.	Thiel College (PA)	25	3.0	65%	44%	46%[6]	N/A	N/A	12/1[4]	890-1150[3]	29%	79%	N/A
31.	Keystone College (PA)	24	2.6	64%	35%	46%	68%	0.3%	13/1	880-1070[2]	N/A	79%	3%
31.	Univ. of Pittsburgh–Johnstown[1]*	24	3.1	73%[8]	48%	48%[6]	N/A	N/A	17/1[4]	1020-1200[4]	N/A	65%[4]	N/A
33.	University of Valley Forge (PA)	22	2.8	73%	40%	44%	45%	2%	10/1	950-1180[2]	19%	63%	2%
34.	Dean College (MA)	20	2.8	71%	43%	48%	46%	0%	17/1	910-1105[2]	N/A	69%	5%
34.	Fisher College (MA)	20	2.5	62%	30%	34%	64%	0%	14/1	830-1030[2]	N/A	69%	N/A
34.	Mount Aloysius College (PA)	20	2.7	72%[8]	35%	35%[6]	77%	0%	11/1	943-1120[4]	N/A	95%	N/A
37.	University of Maine–Fort Kent*	19	3.1	66%	34%	36%	58%	2%	15/1	880-1070[9]	13%[4]	99%	4%

Note: Key to footnotes, Page 60.

Rank	School (State) (*Public)	Overall score	Peer assessment score (5.0=highest)	Average first-year student retention rate	2019 graduation rate Predicted	Actual	% of classes under 20 ('19)	% of classes of 50 or more ('19)	Student/ faculty ratio ('19)	SAT/ACT 25th-75th percentile ('19)	Freshmen in top 25% of HS class ('19)	Accept-ance rate ('19)	Average alumni giving rate
38.	CUNY–York College*	18	2.8	68%	29%	35%	29%	8%	19/1	880-1040	N/A	73%	N/A
39.	CUNY–New York City Col. of Tech.*	17	3.0	73%	28%	32%	28%	0%	18/1[4]	N/A[2]	N/A	88%	N/A
40.	Hilbert College[1] (NY)	15	2.6	70%[8]	44%	50%[6]	N/A	N/A	12/1[4]	N/A[2]	N/A	84%[4]	N/A

School (State) (*Public)	Peer assessment score (5.0=highest)	Average first-year student retention rate	2019 graduation rate Predicted	Actual	% of classes under 20 ('19)	% of classes of 50 or more ('19)	Student/ faculty ratio ('19)	SAT/ACT 25th-75th percentile ('19)	Freshmen in top 25% of HS class ('19)	Accept-ance rate ('19)	Average alumni giving rate
SCHOOLS RANKED 41 THROUGH 53 ARE LISTED HERE ALPHABETICALLY											
Bay State College[1] (MA)	2.4	56%[8]	41%	41%[6]	88%[4]	0%[4]	14/1[4]	N/A[2]	N/A	70%[4]	N/A
Becker College[1] (MA)	2.3	71%[8]	47%	41%[6]	N/A	N/A	16/1[4]	980-1180[4]	N/A	66%[4]	N/A
Berkeley College (NJ)	2.7	61%	29%	33%	71%	0%	14/1	N/A[2]	N/A	98%	N/A
Boricua College (NY)	2.3	50%[8]	23%	32%[6]	N/A	N/A	20/1[4]	N/A[2]	N/A	N/A	N/A
Central Penn College[1]	2.7	50%[8]	37%	34%[8]	78%[4]	0%[4]	9/1[4]	660-910[4]	N/A	72%[4]	1%[4]
The College of Westchester[1] (NY)	2.6	64%[8]	29%	44%[6]	N/A	N/A	18/1[4]	N/A[2]	N/A	97%[4]	N/A
CUNY–Medgar Evers College*	2.7	67%	26%	26%	26%	0%	14/1	810-1000[9]	N/A	90%	N/A
Eastern Nazarene College (MA)	2.6	68%	44%	40%	N/A	N/A	10/1[4]	880-1110	N/A	59%	N/A
Five Towns College (NY)	2.3	71%[8]	42%	48%	79%	0%	11/1	N/A[2]	N/A	34%	N/A
Mitchell College[1] (CT)	2.2	61%[8]	52%	43%[6]	N/A	N/A	15/1[4]	N/A[2]	N/A	83%[4]	N/A
University of Maine–Augusta[1]*	3.3	56%[8]	27%	15%[6]	N/A	N/A	16/1[4]	N/A[2]	N/A	N/A	N/A
Villa Maria College[1] (NY)	2.4	65%[8]	33%	34%[6]	N/A	N/A	8/1[4]	N/A[2]	N/A	75%[4]	N/A
Wesley College[1] (DE)	2.8	55%[8]	33%	23%[6]	N/A	N/A	12/1[4]	820-1023[4]	N/A	62%[4]	N/A

SOUTH ▶

Rank	School (State) (*Public)	Overall score	Peer assessment score (5.0=highest)	Average first-year student retention rate	2019 graduation rate Predicted	Actual	% of classes under 20 ('19)	% of classes of 50 or more ('19)	Student/ faculty ratio ('19)	SAT/ACT 25th-75th percentile ('19)	Freshmen in top 25% of HS class ('19)	Accept-ance rate ('19)	Average alumni giving rate
1.	High Point University (NC)	100	3.9	81%	61%	65%	49%	1%	15/1	1090-1260[2]	43%	74%	11%
2.	Ouachita Baptist University (AR)	91	3.4	81%	64%	63%	54%	2%	14/1	21-28	60%	61%	16%
3.	Maryville College (TN)	86	3.3	74%	55%	51%	60%	1%	12/1	21-27	52%	56%	16%[4]
4.	Flagler College (FL)	85	3.6	72%	52%	53%	63%	0%	15/1	1030-1210[2]	N/A	65%	11%
5.	LaGrange College (GA)	76	3.2	65%	52%	41%	72%	1%	11/1	1000-1148	42%	49%	12%
5.	University of the Ozarks (AR)	76	3.3	67%[8]	54%	52%	54%	0%	15/1	18-23[2]	10%	91%	13%
7.	Catawba College (NC)	75	3.1	76%[8]	47%	51%	60%	0%	12/1	930-1120[9]	31%	59%	10%
7.	Erskine College (SC)	75	2.8	62%	50%	54%	78%	0.3%	12/1	920-1140	28%	70%	16%
9.	Claflin University (SC)	74	2.6	76%	34%	51%	64%	1%	13/1	880-1040	33%	55%	40%
10.	Barton College (NC)	72	2.9	68%	45%	55%	58%	1%	12/1	940-1130	37%	45%	5%
11.	Newberry College (SC)	69	2.8	65%	44%	53%	68%	0.2%	13/1	870-1100	26%	63%	14%
12.	Univ. of South Carolina–Aiken*	68	3.2	67%	44%	39%	60%	1%	14/1	960-1140	44%	56%	4%
12.	U. of South Carolina–Upstate*	68	3.0	69%	41%	48%	60%	1%	16/1	920-1110	35%	47%	1%[4]
14.	Blue Mountain College (MS)	67	2.8	71%	44%	48%	65%	1%	16/1	18-23	38%	96%	5%
14.	Huntingdon College (AL)	67	2.9	64%	50%	49%	50%	0.4%	13/1	19-24	47%	59%	28%
16.	Florida National U.–Main Campus	66	2.1	91%	20%	73%	60%	0%	24/1	N/A[2]	N/A	99%	N/A
16.	University of Mobile (AL)	66	2.9	73%	52%	55%	71%	1%	12/1	20-27[2]	62%	46%	2%
18.	Averett University (VA)	65	2.8	62%	42%	41%	80%	0%	10/1	860-1060	19%	65%	3%
18.	Belmont Abbey College (NC)	65	3.0	63%	47%	45%	66%	0.2%	16/1	970-1220[2]	28%	81%	7%
18.	Kentucky Wesleyan College	65	3.0	68%	47%	45%	72%	0%	14/1	20-26	N/A	62%	8%
18.	University of Puerto Rico–Humacao[1]*	65	2.8	84%[8]	35%	47%[6]	N/A	N/A	16/1[4]	N/A[2]	N/A	42%[4]	N/A
18.	Welch College (TN)	65	2.6	76%	47%	55%	83%	2%	8/1	20-26	55%	66%	14%
23.	Tennessee Wesleyan University	64	3.1	69%	42%	42%	62%	5%	12/1	19-25	35%[4]	63%	3%
24.	Brevard College (NC)	62	3.2	59%[8]	49%	37%[6]	78%	0.1%	11/1	18-22[2]	19%	59%	N/A
24.	William Peace University (NC)	62	2.9	66%	42%	42%	72%	0.3%	12/1	920-1140	25%[4]	46%	2%
26.	Alice Lloyd College (KY)	61	2.9	59%	42%	44%	55%	2%	16/1	18-22	8%	7%	46%
26.	Lees-McRae College (NC)	61	2.8	62%	43%	46%	84%	0%	11/1	18-24[2]	N/A	55%	5%
26.	Mars Hill University (NC)	61	2.9	60%	41%	30%	80%	0%	9/1	18-23	27%	63%	8%
26.	Toccoa Falls College (GA)	61	2.7	66%	46%	45%	69%	0%	16/1	920-1150	36%	60%	2%

SOUTH ▶

Rank	School (State) (*Public)	Overall score	Peer assessment score (5.0=highest)	Average first-year student retention rate	2019 graduation rate		% of classes under 20 ('19)	% of classes of 50 or more ('19)	Student/ faculty ratio ('19)	SAT/ACT 25th-75th percentile ('19)	Freshmen in top 25% of HS class ('19)	Accept-ance rate ('19)	Average alumni giving rate
					Predicted	Actual							
30.	Pensacola State College (FL)*	60	2.7	76%	36%	46%	58%	1%	17/1	18-23[2]	N/A	52%	9%
31.	Beacon College[1] (FL)	59	2.4	81%[8]	60%	64%[6]	N/A	N/A	11/1[4]	N/A[2]	N/A	51%[4]	N/A
31.	University of Puerto Rico–Aguadilla[1]*	59	2.6	80%[8]	35%	45%[8]	28%[4]	0%[4]	20/1[4]	927-1130[4]	N/A	28%[4]	N/A
33.	Brescia University (KY)	57	2.9	65%	45%	34%	85%	0%	13/1	20-26	N/A	42%	9%
33.	Emmanuel College (GA)	57	2.8	61%	40%	40%	68%	0%	15/1	920-1120	N/A	46%	7%
33.	South Florida State College*	57	2.6	58%	35%	49%	70%[4]	0%[4]	17/1[4]	17-18[9]	19%	100%	N/A
36.	Elizabeth City State University (NC)*	56	2.3	71%	33%	39%[6]	56%	1%	15/1	875-1050	5%	66%	N/A
36.	Greensboro College (NC)	56	2.6	62%	38%	33%	87%	0.3%	7/1	900-1090	25%	45%	15%
36.	Kentucky State University*	56	2.8	62%	35%	26%	67%	1%	11/1	18-22	N/A	81%	N/A
36.	Martin Methodist College (TN)	56	2.7	54%	33%	35%	69%	0%	13/1	17-22	N/A	99%	8%
36.	University of the Virgin Islands*	56	2.6	71%	34%	32%	78%	0.3%	12/1	792-1027[2]	32%	98%	N/A
41.	Lander University (SC)*	55	2.8	66%	37%	45%	42%	4%	17/1	940-1130	38%	43%	5%
42.	University of Arkansas–Pine Bluff*	54	2.7	71%	35%	33%	60%	2%	14/1	16-20	30%	44%	10%
43.	Davis and Elkins College (WV)	52	2.5	69%[8]	39%	43%	N/A	N/A	12/1	930-1110	N/A	43%	7%
43.	Philander Smith College (AR)	52	2.5	66%	38%	44%	69%	0.3%	15/1	15-21	29%	35%	7%
43.	University of Puerto Rico–Arecibo*	52	2.4	81%	31%	47%[8]	33%	0.3%	22/1	N/A[2]	N/A	55%	N/A
43.	University of Puerto Rico–Bayamon[1]*	52	2.7	83%[8]	36%	39%[6]	47%[4]	0.3%[4]	21/1[4]	N/A[2]	N/A	70%[4]	N/A
47.	North Carolina Wesleyan College	51	2.7	62%	31%	41%	72%	0%	20/1	860-1070[2]	15%	62%	3%
47.	Oakwood University[1] (AL)	51	2.5	71%[8]	46%	48%[6]	N/A	N/A	11/1[4]	16-22[4]	N/A	66%[4]	N/A
47.	Truett McConnell University (GA)	51	2.8	64%	41%	40%	62%	2%	18/1	930-1150	42%	94%	1%
50.	Bluefield State College (WV)*	50	2.5	64%	29%	32%	90%	0%	13/1	16-21	48%	94%	6%[4]
50.	Ferrum College (VA)	50	2.8	53%	35%	29%	71%	0%	13/1	860-1060[2]	1%[4]	73%	4%[4]
50.	Middle Georgia State University*	50	2.9	61%	33%	30%[8]	48%	1%	22/1	880-1090	N/A	94%	1%
50.	Point University[1] (GA)	50	2.6	57%[8]	39%	31%[6]	69%[4]	1%[4]	17/1[4]	880-1085[4]	22%[4]	53%[4]	N/A
54.	Florida Memorial University[1]	49	2.5	66%[8]	31%	37%[6]	N/A	N/A	14/1[4]	N/A[2]	N/A	N/A	N/A
55.	Alderson Broaddus University (WV)	46	2.4	53%	43%	39%	70%	4%	15/1	860-1060	22%	47%	6%
55.	Glenville State College (WV)*	46	2.2	63%	29%	48%	69%	1%	15/1	840-1040	24%	100%	5%
55.	Limestone University (SC)	46	2.5	55%	36%	30%	72%	0.2%	14/1	880-1060[2]	23%	14%	3%
55.	Voorhees College (SC)	46	2.3	57%[8]	28%	41%	61%	2%	10/1	17[4]	N/A	64%	N/A
59.	Bluefield College[1] (VA)	45	2.8	55%[8]	35%	27%[8]	75%[4]	0%[4]	14/1[4]	898-1063[4]	16%[4]	94%[4]	7%[4]
59.	West Virginia State University[1]*	45	2.9	57%[8]	38%	28%[6]	N/A	N/A	19/1[4]	17-22[4]	N/A	94%[4]	N/A
61.	Gordon State College[1] (GA)*	44	2.4	49%[8]	27%	50%[6]	N/A	N/A	20/1[4]	850-1040[4]	N/A	71%[4]	N/A
61.	University of Arkansas–Fort Smith[1]*	44	2.8	65%[8]	37%	30%[6]	N/A	N/A	17/1[4]	N/A	N/A	N/A	N/A
63.	Central Baptist College (AR)	43	2.5	64%	39%	25%	73%	1%	11/1	17-22	22%[4]	56%	7%
63.	Warner University (FL)	43	2.4	58%	34%	35%	71%	0.4%	14/1	870-1090[2]	19%	46%	3%
65.	St. Augustine's University[1] (NC)	42	2.2	55%[8]	30%	28%[6]	75%[4]	1%[4]	9/1[4]	768-940[4]	N/A	63%[4]	9%[4]
66.	Florida College[1]	41	2.6	62%[8]	54%	26%[6]	68%[4]	8%[4]	13/1[4]	20-26[4]	N/A	74%[4]	N/A
66.	Georgia Gwinnett College*	41	2.9	67%	33%	21%	33%	0%	19/1	910-1100[2]	15%	94%	4%
68.	Kentucky Christian University[1]	40	2.7	59%[8]	42%	32%[6]	N/A	N/A	10/1[4]	17-21[4]	N/A	37%[4]	N/A
68.	St. Petersburg College (FL)*	40	2.9	70%	38%	33%	34%	1%	22/1	920-1130[2]	N/A	100%	1%

School (State) (*Public)	Peer assessment score (5.0=highest)	Average first-year student retention rate	2019 graduation rate		% of classes under 20 ('19)	% of classes of 50 or more ('19)	Student/ faculty ratio ('19)	SAT/ACT 25th-75th percentile ('19)	Freshmen in top 25% of HS class ('19)	Accept-ance rate ('19)	Average alumni giving rate
			Predicted	Actual							
SCHOOLS RANKED 70 THROUGH 91 ARE LISTED HERE ALPHABETICALLY											
Abraham Baldwin Agricultural College[1] (GA)*	2.5	65%[8]	33%	24%[6]	N/A	N/A	18/1[4]	930-1130[4]	N/A	69%[4]	N/A
American University of Puerto Rico–Bayamon[1]	2.1	67%[8]	31%	35%[6]	N/A	N/A	15/1[4]	N/A[2]	N/A	N/A	N/A
American University of Puerto Rico–Manati[1]	1.9	74%[8]	30%	42%[6]	N/A	N/A	20/1[4]	N/A[2]	N/A	N/A	N/A
Arkansas Baptist College	2.4	44%[8]	27%	4%[6]	68%	0%	23/1[4]	N/A[2]	N/A	26%	N/A
Benedict College[1] (SC)	2.4	55%[8]	27%	26%[6]	N/A	N/A	17/1[4]	N/A[2]	N/A	N/A	N/A
Colegio Universitario de San Juan[1] (PR)*	1.9	52%[8]	19%	20%[6]	N/A	N/A	20/1[4]	N/A[2]	N/A	94%[4]	N/A
College of Coastal Georgia*	2.7	58%	33%	27%	37%	2%	19/1	910-1100	N/A	87%	1%
Crowley's Ridge College[1] (AR)	2.0	54%[8]	38%	40%[6]	N/A	N/A	8/1[4]	N/A[2]	N/A	N/A	N/A
Dalton State College[1] (GA)*	2.8	76%[8]	27%	25%[6]	N/A	N/A	23/1[4]	N/A	N/A	N/A	N/A
Edward Waters College[1] (FL)	2.3	57%[8]	23%	26%[6]	N/A	N/A	23/1[4]	830-1040[4]	N/A	56%[4]	N/A
LeMoyne-Owen College (TN)	2.2	55%	25%	14%	78%	0%	13/1	15-17	N/A	41%	N/A
Livingstone College (NC)	2.2	50%	28%	25%[6]	54%	0%	16/1	710-855	5%	56%	8%
Miles College[1] (AL)	2.5	55%[8]	29%	21%[6]	N/A	N/A	16/1[4]	N/A[2]	N/A	N/A	N/A
Morris College[1] (SC)	2.1	49%[8]	25%	25%[6]	N/A	N/A	15/1[4]	N/A	N/A	N/A	N/A

Note: Key to footnotes, Page 60.

School (State) (*Public)	Peer assessment score (5.0=highest)	Average first-year student retention rate	2019 graduation rate Predicted	2019 graduation rate Actual	% of classes under 20 ('19)	% of classes of 50 or more ('19)	Student/faculty ratio ('19)	SAT/ACT 25th-75th percentile ('19)	Freshmen in top 25% of HS class ('19)	Acceptance rate ('19)	Average alumni giving rate
CONTINUED (SCHOOLS RANKED 70 THROUGH 91 ARE LISTED HERE ALPHABETICALLY)											
Ohio Valley University (WV)	2.2	52%	43%	30%	79%	0%	10/1	17-23[2]	N/A	43%	8%
Paine College[1] (GA)	1.9	50%[8]	32%	21%[6]	N/A	N/A	10/1[4]	780-980[4]	N/A	40%[4]	N/A
Seminole State College of Florida*	2.4	67%[8]	38%	41%	31%	0.4%	23/1	N/A[2]	N/A	75%	N/A
Shaw University (NC)	2.3	49%	23%	17%	58%	0%	15/1	737-902	6%	63%	N/A
Universidad Adventista de las Antillas[1] (PR)	2.1	72%[8]	26%	49%[6]	N/A	N/A	19/1[4]	N/A[2]	N/A	99%[4]	N/A
University of Puerto Rico–Utuado[1]*	2.5	56%[8]	33%	13%[8]	49%[4]	0%[4]	15/1[4]	N/A[2]	N/A	40%[4]	0%[4]
Webber International University (FL)	2.4	49%	39%	38%	50%	0%	24/1	900-1050	52%	42%	N/A
West Virginia University–Parkersburg[1]*	2.5	N/A	30%	32%[6]	N/A	N/A	15/1[4]	N/A[2]	N/A	N/A	N/A

MIDWEST ▶

Rank School (State) (*Public)	Overall score	Peer assessment score (5.0=highest)	Average first-year student retention rate	2019 graduation rate Predicted	2019 graduation rate Actual	% of classes under 20 ('19)	% of classes of 50 or more ('19)	Student/faculty ratio ('19)	SAT/ACT 25th-75th percentile ('19)	Freshmen in top 25% of HS class ('19)	Acceptance rate ('19)	Average alumni giving rate
1. **Cottey College** (MO)	100	3.0	69%	57%	64%	99%	0%	6/1	19-24	52%	85%	6%
2. **Taylor University** (IN)	99	3.7	87%	74%	77%	66%	4%	13/1	1080-1310	59%	68%	16%
3. **Ohio Northern University**	92	3.5	85%	70%	71%	58%	1%	11/1	23-28	57%[5]	70%	10%
4. **College of the Ozarks** (MO)	91	3.7	76%	49%	71%	52%	1%	15/1	21-26	66%	9%	20%
4. **Dordt University** (IA)	91	3.4	82%	65%	75%	69%	5%	12/1	22-28[2]	49%	74%	19%
6. **Northwestern College** (IA)	88	3.4	78%	65%	68%	71%	1%	10/1	21-27	49%	70%	18%
7. **Goshen College** (IN)	87	3.4	77%	61%	64%	66%	2%	10/1	1010-1210	53%	63%	18%
8. **Marietta College** (OH)	86	3.2	71%	60%	58%	84%	0.2%	8/1	20-26	47%[4]	71%	15%
8. **William Jewell College** (MO)	86	3.2	77%	69%	63%	82%	0%	10/1	22-27[2]	61%	46%	7%
10. **Alma College** (MI)	82	3.2	78%	61%	67%	59%	1%	14/1	1030-1230[9]	29%	61%	15%
10. **University of Mount Union** (OH)	82	3.2	76%	50%	66%	63%	0.4%	12/1	20-25	61%[5]	78%	15%
12. **Carthage College** (WI)	81	3.5	78%	62%	66%	53%	0%	12/1	20-27[2]	50%	68%	13%
12. **Millikin University** (IL)	81	3.4	75%	56%	59%	68%	0.4%	10/1	950-1200[2]	43%	71%	9%
14. **Benedictine College** (KS)	78	3.4	80%	62%	64%	63%	2%	14/1	21-28	42%	97%	21%
15. **Hiram College** (OH)	77	3.2	71%	51%	54%	81%	0%	12/1	18-25[2]	27%	60%	9%
16. **Loras College** (IA)	76	3.2	78%	59%	66%	48%	0%	12/1	20-25	N/A	75%	16%
17. **Adrian College** (MI)	74	3.3	67%	52%	45%	69%	1%	13/1	960-1163	29%	56%	13%
18. **Northland College** (WI)	70	2.7	72%	60%	54%	74%	0%	11/1	18-27[2]	43%	67%	11%

MIDWEST ▶

Rank School (State) (*Public)	Overall score	Peer assessment score (5.0=highest)	Average first-year student retention rate	2019 graduation rate		% of classes under 20 ('19)	% of classes of 50 or more ('19)	Student/ faculty ratio ('19)	SAT/ACT 25th-75th percentile ('19)	Freshmen in top 25% of HS class ('19)	Accept-ance rate ('19)	Average alumni giving rate
				Predicted	Actual							
18. Wisconsin Lutheran College	70	2.9	77%	63%	59%	60%	1%	12/1	21-27	46%	89%	16%
20. Hastings College (NE)	69	3.1	67%	60%	59%	64%	0%	13/1	18-24[3]	45%[4]	67%	15%
21. Heidelberg University (OH)	68	3.2	71%	50%	51%	N/A	N/A	13/1	19-25	N/A	73%	9%
21. Trinity Christian College (IL)	68	2.8	82%	52%	66%	66%	1%	10/1	970-1150	16%	69%	9%
23. Dakota Wesleyan University (SD)	66	3.2	69%	50%	52%	69%	2%	11/1	19-24	38%	67%	4%
24. Manchester University[1] (IN)	65	3.0	64%[8]	50%	55%[6]	56%[4]	0%[4]	12/1[4]	N/A[2]	40%[4]	59%[4]	18%[4]
25. Dunwoody College of Tech. (MN)	64	2.5	86%[8]	43%	67%[6]	86%	0%	11/1	N/A[2]	30%	65%	3%
26. Bethel College (KS)	63	2.8	62%	53%	44%	77%	2%	9/1	18-24	42%	57%	14%
27. University of Minnesota–Crookston[1]*	61	2.9	70%[8]	51%	52%[8]	72%[4]	0.4%[4]	16/1[4]	19-24[4]	34%[4]	66%[4]	4%[4]
28. Bluffton University (OH)	60	2.8	64%	51%	54%	71%	1%	11/1	18-23	16%	57%	7%
28. Oakland City University (IN)	60	2.4	67%	40%	62%	87%	0%	12/1	920-1130[2]	38%	55%	5%
28. Quincy University (IL)	60	2.7	65%[8]	49%	53%	75%	0%	14/1	19-25[2]	51%	62%	11%
31. Central Methodist University (MO)	59	2.7	69%	48%	47%	59%	2%	12/1	19-25	39%	94%	12%
31. McPherson College (KS)	59	3.0	65%	49%	41%	70%	0%	14/1	19-23[2]	21%	53%	10%
33. Eureka College (IL)	58	2.7	65%	49%	49%	77%	0%	12/1	910-1140	25%	62%	11%
34. Briar Cliff University (IA)	57	2.8	67%	52%	40%	76%	1%	11/1	19-23	15%	77%	11%
34. Holy Cross Col. at Notre Dame, Indiana	57	3.0	45%	55%	39%	72%	0%	12/1	1050-1380	47%	94%	22%
36. Culver-Stockton College (MO)	56	2.8	64%	43%	52%	71%	0%	14/1	18-22	23%	52%	20%
36. Maranatha Baptist University (WI)	56	2.5	74%	48%	66%	81%	1%	10/1	19-26	52%	74%	N/A
38. Kansas Wesleyan University	55	2.9	60%	52%	42%	79%	0%	11/1	19-24	34%	59%	10%
38. Union College (NE)	55	2.6	77%	58%	47%	73%	0%	8/1	18-26[3]	N/A	70%	N/A
38. University of Jamestown (ND)	55	2.8	70%	54%	45%	57%	2%	10/1	19-25[3]	35%	69%	14%
38. Wilmington College (OH)	55	2.6	68%	46%	55%	58%	1%	15/1	18-23	42%	78%	11%
42. Grand View University (IA)	54	2.7	68%	49%	55%	66%	1%	12/1	17-22	38%	96%	3%
42. St. Augustine College[1] (IL)	54	2.8	N/A	19%	42%[6]	N/A	N/A	14/1[4]	N/A[2]	N/A	N/A	N/A
44. Dickinson State University (ND)*	53	2.8	64%	51%	41%	77%	1%	12/1	18-23[2]	N/A	100%	4%
45. York College (NE)	52	2.5	58%	49%	46%	71%	1%	12/1	17-21	43%	57%	16%
46. Lake Superior State University (MI)*	51	2.7	70%	52%	49%	54%	4%	15/1	970-1160[2]	29%	57%	1%
46. Olivet College[1] (MI)	51	2.8	63%[8]	43%	50%[6]	69%[4]	2%[4]	16/1[4]	850-1070[4]	N/A	71%[4]	N/A
46. Sterling College (KS)	51	2.6	58%[8]	48%	53%	79%	2%	11/1	18-23	22%	40%	N/A
49. Defiance College (OH)	49	2.7	55%	46%	35%	75%	0%	9/1	17-21	23%	50%	7%
49. Ottawa University (KS)	49	2.8	60%	54%	51%	62%	1%	10/1	16-22[2]	21%	14%	11%
49. Tabor College (KS)	49	2.9	60%	49%	44%	65%	2%	13/1	17-22	16%	56%	N/A
49. Valley City State University (ND)*	49	2.7	71%	53%	50%	70%	0.4%	13/1	18-23	N/A	77%	9%
53. North Central University (MN)	43	2.7	77%	57%	50%	57%	8%	16/1	18-24[3]	27%	90%	2%
54. Mayville State University (ND)*	42	2.5	61%[8]	49%	30%[6]	75%	1%	12/1	18-25[4]	N/A	N/A	N/A
54. Rochester University (MI)	42	2.6	64%[8]	47%	50%	69%	0%	9/1	850-1070	N/A	100%	N/A
56. Kuyper College[1] (MI)	41	2.3	71%[8]	50%	44%[6]	N/A	N/A	11/1[4]	850-1050[4]	N/A	68%[4]	N/A
57. Missouri Southern State University*	39	2.8	63%	37%	33%	49%	1%	17/1	18-24	40%	94%	3%

School (State) (*Public)		Peer assessment score (5.0=highest)	Average first-year student retention rate	2019 graduation rate		% of classes under 20 ('19)	% of classes of 50 or more ('19)	Student/ faculty ratio ('19)	SAT/ACT 25th-75th percentile ('19)	Freshmen in top 25% of HS class ('19)	Accept-ance rate ('19)	Average alumni giving rate
				Predicted	Actual							
SCHOOLS RANKED 58 THROUGH 76 ARE LISTED HERE ALPHABETICALLY												
Bethany College (KS)		2.6	58%	47%	39%[6]	65%[4]	2%[4]	14/1	18-23[4]	N/A	N/A	N/A
Central Christian College (KS)		2.1	59%	38%	44%	85%	1%	13/1	15-20[2]	14%	99%	4%
Central State University (OH)*		2.1	47%	29%	28%	56%	1%	14/1	14-17[2]	23%[4]	57%	34%
Donnelly College (KS)		2.2	69%[8]	28%	19%	N/A	N/A	11/1[4]	N/A[2]	N/A	N/A	N/A
Finlandia University[1] (MI)		2.3	48%[8]	43%	25%[6]	N/A	N/A	9/1[4]	890-1080[4]	N/A	32%[4]	N/A
Hannibal-LaGrange University[1] (MO)		2.5	56%[8]	44%	45%[6]	N/A	N/A	12/1[4]	N/A	N/A	54%[4]	N/A
Harris-Stowe State University (MO)*		2.3	55%	26%	17%	N/A	N/A	18/1	15-19	N/A	52%	N/A
Indiana University–Kokomo*		2.3	62%	35%	38%	48%	2%	15/1	970-1130[2]	33%	74%	6%
Iowa Wesleyan University		2.4	56%	42%	31%	73%	0%	10/1	18-21	15%	68%	5%
Lincoln College[1] (IL)		2.3	50%[8]	32%	8%[6]	N/A	N/A	14/1[4]	700-810[4]	N/A	80%[4]	N/A
Lincoln University (MO)*		2.3	51%	33%	26%	53%	0.3%	15/1	14-19	13%	N/A	4%
Martin University[1] (IN)		2.1	64%[8]	22%	5%[6]	N/A	N/A	17/1[4]	N/A[2]	N/A	N/A	N/A
Missouri Valley College		2.3	43%[8]	34%	27%	62%	0.3%	13/1	12-27[2]	47%	54%	N/A
Ranken Technical College[1] (MO)		2.4	61%[8]	43%	46%[6]	N/A	N/A	11/1[4]	N/A[2]	N/A	N/A	N/A
University of Northwestern Ohio[1]		2.2	57%[8]	36%	40%[6]	N/A	N/A	24/1[4]	N/A[2]	N/A	N/A	N/A
University of Rio Grande[1] (OH)		2.4	54%[8]	31%	19%[6]	N/A	N/A	17/1[4]	N/A[2]	N/A	N/A	N/A

Note: Key to footnotes, Page 60.

School (State) (*Public)	Peer assessment score (5.0=highest)	Average first-year student retention rate	2019 graduation rate		% of classes under 20 ('19)	% of classes of 50 or more ('19)	Student/ faculty ratio ('19)	SAT/ACT 25th-75th percentile ('19)	Freshmen in top 25% of HS class ('19)	Accept-ance rate ('19)	Average alumni giving rate
			Predicted	Actual							
CONTINUED (SCHOOLS RANKED 58 THROUGH 76 ARE LISTED HERE ALPHABETICALLY)											
Vincennes University (IN)*	2.7	47%[8]	33%	21%	86%	0%	21/1	N/A[2]	N/A	77%	N/A
Wilberforce University[1] (OH)	2.4	42%[8]	31%	22%[6]	N/A	N/A	11/1[4]	14-19[4]	N/A	67%[4]	N/A
William Penn University[1] (IA)	2.4	52%[8]	35%	32%[6]	N/A	N/A	16/1[4]	N/A[2]	N/A	55%[4]	N/A

WEST ▶

Rank School (State) (*Public)	Overall score	Peer assessment score (5.0=highest)	Average first-year student retention rate	2019 graduation rate		% of classes under 20 ('19)	% of classes of 50 or more ('19)	Student/ faculty ratio ('19)	SAT/ACT 25th-75th percentile ('19)	Freshmen in top 25% of HS class ('19)	Accept-ance rate ('19)	Average alumni giving rate
				Predicted	Actual							
1. Carroll College (MT)	100	3.5	81%	68%	63%	64%	2%	12/1	21-26[2]	72%	69%	11%
2. California State U.–Maritime Academy*	97	3.7	80%	62%	67%	39%	1%	13/1	1068-1263	N/A	76%	N/A
2. William Jessup University (CA)	97	3.7	78%	53%	63%	66%	1%	10/1	950-1210	43%	65%	5%
4. Texas Lutheran University	88	3.5	71%	56%	55%	53%	0.2%	14/1	990-1160	48%	56%	11%
5. Oral Roberts University (OK)	83	3.5	82%	56%	51%	50%	7%	17/1	18-25	43%	68%	7%
5. Oregon Tech*	83	3.6	78%	51%	46%	57%	2%	15/1	1000-1200	50%	97%	4%
7. Schreiner University (TX)	79	3.3	66%	49%	45%	65%	0.3%	14/1	920-1110	32%	93%	8%
8. Oklahoma Baptist University	77	3.2	74%[8]	62%	41%	68%	5%	11/1	20-26	21%	57%	5%
9. Warner Pacific University (OR)	76	2.9	66%	47%	45%	86%	0%	11/1	15-20	45%	97%	2%
10. Brigham Young University–Hawaii[1]	75	3.5	63%[8]	63%	45%[6]	N/A	N/A	17/1[4]	21-26[4]	N/A	45%[4]	N/A
11. Corban University[1] (OR)	72	3.2	79%[8]	58%	58%[6]	N/A	N/A	12/1[4]	1030-1200[4]	N/A	91%[4]	N/A
11. Southwestern Adventist Univ.[1] (TX)	72	2.9	72%[8]	47%	44%[6]	79%[4]	0.4%[4]	15/1[4]	900-1145[4]	23%[4]	55%[4]	2%[4]
13. McMurry University (TX)	71	3.2	62%	45%	33%	76%	0.3%	10/1	940-1100	39%	45%	7%
14. Arizona Christian University (AZ)	70	3.1	57%[8]	55%	50%	72%	2%	16/1	15-21	N/A	65%	N/A
15. East Texas Baptist University	68	3.1	62%	47%	44%	57%	0.3%	14/1	17-22	41%	59%	4%
16. Brigham Young University–Idaho[1]	66	3.6	72%[8]	51%	47%[6]	N/A	N/A	22/1[4]	20-26[4]	N/A	97%[4]	N/A
16. University of Hawaii–West Oahu*	66	3.2	71%	43%	28%	49%	0%	18/1	16-21[2]	40%	84%	2%
18. Lewis-Clark State College[7] (ID)*	65	3.3	60%[8]	35%	40%	77%	1%	12/1	890-1110[9]	24%	100%	N/A
18. San Diego Christian College[1]	65	3.1	65%[8]	48%	51%[6]	N/A	N/A	8/1[4]	973-1140[4]	N/A	60%[4]	N/A
20. Okla. State U. Inst. of Tech.–Okmulgee*	64	3.5	60%	32%	37%	63%	0%	16/1	15-20[3]	24%	29%	1%
21. Howard Payne University (TX)	61	3.0	48%	44%	35%	N/A	N/A	10/1	940-1110	29%	54%	1%
22. Life Pacific College[1] (CA)	57	2.9	68%[8]	42%	43%[6]	N/A	N/A	14/1[4]	900-1096[4]	N/A	96%[4]	4%
23. Oklahoma Panhandle State Univ.*	54	2.7	55%[8]	35%	48%	62%	4%	16/1	7-22[2]	21%	90%	4%
24. Dixie State University[1] (UT)*	51	3.2	55%[8]	40%	21%[6]	39%[4]	4%[4]	20/1[4]	17-24[4]	30%[4]	100%[4]	14%[4]
24. Northern New Mexico College[1]*	51	2.9	54%[8]	25%	25%[6]	N/A	N/A	12/1[4]	N/A[2]	N/A	N/A	N/A

School (State) (*Public)	Peer assessment score (5.0=highest)	Average first-year student retention rate	2019 graduation rate		% of classes under 20 ('19)	% of classes of 50 or more ('19)	Student/ faculty ratio ('19)	SAT/ACT 25th-75th percentile ('19)	Freshmen in top 25% of HS class ('19)	Accept-ance rate ('19)	Average alumni giving rate
			Predicted	Actual							
SCHOOLS RANKED 26 THROUGH 33 ARE LISTED HERE ALPHABETICALLY											
Bacone College[1] (OK)	1.4	31%[8]	29%	7%[6]	N/A	N/A	7/1[4]	14-19[4]	N/A	15%[4]	N/A
Huston-Tillotson University (TX)	2.5	60%[8]	28%	28%	76%	0%	18/1	800-980	N/A[5]	63%	N/A
Jarvis Christian College[1] (TX)	2.6	49%[8]	24%	18%[6]	56%[4]	2%[4]	20/1[4]	800-980[4]	N/A	14%[4]	5%[4]
Oklahoma State University–Oklahoma City[1]*	3.5	51%[8]	39%	6%[8]	N/A	N/A	22/1[4]	N/A[2]	N/A	N/A	N/A
Paul Quinn College[1] (TX)	2.9	65%[8]	26%	20%[6]	N/A	N/A	22/1[4]	712-928[4]	N/A	90%[4]	N/A
Rogers State University (OK)*	2.8	67%	35%	35%	48%	2%	19/1	16-20	18%	89%	N/A
Southwestern Christian University (OK)	2.8	49%	41%	23%	79%	0%	11/1	16-20	N/A	62%	N/A
Wiley College[1] (TX)	2.2	54%[8]	24%	22%[6]	N/A	N/A	14/1[4]	N/A[2]	N/A	N/A	N/A

The Top Public Regional Colleges ▶

NORTH
Rank School (State)
1. U.S. Coast Guard Academy (CT)
2. U.S. Merchant Marine Acad. (NY)
3. Maine Maritime Academy
4. Massachusetts Maritime Academy
5. University of Maine–Farmington

SOUTH
Rank School (State)
1. Univ. of South Carolina–Aiken
1. U. of South Carolina–Upstate
3. University of Puerto Rico–Humacao
4. Pensacola State College (FL)
5. University of Puerto Rico–Aguadilla

MIDWEST
Rank School (State)
1. University of Minnesota–Crookston
2. Dickinson State University (ND)
3. Lake Superior State University (MI)
4. Valley City State University (ND)
5. Mayville State University (ND)

WEST
Rank School (State)
1. California State U.–Maritime Acad.
2. Oregon Tech
3. University of Hawaii–West Oahu
4. Lewis-Clark State College[7] (ID)
5. Oklahoma State U. Inst. of Tech.– Okmulgee

Best
Historically Black Colleges

INCREASINGLY, **THE NATION'S TOP** historically Black colleges and universities are an appealing option for applicants of all races; many HBCUs, in fact, actively recruit Hispanic, international and white students in addition to African American high school grads. Which offer the best undergraduate education? U.S. News each year surveys administrators at the HBCUs, asking the president, provost and admissions dean to rate the academic quality of all other HBCUs with which they are familiar.

In addition to the two most recent years of survey results reflected in the peer assessment score, the rankings are based on nearly all the indicators (although weighted slightly differently) as those used in ranking the regional universities: graduation and retention rates, social mobility, high school class standing, graduate indebtedness (new

this year), admission test scores, and the strength of the faculty, among others. We gave more weight this year to outcomes measures (from 30% previously to 40%) and slightly less to peer assessment, student excellence and alumni giving.

To be part of the universe, a school must be designated by the Department of Education as an HBCU, be a baccalaureate-granting institution that enrolls primarily first-year, first-time students, and have been part of this year's Best Colleges ranking process. If an HBCU is unranked in the 2021 Best Colleges rankings, it is unranked here; reasons that schools are not ranked vary.

Of 79 HBCUs, 77 were ranked. HBCUs in the top three-quarters are numerically ranked; those in the bottom quarter appear alphabetically. For more detail on the methodology and changes made for this ranking, visit **usnews.com/hbcu**.

Key Measures

Measure	Weight
Outcomes	40%
Peer Assessment	20%
Faculty Resources	20%
Financial Resources	10%
Student Excellence	7%
Alumni Giving	3%

Rank School (State) (*Public)	Overall score	Peer assessment score (5.0=highest)	Average first-year student retention rate	Average graduation rate	% of classes under 20 ('19)	% of classes of 50 or more ('19)	Student/ faculty ratio ('19)	% of faculty who are full time ('19)	SAT/ACT 25th-75th percentile ('19)	Freshmen in top 25% of HS class ('19)	Accept-ance rate ('19)	Average alumni giving rate
1. Spelman College (GA)	100	4.7	90%	75%[6]	62%	1%	10/1	86%	1080-1230	56%	43%	28%
2. Howard University (DC)	98	4.4	88%	63%	52%	6%	10/1	92%	1130-1280	63%	36%	11%
3. Xavier University of Louisiana	74	4.3	72%	46%	53%	3%	15/1	95%	20-26	59%	60%	17%
4. Tuskegee University (AL)	73	3.9	71%	48%[6]	54%	6%	10/1	100%	18-23	79%	57%	24%
5. Hampton University (VA)	72	4.2	77%	57%[6]	71%	9%	12/1	91%	20-25[2]	25%	36%	17%
6. Morehouse College (GA)	68	4.3	80%	53%	45%	1%	13/1	85%	995-1180[3]	11%[4]	51%	12%
7. Florida A&M University	67	4.1	82%	48%	38%	11%	15/1	91%	1030-1160	30%	36%	3%
7. North Carolina A&T State Univ.	67	4.4	78%	48%[6]	25%	7%	19/1	80%	960-1130	38%	58%	9%
9. Claflin University (SC)	59	3.8	76%	53%	64%	1%	13/1	84%	880-1040	33%	55%	40%
10. Fisk University (TN)	57	3.5	80%	45%	64%	2%	13/1	88%	18-24	45%	93%	31%
11. Delaware State University	56	3.6	72%	41%	46%	3%	16/1	84%	820-1020	29%	53%	11%
11. North Carolina Central Univ.	56	3.8	79%	46%	41%	5%	16/1	84%	890-1050	24%	68%	8%
13. Morgan State University (MD)	54	3.8	73%	38%[6]	48%	2%	13/1	86%	920-1070	22%	68%	16%
14. Tougaloo College[1] (MS)	52	3.2	72%[8]	42%[8]	75%[4]	0.4%[4]	11/1[4]	87%[4]	16-23[4]	30%[4]	91%[4]	28%[4]
15. Clark Atlanta University	49	3.6	70%	42%[6]	37%	5%	19/1	81%	940-1080	31%	55%	10%
16. Jackson State University[1] (MS)	48	3.6	62%[8]	38%[6]	N/A	N/A	15/1[4]	85%[4]	17-22[4]	N/A	69%[4]	N/A
16. Winston-Salem State Univ.[1] (NC)	48	3.4	77%[8]	48%[6]	N/A	N/A	14/1[4]	86%[4]	890-1030[4]	N/A	65%[4]	N/A
18. Univ. of Maryland Eastern Shore	47	3.3	62%	39%	68%	2%	11/1	87%	850-1030[2]	N/A	65%	1%
19. Alcorn State University (MS)	44	3.3	75%	36%[6]	N/A	N/A	17/1	88%	17-24	24%	58%	8%
20. Lincoln University (PA)	43	3.0	73%	46%	53%	0.4%	15/1	74%	870-1010	16%	83%	15%
20. Norfolk State University (VA)	43	3.5	73%	37%	57%	2%	16/1	85%	860-1040	20%	90%	N/A
22. Dillard University[1] (LA)	42	3.5	70%[8]	40%[6]	N/A	N/A	14/1[4]	80%[4]	N/A	N/A	61%[4]	N/A
22. Elizabeth City State University (NC)	42	2.9	71%	39%[6]	56%	1%	15/1	93%	875-1050	5%	66%	N/A
24. Fayetteville State University (NC)	41	3.2	72%	34%[6]	39%	1%	18/1	92%	870-1010	27%	69%	2%
24. Virginia State University[1]	41	3.4	70%[8]	42%[6]	N/A	N/A	13/1[4]	86%[4]	840-1010[4]	17%[4]	91%[4]	N/A
26. Bowie State University (MD)	40	3.3	71%	41%	46%	2%	15/1	70%	860-1030	N/A	80%	5%
26. Prairie View A&M University (TX)	40	3.7	70%	34%	18%	8%	17/1	94%	870-1040	25%	80%	N/A
26. Univ. of the District of Columbia	40	3.0	64%	37%	70%	0%	9/1	59%	N/A	N/A	74%	N/A
29. Kentucky State University	39	3.1	62%	22%	67%	1%	11/1	89%	18-22	N/A	81%	N/A
30. Oakwood University[1] (AL)	38	3.1	71%[8]	48%[6]	N/A	N/A	11/1[4]	84%[4]	16-22[4]	N/A	66%[4]	N/A

Note: Key to footnotes, Page 60.

Rank	School (State) (*Public)	Overall score	Peer assessment score (5.0=highest)	Average first-year student retention rate	Average graduation rate	% of classes under 20 ('19)	% of classes of 50 or more ('19)	Student/faculty ratio ('19)	% of faculty who are full time ('19)	SAT/ACT 25th-75th percentile ('19)	Freshmen in top 25% of HS class ('19)	Acceptance rate ('19)	Average alumni giving rate
31.	South Carolina State University	37	3.1	68%	36%	58%	1%	15/1	87%	15-17	25%	66%	6%
31.	Tennessee State University[7]	37	3.6	55%	35%[6]	60%[4]	2%[4]	18/1	90%	17-21[3]	N/A	66%	N/A
33.	University of Arkansas–Pine Bluff	36	3.0	71%	29%	60%	2%	14/1	92%	16-20	30%	44%	10%
34.	Southern U. and A&M College (LA)	34	3.3	64%	30%[6]	38%	5%	21/1	87%	17-20	14%	35%	15%
34.	Talladega College (AL)	34	3.1	64%	38%[6]	48%	6%	20/1	75%	20-24	N/A	63%	9%
36.	Johnson C. Smith University[1] (NC)	33	3.0	68%[8]	44%[6]	70%[4]	0%[4]	12/1	73%	803-960	N/A	47%	N/A
37.	Alabama Agricultural & Mechanical U.	32	3.6	58%	27%	36%	5%	20/1	87%	15-18	N/A	92%	14%
38.	Alabama State University	30	3.2	60%	28%	60%	0.3%	15/1	84%	15-20	N/A[5]	97%	6%
38.	Bennett College[1] (NC)	30	2.6	47%[8]	37%[8]	66%[4]	1%[4]	11/1[4]	81%[4]	800-1000[4]	32%[4]	96%[4]	17%[4]
38.	Central State University (OH)	30	3.0	47%	24%	56%	1%	14/1	72%	14-17[2]	23%[4]	57%	34%
38.	Fort Valley State University (GA)	30	3.0	75%	29%[6]	50%	2%	27/1	100%	850-960	14%	55%	9%
38.	Mississippi Valley State Univ.	30	2.9	61%[8]	31%[6]	65%	1%	15/1	87%	16-21	N/A	65%	N/A
43.	Coppin State University[1] (MD)	29	2.9	64%[8]	22%[6]	60%[4]	0.3%[4]	13/1[4]	73%[4]	880-1030[4]	N/A	38%[4]	N/A
44.	Bethune-Cookman University (FL)	28	2.9	63%	34%	55%	3%	14/1	89%	840-1010	33%	84%	4%
44.	Philander Smith College (AR)	28	2.6	66%	39%	69%	0.3%	15/1	75%	15-21	29%	35%	7%
46.	Florida Memorial University[1]	27	2.7	66%[8]	37%[6]	N/A	N/A	14/1[4]	88%[4]	N/A[2]	N/A	N/A	N/A
46.	Grambling State University[1] (LA)	27	3.2	67%[8]	34%[6]	33%[4]	9%[4]	25/1[4]	94%[4]	16-19[4]	14%[4]	96%[4]	N/A
46.	Stillman College (AL)	27	2.9	66%[8]	26%[6]	N/A	N/A	18/1	89%	N/A	N/A	33%	9%
46.	Texas Southern University	27	3.2	54%	21%[6]	33%	9%	16/1	79%	840-1000	19%	91%	4%
50.	Langston University[1] (OK)	26	2.8	57%[8]	20%[6]	51%[4]	7%[4]	16/1[4]	94%[4]	17-26[4]	N/A	55%[4]	N/A
50.	Savannah State University[7] (GA)	26	3.0	60%	28%[8]	44%	1%	16/1	96%	900-1030[3]	N/A	33%	5%[4]
50.	Voorhees College (SC)	26	2.6	57%[8]	35%[6]	61%	2%	10/1	85%	17[4]	N/A	64%	N/A
50.	West Virginia State University[1]	26	2.9	57%[8]	28%[6]	N/A	N/A	19/1[4]	79%[4]	17-22[4]	N/A	94%[4]	N/A
54.	Bluefield State College (WV)	25	2.6	64%	26%[6]	90%	0%	13/1	85%	16-21	48%	94%	6%[4]
55.	Cheyney U. of Pennsylvania[1]	24	2.4	52%[8]	19%[6]	N/A	N/A	12/1[4]	84%[4]	N/A	N/A	N/A	N/A
55.	Virginia Union University	24	2.9	63%	31%	69%	1%	16/1	75%	770-929[2]	11%	63%	7%
57.	Albany State University[1] (GA)	23	3.0	62%[8]	33%[6]	46%[4]	1%[4]	18/1[4]	82%[4]	750-900[4]	21%[4]	89%[4]	0.4%[4]
58.	St. Augustine's University[1] (NC)	19	2.5	55%[8]	28%[6]	75%[4]	1%[4]	9/1[4]	84%[4]	768-940[4]	N/A	63%[4]	9%[4]

School (State) (*Public)	Peer assessment score (5.0=highest)	Average first-year student retention rate	Average graduation rate	% of classes under 20 ('19)	% of classes of 50 or more ('19)	Student/faculty ratio ('19)	% of faculty who are full time ('19)	SAT/ACT 25th-75th percentile ('19)	Freshmen in top 25% of HS class ('19)	Acceptance rate ('19)	Average alumni giving rate
SCHOOLS RANKED 59 THROUGH 77 ARE LISTED HERE ALPHABETICALLY											
Allen University[1] (SC)	2.4	40%[8]	24%[6]	N/A	N/A	16/1[4]	93%[4]	N/A[2]	N/A	N/A	N/A
Arkansas Baptist College	2.2	44%[8]	4%[6]	68%	0%	23/1[4]	48%	N/A[2]	N/A	26%	N/A
Benedict College[1] (SC)	2.8	55%[8]	26%[6]	N/A	N/A	17/1[4]	84%[4]	N/A[2]	N/A	N/A	N/A
Edward Waters College[1] (FL)	2.5	57%[8]	26%[6]	N/A	N/A	23/1[4]	79%[4]	830-1040[4]	N/A	56%[4]	N/A
Harris-Stowe State University (MO)	2.7	55%	10%	N/A	N/A	18/1	43%	15-19	N/A	52%	N/A
Huston-Tillotson University (TX)	2.8	60%[8]	24%[6]	76%	0%	18/1	74%	800-980	N/A[5]	63%	N/A
Jarvis Christian College[1] (TX)	2.5	49%[8]	18%[6]	56%[4]	2%[4]	20/1[4]	72%[4]	800-980[4]	N/A	14%[4]	5%[4]
Lane College (TN)	2.6	55%	22%[6]	43%	0.3%	20/1	97%	14-17[2]	N/A	61%	N/A
LeMoyne-Owen College (TN)	2.4	55%	14%[6]	78%	0%	13/1	72%	15-17	N/A	41%	N/A
Lincoln University (MO)	2.8	51%	21%[6]	53%	0.3%	15/1	86%	14-19	13%	N/A	4%
Livingstone College (NC)	2.5	50%	25%[6]	54%	0%	16/1	93%	710-855	5%	56%	8%
Miles College[1] (AL)	2.8	55%[8]	21%[6]	N/A	N/A	16/1[4]	88%[4]	N/A[2]	N/A	N/A	N/A
Morris College[1] (SC)	2.4	49%[8]	25%[6]	N/A	N/A	15/1[4]	89%[4]	N/A	N/A	N/A	N/A
Paine College[1] (GA)	2.3	50%[8]	21%[6]	N/A	N/A	10/1[4]	91%[4]	780-980[4]	N/A	40%[4]	N/A
Rust College[1] (MS)	2.5	71%[8]	34%[6]	55%[4]	0%[4]	19/1[4]	97%[4]	14-15[4]	N/A	53%[4]	N/A
Shaw University (NC)	2.7	49%	17%[6]	58%	0%	15/1	78%	737-902	6%	63%	N/A
Southern University–New Orleans	2.9	50%[8]	21%[6]	47%	0.3%	21/1	81%	15-18	27%	60%	N/A
Wilberforce University[1] (OH)	2.6	42%[8]	22%[6]	N/A	N/A	11/1[4]	60%[4]	14-19[4]	N/A	67%[4]	N/A
Wiley College[1] (TX)	2.7	54%[8]	22%[6]	N/A	N/A	14/1[4]	81%[4]	N/A[2]	N/A	N/A	N/A

Sources: Statistical data from the schools. The 2020 peer assessment data were collected by U.S. News.

Best
Business Programs

Each year, U.S. News ranks undergraduate business programs accredited by AACSB International; the results are based solely on surveys of B-school deans and senior faculty. Participants were asked to rate the quality of business programs with which they're familiar on a scale of 1 (marginal) to 5 (distinguished); 52% of those canvassed responded to the most recent survey conducted in the spring of 2020. Two years of data were used to calculate the peer assessment score. Deans and faculty members also were asked to nominate up to 15 programs they consider best in a number of specialty areas; the five schools receiving the most mentions in the 2020 survey appear on page 101.

▶ Top Programs

Rank	School (B-school) (State) (*Public)	Peer assessment score (5.0=highest)
1.	University of Pennsylvania (Wharton)	4.8
2.	Massachusetts Institute of Technology (Sloan)	4.7
3.	University of California–Berkeley (Haas)*	4.6
3.	University of Michigan–Ann Arbor (Ross)*	4.6
5.	New York University (Stern)	4.4
5.	University of Texas at Austin (McCombs)*	4.4
7.	Carnegie Mellon University (Tepper) (PA)	4.3
7.	Cornell University (Dyson) (NY)	4.3
7.	U. of N. Carolina–Chapel Hill (Kenan-Flagler)*	4.3
7.	University of Virginia (McIntire)*	4.3
11.	Indiana University–Bloomington (Kelley)*	4.2
12.	Emory University (Goizueta) (GA)	4.1
12.	University of Notre Dame (Mendoza) (IN)	4.1
12.	University of Southern California (Marshall)	4.1
12.	Washington University in St. Louis (Olin)	4.1
16.	Georgetown University (McDonough) (DC)	4.0
16.	Ohio State University–Columbus (Fisher)*	4.0
16.	Univ. of Wisconsin–Madison*	4.0
19.	Georgia Institute of Technology (Scheller)*	3.9
19.	U. of Illinois–Urbana-Champaign (Gies)*	3.9
19.	Univ. of Maryland–College Park (Smith)*	3.9
19.	U. of Minnesota–Twin Cities (Carlson)*	3.9
19.	University of Washington (Foster)*	3.9
24.	Arizona State University–Tempe (Carey)*	3.8
24.	Boston College (Carroll)	3.8
24.	Michigan State University (Broad)*	3.8
24.	Pennsylvania State U.–Univ. Park (Smeal)*	3.8
24.	Purdue U.–West Lafayette (Krannert) (IN)*	3.8
24.	Texas A&M University (Mays)*	3.8
24.	University of Florida (Warrington)*	3.8
24.	University of Georgia (Terry)*	3.8
32.	Babson College (Olin) (MA)	3.7
32.	Johns Hopkins University (MD)	3.7
32.	University of Arizona (Eller)*	3.7
32.	University of California–Irvine (Merage)*	3.7
32.	University of Colorado Boulder (Leeds)*	3.7
32.	University of Iowa (Tippie)*	3.7
38.	Brigham Young Univ.–Provo (Marriott) (UT)	3.6
38.	Case Western Reserve U. (Weatherhead) (OH)	3.6
38.	University of Pittsburgh*	3.6
38.	Univ. of South Carolina (Moore)*	3.6
38.	Virginia Tech (Pamplin)*	3.6
38.	Wake Forest University (NC)	3.6
44.	Boston University (Questrom)	3.5
44.	Florida State University*	3.5
44.	George Washington University (DC)	3.5
44.	Tulane University (Freeman) (LA)	3.5
44.	University of Alabama (Culverhouse)*	3.5
44.	University of Arkansas (Walton)*	3.5
44.	University of Oregon (Lundquist)*	3.5
44.	University of Tennessee (Haslam)*	3.5

Rank	School (B-school) (State) (*Public)	Peer assessment score (5.0=highest)
44.	University of Utah (Eccles)*	3.5
53.	Auburn University (Harbert) (AL)*	3.4
53.	Georgia State University (Robinson)*	3.4
53.	Northeastern U. (D'Amore-McKim) (MA)	3.4
53.	Pepperdine University (CA)	3.4
53.	Southern Methodist University (Cox) (TX)	3.4
53.	Syracuse University (Whitman) (NY)	3.4
53.	University of California–San Diego (Rady)*	3.4
53.	University of Connecticut*	3.4
53.	U. of Massachusetts–Amherst (Isenberg)*	3.4
53.	University of Miami (FL)	3.4
53.	Univ. of Nebraska–Lincoln*	3.4
53.	University of Oklahoma (Price)*	3.4
53.	Villanova University (PA)	3.4
53.	William & Mary (Mason) (VA)*	3.4
67.	Baylor University (Hankamer) (TX)	3.3
67.	Bentley University (MA)	3.3
67.	Clemson University (SC)*	3.3
67.	Fordham University (Gabelli) (NY)	3.3
67.	Iowa State University (Ivy)*	3.3
67.	Miami University–Oxford (Farmer) (OH)*	3.3
67.	Rochester Inst. of Technology (Saunders) (NY)	3.3
67.	Rutgers University–New Brunswick (NJ)*	3.3
67.	Santa Clara University (Leavey) (CA)	3.3
67.	United States Air Force Academy (CO)*	3.3
67.	University of Kansas*	3.3
67.	University of Kentucky (Gatton)*	3.3
67.	University of Texas at Dallas (Jindal)*	3.3
67.	Washington State University (Carson)*	3.3
81.	Brandeis University (MA)	3.2
81.	CUNY–Baruch College (Zicklin)*	3.2
81.	George Mason University (VA)*	3.2
81.	Lehigh University (PA)	3.2
81.	Louisiana State U.–Baton Rouge (Ourso)*	3.2
81.	Loyola University Chicago (Quinlan)	3.2
81.	Marquette University (WI)	3.2
81.	North Carolina State U. (Poole)*	3.2
81.	Oklahoma State University (Spears)*	3.2
81.	Rensselaer Polytechnic Inst. (Lally) (NY)	3.2
81.	San Diego State University (Fowler)*	3.2
81.	Texas Christian University (Neeley)	3.2
81.	University at Buffalo–SUNY*	3.2
81.	University of Houston (Bauer)*	3.2
81.	University of Illinois–Chicago*	3.2
81.	Univ. of Missouri (Trulaske)*	3.2
97.	American University (Kogod) (DC)	3.1
97.	Colorado State University*	3.1
97.	Creighton University (Heider) (NE)	3.1
97.	DePaul University (Driehaus) (IL)	3.1
97.	Drexel University (LeBow) (PA)	3.1
97.	Gonzaga University (WA)	3.1

Rank	School (B-school) (State) (*Public)	Peer assessment score (5.0=highest)
97.	James Madison University (VA)*	3.1
97.	Loyola Marymount University (CA)	3.1
97.	Saint Louis University (Cook)	3.1
97.	Temple University (Fox) (PA)*	3.1
97.	Texas Tech University (Rawls)*	3.1
97.	University of California–Riverside*	3.1
97.	University of Cincinnati (Lindner)*	3.1
97.	University of Delaware (Lerner)*	3.1
97.	University of Denver (Daniels)	3.1
97.	University of Louisville (KY)*	3.1
97.	University of Mississippi*	3.1
97.	University of Richmond (Robins) (VA)	3.1
97.	University of San Diego	3.1
116.	Binghamton University–SUNY*	3.0
116.	Cal. Polytech. State U.–San Luis Obispo (Orfalea)*	3.0
116.	Florida International University*	3.0
116.	Howard University (DC)	3.0
116.	Kansas State University*	3.0
116.	Loyola University Maryland (Sellinger)	3.0
116.	Oregon State University*	3.0
116.	Rutgers University–Newark (NJ)*	3.0
116.	Seton Hall University (Stillman) (NJ)	3.0
116.	University of Alabama at Birmingham (Collat)*	3.0
116.	University of Central Florida*	3.0
116.	University of Hawaii–Manoa (Shidler)*	3.0
116.	U. of North Carolina–Charlotte (Belk)*	3.0
116.	Univ. of Wisconsin–Milwaukee (Lubar)*	3.0
116.	Virginia Commonwealth University*	3.0
116.	Washington and Lee University (Williams) (VA)	3.0
132.	Bucknell University (PA)	2.9
132.	Butler University (IN)	2.9
132.	California State University–Los Angeles*	2.9
132.	Elon University (Love) (NC)	2.9
132.	Hofstra University (Zarb) (NY)	2.9
132.	Kennesaw State University (Coles) (GA)*	2.9
132.	Mississippi State University*	2.9
132.	Ohio University*	2.9
132.	Rutgers University–Camden (NJ)*	2.9
132.	Saint Joseph's University (Haub) (PA)	2.9
132.	Seattle University (Albers)	2.9
132.	United States Coast Guard Academy (CT)*	2.9
132.	University at Albany–SUNY*	2.9
132.	University of Colorado Denver*	2.9
132.	University of Memphis (Fogelman)*	2.9
132.	University of Nevada–Las Vegas (Lee)*	2.9
132.	University of New Mexico (Anderson)*	2.9
132.	U. of North Carolina–Greensboro (Bryan)*	2.9
132.	University of San Francisco	2.9
132.	University of South Florida (Muma)*	2.9
132.	University of Texas at Arlington*	2.9
132.	University of Vermont*	2.9

▶ Top Programs

Rank School (B-school) (State) (*Public)	Peer assessment score (5.0=highest)
132. Utah State University (Huntsman)*	2.9
132. West Virginia University*	2.9
132. Xavier University (Williams) (OH)	2.9
157. Ball State University (Miller) (IN)*	2.8
157. Boise State University (ID)*	2.8
157. John Carroll University (Boler) (OH)	2.8
157. Kent State University (OH)*	2.8
157. Northern Illinois University*	2.8
157. Quinnipiac University (CT)	2.8
157. Rollins College (FL)	2.8
157. San Jose State University (Lucas) (CA)*	2.8
157. Stevens Institute of Technology (NJ)	2.8
157. St. John's University (Tobin) (NY)	2.8
157. University of Alabama–Huntsville*	2.8
157. University of Colorado–Colorado Springs*	2.8
157. University of Dayton (OH)	2.8
157. University of Idaho*	2.8
157. University of Maine*	2.8
157. Univ. of Massachusetts–Boston*	2.8
157. Univ. of Missouri–Kansas City (Bloch)*	2.8
157. University of Montana*	2.8
157. University of New Hampshire (Paul)*	2.8
157. University of Portland (Pamplin) (OR)	2.8
157. University of Rhode Island*	2.8
157. University of Tampa (Sykes) (FL)	2.8
157. University of Wyoming*	2.8
180. Bowling Green State University (OH)*	2.7
180. California State Polytechnic U.–Pomona*	2.7
180. California State U.–Fullerton (Mihaylo)*	2.7
180. Chapman University (Argyros) (CA)	2.7
180. The Citadel, Military Coll. of SC*	2.7
180. Duquesne University (Palumbo) (PA)	2.7
180. Fairfield University (Dolan) (CT)	2.7
180. Florida Atlantic University*	2.7
180. Loyola University New Orleans	2.7
180. Old Dominion University (Strome) (VA)*	2.7
180. Pace University (Lubin) (NY)	2.7
180. San Francisco State University*	2.7
180. Southern Illinois University–Carbondale*	2.7
180. University of Dallas (Gupta)	2.7
180. U. of Massachusetts–Dartmouth (Charlton)*	2.7
180. University of Minnesota–Duluth (Labovitz)*	2.7
180. University of Nebraska–Omaha*	2.7
180. University of North Texas (Ryan)*	2.7
180. University of St. Thomas (Opus) (MN)	2.7
180. University of Tennessee–Chattanooga*	2.7
180. Worcester Polytechnic Inst. (MA)	2.7
201. Appalachian State University (Walker) (NC)*	2.6
201. Belmont University (TN)	2.6
201. Bradley University (Foster) (IL)	2.6
201. Bryant University (RI)	2.6
201. Clarkson University (NY)	2.6
201. Clark University (MA)	2.6
201. Georgia College & State University (Bunting)*	2.6
201. Idaho State University*	2.6
201. Illinois State University*	2.6
201. Ithaca College (NY)	2.6
201. Montana State University*	2.6
201. Morehouse College (GA)	2.6
201. New Jersey Inst. of Technology*	2.6
201. New Mexico State University*	2.6
201. Northern Arizona University (Franke)*	2.6
201. Portland State University (OR)*	2.6
201. Providence College (RI)	2.6
201. Purdue University–Fort Wayne (Doermer)*	2.6
201. Trinity University (TX)	2.6
201. University of Arkansas at Little Rock*	2.6
201. University of Hartford (Barney) (CT)	2.6
201. Univ. of Massachusetts–Lowell (Manning)*	2.6
201. University of Michigan–Dearborn*	2.6
201. Univ. of Missouri–St. Louis*	2.6
201. University of Nevada–Reno*	2.6
201. University of North Dakota*	2.6
201. University of Scranton (Kania) (PA)	2.6
201. University of South Dakota (Beacom)*	2.6
201. University of Texas at San Antonio*	2.6
201. University of Washington–Tacoma*	2.6
201. Valparaiso University (IN)	2.6
201. Wayne State University (MI)*	2.6
201. Western Michigan University (Haworth)*	2.6
201. Wichita State University (Barton) (KS)*	2.6

Note: Peer assessment surveys in 2020 conducted by U.S. News. To be ranked in a specialty, an undergraduate business school may have either a program or course offerings in that subject area. Extended undergraduate business rankings can be found at usnews.com/bestcolleges. U.S. News surveyed 511 business programs.

▶ Best in the Specialties (*Public)

ACCOUNTING
1. University of Texas–Austin (McCombs)*
2. Brigham Young Univ.–Provo (Marriott) (UT)
3. University of Illinois–Urbana-Champaign (Gies)*
4. University of Pennsylvania (Wharton)
5. University of Michigan–Ann Arbor (Ross)*

BUSINESS ANALYTICS
1. Massachusetts Institute of Technology (Sloan)
2. Carnegie Mellon University (Tepper) (PA)
3. Georgia Institute of Technology (Scheller)*
4. University of Pennsylvania (Wharton)
5. University of Texas–Austin (McCombs)*

ENTREPRENEURSHIP
1. Babson College (Olin) (MA)
2. Massachusetts Institute of Technology (Sloan)
3. University of California–Berkeley (Haas)*
4. Indiana University–Bloomington (Kelley)*
5. University of Pennsylvania (Wharton)

FINANCE
1. University of Pennsylvania (Wharton)
2. New York University (Stern)
3. University of Michigan–Ann Arbor (Ross)*
4. Massachusetts Institute of Technology (Sloan)
5. University of Texas–Austin (McCombs)*

INSURANCE/RISK MANAGEMENT
1. University of Georgia (Terry)*
2. Temple University (Fox) (PA)*
3. University of Wisconsin–Madison*
4. Georgia State University (Robinson)*
5. Florida State University*
5. University of Pennsylvania (Wharton)

INTERNATIONAL BUSINESS
1. Univ. of South Carolina (Moore)*
2. Florida International University*
3. New York University (Stern)
4. Georgetown University (McDonough) (DC)
5. University of Pennsylvania (Wharton)

MANAGEMENT
1. University of Michigan–Ann Arbor (Ross)*
2. University of Pennsylvania (Wharton)
3. University of Virginia (McIntire)*
4. University of Texas–Austin (McCombs)*
5. University of California–Berkeley (Haas)*

MANAGEMENT INFORMATION SYSTEMS
1. Carnegie Mellon University (Tepper) (PA)
2. Massachusetts Institute of Technology (Sloan)
3. Georgia Institute of Technology (Scheller)*
4. University of Arizona (Eller)*
5. University of Texas–Austin (McCombs)*

MARKETING
1. University of Michigan–Ann Arbor (Ross)*
2. University of Pennsylvania (Wharton)
3. New York University (Stern)
3. University of Texas–Austin (McCombs)*
5. Indiana University–Bloomington (Kelley)*

PRODUCTION/OPERATIONS MANAGEMENT
1. Massachusetts Institute of Technology (Sloan)
2. Carnegie Mellon University (Tepper) (PA)
2. University of Pennsylvania (Wharton)
4. University of Michigan–Ann Arbor (Ross)*
5. Ohio State University–Columbus (Fisher)*

QUANTITATIVE ANALYSIS/METHODS
1. Massachusetts Institute of Technology (Sloan)
2. Carnegie Mellon University (Tepper) (PA)
3. University of Pennsylvania (Wharton)
4. Georgia Institute of Technology (Scheller)*
4. University of Michigan–Ann Arbor (Ross)*

REAL ESTATE
1. University of Pennsylvania (Wharton)
2. Univ. of Wisconsin–Madison*
3. New York University (Stern)
4. University of California–Berkeley (Haas)*
4. University of Southern California (Marshall)

SUPPLY CHAIN MANAGEMENT/LOGISTICS
1. Michigan State University (Broad)*
2. Pennsylvania State U.–Univ. Park (Smeal)*
3. Arizona State University–Tempe (Carey)*
4. Massachusetts Institute of Technology (Sloan)
5. University of Tennessee (Haslam)*

Best
Engineering Programs

O N THESE PAGES, U.S. News ranks undergraduate engineering programs accredited by ABET. Rankings are based solely on surveys of engineering deans and senior faculty at accredited programs. Participants were asked to rate programs with which they're familiar on a scale from 1 (marginal) to 5 (distinguished); the two most recent years' results were used to calculate the peer assessment score. Students who prefer a program focused on its undergrads can use the list of top institutions whose terminal degree is a bachelor's or master's; universities that grant doctorates in engineering, whose programs are ranked separately, may boast more offerings at the undergraduate level. For the 2020 surveys, 48.3% of those canvassed returned ratings of schools below; 61.6% did so for the doctorate group. Respondents were also asked to name up to 15 top programs in specialty areas; those mentioned most often in the 2020 survey alone appear here.

Top Programs ▶ AT ENGINEERING SCHOOLS WHOSE HIGHEST DEGREE IS A BACHELOR'S OR MASTER'S

Rank	School (State) (*Public)	Peer assessment score (5.0=highest)
1.	Rose-Hulman Institute of Technology (IN)	4.6
2.	Harvey Mudd College (CA)	4.5
3.	Franklin W. Olin College of Engineering (MA)	4.4
4.	United States Military Academy (NY)*	4.3
5.	United States Air Force Academy (CO)*	4.2
5.	United States Naval Academy (MD)*	4.2
7.	Bucknell University (PA)	4.1
8.	Cal. Polytech. State U.–San Luis Obispo*	4.0
9.	Milwaukee School of Engineering	3.9
10.	Cooper Union for Adv. of Sci. and Art (NY)	3.8
11.	California State Polytechnic U.–Pomona*	3.7
11.	United States Coast Guard Academy (CT)*	3.7
13.	Embry-Riddle Aeronautical U.–Prescott (AZ)	3.6
13.	Lafayette College (PA)	3.6
13.	University of San Diego	3.6
13.	Valparaiso University (IN)	3.6
17.	The Citadel, Military Coll. of SC*	3.5
17.	Kettering University (MI)	3.5
17.	Rowan University (NJ)*	3.5
17.	San Jose State University (CA)*	3.5

Rank	School (State) (*Public)	Peer assessment score (5.0=highest)
17.	Smith College (MA)	3.5
17.	Swarthmore College (PA)	3.5
23.	California State University–Los Angeles*	3.4
23.	Gonzaga University (WA)	3.4
23.	Union College (NY)	3.4
26.	James Madison University (VA)*	3.3
26.	Loyola Marymount University (CA)	3.3
26.	U.S. Merchant Marine Acad. (NY)*	3.3
29.	Bradley University (IL)	3.2
29.	Miami University–Oxford (OH)*	3.2
29.	Ohio Northern University	3.2
29.	Virginia Military Institute*	3.2
33.	California State University–Fullerton*	3.1
33.	California State University–Northridge*	3.1
33.	Hofstra University (NY)	3.1
33.	LeTourneau University (TX)	3.1
33.	Massachusetts Maritime Academy*	3.1
33.	Northern Illinois University*	3.1
33.	Purdue University–Fort Wayne*	3.1
33.	Seattle University	3.1

Rank	School (State) (*Public)	Peer assessment score (5.0=highest)
33.	Texas Christian University	3.1
33.	Trinity University (TX)	3.1
33.	University of Portland (OR)	3.1
33.	University of St. Thomas (MN)	3.1
33.	Wentworth Inst. of Technology (MA)	3.1
46.	Brigham Young University–Idaho	3.0
46.	California State U.–Maritime Academy*	3.0
46.	California State University–Sacramento*	3.0
46.	Calvin University (MI)	3.0
46.	Cedarville University (OH)	3.0
46.	Manhattan College (NY)	3.0
46.	New York Inst. of Technology	3.0
46.	Northern Arizona University*	3.0
46.	Oregon Tech*	3.0
46.	Penn State Univ.–Erie, Behrend Col.*	3.0
46.	San Francisco State University*	3.0
46.	Univ. of Massachusetts–Boston*	3.0
46.	University of Minnesota–Duluth*	3.0
46.	Univ. of Wisconsin–Platteville*	3.0

Best in the Specialties ▶

(*Public)

AEROSPACE/AERONAUTICAL/ASTRONAUTICAL
1. Embry-Riddle Aeronautical University–Prescott (AZ)
2. California Polytechnic State University–San Luis Obispo*
3. California State Polytechnic University–Pomona*
3. United States Air Force Academy (CO)*
5. United States Naval Academy (MD)*

BIOMEDICAL/BIOMEDICAL ENGINEERING
1. Bucknell University (PA)
2. Rose-Hulman Institute of Technology (IN)
3. California Polytechnic State University–San Luis Obispo*
4. Lafayette College (PA)

CIVIL
1. Rose-Hulman Institute of Technology (IN)
2. California Polytechnic State University–San Luis Obispo*
3. United States Military Academy (NY)*
4. Bucknell University (PA)
4. Harvey Mudd College (CA)

COMPUTER ENGINEERING
1. Rose-Hulman Institute of Technology (IN)
2. California Polytechnic State U.–San Luis Obispo*
3. California State University–Fullerton*
4. California State Polytechnic University–Pomona*
4. Harvey Mudd College (CA)
4. Milwaukee School of Engineering

ELECTRICAL/ELECTRONIC/COMMUNICATIONS
1. Rose-Hulman Institute of Technology (IN)
2. California Polytechnic State University–San Luis Obispo*
3. Harvey Mudd College (CA)
4. Bucknell University (PA)
5. Milwaukee School of Engineering

MECHANICAL
1. Rose-Hulman Institute of Technology (IN)
2. Harvey Mudd College (CA)
3. California Polytechnic State University–San Luis Obispo*
4. Bucknell University (PA)
4. Franklin W. Olin College of Engineering (MA)

Top Programs ▶ AT ENGINEERING SCHOOLS WHOSE HIGHEST DEGREE IS A DOCTORATE

Rank	School (State) (*Public)	Peer assessment score (5.0=highest)
1.	Massachusetts Institute of Technology	4.9
2.	Stanford University (CA)	4.7
2.	University of California–Berkeley*	4.7
4.	Georgia Institute of Technology*	4.6
5.	California Institute of Technology	4.5
6.	Carnegie Mellon University (PA)	4.4
6.	University of Illinois–Urbana-Champaign*	4.4
6.	University of Michigan–Ann Arbor*	4.4
9.	Cornell University (NY)	4.3
9.	Purdue University–West Lafayette (IN)*	4.3
11.	University of Texas at Austin*	4.2
12.	Princeton University (NJ)	4.1
13.	Columbia University (NY)	3.9
13.	Johns Hopkins University (MD)	3.9
13.	Northwestern University (IL)	3.9
13.	Texas A&M University*	3.9
13.	Univ. of Wisconsin–Madison*	3.9
13.	Virginia Tech*	3.9
19.	Rice University (TX)	3.8
19.	University of California–Los Angeles*	3.8
19.	University of Washington*	3.8

Rank	School (State) (*Public)	Peer assessment score (5.0=highest)
22.	Duke University (NC)	3.7
22.	Harvard University (MA)	3.7
22.	Pennsylvania State U.–Univ. Park*	3.7
22.	University of California–San Diego*	3.7
22.	Univ. of Maryland–College Park*	3.7
22.	University of Pennsylvania	3.7
28.	Ohio State University–Columbus*	3.6
28.	University of California–Davis*	3.6
28.	University of Colorado Boulder*	3.6
28.	University of Minnesota–Twin Cities*	3.6
32.	North Carolina State U.*	3.5
32.	Rensselaer Polytechnic Inst. (NY)	3.5
32.	University of Florida*	3.5
32.	University of Southern California	3.5
32.	Yale University (CT)	3.5
37.	Brown University (RI)	3.4
37.	University of California–Irvine*	3.4
37.	University of California–Santa Barbara*	3.4
37.	University of Virginia*	3.4
37.	Vanderbilt University (TN)	3.4
42.	Arizona State University–Tempe*	3.3

Rank	School (State) (*Public)	Peer assessment score (5.0=highest)
42.	Case Western Reserve Univ. (OH)	3.3
42.	Colorado School of Mines*	3.3
42.	Iowa State University*	3.3
42.	University of Notre Dame (IN)	3.3
42.	Washington University in St. Louis	3.3
48.	Dartmouth College (NH)	3.2
48.	Lehigh University (PA)	3.2
48.	Michigan State University*	3.2
48.	Northeastern University (MA)	3.2
48.	Rutgers University–New Brunswick (NJ)*	3.2
53.	Auburn University (AL)*	3.1
53.	Boston University	3.1
53.	Drexel University (PA)	3.1
53.	University of Arizona*	3.1
53.	University of Delaware*	3.1
53.	University of Pittsburgh*	3.1
59.	Clemson University (SC)*	3.0
59.	Rochester Inst. of Technology (NY)	3.0
59.	Tufts University (MA)	3.0
59.	U. of North Carolina–Chapel Hill*	3.0

Best in the Specialties ▶

(*Public)

AEROSPACE/AERONAUTICAL/ASTRONAUTICAL
1. Massachusetts Institute of Technology
2. Georgia Institute of Technology*
3. California Institute of Technology
4. University of Michigan–Ann Arbor*
5. Purdue University–West Lafayette (IN)*
5. Stanford University (CA)

BIOLOGICAL/AGRICULTURAL
1. Purdue University–West Lafayette (IN)*
2. Cornell University (NY)
2. Iowa State University*
2. Texas A&M University*
5. Michigan State University*

BIOMEDICAL/BIOMEDICAL ENGINEERING
1. Johns Hopkins University (MD)
2. Georgia Institute of Technology*
3. Massachusetts Institute of Technology
4. Duke University (NC)
5. Stanford University (CA)

CHEMICAL
1. Massachusetts Institute of Technology
2. Georgia Institute of Technology*
3. University of California–Berkeley*
4. California Institute of Technology
4. University of Michigan–Ann Arbor*

CIVIL
1. Georgia Institute of Technology*
2. University of California–Berkeley*
3. Massachusetts Institute of Technology
3. Purdue University–West Lafayette (IN)*
5. University of Texas at Austin*

COMPUTER ENGINEERING
1. Carnegie Mellon University (PA)
2. Massachusetts Institute of Technology
3. University of California–Berkeley*
4. Stanford University (CA)
5. Georgia Institute of Technology*

ELECTRICAL/ELECTRONIC/COMMUNICATIONS
1. Massachusetts Institute of Technology
2. University of California–Berkeley*
3. California Institute of Technology
4. Georgia Institute of Technology*
5. Stanford University (CA)

ENVIRONMENTAL/ENVIRONMENTAL HEALTH
1. University of California–Berkeley*
2. Stanford University (CA)
2. University of Michigan–Ann Arbor*
4. Georgia Institute of Technology*
4. University of Texas at Austin*

INDUSTRIAL/MANUFACTURING
1. Georgia Institute of Technology*
2. Purdue University–West Lafayette (IN)*
3. University of Michigan–Ann Arbor*
4. Virginia Tech*
5. Cornell University (NY)

MATERIALS
1. Massachusetts Institute of Technology
2. University of California–Berkeley*
2. University of Illinois–Urbana-Champaign*
4. Georgia Institute of Technology*
5. Northwestern University (IL)

MECHANICAL
1. Massachusetts Institute of Technology
2. Georgia Institute of Technology*
3. Stanford University (CA)
4. University of Michigan–Ann Arbor*
5. University of California–Berkeley*

PETROLEUM
1. Texas A&M University*
2. Louisiana State University–Baton Rouge*
2. University of Texas at Austin*
4. Texas Tech University*
5. Pennsylvania State University–University Park*

Note: Peer assessment survey in 2020 conducted by U.S. News. To be ranked in a specialty, a school may have either a program or course offerings in that subject area; ABET accreditation of that program is not needed. Extended rankings can be found at usnews.com/bestcolleges. U.S. News surveyed 206 undergraduate engineering programs at colleges that offer doctoral degrees in engineering and 220 engineering programs at colleges where the terminal degree in engineering is a bachelor's or master's.

Best
Computer Science Programs

THIS YEAR, U.S. NEWS introduces its first ranking of undergraduate computer science programs. To be eligible, programs must be accredited by ABET or be housed in an engineering school that grants Ph.D.s in engineering or computer science or have granted at least 20 computer science bachelor's degrees, according to U.S. Department of Education data. Results are based solely on surveys conducted in 2020 of computer science deans and senior faculty, who were asked to rate the quality of programs with which they're familiar on a scale of 1 (marginal) to 5 (distinguished); 38.8% responded. They also were asked to nominate up to 15 programs they consider best in specialty areas; the five receiving the most mentions appear.

▶ Top Programs

Rank	School (State) (*Public)	Peer assessment score (5.0=highest)
1.	Massachusetts Institute of Technology	5.0
2.	Carnegie Mellon University (PA)	4.9
2.	Stanford University (CA)	4.9
2.	University of California–Berkeley*	4.9
5.	California Institute of Technology	4.6
5.	Cornell University (NY)	4.6
5.	Georgia Institute of Technology*	4.6
5.	Princeton University (NJ)	4.6
5.	University of Illinois–Urbana-Champaign*	4.6
5.	University of Washington*	4.6
11.	University of Texas at Austin*	4.5
12.	University of Michigan–Ann Arbor*	4.4
13.	Columbia University (NY)	4.3
13.	Harvard University (MA)	4.3
13.	University of California–Los Angeles*	4.3
16.	University of California–San Diego*	4.2
16.	Univ. of Maryland–College Park*	4.2
16.	University of Pennsylvania	4.2
16.	Univ. of Wisconsin–Madison*	4.2
20.	Harvey Mudd College (CA)	4.1
20.	Johns Hopkins University (MD)	4.1
20.	Purdue University–West Lafayette (IN)*	4.1
20.	Rice University (TX)	4.1
20.	Yale University (CT)	4.1
25.	Brown University (RI)	4.0
25.	Duke University (NC)	4.0
25.	Northwestern University (IL)	4.0
25.	University of California–Irvine*	4.0
25.	University of Chicago	4.0
25.	University of Southern California	4.0
31.	University of Colorado Boulder*	3.9
31.	University of Massachusetts–Amherst*	3.9
31.	University of North Carolina–Chapel Hill*	3.9
31.	University of Virginia*	3.9
31.	Virginia Tech*	3.9
36.	New York University	3.8
36.	Texas A&M University*	3.8
36.	University of California–Davis*	3.8
36.	University of California–Santa Barbara*	3.8
36.	University of Minnesota–Twin Cities*	3.8
41.	Dartmouth College (NH)	3.7
41.	Northeastern University (MA)	3.7
41.	Ohio State University–Columbus*	3.7
41.	Rensselaer Polytechnic Inst. (NY)	3.7
41.	Rutgers University–New Brunswick (NJ)*	3.7
41.	Vanderbilt University (TN)	3.7
41.	Washington University in St. Louis	3.7
48.	Pennsylvania State U.–Univ. Park*	3.6
48.	Stony Brook–SUNY*	3.6
48.	University of Florida*	3.6
48.	University of Utah*	3.6
52.	Michigan State University*	3.5
52.	North Carolina State U.*	3.5
52.	Rochester Inst. of Technology (NY)	3.5
52.	Rose-Hulman Institute of Technology (IN)	3.5
52.	University of Arizona*	3.5
52.	University of California–Riverside*	3.5
52.	University of California–Santa Cruz*	3.5
52.	University of Notre Dame (IN)	3.5
52.	University of Pittsburgh*	3.5
61.	Arizona State University–Tempe*	3.4
61.	Boston University	3.4
61.	Indiana University–Bloomington*	3.4
61.	Iowa State University*	3.4
61.	Tufts University (MA)	3.4
61.	University at Buffalo–SUNY*	3.4
61.	University of Rochester (NY)	3.4
68.	Colorado School of Mines*	3.3
68.	Georgetown University (DC)	3.3
68.	William & Mary (VA)*	3.3
71.	Case Western Reserve Univ. (OH)	3.2
71.	Clemson University (SC)*	3.2
71.	Emory University (GA)	3.2
71.	George Mason University (VA)*	3.2
71.	George Washington University (DC)	3.2
71.	Oregon State University*	3.2
71.	Pomona College (CA)	3.2
71.	Stevens Institute of Technology (NJ)	3.2
71.	Syracuse University (NY)	3.2
71.	United States Military Academy (NY)*	3.2
71.	United States Naval Academy (MD)*	3.2
71.	University of Central Florida*	3.2
71.	University of Illinois–Chicago*	3.2
71.	University of Iowa*	3.2
71.	University of Tennessee*	3.2
71.	Worcester Polytechnic Inst. (MA)	3.2
87.	Auburn University (AL)*	3.1
87.	California Polytechnic State U.–San Luis Obispo*	3.1
87.	Colorado State University*	3.1
87.	Drexel University (PA)	3.1
87.	United States Air Force Academy (CO)*	3.1
87.	University of Connecticut*	3.1
87.	University of Kansas*	3.1
87.	University of Oregon*	3.1
87.	University of Texas at Dallas*	3.1
96.	Boston College	3.0
96.	Michigan Technological University*	3.0
96.	University of Alabama*	3.0
96.	University of Delaware*	3.0
96.	Univ. of Maryland–Baltimore County*	3.0
96.	Univ. of Nebraska–Lincoln*	3.0
96.	University of Texas at Arlington*	3.0
96.	Washington State University*	3.0
104.	Amherst College (MA)	2.9
104.	Brandeis University (MA)	2.9
104.	California State Polytechnic U.–Pomona*	2.9
104.	CUNY–City College*	2.9
104.	Florida State University*	2.9
104.	Grinnell College (IA)	2.9
104.	Illinois Institute of Technology	2.9
104.	Lehigh University (PA)	2.9
104.	New Jersey Inst. of Technology*	2.9
104.	San Diego State University*	2.9
104.	Smith College (MA)	2.9
104.	Tulane University (LA)	2.9
104.	University of Georgia*	2.9
104.	University of Houston*	2.9
104.	University of New Mexico*	2.9
104.	U. of North Carolina–Charlotte*	2.9
104.	Williams College (MA)	2.9
121.	Baylor University (TX)	2.8
121.	Brigham Young Univ.–Provo (UT)	2.8
121.	California State University–Los Angeles*	2.8
121.	Carleton College (MN)	2.8
121.	Howard University (DC)	2.8
121.	Kansas State University*	2.8
121.	Mississippi State University*	2.8
121.	Missouri U. of Science and Technology*	2.8
121.	Temple University (PA)*	2.8
121.	University of Kentucky*	2.8
121.	Univ. of Missouri*	2.8
121.	University of Oklahoma*	2.8
121.	University of San Diego	2.8
121.	Univ. of South Carolina*	2.8
121.	University of South Florida*	2.8
121.	University of Texas at San Antonio*	2.8
121.	Wake Forest University (NC)	2.8
138.	Binghamton University–SUNY*	2.7
138.	Bucknell University (PA)	2.7
138.	Louisiana State University–Baton Rouge*	2.7
138.	Montana State University*	2.7
138.	Oklahoma State University*	2.7
138.	San Jose State University (CA)*	2.7
138.	Santa Clara University (CA)	2.7
138.	Texas Tech University*	2.7
138.	University at Albany–SUNY*	2.7
138.	University of Alabama at Birmingham*	2.7

►Top Programs

Rank	School (State) (*Public)	Peer assessment score (5.0=highest)
138.	University of Arkansas*	2.7
138.	University of Colorado–Colorado Springs*	2.7
138.	Univ. of Massachusetts–Lowell*	2.7
138.	University of Miami (FL)	2.7
138.	University of Vermont*	2.7
138.	Wesleyan University (CT)	2.7
154.	Georgia State University*	2.6
154.	Mount Holyoke College (MA)	2.6
154.	Ohio University*	2.6
154.	Old Dominion University (VA)*	2.6
154.	Portland State University (OR)*	2.6
154.	Tennessee Technological Univ.*	2.6
154.	University of Alabama–Huntsville*	2.6
154.	University of Cincinnati*	2.6
154.	University of Colorado Denver*	2.6
154.	Univ. of Massachusetts–Boston*	2.6
154.	Univ. of Massachusetts–Dartmouth*	2.6
154.	University of Mississippi*	2.6
154.	University of New Hampshire*	2.6
154.	Univ. of Wisconsin–Milwaukee*	2.6
154.	Villanova University (PA)	2.6
154.	Virginia Commonwealth University*	2.6
154.	West Virginia University*	2.6
171.	Boise State University (ID)*	2.5
171.	Embry-Riddle Aeronautical University (FL)	2.5
171.	Florida Institute of Technology	2.5
171.	Florida International University*	2.5
171.	Loyola University Maryland	2.5
171.	Marquette University (WI)	2.5
171.	Miami University–Oxford (OH)*	2.5
171.	Middlebury College (VT)	2.5
171.	New Mexico State University*	2.5
171.	S.D. School of Mines and Tech.*	2.5
171.	Southern Methodist University (TX)	2.5

Rank	School (State) (*Public)	Peer assessment score (5.0=highest)
171.	University of Hawaii–Manoa*	2.5
171.	University of Louisiana at Lafayette*	2.5
171.	University of Maine*	2.5
171.	University of Minnesota–Duluth*	2.5
171.	University of Nevada–Las Vegas*	2.5
171.	University of Rhode Island*	2.5
171.	University of Texas–El Paso*	2.5
171.	University of Wyoming*	2.5
171.	Wayne State University (MI)*	2.5
191.	Clarkson University (NY)	2.4
191.	Colgate University (NY)	2.4
191.	CUNY–Hunter College*	2.4
191.	DePaul University (IL)	2.4
191.	Florida Atlantic University*	2.4
191.	Indiana U.-Purdue University–Indianapolis*	2.4
191.	Kennesaw State University (GA)*	2.4
191.	Saint Louis University	2.4
191.	San Francisco State University*	2.4
191.	University of Arkansas at Little Rock*	2.4
191.	University of Dayton (OH)	2.4
191.	University of Denver	2.4
191.	University of Idaho*	2.4
191.	University of Memphis*	2.4
191.	University of San Francisco	2.4
191.	University of Tulsa (OK)	2.4
191.	Utah State University*	2.4
191.	Wichita State University (KS)*	2.4
191.	Wright State University (OH)*	2.4
210.	Bowdoin College (ME)	2.3
210.	The Citadel, Military Coll. of SC*	2.3
210.	Dakota State University (SD)*	2.3
210.	Gonzaga University (WA)	2.3
210.	Lafayette College (PA)	2.3
210.	Lawrence Technological Univ. (MI)	2.3

Rank	School (State) (*Public)	Peer assessment score (5.0=highest)
210.	Louisiana Tech University*	2.3
210.	North Carolina A&T State Univ.*	2.3
210.	Purdue University–Fort Wayne*	2.3
210.	Seattle University	2.3
210.	Southern Illinois University–Carbondale*	2.3
210.	Towson University (MD)*	2.3
210.	University of Alaska–Fairbanks*	2.3
210.	University of Michigan–Dearborn*	2.3
210.	Univ. of Missouri–Kansas City*	2.3
210.	University of Nebraska–Omaha*	2.3
210.	University of Nevada–Reno*	2.3
210.	University of North Texas*	2.3
210.	University of South Dakota*	2.3
210.	Virginia Military Institute*	2.3
230.	Bowling Green State University (OH)*	2.2
230.	California State University–Fullerton*	2.2
230.	California State University–Long Beach*	2.2
230.	Florida A&M University*	2.2
230.	Idaho State University*	2.2
230.	Kent State University (OH)*	2.2
230.	N.M. Inst. of Mining and Tech.*	2.2
230.	New York Inst. of Technology	2.2
230.	North Dakota State University*	2.2
230.	Northern Arizona University*	2.2
230.	Oakland University (MI)*	2.2
230.	University of Akron (OH)*	2.2
230.	Univ. of Missouri–St. Louis*	2.2
230.	University of New Haven (CT)	2.2
230.	University of New Orleans*	2.2
230.	U. of North Carolina–Greensboro*	2.2
230.	University of North Dakota*	2.2
230.	University of Puerto Rico–Mayaguez*	2.2
230.	Western Michigan University*	2.2

Note: Peer assessment surveys in 2020 conducted by U.S. News. To be ranked in a specialty, a school may have either a program or course offerings in that subject area. Extended undergraduate computer science rankings can be found at usnews.com/bestcolleges. U.S. News surveyed and ranked 481 computer science programs.

► Best in the Specialties (*Public)

ARTIFICIAL INTELLIGENCE
1. Carnegie Mellon University (PA)
2. Massachusetts Institute of Technology
3. Stanford University (CA)
4. University of California–Berkeley*
5. University of Texas–Austin*

BIOCOMPUTING/BIOINFORMATICS/BIOTECHNOLOGY
1. Massachusetts Institute of Technology
2. Carnegie Mellon University (PA)
2. University of California–San Diego*
4. Stanford University (CA)
4. University of California–Berkeley*

COMPUTER SYSTEMS
1. University of California–Berkeley*
2. Massachusetts Institute of Technology
3. Carnegie Mellon University (PA)
3. University of Illinois–Urbana-Champaign*
5. Stanford University (CA)

CYBERSECURITY
1. Carnegie Mellon University (PA)
1. Georgia Institute of Technology*
3. University of California–Berkeley*
4. Massachusetts Institute of Technology
5. University of Illinois–Urbana-Champaign*

DATA ANALYTICS/SCIENCE
1. University of California–Berkeley*
2. Massachusetts Institute of Technology
3. Carnegie Mellon University (PA)
4. Stanford University (CA)
5. University of Michigan–Ann Arbor*
5. University of Washington*

MOBILE/WEB APPLICATIONS
1. Carnegie Mellon University (PA)
2. Massachusetts Institute of Technology
2. Stanford University (CA)
4. University of California–Berkeley*
4. University of Illinois–Urbana-Champaign*
4. University of Washington*

PROGRAMMING LANGUAGES
1. Massachusetts Institute of Technology
2. Carnegie Mellon University (PA)
2. Stanford University (CA)
4. University of Illinois–Urbana-Champaign*
5. University of California–Berkeley*

SOFTWARE ENGINEERING
1. Carnegie Mellon University (PA)
2. Georgia Institute of Technology*
2. University of California–Berkeley*
2. University of Illinois–Urbana-Champaign*
5. University of Texas–Austin*

THEORY
1. Massachusetts Institute of Technology
2. University of California–Berkeley*
3. Carnegie Mellon University (PA)
4. Stanford University (CA)
5. Princeton University (NJ)

Best
Online Degree Programs

WHEN WE SURVEYED COLLEGES IN 2019 about their online options, more than 360 schools reported having bachelor's programs that can be completed without showing up in person for class (though attendance may be required for testing, orientations and support services). These offerings, typically degree-completion programs aimed at working adults and community college grads, were evaluated on their success at engaging students, the credentials of their faculty, and the services and technologies made available remotely. The table below features some of the most significant ranking factors, such as the prevalence

of faculty holding a Ph.D. or other terminal degree, class size, the percentages of new entrants who stayed enrolled and later graduated, and the debt loads of recent graduates. The top half of programs are listed here. Ranks are determined by the institutions' rounded overall program scores, displayed below. To see the rest of the ranked online bachelor's programs and to read the full details about the methodology, visit usnews.com/online. There you'll also find detail-rich profile pages for each of the schools and (in case you want to plan ahead) rankings of online MBA programs and graduate programs in engineering, nursing, education and more.

(*Public, **For profit)

Rank	School	Overall program score	Average peer assessment score (5.0=highest)	'19 total program enrollment	'19 - '20 tuition[1]	'19 full-time faculty with Ph.D.	'19 average class size	'19 retention rate	'19 graduation rate[2]	% graduates with debt ('19)	Average debt of graduates ('19)
1.	Ohio State University–Columbus*	100	3.7	456	$359	85%	39	100%	92%	48%	$12,356
2.	Embry-Riddle Aeronautical U.–Worldwide (FL)	99	3.6	15,511	$413	62%	20	81%	28%	10%	$7,953
3.	University of Illinois–Chicago*	98	3.5	250	$462	46%	21	92%	87%	49%	$17,333
4.	University of Florida*	95	3.8	3,054	$500	81%	29	87%	65%	43%	$18,146
5.	Oregon State University*	94	3.9	6,328	$309	67%	34	87%	40%	59%	$24,873
6.	Arizona State University*	93	3.9	44,579	$530	73%	48	86%	50%	66%	$23,874
7.	University of Oklahoma*	91	3.7	1,023	$672	76%	16	81%	42%	58%	$23,209
8.	Loyola University Chicago (IL)	90	3.6	404	$693	69%	13	83%	81%	71%	$25,100
8.	Pennsylvania State University–World Campus*	90	4.2	9,198	$555	65%	28	77%	39%	70%	$37,228
8.	University of North Carolina–Wilmington*	90	3.3	2,175	$644	65%	26	95%	86%	34%	$15,466
11.	Charleston Southern University (SC)	89	2.6	269	$490	74%	10	65%	73%	26%	$15,926
11.	Colorado State University*	89	3.5	804	$476	64%	11	83%	67%	62%	$28,788
11.	Colorado State University–Global Campus*	89	3.4	11,594	$350	97%	14	66%	45%	66%	$25,548
11.	University of Arizona*	89	3.5	2,264	$525	76%	11	86%	N/A	61%	$29,099
11.	University of Georgia*	89	3.7	32	$326	100%	15	89%	93%	60%	$21,216
16.	CUNY School of Professional Studies*	88	3.2	2,422	$295	73%	18	65%	35%	31%	$13,968
16.	Concordia University Wisconsin & Ann Arbor	88	2.8	374	$512	100%	12	72%	82%	83%	$11,692
16.	University of Central Florida*	88	3.9	12,573	$616	72%	71	85%	74%	57%	$21,597
16.	West Texas A&M University*	88	3.0	1,420	$345	73%	39	85%	75%	52%	$14,800
20.	George Washington University (DC)	87	3.7	373	$615	75%	15	81%	49%	29%	$25,766
20.	University of Alabama–Birmingham*	87	3.4	1,699	$441	82%	42	69%	41%	56%	$27,610
20.	Western Kentucky University*	87	3.3	3,350	$540	77%	19	81%	49%	67%	$26,586
23.	Illinois State University*	86	3.2	92	$838	45%	13	86%	N/A	5%	$20,500
23.	Indiana University–Online*	86	3.5	2,883	$331	65%	22	76%	62%	71%	$24,318
23.	University at Buffalo–SUNY*	86	3.6	95	$353	88%	30	92%	45%	41%	$12,212
23.	University of Massachusetts–Amherst*	86	3.6	1,506	$460	73%	23	69%	62%	63%	$23,716
23.	Utah State University*	86	3.5	1,628	$414	57%	88	85%	64%	49%	$18,021
23.	Washington State University*	86	3.6	2,326	$578	74%	26	71%	48%	70%	$26,834
29.	Ball State University* (IN)	85	3.3	1,283	$543	72%	27	81%	36%	64%	$29,178
29.	Daytona State College* (FL)	85	2.5	1,843	$550	67%	26	75%	51%	43%	$24,702
29.	University of Arkansas*	85	3.3	987	$252	52%	30	75%	69%	56%	$22,143
29.	University of Massachusetts–Lowell*	85	3.4	2,162	$380	81%	25	80%	42%	54%	$23,401
33.	Pace University (NY)	84	3.0	231	$555	94%	12	80%	70%	48%	$34,745
33.	Siena Heights University (MI)	84	2.4	1,463	$530	59%	13	82%	83%	70%	$19,770
33.	University of Illinois–Springfield*	84	3.6	996	$359	85%	20	79%	43%	58%	$19,937
33.	University of North Carolina–Charlotte*	84	3.5	530	$583	69%	25	93%	87%	34%	$13,738
37.	Dakota Wesleyan University (SD)	83	2.6	72	$375	0%	12	89%	N/A	14%	$18,421
37.	Maranatha Baptist University (WI)	83	2.2	139	$430	56%	8	85%	N/A	25%	$8,056
39.	City University of Seattle (WA)	82	2.8	1,819	$456	0%	9	70%	52%	14%	$19,292
39.	Clarion University of Pennsylvania*	82	2.6	759	$347	92%	25	76%	61%	69%	$22,776
39.	North Carolina State University–Raleigh*	82	3.4	65	$900	100%	18	90%	79%	41%	$14,148
39.	Purdue University–Northwest* (IN)	82	3.1	1,673	$367	100%	26	85%	81%	36%	$10,748

N/A=Data were not provided by the school. **1.** Tuition is reported on a per-credit-hour basis. Out-of-state tuition is listed for public institutions. **2.** Displayed here for standardization are six-year graduation rates.

Rank	School	Overall program score	Average peer assessment score (5.0=highest)	'19 total program enrollment	'19 - '20 tuition[1]	'19 full-time faculty with Ph.D.	'19 average class size	'19 retention rate	'19 graduation rate[2]	% graduates with debt ('19)	Average debt of graduates ('19)
39.	Rutgers University–Camden* (NJ)	82	3.5	405	$550	89%	36	80%	N/A	71%	$28,232
39.	Sam Houston State University* (TX)	82	2.9	1,246	$244	89%	29	N/A	N/A	58%	$27,166
39.	Texas A&M University–Commerce*	82	3.1	1,871	$575	69%	24	78%	48%	55%	$19,357
39.	University of North Florida*	82	3.1	218	$285	86%	45	87%	N/A	25%	$6,675
39.	University of West Florida*	82	3.1	1,965	$342	85%	29	74%	51%	39%	$15,542
48.	Concordia University Chicago (IL)	81	2.4	284	$505	79%	10	N/A	100%	N/A	N/A
48.	Creighton University (NE)	81	3.5	112	$470	90%	13	75%	33%	70%	$35,318
48.	University of Wisconsin–Milwaukee*	81	3.3	4,129	$337	77%	35	80%	33%	74%	$32,390
48.	University of Wisconsin–Whitewater*	81	3.2	229	$389	69%	30	80%	59%	63%	N/A
52.	California Baptist University	80	2.9	2,345	$613	79%	20	83%	51%	85%	$27,965
52.	Florida International University*	80	3.2	5,514	$247	79%	49	95%	43%	62%	$22,604
52.	Troy University* (AL)	80	2.9	4,320	$338	80%	36	60%	24%	24%	$14,803
52.	University of Memphis* (TN)	80	3.0	2,312	$463	67%	30	77%	48%	65%	$28,936
52.	University of Missouri–St. Louis*	80	3.2	54	$452	100%	19	75%	77%	44%	$16,103
52.	University of the Incarnate Word (TX)	80	2.6	1,332	$530	100%	19	69%	58%	80%	$24,347
58.	Eastern Kentucky University*	79	3.1	2,400	$409	71%	18	76%	48%	62%	$33,995
58.	Kansas State University*	79	3.5	449	$436	59%	30	74%	N/A	73%	$34,686
58.	Marist College (NY)	79	2.9	127	$730	65%	15	90%	50%	68%	$25,037
58.	Regent University (VA)	79	2.6	4,808	$395	73%	18	70%	39%	70%	$27,657
58.	Sacred Heart University (CT)	79	2.6	327	$590	100%	13	77%	47%	59%	$21,026
58.	Savannah College of Art and Design (GA)	79	3.1	592	$835	22%	19	70%	29%	60%	$37,549
58.	St. Petersburg College* (FL)	79	N/A	5,386	$426	69%	25	85%	58%	54%	$27,675
58.	University of St. Francis (IL)	79	2.8	258	$399	73%	13	81%	60%	56%	$26,110
66.	Cornerstone University (MI)	78	2.4	283	$450	60%	9	86%	100%	84%	$23,849
66.	Lee University (TN)	78	2.8	894	$259	74%	7	85%	34%	72%	$26,629
66.	University of North Carolina–Pembroke*	78	2.9	1,205	$188	73%	21	65%	49%	73%	$18,171
66.	University of North Texas*	78	3.3	1,626	$715	75%	40	84%	70%	47%	$17,984
66.	University of Northern Colorado*	78	3.0	509	$432	76%	21	85%	64%	50%	$14,758
66.	University of South Carolina–Aiken*	78	2.8	344	$869	71%	17	82%	73%	63%	$24,315
66.	Utica College (NY)	78	3.1	1,135	$475	59%	15	83%	59%	51%	$15,869
73.	Florida Atlantic University*	77	3.3	580	$750	66%	9	91%	67%	40%	$16,624
73.	Old Dominion University* (VA)	77	3.1	7,050	$407	69%	38	84%	65%	N/A	N/A
73.	Pensacola State College* (FL)	77	2.6	288	$486	100%	20	74%	39%	N/A	N/A
73.	University of Cincinnati*	77	3.3	N/A	$431	67%	33	88%	55%	64%	$17,167
73.	University of Denver*	77	3.2	278	$668	75%	10	77%	45%	63%	$46,149
73.	University of North Dakota*	77	3.4	631	$399	71%	19	62%	38%	69%	$29,446
73.	University of South Alabama*	77	3.1	41	$328	50%	16	28%	94%	100%	$4,000
80.	Anderson University (SC)	76	2.6	383	$450	65%	13	61%	64%	86%	$25,893
80.	Berkeley College** (NY)	76	2.7	1,432	$855	62%	20	55%	47%	86%	$31,869
80.	Bowling Green State University* (OH)	76	3.1	481	$390	73%	16	83%	54%	45%	$25,364
80.	Fort Hays State University* (KS)	76	3.0	4,660	$219	62%	20	82%	32%	62%	$24,327
80.	Kentucky Wesleyan College	76	2.4	50	$455	71%	11	66%	78%	91%	$27,650
80.	Linfield College (OR)	76	2.5	351	$495	73%	10	80%	73%	54%	$22,599
80.	McKendree University (IL)	76	2.5	368	$390	87%	12	86%	77%	55%	$20,278
80.	Northern Arizona University*	76	3.2	4,322	$435	58%	30	87%	61%	65%	$20,136
80.	Saint Leo University (FL)	76	2.8	5,384	$370	83%	18	76%	29%	64%	$30,340
80.	University of Houston–Downtown*	76	3.0	253	$655	100%	27	79%	64%	57%	$14,292
80.	University of Louisville* (KY)	76	3.4	616	$539	70%	18	63%	27%	56%	$23,275
80.	University of Nebraska–Omaha*	76	3.4	786	$475	75%	23	90%	70%	61%	$32,812
80.	Westfield State University* (MA)	76	2.4	261	$320	93%	18	73%	21%	62%	$19,423
93.	California State University–Dominguez Hills*	75	2.7	444	$809	92%	16	83%	58%	30%	$13,861
93.	Herzing University (WI)	75	2.2	1,318	$570	63%	15	83%	34%	79%	$19,101
93.	New England Col. of Business and Finance** (MA)	75	2.0	817	$423	63%	14	90%	44%	50%	$22,355
93.	SUNY College of Technology–Delhi*	75	2.9	801	$353	45%	16	70%	45%	50%	$21,575
93.	University of Massachusetts–Boston*	75	3.4	44	$575	N/A	24	60%	N/A	67%	$30,861
93.	University of Southern Mississippi*	75	3.2	3,783	$371	61%	33	75%	N/A	84%	$26,743
99.	Central Washington University*	74	3.0	1,595	$511	74%	21	90%	62%	64%	$18,155
99.	Drexel University (PA)	74	3.5	1,606	$513	74%	20	79%	39%	59%	$33,878
99.	Moody Bible Institute (IL)	74	2.6	901	$350	82%	15	70%	33%	31%	$14,944
99.	Ohio University*	74	3.4	8,219	$243	71%	39	85%	70%	49%	$17,308
99.	University of Alaska–Fairbanks*	74	3.0	5,718	$246	54%	21	N/A	N/A	44%	$25,985
99.	University of Maine–Augusta*	74	2.9	2,926	$299	72%	23	80%	29%	72%	$25,927
99.	University of Missouri*	74	3.5	562	$382	73%	25	77%	N/A	43%	$15,201
106.	Appalachian State University* (NC)	73	3.0	481	$643	69%	24	84%	76%	38%	$11,248
106.	Brandman University (CA)	73	2.6	2,643	$500	88%	25	92%	54%	71%	$34,807

(*Public, **For profit)

Rank	School	Overall program score	Average peer assessment score (5.0=highest)	'19 total program enrollment	'19 - '20 tuition[1]	'19 full-time faculty with Ph.D.	'19 average class size	'19 retention rate	'19 graduation rate[2]	% graduates with debt ('19)	Average debt of graduates ('19)
106.	California State University–Chico*	73	3.1	483	$657	88%	32	93%	63%	57%	$15,392
106.	Granite State College* (NH)	73	2.4	2,029	$365	36%	13	82%	40%	62%	$20,597
106.	Lynn University (FL)	73	2.6	293	$300	3%	11	67%	61%	48%	$35,677
106.	Saint Joseph's University (PA)	73	3.1	75	$584	67%	13	80%	48%	N/A	N/A
106.	University of Louisiana–Lafayette*	73	2.9	1,510	$380	49%	34	62%	58%	N/A	N/A
113.	Auburn University–Montgomery* (AL)	72	3.0	100	$342	0%	20	90%	N/A	40%	$11,358
113.	Central Michigan University*	72	3.2	1,539	$430	77%	26	60%	38%	71%	$21,160
113.	Duquesne University (PA)	72	3.3	84	$965	75%	10	69%	N/A	65%	$28,022
113.	Ferris State University* (MI)	72	2.9	741	$452	76%	17	79%	51%	52%	$19,420
113.	Johnson & Wales University (RI)	72	2.8	1,455	$330	44%	18	60%	54%	88%	N/A
113.	Oakland University* (MI)	72	2.8	281	$495	88%	28	74%	47%	53%	$26,056
113.	Robert Morris University (PA)	72	2.6	403	$780	100%	14	72%	46%	54%	$34,798
113.	SUNY College of Technology–Canton*	72	2.9	1,148	$353	62%	21	80%	48%	75%	$27,431
113.	University of Massachusetts–Dartmouth*	72	3.3	449	$332	78%	15	66%	44%	60%	$27,261
113.	Western Illinois University*	72	2.8	1,675	$296	77%	22	77%	51%	67%	$30,788
123.	Bluefield College (VA)	71	2.4	475	$365	53%	13	62%	59%	76%	$25,232
123.	La Salle University (PA)	71	3.1	141	$507	94%	15	100%	N/A	50%	$20,165
123.	Lindenwood University (MO)	71	2.4	380	$495	70%	19	69%	N/A	84%	$31,406
123.	Marian University (IN)	71	2.6	910	$825	35%	25	89%	N/A	81%	$47,370
123.	Mount Mercy University (IA)	71	N/A	238	$530	71%	16	61%	N/A	73%	$24,783
123.	Northwestern College (IA)	71	2.9	92	$335	94%	15	76%	N/A	N/A	N/A
123.	Southeast Missouri State University*	71	2.8	871	$300	0%	26	68%	55%	75%	$23,607
123.	Southwestern College (KS)	71	2.5	1,182	$527	88%	8	81%	44%	29%	$24,823
123.	The Citadel* (SC)	71	N/A	212	$665	86%	17	61%	N/A	51%	$22,365
123.	Western Carolina University* (NC)	71	3.0	1,562	$189	68%	21	76%	63%	N/A	N/A
133.	Campbell University (NC)	70	2.5	594	$450	89%	12	65%	N/A	54%	$21,687
133.	Eastern Oregon University*	70	2.6	2,410	$252	59%	19	84%	42%	68%	$25,357
133.	Florida Institute of Technology	70	2.9	1,781	$510	79%	17	75%	15%	76%	$40,179
133.	Neumann University (PA)	70	2.1	192	$550	N/A	14	80%	71%	42%	$20,295
133.	Northeastern State University* (OK)	70	2.7	965	$477	62%	21	79%	56%	N/A	N/A
133.	Oregon Health and Science University*	70	2.9	136	$288	45%	28	90%	N/A	62%	$16,447
133.	St. Joseph's College New York (NY)	70	2.9	307	$625	83%	15	60%	6%	63%	$21,661
133.	Syracuse University (NY)	70	3.6	47	$695	100%	16	92%	N/A	N/A	N/A
133.	Texas Tech University*	70	3.5	2,430	$268	88%	31	N/A	N/A	69%	$31,339
133.	University of La Verne (CA)	70	2.3	340	$645	100%	16	83%	47%	73%	$32,297
143.	Ashland University (OH)	69	2.4	219	$530	71%	16	70%	N/A	69%	$28,237
143.	Campbellsville University (KY)	69	2.4	515	$399	62%	18	75%	N/A	60%	$33,442
143.	Concordia University–St. Paul (MN)	69	2.4	1,560	$420	74%	14	83%	69%	74%	$24,014
143.	Houston Baptist University (TX)	69	2.7	395	$415	81%	18	58%	N/A	57%	$17,890

JURGITA VAICIKEVICIENE / EYEEM – GETTY IMAGES

Rank	School	Overall program score	Average peer assessment score (5.0=highest)	'19 total program enrollment	'19 - '20 tuition[1]	'19 full-time faculty with Ph.D.	'19 average class size	'19 retention rate	'19 graduation rate[2]	% graduates with debt ('19)	Average debt of graduates ('19)
143.	Loyola University New Orleans (LA)	69	3.1	293	$450	87%	12	70%	N/A	N/A	N/A
143.	Millersville University of Pennsylvania*	69	2.5	461	$398	93%	19	77%	N/A	43%	$17,796
143.	Purdue University–Fort Wayne*	69	3.0	177	$687	74%	21	58%	37%	64%	$25,711
143.	Southwestern Oklahoma State University*	69	2.6	578	$442	33%	19	90%	63%	45%	$16,509
143.	Valdosta State University* (GA)	69	2.9	1,064	$202	79%	14	63%	N/A	67%	$25,012
152.	Arkansas State University*	68	2.8	1,264	$210	40%	23	27%	N/A	77%	$25,450
152.	Champlain College (VT)	68	2.7	2,086	$318	0%	13	80%	49%	52%	$26,774
152.	Colorado Technical University**	68	2.5	30,883	$340	69%	32	84%	23%	77%	$20,756
152.	Florida State University*	68	3.5	567	$721	45%	32	N/A	71%	N/A	N/A
152.	Georgia Southern University*	68	2.9	683	$204	0%	37	64%	44%	73%	$27,681
152.	Graceland University (IA)	68	2.1	140	$430	50%	10	70%	78%	72%	$17,215
152.	Maryville University of St. Louis (MO)	68	2.7	1,272	$500	0%	15	N/A	N/A	N/A	N/A
152.	Midwestern Baptist Theological Seminary (MO)	68	2.4	308	$360	65%	20	73%	33%	56%	$24,583
152.	Nicholls State University* (LA)	68	2.5	675	$275	56%	10	N/A	N/A	29%	$4,808
152.	Slippery Rock University of Pennsylvania*	68	2.6	225	$328	100%	12	63%	72%	43%	$19,633
152.	Union Institute & University (OH)	68	2.2	935	$545	64%	8	79%	72%	61%	$38,290
152.	University of Colorado–Colorado Springs*	68	3.2	3,013	$514	70%	23	73%	N/A	58%	$19,925
152.	University of North Carolina–Greensboro*	68	N/A	1,164	$928	83%	47	78%	N/A	88%	$22,767
152.	University of Tennessee–Martin*	68	2.9	557	$399	73%	21	83%	N/A	68%	$24,501
166.	College of Coastal Georgia*	67	2.3	82	$115	72%	22	58%	45%	56%	$25,560
166.	Limestone University (SC)	67	2.1	761	$441	68%	16	73%	63%	91%	$28,888
166.	Northwest University (WA)	67	2.7	149	$446	65%	11	77%	N/A	78%	$25,650
166.	Toccoa Falls College (GA)	67	2.3	288	$333	82%	16	68%	37%	67%	$17,063
166.	University of Toledo* (OH)	67	3.0	2,650	$758	62%	34	71%	55%	66%	$16,175
171.	Iowa Wesleyan University	66	2.4	68	$435	45%	8	100%	0%	53%	$25,518
171.	Lamar University* (TX)	66	2.7	1,543	$248	51%	18	68%	N/A	N/A	N/A
171.	Portland State University* (OR)	66	3.2	4,278	$633	66%	41	N/A	N/A	46%	$8,091
171.	SUNY Polytechnic Institute*	66	3.0	65	$353	50%	11	N/A	N/A	63%	$21,676
171.	Upper Iowa University	66	2.5	1,813	$471	39%	15	80%	50%	63%	$33,223

(*Public, **For profit)

▶ Best Online Bachelor's Programs For Veterans

WHICH PROGRAMS OFFER MILITARY VETERANS and active-duty service members the best distance education? To ensure academic quality, all schools included in this ranking had to first qualify for a spot by being in the top half of the Best Online Degree Programs ranking, above. They had to be housed in a regionally accredited institution and were judged on a multitude of factors, including program reputation, faculty credentials, student graduation rate and graduate debt load. Secondly, because veterans and active-duty members often wish to take full advantage of federal benefits designed to make their coursework less expensive, programs also had to be certified for the GI Bill and participate in the Yellow Ribbon Program or charge in-state tuition that can be fully covered by the GI Bill to veterans from out of state. A third criterion for being ranked is that a program must have enrolled a critical mass of students with military backgrounds. The undergraduate-level rankings require a total of 25 veterans and active-duty service members to be included. Qualifying programs were ranked in descending order based on their spot in the overall ranking.

Rank School (State)

1. Embry-Riddle Aeronautical University–Worldwide (FL)
2. University of Florida*
3. Oregon State University*
4. Arizona State University*
5. University of Oklahoma*
6. Pennsylvania State University–World Campus*
6. University of North Carolina–Wilmington*
8. University of Arizona*
8. Charleston Southern University (SC)
8. Colorado State University–Global Campus*
8. Colorado State University*
12. CUNY School of Professional Studies*

12. University of Central Florida*
12. West Texas A&M University*
15. Western Kentucky University*
15. University of Alabama–Birmingham*
15. George Washington University (DC)
18. University of Massachusetts–Amherst*
18. Utah State University*
18. Indiana University–Online*
18. Washington State University*
22. Daytona State College* (FL)
22. University of Arkansas*
22. Ball State University* (IN)
22. University of Massachusetts–Lowell*
26. University of Illinois–Springfield*
26. Siena Heights University (MI)

28. University of West Florida*
28. Sam Houston State University* (TX)
28. City University of Seattle (WA)
31. University of Wisconsin–Milwaukee*
31. Concordia University Chicago (IL)
31. University of Wisconsin–Whitewater*
34. Troy University* (AL)
34. University of Memphis* (TN)
34. University of the Incarnate Word (TX)
34. California Baptist University
34. Florida International University*
39. Eastern Kentucky University*
39. Regent University (VA)
39. Kansas State University*
39. St. Petersburg College* (FL)

43. University of North Carolina–Pembroke*
43. University of Northern Colorado*
43. Lee University (TN)
43. Utica College (NY)
47. Old Dominion University* (VA)
47. University of North Dakota*
49. University of Louisville* (KY)
49. Saint Leo University (FL)
49. Northern Arizona University*
49. Fort Hays State University* (KS)
49. University of Nebraska–Omaha*
49. Bowling Green State University* (OH)
49. McKendree University (IL)
49. Berkeley College (NY)
49. Westfield State University* (MA)

Note: Key to footnotes, Page 106.

Best
Colleges for Social Mobility

ECONOMICALLY DISADVANTAGED STUDENTS are less likely than others to finish college. This ranking reveals which schools stand out among their peers at serving recipients of Pell Grants, federal awards that go to students with exceptional financial need – what U.S. News defines as advancing social mobility. The ranking is based on an average of the six-year graduation rates of students entering in fall 2012 and 2013 (though we show actual data for those entering in 2013 below) and how that performance compares with the rates of all other students. Scores were adjusted by the proportion of the classes awarded Pell Grants, because achieving great results among low-income students is more challenging with a larger proportion of such students enrolled. Find additional schools doing a good job at usnews.com, and see page 58 for more on the methodology.

▶ National Universities

Rank	School (State) (*Public)	% of Pell recipients (entering 2013)	Pell graduation rate
1.	University of California–Riverside*	55%	75%
2.	University of California–Irvine*	47%	84%
3.	Rutgers University–Newark (NJ)*	52%	71%
4.	University of California–Santa Cruz*	49%	74%
5.	University of California–Merced*	63%	68%
6.	University of La Verne (CA)	47%	71%
6.	University of Puerto Rico–Rio Piedras*	N/A	N/A
8.	Russell Sage College (NY)	59%	69%
9.	Georgia State University*	65%	55%
10.	University of Illinois–Chicago*	56%	59%
11.	Howard University (DC)	50%	60%
11.	Keiser University (FL)	68%	61%
13.	University of California–Los Angeles*	37%	89%
13.	University of California–Santa Barbara*	36%	84%
15.	University of California–Davis*	37%	83%
15.	William Carey University (MS)	51%	48%
17.	CUNY–City College*	N/A	N/A
17.	University of South Florida*	39%	72%
19.	Florida International University*	42%	64%
20.	Florida A&M University*	69%	52%
20.	Metropolitan State University (MN)*	N/A	N/A
20.	Montclair State University (NJ)*	40%	66%
23.	U. of North Carolina–Greensboro*	48%	57%
24.	Gallaudet University (DC)	58%	49%
24.	University of Findlay (OH)	31%	78%
26.	California State University–Fresno*	68%	53%
26.	Rutgers University–Camden (NJ)*	47%	64%
26.	University of Texas at Arlington*	44%	50%
29.	Chatham University (PA)	46%	62%
29.	Mary Baldwin University (VA)	59%	46%
29.	Stony Brook–SUNY*	32%	80%
29.	University at Albany–SUNY*	37%	63%
33.	East Carolina University (NC)*	41%	62%
33.	Florida Atlantic University*	41%	52%
33.	University of California–San Diego*	32%	85%
36.	Univ. of Massachusetts–Boston*	43%	48%
36.	University of Texas–Rio Grande Valley*	N/A	N/A
36.	University of the Pacific (CA)	40%	63%
39.	Grand Canyon University (AZ)	N/A	N/A
39.	Lincoln Memorial University (TN)	52%	54%
39.	St. Catherine University (MN)	44%	53%
39.	St. John's University (NY)	42%	57%
39.	Univ. of Maryland Eastern Shore*	59%	42%
44.	Portland State University (OR)*	44%	45%
44.	University of North Texas*	47%	55%
44.	University of Texas at San Antonio*	44%	44%
44.	University of the Incarnate Word (TX)	47%	48%
48.	North Carolina A&T State Univ.*	67%	47%

Rank	School (State) (*Public)	% of Pell recipients (entering 2013)	Pell graduation rate
48.	University of Florida*	29%	86%
48.	University of Houston*	39%	58%
48.	University of West Georgia*	55%	43%
52.	Edgewood College (WI)	41%	55%
52.	Hampton University (VA)	40%	50%
54.	Clarke University (IA)	34%	65%
54.	Husson University (ME)	50%	50%
54.	Jackson State University (MS)*	N/A	N/A
54.	Our Lady of the Lake University (TX)	68%	41%
54.	Sam Houston State University (TX)*	46%	50%
59.	Delaware State University*	53%	42%
59.	Rutgers University–New Brunswick (NJ)*	30%	80%
59.	San Diego State University*	33%	70%
62.	Trinity International University (IL)	N/A	N/A
62.	University at Buffalo–SUNY*	33%	71%
62.	University of Central Florida*	32%	70%
62.	U. of North Carolina–Charlotte*	34%	63%
66.	Long Island University (NY)	58%	41%
66.	New Jersey Inst. of Technology*	37%	63%
68.	Carson-Newman University (TN)	43%	48%
68.	Clark Atlanta University	72%	42%
68.	University of Texas at Dallas*	32%	67%
71.	Azusa Pacific University (CA)	N/A	N/A
71.	Benedictine University (IL)	44%	40%
71.	Stephen F. Austin State University (TX)*	N/A	N/A
71.	University of New Mexico*	45%	46%
71.	William Woods University (MO)	N/A	N/A
76.	Regis University (CO)	30%	66%
76.	University of Arizona*	36%	59%
76.	University of California–Berkeley*	24%	88%
76.	Univ. of Massachusetts–Dartmouth*	40%	54%
80.	Adelphi University (NY)	34%	65%
80.	Florida State University*	27%	81%
80.	Kennesaw State University (GA)*	37%	41%
80.	Middle Tennessee State Univ.*	49%	41%
80.	Pontifical Catholic U. of Puerto Rico–Ponce	N/A	N/A
80.	Simmons University (MA)	28%	80%
80.	Texas A&M University*	29%	76%
80.	University of Hawaii–Hilo*	46%	42%
80.	University of San Francisco	27%	76%
80.	Virginia Commonwealth University*	27%	63%
90.	D'Youville College (NY)	41%	53%
90.	Illinois Institute of Technology	30%	66%
90.	Missouri State University*	N/A	N/A
90.	Morgan State University (MD)*	58%	38%
90.	Pace University (NY)	36%	48%
90.	St. John Fisher College (NY)	29%	74%
90.	University of New Orleans*	44%	42%

N/A=Data for 2013 were not provided by the school. Rank is based on 2012 data from the school or the federal government or, in some cases, on U.S. News estimates.

Rank	School (State) (*Public)	% of Pell recipients (entering 2013)	Pell graduation rate
90.	University of Texas–El Paso*	67%	34%
98.	Binghamton University–SUNY*	25%	81%
98.	Biola University (CA)	27%	66%
98.	Clarkson University (NY)	25%	77%
98.	Syracuse University (NY)	24%	81%
98.	University of Memphis*	48%	45%
103.	Rochester Inst. of Technology (NY)	29%	66%
103.	University of St. Francis (IL)	39%	53%
103.	Wayne State University (MI)*	53%	42%
106.	Barry University (FL)	63%	32%
106.	Roosevelt University (IL)	47%	37%
106.	Texas A&M University–Commerce*	54%	43%
106.	University of Colorado Denver*	36%	50%
106.	University of Idaho*	40%	49%
106.	Univ. of Missouri–St. Louis*	45%	45%
106.	Western Michigan University*	42%	49%

▶ National Liberal Arts Colleges

Rank	School (State) (*Public)	% of Pell recipients (entering 2013)	Pell graduation rate
1.	College of Idaho	48%	62%
2.	Lake Forest College (IL)	42%	81%
3.	Thomas Aquinas College (CA)	41%	89%
4.	Spelman College (GA)	49%	67%
5.	University of Puerto Rico–Cayey*	N/A	N/A
6.	Agnes Scott College (GA)	41%	73%
6.	University of Virginia–Wise*	N/A	N/A
8.	Pine Manor College (MA)	79%	40%
9.	Berea College (KY)	93%	67%
10.	College of the Atlantic (ME)	50%	47%
10.	Cornell College (IA)	34%	65%
10.	Houghton College (NY)	40%	67%
10.	Salem College (NC)	51%	52%
14.	Wells College (NY)	53%	51%
14.	Westminster College (PA)	43%	66%
16.	Dillard University (LA)	N/A	N/A
16.	Tougaloo College (MS)	N/A	N/A
18.	University of Puerto Rico–Ponce*	N/A	N/A
19.	Blackburn College (IL)	47%	44%
19.	Vassar College (NY)	28%	91%
21.	Hollins University (VA)	43%	60%
21.	Whittier College (CA)	33%	81%
23.	Morehouse College (GA)	51%	49%
23.	Stillman College (AL)	73%	33%
23.	Virginia Union University	68%	33%
26.	Soka University of America (CA)	33%	92%
26.	Talladega College (AL)	83%	39%
28.	Warren Wilson College (NC)	39%	48%
29.	Bethune-Cookman University (FL)	81%	34%
29.	Bryn Athyn Col. of New Church (PA)	N/A	N/A
29.	Lycoming College (PA)	32%	65%
29.	Monmouth College (IL)	46%	51%
29.	U. of North Carolina Asheville*	35%	59%
34.	Illinois College	47%	55%
34.	Knox College (IL)	34%	76%
34.	Marymount California University	38%	51%
37.	Bennett College (NC)	N/A	N/A
37.	Franklin College (IN)	42%	58%
37.	Hartwick College (NY)	39%	59%
40.	Albright College (PA)	N/A	N/A
40.	Covenant College (GA)	28%	69%
42.	Bloomfield College (NJ)	N/A	N/A
42.	Mansfield University of Pennsylvania*	40%	47%

Rank	School (State) (*Public)	% of Pell recipients (entering 2013)	Pell graduation rate
42.	Massachusetts Col. of Liberal Arts*	46%	52%
45.	Drew University (NJ)	32%	74%
45.	Lyon College (AR)	36%	66%
45.	Purchase College–SUNY*	35%	60%
48.	Hanover College (IN)	28%	64%
49.	Grinnell College (IA)	25%	91%
49.	Wabash College (IN)	29%	73%
51.	Concordia College–Moorhead (MN)	30%	67%
51.	Gustavus Adolphus College (MN)	27%	75%
51.	Ripon College (WI)	37%	57%
51.	Simpson College (IA)	32%	67%
55.	Coe College (IA)	30%	61%
55.	Guilford College (NC)	37%	52%
55.	Moravian College (PA)	31%	63%
58.	Austin College (TX)	29%	67%
58.	Beloit College (WI)	29%	74%
58.	Ohio Wesleyan University	38%	60%
61.	University of the West (CA)	N/A	N/A
61.	Virginia Wesleyan University	42%	44%
63.	Amherst College (MA)	24%	95%
63.	Cheyney U. of Pennsylvania*	N/A	N/A
63.	Meredith College (NC)	32%	60%
63.	Oglethorpe University (GA)	37%	41%
63.	Presbyterian College (SC)	31%	69%
63.	Saint Vincent College (PA)	26%	63%
63.	Southern Virginia University	N/A	N/A
63.	Susquehanna University (PA)	28%	67%
63.	University of Maine–Machias*	59%	30%
63.	Wellesley College (MA)	24%	90%

▶ Regional Universities

Rank	School (State) (*Public)	% of Pell recipients (entering 2013)	Pell graduation rate
NORTH			
1.	Monroe College (NY)	80%	73%
2.	CUNY–Baruch College*	45%	71%
3.	CUNY–Hunter College*	50%	58%
4.	Saint Elizabeth University (NJ)	73%	53%
4.	St. Joseph's College–Brooklyn	41%	61%
6.	CUNY–Brooklyn College*	58%	52%
7.	Elms College (MA)	49%	70%
7.	SUNY College–Old Westbury*	N/A	N/A
7.	Thomas College (ME)	N/A	N/A
10.	SUNY Polytechnic Institute–Albany/Utica*	46%	60%
11.	Manhattanville College (NY)	44%	62%
11.	Notre Dame of Maryland University	49%	65%
13.	CUNY–John Jay Col. of Crim. Justice*	N/A	N/A
14.	CUNY–Queens College*	49%	54%
15.	Rosemont College (PA)	65%	53%
16.	SUNY Buffalo State*	57%	46%
17.	Mercy College (NY)	71%	43%
18.	Cedar Crest College (PA)	59%	47%
19.	Caldwell University (NJ)	47%	61%
20.	Felician University (NJ)	71%	44%
20.	Saint Peter's University (NJ)	67%	56%
22.	College of Mount St. Vincent (NY)	53%	46%
22.	New Jersey City University*	74%	40%
22.	Washington Adventist University (MD)	N/A	N/A
25.	CUNY–Lehman College*	76%	49%
26.	Anna Maria College (MA)	N/A	N/A
26.	Carlow University (PA)	52%	52%
26.	Chestnut Hill College (PA)	47%	53%
26.	SUNY Brockport*	40%	61%

▶ Regional Universities (continued)

Rank	School (State) (*Public)	% of Pell recipients (entering 2013)	Pell graduation rate
26.	SUNY–Fredonia*	37%	61%
31.	La Roche University (PA)	36%	54%
31.	Roberts Wesleyan College (NY)	43%	56%
31.	St. Thomas Aquinas College (NY)	38%	54%
31.	Suffolk University (MA)	38%	58%
31.	Utica College (NY)	52%	51%
36.	Alfred University (NY)	42%	54%
36.	Salem State University (MA)*	39%	55%
38.	Albertus Magnus College (CT)	44%	55%
38.	Southern New Hampshire University	36%	64%
38.	SUNY College–Potsdam*	43%	52%
38.	William Paterson Univ. of N.J.*	45%	53%
42.	Dominican College (NY)	46%	42%
42.	Kean University (NJ)*	53%	44%
42.	La Salle University (PA)	40%	60%
42.	Lincoln University (PA)*	66%	43%
42.	SUNY Empire State College*	N/A	N/A
47.	Trinity Washington University (DC)	N/A	N/A
48.	Centenary University (NJ)	47%	46%
48.	Fairleigh Dickinson University (NJ)	45%	52%
48.	Rhode Island College*	49%	45%
51.	Frostburg State University (MD)*	N/A	N/A
51.	SUNY–Oswego*	36%	61%
51.	SUNY–Plattsburgh*	36%	66%

SOUTH

Rank	School (State) (*Public)	% of Pell recipients (entering 2013)	Pell graduation rate
1.	EDP U. of Puerto Rico Inc–San Juan (PR)	N/A	N/A
2.	Christian Brothers University (TN)	48%	57%
3.	Shorter University (GA)	46%	62%
4.	Columbia International Univ. (SC)	48%	56%
4.	North Carolina Central Univ.*	79%	48%
6.	Bob Jones University (SC)	60%	64%
6.	Winston-Salem State Univ. (NC)*	N/A	N/A
8.	Southern Adventist University (TN)	N/A	N/A
9.	Columbia College (SC)	54%	56%
10.	Midway University (KY)	51%	38%
10.	West Liberty University (WV)*	N/A	N/A
12.	Grambling State University (LA)*	N/A	N/A
12.	Southern Wesleyan University (SC)	N/A	N/A
14.	Saint Leo University (FL)	51%	44%
14.	University of Mount Olive (NC)	49%	47%
14.	University of Puerto Rico–Mayaguez*	N/A	N/A
17.	University of the Sacred Heart (PR)	N/A	N/A
18.	Brenau University (GA)	58%	42%
18.	North Greenville University (SC)	42%	57%
18.	Piedmont College (GA)	51%	43%
18.	U. of North Carolina–Pembroke*	60%	39%
18.	Western Carolina University (NC)*	41%	54%
23.	Mississippi Valley State Univ.*	87%	32%
23.	Norfolk State University (VA)*	69%	39%
23.	Winthrop University (SC)*	44%	56%
26.	Everglades University (FL)	N/A	N/A
26.	Reinhardt University (GA)	48%	41%
28.	Alcorn State University (MS)*	83%	39%
28.	Fort Valley State University (GA)*	81%	35%
28.	King University (TN)	46%	56%
28.	Universidad Ana G. Mendez–Cupey Campus (PR)	N/A	N/A
32.	Fayetteville State University (NC)*	78%	34%
33.	Asbury University (KY)	35%	57%
33.	Jacksonville University (FL)	42%	42%
33.	Universidad Ana G. Mendez–Carolina Campus (PR)	N/A	N/A

Rank	School (State) (*Public)	% of Pell recipients (entering 2013)	Pell graduation rate
36.	Clayton State University (GA)*	73%	33%
36.	Milligan University (TN)	33%	59%
36.	Pfeiffer University (NC)	N/A	N/A
39.	Tuskegee University (AL)	76%	44%
39.	University of West Florida*	40%	39%

MIDWEST

Rank	School (State) (*Public)	% of Pell recipients (entering 2013)	Pell graduation rate
1.	Ohio Christian University	51%	88%
2.	Dominican University (IL)	61%	59%
3.	Mount Mary University (WI)	66%	66%
3.	Stephens College (MO)	N/A	N/A
5.	Bethel University (IN)	42%	61%
5.	Maharishi University of Management (IA)	N/A	N/A
7.	Augsburg University (MN)	47%	53%
7.	MidAmerica Nazarene University (KS)	N/A	N/A
9.	Lakeland University (WI)	N/A	N/A
10.	Herzing University (WI)	N/A	N/A
11.	Spring Arbor University (MI)	47%	51%
12.	Crown College (MN)	N/A	N/A
13.	Univ. of Northwestern–St. Paul (MN)	32%	62%
14.	North Park University (IL)	45%	58%
15.	Drury University (MO)	40%	54%
15.	Saint Xavier University (IL)	59%	50%
17.	Bemidji State University (MN)*	N/A	N/A
18.	Elmhurst University (IL)	34%	64%
18.	Grace College and Seminary (IN)	N/A	N/A
18.	Lewis University (IL)	33%	63%
18.	Univ. of Illinois–Springfield*	46%	46%
22.	Greenville University (IL)	38%	55%
22.	Hamline University (MN)	37%	62%
22.	University of Michigan–Dearborn*	40%	50%
25.	Buena Vista University (IA)	40%	53%
25.	Mount Mercy University (IA)	30%	63%
25.	Mount Vernon Nazarene U. (OH)	42%	59%
28.	Northeastern Illinois University*	63%	23%
29.	Avila University (MO)	N/A	N/A
29.	Concordia University Chicago	49%	41%
29.	Indiana University East*	54%	35%
29.	Univ. of Wisconsin–Eau Claire*	31%	62%
33.	Calumet College of St. Joseph (IN)	56%	26%
33.	Cornerstone University (MI)	37%	53%
33.	Evangel University (MO)	N/A	N/A
33.	Saint Mary-of-the-Woods College (IN)	61%	51%
33.	Silver Lake College (WI)	N/A	N/A
38.	Muskingum University (OH)	46%	42%
38.	Southeast Missouri State Univ.*	43%	44%
40.	Morningside College (IA)	36%	55%
40.	Univ. of Wisconsin–Stevens Point*	31%	52%
40.	Ursuline College (OH)	46%	43%
40.	Winona State University (MN)*	32%	54%
44.	Ashland University (OH)	39%	56%
44.	Baldwin Wallace University (OH)	36%	56%
44.	Huntington University (IN)	34%	68%
44.	University of Minnesota–Duluth*	30%	56%
44.	Univ. of Nebraska–Kearney*	38%	47%
44.	University of Saint Francis (IN)	46%	43%

WEST

Rank	School (State) (*Public)	% of Pell recipients (entering 2013)	Pell graduation rate
1.	Mount Saint Mary's University (CA)	64%	69%
2.	California State University–Long Beach*	50%	72%
3.	Fresno Pacific University (CA)	43%	68%

Rank	School (State) (*Public)	% of Pell recipients (entering 2013)	Pell graduation rate
3.	San Jose State University (CA)*	50%	63%
5.	California State Polytechnic U.–Pomona*	48%	67%
5.	California State U.–Monterey Bay*	53%	62%
7.	California State University–Stanislaus*	61%	58%
8.	University of Washington–Tacoma*	N/A	N/A
9.	California State University–Fullerton*	47%	66%
9.	Texas A&M International University*	78%	48%
11.	California State University–San Bernardino*	71%	53%
12.	San Francisco State University*	47%	56%
13.	Alaska Pacific University	N/A	N/A
13.	California State University–Los Angeles*	78%	50%
13.	California State Univ.–San Marcos*	47%	53%
13.	Mills College (CA)	50%	53%
17.	California State University–Dominguez Hills*	74%	45%
17.	La Sierra University (CA)	54%	44%
19.	California State University–Sacramento*	60%	52%
20.	University of Washington–Bothell*	N/A	N/A
21.	California State University–Channel Islands*	N/A	N/A
21.	California State University–Northridge*	61%	51%
21.	Prescott College (AZ)	N/A	N/A
21.	Vanguard University of Southern California	44%	53%
25.	Hope International University (CA)	50%	59%
25.	St. Mary's Univ. of San Antonio	59%	56%
25.	Woodbury University (CA)	44%	50%
28.	California State University–East Bay*	58%	46%
28.	Midwestern State University (TX)*	50%	43%
30.	University of Alaska–Southeast*	43%	46%
31.	California State Univ.–Bakersfield*	N/A	N/A
31.	Univ. of Mary Hardin-Baylor (TX)	49%	49%
33.	University of St. Thomas (TX)	39%	63%
34.	Humboldt State University (CA)*	55%	45%
34.	Sierra Nevada University (NV)	N/A	N/A

▶ Regional Colleges

Rank	School (State) (*Public)	% of Pell recipients (entering 2013)	Pell graduation rate
NORTH			
1.	Unity College (ME)	N/A	N/A
2.	Elmira College (NY)	N/A	N/A
3.	St. Francis College (NY)	45%	54%
4.	Keystone College (PA)	59%	42%
5.	University of Maine–Farmington*	51%	54%
6.	Cazenovia College (NY)	48%	55%
6.	SUNY Cobleskill*	51%	53%
6.	SUNY Morrisville (NY)*	52%	45%
9.	Colby-Sawyer College (NH)	39%	61%
9.	Univ. of Pittsburgh at Bradford*	50%	41%
11.	Mitchell College (CT)	N/A	N/A
12.	New England Institute of Technology (RI)	55%	47%
13.	Fisher College (MA)	62%	32%
14.	CUNY–New York City Col. of Tech.*	67%	32%
14.	Hilbert College (NY)	N/A	N/A
SOUTH			
1.	Pensacola State College (FL)*	57%	62%
2.	Universidad Adventista de las Antillas (PR)	N/A	N/A
3.	University of Puerto Rico–Humacao*	N/A	N/A
4.	Florida National University–Main Campus	89%	79%
5.	University of Puerto Rico–Aguadilla*	N/A	N/A
6.	Newberry College (SC)	49%	53%

Rank	School (State) (*Public)	% of Pell recipients (entering 2013)	Pell graduation rate
7.	University of Puerto Rico–Arecibo*	N/A	N/A
8.	Crowley's Ridge College (AR)	N/A	N/A
8.	Erskine College (SC)	43%	53%
10.	Toccoa Falls College (GA)	53%	43%
10.	Voorhees College (SC)	99%	40%
12.	Alice Lloyd College (KY)	65%	47%
13.	U. of South Carolina–Upstate*	54%	45%
14.	Claflin University (SC)	79%	50%
14.	Elizabeth City State University (NC)*	N/A	N/A
16.	Averett University (VA)	51%	37%
17.	Point University (GA)	N/A	N/A
18.	Catawba College (NC)	54%	46%
19.	Barton College (NC)	47%	49%
20.	Maryville College (TN)	49%	44%
21.	Morris College (SC)	N/A	N/A
21.	Welch College (TN)	60%	61%
23.	William Peace University (NC)	59%	40%
24.	Central Baptist College (AR)	45%	29%
24.	Edward Waters College (FL)	N/A	N/A
MIDWEST			
1.	College of the Ozarks (MO)	58%	69%
2.	Sterling College (KS)	62%	53%
3.	Cottey College (MO)	64%	57%
3.	St. Augustine College (IL)	N/A	N/A
5.	Oakland City University (IN)	31%	67%
6.	Dordt University (IA)	29%	70%
7.	Maranatha Baptist University (WI)	34%	58%
8.	York College (NE)	56%	40%
9.	Central Christian College (KS)	57%	54%
10.	Olivet College (MI)	N/A	N/A
11.	Hiram College (OH)	52%	45%
12.	Finlandia University (MI)	N/A	N/A
13.	Bluffton University (OH)	44%	52%
13.	Heidelberg University (OH)	42%	44%
13.	McPherson College (KS)	52%	35%
13.	North Central University (MN)	41%	45%
13.	Wilmington College (OH)	46%	50%
18.	Goshen College (IN)	43%	48%
18.	University of Minnesota–Crookston*	N/A	N/A
20.	Marietta College (OH)	41%	54%
20.	Quincy University (IL)	45%	43%
20.	Union College (NE)	50%	52%
WEST			
1.	William Jessup University (CA)	46%	61%
2.	Southwestern Adventist Univ. (TX)	N/A	N/A
3.	Arizona Christian University (AZ)	49%	51%
4.	Corban University (OR)	N/A	N/A
5.	San Diego Christian College	N/A	N/A
6.	Warner Pacific University (OR)	63%	43%
7.	Oklahoma Panhandle State Univ.*	34%	52%
8.	Oklahoma State U. Inst. of Tech.–Okmulgee*	59%	33%
9.	Life Pacific College (CA)	N/A	N/A
9.	McMurry University (TX)	48%	33%

Claremont McKenna College
BRETT ZIEGLER FOR USN&WR

Getting In

116 **Debunking 6 Myths About Admissions**

122 **We Did It! How 8 Students Got Accepted**

128 **A+ Schools for B Students**

132 **Your College Search To-Do List**

Debunking 6 Myths About Admissions

Get a feel for how much grades, tests and your résumé
really matter from those who review the applications

by **Stacey Colino**

WHEN APPLYING TO COLLEGE, many students think they know which strategies will help them attract the attention (in a good way) of admission officers. But there's often a gap between perception and reality about what actually matters – and what matters most – when it comes to grades, test scores, extracurricular activities and other factors. And what holds true in this unprecedented time will differ in some ways from the norm. Many colleges report that they take a multifaceted approach to reviewing applicants, factoring in grades and scores on the SAT or ACT, but also aiming "to evaluate them beyond what is seen on a transcript," says Joe Shields, an admissions counselor at Goucher College in Baltimore. "A holistic admissions review process allows a student to demonstrate their best qualities and discuss how they would be a good fit for that college."

Another promising and often misunderstood fact: It's not as difficult as many students think to get admitted to a college, beyond the most selective schools. On average, two-thirds of first-time, freshman applicants were offered admission to a four-year school in the U.S., according to a 2019 report from the National Association for College Admission Counseling. Some 80% of places accepted 50% or more. "There are many good colleges you may not have heard of," says Hannah Serota, founder and CEO of Creative College Connections, a consulting practice that's dedicated to helping applicants find the right fit. Read on for a look at several other persistent myths about admissions:

MYTH #1

Getting all A's is the most important thing.

OF COURSE, YOUR GRADES MATTER. But what that means depends on a given college's level of selectivity as well as the classes you took, based on the offerings at your high school. After all, some places offer more honors, Advanced Placement or International Baccalaureate courses than others, and an A in one of these more challenging courses can signify mastery of more rigorous content than an A in a grade-level class at a school that offers both. College admissions officers are often well aware of how different high school curricula are because they work with many of the same schools every year and receive detailed profiles of the course offerings, along with context about the student body. "GPAs can present very differently from each institution to the next," says Janine Bissic, former director of admission at Whittier College in California.

Spring semester junior year grades are typically a crucial

metric, but this cycle will be different, thanks to the varied experiences students have had studying from home during the pandemic. Admissions officers say they'll be forgiving to those who didn't receive letter grades, for instance. Everyone evaluating applicants is in the same boat, says Todd Rinehart, vice chancellor for enrollment at the University of Denver. But expect fall of senior year to get a close look, along with your earlier performances.

At Vanderbilt University in Nashville, Tennessee, "we would expect the most rigorous schedule that's appropriate for the student and the highest grades – we would be looking for both," says Douglas Christiansen, vice provost for university

enrollment affairs and dean of admissions and financial aid. Being able to handle a challenging course load while maintaining strong marks is a signal that you have the academic grit and discipline to succeed at college.

Balance is also key. Taking a handful of AP or advanced classes can help you look good, but more isn't always better; the idea is to take the most rigorous set of courses that makes sense given your abilities. While a B in an AP English lit class may be more impressive than an A in a grade-level English class, a C or D isn't likely to wow anyone. "Challenge yourself where you are strong, and then work hard and do well in all of your courses," says Clark Brigger, executive director of admissions at the University of Colorado–Boulder. Has the pandemic quashed your plans to take AP courses this semester? "If the school says, 'We're going to limit the AP classes,' then colleges are going to understand," says Serota.

"When a student takes a challenging course and does well, it is predictive of how they will perform in college," Brigger adds. "However, there are always some students who stretch too far and then struggle with their performance and subsequently their health." If your grades dropped during a semester when you had health problems or personal hardships (such as a parent's job loss or a serious illness or death in the family), it's wise to explain the reason somewhere in your application. If the issue is coronavirus-related, the Common App and Coalition Application have added optional special sections where applicants can elaborate.

But don't be discouraged if your grades aren't where you'd like them to be early in high school. Many admissions officers look for upward trends in grades, improvements over time that enable a student to finish strong. "At the end of the day, we want to feel confident that if we admit a student, they can handle the rigor of the courses here," says Yvonne Romero da Silva, vice president for enrollment at Rice University in Houston.

MYTH #2

Your test scores can make or break your chances of getting in.

ON THE CONTRARY, THEY'RE JUST ONE element of the application package. "There are many students we've denied with perfect test scores because they didn't have anything else to set them apart," Christiansen says. Even in normal times, different institutions place varying levels of importance on standardized tests. This year, more than half of all colleges and universities, including Harvard and Yale, will be test-optional for fall 2021 admissions; in many cases, schools are extending this beyond next fall. The University of Maryland–College Park is one of many state flagships temporarily suspending their test requirements. The University of California system is test-optional for fall 2021 and 2022 entrants, and it will create its own test to use for admission on a trial basis.

Even before the pandemic, many schools were shifting

their test policies to optional, including Ohio Wesleyan University, the University of Denver and the University of Chicago. Bowdoin College in Maine has been test-optional for more than half a century. This trend is partly because admissions officers recognize that many applicants have intellectual abilities and academic strengths that aren't reflected in exam scores.

But before you decide to skip the tests, consider whether you'll be applying for scholarships, some of which depend on test scores to qualify applicants, and whether having good results might be beneficial even at a test-optional school. Colleges and universities publish the data related to the average test scores of their incoming classes online, so officials suggest that students can use that data to benchmark their own exam results and weigh whether it might enhance their application to submit scores.

Taking the SAT or ACT more than once generally improves scores, especially if the testing dates are spaced out appropriately (that is, by months, not weeks), because "the test scores are merely an assessment of a student's capabilities at the time of the assessment," Romero da Silva explains. For those who might have been nervous or encountered unfamiliar questions, deciding on a redo could be beneficial. Additional exposure to the test does generally improve a student's score, but typically not after two attempts, says Stacey Kostell, chief executive officer for the Coalition for College, a group of more than 150 colleges and universities dedicated to increasing students' access to higher education.

Among colleges that do require the SAT or ACT, many will "superscore," which means they use your best section-level scores even if they're from different test dates. In other words, if your SAT reading score was 70 points higher the second time you took the test but your math score was 50 points higher on the first, you share the better of both attempts with the admissions office for review.

MYTH #3

The more clubs and activities you have on your résumé, the better.

THE QUALITY OF YOUR INVOLVEMENT counts more than the quantity of your activities. "Being passionate about key interests is more important than joining a lot of clubs," says Christiansen. "We're looking for depth and progression of leadership, not just participation." David Senter of Oak Ridge, Tennessee, thinks his experience swimming competitively and working his way up to varsity team captain helped demonstrate his dedication and added something important to his strong academic record, along with his participation on the academic quiz bowl team. "You have to show you care," says

Senter, a 2020 Rice grad. "I was never the fastest, and I never went to the state championships, but I showed up every day and bonded with the team."

When reviewing extracurricular activities on an application, admissions officers really want to know things like: What did you do in high school that made whatever you participated in better and helped you grow? or What are you doing with your time that would contribute to our campus in a meaningful way if you came here? "Colleges are looking for a well-rounded student body, not necessarily a well-rounded student," says Serota.

These days, college admissions officers are also typically sensitive to the fact that some students don't have time for extracurricular activities. Rather, they might need to take care of younger siblings after school or hold a job. If that's the case, prospective students would do well to be honest about their situation and to focus on the qualities that emerge from those experiences and what they get out of them, Kostell says.

#4 MYTH

You should only ask for a recommendation from a teacher who gave you an A.

WRONG AGAIN. INSTEAD, IT'S BETTER to consider whether a teacher can help admissions officers get to know a different side of you and understand who you are. It could be from the

teacher who taught your most difficult class or a class you thought you wouldn't like but did. Students "should really be looking for recommendations from teachers and mentors who know them especially well and can give rich context to their work ethic, character, persistence and growth," Bissic says.

Shields agrees: "If you struggled with a subject and had a good rapport with the teacher, you can get a helpful recommendation if the teacher can talk about how you came for extra help or you were able to advocate for yourself."

MYTH #5

It's a mistake to get creative with your essay.

ON THE CONTRARY, BEING CLEVER and original can help you stand out from the crowd – but only if you can pull it off. If you're not funny, don't try to be. If you're not impassioned about a controversial subject, don't pretend to be. "You need to make the case for why you care about something and what you're doing about it," advises Serota. But do think carefully about what you choose to share, such as a mental health issue or a gambling or drug problem. "Be careful about revealing things that would make the reader feel a sense of caution about you," Serota says.

And while you may be tempted to write about how the pandemic affected you and your family, consider that admissions officers will likely be inundated with essays on the topic. "It's immediately likely to blend in, and it becomes that much more difficult to stand out," says Ethan Sawyer, author of "College Admission Essentials" and "College Essay Essentials." He encourages students to instead use the extra space provided by the Common and Coalition applications to describe the effects of the pandemic on their families. And he says it's not necessary to worry about making that section of your app sing. "Students shouldn't be shy about bullet points," Sawyer says. "Value information over poetry."

An essay's most important quality is that it feels authentic, Serota and others say. Make sure that it addresses the prompt, but also think of your essay as an opportunity to reveal your true voice and to highlight who you really are. Admissions folks are experts at distinguishing between viewpoints that feel genuine and those that don't. The most compelling essays reveal something about an applicant's personality, Kostell says.

Moe de La Viez of Frederick, Maryland, thought her voice and interests would come through most clearly in a visual essay, which she submitted to Goucher when she applied in 2015. "I felt like I could personalize my application more if I did it myself on video," explains de La Viez, a 2019 Goucher grad who got interested in video production in high school and ultimately crafted an interdisciplinary major at the college involving communications, creative writing and studio art under the umbrella of video production.

When it comes to large universities in particular, it may be hard to believe that there are human beings who are actually reading and giving careful consideration to your app, but it's true. During the review process, "multiple sets of eyes read every piece of the application, essay and letters of recommendation," says Brigger, whose university reviews more than 44,000 first-year applications per year.

"Admissions officers and university faculty and staff are the ones making admissions decisions, not a computer or automated process." The essay is your opportunity to connect and make an impression.

MYTH #6

To make yourself memorable, you need to visit the campus.

SINCE THE CORONAVIRUS BROUGHT visits to a screeching halt last spring, schools have introduced a wide range of virtual tools, from informal chats to tours that are meant to offer students a taste of campus life. Many competitive colleges are using these new options to gauge an applicant's "demonstrated interest." This can be shown in various ways: by calling or emailing with questions, requesting a virtual interview, contacting alumni or interacting with a representative on social media or, when possible, at a college fair. Some 40% of colleges indicate that demonstrated interest is a moderately or considerably important factor in decisions, according to the most recent NACAC data.

Admissions officers can track how many contacts you've

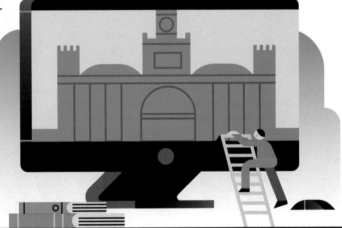

had with their institution – and they can even see if you've opened or engaged with emails.

Once campuses are fully reopened and old opportunities resume, spending a day on campus visiting class and talking with students, or perhaps attending a summer program for high schoolers at a college that appeals to you, can both signal your interest and help you (and the admissions office) establish that you'll be a good fit. That's key. "Fit continues to be the most important factor to us – we want students to succeed here," says Marc Harding, vice provost for enrollment at the University of Pittsburgh. Participating in such a program also shows that you're passionate and curious enough about a subject to take it to the next level. And that says a lot about your college readiness. ●

With Zackary Bennett and Margaret Loftus

We Did It!

How 8 Missouri high school seniors got to college

by **Zackary Bennett**

LIKE MILLIONS OF STUDENTS across the country, the class of 2020 at Clayton High School in Missouri navigated a turbulent end to the school year. In mid-March, the COVID-19 pandemic suspended in-person classes at the public high school about a 20-minute drive from St. Louis, and students began virtual learning on March 23. Sports seasons and extracurricular activities were cut short, and a socially distanced graduation ceremony was held in late June.

Through it all, Clayton's seniors completed their college search and decision-making process. The school is home to around 900 students, about 97% of whom typically continue their education after graduation. Some 60% of students are white, 20% are Black, 13% are Asian and 4% are Hispanic. Around 28% of students take Advanced Placement classes, and more than 90% of those pass their AP exams. U.S. News spoke with eight recent Clayton grads about their college searches and collected advice they had to share.

Graduates distanced, while parents watched the ceremony from their cars.

Mason Sharon

Whether starring as the Wicked Witch of the West in "The Wizard of Oz," performing in the dance ensemble or serving as theater house manager, Mason Sharon made it a point to be involved in school performances. And she settled on studying theater education in college.

She applied to half a dozen schools offering theater education programs: the all-women Stephens College in Columbia, Missouri, which required that she audition; Saint Louis University; Millikin University in Illinois; Ball State University in Indiana; Loyola University Chicago and Columbia College Chicago.

She was accepted by all and eventually settled on Ball State, a public institution of about 16,000 undergrads in Muncie. When Sharon stepped on campus the first time for a visit, she "loved everything about it so much." She likes that the program is "super well-oiled" and that students are assured they will get into the classes they need to graduate in eight semesters.

GPA: 3.5

ACT: 30

Extracurriculars: Theater, vice president of the thespian troupe, president of show choir, feminist club, founder of the creative writing club; worked at a local ice cream shop and candy store

Essay: None were required.

Good move: Whenever her family took a vacation, they would plan to visit colleges in the area. She advises setting up appointments with department heads, financial aid counselors and others. "Figure out what you want and then ask about it."

Cost: Ball State awarded her an annual merit scholarship of about $14,000, and she earned another scholarship from an organization supporting those studying theater education. Sharon's mom works at Washington University

MASON SHARON

in St. Louis, and the school will provide a partial tuition remission benefit. Her family will shoulder the rest of Ball State's roughly $27,000 out-of-state tuition and fees.

Lailah Hall

Originally Lailah Hall had her sights set on a traditional business degree. But the summer before senior year, her interest in food insecurity and disparities between communities caused her to narrow her focus to agribusiness.

One thing that didn't change

was her interest in attending a historically Black college or university, and Hall eventually landed on Florida A&M University in Tallahassee. She cast an extremely wide net, applying to 26 schools in total, and was accepted by 25, including North Carolina A&T State University, Hampton University in Virginia, Xavier University of Louisiana, Baylor University in Texas and Howard University in Washington, D.C. The only school not to accept her was WashU.

Hall dreams of owning her own farm or being otherwise involved in the food industry. "I'm not totally sure yet, but [my future] has something to do with food manufacturing and food production," she says. "I like food a lot!"

GPA: 3.6

ACT: 30

Extracurriculars: Volleyball (junior varsity player, varsity manager), presi-

LAILAH HALL

dent of the Black Student Union, student council, treasurer of Best Buddies (dedicated to creating opportunities for students with disabilities), board member of Clayton Conversations, Chinese Culture Club, feminist club

Essay: The one that helped her secure a spot at Florida A&M was focused on how her own family deals with food insecurity in metropolitan St. Louis, where she says many residents lack access to healthy and affordable meals.

Advice: Be involved and do productive things during high school that can enhance your résumé. Be a club leader, not just "a member."

Cost: Hall will cover her $17,000-plus in out-of-state tuition at Florida A&M through the various merit scholarships she has earned.

Koji Barrette

Having been a competitive swimmer since first grade, Koji Barrette found the question of whether he'd pursue athletics in college to be a huge decision. He saw success on Clayton's team, finishing in the top five at a state meet and qualifying for a junior national meet (canceled due to COVID-19). "That was my greatest dilemma: Did I want to swim in college?" To cover his bases, Barrette spoke with coaches and applied to schools where he could swim as well as ones where he couldn't. His only in-state selection was WashU, where his parents are faculty physicians. In total he applied to 15 schools, sending early applications to Pomona College in California, Case Western Reserve University in Cleveland and WashU. He submitted regular decision apps to Amherst Col-

lege and Tufts University in Massachusetts, Colby College in Maine, Connecticut College and multiple University of California schools, including UC–Berkeley, UCLA and UC–Davis.

His first two decisions were a rejection from Pomona and a deferral from Case Western Reserve. WashU accepted his early decision application and he withdrew all others. "I had found my true love in a school," he says.

Barrette wants to go into a medical field like his parents, most likely pediatrics, and is considering majoring in chemistry or biochemistry. He thinks the chances of swimming with the university's NCAA Division III team are "quite low" but plans to pursue swimming through club athletics.

GPA: 3.81
ACT: 34
Extracurriculars: Varsity swimming, played French horn in the concert and symphonic bands as well as trumpet in jazz band and mellophone in pep band, volunteered for a swimming program for youth with disabilities.
Essay: Barrette wrote about a three-week summer program in which he rode a bicycle nearly 550 miles from Eugene, Oregon, to San Francisco, camping along the way. For a supplemental essay, he wrote about being half Japanese on his mother's side and how Japanese culture has always been hugely important to him.
Advice: "When you're searching for colleges, don't stress so much about a specific major," he says. "The next four years could change your mind several different times over."
Cost: Since his parents are both employed by WashU, he will receive a benefit that will totally cover his tuition.

Jillian Beck

At first, Jillian Beck had her sights set on a historically Black college or the University of Missouri. She applied to Mizzou, Jackson State University in Mississippi, Langston University in Oklahoma and Alabama State University. She was initially wait-listed at some places, but in the end accepted by all.

Beck planned to attend Mizzou, but then had some discussions with her parents about her long-term plans. She began looking into com-

KOJI BARRETTE

munity college in an effort to save money in the early years and set herself up for the most prosperous possible educational and financial future. With some help from her guidance counselor, Beck found that her grades and test scores qualified her for the A+ Program, which will pay her way through community college. After she earns her associate degree, she plans to transfer to a four-year school, probably Mizzou. At St. Charles Community College,

a half-hour from home, she'll study psychology.

Initially, she says, "I felt like there wouldn't be excitement in me 'going to college' two years later." But COVID-19 gave her family pause. "We weren't sure if I'd be having normal classes and still paying that much – it just didn't make sense to us."
GPA: 3.42
ACT: 24
Extracurriculars: Varsity volleyball, track and field and soccer, Girl Scout for 13 years
Essay: Beck didn't have to write any essays.
Good move: Going to a college fair (prior to the pandemic). Beck got to talk to a number of college reps, which gave her a feel for how the schools differed from each other.
Advice: "Don't focus on how others view where you want to go," she says.

Rosalinda Christopher

Above all else, Rosalinda Christopher was focused on finding the right fit in a college. She credits her parents with giving her that guidance. "You should listen to the adults around you who give you advice about what they went through," she says, adding that her parents "went to Saint Louis University here, and my parents turned out great."

Christopher didn't want to go to a huge university, but she didn't want to go to a tiny school either. She applied to a number of smaller and medium-sized colleges, including SLU, Creighton University in Nebraska, and the University of Dayton and Xavier in Ohio. She was accepted by all and ultimately chose Xavier. Her experiences when touring the private Jesuit university in Cincinnati really struck a chord. The message was

JILLIAN BECK

"that it's not about the grades, it's more about the person," she says.
GPA: 3.63
ACT: 24
Extracurriculars: Played clarinet in the band, managed the volleyball team, completed community service hours and volunteered with children with disabilities.
Essay: Christopher chose to write about a severe knee injury (torn ACL and meniscus) caused by a fall during gym class. She needed surgery, and her recovery was hampered when a second fall reinjured her knee and required another procedure.
Good move: Don't get caught up in thinking you have to go to the "best" schools or schools where your friends are going. "Find the place that fits you best."
Regrets: "I would've probably joined more clubs in high school, just to get a feel of different things," she says. She also wishes that she had started thinking about college more thoroughly during junior year.
Cost: She received a renewable scholarship, but most of her $42,460 tuition expenses will be shouldered by her parents. She doesn't expect to graduate with any debt.

Sarah Jane Baker

Even before she knew where she would be going to college, Sarah Jane Baker spent a lot of time applying for institutional scholarships. That advance planning paid off (literally) when she got the news that she'd been awarded the Belk Scholarship at Davidson College in North Carolina, her No. 1 choice.

In addition to carefully considering costs, Baker prioritized finding a place that felt like home and had a tightknit community. She also sent applications to McGill University in Montreal, the University of Missouri, Denison University in Ohio, Elon University in North Carolina, the University of Iowa, Rhodes College in Tennessee and the University of South Carolina.

Even before she received the Belk, Baker knew she wanted to end up at Davidson. "I could just see how much the school cared about people," she says, pointing especially to how the liberal arts college handled the emerging COVID-19 pandemic. For example, Davidson

announced that students and families could have the option of deferring their tuition payment for up to one year while still attending classes.

"I think how a school deals with that kind of crisis really says something," Baker says.

She was invited to participate in "Belk Weekend," an opportunity for all candidates for the scholarship to travel to campus to tour and meet people. The pandemic put a stop to those plans, but Baker appreciated that Davidson offered a virtual weekend instead.

GPA: 3.8
ACT: 31
Extracurriculars: Baker helped found Clayton's Best Buddies chapter; participated in Challenger Baseball (for people with disabilities); Planned Parenthood's Teen Advocates for Sexual Health (she became a certified sex educator); volunteered at her synagogue in the homeless outreach program; worked at Noodles & Company.

Essay: She wrote about how her role with Planned Parenthood taught her to use her voice for advocacy and how her Best Buddies experience taught her to help other people be heard.
Good move: Getting applications in as early as possible

SARAH JANE BAKER

to reduce stress. Soon after senior year started she began writing her Common Application essay and preparing early action applications.
Regrets: Underestimating the amount of time and effort required to apply to so many schools. "My applications were on time but cramming on applications or essays is tough."
Advice: Don't be afraid to let go of things that aren't bringing meaning to your life. She made the careful decision to stop playing field hockey to spend her time on Planned Parenthood and Best Buddies.
Cost: As a Belk Scholar, she will have her expenses covered. Plus, she'll be receiving two $3,000 special study stipends. (One past Belk Scholar used the stipend to go to Guatemala for a photojournalism project; another spent a summer in South Africa at an innovation lab focusing on local shelter problems.)

Brooke Becker

During her early high school years, Brooke Becker quietly began her college search while tagging along on her older sister's campus tours. Her sister ended up at Arizona State, but Becker wasn't sure that would be quite the right fit for her. Still, she was leaning toward a larger school with a strong honors college and engineering program. She ended up applying to Arizona State, Colorado State, Michigan State, Indiana University, Purdue University (also in Indiana), Ohio State, the University of South Carolina and the University of Missouri. She was accepted everywhere, often with an honors college spot.

Because the COVID-19 pandemic limited touring opportunities, Becker found her decision-making tougher. She resorted to taking virtual tours and finding other ways to make comparisons. Her experiences touring with her sister had given her an idea of where she would be happy, and she ended up picking close-to-home Mizzou without being able to visit. "Everybody applies there," Becker says. "My dad was like, 'You've got to apply to Mizzou, just in case.' Thank goodness I did."

Along with the diversity of Mizzou's student body, affordability played a big role in her choice. She will be studying mechanical engineering.
GPA: 3.71
SAT: 1320
Extracurriculars: Varsity volleyball captain, varsity diving, Chinese Culture Club president, National Honor Society, Society of Women Engineers, principal's advisory council; worked at Flying Tiger Motorcycles; volunteered at a local pet shop's cat adoption events; community organizer. Becker participated in a climate change walkout at Clayton, a reproductive rights protest and the Black Lives Matter movement.
Essay: "My mom's half

ROSALINDA CHRISTOPHER

Black and half white, and my dad's white," she says. She wrote about experiencing microaggressions based on society's perceiving her as Black (unlike her sisters, who are seen as white) and how she grew from those experiences.

Regrets: Thinking the ACT was her only option and not trying the SAT earlier. It ended up being a better fit for her. "If one test doesn't work for you, try the other test."

Advice: "I definitely would recommend talking to a senior who has recently gone through all this." She also suggests talking to coaches, family friends or anyone with a connection to a recent or current college student to learn about their experiences.

Cost: She'll be paying for a portion of her $12,600 in-state tuition with a $3,500 scholarship from Mizzou. Her parents will be covering the rest, but she plans to contribute herself if costs rise.

Emilio Rosas Linhard

Growing up as the son of two professors at WashU, Emilio Rosas Linhard got a clear sense of the college experience but didn't grow up with a "dream school" in mind.

His first instinct was to apply to WashU, given the tuition benefits for children of employees. But he ended up realizing he wanted to go somewhere away from home. He toured the Massachusetts Institute of Technology while visiting family in Boston, and he did a fly-in program at Rice University in Houston. During the summer before senior year, he spent three weeks at a University of Chicago academic session.

Rosas Linhard ended up applying early action to UChicago, MIT, Tulane University in New Orleans and the University of Miami.

BROOKE BECKER

He also sent applications to WashU, Rice, Vanderbilt University in Tennessee and a joint program between Columbia University in New York and a school in France.

He was wait-listed at MIT, deferred at Tulane, rejected by the Columbia joint program and accepted everywhere else.

UChicago's acceptance was the first to arrive, and it came with a sizable merit scholarship. He and his family concluded that they could afford it and that UChicago felt like the best fit; its core curriculum appealed since he wasn't settled on what he wanted to study. He's interested in the social sciences and maybe economics, and he has known for sure that he wants to study German since he visited Berlin

(his mom's hometown) back in eighth grade.

GPA: 4.18

ACT: 35

Extracurriculars: Varsity cross country and track, captain and board member of the speech and debate team, science and engineering academic teams, co-founder of the Latin American Culture Club, Clayton Connect volunteer tutor for elementary students, host at a brunch restaurant

Essay: Rosas Linhard appreciated UChicago's creative essay prompts, and he chose one instructing him to pick any program at the school and remove or add a letter to its title. He changed the program "big problems" to "pig problems" and wrote about a pig attending the uni-

versity. For his more traditional Common App essay, he wrote about his name and its blended history. He was born in Mexico City to a Mexican father and a German mother prior to moving to Clayton before his second birthday.

Regrets: "I think I should've spent more time finding things I truly enjoy and spent more time with friends," he says. That said, he's happy with his time at Clayton and thinks he struck a good balance; he wasn't constantly up until 3 a.m. studying, but also wasn't one to shrug off academic responsibilities.

Advice: Focus on quality over quantity. Rosas Linhard thinks it is clear when applicants spread themselves too thin across activities. He says he's very happy about his development in cross country and track, "but with speech and debate, I think I could've chilled out a little bit." Don't make your entire high school experience focused on getting into college, he says.

Cost: With help from his parents and the tuition benefit for kids of WashU faculty, plus merit scholarships from UChicago, his tuition of roughly $59,300 will be covered with no loans. Rosas Linhard says he plans to find a job once he's settled in at UChicago to earn some money and help out with fees and other expenses where he can. ●

EMILIO ROSAS LINHARD

U.S. News Student Connect

Introducing a new, higher education marketing solution to connect with students through the U.S. News Best Colleges platform.

BENEFITS

Engage with students and parents seeking guidance on a college decision.

Elevate your school's brand.

Enhance the user experience on your school's Best Colleges profile.

Ability to **own** the messaging on your school's profile.

PREMIUM FEATURES

1 Premium Profile Design: Custom Photo

2 Integration of Slate CRM Tool
Use your own Slate web form, or upload a CSV file to your own CRM, to connect with students/parents visiting usnews.com.

3 Custom Video
Amplify your school's messaging in an interacive format.

4 100,000 Premium Impressions
Across Best Colleges and your school's profile.

5 Premium Profile Design: Custom Messaging

For more information contact:

Shannon Tkach
Director, Education Advertising
stkach@usnews.com
(202) 955-2134

Michael Zee
Account Executive
mzee@usnews.com
(212) 916-8764

A+ Schools for B Students

S O YOU'RE A SCHOLAR WITH LOTS to offer and the GPA of a B student, and your heart is set on going to a great college. No problem. U.S. News has screened the universe of colleges and universities to identify those where nonsuperstars have a decent shot at being accepted and thriving – where spirit and hard work could make all the difference to the admissions office.

To make this list, which is presented alphabetically, schools had to admit a meaningful proportion of applicants whose test scores and class standing put them in non-A territory (methodology, Page 131). Since many truly seek a broad and engaged student body, be sure to display your individuality and seriousness of purpose as you apply.

▶ National Universities

School (State) (*Public)	SAT/ACT 25th-75th percentile ('19)	Average high school GPA ('19)	Freshmen in top 25% of class ('19)
Adelphi University (NY)	1090-1270[9]	3.5	61%[5]
Arizona State University–Tempe*	22-28[2]	3.5	61%
Baker University (KS)	20-25	3.5	44%
Belmont University (TN)	24-29	3.8	61%
Bethel University (MN)	21-27	3.6	52%
Biola University (CA)	1080-1310	3.6	69%
Bowling Green State University (OH)*	20-25	3.5	42%
Chatham University (PA)	1050-1270[2]	3.7	52%
Clarkson University (NY)	1160-1350[2]	3.7	69%
College of St. Scholastica (MN)	22-26[9]	3.5	48%
Colorado State University*	1070-1290	3.7	48%
Concordia University Wisconsin	21-26	3.4	61%
Creighton University (NE)	23-29[2]	3.8	66%
Duquesne University (PA)	1130-1300[2]	3.7	55%
Edgewood College (WI)	20-25	3.5	50%
Elon University (NC)	1160-1320[2]	3.8	56%
Florida Atlantic University*	1080-1240	3.7	48%
Florida International University*	1110-1280	3.9	63%[5]
Florida State University*	1200-1340	3.9	73%
Gannon University (PA)	1030-1240	3.6	63%[5]
George Fox University (OR)	1030-1270	3.7	60%
George Mason University (VA)*	1110-1320[2]	3.7	44%
Harding University (AR)	21-29	3.7	53%
Hofstra University (NY)	1160-1340[2]	3.7	60%
Howard University (DC)	1130-1280	3.6	63%
Iowa State University*	22-28	3.7	62%
Kansas State University*	22-28	3.6	52%
Kent State University[7] (OH)*	20-26	3.5	43%
Lipscomb University (TN)	23-29	3.7	60%
Long Island University (NY)	1080-1290	3.4	47%
Louisiana State University–Baton Rouge*	23-29	3.4	48%
Loyola University Chicago	25-30	3.7	68%
Loyola University New Orleans	22-28[2]	3.4	41%[5]
Marquette University (WI)	24-29	N/A	63%
Maryville University of St. Louis	20-25[2]	3.6	55%
Mercer University (GA)	1170-1340	3.8	68%
Michigan State University*	1100-1320	3.8	65%
Misericordia University (PA)	1050-1220	3.4	49%
Mississippi State University*	22-30	3.5	57%
Montana State University*	21-27	3.5	46%
North Dakota State University*	21-26[3]	3.5	40%
Nova Southeastern University (FL)	1020-1250	3.9	69%
Ohio University*	21-26	3.6	47%
Oklahoma State University*	21-28	3.5	54%
Oregon State University*	1080-1320	3.6	55%
Pace University (NY)	1050-1230[2]	3.2	47%

School (State) (*Public)	SAT/ACT 25th-75th percentile ('19)	Average high school GPA ('19)	Freshmen in top 25% of class ('19)
Regis University (CO)	1030-1240	3.8	60%
Robert Morris University (PA)	1020-1210	3.5	42%
Rutgers University–Camden (NJ)*	980-1170	N/A	45%
Rutgers University–Newark (NJ)*	1020-1200	N/A	51%
Saint Louis University	25-30	3.9	72%
Samford University (AL)	23-29	3.8	61%
San Diego State University*	1110-1320	3.8	70%
Seattle University	1150-1330	3.7	64%
Seton Hall University (NJ)	1150-1330	3.6	60%
Simmons University (MA)	1110-1290	3.8	69%
St. John Fisher College (NY)	1070-1260	3.5	55%
St. John's University (NY)	1080-1300[2]	3.5	48%
SUNY Col. of Environmental Science & Forestry*	1120-1300	3.6	63%
Temple University (PA)*	1120-1320[2]	3.5	76%
Tennessee Technological University*	21-27[2]	3.6	57%
Texas Tech University*	1070-1260	3.6	53%
Thomas Jefferson University (PA)	1070-1270	3.6	55%
Towson University (MD)*	1060-1220	3.6	42%
Union University (TN)	22-30	3.7	61%
University at Albany–SUNY*	1090-1250	3.3	46%
University at Buffalo–SUNY*	1160-1340	3.7	65%
University of Alabama at Birmingham*	22-29	3.8	57%
University of Arkansas*	23-30	3.7	52%
University of Central Florida*	1170-1340	3.9	74%
University of Cincinnati*	23-29	3.7	51%
University of Dayton (OH)	23-29[3]	3.7	59%
University of Detroit Mercy	1060-1250	3.6	53%
University of Findlay (OH)	21-26	3.6	58%
University of Hawaii–Manoa*	1070-1270[3]	3.7	52%
University of Houston*	1140-1310	3.7	64%
University of Idaho*	1010-1240	3.4	44%
University of Illinois–Chicago*	1030-1260	3.4	59%
University of Iowa*	22-29	3.8	63%
University of Kansas*	22-29	3.6	55%
University of Kentucky*	22-29	3.5	59%
University of La Verne (CA)	1040-1190[2]	3.5	54%
University of Louisville (KY)*	22-29[3]	3.6	54%
University of Maine*	1050-1260	3.3	46%
University of Massachusetts–Boston*	1010-1220[2]	3.3	41%
University of Massachusetts–Lowell*	1150-1320[2]	3.6	56%
University of Mississippi*	21-29[2]	3.6	49%
University of Missouri*	23-29	N/A	63%
University of Missouri–St. Louis*	21-27	3.4	64%
University of Nebraska–Lincoln*	22-28	3.6	56%
University of Nevada–Reno*	21-26	3.4	57%
University of New Hampshire*	1070-1270[2]	3.5	49%

Note: Key to footnotes, Page 60.

School (State) (*Public)	SAT/ACT 25th-75th percentile ('19)	Average high school GPA ('19)	Freshmen in top 25% of class ('19)
University of North Carolina–Charlotte*	1120-1290	3.5	49%
University of North Carolina–Wilmington*	22-27	3.9	63%
University of North Dakota*	20-26	3.5	44%
University of North Florida*	1090-1260	3.9	40%
University of North Texas*	1060-1260	N/A	53%
University of Oklahoma*	23-29	3.6	61%
University of Oregon*	1100-1310[2]	3.6	57%[5]
University of Rhode Island*	1080-1260[3]	3.5	49%
University of San Francisco	1130-1330[2]	3.5	66%
University of South Florida*	1170-1330	3.9	68%
University of St. Joseph (CT)	1030-1210[2]	3.3	50%
University of St. Thomas (MN)	24-29	3.6	49%
University of Tennessee*	24-30	3.8	63%
University of Wyoming*	22-28	3.5	51%
Valparaiso University (IN)	1070-1290	3.8	65%
Virginia Commonwealth University*	1070-1260[2]	3.6	45%
Western New England University (MA)	1080-1242[2]	3.6	52%
Wilkes University (PA)	1020-1218	3.6	47%
William Carey University (MS)	20-28	3.6	53%

▶ National Liberal Arts Colleges

School (State) (*Public)	SAT/ACT 25th-75th percentile ('19)	Average high school GPA ('19)	Freshmen in top 25% of class ('19)
Agnes Scott College (GA)	1130-1340[2]	3.8	67%
Augustana College (IL)	1090-1320[2]	3.4	64%
Austin College (TX)	1110-1310[2]	3.6	59%
Berea College (KY)	23-27	3.6	72%
Birmingham-Southern College (AL)	22-29[2]	3.7	49%
Coe College (IA)	21-27	3.6	55%
College of St. Benedict (MN)	22-28	3.6	62%
College of the Atlantic (ME)	1170-1340[2]	3.6	53%
Concordia College–Moorhead (MN)	21-27	3.6	50%
Cornell College (IA)	23-29[2]	3.5	47%
Covenant College (GA)	23-29	3.7	50%
Drew University (NJ)	1105-1300[2]	3.5	49%
Elizabethtown College (PA)	1080-1290	N/A	61%
Gordon College (MA)	1060-1310	3.6	51%
Goucher College (MD)	1030-1260[2]	3.2	44%
Gustavus Adolphus College (MN)	25-30[2]	3.7	62%
Hanover College (IN)	1030-1240[2]	3.7	59%
Hollins University (VA)	1070-1300[3]	3.6	56%
Hope College (MI)	1130-1330	3.9	71%
Houghton College (NY)	1060-1320[2]	3.5	50%
Illinois Wesleyan University	24-29	3.8	72%
Juniata College (PA)	1118-1320[2]	3.7	62%
Knox College (IL)	1090-1350[2]	N/A	69%
Lake Forest College (IL)	1080-1280[2]	3.7	63%
Luther College (IA)	22-28	3.6	51%
Lycoming College (PA)	1040-1220[2]	3.5	43%
Meredith College (NC)	1020-1220	3.5	45%
Moravian College (PA)	1040-1210[3]	3.5	51%
Muhlenberg College (PA)	1150-1340[2]	3.4	72%
Oglethorpe University (GA)	1110-1280	3.7	55%
Ohio Wesleyan University	22-28[2]	3.5	60%
Presbyterian College (SC)	1000-1230[2]	3.3	53%
Principia College (IL)	1010-1218	3.4	57%[5]
Randolph-Macon College (VA)	1050-1240	3.7	50%

School (State) (*Public)	SAT/ACT 25th-75th percentile ('19)	Average high school GPA ('19)	Freshmen in top 25% of class ('19)
Roanoke College (VA)	1050-1260[2]	3.6	46%
Saint Anselm College (NH)	1140-1300[2]	3.4	61%
Saint Mary's College (IN)	1060-1250[2]	3.8	69%
Saint Michael's College (VT)	1155-1310[2]	3.4	49%
Saint Vincent College (PA)	1030-1240	3.5	46%
Southwestern University (TX)	1140-1320[2]	3.5	67%
Spelman College (GA)	1080-1230	3.8	56%
St. John's University (MN)	22-27	3.3	43%
St. Lawrence University (NY)	1160-1350[2]	3.6	77%
St. Mary's College of Maryland*	1060-1290[2]	3.4	55%
St. Norbert College (WI)	21-27	3.5	47%
Stonehill College (MA)	1120-1290[2]	3.3	51%
Susquehanna University (PA)	1100-1290[2]	3.6	63%
Transylvania University (KY)	23-30[2]	3.7	61%
University of Minnesota Morris*	21-28	3.7	52%
The University of the South (TN)	25-30[2]	N/A	60%
Ursinus College (PA)	1150-1350[2]	3.4	50%
Wabash College (IN)	1120-1320	3.8	60%
Wartburg College (IA)	21-26[3]	3.6	56%
Washington and Jefferson College (PA)	1090-1280[9]	3.7	48%
Washington College (MD)	1090-1300	3.6	53%
Westmont College (CA)	1100-1330	3.5	56%
Wheaton College (MA)	1150-1340[2]	3.4	53%
Willamette University (OR)	1140-1340[2]	3.9	78%
Wofford College (SC)	1190-1350[2]	3.7	70%

▶ Regional Universities

School (State) (*Public)	SAT/ACT 25th-75th percentile ('19)	Average high school GPA ('19)	Freshmen in top 25% of class ('19)
NORTH			
Arcadia University (PA)	1030-1260[2]	3.7	47%
Assumption University (MA)	1090-1238[2]	3.4	41%
Bryant University (RI)	1130-1300[2]	3.4	48%
Canisius College (NY)	1030-1270	3.5	45%
CUNY–Baruch College*	1130-1330	3.3	74%
Eastern University (PA)	1030-1230[2]	3.6	58%
Endicott College (MA)	1090-1240[2]	3.4	45%
Fairfield University (CT)	1210-1350[2]	3.6	73%
Fairleigh Dickinson University (NJ)	1000-1180[2]	3.5	42%
Geneva College (PA)	1020-1240	3.5	51%
Ithaca College (NY)	1160-1350[2]	N/A	57%
Le Moyne College (NY)	1073-1280[2]	3.5	53%
Loyola University Maryland	1143-1320[2]	3.6	60%[5]
Manhattan College (NY)	1060-1280[3]	N/A	52%
Marist College (NY)	1150-1330[2]	3.3	57%
Marywood University (PA)	1000-1190	3.5	49%
McDaniel College (MD)	988-1190[2]	3.5	44%
Messiah University (PA)	1090-1310[2]	3.8	64%
Molloy College (NY)	1020-1220	3.0	56%
Monmouth University (NJ)	1030-1210	3.5	42%
Nazareth College (NY)	1100-1290[2]	3.5	59%
Niagara University (NY)	1020-1230[2]	3.4	40%
Providence College (RI)	1210-1350[2]	3.5	75%
Ramapo College of New Jersey*	1030-1220	3.4	41%
Roberts Wesleyan College (NY)	1020-1270[2]	3.5	47%
Saint Joseph's University (PA)	1120-1300[2]	3.7	52%
Salisbury University (MD)*	1120-1280[2]	3.7	45%

▶ Regional Universities (continued)

School (State) (*Public)	SAT/ACT 25th-75th percentile ('19)	Average high school GPA ('19)	Freshmen in top 25% of class ('19)
Salve Regina University (RI)	1100-1260[2]	3.4	43%
Seton Hill University (PA)	1000-1220[2]	3.7	44%
Siena College (NY)	1070-1280[2]	3.5	51%
Stevenson University (MD)	1010-1190	3.1	44%
St. Francis University (PA)	1030-1250	3.6	52%
Stockton University (NJ)*	1020-1210[2]	N/A	41%
Suffolk University (MA)	1020-1210	3.3	43%
SUNY College–Cortland*	1090-1230[9]	3.4	45%
SUNY–Fredonia*	990-1200	3.2	41%
SUNY–Geneseo*	1120-1310	3.6	63%
SUNY–New Paltz*	1090-1280[3]	3.6	58%[5]
SUNY–Oswego*	1040-1220	3.3	53%

School (State) (*Public)	SAT/ACT 25th-75th percentile ('19)	Average high school GPA ('19)	Freshmen in top 25% of class ('19)
University of New Haven (CT)	1030-1220[2]	3.5	42%
University of Scranton (PA)	1120-1310	3.6	68%
Wagner College (NY)	1070-1270[2]	3.5	51%
Wentworth Inst. of Technology (MA)	1060-1270[2]	3.1	41%
SOUTH			
Anderson University (SC)	1060-1250	3.6	62%
Appalachian State University (NC)*	21-26	3.9	52%
Asbury University (KY)	21-28[2]	3.7	48%
Berry College (GA)	1090-1320	3.7	61%
Christian Brothers University (TN)	22-27	3.7	59%
Christopher Newport University (VA)*	1110-1280[2]	3.8	48%

SUNY–Geneseo

School (State) (*Public)	SAT/ACT 25th-75th percentile ('19)	Average high school GPA ('19)	Freshmen in top 25% of class ('19)
College of Charleston (SC)*	1080-1260	3.9	52%
Florida Gulf Coast University*	1060-1210[3]	3.9	43%
Florida Southern College	1120-1265	3.7	58%
Freed-Hardeman University (TN)	21-28	3.7	56%
John Brown University (AR)	23-29[2]	3.8	70%
Lee University (TN)	21-28	3.7	49%
Murray State University (KY)*	21-28[2]	3.6	51%
Queens University of Charlotte (NC)	1040-1240[2]	N/A	41%
Rollins College (FL)	1160-1340[2]	3.4	59%
Stetson University (FL)	1110-1300[2]	3.8	56%
University of Mary Washington (VA)*	1080-1280[2]	3.6	41%
University of North Alabama*	20-26	3.5	46%
University of North Georgia*	1070-1230	3.6	48%
University of Tampa (FL)	1100-1250	3.4	47%
University of West Florida*	22-27	3.8	42%

MIDWEST

School (State) (*Public)	SAT/ACT 25th-75th percentile ('19)	Average high school GPA ('19)	Freshmen in top 25% of class ('19)
Augustana University (SD)	23-29[2]	3.7	64%
Baldwin Wallace University (OH)	21-27[2]	N/A	48%
Bradley University (IL)	1070-1270[2]	3.8	60%
Butler University (IN)	1150-1330	3.9	77%
Calvin University (MI)	1130-1350[2]	3.8	62%
Capital University (OH)	20-26[3]	3.6	47%
Cedarville University (OH)	23-29	3.8	62%
Concordia University (NE)	20-26	3.5	46%
Dominican University (IL)	1000-1200	3.8	58%
Drury University (MO)	22-28	3.8	60%
Elmhurst University (IL)	990-1210	3.6	52%
Franciscan U. of Steubenville (OH)	1090-1300	3.8	74%[5]
Grand Valley State University (MI)*	1040-1250	3.7	46%
Indiana Wesleyan University–Marion	1020-1220	3.6	60%
John Carroll University (OH)	22-28	3.6	49%
Lawrence Technological U. (MI)	1020-1270	3.5	40%[5]
Lewis University (IL)	1010-1200	3.5	46%
Mount Vernon Nazarene U. (OH)	20-25	3.5	48%
Nebraska Wesleyan University	22-28[2]	3.7	53%
North Central College (IL)	1030-1260	3.6	55%
Otterbein University (OH)	20-27	3.6	56%
Rockhurst University (MO)	21-27	3.7	59%
Spring Arbor University (MI)	980-1220	3.6	50%
St. Ambrose University (IA)	20-25[3]	3.3	56%
University of Evansville (IN)	1090-1288[2]	3.8	75%
University of Illinois–Springfield*	995-1220	3.6	45%
University of Minnesota–Duluth*	21-26	3.6	48%
University of Nebraska–Kearney*	20-26	3.5	45%
University of Northern Iowa*	20-26	3.6	45%
U. of Northwestern–St. Paul (MN)	21-28[2]	3.5	46%
University of Wisconsin–Eau Claire*	21-26	3.4	48%
University of Wisconsin–La Crosse*	23-27	N/A	57%
Viterbo University (WI)	21-25[2]	3.6	47%
Xavier University (OH)	22-28[9]	3.6	52%

WEST

School (State) (*Public)	SAT/ACT 25th-75th percentile ('19)	Average high school GPA ('19)	Freshmen in top 25% of class ('19)
Abilene Christian University (TX)	21-28[2]	3.6	56%
California Baptist University	990-1210	3.5	40%
California Lutheran University	1070-1250	3.7	65%
California State University–Fullerton*	1030-1200	3.7	63%
Chaminade University of Honolulu	980-1150	3.5	41%
Concordia University (CA)	990-1210	3.4	44%

School (State) (*Public)	SAT/ACT 25th-75th percentile ('19)	Average high school GPA ('19)	Freshmen in top 25% of class ('19)
Dominican University of California	1030-1220[2]	3.6	54%
LeTourneau University (TX)	1090-1310[2]	3.6	53%
The Master's U. and Seminary (CA)	990-1320	3.9	61%
Montana Technological University*	21-26	3.6	55%
New Mexico Inst. of Mining & Technology*	23-29	3.7	68%
Oklahoma Christian University	21-27	3.6	51%
Point Loma Nazarene University (CA)	1140-1310	3.7	78%
St. Edward's University (TX)	1060-1245	N/A	51%
University of Redlands (CA)	1080-1270	N/A	73%
University of St. Thomas (TX)	1057-1242	3.7	48%
Western Washington University*	1060-1280	3.4	51%
Whitworth University (WA)	1050-1290[2]	3.6	64%

▶ Regional Colleges

School (State) (*Public)	SAT/ACT 25th-75th percentile ('19)	Average high school GPA ('19)	Freshmen in top 25% of class ('19)
NORTH			
Maine Maritime Academy*	1010-1200	3.3	40%
SOUTH			
High Point University (NC)	1090-1260[2]	3.3	43%
Ouachita Baptist University (AR)	21-28	3.7	60%
Welch College (TN)	20-26	3.6	55%
MIDWEST			
Benedictine College (KS)	21-28	3.6	42%
Carthage College (WI)	20-27[2]	3.3	50%
College of the Ozarks (MO)	21-26	3.7	66%
Dordt University (IA)	22-28[2]	3.7	49%
Goshen College (IN)	1010-1210	3.6	53%
Northwestern College (IA)	21-27	3.6	49%
Ohio Northern University	23-28	3.7	57%[5]
Taylor University (IN)	1080-1310	3.8	59%
University of Mount Union (OH)	20-25	3.5	61%[5]
William Jewell College (MO)	22-27[2]	3.6	61%
Wisconsin Lutheran College	21-27	3.5	46%
WEST			
Carroll College (MT)	21-26[2]	3.7	72%
Oregon Tech*	1000-1200	3.5	50%

Methodology: To be eligible, national universities, liberal arts colleges, regional universities and regional colleges all had to be numerically ranked among the top three-quarters of their peer groups in the 2021 Best Colleges rankings. They had to admit a meaningful proportion of non-A students, as indicated by fall 2019 admissions data on SAT Evidence-based Reading and Writing and Math scores or Composite ACT scores and high school class standing. The cutoffs were: The 75th percentile for the SAT had to be less than or equal to 1,350; the 25th percentile, greater than or equal to 980. The ACT composite range: less than or equal to 30 and greater than or equal to 20. The proportion of freshmen from the top 10% of their high school class had to be less than or equal to 50% (for national universities and liberal arts colleges only); for all schools, the proportion of freshmen from the top 25% of their high school class had to be less than or equal to 80%, and greater than or equal to 40% Average freshman retention rates for all schools had to be greater than or equal to 75%. Average high school GPA itself was not used in the calculations identifying the A-plus schools. N/A means not available.

Your College Search:
A To-Do List

PREPARE FOR A GREAT HIGH SCHOOL EXPERIENCE. *You'll be able to grow inside and outside the classroom, while making sure you're ready to apply to college in a few years. Although the pandemic has disrupted opportunities for standardized tests and shifted many college visits from campus to online for now, you can remain curious, investigate virtually, and continue to work toward your future goals. Careful planning and good choices over time make for strong options later. Ready, set, go! –by* **Ned Johnson**

Freshman Year

LISTEN AND OBSERVE. Faced with more challenging high school class work, you'll need to pay attention to what your new teachers expect from you and look for ways to work harder and smarter. Grades are important in ninth grade, but seek balance so that you are challenged though not overwhelmed. Don't be afraid to ask for help if you need it.

☐ **Get involved.** High school is not a four-year audition for college but rather a critical period to develop yourself. Grades are important, but so are social connections and extracurriculars. Use part-time jobs, community service, arts and music, robotics clubs and other activities to engage with others.

☐ **Read voraciously.** Dive into books, newspapers, magazines and blogs. Explore subjects that engage you. Additionally, check out TED Talks, YouTube videos and free online courses.

☐ **Find mentors.** Look for knowledgeable people who can offer helpful advice: teachers, coaches, counselors and friends. These relationships can pay off in other ways, too: People like to help students they know.

☐ **Schedule downtime.** That means turning off electronic devices. No phones. No screens. We all need time to daydream and think about ourselves and our place in the world.

☐ **Identify ways to relieve stress.** For school and college, you'll need a model for success that is sustainable and that includes finding healthy ways to manage stress and getting enough rest.

Sophomore Year

KEEP EVOLVING AS A LEARNER. Focus on better understanding your strengths and interests – and how to develop them.

☐ **Challenge yourself (wisely).** Strive for strong grades and take on new challenges, but ask for help when needed and avoid overtaxing yourself. Balance is your goal.

☐ **Speak up in class.** Learning at the college level is about an exchange of ideas between professors and peers. Critical thinking and the ability to articulate your thoughts and ideas are skills that contribute to college success.

☐ **Sleep.** The typical 15-year-old brain needs eight to 10 hours of sleep to function at 100%, so that should be your goal.

☐ **Refine your route.** Look ahead to the 11th- and 12th-grade courses you might be interested in taking and plan to work any prerequisites into your schedule. Take advantage of special courses, particularly rigorous ones that are in line with your academic interests.

☐ **Learn from the masters.** As you take inventory of your own interests, find people who work in related areas. Listen to their stories and consider opportunities for gaining firsthand experience. A 20-minute conversation with a professional could even turn into a fruitful internship opportunity.

Put together an activities list. Start keeping track of your hobbies, jobs, extracurricular activities and accomplishments. This will form the basis of your résumé and will be essential in preparing for college interviews and applications as well as for possible jobs, internships and summer programs.

Make your summer matter. Work, volunteer, play sports, travel or take a class. Research summer programs and internships to give yourself the chance to move beyond the scope of your regular high school courses. Plunge into an activity that excites you or one that builds on a special interest.

Settle on a testing strategy. Use your PSAT scores and other practice tests to help you identify the right test for you (i.e., SAT vs. ACT). Set up a test-prep plan.

Junior Year

ESSAYS, TESTS AND APS, OH MY!
Your grades, test scores and activities this year form a large part of what colleges consider for admission. Prepare for your exams, do your best in class, and stay active and involved.

Plot out your calendar. Talk with your parents and guidance counselor about which exams to take and when. If your 10th-grade PSAT scores put you in reach of a National Merit Scholarship, concentrated prep time might be worth it. Then, take the SAT or ACT. In May or June, the SAT Subject Tests (required by some colleges) are also an option in areas where you shine. If you're enrolled in an AP or honors course now, consider taking a College Board practice test.

Immerse yourself in activities. Look for extracurriculars both in and out of school that you enjoy and that show you are dedicated, play well with others, and can assume leadership roles. High school is your time to discover what you like, to grow intellectually and socially, and to sharpen skills you'll use after high school.

Build your college list in the spring. Once you get your test scores, talk to a counselor and assemble a list of target, reach and likely schools. Use tools to aid your research. Explore college websites and other resources such as ed.gov/finaid and usnews.com/bestcolleges. And clean up social media (e.g., Instagram, Facebook, Twitter) since admissions folks may check it out.

Visit schools if you can. Spring break and summer vacation are ideal times to check out a few campuses.

Connect digitally. Too busy or unable to visit schools? Attend college fairs and information sessions. Grab the admissions rep's card at an info session and follow up via email with a thank-you note or with questions whose answers aren't already available on the college website.

Get recommendations. Right after spring break, ask two teachers with different perspectives on your performance if they will write letters for you. Choose teachers who will effectively communicate your academic and personal qualities.

Write. Reflect on your experiences and strengths as you prepare to write your college essay. Procrastination causes stress, so aim to have first drafts done by Labor Day of senior year. Share them with an English teacher, parent or counselor.

Senior Year

DON'T SLACK OFF. Colleges look at senior-year transcripts, so keep working hard in your classes.

Finish testing. If necessary, you can retake the SAT, ACT or SAT Subject Tests in the early fall. Check deadlines and the admissions testing policies of your schools. Are they test-optional or do they require the SAT or ACT? If so, do you also need the optional written essays? What about the SAT Subject Tests?

Know your deadlines. Many colleges have multiple deadline options. Consider the implications of early action and early, rolling or regular decision – and confirm the rules and deadlines for aid – so you can plan accordingly.

Apply. Craft your essays with a well-thought-out narrative. Fill out applications carefully. Review a copy of your transcript. Have you displayed an upward trend that should be discussed? Does an anomaly need context? Discuss any issues with your counselor. Leave yourself time to reread essays to clean up any errors.

Follow up. Check that your colleges have received records and recs from your high school and your SAT or ACT scores from the testing organization. A month after you submit your application, call the college and confirm that your file is complete.

Confirm aid rules. Check with each college for specific financial aid application requirements. Dates and forms may vary.

Make a choice. Try to visit or even revisit the colleges where you've been accepted before committing. Talk with alumni; attend an accepted-student reception. Then, make your college choice official by sending in your deposit. Congrats! •

Ned Johnson is founder of and tutor-geek at PrepMatters (prepmatters.com) where, along with colleagues, he torments teens with test prep, educational counseling and general attempts to help them thrive. He is also co-author with Dr. William Stixrud of "The Self-Driven Child: The Science and Sense of Giving Your Kids More Control Over Their Lives."

Find
the Money

136 How to Maximize Your Financial Aid

142 Need a Loan? Borrow Wisely

146 Great Schools at Great Prices

148 Whose Grads Borrow Most (and Least)?

150 The Case for a Credit Card in College

5 FIND THE MONEY

Smart **Money** Moves

Researching the wealth of
scholarship opportunities can be
a great investment of your time

by **Elizabeth Gardner**

NEWS YOU CAN USE

DEVIN KEENEY'S INTENSE interest in robotics
is saving $25,000 a year off the cost of attending
Chicago's Illinois Institute of Technology, in the form
of a merit scholarship from the school for participating in the FIRST Robotics Competition in high
school in Shawnee Mission, Kansas. "At competi-
tions, Illinois Tech was always at the top" of the video showcasing the
sponsors, and the scholarship "made me look into the school more,"
Keeney says. Between the FIRST scholarship and several smaller merit
awards, Keeney, now a junior computer engineering major and president of the student organization Illinois Tech Robotics, is paying about
70% less than the school's list price.

Most students hoping to graduate from college with little or no debt
will need financial aid awarded as scholarships and grants. There are
two categories: need-based and merit aid. To receive need-based awards,
families must fill out the Free Application for Federal Student Aid (box,
Page 138), which schools use to evaluate a family's ability to contribute

GRAHAM WEBB
Washington University in St. Louis

ONE STUDENT'S STRATEGY:
Join the Army

● **JOINING THE MILITARY** hadn't occurred
to Graham Webb until he happened upon
the Army ROTC booth at the activity
fair freshman year at WashU. "I thought
it was very cool," says Webb, a second
lieutenant in the Army's CyberCorps,
which defends military networks and
conducts electronic warfare. The Darien,
Connecticut, native graduated last spring
with a major in systems engineering.
The scholarship, which fully funds a

Start your journey with free money

Find scholarship opportunities with Sallie Mae® Scholarship Search

Don't miss out on free money
In academic year 2019 – 20, 24,000 users of Sallie Mae Scholarship Search won at least one scholarship, for a combined total of more than $67 million.

Turn the things you love into scholarships
It's easy. Create a profile and you'll get alerts letting you know which scholarships match your skills, activities, and interests. Plus, new ones are added every day.

You could win $1,000 for college
When you register, you can enter for a chance to win $1,000 in our monthly sweepstakes.[1]

Register for Scholarship Search at
salliemae.com/scholarship

sallie mae®

to the cost of a college education. Need-based aid depends on the gap between the so-called expected family contribution and the cost of attendance; it may change when one's financial situation alters, as has been the case for so many families affected by job losses and pay cuts during the coronavirus pandemic. (Aid offices were recently surveyed by the National Association of Student Financial Aid Administrators, and 90% of respondents predicted that they would receive an increased number of requests for more help from current students by this fall compared to last year.)

THE MERIT ADVANTAGE. Merit aid is different. Thousands of students every year score significant discounts off tuition – sometimes even earning a full ride – regardless of need, especially if a school wants them badly. These awards may be based on GPA and test scores, or on special achievements or talents, or, as with Keeney, on a deep interest in a particular field. While merit aid budgets will likely be adversely affected at many less wealthy colleges this year, the inverse may be true on campuses with healthy endowments. "I could see a scenario where they would start to bump up merit aid because they need to enroll students," says Hannah Serota, founder and CEO of Creative College Connections.

Jim Franko, a guidance counselor at Riverside Brookfield High School in Illinois, recommends that students take stock of their value as potential assets to each college they target. A highly selective school might admit you but offer no merit aid, notes Franko, who steers about 80 teens per year through the application process. Yet others "would love to have you" and can be more generous, especially if your GPA and test scores put you at or above the 75th percentile for students at the school.

The National Center for Education Statistics has a wealth of useful information for families researching financial aid at its College Navigator website (nces.ed.gov/collegenavigator). For each school, it lists (among other things) the total cost of attendance, how many students receive aid and whether it comes from federal or school sources, and the average net cost of attendance per student (further broken down by household income). You'll want to go through all the

Cracking the Financial Aid Code

COLLEGE CAN DELIVER A BRUTAL WALLOP to family finances. But with a smart strategy, you may be able to soften the blow. Your first move is to tap Uncle Sam's rich resources, including federal grants and loans. For that, you must start by filling out the Free Application for Federal Student Aid – better known as the FAFSA – as early as possible. The deadline for the 2021-22 school year is June 30, but you can file as early as Oct. 1 of senior year. Colleges use the form to allocate their own money, too. They all may have different deadlines, so stay on top of the key dates.

The FAFSA crunches your family's financial data to determine your "expected family contribution," which is one way that colleges use to figure out how much a family can pay toward higher ed costs. But schools assemble their aid packages based on multiple factors, including how badly they want you and whether they commit to meeting every student's full demonstrated need, meaning the gap between how much the FAFSA determines you can pay and the total cost of attending. Some colleges resort to "gapping," a practice where they offer a package that falls short of the full need of some applicants, perhaps those who are not in their top tier.

Some schools have to be "need-aware" when weighing candidates, meaning that they consider how much aid will be required. With college budgets squeezed and many families suffering financial reversals since the pandemic began, that may be more true than ever this year. But in normal times, at least, an applicant often brings "other things to the table that outweigh cost," such as geographic diversity or a strong interest in theater, notes Sean Martin, director of financial aid services at Connecticut College. A good tactic is to apply to at least some colleges where you beat the average of previously admitted students on measures like GPA and test scores.

THE PACKAGE. After students are admitted, universities typically bundle a mix of federal grants and need-based loans, plus scholarships from the school based on need, academic merit and/or special talents. Some students will also receive work-study jobs. Many places – particularly those that commit to meeting every student's full need – will expect you to file a supplemental form known as the CSS Profile, available on the College Board's website. Far more detailed than the FAFSA, the CSS collects data about the amount of equity your family has in your home, for example, and how much income is from a family-held business. If one's parents are divorced or separated, financial information about both may be needed – and new spouses, if applicable.

When comparing aid packages, note that some may be more heavily tilted toward loans. It can be useful to subtract the value of grants, scholarships and other so-called gift aid; the amount left over is what you'll have to pay out of pocket, which may or may not include loans.

Is it OK to ask for more? Yes, in certain circumstances. If your financial situation has changed since you submitted the FAFSA, schools want to hear from you. But make your case with facts and be personable with financial aid officers, suggests Charlie Javice, founder and CEO of Frank, an online tool designed to help college students with the admissions and financial aid process. They'll "work with you," she says, as they're reluctant to lose out on good students. *-Arlene Weintraub*

An ROTC scholarship helped put Graham Webb through WashU.

cadet's college education in exchange for a four-year commitment in the Army (some serve in the reserves for a longer period), appealed to Webb. Mainly, it would lift a burden from his parents, who had taken out loans and remortgaged their house to cover the school's sticker price of about $50,000 plus over $10,000 in room and board. And there would be a "cool job" waiting when he graduated, he says.

Getting accepted proved more difficult than Webb had anticipated. He struggled in his original course of study, biomedical engineering, earning a 2.2 grade point average freshman year. (The Army requires a minimum GPA of 2.5, but in Webb's case, recruiters were looking for a 3.3 or 3.4 thanks to stiff competition for the scholar-

ship.) Passing the physical fitness test was also a challenge. Over the course of the next year, he switched his major to systems engineering and embarked on a self-improvement program, buckling down on academics and working out regularly to get fit. His grades improved steadily (reaching a 3.79 for a 21-credit course load senior year). By junior year, he was able to hike 24 miles in the mountains of New Mexico with a 45-pound backpack.

THE PAYOFF. The effort bore results when he reapplied to ROTC sophomore year. In addition to covering tuition, room and board and books, Webb received a stipend of $420 month, plus $250 per credit hour in "critical language incentive pay" for taking Mandarin, amounting to

about $1,250 a semester. He also received a $5,000 grant from a Chicago law firm for those studying engineering and Mandarin.

Now stationed in Fort Gordon, Georgia, for a nine-month course for officers, Webb feels fortunate for the way things turned out. Having to juggle his ROTC duties, including 5 a.m. workouts, military science classes and weekly labs, a summer internship at the Army Cyber Institute at the U.S. Military Academy, and informal mentoring of younger cadets, taught him time-management, organizational and leadership skills. His only regret is that he didn't apply earlier. "It's much easier to get the scholarship while you're still in high school," he says. "Otherwise you're fighting for leftover funds." *–Margaret Loftus*

GRACE ITIRA YOUNG
Tennessee Technological University

ONE STUDENT'S STRATEGY:
Take advantage of tuition-free
community college

● **IF THERE'S ONE QUALITY** that Grace Itira Young admits to having in spades, it's perseverance. Apprehensive about taking her first math course in college, the McMinnville, Tennessee, native ordered the textbook and taught herself the material before stepping into the classroom. And when it became clear that she couldn't rely on her parents for financial support, she doggedly searched for money to pay for college without having to take out loans.

The foundation of her strategy was the Tennessee Promise program, which covers the cost of tuition and fees (after other financial aid) for up to two years at community colleges and other associate-degree-granting schools in the state for eligible residents. One requirement: a commitment to do community service. Young was already volunteering at a church, painting and running a food bank, and she also helped build a house for Habitat for Humanity. "Tennessee Promise gave me hope and introduced me to what was possible," she says. As a freshman at Motlow State Community College-McMinnville, Young forced herself to get involved in extracurricular activities that could boost her résumé and that turned out to be good sources of additional scholarship money.

SUCCESS. Her plan worked. Young became executive vice president of the student government, which provided a grant that paid for her books. Her position on Phi Beta Kappa's statewide academic team netted a $5,000 scholarship, enabling her to transfer to Tennessee Technological University, where she's now a senior in an interdisciplinary program focused on human resources and leadership. This semester she also received a $1,998 Pell Grant, $2,250 from a merit-based Tennessee HOPE Scholarship and two other awards, and she expects to cover her annual $11,000 tuition with cash left over.

Another major contributor: her full-time job. Young works as a legal secretary while taking a full load of accelerated courses in the evenings. She earns $12.50 an hour, lives at home and spends as little as possible so she can save and help her parents. Little wonder that she's a stickler for time management. "Every week, I have a schedule of what time I devote to work, class, homework, housework, and down time – which is limited," she says.

Another tactic she recommends is appealing to a school's financial aid office if the first package doesn't meet your needs. When considering four-year colleges, she successfully negotiated a revised offer from Lee University in Cleveland, Tennessee, but ultimately chose Tennessee Tech based on cost. "I still would have had to take out a loan to go to Lee," she says. "And there wasn't that much difference between the schools." She plans to graduate with no debt and money in the bank. No surprise there. *-Margaret Loftus*

numbers and assess what percentage of the typical aid package is made up of grants or scholarships as opposed to loans (story, Page 142).

GRANTS VS. LOANS. For example, while school X might offer higher average awards than school Y, school X's total costs or percentage of loans may be higher, so the place with the more modest package may still end up having the lower price tag. Also, pay attention to how many incoming students receive aid: It might be 100% at a less selective school and 50% or less at a more selective one. If there are large differences in average cost of attendance based on family income, that's a sign that financial need, rather than merit, determines most of the awards. While public institutions generally have lower tuition, private colleges tend to meet more need and have larger scholarship programs. "If your academic record puts you at the top of our applicant pool, you'll be competitive for a half-tuition scholarship just in merit aid, and you might qualify for a need-based award on top of that," says Todd Rinehart, vice chancellor for enrollment at the private University of Denver.

Joe Orsolini, a principal with College Aid Planners in Glen Ellyn, Illinois, typically recommends applying to six to eight colleges, and paying attention to the relationships between them, to gain maximum leverage for merit aid. "If I know a kid is looking at a school, I will recommend throwing an application to a rival school" in the same general geographic area or in the same athletic conference, he says. "A school might try a little harder when it knows it's competing against a rival." This year, however, he suggests casting an even wider net in light of the uncertainty surrounding merit aid. "Don't put all your eggs in one basket. Add another two to three schools to the mix."

When comparing offers, Rinehart advises students to pay careful attention to fine print. For example, when tuition goes up, will your merit or need-based award go up, too? Often it doesn't, Rinehart says. Keeping a scholarship beyond the first year may require making satisfactory progress toward a degree, maintaining a certain GPA or sticking with an activity or academic area.

As a public institution, the University of Arizona has established set merit scholarship award offers based on high school GPA, test scores and state residency status. There's no wiggle room in that basic amount, says Meghan McKenney, director of counseling in the Office of Scholarships and Financial Aid. But the school created Scholarship Universe (financialaid.arizona.edu/scholarshipuniverse) to help admitted students find additional scholarships, merit-based and otherwise, at UA and elsewhere. They include scholarships from individual academic departments, donors and external sources. UA has also licensed the platform to CampusLogic to distribute more broadly.

EXPAND YOUR SEARCH. Besides exhausting aid sources through their chosen school, students can find plenty of other resources online – either free or at modest subscription prices – to search for scholarship money. They include Scholly, a website and mobile app accessible at myscholly.com; Scholarships.com; and Fastweb.com, among many others. The U.S. Department of Education also offers information and scholarship advice at studentaid.gov.

Investigate organizations that you or your family are involved with: church, scouting, companies that employ you or your parents, hobby-based organizations (like FIRST Robotics, say, or the Amateur Trapshooting Association), and civic groups like the Benevolent and Protective Order of Elks or a local chamber of commerce. For example, the Taco Bell Foundation awards $6 million in scholarships every year, with separate programs for Taco Bell employees and nonemployees. The CVS Health Foundation offers scholarships to children of full-time CVS employees.

Opportunities lurk in unexpected places: The Tall Clubs International social organization offers scholarships for tall people, for example, while the Mayflower Society has college money earmarked for proven descendants of families who came to America on the Mayflower.

Bobbi Lehman, director of financial aid compliance at the University of Arizona, urges applicants to go after every scholarship for which they're eligible. She recalls meeting a student who had been particularly determined in his search and won so many awards that he exceeded his cost of attendance. "They were just a few hundred dollars each," Lehman says, "but he treated it like a job and just kept applying." •

5 FIND THE MONEY

Be a Better Borrower

Here's some expert guidance on keeping your debt level down

by **Alison Murtagh**

Tess Kerkhof in Grinnell's campus garden, where she has worked in the summer

TESS KERKHOF GREW UP working on her family's farm in Wilton, Iowa, and when it came time to apply to college, she was laser-focused on reducing her costs. "Both of my parents are extremely debt-averse," she says, and "the mindset of financial autonomy has always been very important to me." After zeroing in on Grinnell College, a liberal arts school about 90 miles from home, she and her parents met with financial aid counselors to understand how to afford the roughly $54,000 annual tuition plus $13,000 in room and board.

After applying early decision, Kerkhof successfully negotiated with the aid office to boost her initial offer with additional grant money. She also brought along several scholarships and nabbed a work-study job as a live-in community adviser in a campus residence hall, which covers housing costs. She found work during summers as well. As a result, Kerkhof expects to graduate in 2021 with less than $20,000 in student loan debt,

which she thinks will give her the "freedom to do what I want to do" without a huge payment. Thanks to the many undergrads who borrow to finance a bachelor's, the total student loan burden has topped $1.6 trillion; the average grad who borrows leaves campus owing about $30,000.

In general, experts suggest that prospective borrowers consider their future career path and potential earnings to ensure that they take on a manageable amount of debt. A good rule of thumb is to try to borrow no more than "the amount that you expect to earn in a first-year-out-of-school salary," says Gail Holt, dean of financial aid at Amherst College in Massachusetts. A loan repayment calculator can give you a sense of the potential monthly tab. For example, borrowing $20,000 at 4.5% interest would mean you pay about $207 per month over 10 years. To limit borrowing, a student "should meet with a financial aid counselor to discuss strategies for working and budgeting and other campus resources,"

Holt adds. Advance planning is key because debt "can really hamper" plans after college for buying a car or a house or getting a graduate degree, for instance, says Andrew Belasco, chief executive officer of College Transitions, an admissions consulting company.

CHECKUP. During college, it can be helpful to do "an annual financial checkup" of where your debt stands, whether and how much you need to borrow again, and if any changes in your financial picture might make a difference in your overall aid situation, says Megan Coval, vice president of policy and federal relations at the National Association of Student Financial Aid Administrators.

To start, after exhausting any college savings and scholarships, aid specialists recommend exploring federal loan options. Schools use the Free Application for Federal Student Aid to calculate their financial aid awards, and some private lenders also look at the FAFSA when determining loan eligibility.

Direct loans extended by Uncle Sam allow dependent students to borrow up to $5,500 for their first year, $6,500 for year two, and $7,500 for their third year and beyond, capped at $31,000 total. These loans can either be subsidized (for those with financial need, the government pays interest during school) or unsubsidized (interest starts accruing right away and the borrower must pay it). For 2020-21, direct loans for undergrads have an interest rate of 2.75%; the rate for future

> # Debt 'can really hamper' plans after college to **buy a car or house** or get a graduate degree.

loans is readjusted each summer.

If direct loans don't cover the bill, parent PLUS loans are available up to the full cost of attendance (after other aid) as determined by the school. PLUS loans carry an interest rate of 5.3%.

Besides fixed interest rates, federal loans carry a number of benefits, such as a six-month grace period after graduation before one has to start paying off debt. There is also a choice of repayment plans. Under income-based repayment, for instance, borrowers can adjust their monthly bills to a percentage of their discretionary income. Those who work in a qualifying job, such as for the government or a nonprofit, can apply to have their outstanding balance forgiven after 10 years of payments.

Many private lenders now offer both fixed rates and variable ones, which can swing based on market conditions. For example, Sallie Mae currently offers loans with fixed rates of between about 4.25% and 12.35% and variable rates from 1.25% to 11.15%. Securing the most favorable option typically requires evidence of creditworthiness, and some lenders insist upon a co-signer. With a wide range in variable rates, borrowers could see their bills fluctuate toward a much higher rate than when they took out a loan. Protections vary by lender, but private loans generally don't have the same safeguards as federal ones, experts say. ●

With Mariya Greeley

A Glossary of Financial Aid Terms

Expected family contribution. Determined by the info you enter in the FAFSA (see next entry), this is a figure the government provides for schools to determine how much a family should plan to contribute to college costs.

FAFSA. Anyone seeking financial aid must fill out the Free Application for Federal Student Aid, which crunches family income, assets and other personal info. Schools use this to assemble an aid package, and those who wish to receive aid must complete it every year.

Federal direct loans. There are two basic types: subsidized loans for undergrads with financial need and unsubsidized loans (see final entry). The loans carry a fixed rate – those taken out in 2020-21 have a 2.75% interest rate – and repayment starts six months after graduation.

Fixed- vs. variable-rate loans. The interest on a fixed-rate loan will never change during its term, whereas a variable rate might rise or fall from year to year based on market conditions. While all federal student loans carry fixed rates, most private loans offer a choice.

Grants/scholarships. This so-called gift aid can come from colleges, the government, foundations and other sources. You don't need to pay it back, though you might owe tax on it and it can come with strings attached, like maintaining a certain GPA or pursuing a major or career in a particular field.

Income-based repayment. A federal government option where monthly loan payments are reduced based on salary. This approach will typically extend the time of repayment from the standard 10 years to 20 or 25.

Loan forgiveness. Eligible borrowers' student loan debt may be erased after 10 years of consistent payments if they work for nonprofits, the government or certain public service organizations like the Peace Corps.

Meet full need. The college pledges to meet 100% of one's "demonstrated financial need," which is the difference between the cost of attendance and the expected family contribution.

Need-based vs. merit-based aid. Need-based aid is given out based on a family's financial circumstances, while merit aid is awarded for academic, extracurricular or other achievements.

Need-blind vs. need-aware. A need-blind college says it does not consider finances at all when making an admissions decision, while a need-aware school might.

Parent PLUS loans. Parents can take out these loans from the government up to the cost of attendance (minus other aid). The loans are unsubsidized, and for 2020-21, they carry a 5.3% interest rate.

Pell Grant. A federal grant for undergrads who display exceptional financial need. For 2020-21, the maximum award is $6,345.

Subsidized vs. unsubsidized loans. Subsidized loans are for students with need; the government pays the interest while a student is enrolled at least half-time and during a six-month grace period after completing school. Students without need can take out an unsubsidized loan (and are responsible for the accumulating interest). –*Michael Morella*

EQUITABLE

Scholarships in the amount of

$2,500
$10,000
$25,000

Get up to $25K for college!

We want the changemakers. We want those who push the boundaries of what's possible. We want individuals who embody courage, strength and wisdom in their words and actions.

Every year, Equitable Foundation recognizes outstanding, dedicated students through our Equitable Excellence℠ program. We award $1.4 million in scholarships to deserving high schoolers who have made a positive and lasting impact in their community and beyond. In addition, to honor the invaluable role educators play in guiding these students on their path to success, each winner's school receives a $1,000 grant.

The deadline for submitting applications is December 15, 2020.

EQUITABLE EXCELLENCE

Visit Equitable.com/foundation to learn more and apply online.

Great Schools, Great Prices

WHICH SCHOOLS offer students the best value? The calculation used here takes into account a school's academic quality based on its Best Colleges ranking, the 2019-20 net cost of attendance for a student who received the average level of need-based financial aid, and the proportion of aid recipients who also received a scholarship or grant. The higher the quality of the program and the lower the cost, the better the deal. Only schools in the top half of their U.S. News ranking categories are included because U.S. News considers the most significant values to be among colleges that perform well academically.

▶ National Universities

Rank School (State) (*Public)	% students receiving grants based on need ('19)	% aid recipients receiving grants ('19)	Average cost after grants ('19)
1. Harvard University (MA)	52%	100%	$14,898
2. Princeton University (NJ)	62%	100%	$16,014
3. Gallaudet University (DC)	89%	94%	$11,493
4. Yale University (CT)	54%	100%	$17,718
5. Massachusetts Institute of Technology	62%	98%	$20,350
6. Columbia University (NY)	49%	99%	$20,517
7. Stanford University (CA)	50%	97%	$21,070
8. Rice University (TX)	42%	99%	$19,102
9. Vanderbilt University (TN)	49%	99%	$20,906
10. Dartmouth College (NH)	48%	95%	$23,279
11. Brigham Young Univ.–Provo (UT)	39%	84%	$13,524
12. California Institute of Technology	50%	100%	$24,705
13. Duke University (NC)	44%	96%	$23,874
14. U. of North Carolina–Chapel Hill*	36%	95%	$19,508
15. Northwestern University (IL)	45%	98%	$25,970
16. Johns Hopkins University (MD)	51%	99%	$26,855
17. University of Pennsylvania	45%	99%	$26,783
18. Brown University (RI)	42%	100%	$25,476
19. University of Chicago	40%	100%	$27,806
20. Washington University in St. Louis	41%	98%	$26,185
21. Lehigh University (PA)	41%	99%	$23,720
22. University of Rochester (NY)	55%	100%	$28,629
23. Emory University (GA)	46%	96%	$28,945
24. Wake Forest University (NC)	28%	97%	$25,902
25. Cornell University (NY)	46%	96%	$31,312
26. University of Notre Dame (IN)	46%	97%	$31,811
27. Clark University (MA)	63%	100%	$27,761
28. Tufts University (MA)	34%	95%	$28,846
29. Georgetown University (DC)	36%	95%	$30,557
30. Carnegie Mellon University (PA)	38%	98%	$31,616
31. Simmons University (MA)	76%	100%	$30,796
32. University of Virginia*	33%	94%	$29,770
33. Rochester Inst. of Technology (NY)	71%	97%	$30,854
34. University of Detroit Mercy	63%	99%	$24,437
35. Mercer University (GA)	67%	99%	$28,009
36. Clarkson University (NY)	80%	99%	$35,515
37. University of Idaho*	80%	95%	$27,952
38. Valparaiso University (IN)	77%	99%	$31,128
39. Illinois Institute of Technology	66%	100%	$31,598
40. Rensselaer Polytechnic Inst. (NY)	56%	100%	$35,007
41. University of St. Joseph (CT)	79%	90%	$29,494
42. Boston College	38%	90%	$31,462
43. Brandeis University (MA)	43%	96%	$32,795
44. St. John Fisher College (NY)	78%	100%	$31,265
45. University of Dayton (OH)	56%	99%	$29,669
46. Pepperdine University (CA)	52%	100%	$36,244
47. Boston University	41%	98%	$34,033
48. Saint Louis University	59%	98%	$32,724
49. Case Western Reserve Univ. (OH)	45%	97%	$34,454
50. University of Michigan–Ann Arbor*	29%	85%	$31,813

▶ National Liberal Arts Colleges

Rank School (State) (*Public)	% students receiving grants based on need ('19)	% aid recipients receiving grants ('19)	Average cost after grants ('19)
1. Williams College (MA)	52%	100%	$18,732
2. Pomona College (CA)	55%	100%	$18,232
3. Amherst College (MA)	57%	99%	$18,990
4. Swarthmore College (PA)	54%	100%	$19,715
5. Principia College (IL)	71%	100%	$15,305
6. Soka University of America (CA)	86%	100%	$24,170
7. Grinnell College (IA)	65%	100%	$24,864
8. Smith College (MA)	60%	99%	$24,130
9. College of the Atlantic (ME)	85%	99%	$19,059
10. Colby College (ME)	45%	100%	$22,532
11. Davidson College (NC)	50%	100%	$23,394
12. Bowdoin College (ME)	49%	100%	$24,676
13. Wellesley College (MA)	53%	95%	$23,822
14. Vassar College (NY)	60%	100%	$25,829
15. Colgate University (NY)	32%	100%	$21,444
16. Washington and Lee University (VA)	45%	100%	$24,155
17. Hamilton College (NY)	52%	100%	$25,545
18. Haverford College (PA)	45%	100%	$24,307
19. Claremont McKenna College (CA)	41%	98%	$24,637
20. Knox College (IL)	79%	99%	$22,758
21. Middlebury College (VT)	44%	96%	$24,456
22. Wabash College (IN)	75%	99%	$24,393
23. Wesleyan University (CT)	41%	99%	$24,634
24. Agnes Scott College (GA)	78%	100%	$25,530
25. University of Richmond (VA)	38%	98%	$23,831
26. St. Olaf College (MN)	77%	100%	$25,634
27. Centre College (KY)	58%	100%	$23,258
28. Carleton College (MN)	56%	100%	$29,501
29. Earlham College (IN)	91%	100%	$26,631
30. Macalester College (MN)	66%	99%	$28,779
31. Bates College (ME)	43%	100%	$26,469
32. Hendrix College (AR)	77%	100%	$24,766
33. Lake Forest College (IL)	73%	100%	$24,290
34. Franklin & Marshall College (PA)	55%	100%	$26,183
35. Bryn Mawr College (PA)	52%	100%	$27,543
36. Lawrence University (WI)	62%	100%	$25,166
37. Hanover College (IN)	76%	100%	$23,629
38. Kalamazoo College (MI)	71%	99%	$26,179
39. St. John's College (MD)	69%	100%	$25,478
40. Bard College (NY)	71%	98%	$27,394

Methodology: The rankings were based on four variables: **1.** Ratio of quality to price: a school's overall score in the Best Colleges rankings divided by the net cost to a student receiving the average need-based scholarship or grant. The higher the ratio of rank to the discounted cost (tuition, fees, room and board, and other expenses less average need-based scholarship or grant), the better the value. **2.** Percentage of undergrads receiving need-based scholarships or grants during the 2019-20 school year. **3.** New this year: proportion of aid recipients receiving a need-based scholarship or grant. **4.** Average discount: percentage of a school's total costs for 2019-20 school year covered by the average need-based scholarship or grant to undergrads. For public institutions, 2019-20 out-of-state tuition and percentage of out-of-state students receiving scholarships or grants were used. Only schools in the top half of their U.S. News ranking categories were considered. Ratio of quality to price accounted for 50% of the overall score; percentage of undergrads receiving need-based grants, for 20%; proportion of aid recipients receiving scholarships or grants, for 20%; and average discount, for 10%. The school with the most total weighted points became No. 1 in its category.

Regional Universities

NORTH

Rank School (State) (*Public)	% students receiving grants based on need ('19)	% aid recipients receiving grants ('19)	Average cost after grants ('19)
1. McDaniel College (MD)	76%	100%	$22,994
2. Bentley University (MA)	45%	98%	$34,268
3. Canisius College (NY)	69%	99%	$24,989
4. Waynesburg University (PA)	80%	98%	$21,819
5. SUNY Polytechnic Inst.–Albany/Utica*	71%	88%	$27,730
6. St. Bonaventure University (NY)	75%	100%	$26,181
7. Niagara University (NY)	66%	98%	$25,233
8. Le Moyne College (NY)	80%	100%	$28,597
9. SUNY–Oswego*	62%	98%	$22,712
10. Providence College (RI)	48%	100%	$37,414
11. Saint Peter's University (NJ)	89%	100%	$24,476
12. Ithaca College (NY)	68%	99%	$34,447
13. Alfred University (NY)	87%	98%	$27,550
14. Caldwell University (NJ)	77%	99%	$25,408
15. Siena College (NY)	76%	100%	$32,689

SOUTH

Rank School (State) (*Public)	% students receiving grants based on need ('19)	% aid recipients receiving grants ('19)	Average cost after grants ('19)
1. Berry College (GA)	69%	100%	$25,683
2. Bob Jones University (SC)	70%	100%	$18,008
3. King University (TN)	71%	87%	$16,048
4. Saint Leo University (FL)	69%	100%	$20,751
5. Milligan University (TN)	77%	99%	$23,300
6. Coastal Carolina University (SC)*	21%	43%	$14,339
7. Christian Brothers University (TN)	66%	98%	$22,621
8. Freed-Hardeman University (TN)	72%	98%	$20,609
9. Western Carolina University (NC)*	47%	92%	$19,033
10. Columbia International Univ. (SC)	83%	99%	$21,605
11. The Citadel, Military Coll. of SC*	44%	85%	$28,868
12. Asbury University (KY)	76%	100%	$27,424
13. Lee University (TN)	66%	93%	$20,816
14. Rollins College (FL)	53%	100%	$34,746
15. Stetson University (FL)	66%	99%	$32,134

MIDWEST

Rank School (State) (*Public)	% students receiving grants based on need ('19)	% aid recipients receiving grants ('19)	Average cost after grants ('19)
1. Truman State University (MO)*	37%	93%	$21,327
2. Olivet Nazarene University (IL)	81%	100%	$18,714
3. Buena Vista University (IA)	88%	100%	$21,178
4. Dominican University (IL)	81%	98%	$24,797
5. Marian University (IN)	78%	99%	$22,894
6. Bradley University (IL)	71%	99%	$28,136
7. Augustana University (SD)	59%	98%	$23,962
8. University of Evansville (IN)	65%	95%	$28,633
9. Drury University (MO)	67%	100%	$23,298
10. Franciscan Univ. of Steubenville (OH)	65%	100%	$24,595
11. Univ. of Nebraska–Kearney*	39%	95%	$20,011
12. Milwaukee School of Engineering	80%	100%	$30,137
13. Calvin University (MI)	57%	100%	$30,818
14. Hamline University (MN)	85%	100%	$28,107
15. Augsburg University (MN)	81%	100%	$27,549

WEST

Rank School (State) (*Public)	% students receiving grants based on need ('19)	% aid recipients receiving grants ('19)	Average cost after grants ('19)
1. Mills College (CA)	77%	94%	$9,573
2. Trinity University (TX)	44%	100%	$26,959
3. Whitworth University (WA)	71%	99%	$28,235
4. St. Mary's Univ. of San Antonio	73%	97%	$24,993
5. University of St. Thomas (TX)	68%	99%	$22,773
6. University of Dallas	61%	98%	$27,748
7. Pacific Lutheran University (WA)	74%	100%	$27,285
8. Westminster College (UT)	63%	99%	$25,707
9. Abilene Christian University (TX)	67%	100%	$29,810
10. Saint Martin's University (WA)	74%	100%	$26,344
11. California State U.–Los Angeles*	84%	98%	$26,810
12. Rocky Mountain College (MT)	74%	99%	$21,659
13. California Lutheran University	70%	99%	$35,064
14. Northwest University (WA)	78%	100%	$23,762
15. LeTourneau University (TX)	67%	98%	$26,948

Regional Colleges

NORTH

Rank School (State) (*Public)	% students receiving grants based on need ('19)	% aid recipients receiving grants ('19)	Average cost after grants ('19)
1. Cooper Union for Adv. of Sci. & Art (NY)	57%	100%	$24,223
2. Cazenovia College (NY)	78%	98%	$18,410
3. Elmira College (NY)	82%	100%	$24,476
4. University of Maine–Farmington*	66%	75%	$21,670
5. Colby-Sawyer College (NH)	81%	100%	$29,188
6. Massachusetts Maritime Academy*	10%	83%	$23,581
7. SUNY College of Technology at Alfred*	63%	86%	$25,709
8. St. Francis College (NY)	70%	96%	$29,577
9. Keene State College (NH)*	52%	83%	$30,810
10. Maine Maritime Academy*	13%	62%	$37,567

SOUTH

Rank School (State) (*Public)	% students receiving grants based on need ('19)	% aid recipients receiving grants ('19)	Average cost after grants ('19)
1. Kentucky State University*	87%	100%	$9,201
2. University of the Ozarks (AR)	65%	100%	$15,770
3. Blue Mountain College (MS)	76%	97%	$14,847
4. Alice Lloyd College (KY)	88%	100%	$16,343
5. Ouachita Baptist University (AR)	61%	96%	$21,026
6. Newberry College (SC)	85%	100%	$21,187
7. Maryville College (TN)	82%	99%	$25,767
8. Barton College (NC)	83%	100%	$26,473
9. Emmanuel College (GA)	75%	100%	$19,432
10. Huntingdon College (AL)	77%	100%	$23,666

MIDWEST

Rank School (State) (*Public)	% students receiving grants based on need ('19)	% aid recipients receiving grants ('19)	Average cost after grants ('19)
1. Cottey College (MO)	75%	100%	$13,382
2. College of the Ozarks (MO)	91%	100%	$17,446
3. Marietta College (OH)	78%	98%	$20,121
4. Ohio Northern University	82%	100%	$24,319
5. Goshen College (IN)	76%	100%	$22,527
6. William Jewell College (MO)	71%	100%	$23,044
7. Alma College (MI)	85%	100%	$26,561
8. Heidelberg University (OH)	87%	100%	$22,695
9. Northland College (WI)	83%	98%	$22,542
10. Loras College (IA)	81%	100%	$23,644

WEST

Rank School (State) (*Public)	% students receiving grants based on need ('19)	% aid recipients receiving grants ('19)	Average cost after grants ('19)
1. Oral Roberts University (OK)	69%	100%	$19,277
2. Texas Lutheran University	79%	100%	$21,882
3. Carroll College (MT)	63%	99%	$27,272
4. William Jessup University (CA)	75%	99%	$29,319
5. McMurry University (TX)	79%	98%	$24,400
6. Warner Pacific University (OR)	63%	75%	$25,428
7. Oklahoma Baptist University	62%	84%	$33,760
8. Schreiner University (TX)	60%	78%	$36,291
9. Arizona Christian University (AZ)	48%	98%	$37,215
10. East Texas Baptist University	59%	71%	$33,360

The Payback Picture

WITH TUITION RISING and financial aid budgets shrinking, many students must borrow their way to a degree. U.S. News has compiled a list of the schools whose bachelor's degree grads of 2018 carried the heaviest and lightest debt loads. The data include loans taken out by students from the federal government – private loans, state and local government loans, and loans directly to parents are not included. The first column of data indicates what percentage of the class graduated owing money and, by extrapolation, what percentage graduated debt-free. "Median amount of debt" is the 50th percentile amount of cumulative federal borrowing by graduates who incurred debt; it does not reflect all graduates, just those with debt.

MOST DEBT

▶ National Universities

School (State) (*Public)	% of grads with debt	Median amount of debt
Jackson State University (MS)*	70%	$30,500
Morgan State University (MD)*	66%	$30,500
Texas Southern University*	66%	$30,347
Clark Atlanta University	83%	$28,500
Barry University (FL)	56%	$28,386
North Carolina A&T State Univ.*	76%	$28,360
Cardinal Stritch University (WI)	58%	$28,354
Tennessee State University*	66%	$28,017
Univ. of Maryland Eastern Shore*	64%	$28,000
Colorado Technical University	75%	$27,871
University of the Incarnate Word (TX)	73%	$27,666
Central Michigan University*	71%	$27,000
Clarke University (IA)	82%	$27,000
Delaware State University*	66%	$27,000
Duquesne University (PA)	68%	$27,000
Florida Institute of Technology	35%	$27,000
Gannon University (PA)	58%	$27,000
Husson University (ME)	78%	$27,000
Immaculata University (PA)	68%	$27,000
Indiana Univ. of Pennsylvania*	72%	$27,000
Lindenwood University (MO)	63%	$27,000
Mary Baldwin University (VA)	70%	$27,000
Robert Morris University (PA)	64%	$27,000
Rochester Inst. of Technology (NY)	61%	$27,000
Syracuse University (NY)	47%	$27,000
University of Hartford (CT)	63%	$27,000
University of Michigan–Flint*	52%	$27,000
University of New Hampshire*	65%	$27,000
University of St. Joseph (CT)	73%	$27,000
Valparaiso University (IN)	67%	$27,000
Widener University (PA)	69%	$27,000
Worcester Polytechnic Inst. (MA)	52%	$27,000

▶ National Liberal Arts Colleges

School (State) (*Public)	% of grads with debt	Median amount of debt
Lane College (TN)	92%	$37,621
Chowan University (NC)	87%	$35,579
Tougaloo College (MS)	82%	$34,874
Bennett College (NC)	79%	$34,500
Bethune-Cookman University (FL)	82%	$34,500
Stillman College (AL)	92%	$33,500
Dillard University (LA)	88%	$32,960
Talladega College (AL)	83%	$32,039
Allen University (SC)	90%	$31,446
Johnson C. Smith University (NC)	87%	$31,000
Virginia Union University	75%	$31,000
Bloomfield College (NJ)	76%	$29,375
Pine Manor College (MA)	53%	$28,722
Brewton-Parker College (GA)	48%	$28,348
Rust College (MS)	87%	$28,289

▶ Regional Universities

School (State) (*Public)	% of grads with debt	Median amount of debt
NORTH		
Strayer University (DC)	74%	$37,500
Lincoln University (PA)*	81%	$31,000
Trinity Washington University (DC)	67%	$29,500
Metropolitan College of New York	71%	$29,250
Post University (CT)	71%	$28,500
SOUTH		
Everglades University (FL)	43%	$40,802
Grambling State University (LA)*	86%	$38,500
Fort Valley State University (GA)*	85%	$37,500
Alabama Agricultural and Mechanical University*	75%	$34,500
Alabama State University*	78%	$32,637
MIDWEST		
Chicago State University*	82%	$31,250
DeVry University (IL)	76%	$31,206
Alverno College (WI)	82%	$31,000
Maharishi University of Management (IA)	61%	$30,500
Kettering University (MI)	59%	$28,726
WEST		
Academy of Art University (CA)	46%	$31,365
Prairie View A&M University (TX)*	74%	$29,902
Woodbury University (CA)	62%	$29,250
Colorado Christian University	51%	$27,523
La Sierra University (CA)	59%	$27,500

▶ Regional Colleges

School (State) (*Public)	% of grads with debt	Median amount of debt
NORTH		
Peirce College (PA)	71%	$33,373
Wesley College (DE)	80%	$31,000
SOUTH		
Benedict College (SC)	87%	$40,000
Shaw University (NC)	87%	$38,479
Livingstone College (NC)	91%	$35,000
St. Augustine's University (NC)	88%	$35,000
Paine College (GA)	72%	$34,807
MIDWEST		
Martin University (IN)	90%	$46,769
Harris-Stowe State University (MO)*	74%	$32,786
Central State University (OH)*	88%	$31,250
WEST		
Jarvis Christian College (TX)	86%	$30,156
Wiley College (TX)	72%	$29,000
Bacone College (OK)	68%	$28,931
McMurry University (TX)	72%	$27,250
Warner Pacific University (OR)	69%	$27,000

Note: Student debt data are from the U.S. Department of Education College Scorecard

LEAST DEBT

▶ National Universities

School (State) (*Public)	% of grads with debt	Median amount of debt
California Institute of Technology	5%	$8,700
Princeton University (NJ)	4%	$9,850
Stanford University (CA)	8%	$11,341
Duke University (NC)	20%	$11,500
University of Texas–Rio Grande Valley*	37%	$11,661
Rice University (TX)	16%	$11,989
Brigham Young Univ.–Provo (UT)	15%	$12,100
Alliant International University (CA)	8%	$12,500
CUNY–City College*	13%	$12,500
Dartmouth College (NH)	26%	$12,500
Massachusetts Institute of Technology	11%	$12,500
University of California–Davis*	34%	$13,000
Yale University (CT)	8%	$13,000
University of California–Berkeley*	22%	$13,750
Harvard University (MA)	2%	$13,875
Cornell University (NY)	31%	$14,000
Utah State University*	29%	$14,000
California State University–Fresno*	30%	$15,000
Northwestern University (IL)	21%	$15,000
Touro College (NY)	28%	$15,000
University of California–Los Angeles*	32%	$15,000
University of Washington*	26%	$15,000
Vanderbilt University (TN)	12%	$15,000
University of California–Santa Barbara*	35%	$15,306
San Diego State University*	28%	$15,340

▶ National Liberal Arts Colleges

School (State) (*Public)	% of grads with debt	Median amount of debt
Berea College (KY)	15%	$5,600
Pomona College (CA)	12%	$10,040
Wellesley College (MA)	24%	$10,600
Williams College (MA)	24%	$12,702
Bates College (ME)	22%	$12,725
Amherst College (MA)	17%	$12,896
Reed College (OR)	39%	$13,465
Middlebury College (VT)	24%	$13,750
Carleton College (MN)	44%	$13,834
Scripps College (CA)	33%	$13,900
Claremont McKenna College (CA)	22%	$14,250
Pitzer College (CA)	38%	$14,625
Haverford College (PA)	18%	$15,000
Bowdoin College (ME)	18%	$15,850
New College of Florida*	32%	$16,000
Colorado College	23%	$16,043
Colgate University (NY)	24%	$16,125
Hamilton College (NY)	33%	$16,250
Grinnell College (IA)	40%	$17,000
Sarah Lawrence College (NY)	44%	$17,000
Whitman College (WA)	36%	$17,175
Wesleyan University (CT)	26%	$17,231
Barnard College (NY)	30%	$17,500
Vassar College (NY)	43%	$17,695
Kenyon College (OH)	30%	$18,000
Thomas Aquinas College (CA)	69%	$18,000

▶ Regional Universities

School (State) (*Public)	% of grads with debt	Median amount of debt
NORTH		
CUNY–John Jay Col. of Crim. Justice*	12%	$10,500
CUNY–Lehman College*	19%	$10,500
CUNY–Baruch College*	12%	$11,500
CUNY–Brooklyn College*	13%	$11,819
CUNY–Queens College*	11%	$12,000
SOUTH		
Mississippi Univ. fur Women*	55%	$15,020
University of Arkansas–Monticello*	60%	$16,001
Salem University (WV)	80%	$17,795
Lynn University (FL)	30%	$18,000
University of North Georgia*	33%	$18,000
MIDWEST		
Northeastern Illinois University*	40%	$15,000
MidAmerica Nazarene University (KS)	64%	$16,275
Siena Heights University (MI)	65%	$17,250
Waldorf University (IA)	74%	$18,191
Univ. of Illinois–Springfield*	46%	$18,532
WEST		
Southern Utah University*	86%	$11,437
University of North Texas–Dallas*	43%	$12,500
California State University–Los Angeles*	29%	$13,381
California State U.–Monterey Bay*	42%	$13,521
New Mexico Highlands University*	31%	$13,750

▶ Regional Colleges

School (State) (*Public)	% of grads with debt	Median amount of debt
NORTH		
Boricua College (NY)	17%	$4,500
CUNY–Medgar Evers College*	19%	$9,250
CUNY–York College*	8%	$9,913
CUNY–New York City Col. of Tech.*	8%	$10,342
U.S. Merchant Marine Acad. (NY)*	8%	$12,000
SOUTH		
Pensacola State College (FL)*	7%	$5,500
South Florida State College*	5%	$8,200
Seminole State College of Florida*	19%	$10,500
Florida College	65%	$12,000
West Virginia University–Parkersburg*	44%	$13,407
MIDWEST		
St. Augustine College (IL)	N/A	$2,735
Donnelly College (KS)	41%	$9,373
Cottey College (MO)	57%	$12,000
Ranken Technical College (MO)	65%	$12,000
Vincennes University (IN)*	14%	$13,000
WEST		
Brigham Young University–Hawaii	12%	$9,016
Northern New Mexico College*	13%	$9,250
Oklahoma State U. Institute of Technology–Okmulgee*	47%	$12,000
Brigham Young University–Idaho	15%	$12,601
Oklahoma State University–Oklahoma City*	27%	$15,184

A Credit Card in College?

The idea may sound risky, but there are benefits to building a credit history

by **Bob Musinski**

PARENTS MIGHT be apprehensive about giving their college student a credit card, but if they don't, it could cause problems later. Those who delay building a strong credit history may have trouble qualifying for credit cards and loans or even renting an apartment after graduation. With planning and education, students can use credit cards to build a strong record in college and graduate ready for real-world financial situations.

Building credit during the college years allows students "to make small mistakes when the stakes are small, so they can learn lessons that will help them in the future, when the stakes get higher," says Matt Schulz, chief credit analyst at personal finance site Lending Tree and a former U.S. News contributor. Currently some 57% of college students have their own credit cards, according to a 2019 survey from Sallie Mae – in fact, they have 5.2 of them, on average. And 58% say they use the cards as a way to build credit.

For parents, there is no one way to figure out whether your young adult is ready. A common starting point is to allow a high schooler to use a debit card as a method of payment, which could carry over into the first couple years of college. In fact, 85% of college students surveyed by Sallie Mae had debit cards.

Top-rated Student Credit Cards

Student credit cards are designed for college students who have little or no credit history. These cards usually offer low credit limits, and most don't charge annual fees. If you're new to credit cards and want to learn how to use them responsibly, a student card may be the right choice. U.S. News rates credit cards available to students from major credit card issuers on a regular basis. We identify cards offering the best overall value for students based on customer satisfaction, cost and rewards programs. As the semester began, these were top-rated student credit cards to consider:

▶ **Bank of America Cash Rewards Credit Card for Students**
▶ **Bank of America Travel Rewards Credit Card for Students**
▶ **Chase Freedom Unlimited**
▶ **Journey Student Rewards from Capital One**
▶ **Wells Fargo Cash Back College Card**

Visit usnews.com/creditcards for more information and updates.

"When you're just getting started, it's really important to know yourself or, if you're a parent, know your kid and understand whether they are someone who is likely to handle this credit limit without going on a spending spree," Schulz says. "Are they somebody who is able to make payments every month without forgetting or being late?"

Many parents believe their children are showing fiscal responsibility if they have no credit card during college. While limiting the chance for significant

debt is wise, students might graduate and need a parent to co-sign for an apartment if they don't have a credit file, says Tim Ranzetta, co-founder of Next Gen Personal Finance, a nonprofit that offers resources for teaching personal finance in schools.

The most common ways to get a student started with a credit card are by adding them as an authorized user on a parent's account or encouraging them to get a secured credit card or an unsecured student card. Making a student an authorized user on a parent's credit card can allow the student to pay for items without the responsibility of monthly balance payments. If this arrangement is made in high school, the student can become comfortable with using the card while his or her parents are around to answer questions, Ranzetta says. Parents also get to see what is being purchased.

Making children authorized users can help them build a strong credit history provided that the card issuer reports that information to credit bureaus. If you use your card account responsibly and make a child an authorized user on your account, you can "transfer the good history on that card to the authorized user's credit. That can be a good jump-start," Schulz says.

On the negative side, an authorized user has buy-ing power without ultimate responsibility for payment. That can be a problem if a student racks up huge charges. "An authorized user legally isn't liable for those balances," Schulz says. "Mom and Dad are the ones legally stuck with that bill."

Parents should talk to their kids about the responsible use of credit before allowing them to become authorized users. Discuss credit limits, and most importantly, make a plan for how they'll pay off their charges each month. It's important to know that the kids benefit from the strong credit history only as long as they're authorized users of the card. If the user is removed, that history goes away, Schulz says.

TRAINING WHEELS. Secured credit cards are backed with a cash deposit made by the cardholder, and are designed for consumers who likely can't get an unsecured card because they have no (or a bad) credit history. They can be ideal for college students who wouldn't otherwise be approved. "Secured cards minimize the risk for pretty much everybody involved," Schulz says. "You put a little bit of money down, you get a credit card account and start using it to build up your credit. Because the credit limit isn't going to be very high, there is only so much damage that you're going to be able to do. It's a good set of training wheels to help you get more comfortable with credit."

Deposits on these cards are usually about $200 to $500, which often matches the credit limit on the card. These are not prepaid cards, though; the owner still has to make monthly payments while the security deposit acts as a backup in case of

"Students can make small mistakes when the stakes are small."

default. Secured cards often have an annual fee as well. "Beyond the deposit, most of these secured cards act exactly like any other credit card would," Schulz says. But it is important to make sure the credit card issuer will submit the payment history to credit reporting bureaus. Some secured cards offer tools such as text alerts or reminders of payment due dates that help students learn how to responsibly use the card, Schulz says.

Another option is an unsecured student credit card. These cards often accept students who have limited or no credit history, and while they don't require a security deposit, they may have lower credit limits than other types of cards to lessen the risk of racking up debt. And they usually don't have annual fees. Typically, such cards are designed to help students get experience with credit and may have credit-building tools available, such as free FICO score and credit report access. Some offer cash back, travel rewards and even a statement credit for good grades.

Determining when a student is ready for a credit card may not be easy, but testing some combination of approaches can help, experts say. "You have to know your child," says Ranzetta. You can watch how a child handles an allowance or earnings from a part-time job to get a feel for his or her habits.

Schulz compares the credit card decision to the issue of whether to give a young person the family car. "If you have one kid who always fills the tank up with gas and never misses curfew, you'll probably give him the keys again," he says. "If a kid always comes home late with scratches on the car, it's probably good to keep the keys from him." ●

5 Ways Students Go Wrong With Credit Cards

YOU'RE AWAY FROM home, and you have a credit card. It might seem like a dream come true right now, but it can quickly turn into a nightmare if you use your card the wrong way. Here are some of the biggest mistakes college students make (so that you can avoid them):

1 THEY DON'T THINK CREDIT IS IMPORTANT. In the world after college, credit matters a lot. People with excellent credit often get the best interest rates on mortgages, lower premiums on car insurance and the best offers for rewards credit cards.

2 THEY SHRUG OFF A LATE PAYMENT. For young people, a credit report won't include a lot of information, so a negative item is going to stick out. If you keep ignoring a late payment, after 120 days or so, your issuer might sell your account to a collection agency. If

that happens, you'll see both the late payment and the defaulted account on your credit report. Those two negative items plus a short credit history equal a really bad credit score.

3 THEY DON'T KNOW WHAT THEY SPENT (OR WHERE THEY SPENT IT). This is the mistake that not only messes up your credit score but also gets you into debt. You don't want to leave college with credit card debt, especially as you might already have student loan debt hanging over your head. Don't use your new credit card until you have a budget and a tracking system in place, such as through a money management website or an app like Mint.

4 THEY DON'T UNDERSTAND THAT COMPOUND INTEREST IS BAD. Let's say you have a $5,000 balance on a credit card that has a 20% annual percentage rate. The minimum payment on this debt is $133.33. If you only make the

minimum payment, it will take you 277 months (or just over 23 years) to get rid of your debt. You end up paying $7,732.49 in interest on your original $5,000 balance. If you do get in over your head, pay more than the minimum. Don't relax until your balance is zero again.

5 THEY DON'T UNDERSTAND THE CONNECTION BETWEEN THEIR CREDIT CARDS AND THEIR CREDIT SCORE. A credit utilization ratio is the amount of credit you've used compared with the amount of credit you have available. Simply put, if you keep high balances on your credit cards, your score will go down. Your credit utilization accounts for 30% of your FICO score. If you have a $1,000 credit limit, don't use the card to purchase more than $300 during the month. This gives you a 30% ratio , which is acceptable. The lower the ratio, the better. *-Beverly Harzog*

DIRECTORY
OF
COLLEGES
AND
UNIVERSITIES

INSIDE

The latest facts and figures on over
1,600 American colleges and universities,
including schools' U.S. News rankings

New data on tuition, admissions, the
makeup of the undergraduate student body,
popular majors and financial aid

Statistical profiles of freshman classes, including entrance
exam scores and high school class standing

Using the Directory

How to interpret the statistics in the following entries on more than 1,600 American colleges and universities – and how to get the most out of them

THE SNAPSHOTS OF colleges and universities presented here, alphabetized by state, contain a wealth of information on everything from the most popular majors offered to the stats on the freshman class that arrived in the fall of 2019. The statistics were collected in 2020 and are as of Aug. 26, 2020; they are explained in detail below. A school whose name has been footnoted with a 1 did not return the U.S. News statistical questionnaire, so limited data appear; a 7 means the school declined to have an official verify the data's accuracy. If a college did not reply to a particular question, you'll see N/A, for "not available." Our online directory allows you to search our database for schools based on major, location and other criteria (go to usnews.com/collegesearch). To find a school of interest in the rankings tables, consult the index at the back of the book.

1. TELEPHONE NUMBER
This number reaches the admissions office.

2. U.S. NEWS RANKING
The abbreviation indicates which category of institution the school falls into: National Universities (Nat. U.), National Liberal Arts Colleges (Nat. Lib. Arts), Regional Universities (Reg. U.), or Regional Colleges (Reg. Coll.). The regional universities and regional colleges are further divided by region: North (N), South (S), Midwest (Mid. W), and West (W). "Business" refers to business specialty schools, and "Engineering" refers to engineering specialty schools. "Arts" refers to schools devoted to the fine and performing arts.

Next, you'll find the school's 2021 rank within its category. Schools falling in the top three-fourths of their categories are ranked numerically. (Those ranked in the bottom 25% of their category are listed alphabetically in the ranking tables.) You cannot compare ranks of schools in different categories; U.S. News ranks schools only against their peers. Specialty schools that focus on business, engineering and the arts aren't ranked. Also unranked are schools with fewer than 200 students, those with a high percentage of older or part-time students, those that don't admit freshmen, and those that received a very small number of peer assessment votes in the U.S. News peer surveys conducted in 2019 and 2020.

3. WEBSITE
Visit the school's website to research programs, take a virtual tour, or submit an application.

4. ADMISSIONS EMAIL
You can use this email address to request information or to submit an application.

5. TYPE/AFFILIATION
Is the school public, private or for-profit? Affiliated with a religious denomination?

6. FRESHMAN ADMISSIONS
How competitive is the admissions process at this institution? Schools are designated "most selective," "more selective," "selective," "less selective" or "least selective." The more selective a school, the harder it will probably be to get in. All of the admissions statistics reported are for the class that entered in the fall of 2019. The 25/75 percentiles for the SAT Evidence-Based Reading and Writing and Math or ACT Composite scores show the range in which half the students scored: 25% of students scored at or below the lower end, and 75% scored at or below the upper end. If a school reported the averages and not the 25/75 percentiles, the average score is listed. The test score that is published represents the test that the greatest percentage of entering students took.

7. EARLY DECISION/ EARLY ACTION DEADLINES
Applicants who plan to take the early decision route to fall 2021 enrollment will have to meet the deadline listed for the school. If the school offers an early action option, the application deadline and notification date are also shown.

8. APPLICATION DEADLINE
The date shown is the regular admission deadline for the academic year starting in the fall of 2021. "Rolling" means the school makes admissions decisions as applications come in until the class is filled.

9. UNDERGRADUATE STUDENT BODY
This section gives the breakdown of full-time vs. part-time students and male and female enrollment, the ethnic makeup of the student body, proportions of in-state and out-of-state students, percentage living on campus, and percentage in fraternities and sororities. Figures are for 2019-2020.

10. MOST POPULAR MAJORS
The five most popular majors appear, along with the percentage majoring in each among 2019 graduates with a bachelor's degree.

11. EXPENSES
The first figure represents tuition (including required fees); next is total room and board. Figures are for the 2020-2021 academic year; if data are not available, we use figures for the 2019-2020 academic year. For public schools, we list both in-state and out-of-state tuition.

12. FINANCIAL AID
The percentage of undergrads determined to have financial need and the amount of the average package (grants, loans and jobs) in 2019-2020. We also provide the phone number of the financial aid office.

ALABAMA

Alabama Agricultural and Mechanical University
Normal AL
(256) 372-5245
U.S. News ranking: Reg. U. (S), second tier
Website: www.aamu.edu/admissions/undergraduateadmissions/pages/default.aspx
Admissions email: admissions@aamu.edu
Public; founded 1875
Freshman admissions: less selective; 2019-2020: 9,579 applied, 8,789 accepted. Either SAT or ACT required. ACT 25/75 percentile: 15-18. High school rank: N/A
Early decision deadline: N/A, notification date: N/A
Early action deadline: N/A, notification date: N/A
Application deadline (fall): 7/15
Undergraduate student body: 4,975 full time, 298 part time; 40% male, 60% female; 0% American Indian, 0% Asian, 91% Black, 1% Hispanic, 1% multiracial, 0% Pacific Islander, 1% white, 1% international; 59% from in state; 57% live on campus; N/A of students in fraternities, N/A in sororities
Most popular majors: 10% Biology/Biological Sciences, General, 8% Business Administration and Management, General, 7% Criminal Justice/Law Enforcement Administration, 6% Electrical and Electronics Engineering, 6% Radio and Television Broadcasting Technology/Technician
Expenses: 2019-2020: $10,024 in state, $18,634 out of state; room/board: $7,522
Financial aid: (256) 372-5400; 94% of undergrads determined to have financial need; average aid package $11,654

Alabama State University
Montgomery AL
(334) 229-4291
U.S. News ranking: Reg. U. (S), No. 94
Website: www.alasu.edu
Admissions email: admissions@alasu.edu
Public; founded 1867
Freshman admissions: least selective; 2019-2020: 6,674 applied, 6,467 accepted. Either SAT or ACT required. ACT 25/75 percentile: 15-20. High school rank: 8% in top tenth, 31% in top quarter, 39% in top half
Early decision deadline: N/A, notification date: N/A
Early action deadline: N/A, notification date: N/A
Application deadline (fall): 7/30
Undergraduate student body: 3,446 full time, 304 part time; 37% male, 63% female; 0% American Indian, 0% Asian, 93% Black, 1% Hispanic, 1% multiracial, 0% Pacific Islander, 2% white, 1% international; 64% from in state; N/A live on campus;

3% of students in fraternities, 5% in sororities
Most popular majors: 14% Health Information/Medical Records Administration/Administrator, 12% Business Administration and Management, General, 11% Criminal Justice/Safety Studies, 10% Elementary Education and Teaching, 9% Speech Communication and Rhetoric
Expenses: 2020-2021: $11,068 in state, $19,396 out of state; room/board: $6,050
Financial aid: (334) 229-4712; 95% of undergrads determined to have financial need; average aid package $16,730

Auburn University
Auburn AL
(334) 844-6425
U.S. News ranking: Nat. U., No. 97
Website: www.auburn.edu
Admissions email: admissions@auburn.edu
Public; founded 1856
Freshman admissions: more selective; 2019-2020: 20,205 applied, 16,300 accepted. Either SAT or ACT required. ACT 25/75 percentile: 25-31. High school rank: 33% in top tenth, 63% in top quarter, 89% in top half
Early decision deadline: N/A, notification date: N/A
Early action deadline: N/A, notification date: N/A
Undergraduate student body: 22,527 full time, 2,067 part time; 52% male, 48% female; 0% American Indian, 2% Asian, 5% Black, 3% Hispanic, 3% multiracial, 0% Pacific Islander, 80% white, 6% international; 63% from in state; 19% live on campus; 23% of students in fraternities, 42% in sororities
Most popular majors: 22% Business, Management, Marketing, and Related Support Services, 18% Biological and Biomedical Sciences, 6% Health Professions and Related Programs, 5% Education
Expenses: 2020-2021: $11,796 in state, $31,956 out of state; room/board: $13,778
Financial aid: (334) 844-4634; 34% of undergrads determined to have financial need; average aid package $11,097

Auburn University at Montgomery
Montgomery AL
(334) 244-3615
U.S. News ranking: Reg. U. (S), No. 73
Website: www.aum.edu
Admissions email: admissions@aum.edu
Public; founded 1967
Freshman admissions: selective; 2019-2020: 4,109 applied, 3,716 accepted. Either SAT or ACT required. ACT 25/75 percentile: 19-23. High school rank: 20% in top tenth, 46% in top quarter, 78% in top half
Early decision deadline: N/A, notification date: N/A
Early action deadline: N/A, notification date: N/A

Application deadline (fall): 8/1
Undergraduate student body: 3,505 full time, 1,018 part time; 35% male, 65% female; 0% American Indian, 2% Asian, 42% Black, 1% Hispanic, 4% multiracial, 0% Pacific Islander, 44% white, 6% international; 94% from in state; 29% live on campus; 0% of students in fraternities, 2% in sororities
Most popular majors: 30% Health Professions and Related Programs, 17% Business, Management, Marketing, and Related Support Services, 7% Computer and Information Sciences and Support Services, 7% Education, 6% Psychology
Expenses: 2020-2021: $8,860 in state, $18,820 out of state; room/board: $7,268
Financial aid: (334) 244-3571; 69% of undergrads determined to have financial need; average aid package $9,520

Birmingham-Southern College
Birmingham AL
(205) 226-4696
U.S. News ranking: Nat. Lib. Arts, No. 130
Website: www.bsc.edu
Admissions email: admiss@bsc.edu
Private; founded 1856
Affiliation: United Methodist
Freshman admissions: more selective; 2019-2020: 3,384 applied, 1,821 accepted. Neither SAT nor ACT required. ACT 25/75 percentile: 22-29. High school rank: 24% in top tenth, 49% in top quarter, 77% in top half
Early decision deadline: 11/1, notification date: 12/1
Early action deadline: 11/15, notification date: 12/15
Application deadline (fall): rolling
Undergraduate student body: 1,201 full time, 8 part time; 47% male, 53% female; 0% American Indian, 2% Asian, 14% Black, 3% Hispanic, 1% multiracial, 0% Pacific Islander, 79% white, 1% international; 64% from in state; 78% live on campus; 38% of students in fraternities, 52% in sororities
Most popular majors: 20% Business Administration and Management, General, 11% Biology/Biological Sciences, General, 11% Psychology, General, 7% Accounting, 6% Teacher Education, Multiple Levels
Expenses: 2020-2021: $18,900; room/board: $12,900
Financial aid: (205) 226-4688; 50% of undergrads determined to have financial need; average aid package $17,460

Faulkner University[1]
Montgomery AL
(334) 386-7200
U.S. News ranking: Reg. U. (S), second tier
Website: www.faulkner.edu
Admissions email: admissions@faulkner.edu
Private; founded 1942
Affiliation: Churches of Christ
Application deadline (fall): 8/1

Undergraduate student body: N/A full time, N/A part time
Expenses: 2020-2021: $22,990; room/board: $7,700
Financial aid: (334) 386-7195

Huntingdon College
Montgomery AL
(334) 833-4497
U.S. News ranking: Reg. Coll. (S), No. 14
Website: www.huntingdon.edu
Admissions email: admiss@hawks.huntingdon.edu
Private; founded 1854
Affiliation: United Methodist
Freshman admissions: selective; 2019-2020: 2,336 applied, 1,385 accepted. Either SAT or ACT required. ACT 25/75 percentile: 19-24. High school rank: 17% in top tenth, 47% in top quarter, 76% in top half
Early decision deadline: N/A, notification date: N/A
Early action deadline: N/A, notification date: N/A
Application deadline (fall): rolling
Undergraduate student body: 830 full time, 177 part time; 49% male, 51% female; 1% American Indian, 1% Asian, 19% Black, 5% Hispanic, 4% multiracial, 0% Pacific Islander, 68% white, 0% international
Most popular majors: Information not available
Expenses: 2020-2021: $27,900; room/board: $10,150
Financial aid: (334) 833-4428; 77% of undergrads determined to have financial need; average aid package $19,578

Jacksonville State University[1]
Jacksonville AL
(256) 782-5268
U.S. News ranking: Reg. U. (S), No. 62
Website: www.jsu.edu
Admissions email: info@jsu.edu
Public; founded 1883
Application deadline (fall): rolling
Undergraduate student body: N/A full time, N/A part time
Expenses: 2019-2020: $10,704 in state, $20,424 out of state; room/board: $7,494
Financial aid: (256) 782-5006

Judson College
Marion AL
(800) 447-9472
U.S. News ranking: Nat. Lib. Arts, second tier
Website: www.judson.edu/
Admissions email: admissions@judson.edu
Private; founded 1838
Affiliation: Southern Baptist
Freshman admissions: less selective; 2019-2020: 478 applied, 178 accepted. Neither SAT nor ACT required. ACT 25/75 percentile: 17-21. High school rank: N/A
Early decision deadline: N/A, notification date: N/A
Early action deadline: N/A, notification date: N/A
Application deadline (fall): rolling
Undergraduate student body: 196 full time, 54 part time;

1% male, 99% female; 1% American Indian, 0% Asian, 19% Black, 2% Hispanic, 0% multiracial, 0% Pacific Islander, 71% white, 0% international; N/A from in state; 62% live on campus; N/A of students in fraternities, N/A in sororities
Most popular majors: 20% Psychology, 17% Biological and Biomedical Sciences, 14% Education, 11% Agriculture, Agriculture Operations, and Related Sciences, 9% Physical Sciences
Expenses: 2019-2020: $18,540; room/board: $10,910
Financial aid: N/A

Miles College[1]
Birmingham AL
(205) 929-1000
U.S. News ranking: Reg. Coll. (S), second tier
Website: www.miles.edu
Admissions email: admissions@mail.miles.edu
Private
Application deadline (fall): N/A
Undergraduate student body: N/A full time, N/A part time
Expenses: 2019-2020: $12,464; room/board: $7,348
Financial aid: N/A

Oakwood University[1]
Huntsville AL
(256) 726-7356
U.S. News ranking: Reg. Coll. (S), No. 47
Website: www.oakwood.edu
Admissions email: admissions@oakwood.edu
Private; founded 1896
Affiliation: Seventh Day Adventist
Application deadline (fall): N/A
Undergraduate student body: N/A full time, N/A part time
Expenses: 2019-2020: $19,990; room/board: $9,374
Financial aid: N/A

Samford University
Birmingham AL
(205) 726-2011
U.S. News ranking: Nat. U., No. 143
Website: www.samford.edu
Admissions email: admission@samford.edu
Private; founded 1841
Affiliation: Baptist
Freshman admissions: more selective; 2019-2020: 3,912 applied, 3,259 accepted. Either SAT or ACT required. ACT 25/75 percentile: 23-29. High school rank: 33% in top tenth, 61% in top quarter, 86% in top half
Early decision deadline: N/A, notification date: N/A
Early action deadline: N/A, notification date: N/A
Undergraduate student body: 3,509 full time, 82 part time; 33% male, 67% female; 0% American Indian, 1% Asian, 7% Black, 3% Hispanic, 2% multiracial, 0% Pacific Islander, 85% white, 1% international; 32% from in state; 65% live on campus; 35% of students in fraternities, 56% in sororities

Most popular majors: 35% Health Professions and Related Programs, 21% Business, Management, Marketing, and Related Support Services, 7% Communication, Journalism, and Related Programs, 6% Visual and Performing Arts, 5% Family and Consumer Sciences/Human Sciences
Expenses: 2020-2021: $34,198; room/board: $11,260
Financial aid: (205) 726-2905; 40% of undergrads determined to have financial need; average aid package $21,884

Spring Hill College
Mobile AL
(251) 380-3030
U.S. News ranking: Nat. Lib. Arts, second tier
Website: www.shc.edu
Admissions email: admit@shc.edu
Private; founded 1830
Freshman admissions: selective; 2019-2020: 7,616 applied, 3,791 accepted. Either SAT or ACT required. ACT 25/75 percentile: 20-25. High school rank: 17% in top tenth, 45% in top quarter, 80% in top half
Early decision deadline: N/A, notification date: N/A
Early action deadline: N/A, notification date: N/A
Application deadline (fall): 7/15
Undergraduate student body: 1,170 full time, 17 part time; 37% male, 63% female; 0% American Indian, 1% Asian, 14% Black, 4% Hispanic, 3% multiracial, 0% Pacific Islander, 68% white, 4% international; N/A from in state; 70% live on campus; N/A of students in fraternities, N/A in sororities
Most popular majors: 28% Business, Management, Marketing, and Related Support Services, 13% Health Professions and Related Programs, 11% Biological and Biomedical Sciences, 9% Communication, Journalism, and Related Programs, 9% Social Sciences
Expenses: 2020-2021: $41,868; room/board: $14,062
Financial aid: (800) 548-7886; 73% of undergrads determined to have financial need; average aid package $36,757

Stillman College
Tuscaloosa AL
(205) 366-8817
U.S. News ranking: Nat. Lib. Arts, second tier
Website: www.stillman.edu
Admissions email: admissions@stillman.edu
Private; founded 1876
Affiliation: Presbyterian Church (USA)
Freshman admissions: less selective; 2019-2020: 2,697 applied, 889 accepted. Either SAT or ACT required. SAT 25/75 percentile: N/A. High school rank: N/A
Early decision deadline: N/A, notification date: N/A
Early action deadline: N/A, notification date: N/A
Application deadline (fall): rolling

Undergraduate student body: 795 full time, 66 part time; 47% male, 53% female; 0% American Indian, 0% Asian, 86% Black, 0% Hispanic, 0% multiracial, 0% Pacific Islander, 4% white, 0% international
Most popular majors: 25% Psychology, General, 22% Business/Commerce, General, 17% Biology/Biological Sciences, General, 12% Physical Education Teaching and Coaching, 5% Journalism
Expenses: 2020-2021: $11,292; room/board: $8,840
Financial aid: (205) 366-8817

Talladega College
Talladega AL
(256) 761-6235
U.S. News ranking: Nat. Lib. Arts, second tier
Website: www.talladega.edu
Admissions email: admissions@talladega.edu
Private; founded 1867
Affiliation: United Church of Christ
Freshman admissions: less selective; 2019-2020: 7,447 applied, 4,674 accepted. Either SAT or ACT required. ACT 25/75 percentile: 20-24. High school rank: N/A
Early decision deadline: N/A, notification date: N/A
Early action deadline: N/A, notification date: N/A
Application deadline (fall): N/A
Undergraduate student body: 1,082 full time, 148 part time; 46% male, 54% female; 0% American Indian, 0% Asian, 89% Black, 3% Hispanic, 2% multiracial, 0% Pacific Islander, 2% white, 3% international; 1230% from in state; N/A live on campus; N/A of students in fraternities, N/A in sororities
Most popular majors: 35% Business Administration and Management, General, 12% Criminal Justice/Law Enforcement Administration, 12% Sociology, 10% Psychology, General, 10% Social Work
Expenses: 2020-2021: $13,571; room/board: $6,704
Financial aid: (256) 761-6237; 98% of undergrads determined to have financial need; average aid package $20,341

Troy University
Troy AL
(334) 670-3179
U.S. News ranking: Reg. U. (S), No. 51
Website: www.troy.edu
Admissions email: ask@troy.edu
Public; founded 1887
Freshman admissions: selective; 2019-2020: 6,146 applied, 5,382 accepted. Either SAT or ACT required. ACT 25/75 percentile: 18-24. High school rank: N/A
Early decision deadline: N/A, notification date: N/A
Early action deadline: N/A, notification date: N/A
Application deadline (fall): rolling
Undergraduate student body: 8,741 full time, 4,254 part time; 37% male, 63% female; 0% American

Indian, 1% Asian, 31% Black, 4% Hispanic, 3% multiracial, 0% Pacific Islander, 53% white, 5% international; 60% from in state; 15% live on campus; 9% of students in fraternities, 12% in sororities
Most popular majors: 15% Business Administration and Management, General, 11% Psychology, General, 10% Criminal Justice/Safety Studies, 5% Registered Nursing/Registered Nurse, 5% Social Work
Expenses: 2020-2021: $11,110 in state, $20,860 out of state; room/board: $6,904
Financial aid: (334) 808-6261; 63% of undergrads determined to have financial need; average aid package $5,229

Tuskegee University
Tuskegee AL
(334) 727-8500
U.S. News ranking: Reg. U. (S), No. 20
Website: www.tuskegee.edu
Admissions email: admissions@tuskegee.edu
Private; founded 1881
Freshman admissions: selective; 2019-2020: 11,133 applied, 6,352 accepted. Either SAT or ACT required. ACT 25/75 percentile: 18-23. High school rank: 21% in top tenth, 79% in top quarter, 100% in top half
Early decision deadline: N/A, notification date: N/A
Early action deadline: N/A, notification date: N/A
Application deadline (fall): rolling
Undergraduate student body: 2,254 full time, 140 part time; 36% male, 64% female; 0% American Indian, 1% Asian, 89% Black, 1% Hispanic, 2% multiracial, 1% Pacific Islander, 0% white, 0% international; 28% from in state; 65% live on campus; 0% of students in fraternities, 0% in sororities
Most popular majors: 12% Mechanical Engineering, 10% Biology/Biological Sciences, General, 7% Psychology, General, 6% Registered Nursing/Registered Nurse, 4% Sales, Distribution, and Marketing Operations, General
Expenses: 2020-2021: $22,679; room/board: $9,844
Financial aid: (334) 727-8088; 96% of undergrads determined to have financial need; average aid package $24,750

University of Alabama
Tuscaloosa AL
(205) 348-5666
U.S. News ranking: Nat. U., No. 143
Website: www.ua.edu
Admissions email: admissions@ua.edu
Public; founded 1831
Freshman admissions: more selective; 2019-2020: 38,505 applied, 31,835 accepted. Either SAT or ACT required. ACT 25/75 percentile: 23-31. High school rank: 40% in top tenth, 61% in top quarter, 84% in top half
Early decision deadline: N/A, notification date: N/A

Early action deadline: N/A, notification date: N/A
Application deadline (fall): rolling
Undergraduate student body: 29,135 full time, 3,660 part time; 44% male, 56% female; 0% American Indian, 1% Asian, 10% Black, 5% Hispanic, 4% multiracial, 0% Pacific Islander, 77% white, 2% international; 39% from in state; 25% live on campus; 28% of students in fraternities, 42% in sororities
Most popular majors: 29% Business, Management, Marketing, and Related Support Services, 12% Engineering, 10% Communication, Journalism, and Related Programs, 8% Health Professions and Related Programs, 7% Family and Consumer Sciences/Human Sciences
Expenses: 2020-2021: $11,620 in state, $31,090 out of state; room/board: $11,012
Financial aid: (205) 348-6756; 42% of undergrads determined to have financial need; average aid package $15,049

University of Alabama at Birmingham
Birmingham AL
(205) 934-8221
U.S. News ranking: Nat. U., No. 153
Website: www.uab.edu
Admissions email: chooseuab@uab.edu
Public; founded 1969
Freshman admissions: more selective; 2019-2020: 8,298 applied, 6,112 accepted. Either SAT or ACT required. ACT 25/75 percentile: 22-29. High school rank: 29% in top tenth, 57% in top quarter, 86% in top half
Early decision deadline: N/A, notification date: N/A
Early action deadline: N/A, notification date: N/A
Application deadline (fall): rolling
Undergraduate student body: 10,315 full time, 3,521 part time; 39% male, 61% female; 0% American Indian, 7% Asian, 24% Black, 6% Hispanic, 4% multiracial, 0% Pacific Islander, 56% white, 2% international; N/A from in state; 23% live on campus; 7% of students in fraternities, 9% in sororities
Most popular majors: 22% Health Professions and Related Programs, 19% Business, Management, Marketing, and Related Support Services, 9% Biological and Biomedical Sciences, 7% Education, 7% Psychology
Expenses: 2020-2021: $10,710 in state, $25,380 out of state; room/board: $12,307
Financial aid: (205) 934-8223; 59% of undergrads determined to have financial need; average aid package $12,330

University of Alabama–Huntsville
Huntsville AL
(256) 824-6070
U.S. News ranking: Nat. U., No. 272
Website: www.uah.edu/

Admissions email: admissions@uah.edu
Public; founded 1969
Freshman admissions: more selective; 2019-2020: 5,420 applied, 4,410 accepted. Either SAT or ACT required. ACT 25/75 percentile: 25-31. High school rank: 38% in top tenth, 66% in top quarter, 82% in top half
Early decision deadline: N/A, notification date: N/A
Early action deadline: N/A, notification date: N/A
Application deadline (fall): 8/17
Undergraduate student body: 6,749 full time, 1,240 part time; 58% male, 42% female; 1% American Indian, 3% Asian, 9% Black, 6% Hispanic, 4% multiracial, 0% Pacific Islander, 72% white, 2% international; 82% from in state; 28% live on campus; 6% of students in fraternities, 7% in sororities
Most popular majors: 29% Engineering, 18% Business, Management, Marketing, and Related Support Services, 16% Health Professions and Related Programs, 8% Computer and Information Sciences and Support Services, 7% Biological and Biomedical Sciences
Expenses: 2020-2021: $11,122 in state, $23,518 out of state; room/board: $10,400
Financial aid: (256) 824-6650; 50% of undergrads determined to have financial need; average aid package $17,708

University of Mobile
Mobile AL
(251) 442-2222
U.S. News ranking: Reg. Coll. (S), No. 16
Website: www.umobile.edu
Admissions email: umenrollment@umobile.edu
Private; founded 1961
Affiliation: Baptist
Freshman admissions: more selective; 2019-2020: 2,696 applied, 1,231 accepted. Neither SAT nor ACT required. ACT 25/75 percentile: 20-27. High school rank: 27% in top tenth, 62% in top quarter, 90% in top half
Early decision deadline: N/A, notification date: N/A
Early action deadline: N/A, notification date: N/A
Application deadline (fall): rolling
Undergraduate student body: 1,106 full time, 663 part time; 36% male, 64% female; 2% American Indian, 2% Asian, 17% Black, 1% Hispanic, 2% multiracial, 0% Pacific Islander, 68% white, 4% international; 87% from in state; N/A live on campus; N/A of students in fraternities, N/A in sororities
Most popular majors: 11% Business Administration and Management, General, 11% Registered Nursing/Registered Nurse, 7% Health and Physical Education/Fitness, General, 5% Elementary Education and Teaching, 5% Religious/Sacred Music
Expenses: 2020-2021: $24,050; room/board: $9,886

Financial aid: (251) 442-2222; 76% of undergrads determined to have financial need; average aid package $21,326

University of Montevallo

Montevallo AL
(205) 665-6030
U.S. News ranking: Reg. U. (S), No. 26
Website: www.montevallo.edu
Admissions email: admissions@montevallo.edu
Public; founded 1896
Freshman admissions: selective; 2019-2020: 5,553 applied, 2,955 accepted. Either SAT or ACT required. ACT 25/75 percentile: 20-25. High school rank: N/A
Early decision deadline: N/A, notification date: N/A
Early action deadline: N/A, notification date: N/A
Application deadline (fall): 8/15
Undergraduate student body: 1,997 full time, 245 part time; 35% male, 65% female; 0% American Indian, 1% Asian, 16% Black, 5% Hispanic, 4% multiracial, 0% Pacific Islander, 68% white, 3% international; N/A from in state; 55% live on campus; N/A of students in fraternities, N/A in sororities
Most popular majors: Information not available
Expenses: 2020-2021: $13,710 in state, $26,730 out of state; room/board: $9,810
Financial aid: (205) 665-6050; 68% of undergrads determined to have financial need; average aid package $12,666

University of North Alabama

Florence AL
(256) 765-4608
U.S. News ranking: Reg. U. (S), No. 40
Website: www.una.edu
Admissions email: admissions@una.edu
Public; founded 1830
Freshman admissions: selective; 2019-2020: 3,583 applied, 2,390 accepted. Either SAT or ACT required. ACT 25/75 percentile: 20-26. High school rank: 22% in top tenth, 46% in top quarter, 77% in top half
Early decision deadline: N/A, notification date: N/A
Early action deadline: N/A, notification date: N/A
Application deadline (fall): rolling
Undergraduate student body: 4,942 full time, 1,397 part time; 39% male, 61% female; 1% American Indian, 1% Asian, 13% Black, 3% Hispanic, 3% multiracial, 0% Pacific Islander, 74% white, 4% international; 82% from in state; 26% live on campus; 14% of students in fraternities, 18% in sororities
Most popular majors: 22% Business, Management, Marketing, and Related Support Services, 12% Health Professions and Related Programs, 11% Education, 7% Parks, Recreation, Leisure, and Fitness Studies,

6% Visual and Performing Arts
Expenses: 2020-2021: $10,800 in state, $20,400 out of state; room/board: $4,846
Financial aid: (256) 765-4278; 62% of undergrads determined to have financial need; average aid package $10,212

University of South Alabama

Mobile AL
(251) 460-6141
U.S. News ranking: Nat. U., second tier
Website: www.southalabama.edu
Admissions email: recruitment@southalabama.edu
Public; founded 1963
Freshman admissions: selective; 2019-2020: 6,465 applied, 5,047 accepted. Neither SAT nor ACT required. ACT 25/75 percentile: 20-27. High school rank: N/A
Early decision deadline: 8/1, notification date: 10/1
Early action deadline: N/A, notification date: N/A
Application deadline (fall): 7/15
Undergraduate student body: 8,065 full time, 1,536 part time; 40% male, 60% female; 1% American Indian, 3% Asian, 22% Black, 4% Hispanic, 4% multiracial, 0% Pacific Islander, 61% white, 2% international; 18% from in state; 21% live on campus; N/A of students in fraternities, N/A in sororities
Most popular majors: 27% Health Professions and Related Programs, 12% Business, Management, Marketing, and Related Support Services, 11% Engineering, 9% Education, 7% Biological and Biomedical Sciences
Expenses: 2020-2021: $10,294 in state, $20,164 out of state; room/board: $7,800
Financial aid: (251) 460-6231; 65% of undergrads determined to have financial need; average aid package $10,766

University of West Alabama

Livingston AL
(205) 652-3578
U.S. News ranking: Reg. U. (S), second tier
Website: www.uwa.edu
Admissions email: admissions@uwa.edu
Public; founded 1835
Freshman admissions: selective; 2019-2020: 7,569 applied, 2,644 accepted. Either SAT or ACT required. ACT 25/75 percentile: 18-22. High school rank: N/A
Early decision deadline: N/A, notification date: N/A
Early action deadline: N/A, notification date: N/A
Application deadline (fall): rolling
Undergraduate student body: 1,883 full time, 356 part time; 39% male, 61% female; 0% American Indian, 0% Asian, 41% Black, 2% Hispanic, 2% multiracial, 0% Pacific Islander, 45% white, 4% international; 82% from in state; 50% live on campus;

10% of students in fraternities, 12% in sororities
Most popular majors: 17% Multi-/Interdisciplinary Studies, Other, 7% Biology/ Biological Sciences, General, 7% Business Administration and Management, General, 7% Kinesiology and Exercise Science, 6% Communication and Media Studies, Other
Expenses: 2020-2021: $10,990 in state, $20,090 out of state; room/board: $8,350
Financial aid: (205) 652-3576; 80% of undergrads determined to have financial need; average aid package $10,889

ALASKA

Alaska Pacific University

Anchorage AK
(800) 252-7528
U.S. News ranking: Reg. U. (W), No. 88
Website: www.alaskapacific.edu
Admissions email: admissions@alaskapacific.edu
Private; founded 1959
Freshman admissions: less selective; 2019-2020: 353 applied, 315 accepted. Neither SAT nor ACT required. SAT 25/75 percentile: N/A. High school rank: N/A
Early decision deadline: N/A, notification date: N/A
Early action deadline: N/A, notification date: N/A
Application deadline (fall): 8/15
Undergraduate student body: 244 full time, 93 part time; 29% male, 71% female; 25% American Indian, 2% Asian, 3% Black, 8% Hispanic, 12% multiracial, 2% Pacific Islander, 37% white, 0% international
Most popular majors: Information not available
Expenses: 2020-2021: $20,760; room/board: $8,400
Financial aid: (907) 564-8342

University of Alaska–Anchorage

Anchorage AK
(907) 786-1480
U.S. News ranking: Reg. U. (W), No. 75
Website: www.uaa.alaska.edu
Admissions email: futureseawolf@alaska.edu
Public; founded 1954
Freshman admissions: selective; 2019-2020: 3,673 applied, 3,047 accepted. Neither SAT nor ACT required. SAT 25/75 percentile: 1020-1220. High school rank: 12% in top tenth, 35% in top quarter, 65% in top half
Early decision deadline: N/A, notification date: N/A
Early action deadline: N/A, notification date: N/A
Application deadline (fall): 7/15
Undergraduate student body: 5,522 full time, 6,680 part time; 41% male, 59% female; 5% American Indian, 8% Asian, 3% Black, 8% Hispanic, 13% multiracial, 3% Pacific Islander, 52% white,

2% international; 91% from in state; N/A live on campus; N/A of students in fraternities, N/A in sororities
Most popular majors: 20% Business, Management, Marketing, and Related Support Services, 19% Health Professions and Related Programs, 9% Engineering, 5% Multi/ Interdisciplinary Studies, 5% Social Sciences
Expenses: 2020-2021: $8,418 in state, $25,398 out of state; room/board: $12,662
Financial aid: (907) 786-6170; 53% of undergrads determined to have financial need; average aid package $10,955

University of Alaska–Fairbanks[1]

Fairbanks AK
(800) 478-1823
U.S. News ranking: Nat. U., second tier
Website: www.uaf.edu
Admissions email: admissions@uaf.edu
Public; founded 1917
Application deadline (fall): 6/15
Undergraduate student body: N/A full time, N/A part time
Expenses: 2019-2020: $7,080 in state, $21,216 out of state; room/board: $10,440
Financial aid: (907) 474-7256

University of Alaska–Southeast[7]

Juneau AK
(907) 796-6100
U.S. News ranking: Reg. U. (W), No. 88
Website: www.uas.alaska.edu
Admissions email: admissions@uas.alaska.edu
Public; founded 1983
Freshman admissions: less selective; 2019-2020: 492 applied, 298 accepted. Neither SAT nor ACT required. SAT 25/75 percentile: N/A. High school rank: N/A
Early decision deadline: N/A, notification date: N/A
Early action deadline: N/A, notification date: N/A
Application deadline (fall): 8/15
Undergraduate student body: 588 full time, 1,298 part time
Most popular majors: 23% Business, Management, Marketing, and Related Support Services, 18% Education, 17% Multi/Interdisciplinary Studies, 15% Social Sciences, 5% English Language and Literature/Letters
Expenses: 2019-2020: $6,696 in state, $20,832 out of state; room/board: $9,200
Financial aid: N/A

AMERICAN SAMOA

American Samoa Community College[1]

Pago Pago AS
(684) 699-9155
U.S. News ranking: Reg. Coll. (W), unranked
Website: WWW.amsamoa.edu

Admissions email: Admissions@amsamoa.edu
Public; founded 1970
Undergraduate student body: 585 full time, 450 part time
Expenses: 2019-2020: $3,950 in state, $4,250 out of state; room/board: $3,000
Financial aid: N/A

ARIZONA

Arizona Christian University

Glendale AZ
(602) 489-5300
U.S. News ranking: Reg. Coll. (W), No. 14
Website: arizonachristian.edu/
Admissions email: admissions@ arizonachristian.edu
Private; founded 1960
Affiliation: Undenominational
Freshman admissions: selective; 2019-2020: 421 applied, 274 accepted. Either SAT or ACT required. ACT 25/75 percentile: 15-21. High school rank: N/A
Early decision deadline: N/A, notification date: N/A
Early action deadline: N/A, notification date: N/A
Application deadline (fall): 8/24
Undergraduate student body: 713 full time, 157 part time; 62% male, 38% female; 1% American Indian, 1% Asian, 15% Black, 24% Hispanic, 5% multiracial, 0% Pacific Islander, 46% white, 4% international; N/A from in state; 50% live on campus; N/A of students in fraternities, N/A in sororities
Most popular majors: 38% Business, Management, Marketing, and Related Support Services, 21% Theology and Religious Vocations, 16% Psychology, 9% Education, 6% Communication, Journalism, and Related Programs
Expenses: 2020-2021: $29,250; room/board: $12,000
Financial aid: (602) 386-4115; 69% of undergrads determined to have financial need; average aid package $9,070

Arizona State University–Tempe

Tempe AZ
(480) 965-7788
U.S. News ranking: Nat. U., No. 103
Website: www.asu.edu
Admissions email: admissions@asu.edu
Public; founded 1885
Freshman admissions: more selective; 2019-2020: 34,188 applied, 29,562 accepted. Neither SAT nor ACT required. ACT 25/75 percentile: 22-28. High school rank: 31% in top tenth, 61% in top quarter, 88% in top half
Early decision deadline: N/A, notification date: N/A
Early action deadline: N/A, notification date: N/A
Application deadline (fall): rolling
Undergraduate student body: 41,182 full time, 3,279 part time; 55% male, 45% female; 1% American Indian, 9% Asian,

4% Black, 23% Hispanic, 5% multiracial, 0% Pacific Islander, 49% white, 9% international; 73% from in state; 27% live on campus; 10% of students in fraternities, 16% in sororities
Most popular majors: 27% Business, Management, Marketing, and Related Support Services, 13% Engineering, 9% Biological and Biomedical Sciences, 8% Social Sciences, 6% Visual and Performing Arts
Expenses: 2020-2021: $11,338 in state, $29,428 out of state; room/board: $13,150
Financial aid: (855) 278-5080; 54% of undergrads determined to have financial need; average aid package $15,864

Arizona State University–West
Tempe AZ
(480) 965-7788
U.S. News ranking: Unranked
Website: campus.asu.edu/west
Admissions email: admissions@asu.edu
Public; founded 1984
Freshman admissions: N/A; 2019-2020: 3,376 applied, 2,760 accepted. Neither SAT nor ACT required. ACT 25/75 percentile: 19-25. High school rank: 32% in top tenth, 66% in top quarter, 92% in top half
Early decision deadline: N/A, notification date: N/A
Early action deadline: N/A, notification date: N/A
Application deadline (fall): rolling
Undergraduate student body: 4,076 full time, 525 part time; 38% male, 62% female; 1% American Indian, 6% Asian, 5% Black, 38% Hispanic, 3% multiracial, 0% Pacific Islander, 41% white, 4% international; 86% from in state; 15% live on campus; N/A of students in fraternities, N/A in sororities
Most popular majors: 28% Business, Management, Marketing, and Related Support Services, 15% Psychology, 10% Biological and Biomedical Sciences, 9% Education, 6% Communication, Journalism, and Related Programs
Expenses: 2020-2021: $11,338 in state, $29,428 out of state; room/board: $12,364
Financial aid: (855) 278-5080; 73% of undergrads determined to have financial need; average aid package $13,850

Embry-Riddle Aeronautical University–Prescott
Prescott AZ
(928) 777-6600
U.S. News ranking: Unranked
Website: prescott.erau.edu/index.html
Admissions email: Prescott@erau.edu
Private; founded 1926
Freshman admissions: N/A; 2019-2020: 3,752 applied, 2,465 accepted. Neither SAT nor ACT required. SAT 25/75 percentile: 1150-1360. High school rank:

29% in top tenth, 57% in top quarter, 87% in top half
Early decision deadline: N/A, notification date: N/A
Early action deadline: N/A, notification date: N/A
Application deadline (fall): rolling
Undergraduate student body: 2,773 full time, 121 part time; 74% male, 26% female; 0% American Indian, 6% Asian, 1% Black, 14% Hispanic, 6% multiracial, 1% Pacific Islander, 62% white, 7% international
Most popular majors: 37% Engineering, 26% Transportation and Materials Moving, 16% Social Sciences, 8% Business, Management, Marketing, and Related Support Services, 8% Homeland Security, Law Enforcement, Firefighting and Related Protective Services
Expenses: 2020-2021: $37,864; room/board: $12,174
Financial aid: (800) 888-3728; 91% of undergrads determined to have financial need; average aid package $17,021

Grand Canyon University[1]
Phoenix AZ
(800) 800-9776
U.S. News ranking: Nat. U., second tier
Website: apply.gcu.edu
Admissions email: golopes@gcu.edu
For-profit; founded 1949
Application deadline (fall): rolling
Undergraduate student body: N/A full time, N/A part time
Expenses: 2019-2020: $17,800; room/board: $7,800
Financial aid: (602) 639-6600

Northern Arizona University
Flagstaff AZ
(928) 523-5511
U.S. News ranking: Nat. U., No. 284
Website: www.nau.edu
Admissions email: admissions@nau.edu
Public; founded 1899
Freshman admissions: selective; 2019-2020: 36,855 applied, 31,313 accepted. Neither SAT nor ACT required. ACT 25/75 percentile: 19-25. High school rank: 21% in top tenth, 51% in top quarter, 84% in top half
Early decision deadline: N/A, notification date: N/A
Early action deadline: N/A, notification date: N/A
Application deadline (fall): 8/1
Undergraduate student body: 21,731 full time, 4,782 part time; 39% male, 61% female; 3% American Indian, 2% Asian, 3% Black, 25% Hispanic, 6% multiracial, 0% Pacific Islander, 55% white, 4% international; 69% from in state; 37% live on campus; 7% of students in fraternities, 8% in sororities
Most popular majors: 18% Business, Management, Marketing, and Related Support Services, 14% Health Professions and Related Programs, 9% Education, 9% Liberal Arts and

Sciences, General Studies and Humanities, 8% Social Sciences
Expenses: 2020-2021: $11,896 in state, $26,642 out of state; room/board: $11,106
Financial aid: (928) 523-4951; 62% of undergrads determined to have financial need; average aid package $13,228

Prescott College[1]
Prescott AZ
(877) 350-2100
U.S. News ranking: Reg. U. (W), second tier
Website: www.prescott.edu/
Admissions email: admissions@prescott.edu
Private; founded 1966
Application deadline (fall): 8/15
Undergraduate student body: N/A full time, N/A part time
Expenses: 2019-2020: $32,553; room/board: $9,520
Financial aid: (928) 350-1104

Southwest University of Visual Arts[1]
Tucson AZ
(520) 325-0123
U.S. News ranking: Arts, unranked
Website: www.suva.edu/
Admissions email: N/A
Private
Application deadline (fall): N/A
Undergraduate student body: N/A full time, N/A part time
Expenses: 2019-2020: $23,069; room/board: $12,660
Financial aid: N/A

University of Arizona
Tucson AZ
(520) 621-3237
U.S. News ranking: Nat. U., No. 97
Website: www.arizona.edu
Admissions email: admissions@arizona.edu
Public; founded 1885
Freshman admissions: more selective; 2019-2020: 40,854 applied, 34,558 accepted. Neither SAT nor ACT required. SAT 25/75 percentile: 1110-1360. High school rank: 36% in top tenth, 65% in top quarter, 88% in top half
Early decision deadline: N/A, notification date: N/A
Early action deadline: N/A, notification date: N/A
Application deadline (fall): 5/1
Undergraduate student body: 29,454 full time, 6,347 part time; 47% male, 53% female; 1% American Indian, 5% Asian, 4% Black, 27% Hispanic, 5% multiracial, 0% Pacific Islander, 49% white, 6% international; 67% from in state; 20% live on campus; 10% of students in fraternities, 20% in sororities
Most popular majors: 16% Business, Management, Marketing, and Related Support Services, 9% Biological and Biomedical Sciences, 8% Engineering, 8% Health Professions and Related Programs, 7% Social Sciences
Expenses: 2020-2021: $12,402 in state, $36,738 out of state; room/board: $13,050

Financial aid: (520) 621-1858; 51% of undergrads determined to have financial need; average aid package $14,300

University of Phoenix[1]
Phoenix AZ
(866) 766-0766
U.S. News ranking: Nat. U., second tier
Website: www.phoenix.edu
Admissions email: N/A
For-profit
Application deadline (fall): N/A
Undergraduate student body: N/A full time, N/A part time
Expenses: 2019-2020: $9,552; room/board: $5,250
Financial aid: N/A

ARKANSAS

Arkansas Baptist College
Little Rock AR
(501) 420-1234
U.S. News ranking: Reg. Coll. (S), second tier
Website: www.arkansasbaptist.edu
Admissions email: admissions@arkansasbaptist.edu
Private; founded 1884
Affiliation: Baptist
Freshman admissions: less selective; 2019-2020: 890 applied, 229 accepted. Neither SAT nor ACT required. SAT 25/75 percentile: N/A. High school rank: N/A
Early decision deadline: 5/1, notification date: 5/1
Early action deadline: 5/1, notification date: 5/1
Application deadline (fall): 8/3
Undergraduate student body: 460 full time, 71 part time; 77% male, 23% female; N/A American Indian, N/A Asian, N/A Black, N/A Hispanic, N/A multiracial, N/A Pacific Islander, N/A white, N/A international; 33% from in state; N/A live on campus; N/A of students in fraternities, N/A in sororities
Most popular majors: 15% Public Administration and Social Service Professions, 14% Business Administration, Management and Operations, 10% Urban Education and Leadership, 5% Corrections and Criminal Justice, Other, 2% Religion/Religious Studies
Expenses: 2020-2021: $20,882; room/board: $8,826
Financial aid: (501) 420-1222

Arkansas State University
State University AR
(870) 972-2782
U.S. News ranking: Nat. U., second tier
Website: www.astate.edu
Admissions email: admissions@astate.edu
Public; founded 1909
Freshman admissions: more selective; 2019-2020: 4,689 applied, 3,747 accepted. Neither SAT nor ACT required. ACT 25/75 percentile: 21-27. High school rank: 23% in top tenth, 57% in top quarter, 90% in top half

Early decision deadline: N/A, notification date: N/A
Early action deadline: N/A, notification date: N/A
Application deadline (fall): 8/22
Undergraduate student body: 6,439 full time, 2,489 part time; 40% male, 60% female; 0% American Indian, 1% Asian, 13% Black, 4% Hispanic, 2% multiracial, 0% Pacific Islander, 74% white, 5% international
Most popular majors: 12% Registered Nursing/Registered Nurse, 10% General Studies, 6% Business Administration and Management, General, 5% Early Childhood Education and Teaching, 4% Biology/Biological Sciences, General
Expenses: 2020-2021: $8,900 in state, $16,070 out of state; room/board: $10,022
Financial aid: (870) 972-2310; 67% of undergrads determined to have financial need; average aid package $12,941

Arkansas Tech University
Russellville AR
(479) 968-0343
U.S. News ranking: Reg. U. (S), No. 80
Website: www.atu.edu
Admissions email: tech.enroll@atu.edu
Public; founded 1909
Freshman admissions: selective; 2019-2020: 7,228 applied, 6,848 accepted. Either SAT or ACT required. ACT 25/75 percentile: 18-25. High school rank: 15% in top tenth, 36% in top quarter, 68% in top half
Early decision deadline: N/A, notification date: N/A
Early action deadline: N/A, notification date: N/A
Application deadline (fall): rolling
Undergraduate student body: 6,584 full time, 4,431 part time; 45% male, 55% female; 1% American Indian, 1% Asian, 8% Black, 8% Hispanic, 5% multiracial, 0% Pacific Islander, 74% white, 3% international; N/A from in state; 30% live on campus; 9% of students in fraternities, 7% in sororities
Most popular majors: 15% Health Professions and Related Programs, 14% Business, Management, Marketing, and Related Support Services, 12% Education, 10% Engineering, 10% Multi/Interdisciplinary Studies
Expenses: 2020-2021: $9,585 in state, $16,545 out of state; room/board: $8,754
Financial aid: (479) 968-0399; 69% of undergrads determined to have financial need; average aid package $10,702

Central Baptist College
Conway AR
(501) 329-6873
U.S. News ranking: Reg. Coll. (S), No. 63
Website: www.cbc.edu
Admissions email: admissions@cbc.edu

Private; founded 1952
Affiliation: Baptist
Freshman admissions: selective;
2019-2020: 519 applied, 292
accepted. Either SAT or ACT
required. ACT 25/75 percentile:
17-22. High school rank: N/A
Early decision deadline: N/A,
notification date: N/A
Early action deadline: N/A,
notification date: N/A
Application deadline (fall): 8/15
Undergraduate student body: 559
full time, 44 part time; 53%
male, 47% female; 2% American
Indian, 1% Asian, 17% Black,
4% Hispanic, 3% multiracial,
0% Pacific Islander, 68% white,
3% international; 62% from in
state; 28% live on campus; 0%
of students in fraternities, 0% in
sororities
Most popular majors: 19%
Business, Management,
Marketing, and Related Support
Services, Other, 11% Psychology,
General, 10% Kinesiology and
Exercise Science, 8% Bible/
Biblical Studies, 4% Human
Resources Management/Personnel
Administration, General
Expenses: 2020-2021: $17,100;
room/board: $7,500
Financial aid: (501) 205-8809;
80% of undergrads determined to
have financial need; average aid
package $13,851

Crowley's Ridge College[1]
Paragould AR
(870) 236-6901
U.S. News ranking: Reg. Coll. (S),
second tier
Admissions email: N/A
Private
Application deadline (fall): N/A
Undergraduate student body: N/A
full time, N/A part time
Expenses: 2019-2020: $14,500;
room/board: $6,350
Financial aid: N/A

Harding University
Searcy AR
(800) 477-4407
U.S. News ranking: Nat. U.,
No. 249
Website: www.harding.edu
Admissions email:
admissions@harding.edu
Private; founded 1924
Affiliation: Churches of Christ
Freshman admissions: more
selective; 2019-2020: 1,836
applied, 1,125 accepted. Either
SAT or ACT required. ACT 25/75
percentile: 21-29. High school
rank: 28% in top tenth, 53% in
top quarter, 80% in top half
Early decision deadline: N/A,
notification date: N/A
Early action deadline: N/A,
notification date: N/A
Application deadline (fall): rolling
Undergraduate student body: 3,533
full time, 246 part time; 45%
male, 55% female; 0% American
Indian, 1% Asian, 5% Black,
4% Hispanic, 3% multiracial,
0% Pacific Islander, 81% white,
6% international; 30% from in
state; 90% live on campus; 0%
of students in fraternities, 0% in
sororities

Most popular majors: 18%
Business, Management,
Marketing, and Related Support
Services, 14% Education, 12%
Health Professions and Related
Programs, 7% Liberal Arts and
Sciences, General Studies and
Humanities, 5% Computer and
Information Sciences and Support
Services
Expenses: 2020-2021: $21,540;
room/board: $7,438
Financial aid: (501) 279-4257;
58% of undergrads determined to
have financial need; average aid
package $13,594

Henderson State University[1]
Arkadelphia AR
(870) 230-5028
U.S. News ranking: Reg. U. (S),
No. 86
Website: www.hsu.edu/pages/
future-students/admissions/
Admissions email:
admissions@hsu.edu
Public; founded 1890
Application deadline (fall): rolling
Undergraduate student body: N/A
full time, N/A part time
Expenses: 2019-2020: $8,811 in
state, $10,521 out of state; room/
board: $8,440
Financial aid: (870) 230-5148

Hendrix College
Conway AR
(800) 277-9017
U.S. News ranking: Nat. Lib. Arts,
No. 93
Website: www.hendrix.edu
Admissions email:
adm@hendrix.edu
Private; founded 1876
Affiliation: United Methodist
Freshman admissions: more
selective; 2019-2020: 1,628
applied, 1,139 accepted. Neither
SAT nor ACT required. ACT 25/75
percentile: 25-31. High school
rank: 36% in top tenth, 74% in
top quarter, 93% in top half
Early decision deadline: N/A,
notification date: N/A
Early action deadline: 11/15,
notification date: 12/15
Application deadline (fall): 6/1
Undergraduate student body:
1,101 full time, 8 part time; 48%
male, 52% female; 0% American
Indian, 3% Asian, 7% Black,
7% Hispanic, 3% multiracial,
0% Pacific Islander, 61% white,
2% international
Most popular majors: Information
not available
Expenses: 2020-2021: $49,490;
room/board: $12,820
Financial aid: (501) 450-1368;
77% of undergrads determined to
have financial need; average aid
package $42,816

John Brown University
Siloam Springs AR
(479) 524-9500
U.S. News ranking: Reg. U. (S),
No. 12
Website: www.jbu.edu
Admissions email: jbuinfo@jbu.edu
Private; founded 1919
Affiliation: Interdenominational

Freshman admissions: more
selective; 2019-2020: 1,176
applied, 891 accepted. Neither
SAT nor ACT required. ACT 25/75
percentile: 23-29. High school
rank: 40% in top tenth, 70% in
top quarter, 91% in top half
Early decision deadline: N/A,
notification date: N/A
Early action deadline: N/A,
notification date: N/A
Application deadline (fall): rolling
Undergraduate student body: 1,262
full time, 346 part time; 43%
male, 57% female; 1% American
Indian, 1% Asian, 1% Black,
8% Hispanic, 5% multiracial,
0% Pacific Islander, 73% white,
8% international; N/A from in
state; 68% live on campus; 0%
of students in fraternities, 0% in
sororities
Most popular majors: 30%
Business, Management,
Marketing, and Related Support
Services, 10% Visual and
Performing Arts, 8% Psychology,
7% Education, 7% Family and
Consumer Sciences/Human
Sciences
Expenses: 2020-2021: $28,288;
room/board: $9,554
Financial aid: (479) 524-7427

Lyon College
Batesville AR
(800) 423-2542
U.S. News ranking: Nat. Lib. Arts,
No. 166
Website: www.lyon.edu
Admissions email:
admissions@lyon.edu
Private; founded 1872
Affiliation:
Presbyterian Church (USA)
Freshman admissions: more
selective; 2019-2020: 2,394
applied, 1,063 accepted. Either
SAT or ACT required. ACT 25/75
percentile: 21-26. High school
rank: 20% in top tenth, 49% in
top quarter, 79% in top half
Early decision deadline: N/A,
notification date: N/A
Early action deadline: 1/15,
notification date: 3/15
Application deadline (fall): rolling
Undergraduate student body: 645
full time, 17 part time; 56%
male, 44% female; 3% American
Indian, 5% Asian, 9% Black,
6% Hispanic, 0% multiracial,
0% Pacific Islander, 55% white,
1% international
Most popular majors: Information
not available
Expenses: 2020-2021: $29,415;
room/board: $10,330
Financial aid: (870) 307-7250;
77% of undergrads determined to
have financial need; average aid
package $23,670

Ouachita Baptist University
Arkadelphia AR
(870) 245-5110
U.S. News ranking: Reg. Coll. (S),
No. 2
Website: www.obu.edu
Admissions email:
admissions@obu.edu
Private; founded 1886
Affiliation: Southern Baptist

Freshman admissions: more
selective; 2019-2020: 2,538
applied, 1,559 accepted. Either
SAT or ACT required. ACT 25/75
percentile: 21-28. High school
rank: 32% in top tenth, 60% in
top quarter, 88% in top half
Early decision deadline: N/A,
notification date: N/A
Early action deadline: N/A,
notification date: N/A
Application deadline (fall): rolling
Undergraduate student body: 1,506
full time, 127 part time;
43% male, 57% female; 0%
American Indian, 1% Asian,
7% Black, 6% Hispanic, 3%
multiracial, 0% Pacific Islander,
80% white, 2% international;
62% from in state; 95% live
on campus; 14% of students in
fraternities, 33% in sororities
Most popular majors: 23%
Business, Management,
Marketing, and Related Support
Services, 10% Education, 9%
Biological and Biomedical
Sciences, 8% Theology and
Religious Vocations, 8% Visual
and Performing Arts
Expenses: 2020-2021: $29,120;
room/board: $8,000
Financial aid: (870) 245-5570;
64% of undergrads determined to
have financial need; average aid
package $29,837

Philander Smith College
Little Rock AR
(501) 370-5221
U.S. News ranking: Reg. Coll. (S),
No. 43
Website: www.philander.edu
Admissions email:
admissions@philander.edu
Private; founded 1877
Affiliation: United Methodist
Freshman admissions: less
selective; 2019-2020: 5,932
applied, 2,075 accepted. Either
SAT or ACT required. ACT 25/75
percentile: 15-21. High school
rank: 12% in top tenth, 29% in
top quarter, 58% in top half
Early decision deadline: N/A,
notification date: N/A
Early action deadline: N/A,
notification date: N/A
Application deadline (fall): rolling
Undergraduate student body: 951
full time, 45 part time; 36%
male, 64% female; 0% American
Indian, 0% Asian, 92% Black,
1% Hispanic, 2% multiracial, 0%
Pacific Islander, 0% white, 3%
international
Most popular majors: 36%
Business/Commerce, General,
11% Health and Physical
Education/Fitness, General,
11% Social Work, 9% Biology/
Biological Sciences, General, 9%
Psychology, General
Expenses: 2019-2020: $13,014;
room/board: $8,250
Financial aid: (501) 370-5380

Southern Arkansas University
Magnolia AR
(870) 235-4040
U.S. News ranking: Reg. U. (S),
No. 99
Website: www.saumag.edu

Admissions email:
muleriders@saumag.edu
Public; founded 1909
Freshman admissions: selective;
2019-2020: 3,870 applied,
2,518 accepted. Either SAT
or ACT required. ACT 25/75
percentile: 18-24. High school
rank: 14% in top tenth, 37% in
top quarter, 68% in top half
Early decision deadline: N/A,
notification date: N/A
Early action deadline: N/A,
notification date: N/A
Application deadline (fall): 8/27
Undergraduate student body: 3,003
full time, 582 part time; 44%
male, 56% female; 1% American
Indian, 1% Asian, 25% Black,
4% Hispanic, 0% multiracial,
0% Pacific Islander, 67% white,
2% international; 74% from in
state; 54% live on campus;
1% of students in fraternities,
1% in sororities
Most popular majors: 19%
Business, Management,
Marketing, and Related Support
Services, 11% Education, 10%
Liberal Arts and Sciences, General
Studies and Humanities, 8%
Health Professions and Related
Programs, 8% Psychology
Expenses: 2020-2021: $8,980 in
state, $14,020 out of state; room/
board: $6,624
Financial aid: (870) 235-4023

University of Arkansas
Fayetteville AR
(800) 377-8632
U.S. News ranking: Nat. U.,
No. 160
Website: www.uark.edu
Admissions email: uofa@uark.edu
Public; founded 1871
Freshman admissions: more
selective; 2019-2020: 17,913
applied, 13,809 accepted. Either
SAT or ACT required. ACT 25/75
percentile: 23-30. High school
rank: 25% in top tenth, 52% in
top quarter, 83% in top half
Early decision deadline: N/A,
notification date: N/A
Early action deadline: 11/1,
notification date: 12/15
Application deadline (fall): 8/1
Undergraduate student body:
20,559 full time, 2,466 part
time; 46% male, 54% female;
1% American Indian, 3% Asian,
4% Black, 9% Hispanic, 4%
multiracial, 0% Pacific Islander,
76% white, 3% international;
54% from in state; 25% live
on campus; 23% of students in
fraternities, 37% in sororities
Most popular majors: 28%
Business, Management,
Marketing, and Related Support
Services, 10% Engineering, 9%
Health Professions and Related
Programs, 6% Communication,
Journalism, and Related Programs,
6% Social Sciences
Expenses: 2020-2021: $9,384 in
state, $25,872 out of state; room/
board: $11,330
Financial aid: (479) 575-3806;
41% of undergrads determined to
have financial need; average aid
package $10,337

University of Arkansas at Little Rock

Little Rock AR
(501) 569-3127
U.S. News ranking: Nat. U., second tier
Website: www.ualr.edu/
Admissions email: admissions@ualr.edu
Public; founded 1927
Freshman admissions: selective; 2019-2020: 2,325 applied, 1,481 accepted. Either SAT or ACT required. ACT 25/75 percentile: 19-25. High school rank: N/A
Early decision deadline: N/A, notification date: N/A
Early action deadline: N/A, notification date: N/A
Application deadline (fall): 8/17
Undergraduate student body: 3,847 full time, 3,768 part time; 36% male, 64% female; 0% American Indian, 2% Asian, 27% Black, 4% Hispanic, 13% multiracial, 0% Pacific Islander, 50% white, 4% international
Most popular majors: 19% Health Professions and Related Programs, 14% Business, Management, Marketing, and Related Support Services, 8% Homeland Security, Law Enforcement, Firefighting and Related Protective Services, 6% Communication, Journalism, and Related Programs, 5% Biological and Biomedical Sciences
Expenses: 2019-2020: $9,544 in state, $21,754 out of state; room/board: $8,556
Financial aid: (501) 569-3035

University of Arkansas–Fort Smith[1]

Fort Smith AR
(479) 788-7120
U.S. News ranking: Reg. Coll. (S), No. 61
Website: www.uafortsmith.edu/Home/Index
Admissions email: N/A
Public; founded 1928
Application deadline (fall): rolling
Undergraduate student body: N/A full time, N/A part time
Expenses: 2019-2020: $5,754 in state, $13,026 out of state; room/board: $9,039
Financial aid: N/A

University of Arkansas–Monticello[1]

Monticello AR
(870) 367-6811
U.S. News ranking: Reg. U. (S), second tier
Website: www.uamont.edu
Admissions email: admissions@uamont.edu
Public
Application deadline (fall): N/A
Undergraduate student body: N/A full time, N/A part time
Expenses: 2019-2020: $7,909 in state, $13,759 out of state; room/board: $7,058
Financial aid: N/A

University of Arkansas–Pine Bluff

Pine Bluff AR
(870) 575-8492
U.S. News ranking: Reg. Coll. (S), No. 42
Website: www.uapb.edu/
Admissions email: owasoyop@uapb.edu
Public; founded 1873
Freshman admissions: less selective; 2019-2020: 5,136 applied, 2,257 accepted. Either SAT or ACT required. ACT 25/75 percentile: 16-20. High school rank: 13% in top tenth, 30% in top quarter, 60% in top half
Early decision deadline: N/A, notification date: N/A
Early action deadline: N/A, notification date: N/A
Application deadline (fall): rolling
Undergraduate student body: 2,161 full time, 221 part time; 41% male, 59% female; 0% American Indian, 0% Asian, 90% Black, 2% Hispanic, 2% multiracial, 0% Pacific Islander, 3% white, 1% international; 62% from in state; N/A live on campus; N/A of students in fraternities, N/A in sororities
Most popular majors: 11% Biology/Biological Sciences, General, 10% Business Administration and Management, General, 9% Criminal Justice/Safety Studies, 8% General Studies, 8% Industrial Technology/Technician
Expenses: 2019-2020: $8,248 in state, $14,908 out of state; room/board: $8,472
Financial aid: (870) 575-8302

University of Central Arkansas

Conway AR
(501) 450-3128
U.S. News ranking: Nat. U., second tier
Website: www.uca.edu
Admissions email: admissions@uca.edu
Public; founded 1907
Freshman admissions: selective; 2019-2020: 5,397 applied, 4,880 accepted. Either SAT or ACT required. ACT 25/75 percentile: 21-27. High school rank: 22% in top tenth, 50% in top quarter, 81% in top half
Early decision deadline: N/A, notification date: N/A
Early action deadline: N/A, notification date: N/A
Application deadline (fall): rolling
Undergraduate student body: 7,634 full time, 1,500 part time; 40% male, 60% female; 1% American Indian, 2% Asian, 16% Black, 6% Hispanic, 4% multiracial, 0% Pacific Islander, 66% white, 4% international; N/A from in state; 38% live on campus; 10% of students in fraternities, 15% in sororities
Most popular majors: 20% Business, Management, Marketing, and Related Support Services, 19% Health Professions and Related Programs, 7% Education, 7% Psychology, 6% Visual and Performing Arts

Expenses: 2020-2021: $9,338 in state, $16,148 out of state; room/board: $7,554
Financial aid: (501) 450-3140

University of the Ozarks

Clarksville AR
(479) 979-1227
U.S. News ranking: Reg. Coll. (S), No. 5
Website: www.ozarks.edu
Admissions email: admiss@ozarks.edu
Private; founded 1834
Affiliation: Presbyterian Church (USA)
Freshman admissions: less selective; 2019-2020: 1,009 applied, 923 accepted. Neither SAT nor ACT required. ACT 25/75 percentile: 18-23. High school rank: 3% in top tenth, 10% in top quarter, 35% in top half
Early decision deadline: N/A, notification date: N/A
Early action deadline: N/A, notification date: N/A
Application deadline (fall): rolling
Undergraduate student body: 813 full time, 11 part time; 50% male, 50% female; 1% American Indian, 1% Asian, 7% Black, 11% Hispanic, 4% multiracial, 0% Pacific Islander, 44% white, 26% international; 44% from in state; 65% live on campus; 0% of students in fraternities, 0% in sororities
Most popular majors: 15% Biology/Biological Sciences, General, 14% Public Health Education and Promotion, 7% General Studies, 7% Marketing/Marketing Management, General, 5% Political Science and Government, General
Expenses: 2020-2021: $25,950; room/board: $7,800
Financial aid: (479) 979-1201; 65% of undergrads determined to have financial need; average aid package $26,931

Williams Baptist University

Walnut Ridge AR
(800) 722-4434
U.S. News ranking: Nat. Lib. Arts, second tier
Website: williamsbu.edu/
Admissions email: admissions@williamsbu.edu
Private; founded 1941
Affiliation: Southern Baptist
Freshman admissions: selective; 2019-2020: 1,036 applied, 609 accepted. Either SAT or ACT required. ACT 25/75 percentile: 18-23. High school rank: 11% in top tenth, 30% in top quarter, 72% in top half
Early decision deadline: N/A, notification date: N/A
Early action deadline: N/A, notification date: N/A
Application deadline (fall): rolling
Undergraduate student body: 507 full time, 19 part time; 53% male, 47% female; 0% American Indian, 0% Asian, 13% Black, 4% Hispanic, 2% multiracial, 0% Pacific Islander, 73% white, 7% international

Most popular majors: 23% Liberal Arts and Sciences/Liberal Studies, 13% Business Administration and Management, General, 11% Psychology, General, 8% Physical Education Teaching and Coaching, 7% Bible/Biblical Studies
Expenses: 2020-2021: $18,500; room/board: $8,200
Financial aid: (870) 759-4112; 82% of undergrads determined to have financial need; average aid package $17,709

CALIFORNIA

Academy of Art University

San Francisco CA
(800) 544-2787
U.S. News ranking: Reg. U. (W), second tier
Website: www.academyart.edu/
Admissions email: admissions@academyart.edu
For-profit; founded 1929
Freshman admissions: least selective; 2019-2020: 2,396 applied, 2,396 accepted. Neither SAT nor ACT required. SAT 25/75 percentile: N/A. High school rank: N/A
Early decision deadline: N/A, notification date: N/A
Early action deadline: N/A, notification date: N/A
Application deadline (fall): rolling
Undergraduate student body: 3,758 full time, 2,936 part time; 43% male, 57% female; 0% American Indian, 5% Asian, 6% Black, 11% Hispanic, 3% multiracial, 1% Pacific Islander, 15% white, 26% international; 61% from in state; 14% live on campus; N/A of students in fraternities, N/A in sororities
Most popular majors: 38% Visual and Performing Arts, 21% Computer and Information Sciences and Support Services, 13% Communications Technologies/Technicians and Support Services, 13% Engineering Technologies and Engineering-Related Fields, 6% Family and Consumer Sciences/Human Sciences
Expenses: 2020-2021: $30,630; room/board: $18,386
Financial aid: (415) 618-6190; 45% of undergrads determined to have financial need; average aid package $14,188

Alliant International University[1]

San Diego CA
(858) 635-4772
U.S. News ranking: Nat. U., second tier
Website: www.alliant.edu
Admissions email: admissions@alliant.edu
For-profit; founded 1969
Application deadline (fall): rolling
Undergraduate student body: N/A full time, N/A part time
Expenses: 2019-2020: $18,510; room/board: N/A
Financial aid: (858) 635-4700

American Jewish University[1]

Bel-Air CA
(310) 440-1247
U.S. News ranking: Nat. Lib. Arts, unranked
Website: www.aju.edu
Admissions email: admissions@aju.edu
Private; founded 1947
Application deadline (fall): rolling
Undergraduate student body: N/A full time, N/A part time
Expenses: 2020-2021: $32,404; room/board: $14,764
Financial aid: (310) 476-9777

Antelope Valley College[1]

Lancaster CA
(661) 722-6300
U.S. News ranking: Reg. Coll. (W), unranked
Website: www.avc.edu
Admissions email: N/A
Public
Application deadline (fall): N/A
Undergraduate student body: N/A full time, N/A part time
Expenses: 2019-2020: $1,124 in state, $6,380 out of state; room/board: $10,000
Financial aid: N/A

ArtCenter College of Design

Pasadena CA
(626) 396-2373
U.S. News ranking: Arts, unranked
Website: www.artcenter.edu
Admissions email: admissions@artcenter.edu
Private; founded 1930
Freshman admissions: least selective; 2019-2020: N/A applied, N/A accepted. Neither SAT nor ACT required. SAT 25/75 percentile: N/A. High school rank: N/A
Early decision deadline: N/A, notification date: N/A
Early action deadline: N/A, notification date: N/A
Application deadline (fall): rolling
Undergraduate student body: 1,793 full time, 269 part time; 43% male, 57% female; 0% American Indian, 33% Asian, 1% Black, 10% Hispanic, 3% multiracial, 0% Pacific Islander, 12% white, 39% international
Most popular majors: 64% Visual and Performing Arts, 25% Engineering Technologies and Engineering-Related Fields, 4% Architecture and Related Services, 4% Communications Technologies/Technicians and Support Services, 3% Computer and Information Sciences and Support Services
Expenses: 2020-2021: $44,932; room/board: N/A
Financial aid: (626) 396-2215

Azusa Pacific University[1]

Azusa CA
(800) 825-5278
U.S. News ranking: Nat. U., No. 227
Website: www.apu.edu

Admissions email:
admissions@apu.edu
Private; founded 1899
Affiliation: Evangelical Christian
Application deadline (fall): 6/1
Undergraduate student body: N/A
full time, N/A part time
Expenses: 2019-2020: $38,880;
room/board: $10,076
Financial aid: (800) 825-5278

Bakersfield College[1]

Bakersfield CA
(661) 395-4011
U.S. News ranking: Reg. Coll. (W),
unranked
Website:
www.bakersfieldcollege.edu/
Admissions email: N/A
Public
Application deadline (fall): N/A
Undergraduate student body: N/A
full time, N/A part time
Expenses: 2019-2020: $1,325 in
state, $7,737 out of state; room/
board: $14,189
Financial aid: N/A

Biola University

La Mirada CA
(562) 903-4752
U.S. News ranking: Nat. U.,
No. 187
Website: www.biola.edu
Admissions email:
admissions@biola.edu
Private; founded 1908
Affiliation: Multiple Protestant
Denominations
Freshman admissions: more
selective; 2019-2020: 4,149
applied, 2,927 accepted. Either
SAT or ACT required. SAT 25/75
percentile: 1080-1310. High
school rank: 45% in top tenth,
69% in top quarter, 86% in
top half
Early decision deadline: 11/15,
notification date: 1/15
Early action deadline: 11/15,
notification date: 1/15
Application deadline (fall): rolling
Undergraduate student body: 3,772
full time, 271 part time; 37%
male, 63% female; N/A American
Indian, N/A Asian, N/A Black, N/A
Hispanic, N/A multiracial, N/A
Pacific Islander, N/A white, N/A
international
Most popular majors: Information
not available
Expenses: 2020-2021: $41,976;
room/board: $11,514
Financial aid: (562) 903-4742;
68% of undergrads determined to
have financial need; average aid
package $25,339

California Baptist University

Riverside CA
(877) 228-8866
U.S. News ranking: Reg. U. (W),
No. 40
Website: www.calbaptist.edu
Admissions email:
admissions@calbaptist.edu
Private; founded 1950
Affiliation: Southern Baptist
Freshman admissions: selective;
2019-2020: 8,241 applied,
6,451 accepted. Either SAT
or ACT required. SAT 25/75
percentile: 990-1210. High school

rank: 16% in top tenth, 40% in
top quarter, 77% in top half
Early decision deadline: N/A,
notification date: N/A
Early action deadline: 12/15,
notification date: 1/31
Application deadline (fall): rolling
Undergraduate student body: 7,333
full time, 857 part time; 38%
male, 62% female; 1% American
Indian, 6% Asian, 6% Black,
36% Hispanic, 6% multiracial,
1% Pacific Islander, 39% white,
2% international; 90% from in
state; 42% live on campus; N/A
of students in fraternities, N/A in
sororities
Most popular majors: 10%
Business/Commerce, General,
10% Registered Nursing/
Registered Nurse, 9% Psychology,
General, 7% Kinesiology and
Exercise Science, 6% Liberal Arts
and Sciences/Liberal Studies
Expenses: 2020-2021: $36,340;
room/board: $11,680
Financial aid: (951) 343-4235;
85% of undergrads determined to
have financial need; average aid
package $21,442

California College of the Arts[1]

San Francisco CA
(800) 447-1278
U.S. News ranking: Arts, unranked
Website: www.cca.edu
Admissions email: enroll@cca.edu
Private; founded 1907
Application deadline (fall): rolling
Undergraduate student body: 1,401
full time, 65 part time
Expenses: 2020-2021: $53,328;
room/board: $18,593
Financial aid: (415) 338-9538;
65% of undergrads determined to
have financial need; average aid
package $32,590

California Institute of Technology

Pasadena CA
(626) 395-6341
U.S. News ranking: Nat. U., No. 9
Website: www.caltech.edu
Admissions email:
ugadmissions@caltech.edu
Private; founded 1891
Freshman admissions: most
selective; 2019-2020: 8,367
applied, 537 accepted. Either
SAT or ACT required. SAT 25/75
percentile: 1530-1560. High
school rank: 99% in top tenth,
100% in top quarter, 100% in
top half
Early decision deadline: N/A,
notification date: N/A
Early action deadline: 11/1,
notification date: 12/15
Application deadline (fall): 1/3
Undergraduate student body:
938 full time, 0 part time; 55%
male, 45% female; 0% American
Indian, 37% Asian, 2% Black,
17% Hispanic, 9% multiracial,
0% Pacific Islander, 27% white,
8% international; 32% from in
state; 94% live on campus; 0%
of students in fraternities, 0% in
sororities

Most popular majors: 35%
Engineering, 27% Computer and
Information Sciences and Support
Services, 22% Physical Sciences,
10% Mathematics and Statistics,
5% Biological and Biomedical
Sciences
Expenses: 2020-2021: $56,862;
room/board: $17,337
Financial aid: (626) 395-6280;
50% of undergrads determined to
have financial need; average aid
package $53,090

California Institute of the Arts[1]

Valencia CA
(661) 255-1050
U.S. News ranking: Arts, unranked
Website: www.calarts.edu
Admissions email:
admissions@calarts.edu
Private; founded 1961
Application deadline (fall): N/A
Undergraduate student body: N/A
full time, N/A part time
Expenses: 2019-2020: $51,466;
room/board: $12,524
Financial aid: (661) 253-7869

California Lutheran University

Thousand Oaks CA
(877) 258-3678
U.S. News ranking: Reg. U. (W),
No. 10
Website: www.callutheran.edu
Admissions email:
admissions@callutheran.edu
Private; founded 1959
Affiliation:
Evangelical Lutheran Church
Freshman admissions: more
selective; 2019-2020: 6,175
applied, 4,406 accepted. Either
SAT or ACT required. SAT 25/75
percentile: 1070-1250. High
school rank: 33% in top tenth,
65% in top quarter, 94% in
top half
Early decision deadline: N/A,
notification date: N/A
Early action deadline: 11/1,
notification date: 1/15
Application deadline (fall): N/A
Undergraduate student body: 2,971
full time, 107 part time; 44%
male, 56% female; 0% American
Indian, 5% Asian, 4% Black,
37% Hispanic, 7% multiracial,
0% Pacific Islander, 41% white,
3% international; 11% from in
state; 53% live on campus; N/A
of students in fraternities, N/A in
sororities
Most popular majors: 24%
Business Administration and
Management, General, 13%
Psychology, General, 12% Speech
Communication and Rhetoric,
11% Criminology, 8% Biology/
Biological Sciences, General
Expenses: 2020-2021: $45,982;
room/board: $14,596
Financial aid: (805) 493-3139;
71% of undergrads determined to
have financial need; average aid
package $33,112

California Polytechnic State University– San Luis Obispo

San Luis Obispo CA
(805) 756-2311
U.S. News ranking: Reg. U. (W),
No. 3
Website: www.calpoly.edu/
Admissions email:
admissions@calpoly.edu
Public; founded 1901
Freshman admissions: more
selective; 2019-2020: 54,072
applied, 15,366 accepted. Either
SAT or ACT required. SAT 25/75
percentile: 1240-1440. High
school rank: 54% in top tenth,
85% in top quarter, 98% in
top half
Early decision deadline: N/A,
notification date: N/A
Early action deadline: N/A,
notification date: N/A
Application deadline (fall): 11/30
Undergraduate student body:
19,635 full time, 819 part time;
52% male, 48% female; 0%
American Indian, 14% Asian,
1% Black, 18% Hispanic, 8%
multiracial, 0% Pacific Islander,
54% white, 2% international;
N/A from in state; 35% live
on campus; 6% of students in
fraternities, 10% in sororities
Most popular majors: 27%
Engineering, 13% Business,
Management, Marketing, and
Related Support Services,
12% Agriculture, Agriculture
Operations, and Related Sciences,
6% Biological and Biomedical
Sciences, 5% Social Sciences
Expenses: 2020-2021: $9,948 in
state, $21,828 out of state; room/
board: $15,706
Financial aid: (805) 756-2927;
41% of undergrads determined to
have financial need; average aid
package $10,774

California State Polytechnic University–Pomona

Pomona CA
(909) 869-5299
U.S. News ranking: Reg. U. (W),
No. 10
Website: www.cpp.edu
Admissions email:
admissions@cpp.edu
Public; founded 1938
Freshman admissions: selective;
2019-2020: 39,726 applied,
21,687 accepted. Either SAT
or ACT required. SAT 25/75
percentile: 1010-1270. High
school rank: N/A
Early decision deadline: N/A,
notification date: N/A
Early action deadline: N/A,
notification date: N/A
Application deadline (fall): 11/30
Undergraduate student body:
23,592 full time, 2,857 part
time; 53% male, 47% female;
0% American Indian, 22% Asian,
3% Black, 47% Hispanic, 4%
multiracial, 0% Pacific Islander,
15% white, 6% international;
98% from in state; 10% live
on campus; 2% of students in
fraternities, 1% in sororities
Most popular majors: 25%
Business Administration and
Management, General,

6% Hospitality Administration/
Management, General, 4%
Civil Engineering, General,
4% Computer Science, 4%
Mechanical Engineering
Expenses: 2020-2021: $7,396 in
state, $19,276 out of state; room/
board: $15,791
Financial aid: (909) 869-3700;
68% of undergrads determined to
have financial need; average aid
package $10,938

California State University– Bakersfield

Bakersfield CA
(661) 654-3036
U.S. News ranking: Reg. U. (W),
No. 52
Website: www.csub.edu
Admissions email:
admissions@csub.edu
Public
Freshman admissions: less
selective; 2019-2020: 10,931
applied, 8,661 accepted. Neither
SAT nor ACT required. SAT 25/75
percentile: 880-1080. High
school rank: N/A
Early decision deadline: N/A,
notification date: N/A
Early action deadline: N/A,
notification date: N/A
Application deadline (fall): 3/1
Undergraduate student body: 8,386
full time, 1,410 part time;
38% male, 62% female; 0%
American Indian, 6% Asian,
5% Black, 60% Hispanic, 2%
multiracial, 0% Pacific Islander,
14% white, 4% international; N/A
from in state; 4% live on campus;
4% of students in fraternities, 3%
in sororities
Most popular majors: 20%
Business, Management,
Marketing, and Related Support
Services, 14% Liberal Arts and
Sciences, General Studies and
Humanities, 8% Psychology,
7% Homeland Security, Law
Enforcement, Firefighting and
Related Protective Services, 7%
Social Sciences
Expenses: 2020-2021: $10,832
in state, $1,760 out of state;
room/board: $12,900
Financial aid: (661) 654-3016;
85% of undergrads determined to
have financial need; average aid
package $11,343

California State University– Channel Islands[1]

Camarillo CA
(805) 437-8500
U.S. News ranking: Reg. U. (W),
No. 43
Website: www.csuci.edu
Admissions email: N/A
Public
Application deadline (fall): N/A
Undergraduate student body: N/A
full time, N/A part time
Expenses: 2019-2020: $6,802 in
state, $18,682 out of state; room/
board: $16,954
Financial aid: N/A

California State University–Chico

Chico CA
(530) 898-6322
U.S. News ranking: Reg. U. (W), No. 26
Website: www.csuchico.edu
Admissions email: info@csuchico.edu
Public; founded 1887
Freshman admissions: selective; 2019-2020: 25,908 applied, 18,740 accepted. Either SAT or ACT required. SAT 25/75 percentile: 990-1180. High school rank: N/A
Early decision deadline: N/A, notification date: N/A
Early action deadline: N/A, notification date: N/A
Application deadline (fall): 11/30
Undergraduate student body: 14,979 full time, 1,115 part time; 47% male, 53% female; 0% American Indian, 5% Asian, 3% Black, 35% Hispanic, 7% multiracial, 0% Pacific Islander, 44% white, 3% international; 0% from in state; 2% live on campus; 1% of students in fraternities, 1% in sororities
Most popular majors: 16% Business, Management, Marketing, and Related Support Services, 15% Computer and Information Sciences and Support Services, 7% Health Professions and Related Programs, 5% Communication, Journalism, and Related Programs, 5% Psychology
Expenses: 2020-2021: $7,814 in state, $19,694 out of state; room/board: $11,360
Financial aid: (530) 898-6451; 66% of undergrads determined to have financial need; average aid package $12,607

California State University–Dominguez Hills

Carson CA
(310) 243-3300
U.S. News ranking: Reg. U. (W), No. 58
Website: www.csudh.edu
Admissions email: info@csudh.edu
Public; founded 1960
Freshman admissions: less selective; 2019-2020: 20,351 applied, 16,066 accepted. Neither SAT nor ACT required. SAT 25/75 percentile: 850-1030. High school rank: N/A
Early decision deadline: N/A, notification date: N/A
Early action deadline: N/A, notification date: N/A
Application deadline (fall): rolling
Undergraduate student body: 12,094 full time, 3,221 part time; 38% male, 62% female; 0% American Indian, 7% Asian, 11% Black, 66% Hispanic, 3% multiracial, 0% Pacific Islander, 5% white, 5% international; 100% from in state; 4% live on campus; 1% of students in fraternities, 1% in sororities
Most popular majors: 18% Business, Management, Marketing, and Related Support Services, 12% Psychology, 11% Health Professions and Related Programs, 10% Social Sciences,

6% Communication, Journalism, and Related Programs
Expenses: 2020-2021: $8,140 in state, $17,644 out of state; room/board: $13,984
Financial aid: (310) 243-3189; 71% of undergrads determined to have financial need; average aid package $6,247

California State University–East Bay

Hayward CA
(510) 885-3500
U.S. News ranking: Reg. U. (W), No. 80
Website: www.csueastbay.edu
Admissions email: admissions@csueastbay.edu
Public; founded 1957
Freshman admissions: less selective; 2019-2020: 16,196 applied, 12,341 accepted. Neither SAT nor ACT required. SAT 25/75 percentile: 900-1100. High school rank: N/A
Early decision deadline: N/A, notification date: N/A
Early action deadline: N/A, notification date: N/A
Application deadline (fall): 11/30
Undergraduate student body: 10,397 full time, 2,210 part time; 40% male, 60% female; 0% American Indian, 23% Asian, 10% Black, 37% Hispanic, 5% multiracial, 1% Pacific Islander, 14% white, 5% international
Most popular majors: 21% Business Administration and Management, General, 16% Health Professions and Related Programs, 10% Psychology, General, 10% Social Sciences, 6% Family and Consumer Economics and Related Services, Other
Expenses: 2019-2020: $6,984 in state, $18,864 out of state; room/board: $14,558
Financial aid: (510) 885-2784

California State University–Fresno

Fresno CA
(559) 278-2191
U.S. News ranking: Nat. U., No. 196
Website: www.csufresno.edu
Admissions email: lyager@csufresno.edu
Public; founded 1911
Freshman admissions: selective; 2019-2020: 18,122 applied, 10,500 accepted. Either SAT or ACT required. SAT 25/75 percentile: 940-1130. High school rank: 15% in top tenth, 80% in top quarter, 100% in top half
Early decision deadline: N/A, notification date: N/A
Early action deadline: N/A, notification date: N/A
Application deadline (fall): 11/30
Undergraduate student body: 18,838 full time, 2,624 part time; 41% male, 59% female; 0% American Indian, 13% Asian, 3% Black, 55% Hispanic, 3% multiracial, 0% Pacific Islander, 18% white, 5% international; N/A from in state; 5% live on campus; 3% of students in fraternities, 3% in sororities

Most popular majors: 14% Business, Management, Marketing, and Related Support Services, 9% Health Professions and Related Programs, 9% Liberal Arts and Sciences, General Studies and Humanities, 8% Homeland Security, Law Enforcement, Firefighting and Related Protective Services, 8% Psychology
Expenses: 2020-2021: $6,643 in state, $12,781 out of state; room/board: $10,904
Financial aid: (559) 278-2182; 76% of undergrads determined to have financial need; average aid package $9,982

California State University–Fullerton

Fullerton CA
(657) 278-7788
U.S. News ranking: Reg. U. (W), No. 16
Website: www.fullerton.edu
Admissions email: admissions@fullerton.edu
Public; founded 1957
Freshman admissions: selective; 2019-2020: 50,105 applied, 26,398 accepted. Either SAT or ACT required. SAT 25/75 percentile: 1030-1200. High school rank: 22% in top tenth, 63% in top quarter, 93% in top half
Early decision deadline: N/A, notification date: N/A
Early action deadline: N/A, notification date: N/A
Application deadline (fall): 11/30
Undergraduate student body: 28,769 full time, 6,400 part time; 43% male, 57% female; 0% American Indian, 21% Asian, 2% Black, 46% Hispanic, 4% multiracial, 0% Pacific Islander, 18% white, 6% international; N/A from in state; 2% live on campus; 1% of students in fraternities, 2% in sororities
Most popular majors: 25% Business, Management, Marketing, and Related Support Services, 11% Communication, Journalism, and Related Programs, 10% Health Professions and Related Programs, 7% Psychology, 6% Social Sciences
Expenses: 2020-2021: $6,952 in state, $16,456 out of state; room/board: $16,296
Financial aid: (657) 278-5256; 70% of undergrads determined to have financial need; average aid package $10,485

California State University–Long Beach

Long Beach CA
(562) 985-5471
U.S. News ranking: Reg. U. (W), No. 14
Website: www.csulb.edu
Admissions email: eslb@csulb.edu
Public; founded 1949
Freshman admissions: selective; 2019-2020: 71,297 applied, 28,019 accepted. Either SAT or ACT required. SAT 25/75 percentile: 1040-1250. High school rank: N/A

Early decision deadline: N/A, notification date: N/A
Early action deadline: N/A, notification date: N/A
Application deadline (fall): rolling
Undergraduate student body: 28,584 full time, 4,200 part time; 43% male, 57% female; 0% American Indian, 21% Asian, 4% Black, 45% Hispanic, 5% multiracial, 0% Pacific Islander, 17% white, 5% international; N/A from in state; 8% live on campus; N/A of students in fraternities, N/A in sororities
Most popular majors: 18% Business, Management, Marketing, and Related Support Services, 10% Visual and Performing Arts, 8% Family and Consumer Sciences/Human Sciences, 8% Health Professions and Related Programs, 8% Social Sciences
Expenses: 2020-2021: $6,846 in state, $17,142 out of state; room/board: $13,070
Financial aid: (562) 985-8403; 78% of undergrads determined to have financial need; average aid package $14,185

California State University–Los Angeles

Los Angeles CA
(323) 343-3901
U.S. News ranking: Reg. U. (W), No. 26
Website: www.calstatela.edu
Admissions email: admission@calstatela.edu
Public; founded 1947
Freshman admissions: less selective; 2019-2020: 33,641 applied, 16,084 accepted. Either SAT or ACT required. SAT 25/75 percentile: 890-1080. High school rank: N/A
Early decision deadline: N/A, notification date: N/A
Early action deadline: N/A, notification date: N/A
Application deadline (fall): 12/15
Undergraduate student body: 19,609 full time, 3,017 part time; 42% male, 58% female; 0% American Indian, 12% Asian, 3% Black, 70% Hispanic, 1% multiracial, 0% Pacific Islander, 5% white, 6% international; N/A from in state; 4% live on campus; 1% of students in fraternities, 1% in sororities
Most popular majors: 19% Business, Management, Marketing, and Related Support Services, 11% Health Professions and Related Programs, 10% Social Sciences, 6% Engineering, 6% Homeland Security, Law Enforcement, Firefighting and Related Protective Services
Expenses: 2020-2021: $6,768 in state, $18,648 out of state; room/board: $16,932
Financial aid: (323) 343-6260; 89% of undergrads determined to have financial need; average aid package $12,384

California State University–Maritime Academy

Vallejo CA
(707) 654-1330
U.S. News ranking: Regl. Coll. (W), No. 2
Website: www.csum.edu
Admissions email: admission@csum.edu
Public; founded 1929
Freshman admissions: selective; 2019-2020: 1,418 applied, 1,084 accepted. Either SAT or ACT required. SAT 25/75 percentile: 1068-1263. High school rank: N/A
Early decision deadline: N/A, notification date: N/A
Early action deadline: 10/31, notification date: 12/15
Application deadline (fall): 11/30
Undergraduate student body: 888 full time, 23 part time; 83% male, 17% female; 1% American Indian, 10% Asian, 3% Black, 22% Hispanic, 11% multiracial, 2% Pacific Islander, 45% white, 1% international; N/A from in state; 77% live on campus; N/A of students in fraternities, N/A in sororities
Most popular majors: 29% Transportation and Materials Moving, 22% Engineering Technologies and Engineering-Related Fields, 20% Business, Management, Marketing, and Related Support Services, 16% Engineering, 13% Multi/Interdisciplinary Studies
Expenses: 2020-2021: $18,643 in state, $18,643 out of state; room/board: $12,828
Financial aid: N/A; 51% of undergrads determined to have financial need; average aid package $12,576

California State University–Monterey Bay

Seaside CA
(831) 582-3783
U.S. News ranking: Reg. U. (W), No. 25
Website: www.csumb.edu
Admissions email: admissions@csumb.edu
Public; founded 1994
Freshman admissions: selective; 2019-2020: 12,327 applied, 9,280 accepted. Either SAT or ACT required. SAT 25/75 percentile: 960-1170. High school rank: 12% in top tenth, 44% in top quarter, 86% in top half
Early decision deadline: N/A, notification date: N/A
Early action deadline: N/A, notification date: N/A
Application deadline (fall): 11/30
Undergraduate student body: 6,052 full time, 742 part time; 39% male, 61% female; 1% American Indian, 6% Asian, 4% Black, 42% Hispanic, 8% multiracial, 1% Pacific Islander, 27% white, 6% international; N/A from in state; N/A live on campus; 3% of students in fraternities, 2% in sororities

Most popular majors: 15% Business, Management, Marketing, and Related Support Services, 12% Liberal Arts and Sciences, General Studies and Humanities, 12% Psychology, 9% Computer and Information Sciences and Support Services, 9% Parks, Recreation, Leisure, and Fitness Studies
Expenses: 2020-2021: $7,143 in state, $19,023 out of state; room/board: N/A
Financial aid: N/A; 69% of undergrads determined to have financial need; average aid package $11,365

California State University–Northridge
Northridge CA
(818) 677-3700
U.S. News ranking: Reg. U. (W), No. 40
Website: www.csun.edu
Admissions email: admissions.records@csun.edu
Public; founded 1958
Freshman admissions: selective; 2019-2020: 58,001 applied, 33,245 accepted. Either SAT or ACT required. SAT 25/75 percentile: 910-1130. High school rank: N/A
Early decision deadline: N/A, notification date: N/A
Early action deadline: N/A, notification date: N/A
Application deadline (fall): 11/30
Undergraduate student body: 29,275 full time, 5,358 part time; 45% male, 55% female; 0% American Indian, 9% Asian, 5% Black, 52% Hispanic, 3% multiracial, 0% Pacific Islander, 20% white, 7% international; 96% from in state; 9% live on campus; N/A of students in fraternities, N/A in sororities
Most popular majors: 17% Business, Management, Marketing, and Related Support Services, 11% Education, 9% Social Sciences, 8% Communication, Journalism, and Related Programs, 8% Psychology
Expenses: 2020-2021: $6,992 in state, $18,872 out of state; room/board: $11,662
Financial aid: (818) 677-4085; 82% of undergrads determined to have financial need; average aid package $11,686

California State University–Sacramento
Sacramento CA
(916) 278-1000
U.S. News ranking: Reg. U. (W), No. 43
Website: www.csus.edu
Admissions email: admissions@csus.edu
Public; founded 1947
Freshman admissions: selective; 2019-2020: 27,576 applied, 22,685 accepted. Neither SAT nor ACT required. SAT 25/75 percentile: 940-1140. High school rank: N/A
Early decision deadline: N/A, notification date: N/A

Early action deadline: N/A, notification date: 12/1
Application deadline (fall): 11/30
Undergraduate student body: 23,907 full time, 4,344 part time; 45% male, 55% female; 0% American Indian, 20% Asian, 6% Black, 35% Hispanic, 6% multiracial, 1% Pacific Islander, 25% white, 3% international; 99% from in state; 7% live on campus; N/A of students in fraternities, N/A in sororities
Most popular majors: 13% Business, Management, Marketing, and Related Support Services, 10% Family and Consumer Sciences/Human Sciences, 10% Social Sciences, 9% Communication, Journalism, and Related Programs, 8% Health Professions and Related Programs
Expenses: 2020-2021: $7,418 in state, $11,180 out of state; room/board: $15,202
Financial aid: (916) 278-1000; 87% of undergrads determined to have financial need; average aid package $11,216

California State University–San Bernardino
San Bernardino CA
(909) 537-5188
U.S. News ranking: Reg. U. (W), No. 40
Website: www.csusb.edu
Admissions email: moreinfo@csusb.edu
Public; founded 1962
Freshman admissions: less selective; 2019-2020: 16,307 applied, 11,180 accepted. Neither SAT nor ACT required. SAT 25/75 percentile: 910-1090. High school rank: N/A
Early decision deadline: N/A, notification date: N/A
Early action deadline: N/A, notification date: 5/1
Application deadline (fall): rolling
Undergraduate student body: 16,432 full time, 1,682 part time; 39% male, 61% female; 0% American Indian, 5% Asian, 5% Black, 66% Hispanic, 2% multiracial, 0% Pacific Islander, 11% white, 7% international; N/A from in state; 6% live on campus; 3% of students in fraternities, 3% in sororities
Most popular majors: 25% Business, Management, Marketing, and Related Support Services, 14% Psychology, 10% Social Sciences, 7% Health Professions and Related Programs, 6% Homeland Security, Law Enforcement, Firefighting and Related Protective Services
Expenses: 2020-2021: $6,956 in state, $13,094 out of state; room/board: $12,142
Financial aid: (909) 537-5227; 85% of undergrads determined to have financial need; average aid package $9,640

California State University–San Marcos
San Marcos CA
(760) 750-4848
U.S. News ranking: Reg. U. (W), No. 60
Website: www.csusm.edu/admissions/
Admissions email: apply@csusm.edu
Public; founded 1989
Freshman admissions: selective; 2019-2020: 17,343 applied, 10,696 accepted. Either SAT or ACT required. SAT 25/75 percentile: 930-1130. High school rank: N/A
Early decision deadline: N/A, notification date: N/A
Early action deadline: N/A, notification date: N/A
Application deadline (fall): 11/30
Undergraduate student body: 11,445 full time, 2,434 part time; 40% male, 60% female; 0% American Indian, 9% Asian, 3% Black, 48% Hispanic, 5% multiracial, 0% Pacific Islander, 26% white, 4% international
Most popular majors: 19% Health Professions and Related Programs, 16% Social Sciences, 13% Business, Management, Marketing, and Related Support Services, 8% Family and Consumer Sciences/Human Sciences, 7% Psychology
Expenses: 2020-2021: $7,712 in state, $17,216 out of state; room/board: $13,150
Financial aid: (760) 750-4881; 73% of undergrads determined to have financial need; average aid package $11,056

California State University–Stanislaus
Turlock CA
(209) 667-3070
U.S. News ranking: Reg. U. (W), No. 29
Website: www.csustan.edu
Admissions email: Outreach_Help_Desk@csustan.edu
Public; founded 1957
Freshman admissions: less selective; 2019-2020: 8,764 applied, 7,825 accepted. Neither SAT nor ACT required. SAT 25/75 percentile: 890-1070. High school rank: N/A
Early decision deadline: N/A, notification date: N/A
Early action deadline: N/A, notification date: N/A
Application deadline (fall): 11/30
Undergraduate student body: 8,262 full time, 1,461 part time; 35% male, 65% female; 0% American Indian, 9% Asian, 2% Black, 56% Hispanic, 3% multiracial, 0% Pacific Islander, 20% white, 4% international; 100% from in state; 7% live on campus; 1% of students in fraternities, 3% in sororities
Most popular majors: 19% Business Administration and Management, General, 14% Psychology, General, 12% Sociology, 9% Criminal Justice/Safety Studies, 8% Liberal Arts and Sciences/Liberal Studies

Expenses: 2020-2021: $7,584 in state, $21,306 out of state; room/board: $10,950
Financial aid: (209) 667-3337; 82% of undergrads determined to have financial need; average aid package $17,184

Chapman University
Orange CA
(888) 282-7759
U.S. News ranking: Nat. U., No. 124
Website: www.chapman.edu
Admissions email: admit@chapman.edu
Private; founded 1861
Affiliation: Christian Church (Disciples of Christ)
Freshman admissions: more selective; 2019-2020: 14,273 applied, 7,943 accepted. Neither SAT nor ACT required. SAT 25/75 percentile: 1190-1380. High school rank: 36% in top tenth, 75% in top quarter, 94% in top half
Early decision deadline: 11/1, notification date: 12/20
Early action deadline: 11/1, notification date: 12/20
Application deadline (fall): 1/15
Undergraduate student body: 7,046 full time, 456 part time; 40% male, 60% female; 0% American Indian, 14% Asian, 2% Black, 16% Hispanic, 8% multiracial, 0% Pacific Islander, 52% white, 4% international; 67% from in state; 47% live on campus; 30% of students in fraternities, 36% in sororities
Most popular majors: 25% Business Administration and Management, General, 11% Cinematography and Film/Video Production, 6% Psychology, General, 5% Business/Corporate Communications, 5% Political Science and Government, General
Expenses: 2019-2020: $54,924; room/board: $17,818
Financial aid: (714) 997-6741

Claremont McKenna College
Claremont CA
(909) 621-8088
U.S. News ranking: Nat. Lib. Arts, No. 6
Website: www.claremontmckenna.edu
Admissions email: admission@cmc.edu
Private; founded 1946
Freshman admissions: most selective; 2019-2020: 6,066 applied, 625 accepted. Either SAT or ACT required. SAT 25/75 percentile: 1360-1510. High school rank: 83% in top tenth, 100% in top quarter, 100% in top half
Early decision deadline: 11/1, notification date: 12/15
Early action deadline: N/A, notification date: N/A
Application deadline (fall): 1/5
Undergraduate student body: 1,340 full time, 3 part time; 51% male, 49% female; 0% American Indian, 12% Asian, 4% Black, 15% Hispanic, 7% multiracial, 0% Pacific Islander, 41% white, 16% international; 38% from in

state; 96% live on campus; N/A of students in fraternities, N/A in sororities
Most popular majors: 33% Econometrics and Quantitative Economics, 12% Political Science and Government, General, 11% Experimental Psychology, 10% International Relations and Affairs, 8% Accounting
Expenses: 2020-2021: $56,475; room/board: $17,300
Financial aid: (909) 621-8356; 42% of undergrads determined to have financial need; average aid package $57,151

Cogswell University of Silicon Valley
San Jose CA
(408) 498-5160
U.S. News ranking: Reg. Coll. (W), unranked
Website: www. cogswell.edu
Admissions email: admissions@cogswell.edu
For-profit; founded 1887
Freshman admissions: selective; 2019-2020: 167 applied, 57 accepted. Neither SAT nor ACT required. SAT 25/75 percentile: 1000-1220. High school rank: N/A
Early decision deadline: N/A, notification date: N/A
Early action deadline: 12/1, notification date: 12/1
Application deadline (fall): rolling
Undergraduate student body: 424 full time, 118 part time; 68% male, 32% female; 1% American Indian, 22% Asian, 8% Black, 22% Hispanic, 5% multiracial, 0% Pacific Islander, 28% white, 2% international; 92% from in state; 30% live on campus; 0% of students in fraternities, 0% in sororities
Most popular majors: 41% Animation, Interactive Technology, Video Graphics and Special Effects, 21% Modeling, Virtual Environments and Simulation, 13% Music Performance, General, 11% Game and Interactive Media Design, 9% Computer Programming/Programmer, General
Expenses: 2020-2021: $26,980; room/board: $12,790
Financial aid: (408) 498-5145; 69% of undergrads determined to have financial need; average aid package $10,492

Columbia College Hollywood[1]
Tarzana CA
(818) 345-8414
U.S. News ranking: Arts, unranked
Website: flashpoint.columbiacollege.edu/
Admissions email: admissions@columbiacollege.edu
Private; founded 1953
Application deadline (fall): rolling
Undergraduate student body: N/A full time, N/A part time
Expenses: 2019-2020: $24,495; room/board: N/A
Financial aid: (818) 345-8414

Concordia University

Irvine CA
(949) 214-3010
U.S. News ranking: Reg. U. (W), No. 49
Website: www.cui.edu
Admissions email: admission@cui.edu
Private; founded 1972
Affiliation: Lutheran Church–Missouri Synod
Freshman admissions: selective; 2019-2020: 3,727 applied, 2,639 accepted. Either SAT or ACT required. SAT 25/75 percentile: 990-1210. High school rank: 15% in top tenth, 44% in top quarter, 77% in top half
Early decision deadline: N/A, notification date: N/A
Early action deadline: 12/1, notification date: 12/15
Application deadline (fall): 8/1
Undergraduate student body: 1,594 full time, 144 part time; 39% male, 61% female; 0% American Indian, 10% Asian, 4% Black, 25% Hispanic, 7% multiracial, 0% Pacific Islander, 48% white, 5% international; 79% from in state; 45% live on campus; N/A of students in fraternities, N/A in sororities
Most popular majors: 27% Health Professions and Related Programs, 18% Business, Management, Marketing, and Related Support Services, 8% Liberal Arts and Sciences, General Studies and Humanities, 8% Psychology, 7% Multi/Interdisciplinary Studies
Expenses: 2020-2021: $38,000; room/board: $12,270
Financial aid: (949) 214-3066; 69% of undergrads determined to have financial need; average aid package $24,613

Cypress College[1]

Cypress CA
(714) 484-7000
U.S. News ranking: Reg. Coll. (W), unranked
Website: www.cypresscollege.edu
Admissions email: N/A
Public
Application deadline (fall): N/A
Undergraduate student body: N/A full time, N/A part time
Expenses: 2019-2020: $1,142 in state, $6,878 out of state; room/board: $17,374
Financial aid: N/A

Design Institute of San Diego[1]

San Diego CA
(858) 566-1200
U.S. News ranking: Arts, unranked
Website: www.disd.edu
Admissions email: admissions@disd.edu
For-profit; founded 1977
Application deadline (fall): N/A
Undergraduate student body: N/A full time, N/A part time
Expenses: 2019-2020: $23,999; room/board: $0
Financial aid: (858) 566-1200

Dominican University of California

San Rafael CA
(415) 485-3204
U.S. News ranking: Reg. U. (W), No. 24
Website: www.dominican.edu
Admissions email: enroll@dominican.edu
Private; founded 1890
Freshman admissions: selective; 2019-2020: 2,041 applied, 1,857 accepted. Neither SAT nor ACT required. SAT 25/75 percentile: 1030-1220. High school rank: 21% in top tenth, 54% in top quarter, 84% in top half
Early decision deadline: N/A, notification date: N/A
Early action deadline: N/A, notification date: N/A
Application deadline (fall): rolling
Undergraduate student body: 1,241 full time, 220 part time; 31% male, 69% female; 0% American Indian, 27% Asian, 5% Black, 26% Hispanic, 6% multiracial, 0% Pacific Islander, 29% white, 1% international; N/A from in state; 35% live on campus; 0% of students in fraternities, 0% in sororities
Most popular majors: 46% Health Professions and Related Programs, 15% Business, Management, Marketing, and Related Support Services, 9% Biological and Biomedical Sciences, 7% Communications Technologies/Technicians and Support Services, 6% Psychology
Expenses: 2020-2021: $47,910; room/board: $15,634
Financial aid: (415) 257-1350; 74% of undergrads determined to have financial need; average aid package $33,948

Fashion Institute of Design & Merchandising

Los Angeles CA
(800) 624-1200
U.S. News ranking: Arts, unranked
Website: fidm.edu/
Admissions email: admissions@fidm.edu
For-profit; founded 1969
Freshman admissions: least selective; 2019-2020: 2,014 applied, 737 accepted. Neither SAT nor ACT required. SAT 25/75 percentile: N/A. High school rank: N/A
Early decision deadline: N/A, notification date: N/A
Early action deadline: N/A, notification date: N/A
Application deadline (fall): rolling
Undergraduate student body: 2,147 full time, 236 part time; 17% male, 83% female; 1% American Indian, 11% Asian, 7% Black, 22% Hispanic, 1% multiracial, 1% Pacific Islander, 32% white, 19% international; 50% from in state; 0% live on campus; 0% of students in fraternities, 0% in sororities
Most popular majors: 29% Fashion Merchandising, 16% Business, Management, Marketing, and Related Support Services, Other, 15% Fashion/Apparel Design, 13% Design and Visual Communications, General
Expenses: 2020-2021: $31,870; room/board: N/A
Financial aid: (213) 624-1200

Feather River Community College District

Quincy CA
(530) 283-0202
U.S. News ranking: Reg. Coll. (W), unranked
Website: www.frc.edu
Admissions email: N/A
Public
Freshman admissions: least selective; 2019-2020: 304 applied, 304 accepted. Neither SAT nor ACT required. SAT 25/75 percentile: N/A. High school rank: N/A
Early decision deadline: N/A, notification date: N/A
Early action deadline: N/A, notification date: N/A
Application deadline (fall): N/A
Undergraduate student body: 460 full time, 1,530 part time; 48% male, 52% female; N/A American Indian, N/A Asian, N/A Black, N/A Hispanic, N/A multiracial, N/A Pacific Islander, N/A white, N/A international; N/A from in state; 20% live on campus; N/A of students in fraternities, N/A in sororities
Most popular majors: Information not available
Expenses: 2019-2020: $1,461 in state, $9,441 out of state; room/board: $10,129
Financial aid: N/A

Foothill College[1]

Los Altos Hills CA
(650) 949-7777
U.S. News ranking: Reg. Coll. (W), unranked
Website: www.foothill.edu
Admissions email: N/A
Public
Application deadline (fall): N/A
Undergraduate student body: N/A full time, N/A part time
Expenses: 2019-2020: $1,563 in state, $9,528 out of state; room/board: $15,804
Financial aid: N/A

Fresno Pacific University

Fresno CA
(559) 453-2039
U.S. News ranking: Reg. U. (W), No. 37
Website: www.fresno.edu
Admissions email: ugadmis@fresno.edu
Private; founded 1944
Affiliation: Mennonite Brethren Church
Freshman admissions: less selective; 2019-2020: 981 applied, 642 accepted. Either SAT or ACT required. SAT 25/75 percentile: 870-980. High school rank: 24% in top tenth, 55% in top quarter, 91% in top half
Early decision deadline: N/A, notification date: N/A
Early action deadline: N/A, notification date: N/A

Application deadline (fall): 7/31
Undergraduate student body: 2,438 full time, 468 part time; 26% male, 74% female; 1% American Indian, 4% Asian, 5% Black, 56% Hispanic, 0% multiracial, 0% Pacific Islander, 26% white, 2% international; 98% from in state; 12% live on campus; 0% of students in fraternities, 0% in sororities
Most popular majors: 28% Liberal Arts and Sciences, General Studies and Humanities, 20% Business, Management, Marketing, and Related Support Services, 15% Family and Consumer Sciences/Human Sciences, 12% Public Administration and Social Service Professions, 6% Health Professions and Related Programs
Expenses: 2020-2021: $32,977; room/board: $8,954
Financial aid: (559) 453-7195; 88% of undergrads determined to have financial need; average aid package $14,472

Harvey Mudd College

Claremont CA
(909) 621-8011
U.S. News ranking: Nat. Lib. Arts, No. 25
Website: www.hmc.edu
Admissions email: admission@hmc.edu
Private; founded 1955
Freshman admissions: most selective; 2019-2020: 4,045 applied, 553 accepted. Either SAT or ACT required. SAT 25/75 percentile: 1490-1570. High school rank: N/A
Early decision deadline: 11/5, notification date: 12/15
Early action deadline: N/A, notification date: N/A
Application deadline (fall): 1/5
Undergraduate student body: 894 full time, 1 part time; 50% male, 50% female; 0% American Indian, 20% Asian, 4% Black, 20% Hispanic, 11% multiracial, 1% Pacific Islander, 31% white, 8% international; 54% from in state; 98% live on campus; 0% of students in fraternities, 0% in sororities
Most popular majors: 39% Engineering, 22% Multi/Interdisciplinary Studies, 20% Computer and Information Sciences and Support Services, 11% Physical Sciences, 4% Mathematics and Statistics
Expenses: 2020-2021: $58,660; room/board: $18,679
Financial aid: (909) 621-8055; 48% of undergrads determined to have financial need; average aid package $47,348

Holy Names University

Oakland CA
(510) 436-1351
U.S. News ranking: Reg. U. (W), No. 64
Website: www.hnu.edu
Admissions email: admissions@hnu.edu
Private; founded 1868
Affiliation: Roman Catholic
Freshman admissions: least selective; 2019-2020: 2,441

applied, 1,544 accepted. Either SAT or ACT required. SAT 25/75 percentile: 720-880. High school rank: 7% in top tenth, 19% in top quarter, 39% in top half
Early decision deadline: N/A, notification date: N/A
Early action deadline: N/A, notification date: N/A
Application deadline (fall): rolling
Undergraduate student body: 589 full time, 40 part time; 36% male, 64% female; 0% American Indian, 11% Asian, 16% Black, 41% Hispanic, 5% multiracial, 1% Pacific Islander, 14% white, 3% international
Most popular majors: Information not available
Expenses: 2020-2021: $40,904; room/board: $13,994
Financial aid: (510) 436-1089; 89% of undergrads determined to have financial need; average aid package $37,762

Hope International University

Fullerton CA
(888) 352-4673
U.S. News ranking: Reg. U. (W), No. 84
Website: www.hiu.edu
Admissions email: admissions@hiu.edu
Private; founded 1928
Affiliation: Christian Churches and Churches of Christ
Freshman admissions: selective; 2019-2020: 685 applied, 252 accepted. Either SAT or ACT required. SAT 25/75 percentile: 910-1070. High school rank: 5% in top tenth, 27% in top quarter, 72% in top half
Early decision deadline: N/A, notification date: N/A
Early action deadline: N/A, notification date: N/A
Application deadline (fall): rolling
Undergraduate student body: 538 full time, 113 part time; 45% male, 55% female; 1% American Indian, 5% Asian, 8% Black, 29% Hispanic, 12% multiracial, 2% Pacific Islander, 36% white, 0% international; 82% from in state; 48% live on campus; N/A of students in fraternities, N/A in sororities
Most popular majors: 32% Business Administration and Management, General, 14% Education, General, 14% Psychology, General, 12% Human Development and Family Studies, General, 12% Theological and Ministerial Studies, Other
Expenses: 2020-2021: $34,450; room/board: $11,050
Financial aid: (714) 879-3901; 71% of undergrads determined to have financial need; average aid package $23,008

Hult International Business School

Cambridge CA
(617) 746-1990
U.S. News ranking: Business, unranked
Website: www.hult.edu
Admissions email: undergraduate.info@hult.edu

Private; founded 1964
Freshman admissions: least selective; 2019-2020: 3,856 applied, 1,455 accepted. Neither SAT nor ACT required. SAT 25/75 percentile: N/A. High school rank: N/A
Early decision deadline: 11/1, notification date: 12/15
Early action deadline: N/A, notification date: N/A
Application deadline (fall): rolling
Undergraduate student body: 1,636 full time, 0 part time; 62% male, 38% female; 0% American Indian, 1% Asian, 1% Black, 1% Hispanic, 0% multiracial, 0% Pacific Islander, 1% white, 96% international
Most popular majors: Information not available
Expenses: 2020-2021: $49,950; room/board: $17,500
Financial aid: N/A; 72% of undergrads determined to have financial need; average aid package $15,894

Humboldt State University
Arcata CA
(707) 826-4402
U.S. News ranking: Reg. U. (W), No. 37
Website: www.humboldt.edu
Admissions email: hsuinfo@humboldt.edu
Public; founded 1913
Freshman admissions: selective; 2019-2020: 16,355 applied, 14,862 accepted. Neither SAT nor ACT required. SAT 25/75 percentile: 970-1200. High school rank: 5% in top tenth, 31% in top quarter, 71% in top half
Early decision deadline: N/A, notification date: N/A
Early action deadline: N/A, notification date: N/A
Application deadline (fall): 11/30
Undergraduate student body: 6,038 full time, 405 part time; 43% male, 57% female; 1% American Indian, 3% Asian, 3% Black, 35% Hispanic, 7% multiracial, 0% Pacific Islander, 44% white, 1% international; 94% from in state; 28% live on campus; 1% of students in fraternities, 1% in sororities
Most popular majors: 9% Business Administration and Management, General, 9% Psychology, General, 8% Biology/Biological Sciences, General, 7% Environmental Science, 6% Health and Physical Education/Fitness, General
Expenses: 2020-2021: $7,858 in state, $19,738 out of state; room/board: $13,390
Financial aid: (707) 826-4321; 78% of undergrads determined to have financial need; average aid package $15,980

Humphreys College[1]
Stockton CA
(209) 478-0800
U.S. News ranking: Reg. Coll. (W), unranked
Website: www.humphreys.edu
Admissions email: ugadmission@humphreys.edu
Private
Application deadline (fall): N/A

Undergraduate student body: N/A full time, N/A part time
Expenses: 2019-2020: $14,580; room/board: $15,084
Financial aid: N/A

John Paul the Great Catholic University
Escondido CA
(858) 653-6740
U.S. News ranking: Reg. Coll. (W), unranked
Website: jpcatholic.edu/
Admissions email: N/A
Private; founded 2006
Affiliation: Roman Catholic
Freshman admissions: selective; 2019-2020: 350 applied, 255 accepted. Either SAT or ACT required. SAT 25/75 percentile: 1025-1223. High school rank: N/A
Early decision deadline: N/A, notification date: N/A
Early action deadline: N/A, notification date: N/A
Application deadline (fall): rolling
Undergraduate student body: 262 full time, 10 part time; 49% male, 51% female; 0% American Indian, 4% Asian, 2% Black, 28% Hispanic, 6% multiracial, 1% Pacific Islander, 44% white, 0% international; 51% from in state; 83% live on campus; N/A of students in fraternities, N/A in sororities
Most popular majors: 68% Visual and Performing Arts, 16% Business, Management, Marketing, and Related Support Services, 16% Liberal Arts and Sciences, General Studies and Humanities
Expenses: 2020-2021: $27,000; room/board: $7,710
Financial aid: (858) 653-6740

Laguna College of Art and Design[1]
Laguna Beach CA
(949) 376-6000
U.S. News ranking: Arts, unranked
Website: www.lcad.edu/
Admissions email: admissions@lcad.edu
Private; founded 1961
Application deadline (fall): 8/1
Undergraduate student body: N/A full time, N/A part time
Expenses: 2019-2020: $31,600; room/board: $17,086
Financial aid: (949) 376-6000

La Sierra University
Riverside CA
(951) 785-2176
U.S. News ranking: Reg. U. (W), No. 68
Website: lasierra.edu/about/
Admissions email: Admissions@lasierra.edu
Private; founded 1922
Affiliation: Seventh Day Adventist
Freshman admissions: selective; 2019-2020: 5,403 applied, 2,975 accepted. Either SAT or ACT required. SAT 25/75 percentile: 910-1160. High school rank: 14% in top tenth, 34% in top quarter, 71% in top half
Early decision deadline: N/A, notification date: N/A

Early action deadline: N/A, notification date: N/A
Application deadline (fall): 7/15
Undergraduate student body: 1,480 full time, 266 part time; 40% male, 60% female; 0% American Indian, 16% Asian, 7% Black, 50% Hispanic, 4% multiracial, 1% Pacific Islander, 12% white, 9% international; 77% from in state; 36% live on campus; 0% of students in fraternities, 0% in sororities
Most popular majors: 15% Business Administration and Management, General, 9% Criminal Justice/Safety Studies, 7% Kinesiology and Exercise Science, 5% Pre-Nursing Studies, 4% Social Work
Expenses: 2020-2021: $35,208; room/board: $8,790
Financial aid: (951) 785-2175; 80% of undergrads determined to have financial need; average aid package $25,025

Life Pacific College[1]
San Dimas CA
(909) 599-5433
U.S. News ranking: Reg. Coll. (W), No. 22
Website: www.lifepacific.edu
Admissions email: adm@lifepacific.edu
Private
Application deadline (fall): N/A
Undergraduate student body: N/A full time, N/A part time
Expenses: 2019-2020: $16,592; room/board: $15,084
Financial aid: N/A

Loyola Marymount University
Los Angeles CA
(310) 338-2750
U.S. News ranking: Nat. U., No. 66
Website: www.lmu.edu
Admissions email: admission@lmu.edu
Private; founded 1911
Affiliation: Roman Catholic
Freshman admissions: more selective; 2019-2020: 18,592 applied, 8,150 accepted. Either SAT or ACT required. SAT 25/75 percentile: 1230-1410. High school rank: 47% in top tenth, 79% in top quarter, 98% in top half
Early decision deadline: 11/1, notification date: 12/1
Early action deadline: 11/1, notification date: 12/20
Application deadline (fall): 1/15
Undergraduate student body: 6,548 full time, 230 part time; 45% male, 55% female; 0% American Indian, 10% Asian, 7% Black, 23% Hispanic, 7% multiracial, 0% Pacific Islander, 43% white, 11% international; N/A from in state; 47% live on campus; 20% of students in fraternities, 26% in sororities
Most popular majors: 25% Business, Management, Marketing, and Related Support Services, 15% Social Sciences, 14% Visual and Performing Arts, 10% Communication, Journalism, and Related Programs, 8% Psychology

Expenses: 2020-2021: $52,577; room/board: $16,165
Financial aid: (310) 338-2753; 49% of undergrads determined to have financial need; average aid package $32,326

Marymount California University
Rancho Palos Verdes CA
(310) 303-7311
U.S. News ranking: Nat. Lib. Arts, second tier
Website: www.marymountcalifornia.edu
Admissions email: admissions@marymountcalifornia.edu
Private; founded 1933
Affiliation: Roman Catholic
Freshman admissions: less selective; 2019-2020: 1,481 applied, 1,267 accepted. Neither SAT nor ACT required. SAT 25/75 percentile: 920-1090. High school rank: N/A
Early decision deadline: N/A, notification date: N/A
Early action deadline: N/A, notification date: N/A
Application deadline (fall): rolling
Undergraduate student body: 586 full time, 15 part time; 50% male, 50% female; 0% American Indian, 5% Asian, 7% Black, 44% Hispanic, 6% multiracial, 0% Pacific Islander, 21% white, 14% international; N/A from in state; 36% live on campus; N/A of students in fraternities, N/A in sororities
Most popular majors: 34% Business Administration and Management, General, 23% Psychology, General, 21% Liberal Arts and Sciences/Liberal Studies, 10% Criminal Justice/Safety Studies, 9% Digital Arts
Expenses: 2019-2020: $36,134; room/board: $14,666
Financial aid: (310) 303-7217

The Master's University and Seminary
Santa Clarita CA
(800) 568-6248
U.S. News ranking: Reg. U. (W), No. 52
Website: www.masters.edu
Admissions email: admissions@masters.edu
Private; founded 1927
Affiliation: Other
Freshman admissions: more selective; 2019-2020: 660 applied, 443 accepted. Either SAT or ACT required. SAT 25/75 percentile: 990-1320. High school rank: 44% in top tenth, 61% in top quarter, 100% in top half
Early decision deadline: N/A, notification date: N/A
Early action deadline: 11/15, notification date: 12/22
Application deadline (fall): rolling
Undergraduate student body: 975 full time, 386 part time; 52% male, 48% female; 0% American Indian, 5% Asian, 2% Black, 5% Hispanic, 9% multiracial, 0% Pacific Islander, 67% white, 1% international; 67% from in

state; 75% live on campus; N/A of students in fraternities, N/A in sororities
Most popular majors: 24% Business, Management, Marketing, and Related Support Services, 17% Theology and Religious Vocations, 10% Communication, Journalism, and Related Programs, 9% Biological and Biomedical Sciences, 9% Liberal Arts and Sciences, General Studies and Humanities
Expenses: 2020-2021: $28,740; room/board: $11,500
Financial aid: (661) 362-2290; 68% of undergrads determined to have financial need; average aid package $4,062

Menlo College[1]
Atherton CA
(800) 556-3656
U.S. News ranking: Business, unranked
Website: www.menlo.edu
Admissions email: admissions@menlo.edu
Private; founded 1927
Application deadline (fall): 4/1
Undergraduate student body: N/A full time, N/A part time
Expenses: 2019-2020: $44,035; room/board: $14,796
Financial aid: N/A

Mills College
Oakland CA
(510) 430-2135
U.S. News ranking: Reg. U. (W), No. 12
Website: www.mills.edu
Admissions email: admission@mills.edu
Private; founded 1852
Freshman admissions: selective; 2019-2020: 1,057 applied, 809 accepted. Neither SAT nor ACT required. SAT 25/75 percentile: 1008-1240. High school rank: 31% in top tenth, 52% in top quarter, 90% in top half
Early decision deadline: N/A, notification date: N/A
Early action deadline: 11/15, notification date: 12/1
Application deadline (fall): rolling
Undergraduate student body: 674 full time, 33 part time; 0% male, 100% female; 1% American Indian, 8% Asian, 10% Black, 33% Hispanic, 11% multiracial, 0% Pacific Islander, 37% white, 0% international; N/A from in state; 58% live on campus; N/A of students in fraternities, N/A in sororities
Most popular majors: 26% Social Sciences, 13% Business, Management, Marketing, and Related Support Services, 9% English Language and Literature/Letters, 8% Psychology, 7% Multi/Interdisciplinary Studies
Expenses: 2020-2021: $31,512; room/board: $14,370
Financial aid: (510) 430-2039; 83% of undergrads determined to have financial need; average aid package $53,604

MiraCosta College[1]

Oceanside CA
(760) 757-2121
U.S. News ranking: Reg. Coll. (W), unranked
Website: www.miracosta.edu
Admissions email: N/A
Public
Application deadline (fall): N/A
Undergraduate student body: N/A full time, N/A part time
Expenses: 2019-2020: $1,152 in state, $7,512 out of state; room/board: $15,084
Financial aid: N/A

Modesto Junior College[1]

Modesto CA
(209) 575-6550
U.S. News ranking: Reg. Coll. (W), unranked
Website: www.mjc.edu
Admissions email: N/A
Public
Application deadline (fall): N/A
Undergraduate student body: N/A full time, N/A part time
Expenses: 2019-2020: $1,176 in state, $7,536 out of state; room/board: $15,084
Financial aid: N/A

Mount Saint Mary's University

Los Angeles CA
(310) 954-4250
U.S. News ranking: Reg. U. (W), No. 16
Website: www.msmu.edu
Admissions email: admissions@msmu.edu
Private; founded 1925
Affiliation: Roman Catholic
Freshman admissions: selective; 2019-2020: 2,165 applied, 1,941 accepted. Neither SAT nor ACT required. SAT 25/75 percentile: 920-1170. High school rank: 20% in top tenth, 49% in top quarter, 81% in top half
Early decision deadline: N/A, notification date: N/A
Early action deadline: 12/1, notification date: 1/30
Application deadline (fall): 8/1
Undergraduate student body: 1,745 full time, 482 part time; 7% male, 93% female; 0% American Indian, 15% Asian, 7% Black, 59% Hispanic, 2% multiracial, 1% Pacific Islander, 8% white, 0% international; N/A from in state; 26% live on campus; N/A of students in fraternities, 1% in sororities
Most popular majors: 36% Health Professions and Related Programs, 13% Business, Management, Marketing, and Related Support Services, 13% Psychology, 9% Social Sciences, 7% Liberal Arts and Sciences, General Studies and Humanities
Expenses: 2020-2021: $44,474; room/board: $12,704
Financial aid: (310) 954-4190; 91% of undergrads determined to have financial need; average aid package $31,778

National University

La Jolla CA
(844) 873-1037
U.S. News ranking: Reg. U. (W), second tier
Website: www.nu.edu/
Admissions email: advisor@nu.edu
Private; founded 1971
Freshman admissions: less selective; 2019-2020: 171 applied, 153 accepted. Neither SAT nor ACT required. SAT 25/75 percentile: N/A. High school rank: N/A
Early decision deadline: N/A, notification date: N/A
Early action deadline: N/A, notification date: N/A
Application deadline (fall): rolling
Undergraduate student body: 2,856 full time, 4,500 part time; 44% male, 56% female; 1% American Indian, 8% Asian, 8% Black, 28% Hispanic, 6% multiracial, 1% Pacific Islander, 34% white, 1% international; 88% from in state; N/A live on campus; N/A of students in fraternities, N/A in sororities
Most popular majors: 19% Registered Nursing/Registered Nurse, 14% Business Administration and Management, General, 8% Teacher Education and Professional Development, Specific Levels and Methods, 7% Psychology, General, 5% Criminal Justice/Law Enforcement Administration
Expenses: 2020-2021: $13,320; room/board: $0
Financial aid: (858) 642-8500; 77% of undergrads determined to have financial need; average aid package $8,637

NewSchool of Architecture and Design[1]

San Diego CA
(619) 684-8828
U.S. News ranking: Arts, unranked
Website: newschoolarch.edu/
Admissions email: fguidali@newschoolarch.edu
For-profit; founded 1980
Application deadline (fall): rolling
Undergraduate student body: N/A full time, N/A part time
Expenses: 2019-2020: $28,386; room/board: $11,880
Financial aid: (619) 684-8803

Notre Dame de Namur University[1]

Belmont CA
(650) 508-3600
U.S. News ranking: Reg. U. (W), No. 64
Website: www.ndnu.edu
Admissions email: admissions@ndnu.edu
Private; founded 1851
Affiliation: Roman Catholic
Application deadline (fall): rolling
Undergraduate student body: N/A full time, N/A part time
Expenses: 2019-2020: $36,596; room/board: $14,766
Financial aid: (650) 508-3741

Occidental College

Los Angeles CA
(323) 259-2700
U.S. News ranking: Nat. Lib. Arts, No. 40
Website: www.oxy.edu
Admissions email: admission@oxy.edu
Private; founded 1887
Freshman admissions: more selective; 2019-2020: 7,501 applied, 2,752 accepted. Either SAT or ACT required. SAT 25/75 percentile: 1300-1480. High school rank: 53% in top tenth, 87% in top quarter, 97% in top half
Early decision deadline: 11/15, notification date: 12/15
Early action deadline: N/A, notification date: N/A
Application deadline (fall): 1/10
Undergraduate student body: 2,058 full time, 23 part time; 42% male, 58% female; 0% American Indian, 15% Asian, 4% Black, 14% Hispanic, 9% multiracial, 0% Pacific Islander, 49% white, 6% international; 41% from in state; 82% live on campus; N/A of students in fraternities, N/A in sororities
Most popular majors: 16% Economics, General, 8% Biology/Biological Sciences, General, 8% International Relations and Affairs, 6% Psychology, General, 6% Sociology
Expenses: 2020-2021: $56,576; room/board: $16,600
Financial aid: (323) 259-2548; 56% of undergrads determined to have financial need; average aid package $52,583

Otis College of Art and Design

Los Angeles CA
(310) 665-6820
U.S. News ranking: Arts, unranked
Website: www.otis.edu
Admissions email: admissions@otis.edu
Private; founded 1918
Freshman admissions: selective; 2019-2020: 2,442 applied, 1,909 accepted. Neither SAT nor ACT required. ACT 25/75 percentile: 23-29. High school rank: 18% in top tenth, 40% in top quarter, 66% in top half
Early decision deadline: N/A, notification date: N/A
Early action deadline: 11/15, notification date: N/A
Application deadline (fall): N/A
Undergraduate student body: 1,109 full time, 16 part time; 31% male, 69% female; 0% American Indian, 21% Asian, 5% Black, 16% Hispanic, 6% multiracial, 1% Pacific Islander, 23% white, 25% international; 63% from in state; 37% live on campus; N/A of students in fraternities, N/A in sororities
Most popular majors: 31% Digital Arts, 20% Fashion/Apparel Design, 15% Design and Visual Communications, General, 12% Fine/Studio Arts, General, 9% Design and Applied Arts, Other
Expenses: 2020-2021: $49,680; room/board: $15,340

Pacific Union College

Angwin CA
(707) 965-6336
U.S. News ranking: Reg. Coll. (W), unranked
Website: www.puc.edu
Admissions email: admissions@puc.edu
Private; founded 1882
Affiliation: Seventh Day Adventist
Freshman admissions: selective; 2019-2020: 1,572 applied, 867 accepted. Either SAT or ACT required. SAT 25/75 percentile: 930-1190. High school rank: N/A
Early decision deadline: N/A, notification date: N/A
Early action deadline: 12/15, notification date: 11/15
Application deadline (fall): rolling
Undergraduate student body: 822 full time, 84 part time; 40% male, 60% female; 0% American Indian, 23% Asian, 5% Black, 27% Hispanic, 9% multiracial, 1% Pacific Islander, 22% white, 3% international; 90% from in state; 71% live on campus; N/A of students in fraternities, N/A in sororities
Most popular majors: 25% Registered Nursing/Registered Nurse, 18% Business/Commerce, General, 8% Biology/Biological Sciences, General, 5% Health Communication, 5% Psychology, General
Expenses: 2020-2021: $32,016; room/board: $8,517
Financial aid: (707) 965-7200; 76% of undergrads determined to have financial need; average aid package $25,290

Pepperdine University

Malibu CA
(310) 506-4392
U.S. News ranking: Nat. U., No. 49
Website: www.pepperdine.edu
Admissions email: admission-seaver@pepperdine.edu
Private; founded 1937
Affiliation: Churches of Christ
Freshman admissions: more selective; 2019-2020: 12,764 applied, 4,049 accepted. Either SAT or ACT required. SAT 25/75 percentile: 1230-1450. High school rank: 46% in top tenth, 77% in top quarter, 97% in top half
Early decision deadline: N/A, notification date: N/A
Early action deadline: 11/1, notification date: 1/10
Application deadline (fall): 1/15
Undergraduate student body: 3,320 full time, 263 part time; 42% male, 58% female; 0% American Indian, 11% Asian, 5% Black, 14% Hispanic, 7% multiracial, 0% Pacific Islander, 49% white, 12% international; 55% from in state; 60% live on campus; 18% of students in fraternities, 27% in sororities
Most popular majors: 32% Business, Management, Marketing, and Related Support Services, 20% Communication,

Financial aid: (310) 665-6999; 89% of undergrads determined to have financial need; average aid package $22,854

Journalism, and Related Programs, 9% Social Sciences, 7% Parks, Recreation, Leisure, and Fitness Studies, 7% Psychology
Expenses: 2020-2021: $58,002; room/board: $16,160
Financial aid: (310) 506-4301; 52% of undergrads determined to have financial need; average aid package $42,854

Pitzer College

Claremont CA
(909) 621-8129
U.S. News ranking: Nat. Lib. Arts, No. 36
Website: www.pitzer.edu
Admissions email: admission@pitzer.edu
Private; founded 1963
Freshman admissions: more selective; 2019-2020: 4,415 applied, 605 accepted. Neither SAT nor ACT required. SAT 25/75 percentile: 1348-1480. High school rank: 59% in top tenth, 82% in top quarter, 100% in top half
Early decision deadline: 11/15, notification date: 12/18
Early action deadline: N/A, notification date: N/A
Application deadline (fall): 1/1
Undergraduate student body: 1,094 full time, 25 part time; 43% male, 57% female; 0% American Indian, 8% Asian, 6% Black, 15% Hispanic, 9% multiracial, 0% Pacific Islander, 49% white, 8% international; 44% from in state; 75% live on campus; 0% of students in fraternities, 0% in sororities
Most popular majors: 18% Social Sciences, 11% Multi/Interdisciplinary Studies, 10% Natural Resources and Conservation, 9% Business, Management, Marketing, and Related Support Services, 8% Psychology
Expenses: 2020-2021: $55,878; room/board: $9,265
Financial aid: (909) 621-8208

Point Loma Nazarene University

San Diego CA
(619) 849-2273
U.S. News ranking: Reg. U. (W), No. 13
Website: www.pointloma.edu
Admissions email: admissions@pointloma.edu
Private; founded 1902
Affiliation: Church of the Nazarene
Freshman admissions: more selective; 2019-2020: 3,277 applied, 2,414 accepted. Either SAT or ACT required. SAT 25/75 percentile: 1140-1310. High school rank: 40% in top tenth, 78% in top quarter, 96% in top half
Early decision deadline: N/A, notification date: N/A
Early action deadline: 11/15, notification date: 12/21
Application deadline (fall): 2/15
Undergraduate student body: 2,611 full time, 592 part time; 35% male, 65% female; 0% American Indian, 7% Asian, 2% Black, 26% Hispanic, 8% multiracial, 1% Pacific Islander, 53% white,

1% international; 82% from in state; 55% live on campus; N/A of students in fraternities, N/A in sororities
Most popular majors: 25% Health Professions and Related Programs, 21% Business, Management, Marketing, and Related Support Services, 10% Family and Consumer Sciences/Human Sciences, 7% Psychology, 6% Social Sciences
Expenses: 2020-2021: $38,300; room/board: $10,900
Financial aid: (619) 849-2538; 65% of undergrads determined to have financial need; average aid package $25,229

Pomona College
Claremont CA
(909) 621-8134
U.S. News ranking: Nat. Lib. Arts, No. 4
Website: www.pomona.edu
Admissions email: admissions@pomona.edu
Private; founded 1887
Freshman admissions: most selective; 2019-2020: 10,401 applied, 770 accepted. Neither SAT nor ACT required. SAT 25/75 percentile: 1390-1540. High school rank: 93% in top tenth, 100% in top quarter, 100% in top half
Early decision deadline: 11/15, notification date: 12/15
Early action deadline: N/A, notification date: N/A
Application deadline (fall): 1/8
Undergraduate student body: 1,696 full time, 21 part time; 47% male, 53% female; 0% American Indian, 16% Asian, 10% Black, 17% Hispanic, 7% multiracial, 0% Pacific Islander, 34% white, 11% international
Most popular majors: 20% Social Sciences, 12% Multi/Interdisciplinary Studies, 9% Mathematics and Statistics, 8% Computer and Information Sciences and Support Services, 7% Physical Sciences
Expenses: 2020-2021: $54,774; room/board: $17,820
Financial aid: (909) 621-8205; 55% of undergrads determined to have financial need; average aid package $59,966

Providence Christian College[1]
Pasadena CA
(866) 323-0233
U.S. News ranking: Nat. Lib. Arts, second tier
Website: www.providencecc.net/
Admissions email: N/A
Private; founded 2003
Application deadline (fall): rolling
Undergraduate student body: N/A full time, N/A part time
Expenses: 2019-2020: $31,846; room/board: $10,490
Financial aid: N/A

Rio Hondo College[1]
Whittier CA
(562) 692-0921
U.S. News ranking: Reg. Coll. (W), unranked
Website: www.riohondo.edu
Admissions email: N/A
Public
Application deadline (fall): N/A
Undergraduate student body: N/A full time, N/A part time
Expenses: 2019-2020: $1,360 in state, $8,584 out of state; room/board: $15,084
Financial aid: N/A

San Diego Christian College[1]
Santee CA
(800) 676-2242
U.S. News ranking: Reg. Coll. (W), No. 18
Website: www.sdcc.edu/
Admissions email: admissions@sdcc.edu
Private; founded 1970
Affiliation: Undenominational
Application deadline (fall): rolling
Undergraduate student body: N/A full time, N/A part time
Expenses: 2019-2020: $32,346; room/board: $12,222
Financial aid: N/A

San Diego Mesa College[1]
San Diego CA
(619) 388-2604
U.S. News ranking: Reg. Coll. (W), unranked
Website: www.sdmesa.edu/
Admissions email: N/A
Public
Application deadline (fall): N/A
Undergraduate student body: N/A full time, N/A part time
Expenses: 2019-2020: $1,144 in state, $7,480 out of state; room/board: $15,084
Financial aid: N/A

San Diego State University
San Diego CA
(619) 594-6336
U.S. News ranking: Nat. U., No. 143
Website: www.sdsu.edu
Admissions email: admissions@sdsu.edu
Public; founded 1897
Freshman admissions: more selective; 2019-2020: 69,842 applied, 23,767 accepted. Either SAT or ACT required. SAT 25/75 percentile: 1110-1320. High school rank: 33% in top tenth, 70% in top quarter, 94% in top half
Early decision deadline: N/A, notification date: N/A
Early action deadline: N/A, notification date: N/A
Application deadline (fall): 11/30
Undergraduate student body: 27,575 full time, 3,019 part time; 45% male, 55% female; 0% American Indian, 13% Asian, 4% Black, 32% Hispanic, 6% multiracial, 0% Pacific Islander, 34% white, 7% international;

84% from in state; 23% live on campus; 15% of students in fraternities, 17% in sororities
Most popular majors: 20% Business Administration and Management, General, 7% Psychology, General, 5% Criminal Justice/Safety Studies, 5% Health and Physical Education/Fitness, General, 4% Biology/Biological Sciences, General
Expenses: 2020-2021: $7,720 in state, $19,600 out of state; room/board: $18,531
Financial aid: (619) 594-6323; 52% of undergrads determined to have financial need; average aid package $10,000

San Francisco Conservatory of Music[1]
San Francisco CA
(800) 899-7326
U.S. News ranking: Arts, unranked
Website: www.sfcm.edu
Admissions email: admit@sfcm.edu
Private; founded 1917
Affiliation: Other
Application deadline (fall): 12/1
Undergraduate student body: N/A full time, N/A part time
Expenses: 2019-2020: $47,560; room/board: $18,100
Financial aid: (415) 503-6214

San Francisco State University
San Francisco CA
(415) 338-6486
U.S. News ranking: Reg. U. (W), No. 29
Website: www.sfsu.edu
Admissions email: ugadmit@sfsu.edu
Public; founded 1899
Freshman admissions: selective; 2019-2020: 34,629 applied, 23,308 accepted. Either SAT or ACT required. SAT 25/75 percentile: 940-1150. High school rank: N/A
Early decision deadline: N/A, notification date: N/A
Early action deadline: N/A, notification date: N/A
Application deadline (fall): 11/30
Undergraduate student body: 21,663 full time, 4,237 part time; 45% male, 55% female; 0% American Indian, 26% Asian, 6% Black, 35% Hispanic, 6% multiracial, 1% Pacific Islander, 17% white, 7% international
Most popular majors: 24% Business, Management, Marketing, and Related Support Services, 11% Communication, Journalism, and Related Programs, 8% Social Sciences, 8% Visual and Performing Arts, 6% Psychology
Expenses: 2020-2021: $7,436 in state, $19,316 out of state; room/board: $15,201
Financial aid: (415) 338-7000; 70% of undergrads determined to have financial need; average aid package $15,435

San Joaquin Valley College—Visalia[1]
Visalia CA
(559) 734-9000
U.S. News ranking: Reg. Coll. (W), unranked
Website: www.sjvc.edu
Admissions email: N/A
For-profit
Application deadline (fall): N/A
Undergraduate student body: N/A full time, N/A part time
Expenses: 2019-2020: $43,990; room/board: N/A
Financial aid: N/A

San Jose State University
San Jose CA
(408) 283-7500
U.S. News ranking: Reg. U. (W), No. 22
Website: www.sjsu.edu/Admissions/
Admissions email: admissions@sjsu.edu
Public; founded 1857
Freshman admissions: selective; 2019-2020: 35,307 applied, 22,446 accepted. Either SAT or ACT required. SAT 25/75 percentile: 1030-1260. High school rank: N/A
Early decision deadline: N/A, notification date: N/A
Early action deadline: N/A, notification date: N/A
Application deadline (fall): 11/30
Undergraduate student body: 23,593 full time, 4,312 part time; 50% male, 50% female; 0% American Indian, 36% Asian, 3% Black, 29% Hispanic, 5% multiracial, 1% Pacific Islander, 14% white, 8% international; 99% from in state; 14% live on campus; N/A of students in fraternities, N/A in sororities
Most popular majors: 26% Business, Management, Marketing, and Related Support Services, 14% Engineering, 7% Health Professions and Related Programs, 7% Visual and Performing Arts, 6% Psychology
Expenses: 2020-2021: $7,852 in state, $19,466 out of state; room/board: $16,946
Financial aid: (408) 924-6086; 65% of undergrads determined to have financial need; average aid package $19,319

Santa Ana College[1]
Santa Ana CA
(714) 564-6000
U.S. News ranking: Reg. Coll. (W), unranked
Website: www.sac.edu
Admissions email: N/A
Public
Application deadline (fall): N/A
Undergraduate student body: N/A full time, N/A part time
Expenses: 2019-2020: $1,160 in state, $8,360 out of state; room/board: $15,084
Financial aid: N/A

Santa Clara University
Santa Clara CA
(408) 554-4700
U.S. News ranking: Nat. U., No. 53
Website: www.scu.edu
Admissions email: Admission@scu.edu
Private; founded 1851
Affiliation: Roman Catholic
Freshman admissions: more selective; 2019-2020: 16,300 applied, 7,958 accepted. Either SAT or ACT required. SAT 25/75 percentile: 1280-1440. High school rank: 52% in top tenth, 88% in top quarter, 99% in top half
Early decision deadline: 11/1, notification date: 12/31
Early action deadline: 11/1, notification date: 12/31
Application deadline (fall): 1/7
Undergraduate student body: 5,586 full time, 108 part time; 50% male, 50% female; 0% American Indian, 18% Asian, 3% Black, 18% Hispanic, 8% multiracial, 0% Pacific Islander, 47% white, 4% international; 58% from in state; 58% live on campus; 0% of students in fraternities, 0% in sororities
Most popular majors: 24% Business, Management, Marketing, and Related Support Services, 16% Social Sciences, 14% Engineering, 9% Communication, Journalism, and Related Programs, 6% Psychology
Expenses: 2020-2021: $55,629; room/board: $15,972
Financial aid: (408) 551-1000; 45% of undergrads determined to have financial need; average aid package $39,105

Santa Monica College[1]
Santa Monica CA
(310) 434-4000
U.S. News ranking: Reg. Coll. (W), unranked
Website: www.smc.edu
Admissions email: N/A
Public
Application deadline (fall): N/A
Undergraduate student body: N/A full time, N/A part time
Expenses: 2019-2020: $1,144 in state, $8,840 out of state; room/board: $11,556
Financial aid: N/A

Scripps College
Claremont CA
(909) 621-8149
U.S. News ranking: Nat. Lib. Arts, No. 28
Website: www.scrippscollege.edu/
Admissions email: admission@scrippscollege.edu
Private; founded 1926
Freshman admissions: more selective; 2019-2020: 3,022 applied, 967 accepted. Either SAT or ACT required. SAT 25/75 percentile: 1333-1490. High school rank: 78% in top tenth, 98% in top quarter, 100% in top half
Early decision deadline: 11/15, notification date: 12/15
Early action deadline: N/A, notification date: N/A

Application deadline (fall): 1/3
Undergraduate student body: 1,082 full time, 7 part time; 0% male, 100% female; 0% American Indian, 16% Asian, 4% Black, 14% Hispanic, 7% multiracial, 0% Pacific Islander, 53% white, 5% international; N/A from in state; 94% live on campus; N/A of students in fraternities, N/A in sororities
Most popular majors: 22% Biological and Biomedical Sciences, 15% Social Sciences, 9% Psychology, 7% Communication, Journalism, and Related Programs, 7% Natural Resources and Conservation
Expenses: 2020-2021: $59,410; room/board: $18,286
Financial aid: (909) 621-8275; 36% of undergrads determined to have financial need; average aid package $49,446

Shasta College[1]
Redding CA
(530) 242-7500
U.S. News ranking: Reg. Coll. (W), unranked
Website: www.shastacollege.edu
Admissions email: N/A
Public
Application deadline (fall): N/A
Undergraduate student body: N/A full time, N/A part time
Expenses: 2019-2020: $1,186 in state, $6,802 out of state; room/board: $5,290
Financial aid: N/A

Simpson University[1]
Redding CA
(530) 226-4606
U.S. News ranking: Reg. U. (W), No. 92
Website: www.simpsonu.edu
Admissions email: admissions@simpsonu.edu
Private; founded 1921
Affiliation: Christ and Missionary Alliance Church
Application deadline (fall): 8/1
Undergraduate student body: N/A full time, N/A part time
Expenses: 2019-2020: $31,910; room/board: $9,380
Financial aid: (530) 226-4621

Skyline College[1]
San Bruno CA
(650) 738-4100
U.S. News ranking: Reg. Coll. (W), unranked
Website: skylinecollege.edu
Admissions email: N/A
Public
Application deadline (fall): N/A
Undergraduate student body: N/A full time, N/A part time
Expenses: 2019-2020: $1,464 in state, $9,654 out of state; room/board: $15,084
Financial aid: N/A

Soka University of America
Aliso Viejo CA
(888) 600-7652
U.S. News ranking: Nat. Lib. Arts, No. 28
Website: www.soka.edu

Admissions email: admission@soka.edu
Private; founded 1987
Freshman admissions: more selective; 2019-2020: 504 applied, 202 accepted. Either SAT or ACT required. SAT 25/75 percentile: 1240-1430. High school rank: 62% in top tenth, 76% in top quarter, 95% in top half
Early decision deadline: N/A, notification date: N/A
Early action deadline: 11/1, notification date: 12/1
Application deadline (fall): 1/15
Undergraduate student body: 406 full time, 0 part time; 35% male, 65% female; 0% American Indian, 15% Asian, 3% Black, 12% Hispanic, 5% multiracial, 1% Pacific Islander, 17% white, 45% international; 48% from in state; 99% live on campus; 0% of students in fraternities, 0% in sororities
Most popular majors: 100% Liberal Arts and Sciences/Liberal Studies
Expenses: 2020-2021: $33,962; room/board: $13,032
Financial aid: (949) 480-4000; 86% of undergrads determined to have financial need; average aid package $38,037

Solano Community College[1]
Fairfield CA
(707) 864-7000
U.S. News ranking: Reg. Coll. (W), unranked
Website: www.solano.edu
Admissions email: N/A
Public
Application deadline (fall): N/A
Undergraduate student body: N/A full time, N/A part time
Expenses: 2019-2020: $1,163 in state, $6,607 out of state; room/board: $15,084
Financial aid: N/A

Sonoma State University
Rohnert Park CA
(707) 664-2778
U.S. News ranking: Reg. U. (W), No. 33
Website: www.sonoma.edu
Admissions email: student.outreach@sonoma.edu
Public; founded 1960
Freshman admissions: selective; 2019-2020: 15,093 applied, 13,764 accepted. Neither SAT nor ACT required. SAT 25/75 percentile: 980-1170. High school rank: N/A
Early decision deadline: N/A, notification date: N/A
Early action deadline: N/A, notification date: N/A
Application deadline (fall): 11/30
Undergraduate student body: 7,380 full time, 652 part time; 38% male, 62% female; 0% American Indian, 5% Asian, 2% Black, 35% Hispanic, 7% multiracial, 0% Pacific Islander, 43% white, 3% international
Most popular majors: Information not available
Expenses: 2020-2021: $7,952 in state, $19,832 out of state; room/board: $14,282

Financial aid: (707) 664-2389; 56% of undergrads determined to have financial need; average aid package $10,634

Southern California Institute of Architecture[1]
Los Angeles CA
(213) 613-2200
U.S. News ranking: Arts, unranked
Website: www.sciarc.edu
Admissions email: admissions@sciarc.edu
Private
Application deadline (fall): N/A
Undergraduate student body: N/A full time, N/A part time
Expenses: 2019-2020: $45,892; room/board: N/A
Financial aid: N/A

Stanford University
Stanford CA
(650) 723-2091
U.S. News ranking: Nat. U., No. 6
Website: www.stanford.edu
Admissions email: admission@stanford.edu
Private; founded 1885
Freshman admissions: most selective; 2019-2020: 47,498 applied, 2,062 accepted. Either SAT or ACT required. SAT 25/75 percentile: 1440-1570. High school rank: 98% in top tenth, 100% in top quarter, 100% in top half
Early decision deadline: N/A, notification date: N/A
Early action deadline: 11/1, notification date: 12/15
Application deadline (fall): 1/2
Undergraduate student body: 6,996 full time, 0 part time; 50% male, 50% female; 1% American Indian, 23% Asian, 7% Black, 17% Hispanic, 9% multiracial, 0% Pacific Islander, 32% white, 11% international; N/A from in state; 93% live on campus; 18% of students in fraternities, 24% in sororities
Most popular majors: 19% Engineering, 17% Computer and Information Sciences and Support Services, 15% Multi/Interdisciplinary Studies, 13% Social Sciences, 5% Mathematics and Statistics
Expenses: 2020-2021: $56,169; room/board: $17,255
Financial aid: (650) 723-3058; 52% of undergrads determined to have financial need; average aid package $57,500

St. Mary's College of California
Moraga CA
(925) 631-4224
U.S. News ranking: Reg. U. (W), No. 6
Website: www.stmarys-ca.edu
Admissions email: smcadmit@stmarys-ca.edu
Private; founded 1863
Affiliation: Roman Catholic
Freshman admissions: selective; 2019-2020: 6,069 applied, 4,916 accepted. Either SAT or ACT required. SAT 25/75

percentile: 1060-1250. High school rank: N/A
Early decision deadline: N/A, notification date: N/A
Early action deadline: 11/15, notification date: 1/1
Application deadline (fall): 1/15
Undergraduate student body: 2,495 full time, 151 part time; 43% male, 57% female; 0% American Indian, 11% Asian, 4% Black, 28% Hispanic, 8% multiracial, 2% Pacific Islander, 42% white, 3% international; 87% from in state; 55% live on campus; 0% of students in fraternities, 0% in sororities
Most popular majors: 27% Business, Management, Marketing, and Related Support Services, 11% Psychology, 9% Liberal Arts and Sciences, General Studies and Humanities, 9% Social Sciences, 7% Parks, Recreation, Leisure, and Fitness Studies
Expenses: 2020-2021: $50,660; room/board: $15,706
Financial aid: (925) 631-4370; 71% of undergrads determined to have financial need; average aid package $37,988

Thomas Aquinas College
Santa Paula CA
(805) 525-4417
U.S. News ranking: Nat. Lib. Arts, No. 40
Website: www.thomasaquinas.edu
Admissions email: admissions@thomasaquinas.edu
Private; founded 1971
Affiliation: Roman Catholic
Freshman admissions: more selective; 2019-2020: 204 applied, 161 accepted. Either SAT or ACT required. SAT 25/75 percentile: 1150-1390. High school rank: 29% in top tenth, 64% in top quarter, 86% in top half
Early decision deadline: N/A, notification date: N/A
Early action deadline: N/A, notification date: N/A
Application deadline (fall): rolling
Undergraduate student body: 439 full time, 0 part time; 47% male, 53% female; 1% American Indian, 3% Asian, 0% Black, 15% Hispanic, 4% multiracial, 0% Pacific Islander, 76% white, 1% international; 39% from in state; 99% live on campus; 0% of students in fraternities, 0% in sororities
Most popular majors: 100% Liberal Arts and Sciences/Liberal Studies
Expenses: 2020-2021: $26,000; room/board: $9,400
Financial aid: (805) 421-5936; 71% of undergrads determined to have financial need; average aid package $21,662

United States University[1]
Chula Vista CA
(800) 316-6314
U.S. News ranking: Reg. U. (W), unranked
Admissions email: N/A
For-profit
Application deadline (fall): N/A

Undergraduate student body: N/A full time, N/A part time
Expenses: 2019-2020: $6,480; room/board: N/A
Financial aid: N/A

University of Antelope Valley[1]
Lancaster CA
(661) 726-1911
U.S. News ranking: Reg. Coll. (W), unranked
Website: www.uav.edu
Admissions email: N/A
For-profit
Application deadline (fall): N/A
Undergraduate student body: N/A full time, N/A part time
Expenses: 2019-2020: N/A; room/board: $4,414
Financial aid: N/A

University of California–Berkeley
Berkeley CA
(510) 642-3175
U.S. News ranking: Nat. U., No. 22
Website: www.berkeley.edu
Admissions email: N/A
Public; founded 1868
Freshman admissions: most selective; 2019-2020: 87,398 applied, 14,676 accepted. Either SAT or ACT required. SAT 25/75 percentile: 1310-1530. High school rank: 97% in top tenth, 100% in top quarter, 100% in top half
Early decision deadline: N/A, notification date: N/A
Early action deadline: N/A, notification date: N/A
Application deadline (fall): 11/30
Undergraduate student body: 30,067 full time, 1,462 part time; 46% male, 54% female; 0% American Indian, 36% Asian, 2% Black, 16% Hispanic, 6% multiracial, 0% Pacific Islander, 24% white, 13% international; 84% from in state; 27% live on campus; 3% of students in fraternities, 9% in sororities
Most popular majors: 20% Social Sciences, 11% Engineering, 10% Biological and Biomedical Sciences, 8% Computer and Information Sciences and Support Services, 7% Multi/Interdisciplinary Studies
Expenses: 2020-2021: $14,226 in state, $43,980 out of state; room/board: $19,556
Financial aid: (510) 642-7117; 45% of undergrads determined to have financial need; average aid package $26,153

University of California–Davis
Davis CA
(530) 752-2971
U.S. News ranking: Nat. U., No. 39
Website: www.ucdavis.edu
Admissions email: undergraduateadmissions@ucdavis.edu
Public; founded 1905
Freshman admissions: most selective; 2019-2020: 77,152 applied, 30,001 accepted. Either SAT or ACT required. SAT 25/75 percentile: 1150-1420. High

school rank: 100% in top tenth, 100% in top quarter, 100% in top half
Early decision deadline: N/A, notification date: N/A
Early action deadline: N/A, notification date: N/A
Application deadline (fall): 11/30
Undergraduate student body: 30,171 full time, 811 part time; 39% male, 61% female; 0% American Indian, 28% Asian, 2% Black, 23% Hispanic, 6% multiracial, 0% Pacific Islander, 23% white, 17% international
Most popular majors: 15% Social Sciences, 14% Biological and Biomedical Sciences, 13% Psychology, 10% Engineering, 6% Agriculture, Agriculture Operations, and Related Sciences
Expenses: 2020-2021: $14,653 in state, $44,407 out of state; room/board: $16,100
Financial aid: (530) 752-2396; 58% of undergrads determined to have financial need; average aid package $21,768

University of California–Irvine
Irvine CA
(949) 824-6703
U.S. News ranking: Nat. U., No. 35
Website: www.uci.edu
Admissions email: admissions@uci.edu
Public; founded 1965
Freshman admissions: most selective; 2019-2020: 95,568 applied, 25,361 accepted. Either SAT or ACT required. SAT 25/75 percentile: 1160-1440. High school rank: 99% in top tenth, 100% in top quarter, 100% in top half
Early decision deadline: N/A, notification date: N/A
Early action deadline: N/A, notification date: N/A
Application deadline (fall): 11/30
Undergraduate student body: 29,796 full time, 586 part time; 48% male, 52% female; 0% American Indian, 36% Asian, 2% Black, 26% Hispanic, 4% multiracial, 0% Pacific Islander, 13% white, 17% international; N/A from in state; 41% live on campus; 8% of students in fraternities, 9% in sororities
Most popular majors: 17% Social Sciences, 12% Business, Management, Marketing, and Related Support Services, 11% Engineering, 11% Psychology, 9% Biological and Biomedical Sciences
Expenses: 2020-2021: $13,932 in state, $43,686 out of state; room/board: $16,561
Financial aid: (949) 824-5337; 60% of undergrads determined to have financial need; average aid package $24,209

University of California– Los Angeles
Los Angeles CA
(310) 825-3101
U.S. News ranking: Nat. U., No. 20
Website: www.ucla.edu/

Admissions email: ugadm@saonet.ucla.edu
Public; founded 1919
Freshman admissions: most selective; 2019-2020: 111,322 applied, 13,720 accepted. Either SAT or ACT required. SAT 25/75 percentile: 1280-1530. High school rank: 97% in top tenth, 100% in top quarter, 100% in top half
Early decision deadline: N/A, notification date: N/A
Early action deadline: N/A, notification date: N/A
Application deadline (fall): 11/30
Undergraduate student body: 30,872 full time, 571 part time; 42% male, 58% female; 0% American Indian, 28% Asian, 3% Black, 22% Hispanic, 6% multiracial, 0% Pacific Islander, 26% white, 11% international; 78% from in state; 48% live on campus; 11% of students in fraternities, 13% in sororities
Most popular majors: 26% Social Sciences, 14% Biological and Biomedical Sciences, 11% Psychology, 7% Engineering, 7% Mathematics and Statistics
Expenses: 2020-2021: $13,226 in state, $42,980 out of state; room/board: $16,104
Financial aid: (310) 206-0401; 51% of undergrads determined to have financial need; average aid package $24,808

University of California–Merced
Merced CA
(866) 270-7301
U.S. News ranking: Nat. U., No. 97
Website: www.ucmerced.edu
Admissions email: admissions@ucmerced.edu
Public; founded 2005
Freshman admissions: selective; 2019-2020: 25,424 applied, 18,291 accepted. Either SAT or ACT required. SAT 25/75 percentile: 980-1180. High school rank: N/A
Early decision deadline: N/A, notification date: N/A
Early action deadline: N/A, notification date: N/A
Application deadline (fall): 11/30
Undergraduate student body: 8,080 full time, 71 part time; 48% male, 52% female; 0% American Indian, 19% Asian, 4% Black, 56% Hispanic, 3% multiracial, 1% Pacific Islander, 9% white, 8% international; 99% from in state; 44% live on campus; N/A of students in fraternities, N/A in sororities
Most popular majors: 23% Biological and Biomedical Sciences, 21% Engineering, 15% Psychology, 12% Social Sciences, 11% Business, Management, Marketing, and Related Support Services
Expenses: 2020-2021: $13,538 in state, $43,292 out of state; room/board: $18,267
Financial aid: (209) 228-7178; 90% of undergrads determined to have financial need; average aid package $26,288

University of California–Riverside
Riverside CA
(951) 827-3411
U.S. News ranking: Nat. U., No. 88
Website: www.ucr.edu
Admissions email: admissions@ucr.edu
Public; founded 1954
Freshman admissions: more selective; 2019-2020: 49,518 applied, 28,224 accepted. Neither SAT nor ACT required. SAT 25/75 percentile: 1110-1340. High school rank: 94% in top tenth, 100% in top quarter, 100% in top half
Early decision deadline: N/A, notification date: N/A
Early action deadline: N/A, notification date: N/A
Application deadline (fall): 11/30
Undergraduate student body: 21,429 full time, 398 part time; 46% male, 54% female; 0% American Indian, 34% Asian, 3% Black, 42% Hispanic, 6% multiracial, 0% Pacific Islander, 11% white, 4% international; N/A from in state; 28% live on campus; 4% of students in fraternities, 6% in sororities
Most popular majors: 19% Social Sciences, 16% Business, Management, Marketing, and Related Support Services, 15% Biological and Biomedical Sciences, 10% Psychology, 8% Engineering
Expenses: 2020-2021: $13,859 in state, $43,613 out of state; room/board: $16,927
Financial aid: (951) 827-3878; 77% of undergrads determined to have financial need; average aid package $21,726

University of California–San Diego
La Jolla CA
(858) 534-4831
U.S. News ranking: Nat. U., No. 35
Website: www.ucsd.edu/
Admissions email: admissionsreply@ucsd.edu
Public; founded 1960
Freshman admissions: most selective; 2019-2020: 99,133 applied, 32,062 accepted. Either SAT or ACT required. SAT 25/75 percentile: 1230-1490. High school rank: 100% in top tenth, 100% in top quarter, 100% in top half
Early decision deadline: N/A, notification date: N/A
Early action deadline: N/A, notification date: N/A
Application deadline (fall): 11/30
Undergraduate student body: 30,114 full time, 531 part time; 50% male, 50% female; 0% American Indian, 36% Asian, 3% Black, 21% Hispanic, 0% multiracial, 0% Pacific Islander, 19% white, 18% international; 76% from in state; 38% live on campus; 14% of students in fraternities, 14% in sororities
Most popular majors: 20% Biology, General, 10% Mathematics, 8% Economics, 7% International/ Global Studies, 6% Computer Science

Expenses: 2020-2021: $14,451 in state, $44,205 out of state; room/board: $14,680
Financial aid: (858) 534-3800; 55% of undergrads determined to have financial need; average aid package $24,977

University of California– Santa Barbara
Santa Barbara CA
(805) 893-2881
U.S. News ranking: Nat. U., No. 30
Website: www.ucsb.edu/
Admissions email: admissions@sa.ucsb.edu
Public; founded 1909
Freshman admissions: most selective; 2019-2020: 93,457 applied, 27,626 accepted. Either SAT or ACT required. SAT 25/75 percentile: 1240-1490. High school rank: 100% in top tenth, 100% in top quarter, 100% in top half
Early decision deadline: N/A, notification date: N/A
Early action deadline: N/A, notification date: N/A
Application deadline (fall): 11/30
Undergraduate student body: 22,777 full time, 497 part time; 45% male, 55% female; 0% American Indian, 19% Asian, 2% Black, 26% Hispanic, 6% multiracial, 0% Pacific Islander, 31% white, 14% international; N/A from in state; 39% live on campus; 10% of students in fraternities, 7% in sororities
Most popular majors: 26% Social Sciences, 9% Biological and Biomedical Sciences, 8% Multi/ Interdisciplinary Studies, 8% Psychology, 7% Mathematics and Statistics
Expenses: 2020-2021: $14,391 in state, $44,145 out of state; room/board: $15,389
Financial aid: (805) 893-2432; 54% of undergrads determined to have financial need; average aid package $29,936

University of California–Santa Cruz
Santa Cruz CA
(831) 459-4008
U.S. News ranking: Nat. U., No. 97
Website: www.ucsc.edu
Admissions email: admissions@ucsc.edu
Public; founded 1965
Freshman admissions: more selective; 2019-2020: 55,866 applied, 28,808 accepted. Either SAT or ACT required. SAT 25/75 percentile: 1190-1390. High school rank: 96% in top tenth, 100% in top quarter, 100% in top half
Early decision deadline: N/A, notification date: N/A
Early action deadline: N/A, notification date: N/A
Application deadline (fall): 11/30
Undergraduate student body: 16,994 full time, 523 part time; 52% male, 48% female; 0% American Indian, 22% Asian, 2% Black, 26% Hispanic, 8% multiracial, 0% Pacific Islander, 31% white, 9% international;

89% from in state; 50% live on campus; 7% of students in fraternities, 8% in sororities
Most popular majors: 10% Computer and Information Sciences, General, 9% Psychology, General, 7% Business/ Managerial Economics, 5% Cell/ Cellular and Molecular Biology, 5% Sociology
Expenses: 2020-2021: $14,054 in state, $43,808 out of state; room/board: $16,641
Financial aid: (831) 459-2963; 56% of undergrads determined to have financial need; average aid package $25,453

University of La Verne
La Verne CA
(800) 876-4858
U.S. News ranking: Nat. U., No. 112
Website: www.laverne.edu
Admissions email: admission@laverne.edu
Private; founded 1891
Freshman admissions: selective; 2019-2020: 6,864 applied, 3,763 accepted. Neither SAT nor ACT required. SAT 25/75 percentile: 1040-1190. High school rank: 21% in top tenth, 54% in top quarter, 88% in top half
Early decision deadline: N/A, notification date: N/A
Early action deadline: N/A, notification date: N/A
Application deadline (fall): rolling
Undergraduate student body: 2,412 full time, 97 part time; 43% male, 57% female; 0% American Indian, 5% Asian, 5% Black, 57% Hispanic, 5% multiracial, 0% Pacific Islander, 17% white, 8% international; N/A from in state; 32% live on campus; 3% of students in fraternities, 6% in sororities
Most popular majors: 25% Business, Management, Marketing, and Related Support Services, 16% Social Sciences, 10% Education, 9% Psychology, 8% Communication, Journalism, and Related Programs
Expenses: 2020-2021: $45,850; room/board: $13,800
Financial aid: (800) 649-0160; 84% of undergrads determined to have financial need; average aid package $32,544

University of Redlands
Redlands CA
(800) 455-5064
U.S. News ranking: Reg. U. (W), No. 5
Website: www.redlands.edu
Admissions email: admissions@redlands.edu
Private; founded 1907
Freshman admissions: more selective; 2019-2020: 4,621 applied, 3,531 accepted. Either SAT or ACT required. SAT 25/75 percentile: 1080-1270. High school rank: 34% in top tenth, 73% in top quarter, 95% in top half
Early decision deadline: N/A, notification date: N/A

Early action deadline: 11/15, notification date: 1/15
Application deadline (fall): 1/15
Undergraduate student body: 2,650 full time, 540 part time; 39% male, 61% female; 1% American Indian, 6% Asian, 4% Black, 37% Hispanic, 5% multiracial, 0% Pacific Islander, 39% white, 2% international
Most popular majors: Information not available
Expenses: 2020-2021: $52,650; room/board: $15,109
Financial aid: (909) 748-8047; 78% of undergrads determined to have financial need; average aid package $52,070

University of San Diego
San Diego CA
(619) 260-4506
U.S. News ranking: Nat. U., No. 88
Website: www.SanDiego.edu
Admissions email: admissions@SanDiego.edu
Private; founded 1949
Affiliation: Roman Catholic
Freshman admissions: more selective; 2019-2020: 13,755 applied, 6,697 accepted. Neither SAT nor ACT required. SAT 25/75 percentile: 1190-1370. High school rank: 33% in top tenth, 74% in top quarter, 97% in top half
Early decision deadline: N/A, notification date: N/A
Early action deadline: N/A, notification date: N/A
Application deadline (fall): 12/15
Undergraduate student body: 5,761 full time, 158 part time; 44% male, 56% female; 0% American Indian, 7% Asian, 3% Black, 21% Hispanic, 7% multiracial, 0% Pacific Islander, 50% white, 9% international; 55% from in state; 44% live on campus; 18% of students in fraternities, 32% in sororities
Most popular majors: 41% Business, Management, Marketing, and Related Support Services, 12% Biological and Biomedical Sciences, 10% Social Sciences, 9% Engineering, 8% Communication, Journalism, and Related Programs
Expenses: 2020-2021: $52,864; room/board: $15,156
Financial aid: (619) 260-2700; 54% of undergrads determined to have financial need; average aid package $40,082

University of San Francisco
San Francisco CA
(415) 422-6563
U.S. News ranking: Nat. U., No. 103
Website: www.usfca.edu
Admissions email: admission@usfca.edu
Private; founded 1855
Affiliation: Roman Catholic
Freshman admissions: more selective; 2019-2020: 21,867 applied, 14,086 accepted. Neither SAT nor ACT required. SAT 25/75 percentile: 1130-1330. High school rank: 32% in top

tenth, 66% in top quarter, 95% in top half
Early decision deadline: 11/1, notification date: 12/1
Early action deadline: 11/1, notification date: 12/14
Application deadline (fall): 1/15
Undergraduate student body: 6,345 full time, 232 part time; 38% male, 62% female; 0% American Indian, 24% Asian, 5% Black, 22% Hispanic, 9% multiracial, 1% Pacific Islander, 25% white, 13% international; 62% from in state; 34% live on campus; 5% of students in fraternities, 10% in sororities
Most popular majors: 36% Business, Management, Marketing, and Related Support Services, 14% Health Professions and Related Programs, 9% Communication, Journalism, and Related Programs, 9% Social Sciences, 7% Psychology
Expenses: 2020-2021: $52,482; room/board: $15,990
Financial aid: (415) 422-3387; 59% of undergrads determined to have financial need; average aid package $35,618

University of Southern California
Los Angeles CA
(213) 740-1111
U.S. News ranking: Nat. U., No. 24
Website: www.usc.edu/
Admissions email: admitusc@usc.edu
Private; founded 1880
Freshman admissions: most selective; 2019-2020: 66,198 applied, 7,558 accepted. Either SAT or ACT required. SAT 25/75 percentile: 1360-1530. High school rank: N/A
Early decision deadline: N/A, notification date: N/A
Early action deadline: N/A, notification date: N/A
Application deadline (fall): 1/15
Undergraduate student body: 19,622 full time, 729 part time; 48% male, 52% female; 0% American Indian, 21% Asian, 5% Black, 16% Hispanic, 6% multiracial, 0% Pacific Islander, 37% white, 13% international; 50% from in state; 30% live on campus; 26% of students in fraternities, 27% in sororities
Most popular majors: 25% Business, Management, Marketing, and Related Support Services, 12% Social Sciences, 12% Visual and Performing Arts, 9% Engineering, 8% Communication, Journalism, and Related Programs
Expenses: 2020-2021: $59,072; room/board: $15,916
Financial aid: (213) 740-4444; 37% of undergrads determined to have financial need; average aid package $53,612

University of the Pacific
Stockton CA
(209) 946-2011
U.S. News ranking: Nat. U., No. 133
Website: www.pacific.edu

Admissions email: admissions@pacific.edu
Private; founded 1851
Freshman admissions: more selective; 2019-2020: 13,096 applied, 8,592 accepted. Either SAT or ACT required. SAT 25/75 percentile: 1120-1360. High school rank: 37% in top tenth, 66% in top quarter, 93% in top half
Early decision deadline: N/A, notification date: N/A
Early action deadline: 11/15, notification date: 1/15
Application deadline (fall): 1/15
Undergraduate student body: 3,536 full time, 104 part time; 48% male, 52% female; 0% American Indian, 38% Asian, 3% Black, 21% Hispanic, 4% multiracial, 1% Pacific Islander, 23% white, 7% international; N/A from in state; 47% live on campus; 7% of students in fraternities, 5% in sororities
Most popular majors: 20% Business, Management, Marketing, and Related Support Services, 16% Biological and Biomedical Sciences, 9% Engineering, 8% Health Professions and Related Programs, 8% Multi/Interdisciplinary Studies
Expenses: 2020-2021: $51,094; room/board: $13,740
Financial aid: (209) 946-2421; 71% of undergrads determined to have financial need; average aid package $38,616

University of the West[1]
Rosemead CA
(855) 468-9378
U.S. News ranking: Nat. Lib. Arts, second tier
Website: www.uwest.edu
Admissions email: admission@uwest.edu
Private; founded 1991
Application deadline (fall): 5/1
Undergraduate student body: N/A full time, N/A part time
Expenses: 2019-2020: $12,956; room/board: $7,996
Financial aid: (626) 571-8811

Vanguard University of Southern California
Costa Mesa CA
(800) 722-6279
U.S. News ranking: Reg. U. (W), No. 52
Website: www.vanguard.edu
Admissions email: admissions@vanguard.edu
Private; founded 1920
Affiliation:
Assemblies of God Church
Freshman admissions: selective; 2019-2020: 3,976 applied, 1,966 accepted. Either SAT or ACT required. SAT 25/75 percentile: 980-1170. High school rank: 21% in top tenth, 46% in top quarter, 75% in top half
Early decision deadline: N/A, notification date: N/A
Early action deadline: 12/1, notification date: 1/15
Application deadline (fall): 8/1
Undergraduate student body: 1,668 full time, 201 part time; 33% male, 67% female; 0% American

Indian, 6% Asian, 5% Black, 43% Hispanic, 2% multiracial, 1% Pacific Islander, 34% white, 1% international; 88% from in state; 59% live on campus; 0% of students in fraternities, 1% in sororities
Most popular majors: 18% Psychology, General, 16% Business Administration and Management, General, 10% Nursing Administration, 6% Education, General, 6% Speech Communication and Rhetoric
Expenses: 2020-2021: $36,550; room/board: $12,222
Financial aid: (714) 619-6691; 89% of undergrads determined to have financial need; average aid package $15,700

Westcliff University[1]
Irvine, CA
(888) 491-8686
U.S. News ranking: Business, unranked
Admissions email: N/A
For-profit
Application deadline (fall): N/A
Undergraduate student body: N/A full time, N/A part time
Expenses: 2019-2020: $8,700; room/board: $10,248
Financial aid: N/A

West Los Angeles College[1]
Culver City CA
(310) 287-4501
U.S. News ranking: Reg. Coll. (W), unranked
Website: www.wlac.edu
Admissions email: N/A
Public; founded 1969
Application deadline (fall): N/A
Undergraduate student body: N/A full time, N/A part time
Expenses: 2019-2020: $1,220 in state, $8,110 out of state; room/board: $15,084
Financial aid: N/A

Westmont College
Santa Barbara CA
(805) 565-6000
U.S. News ranking: Nat. Lib. Arts, No. 113
Website: www.westmont.edu
Admissions email: admissions@westmont.edu
Private; founded 1937
Affiliation: Undenominational
Freshman admissions: more selective; 2019-2020: 3,074 applied, 1,992 accepted. Either SAT or ACT required. SAT 25/75 percentile: 1100-1330. High school rank: 33% in top tenth, 56% in top quarter, 81% in top half
Early decision deadline: N/A, notification date: N/A
Early action deadline: 12/1, notification date: 12/1
Application deadline (fall): rolling
Undergraduate student body: 1,312 full time, 13 part time; 40% male, 60% female; 0% American Indian, 7% Asian, 2% Black, 20% Hispanic, 6% multiracial, 1% Pacific Islander, 55% white, 2% international; 63% from in state; 90% live on campus; N/A of students in fraternities, N/A in sororities

Most popular majors: 16% Business, Management, Marketing, and Related Support Services, 16% Parks, Recreation, Leisure, and Fitness Studies, 12% Biological and Biomedical Sciences, 9% Psychology, 8% Communication, Journalism, and Related Programs
Expenses: 2020-2021: $48,180; room/board: $15,040
Financial aid: (805) 565-6063; 68% of undergrads determined to have financial need; average aid package $37,908

Whittier College
Whittier CA
(562) 907-4200
U.S. News ranking: Nat. Lib. Arts, No. 102
Admissions email: N/A
Private; founded 1887
Freshman admissions: selective; 2019-2020: 7,233 applied, 4,131 accepted. Neither SAT nor ACT required. SAT 25/75 percentile: 1038-1220. High school rank: 20% in top tenth, 33% in top quarter, 91% in top half
Early decision deadline: N/A, notification date: N/A
Early action deadline: 11/15, notification date: 12/20
Application deadline (fall): rolling
Undergraduate student body: 1,748 full time, 28 part time; 44% male, 56% female; 0% American Indian, 7% Asian, 5% Black, 51% Hispanic, 7% multiracial, 0% Pacific Islander, 25% white, 3% international
Most popular majors: Information not available
Expenses: 2020-2021: $49,314; room/board: $14,438
Financial aid: (562) 907-4285; 76% of undergrads determined to have financial need; average aid package $39,393

William Jessup University
Rocklin CA
(916) 577-2222
U.S. News ranking: Reg. Coll. (W), No. 2
Website: www.jessup.edu
Admissions email: admissions@jessup.edu
Private; founded 1939
Affiliation: Protestant, not specified
Freshman admissions: selective; 2019-2020: 773 applied, 502 accepted. Either SAT or ACT required. SAT 25/75 percentile: 950-1210. High school rank: 16% in top tenth, 43% in top quarter, 68% in top half
Early decision deadline: N/A, notification date: N/A
Early action deadline: N/A, notification date: N/A
Application deadline (fall): rolling
Undergraduate student body: 1,078 full time, 183 part time; 41% male, 59% female; 1% American Indian, 5% Asian, 6% Black, 19% Hispanic, 1% multiracial, 1% Pacific Islander, 52% white, 7% international; 91% from in state; 58% live on campus; 0% of students in fraternities, 0% in sororities

Most popular majors: 27% Business, Management, Marketing, and Related Support Services, 23% Psychology, 12% Education, 12% Theology and Religious Vocations, 7% Parks, Recreation, Leisure, and Fitness Studies
Expenses: 2020-2021: $36,750; room/board: $12,160
Financial aid: (916) 577-2232; 76% of undergrads determined to have financial need; average aid package $26,018

Woodbury University
Burbank CA
(818) 252-5221
U.S. News ranking: Reg. U. (W), No. 50
Website: woodbury.edu/
Admissions email: info@woodbury.edu
Private; founded 1884
Freshman admissions: selective; 2019-2020: 1,907 applied, 1,265 accepted. Neither SAT nor ACT required. SAT 25/75 percentile: 940-1220. High school rank: N/A
Early decision deadline: N/A, notification date: N/A
Early action deadline: N/A, notification date: N/A
Application deadline (fall): rolling
Undergraduate student body: 1,064 full time, 54 part time; 48% male, 52% female; 0% American Indian, 10% Asian, 4% Black, 38% Hispanic, 3% multiracial, 0% Pacific Islander, 34% white, 11% international; N/A from in state; 17% live on campus; N/A of students in fraternities, N/A in sororities
Most popular majors: Information not available
Expenses: 2020-2021: $42,596; room/board: $13,331
Financial aid: (818) 252-5273; 75% of undergrads determined to have financial need; average aid package $32,723

COLORADO

Adams State University[1]
Alamosa CO
(800) 824-6494
U.S. News ranking: Reg. U. (W), second tier
Website: www.adams.edu
Admissions email: ascadmit@adams.edu
Public
Application deadline (fall): N/A
Undergraduate student body: N/A full time, N/A part time
Expenses: 2019-2020: $9,440 in state, $20,864 out of state; room/board: $8,760
Financial aid: N/A

Colorado Christian University
Lakewood CO
(303) 963-3200
U.S. News ranking: Reg. U. (W), No. 68
Website: www.ccu.edu
Admissions email: admission@ccu.edu

Private; founded 1914
Affiliation: Interdenominational
Freshman admissions: selective; 2019-2020: 2,328 applied, 1,475 accepted. Neither SAT nor ACT required. ACT 25/75 percentile: 22-28. High school rank: N/A
Early decision deadline: N/A, notification date: N/A
Early action deadline: N/A, notification date: N/A
Application deadline (fall): N/A
Undergraduate student body: 1,737 full time, 4,802 part time; 34% male, 66% female; 1% American Indian, 2% Asian, 12% Black, 18% Hispanic, 4% multiracial, 0% Pacific Islander, 62% white, 0% international; N/A from in state; N/A live on campus; 0% of students in fraternities, 0% in sororities
Most popular majors: 14% Psychology, General, 9% Business Administration and Management, General, 7% Bible/Biblical Studies, 7% Registered Nursing, Nursing Administration, Nursing Research and Clinical Nursing, 6% Health and Medical Administrative Services
Expenses: 2020-2021: $34,750; room/board: $11,694
Financial aid: N/A

Colorado College
Colorado Springs CO
(719) 389-6344
U.S. News ranking: Nat. Lib. Arts, No. 25
Website: www.ColoradoCollege.edu
Admissions email: admission@ColoradoCollege.edu
Private; founded 1874
Freshman admissions: most selective; 2019-2020: 9,456 applied, 1,277 accepted. Neither SAT nor ACT required. SAT 25/75 percentile: 1300-1480. High school rank: 82% in top tenth, 98% in top quarter, 100% in top half
Early decision deadline: 11/10, notification date: 12/15
Early action deadline: 11/1, notification date: 12/20
Application deadline (fall): 1/15
Undergraduate student body: 2,089 full time, 10 part time; 45% male, 55% female; 0% American Indian, 5% Asian, 3% Black, 9% Hispanic, 8% multiracial, 0% Pacific Islander, 65% white, 8% international; 83% from in state; 83% live on campus; N/A of students in fraternities, N/A in sororities
Most popular majors: 7% Ecology and Evolutionary Biology, 7% Economics, General, 6% Sociology, 5% Cell/Cellular and Molecular Biology, 5% Political Science and Government, General
Expenses: 2020-2021: $60,864; room/board: $13,392
Financial aid: (719) 389-6651; 40% of undergrads determined to have financial need; average aid package $47,954

Colorado Mesa University
Grand Junction CO
(970) 248-1875
U.S. News ranking: Reg. U. (W), second tier
Website: www.coloradomesa.edu
Admissions email: admissions@coloradomesa.edu
Public; founded 1925
Freshman admissions: selective; 2019-2020: 8,845 applied, 6,917 accepted. Either SAT or ACT required. SAT 25/75 percentile: 930-1170. High school rank: 11% in top tenth, 29% in top quarter, 59% in top half
Early decision deadline: N/A, notification date: N/A
Early action deadline: N/A, notification date: N/A
Application deadline (fall): rolling
Undergraduate student body: 6,972 full time, 2,267 part time; 46% male, 54% female; 1% American Indian, 1% Asian, 2% Black, 21% Hispanic, 4% multiracial, 1% Pacific Islander, 67% white, 1% international; N/A from in state; 25% live on campus; 1% of students in fraternities, 1% in sororities
Most popular majors: 21% Business/Commerce, General, 19% Registered Nursing/Registered Nurse, 14% Kinesiology and Exercise Science, 7% Criminal Justice/Safety Studies, 4% Biology/Biological Sciences, General
Expenses: 2020-2021: $9,306 in state, $23,163 out of state; room/board: $11,168
Financial aid: (970) 248-1396; 63% of undergrads determined to have financial need; average aid package $10,393

Colorado Mountain College[1]
Glenwood Springs CO
(970) 945-8691
U.S. News ranking: Reg. Coll. (W), unranked
Admissions email: joinus@coloradomtn.edu
Public; founded 1967
Application deadline (fall): rolling
Undergraduate student body: N/A full time, N/A part time
Expenses: 2019-2020: $4,620 in state, $11,172 out of state; room/board: $9,658
Financial aid: N/A

Colorado School of Mines
Golden CO
(303) 273-3220
U.S. News ranking: Nat. U., No. 88
Website: www.mines.edu
Admissions email: admissions@mines.edu
Public; founded 1874
Freshman admissions: more selective; 2019-2020: 11,756 applied, 6,240 accepted. Either SAT or ACT required. SAT 25/75 percentile: 1260-1460. High school rank: 50% in top tenth, 81% in top quarter, 98% in top half
Early decision deadline: N/A, notification date: N/A

Early action deadline: N/A, notification date: N/A
Application deadline (fall): 5/1
Undergraduate student body: 4,928 full time, 226 part time; 69% male, 31% female; 0% American Indian, 5% Asian, 1% Black, 11% Hispanic, 6% multiracial, 0% Pacific Islander, 70% white, 5% international; 55% from in state; 11% live on campus; 15% of students in fraternities, 22% in sororities
Most popular majors: 85% Engineering, 9% Computer and Information Sciences and Support Services, 3% Mathematics and Statistics, 2% Physical Sciences, 1% Social Sciences
Expenses: 2020-2021: $19,100 in state, $39,800 out of state; room/board: $14,720
Financial aid: (303) 273-3301; 46% of undergrads determined to have financial need; average aid package $16,918

Colorado State University
Fort Collins CO
(970) 491-6909
U.S. News ranking: Nat. U., No. 153
Website: www.colostate.edu
Admissions email: admissions@colostate.edu
Public; founded 1870
Freshman admissions: more selective; 2019-2020: 28,319 applied, 23,038 accepted. Either SAT or ACT required. SAT 25/75 percentile: 1070-1290. High school rank: 21% in top tenth, 48% in top quarter, 83% in top half
Early decision deadline: N/A, notification date: N/A
Early action deadline: 12/1, notification date: 1/1
Application deadline (fall): 7/1
Undergraduate student body: 22,388 full time, 4,171 part time; 47% male, 53% female; 0% American Indian, 3% Asian, 2% Black, 15% Hispanic, 5% multiracial, 0% Pacific Islander, 70% white, 4% international; N/A from in state; 24% live on campus; 5% of students in fraternities, 7% in sororities
Most popular majors: 14% Business, Management, Marketing, and Related Support Services, 13% Biological and Biomedical Sciences, 11% Engineering, 9% Social Sciences, 6% Parks, Recreation, Leisure, and Fitness Studies
Expenses: 2020-2021: $12,260 in state, $31,540 out of state; room/board: $12,440
Financial aid: (970) 491-6321; 48% of undergrads determined to have financial need; average aid package $11,515

Colorado State University–Pueblo
Pueblo CO
(719) 549-2462
U.S. News ranking: Reg. U. (W), No. 93
Website: www.csupueblo.edu
Admissions email: info@csupueblo.edu

Public; founded 1933
Freshman admissions: selective; 2019-2020: 2,885 applied, 2,684 accepted. Either SAT or ACT required. SAT 25/75 percentile: 940-1130. High school rank: 10% in top tenth, 34% in top quarter, 71% in top half
Early decision deadline: N/A, notification date: N/A
Early action deadline: N/A, notification date: N/A
Application deadline (fall): 8/1
Undergraduate student body: 2,985 full time, 1,325 part time; 46% male, 54% female; 0% American Indian, 1% Asian, 6% Black, 36% Hispanic, 6% multiracial, 0% Pacific Islander, 45% white, 2% international; 87% from in state; 19% live on campus; 1% of students in fraternities, 2% in sororities
Most popular majors: 13% Registered Nursing/Registered Nurse, 9% Business/Commerce, General, 8% Social Work, 7% Psychology, General, 7% Sociology
Expenses: 2020-2021: $10,445 in state, $18,643 out of state; room/board: $10,930
Financial aid: (719) 549-2753; 76% of undergrads determined to have financial need; average aid package $11,821

Colorado Technical University[1]
Colorado Springs CO
(888) 404-7555
U.S. News ranking: Nat. U., second tier
Website: www.coloradotech.edu
Admissions email: info@ctuonline.edu
For-profit
Application deadline (fall): N/A
Undergraduate student body: N/A full time, N/A part time
Expenses: 2019-2020: $12,529; room/board: N/A
Financial aid: N/A

Community College of Denver[1]
Denver CO
(303) 556-2600
U.S. News ranking: Reg. Coll. (W), unranked
Website: www.ccd.edu
Admissions email: N/A
Public
Application deadline (fall): N/A
Undergraduate student body: N/A full time, N/A part time
Expenses: 2019-2020: $4,831 in state, $15,911 out of state; room/board: $11,799
Financial aid: N/A

Fort Lewis College
Durango CO
(877) 352-2656
U.S. News ranking: Nat. Lib. Arts, second tier
Website: www.fortlewis.edu
Admissions email: admission@fortlewis.edu
Public; founded 1911
Freshman admissions: selective; 2019-2020: 3,757 applied, 3,433 accepted. Either SAT or ACT required. ACT 25/75

percentile: 17-23. High school rank: 13% in top tenth, 20% in top quarter, 67% in top half
Early decision deadline: N/A, notification date: N/A
Early action deadline: 11/15, notification date: 12/24
Application deadline (fall): 8/1
Undergraduate student body: 2,865 full time, 364 part time; 46% male, 54% female; 30% American Indian, 1% Asian, 1% Black, 12% Hispanic, 11% multiracial, 0% Pacific Islander, 44% white, 1% international; N/A from in state; 43% live on campus; 0% of students in fraternities, 0% in sororities
Most popular majors: 20% Business, Management, Marketing, and Related Support Services, 13% Homeland Security, Law Enforcement, Firefighting and Related Protective Services, 11% Parks, Recreation, Leisure, and Fitness Studies, 9% Psychology, 7% Visual and Performing Arts
Expenses: 2020-2021: $8,872 in state, $19,528 out of state; room/board: $10,076
Financial aid: (970) 247-7142; 58% of undergrads determined to have financial need; average aid package $19,273

Metropolitan State University of Denver[7]
Denver CO
(303) 556-3058
U.S. News ranking: Reg. U. (W), second tier
Website: www.msudenver.edu
Admissions email: askmetro@msudenver.edu
Public; founded 1963
Freshman admissions: less selective; 2019-2020: 13,526 applied, 8,270 accepted. Either SAT or ACT required. SAT 25/75 percentile: 880-1110. High school rank: 2% in top tenth, 14% in top quarter, 47% in top half
Early decision deadline: N/A, notification date: N/A
Early action deadline: N/A, notification date: N/A
Application deadline (fall): 7/1
Undergraduate student body: 12,250 full time, 6,944 part time
Most popular majors: 21% Business, Management, Marketing, and Related Support Services, 8% Health Professions and Related Programs, 8% Multi/Interdisciplinary Studies, 7% Psychology, 6% Biological and Biomedical Sciences
Expenses: 2019-2020: $7,666 in state, $20,847 out of state; room/board: N/A
Financial aid: (303) 605-5504; 69% of undergrads determined to have financial need; average aid package $9,373

Naropa University
Boulder CO
(303) 546-3572
U.S. News ranking: Reg. U. (W), second tier
Website: www.naropa.edu
Admissions email: admissions@naropa.edu
Private; founded 1974

Freshman admissions: least selective; 2019-2020: 135 applied, 133 accepted. Neither SAT nor ACT required. SAT 25/75 percentile: N/A. High school rank: N/A
Early decision deadline: N/A, notification date: N/A
Early action deadline: N/A, notification date: N/A
Application deadline (fall): rolling
Undergraduate student body: 354 full time, 27 part time; 29% male, 71% female; 0% American Indian, 2% Asian, 1% Black, 14% Hispanic, 6% multiracial, 0% Pacific Islander, 69% white, 1% international; 41% from in state; 18% live on campus; 0% of students in fraternities, 0% in sororities
Most popular majors: 31% Psychology, 14% Multi/Interdisciplinary Studies, 12% Health Professions and Related Programs, 11% Visual and Performing Arts, 10% English Language and Literature/Letters
Expenses: 2019-2020: $33,070; room/board: $10,957
Financial aid: (303) 546-3509

Pueblo Community College[1]
Pueblo CO
(719) 549-3200
U.S. News ranking: Reg. Coll. (W), unranked
Website: www.pueblocc.edu
Admissions email: N/A
Public
Application deadline (fall): N/A
Undergraduate student body: N/A full time, N/A part time
Expenses: 2019-2020: $5,179 in state, $16,262 out of state; room/board: $10,641
Financial aid: N/A

Red Rocks Community College[1]
Lakewood CO
(303) 914-6600
U.S. News ranking: Reg. Coll. (W), unranked
Website: www.rrcc.edu
Admissions email: N/A
Public
Application deadline (fall): N/A
Undergraduate student body: N/A full time, N/A part time
Expenses: 2019-2020: $4,263 in state, $15,350 out of state; room/board: $11,637
Financial aid: N/A

Regis University
Denver CO
(303) 458-4900
U.S. News ranking: Nat. U., No. 217
Website: www.regis.edu
Admissions email: ruadmissions@regis.edu
Private; founded 1877
Affiliation: Roman Catholic
Freshman admissions: selective; 2019-2020: 6,910 applied, 4,903 accepted. Either SAT or ACT required. SAT 25/75 percentile: 1030-1240. High school rank: 28% in top tenth, 60% in top quarter, 91% in top half

Early decision deadline: N/A, notification date: N/A
Early action deadline: N/A, notification date: N/A
Application deadline (fall): 8/1
Undergraduate student body: 2,191 full time, 1,309 part time; 39% male, 61% female; 1% American Indian, 6% Asian, 4% Black, 25% Hispanic, 5% multiracial, 0% Pacific Islander, 54% white, 1% international
Most popular majors: 31% Health Professions and Related Programs, 22% Business, Management, Marketing, and Related Support Services, 10% Liberal Arts and Sciences, General Studies and Humanities, 7% Computer and Information Sciences and Support Services, 6% Biological and Biomedical Sciences
Expenses: 2020-2021: $38,558; room/board: $12,838
Financial aid: (303) 458-4126; 71% of undergrads determined to have financial need; average aid package $31,006

Rocky Mountain College of Art and Design[1]
Lakewood CO
(303) 753-6046
U.S. News ranking: Arts, unranked
Website: www.rmcad.edu/
Admissions email: admissions@rmcad.edu
For-profit; founded 1963
Application deadline (fall): N/A
Undergraduate student body: N/A full time, N/A part time
Expenses: 2019-2020: $19,670; room/board: N/A
Financial aid: (303) 225-8551

United States Air Force Academy
USAF Academy CO
(800) 443-9266
U.S. News ranking: Nat. Lib. Arts, No. 28
Website: academyadmissions.com
Admissions email: rr_webmail@usafa.edu
Public; founded 1954
Freshman admissions: more selective; 2019-2020: 10,354 applied, 1,147 accepted. Either SAT or ACT required. ACT 25/75 percentile: 28-33. High school rank: 54% in top tenth, 82% in top quarter, 97% in top half
Early decision deadline: N/A, notification date: N/A
Early action deadline: N/A, notification date: N/A
Application deadline (fall): 12/31
Undergraduate student body: 4,304 full time, 0 part time; 72% male, 28% female; 0% American Indian, 6% Asian, 7% Black, 11% Hispanic, 7% multiracial, 1% Pacific Islander, 64% white, 1% international; 8% from in state; 100% live on campus; 0% of students in fraternities, 0% in sororities
Most popular majors: 25% Engineering, 22% Business, Management, Marketing, and Related Support Services, 13% Social Sciences, 12% Multi/Interdisciplinary Studies,

6% Biological and Biomedical Sciences
Expenses: N/A
Financial aid: N/A

University of Colorado Boulder
Boulder CO
(303) 492-6301
U.S. News ranking: Nat. U., No. 103
Website: www.colorado.edu
Admissions email: apply@colorado.edu
Public; founded 1876
Freshman admissions: more selective; 2019-2020: 40,740 applied, 31,933 accepted. Either SAT or ACT required. SAT 25/75 percentile: 1140-1360. High school rank: 26% in top tenth, 56% in top quarter, 86% in top half
Early decision deadline: N/A, notification date: N/A
Early action deadline: 11/15, notification date: 2/1
Application deadline (fall): 1/15
Undergraduate student body: 28,834 full time, 2,267 part time; 55% male, 45% female; 0% American Indian, 6% Asian, 2% Black, 13% Hispanic, 6% multiracial, 0% Pacific Islander, 67% white, 6% international; 61% from in state; 28% live on campus; 12% of students in fraternities, 22% in sororities
Most popular majors: 15% Business, Management, Marketing, and Related Support Services, 13% Biological and Biomedical Sciences, 12% Engineering, 12% Social Sciences, 10% Communication, Journalism, and Related Programs
Expenses: 2020-2021: $12,466 in state, $38,284 out of state; room/board: $15,220
Financial aid: (303) 492-5091; 35% of undergrads determined to have financial need; average aid package $17,962

University of Colorado–Colorado Springs
Colorado Springs CO
(719) 255-3084
U.S. News ranking: Nat. U., second tier
Website: www.uccs.edu
Admissions email: go@uccs.edu
Public; founded 1965
Freshman admissions: selective; 2019-2020: 10,834 applied, 9,597 accepted. Either SAT or ACT required. SAT 25/75 percentile: 1020-1230. High school rank: 15% in top tenth, 36% in top quarter, 73% in top half
Early decision deadline: N/A, notification date: N/A
Early action deadline: N/A, notification date: N/A
Application deadline (fall): rolling
Undergraduate student body: 8,181 full time, 2,015 part time; 48% male, 52% female; 0% American Indian, 3% Asian, 4% Black, 19% Hispanic, 8% multiracial, 0% Pacific Islander, 63% white, 1% international; 87% from in

state; 15% live on campus; N/A of students in fraternities, N/A in sororities
Most popular majors: 18% Business, Management, Marketing, and Related Support Services, 14% Health Professions and Related Programs, 10% Biological and Biomedical Sciences, 9% Social Sciences, 8% Engineering
Expenses: 2020-2021: $10,480 in state, $25,600 out of state; room/board: $11,158
Financial aid: (719) 255-3460; 59% of undergrads determined to have financial need; average aid package $9,398

University of Colorado Denver
Denver CO
(303) 556-2704
U.S. News ranking: Nat. U., No. 227
Website: www.ucdenver.edu
Admissions email: admissions@ucdenver.edu
Public; founded 1912
Freshman admissions: selective; 2019-2020: 9,565 applied, 6,438 accepted. Either SAT or ACT required. SAT 25/75 percentile: 1000-1220. High school rank: 20% in top tenth, 50% in top quarter, 82% in top half
Early decision deadline: N/A, notification date: N/A
Early action deadline: N/A, notification date: N/A
Application deadline (fall): rolling
Undergraduate student body: 8,857 full time, 6,961 part time; 45% male, 55% female; 0% American Indian, 10% Asian, 5% Black, 25% Hispanic, 6% multiracial, 0% Pacific Islander, 44% white, 8% international
Most popular majors: 16% Business, Management, Marketing, and Related Support Services, 15% Health Professions and Related Programs, 12% Social Sciences, 8% Biological and Biomedical Sciences, 8% Psychology
Expenses: 2020-2021: $11,395 in state, $32,005 out of state; room/board: $11,547
Financial aid: (303) 315-1850; 61% of undergrads determined to have financial need; average aid package $10,728

University of Denver
Denver CO
(303) 871-2036
U.S. News ranking: Nat. U., No. 80
Website: www.du.edu
Admissions email: admission@du.edu
Private; founded 1864
Freshman admissions: more selective; 2019-2020: 21,028 applied, 12,345 accepted. Neither SAT nor ACT required. ACT 25/75 percentile: 26-31. High school rank: 39% in top tenth, 73% in top quarter, 94% in top half
Early decision deadline: 11/1, notification date: 12/15
Early action deadline: 11/1, notification date: 1/15

Application deadline (fall): 1/15
Undergraduate student body: 5,478 full time, 296 part time; 46% male, 54% female; 0% American Indian, 4% Asian, 2% Black, 12% Hispanic, 5% multiracial, 0% Pacific Islander, 68% white, 6% international; 36% from in state; 48% live on campus; 25% of students in fraternities, 28% in sororities
Most popular majors: 35% Business, Management, Marketing, and Related Support Services, 15% Social Sciences, 10% Biological and Biomedical Sciences, 7% Communication, Journalism, and Related Programs, 7% Psychology
Expenses: 2020-2021: $53,775; room/board: $14,178
Financial aid: (303) 871-4020; 43% of undergrads determined to have financial need; average aid package $42,918

University of Northern Colorado
Greeley CO
(970) 351-2881
U.S. News ranking: Nat. U., second tier
Website: www.unco.edu
Admissions email: admissions@unco.edu
Public; founded 1890
Freshman admissions: selective; 2019-2020: 9,275 applied, 8,425 accepted. Either SAT or ACT required. SAT 25/75 percentile: 970-1200. High school rank: 13% in top tenth, 37% in top quarter, 73% in top half
Early decision deadline: N/A, notification date: N/A
Early action deadline: N/A, notification date: N/A
Application deadline (fall): 8/1
Undergraduate student body: 7,752 full time, 2,058 part time; 34% male, 66% female; 0% American Indian, 2% Asian, 4% Black, 24% Hispanic, 5% multiracial, 0% Pacific Islander, 63% white, 1% international; 86% from in state; 34% live on campus; 11% of students in fraternities, 8% in sororities
Most popular majors: 18% Health Professions and Related Programs, 13% Education, 10% Business, Management, Marketing, and Related Support Services, 9% Parks, Recreation, Leisure, and Fitness Studies, 8% Visual and Performing Arts
Expenses: 2020-2021: $10,188 in state, $22,260 out of state; room/board: $11,204
Financial aid: (970) 351-2502; 63% of undergrads determined to have financial need; average aid package $15,328

Western Colorado University
Gunnison CO
(970) 943-2119
U.S. News ranking: Reg. U. (W), No. 75
Website: www.western.edu
Admissions email: admissions@western.edu
Public; founded 1901

Freshman admissions: selective; 2019-2020: 2,504 applied, 2,107 accepted. Either SAT or ACT required. SAT 25/75 percentile: 1000-1200. High school rank: 6% in top tenth, 17% in top quarter, 37% in top half
Early decision deadline: N/A, notification date: N/A
Early action deadline: 11/1, notification date: N/A
Application deadline (fall): rolling
Undergraduate student body: 1,762 full time, 1,278 part time; 51% male, 49% female; 0% American Indian, 1% Asian, 3% Black, 11% Hispanic, 4% multiracial, 0% Pacific Islander, 70% white, 0% international; 71% from in state; 57% live on campus; N/A of students in fraternities, N/A in sororities
Most popular majors: 26% Business, Management, Marketing, and Related Support Services, 19% Parks, Recreation, Leisure, and Fitness Studies, 11% Biological and Biomedical Sciences, 10% Social Sciences, 7% Psychology
Expenses: 2020-2021: $10,437 in state, $21,909 out of state; room/board: $9,704
Financial aid: (970) 943-7015; 57% of undergrads determined to have financial need; average aid package $12,280

CONNECTICUT

Albertus Magnus College
New Haven CT
(800) 578-9160
U.S. News ranking: Reg. U. (N), No. 88
Website: www.albertus.edu
Admissions email: admissions@albertus.edu
Private; founded 1925
Affiliation: Roman Catholic
Freshman admissions: less selective; 2019-2020: 1,425 applied, 1,074 accepted. Neither SAT nor ACT required. SAT 25/75 percentile: 850-1080. High school rank: N/A
Early decision deadline: N/A, notification date: N/A
Early action deadline: N/A, notification date: N/A
Application deadline (fall): 8/28
Undergraduate student body: 985 full time, 131 part time; 37% male, 63% female; 1% American Indian, 1% Asian, 32% Black, 20% Hispanic, 1% multiracial, 0% Pacific Islander, 33% white, 3% international; 89% from in state; 25% live on campus; 0% of students in fraternities, 0% in sororities
Most popular majors: 38% Business, Management, Marketing, and Related Support Services, 11% Homeland Security, Law Enforcement, Firefighting and Related Protective Services, 10% Psychology, 9% Public Administration and Social Service Professions, 7% Health Professions and Related Programs
Expenses: 2020-2021: $35,410; room/board: $14,464

Financial aid: (203) 773-8508; 88% of undergrads determined to have financial need; average aid package $19,337

Central Connecticut State University
New Britain CT
(860) 832-2278
U.S. News ranking: Reg. U. (N), No. 105
Website: www.ccsu.edu/admissions
Admissions email: admissions@ccsu.edu
Public; founded 1849
Freshman admissions: selective; 2019-2020: 7,807 applied, 5,124 accepted. Neither SAT nor ACT required. SAT 25/75 percentile: 970-1160. High school rank: 7% in top tenth, 28% in top quarter, 64% in top half
Early decision deadline: N/A, notification date: N/A
Early action deadline: N/A, notification date: N/A
Application deadline (fall): 5/1
Undergraduate student body: 7,253 full time, 1,792 part time; 53% male, 47% female; 0% American Indian, 4% Asian, 12% Black, 16% Hispanic, 3% multiracial, 0% Pacific Islander, 59% white, 1% international; 96% from in state; 24% live on campus; N/A of students in fraternities, N/A in sororities
Most popular majors: 28% Business, Management, Marketing, and Related Support Services, 12% Social Sciences, 8% Psychology, 7% Biological and Biomedical Sciences, 6% Communication, Journalism, and Related Programs
Expenses: 2020-2021: $11,502 in state, $23,776 out of state; room/board: $12,716
Financial aid: (860) 832-2200; 68% of undergrads determined to have financial need; average aid package $9,868

Connecticut College
New London CT
(860) 439-2200
U.S. News ranking: Nat. Lib. Arts, No. 51
Website: www.conncoll.edu
Admissions email: admission@conncoll.edu
Private; founded 1911
Freshman admissions: more selective; 2019-2020: 6,784 applied, 2,538 accepted. Neither SAT nor ACT required. SAT 25/75 percentile: 1310-1450. High school rank: 45% in top tenth, 81% in top quarter, 96% in top half
Early decision deadline: 11/15, notification date: 12/15
Early action deadline: N/A, notification date: N/A
Application deadline (fall): 1/1
Undergraduate student body: 1,819 full time, 42 part time; 38% male, 62% female; 0% American Indian, 4% Asian, 4% Black, 10% Hispanic, 4% multiracial, 0% Pacific Islander, 67% white, 9% international; 16% from in

state; 99% live on campus; 0% of students in fraternities, 0% in sororities
Most popular majors: 13% Economics, General, 13% Psychology, General, 9% Political Science and Government, General, 7% Biology/Biological Sciences, General, 7% International Relations and Affairs
Expenses: 2020-2021: $59,025; room/board: $16,290
Financial aid: (860) 439-2058; 59% of undergrads determined to have financial need; average aid package $46,607

Eastern Connecticut State University
Willimantic CT
(860) 465-5286
U.S. News ranking: Reg. U. (N), No. 90
Website: www.easternct.edu
Admissions email: admissions@easternct.edu
Public; founded 1889
Freshman admissions: selective; 2019-2020: 5,590 applied, 3,554 accepted. Neither SAT nor ACT required. SAT 25/75 percentile: 1010-1190. High school rank: 12% in top tenth, 35% in top quarter, 72% in top half
Early decision deadline: N/A, notification date: N/A
Early action deadline: N/A, notification date: N/A
Application deadline (fall): rolling
Undergraduate student body: 4,063 full time, 737 part time; 42% male, 58% female; 0% American Indian, 3% Asian, 10% Black, 13% Hispanic, 4% multiracial, 0% Pacific Islander, 64% white, 1% international; 89% from in state; 53% live on campus; N/A of students in fraternities, N/A in sororities
Most popular majors: 18% Business, Management, Marketing, and Related Support Services, 11% Liberal Arts and Sciences, General Studies and Humanities, 9% Communication, Journalism, and Related Programs, 9% Psychology, 8% Social Sciences
Expenses: 2020-2021: $12,304 in state, $24,578 out of state; room/board: $14,394
Financial aid: (860) 465-5775; 65% of undergrads determined to have financial need; average aid package $11,141

Fairfield University
Fairfield CT
(203) 254-4100
U.S. News ranking: Reg. U. (N), No. 3
Website: www.fairfield.edu
Admissions email: admis@fairfield.edu
Private; founded 1942
Affiliation: Roman Catholic
Freshman admissions: more selective; 2019-2020: 12,315 applied, 7,035 accepted. Neither SAT nor ACT required. SAT 25/75 percentile: 1210-1350. High school rank: 41% in top tenth, 73% in top quarter, 97% in top half

Early decision deadline: 11/15, notification date: 12/15
Early action deadline: 11/1, notification date: 12/20
Application deadline (fall): 1/15
Undergraduate student body: 4,160 full time, 143 part time; 41% male, 59% female; 0% American Indian, 3% Asian, 2% Black, 7% Hispanic, 2% multiracial, 0% Pacific Islander, 77% white, 4% international; 26% from in state; 73% live on campus; N/A of students in fraternities, N/A in sororities
Most popular majors: 38% Business, Management, Marketing, and Related Support Services, 14% Health Professions and Related Programs, 11% Communication, Journalism, and Related Programs, 8% Social Sciences, 6% Engineering
Expenses: 2020-2021: $51,325; room/board: $15,610
Financial aid: (203) 254-4000; 40% of undergrads determined to have financial need; average aid package $33,292

Mitchell College[1]
New London CT
(860) 701-5000
U.S. News ranking: Reg. Coll. (N), second tier
Website: www.mitchell.edu
Admissions email: admissions@mitchell.edu
Private
Application deadline (fall): N/A
Undergraduate student body: N/A full time, N/A part time
Expenses: 2019-2020: $34,050; room/board: $13,500
Financial aid: N/A

Post University
Waterbury CT
(800) 660-6615
U.S. News ranking: Reg. U. (N), second tier
Website: www.post.edu
Admissions email: admissions@post.edu
For-profit; founded 1890
Freshman admissions: least selective; 2019-2020: 14,281 applied, 9,118 accepted. Neither SAT nor ACT required. SAT 25/75 percentile: 900-900. High school rank: N/A
Early decision deadline: N/A, notification date: N/A
Early action deadline: N/A, notification date: N/A
Application deadline (fall): rolling
Undergraduate student body: 2,293 full time, 7,436 part time; 29% male, 71% female; 1% American Indian, 1% Asian, 26% Black, 8% Hispanic, 10% multiracial, 0% Pacific Islander, 37% white, 1% international; 20% from in state; 4% live on campus; 0% of students in fraternities, 0% in sororities
Most popular majors: 63% Business Administration and Management, General, 10% Criminal Justice/Safety Studies, 7% Management Information Systems, General, 6% Accounting, 6% Public Administration and Social Service Professions

Expenses: 2020-2021: $17,810; room/board: $11,600
Financial aid: (800) 345-2562; 82% of undergrads determined to have financial need; average aid package $9,562

Quinnipiac University[1]
Hamden CT
(203) 582-8600
U.S. News ranking: Nat. U., No. 153
Website: www.qu.edu
Admissions email: admissions@qu.edu
Private; founded 1929
Affiliation: Undenominational
Application deadline (fall): 2/1
Undergraduate student body: N/A full time, N/A part time
Expenses: 2019-2020: $49,280; room/board: $15,140
Financial aid: (203) 582-8750

Sacred Heart University
Fairfield CT
(203) 371-7880
U.S. News ranking: Nat. U., No. 217
Website: www.sacredheart.edu
Admissions email: enroll@sacredheart.edu
Private; founded 1963
Affiliation: Roman Catholic
Freshman admissions: selective; 2019-2020: 11,717 applied, 7,489 accepted. Neither SAT nor ACT required. SAT 25/75 percentile: 1120-1260. High school rank: 10% in top tenth, 35% in top quarter, 69% in top half
Early decision deadline: 12/1, notification date: 12/15
Early action deadline: 12/15, notification date: 1/31
Application deadline (fall): rolling
Undergraduate student body: 5,348 full time, 810 part time; 34% male, 66% female; 0% American Indian, 2% Asian, 5% Black, 12% Hispanic, 2% multiracial, 0% Pacific Islander, 73% white, 1% international; 36% from in state; 50% live on campus; 32% of students in fraternities, 55% in sororities
Most popular majors: 30% Health Professions and Related Programs, 29% Business, Management, Marketing, and Related Support Services, 8% Psychology, 5% Communication, Journalism, and Related Programs, 4% Biological and Biomedical Sciences
Expenses: 2020-2021: $44,350; room/board: $16,492
Financial aid: (203) 371-7980; 64% of undergrads determined to have financial need; average aid package $22,356

Southern Connecticut State University
New Haven CT
(203) 392-5644
U.S. News ranking: Reg. U. (N), No. 121
Website: www.southernct.edu/
Admissions email: admissions@southernct.edu
Public; founded 1893

Freshman admissions: less selective; 2019-2020: 9,156 applied, 6,351 accepted. Either SAT or ACT required. SAT 25/75 percentile: 910-1090. High school rank: 9% in top tenth, 28% in top quarter, 63% in top half
Early decision deadline: N/A, notification date: N/A
Early action deadline: N/A, notification date: N/A
Application deadline (fall): 8/16
Undergraduate student body: 6,801 full time, 1,161 part time; 39% male, 61% female; 0% American Indian, 3% Asian, 19% Black, 12% Hispanic, 4% multiracial, 0% Pacific Islander, 53% white, 1% international; 97% from in state; 30% live on campus; 1% of students in fraternities, 3% in sororities
Most popular majors: 17% Liberal Arts and Sciences/Liberal Studies, 15% Business Administration and Management, General, 9% Psychology, General, 6% Registered Nursing/Registered Nurse, 5% Public Health, General
Expenses: 2020-2021: $11,842 in state, $24,116 out of state; room/board: $13,270
Financial aid: N/A; 77% of undergrads determined to have financial need; average aid package $8,775

Trinity College
Hartford CT
(860) 297-2180
U.S. News ranking: Nat. Lib. Arts, No. 44
Website: www.trincoll.edu
Admissions email: admissions.office@trincoll.edu
Private; founded 1823
Affiliation: Undenominational
Freshman admissions: more selective; 2019-2020: 6,080 applied, 2,036 accepted. Neither SAT nor ACT required. SAT 25/75 percentile: 1298-1450. High school rank: 46% in top tenth, 75% in top quarter, 95% in top half
Early decision deadline: 11/15, notification date: 12/15
Early action deadline: N/A, notification date: N/A
Application deadline (fall): 1/15
Undergraduate student body: 2,128 full time, 67 part time; 50% male, 50% female; 0% American Indian, 4% Asian, 7% Black, 8% Hispanic, 3% multiracial, 0% Pacific Islander, 63% white, 13% international; 17% from in state; 87% live on campus; 29% of students in fraternities, 17% in sororities
Most popular majors: 32% Social Sciences, 9% Biological and Biomedical Sciences, 7% English Language and Literature/Letters, 6% Area, Ethnic, Cultural, Gender, and Group Studies, 6% Public Administration and Social Service Professions
Expenses: 2020-2021: $58,620; room/board: $15,300
Financial aid: (860) 297-2046; 52% of undergrads determined to have financial need; average aid package $54,346

United States Coast Guard Academy
New London CT
(800) 883-8724
U.S. News ranking: Reg. Coll. (N), No. 1
Website: www.uscga.edu
Admissions email: admissions@uscga.edu
Public; founded 1876
Freshman admissions: more selective; 2019-2020: 1,930 applied, 392 accepted. Either SAT or ACT required. SAT 25/75 percentile: 1212-1400. High school rank: 46% in top tenth, 84% in top quarter, 99% in top half
Early decision deadline: N/A, notification date: N/A
Early action deadline: 10/15, notification date: 12/24
Application deadline (fall): 1/15
Undergraduate student body: 1,069 full time, 0 part time; 62% male, 38% female; 0% American Indian, 7% Asian, 6% Black, 11% Hispanic, 10% multiracial, 0% Pacific Islander, 63% white, 3% international
Most popular majors: 38% Engineering, 21% Social Sciences, 16% Business, Management, Marketing, and Related Support Services, 13% Biological and Biomedical Sciences, 12% Mathematics and Statistics
Expenses: 2020-2021: $0 in state, $0 out of state; room/board: $0
Financial aid: N/A

University of Bridgeport[1]
Bridgeport CT
(203) 576-4552
U.S. News ranking: Nat. U., second tier
Website: www.bridgeport.edu
Admissions email: admit@bridgeport.edu
Private; founded 1927
Application deadline (fall): rolling
Undergraduate student body: N/A full time, N/A part time
Expenses: 2019-2020: $34,100; room/board: $15,950
Financial aid: (203) 576-4568

University of Connecticut
Storrs CT
(860) 486-3137
U.S. News ranking: Nat. U., No. 63
Website: www.uconn.edu
Admissions email: beahusky@uconn.edu
Public; founded 1881
Freshman admissions: more selective; 2019-2020: 35,096 applied, 17,346 accepted. Either SAT or ACT required. SAT 25/75 percentile: 1190-1390. High school rank: 55% in top tenth, 88% in top quarter, 98% in top half
Early decision deadline: N/A, notification date: N/A
Early action deadline: N/A, notification date: N/A
Application deadline (fall): 1/15

Undergraduate student body: 18,229 full time, 618 part time; 49% male, 51% female; 0% American Indian, 11% Asian, 7% Black, 12% Hispanic, 3% multiracial, 0% Pacific Islander, 55% white, 10% international; 81% from in state; 65% live on campus; 10% of students in fraternities, 12% in sororities
Most popular majors: 6% Economics, General, 6% Psychology, General, 6% Speech Communication and Rhetoric, 5% Registered Nursing/Registered Nurse, 4% Biology/Biological Sciences, General
Expenses: 2020-2021: $17,834 in state, $40,502 out of state; room/board: $13,258
Financial aid: (860) 486-2819; 53% of undergrads determined to have financial need; average aid package $16,196

University of Hartford
West Hartford CT
(860) 768-4296
U.S. News ranking: Nat. U., No. 217
Website: www.hartford.edu
Admissions email: admission@hartford.edu
Private; founded 1877
Freshman admissions: selective; 2019-2020: 13,233 applied, 10,103 accepted. Neither SAT nor ACT required. SAT 25/75 percentile: 1030-1230. High school rank: N/A
Early decision deadline: N/A, notification date: N/A
Early action deadline: 11/15, notification date: 12/1
Application deadline (fall): rolling
Undergraduate student body: 4,247 full time, 546 part time; 48% male, 52% female; 0% American Indian, 4% Asian, 15% Black, 13% Hispanic, 4% multiracial, 0% Pacific Islander, 53% white, 6% international; 50% from in state; 63% live on campus; N/A of students in fraternities, N/A in sororities
Most popular majors: 18% Business, Management, Marketing, and Related Support Services, 16% Visual and Performing Arts, 14% Health Professions and Related Programs, 13% Engineering, 7% Engineering Technologies and Engineering-Related Fields
Expenses: 2020-2021: $43,560; room/board: $13,200
Financial aid: (860) 768-4296; 73% of undergrads determined to have financial need; average aid package $30,839

University of New Haven
West Haven CT
(203) 932-7319
U.S. News ranking: Reg. U. (N), No. 59
Website: www.newhaven.edu
Admissions email: admissions@newhaven.edu
Private; founded 1920
Freshman admissions: selective; 2019-2020: 10,997 applied, 9,126 accepted. Neither SAT nor ACT required. SAT 25/75

percentile: 1030-1220. High school rank: 17% in top tenth, 42% in top quarter, 75% in top half
Early decision deadline: 12/1, notification date: 12/15
Early action deadline: N/A, notification date: N/A
Application deadline (fall): rolling
Undergraduate student body: 4,625 full time, 287 part time; 44% male, 56% female; 0% American Indian, 4% Asian, 12% Black, 13% Hispanic, 1% multiracial, 0% Pacific Islander, 64% white, 3% international
Most popular majors: 44% Homeland Security, Law Enforcement, Firefighting and Related Protective Services, 10% Business, Management, Marketing, and Related Support Services, 10% Engineering, 8% Visual and Performing Arts, 7% Biological and Biomedical Sciences
Expenses: 2020-2021: $41,654; room/board: $16,860
Financial aid: (203) 932-7220

University of St. Joseph
West Hartford CT
(860) 231-5216
U.S. News ranking: Nat. U., No. 176
Website: www.usj.edu
Admissions email: admissions@usj.edu
Private; founded 1932
Affiliation: Roman Catholic
Freshman admissions: selective; 2019-2020: 1,644 applied, 1,261 accepted. Neither SAT nor ACT required. SAT 25/75 percentile: 1030-1210. High school rank: 17% in top tenth, 50% in top quarter, 79% in top half
Early decision deadline: N/A, notification date: N/A
Early action deadline: N/A, notification date: N/A
Application deadline (fall): rolling
Undergraduate student body: 794 full time, 110 part time; 19% male, 81% female; 0% American Indian, 6% Asian, 14% Black, 15% Hispanic, 3% multiracial, 0% Pacific Islander, 57% white, 1% international; N/A from in state; 35% live on campus; N/A of students in fraternities, N/A in sororities
Most popular majors: 46% Health Professions and Related Programs, 13% Public Administration and Social Service Professions, 11% Psychology, 10% Biological and Biomedical Sciences, 6% Family and Consumer Sciences/Human Sciences
Expenses: 2020-2021: $40,286; room/board: $11,771
Financial aid: (860) 231-5223; 88% of undergrads determined to have financial need; average aid package $28,474

Wesleyan University
Middletown CT
(860) 685-3000
U.S. News ranking: Nat. Lib. Arts, No. 20
Website: www.wesleyan.edu

Admissions email:
admission@wesleyan.edu
Private; founded 1831
Freshman admissions: most selective; 2019-2020: 13,264 applied, 2,186 accepted. Neither SAT nor ACT required. SAT 25/75 percentile: 1320-1510. High school rank: 67% in top tenth, 86% in top quarter, 94% in top half
Early decision deadline: 11/15, notification date: 12/15
Early action deadline: N/A, notification date: N/A
Application deadline (fall): 1/1
Undergraduate student body: 2,937 full time, 81 part time; 46% male, 54% female; 0% American Indian, 7% Asian, 5% Black, 11% Hispanic, 6% multiracial, 0% Pacific Islander, 54% white, 14% international; 8% from in state; 99% live on campus; 4% of students in fraternities, 1% in sororities
Most popular majors: 24% Social Sciences, 16% Psychology, 14% Area, Ethnic, Cultural, Gender, and Group Studies, 12% Visual and Performing Arts, 8% English Language and Literature/Letters
Expenses: 2020-2021: $59,386; room/board: $16,384
Financial aid: (860) 685-2800; 41% of undergrads determined to have financial need; average aid package $58,719

Western Connecticut State University

Danbury CT
(203) 837-9000
U.S. News ranking: Reg. U. (N), No. 130
Website: www.wcsu.edu
Admissions email:
admissions@wcsu.edu
Public; founded 1903
Freshman admissions: selective; 2019-2020: 5,388 applied, 4,084 accepted. Neither SAT nor ACT required. SAT 25/75 percentile: 1020-1220. High school rank: 8% in top tenth, 28% in top quarter, 67% in top half
Early decision deadline: N/A, notification date: N/A
Early action deadline: N/A, notification date: N/A
Application deadline (fall): rolling
Undergraduate student body: 4,078 full time, 904 part time; 47% male, 53% female; 0% American Indian, 5% Asian, 9% Black, 22% Hispanic, 3% multiracial, 0% Pacific Islander, 59% white, 0% international; 84% from in state; 24% live on campus; 3% of students in fraternities, 5% in sororities
Most popular majors: 24% Business, Management, Marketing, and Related Support Services, 16% Health Professions and Related Programs, 10% Visual and Performing Arts, 9% Homeland Security, Law Enforcement, Firefighting and Related Protective Services, 9% Psychology
Expenses: 2020-2021: $11,781 in state, $24,055 out of state; room/board: $13,921
Financial aid: (203) 837-8580; 54% of undergrads determined to

have financial need; average aid package $9,582

Yale University

New Haven CT
(203) 432-9300
U.S. News ranking: Nat. U., No. 4
Website: www.yale.edu/
Admissions email:
student.questions@yale.edu
Private; founded 1701
Freshman admissions: most selective; 2019-2020: 36,844 applied, 2,241 accepted. Either SAT or ACT required. SAT 25/75 percentile: 1460-1570. High school rank: 92% in top tenth, 98% in top quarter, 100% in top half
Early decision deadline: N/A, notification date: N/A
Early action deadline: 11/1, notification date: 12/15
Application deadline (fall): 1/2
Undergraduate student body: 6,088 full time, 4 part time; 49% male, 51% female; 0% American Indian, 20% Asian, 8% Black, 14% Hispanic, 7% multiracial, 0% Pacific Islander, 40% white, 10% international; N/A from in state; 84% live on campus; N/A of students in fraternities, N/A in sororities
Most popular majors: 24% Social Sciences, 11% Biological and Biomedical Sciences, 8% History, 7% Engineering, 7% Mathematics and Statistics
Expenses: 2020-2021: $57,700; room/board: $17,200
Financial aid: (203) 432-2700; 54% of undergrads determined to have financial need; average aid package $61,315

DELAWARE

Delaware State University

Dover DE
(302) 857-6353
U.S. News ranking: Nat. U., No. 284
Website: www.desu.edu
Admissions email:
admissions@desu.edu
Public; founded 1891
Freshman admissions: less selective; 2019-2020: 9,084 applied, 4,794 accepted. Either SAT or ACT required. SAT 25/75 percentile: 820-1020. High school rank: 11% in top tenth, 29% in top quarter, 64% in top half
Early decision deadline: N/A, notification date: N/A
Early action deadline: N/A, notification date: N/A
Application deadline (fall): rolling
Undergraduate student body: 3,790 full time, 525 part time; 34% male, 66% female; 0% American Indian, 0% Asian, 72% Black, 7% Hispanic, 6% multiracial, 0% Pacific Islander, 9% white, 6% international; N/A from in state; N/A live on campus; 3% of students in fraternities, 3% in sororities
Most popular majors: 13% Parks, Recreation, Leisure, and Fitness Studies, 12% Communication, Journalism, and Related Programs,

11% Business, Management, Marketing, and Related Support Services, 10% Social Sciences, 7% Biological and Biomedical Sciences
Expenses: 2020-2021: $8,258 in state, $17,294 out of state; room/board: $11,984
Financial aid: (302) 857-6250; 80% of undergrads determined to have financial need; average aid package $20,520

Delaware Technical Community College–Terry[1]

Dover DE
(302) 857-1000
U.S. News ranking: Reg. Coll. (N), unranked
Website: www.dtcc.edu/our-campuses/dover
Admissions email: N/A
Public
Application deadline (fall): N/A
Undergraduate student body: N/A full time, N/A part time
Expenses: 2019-2020: $4,945 in state, $11,808 out of state; room/board: $8,400
Financial aid: N/A

Goldey-Beacom College[1]

Wilmington DE
(302) 998-8814
U.S. News ranking: Business, unranked
Website: www.gbc.edu
Admissions email:
admissions@gbc.edu
Private; founded 1886
Application deadline (fall): N/A
Undergraduate student body: N/A full time, N/A part time
Expenses: 2019-2020: $24,780; room/board: $8,482
Financial aid: (302) 225-6265

University of Delaware

Newark DE
(302) 831-8123
U.S. News ranking: Nat. U., No. 97
Website: www.udel.edu/
Admissions email:
admissions@udel.edu
Public; founded 1743
Freshman admissions: more selective; 2019-2020: 26,500 applied, 18,106 accepted. Neither SAT nor ACT required. SAT 25/75 percentile: 1170-1360. High school rank: 30% in top tenth, 64% in top quarter, 93% in top half
Early decision deadline: N/A, notification date: N/A
Early action deadline: N/A, notification date: N/A
Application deadline (fall): 1/15
Undergraduate student body: 17,509 full time, 1,257 part time; 42% male, 58% female; 0% American Indian, 5% Asian, 5% Black, 8% Hispanic, 3% multiracial, 0% Pacific Islander, 69% white, 6% international; 38% from in state; 40% live on campus; 18% of students in fraternities, 23% in sororities

Most popular majors: 22% Business, Management, Marketing, and Related Support Services, 12% Social Sciences, 11% Health Professions and Related Programs, 10% Engineering, 6% Education
Expenses: 2020-2021: $14,412 in state, $35,842 out of state; room/board: $13,472
Financial aid: (302) 831-2126; 51% of undergrads determined to have financial need; average aid package $14,188

Wesley College[1]

Dover DE
(302) 736-2400
U.S. News ranking: Reg. Coll. (N), second tier
Website: www.wesley.edu
Admissions email:
admissions@wesley.edu
Private; founded 1873
Affiliation: United Methodist
Application deadline (fall): 4/30
Undergraduate student body: N/A full time, N/A part time
Expenses: 2019-2020: $26,756; room/board: $11,864
Financial aid: (302) 736-2483

Wilmington University

New Castle DE
(302) 328-9407
U.S. News ranking: Nat. U., second tier
Website: www.wilmu.edu
Admissions email:
undergradadmissions@wilmu.edu
Private; founded 1968
Freshman admissions: least selective; 2019-2020: 1,681 applied, 1,681 accepted. Neither SAT nor ACT required. SAT 25/75 percentile: N/A. High school rank: N/A
Early decision deadline: N/A, notification date: N/A
Early action deadline: N/A, notification date: N/A
Application deadline (fall): rolling
Undergraduate student body: 2,968 full time, 6,129 part time; 37% male, 63% female; 1% American Indian, 2% Asian, 22% Black, 10% Hispanic, 3% multiracial, 0% Pacific Islander, 53% white, 5% international
Most popular majors: 23% Registered Nursing/Registered Nurse, 11% Behavioral Sciences, 10% Business Administration and Management, General, 7% Criminal Justice/Law Enforcement Administration, 7% Psychology, General
Expenses: 2019-2020: $11,480; room/board: N/A
Financial aid: (302) 356-4636

DISTRICT OF COLUMBIA

American University

Washington DC
(202) 885-6000
U.S. News ranking: Nat. U., No. 76
Website: www.american.edu
Admissions email:
admissions@american.edu
Private; founded 1893
Affiliation: United Methodist

Freshman admissions: more selective; 2019-2020: 18,545 applied, 6,691 accepted. Neither SAT nor ACT required. SAT 25/75 percentile: 1210-1390. High school rank: 32% in top tenth, 67% in top quarter, 93% in top half
Early decision deadline: 11/15, notification date: 12/31
Early action deadline: N/A, notification date: N/A
Application deadline (fall): 1/15
Undergraduate student body: 8,207 full time, 320 part time; 39% male, 61% female; 0% American Indian, 6% Asian, 7% Black, 13% Hispanic, 5% multiracial, 0% Pacific Islander, 55% white, 10% international; N/A from in state; N/A live on campus; 14% of students in fraternities, 16% in sororities
Most popular majors: 38% Social Sciences, 11% Communication, Journalism, and Related Programs, 5% Health Professions and Related Programs, 5% Multi/Interdisciplinary Studies, 5% Visual and Performing Arts
Expenses: 2020-2021: $51,335; room/board: $14,980
Financial aid: (202) 885-6500; 46% of undergrads determined to have financial need; average aid package $35,880

The Catholic University of America

Washington DC
(800) 673-2772
U.S. News ranking: Nat. U., No. 143
Website: www.catholic.edu/
Admissions email:
cua-admissions@cua.edu
Private; founded 1887
Affiliation: Roman Catholic
Freshman admissions: selective; 2019-2020: 5,668 applied, 4,838 accepted. Neither SAT nor ACT required. SAT 25/75 percentile: 1130-1330. High school rank: N/A
Early decision deadline: 11/15, notification date: 12/17
Early action deadline: 11/1, notification date: 1/15
Application deadline (fall): 1/15
Undergraduate student body: 3,168 full time, 111 part time; 45% male, 55% female; 0% American Indian, 3% Asian, 4% Black, 14% Hispanic, 4% multiracial, 0% Pacific Islander, 67% white, 5% international; 4% from in state; N/A live on campus; N/A of students in fraternities, N/A in sororities
Most popular majors: 9% Registered Nursing/Registered Nurse, 8% Marketing/Marketing Management, General, 8% Political Science and Government, General, 8% Psychology, General, 7% Architecture
Expenses: 2020-2021: $49,416; room/board: $15,820
Financial aid: (202) 319-5307; 55% of undergrads determined to have financial need; average aid package $33,655

Gallaudet University
Washington DC
(202) 651-5750
U.S. News ranking: Nat. U., No. 124
Website: www.gallaudet.edu
Admissions email: admissions.office@gallaudet.edu
Private; founded 1864
Freshman admissions: less selective; 2019-2020: 477 applied, 292 accepted. Either SAT or ACT required. ACT 25/75 percentile: 14-19. High school rank: N/A
Early decision deadline: N/A, notification date: N/A
Early action deadline: N/A, notification date: N/A
Application deadline (fall): rolling
Undergraduate student body: 1,005 full time, 70 part time; 46% male, 54% female; 1% American Indian, 5% Asian, 17% Black, 15% Hispanic, 3% multiracial, 1% Pacific Islander, 47% white, 5% international; N/A from in state; 85% live on campus; 1% of students in fraternities, 1% in sororities
Most popular majors: 17% Business, Management, Marketing, and Related Support Services, 13% Foreign Languages, Literatures, and Linguistics, 10% Area, Ethnic, Cultural, Gender, and Group Studies, 9% Parks, Recreation, Leisure, and Fitness Studies, 9% Public Administration and Social Service Professions
Expenses: 2020-2021: $17,038; room/board: $14,800
Financial aid: (202) 651-5290; 95% of undergrads determined to have financial need; average aid package $25,111

Georgetown University
Washington DC
(202) 687-3600
U.S. News ranking: Nat. U., No. 23
Website: www.georgetown.edu
Admissions email: guadmiss@georgetown.edu
Private; founded 1789
Affiliation: Roman Catholic
Freshman admissions: most selective; 2019-2020: 22,764 applied, 3,269 accepted. Either SAT or ACT required. SAT 25/75 percentile: 1380-1550. High school rank: 85% in top tenth, 96% in top quarter, 99% in top half
Early decision deadline: N/A, notification date: N/A
Early action deadline: 11/1, notification date: 12/15
Application deadline (fall): 1/10
Undergraduate student body: 7,029 full time, 484 part time; 44% male, 56% female; 0% American Indian, 11% Asian, 6% Black, 10% Hispanic, 5% multiracial, 0% Pacific Islander, 51% white, 14% international; 2% from in state; 77% live on campus; N/A of students in fraternities, N/A in sororities
Most popular majors: 33% Social Sciences, 26% Business, Management, Marketing, and Related Support Services, 7% Multi/Interdisciplinary Studies,

4% Biological and Biomedical Sciences, 4% Psychology
Expenses: 2020-2021: $57,928; room/board: $17,498
Financial aid: (202) 687-4547; 38% of undergrads determined to have financial need; average aid package $50,261

George Washington University
Washington DC
(202) 994-6040
U.S. News ranking: Nat. U., No. 66
Website: www.gwu.edu
Admissions email: gwadm@gwu.edu
Private; founded 1821
Freshman admissions: more selective; 2019-2020: 26,978 applied, 11,019 accepted. Neither SAT nor ACT required. SAT 25/75 percentile: 1280-1470. High school rank: 53% in top tenth, 83% in top quarter, 96% in top half
Early decision deadline: 11/1, notification date: 12/15
Early action deadline: N/A, notification date: N/A
Application deadline (fall): 1/1
Undergraduate student body: 11,102 full time, 1,382 part time; 38% male, 62% female; 0% American Indian, 11% Asian, 8% Black, 11% Hispanic, 4% multiracial, 0% Pacific Islander, 50% white, 12% international; 4% from in state; 58% live on campus; 5% of students in fraternities, 9% in sororities
Most popular majors: 34% Social Sciences, 16% Health Professions and Related Programs, 15% Business, Management, Marketing, and Related Support Services, 6% Engineering, 5% Communication, Journalism, and Related Programs
Expenses: 2020-2021: $58,640; room/board: $14,711
Financial aid: (202) 994-6620; 46% of undergrads determined to have financial need; average aid package $48,579

Howard University
Washington DC
(202) 806-2755
U.S. News ranking: Nat. U., No. 80
Website: www.howard.edu
Admissions email: admission@howard.edu
Private; founded 1867
Freshman admissions: more selective; 2019-2020: 21,006 applied, 7,578 accepted. Either SAT or ACT required. SAT 25/75 percentile: 1130-1280. High school rank: 28% in top tenth, 63% in top quarter, 92% in top half
Early decision deadline: 11/1, notification date: 12/18
Early action deadline: 11/1, notification date: 12/18
Application deadline (fall): 2/15
Undergraduate student body: 6,269 full time, 257 part time; 29% male, 71% female; 2% American Indian, 1% Asian, 73% Black, 6% Hispanic, 3% multiracial, 0% Pacific Islander, 1% white, 5% international; 2% from in state; 78% live on campus;

8% of students in fraternities, 6% in sororities
Most popular majors: 15% Communication, Journalism, and Related Programs, 14% Business, Management, Marketing, and Related Support Services, 12% Biological and Biomedical Sciences, 12% Social Sciences, 8% Parks, Recreation, Leisure, and Fitness Studies
Expenses: 2020-2021: $28,440; room/board: $12,380
Financial aid: (202) 806-2747; 81% of undergrads determined to have financial need; average aid package $22,191

Strayer University[1]
Washington DC
(202) 408-2400
U.S. News ranking: Reg. U. (N), second tier
Website: www.strayer.edu
Admissions email: mzm@strayer.edu
For-profit; founded 1892
Application deadline (fall): N/A
Undergraduate student body: N/A full time, N/A part time
Expenses: 2019-2020: $13,515; room/board: N/A
Financial aid: N/A

Trinity Washington University[1]
Washington DC
(202) 884-9400
U.S. News ranking: Reg. U. (N), second tier
Website: www.trinitydc.edu
Admissions email: admissions@trinitydc.edu
Private
Application deadline (fall): N/A
Undergraduate student body: N/A full time, N/A part time
Expenses: 2019-2020: $24,630; room/board: $10,750
Financial aid: N/A

University of the District of Columbia
Washington DC
(202) 274-5010
U.S. News ranking: Reg. U. (N), second tier
Website: www.udc.edu/
Admissions email: N/A
Public; founded 1976
Freshman admissions: less selective; 2019-2020: 3,684 applied, 2,742 accepted. Either SAT or ACT required. SAT 25/75 percentile: N/A. High school rank: N/A
Early decision deadline: N/A, notification date: N/A
Early action deadline: N/A, notification date: N/A
Application deadline (fall): rolling
Undergraduate student body: 1,741 full time, 1,928 part time; 40% male, 60% female; 0% American Indian, 1% Asian, 41% Black, 9% Hispanic, 0% multiracial, 0% Pacific Islander, 3% white, 8% international
Most popular majors: 13% Business Administration, Management and Operations, 8% Biology, General, 7% Computer Science, 6% Political Science

and Government, 4% Accounting and Related Services
Expenses: 2019-2020: $6,020 in state, $12,704 out of state; room/board: $16,781
Financial aid: (202) 274-6053

University of the Potomac[1]
Washington DC
(202) 274-2303
U.S. News ranking: Business, unranked
Website: www.potomac.edu
Admissions email: admissions@potomac.edu
For-profit; founded 1991
Application deadline (fall): rolling
Undergraduate student body: N/A full time, N/A part time
Expenses: 2019-2020: $9,990; room/board: N/A
Financial aid: N/A

FLORIDA

Ave Maria University
Ave Maria FL
(877) 283-8648
U.S. News ranking: Nat. Lib. Arts, second tier
Website: www.avemaria.edu
Admissions email: admissions@avemaria.edu
Private; founded 2003
Affiliation: Roman Catholic
Freshman admissions: selective; 2019-2020: 1,441 applied, 1,222 accepted. Either SAT or ACT required. SAT 25/75 percentile: 1040-1230. High school rank: N/A
Early decision deadline: N/A, notification date: N/A
Early action deadline: N/A, notification date: N/A
Application deadline (fall): rolling
Undergraduate student body: 1,079 full time, 50 part time; 47% male, 53% female; 0% American Indian, 3% Asian, 5% Black, 14% Hispanic, 0% multiracial, 0% Pacific Islander, 63% white, 4% international; 36% from in state; 88% live on campus; 0% of students in fraternities, 0% in sororities
Most popular majors: 11% Behavioral Sciences, 9% Theology and Religious Vocations, 7% Business Administration and Management, General, 6% Accounting, 6% Biochemistry
Expenses: 2020-2021: $23,188; room/board: $12,580
Financial aid: (239) 280-2423; 60% of undergrads determined to have financial need; average aid package $22,513

Barry University
Miami Shores FL
(305) 899-3100
U.S. News ranking: Nat. U., second tier
Website: www.barry.edu
Admissions email: admissions@barry.edu
Private; founded 1940
Affiliation: Roman Catholic
Freshman admissions: selective; 2019-2020: 10,577 applied, 5,415 accepted. Either SAT

or ACT required. SAT 25/75 percentile: 930-1080. High school rank: N/A
Early decision deadline: N/A, notification date: N/A
Early action deadline: N/A, notification date: N/A
Application deadline (fall): rolling
Undergraduate student body: 3,015 full time, 732 part time; 37% male, 63% female; 0% American Indian, 1% Asian, 36% Black, 36% Hispanic, 2% multiracial, 0% Pacific Islander, 17% white, 7% international; 72% from in state; 25% live on campus; N/A of students in fraternities, N/A in sororities
Most popular majors: 31% Business, Management, Marketing, and Related Support Services, 21% Health Professions and Related Programs, 10% Public Administration and Social Service Professions, 7% Biological and Biomedical Sciences, 5% Liberal Arts and Sciences, General Studies and Humanities
Expenses: 2020-2021: $30,014; room/board: $11,474
Financial aid: (305) 899-3673; 78% of undergrads determined to have financial need; average aid package $24,378

Beacon College[1]
Leesburg FL
(352) 787-7660
U.S. News ranking: Reg. Coll. (S), No. 31
Website: www.beaconcollege.edu/
Admissions email: admissions@beaconcollege.edu
Private
Application deadline (fall): N/A
Undergraduate student body: N/A full time, N/A part time
Expenses: 2019-2020: $40,880; room/board: $11,946
Financial aid: N/A

Bethune-Cookman University
Daytona Beach FL
(800) 448-0228
U.S. News ranking: Nat. Lib. Arts, second tier
Website: www.bethune.cookman.edu
Admissions email: admissions@cookman.edu
Private; founded 1904
Affiliation: United Methodist
Freshman admissions: less selective; 2019-2020: 7,081 applied, 5,952 accepted. Either SAT or ACT required. SAT 25/75 percentile: 840-1010. High school rank: 13% in top tenth, 33% in top quarter, 67% in top half
Early decision deadline: N/A, notification date: N/A
Early action deadline: N/A, notification date: N/A
Application deadline (fall): rolling
Undergraduate student body: 2,709 full time, 70 part time; 37% male, 63% female; 0% American Indian, 0% Asian, 79% Black, 4% Hispanic, 3% multiracial, 0% Pacific Islander, 1% white, 3% international
Most popular majors: 17% Psychology, General, 15% Liberal Arts and Sciences/Liberal

Studies, 13% Corrections and Criminal Justice, Other, 10% Business Administration and Management, General, 8% Mass Communication/Media Studies
Expenses: 2019-2020: $14,814; room/board: $9,462
Financial aid: (386) 481-2620; 94% of undergrads determined to have financial need; average aid package $15,144

Broward College[1]
Fort Lauderdale FL
(954) 201-7350
U.S. News ranking: Reg. Coll. (S), unranked
Website: www.broward.edu
Admissions email: N/A
Public; founded 1960
Application deadline (fall): rolling
Undergraduate student body: N/A full time, N/A part time
Expenses: 2019-2020: $3,537 in state, $10,779 out of state; room/board: N/A
Financial aid: (954) 201-2330

Chipola College[1]
Marianna FL
(850) 718-2211
U.S. News ranking: Reg. Coll. (S), unranked
Website: www.chipola.edu
Admissions email: N/A
Public
Application deadline (fall): N/A
Undergraduate student body: N/A full time, N/A part time
Expenses: 2019-2020: $3,120 in state, $8,950 out of state; room/board: $4,560
Financial aid: N/A

College of Central Florida[1]
Ocala FL
(352) 854-2322
U.S. News ranking: Reg. Coll. (S), unranked
Website: www.cf.edu
Admissions email: admissions@cf.edu
Public; founded 1957
Application deadline (fall): 8/12
Undergraduate student body: N/A full time, N/A part time
Expenses: 2019-2020: $2,710 in state, $10,517 out of state; room/board: $7,462
Financial aid: (352) 854-2322

Daytona State College[1]
Daytona Beach FL
(386) 506-3000
U.S. News ranking: Reg. Coll. (S), unranked
Website: www.daytonastate.edu
Admissions email: N/A
Public; founded 1957
Application deadline (fall): N/A
Undergraduate student body: N/A full time, N/A part time
Expenses: 2019-2020: $3,106 in state, $11,994 out of state; room/board: $7,600
Financial aid: N/A

Eastern Florida State College[1]
Cocoa FL
(321) 633-1111
U.S. News ranking: Reg. Coll. (S), unranked
Website: www.easternflorida.edu
Admissions email: N/A
Public; founded 1960
Application deadline (fall): rolling
Undergraduate student body: N/A full time, N/A part time
Expenses: 2019-2020: $2,496 in state, $9,739 out of state; room/board: $6,968
Financial aid: N/A

Eckerd College
St. Petersburg FL
(727) 864-8331
U.S. News ranking: Nat. Lib. Arts, No. 136
Website: www.eckerd.edu
Admissions email: admissions@eckerd.edu
Private; founded 1958
Freshman admissions: selective; 2019-2020: 4,644 applied, 3,132 accepted. Neither SAT nor ACT required. SAT 25/75 percentile: 1090-1280. High school rank: N/A
Early decision deadline: N/A, notification date: N/A
Early action deadline: 11/15, notification date: 12/15
Application deadline (fall): rolling
Undergraduate student body: 1,958 full time, 49 part time; 33% male, 67% female; 1% American Indian, 3% Asian, 3% Black, 9% Hispanic, 4% multiracial, 0% Pacific Islander, 78% white, 3% international; N/A from in state; 87% live on campus; N/A of students in fraternities, N/A in sororities
Most popular majors: 22% Biological and Biomedical Sciences, 14% Social Sciences, 13% Natural Resources and Conservation, 12% Psychology, 11% Business, Management, Marketing, and Related Support Services
Expenses: 2020-2021: $47,704; room/board: $13,482
Financial aid: (727) 864-8334; 60% of undergrads determined to have financial need; average aid package $38,819

Edward Waters College[1]
Jacksonville FL
(904) 470-8200
U.S. News ranking: Reg. Coll. (S), second tier
Website: www.ewc.edu
Admissions email: admissions@ewc.edu
Private
Application deadline (fall): N/A
Undergraduate student body: N/A full time, N/A part time
Expenses: 2019-2020: $14,878; room/board: $8,010
Financial aid: N/A

Embry-Riddle Aeronautical University
Daytona Beach FL
(800) 862-2416
U.S. News ranking: Reg. U. (S), No. 9
Website: www.embryriddle.edu
Admissions email: dbadmit@erau.edu
Private; founded 1926
Freshman admissions: more selective; 2019-2020: 8,551 applied, 5,211 accepted. Neither SAT nor ACT required. SAT 25/75 percentile: 1120-1360. High school rank: 23% in top tenth, 52% in top quarter, 82% in top half
Early decision deadline: N/A, notification date: N/A
Early action deadline: N/A, notification date: N/A
Application deadline (fall): rolling
Undergraduate student body: 6,023 full time, 379 part time; 77% male, 23% female; 0% American Indian, 5% Asian, 5% Black, 14% Hispanic, 4% multiracial, 0% Pacific Islander, 57% white, 12% international; N/A from in state; 43% live on campus; N/A of students in fraternities, N/A in sororities
Most popular majors: 40% Transportation and Materials Moving, 35% Engineering, 8% Business, Management, Marketing, and Related Support Services, 6% Homeland Security, Law Enforcement, Firefighting and Related Protective Services, 4% Psychology
Expenses: 2020-2021: $37,964; room/board: $12,410
Financial aid: (386) 226-6300; 89% of undergrads determined to have financial need; average aid package $17,460

Everglades University
Boca Raton FL
(888) 772-6077
U.S. News ranking: Reg. U. (S), second tier
Website: www.evergladesuniversity.edu
Admissions email: rheintz@ evergladesuniversity.edu
Private; founded 2002
Freshman admissions: less selective; 2019-2020: 1,500 applied, 1,124 accepted. Neither SAT nor ACT required. SAT 25/75 percentile: N/A. High school rank: N/A
Early decision deadline: N/A, notification date: N/A
Early action deadline: N/A, notification date: N/A
Application deadline (fall): rolling
Undergraduate student body: 1,757 full time, 0 part time; 55% male, 45% female; 1% American Indian, 1% Asian, 19% Black, 22% Hispanic, 2% multiracial, 0% Pacific Islander, 45% white, 0% international
Most popular majors: 33% Alternative and Complementary Medicine and Medical Systems, 17% Construction Management, 12% Aeronautics/ Aviation/Aerospace Science and Technology, General,

3% Natural Resources Management and Policy, Other, 2% Business Administration and Management, General
Expenses: 2020-2021: $18,320; room/board: N/A
Financial aid: (561) 912-1211

Flagler College
St. Augustine FL
(800) 304-4208
U.S. News ranking: Reg. Coll. (S), No. 4
Website: www.flagler.edu
Admissions email: admissions@flagler.edu
Private; founded 1968
Freshman admissions: selective; 2019-2020: 4,569 applied, 2,959 accepted. Neither SAT nor ACT required. SAT 25/75 percentile: 1030-1210. High school rank: N/A
Early decision deadline: 11/1, notification date: 12/15
Early action deadline: N/A, notification date: N/A
Application deadline (fall): 3/1
Undergraduate student body: 2,819 full time, 70 part time; 33% male, 67% female; 0% American Indian, 1% Asian, 5% Black, 10% Hispanic, 3% multiracial, 0% Pacific Islander, 74% white, 3% international; N/A from in state; 39% live on campus; 3% of students in fraternities, 4% in sororities
Most popular majors: 28% Business, Management, Marketing, and Related Support Services, 14% Communication, Journalism, and Related Programs, 11% Education, 10% Social Sciences, 10% Visual and Performing Arts
Expenses: 2020-2021: $20,040; room/board: $12,540
Financial aid: (904) 819-6225; 55% of undergrads determined to have financial need; average aid package $13,498

Florida A&M University
Tallahassee FL
(850) 599-3796
U.S. News ranking: Nat. U., No. 241
Website: www.famu.edu
Admissions email: ugrdadmissions@famu.edu
Public; founded 1887
Freshman admissions: selective; 2019-2020: 10,269 applied, 3,665 accepted. Either SAT or ACT required. SAT 25/75 percentile: 1030-1160. High school rank: 12% in top tenth, 30% in top quarter, 77% in top half
Early decision deadline: N/A, notification date: N/A
Early action deadline: N/A, notification date: N/A
Application deadline (fall): 5/1
Undergraduate student body: 6,802 full time, 1,016 part time; 35% male, 65% female; 0% American Indian, 0% Asian, 88% Black, 4% Hispanic, 3% multiracial, 0% Pacific Islander, 3% white, 0% international; 85% from in

state; N/A live on campus; N/A of students in fraternities, N/A in sororities
Most popular majors: 21% Health Professions and Related Programs, 14% Multi/Interdisciplinary Studies, 8% Homeland Security, Law Enforcement, Firefighting and Related Protective Services, 7% Communication, Journalism, and Related Programs, 7% Psychology
Expenses: 2020-2021: $5,785 in state, $17,725 out of state; room/board: $10,986
Financial aid: (850) 599-3730; 88% of undergrads determined to have financial need; average aid package $13,284

Florida Atlantic University
Boca Raton FL
(561) 297-3040
U.S. News ranking: Nat. U., No. 272
Website: www.fau.edu
Admissions email: Admissions@fau.edu
Public; founded 1961
Freshman admissions: selective; 2019-2020: 18,854 applied, 11,932 accepted. Either SAT or ACT required. SAT 25/75 percentile: 1080-1240. High school rank: 16% in top tenth, 48% in top quarter, 85% in top half
Early decision deadline: N/A, notification date: N/A
Early action deadline: N/A, notification date: N/A
Application deadline (fall): 5/1
Undergraduate student body: 16,679 full time, 8,163 part time; 43% male, 57% female; 0% American Indian, 4% Asian, 20% Black, 28% Hispanic, 4% multiracial, 0% Pacific Islander, 40% white, 3% international; N/A from in state; 18% live on campus; 6% of students in fraternities, 10% in sororities
Most popular majors: 20% Business, Management, Marketing, and Related Support Services, 9% Multi/Interdisciplinary Studies, 8% Health Professions and Related Programs, 8% Psychology, 7% Biological and Biomedical Sciences
Expenses: 2020-2021: $6,099 in state, $21,655 out of state; room/board: $12,030
Financial aid: (561) 297-3531; 62% of undergrads determined to have financial need; average aid package $14,639

Florida College[1]
Temple Terrace FL
(800) 326-7655
U.S. News ranking: Reg. Coll. (S), No. 66
Website: www.floridacollege.edu/
Admissions email: admissions@ floridacollege.edu
Private; founded 1946
Application deadline (fall): 8/25
Undergraduate student body: N/A full time, N/A part time
Expenses: 2019-2020: $17,300; room/board: $8,690
Financial aid: (813) 988-5131

Florida Gateway College

Lake City FL
(386) 754-4280
U.S. News ranking: Reg. Coll. (S), unranked
Website: www.fgc.edu
Admissions email: enrollment.services@fgc.edu
Public
Freshman admissions: least selective; 2019-2020: N/A applied, N/A accepted. Neither SAT nor ACT required. SAT 25/75 percentile: N/A. High school rank: N/A
Early decision deadline: N/A, notification date: N/A
Early action deadline: N/A, notification date: N/A
Application deadline (fall): rolling
Undergraduate student body: 1,133 full time, 2,273 part time; 34% male, 66% female; 0% American Indian, 1% Asian, 17% Black, 7% Hispanic, 2% multiracial, 0% Pacific Islander, 72% white, 0% international
Most popular majors: Information not available
Expenses: 2020-2021: $3,099 in state, $10,204 out of state; room/board: $5,400
Financial aid: (386) 754-4296

Florida Gulf Coast University

Fort Myers FL
(239) 590-7878
U.S. News ranking: Reg. U. (S), No. 68
Website: www.fgcu.edu
Admissions email: admissions@fgcu.edu
Public; founded 1991
Freshman admissions: selective; 2019-2020: 13,735 applied, 9,157 accepted. Either SAT or ACT required. SAT 25/75 percentile: 1060-1210. High school rank: 16% in top tenth, 43% in top quarter, 78% in top half
Early decision deadline: N/A, notification date: N/A
Early action deadline: N/A, notification date: N/A
Application deadline (fall): 7/1
Undergraduate student body: 11,194 full time, 2,505 part time; 44% male, 56% female; 0% American Indian, 2% Asian, 7% Black, 23% Hispanic, 3% multiracial, 0% Pacific Islander, 61% white, 2% international; 92% from in state; 35% live on campus; 7% of students in fraternities, 5% in sororities
Most popular majors: 8% Speech Communication and Rhetoric, 7% Psychology, General, 7% Resort Management, 6% Business Administration and Management, General, 5% Criminal Justice/Safety Studies
Expenses: 2020-2021: $6,171 in state, $25,214 out of state; room/board: $10,995
Financial aid: (239) 590-1210; 47% of undergrads determined to have financial need; average aid package $8,630

Florida Institute of Technology

Melbourne FL
(321) 674-8000
U.S. News ranking: Nat. U., No. 206
Website: www.fit.edu
Admissions email: admission@fit.edu
Private; founded 1958
Freshman admissions: more selective; 2019-2020: 9,743 applied, 6,406 accepted. Either SAT or ACT required. SAT 25/75 percentile: 1150-1360. High school rank: 26% in top tenth, 58% in top quarter, 85% in top half
Early decision deadline: N/A, notification date: N/A
Early action deadline: N/A, notification date: N/A
Application deadline (fall): rolling
Undergraduate student body: 3,169 full time, 396 part time; 71% male, 29% female; 0% American Indian, 2% Asian, 6% Black, 10% Hispanic, 3% multiracial, 0% Pacific Islander, 52% white, 24% international; 41% from in state; 48% live on campus; 12% of students in fraternities, 8% in sororities
Most popular majors: 13% Mechanical Engineering, 9% Aeronautics/Aviation/Aerospace Science and Technology, General, 9% Aerospace, Aeronautical and Astronautical/Space Engineering, 6% Computer Science, 5% Electrical and Electronics Engineering
Expenses: 2020-2021: $43,246; room/board: $13,180
Financial aid: (321) 674-8070; 57% of undergrads determined to have financial need; average aid package $36,489

Florida International University

Miami FL
(305) 348-2363
U.S. News ranking: Nat. U., No. 187
Website: www.fiu.edu
Admissions email: admiss@fiu.edu
Public; founded 1972
Freshman admissions: more selective; 2019-2020: 18,492 applied, 10,634 accepted. Either SAT or ACT required. SAT 25/75 percentile: 1110-1280. High school rank: 35% in top tenth, 63% in top quarter, 91% in top half
Early decision deadline: N/A, notification date: N/A
Early action deadline: N/A, notification date: N/A
Undergraduate student body: 28,392 full time, 20,612 part time; 44% male, 56% female; 0% American Indian, 2% Asian, 12% Black, 67% Hispanic, 2% multiracial, 0% Pacific Islander, 9% white, 7% international; 96% from in state; 6% live on campus; N/A of students in fraternities, N/A in sororities
Most popular majors: 26% Business, Management, Marketing, and Related Support Services, 11% Psychology, 9% Multi/Interdisciplinary Studies,

6% Biological and Biomedical Sciences, 6% Communication, Journalism, and Related Programs
Expenses: 2020-2021: $6,566 in state, $18,964 out of state; room/board: $11,136
Financial aid: (305) 348-2333; 68% of undergrads determined to have financial need; average aid package $9,847

Florida Keys Community College[1]

Key West FL
(305) 296-9081
U.S. News ranking: Reg. Coll. (S), unranked
Website: www.fkcc.edu
Admissions email: N/A
Public
Application deadline (fall): N/A
Undergraduate student body: N/A full time, N/A part time
Expenses: 2019-2020: $3,276 in state, $13,162 out of state; room/board: $15,279
Financial aid: N/A

Florida Memorial University[1]

Miami FL
(305) 626-3750
U.S. News ranking: Reg. Coll. (S), No. 54
Website: www.fmuniv.edu/
Admissions email: admit@fmuniv.edu
Private; founded 1879
Affiliation: Baptist
Application deadline (fall): rolling
Undergraduate student body: N/A full time, N/A part time
Expenses: 2019-2020: $16,236; room/board: $7,776
Financial aid: (305) 626-3745

Florida National University– Main Campus

Hialeah FL
(305) 821-3333
U.S. News ranking: Reg. Coll. (S), No. 16
Website: www.fnu.edu/
Admissions email: rlopez@fnu.edu
For-profit; founded 1988
Freshman admissions: least selective; 2019-2020: 1,503 applied, 1,486 accepted. Neither SAT nor ACT required. SAT 25/75 percentile: N/A. High school rank: N/A
Early decision deadline: N/A, notification date: N/A
Early action deadline: N/A, notification date: N/A
Application deadline (fall): N/A
Undergraduate student body: 1,944 full time, 1,085 part time; 28% male, 72% female; 0% American Indian, 0% Asian, 5% Black, 87% Hispanic, 0% multiracial, 0% Pacific Islander, 2% white, 6% international; 99% from in state; 0% live on campus; 0% of students in fraternities, 0% in sororities
Most popular majors: 65% Registered Nursing/Registered Nurse, 13% Nursing Administration, 10% Health Services Administration, 7% Accounting Technology/Technician

and Bookkeeping, 5% Business, Management, Marketing, and Related Support Services, Other
Expenses: 2020-2021: $13,688; room/board: N/A
Financial aid: (305) 821-3333; 90% of undergrads determined to have financial need; average aid package $7,540

Florida Polytechnic University

Lakeland FL
(863) 874-4774
U.S. News ranking: Reg. Coll. (S), unranked
Website: floridapoly.edu/
Admissions email: admissions@floridapoly.edu
Public; founded 2012
Freshman admissions: more selective; 2019-2020: 1,259 applied, 631 accepted. Either SAT or ACT required. SAT 25/75 percentile: 1200-1360. High school rank: 29% in top tenth, 61% in top quarter, 88% in top half
Early decision deadline: N/A, notification date: N/A
Early action deadline: N/A, notification date: N/A
Application deadline (fall): 4/1
Undergraduate student body: 1,135 full time, 153 part time; 85% male, 15% female; 0% American Indian, 4% Asian, 6% Black, 20% Hispanic, 3% multiracial, 0% Pacific Islander, 63% white, 1% international; 95% from in state; 52% live on campus; N/A of students in fraternities, N/A in sororities
Most popular majors: 43% Computer Software and Media Applications, Other, 25% Mechanical Engineering, 12% Electrical and Electronics Engineering, 10% Logistics, Materials, and Supply Chain Management, 5% Data Modeling/Warehousing and Database Administration
Expenses: 2020-2021: $4,940 in state, $21,005 out of state; room/board: $11,471
Financial aid: (863) 874-4774; 48% of undergrads determined to have financial need; average aid package $12,801

Florida Southern College

Lakeland FL
(863) 680-4131
U.S. News ranking: Reg. U. (S), No. 9
Website: www.flsouthern.edu
Admissions email: fscadm@flsouthern.edu
Private; founded 1883
Freshman admissions: more selective; 2019-2020: 8,350 applied, 4,177 accepted. Either SAT or ACT required. SAT 25/75 percentile: 1120-1265. High school rank: 25% in top tenth, 58% in top quarter, 87% in top half
Early decision deadline: 11/1, notification date: 12/1
Early action deadline: N/A, notification date: N/A
Application deadline (fall): rolling

Undergraduate student body: 2,537 full time, 218 part time; 37% male, 63% female; 1% American Indian, 3% Asian, 7% Black, 13% Hispanic, 0% multiracial, 0% Pacific Islander, 71% white, 3% international; 64% from in state; 80% live on campus; 29% of students in fraternities, 35% in sororities
Most popular majors: 17% Business Administration and Management, General, 9% Registered Nursing/Registered Nurse, 6% Accounting, 6% Psychology, General, 5% Biology/Biological Sciences, General
Expenses: 2020-2021: $38,980; room/board: $12,006
Financial aid: (863) 680-4140; 67% of undergrads determined to have financial need; average aid package $31,709

Florida SouthWestern State College

Fort Myers FL
(239) 489-9054
U.S. News ranking: Reg. Coll. (S), unranked
Website: www.fsw.edu
Admissions email: admissions@fsw.edu
Public; founded 1962
Freshman admissions: least selective; 2019-2020: 6,397 applied, 5,084 accepted. Neither SAT nor ACT required. SAT 25/75 percentile: N/A. High school rank: N/A
Early decision deadline: N/A, notification date: N/A
Early action deadline: N/A, notification date: N/A
Application deadline (fall): 7/31
Undergraduate student body: 6,337 full time, 10,335 part time; 36% male, 64% female; 0% American Indian, 2% Asian, 12% Black, 34% Hispanic, 2% multiracial, 0% Pacific Islander, 41% white, 2% international; 93% from in state; 2% live on campus; 0% of students in fraternities, 0% in sororities
Most popular majors: 38% Business, Management, Marketing, and Related Support Services, 35% Health Professions and Related Programs, 20% Education, 7% Homeland Security, Law Enforcement, Firefighting and Related Protective Services
Expenses: 2019-2020: $3,401 in state, $10,715 out of state; room/board: $10,500
Financial aid: (239) 489-9336

Florida State College–Jacksonville[1]

Jacksonville FL
(904) 359-5433
U.S. News ranking: Reg. Coll. (S), unranked
Website: www.fscj.edu
Admissions email: N/A
Public
Application deadline (fall): N/A
Undergraduate student body: N/A full time, N/A part time
Expenses: 2019-2020: $2,878 in state, $9,992 out of state; room/board: $8,496
Financial aid: N/A

Florida State University

Tallahassee FL
(850) 644-6200
U.S. News ranking: Nat. U., No. 58
Website: www.fsu.edu
Admissions email: admissions@admin.fsu.edu
Public; founded 1851
Freshman admissions: more selective; 2019-2020: 58,936 applied, 21,202 accepted. Either SAT or ACT required. SAT 25/75 percentile: 1200-1340. High school rank: 47% in top tenth, 73% in top quarter, 95% in top half
Early decision deadline: N/A, notification date: N/A
Early action deadline: N/A, notification date: N/A
Application deadline (fall): 3/1
Undergraduate student body: 29,879 full time, 3,391 part time; 43% male, 57% female; 0% American Indian, 3% Asian, 9% Black, 22% Hispanic, 4% multiracial, 0% Pacific Islander, 60% white, 2% international; 89% from in state; 20% live on campus; 13% of students in fraternities, 23% in sororities
Most popular majors: 8% Psychology, General, 6% Criminal Justice/Safety Studies, 6% Finance, General, 5% Marketing/Marketing Management, General, 4% English Language and Literature, General
Expenses: 2020-2021: $6,507 in state, $21,673 out of state; room/board: $11,088
Financial aid: (850) 644-5716; 46% of undergrads determined to have financial need; average aid package $18,836

Gulf Coast State College[1]

Panama City FL
(850) 769-1551
U.S. News ranking: Reg. Coll. (S), unranked
Admissions email: N/A
Public
Application deadline (fall): N/A
Undergraduate student body: N/A full time, N/A part time
Expenses: 2020-2021: $2,370 in state, $7,685 out of state; room/board: N/A
Financial aid: (850) 873-3543

Hodges University[1]

Naples FL
(239) 513-1122
U.S. News ranking: Reg. U. (S), second tier
Website: www.hodges.edu
Admissions email: admit@hodges.edu
Private; founded 1990
Application deadline (fall): rolling
Undergraduate student body: N/A full time, N/A part time
Expenses: 2019-2020: $14,300; room/board: N/A
Financial aid: (239) 938-7765

Indian River State College[1]

Fort Pierce FL
(772) 462-7460
U.S. News ranking: Reg. Coll. (S), unranked
Website: www.irsc.edu
Admissions email: records@irsc.edu
Public; founded 1960
Application deadline (fall): rolling
Undergraduate student body: N/A full time, N/A part time
Expenses: 2019-2020: $2,764 in state, $10,201 out of state; room/board: $5,700
Financial aid: (772) 462-7450

Jacksonville University

Jacksonville FL
(800) 225-2027
U.S. News ranking: Reg. U. (S), No. 29
Website: www.ju.edu/index.php
Admissions email: admiss@ju.edu
Private; founded 1934
Freshman admissions: selective; 2019-2020: 5,139 applied, 4,712 accepted. ACT 25/75 nor ACT required. ACT 25/75 percentile: 18-25. High school rank: 16% in top tenth, 44% in top quarter, 78% in top half
Early decision deadline: N/A, notification date: N/A
Early action deadline: N/A, notification date: N/A
Application deadline (fall): 7/1
Undergraduate student body: 2,391 full time, 537 part time; 41% male, 59% female; 0% American Indian, 2% Asian, 20% Black, 12% Hispanic, 3% multiracial, 0% Pacific Islander, 50% white, 7% international; 59% from in state; 47% live on campus; 10% of students in fraternities, 11% in sororities
Most popular majors: 47% Health Professions and Related Programs, 13% Business, Management, Marketing, and Related Support Services, 10% Social Sciences, 7% Visual and Performing Arts, 4% Biological and Biomedical Sciences
Expenses: 2020-2021: $40,800; room/board: $14,810
Financial aid: (904) 256-7062; 68% of undergrads determined to have financial need; average aid package $29,666

Keiser University

Ft. Lauderdale FL
(954) 776-4456
U.S. News ranking: Nat. U., No. 284
Website: www.keiseruniversity.edu/admissions/
Admissions email: N/A
Private; founded 1977
Freshman admissions: less selective; 2019-2020: 3,453 applied, 2,924 accepted. Neither SAT nor ACT required. SAT 25/75 percentile: N/A. High school rank: N/A
Early decision deadline: N/A, notification date: N/A
Early action deadline: N/A, notification date: N/A

Application deadline (fall): rolling
Undergraduate student body: 10,479 full time, 7,011 part time; 30% male, 70% female; 1% American Indian, 3% Asian, 19% Black, 29% Hispanic, 2% multiracial, 0% Pacific Islander, 30% white, 1% international
Most popular majors: 18% Business Administration and Management, General, 12% Multi-/Interdisciplinary Studies, 11% Registered Nursing/Registered Nurse, 10% Psychology, General, 6% Health Services Administration
Expenses: 2020-2021: $33,120; room/board: $11,720
Financial aid: (954) 776-4476; 89% of undergrads determined to have financial need; average aid package $6,972

Lake-Sumter State College[1]

Leesburg FL
(352) 323-3665
U.S. News ranking: Reg. Coll. (S), unranked
Website: www.lssc.edu/future-students/admissions/
Admissions email: AdmissionsOffice@lssc.edu
Public; founded 1962
Application deadline (fall): 8/5
Undergraduate student body: N/A full time, N/A part time
Expenses: 2019-2020: $3,232 in state, $13,336 out of state; room/board: $8,001
Financial aid: (352) 365-3567

Lynn University

Boca Raton FL
(561) 237-7900
U.S. News ranking: Reg. U. (S), No. 53
Website: www.lynn.edu
Admissions email: admission@lynn.edu
Private; founded 1962
Freshman admissions: selective; 2019-2020: 7,385 applied, 5,482 accepted. Neither SAT nor ACT required. SAT 25/75 percentile: 970-1170. High school rank: N/A
Early decision deadline: N/A, notification date: N/A
Early action deadline: 11/15, notification date: 12/15
Application deadline (fall): 3/1
Undergraduate student body: 2,218 full time, 204 part time; 50% male, 50% female; 0% American Indian, 1% Asian, 10% Black, 18% Hispanic, 2% multiracial, 0% Pacific Islander, 46% white, 16% international; 40% from in state; 72% live on campus; 5% of students in fraternities, 4% in sororities
Most popular majors: 43% Business, Management, Marketing, and Related Support Services, 13% Communication, Journalism, and Related Programs, 9% Visual and Performing Arts, 8% Psychology, 6% Biological and Biomedical Sciences
Expenses: 2020-2021: $39,850; room/board: $12,470
Financial aid: (561) 237-7973; 48% of undergrads determined to have financial need; average aid package $24,022

Miami Dade College[1]

Miami FL
(305) 237-8888
U.S. News ranking: Reg. Coll. (S), unranked
Website: www.mdc.edu/
Admissions email: mdcinfo@mdc.edu
Public
Application deadline (fall): N/A
Undergraduate student body: N/A full time, N/A part time
Expenses: 2019-2020: $2,838 in state, $9,661 out of state; room/board: $17,302
Financial aid: N/A

Miami International University of Art & Design[1]

Miami FL
(305) 428-5700
U.S. News ranking: Arts, unranked
Website: www.aimiu.aii.edu/
Admissions email: N/A
For-profit
Application deadline (fall): 9/14
Undergraduate student body: N/A full time, N/A part time
Expenses: 2019-2020: $19,354; room/board: N/A
Financial aid: N/A

New College of Florida

Sarasota FL
(941) 487-5000
U.S. News ranking: Nat. Lib. Arts, No. 84
Website: www.ncf.edu
Admissions email: admissions@ncf.edu
Public; founded 1960
Freshman admissions: more selective; 2019-2020: 1,226 applied, 896 accepted. SAT or ACT required. SAT 25/75 percentile: 1180-1360. High school rank: 22% in top tenth, 50% in top quarter, 88% in top half
Early decision deadline: 11/1, notification date: 12/15
Early action deadline: 11/1, notification date: 12/15
Application deadline (fall): 4/15
Undergraduate student body: 702 full time, 0 part time; 37% male, 63% female; 0% American Indian, 3% Asian, 3% Black, 18% Hispanic, 4% multiracial, 0% Pacific Islander, 69% white, 2% international; 80% from in state; 82% live on campus; 0% of students in fraternities, 0% in sororities
Most popular majors: 47% Liberal Arts and Sciences, General Studies and Humanities, Other, 33% Biological and Physical Sciences, 8% Foreign Languages and Literatures, General, 6% Environmental Studies, 6% International/Global Studies
Expenses: 2020-2021: $6,916 in state, $29,944 out of state; room/board: $9,529
Financial aid: (941) 487-5000; 51% of undergrads determined to have financial need; average aid package $14,896

North Florida Community College[1]

Madison FL
(850) 973-2288
U.S. News ranking: Reg. Coll. (S), unranked
Admissions email: N/A
Public
Application deadline (fall): rolling
Undergraduate student body: N/A full time, N/A part time
Expenses: 2019-2020: $3,054 in state, $11,400 out of state; room/board: $5,400
Financial aid: N/A

Northwest Florida State College[1]

Niceville FL
(850) 678-5111
U.S. News ranking: Reg. Coll. (S), unranked
Website: www.nwfsc.edu/
Admissions email: N/A
Public
Application deadline (fall): rolling
Undergraduate student body: N/A full time, N/A part time
Expenses: 2019-2020: $3,133 in state, $11,940 out of state; room/board: $8,930
Financial aid: (850) 729-5370

Nova Southeastern University

Ft. Lauderdale FL
(954) 262-8000
U.S. News ranking: Nat. U., No. 227
Website: www.nova.edu
Admissions email: admissions@nova.edu
Private; founded 1964
Freshman admissions: more selective; 2019-2020: 11,062 applied, 8,861 accepted. Either SAT or ACT required. SAT 25/75 percentile: 1020-1250. High school rank: 34% in top tenth, 69% in top quarter, 86% in top half
Early decision deadline: 11/1, notification date: N/A
Early action deadline: 11/1, notification date: N/A
Application deadline (fall): 2/1
Undergraduate student body: 4,619 full time, 1,047 part time; 29% male, 71% female; 0% American Indian, 11% Asian, 14% Black, 36% Hispanic, 3% multiracial, 0% Pacific Islander, 27% white, 5% international; N/A from in state; 37% live on campus; 11% of students in fraternities, 10% in sororities
Most popular majors: 40% Health Professions and Related Programs, 21% Biological and Biomedical Sciences, 10% Business, Management, Marketing, and Related Support Services, 5% Psychology, 4% Parks, Recreation, Leisure, and Fitness Studies
Expenses: 2020-2021: $33,430; room/board: $13,656
Financial aid: (800) 806-3680; 73% of undergrads determined to have financial need; average aid package $32,880

Palm Beach Atlantic University

West Palm Beach FL
(888) 468-6722
U.S. News ranking: Nat. U., second tier
Website: www.pba.edu
Admissions email: admit@pba.edu
Private; founded 1968
Affiliation: Interdenominational
Freshman admissions: selective; 2019-2020: 1,534 applied, 1,464 accepted. Either SAT or ACT required. SAT 25/75 percentile: 980-1200. High school rank: N/A
Early decision deadline: N/A, notification date: N/A
Early action deadline: 5/1, notification date: 6/1
Application deadline (fall): rolling
Undergraduate student body: 2,264 full time, 619 part time; 37% male, 63% female; 0% American Indian, 2% Asian, 10% Black, 15% Hispanic, 4% multiracial, 0% Pacific Islander, 61% white, 4% international; N/A from in state; 49% live on campus; N/A of students in fraternities, N/A in sororities
Most popular majors: 25% Business, Management, Marketing, and Related Support Services, 14% Psychology, 12% Health Professions and Related Programs, 9% Theology and Religious Vocations, 7% Visual and Performing Arts
Expenses: 2020-2021: $33,475; room/board: $10,722
Financial aid: (561) 803-2629; 73% of undergrads determined to have financial need; average aid package $23,772

Palm Beach State College[1]

Lake Worth FL
(561) 207-5000
U.S. News ranking: Reg. Coll. (S), unranked
Admissions email: N/A
Public
Application deadline (fall): N/A
Undergraduate student body: N/A full time, N/A part time
Expenses: 2019-2020: $2,444 in state, $2,444 out of state; room/board: N/A
Financial aid: N/A

Pasco-Hernando State College[1]

New Port Richey FL
(727) 847-2727
U.S. News ranking: Reg. Coll. (S), unranked
Website: www.phsc.edu
Admissions email: N/A
Public
Application deadline (fall): N/A
Undergraduate student body: N/A full time, N/A part time
Expenses: 2019-2020: $3,155 in state, $12,032 out of state; room/board: $6,628
Financial aid: N/A

Pensacola State College

Pensacola FL
(850) 484-2544
U.S. News ranking: Reg. Coll. (S), No. 30
Website: www.pensacolastate.edu
Admissions email: askus@pensacolastate.edu
Public; founded 1948
Freshman admissions: less selective; 2019-2020: 2,461 applied, 1,285 accepted. Neither SAT nor ACT required. ACT 25/75 percentile: 18-23. High school rank: N/A
Early decision deadline: N/A, notification date: N/A
Early action deadline: N/A, notification date: N/A
Application deadline (fall): rolling
Undergraduate student body: 3,800 full time, 6,022 part time; 37% male, 63% female; 1% American Indian, 3% Asian, 18% Black, 9% Hispanic, 2% multiracial, 0% Pacific Islander, 63% white, 0% international; 76% from in state; N/A live on campus; N/A of students in fraternities, N/A in sororities
Most popular majors: 41% Liberal Arts and Sciences, General Studies and Humanities, 6% Health Professions and Related Programs, 2% Business, Management, Marketing, and Related Support Services, 1% Computer and Information Sciences and Support Services, 1% Education
Expenses: 2020-2021: $3,467 in state, $12,623 out of state; room/board: N/A
Financial aid: (850) 484-1708; 48% of undergrads determined to have financial need; average aid package $1,419

Polk State College[1]

Winter Haven FL
(863) 297-1000
U.S. News ranking: Reg. Coll. (S), unranked
Admissions email: N/A
Public
Application deadline (fall): N/A
Undergraduate student body: N/A full time, N/A part time
Expenses: 2019-2020: $3,366 in state, $12,272 out of state; room/board: $8,339
Financial aid: N/A

Ringling College of Art and Design

Sarasota FL
(800) 255-7695
U.S. News ranking: Arts, unranked
Website: www.ringling.edu
Admissions email: admissions@ringling.edu
Private; founded 1931
Freshman admissions: least selective; 2019-2020: 2,557 applied, 1,633 accepted. Neither SAT nor ACT required. SAT 25/75 percentile: N/A. High school rank: N/A
Early decision deadline: N/A, notification date: N/A
Early action deadline: 11/1, notification date: 12/15
Application deadline (fall): rolling

Undergraduate student body: 1,606 full time, 52 part time; 30% male, 70% female; 0% American Indian, 9% Asian, 4% Black, 15% Hispanic, 4% multiracial, 0% Pacific Islander, 48% white, 17% international; 43% from in state; 69% live on campus; 0% of students in fraternities, 0% in sororities
Most popular majors: 39% Animation, Interactive Technology, Video Graphics and Special Effects, 31% Illustration, 7% Cinematography and Film/Video Production, 6% Art/Art Studies, General, 5% Graphic Design
Expenses: 2020-2021: $49,540; room/board: $15,710
Financial aid: (941) 359-7532; 61% of undergrads determined to have financial need; average aid package $27,804

Rollins College

Winter Park FL
(407) 646-2161
U.S. News ranking: Reg. U. (S), No. 1
Website: www.rollins.edu
Admissions email: admission@rollins.edu
Private; founded 1885
Affiliation: Undenominational
Freshman admissions: more selective; 2019-2020: 6,167 applied, 3,598 accepted. Neither SAT nor ACT required. SAT 25/75 percentile: 1160-1340. High school rank: 22% in top tenth, 59% in top quarter, 89% in top half
Early decision deadline: 11/15, notification date: 12/15
Early action deadline: N/A, notification date: N/A
Application deadline (fall): 2/1
Undergraduate student body: 2,127 full time, 6 part time; 40% male, 60% female; 0% American Indian, 3% Asian, 4% Black, 18% Hispanic, 5% multiracial, 0% Pacific Islander, 58% white, 10% international; 55% from in state; 57% live on campus; 29% of students in fraternities, 32% in sororities
Most popular majors: 21% Business Administration, Management and Operations, 12% Communication, Journalism, and Related Programs, 11% International Business, 7% Biological and Biomedical Sciences, 6% Social Sciences
Expenses: 2020-2021: $53,716; room/board: $15,200
Financial aid: (407) 646-2395; 54% of undergrads determined to have financial need; average aid package $42,681

Saint Johns River State College[1]

Palatka FL
(904) 276-6800
U.S. News ranking: Reg. Coll. (S), unranked
Admissions email: N/A
Public
Application deadline (fall): N/A
Undergraduate student body: N/A full time, N/A part time

Expenses: 2019-2020: $2,830 in state, $10,347 out of state; room/board: $8,602
Financial aid: N/A

Saint Leo University

Saint Leo FL
(800) 334-5532
U.S. News ranking: Reg. U. (S), No. 26
Website: www.saintleo.edu
Admissions email: admission@saintleo.edu
Private; founded 1889
Affiliation: Roman Catholic
Freshman admissions: selective; 2019-2020: 5,195 applied, 3,745 accepted. Neither SAT nor ACT required. SAT 25/75 percentile: 1040-1190. High school rank: 9% in top tenth, 27% in top quarter, 58% in top half
Early decision deadline: N/A, notification date: N/A
Early action deadline: N/A, notification date: N/A
Application deadline (fall): rolling
Undergraduate student body: 2,223 full time, 59 part time; 42% male, 58% female; 0% American Indian, 1% Asian, 14% Black, 21% Hispanic, 2% multiracial, 0% Pacific Islander, 37% white, 14% international; 74% from in state; 68% live on campus; 13% of students in fraternities, 11% in sororities
Most popular majors: 26% Business, Management, Marketing, and Related Support Services, 15% Homeland Security, Law Enforcement, Firefighting and Related Protective Services, 11% Psychology, 10% Computer and Information Sciences and Support Services, 8% Biological and Biomedical Sciences
Expenses: 2020-2021: $23,750; room/board: $11,250
Financial aid: (800) 240-7658; 69% of undergrads determined to have financial need; average aid package $25,819

Santa Fe College[1]

Gainesville FL
(352) 395-5000
U.S. News ranking: Reg. Coll. (S), unranked
Admissions email: N/A
Public
Application deadline (fall): N/A
Undergraduate student body: N/A full time, N/A part time
Expenses: 2019-2020: $2,563 in state, $9,189 out of state; room/board: $10,008
Financial aid: N/A

Seminole State College of Florida

Sanford FL
(407) 708-2380
U.S. News ranking: Reg. Coll. (S), second tier
Website: www.seminolestate.edu
Admissions email: admissions@seminolestate.edu
Public; founded 1965
Freshman admissions: less selective; 2019-2020: 5,705 applied, 4,284 accepted. Neither SAT nor ACT required. SAT 25/75

percentile: N/A. High school rank: N/A
Early decision deadline: N/A, notification date: N/A
Early action deadline: N/A, notification date: N/A
Application deadline (fall): N/A
Undergraduate student body: 5,752 full time, 12,002 part time; 43% male, 57% female; N/A American Indian, N/A Asian, N/A Black, N/A Hispanic, N/A multiracial, N/A Pacific Islander, N/A white, N/A international
Most popular majors: 28% Business, Management, Marketing, and Related Support Services, 28% Health Professions and Related Programs, 26% Computer and Information Sciences and Support Services, 12% Engineering Technologies and Engineering-Related Fields, 6% Visual and Performing Arts
Expenses: 2020-2021: $3,131 in state, $11,456 out of state; room/board: N/A
Financial aid: N/A

Southeastern University

Lakeland FL
(800) 500-8760
U.S. News ranking: Reg. U. (S), second tier
Website: www.seu.edu
Admissions email: admission@seu.edu
Private; founded 1935
Affiliation: Assemblies of God Church
Freshman admissions: selective; 2019-2020: 5,010 applied, 2,414 accepted. Either SAT or ACT required. SAT 25/75 percentile: 960-1180. High school rank: 9% in top tenth, 27% in top quarter, 56% in top half
Early decision deadline: N/A, notification date: N/A
Early action deadline: N/A, notification date: N/A
Application deadline (fall): 5/1
Undergraduate student body: 4,974 full time, 3,743 part time; 42% male, 58% female; 1% American Indian, 1% Asian, 13% Black, 22% Hispanic, 2% multiracial, 0% Pacific Islander, 58% white, 2% international; N/A from in state; 29% live on campus; N/A of students in fraternities, N/A in sororities
Most popular majors: 22% Theology and Religious Vocations, 16% Business, Management, Marketing, and Related Support Services, 7% Communication, Journalism, and Related Programs, 7% Parks, Recreation, Leisure, and Fitness Studies, 5% Education
Expenses: 2020-2021: $27,520; room/board: $10,380
Financial aid: (863) 667-5306; 77% of undergrads determined to have financial need; average aid package $15,978

South Florida State College

Avon Park FL
(863) 453-6661
U.S. News ranking: Reg. Coll. (S), No. 33
Website: www.southflorida.edu
Admissions email: jonathan.stern@southflorida.edu
Public; founded 1966
Freshman admissions: least selective; 2019-2020: 563 applied, 563 accepted. Neither SAT nor ACT required. ACT 25/75 percentile: 17-18. High school rank: 17% in top tenth, 19% in top quarter, 40% in top half
Early decision deadline: N/A, notification date: N/A
Early action deadline: N/A, notification date: N/A
Application deadline (fall): rolling
Undergraduate student body: 932 full time, 1,877 part time; 37% male, 63% female; 0% American Indian, 2% Asian, 8% Black, 38% Hispanic, 2% multiracial, 0% Pacific Islander, 43% white, 2% international
Most popular majors: Information not available
Expenses: 2019-2020: $3,165 in state, $11,859 out of state; room/board: $5,920
Financial aid: (863) 784-7108

State College of Florida–Manatee-Sarasota[1]

Bradenton FL
(941) 752-5000
U.S. News ranking: Reg. Coll. (S), unranked
Admissions email: N/A
Public
Application deadline (fall): N/A
Undergraduate student body: N/A full time, N/A part time
Expenses: 2019-2020: $3,074 in state, $11,606 out of state; room/board: $18,960
Financial aid: N/A

Stetson University

DeLand FL
(800) 688-0101
U.S. News ranking: Reg. U. (S), No. 4
Website: www.stetson.edu
Admissions email: admissions@stetson.edu
Private; founded 1883
Freshman admissions: more selective; 2019-2020: 13,005 applied, 9,410 accepted. Neither SAT nor ACT required. SAT 25/75 percentile: 1110-1300. High school rank: 23% in top tenth, 56% in top quarter, 87% in top half
Early decision deadline: N/A, notification date: N/A
Early action deadline: 11/1, notification date: N/A
Application deadline (fall): rolling
Undergraduate student body: 3,133 full time, 50 part time; 43% male, 57% female; 0% American Indian, 2% Asian, 8% Black, 18% Hispanic, 5% multiracial, 0% Pacific Islander, 58% white, 6% international; 75% from in state; 65% live on campus; 24%

of students in fraternities, 23% in sororities
Most popular majors: 33% Business, Management, Marketing, and Related Support Services, 10% Social Sciences, 9% Psychology, 9% Visual and Performing Arts, 7% Biological and Biomedical Sciences
Expenses: 2020-2021: $49,500; room/board: $14,540
Financial aid: (386) 822-7120; 67% of undergrads determined to have financial need; average aid package $40,976

St. Petersburg College

St. Petersburg FL
(727) 341-3400
U.S. News ranking: Reg. Coll. (S), No. 68
Website: www.spcollege.edu/
Admissions email: Admissions@SPC.edu
Public; founded 1927
Freshman admissions: less selective; 2019-2020: 4,120 applied, 4,120 accepted. Neither SAT nor ACT required. SAT 25/75 percentile: 920-1130. High school rank: N/A
Early decision deadline: N/A, notification date: N/A
Early action deadline: N/A, notification date: N/A
Application deadline (fall): rolling
Undergraduate student body: 8,841 full time, 20,012 part time; 38% male, 62% female; 0% American Indian, 4% Asian, 14% Black, 16% Hispanic, 4% multiracial, 0% Pacific Islander, 59% white, 1% international; N/A from in state; 0% live on campus; 0% of students in fraternities, 0% in sororities
Most popular majors: 35% Health Professions and Related Programs, 26% Business, Management, Marketing, and Related Support Services, 12% Education, 10% Computer and Information Sciences and Support Services, 7% Homeland Security, Law Enforcement, Firefighting and Related Protective Services
Expenses: 2020-2021: $2,682 in state, $8,513 out of state; room/board: N/A
Financial aid: (727) 791-2485; 88% of undergrads determined to have financial need; average aid package $7,629

St. Thomas University

Miami Gardens FL
(305) 628-6546
U.S. News ranking: Reg. U. (S), No. 94
Website: www.stu.edu
Admissions email: signup@stu.edu
Private; founded 1961
Affiliation: Roman Catholic
Freshman admissions: less selective; 2019-2020: 5,062 applied, 2,785 accepted. Either SAT or ACT required. SAT 25/75 percentile: 890-1090. High school rank: N/A
Early decision deadline: N/A, notification date: N/A
Early action deadline: N/A, notification date: N/A
Application deadline (fall): rolling

Undergraduate student body: 1,246 full time, 1,854 part time; 47% male, 53% female; 0% American Indian, 0% Asian, 34% Black, 39% Hispanic, 3% multiracial, 0% Pacific Islander, 8% white, 11% international
Most popular majors: 44% Business, Management, Marketing, and Related Support Services, 10% Biological and Biomedical Sciences, 10% Homeland Security, Law Enforcement, Firefighting and Related Protective Services, 6% Communication, Journalism, and Related Programs, 5% Psychology
Expenses: 2020-2021: $34,558; room/board: $12,630
Financial aid: (305) 474-6000; 59% of undergrads determined to have financial need; average aid package $12,497

Tallahassee Community College[1]

Tallahassee FL
(850) 201-6200
U.S. News ranking: Reg. Coll. (S), unranked
Website: www.tcc.fl.edu
Admissions email: N/A
Public
Application deadline (fall): N/A
Undergraduate student body: N/A full time, N/A part time
Expenses: 2019-2020: $2,026 in state, $8,062 out of state; room/board: $6,000
Financial aid: N/A

University of Central Florida

Orlando FL
(407) 823-3000
U.S. News ranking: Nat. U., No. 160
Website: www.ucf.edu
Admissions email: admission@ucf.edu
Public; founded 1963
Freshman admissions: more selective; 2019-2020: 45,118 applied, 20,016 accepted. Either SAT or ACT required. SAT 25/75 percentile: 1170-1340. High school rank: 36% in top tenth, 74% in top quarter, 97% in top half
Early decision deadline: N/A, notification date: N/A
Early action deadline: N/A, notification date: N/A
Application deadline (fall): 5/1
Undergraduate student body: 42,467 full time, 17,012 part time; 45% male, 55% female; 0% American Indian, 6% Asian, 11% Black, 28% Hispanic, 4% multiracial, 0% Pacific Islander, 47% white, 3% international; N/A from in state; 18% live on campus; 5% of students in fraternities, 6% in sororities
Most popular majors: 20% Business, Management, Marketing, and Related Support Services, 16% Health Professions and Related Programs, 8% Education, 8% Psychology, 7% Engineering
Expenses: 2020-2021: $6,368 in state, $22,467 out of state; room/board: $9,760

Financial aid: (407) 823-2827; 61% of undergrads determined to have financial need; average aid package $10,852

University of Florida

Gainesville FL
(352) 392-1365
U.S. News ranking: Nat. U., No. 30
Website: www.ufl.edu
Admissions email: webrequests@admissions.ufl.edu
Public; founded 1853
Freshman admissions: most selective; 2019-2020: 38,069 applied, 13,925 accepted. Either SAT or ACT required. SAT 25/75 percentile: 1310-1470. High school rank: 81% in top tenth, 98% in top quarter, 100% in top half
Early decision deadline: N/A, notification date: N/A
Early action deadline: N/A, notification date: N/A
Application deadline (fall): 3/1
Undergraduate student body: 32,157 full time, 3,248 part time; 44% male, 56% female; 0% American Indian, 9% Asian, 6% Black, 23% Hispanic, 4% multiracial, 0% Pacific Islander, 52% white, 2% international; 92% from in state; 24% live on campus; 17% of students in fraternities, 23% in sororities
Most popular majors: 14% Engineering, 13% Business, Management, Marketing, and Related Support Services, 11% Biological and Biomedical Sciences, 10% Social Sciences, 9% Health Professions and Related Programs
Expenses: 2020-2021: $6,380 in state, $28,658 out of state; room/board: $10,590
Financial aid: (352) 294-3226; 41% of undergrads determined to have financial need; average aid package $13,935

University of Miami

Coral Gables FL
(305) 284-4323
U.S. News ranking: Nat. U., No. 49
Website: www.miami.edu
Admissions email: admission@miami.edu
Private; founded 1925
Freshman admissions: more selective; 2019-2020: 38,919 applied, 10,557 accepted. Either SAT or ACT required. SAT 25/75 percentile: 1270-1440. High school rank: 59% in top tenth, 83% in top quarter, 95% in top half
Early decision deadline: 11/1, notification date: 12/15
Early action deadline: 11/1, notification date: 1/31
Application deadline (fall): 1/1
Undergraduate student body: 10,701 full time, 606 part time; 46% male, 54% female; 0% American Indian, 5% Asian, 9% Black, 22% Hispanic, 3% multiracial, 0% Pacific Islander, 42% white, 14% international; 39% from in state; 37% live on campus; 16% of students in fraternities, 18% in sororities

Most popular majors: 21% Business, Management, Marketing, and Related Support Services, 14% Biological and Biomedical Sciences, 13% Health Professions and Related Programs, 10% Engineering, 9% Social Sciences
Expenses: 2020-2021: $53,682; room/board: $15,470
Financial aid: (305) 284-2270; 43% of undergrads determined to have financial need; average aid package $41,057

University of North Florida

Jacksonville FL
(904) 620-2624
U.S. News ranking: Nat. U., No. 272
Website: www.unf.edu
Admissions email: admissions@unf.edu
Public; founded 1965
Freshman admissions: selective; 2019-2020: 16,305 applied, 11,786 accepted. Either SAT or ACT required. SAT 25/75 percentile: 1090-1260. High school rank: 15% in top tenth, 40% in top quarter, 77% in top half
Early decision deadline: N/A, notification date: N/A
Early action deadline: N/A, notification date: N/A
Application deadline (fall): rolling
Undergraduate student body: 10,757 full time, 3,977 part time; 43% male, 57% female; 0% American Indian, 5% Asian, 9% Black, 14% Hispanic, 5% multiracial, 0% Pacific Islander, 64% white, 2% international; N/A from in state; 24% live on campus; N/A of students in fraternities, N/A in sororities
Most popular majors: 19% Business, Management, Marketing, and Related Support Services, 18% Health Professions and Related Programs, 9% Psychology, 7% Communication, Journalism, and Related Programs, 6% Social Sciences
Expenses: 2020-2021: $6,394 in state, $20,112 out of state; room/board: $9,956
Financial aid: (904) 620-5555; 52% of undergrads determined to have financial need; average aid package $9,564

University of South Florida

Tampa FL
(813) 974-3350
U.S. News ranking: Nat. U., No. 103
Website: www.usf.edu
Admissions email: admission@admin.usf.edu
Public; founded 1956
Freshman admissions: more selective; 2019-2020: 36,986 applied, 17,618 accepted. Either SAT or ACT required. SAT 25/75 percentile: 1170-1330. High school rank: 34% in top tenth, 68% in top quarter, 92% in top half
Early decision deadline: N/A, notification date: N/A

Early action deadline: N/A, notification date: N/A
Application deadline (fall): 4/1
Undergraduate student body: 25,457 full time, 7,224 part time; 45% male, 55% female; 0% American Indian, 7% Asian, 10% Black, 22% Hispanic, 4% multiracial, 0% Pacific Islander, 46% white, 7% international; 94% from in state; 15% live on campus; 5% of students in fraternities, 7% in sororities
Most popular majors: 22% Health Professions and Related Programs, 16% Business, Management, Marketing, and Related Support Services, 11% Biological and Biomedical Sciences, 11% Social Sciences, 8% Engineering
Expenses: 2020-2021: $6,410 in state, $17,324 out of state; room/board: $11,836
Financial aid: (813) 974-4700; 58% of undergrads determined to have financial need; average aid package $11,537

University of Tampa
Tampa FL
(888) 646-2738
U.S. News ranking: Reg. U. (S), No. 13
Website: www.ut.edu
Admissions email: admissions@ut.edu
Private; founded 1931
Freshman admissions: more selective; 2019-2020: 24,448 applied, 10,940 accepted. Either SAT or ACT required. SAT 25/75 percentile: 1100-1250. High school rank: 19% in top tenth, 47% in top quarter, 81% in top half
Early decision deadline: N/A, notification date: N/A
Early action deadline: 11/15, notification date: 12/15
Application deadline (fall): rolling
Undergraduate student body: 8,441 full time, 256 part time; 42% male, 58% female; 0% American Indian, 2% Asian, 4% Black, 12% Hispanic, 3% multiracial, 0% Pacific Islander, 61% white, 8% international; 31% from in state; 49% live on campus; 2% of students in fraternities, 5% in sororities
Most popular majors: 8% Finance, General, 7% Business Administration and Management, General, 6% Marketing/Marketing Management, General, 5% Communication and Media Studies, 5% Criminology
Expenses: 2020-2021: $30,884; room/board: $11,526
Financial aid: (813) 253-6219; 57% of undergrads determined to have financial need; average aid package $18,110

University of West Florida
Pensacola FL
(850) 474-2230
U.S. News ranking: Reg. U. (S), No. 36
Website: uwf.edu
Admissions email: admissions@uwf.edu
Public; founded 1963
Affiliation: Undenominational

Freshman admissions: more selective; 2019-2020: 7,194 applied, 2,230 accepted. Either SAT or ACT required. ACT 25/75 percentile: 22-27. High school rank: 15% in top tenth, 42% in top quarter, 80% in top half
Early decision deadline: N/A, notification date: N/A
Early action deadline: N/A, notification date: N/A
Application deadline (fall): 6/30
Undergraduate student body: 6,601 full time, 2,930 part time; 43% male, 57% female; 1% American Indian, 3% Asian, 11% Black, 10% Hispanic, 6% multiracial, 0% Pacific Islander, 66% white, 2% international; 88% from in state; 15% live on campus; N/A of students in fraternities, N/A in sororities
Most popular majors: 23% Registered Nursing/Registered Nurse, 5% Health Professions and Related Programs, 5% Health and Physical Education/Fitness, General, 5% Mass Communication/Media Studies, 5% Psychology, General
Expenses: 2020-2021: $6,360 in state, $18,628 out of state; room/board: $11,268
Financial aid: (850) 474-2398; 29% of undergrads determined to have financial need; average aid package $11,884

Valencia College[1]
Orlando FL
(407) 299-5000
U.S. News ranking: Reg. Coll. (S), unranked
Admissions email: N/A
Public
Application deadline (fall): N/A
Undergraduate student body: N/A full time, N/A part time
Expenses: 2019-2020: $2,474 in state, $9,383 out of state; room/board: $9,366
Financial aid: N/A

Warner University
Lake Wales FL
(800) 309-9563
U.S. News ranking: Reg. Coll. (S), No. 63
Website: www.warner.edu
Admissions email: admissions@warner.edu
Private; founded 1964
Affiliation: Church of God
Freshman admissions: less selective; 2019-2020: 1,256 applied, 575 accepted. Neither SAT nor ACT required. SAT 25/75 percentile: 870-1090. High school rank: 8% in top tenth, 19% in top quarter, 49% in top half
Early decision deadline: N/A, notification date: N/A
Early action deadline: N/A, notification date: N/A
Application deadline (fall): rolling
Undergraduate student body: 796 full time, 74 part time; 54% male, 46% female; 0% American Indian, 0% Asian, 37% Black, 12% Hispanic, 1% multiracial, 0% Pacific Islander, 45% white, 4% international; N/A from in state; 46% live on campus; N/A of students in fraternities, N/A in sororities

Most popular majors: 32% Business, Management, Marketing, and Related Support Services, 25% Education, 14% Parks, Recreation, Leisure, and Fitness Studies, 10% Agriculture, Agriculture Operations, and Related Sciences, 5% Theology and Religious Vocations
Expenses: 2020-2021: $24,750; room/board: $9,200
Financial aid: (863) 638-7203; 89% of undergrads determined to have financial need; average aid package $17,563

Webber International University
Babson Park FL
(800) 741-1844
U.S. News ranking: Reg. Coll. (S), second tier
Website: www.webber.edu
Admissions email: admissions@webber.edu
Private; founded 1927
Freshman admissions: selective; 2019-2020: 1,690 applied, 714 accepted. Either SAT or ACT required. SAT 25/75 percentile: 900-1050. High school rank: 7% in top tenth, 52% in top quarter, 53% in top half
Early decision deadline: N/A, notification date: N/A
Early action deadline: N/A, notification date: N/A
Application deadline (fall): 8/1
Undergraduate student body: 642 full time, 22 part time; 69% male, 31% female; 1% American Indian, 0% Asian, 31% Black, 12% Hispanic, 2% multiracial, 1% Pacific Islander, 39% white, 14% international; 71% from in state; 55% live on campus; N/A of students in fraternities, N/A in sororities
Most popular majors: 50% Business, Management, Marketing, and Related Support Services, 20% Public Administration and Social Service Professions, 16% Homeland Security, Law Enforcement, Firefighting and Related Protective Services, 3% Computer and Information Sciences and Support Services, 2% Legal Professions and Studies
Expenses: 2020-2021: $28,500; room/board: $9,940
Financial aid: (863) 638-2929; 75% of undergrads determined to have financial need; average aid package $20,114

GEORGIA

Abraham Baldwin Agricultural College[1]
Tifton GA
(800) 733-3653
U.S. News ranking: Reg. Coll. (S), second tier
Website: www.abac.edu/
Admissions email: N/A
Public; founded 1908
Application deadline (fall): 8/1
Undergraduate student body: N/A full time, N/A part time

Expenses: 2019-2020: $3,565 in state, $10,471 out of state; room/board: $7,814
Financial aid: (229) 391-4985

Agnes Scott College
Decatur GA
(800) 868-8602
U.S. News ranking: Nat. Lib. Arts, No. 61
Website: www.agnesscott.edu
Admissions email: admission@agnesscott.edu
Private; founded 1889
Affiliation: Presbyterian Church (USA)
Freshman admissions: more selective; 2019-2020: 1,751 applied, 1,135 accepted. Neither SAT nor ACT required. SAT 25/75 percentile: 1130-1340. High school rank: 32% in top tenth, 67% in top quarter, 95% in top half
Early decision deadline: 11/1, notification date: 12/1
Early action deadline: 11/15, notification date: 12/15
Application deadline (fall): 5/1
Undergraduate student body: 990 full time, 15 part time; 0% male, 100% female; 0% American Indian, 8% Asian, 32% Black, 14% Hispanic, 6% multiracial, 0% Pacific Islander, 31% white, 6% international; 60% from in state; 82% live on campus; N/A of students in fraternities, N/A in sororities
Most popular majors: 11% Public Health, General, 7% Neuroscience, 6% Business Administration and Management, General, 6% Psychology, General, 6% Social Sciences, Other
Expenses: 2020-2021: $44,250; room/board: $13,050
Financial aid: (404) 471-6395; 78% of undergrads determined to have financial need; average aid package $38,618

Albany State University[1]
Albany GA
(229) 500-4358
U.S. News ranking: Reg. U. (S), second tier
Website: www.asurams.edu/
Admissions email: admissions@asurams.edu
Public; founded 1903
Application deadline (fall): 7/1
Undergraduate student body: N/A full time, N/A part time
Expenses: 2019-2020: $6,950 in state, $20,352 out of state; room/board: $8,980
Financial aid: (229) 500-4358

Andrew College[1]
Cuthbert GA
(229) 732-5938
U.S. News ranking: Reg. Coll. (S), unranked
Website: www.andrewcollege.edu/
Admissions email: admissions@andrewcollege.edu
Private; founded 1854
Affiliation: United Methodist
Application deadline (fall): N/A
Undergraduate student body: N/A full time, N/A part time

Expenses: 2019-2020: $18,258; room/board: $11,170
Financial aid: N/A

Art Institute of Atlanta[1]
Atlanta GA
(770) 394-8300
U.S. News ranking: Arts, unranked
Website: www.artinstitutes.edu/atlanta/
Admissions email: aiaadm@aii.edu
For-profit
Application deadline (fall): N/A
Undergraduate student body: N/A full time, N/A part time
Expenses: 2019-2020: $19,354; room/board: N/A
Financial aid: N/A

Atlanta Metropolitan State College[1]
Atlanta GA
(404) 756-4004
U.S. News ranking: Reg. Coll. (S), unranked
Website: www.Atlm.edu
Admissions email: admissions@atlm.edu
Public; founded 1974
Application deadline (fall): rolling
Undergraduate student body: N/A full time, N/A part time
Expenses: 2019-2020: $3,505 in state, $10,131 out of state; room/board: $6,480
Financial aid: N/A

Augusta University
Augusta GA
(706) 721-2725
U.S. News ranking: Nat. U., second tier
Website: www.augusta.edu/
Admissions email: admissions@augusta.edu
Public; founded 1828
Freshman admissions: less selective; 2019-2020: 3,374 applied, 2,561 accepted. Either SAT or ACT required. ACT 25/75 percentile: 19-26. High school rank: N/A
Early decision deadline: N/A, notification date: N/A
Early action deadline: N/A, notification date: N/A
Application deadline (fall): N/A
Undergraduate student body: 4,562 full time, 1,042 part time; 35% male, 65% female; 0% American Indian, 6% Asian, 25% Black, 8% Hispanic, 6% multiracial, 0% Pacific Islander, 51% white, 1% international; 91% from in state; N/A live on campus; N/A of students in fraternities, N/A in sororities
Most popular majors: Information not available
Expenses: 2020-2021: $8,832 in state, $24,210 out of state; room/board: $10,666
Financial aid: (706) 737-1524

Berry College
Mount Berry GA
(706) 236-2215
U.S. News ranking: Reg. U. (S), No. 4
Website: www.berry.edu/
Admissions email: admissions@berry.edu

Private; founded 1902
Freshman admissions: more selective; 2019-2020: 4,328 applied, 3,055 accepted. Either SAT or ACT required. SAT 25/75 percentile: 1090-1320. High school rank: 32% in top tenth, 61% in top quarter, 87% in top half
Early decision deadline: 11/1, notification date: 12/1
Early action deadline: 11/1, notification date: 12/15
Application deadline (fall): 7/24
Undergraduate student body: 1,911 full time, 32 part time; 39% male, 61% female; 0% American Indian, 2% Asian, 7% Black, 7% Hispanic, 4% multiracial, 0% Pacific Islander, 78% white, 1% international; 69% from in state; 89% live on campus; 0% of students in fraternities, 0% in sororities
Most popular majors: 18% Biological and Biomedical Sciences, 18% Business, Management, Marketing, and Related Support Services, 8% Education, 8% Psychology, 7% Parks, Recreation, Leisure, and Fitness Studies
Expenses: 2020-2021: $37,946; room/board: $13,370
Financial aid: (706) 236-1714; 70% of undergrads determined to have financial need; average aid package $31,911

Brenau University
Gainesville GA
(770) 534-6100
U.S. News ranking: Reg. U. (S), No. 36
Website: www.brenau.edu
Admissions email: admissions@brenau.edu
Private; founded 1878
Freshman admissions: selective; 2019-2020: 1,912 applied, 1,219 accepted. Neither SAT nor ACT required. SAT 25/75 percentile: 900-1110. High school rank: 14% in top tenth, 37% in top quarter, 72% in top half
Early decision deadline: N/A, notification date: N/A
Early action deadline: N/A, notification date: N/A
Application deadline (fall): rolling
Undergraduate student body: 1,108 full time, 648 part time; 10% male, 90% female; 0% American Indian, 2% Asian, 29% Black, 11% Hispanic, 2% multiracial, 0% Pacific Islander, 46% white, 7% international; 95% from in state; 19% live on campus; 0% of students in fraternities, 9% in sororities
Most popular majors: 28% Health Professions and Related Programs, 22% Business, Management, Marketing, and Related Support Services, 15% Education, 14% Visual and Performing Arts, 7% Psychology
Expenses: 2020-2021: $31,720; room/board: $12,500
Financial aid: (770) 534-6176; 79% of undergrads determined to have financial need; average aid package $20,404

Brewton-Parker College
Mount Vernon GA
(912) 583-3265
U.S. News ranking: Nat. Lib. Arts, second tier
Website: www.bpc.edu
Admissions email: admissions@bpc.edu
Private; founded 1904
Affiliation: Baptist
Freshman admissions: least selective; 2019-2020: 452 applied, 435 accepted. Either SAT or ACT required. SAT 25/75 percentile: 880-1050. High school rank: 4% in top tenth, 18% in top quarter, 51% in top half
Early decision deadline: N/A, notification date: N/A
Early action deadline: N/A, notification date: N/A
Application deadline (fall): rolling
Undergraduate student body: 476 full time, 412 part time; 56% male, 44% female; 1% American Indian, 1% Asian, 35% Black, 3% Hispanic, 1% multiracial, 2% Pacific Islander, 51% white, 4% international; 75% from in state; 46% live on campus; 1% of students in fraternities, 0% in sororities
Most popular majors: 34% General Studies, 11% Business, Management, Marketing, and Related Support Services, Other, 11% Psychology, General, 7% Criminal Justice/Law Enforcement Administration, 7% Sport and Fitness Administration/ Management
Expenses: 2020-2021: $18,900; room/board: $8,230
Financial aid: (912) 583-3215; 86% of undergrads determined to have financial need; average aid package $16,023

Clark Atlanta University
Atlanta GA
(800) 688-3228
U.S. News ranking: Nat. U., second tier
Website: www.cau.edu
Admissions email: cauadmissions@cau.edu
Private; founded 1988
Affiliation: United Methodist
Freshman admissions: selective; 2019-2020: 16,483 applied, 9,036 accepted. Either SAT or ACT required. SAT 25/75 percentile: 940-1080. High school rank: 10% in top tenth, 31% in top quarter, 70% in top half
Early decision deadline: N/A, notification date: N/A
Early action deadline: N/A, notification date: N/A
Application deadline (fall): 4/1
Undergraduate student body: 3,255 full time, 63 part time; 24% male, 76% female; 0% American Indian, 0% Asian, 92% Black, 0% Hispanic, 0% multiracial, 0% Pacific Islander, 0% white, 3% international; 34% from in state; 58% live on campus; 2% of students in fraternities, 3% in sororities
Most popular majors: 26% Business, Management, Marketing, and Related Support

Services, 18% Communication, Journalism, and Related Programs, 11% Homeland Security, Law Enforcement, Firefighting and Related Protective Services, 11% Psychology, 8% Visual and Performing Arts
Expenses: 2020-2021: $24,157; room/board: $11,506
Financial aid: (404) 880-8992; 91% of undergrads determined to have financial need; average aid package $8,362

Clayton State University
Morrow GA
(678) 466-4115
U.S. News ranking: Reg. U. (S), second tier
Website: www.clayton.edu
Admissions email: csuinfo@clayton.edu
Public; founded 1969
Freshman admissions: less selective; 2019-2020: 1,938 applied, 991 accepted. Either SAT or ACT required. SAT 25/75 percentile: 880-1020. High school rank: N/A
Early decision deadline: N/A, notification date: N/A
Early action deadline: N/A, notification date: N/A
Application deadline (fall): 7/1
Undergraduate student body: 3,837 full time, 2,531 part time; 31% male, 69% female; 0% American Indian, 6% Asian, 66% Black, 8% Hispanic, 3% multiracial, 0% Pacific Islander, 13% white, 2% international; 96% from in state; 18% live on campus; N/A of students in fraternities, N/A in sororities
Most popular majors: 13% Community Psychology, 12% Registered Nursing/Registered Nurse, 11% Liberal Arts and Sciences/Liberal Studies, 6% Hospital and Health Care Facilities Administration/Management, 5% Office Management and Supervision
Expenses: 2020-2021: $6,584 in state, $19,986 out of state; room/board: $10,397
Financial aid: (678) 466-4181; 86% of undergrads determined to have financial need; average aid package $11,304

College of Coastal Georgia
Brunswick GA
(912) 279-5730
U.S. News ranking: Reg. Coll. (S), second tier
Website: www.ccga.edu
Admissions email: admiss@ccga.edu
Public; founded 1961
Freshman admissions: less selective; 2019-2020: 1,785 applied, 1,556 accepted. Either SAT or ACT required. SAT 25/75 percentile: 910-1100. High school rank: N/A
Early decision deadline: N/A, notification date: N/A
Early action deadline: N/A, notification date: N/A
Application deadline (fall): 8/5

Undergraduate student body: 1,997 full time, 1,538 part time; 32% male, 68% female; 0% American Indian, 2% Asian, 21% Black, 7% Hispanic, 4% multiracial, 0% Pacific Islander, 63% white, 1% international; 90% from in state; 21% live on campus; 0% of students in fraternities, 0% in sororities
Most popular majors: 23% Business/Commerce, General, 16% Psychology, General, 13% Registered Nursing/Registered Nurse, 9% Biology/Biological Sciences, General, 8% Multi/ Interdisciplinary Studies
Expenses: 2020-2021: $4,774 in state, $13,406 out of state; room/ board: $10,636
Financial aid: (912) 279-5726; 63% of undergrads determined to have financial need; average aid package $11,182

Columbus State University
Columbus GA
(706) 507-8800
U.S. News ranking: Reg. U. (S), No. 73
Website: www.columbusstate.edu
Admissions email: admissions@ columbusstate.edu
Public; founded 1958
Freshman admissions: selective; 2019-2020: 2,881 applied, 2,288 accepted. Either SAT or ACT required. SAT 25/75 percentile: 860-1100. High school rank: 16% in top tenth, 42% in top quarter, 76% in top half
Early decision deadline: N/A, notification date: N/A
Early action deadline: N/A, notification date: N/A
Application deadline (fall): 6/30
Undergraduate student body: 4,554 full time, 1,947 part time; 39% male, 61% female; 0% American Indian, 3% Asian, 40% Black, 7% Hispanic, 1% multiracial, 0% Pacific Islander, 47% white, 1% international; 86% from in state; 23% live on campus; 5% of students in fraternities, 5% in sororities
Most popular majors: 26% Health Professions and Related Programs, 17% Business, Management, Marketing, and Related Support Services, 7% Computer and Information Sciences and Support Services, 7% Visual and Performing Arts, 6% Communication, Journalism, and Related Programs
Expenses: 2020-2021: $7,334 in state, $21,152 out of state; room/ board: $10,150
Financial aid: (706) 507-8800; 72% of undergrads determined to have financial need; average aid package $10,142

Covenant College
Lookout Mountain GA
(706) 820-2398
U.S. News ranking: Nat. Lib. Arts, No. 140
Website: www.covenant.edu
Admissions email: admissions@covenant.edu
Private; founded 1955

Affiliation: The Presbyterian Church in America
Freshman admissions: more selective; 2019-2020: 561 applied, 551 accepted. Either SAT or ACT required. ACT 25/75 percentile: 23-29. High school rank: 33% in top tenth, 50% in top quarter, 71% in top half
Early decision deadline: N/A, notification date: N/A
Early action deadline: 11/15, notification date: 12/1
Application deadline (fall): 2/1
Undergraduate student body: 887 full time, 59 part time; 47% male, 53% female; 1% American Indian, 1% Asian, 3% Black, 1% Hispanic, 5% multiracial, 0% Pacific Islander, 84% white, 3% international; 29% from in state; 82% live on campus; N/A of students in fraternities, N/A in sororities
Most popular majors: 14% Multi/ Interdisciplinary Studies, 12% Social Sciences, 10% Psychology, 9% English Language and Literature/Letters, 9% Visual and Performing Arts
Expenses: 2020-2021: $36,710; room/board: $10,970
Financial aid: (706) 419-1447; 66% of undergrads determined to have financial need; average aid package $30,012

Dalton State College[1]
Dalton GA
(706) 272-4436
U.S. News ranking: Reg. Coll. (S), second tier
Website: www.daltonstate.edu/
Admissions email: N/A
Public
Application deadline (fall): N/A
Undergraduate student body: N/A full time, N/A part time
Expenses: 2019-2020: $3,683 in state, $10,589 out of state; room/ board: $8,430
Financial aid: N/A

East Georgia State College[1]
Swainsboro GA
(478) 289-2017
U.S. News ranking: Reg. Coll. (S), unranked
Website: www.ega.edu/admissions
Admissions email: Ask_EGSC@ega.edu
Public; founded 1973
Application deadline (fall): 8/15
Undergraduate student body: N/A full time, N/A part time
Expenses: 2019-2020: $3,136 in state, $9,488 out of state; room/ board: $9,784
Financial aid: N/A

Emmanuel College
Franklin Springs GA
(800) 860-8800
U.S. News ranking: Reg. Coll. (S), No. 33
Website: www.ec.edu
Admissions email: admissions@ec.edu
Private; founded 1919
Affiliation: Pentecostal Holiness Church
Freshman admissions: selective; 2019-2020: 767 applied, 354

accepted. Either SAT or ACT required. SAT 25/75 percentile: 920-1120. High school rank: N/A
Early decision deadline: N/A, notification date: N/A
Early action deadline: N/A, notification date: N/A
Application deadline (fall): 8/1
Undergraduate student body: 829 full time, 129 part time; 53% male, 47% female; 1% American Indian, 0% Asian, 16% Black, 7% Hispanic, 4% multiracial, 1% Pacific Islander, 61% white, 9% international; 75% from in state; 58% live on campus; N/A of students in fraternities, N/A in sororities
Most popular majors: 26% Business, Management, Marketing, and Related Support Services, 15% Education, 13% Parks, Recreation, Leisure, and Fitness Studies, 11% Communication, Journalism, and Related Programs, 11% Psychology
Expenses: 2020-2021: $21,220; room/board: $8,234
Financial aid: (706) 245-2844; 75% of undergrads determined to have financial need; average aid package $16,881

Emory University
Atlanta GA
(404) 727-6036
U.S. News ranking: Nat. U., No. 21
Website: www.emory.edu
Admissions email: admission@emory.edu
Private; founded 1836
Affiliation: United Methodist
Freshman admissions: most selective; 2019-2020: 30,017 applied, 4,682 accepted. Either SAT or ACT required. SAT 25/75 percentile: 1360-1530. High school rank: 84% in top tenth, 97% in top quarter, 100% in top half
Early decision deadline: 11/1, notification date: 12/15
Early action deadline: N/A, notification date: N/A
Application deadline (fall): 1/1
Undergraduate student body: 7,012 full time, 106 part time; 40% male, 60% female; 0% American Indian, 22% Asian, 8% Black, 11% Hispanic, 4% multiracial, 0% Pacific Islander, 39% white, 15% international; 20% from in state; 63% live on campus; 23% of students in fraternities, 22% in sororities
Most popular majors: 13% Business Administration and Management, General, 10% Biology/Biological Sciences, General, 8% Registered Nursing/Registered Nurse, 6% Economics, General, 6% Psychology, General
Expenses: 2020-2021: $53,868; room/board: $15,242
Financial aid: (404) 727-6039; 48% of undergrads determined to have financial need; average aid package $47,223

Fort Valley State University
Fort Valley GA
(478) 825-6307
U.S. News ranking: Reg. U. (S), second tier
Website: www.fvsu.edu
Admissions email: admissap@mail.fvsu.edu
Public; founded 1895
Freshman admissions: least selective; 2019-2020: 3,473 applied, 1,913 accepted. Either SAT or ACT required. SAT 25/75 percentile: 850-960. High school rank: 5% in top tenth, 14% in top quarter, 47% in top half
Early decision deadline: N/A, notification date: N/A
Early action deadline: N/A, notification date: N/A
Application deadline (fall): 7/19
Undergraduate student body: 2,059 full time, 234 part time; 39% male, 61% female; 0% American Indian, 0% Asian, 92% Black, 2% Hispanic, 3% multiracial, 0% Pacific Islander, 2% white, 0% international; 93% from in state; 53% live on campus; N/A of students in fraternities, N/A in sororities
Most popular majors: 44% Psychology, 18% Homeland Security, Law Enforcement, Firefighting and Related Protective Services, 15% Health Professions and Related Programs, 9% Biological and Biomedical Sciences, 5% Physical Sciences
Expenses: 2020-2021: $6,848 in state, $20,250 out of state; room/board: $9,632
Financial aid: (478) 825-6363; 94% of undergrads determined to have financial need; average aid package $7,801

Georgia College & State University
Milledgeville GA
(478) 445-1283
U.S. News ranking: Reg. U. (S), No. 21
Website: www.gcsu.edu
Admissions email: admissions@gcsu.edu
Public; founded 1889
Freshman admissions: selective; 2019-2020: 4,386 applied, 3,490 accepted. Either SAT or ACT required. SAT 25/75 percentile: 1110-1260. High school rank: N/A
Early decision deadline: N/A, notification date: N/A
Early action deadline: 11/1, notification date: 12/1
Application deadline (fall): 4/1
Undergraduate student body: 5,364 full time, 480 part time; 36% male, 64% female; 0% American Indian, 1% Asian, 5% Black, 6% Hispanic, 3% multiracial, 0% Pacific Islander, 83% white, 0% international; 99% from in state; 36% live on campus; 8% of students in fraternities, 13% in sororities
Most popular majors: 8% Business Administration and Management, General, 8% Registered Nursing/Registered Nurse, 7% Marketing/Marketing Management, General,

7% Research and Experimental Psychology, Other, 6% Journalism
Expenses: 2020-2021: $9,524 in state, $28,704 out of state; room/board: $11,318
Financial aid: (478) 445-5149; 48% of undergrads determined to have financial need; average aid package $11,322

Georgia Gwinnett College
Lawrenceville GA
(678) 407-5313
U.S. News ranking: Reg. Coll. (S), No. 66
Website: www.ggc.edu
Admissions email: ggcadmissions@ggc.edu
Public; founded 2005
Freshman admissions: less selective; 2019-2020: 4,853 applied, 4,559 accepted. Neither SAT nor ACT required. SAT 25/75 percentile: 910-1100. High school rank: 4% in top tenth, 15% in top quarter, 41% in top half
Early decision deadline: N/A, notification date: N/A
Early action deadline: N/A, notification date: N/A
Application deadline (fall): 5/1
Undergraduate student body: 8,556 full time, 4,275 part time; 43% male, 57% female; 0% American Indian, 10% Asian, 33% Black, 23% Hispanic, 4% multiracial, 0% Pacific Islander, 26% white, 2% international; 96% from in state; 7% live on campus; N/A of students in fraternities, N/A in sororities
Most popular majors: 32% Business, Management, Marketing, and Related Support Services, 12% Computer and Information Sciences and Support Services, 12% Psychology, 9% Biological and Biomedical Sciences, 9% Education
Expenses: 2020-2021: $5,762 in state, $16,744 out of state; room/board: $13,616
Financial aid: (678) 407-5701; 74% of undergrads determined to have financial need; average aid package $12,331

Georgia Highlands College[1]
Rome GA
(706) 802-5000
U.S. News ranking: Reg. Coll. (S), unranked
Admissions email: N/A
Public
Application deadline (fall): N/A
Undergraduate student body: N/A full time, N/A part time
Expenses: 2019-2020: $3,344 in state, $9,696 out of state; room/board: $8,372
Financial aid: N/A

Georgia Institute of Technology
Atlanta GA
(404) 894-4154
U.S. News ranking: Nat. U., No. 35
Website: admission.gatech.edu
Admissions email: admission@gatech.edu

Public; founded 1885
Freshman admissions: most selective; 2019-2020: 36,856 applied, 7,584 accepted. Either SAT or ACT required. SAT 25/75 percentile: 1370-1530. High school rank: 90% in top tenth, 98% in top quarter, 99% in top half
Early decision deadline: N/A, notification date: N/A
Early action deadline: 10/15, notification date: 1/18
Application deadline (fall): 1/6
Undergraduate student body: 14,309 full time, 1,655 part time; 61% male, 39% female; 0% American Indian, 23% Asian, 7% Black, 7% Hispanic, 4% multiracial, 0% Pacific Islander, 47% white, 10% international; N/A from in state; 50% live on campus; 22% of students in fraternities, 26% in sororities
Most popular majors: 59% Engineering, 17% Computer and Information Sciences and Support Services, 10% Business, Management, Marketing, and Related Support Services, 4% Biological and Biomedical Sciences, 2% Physical Sciences
Expenses: 2020-2021: $12,682 in state, $33,794 out of state; room/board: $14,830
Financial aid: (404) 894-4160; 40% of undergrads determined to have financial need; average aid package $14,565

Georgia Military College[1]
Milledgeville GA
(478) 387-4900
U.S. News ranking: Reg. Coll. (S), unranked
Website: www.hfcc.edu
Admissions email: N/A
Public
Application deadline (fall): N/A
Undergraduate student body: N/A full time, N/A part time
Expenses: 2019-2020: $6,525 in state, $6,525 out of state; room/board: $7,500
Financial aid: N/A

Georgia Southern University
Statesboro GA
(912) 478-5391
U.S. News ranking: Nat. U., second tier
Website: www.georgiasouthern.edu/
Admissions email: admissions@georgiasouthern.edu
Public; founded 1906
Freshman admissions: selective; 2019-2020: 13,858 applied, 7,549 accepted. Either SAT or ACT required. SAT 25/75 percentile: 1050-1200. High school rank: 17% in top tenth, 44% in top quarter, 77% in top half
Early decision deadline: N/A, notification date: N/A
Early action deadline: N/A, notification date: N/A
Application deadline (fall): 5/1
Undergraduate student body: 19,156 full time, 3,559 part time; 44% male, 56% female; 0% American Indian, 2% Asian,

25% Black, 7% Hispanic, 4% multiracial, 0% Pacific Islander, 59% white, 1% international; 80% from in state; 25% live on campus; 20% of students in fraternities, 15% in sororities
Most popular majors: 17% Business, Management, Marketing, and Related Support Services, 15% Health Professions and Related Programs, 7% Engineering, 7% Parks, Recreation, Leisure, and Fitness Studies, 6% Education
Expenses: 2020-2021: $7,578 in state, $21,396 out of state; room/board: $10,216
Financial aid: (912) 478-5413; 64% of undergrads determined to have financial need; average aid package $11,471

Georgia Southwestern State University
Americus GA
(229) 928-1273
U.S. News ranking: Reg. U. (S), second tier
Website: www.gsw.edu
Admissions email: admissions@gsw.edu
Public; founded 1906
Freshman admissions: selective; 2019-2020: 1,783 applied, 1,040 accepted. Either SAT or ACT required. SAT 25/75 percentile: 940-1120. High school rank: 15% in top tenth, 37% in top quarter, 70% in top half
Early decision deadline: N/A, notification date: N/A
Early action deadline: N/A, notification date: N/A
Application deadline (fall): 7/21
Undergraduate student body: 1,648 full time, 850 part time; 38% male, 62% female; 0% American Indian, 1% Asian, 28% Black, 6% Hispanic, 3% multiracial, 0% Pacific Islander, 60% white, 2% international; N/A from in state; 30% live on campus; 11% of students in fraternities, 10% in sororities
Most popular majors: 16% Business Administration and Management, General, 14% Accounting, 12% Registered Nursing/Registered Nurse, 10% Psychology, General, 9% Elementary Education and Teaching
Expenses: 2020-2021: $6,516 in state, $19,918 out of state; room/board: N/A
Financial aid: (229) 928-1378; 72% of undergrads determined to have financial need; average aid package $10,505

Georgia State University
Atlanta GA
(404) 413-2500
U.S. News ranking: Nat. U., No. 206
Website: www.gsu.edu
Admissions email: admissions@gsu.edu
Public; founded 1913
Freshman admissions: selective; 2019-2020: 20,949 applied, 12,028 accepted. Either SAT or ACT required. SAT 25/75

percentile: 990-1190. High school rank: N/A
Early decision deadline: N/A, notification date: N/A
Early action deadline: 11/15, notification date: 12/15
Application deadline (fall): 6/1
Undergraduate student body: 21,978 full time, 5,991 part time; 41% male, 59% female; 0% American Indian, 15% Asian, 41% Black, 12% Hispanic, 6% multiracial, 0% Pacific Islander, 22% white, 3% international; 95% from in state; 21% live on campus; N/A of students in fraternities, N/A in sororities
Most popular majors: 21% Business, Management, Marketing, and Related Support Services, 10% Social Sciences, 9% Computer and Information Sciences and Support Services, 9% Psychology, 8% Biological and Biomedical Sciences
Expenses: 2020-2021: $11,076 in state, $30,114 out of state; room/board: $14,958
Financial aid: (404) 413-2600; 76% of undergrads determined to have financial need; average aid package $10,976

Gordon State College[1]
Barnesville GA
(678) 359-5021
U.S. News ranking: Reg. Coll. (S), No. 61
Website: www.gordonstate.edu/
Admissions email: admissions@gordonstate.edu
Public; founded 1852
Application deadline (fall): rolling
Undergraduate student body: N/A full time, N/A part time
Expenses: 2019-2020: $4,084 in state, $11,946 out of state; room/board: $8,666
Financial aid: (678) 359-5990

Kennesaw State University
Kennesaw GA
(770) 423-6300
U.S. News ranking: Nat. U., second tier
Website: www.kennesaw.edu
Admissions email: KSUAdmit@kennesaw.edu
Public; founded 1963
Freshman admissions: selective; 2019-2020: 15,691 applied, 11,803 accepted. Either SAT or ACT required. SAT 25/75 percentile: 1050-1230. High school rank: 15% in top tenth, 41% in top quarter, 76% in top half
Early decision deadline: N/A, notification date: N/A
Early action deadline: N/A, notification date: N/A
Application deadline (fall): 6/1
Undergraduate student body: 25,745 full time, 8,754 part time; 52% male, 48% female; 0% American Indian, 5% Asian, 22% Black, 12% Hispanic, 5% multiracial, 0% Pacific Islander, 53% white, 2% international; N/A from in state; 15% live on campus; 4% of students in fraternities, 7% in sororities
Most popular majors: 20% Business, Management,

Marketing, and Related Support Services, 10% Computer and Information Sciences and Support Services, 10% Engineering, 7% Psychology, 6% Multi/Interdisciplinary Studies
Expenses: 2020-2021: $7,548 in state, $21,616 out of state; room/board: $12,947
Financial aid: (770) 423-6074; 70% of undergrads determined to have financial need; average aid package $11,585

LaGrange College
LaGrange GA
(706) 880-8005
U.S. News ranking: Reg. Coll. (S), No. 5
Website: www.lagrange.edu
Admissions email: admissions@lagrange.edu
Private; founded 1831
Affiliation: United Methodist
Freshman admissions: selective; 2019-2020: 1,694 applied, 825 accepted. Either SAT or ACT required. SAT 25/75 percentile: 1000-1148. High school rank: 15% in top tenth, 42% in top quarter, 77% in top half
Early decision deadline: N/A, notification date: N/A
Early action deadline: N/A, notification date: N/A
Application deadline (fall): 8/31
Undergraduate student body: 847 full time, 25 part time; 51% male, 49% female; 1% American Indian, 1% Asian, 22% Black, 2% Hispanic, 2% multiracial, 0% Pacific Islander, 71% white, 1% international; 83% from in state; 63% live on campus; 17% of students in fraternities, 31% in sororities
Most popular majors: 23% Registered Nursing/Registered Nurse, 17% Business Administration and Management, General, 9% Kinesiology and Exercise Science, 6% Biology/Biological Sciences, General, 5% Psychology, General
Expenses: 2020-2021: $32,350; room/board: $12,260
Financial aid: (706) 880-8249; 89% of undergrads determined to have financial need; average aid package $27,550

Mercer University
Macon GA
(478) 301-2650
U.S. News ranking: Nat. U., No. 160
Website: www.mercer.edu
Admissions email: admissions@mercer.edu
Private; founded 1833
Freshman admissions: more selective; 2019-2020: 5,034 applied, 3,736 accepted. Either SAT or ACT required. SAT 25/75 percentile: 1170-1340. High school rank: 36% in top tenth, 68% in top quarter, 92% in top half
Early decision deadline: N/A, notification date: N/A
Early action deadline: 10/15, notification date: 1/5
Application deadline (fall): 7/1
Undergraduate student body: 4,260 full time, 605 part time; 37%

male, 63% female; 0% American Indian, 8% Asian, 28% Black, 7% Hispanic, 4% multiracial, 0% Pacific Islander, 47% white, 2% international; 84% from in state; 78% live on campus; 23% of students in fraternities, 26% in sororities
Most popular majors: 20% Business, Management, Marketing, and Related Support Services, 16% Engineering, 14% Biological and Biomedical Sciences, 7% Communication, Journalism, and Related Programs, 6% Social Sciences
Expenses: 2020-2021: $37,808; room/board: $13,070
Financial aid: (478) 301-2670; 67% of undergrads determined to have financial need; average aid package $37,583

Middle Georgia State University
Macon GA
(478) 471-2725
U.S. News ranking: Reg. Coll. (S), No. 50
Website: www.mga.edu/
Admissions email: admissions@mga.edu
Public; founded 2013
Freshman admissions: less selective; 2019-2020: 2,759 applied, 2,598 accepted. Either SAT or ACT required. SAT 25/75 percentile: 880-1090. High school rank: N/A
Early decision deadline: N/A, notification date: N/A
Early action deadline: N/A, notification date: N/A
Application deadline (fall): rolling
Undergraduate student body: 4,906 full time, 2,882 part time; 43% male, 57% female; 0% American Indian, 2% Asian, 36% Black, 5% Hispanic, 4% multiracial, 0% Pacific Islander, 50% white, 2% international; 96% from in state; 22% live on campus; N/A of students in fraternities, N/A in sororities
Most popular majors: 21% Registered Nursing/Registered Nurse, 17% Business Administration and Management, General, 16% Computer and Information Sciences, General, 8% Aviation/Airway Management and Operations, 8% Psychology, General
Expenses: 2020-2021: $4,742 in state, $13,926 out of state; room/board: $9,560
Financial aid: (877) 238-8664; 100% of undergrads determined to have financial need; average aid package $8,223

Morehouse College
Atlanta GA
(844) 512-6672
U.S. News ranking: Nat. Lib. Arts, No. 155
Website: www.morehouse.edu
Admissions email: admissions@morehouse.edu
Private; founded 1867
Freshman admissions: selective; 2019-2020: 3,659 applied, 1,864 accepted. Either SAT or ACT required. SAT 25/75

percentile: 995-1180. High school rank: N/A
Early decision deadline: 11/1, notification date: 12/15
Early action deadline: 11/1, notification date: 12/15
Application deadline (fall): 2/15
Undergraduate student body: 2,145 full time, 93 part time; 100% male, 0% female; 0% American Indian, 0% Asian, 72% Black, 0% Hispanic, 2% multiracial, 0% Pacific Islander, 0% white, 1% international; N/A from in state; 66% live on campus; N/A of students in fraternities, N/A in sororities
Most popular majors: 21% Business, Management, Marketing, and Related Support Services, 8% Biological and Biomedical Sciences, 7% English Language and Literature/Letters, 7% Political Science and Government, 6% Sociology
Expenses: 2020-2021: $28,847; room/board: $14,041
Financial aid: (844) 512-6672; 83% of undergrads determined to have financial need

Oglethorpe University
Atlanta GA
(404) 364-8307
U.S. News ranking: Nat. Lib. Arts, No. 166
Website: oglethorpe.edu
Admissions email: admission@oglethorpe.edu
Private; founded 1835
Freshman admissions: more selective; 2019-2020: 2,327 applied, 1,572 accepted. Either SAT or ACT required. SAT 25/75 percentile: 1110-1280. High school rank: 23% in top tenth, 55% in top quarter, 88% in top half
Early decision deadline: N/A, notification date: N/A
Early action deadline: 11/15, notification date: 12/1
Application deadline (fall): 11/15
Undergraduate student body: 1,328 full time, 57 part time; 41% male, 59% female; 1% American Indian, 5% Asian, 24% Black, 13% Hispanic, 1% multiracial, 0% Pacific Islander, 44% white, 9% international; N/A from in state; 55% live on campus; 17% of students in fraternities, 17% in sororities
Most popular majors: 27% Business, Management, Marketing, and Related Support Services, 13% Communication, Journalism, and Related Programs, 11% Biological and Biomedical Sciences, 10% Psychology, 8% Multi/Interdisciplinary Studies
Expenses: 2020-2021: $41,160; room/board: $13,800
Financial aid: (404) 504-1500; 71% of undergrads determined to have financial need; average aid package $34,660

Paine College[1]
Augusta GA
(706) 821-8320
U.S. News ranking: Reg. Coll. (S), second tier
Website: www.paine.edu

Admissions email: admissions@paine.edu
Private; founded 1882
Application deadline (fall): 7/15
Undergraduate student body: N/A full time, N/A part time
Expenses: 2019-2020: $16,096; room/board: $6,662
Financial aid: N/A

Piedmont College
Demorest GA
(800) 277-7020
U.S. News ranking: Reg. U. (S), No. 53
Website: www.piedmont.edu
Admissions email: ugrad@piedmont.edu
Private; founded 1897
Affiliation: United Church of Christ
Freshman admissions: selective; 2019-2020: 1,910 applied, 1,031 accepted. Either SAT or ACT required. SAT 25/75 percentile: 960-1160. High school rank: 11% in top tenth, 36% in top quarter, 75% in top half
Early decision deadline: N/A, notification date: N/A
Early action deadline: N/A, notification date: N/A
Application deadline (fall): 7/15
Undergraduate student body: 1,155 full time, 128 part time; 35% male, 65% female; 0% American Indian, 1% Asian, 11% Black, 7% Hispanic, 1% multiracial, 0% Pacific Islander, 70% white, 1% international; 90% from in state; 75% live on campus; 3% of students in fraternities, 6% in sororities
Most popular majors: 34% Health Professions and Related Programs, 14% Education, 13% Business, Management, Marketing, and Related Support Services, 7% Visual and Performing Arts, 5% Social Sciences
Expenses: 2020-2021: $27,500; room/board: $10,850
Financial aid: (706) 776-0114; 83% of undergrads determined to have financial need; average aid package $21,690

Point University[1]
West Point GA
(706) 385-1202
U.S. News ranking: Reg. Coll. (S), No. 50
Website: www.point.edu
Admissions email: admissions@point.edu
Private; founded 1937
Affiliation: Christian Churches and Churches of Christ
Application deadline (fall): 8/1
Undergraduate student body: N/A full time, N/A part time
Expenses: 2019-2020: $21,185; room/board: $8,500
Financial aid: (706) 385-1462

Reinhardt University
Waleska GA
(770) 720-5526
U.S. News ranking: Reg. U. (S), No. 89
Website: www.reinhardt.edu/
Admissions email: admissions@reinhardt.edu
Private; founded 1883

Affiliation: United Methodist
Freshman admissions: selective; 2019-2020: 1,128 applied, 1,035 accepted. Either SAT or ACT required. SAT 25/75 percentile: 970-1180. High school rank: 8% in top tenth, 30% in top quarter, 61% in top half
Early decision deadline: N/A, notification date: N/A
Early action deadline: N/A, notification date: N/A
Application deadline (fall): 8/20
Undergraduate student body: 1,270 full time, 162 part time; 51% male, 49% female; 0% American Indian, 1% Asian, 17% Black, 9% Hispanic, 3% multiracial, 0% Pacific Islander, 61% white, 3% international; N/A from in state; 49% live on campus; 1% of students in fraternities, 1% in sororities
Most popular majors: 30% Business, Management, Marketing, and Related Support Services, 13% Homeland Security, Law Enforcement, Firefighting and Related Protective Services, 11% Education, 11% Parks, Recreation, Leisure, and Fitness Studies, 7% Health Professions and Related Programs
Expenses: 2020-2021: $25,228; room/board: $10,920
Financial aid: (770) 720-5667; 82% of undergrads determined to have financial need; average aid package $17,227

Savannah College of Art and Design
Savannah GA
(912) 525-5100
U.S. News ranking: Arts, unranked
Website: www.scad.edu
Admissions email: admission@scad.edu
Private; founded 1978
Freshman admissions: selective; 2019-2020: 15,236 applied, 11,079 accepted. Neither SAT nor ACT required. SAT 25/75 percentile: 1050-1250. High school rank: N/A
Early decision deadline: N/A, notification date: N/A
Early action deadline: N/A, notification date: N/A
Application deadline (fall): rolling
Undergraduate student body: 10,801 full time, 2,066 part time; 32% male, 68% female; 1% American Indian, 5% Asian, 10% Black, 7% Hispanic, 0% multiracial, 0% Pacific Islander, 52% white, 21% international; 15% from in state; 44% live on campus; N/A of students in fraternities, N/A in sororities
Most popular majors: 54% Visual and Performing Arts, 18% Communications Technologies/ Technicians and Support Services, 15% Communication, Journalism, and Related Programs, 7% Family and Consumer Sciences/Human Sciences, 3% Architecture and Related Services
Expenses: 2020-2021: $37,575; room/board: $14,979
Financial aid: (912) 525-5100; 48% of undergrads determined to have financial need; average aid package $16,860

Savannah State University[7]
Savannah GA
(912) 358-4338
U.S. News ranking: Reg. U. (S), second tier
Website: www. savannahstate.edu
Admissions email: admissions@ savannahstate.edu
Public; founded 1890
Freshman admissions: less selective; 2019-2020: 8,207 applied, 2,725 accepted. Either SAT or ACT required. SAT 25/75 percentile: 900-1030. High school rank: N/A
Early decision deadline: N/A, notification date: N/A
Early action deadline: N/A, notification date: N/A
Application deadline (fall): 7/15
Undergraduate student body: 2,970 full time, 533 part time
Most popular majors: Information not available
Expenses: 2019-2020: $5,999 in state, $19,401 out of state; room/board: $7,762
Financial aid: (912) 358-4162

Shorter University
Rome GA
(800) 868-6980
U.S. News ranking: Reg. U. (S), No. 53
Website: www.shorter.edu/
Admissions email: admissions@shorter.edu
Private; founded 1873
Affiliation: Baptist
Freshman admissions: selective; 2019-2020: 1,643 applied, 991 accepted. Either SAT or ACT required. SAT 25/75 percentile: 930-1130. High school rank: N/A
Early decision deadline: N/A, notification date: N/A
Early action deadline: N/A, notification date: N/A
Application deadline (fall): rolling
Undergraduate student body: 1,112 full time, 282 part time; 44% male, 56% female; N/A American Indian, N/A Asian, N/A Black, N/A Hispanic, N/A multiracial, N/A Pacific Islander, N/A white, N/A international
Most popular majors: 17% Business, Management, Marketing, and Related Support Services, 10% Health Professions and Related Programs, 8% Parks, Recreation, Leisure, and Fitness Studies, 8% Public Administration and Social Service Professions, 5% Homeland Security, Law Enforcement, Firefighting and Related Protective Services
Expenses: 2020-2021: $22,810; room/board: $5,050
Financial aid: (706) 233-7227; 76% of undergrads determined to have financial need

South Georgia State College[1]
Douglas GA
(912) 260-4206
U.S. News ranking: Reg. Coll. (S), unranked
Website: www.sgsc.edu
Admissions email: admissions@sgsc.edu
Public

Application deadline (fall): rolling
Undergraduate student body: N/A full time, N/A part time
Expenses: 2019-2020: $3,360 in state, $9,662 out of state; room/board: $8,640
Financial aid: N/A

Spelman College
Atlanta GA
(800) 982-2411
U.S. News ranking: Nat. Lib. Arts, No. 54
Website: www.spelman.edu
Admissions email: admiss@spelman.edu
Private; founded 1881
Freshman admissions: more selective; 2019-2020: 9,106 applied, 3,956 accepted. Either SAT or ACT required. SAT 25/75 percentile: 1080-1230. High school rank: 24% in top tenth, 56% in top quarter, 91% in top half
Early decision deadline: 11/1, notification date: 12/15
Early action deadline: 11/15, notification date: 12/31
Application deadline (fall): 2/1
Undergraduate student body: 2,080 full time, 40 part time; 0% male, 100% female; 1% American Indian, 0% Asian, 97% Black, 0% Hispanic, 0% multiracial, 0% Pacific Islander, 0% white, 1% international; 26% from in state; 66% live on campus; N/A of students in fraternities, 2% in sororities
Most popular majors: 13% Psychology, General, 12% Biology/ Biological Sciences, General, 12% Political Science and Government, Other, 11% Economics, General, 8% English Language and Literature, General
Expenses: 2020-2021: $29,972; room/board: $14,338
Financial aid: (404) 270-5212; 80% of undergrads determined to have financial need; average aid package $17,700

Thomas University[1]
Thomasville GA
(229) 227-6934
U.S. News ranking: Reg. U. (S), second tier
Website: www.thomasu.edu
Admissions email: rgagliano@thomasu.edu
Private; founded 1950
Application deadline (fall): rolling
Undergraduate student body: N/A full time, N/A part time
Expenses: 2019-2020: $16,940; room/board: $7,040
Financial aid: (229) 226-1621

Toccoa Falls College
Toccoa Falls GA
(888) 785-5624
U.S. News ranking: Reg. Coll. (S), No. 26
Website: tfc.edu
Admissions email: admissions@tfc.edu
Private; founded 1907
Affiliation: Christ and Missionary Alliance Church
Freshman admissions: selective; 2019-2020: 1,176 applied, 703 accepted. Either SAT or ACT

required. SAT 25/75 percentile: 920-1150. High school rank: 17% in top tenth, 36% in top quarter, 65% in top half
Early decision deadline: N/A, notification date: N/A
Early action deadline: N/A, notification date: N/A
Application deadline (fall): rolling
Undergraduate student body: 911 full time, 922 part time; 40% male, 60% female; 0% American Indian, 5% Asian, 10% Black, 5% Hispanic, 3% multiracial, 0% Pacific Islander, 75% white, 1% international; 70% from in state; 52% live on campus; 0% of students in fraternities, 0% in sororities
Most popular majors: 19% Counseling Psychology, 15% Registered Nursing/Registered Nurse, 11% Business Administration and Management, General, 8% Bible/Biblical Studies, 7% Missions/Missionary Studies and Missiology
Expenses: 2020-2021: $21,120; room/board: $8,500
Financial aid: (706) 886-7299; 87% of undergrads determined to have financial need; average aid package $18,146

Truett McConnell University
Cleveland GA
(706) 865-2134
U.S. News ranking: Reg. Coll. (S), No. 47
Website: truett.edu/
Admissions email: admissions@truett.edu
Private; founded 1946
Affiliation: Southern Baptist
Freshman admissions: selective; 2019-2020: 611 applied, 575 accepted. Either SAT or ACT required. SAT 25/75 percentile: 930-1150. High school rank: 16% in top tenth, 42% in top quarter, 74% in top half
Early decision deadline: N/A, notification date: N/A
Early action deadline: N/A, notification date: N/A
Application deadline (fall): 8/1
Undergraduate student body: 852 full time, 2,131 part time; 44% male, 56% female; 1% American Indian, 0% Asian, 6% Black, 4% Hispanic, 0% multiracial, 0% Pacific Islander, 79% white, 3% international; 87% from in state; 71% live on campus; N/A of students in fraternities, N/A in sororities
Most popular majors: 24% Business Administration and Management, General, 21% Psychology, General, 18% Registered Nursing/Registered Nurse, 8% Elementary Education and Teaching, 7% Bible/Biblical Studies
Expenses: 2020-2021: $21,938; room/board: $8,160
Financial aid: (706) 865-2134; 79% of undergrads determined to have financial need; average aid package $16,161

University of Georgia
Athens GA
(706) 542-8776
U.S. News ranking: Nat. U., No. 47
Website: www.admissions.uga.edu
Admissions email: adm-info@uga.edu
Public; founded 1785
Freshman admissions: more selective; 2019-2020: 29,065 applied, 13,261 accepted. Either SAT or ACT required. SAT 25/75 percentile: 1240-1420. High school rank: 60% in top tenth, 92% in top quarter, 99% in top half
Early decision deadline: N/A, notification date: N/A
Early action deadline: 10/15, notification date: 12/1
Application deadline (fall): 1/1
Undergraduate student body: 28,147 full time, 1,662 part time; 43% male, 57% female; 0% American Indian, 11% Asian, 8% Black, 7% Hispanic, 4% multiracial, 0% Pacific Islander, 69% white, 1% international; 88% from in state; 32% live on campus; 20% of students in fraternities, 31% in sororities
Most popular majors: 8% Finance, General, 6% Psychology, General, 5% Biology/Biological Sciences, General, 4% Marketing/Marketing Management, General, 3% International Relations and Affairs
Expenses: 2020-2021: $12,080 in state, $31,120 out of state; room/board: $10,328
Financial aid: (706) 542-6147; 41% of undergrads determined to have financial need; average aid package $12,934

University of North Georgia
Dahlonega GA
(706) 864-1800
U.S. News ranking: Reg. U. (S), No. 36
Website: ung.edu/
Admissions email: admissions-dah@ung.edu
Public; founded 1873
Freshman admissions: selective; 2019-2020: 6,224 applied, 4,729 accepted. Either SAT or ACT required. SAT 25/75 percentile: 1070-1230. High school rank: 17% in top tenth, 48% in top quarter, 85% in top half
Early decision deadline: N/A, notification date: N/A
Early action deadline: 11/15, notification date: 12/15
Application deadline (fall): 2/15
Undergraduate student body: 13,103 full time, 5,933 part time; 43% male, 57% female; 0% American Indian, 3% Asian, 4% Black, 14% Hispanic, 3% multiracial, 0% Pacific Islander, 73% white, 1% international; N/A from in state; 14% live on campus; 3% of students in fraternities, 5% in sororities
Most popular majors: 24% Business, Management, Marketing, and Related Support Services, 9% Education, 9% Health Professions and Related Programs, 7% Psychology, 6% Biological and Biomedical Sciences

Expenses: 2020-2021: $7,462 in state, $21,620 out of state; room/board: $11,510
Financial aid: (706) 864-1412; 59% of undergrads determined to have financial need; average aid package $10,186

University of West Georgia
Carrollton GA
(678) 839-5600
U.S. News ranking: Nat. U., second tier
Website: www.westga.edu
Admissions email: admiss@westga.edu
Public; founded 1906
Freshman admissions: selective; 2019-2020: 7,272 applied, 4,312 accepted. Either SAT or ACT required. SAT 25/75 percentile: 965-1080. High school rank: N/A
Early decision deadline: N/A, notification date: N/A
Early action deadline: N/A, notification date: N/A
Application deadline (fall): 6/1
Undergraduate student body: 8,090 full time, 2,321 part time; 36% male, 64% female; 0% American Indian, 1% Asian, 37% Black, 8% Hispanic, 4% multiracial, 0% Pacific Islander, 47% white, 1% international; 95% from in state; 25% live on campus; 2% of students in fraternities, 3% in sororities
Most popular majors: 24% Business, Management, Marketing, and Related Support Services, 17% Social Sciences, 12% Health Professions and Related Programs, 11% Psychology, 8% Education
Expenses: 2020-2021: $7,488 in state, $21,306 out of state; room/board: $10,340
Financial aid: (678) 839-6421; 72% of undergrads determined to have financial need; average aid package $8,186

Valdosta State University
Valdosta GA
(229) 333-5791
U.S. News ranking: Nat. U., second tier
Website: www.valdosta.edu
Admissions email: admissions@valdosta.edu
Public; founded 1906
Freshman admissions: selective; 2019-2020: 7,563 applied, 4,324 accepted. Either SAT or ACT required. SAT 25/75 percentile: 990-1140. High school rank: N/A
Early decision deadline: N/A, notification date: N/A
Early action deadline: N/A, notification date: N/A
Application deadline (fall): 6/15
Undergraduate student body: 6,797 full time, 1,793 part time; 36% male, 64% female; 0% American Indian, 1% Asian, 39% Black, 7% Hispanic, 4% multiracial, 0% Pacific Islander, 45% white, 1% international; 82% from in state; 30% live on campus; 2% of students in fraternities, 3% in sororities

Most popular majors: 26% Business, Management, Marketing, and Related Support Services, 14% Health Professions and Related Programs, 7% Communication, Journalism, and Related Programs, 7% Education, 7% Psychology
Expenses: 2020-2021: $6,583 in state, $17,638 out of state; room/board: $8,332
Financial aid: (229) 333-5935; 75% of undergrads determined to have financial need; average aid package $15,965

Wesleyan College
Macon GA
(800) 447-6610
U.S. News ranking: Nat. Lib. Arts, No. 149
Website: www.wesleyancollege.edu
Admissions email: admissions@wesleyancollege.edu
Private; founded 1836
Affiliation: United Methodist
Freshman admissions: selective; 2019-2020: 737 applied, 323 accepted. Either SAT or ACT required. SAT 25/75 percentile: 940-1120. High school rank: N/A
Early decision deadline: N/A, notification date: N/A
Early action deadline: N/A, notification date: N/A
Application deadline (fall): rolling
Undergraduate student body: 476 full time, 278 part time; 8% male, 92% female; 0% American Indian, 1% Asian, 36% Black, 5% Hispanic, 4% multiracial, 0% Pacific Islander, 45% white, 7% international; 93% from in state; 55% live on campus; 0% of students in fraternities, 0% in sororities
Most popular majors: 22% Business Administration and Management, General, 16% Economics, General, 15% Psychology, General, 13% Registered Nursing/Registered Nurse, 9% Biology/Biological Sciences, General
Expenses: 2020-2021: $25,190; room/board: $10,365
Financial aid: (478) 757-5146; 81% of undergrads determined to have financial need; average aid package $22,597

Young Harris College
Young Harris GA
(706) 379-3111
U.S. News ranking: Nat. Lib. Arts, second tier
Website: www.yhc.edu
Admissions email: admissions@yhc.edu
Private; founded 1886
Affiliation: United Methodist
Freshman admissions: selective; 2019-2020: 1,488 applied, 962 accepted. Neither SAT nor ACT required. SAT 25/75 percentile: 950-1130. High school rank: 4% in top tenth, 18% in top quarter, 61% in top half
Early decision deadline: N/A, notification date: N/A
Early action deadline: N/A, notification date: N/A
Application deadline (fall): rolling

Undergraduate student body: 927 full time, 471 part time; 45% male, 55% female; 0% American Indian, 1% Asian, 11% Black, 5% Hispanic, 3% multiracial, 0% Pacific Islander, 68% white, 7% international; 90% from in state; 86% live on campus; 0% of students in fraternities, 0% in sororities
Most popular majors: 22% Business, Management, Marketing, and Related Support Services, 16% Psychology, 11% Biological and Biomedical Sciences, 11% Visual and Performing Arts, 9% Multi/Interdisciplinary Studies
Expenses: 2019-2020: $29,067; room/board: N/A
Financial aid: N/A

GUAM

University of Guam
Mangilao GU
(671) 735-2201
U.S. News ranking: Reg. U. (W), No. 84
Website: www.uog.edu
Admissions email: admitme@triton.uog.edu
Public; founded 1952
Freshman admissions: less selective; 2019-2020: 503 applied, 455 accepted. Neither SAT nor ACT required. SAT 25/75 percentile: N/A. High school rank: 24% in top tenth, 44% in top quarter, 68% in top half
Early decision deadline: N/A, notification date: N/A
Early action deadline: N/A, notification date: N/A
Application deadline (fall): 6/1
Undergraduate student body: 2,578 full time, 637 part time; 44% male, 56% female; 0% American Indian, 48% Asian, 0% Black, 1% Hispanic, 0% multiracial, 44% Pacific Islander, 2% white, 1% international; 98% from in state; 5% live on campus; 0% of students in fraternities, 0% in sororities
Most popular majors: 20% Business Administration and Management, General, 10% Criminal Justice/Safety Studies, 7% Accounting, 7% English Language and Literature, General, 6% Registered Nursing, Nursing Administration, Nursing Research and Clinical Nursing, Other
Expenses: 2020-2021: $5,846 in state, $10,886 out of state; room/board: $3,868
Financial aid: (671) 735-2288; 53% of undergrads determined to have financial need; average aid package $2,173

HAWAII

Brigham Young University–Hawaii[1]
Laie Oahu HI
(808) 293-3738
U.S. News ranking: Reg. Coll. (W), No. 10
Website: www.byuh.edu
Admissions email: admissions@byuh.edu

Private
Application deadline (fall): N/A
Undergraduate student body: N/A full time, N/A part time
Expenses: 2019-2020: $5,720; room/board: $6,708
Financial aid: N/A

Chaminade University of Honolulu
Honolulu HI
(808) 735-8340
U.S. News ranking: Reg. U. (W), No. 29
Website: chaminade.edu/
Admissions email: admissions@chaminade.edu
Private; founded 1955
Affiliation: Roman Catholic
Freshman admissions: selective; 2019-2020: 1,490 applied, 1,405 accepted. Either SAT or ACT required. SAT 25/75 percentile: 980-1150. High school rank: 18% in top tenth, 41% in top quarter, 77% in top half
Early decision deadline: N/A, notification date: N/A
Early action deadline: N/A, notification date: N/A
Application deadline (fall): rolling
Undergraduate student body: 1,063 full time, 36 part time; 25% male, 75% female; 1% American Indian, 37% Asian, 3% Black, 4% Hispanic, 8% multiracial, 30% Pacific Islander, 12% white, 2% international; 74% from in state; 23% live on campus; N/A of students in fraternities, N/A in sororities
Most popular majors: 23% Registered Nursing/Registered Nurse, 14% Criminal Justice/Safety Studies, 10% Business Administration and Management, General, 9% Psychology, General, 7% Biology/Biological Sciences, General
Expenses: 2020-2021: $26,914; room/board: $14,610
Financial aid: (808) 735-4780; 65% of undergrads determined to have financial need; average aid package $22,052

Hawaii Pacific University[1]
Honolulu HI
(808) 544-0238
U.S. News ranking: Reg. U. (W), No. 62
Website: www.hpu.edu/
Admissions email: admissions@hpu.edu
Private; founded 1965
Application deadline (fall): 8/15
Undergraduate student body: N/A full time, N/A part time
Expenses: 2019-2020: $27,350; room/board: $19,200
Financial aid: (808) 544-0253

University of Hawaii–Hilo
Hilo HI
(800) 897-4456
U.S. News ranking: Nat. U., second tier
Website: www.uhh.hawaii.edu
Admissions email: uhhadm@hawaii.edu

Public; founded 1947
Freshman admissions: selective; 2019-2020: 4,161 applied, 2,148 accepted. Either SAT or ACT required. ACT 25/75 percentile: 17-23. High school rank: 16% in top tenth, 41% in top quarter, 76% in top half
Early decision deadline: N/A, notification date: N/A
Early action deadline: N/A, notification date: N/A
Application deadline (fall): 7/1
Undergraduate student body: 2,204 full time, 614 part time; 37% male, 63% female; 1% American Indian, 15% Asian, 1% Black, 16% Hispanic, 34% multiracial, 9% Pacific Islander, 20% white, 5% international; N/A from in state; 31% live on campus; N/A of students in fraternities, N/A in sororities
Most popular majors: 17% Health Professions and Related Programs, 10% Social Sciences, 9% Biological and Biomedical Sciences, 9% Business, Management, Marketing, and Related Support Services, 8% Communication, Journalism, and Related Programs
Expenses: 2020-2021: $7,792 in state, $20,752 out of state; room/board: $12,206
Financial aid: (808) 932-7449

University of Hawaii–Manoa
Honolulu HI
(808) 956-8975
U.S. News ranking: Nat. U., No. 170
Website: www.manoa.hawaii.edu/
Admissions email: manoa.admissions@hawaii.edu
Public; founded 1907
Freshman admissions: selective; 2019-2020: 16,244 applied, 9,493 accepted. Either SAT or ACT required. SAT 25/75 percentile: 1070-1270. High school rank: 24% in top tenth, 52% in top quarter, 84% in top half
Early decision deadline: N/A, notification date: N/A
Early action deadline: N/A, notification date: N/A
Application deadline (fall): 3/1
Undergraduate student body: 10,560 full time, 2,071 part time; 42% male, 58% female; 0% American Indian, 39% Asian, 2% Black, 2% Hispanic, 16% multiracial, 17% Pacific Islander, 21% white, 3% international; 66% from in state; 23% live on campus; 1% of students in fraternities, 1% in sororities
Most popular majors: 22% Business, Management, Marketing, and Related Support Services, 9% Engineering, 8% Biological and Biomedical Sciences, 8% Social Sciences, 7% Health Professions and Related Programs
Expenses: 2020-2021: $12,186 in state, $34,218 out of state; room/board: $11,374
Financial aid: (808) 956-7251; 54% of undergrads determined to have financial need; average aid package $15,499

University of Hawaii–Maui College[1]

Kahului HI
(808) 984-3267
U.S. News ranking: Reg. Coll. (W), unranked
Website: www.maui.hawaii.edu/
Admissions email: N/A
Public
Application deadline (fall): N/A
Undergraduate student body: N/A full time, N/A part time
Expenses: 2019-2020: $3,278 in state, $8,414 out of state; room/board: $15,302
Financial aid: N/A

University of Hawaii–West Oahu

Kapolei HI
(808) 689-2900
U.S. News ranking: Reg. Coll. (W), No. 16
Website: westoahu.hawaii.edu/
Admissions email: uhwo.admissions@hawaii.edu
Public; founded 1976
Freshman admissions: selective; 2019-2020: 693 applied, 585 accepted. Neither SAT nor ACT required. ACT 25/75 percentile: 16-21. High school rank: 14% in top tenth, 40% in top quarter, 72% in top half
Early decision deadline: N/A, notification date: N/A
Early action deadline: N/A, notification date: N/A
Application deadline (fall): 7/1
Undergraduate student body: 1,656 full time, 1,328 part time; 34% male, 66% female; 1% American Indian, 40% Asian, 2% Black, 1% Hispanic, 15% multiracial, 30% Pacific Islander, 11% white, 0% international; 98% from in state; N/A live on campus; N/A of students in fraternities, N/A in sororities
Most popular majors: 37% Business Administration and Management, General, 23% Public Administration, 17% Social Sciences, General, 14% Multi-/Interdisciplinary Studies, Other, 5% Humanities/Humanistic Studies
Expenses: 2020-2021: $7,584 in state, $20,544 out of state; room/board: N/A
Financial aid: (808) 689-2900; 41% of undergrads determined to have financial need; average aid package $8,741

IDAHO

Boise State University

Boise ID
(208) 426-1156
U.S. News ranking: Nat. U., second tier
Website: www.boisestate.edu
Admissions email: admissions@boisestate.edu
Public; founded 1932
Freshman admissions: selective; 2019-2020: 15,030 applied, 11,639 accepted. Neither SAT nor ACT required. SAT 25/75 percentile: 1030-1230. High school rank: 15% in top tenth, 40% in top quarter, 74% in top half

Early decision deadline: N/A, notification date: N/A
Early action deadline: N/A, notification date: N/A
Application deadline (fall): 8/1
Undergraduate student body: 13,104 full time, 9,835 part time; 43% male, 57% female; 0% American Indian, 3% Asian, 2% Black, 14% Hispanic, 5% multiracial, 0% Pacific Islander, 74% white, 1% international
Most popular majors: 22% Health Professions and Related Programs, 19% Business, Management, Marketing, and Related Support Services, 6% Communication, Journalism, and Related Programs, 6% Engineering, 6% Multi/Interdisciplinary Studies
Expenses: 2020-2021: $8,068 in state, $24,988 out of state; room/board: $12,347
Financial aid: (208) 426-1664; 56% of undergrads determined to have financial need; average aid package $11,230

Brigham Young University–Idaho[1]

Rexburg ID
(208) 496-1036
U.S. News ranking: Reg. Coll. (W), No. 16
Website: www.byui.edu
Admissions email: admissions@byui.edu
Private
Application deadline (fall): N/A
Undergraduate student body: N/A full time, N/A part time
Expenses: 2019-2020: $4,208; room/board: $4,368
Financial aid: N/A

College of Idaho

Caldwell ID
(208) 459-5011
U.S. News ranking: Nat. Lib. Arts, No. 120
Website: www.collegeofidaho.edu
Admissions email: admissions@collegeofidaho.edu
Private; founded 1891
Freshman admissions: selective; 2019-2020: 3,159 applied, 1,808 accepted. Neither SAT nor ACT required. SAT 25/75 percentile: 1020-1240. High school rank: N/A
Early decision deadline: N/A, notification date: N/A
Early action deadline: 11/16, notification date: 12/21
Application deadline (fall): 2/16
Undergraduate student body: 1,051 full time, 26 part time; 49% male, 51% female; 1% American Indian, 2% Asian, 2% Black, 13% Hispanic, 5% multiracial, 1% Pacific Islander, 57% white, 18% international; N/A from in state; 65% live on campus; 13% of students in fraternities, 11% in sororities
Most popular majors: Information not available
Expenses: 2020-2021: $32,855; room/board: $10,600
Financial aid: (208) 459-5307; 59% of undergrads determined to have financial need; average aid package $23,045

Idaho State University[1]

Pocatello ID
(208) 282-0211
U.S. News ranking: Nat. U., second tier
Website: www.isu.edu
Admissions email: info@isu.edu
Public
Application deadline (fall): N/A
Undergraduate student body: N/A full time, N/A part time
Expenses: 2019-2020: $7,872 in state, $24,168 out of state; room/board: $7,454
Financial aid: N/A

Lewis-Clark State College[7]

Lewiston ID
(208) 792-2210
U.S. News ranking: Reg. Coll. (W), No. 18
Website: www.lcsc.edu
Admissions email: admissions@lcsc.edu
Public; founded 1893
Freshman admissions: less selective; 2019-2020: 1,867 applied, 1,865 accepted. Neither SAT nor ACT required. SAT 25/75 percentile: 890-1110. High school rank: 9% in top tenth, 24% in top quarter, 52% in top half
Early decision deadline: N/A, notification date: N/A
Early action deadline: N/A, notification date: N/A
Application deadline (fall): 8/8
Undergraduate student body: 2,209 full time, 1,475 part time
Most popular majors: 18% Health Professions and Related Programs, 11% Business, Management, Marketing, and Related Support Services, 4% Education, 4% Parks, Recreation, Leisure, and Fitness Studies, 4% Public Administration and Social Service Professions
Expenses: 2020-2021: $6,982 in state, $20,238 out of state; room/board: $7,680
Financial aid: (208) 792-2224; 71% of undergrads determined to have financial need; average aid package $9,575

Northwest Nazarene University

Nampa ID
(208) 467-8000
U.S. News ranking: Reg. U. (W), No. 50
Website: www.nnu.edu
Admissions email: Admissions@nnu.edu
Private; founded 1913
Freshman admissions: selective; 2019-2020: 1,666 applied, 1,425 accepted. Either SAT or ACT required. SAT 25/75 percentile: 990-1190. High school rank: N/A
Early decision deadline: N/A, notification date: N/A
Early action deadline: 1/15, notification date: 9/15
Application deadline (fall): 8/15
Undergraduate student body: 1,066 full time, 159 part time; 40% male, 60% female; 0% American Indian, 2% Asian, 1% Black, 13% Hispanic, 3% multiracial,

0% Pacific Islander, 77% white, 2% international; N/A from in state; 66% live on campus; N/A of students in fraternities, N/A in sororities
Most popular majors: 25% Business, Management, Marketing, and Related Support Services, 13% Health Professions and Related Programs, 8% Education, 7% Engineering, 7% Liberal Arts and Sciences, General Studies and Humanities
Expenses: 2020-2021: $32,630; room/board: $8,800
Financial aid: (208) 467-8347

University of Idaho

Moscow ID
(888) 884-3246
U.S. News ranking: Nat. U., No. 170
Website: www.uidaho.edu/admissions
Admissions email: admissions@uidaho.edu
Public; founded 1889
Freshman admissions: selective; 2019-2020: 8,071 applied, 6,276 accepted. Either SAT or ACT required. SAT 25/75 percentile: 1010-1240. High school rank: 18% in top tenth, 44% in top quarter, 75% in top half
Early decision deadline: N/A, notification date: N/A
Early action deadline: N/A, notification date: N/A
Application deadline (fall): 8/1
Undergraduate student body: 6,788 full time, 2,604 part time; 49% male, 51% female; 1% American Indian, 2% Asian, 1% Black, 11% Hispanic, 4% multiracial, 0% Pacific Islander, 75% white, 4% international; 74% from in state; 39% live on campus; 21% of students in fraternities, 22% in sororities
Most popular majors: 7% Psychology, General, 5% Mechanical Engineering, 4% Electrical and Electronics Engineering, 3% Finance, General, 3% General Studies
Expenses: 2020-2021: $8,304 in state, $27,540 out of state; room/board: $9,080
Financial aid: (208) 885-6312; 62% of undergrads determined to have financial need; average aid package $13,613

ILLINOIS

American Academy of Art[1]

Chicago IL
(312) 461-0600
U.S. News ranking: Arts, unranked
Website: www.aaart.edu
Admissions email: N/A
Private
Application deadline (fall): N/A
Undergraduate student body: N/A full time, N/A part time
Expenses: 2019-2020: $35,270; room/board: N/A
Financial aid: N/A

Augustana College

Rock Island IL
(800) 798-8100
U.S. News ranking: Nat. Lib. Arts, No. 96
Website: www.augustana.edu
Admissions email: admissions@augustana.edu
Private; founded 1860
Affiliation: Evangelical Lutheran Church
Freshman admissions: more selective; 2019-2020: 6,757 applied, 3,826 accepted. Neither SAT nor ACT required. SAT 25/75 percentile: 1090-1320. High school rank: 31% in top tenth, 64% in top quarter, 91% in top half
Early decision deadline: 11/1, notification date: 11/15
Early action deadline: 11/1, notification date: 12/20
Application deadline (fall): rolling
Undergraduate student body: 2,537 full time, 9 part time; 44% male, 56% female; 0% American Indian, 3% Asian, 4% Black, 11% Hispanic, 4% multiracial, 0% Pacific Islander, 66% white, 12% international; 72% from in state; 73% live on campus; 29% of students in fraternities, 46% in sororities
Most popular majors: 22% Biology/Biological Sciences, General, 21% Marketing/Marketing Management, General, 8% Pre-Medicine/Pre-Medical Studies, 7% Social Sciences, Other, 6% Psychology, General
Expenses: 2020-2021: $45,136; room/board: $11,216
Financial aid: (309) 794-7207; 72% of undergrads determined to have financial need; average aid package $34,313

Aurora University[1]

Aurora IL
(800) 742-5281
U.S. News ranking: Nat. U., second tier
Website: www.aurora.edu
Admissions email: admission@aurora.edu
Private
Application deadline (fall): N/A
Undergraduate student body: N/A full time, N/A part time
Expenses: 2019-2020: $25,060; room/board: $9,866
Financial aid: N/A

Benedictine University

Lisle IL
(630) 829-6300
U.S. News ranking: Nat. U., second tier
Website: www.ben.edu
Admissions email: admissions@ben.edu
Private; founded 1887
Affiliation: Roman Catholic
Freshman admissions: selective; 2019-2020: 4,850 applied, 2,023 accepted. Either SAT or ACT required. ACT 25/75 percentile: 19-25. High school rank: 13% in top tenth, 36% in top quarter, 72% in top half
Early decision deadline: N/A, notification date: N/A

Early action deadline: N/A,
notification date: N/A
Application deadline (fall): rolling
Undergraduate student body: 2,131
full time, 362 part time; 46%
male, 54% female; 1% American
Indian, 16% Asian, 9% Black,
18% Hispanic, 0% multiracial,
0% Pacific Islander, 43% white,
2% international; N/A from in
state; 22% live on campus; 3%
of students in fraternities, 3% in
sororities
Most popular majors: 35%
Business, Management,
Marketing, and Related Support
Services, 21% Health Professions
and Related Programs, 8%
Biological and Biomedical
Sciences, 8% Psychology, 4%
Social Sciences
Expenses: 2020-2021: $34,290;
room/board: $8,210
Financial aid: (630) 829-6100;
77% of undergrads determined to
have financial need; average aid
package $25,511

Blackburn College

Carlinville IL
(800) 233-3550
U.S. News ranking: Nat. Lib. Arts,
second tier
Website: www.blackburn.edu
Admissions email:
denny.bardos@blackburn.edu
Private; founded 1837
Affiliation:
Presbyterian Church (USA)
Freshman admissions: selective;
2019-2020: 630 applied, 360
accepted. Either SAT or ACT
required. SAT 25/75 percentile:
910-1110. High school rank: 7%
in top tenth, 23% in top quarter,
64% in top half
Early decision deadline: N/A,
notification date: N/A
Early action deadline: N/A,
notification date: N/A
Application deadline (fall): rolling
Undergraduate student body: 467
full time, 19 part time; 44%
male, 56% female; 0% American
Indian, 1% Asian, 9% Black,
4% Hispanic, 3% multiracial,
0% Pacific Islander, 79% white,
2% international; 88% from in
state; 67% live on campus; 0%
of students in fraternities, 0% in
sororities
Most popular majors: 23%
Business, Management,
Marketing, and Related Support
Services, 15% Biological and
Biomedical Sciences, 13%
Education, 10% Homeland
Security, Law Enforcement,
Firefighting and Related Protective
Services, 10% Visual and
Performing Arts
Expenses: 2020-2021: $24,950;
room/board: $8,600
Financial aid: (217) 854-5774;
93% of undergrads determined to
have financial need; average aid
package $23,075

Bradley University

Peoria IL
(309) 677-1000
U.S. News ranking: Reg. U.
(Mid. W), No. 5
Website: www.bradley.edu

Admissions email:
admissions@bradley.edu
Private; founded 1897
Freshman admissions: more
selective; 2019-2020: 10,708
applied, 7,518 accepted. Neither
SAT nor ACT required. SAT
25/75 percentile: 1070-1270.
High school rank: 25% in top
tenth, 60% in top quarter, 87%
in top half
Early decision deadline: N/A,
notification date: N/A
Early action deadline: 10/15,
notification date: N/A
Application deadline (fall): rolling
Undergraduate student body: 4,508
full time, 128 part time; 49%
male, 51% female; 0% American
Indian, 4% Asian, 7% Black,
11% Hispanic, 3% multiracial,
0% Pacific Islander, 71% white,
2% international; 82% from in
state; 64% live on campus; 8%
of students in fraternities, 7% in
sororities
Most popular majors: 24%
Business, Management,
Marketing, and Related Support
Services, 17% Engineering, 13%
Health Professions and Related
Programs, 9% Communication,
Journalism, and Related Programs,
6% Education
Expenses: 2020-2021: $35,480;
room/board: $11,280
Financial aid: (309) 677-3089;
72% of undergrads determined to
have financial need; average aid
package $25,827

Chicago State University[1]

Chicago IL
(773) 995-2513
U.S. News ranking: Reg. U.
(Mid. W), second tier
Website: www.csu.edu
Admissions email:
ug-admissions@csu.edu
Public; founded 1867
Application deadline (fall): rolling
Undergraduate student body: N/A
full time, N/A part time
Expenses: 2019-2020: $11,366
in state, $18,734 out of state;
room/board: $8,724
Financial aid: N/A

Columbia College Chicago

Chicago IL
(312) 369-7130
U.S. News ranking: Reg. U.
(Mid. W), No. 103
Website: www.colum.edu/
Admissions email:
admissions@colum.edu
Private; founded 1890
Freshman admissions: selective;
2019-2020: 7,430 applied,
6,703 accepted. Neither SAT
nor ACT required. SAT 25/75
percentile: 960-1200. High school
rank: 12% in top tenth, 38% in
top quarter, 73% in top half
Early decision deadline: N/A,
notification date: N/A
Early action deadline: N/A,
notification date: N/A
Application deadline (fall): 8/15
Undergraduate student body: 6,252
full time, 456 part time; 42%
male, 58% female; 0% American
Indian, 4% Asian, 14% Black,

19% Hispanic, 5% multiracial,
0% Pacific Islander, 51% white,
4% international; 57% from in
state; 35% live on campus; N/A
of students in fraternities, N/A in
sororities
Most popular majors: 10%
Cinematography and Film/
Video Production, 6% Graphic
Design, 4% Music Management,
4% Recording Arts Technology/
Technician, 4% Retail
Management
Expenses: 2020-2021: $28,318;
room/board: $16,456
Financial aid: (312) 369-7140;
64% of undergrads determined to
have financial need; average aid
package $14,717

Concordia University Chicago

River Forest IL
(877) 282-4422
U.S. News ranking: Reg. U.
(Mid. W), No. 74
Website: www.cuchicago.edu/
Admissions email:
admission@cuchicago.edu
Private; founded 1864
Affiliation: Lutheran Church–
Missouri Synod
Freshman admissions: selective;
2019-2020: 6,597 applied,
5,460 accepted. Either SAT
or ACT required. SAT 25/75
percentile: 1010-1180. High
school rank: N/A
Early decision deadline: N/A,
notification date: N/A
Early action deadline: N/A,
notification date: N/A
Application deadline (fall): rolling
Undergraduate student body: 1,376
full time, 139 part time; 42%
male, 58% female; 0% American
Indian, 2% Asian, 11% Black,
31% Hispanic, 4% multiracial,
0% Pacific Islander, 47% white,
3% international; 71% from in
state; 38% live on campus; 0%
of students in fraternities, 0% in
sororities
Most popular majors: 31%
Business, Management,
Marketing, and Related Support
Services, 18% Education, 12%
Health Professions and Related
Programs, 6% Parks, Recreation,
Leisure, and Fitness Studies, 6%
Visual and Performing Arts
Expenses: 2020-2021: $33,636;
room/board: $10,226
Financial aid: (708) 209-3113;
84% of undergrads determined to
have financial need; average aid
package $24,688

DePaul University

Chicago IL
(312) 362-8300
U.S. News ranking: Nat. U.,
No. 124
Website: www.depaul.edu/
Admissions email:
admission@depaul.edu
Private; founded 1898
Affiliation: Roman Catholic
Freshman admissions: selective;
2019-2020: 26,895 applied,
18,348 accepted. Neither SAT
nor ACT required. SAT 25/75
percentile: 1070-1290. High
school rank: N/A

Early decision deadline: N/A,
notification date: N/A
Early action deadline: 11/15,
notification date: 1/15
Application deadline (fall): 2/1
Undergraduate student body:
12,784 full time, 1,430 part
time; 47% male, 53% female;
0% American Indian, 11% Asian,
8% Black, 20% Hispanic, 4%
multiracial, 0% Pacific Islander,
52% white, 3% international;
75% from in state; 19% live
on campus; 6% of students in
fraternities, 11% in sororities
Most popular majors: 29%
Business, Management,
Marketing, and Related Support
Services, 13% Communication,
Journalism, and Related Programs,
10% Visual and Performing Arts,
9% Computer and Information
Sciences and Support Services,
8% Liberal Arts and Sciences,
General Studies and Humanities
Expenses: 2020-2021: $41,202;
room/board: $15,093
Financial aid: (312) 362-8520;
71% of undergrads determined to
have financial need; average aid
package $26,194

DeVry University[1]

Downers Grove IL
(630) 515-3000
U.S. News ranking: Reg. U.
(Mid. W), second tier
Website: www.devry.edu
Admissions email: N/A
For-profit; founded 1931
Application deadline (fall): rolling
Undergraduate student body: N/A
full time, N/A part time
Expenses: 2019-2020: $17,798;
room/board: N/A
Financial aid: N/A

Dominican University

River Forest IL
(708) 524-6800
U.S. News ranking: Reg. U.
(Mid. W), No. 10
Website: www.dom.edu/
Admissions email:
domadmis@dom.edu
Private; founded 1901
Affiliation: Roman Catholic
Freshman admissions: selective;
2019-2020: 5,188 applied,
3,338 accepted. Either SAT
or ACT required. SAT 25/75
percentile: 1000-1200. High
school rank: 27% in top tenth,
58% in top quarter, 86% in
top half
Early decision deadline: N/A,
notification date: N/A
Early action deadline: N/A,
notification date: N/A
Application deadline (fall): 8/26
Undergraduate student body: 2,011
full time, 140 part time; 32%
male, 68% female; 0% American
Indian, 4% Asian, 5% Black,
58% Hispanic, 1% multiracial,
0% Pacific Islander, 27% white,
1% international; 92% from in
state; 23% live on campus; 0%
of students in fraternities, 0% in
sororities
Most popular majors: 18%
Business, Management,
Marketing, and Related Support
Services, 14% Health Professions
and Related Programs, 14%

Social Sciences, 10% Multi/
Interdisciplinary Studies, 9%
Biological and Biomedical
Sciences
Expenses: 2020-2021: $35,420;
room/board: $10,865
Financial aid: (708) 524-6950;
83% of undergrads determined to
have financial need; average aid
package $26,039

Eastern Illinois University

Charleston IL
(877) 581-2348
U.S. News ranking: Reg. U.
(Mid. W), No. 51
Website: www.eiu.edu
Admissions email:
admissions@eiu.edu
Public; founded 1895
Freshman admissions: selective;
2019-2020: 8,859 applied,
4,651 accepted. Either SAT
or ACT required. ACT 25/75
percentile: 18-23. High school
rank: 13% in top tenth, 37% in
top quarter, 74% in top half
Early decision deadline: N/A,
notification date: N/A
Early action deadline: N/A,
notification date: N/A
Undergraduate student body: 3,990
full time, 2,239 part time; 43%
male, 57% female; 0% American
Indian, 1% Asian, 22% Black,
9% Hispanic, 3% multiracial,
0% Pacific Islander, 59% white,
3% international; 93% from in
state; 32% live on campus; 10%
of students in fraternities, 12%
in sororities
Most popular majors: 14%
Business, Management,
Marketing, and Related Support
Services, 10% Education, 10%
Liberal Arts and Sciences, General
Studies and Humanities, 8%
Communication, Journalism, and
Related Programs, 8% Psychology
Expenses: 2020-2021: $12,136
in state, $14,447 out of state;
room/board: $10,262
Financial aid: (217) 581-3713;
73% of undergrads determined to
have financial need; average aid
package $14,088

East-West University[1]

Chicago IL
(312) 939-0111
U.S. News ranking: Nat. Lib. Arts,
second tier
Website: www.eastwest.edu
Admissions email:
seeyou@eastwest.edu
Private; founded 1980
Application deadline (fall): rolling
Undergraduate student body: N/A
full time, N/A part time
Expenses: 2019-2020: $22,650;
room/board: N/A
Financial aid: N/A

Elmhurst University

Elmhurst IL
(630) 617-3400
U.S. News ranking: Reg. U.
(Mid. W), No. 15
Website: www.elmhurst.edu/
Admissions email:
admit@elmhurst.edu
Private; founded 1871
Affiliation: United Church of Christ

Freshman admissions: selective; 2019-2020: 4,170 applied, 2,825 accepted. Either SAT or ACT required. SAT 25/75 percentile: 990-1210. High school rank: 20% in top tenth, 52% in top quarter, 82% in top half
Early decision deadline: N/A, notification date: N/A
Early action deadline: 11/1, notification date: 12/1
Application deadline (fall): rolling
Undergraduate student body: 2,722 full time, 169 part time; 38% male, 62% female; 0% American Indian, 6% Asian, 5% Black, 25% Hispanic, 3% multiracial, 0% Pacific Islander, 58% white, 1% international; 91% from in state; 33% live on campus; 8% of students in fraternities, 12% in sororities
Most popular majors: 22% Business, Management, Marketing, and Related Support Services, 12% Health Professions and Related Programs, 12% Psychology, 10% Education, 6% Parks, Recreation, Leisure, and Fitness Studies
Expenses: 2020-2021: $38,654; room/board: $10,952
Financial aid: (630) 617-3015; 75% of undergrads determined to have financial need; average aid package $29,218

Eureka College

Eureka IL
(309) 467-6350
U.S. News ranking: Reg. Coll. (Mid. W), No. 33
Website: www.eureka.edu
Admissions email: admissions@eureka.edu
Private; founded 1855
Affiliation: Christian Church (Disciples of Christ)
Freshman admissions: selective; 2019-2020: 815 applied, 504 accepted. Either SAT or ACT required. SAT 25/75 percentile: 910-1140. High school rank: 4% in top tenth, 25% in top quarter, 53% in top half
Early decision deadline: N/A, notification date: N/A
Early action deadline: N/A, notification date: N/A
Application deadline (fall): 8/15
Undergraduate student body: 480 full time, 33 part time; 53% male, 47% female; 1% American Indian, 1% Asian, 9% Black, 3% Hispanic, 3% multiracial, 0% Pacific Islander, 80% white, 1% international; 95% from in state; 60% live on campus; 20% of students in fraternities, 25% in sororities
Most popular majors: 25% Business, Management, Marketing, and Related Support Services, 12% Psychology, 10% Homeland Security, Law Enforcement, Firefighting and Related Protective Services, 9% Education, 8% Parks, Recreation, Leisure, and Fitness Studies
Expenses: 2020-2021: $28,110; room/board: $10,005
Financial aid: (309) 467-6310; 81% of undergrads determined to have financial need; average aid package $18,196

Governors State University

University Park IL
(708) 534-4490
U.S. News ranking: Reg. U. (Mid. W), unranked
Website: www.govst.edu/
Admissions email: admissions@govst.edu
Public; founded 1969
Freshman admissions: less selective; 2019-2020: 1,434 applied, 654 accepted. Either SAT or ACT required. ACT 25/75 percentile: 17-22. High school rank: 8% in top tenth, 27% in top quarter, 65% in top half
Early decision deadline: 11/15, notification date: 12/15
Early action deadline: N/A, notification date: N/A
Application deadline (fall): 4/1
Undergraduate student body: 1,926 full time, 1,306 part time; 37% male, 63% female; 0% American Indian, 2% Asian, 40% Black, 15% Hispanic, 3% multiracial, 0% Pacific Islander, 30% white, 1% international; 0% from in state; 8% live on campus; 0% of students in fraternities, 0% in sororities
Most popular majors: 19% Business, Management, Marketing, and Related Support Services, 17% Health Professions and Related Programs, 14% Liberal Arts and Sciences, General Studies and Humanities, 12% Psychology, 8% Homeland Security, Law Enforcement, Firefighting and Related Protective Services
Expenses: 2020-2021: $12,616 in state, $22,006 out of state; room/board: $9,102
Financial aid: (708) 534-4480; 78% of undergrads determined to have financial need; average aid package $12,133

Greenville University

Greenville IL
(618) 664-7100
U.S. News ranking: Reg. U. (Mid. W), No. 91
Website: www.greenville.edu
Admissions email: admissions@greenville.edu
Private; founded 1892
Affiliation: Free Methodist
Freshman admissions: selective; 2019-2020: 1,304 applied, 744 accepted. Either SAT or ACT required. SAT 25/75 percentile: 960-1180. High school rank: N/A
Early decision deadline: N/A, notification date: N/A
Early action deadline: N/A, notification date: N/A
Application deadline (fall): rolling
Undergraduate student body: 838 full time, 75 part time; 56% male, 44% female; 0% American Indian, 0% Asian, 13% Black, 7% Hispanic, 3% multiracial, 0% Pacific Islander, 66% white, 9% international; 61% from in state; 92% live on campus; 0% of students in fraternities, 0% in sororities
Most popular majors: 10% Organizational Behavior Studies, 7% Business Administration and Management, General,

7% Elementary Education and Teaching, 6% Biology/Biological Sciences, General, 6% Digital Arts
Expenses: 2020-2021: $28,956; room/board: $9,348
Financial aid: (618) 664-7108; 81% of undergrads determined to have financial need; average aid package $22,943

Illinois College

Jacksonville IL
(217) 245-3030
U.S. News ranking: Nat. Lib. Arts, No. 140
Website: www.ic.edu
Admissions email: admissions@mail.ic.edu
Private; founded 1829
Freshman admissions: selective; 2019-2020: 3,725 applied, 2,907 accepted. Neither SAT nor ACT required. SAT 25/75 percentile: 960-1180. High school rank: 21% in top tenth, 50% in top quarter, 75% in top half
Early decision deadline: N/A, notification date: N/A
Early action deadline: 12/1, notification date: 12/23
Application deadline (fall): rolling
Undergraduate student body: 1,046 full time, 11 part time; 48% male, 52% female; 0% American Indian, 1% Asian, 11% Black, 7% Hispanic, 4% multiracial, 0% Pacific Islander, 73% white, 5% international; N/A from in state; 87% live on campus; 0% of students in fraternities, 0% in sororities
Most popular majors: 27% Business, Management, Marketing, and Related Support Services, 13% Biological and Biomedical Sciences, 10% Psychology, 8% Social Sciences, 7% English Language and Literature/Letters
Expenses: 2020-2021: $34,620; room/board: $9,374
Financial aid: (217) 245-3035; 83% of undergrads determined to have financial need; average aid package $30,285

Illinois Institute of Technology

Chicago IL
(800) 448-2329
U.S. News ranking: Nat. U., No. 124
Website: admissions.iit.edu/ undergraduate/apply
Admissions email: admission@iit.edu
Private; founded 1890
Freshman admissions: more selective; 2019-2020: 5,049 applied, 3,041 accepted. Either SAT or ACT required. SAT 25/75 percentile: 1190-1400. High school rank: 47% in top tenth, 80% in top quarter, 97% in top half
Early decision deadline: N/A, notification date: N/A
Early action deadline: N/A, notification date: N/A
Application deadline (fall): 8/1
Undergraduate student body: 2,882 full time, 262 part time; 68% male, 32% female; 0% American Indian, 16% Asian, 5% Black, 18% Hispanic, 4% multiracial,

0% Pacific Islander, 38% white, 17% international
Most popular majors: 52% Engineering, 21% Computer and Information Sciences and Support Services, 9% Architecture and Related Services, 4% Business, Management, Marketing, and Related Support Services, 4% Engineering Technologies and Engineering-Related Fields
Expenses: 2020-2021: $50,490; room/board: $15,328
Financial aid: (312) 567-7219; 66% of undergrads determined to have financial need; average aid package $42,020

Illinois State University

Normal IL
(309) 438-2181
U.S. News ranking: Nat. U., No. 206
Website: illinoisstate.edu/
Admissions email: admissions@ilstu.edu
Public; founded 1857
Freshman admissions: selective; 2019-2020: 16,151 applied, 13,234 accepted. Either SAT or ACT required. SAT 25/75 percentile: 1020-1220. High school rank: N/A
Early decision deadline: N/A, notification date: N/A
Early action deadline: N/A, notification date: N/A
Application deadline (fall): 4/1
Undergraduate student body: 17,092 full time, 1,158 part time; 45% male, 55% female; 0% American Indian, 2% Asian, 9% Black, 12% Hispanic, 3% multiracial, 0% Pacific Islander, 72% white, 1% international; 98% from in state; 30% live on campus; 4% of students in fraternities, 7% in sororities
Most popular majors: 23% Business, Management, Marketing, and Related Support Services, 14% Education, 9% Health Professions and Related Programs, 7% Communication, Journalism, and Related Programs, 5% Social Sciences
Expenses: 2020-2021: $14,832 in state, $26,356 out of state; room/board: $9,850
Financial aid: (309) 438-2231; 63% of undergrads determined to have financial need; average aid package $12,087

Illinois Wesleyan University

Bloomington IL
(800) 332-2498
U.S. News ranking: Nat. Lib. Arts, No. 80
Website: www.iwu.edu
Admissions email: iwuadmit@iwu.edu
Private; founded 1850
Freshman admissions: more selective; 2019-2020: 3,719 applied, 2,261 accepted. Either SAT or ACT required. ACT 25/75 percentile: 24-29. High school rank: 38% in top tenth, 72% in top quarter, 95% in top half
Early decision deadline: N/A, notification date: N/A

Early action deadline: 11/15, notification date: 12/15
Application deadline (fall): rolling
Undergraduate student body: 1,616 full time, 13 part time; 48% male, 52% female; 0% American Indian, 7% Asian, 7% Black, 9% Hispanic, 2% multiracial, 0% Pacific Islander, 70% white, 4% international; 79% from in state; 85% live on campus; 34% of students in fraternities, 32% in sororities
Most popular majors: 16% Accounting, 9% Biology/Biological Sciences, General, 9% Business/Commerce, General, 8% Registered Nursing/Registered Nurse, 6% Psychology, General
Expenses: 2020-2021: $51,336; room/board: $11,840
Financial aid: (309) 556-3096; 72% of undergrads determined to have financial need; average aid package $37,608

Judson University

Elgin IL
(847) 628-2510
U.S. News ranking: Reg. U. (Mid. W), No. 80
Website: www.judsonu.edu
Admissions email: admissions@judsonu.edu
Private; founded 1963
Affiliation: American Baptist
Freshman admissions: selective; 2019-2020: 1,615 applied, 602 accepted. Either SAT or ACT required. SAT 25/75 percentile: 890-1100. High school rank: 4% in top tenth, 21% in top quarter, 52% in top half
Early decision deadline: N/A, notification date: N/A
Early action deadline: N/A, notification date: N/A
Application deadline (fall): rolling
Undergraduate student body: 944 full time, 102 part time; 43% male, 57% female; 0% American Indian, 2% Asian, 14% Black, 23% Hispanic, 2% multiracial, 0% Pacific Islander, 45% white, 4% international; 84% from in state; 41% live on campus; 0% of students in fraternities, 0% in sororities
Most popular majors: 14% Business Administration and Management, General, 9% Architecture, 9% Psychology, General, 7% Public Administration and Social Service Professions, 6% Business Administration and Management, General
Expenses: 2020-2021: $29,870; room/board: $10,790
Financial aid: (847) 628-2531; 80% of undergrads determined to have financial need; average aid package $20,982

Knox College

Galesburg IL
(800) 678-5669
U.S. News ranking: Nat. Lib. Arts, No. 72
Website: www.knox.edu
Admissions email: admission@knox.edu
Private; founded 1837
Freshman admissions: more selective; 2019-2020: 3,397 applied, 2,321 accepted. Neither

SAT nor ACT required. SAT 25/75 percentile: 1090-1350. High school rank: 35% in top tenth, 69% in top quarter, 97% in top half
Early decision deadline: 11/1, notification date: 11/15
Early action deadline: 11/1, notification date: 12/15
Application deadline (fall): 1/15
Undergraduate student body: 1,222 full time, 36 part time; 43% male, 57% female; 0% American Indian, 5% Asian, 8% Black, 14% Hispanic, 6% multiracial, 0% Pacific Islander, 46% white, 19% international; 44% from in state; 82% live on campus; 28% of students in fraternities, 16% in sororities
Most popular majors: 12% Biology/Biological Sciences, General, 10% Creative Writing, 10% Econometrics and Quantitative Economics, 8% Sociology and Anthropology, 7% Research and Experimental Psychology, Other
Expenses: 2020-2021: $49,974; room/board: $10,170
Financial aid: (309) 341-7149; 81% of undergrads determined to have financial need; average aid package $41,335

Lake Forest College
Lake Forest IL
(847) 735-5000
U.S. News ranking: Nat. Lib. Arts, No. 84
Website: www.lakeforest.edu
Admissions email: admissions@lakeforest.edu
Private; founded 1857
Freshman admissions: more selective; 2019-2020: 4,739 applied, 2,616 accepted. Neither SAT nor ACT required. SAT 25/75 percentile: 1080-1280. High school rank: 40% in top tenth, 63% in top quarter, 87% in top half
Early decision deadline: 11/1, notification date: 12/15
Early action deadline: 11/1, notification date: 12/15
Application deadline (fall): 2/15
Undergraduate student body: 1,517 full time, 21 part time; 42% male, 58% female; 0% American Indian, 5% Asian, 5% Black, 14% Hispanic, 4% multiracial, 0% Pacific Islander, 55% white, 11% international; 62% from in state; 82% live on campus; 15% of students in fraternities, 14% in sororities
Most popular majors: 18% Social Sciences, 17% Business, Management, Marketing, and Related Support Services, 10% Biological and Biomedical Sciences, 9% Psychology, 8% Communication, Journalism, and Related Programs
Expenses: 2020-2021: $49,822; room/board: $10,954
Financial aid: (847) 735-5104; 73% of undergrads determined to have financial need; average aid package $43,010

Lewis University
Romeoville IL
(800) 897-9000
U.S. News ranking: Reg. U. (Mid. W), No. 24
Website: www.lewisu.edu
Admissions email: admissions@lewisu.edu
Private; founded 1932
Affiliation: Roman Catholic
Freshman admissions: selective; 2019-2020: 6,674 applied, 4,265 accepted. Either SAT or ACT required. SAT 25/75 percentile: 1010-1200. High school rank: 18% in top tenth, 46% in top quarter, 84% in top half
Early decision deadline: N/A, notification date: N/A
Early action deadline: N/A, notification date: N/A
Application deadline (fall): rolling
Undergraduate student body: 3,542 full time, 732 part time; 50% male, 50% female; 0% American Indian, 5% Asian, 6% Black, 22% Hispanic, 2% multiracial, 0% Pacific Islander, 59% white, 2% international; 92% from in state; 26% live on campus; 3% of students in fraternities, 3% in sororities
Most popular majors: 12% Registered Nursing/Registered Nurse, 8% Computer Science, 8% Criminal Justice/Safety Studies, 7% Business Administration and Management, General, 6% Psychology, General
Expenses: 2020-2021: $34,478; room/board: $11,050
Financial aid: (815) 836-5263; 75% of undergrads determined to have financial need; average aid package $28,523

Lincoln College[1]
Lincoln IL
(800) 569-0556
U.S. News ranking: Reg. Coll. (Mid. W), second tier
Website: www.lincolncollege.edu
Admissions email: admission@lincolncollege.edu
Private; founded 1865
Application deadline (fall): rolling
Undergraduate student body: N/A full time, N/A part time
Expenses: 2019-2020: $19,000; room/board: $7,900
Financial aid: (217) 732-3155

Loyola University Chicago
Chicago IL
(800) 262-2373
U.S. News ranking: Nat. U., No. 112
Website: www.luc.edu
Admissions email: admission@luc.edu
Private; founded 1870
Affiliation: Roman Catholic
Freshman admissions: more selective; 2019-2020: 25,583 applied, 17,198 accepted. Either SAT or ACT required. ACT 25/75 percentile: 25-30. High school rank: 35% in top tenth, 68% in top quarter, 93% in top half
Early decision deadline: N/A, notification date: N/A

McKendree University
Lebanon IL
(618) 537-6831
U.S. News ranking: Reg. U. (Mid. W), No. 51
Website: www.mckendree.edu
Admissions email: inquiry@mckendree.edu
Private; founded 1828
Affiliation: United Methodist
Freshman admissions: selective; 2019-2020: 1,997 applied, 1,265 accepted. Neither SAT nor ACT required. SAT 25/75 percentile: 859-1268. High school rank: 11% in top tenth, 35% in top quarter, 75% in top half
Early decision deadline: N/A, notification date: N/A
Early action deadline: N/A, notification date: N/A
Application deadline (fall): rolling
Undergraduate student body: 1,484 full time, 304 part time; 48% male, 52% female; 0% American Indian, 1% Asian, 12% Black, 5% Hispanic, 4% multiracial, 0% Pacific Islander, 61% white, 5% international; N/A from in state; 73% live on campus; 4% of students in fraternities, 21% in sororities
Most popular majors: 14% Business Administration and Management, General, 14% Registered Nursing/Registered Nurse, 9% Sociology, 8% Psychology, General, 7% Human Resources Management/Personnel Administration, General
Expenses: 2020-2021: $32,200; room/board: $10,970
Financial aid: (618) 537-6532; 62% of undergrads determined to have financial need; average aid package $22,963

Millikin University
Decatur IL
(217) 424-6210
U.S. News ranking: Reg. Coll. (Mid. W), No. 12
Website: millikin.edu
Admissions email: admis@millikin.edu
Private; founded 1901
Freshman admissions: selective; 2019-2020: 3,531 applied,

2,516 accepted. Neither SAT nor ACT required. SAT 25/75 percentile: 950-1200. High school rank: 20% in top tenth, 43% in top quarter, 68% in top half
Early decision deadline: N/A, notification date: N/A
Early action deadline: N/A, notification date: N/A
Application deadline (fall): rolling
Undergraduate student body: 1,918 full time, 77 part time; 45% male, 55% female; 0% American Indian, 2% Asian, 14% Black, 5% Hispanic, 4% multiracial, 0% Pacific Islander, 68% white, 4% international; 78% from in state; 60% live on campus; 17% of students in fraternities, 26% in sororities
Most popular majors: 22% Business, Management, Marketing, and Related Support Services, 18% Visual and Performing Arts, 11% Education, 11% Health Professions and Related Programs, 6% Parks, Recreation, Leisure, and Fitness Studies
Expenses: 2020-2021: $39,592; room/board: $11,450
Financial aid: (217) 424-6317; 81% of undergrads determined to have financial need; average aid package $29,620

Monmouth College
Monmouth IL
(800) 747-2687
U.S. News ranking: Nat. Lib. Arts, No. 127
Website: www.monmouthcollege.edu/admissions
Admissions email: admissions@monmouthcollege.edu
Private; founded 1853
Freshman admissions: selective; 2019-2020: 2,322 applied, 1,548 accepted. Either SAT or ACT required. SAT 25/75 percentile: 990-1220. High school rank: 13% in top tenth, 40% in top quarter, 79% in top half
Early decision deadline: N/A, notification date: N/A
Early action deadline: N/A, notification date: N/A
Application deadline (fall): rolling
Undergraduate student body: 900 full time, 7 part time; 50% male, 50% female; N/A American Indian, N/A Asian, N/A Black, N/A Hispanic, N/A multiracial, N/A Pacific Islander, N/A white, N/A international; 76% from in state; 92% live on campus; N/A of students in fraternities, N/A in sororities
Most popular majors: Information not available
Expenses: 2020-2021: $41,330; room/board: $9,630
Financial aid: (309) 457-2129; 84% of undergrads determined to have financial need; average aid package $35,268

National Louis University
Chicago IL
(888) 658-8632
U.S. News ranking: Nat. U., second tier
Website: www.nl.edu
Admissions email: nluinfo@nl.edu

Private
Freshman admissions: least selective; 2019-2020: 2,665 applied, 2,603 accepted. Neither SAT nor ACT required. ACT 25/75 percentile: 15-18. High school rank: N/A
Early decision deadline: N/A, notification date: N/A
Early action deadline: N/A, notification date: N/A
Application deadline (fall): N/A
Undergraduate student body: 2,370 full time, 993 part time; 27% male, 73% female; 0% American Indian, 3% Asian, 20% Black, 48% Hispanic, 2% multiracial, 0% Pacific Islander, 16% white, 3% international; 96% from in state; N/A live on campus; N/A of students in fraternities, N/A in sororities
Most popular majors: 19% Multi-/Interdisciplinary Studies, Other, 16% Early Childhood Education and Teaching, 15% Management Science, 11% Hospitality Administration/Management, General, 6% Health and Medical Administrative Services, Other
Expenses: 2019-2020: $11,010; room/board: $3,500
Financial aid: N/A

North Central College
Naperville IL
(630) 637-5800
U.S. News ranking: Reg. U. (Mid. W), No. 10
Website: www.northcentralcollege.edu
Admissions email: admissions@noctrl.edu
Private; founded 1861
Affiliation: United Methodist
Freshman admissions: more selective; 2019-2020: 6,847 applied, 3,673 accepted. Either SAT or ACT required. SAT 25/75 percentile: 1030-1260. High school rank: 29% in top tenth, 55% in top quarter, 88% in top half
Early decision deadline: N/A, notification date: N/A
Early action deadline: N/A, notification date: N/A
Application deadline (fall): rolling
Undergraduate student body: 2,538 full time, 77 part time; 46% male, 54% female; 0% American Indian, 3% Asian, 4% Black, 16% Hispanic, 3% multiracial, 0% Pacific Islander, 66% white, 3% international; 90% from in state; 48% live on campus; 0% of students in fraternities, 0% in sororities
Most popular majors: 12% Psychology, General, 7% Marketing/Marketing Management, General, 5% Accounting, 4% Business Administration, Management and Operations, Other, 4% Kinesiology and Exercise Science
Expenses: 2020-2021: $41,180; room/board: $11,782
Financial aid: (630) 637-5600; 75% of undergrads determined to have financial need; average aid package $29,840

Northeastern Illinois University

Chicago IL
(773) 442-4000
U.S. News ranking: Reg. U. (Mid. W), second tier
Website: www.neiu.edu
Admissions email: admrec@neiu.edu
Public; founded 1867
Freshman admissions: less selective; 2019-2020: 4,711 applied, 2,755 accepted. Either SAT or ACT required. SAT 25/75 percentile: 830-1020. High school rank: 4% in top tenth, 11% in top quarter, 41% in top half
Early decision deadline: N/A, notification date: N/A
Early action deadline: N/A, notification date: N/A
Application deadline (fall): 7/15
Undergraduate student body: 3,294 full time, 2,406 part time; 43% male, 57% female; 0% American Indian, 9% Asian, 11% Black, 40% Hispanic, 2% multiracial, 0% Pacific Islander, 27% white, 2% international; 100% from in state; 3% live on campus; 0% of students in fraternities, 0% in sororities
Most popular majors: 23% Business, Management, Marketing, and Related Support Services, 11% Liberal Arts and Sciences, General Studies and Humanities, 9% Public Administration and Social Service Professions, 8% Psychology, 7% Computer and Information Sciences and Support Services
Expenses: 2020-2021: $11,826 in state, $21,719 out of state; room/board: $8,768
Financial aid: (773) 442-5016; 73% of undergrads determined to have financial need; average aid package $11,090

Northern Illinois University

DeKalb IL
(815) 753-0446
U.S. News ranking: Nat. U., second tier
Website: www.niu.edu/
Admissions email: admissions@niu.edu
Public; founded 1895
Freshman admissions: selective; 2019-2020: 15,693 applied, 7,588 accepted. Either SAT or ACT required. SAT 25/75 percentile: 940-1180. High school rank: 14% in top tenth, 39% in top quarter, 72% in top half
Early decision deadline: N/A, notification date: N/A
Early action deadline: N/A, notification date: N/A
Application deadline (fall): 8/1
Undergraduate student body: 10,567 full time, 1,564 part time; 49% male, 51% female; 0% American Indian, 6% Asian, 17% Black, 19% Hispanic, 4% multiracial, 0% Pacific Islander, 51% white, 2% international; 97% from in state; 30% live on campus; 3% in fraternities, 3% in sororities
Most popular majors: 6% Speech Communication and Rhetoric, 5% Accounting, 5% Health/Medical

Preparatory Programs, Other, 5% Mechanical Engineering, 5% Psychology, General
Expenses: 2020-2021: $12,352 in state, $12,352 out of state; room/board: $10,880
Financial aid: (815) 753-1300; 72% of undergrads determined to have financial need; average aid package $14,067

North Park University

Chicago IL
(773) 244-5500
U.S. News ranking: Reg. U. (Mid. W), No. 39
Website: www.northpark.edu
Admissions email: admissions@northpark.edu
Private; founded 1891
Affiliation: Evangelical Covenant Church of America
Freshman admissions: selective; 2019-2020: 4,435 applied, 2,113 accepted. Either SAT or ACT required. SAT 25/75 percentile: 970-1180. High school rank: N/A
Early decision deadline: N/A, notification date: N/A
Early action deadline: N/A, notification date: N/A
Application deadline (fall): 7/1
Undergraduate student body: 1,721 full time, 188 part time; 39% male, 61% female; 0% American Indian, 9% Asian, 9% Black, 30% Hispanic, 3% multiracial, 1% Pacific Islander, 39% white, 6% international
Most popular majors: 19% Registered Nursing/Registered Nurse, 18% Business Administration and Management, General, 8% Psychology, General, 7% Biology/Biological Sciences, General, 4% Health and Physical Education/Fitness, General
Expenses: 2019-2020: $31,030; room/board: $9,720
Financial aid: N/A

Northwestern University

Evanston IL
(847) 491-7271
U.S. News ranking: Nat. U., No. 9
Website: www.northwestern.edu
Admissions email: ug-admission@northwestern.edu
Private; founded 1851
Freshman admissions: most selective; 2019-2020: 40,585 applied, 3,673 accepted. Either SAT or ACT required. SAT 25/75 percentile: 1440-1550. High school rank: 92% in top tenth, 98% in top quarter, 100% in top half
Early decision deadline: 11/1, notification date: 12/15
Early action deadline: N/A, notification date: N/A
Application deadline (fall): 1/1
Undergraduate student body: 8,186 full time, 141 part time; 49% male, 51% female; 0% American Indian, 18% Asian, 6% Black, 12% Hispanic, 6% multiracial, 0% Pacific Islander, 44% white, 10% international; 32% from in state; 60% live on campus; 27% of students in fraternities, 34% in sororities

Most popular majors: 13% Econometrics and Quantitative Economics, 6% Journalism, 6% Psychology, General, 4% Neuroscience, 4% Political Science and Government, General
Expenses: 2020-2021: $58,701; room/board: $17,616
Financial aid: (847) 491-7400; 46% of undergrads determined to have financial need; average aid package $54,473

Olivet Nazarene University

Bourbonnais IL
(815) 939-5011
U.S. News ranking: Reg. U. (Mid. W), No. 60
Website: www.olivet.edu
Admissions email: admissions@olivet.edu
Private; founded 1907
Affiliation: Church of the Nazarene
Freshman admissions: selective; 2019-2020: 5,019 applied, 2,899 accepted. Neither SAT nor ACT required. SAT 25/75 percentile: 960-1180. High school rank: 14% in top tenth, 41% in top quarter, 75% in top half
Early decision deadline: N/A, notification date: N/A
Early action deadline: N/A, notification date: N/A
Application deadline (fall): 8/1
Undergraduate student body: 2,855 full time, 255 part time; 41% male, 59% female; 0% American Indian, 2% Asian, 9% Black, 10% Hispanic, 3% multiracial, 0% Pacific Islander, 72% white, 1% international; 66% from in state; 72% live on campus; 0% of students in fraternities, 0% in sororities
Most popular majors: 24% Registered Nursing/Registered Nurse, 10% Business Administration and Management, General, 7% Engineering, General, 5% Criminal Justice/Safety Studies, 4% Biology/Biological Sciences, General
Expenses: 2020-2021: $36,950; room/board: $8,990
Financial aid: (815) 939-5249; 81% of undergrads determined to have financial need; average aid package $32,250

Principia College

Elsah IL
(618) 374-5181
U.S. News ranking: Nat. Lib. Arts, No. 93
Website: www.principiacollege.edu
Admissions email: collegeadmissions@principia.edu
Private; founded 1910
Affiliation: Other
Freshman admissions: selective; 2019-2020: 105 applied, 96 accepted. Either SAT or ACT required. SAT 25/75 percentile: 1010-1218. High school rank: 29% in top tenth, 57% in top quarter, 100% in top half
Early decision deadline: N/A, notification date: N/A
Early action deadline: N/A, notification date: N/A
Application deadline (fall): 7/1

Undergraduate student body: 388 full time, 16 part time; 52% male, 48% female; 0% American Indian, 3% Asian, 2% Black, 5% Hispanic, 2% multiracial, 0% Pacific Islander, 69% white, 17% international; 15% from in state; 99% live on campus; 0% of students in fraternities, 0% in sororities
Most popular majors: 18% Sociology and Anthropology, 16% Fine/Studio Arts, General, 15% Business Administration and Management, General, 12% Mass Communication/Media Studies, 8% Biology/Biological Sciences, General
Expenses: 2020-2021: $30,720; room/board: $12,270
Financial aid: (618) 374-5187; 71% of undergrads determined to have financial need; average aid package $33,447

Quincy University

Quincy IL
(217) 228-5210
U.S. News ranking: Reg. Coll. (Mid. W), No. 28
Website: www.quincy.edu
Admissions email: admissions@quincy.edu
Private; founded 1860
Affiliation: Roman Catholic
Freshman admissions: selective; 2019-2020: 1,242 applied, 767 accepted. Neither SAT nor ACT required. ACT 25/75 percentile: 19-25. High school rank: 35% in top tenth, 51% in top quarter, 79% in top half
Early decision deadline: N/A, notification date: N/A
Early action deadline: 11/15, notification date: 12/15
Application deadline (fall): rolling
Undergraduate student body: 934 full time, 108 part time; 48% male, 52% female; 0% American Indian, 1% Asian, 12% Black, 4% Hispanic, 0% multiracial, 0% Pacific Islander, 72% white, 3% international; 60% from in state; 58% live on campus; N/A of students in fraternities, N/A in sororities
Most popular majors: 28% Business, Management, Marketing, and Related Support Services, 24% Health Professions and Related Programs, 7% Biological and Biomedical Sciences, 6% Education, 6% Public Administration and Social Service Professions
Expenses: 2020-2021: $31,160; room/board: $11,050
Financial aid: (217) 228-5260; 78% of undergrads determined to have financial need; average aid package $25,245

Rockford University

Rockford IL
(815) 226-4050
U.S. News ranking: Reg. U. (Mid. W), second tier
Website: www.rockford.edu
Admissions email: Admissions@Rockford.edu
Private; founded 1847
Freshman admissions: selective; 2019-2020: 2,297 applied, 1,246 accepted. Either SAT

or ACT required. SAT 25/75 percentile: 960-1140. High school rank: 16% in top tenth, 34% in top quarter, 65% in top half
Early decision deadline: N/A, notification date: N/A
Early action deadline: N/A, notification date: N/A
Application deadline (fall): 8/15
Undergraduate student body: 912 full time, 70 part time; 43% male, 57% female; 0% American Indian, 3% Asian, 10% Black, 19% Hispanic, 3% multiracial, 0% Pacific Islander, 55% white, 9% international
Most popular majors: 25% Business Administration and Management, General, 20% Registered Nursing/Registered Nurse, 7% Education, Other, 6% Psychology, General, 5% Computer Science
Expenses: 2020-2021: $33,300; room/board: $9,770
Financial aid: (815) 226-3385; 87% of undergrads determined to have financial need; average aid package $22,673

Roosevelt University

Chicago IL
(877) 277-5978
U.S. News ranking: Nat. U., second tier
Website: www.roosevelt.edu
Admissions email: admission@roosevelt.edu
Private; founded 1945
Freshman admissions: selective; 2019-2020: 4,966 applied, 3,342 accepted. Either SAT or ACT required. SAT 25/75 percentile: 1010-1230. High school rank: 8% in top tenth, 46% in top quarter, 62% in top half
Early decision deadline: N/A, notification date: N/A
Early action deadline: N/A, notification date: N/A
Application deadline (fall): rolling
Undergraduate student body: 1,963 full time, 358 part time; 34% male, 66% female; 0% American Indian, 5% Asian, 15% Black, 26% Hispanic, 3% multiracial, 0% Pacific Islander, 43% white, 4% international; 78% from in state; 22% live on campus; 0% of students in fraternities, 2% in sororities
Most popular majors: 16% Psychology, General, 8% Biology/Biological Sciences, General, 6% Hospitality Administration/Management, General, 6% Management Science, 5% Business/Corporate Communications
Expenses: 2020-2021: $31,493; room/board: $12,000
Financial aid: (312) 341-3868; 88% of undergrads determined to have financial need; average aid package $28,000

Saint Xavier University

Chicago IL
(773) 298-3050
U.S. News ranking: Reg. U. (Mid. W), No. 60
Website: www.sxu.edu/admissions/
Admissions email: admission@sxu.edu

Private; founded 1846
Affiliation: Roman Catholic
Freshman admissions: selective;
2019-2020: 8,080 applied,
5,872 accepted. Either SAT
or ACT required. SAT 25/75
percentile: 960-1140. High school
rank: 18% in top tenth, 49% in
top quarter, 83% in top half
Early decision deadline: N/A,
notification date: N/A
Early action deadline: N/A,
notification date: N/A
Application deadline (fall): rolling
Undergraduate student body: 2,725
full time, 232 part time; 38%
male, 62% female; 0% American
Indian, 3% Asian, 11% Black,
42% Hispanic, 2% multiracial,
0% Pacific Islander, 40% white,
0% international; 96% from in
state; 17% live on campus; 0%
of students in fraternities, 0% in
sororities
Most popular majors: 27%
Business, Management,
Marketing, and Related Support
Services, 23% Health Professions
and Related Programs, 14%
Psychology, 6% Biological
and Biomedical Sciences, 5%
Education
Expenses: 2020-2021: $34,730;
room/board: $11,540
Financial aid: (773) 298-3073;
87% of undergrads determined to
have financial need; average aid
package $29,881

School of the Art Institute of Chicago

Chicago IL
(312) 629-6100
U.S. News ranking: Arts, unranked
Website: www.saic.edu
Admissions email:
admiss@saic.edu
Private; founded 1866
Freshman admissions: selective;
2019-2020: 6,410 applied,
3,656 accepted. Either SAT
or ACT required. SAT 25/75
percentile: 1120-1360. High
school rank: N/A
Early decision deadline: N/A,
notification date: N/A
Early action deadline: 11/15,
notification date: 12/25
Application deadline (fall): 4/15
Undergraduate student body: 2,783
full time, 176 part time; 26%
male, 74% female; 0% American
Indian, 9% Asian, 4% Black, 11%
Hispanic, 3% multiracial, 0%
Pacific Islander, 34% white, 33%
international
Most popular majors: 45% Fine/
Studio Arts, General, 10%
Art History, Criticism and
Conservation, 10% Art Therapy/
Therapist, 9% Architecture, 5%
Art Teacher Education
Expenses: 2020-2021: $52,200;
room/board: $16,700
Financial aid: (312) 629-6600

Southern Illinois University–Carbondale

Carbondale IL
(618) 536-4405
U.S. News ranking: Nat. U.,
No. 258
Website: www.siu.edu
Admissions email:
admissions@siu.edu
Public; founded 1869
Freshman admissions: selective;
2019-2020: 5,377 applied,
3,569 accepted. Either SAT
or ACT required. SAT 25/75
percentile: 1070-1420. High
school rank: 20% in top tenth,
47% in top quarter, 79% in
top half
Early decision deadline: N/A,
notification date: N/A
Early action deadline: N/A,
notification date: N/A
Application deadline (fall): rolling
Undergraduate student body: 7,107
full time, 1,294 part time; 53%
male, 47% female; 0% American
Indian, 2% Asian, 14% Black,
10% Hispanic, 3% multiracial,
0% Pacific Islander, 68% white,
3% international; 82% from in
state; 33% live on campus; 9%
of students in fraternities, 7% in
sororities
Most popular majors: 11%
Business, Management,
Marketing, and Related Support
Services, 11% Education, 8%
Engineering Technologies and
Engineering-Related Fields, 8%
Health Professions and Related
Programs, 7% Engineering
Expenses: 2020-2021: $14,904
in state, $14,904 out of state;
room/board: $10,622
Financial aid: (618) 453-4613;
68% of undergrads determined to
have financial need; average aid
package $16,031

Southern Illinois University Edwardsville

Edwardsville IL
(618) 650-3705
U.S. News ranking: Nat. U.,
second tier
Website: www.siue.edu
Admissions email:
admissions@siue.edu
Public; founded 1957
Affiliation: Undenominational
Freshman admissions: selective;
2019-2020: 7,306 applied,
6,259 accepted. Either SAT
or ACT required. ACT 25/75
percentile: 20-26. High school
rank: 20% in top tenth, 48% in
top quarter, 79% in top half
Early decision deadline: N/A,
notification date: N/A
Early action deadline: N/A,
notification date: N/A
Application deadline (fall): 5/1
Undergraduate student body: 8,615
full time, 1,785 part time; 46%
male, 54% female; 0% American
Indian, 2% Asian, 14% Black,
5% Hispanic, 4% multiracial,
0% Pacific Islander, 73% white,
1% international; 84% from in
state; 24% live on campus; N/A
of students in fraternities, N/A in
sororities

Most popular majors: 18%
Registered Nursing/Registered
Nurse, 9% Business
Administration and Management,
General, 5% Biology/Biological
Sciences, General, 5% Criminal
Justice/Safety Studies, 5%
Psychology, General
Expenses: 2020-2021: $12,219
in state, $12,219 out of state;
room/board: $9,881
Financial aid: (618) 650-3879;
63% of undergrads determined to
have financial need; average aid
package $12,515

St. Augustine College[1]

Chicago IL
(773) 878-8756
U.S. News ranking: Reg. Coll.
(Mid. W), No. 42
Website: www.
staugustinecollege.edu/index.asp
Admissions email:
info@staugustine.edu
Private
Application deadline (fall): N/A
Undergraduate student body: N/A
full time, N/A part time
Expenses: 2019-2020: $11,736;
room/board: N/A
Financial aid: N/A

Trinity Christian College

Palos Heights IL
(800) 748-0085
U.S. News ranking: Reg. Coll.
(Mid. W), No. 21
Website: www.trnty.edu
Admissions email:
admissions@trnty.edu
Private; founded 1959
Affiliation: Other
Freshman admissions: selective;
2019-2020: 973 applied, 672
accepted. Either SAT or ACT
required. SAT 25/75 percentile:
970-1150. High school rank:
15% in top tenth, 16% in top
quarter, 73% in top half
Early decision deadline: N/A,
notification date: N/A
Early action deadline: N/A,
notification date: N/A
Application deadline (fall): rolling
Undergraduate student body: 837
full time, 168 part time; 33%
male, 67% female; 1% American
Indian, 2% Asian, 10% Black,
15% Hispanic, 1% multiracial,
0% Pacific Islander, 64% white,
4% international; 69% from in
state; 42% live on campus; 0%
of students in fraternities, 0% in
sororities
Most popular majors: 21%
Education, 17% Business,
Management, Marketing, and
Related Support Services, 15%
Health Professions and Related
Programs, 15% Psychology, 6%
Public Administration and Social
Service Professions
Expenses: 2020-2021: $32,000;
room/board: $10,100
Financial aid: (708) 239-4872;
65% of undergrads determined to
have financial need; average aid
package $24,706

Trinity International University[1]

Deerfield IL
(800) 822-3225
U.S. News ranking: Nat. U.,
second tier
Website: www.tiu.edu
Admissions email:
tcadmissions@tiu.edu
Private; founded 1897
Affiliation: Evangelical Free Church
of America
Application deadline (fall): rolling
Undergraduate student body: N/A
full time, N/A part time
Expenses: 2020-2021: $33,298;
room/board: $10,800
Financial aid: (847) 317-8060;
77% of undergrads determined to
have financial need; average aid
package $29,258

University of Chicago

Chicago IL
(773) 702-8650
U.S. News ranking: Nat. U., No. 6
Website: www.uchicago.edu
Admissions email:
collegeadmissions@uchicago.edu
Private; founded 1890
Freshman admissions: most
selective; 2019-2020: 34,641
applied, 2,137 accepted. Neither
SAT nor ACT required. SAT 25/75
percentile: 1500-1570. High
school rank: 99% in top tenth,
100% in top quarter, 100% in
top half
Early decision deadline: 11/1,
notification date: 12/18
Early action deadline: 11/1,
notification date: 12/18
Application deadline (fall): 1/4
Undergraduate student body:
6,727 full time, 7 part time; 51%
male, 49% female; 0% American
Indian, 19% Asian, 6% Black,
14% Hispanic, 7% multiracial,
0% Pacific Islander, 37% white,
15% international; N/A from in
state; 52% live on campus; N/A
of students in fraternities, N/A in
sororities
Most popular majors: 30% Social
Sciences, 13% Mathematics
and Statistics, 8% Biological
and Biomedical Sciences, 7%
Physical Sciences, 7% Public
Administration and Social Service
Professions
Expenses: 2020-2021: $59,298;
room/board: $17,004
Financial aid: (773) 702-8666;
40% of undergrads determined to
have financial need; average aid
package $57,464

University of Illinois–Chicago

Chicago IL
(312) 996-4350
U.S. News ranking: Nat. U.,
No. 112
Website: www.uic.edu
Admissions email:
admissions@uic.edu
Public; founded 1965
Freshman admissions: selective;
2019-2020: 22,696 applied,
16,501 accepted. Either SAT
or ACT required. SAT 25/75
percentile: 1030-1260. High
school rank: 28% in top tenth,

59% in top quarter, 90% in
top half
Early decision deadline: N/A,
notification date: N/A
Early action deadline: 11/1,
notification date: 12/1
Application deadline (fall): 1/15
Undergraduate student body:
20,195 full time, 1,446 part
time; 48% male, 52% female;
0% American Indian, 21% Asian,
8% Black, 34% Hispanic, 3%
multiracial, 0% Pacific Islander,
27% white, 6% international;
90% from in state; 14% live
on campus; 5% of students in
fraternities, 5% in sororities
Most popular majors: 16%
Business, Management,
Marketing, and Related Support
Services, 13% Biological and
Biomedical Sciences, 12%
Engineering, 11% Health
Professions and Related Programs,
10% Psychology
Expenses: 2020-2021: $15,008
in state, $29,358 out of state;
room/board: $12,000
Financial aid: (312) 996-5563;
73% of undergrads determined to
have financial need; average aid
package $15,635

University of Illinois–Springfield

Springfield IL
(217) 206-4847
U.S. News ranking: Reg. U.
(Mid. W), No. 31
Website: www.uis.edu
Admissions email:
admissions@uis.edu
Public; founded 1969
Freshman admissions: selective;
2019-2020: 2,117 applied,
1,626 accepted. Either SAT
or ACT required. SAT 25/75
percentile: 995-1220. High school
rank: 21% in top tenth, 45% in
top quarter, 82% in top half
Early decision deadline: N/A,
notification date: N/A
Early action deadline: N/A,
notification date: N/A
Application deadline (fall): 8/24
Undergraduate student body: 1,853
full time, 821 part time; 49%
male, 51% female; 0% American
Indian, 4% Asian, 15% Black,
11% Hispanic, 4% multiracial,
0% Pacific Islander, 63% white,
3% international; 85% from in
state; 35% live on campus; 2%
of students in fraternities, 4% in
sororities
Most popular majors: 16%
Business Administration and
Management, General, 12%
Computer Science, 10%
Psychology, General, 8%
Accounting, 7% Communication
and Media Studies
Expenses: 2020-2021: $11,921
in state, $21,536 out of state;
room/board: $9,760
Financial aid: (217) 206-6724;
68% of undergrads determined to
have financial need; average aid
package $15,003

University of Illinois–Urbana-Champaign
Champaign IL
(217) 333-0302
U.S. News ranking: Nat. U., No. 47
Website: illinois.edu
Admissions email:
ugradadmissions@illinois.edu
Public; founded 1867
Freshman admissions: more
selective; 2019-2020: 43,509
applied, 25,684 accepted. Either
SAT or ACT required. SAT 25/75
percentile: 1220-1480. High
school rank: 55% in top tenth,
86% in top quarter, 99% in
top half
Early decision deadline: N/A,
notification date: N/A
Early action deadline: 11/1,
notification date: 12/14
Application deadline (fall): 1/5
Undergraduate student body:
32,854 full time, 1,266 part
time; 54% male, 46% female;
0% American Indian, 19% Asian,
6% Black, 13% Hispanic, 3%
multiracial, 0% Pacific Islander,
43% white, 14% international;
74% from in state; 50% live
on campus; 21% of students in
fraternities, 27% in sororities
Most popular majors: 20%
Engineering, 14% Business,
Management, Marketing, and
Related Support Services, 9%
Social Sciences, 6% Biological
and Biomedical Sciences, 6%
Communication, Journalism, and
Related Programs
Expenses: 2020-2021: $16,862
in state, $34,312 out of state;
room/board: $12,252
Financial aid: (217) 333-0100;
47% of undergrads determined to
have financial need; average aid
package $18,489

University of St. Francis
Joliet IL
(800) 735-7500
U.S. News ranking: Nat. U.,
No. 227
Website: www.stfrancis.edu
Admissions email:
admissions@stfrancis.edu
Private; founded 1920
Affiliation: Roman Catholic
Freshman admissions: selective;
2019-2020: 2,273 applied,
1,039 accepted. Neither SAT
nor ACT required. SAT 25/75
percentile: 1030-1220. High
school rank: N/A
Early decision deadline: N/A,
notification date: N/A
Early action deadline: N/A,
notification date: N/A
Application deadline (fall): 8/1
Undergraduate student body: 1,427
full time, 319 part time; 34%
male, 66% female; 0% American
Indian, 3% Asian, 9% Black,
22% Hispanic, 3% multiracial,
0% Pacific Islander, 58% white,
3% international; 9% from in
state; 23% live on campus; 1%
of students in fraternities, 3% in
sororities
Most popular majors: 45% Health
Professions and Related Programs,
19% Business, Management,
Marketing, and Related Support
Services, 6% Biological

and Biomedical Sciences,
6% Education, 5% Public
Administration and Social Service
Professions
Expenses: 2020-2021: $35,000;
room/board: $10,210
Financial aid: (815) 740-3403;
81% of undergrads determined to
have financial need; average aid
package $26,685

Western Illinois University
Macomb IL
(309) 298-3157
U.S. News ranking: Reg. U.
(Mid. W), No. 60
Website: www.wiu.edu
Admissions email:
admissions@wiu.edu
Public; founded 1899
Freshman admissions: selective;
2019-2020: 7,302 applied,
4,137 accepted. Neither SAT
nor ACT required. SAT 25/75
percentile: 950-1150. High school
rank: 11% in top tenth, 35% in
top quarter, 73% in top half
Early decision deadline: N/A,
notification date: N/A
Early action deadline: N/A,
notification date: N/A
Application deadline (fall): rolling
Undergraduate student body: 5,151
full time, 807 part time; 47%
male, 53% female; 0% American
Indian, 1% Asian, 20% Black,
13% Hispanic, 3% multiracial,
0% Pacific Islander, 61% white,
1% international; 88% from in
state; 43% live on campus; 19%
of students in fraternities, 14%
in sororities
Most popular majors: 22%
Homeland Security, Law
Enforcement, Firefighting and
Related Protective Services,
14% Business, Management,
Marketing, and Related Support
Services, 10% Liberal Arts and
Sciences, General Studies and
Humanities, 6% Agriculture,
Agriculture Operations,
and Related Sciences, 6%
Communication, Journalism, and
Related Programs
Expenses: 2020-2021: $11,724
in state, $11,724 out of state;
room/board: $10,010
Financial aid: (309) 298-2446;
76% of undergrads determined to
have financial need; average aid
package $13,378

Wheaton College
Wheaton IL
(800) 222-2419
U.S. News ranking: Nat. Lib. Arts,
No. 61
Website: www.wheaton.edu
Admissions email:
admissions@wheaton.edu
Private; founded 1860
Affiliation: Protestant, not specified
Freshman admissions: more
selective; 2019-2020: 1,889
applied, 1,602 accepted. Either
SAT or ACT required. SAT 25/75
percentile: 1220-1440. High
school rank: 49% in top tenth,
78% in top quarter, 92% in
top half
Early decision deadline: N/A,
notification date: N/A

Early action deadline: 11/1,
notification date: 12/31
Application deadline (fall): 1/10
Undergraduate student body: 2,328
full time, 67 part time; 46%
male, 54% female; 0% American
Indian, 10% Asian, 3% Black,
7% Hispanic, 5% multiracial,
0% Pacific Islander, 71% white,
4% international; 27% from in
state; 91% live on campus; 0%
of students in fraternities, 0% in
sororities
Most popular majors: 19%
Social Sciences, 10% Business,
Management, Marketing, and
Related Support Services, 7%
Communication, Journalism, and
Related Programs, 7% Psychology,
7% Theology and Religious
Vocations
Expenses: 2020-2021: $39,100;
room/board: $10,990
Financial aid: (630) 752-5021;
62% of undergrads determined to
have financial need; average aid
package $25,684

INDIANA

Anderson University
Anderson IN
(765) 641-4080
U.S. News ranking: Reg. U.
(Mid. W), No. 51
Website: anderson.edu
Admissions email:
info@anderson.edu
Private; founded 1917
Affiliation: Church of God
Freshman admissions: selective;
2019-2020: 3,952 applied,
2,432 accepted. Either SAT
or ACT required. SAT 25/75
percentile: 1000-1160. High
school rank: 18% in top tenth,
38% in top quarter, 74% in
top half
Early decision deadline: N/A,
notification date: N/A
Early action deadline: N/A,
notification date: N/A
Application deadline (fall): rolling
Undergraduate student body: 1,213
full time, 98 part time; 42%
male, 58% female; 0% American
Indian, 0% Asian, 7% Black,
5% Hispanic, 5% multiracial,
0% Pacific Islander, 80% white,
1% international; 21% from in
state; 68% live on campus; 0%
of students in fraternities, 0% in
sororities
Most popular majors: 18%
Business, Management,
Marketing, and Related Support
Services, 12% Health Professions
and Related Programs, 10%
Education, 10% Visual and
Performing Arts, 7% Psychology
Expenses: 2020-2021: $32,100;
room/board: $11,400
Financial aid: (765) 641-4180;
82% of undergrads determined to
have financial need; average aid
package $25,964

Ball State University[1]
Muncie IN
(765) 285-8300
U.S. News ranking: Nat. U.,
No. 284
Website: www.bsu.edu
Admissions email: askus@bsu.edu

Public; founded 1918
Application deadline (fall): 8/10
Undergraduate student body: N/A
full time, N/A part time
Expenses: 2020-2021: $10,144
in state, $27,132 out of state;
room/board: $10,796
Financial aid: (765) 285-5600;
64% of undergrads determined to
have financial need; average aid
package $14,335

Bethel University
Mishawaka IN
(800) 422-4101
U.S. News ranking: Reg. U.
(Mid. W), No. 33
Website: www.betheluniversity.edu
Admissions email: admissions@
betheluniversity.edu
Private; founded 1947
Affiliation: Missionary Church Inc
Freshman admissions: selective;
2019-2020: 1,359 applied,
1,274 accepted. Either SAT
or ACT required. SAT 25/75
percentile: 950-1170. High school
rank: 15% in top tenth, 39% in
top quarter, 71% in top half
Early decision deadline: N/A,
notification date: N/A
Early action deadline: N/A,
notification date: N/A
Application deadline (fall): rolling
Undergraduate student body: 1,015
full time, 205 part time; 38%
male, 62% female; 0% American
Indian, 1% Asian, 10% Black,
11% Hispanic, 7% multiracial,
0% Pacific Islander, 66% white,
3% international; 76% from in
state; 54% live on campus; 0%
of students in fraternities, 0% in
sororities
Most popular majors: 19%
Business, Management,
Marketing, and Related
Support Services, 15% Health
Professions and Related Programs,
10% Education, 8% Multi/
Interdisciplinary Studies, 7%
Theology and Religious Vocations
Expenses: 2020-2021: $29,790;
room/board: $9,310
Financial aid: (574) 807-7239;
80% of undergrads determined to
have financial need; average aid
package $23,506

Butler University
Indianapolis IN
(317) 940-8150
U.S. News ranking: Reg. U.
(Mid. W), No. 1
Website: www.butler.edu
Admissions email:
admission@butler.edu
Private; founded 1855
Freshman admissions: more
selective; 2019-2020: 14,891
applied, 10,896 accepted. Either
SAT or ACT required. SAT 25/75
percentile: 1150-1330. High
school rank: 45% in top tenth,
77% in top quarter, 96% in
top half
Early decision deadline: N/A,
notification date: N/A
Early action deadline: 11/1,
notification date: 12/15
Application deadline (fall): rolling
Undergraduate student body: 4,508
full time, 176 part time; 40%
male, 60% female; 0% American
Indian, 3% Asian, 4% Black,

5% Hispanic, 4% multiracial,
0% Pacific Islander, 83% white,
1% international; 45% from in
state; 70% live on campus; 23%
of students in fraternities, 33%
in sororities
Most popular majors: 34%
Business, Management,
Marketing, and Related Support
Services, 9% Communication,
Journalism, and Related Programs,
8% Health Professions and
Related Programs, 8% Social
Sciences, 6% Education
Expenses: 2020-2021: $43,400;
room/board: $14,380
Financial aid: (317) 940-8200;
53% of undergrads determined to
have financial need; average aid
package $25,549

Calumet College of St. Joseph
Whiting IN
(219) 473-4295
U.S. News ranking: Reg. U.
(Mid. W), second tier
Website: www.ccsj.edu
Admissions email:
admissions@ccsj.edu
Private; founded 1951
Freshman admissions: least
selective; 2019-2020: 953
applied, 386 accepted. Neither
SAT nor ACT required. SAT 25/75
percentile: 810-1000. High
school rank: 6% in top tenth, 14%
in top quarter, 53% in top half
Early decision deadline: N/A,
notification date: N/A
Early action deadline: N/A,
notification date: N/A
Application deadline (fall): rolling
Undergraduate student body: 380
full time, 169 part time; 54%
male, 46% female; 0% American
Indian, 1% Asian, 28% Black,
31% Hispanic, 3% multiracial,
0% Pacific Islander, 36% white,
0% international; 52% from in
state; 0% live on campus; N/A
of students in fraternities, N/A in
sororities
Most popular majors: 49% Criminal
Justice/Safety Studies, 28%
Business Administration and
Management, General, 7% English
Language and Literature, General,
5% Liberal Arts and Sciences,
General Studies and Humanities,
Other, 2% Elementary Education
and Teaching
Expenses: 2020-2021: $20,970;
room/board: $6,000
Financial aid: (219) 473-4296;
71% of undergrads determined to
have financial need; average aid
package $13,753

DePauw University
Greencastle IN
(765) 658-4006
U.S. News ranking: Nat. Lib. Arts,
No. 47
Website: www.depauw.edu
Admissions email:
admission@depauw.edu
Private; founded 1837
Freshman admissions: more
selective; 2019-2020: 4,935
applied, 3,176 accepted. Either
SAT or ACT required. SAT 25/75
percentile: 1130-1360. High
school rank: 43% in top tenth,

77% in top quarter, 98% in top half
Early decision deadline: 11/1, notification date: 12/1
Early action deadline: 12/1, notification date: 1/15
Application deadline (fall): 2/1
Undergraduate student body: 1,943 full time, 29 part time; 48% male, 52% female; 0% American Indian, 3% Asian, 6% Black, 10% Hispanic, 3% multiracial, 0% Pacific Islander, 64% white, 14% international; 43% from in state; 97% live on campus; 68% of students in fraternities, 58% in sororities
Most popular majors: 23% Social Sciences, 15% Communication, Journalism, and Related Programs, 10% Biological and Biomedical Sciences, 9% Computer and Information Sciences and Support Services, 7% Visual and Performing Arts
Expenses: 2020-2021: $53,684; room/board: $13,788
Financial aid: (765) 658-4030; 59% of undergrads determined to have financial need; average aid package $44,766

Earlham College
Richmond IN
(765) 983-1600
U.S. News ranking: Nat. Lib. Arts, No. 84
Website: www.earlham.edu/admissions
Admissions email: admission@earlham.edu
Private; founded 1847
Affiliation: Friends
Freshman admissions: more selective; 2019-2020: 2,070 applied, 1,313 accepted. Neither SAT nor ACT required. SAT 25/75 percentile: 1100-1370. High school rank: 42% in top tenth, 71% in top quarter, 93% in top half
Early decision deadline: 11/1, notification date: 12/15
Early action deadline: 12/1, notification date: 1/15
Application deadline (fall): 2/15
Undergraduate student body: 948 full time, 9 part time; 43% male, 57% female; 0% American Indian, 4% Asian, 7% Black, 8% Hispanic, 5% multiracial, 0% Pacific Islander, 51% white, 23% international; N/A from in state; 95% live on campus; 0% of students in fraternities, 0% in sororities
Most popular majors: 14% Biological and Biomedical Sciences, 12% Social Sciences, 10% Psychology, 9% Business, Management, Marketing, and Related Support Services, 9% Multi/Interdisciplinary Studies
Expenses: 2020-2021: $48,091; room/board: $11,347
Financial aid: (765) 983-1217; 91% of undergrads determined to have financial need; average aid package $42,327

Franklin College
Franklin IN
(317) 738-8062
U.S. News ranking: Nat. Lib. Arts, No. 136
Website: www.franklincollege.edu
Admissions email: admissions@franklincollege.edu
Private; founded 1834
Freshman admissions: selective; 2019-2020: 1,865 applied, 1,516 accepted. Either SAT or ACT required. SAT 25/75 percentile: 970-1180. High school rank: 17% in top tenth, 47% in top quarter, 81% in top half
Early decision deadline: N/A, notification date: N/A
Early action deadline: N/A, notification date: N/A
Application deadline (fall): rolling
Undergraduate student body: 876 full time, 46 part time; 48% male, 52% female; 0% American Indian, 1% Asian, 3% Black, 4% Hispanic, 3% multiracial, 0% Pacific Islander, 87% white, 0% international; 92% from in state; 63% live on campus; 36% of students in fraternities, 37% in sororities
Most popular majors: 21% Business, Management, Marketing, and Related Support Services, 11% Communication, Journalism, and Related Programs, 10% Education, 9% Social Sciences, 8% Parks, Recreation, Leisure, and Fitness Studies
Expenses: 2020-2021: $33,954; room/board: $10,546
Financial aid: (317) 738-8073; 83% of undergrads determined to have financial need; average aid package $27,288

Goshen College
Goshen IN
(574) 535-7535
U.S. News ranking: Reg. Coll. (Mid. W), No. 7
Website: www.goshen.edu
Admissions email: admissions@goshen.edu
Private; founded 1894
Affiliation: Mennonite Church
Freshman admissions: selective; 2019-2020: 1,313 applied, 827 accepted. Either SAT or ACT required. SAT 25/75 percentile: 1010-1210. High school rank: 28% in top tenth, 53% in top quarter, 82% in top half
Early decision deadline: N/A, notification date: N/A
Early action deadline: N/A, notification date: N/A
Application deadline (fall): 7/1
Undergraduate student body: 751 full time, 75 part time; 38% male, 62% female; 0% American Indian, 2% Asian, 4% Black, 24% Hispanic, 2% multiracial, 0% Pacific Islander, 57% white, 7% international; 64% from in state; 57% live on campus; 0% of students in fraternities, 0% in sororities
Most popular majors: 39% Registered Nursing/Registered Nurse, 6% Accounting, 6% Social Work, 5% Business/Commerce, General, 5% Molecular Biology
Expenses: 2020-2021: $35,230; room/board: $10,870

Financial aid: (574) 535-7525; 76% of undergrads determined to have financial need; average aid package $29,993

Grace College and Seminary[1]
Winona Lake IN
(574) 372-5100
U.S. News ranking: Reg. U. (Mid. W), No. 91
Website: www.grace.edu
Admissions email: enroll@grace.edu
Private; founded 1948
Affiliation: Other
Application deadline (fall): 3/1
Undergraduate student body: N/A full time, N/A part time
Expenses: 2019-2020: $26,262; room/board: $9,316
Financial aid: (574) 372-5100

Hanover College
Hanover IN
(812) 866-7021
U.S. News ranking: Nat. Lib. Arts, No. 102
Website: www.hanover.edu
Admissions email: admission@hanover.edu
Private; founded 1827
Affiliation: Presbyterian Church (USA)
Freshman admissions: selective; 2019-2020: 3,127 applied, 2,027 accepted. Neither SAT nor ACT required. SAT 25/75 percentile: 1030-1240. High school rank: 26% in top tenth, 59% in top quarter, 90% in top half
Early decision deadline: N/A, notification date: N/A
Early action deadline: 12/1, notification date: 12/1
Application deadline (fall): rolling
Undergraduate student body: 1,062 full time, 5 part time; 44% male, 56% female; 0% American Indian, 1% Asian, 5% Black, 3% Hispanic, 3% multiracial, 0% Pacific Islander, 75% white, 3% international; 67% from in state; 93% live on campus; 36% of students in fraternities, 32% in sororities
Most popular majors: 20% Social Sciences, 13% Biological and Biomedical Sciences, 12% Parks, Recreation, Leisure, and Fitness Studies, 11% Communication, Journalism, and Related Programs, 9% Psychology
Expenses: 2020-2021: $39,650; room/board: $12,300
Financial aid: (812) 866-7029; 76% of undergrads determined to have financial need; average aid package $34,022

Holy Cross College at Notre Dame, Indiana
Notre Dame IN
(574) 239-8400
U.S. News ranking: Reg. Coll. (Mid. W), No. 34
Website: www.hcc-nd.edu/home
Admissions email: admissions@hcc-nd.edu
Private; founded 1966
Affiliation: Roman Catholic

Freshman admissions: more selective; 2019-2020: 544 applied, 510 accepted. Either SAT or ACT required. SAT 25/75 percentile: 1050-1380. High school rank: 22% in top tenth, 47% in top quarter, 72% in top half
Early decision deadline: N/A, notification date: N/A
Early action deadline: 11/1, notification date: 11/25
Application deadline (fall): 7/28
Undergraduate student body: 446 full time, 42 part time; 62% male, 38% female; 1% American Indian, 1% Asian, 8% Black, 21% Hispanic, 4% multiracial, 0% Pacific Islander, 56% white, 3% international; 49% from in state; 70% live on campus; 0% of students in fraternities, 0% in sororities
Most popular majors: 40% Business/Commerce, General, 15% Communication and Media Studies, 12% Psychology, General, 7% Theology/Theological Studies, 6% Liberal Arts and Sciences/Liberal Studies
Expenses: 2020-2021: $33,250; room/board: $11,650
Financial aid: (574) 239-8400; 63% of undergrads determined to have financial need; average aid package $27,356

Huntington University
Huntington IN
(800) 642-6493
U.S. News ranking: Reg. U. (Mid. W), No. 44
Website: www.huntington.edu
Admissions email: admissions@huntington.edu
Private; founded 1897
Affiliation: Other
Freshman admissions: selective; 2019-2020: 1,036 applied, 804 accepted. Either SAT or ACT required. SAT 25/75 percentile: 960-1140. High school rank: 13% in top tenth, 37% in top quarter, 73% in top half
Early decision deadline: N/A, notification date: N/A
Early action deadline: N/A, notification date: N/A
Application deadline (fall): 8/1
Undergraduate student body: 904 full time, 231 part time; 43% male, 57% female; N/A American Indian, N/A Asian, N/A Black, N/A Hispanic, N/A multiracial, N/A Pacific Islander, N/A white, N/A international
Most popular majors: 15% Business, Management, Marketing, and Related Support Services, 12% Visual and Performing Arts, 11% Education, 11% Health Professions and Related Programs, 10% Communications Technologies/Technicians and Support Services
Expenses: 2020-2021: $26,846; room/board: $8,888
Financial aid: (260) 359-4326; 64% of undergrads determined to have financial need; average aid package $19,829

Indiana State University
Terre Haute IN
(812) 237-2121
U.S. News ranking: Nat. U., second tier
Website: www.indstate.edu/
Admissions email: admissions@indstate.edu
Public; founded 1865
Freshman admissions: selective; 2019-2020: 10,008 applied, 8,964 accepted. Neither SAT nor ACT required. SAT 25/75 percentile: 910-1140. High school rank: 13% in top tenth, 33% in top quarter, 68% in top half
Early decision deadline: N/A, notification date: N/A
Early action deadline: N/A, notification date: N/A
Application deadline (fall): 8/15
Undergraduate student body: 8,105 full time, 2,111 part time; 44% male, 56% female; 0% American Indian, 1% Asian, 18% Black, 5% Hispanic, 4% multiracial, 0% Pacific Islander, 67% white, 2% international; 72% from in state; 30% live on campus; 12% of students in fraternities, 12% in sororities
Most popular majors: 17% Business, Management, Marketing, and Related Support Services, 17% Health Professions and Related Programs, 11% Engineering Technologies and Engineering-Related Fields, 10% Social Sciences, 8% Education
Expenses: 2020-2021: $9,466 in state, $20,570 out of state; room/board: $11,016
Financial aid: (800) 841-4744; 74% of undergrads determined to have financial need; average aid package $11,050

Indiana Tech
Fort Wayne IN
(800) 937-2448
U.S. News ranking: Reg. U. (Mid. W), No. 112
Website: www.indianatech.edu
Admissions email: admissions@indianatech.edu
Private; founded 1930
Freshman admissions: selective; 2019-2020: 3,248 applied, 1,937 accepted. Either SAT or ACT required. SAT 25/75 percentile: 930-1150. High school rank: N/A
Early decision deadline: N/A, notification date: N/A
Early action deadline: N/A, notification date: N/A
Application deadline (fall): 8/1
Undergraduate student body: 1,429 full time, 60 part time; 65% male, 35% female; 0% American Indian, 2% Asian, 18% Black, 6% Hispanic, 4% multiracial, 0% Pacific Islander, 49% white, 15% international; 55% from in state; 42% live on campus; 2% of students in fraternities, 0% in sororities
Most popular majors: 25% Business Administration and Management, General, 10% Industrial Engineering, 8% Mechanical Engineering, 6% Bioengineering and Biomedical Engineering, 6% Psychology, General

Expenses: 2020-2021: $28,000; room/board: $13,236
Financial aid: (260) 422-5561; 75% of undergrads determined to have financial need; average aid package $30,344

Indiana University–Bloomington
Bloomington IN
(812) 855-0661
U.S. News ranking: Nat. U., No. 76
Website: www.indiana.edu
Admissions email: iuadmit@indiana.edu
Public; founded 1820
Freshman admissions: more selective; 2019-2020: 42,902 applied, 33,425 accepted. Either SAT or ACT required. SAT 25/75 percentile: 1150-1360. High school rank: 35% in top tenth, 69% in top quarter, 95% in top half
Early decision deadline: N/A, notification date: N/A
Early action deadline: 11/1, notification date: 1/15
Application deadline (fall): rolling
Undergraduate student body: 31,981 full time, 1,103 part time; 51% male, 49% female; 0% American Indian, 6% Asian, 5% Black, 7% Hispanic, 5% multiracial, 0% Pacific Islander, 69% white, 8% international; 64% from in state; 33% live on campus; 19% of students in fraternities, 24% in sororities
Most popular majors: 26% Business, Management, Marketing, and Related Support Services, 8% Biological and Biomedical Sciences, 8% Communication, Journalism, and Related Programs, 8% Computer and Information Sciences and Support Services, 8% Public Administration and Social Service Professions
Expenses: 2020-2021: $11,221 in state, $37,600 out of state; room/board: N/A
Financial aid: (812) 855-6500; 40% of undergrads determined to have financial need; average aid package $14,756

Indiana University East
Richmond IN
(765) 973-8208
U.S. News ranking: Reg. U. (Mid. W), second tier
Website: www.iue.edu
Admissions email: applynow@iue.edu
Public; founded 1971
Freshman admissions: selective; 2019-2020: 2,316 applied, 1,448 accepted. Neither SAT nor ACT required. SAT 25/75 percentile: 930-1140. High school rank: 12% in top tenth, 35% in top quarter, 69% in top half
Early decision deadline: N/A, notification date: N/A
Early action deadline: N/A, notification date: N/A
Application deadline (fall): rolling
Undergraduate student body: 2,031 full time, 1,469 part time; 36% male, 64% female; 0% American Indian, 1% Asian, 5% Black, 4% Hispanic, 4% multiracial,

0% Pacific Islander, 76% white, 2% international; 72% from in state; 0% live on campus; 0% of students in fraternities, 0% in sororities
Most popular majors: 26% Business, Management, Marketing, and Related Support Services, 16% Health Professions and Related Programs, 14% Psychology, 7% Liberal Arts and Sciences, General Studies and Humanities, 7% Mathematics and Statistics
Expenses: 2020-2021: $7,715 in state, $20,574 out of state; room/board: N/A
Financial aid: (765) 973-8206; 74% of undergrads determined to have financial need; average aid package $9,284

Indiana University–Kokomo
Kokomo IN
(765) 455-9217
U.S. News ranking: Reg. Coll. (Mid. W), second tier
Website: www.iuk.edu
Admissions email: iuadmis@iuk.edu
Public; founded 1945
Freshman admissions: selective; 2019-2020: 2,333 applied, 1,718 accepted. Neither SAT nor ACT required. SAT 25/75 percentile: 970-1130. High school rank: 8% in top tenth, 33% in top quarter, 70% in top half
Early decision deadline: N/A, notification date: N/A
Early action deadline: N/A, notification date: N/A
Application deadline (fall): rolling
Undergraduate student body: 2,315 full time, 654 part time; 35% male, 65% female; 0% American Indian, 1% Asian, 4% Black, 6% Hispanic, 3% multiracial, 0% Pacific Islander, 83% white, 1% international; 97% from in state; 0% live on campus; 0% of students in fraternities, 0% in sororities
Most popular majors: 35% Health Professions and Related Programs, 15% Liberal Arts and Sciences, General Studies and Humanities, 12% Business, Management, Marketing, and Related Support Services, 7% Education, 5% Multi/Interdisciplinary Studies
Expenses: 2020-2021: $7,715 in state, $20,574 out of state; room/board: N/A
Financial aid: (765) 455-9216; 67% of undergrads determined to have financial need; average aid package $8,808

Indiana University Northwest
Gary IN
(219) 980-6991
U.S. News ranking: Reg. U. (Mid. W), second tier
Website: www.iun.edu
Admissions email: admit@iun.edu
Public; founded 1948
Freshman admissions: selective; 2019-2020: 2,486 applied, 1,855 accepted. Either SAT or ACT required. SAT 25/75 percentile: 910-1100. High

school rank: 11% in top tenth, 37% in top quarter, 70% in top half
Early decision deadline: N/A, notification date: N/A
Early action deadline: N/A, notification date: N/A
Application deadline (fall): rolling
Undergraduate student body: 2,515 full time, 939 part time; 28% male, 72% female; 0% American Indian, 3% Asian, 15% Black, 25% Hispanic, 4% multiracial, 0% Pacific Islander, 51% white, 1% international; 96% from in state; 0% live on campus; 0% of students in fraternities, 0% in sororities
Most popular majors: 29% Health Professions and Related Programs, 16% Business, Management, Marketing, and Related Support Services, 9% Liberal Arts and Sciences, General Studies and Humanities, 9% Public Administration and Social Service Professions, 8% Psychology
Expenses: 2020-2021: $7,715 in state, $20,574 out of state; room/board: N/A
Financial aid: (219) 980-6778; 69% of undergrads determined to have financial need; average aid package $9,228

Indiana University-Purdue University–Indianapolis
Indianapolis IN
(317) 274-4591
U.S. News ranking: Nat. U., No. 196
Website: www.iupui.edu
Admissions email: apply@iupui.edu
Public; founded 1969
Freshman admissions: selective; 2019-2020: 15,050 applied, 12,150 accepted. Either SAT or ACT required. SAT 25/75 percentile: 1000-1200. High school rank: 14% in top tenth, 42% in top quarter, 84% in top half
Early decision deadline: N/A, notification date: N/A
Early action deadline: N/A, notification date: N/A
Application deadline (fall): rolling
Undergraduate student body: 17,630 full time, 3,543 part time; 42% male, 58% female; 0% American Indian, 5% Asian, 9% Black, 9% Hispanic, 5% multiracial, 0% Pacific Islander, 67% white, 4% international; 94% from in state; 12% live on campus; 1% of students in fraternities, 2% in sororities
Most popular majors: 19% Health Professions and Related Programs, 18% Business, Management, Marketing, and Related Support Services, 7% Engineering, 6% Liberal Arts and Sciences, General Studies and Humanities, 5% Education
Expenses: 2020-2021: $9,944 in state, $31,626 out of state; room/board: N/A
Financial aid: (317) 274-4162; 65% of undergrads determined to have financial need; average aid package $12,225

Indiana University–South Bend
South Bend IN
(574) 520-4839
U.S. News ranking: Reg. U. (Mid. W), second tier
Website: www.iusb.edu
Admissions email: admissions@iusb.edu
Public; founded 1961
Freshman admissions: selective; 2019-2020: 2,959 applied, 2,299 accepted. Either SAT or ACT required. SAT 25/75 percentile: 950-1130. High school rank: 8% in top tenth, 30% in top quarter, 68% in top half
Early decision deadline: N/A, notification date: N/A
Early action deadline: N/A, notification date: N/A
Application deadline (fall): rolling
Undergraduate student body: 3,481 full time, 1,070 part time; 36% male, 64% female; 0% American Indian, 2% Asian, 8% Black, 14% Hispanic, 5% multiracial, 0% Pacific Islander, 67% white, 3% international; 95% from in state; 9% live on campus; N/A of students in fraternities, N/A in sororities
Most popular majors: 20% Business, Management, Marketing, and Related Support Services, 20% Health Professions and Related Programs, 10% Education, 10% Liberal Arts and Sciences, General Studies and Humanities, 7% Communication, Journalism, and Related Programs
Expenses: 2020-2021: $7,715 in state, $20,574 out of state; room/board: N/A
Financial aid: (574) 520-4357; 70% of undergrads determined to have financial need; average aid package $9,803

Indiana University Southeast
New Albany IN
(812) 941-2212
U.S. News ranking: Reg. U. (Mid. W), second tier
Website: www.ius.edu
Admissions email: admissions@ius.edu
Public; founded 1941
Freshman admissions: selective; 2019-2020: 2,831 applied, 2,319 accepted. Either SAT or ACT required. ACT 25/75 percentile: 17-23. High school rank: 9% in top tenth, 30% in top quarter, 64% in top half
Early decision deadline: N/A, notification date: N/A
Early action deadline: N/A, notification date: N/A
Application deadline (fall): rolling
Undergraduate student body: 3,099 full time, 1,298 part time; 39% male, 61% female; 0% American Indian, 2% Asian, 7% Black, 5% Hispanic, 4% multiracial, 0% Pacific Islander, 81% white, 1% international; 71% from in state; 8% live on campus; N/A of students in fraternities, N/A in sororities
Most popular majors: 19% Business, Management, Marketing, and Related Support Services, 10% Education,

10% Liberal Arts and Sciences, General Studies and Humanities, 10% Psychology, 9% Health Professions and Related Programs
Expenses: 2020-2021: $7,715 in state, $20,574 out of state; room/board: N/A
Financial aid: (812) 941-2100; 64% of undergrads determined to have financial need; average aid package $8,998

Indiana Wesleyan University–Marion
Marion IN
(866) 468-6498
U.S. News ranking: Reg. U. (Mid. W), No. 15
Website: www.indwes.edu
Admissions email: admissions@indwes.edu
Private; founded 1920
Affiliation: Wesleyan
Freshman admissions: selective; 2019-2020: 4,363 applied, 2,923 accepted. Either SAT or ACT required. SAT 25/75 percentile: 1020-1220. High school rank: 28% in top tenth, 60% in top quarter, 84% in top half
Early decision deadline: N/A, notification date: N/A
Early action deadline: N/A, notification date: N/A
Application deadline (fall): rolling
Undergraduate student body: 2,528 full time, 234 part time; 36% male, 64% female; 0% American Indian, 2% Asian, 4% Black, 4% Hispanic, 3% multiracial, 0% Pacific Islander, 83% white, 2% international
Most popular majors: 31% Health Professions and Related Programs, 12% Theology and Religious Vocations, 9% Education, 8% Business, Management, Marketing, and Related Support Services, 6% Biological and Biomedical Sciences
Expenses: 2020-2021: $28,184; room/board: $9,206
Financial aid: (765) 677-2116; 76% of undergrads determined to have financial need; average aid package $31,271

Manchester University[1]
North Manchester IN
(800) 852-3648
U.S. News ranking: Reg. Coll. (Mid. W), No. 24
Website: www.manchester.edu
Admissions email: admitinfo@manchester.edu
Private; founded 1889
Affiliation: Church of Brethren
Application deadline (fall): rolling
Undergraduate student body: N/A full time, N/A part time
Expenses: 2019-2020: $33,624; room/board: $10,050
Financial aid: (260) 982-5237

Marian University
Indianapolis IN
(317) 955-6300
U.S. News ranking: Reg. U. (Mid. W), No. 28
Website: www.marian.edu
Admissions email: admissions@marian.edu

Private; founded 1851
Affiliation: Roman Catholic
Freshman admissions: selective; 2019-2020: 2,525 applied, 1,554 accepted. Neither SAT nor ACT required. SAT 25/75 percentile: 970-1180. High school rank: 25% in top tenth, 51% in top quarter, 79% in top half
Early decision deadline: N/A, notification date: N/A
Early action deadline: N/A, notification date: N/A
Application deadline (fall): 8/1
Undergraduate student body: 2,040 full time, 365 part time; 37% male, 63% female; 0% American Indian, 3% Asian, 12% Black, 7% Hispanic, 4% multiracial, 0% Pacific Islander, 70% white, 2% international; 82% from in state; 47% live on campus; 0% of students in fraternities, 0% in sororities
Most popular majors: 54% Health Professions and Related Programs, 17% Business, Management, Marketing, and Related Support Services, 5% Biological and Biomedical Sciences, 5% Education, 4% Psychology
Expenses: 2020-2021: $36,000; room/board: $11,320
Financial aid: (317) 955-6040; 78% of undergrads determined to have financial need; average aid package $29,534

Martin University[1]

Indianapolis IN
(317) 543-3235
U.S. News ranking: Reg. Coll. (Mid. W), second tier
Website: www.martin.edu
Admissions email: admissions@martin.edu
Private
Application deadline (fall): N/A
Undergraduate student body: N/A full time, N/A part time
Expenses: 2019-2020: $13,200; room/board: N/A
Financial aid: N/A

Oakland City University

Oakland City IN
(800) 737-5125
U.S. News ranking: Reg. Coll. (Mid. W), No. 28
Website: www.oak.edu
Admissions email: admission@oak.edu
Private; founded 1885
Affiliation: General Baptist
Freshman admissions: less selective; 2019-2020: 1,010 applied, 553 accepted. Neither SAT nor ACT required. SAT 25/75 percentile: 920-1130. High school rank: 6% in top tenth, 38% in top quarter, 58% in top half
Early decision deadline: N/A, notification date: N/A
Early action deadline: N/A, notification date: N/A
Application deadline (fall): rolling
Undergraduate student body: 636 full time, 732 part time; 48% male, 52% female; 1% American Indian, 2% Asian, 4% Black, 4% Hispanic, 7% multiracial, 0% Pacific Islander, 63% white, 3% international

Most popular majors: 42% Business, Management, Marketing, and Related Support Services, 23% Homeland Security, Law Enforcement, Firefighting and Related Protective Services, 8% Biological and Biomedical Sciences, 8% Education, 7% Psychology
Expenses: 2020-2021: $24,900; room/board: $10,400
Financial aid: (812) 749-1225; 73% of undergrads determined to have financial need; average aid package $14,000

Purdue University–Fort Wayne

Fort Wayne IN
(260) 481-6812
U.S. News ranking: Reg. U. (Mid. W), No. 112
Website: www.pfw.edu
Admissions email: ask@pfw.edu
Public; founded 1964
Freshman admissions: selective; 2019-2020: 6,376 applied, 5,192 accepted. Either SAT or ACT required. SAT 25/75 percentile: 970-1190. High school rank: 11% in top tenth, 31% in top quarter, 70% in top half
Early decision deadline: N/A, notification date: N/A
Early action deadline: N/A, notification date: N/A
Application deadline (fall): 8/1
Undergraduate student body: 5,370 full time, 4,327 part time; 46% male, 54% female; 0% American Indian, 4% Asian, 7% Black, 8% Hispanic, 5% multiracial, 0% Pacific Islander, 74% white, 3% international; 92% from in state; 15% live on campus; 0% of students in fraternities, 1% in sororities
Most popular majors: 10% Business/Commerce, General, 9% Registered Nursing/Registered Nurse, 8% General Studies, 7% Elementary Education and Teaching, 5% Biology/Biological Sciences, General
Expenses: 2020-2021: $9,970 in state, $22,201 out of state; room/board: $8,748
Financial aid: (260) 481-6820; 68% of undergrads determined to have financial need; average aid package $10,606

Purdue University–Northwest

Hammond IN
(219) 989-2213
U.S. News ranking: Reg. U. (Mid. W), second tier
Website: www.pnw.edu/
Admissions email: admissons@pnw.edu
Public; founded 2016
Affiliation: North American Baptist
Freshman admissions: selective; 2019-2020: 1,761 applied, 1,730 accepted. Either SAT or ACT required. SAT 25/75 percentile: 980-1160. High school rank: 15% in top tenth, 38% in top quarter, 75% in top half
Early decision deadline: N/A, notification date: N/A
Early action deadline: N/A, notification date: N/A

Application deadline (fall): 8/1
Undergraduate student body: 5,558 full time, 2,159 part time; 45% male, 55% female; 0% American Indian, 3% Asian, 10% Black, 21% Hispanic, 3% multiracial, 0% Pacific Islander, 59% white, 2% international; 89% from in state; 7% live on campus; N/A of students in fraternities, N/A in sororities
Most popular majors: 40% Health Professions and Related Programs, 16% Business, Management, Marketing, and Related Support Services, 8% Engineering, 8% Engineering Technologies and Engineering-Related Fields, 4% Education
Expenses: 2020-2021: $7,942 in state, $11,524 out of state; room/board: $7,821
Financial aid: (855) 608-4600; 68% of undergrads determined to have financial need; average aid package $4,826

Purdue University–West Lafayette

West Lafayette IN
(765) 494-1776
U.S. News ranking: Nat. U., No. 53
Website: www.purdue.edu
Admissions email: admissions@purdue.edu
Public; founded 1869
Freshman admissions: more selective; 2019-2020: 54,912 applied, 32,834 accepted. Either SAT or ACT required. SAT 25/75 percentile: 1190-1440. High school rank: 49% in top tenth, 80% in top quarter, 97% in top half
Early decision deadline: N/A, notification date: N/A
Early action deadline: 11/1, notification date: 12/12
Application deadline (fall): rolling
Undergraduate student body: 32,025 full time, 1,621 part time; 57% male, 43% female; 0% American Indian, 9% Asian, 3% Black, 6% Hispanic, 4% multiracial, 0% Pacific Islander, 63% white, 14% international; 60% from in state; 42% live on campus; 18% of students in fraternities, 21% in sororities
Most popular majors: 27% Engineering, 14% Business, Management, Marketing, and Related Support Services, 9% Liberal Arts and Sciences, General Studies and Humanities, 8% Agriculture, Agriculture Operations, and Related Sciences, 7% Engineering Technologies and Engineering-Related Fields
Expenses: 2020-2021: $9,992 in state, $28,794 out of state; room/board: $10,030
Financial aid: (765) 494-5050; 41% of undergrads determined to have financial need; average aid package $14,130

Rose-Hulman Institute of Technology

Terre Haute IN
(812) 877-8213
U.S. News ranking: Engineering, unranked
Website: www.rose-hulman.edu
Admissions email: admissions@rose-hulman.edu
Private; founded 1874
Freshman admissions: more selective; 2019-2020: 4,350 applied, 3,228 accepted. Either SAT or ACT required. SAT 25/75 percentile: 1248-1460. High school rank: 61% in top tenth, 86% in top quarter, 100% in top half
Early decision deadline: N/A, notification date: N/A
Early action deadline: 11/1, notification date: 12/15
Application deadline (fall): 2/1
Undergraduate student body: 1,980 full time, 20 part time; 76% male, 24% female; 0% American Indian, 6% Asian, 4% Black, 5% Hispanic, 5% multiracial, 0% Pacific Islander, 65% white, 14% international; 31% from in state; 57% live on campus; 34% of students in fraternities, 21% in sororities
Most popular majors: 32% Mechanical Engineering, 14% Computer Science, 13% Chemical Engineering, 9% Electrical and Electronics Engineering, 8% Bioengineering and Biomedical Engineering
Expenses: 2020-2021: $50,514; room/board: $15,690
Financial aid: (812) 877-8672; 57% of undergrads determined to have financial need; average aid package $32,356

Saint Mary-of-the-Woods College

St. Mary-of-the-Woods IN
(800) 926-7692
U.S. News ranking: Reg. U. (Mid. W), No. 46
Website: www.smwc.edu
Admissions email: admission@smwc.edu
Private; founded 1840
Affiliation: Roman Catholic
Freshman admissions: less selective; 2019-2020: 714 applied, 480 accepted. Neither SAT nor ACT required. SAT 25/75 percentile: 930-1120. High school rank: N/A
Early decision deadline: N/A, notification date: N/A
Early action deadline: N/A, notification date: N/A
Application deadline (fall): rolling
Undergraduate student body: 629 full time, 138 part time; 14% male, 86% female; 0% American Indian, 1% Asian, 5% Black, 3% Hispanic, 12% multiracial, 0% Pacific Islander, 76% white, 0% international; 86% from in state; 46% live on campus; 0% of students in fraternities, 0% in sororities
Most popular majors: 22% Business, Management, Marketing, and Related Support Services, 20% Health Professions and Related Programs,

15% Education, 14% Psychology, 7% Agriculture, Agriculture Operations, and Related Sciences
Expenses: 2020-2021: $30,500; room/board: $11,240
Financial aid: (812) 535-5110; 100% of undergrads determined to have financial need; average aid package $25,891

Saint Mary's College

Notre Dame IN
(574) 284-4587
U.S. News ranking: Nat. Lib. Arts, No. 96
Website: www.saintmarys.edu
Admissions email: admission@saintmarys.edu
Private; founded 1844
Affiliation: Roman Catholic
Freshman admissions: more selective; 2019-2020: 2,033 applied, 1,651 accepted. Neither SAT nor ACT required. SAT 25/75 percentile: 1060-1250. High school rank: 39% in top tenth, 69% in top quarter, 92% in top half
Early decision deadline: 11/15, notification date: 12/15
Early action deadline: N/A, notification date: N/A
Application deadline (fall): rolling
Undergraduate student body: 1,421 full time, 31 part time; 0% male, 100% female; 0% American Indian, 2% Asian, 2% Black, 15% Hispanic, 3% multiracial, 0% Pacific Islander, 75% white, 1% international; 32% from in state; 84% live on campus; N/A of students in fraternities, 0% in sororities
Most popular majors: 10% Biology/Biological Sciences, General, 10% Registered Nursing/Registered Nurse, 10% Speech Communication and Rhetoric, 9% Business Administration and Management, General, 7% Psychology, General
Expenses: 2020-2021: $45,720; room/board: $13,470
Financial aid: (574) 284-4557; 74% of undergrads determined to have financial need; average aid package $38,653

Taylor University

Upland IN
(765) 998-5134
U.S. News ranking: Reg. Coll. (Mid. W), No. 2
Website: www.taylor.edu
Admissions email: admissions_u@taylor.edu
Private; founded 1846
Affiliation: Interdenominational
Freshman admissions: more selective; 2019-2020: 2,341 applied, 1,595 accepted. Either SAT or ACT required. SAT 25/75 percentile: 1080-1310. High school rank: 28% in top tenth, 59% in top quarter, 89% in top half
Early decision deadline: N/A, notification date: N/A
Early action deadline: N/A, notification date: N/A
Application deadline (fall): 8/1
Undergraduate student body: 1,799 full time, 348 part time; 45% male, 55% female; 0% American Indian, 3% Asian, 3% Black,

4% Hispanic, 1% multiracial, 0% Pacific Islander, 83% white, 5% international; 45% from in state; 90% live on campus; 0% of students in fraternities, 0% in sororities
Most popular majors: 20% Business, Management, Marketing, and Related Support Services, 13% Biological and Biomedical Sciences, 11% Education, 8% Visual and Performing Arts, 5% Computer and Information Sciences and Support Services
Expenses: 2020-2021: $36,535; room/board: $10,299
Financial aid: (765) 998-5358; 64% of undergrads determined to have financial need; average aid package $26,360

Trine University[1]
Angola IN
(260) 665-4100
U.S. News ranking: Reg. U. (Mid. W), No. 60
Website: www.trine.edu
Admissions email: admit@trine.edu
Private; founded 1884
Application deadline (fall): 8/1
Undergraduate student body: N/A full time, N/A part time
Expenses: 2020-2021: $33,490; room/board: $10,880
Financial aid: (260) 665-4438; 83% of undergrads determined to have financial need; average aid package $26,469

University of Evansville
Evansville IN
(812) 488-2468
U.S. News ranking: Reg. U. (Mid. W), No. 4
Website: www.evansville.edu
Admissions email: admission@evansville.edu
Private; founded 1854
Affiliation: United Methodist
Freshman admissions: more selective; 2019-2020: 4,234 applied, 2,992 accepted. Neither SAT nor ACT required. SAT 25/75 percentile: 1090-1288. High school rank: 39% in top tenth, 75% in top quarter, 91% in top half
Early decision deadline: N/A, notification date: N/A
Early action deadline: 12/1, notification date: 12/15
Application deadline (fall): rolling
Undergraduate student body: 1,822 full time, 302 part time; 42% male, 58% female; 0% American Indian, 2% Asian, 4% Black, 4% Hispanic, 3% multiracial, 0% Pacific Islander, 75% white, 11% international; 64% from in state; 55% live on campus; 12% of students in fraternities, 13% in sororities
Most popular majors: 16% Business, Management, Marketing, and Related Support Services, 15% Health Professions and Related Programs, 13% Engineering, 11% Parks, Recreation, Leisure, and Fitness Studies, 10% Visual and Performing Arts
Expenses: 2020-2021: $38,686; room/board: $13,090

Financial aid: (812) 488-2364; 68% of undergrads determined to have financial need; average aid package $32,530

University of Indianapolis
Indianapolis IN
(317) 788-3216
U.S. News ranking: Nat. U., No. 227
Website: www.uindy.edu
Admissions email: admissions@uindy.edu
Private; founded 1902
Affiliation: United Methodist
Freshman admissions: selective; 2019-2020: 8,525 applied, 7,086 accepted. Either SAT or ACT required. SAT 25/75 percentile: 980-1190. High school rank: 17% in top tenth, 48% in top quarter, 83% in top half
Early decision deadline: N/A, notification date: N/A
Early action deadline: N/A, notification date: N/A
Application deadline (fall): rolling
Undergraduate student body: 4,066 full time, 336 part time; 37% male, 63% female; 0% American Indian, 2% Asian, 11% Black, 7% Hispanic, 3% multiracial, 0% Pacific Islander, 65% white, 7% international; 87% from in state; 55% live on campus; 0% of students in fraternities, 0% in sororities
Most popular majors: 17% Registered Nursing/Registered Nurse, 11% Business Administration and Management, General, 10% Psychology, General, 7% Kinesiology and Exercise Science, 5% Biology/Biological Sciences, General
Expenses: 2020-2021: $32,268; room/board: $11,980
Financial aid: (317) 788-3217; 77% of undergrads determined to have financial need; average aid package $26,212

University of Notre Dame
Notre Dame IN
(574) 631-7505
U.S. News ranking: Nat. U., No. 19
Website: www.nd.edu
Admissions email: admissions@nd.edu
Private; founded 1842
Affiliation: Roman Catholic
Freshman admissions: most selective; 2019-2020: 22,200 applied, 3,515 accepted. Either SAT or ACT required. ACT 25/75 percentile: 32-35. High school rank: 90% in top tenth, 99% in top quarter, 100% in top half
Early decision deadline: N/A, notification date: N/A
Early action deadline: 11/1, notification date: 12/15
Application deadline (fall): 1/1
Undergraduate student body: 8,707 full time, 24 part time; 52% male, 48% female; 0% American Indian, 5% Asian, 4% Black, 12% Hispanic, 5% multiracial, 0% Pacific Islander, 67% white, 6% international; 7% from in state; 78% live on campus; 0% of students in fraternities, 0% in sororities

Most popular majors: 8% Economics, General, 8% Finance, General, 7% Political Science and Government, General, 5% Mechanical Engineering, 4% Computer and Information Sciences, General
Expenses: 2020-2021: $57,699; room/board: $15,984
Financial aid: (574) 631-6436; 48% of undergrads determined to have financial need; average aid package $52,593

University of Saint Francis
Fort Wayne IN
(260) 399-8000
U.S. News ranking: Reg. U. (Mid. W), No. 65
Website: www.sf.edu
Admissions email: admis@sf.edu
Private; founded 1890
Affiliation: Roman Catholic
Freshman admissions: selective; 2019-2020: 1,587 applied, 1,527 accepted. Either SAT or ACT required. SAT 25/75 percentile: 948-1170. High school rank: 17% in top tenth, 46% in top quarter, 75% in top half
Early decision deadline: N/A, notification date: N/A
Early action deadline: N/A, notification date: N/A
Application deadline (fall): rolling
Undergraduate student body: 1,497 full time, 248 part time; 30% male, 70% female; 0% American Indian, 2% Asian, 9% Black, 10% Hispanic, 3% multiracial, 0% Pacific Islander, 74% white, 1% international; 89% from in state; 22% live on campus; N/A of students in fraternities, N/A in sororities
Most popular majors: 46% Health Professions and Related Programs, 13% Visual and Performing Arts, 11% Business, Management, Marketing, and Related Support Services, 6% Biological and Biomedical Sciences, 5% Education
Expenses: 2020-2021: $32,420; room/board: $10,490
Financial aid: (260) 399-8003; 85% of undergrads determined to have financial need; average aid package $23,587

University of Southern Indiana
Evansville IN
(812) 464-1765
U.S. News ranking: Reg. U. (Mid. W), No. 98
Website: www.usi.edu
Admissions email: enroll@usi.edu
Public; founded 1965
Freshman admissions: selective; 2019-2020: 4,614 applied, 4,306 accepted. Either SAT or ACT required. SAT 25/75 percentile: 980-1170. High school rank: 14% in top tenth, 38% in top quarter, 75% in top half
Early decision deadline: N/A, notification date: N/A
Early action deadline: N/A, notification date: N/A
Application deadline (fall): 8/15
Undergraduate student body: 6,125 full time, 969 part time; 37% male, 63% female; 0% American

Indian, 1% Asian, 4% Black, 4% Hispanic, 3% multiracial, 0% Pacific Islander, 85% white, 2% international; 84% from in state; 35% live on campus; 9% of students in fraternities, 9% in sororities
Most popular majors: 25% Health Professions and Related Programs, 15% Business, Management, Marketing, and Related Support Services, 9% Education, 7% Parks, Recreation, Leisure, and Fitness Studies, 6% Communication, Journalism, and Related Programs
Expenses: 2020-2021: $8,706 in state, $20,242 out of state; room/board: $10,750
Financial aid: (812) 464-1767; 63% of undergrads determined to have financial need; average aid package $10,422

Valparaiso University
Valparaiso IN
(888) 468-2576
U.S. News ranking: Nat. U., No. 160
Website: www.valpo.edu
Admissions email: undergrad.admission@valpo.edu
Private; founded 1859
Freshman admissions: more selective; 2019-2020: 5,491 applied, 4,714 accepted. Either SAT or ACT required. SAT 25/75 percentile: 1070-1290. High school rank: 36% in top tenth, 65% in top quarter, 93% in top half
Early decision deadline: N/A, notification date: N/A
Early action deadline: N/A, notification date: N/A
Application deadline (fall): rolling
Undergraduate student body: 2,956 full time, 53 part time; 44% male, 56% female; 0% American Indian, 2% Asian, 5% Black, 11% Hispanic, 3% multiracial, 0% Pacific Islander, 72% white, 3% international; 46% from in state; 60% live on campus; 29% of students in fraternities, 29% in sororities
Most popular majors: 21% Health Professions and Related Programs, 14% Business, Management, Marketing, and Related Support Services, 14% Engineering, 6% Education, 6% Social Sciences
Expenses: 2020-2021: $43,286; room/board: $12,620
Financial aid: (219) 464-5015; 78% of undergrads determined to have financial need; average aid package $32,287

Vincennes University
Vincennes IN
(800) 742-9198
U.S. News ranking: Reg. Coll. (Mid. W), second tier
Website: www.vinu.edu
Admissions email: N/A
Public; founded 1801
Freshman admissions: less selective; 2019-2020: 4,631 applied, 3,566 accepted. Neither SAT nor ACT required. SAT 25/75 percentile: N/A. High school rank: N/A
Early decision deadline: N/A, notification date: N/A

Early action deadline: N/A, notification date: N/A
Application deadline (fall): rolling
Undergraduate student body: 9,543 full time, 7,696 part time; 24% male, 76% female; 0% American Indian, 1% Asian, 8% Black, 13% Hispanic, 2% multiracial, 0% Pacific Islander, 72% white, 1% international; N/A from in state; 37% live on campus; N/A of students in fraternities, N/A in sororities
Most popular majors: 41% Homeland Security, Law Enforcement, Firefighting and Related Protective Services, 27% Health Professions and Related Programs, 20% Engineering Technologies and Engineering-Related Fields, 12% Education
Expenses: 2020-2021: $6,251 in state, $14,781 out of state; room/board: $10,590
Financial aid: (812) 888-4361

Wabash College
Crawfordsville IN
(765) 361-6225
U.S. News ranking: Nat. Lib. Arts, No. 54
Website: www.wabash.edu
Admissions email: admissions@wabash.edu
Private; founded 1832
Freshman admissions: more selective; 2019-2020: 1,307 applied, 839 accepted. Either SAT or ACT required. SAT 25/75 percentile: 1120-1320. High school rank: 25% in top tenth, 60% in top quarter, 92% in top half
Early decision deadline: 11/1, notification date: 12/5
Early action deadline: 12/1, notification date: 12/31
Application deadline (fall): 7/1
Undergraduate student body: 866 full time, 1 part time; 100% male, 0% female; 0% American Indian, 1% Asian, 5% Black, 9% Hispanic, 3% multiracial, 0% Pacific Islander, 76% white, 5% international; 80% from in state; 99% live on campus; 64% of students in fraternities, N/A in sororities
Most popular majors: 13% Economics, General, 9% History, General, 9% Political Science and Government, General, 9% Rhetoric and Composition, 7% English Language and Literature, General
Expenses: 2020-2021: $45,850; room/board: $10,900
Financial aid: (765) 361-6370; 76% of undergrads determined to have financial need; average aid package $42,236

IOWA

Briar Cliff University
Sioux City IA
(712) 279-5200
U.S. News ranking: Reg. Coll. (Mid. W), No. 34
Website: www.briarcliff.edu
Admissions email: admissions@briarcliff.edu
Private; founded 1930
Affiliation: Roman Catholic

Freshman admissions: selective; 2019-2020: 1,504 applied, 1,162 accepted. Either SAT or ACT required. ACT 25/75 percentile: 19-23. High school rank: 1% in top tenth, 15% in top quarter, 49% in top half
Early decision deadline: N/A, notification date: N/A
Early action deadline: N/A, notification date: N/A
Application deadline (fall): rolling
Undergraduate student body: 354 full time, 518 part time; 46% male, 54% female; 1% American Indian, 3% Asian, 12% Black, 18% Hispanic, 1% multiracial, 1% Pacific Islander, 57% white, 6% international; 47% from in state; 50% live on campus; 0% of students in fraternities, 0% in sororities
Most popular majors: 27% Registered Nursing/Registered Nurse, 16% Business Administration and Management, General, 11% Social Work, 8% Biology/Biological Sciences, General, 6% Kinesiology and Exercise Science
Expenses: 2019-2020: $32,202; room/board: $9,384
Financial aid: N/A

Buena Vista University

Storm Lake IA
(800) 383-9600
U.S. News ranking: Reg. U. (Mid. W), No. 44
Website: www.bvu.edu
Admissions email: admissions@bvu.edu
Private; founded 1891
Affiliation: Presbyterian Church (USA)
Freshman admissions: selective; 2019-2020: 2,101 applied, 1,205 accepted. Either SAT or ACT required. ACT 25/75 percentile: 19-25. High school rank: 16% in top tenth, 43% in top quarter, 77% in top half
Early decision deadline: N/A, notification date: N/A
Early action deadline: N/A, notification date: N/A
Application deadline (fall): rolling
Undergraduate student body: 1,257 full time, 221 part time; 36% male, 64% female; 1% American Indian, 1% Asian, 2% Black, 8% Hispanic, 2% multiracial, 0% Pacific Islander, 73% white, 1% international; 69% from in state; 92% live on campus; 0% of students in fraternities, 0% in sororities
Most popular majors: 24% Business, Management, Marketing, and Related Support Services, 15% Education, 10% Biological and Biomedical Sciences, 8% Parks, Recreation, Leisure, and Fitness Studies, 5% Psychology
Expenses: 2020-2021: $36,426; room/board: $10,218
Financial aid: (712) 749-2164; 88% of undergrads determined to have financial need; average aid package $32,002

Central College

Pella IA
(641) 628-5286
U.S. News ranking: Nat. Lib. Arts, No. 140
Website: www.central.edu
Admissions email: admission@central.edu
Private; founded 1853
Affiliation: Reformed Church in America
Freshman admissions: selective; 2019-2020: 2,688 applied, 1,749 accepted. Either SAT or ACT required. ACT 25/75 percentile: 19-25. High school rank: 18% in top tenth, 48% in top quarter, 80% in top half
Early decision deadline: N/A, notification date: N/A
Early action deadline: N/A, notification date: N/A
Application deadline (fall): 8/15
Undergraduate student body: 1,120 full time, 43 part time; 52% male, 48% female; 0% American Indian, 1% Asian, 3% Black, 7% Hispanic, 3% multiracial, 0% Pacific Islander, 84% white, 0% international; 67% from in state; 96% live on campus; 1% of students in fraternities, 1% in sororities
Most popular majors: 16% Business Administration and Management, General, 13% Exercise Physiology, 9% Biology/Biological Sciences, General, 9% Elementary Education and Teaching, 9% Psychology, General
Expenses: 2020-2021: $18,600; room/board: $10,280
Financial aid: (641) 628-5336; 81% of undergrads determined to have financial need; average aid package $33,653

Clarke University

Dubuque IA
(563) 588-6316
U.S. News ranking: Nat. U., No. 227
Website: www.clarke.edu
Admissions email: admissions@clarke.edu
Private; founded 1843
Affiliation: Roman Catholic
Freshman admissions: selective; 2019-2020: 1,074 applied, 1,008 accepted. Either SAT or ACT required. ACT 25/75 percentile: 18-23. High school rank: 17% in top tenth, 37% in top quarter, 78% in top half
Early decision deadline: N/A, notification date: N/A
Early action deadline: N/A, notification date: N/A
Application deadline (fall): rolling
Undergraduate student body: 622 full time, 40 part time; 46% male, 54% female; 0% American Indian, 1% Asian, 9% Black, 11% Hispanic, 3% multiracial, 1% Pacific Islander, 69% white, 2% international; 40% from in state; 58% live on campus; N/A of students in fraternities, N/A in sororities
Most popular majors: 30% Health Professions and Related Programs, 15% Psychology, 14% Business, Management, Marketing, and Related Support Services, 10% Education, 8% Biological and Biomedical Sciences

Expenses: 2020-2021: $35,750; room/board: $10,200
Financial aid: (563) 588-6327; 58% of undergrads determined to have financial need; average aid package $30,781

Coe College

Cedar Rapids IA
(319) 399-8500
U.S. News ranking: Nat. Lib. Arts, No. 130
Website: www.coe.edu
Admissions email: admission@coe.edu
Private; founded 1851
Freshman admissions: more selective; 2019-2020: 7,431 applied, 4,706 accepted. Either SAT or ACT required. ACT 25/75 percentile: 21-27. High school rank: 26% in top tenth, 55% in top quarter, 86% in top half
Early decision deadline: N/A, notification date: N/A
Early action deadline: 12/10, notification date: 1/20
Application deadline (fall): 3/1
Undergraduate student body: 1,380 full time, 48 part time; 45% male, 55% female; 0% American Indian, 5% Asian, 7% Black, 12% Hispanic, 3% multiracial, 0% Pacific Islander, 68% white, 1% international; 46% from in state; 86% live on campus; 21% of students in fraternities, 21% in sororities
Most popular majors: 21% Business, Management, Marketing, and Related Support Services, 9% Psychology, 8% Physical Sciences, 7% Biological and Biomedical Sciences, 7% Education
Expenses: 2020-2021: $47,220; room/board: $10,174
Financial aid: (319) 399-8540; 83% of undergrads determined to have financial need; average aid package $39,070

Cornell College

Mount Vernon IA
(800) 747-1112
U.S. News ranking: Nat. Lib. Arts, No. 76
Website: www.cornellcollege.edu
Admissions email: admission@cornellcollege.edu
Private; founded 1853
Affiliation: United Methodist
Freshman admissions: more selective; 2019-2020: 3,118 applied, 1,926 accepted. Neither SAT nor ACT required. ACT 25/75 percentile: 23-29. High school rank: 17% in top tenth, 47% in top quarter, 83% in top half
Early decision deadline: N/A, notification date: N/A
Early action deadline: 11/1, notification date: N/A
Application deadline (fall): rolling
Undergraduate student body: 1,017 full time, 3 part time; 53% male, 47% female; 1% American Indian, 3% Asian, 6% Black, 7% Hispanic, 2% multiracial, 0% Pacific Islander, 71% white, 7% international; 24% from in state; 93% live on campus; 24% of students in fraternities, 36% in sororities

Most popular majors: 11% Biological and Biomedical Sciences, 10% Business, Management, Marketing, and Related Support Services, 10% Social Sciences, 9% Parks, Recreation, Leisure, and Fitness Studies, 8% Education
Expenses: 2020-2021: $45,914; room/board: $10,150
Financial aid: (319) 895-4216; 69% of undergrads determined to have financial need; average aid package $33,307

Dordt University

Sioux Center IA
(800) 343-6738
U.S. News ranking: Reg. Coll. (Mid. W), No. 4
Website: www.dordt.edu
Admissions email: admissions@dordt.edu
Private; founded 1955
Affiliation: Christian Reformed Church
Freshman admissions: more selective; 2019-2020: 1,558 applied, 1,147 accepted. Neither SAT nor ACT required. ACT 25/75 percentile: 22-28. High school rank: 23% in top tenth, 49% in top quarter, 79% in top half
Early decision deadline: N/A, notification date: N/A
Early action deadline: N/A, notification date: N/A
Application deadline (fall): 8/16
Undergraduate student body: 1,319 full time, 67 part time; 54% male, 46% female; 0% American Indian, 3% Asian, 2% Black, 4% Hispanic, 1% multiracial, 0% Pacific Islander, 77% white, 8% international; 44% from in state; 91% live on campus; 0% of students in fraternities, 0% in sororities
Most popular majors: 23% Elementary Education and Teaching, 19% Business/Commerce, General, 9% Engineering, General, 8% Agricultural Business and Management, General, 6% Registered Nursing/Registered Nurse
Expenses: 2020-2021: $32,820; room/board: $10,470
Financial aid: (712) 722-6082; 68% of undergrads determined to have financial need; average aid package $26,434

Drake University

Des Moines IA
(800) 443-7253
U.S. News ranking: Nat. U., No. 124
Website: www.drake.edu
Admissions email: admission@drake.edu
Private; founded 1881
Freshman admissions: more selective; 2019-2020: 6,944 applied, 4,697 accepted. Neither SAT nor ACT required. ACT 25/75 percentile: 24-31. High school rank: 41% in top tenth, 69% in top quarter, 90% in top half
Early decision deadline: N/A, notification date: N/A
Early action deadline: N/A, notification date: N/A

Application deadline (fall): rolling
Undergraduate student body: 2,830 full time, 124 part time; 41% male, 59% female; 0% American Indian, 5% Asian, 6% Black, 7% Hispanic, 3% multiracial, 0% Pacific Islander, 76% white, 4% international; 61% from in state; 70% live on campus; 37% of students in fraternities, 29% in sororities
Most popular majors: 32% Business, Management, Marketing, and Related Support Services, 11% Communication, Journalism, and Related Programs, 6% Biological and Biomedical Sciences, 6% Education, 6% Social Sciences
Expenses: 2020-2021: $44,366; room/board: $11,152
Financial aid: (515) 271-2905; 64% of undergrads determined to have financial need; average aid package $30,942

Graceland University

Lamoni IA
(866) 472-2352
U.S. News ranking: Reg. U. (Mid. W), second tier
Website: www.graceland.edu
Admissions email: admissions@graceland.edu
Private; founded 1895
Affiliation: Other
Freshman admissions: selective; 2019-2020: 2,514 applied, 1,461 accepted. Either SAT or ACT required. ACT 25/75 percentile: 18-24. High school rank: 12% in top tenth, 34% in top quarter, 70% in top half
Early decision deadline: N/A, notification date: N/A
Early action deadline: N/A, notification date: N/A
Application deadline (fall): rolling
Undergraduate student body: 898 full time, 140 part time; 44% male, 56% female; 1% American Indian, 1% Asian, 9% Black, 10% Hispanic, 4% multiracial, 2% Pacific Islander, 62% white, 6% international; 28% from in state; 78% live on campus; N/A of students in fraternities, N/A in sororities
Most popular majors: 27% Health Professions and Related Programs, 18% Business, Management, Marketing, and Related Support Services, 12% Education, 8% Parks, Recreation, Leisure, and Fitness Studies, 4% Psychology
Expenses: 2020-2021: $31,320; room/board: $9,440
Financial aid: (641) 784-5051; 83% of undergrads determined to have financial need; average aid package $22,852

Grand View University

Des Moines IA
(515) 263-2810
U.S. News ranking: Reg. Coll. (Mid. W), No. 42
Website: www.grandview.edu
Admissions email: admissions@grandview.edu
Private; founded 1896
Affiliation: Evangelical Lutheran Church

Freshman admissions: selective; 2019-2020: 1,526 applied, 1,463 accepted. Either SAT or ACT required. ACT 25/75 percentile: 17-22. High school rank: 14% in top tenth, 38% in top quarter, 66% in top half
Early decision deadline: N/A, notification date: N/A
Early action deadline: N/A, notification date: N/A
Application deadline (fall): 8/15
Undergraduate student body: 1,591 full time, 166 part time; 46% male, 54% female; 0% American Indian, 3% Asian, 8% Black, 8% Hispanic, 4% multiracial, 0% Pacific Islander, 64% white, 3% international; 86% from in state; 50% live on campus; 0% of students in fraternities, 0% in sororities
Most popular majors: 29% Business, Management, Marketing, and Related Support Services, 9% Health Professions and Related Programs, 9% Parks, Recreation, Leisure, and Fitness Studies, 8% Psychology, 7% Biological and Biomedical Sciences
Expenses: 2020-2021: $29,960; room/board: $9,614
Financial aid: (515) 263-2853; 80% of undergrads determined to have financial need; average aid package $22,957

Grinnell College
Grinnell IA
(800) 247-0113
U.S. News ranking: Nat. Lib. Arts, No. 13
Website: www.grinnell.edu
Admissions email: admission@grinnell.edu
Private; founded 1846
Freshman admissions: most selective; 2019-2020: 8,004 applied, 1,847 accepted. Either SAT or ACT required. SAT 25/75 percentile: 1370-1530. High school rank: 62% in top tenth, 87% in top quarter, 98% in top half
Early decision deadline: 11/15, notification date: 12/15
Early action deadline: N/A, notification date: N/A
Application deadline (fall): 1/15
Undergraduate student body: 1,700 full time, 33 part time; 47% male, 53% female; 0% American Indian, 8% Asian, 5% Black, 8% Hispanic, 4% multiracial, 0% Pacific Islander, 51% white, 20% international; 9% from in state; 88% live on campus; 0% of students in fraternities, 0% in sororities
Most popular majors: 22% Social Sciences, 15% Biological and Biomedical Sciences, 11% Computer and Information Sciences and Support Services, 9% Foreign Languages, Literatures, and Linguistics, 8% Physical Sciences
Expenses: 2020-2021: $56,680; room/board: $13,864
Financial aid: (641) 269-3250; 65% of undergrads determined to have financial need; average aid package $51,571

Iowa State University
Ames IA
(515) 294-2592
U.S. News ranking: Nat. U., No. 118
Website: www.iastate.edu
Admissions email: admissions@iastate.edu
Public; founded 1858
Freshman admissions: more selective; 2019-2020: 18,246 applied, 16,796 accepted. Either SAT or ACT required. ACT 25/75 percentile: 22-28. High school rank: 28% in top tenth, 62% in top quarter, 93% in top half
Early decision deadline: N/A, notification date: N/A
Early action deadline: N/A, notification date: N/A
Application deadline (fall): rolling
Undergraduate student body: 26,707 full time, 1,587 part time; 57% male, 43% female; 0% American Indian, 4% Asian, 3% Black, 6% Hispanic, 3% multiracial, 0% Pacific Islander, 76% white, 5% international; 63% from in state; 20% live on campus; 14% of students in fraternities, 18% in sororities
Most popular majors: 22% Engineering, 18% Business, Management, Marketing, and Related Support Services, 11% Agriculture, Agriculture Operations, and Related Sciences, 6% Biological and Biomedical Sciences, 4% Education
Expenses: 2020-2021: $9,320 in state, $24,508 out of state; room/board: $9,193
Financial aid: (515) 294-2223; 52% of undergrads determined to have financial need; average aid package $13,440

Iowa Wesleyan University
Mount Pleasant IA
(319) 385-6231
U.S. News ranking: Reg. Coll. (Mid. W), second tier
Website: www.iw.edu
Admissions email: admit@iw.edu
Private; founded 1842
Affiliation: United Methodist
Freshman admissions: selective; 2019-2020: 4,345 applied, 2,974 accepted. Either SAT or ACT required. ACT 25/75 percentile: 18-21. High school rank: 9% in top tenth, 15% in top quarter, 52% in top half
Early decision deadline: N/A, notification date: N/A
Early action deadline: N/A, notification date: N/A
Application deadline (fall): rolling
Undergraduate student body: 560 full time, 31 part time; 48% male, 52% female; 0% American Indian, 1% Asian, 19% Black, 8% Hispanic, 7% multiracial, 1% Pacific Islander, 40% white, 17% international; 35% from in state; 77% live on campus; N/A of students in fraternities, N/A in sororities
Most popular majors: 25% Business, Management, Marketing, and Related Support Services, 15% Homeland Security, Law Enforcement, Firefighting and Related Protective Services, 9% Education, 9% Parks, Recreation,

Leisure, and Fitness Studies, 8% Health Professions and Related Programs
Expenses: 2020-2021: $32,600; room/board: $11,010
Financial aid: (319) 385-6242; 96% of undergrads determined to have financial need; average aid package $26,895

Loras College
Dubuque IA
(800) 245-6727
U.S. News ranking: Reg. Coll. (Mid. W), No. 16
Website: www.loras.edu
Admissions email: admission@loras.edu
Private; founded 1839
Affiliation: Roman Catholic
Freshman admissions: selective; 2019-2020: 1,491 applied, 1,123 accepted. Either SAT or ACT required. ACT 25/75 percentile: 20-25. High school rank: N/A
Early decision deadline: N/A, notification date: N/A
Early action deadline: N/A, notification date: N/A
Application deadline (fall): rolling
Undergraduate student body: 1,264 full time, 53 part time; 57% male, 43% female; 0% American Indian, 1% Asian, 4% Black, 9% Hispanic, 2% multiracial, 0% Pacific Islander, 79% white, 2% international; 41% from in state; 61% live on campus; N/A of students in fraternities, N/A in sororities
Most popular majors: 5% Business Administration and Management, General, 4% Elementary Education and Teaching, 4% Psychology, General, 3% Criminal Justice/Safety Studies, 3% Public Relations/Image Management
Expenses: 2020-2021: $35,218; room/board: $8,600
Financial aid: (563) 588-7817; 81% of undergrads determined to have financial need; average aid package $29,160

Luther College
Decorah IA
(563) 387-1287
U.S. News ranking: Nat. Lib. Arts, No. 102
Website: www.luther.edu
Admissions email: admissions@luther.edu
Private; founded 1861
Affiliation: Evangelical Lutheran Church
Freshman admissions: more selective; 2019-2020: 4,108 applied, 2,558 accepted. Either SAT or ACT required. ACT 25/75 percentile: 22-28. High school rank: 26% in top tenth, 51% in top quarter, 84% in top half
Early decision deadline: N/A, notification date: N/A
Early action deadline: N/A, notification date: N/A
Application deadline (fall): rolling
Undergraduate student body: 1,930 full time, 21 part time; 43% male, 57% female; 0% American Indian, 2% Asian, 2% Black, 6% Hispanic, 2% multiracial, 0% Pacific Islander, 78% white, 9% international; 29% from in

state; 93% live on campus; 1% of students in fraternities, 2% in sororities
Most popular majors: 13% Business Administration and Management, General, 12% Music, General, 11% Biology/Biological Sciences, General, 9% Registered Nursing/Registered Nurse, 8% Research and Experimental Psychology, Other
Expenses: 2020-2021: $45,610; room/board: $10,110
Financial aid: (563) 387-1018

Maharishi International University[1]
Fairfield IA
(641) 472-7000
U.S. News ranking: Reg. U. (Mid. W), second tier
Website: www.mum.edu
Admissions email: admissions@mum.edu
Private
Application deadline (fall): N/A
Undergraduate student body: N/A full time, N/A part time
Expenses: 2019-2020: $16,530; room/board: $7,400
Financial aid: N/A

Morningside College
Sioux City IA
(712) 274-5111
U.S. News ranking: Reg. U. (Mid. W), No. 65
Website: www.morningside.edu
Admissions email: admissions@morningside.edu
Private; founded 1894
Affiliation: United Methodist
Freshman admissions: selective; 2019-2020: 3,717 applied, 2,341 accepted. Either SAT or ACT required. ACT 25/75 percentile: 19-25. High school rank: 17% in top tenth, 40% in top quarter, 69% in top half
Early decision deadline: N/A, notification date: N/A
Early action deadline: N/A, notification date: N/A
Application deadline (fall): rolling
Undergraduate student body: 1,183 full time, 94 part time; 50% male, 50% female; 0% American Indian, 1% Asian, 2% Black, 7% Hispanic, 4% multiracial, 0% Pacific Islander, 73% white, 5% international; 52% from in state; 61% live on campus; N/A of students in fraternities, N/A in sororities
Most popular majors: 17% Business, Management, Marketing, and Related Support Services, 15% Education, 10% Biological and Biomedical Sciences, 9% Health Professions and Related Programs, 8% Psychology
Expenses: 2020-2021: $33,970; room/board: $10,110
Financial aid: (712) 274-5159; 81% of undergrads determined to have financial need; average aid package $27,364

state; 93% live on campus; 1% of students in fraternities, 2% in sororities
Most popular majors: 13% Business Administration and Management, General, 12% Music, General, 11% Biology/Biological Sciences, General, 9% Registered Nursing/Registered Nurse, 8% Research and Experimental Psychology, Other

Mount Mercy University
Cedar Rapids IA
(319) 368-6460
U.S. News ranking: Reg. U. (Mid. W), No. 51
Website: www.mtmercy.edu
Admissions email: admission@mtmercy.edu
Private; founded 1928
Affiliation: Roman Catholic
Freshman admissions: selective; 2019-2020: 1,176 applied, 776 accepted. Either SAT or ACT required. ACT 25/75 percentile: 18-24. High school rank: 18% in top tenth, 41% in top quarter, 81% in top half
Early decision deadline: N/A, notification date: N/A
Early action deadline: N/A, notification date: N/A
Application deadline (fall): rolling
Undergraduate student body: 1,070 full time, 372 part time; 32% male, 68% female; 1% American Indian, 2% Asian, 9% Black, 1% Hispanic, 2% multiracial, 1% Pacific Islander, 76% white, 4% international; 84% from in state; 43% live on campus; 0% of students in fraternities, 0% in sororities
Most popular majors: 30% Registered Nursing/Registered Nurse, 10% Business/Commerce, General, 7% Business Administration and Management, General, 6% Elementary Education and Teaching, 5% Human Resources Management/Personnel Administration, General
Expenses: 2020-2021: $35,574; room/board: $10,112
Financial aid: (319) 368-6467; 58% of undergrads determined to have financial need; average aid package $25,253

Northwestern College
Orange City IA
(800) 747-4757
U.S. News ranking: Reg. Coll. (Mid. W), No. 6
Website: www.nwciowa.edu
Admissions email: admissions@nwciowa.edu
Private; founded 1882
Affiliation: Reformed Church in America
Freshman admissions: more selective; 2019-2020: 1,345 applied, 938 accepted. Either SAT or ACT required. ACT 25/75 percentile: 21-27. High school rank: 23% in top tenth, 49% in top quarter, 75% in top half
Early decision deadline: N/A, notification date: N/A
Early action deadline: N/A, notification date: N/A
Application deadline (fall): rolling
Undergraduate student body: 968 full time, 93 part time; 45% male, 55% female; 0% American Indian, 1% Asian, 2% Black, 5% Hispanic, 2% multiracial, 0% Pacific Islander, 83% white, 3% international; 55% from in state; 83% live on campus; 0% of students in fraternities, 0% in sororities
Most popular majors: 15% Business Administration and

Management, General, 13% Elementary Education and Teaching, 11% Registered Nursing/Registered Nurse, 8% Biology/Biological Sciences, General, 5% Psychology, General
Expenses: 2020-2021: $32,920; room/board: $9,800
Financial aid: (712) 707-7131; 74% of undergrads determined to have financial need; average aid package $26,448

Simpson College
Indianola IA
(515) 961-1624
U.S. News ranking: Nat. Lib. Arts, No. 149
Website: www.simpson.edu
Admissions email: admiss@simpson.edu
Private; founded 1860
Affiliation: United Methodist
Freshman admissions: selective; 2019-2020: 1,611 applied, 1,297 accepted. Neither SAT nor ACT required. ACT 25/75 percentile: 19-25. High school rank: 21% in top tenth, 53% in top quarter, 85% in top half
Early decision deadline: N/A, notification date: N/A
Early action deadline: N/A, notification date: N/A
Application deadline (fall): rolling
Undergraduate student body: 1,159 full time, 146 part time; 47% male, 53% female; 0% American Indian, 2% Asian, 3% Black, 6% Hispanic, 4% multiracial, 0% Pacific Islander, 80% white, 1% international; 81% from in state; 79% live on campus; 22% of students in fraternities, 26% in sororities
Most popular majors: 13% Business Administration and Management, General, 8% Elementary Education and Teaching, 7% Criminal Justice/ Safety Studies, 7% Psychology, General, 6% Accounting
Expenses: 2020-2021: $42,246; room/board: $9,282
Financial aid: (515) 961-1596; 84% of undergrads determined to have financial need; average aid package $34,223

St. Ambrose University
Davenport IA
(563) 333-6300
U.S. News ranking: Reg. U. (Mid. W), No. 27
Website: www.sau.edu
Admissions email: admit@sau.edu
Private; founded 1882
Affiliation: Roman Catholic
Freshman admissions: selective; 2019-2020: 4,877 applied, 3,115 accepted. Either SAT or ACT required. ACT 25/75 percentile: 20-25. High school rank: 27% in top tenth, 56% in top quarter, 84% in top half
Early decision deadline: N/A, notification date: N/A
Early action deadline: N/A, notification date: N/A
Application deadline (fall): rolling
Undergraduate student body: 2,122 full time, 138 part time; 45% male, 55% female; 0% American Indian, 1% Asian, 5% Black,

9% Hispanic, 3% multiracial, 0% Pacific Islander, 74% white, 4% international; 34% from in state; 69% live on campus; 0% of students in fraternities, 0% in sororities
Most popular majors: 30% Business, Management, Marketing, and Related Support Services, 12% Health Professions and Related Programs, 12% Psychology, 9% Parks, Recreation, Leisure, and Fitness Studies, 7% Education
Expenses: 2020-2021: $32,758; room/board: $11,354
Financial aid: (563) 333-6318; 74% of undergrads determined to have financial need; average aid package $24,736

University of Dubuque
Dubuque IA
(563) 589-3200
U.S. News ranking: Reg. U. (Mid. W), No. 98
Website: www.dbq.edu
Admissions email: admssns@dbq.edu
Private; founded 1852
Affiliation: Presbyterian Church (USA)
Freshman admissions: less selective; 2019-2020: 2,054 applied, 1,493 accepted. Either SAT or ACT required. ACT 25/75 percentile: 17-22. High school rank: 8% in top tenth, 19% in top quarter, 49% in top half
Early decision deadline: N/A, notification date: N/A
Early action deadline: N/A, notification date: N/A
Application deadline (fall): rolling
Undergraduate student body: 1,554 full time, 346 part time; 55% male, 45% female; 0% American Indian, 1% Asian, 14% Black, 8% Hispanic, 3% multiracial, 0% Pacific Islander, 63% white, 7% international; 46% from in state; 42% live on campus; N/A of students in fraternities, N/A in sororities
Most popular majors: 30% Business, Management, Marketing, and Related Support Services, 10% Parks, Recreation, Leisure, and Fitness Studies, 9% Health Professions and Related Programs, 9% Homeland Security, Law Enforcement, Firefighting and Related Protective Services, 9% Transportation and Materials Moving
Expenses: 2020-2021: $36,610; room/board: $10,500
Financial aid: (563) 589-3125; 79% of undergrads determined to have financial need; average aid package $31,434

University of Iowa
Iowa City IA
(319) 335-3847
U.S. News ranking: Nat. U., No. 88
Website: www.uiowa.edu
Admissions email: admissions@uiowa.edu
Public; founded 1847
Freshman admissions: more selective; 2019-2020: 25,928 applied, 21,404 accepted. Either SAT or ACT required. ACT 25/75 percentile: 22-29. High school

rank: 32% in top tenth, 63% in top quarter, 93% in top half
Early decision deadline: N/A, notification date: N/A
Early action deadline: N/A, notification date: N/A
Application deadline (fall): 5/1
Undergraduate student body: 21,212 full time, 2,270 part time; 46% male, 54% female; 0% American Indian, 4% Asian, 3% Black, 8% Hispanic, 3% multiracial, 0% Pacific Islander, 74% white, 5% international; 62% from in state; 28% live on campus; 13% of students in fraternities, 17% in sororities
Most popular majors: 22% Business, Management, Marketing, and Related Support Services, 12% Parks, Recreation, Leisure, and Fitness Studies, 9% Social Sciences, 8% Engineering, 6% Communication, Journalism, and Related Programs
Expenses: 2020-2021: $9,605 in state, $31,568 out of state; room/ board: $11,590
Financial aid: (319) 335-1450; 48% of undergrads determined to have financial need; average aid package $12,652

University of Northern Iowa
Cedar Falls IA
(800) 772-2037
U.S. News ranking: Reg. U. (Mid. W), No. 24
Website: uni.edu/
Admissions email: admissions@uni.edu
Public; founded 1876
Affiliation: Undenominational
Freshman admissions: selective; 2019-2020: 4,779 applied, 3,756 accepted. Either SAT or ACT required. ACT 25/75 percentile: 20-26. High school rank: 20% in top tenth, 45% in top quarter, 84% in top half
Early decision deadline: N/A, notification date: N/A
Early action deadline: N/A, notification date: N/A
Application deadline (fall): 8/15
Undergraduate student body: 8,228 full time, 745 part time; 41% male, 59% female; 0% American Indian, 1% Asian, 2% Black, 4% Hispanic, 3% multiracial, 0% Pacific Islander, 83% white, 2% international; 94% from in state; 35% live on campus; 3% of students in fraternities, 5% in sororities
Most popular majors: 21% Business, Management, Marketing, and Related Support Services, 17% Education, 7% Communication, Journalism, and Related Programs, 7% Parks, Recreation, Leisure, and Fitness Studies, 5% Social Sciences
Expenses: 2020-2021: $8,938 in state, $19,480 out of state; room/ board: $9,160
Financial aid: (319) 273-2722; 61% of undergrads determined to have financial need; average aid package $8,442

Upper Iowa University[1]
Fayette IA
(800) 553-4150
U.S. News ranking: Reg. U. (Mid. W), second tier
Website: uiu.edu/
Admissions email: admission@uiu.edu
Private; founded 1857
Application deadline (fall): rolling
Undergraduate student body: N/A full time, N/A part time
Expenses: 2019-2020: $31,685; room/board: $8,706
Financial aid: (563) 425-5299

Waldorf University[1]
Forest City IA
(641) 585-8112
U.S. News ranking: Reg. U. (Mid. W), second tier
Website: www.waldorf.edu
Admissions email: admissions@waldorf.edu
For-profit
Application deadline (fall): N/A
Undergraduate student body: N/A full time, N/A part time
Expenses: 2019-2020: $22,352; room/board: $7,618
Financial aid: N/A

Wartburg College
Waverly IA
(319) 352-8264
U.S. News ranking: Nat. Lib. Arts, No. 162
Website: www.wartburg.edu/
Admissions email: admissions@wartburg.edu
Private; founded 1852
Affiliation: Evangelical Lutheran Church
Freshman admissions: selective; 2019-2020: 4,018 applied, 3,019 accepted. Either SAT or ACT required. ACT 25/75 percentile: 21-26. High school rank: 21% in top tenth, 56% in top quarter, 80% in top half
Early decision deadline: N/A, notification date: N/A
Early action deadline: 12/1, notification date: N/A
Application deadline (fall): rolling
Undergraduate student body: 1,462 full time, 39 part time; 46% male, 54% female; 0% American Indian, 1% Asian, 4% Black, 5% Hispanic, 3% multiracial, 0% Pacific Islander, 78% white, 8% international; 65% from in state; 86% live on campus; N/A of students in fraternities, N/A in sororities
Most popular majors: 20% Business/Commerce, General, 10% Biology/Biological Sciences, General, 6% Accounting, 6% Mass Communication/Media Studies, 6% Music Teacher Education
Expenses: 2020-2021: $45,680; room/board: $9,592
Financial aid: (319) 352-8262; 76% of undergrads determined to have financial need; average aid package $34,888

William Penn University[1]
Oskaloosa IA
(641) 673-1012
U.S. News ranking: Reg. Coll. (Mid. W), second tier
Website: www.wmpenn.edu
Admissions email: admissions@wmpenn.edu
Private
Application deadline (fall): N/A
Undergraduate student body: N/A full time, N/A part time
Expenses: 2019-2020: $26,100; room/board: $7,072
Financial aid: N/A

KANSAS

Baker University
Baldwin City KS
(800) 873-4282
U.S. News ranking: Nat. U., No. 258
Website: www.bakeru.edu
Admissions email: admission@bakeru.edu
Private; founded 1858
Affiliation: United Methodist
Freshman admissions: selective; 2019-2020: 839 applied, 738 accepted. Either SAT or ACT required. ACT 25/75 percentile: 20-25. High school rank: 21% in top tenth, 44% in top quarter, 73% in top half
Early decision deadline: N/A, notification date: N/A
Early action deadline: N/A, notification date: N/A
Application deadline (fall): rolling
Undergraduate student body: 851 full time, 284 part time; 50% male, 50% female; 1% American Indian, 1% Asian, 8% Black, 10% Hispanic, 6% multiracial, 1% Pacific Islander, 70% white, 3% international; 72% from in state; 83% live on campus; 39% of students in fraternities, 43% in sororities
Most popular majors: 21% Business Administration and Management, General, 8% Elementary Education and Teaching, 7% Biology/Biological Sciences, General, 7% Kinesiology and Exercise Science, 7% Psychology, General
Expenses: 2020-2021: $30,670; room/board: $8,350
Financial aid: (785) 594-4595; 78% of undergrads determined to have financial need; average aid package $25,254

Benedictine College
Atchison KS
(800) 467-5340
U.S. News ranking: Reg. Coll. (Mid. W), No. 14
Website: www.benedictine.edu
Admissions email: bcadmiss@benedictine.edu
Private; founded 1858
Affiliation: Roman Catholic
Freshman admissions: selective; 2019-2020: 2,263 applied, 2,198 accepted. Either SAT or ACT required. ACT 25/75 percentile: 21-28. High school rank: 15% in top tenth, 42% in top quarter, 71% in top half

Early decision deadline: N/A, notification date: N/A
Early action deadline: N/A, notification date: N/A
Application deadline (fall): rolling
Undergraduate student body: 1,936 full time, 149 part time; 48% male, 52% female; 1% American Indian, 1% Asian, 3% Black, 9% Hispanic, 4% multiracial, 0% Pacific Islander, 78% white, 2% international; 23% from in state; 80% live on campus; 0% of students in fraternities, 0% in sororities
Most popular majors: 22% Business, Management, Marketing, and Related Support Services, 14% Education, 12% Theology and Religious Vocations, 8% Social Sciences, 5% Health Professions and Related Programs
Expenses: 2020-2021: $31,630; room/board: $10,780
Financial aid: (913) 360-7484; 64% of undergrads determined to have financial need; average aid package $22,806

Bethany College
Lindsborg KS
(800) 826-2281
U.S. News ranking: Reg. Coll. (Mid. W), second tier
Website: www.bethanylb.edu
Admissions email: admissions@bethanylb.edu
Private; founded 1881
Affiliation: Evangelical Lutheran Church
Freshman admissions: less selective; 2019-2020: N/A applied, N/A accepted. Either SAT or ACT required. ACT 25/75 percentile: 18-23. High school rank: N/A
Early decision deadline: N/A, notification date: N/A
Early action deadline: N/A, notification date: N/A
Application deadline (fall): rolling
Undergraduate student body: 753 full time, 62 part time; 54% male, 46% female; N/A American Indian, N/A Asian, N/A Black, N/A Hispanic, N/A multiracial, N/A Pacific Islander, N/A white, N/A international
Most popular majors: Information not available
Expenses: 2020-2021: $30,580; room/board: $12,360
Financial aid: (785) 227-3380

Bethel College
North Newton KS
(800) 522-1887
U.S. News ranking: Reg. Coll. (Mid. W), No. 26
Website: www.bethelks.edu
Admissions email: admissions@bethelks.edu
Private; founded 1887
Affiliation: Mennonite Church
Freshman admissions: selective; 2019-2020: 943 applied, 542 accepted. Either SAT or ACT required. ACT 25/75 percentile: 18-24. High school rank: 15% in top tenth, 42% in top quarter, 77% in top half
Early decision deadline: N/A, notification date: N/A

Early action deadline: N/A, notification date: N/A
Application deadline (fall): N/A
Undergraduate student body: 444 full time, 12 part time; 52% male, 48% female; 1% American Indian, 2% Asian, 18% Black, 10% Hispanic, 2% multiracial, 0% Pacific Islander, 62% white, 5% international; N/A from in state; 70% live on campus; 0% of students in fraternities, 0% in sororities
Most popular majors: 41% Health Professions and Related Programs, 14% Business, Management, Marketing and Related Support Services, 9% Biological and Biomedical Sciences, 6% Psychology, 6% Public Administration and Social Service Professions
Expenses: 2020-2021: $30,264; room/board: $9,670
Financial aid: (316) 284-5232; 90% of undergrads determined to have financial need; average aid package $28,739

Central Christian College
McPherson KS
(620) 241-0723
U.S. News ranking: Reg. Coll. (Mid. W), second tier
Website: www.centralchristian.edu
Admissions email: admissions@centralchristian.edu
Private; founded 2004
Affiliation: Free Methodist
Freshman admissions: less selective; 2019-2020: 164 applied, 162 accepted. Neither SAT nor ACT required. ACT 25/75 percentile: 15-20. High school rank: 2% in top tenth, 14% in top quarter, 49% in top half
Early decision deadline: N/A, notification date: N/A
Early action deadline: N/A, notification date: N/A
Application deadline (fall): rolling
Undergraduate student body: 580 full time, 97 part time; 45% male, 55% female; 2% American Indian, 0% Asian, 17% Black, 15% Hispanic, 4% multiracial, 0% Pacific Islander, 55% white, 3% international; N/A from in state; N/A live on campus; 0% of students in fraternities, 0% in sororities
Most popular majors: 31% Homeland Security, Law Enforcement, Firefighting and Related Protective Services, 22% Business, Management, Marketing, and Related Support Services, 12% Liberal Arts and Sciences, General Studies and Humanities, 5% Parks, Recreation, Leisure, and Fitness Studies, 3% Psychology
Expenses: 2020-2021: $28,725; room/board: $7,500
Financial aid: (620) 241-0723; 89% of undergrads determined to have financial need; average aid package $13,785

Donnelly College
Kansas City KS
(913) 621-8700
U.S. News ranking: Reg. Coll. (Mid. W), second tier
Website: donnelly.edu
Admissions email: admissions@donnelly.edu
Private; founded 1949
Affiliation: Roman Catholic
Freshman admissions: less selective; 2019-2020: N/A applied, N/A accepted. Neither SAT nor ACT required. SAT 25/75 percentile: N/A. High school rank: N/A
Early decision deadline: N/A, notification date: N/A
Early action deadline: N/A, notification date: N/A
Application deadline (fall): rolling
Undergraduate student body: 164 full time, 139 part time; 29% male, 71% female; 2% American Indian, 8% Asian, 35% Black, 37% Hispanic, 3% multiracial, 0% Pacific Islander, 12% white, 1% international
Most popular majors: 41% Licensed Practical/Vocational Nurse Training, 29% Liberal Arts and Sciences/Liberal Studies, 14% Registered Nursing/Registered Nurse, 9% Non-Profit/Public/Organizational Management, 5% Information Technology
Expenses: 2019-2020: $7,740; room/board: N/A
Financial aid: N/A

Emporia State University
Emporia KS
(620) 341-5465
U.S. News ranking: Reg. U. (Mid. W), No. 85
Website: www.emporia.edu
Admissions email: go2esu@emporia.edu
Public; founded 1863
Freshman admissions: selective; 2019-2020: 1,670 applied, 1,414 accepted. Neither SAT nor ACT required. ACT 25/75 percentile: 19-25. High school rank: 15% in top tenth, 38% in top quarter, 73% in top half
Early decision deadline: N/A, notification date: N/A
Early action deadline: N/A, notification date: N/A
Application deadline (fall): rolling
Undergraduate student body: 3,101 full time, 304 part time; 37% male, 63% female; 0% American Indian, 1% Asian, 5% Black, 7% Hispanic, 10% multiracial, 0% Pacific Islander, 70% white, 5% international; 91% from in state; 23% live on campus; 11% of students in fraternities, 8% in sororities
Most popular majors: 26% Education, 19% Business, Management, Marketing, and Related Support Services, 12% Health Professions and Related Programs, 6% Liberal Arts and Sciences, General Studies and Humanities, 6% Psychology
Expenses: 2020-2021: $6,971 in state, $21,221 out of state; room/board: $9,212

Financial aid: (620) 341-5457; 61% of undergrads determined to have financial need; average aid package $9,587

Fort Hays State University
Hays KS
(800) 628-3478
U.S. News ranking: Reg. U. (Mid. W), No. 112
Website: www.fhsu.edu
Admissions email: tigers@fhsu.edu
Public; founded 1902
Freshman admissions: selective; 2019-2020: 2,056 applied, 1,874 accepted. Neither SAT nor ACT required. ACT 25/75 percentile: 17-29. High school rank: 15% in top tenth, 35% in top quarter, 66% in top half
Early decision deadline: N/A, notification date: N/A
Early action deadline: N/A, notification date: N/A
Application deadline (fall): rolling
Undergraduate student body: 5,726 full time, 7,402 part time; 40% male, 60% female; 0% American Indian, 1% Asian, 3% Black, 8% Hispanic, 2% multiracial, 0% Pacific Islander, 50% white, 36% international; 71% from in state; 11% live on campus; 2% of students in fraternities, 2% in sororities
Most popular majors: 39% Business, Management, Marketing, and Related Support Services, 11% Education, 10% Liberal Arts and Sciences, General Studies and Humanities, 8% Health Professions and Related Programs, 8% Social Sciences
Expenses: 2019-2020: $5,280 in state, $15,360 out of state; room/board: $8,210
Financial aid: (785) 628-4408

Friends University
Wichita KS
(316) 295-5100
U.S. News ranking: Reg. U. (Mid. W), No. 98
Website: www.friends.edu
Admissions email: admission@friends.edu
Private; founded 1898
Freshman admissions: selective; 2019-2020: 1,266 applied, 580 accepted. Either SAT or ACT required. ACT 25/75 percentile: 19-25. High school rank: 18% in top tenth, 43% in top quarter, 70% in top half
Early decision deadline: N/A, notification date: N/A
Early action deadline: N/A, notification date: N/A
Application deadline (fall): rolling
Undergraduate student body: 860 full time, 431 part time; 45% male, 55% female; 1% American Indian, 2% Asian, 9% Black, 10% Hispanic, 6% multiracial, 0% Pacific Islander, 59% white, 3% international; 68% from in state; 34% live on campus; 0% of students in fraternities, 0% in sororities
Most popular majors: 37% Business, Management, Marketing, and Related Support Services, 10% Education, 8% Biological and Biomedical

Sciences, 7% Psychology, 6% Computer and Information Sciences and Support Services
Expenses: 2020-2021: $30,120; room/board: $8,350
Financial aid: (316) 295-5200; 79% of undergrads determined to have financial need; average aid package $20,124

Hesston College
Hesston KS
(620) 327-4221
U.S. News ranking: Reg. Coll. (Mid. W), unranked
Website: www.hesston.edu/admissions
Admissions email: admissions@hesston.edu
Private; founded 1909
Affiliation: Mennonite Church
Freshman admissions: selective; 2019-2020: 701 applied, 371 accepted. Either SAT or ACT required. ACT 25/75 percentile: 17-23. High school rank: N/A
Early decision deadline: N/A, notification date: N/A
Early action deadline: N/A, notification date: N/A
Application deadline (fall): rolling
Undergraduate student body: 343 full time, 35 part time; 42% male, 58% female; 1% American Indian, 2% Asian, 6% Black, 13% Hispanic, 2% multiracial, 0% Pacific Islander, 62% white, 15% international; 51% from in state; 71% live on campus; 0% of students in fraternities, 0% in sororities
Most popular majors: 100% Registered Nursing/Registered Nurse
Expenses: 2020-2021: $28,440; room/board: $9,480
Financial aid: (620) 327-8220; 73% of undergrads determined to have financial need; average aid package $22,937

Kansas State University
Manhattan KS
(785) 532-6250
U.S. News ranking: Nat. U., No. 170
Website: www.k-state.edu
Admissions email: k-state@k-state.edu
Public; founded 1863
Freshman admissions: more selective; 2019-2020: 8,140 applied, 7,788 accepted. Either SAT or ACT required. ACT 25/75 percentile: 22-28. High school rank: 28% in top tenth, 52% in top quarter, 81% in top half
Early decision deadline: N/A, notification date: N/A
Early action deadline: N/A, notification date: N/A
Application deadline (fall): rolling
Undergraduate student body: 15,548 full time, 1,662 part time; 52% male, 48% female; 0% American Indian, 2% Asian, 3% Black, 8% Hispanic, 4% multiracial, 0% Pacific Islander, 79% white, 4% international; N/A from in state; 23% live on campus; N/A of students in fraternities, N/A in sororities
Most popular majors: 19% Business, Management,

Marketing, and Related Support Services, 13% Agriculture, Agriculture Operations, and Related Sciences, 13% Engineering, 7% Biological and Biomedical Sciences, 7% Education
Expenses: 2020-2021: $10,320 in state, $26,196 out of state; room/board: $10,100
Financial aid: (785) 532-7626; 49% of undergrads determined to have financial need; average aid package $14,475

Kansas Wesleyan University
Salina KS
(785) 833-4305
U.S. News ranking: Reg. Coll. (Mid. W), No. 38
Website: www.kwu.edu
Admissions email: admissions@kwu.edu
Private; founded 1886
Affiliation: United Methodist
Freshman admissions: selective; 2019-2020: 1,504 applied, 885 accepted. Either SAT or ACT required. ACT 25/75 percentile: 19-24. High school rank: 14% in top tenth, 34% in top quarter, 72% in top half
Early decision deadline: N/A, notification date: N/A
Early action deadline: N/A, notification date: N/A
Application deadline (fall): rolling
Undergraduate student body: 607 full time, 46 part time; 58% male, 42% female; 1% American Indian, 0% Asian, 13% Black, 18% Hispanic, 3% multiracial, 0% Pacific Islander, 63% white, 1% international; 45% from in state; 61% live on campus; 0% of students in fraternities, 0% in sororities
Most popular majors: 23% Business, Management, Marketing, and Related Support Services, 14% Education, 10% Homeland Security, Law Enforcement, Firefighting and Related Protective Services, 10% Parks, Recreation, Leisure, and Fitness Studies, 7% Health Professions and Related Programs
Expenses: 2020-2021: $30,770; room/board: $10,000
Financial aid: (785) 833-4316; 86% of undergrads determined to have financial need; average aid package $23,196

McPherson College
McPherson KS
(800) 365-7402
U.S. News ranking: Reg. Coll. (Mid. W), No. 31
Website: www.mcpherson.edu
Admissions email: admissions@mcpherson.edu
Private; founded 1887
Affiliation: Church of Brethren
Freshman admissions: selective; 2019-2020: 3,229 applied, 1,703 accepted. Neither SAT nor ACT required. ACT 25/75 percentile: 19-23. High school rank: 7% in top tenth, 21% in top quarter, 59% in top half
Early decision deadline: N/A, notification date: N/A

Early action deadline: N/A, notification date: N/A
Application deadline (fall): rolling
Undergraduate student body: 753 full time, 44 part time; 68% male, 32% female; 2% American Indian, 1% Asian, 12% Black, 17% Hispanic, 5% multiracial, 0% Pacific Islander, 52% white, 10% international; 30% from in state; 70% live on campus; 0% of students in fraternities, 0% in sororities
Most popular majors: 26% Mechanical Engineering Related Technologies/Technicians, 23% Business Administration, Management and Operations, 9% Visual and Performing Arts, 8% Health and Physical Education/Fitness, 7% Biology, General
Expenses: 2020-2021: $31,154; room/board: $8,754
Financial aid: (620) 242-0400; 84% of undergrads determined to have financial need; average aid package $27,170

MidAmerica Nazarene University[1]
Olathe KS
(913) 971-3380
U.S. News ranking: Reg. U. (Mid. W), No. 91
Website: www.mnu.edu
Admissions email: admissions@mnu.edu
Private; founded 1966
Affiliation: Church of the Nazarene
Application deadline (fall): N/A
Undergraduate student body: N/A full time, N/A part time
Expenses: 2019-2020: $31,786; room/board: $9,012
Financial aid: (913) 971-3298

Newman University
Wichita KS
(877) 639-6268
U.S. News ranking: Reg. U. (Mid. W), No. 117
Website: www.newmanu.edu
Admissions email: admissions@newmanu.edu
Private; founded 1933
Affiliation: Roman Catholic
Freshman admissions: selective; 2019-2020: 1,078 applied, 727 accepted. Neither SAT nor ACT required. ACT 25/75 percentile: 18-25. High school rank: 23% in top tenth, 50% in top quarter, 78% in top half
Early decision deadline: N/A, notification date: N/A
Early action deadline: N/A, notification date: N/A
Application deadline (fall): 8/15
Undergraduate student body: 944 full time, 1,761 part time; 38% male, 62% female; 1% American Indian, 6% Asian, 5% Black, 14% Hispanic, 3% multiracial, 0% Pacific Islander, 64% white, 5% international; 80% from in state; 21% live on campus; 0% of students in fraternities, 0% in sororities
Most popular majors: 32% Health Professions and Related Programs, 17% Business, Management, Marketing, and Related Support Services, 16% Theology and Religious Vocations, 13% Multi/Interdisciplinary Studies,

5% Liberal Arts and Sciences, General Studies and Humanities
Expenses: 2020-2021: $33,150; room/board: $9,294
Financial aid: (316) 942-4291; 81% of undergrads determined to have financial need; average aid package $23,921

Ottawa University
Ottawa KS
(785) 242-5200
U.S. News ranking: Reg. Coll. (Mid. W), No. 49
Website: www.ottawa.edu
Admissions email: admiss@ottawa.edu
Private; founded 1865
Affiliation: American Baptist
Freshman admissions: selective; 2019-2020: 1,971 applied, 285 accepted. Neither SAT nor ACT required. ACT 25/75 percentile: 16-22. High school rank: 6% in top tenth, 21% in top quarter, 52% in top half
Early decision deadline: N/A, notification date: N/A
Early action deadline: N/A, notification date: N/A
Application deadline (fall): 8/15
Undergraduate student body: 645 full time, 28 part time; 61% male, 39% female; 2% American Indian, 1% Asian, 14% Black, 12% Hispanic, 2% multiracial, 0% Pacific Islander, 58% white, 0% international; 38% from in state; 57% live on campus; N/A of students in fraternities, N/A in sororities
Most popular majors: 21% Business Administration and Management, General, 17% Kinesiology and Exercise Science, 9% Psychology, General, 8% Biology/Biological Sciences, General, 6% Accounting
Expenses: 2020-2021: $31,580; room/board: $11,934
Financial aid: (602) 749-5120; 85% of undergrads determined to have financial need; average aid package $25,021

Pittsburg State University
Pittsburg KS
(800) 854-7488
U.S. News ranking: Reg. U. (Mid. W), No. 86
Website: www.pittstate.edu
Admissions email: psuadmit@pittstate.edu
Public; founded 1903
Freshman admissions: selective; 2019-2020: 1,822 applied, 1,741 accepted. Neither SAT nor ACT required. ACT 25/75 percentile: 19-24. High school rank: 16% in top tenth, 39% in top quarter, 73% in top half
Early decision deadline: N/A, notification date: N/A
Early action deadline: N/A, notification date: N/A
Application deadline (fall): 2/1
Undergraduate student body: 4,650 full time, 531 part time; 50% male, 50% female; 1% American Indian, 1% Asian, 3% Black, 6% Hispanic, 2% multiracial, 0% Pacific Islander, 80% white, 2% international; 29% from in state; N/A live on campus;

N/A of students in fraternities, N/A in sororities
Most popular majors: 22% Business, Management, Marketing, and Related Support Services, 16% Engineering Technologies and Engineering-Related Fields, 12% Education, 11% Health Professions and Related Programs, 7% Psychology
Expenses: 2019-2020: $7,338 in state, $18,682 out of state; room/board: $7,996
Financial aid: (620) 235-4240; 87% of undergrads determined to have financial need; average aid package $6,464

Southwestern College
Winfield KS
(620) 229-6236
U.S. News ranking: Reg. U. (Mid. W), second tier
Website: www.sckans.edu
Admissions email: scadmit@sckans.edu
Private; founded 1885
Affiliation: United Methodist
Freshman admissions: selective; 2019-2020: 914 applied, 466 accepted. Either SAT or ACT required. ACT 25/75 percentile: 18-23. High school rank: 11% in top tenth, 32% in top quarter, 64% in top half
Early decision deadline: N/A, notification date: N/A
Early action deadline: N/A, notification date: N/A
Application deadline (fall): 8/26
Undergraduate student body: 678 full time, 682 part time; 64% male, 36% female; 1% American Indian, 2% Asian, 12% Black, 11% Hispanic, 3% multiracial, 1% Pacific Islander, 41% white, 3% international; 32% from in state; 66% live on campus; N/A of students in fraternities, N/A in sororities
Most popular majors: 10% Business Administration and Management, General, 8% Computer Programming/Programmer, General, 8% Organizational Leadership, 7% Criminal Justice/Safety Studies, 7% Operations Management and Supervision
Expenses: 2020-2021: $33,250; room/board: $8,500
Financial aid: (620) 229-6215; 81% of undergrads determined to have financial need; average aid package $24,519

Sterling College
Sterling KS
(800) 346-1017
U.S. News ranking: Reg. Coll. (Mid. W), No. 46
Website: www.sterling.edu
Admissions email: admissions@sterling.edu
Private; founded 1887
Affiliation: Presbyterian
Freshman admissions: selective; 2019-2020: 1,596 applied, 637 accepted. Either SAT or ACT required. ACT 25/75 percentile: 18-23. High school rank: 3% in top tenth, 22% in top quarter, 57% in top half
Early decision deadline: N/A, notification date: N/A

Early action deadline: N/A, notification date: N/A
Application deadline (fall): rolling
Undergraduate student body: 527 full time, 116 part time; 58% male, 42% female; 2% American Indian, 1% Asian, 16% Black, 15% Hispanic, 4% multiracial, 0% Pacific Islander, 57% white, 4% international; 40% from in state; 76% live on campus; 0% of students in fraternities, 0% in sororities
Most popular majors: 14% Business, Management, Marketing, and Related Support Services, 10% Education, 10% Health Professions and Related Programs, 9% Communication, Journalism, and Related Programs, 9% Psychology
Expenses: 2020-2021: $27,000; room/board: $8,610
Financial aid: (620) 278-4226; 84% of undergrads determined to have financial need; average aid package $23,667

Tabor College
Hillsboro KS
(620) 947-3121
U.S. News ranking: Reg. Coll. (Mid. W), No. 49
Website: www.tabor.edu
Admissions email: admissions@tabor.edu
Private; founded 1908
Affiliation: Mennonite Brethren Church
Freshman admissions: selective; 2019-2020: 812 applied, 454 accepted. Either SAT or ACT required. ACT 25/75 percentile: 17-22. High school rank: 15% in top tenth, 16% in top quarter, 65% in top half
Early decision deadline: N/A, notification date: N/A
Early action deadline: N/A, notification date: N/A
Application deadline (fall): rolling
Undergraduate student body: 481 full time, 93 part time; 58% male, 42% female; N/A American Indian, N/A Asian, N/A Black, N/A Hispanic, N/A multiracial, N/A Pacific Islander, N/A white, N/A international; 49% from in state; 93% live on campus; 0% of students in fraternities, 0% in sororities
Most popular majors: 21% Health Professions and Related Programs, 19% Business, Management, Marketing, and Related Support Services, 16% Parks, Recreation, Leisure, and Fitness Studies, 11% Education, 7% Psychology
Expenses: 2019-2020: $29,360; room/board: $9,975
Financial aid: (620) 947-3121

University of Kansas
Lawrence KS
(785) 864-3911
U.S. News ranking: Nat. U., No. 124
Website: www.ku.edu
Admissions email: adm@ku.edu
Public; founded 1865
Freshman admissions: more selective; 2019-2020: 15,093 applied, 14,052 accepted. Either SAT or ACT required. ACT 25/75 percentile: 22-29. High school

rank: 29% in top tenth, 55% in top quarter, 83% in top half
Early decision deadline: N/A, notification date: N/A
Early action deadline: N/A, notification date: N/A
Application deadline (fall): 8/17
Undergraduate student body: 17,257 full time, 2,410 part time; 48% male, 52% female; 0% American Indian, 5% Asian, 4% Black, 9% Hispanic, 5% multiracial, 0% Pacific Islander, 71% white, 5% international; 65% from in state; 25% live on campus; 18% of students in fraternities, 26% in sororities
Most popular majors: 19% Business, Management, Marketing, and Related Support Services, 12% Health Professions and Related Programs, 9% Communication, Journalism, and Related Programs, 9% Engineering, 7% Social Sciences
Expenses: 2020-2021: $11,166 in state, $28,024 out of state; room/board: $9,900
Financial aid: (785) 864-4700; 46% of undergrads determined to have financial need; average aid package $16,652

University of Saint Mary
Leavenworth KS
(913) 758-5151
U.S. News ranking: Reg. U. (Mid. W), No. 103
Website: www.stmary.edu
Admissions email: admiss@stmary.edu
Private; founded 1923
Affiliation: Roman Catholic
Freshman admissions: selective; 2019-2020: 699 applied, 587 accepted. Either SAT or ACT required. ACT 25/75 percentile: 18-23. High school rank: 10% in top tenth, 26% in top quarter, 65% in top half
Early decision deadline: N/A, notification date: N/A
Early action deadline: N/A, notification date: N/A
Application deadline (fall): rolling
Undergraduate student body: 713 full time, 69 part time; 50% male, 50% female; 1% American Indian, 1% Asian, 14% Black, 15% Hispanic, 5% multiracial, 2% Pacific Islander, 46% white, 1% international; N/A from in state; 39% live on campus; N/A of students in fraternities, N/A in sororities
Most popular majors: 41% Health Professions and Related Programs, 12% Biological and Biomedical Sciences, 11% Business, Management, Marketing, and Related Support Services, 7% Parks, Recreation, Leisure, and Fitness Studies, 7% Psychology
Expenses: 2020-2021: $30,800; room/board: $8,180
Financial aid: (913) 758-6172

Washburn University
Topeka KS
(785) 670-1030
U.S. News ranking: Nat. U., second tier
Website: www.washburn.edu

Admissions email: admissions@washburn.edu
Public; founded 1865
Freshman admissions: selective; 2019-2020: 1,883 applied, 1,748 accepted. ACT required. ACT 25/75 percentile: 18-24. High school rank: 14% in top tenth, 35% in top quarter, 66% in top half
Early decision deadline: N/A, notification date: N/A
Early action deadline: N/A, notification date: N/A
Application deadline (fall): 8/1
Undergraduate student body: 3,597 full time, 1,871 part time; 38% male, 62% female; 1% American Indian, 1% Asian, 7% Black, 12% Hispanic, 5% multiracial, 0% Pacific Islander, 66% white, 4% international
Most popular majors: 34% Health Professions and Related Programs, 10% Business, Management, Marketing, and Related Support Services, 9% Liberal Arts and Sciences, General Studies and Humanities, 7% Legal Professions and Studies, 6% Public Administration and Social Service Professions
Expenses: 2019-2020: $8,704 in state, $19,456 out of state; room/board: $9,399
Financial aid: (785) 670-2770; 62% of undergrads determined to have financial need; average aid package $9,919

Wichita State University
Wichita KS
(316) 978-3085
U.S. News ranking: Nat. U., second tier
Website: www.wichita.edu
Admissions email: admissions@wichita.edu
Public; founded 1895
Freshman admissions: more selective; 2019-2020: 5,947 applied, 3,342 accepted. Neither SAT nor ACT required. ACT 25/75 percentile: 20-27. High school rank: 19% in top tenth, 47% in top quarter, 82% in top half
Early decision deadline: N/A, notification date: N/A
Early action deadline: N/A, notification date: N/A
Application deadline (fall): rolling
Undergraduate student body: 8,994 full time, 4,223 part time; 45% male, 55% female; 1% American Indian, 7% Asian, 6% Black, 13% Hispanic, 5% multiracial, 0% Pacific Islander, 60% white, 6% international; 88% from in state; 13% live on campus; 3% of students in fraternities, 4% in sororities
Most popular majors: 20% Business, Management, Marketing, and Related Support Services, 16% Health Professions and Related Programs, 13% Engineering, 7% Biological and Biomedical Sciences, 7% Education
Expenses: 2020-2021: $8,074 in state, $17,799 out of state; room/board: $12,610

Financial aid: (316) 978-3430; 60% of undergrads determined to have financial need; average aid package $7,950

KENTUCKY

Alice Lloyd College
Pippa Passes KY
(888) 280-4252
U.S. News ranking: Reg. Coll. (S), No. 26
Website: www.alc.edu
Admissions email: admissions@alc.edu
Private; founded 1923
Freshman admissions: selective; 2019-2020: 4,676 applied, 346 accepted. Either SAT or ACT required. ACT 25/75 percentile: 18-22. High school rank: 2% in top tenth, 8% in top quarter, 36% in top half
Early decision deadline: N/A, notification date: N/A
Early action deadline: N/A, notification date: N/A
Application deadline (fall): 7/1
Undergraduate student body: 555 full time, 19 part time; 49% male, 51% female; 0% American Indian, 0% Asian, 3% Black, 1% Hispanic, 0% multiracial, 0% Pacific Islander, 93% white, 1% international
Most popular majors: 25% Biological and Biomedical Sciences, 15% Parks, Recreation, Leisure, and Fitness Studies, 13% Parks, Recreation, Leisure, and Fitness Studies, 11% Social Sciences, 7% Business, Management, Marketing, and Related Support Services
Expenses: 2020-2021: $14,230; room/board: $7,390
Financial aid: (606) 368-6058; 90% of undergrads determined to have financial need; average aid package $14,247

Asbury University
Wilmore KY
(800) 888-1818
U.S. News ranking: Reg. U. (S), No. 9
Website: asbury.edu
Admissions email: admissions@asbury.edu
Private; founded 1890
Affiliation: Wesleyan
Freshman admissions: more selective; 2019-2020: 1,192 applied, 874 accepted. Neither SAT nor ACT required. ACT 25/75 percentile: 21-28. High school rank: 28% in top tenth, 48% in top quarter, 79% in top half
Early decision deadline: N/A, notification date: N/A
Early action deadline: N/A, notification date: N/A
Application deadline (fall): rolling
Undergraduate student body: 1,363 full time, 351 part time; 40% male, 60% female; 1% American Indian, 1% Asian, 5% Black, 7% Hispanic, 1% multiracial, 0% Pacific Islander, 77% white, 6% international; 57% from in state; 60% live on campus; 0% of students in fraternities, 0% in sororities

Most popular majors: 15% Business/Commerce, General, 13% Radio, Television, and Digital Communication, Other, 9% Elementary Education and Teaching, 5% Educational/Instructional Technology, 5% Equestrian/Equine Studies
Expenses: 2020-2021: $32,028; room/board: $7,968
Financial aid: (859) 858-3511; 76% of undergrads determined to have financial need; average aid package $22,279

Bellarmine University
Louisville KY
(502) 272-7100
U.S. News ranking: Nat. U., No. 206
Website: www.bellarmine.edu
Admissions email: admissions@bellarmine.edu
Private; founded 1950
Affiliation: Roman Catholic
Freshman admissions: selective; 2019-2020: 3,799 applied, 3,189 accepted. Either SAT or ACT required. ACT 25/75 percentile: 22-28. High school rank: N/A
Early decision deadline: N/A, notification date: N/A
Early action deadline: 11/1, notification date: 11/15
Application deadline (fall): 8/15
Undergraduate student body: 2,416 full time, 137 part time; 36% male, 64% female; 0% American Indian, 2% Asian, 5% Black, 5% Hispanic, 4% multiracial, 0% Pacific Islander, 78% white, 2% international; 29% from in state; 40% live on campus; 1% of students in fraternities, 1% in sororities
Most popular majors: 23% Health Professions and Related Programs, 12% Business, Management, Marketing, and Related Support Services, 10% Psychology, 9% Biological and Biomedical Sciences, 9% Parks, Recreation, Leisure, and Fitness Studies
Expenses: 2020-2021: $44,620; room/board: $9,030
Financial aid: (502) 272-7300; 79% of undergrads determined to have financial need; average aid package $34,671

Berea College
Berea KY
(859) 985-3500
U.S. News ranking: Nat. Lib. Arts, No. 33
Website: www.berea.edu
Admissions email: admissions@berea.edu
Private; founded 1855
Freshman admissions: more selective; 2019-2020: 1,966 applied, 595 accepted. Either SAT or ACT required. ACT 25/75 percentile: 23-27. High school rank: 25% in top tenth, 72% in top quarter, 97% in top half
Early decision deadline: N/A, notification date: N/A
Early action deadline: N/A, notification date: N/A
Application deadline (fall): 3/31
Undergraduate student body: 1,652 full time, 36 part time; 42% male, 58% female; 0% American

Indian, 3% Asian, 17% Black, 13% Hispanic, 8% multiracial, 0% Pacific Islander, 52% white, 8% international; N/A from in state; 98% live on campus; N/A of students in fraternities, N/A in sororities
Most popular majors: 9% Multi/Interdisciplinary Studies, 8% Mathematics and Statistics, 8% Military Technologies and Applied Sciences, 7% Biological and Biomedical Sciences, 6% Legal Professions and Studies
Expenses: 2019-2020: $44,700; room/board: $6,966
Financial aid: (859) 985-3313; 100% of undergrads determined to have financial need; average aid package $50,865

Brescia University
Owensboro KY
(270) 686-4241
U.S. News ranking: Reg. Coll. (S), No. 33
Website: www.brescia.edu
Admissions email: admissions@brescia.edu
Private; founded 1925
Affiliation: Roman Catholic
Freshman admissions: selective; 2019-2020: 2,688 applied, 1,134 accepted. Either SAT or ACT required. ACT 25/75 percentile: 20-26. High school rank: N/A
Early decision deadline: N/A, notification date: N/A
Early action deadline: N/A, notification date: N/A
Application deadline (fall): rolling
Undergraduate student body: 723 full time, 214 part time; 31% male, 69% female; 1% American Indian, 1% Asian, 12% Black, 8% Hispanic, 1% multiracial, 0% Pacific Islander, 64% white, 1% international
Most popular majors: 49% Social Work, 9% Psychology, General, 7% Accounting, 7% Liberal Arts and Sciences/Liberal Studies
Expenses: 2020-2021: $25,100; room/board: $10,260
Financial aid: (270) 686-4253; 88% of undergrads determined to have financial need; average aid package $18,744

Campbellsville University
Campbellsville KY
(270) 789-5220
U.S. News ranking: Reg. U. (S), No. 94
Website: www.campbellsville.edu
Admissions email: admissions@campbellsville.edu
Private; founded 1906
Freshman admissions: selective; 2019-2020: 4,146 applied, 2,905 accepted. Neither SAT nor ACT required. ACT 25/75 percentile: 18-23. High school rank: 16% in top tenth, 19% in top quarter, 63% in top half
Early decision deadline: N/A, notification date: N/A
Early action deadline: N/A, notification date: N/A
Application deadline (fall): rolling
Undergraduate student body: 2,481 full time, 3,602 part time; 39% male, 61% female; 0% American

Indian, 1% Asian, 15% Black, 4% Hispanic, 2% multiracial, 0% Pacific Islander, 69% white, 7% international; 85% from in state; 42% live on campus; 0% of students in fraternities, 0% in sororities

Most popular majors: 20% Business/Commerce, General, 13% Education, General, 11% Social Work, 8% Criminal Justice/Safety Studies, 7% Registered Nursing, Nursing Administration, Nursing Research and Clinical Nursing, Other

Expenses: 2020-2021: $25,400; room/board: $8,770

Financial aid: (270) 789-5013; 81% of undergrads determined to have financial need; average aid package $20,458

Centre College
Danville KY
(859) 238-5350
U.S. News ranking: Nat. Lib. Arts, No. 52
Website: www.centre.edu
Admissions email: admission@centre.edu
Private; founded 1819
Affiliation: Presbyterian
Freshman admissions: more selective; 2019-2020: 2,220 applied, 1,689 accepted. Either SAT or ACT required. ACT 25/75 percentile: 26-32. High school rank: 52% in top tenth, 80% in top quarter, 97% in top half
Early decision deadline: 11/15, notification date: 12/15
Early action deadline: 12/1, notification date: 1/15
Application deadline (fall): 1/15
Undergraduate student body: 1,410 full time, 1 part time; 48% male, 52% female; 0% American Indian, 4% Asian, 5% Black, 6% Hispanic, 4% multiracial, 0% Pacific Islander, 72% white, 6% international; N/A from in state; 99% live on campus; 37% of students in fraternities, 42% in sororities
Most popular majors: 23% Economics, Other, 10% History, General, 8% Psychology, General, 7% International/Global Studies, 7% Sociology and Anthropology
Expenses: 2020-2021: $44,300; room/board: $11,170
Financial aid: (859) 238-5365; 58% of undergrads determined to have financial need; average aid package $36,841

Eastern Kentucky University
Richmond KY
(859) 622-2106
U.S. News ranking: Reg. U. (S), No. 51
Website: www.eku.edu
Admissions email: admissions@eku.edu
Public; founded 1906
Freshman admissions: selective; 2019-2020: 8,975 applied, 8,421 accepted. Either SAT or ACT required. ACT 25/75 percentile: 20-26. High school rank: 17% in top tenth, 42% in top quarter, 74% in top half

Early decision deadline: N/A, notification date: N/A
Early action deadline: N/A, notification date: N/A
Application deadline (fall): 8/1
Undergraduate student body: 9,908 full time, 2,754 part time; 43% male, 57% female; 0% American Indian, 1% Asian, 6% Black, 4% Hispanic, 3% multiracial, 0% Pacific Islander, 84% white, 1% international; 87% from in state; 36% live on campus; 1% of students in fraternities, 1% in sororities
Most popular majors: 16% Health Professions and Related Programs, 12% Homeland Security, Law Enforcement, Firefighting and Related Protective Services, 11% Business, Management, Marketing, and Related Support Services, 8% Liberal Arts and Sciences, General Studies and Humanities, 6% Psychology
Expenses: 2020-2021: $9,806 in state, $10,713 out of state; room/board: $10,173
Financial aid: (859) 622-2361; 71% of undergrads determined to have financial need; average aid package $12,422

Georgetown College
Georgetown KY
(800) 788-9985
U.S. News ranking: Nat. Lib. Arts, second tier
Website: www.georgetowncollege.edu
Admissions email: admissions@georgetowncollege.edu
Private; founded 1829
Affiliation: Baptist
Freshman admissions: more selective; 2019-2020: 2,791 applied, 1,768 accepted. Either SAT or ACT required. ACT 25/75 percentile: 21-27. High school rank: 22% in top tenth, 52% in top quarter, 85% in top half
Early decision deadline: N/A, notification date: N/A
Early action deadline: N/A, notification date: N/A
Application deadline (fall): 8/20
Undergraduate student body: 932 full time, 51 part time; 45% male, 55% female; 0% American Indian, 1% Asian, 10% Black, 5% Hispanic, 5% multiracial, 0% Pacific Islander, 74% white, 2% international; 73% from in state; 93% live on campus; 18% of students in fraternities, 32% in sororities
Most popular majors: 13% Psychology, General, 10% Biology/Biological Sciences, General, 8% Communication and Media Studies, Other, 8% Health and Wellness, General, 6% Kinesiology and Exercise Science
Expenses: 2020-2021: $40,800; room/board: $10,670
Financial aid: (502) 863-8027; 86% of undergrads determined to have financial need; average aid package $36,964

Kentucky Christian University[1]
Grayson KY
(800) 522-3181
U.S. News ranking: Reg. Coll. (S), No. 68
Website: www.kcu.edu
Admissions email: knights@kcu.edu
Private; founded 1919
Application deadline (fall): 8/1
Undergraduate student body: N/A full time, N/A part time
Expenses: 2019-2020: $20,596; room/board: $8,480
Financial aid: (606) 474-3226

Kentucky State University
Frankfort KY
(800) 633-9415
U.S. News ranking: Reg. Coll. (S), No. 36
Website: www.kysu.edu
Admissions email: admissions@kysu.edu
Public; founded 1886
Freshman admissions: less selective; 2019-2020: 2,185 applied, 1,763 accepted. Either SAT or ACT required. ACT 25/75 percentile: 18-22. High school rank: N/A
Early decision deadline: N/A, notification date: N/A
Early action deadline: N/A, notification date: N/A
Application deadline (fall): 7/31
Undergraduate student body: 1,156 full time, 873 part time; 43% male, 57% female; 0% American Indian, 1% Asian, 74% Black, 3% Hispanic, 4% multiracial, 0% Pacific Islander, 15% white, 1% international; 62% from in state; 39% live on campus; 4% of students in fraternities, 3% in sororities
Most popular majors: 15% Business Administration and Management, General, 14% Criminal Justice/Safety Studies, 10% Physical Education Teaching and Coaching, 8% Biology/Biological Sciences, General, 8% Psychology, General
Expenses: 2020-2021: $9,190 in state, $13,040 out of state; room/board: $6,690
Financial aid: (502) 597-5759; 87% of undergrads determined to have financial need; average aid package $13,132

Kentucky Wesleyan College
Owensboro KY
(800) 999-0592
U.S. News ranking: Reg. Coll. (S), No. 18
Website: kwc.edu/
Admissions email: admissions@kwc.edu
Private; founded 1858
Affiliation: United Methodist
Freshman admissions: selective; 2019-2020: 1,690 applied, 1,047 accepted. Either SAT or ACT required. ACT 25/75 percentile: 20-26. High school rank: N/A
Early decision deadline: N/A, notification date: N/A

Early action deadline: N/A, notification date: N/A
Application deadline (fall): 9/1
Undergraduate student body: 779 full time, 60 part time; 51% male, 49% female; 0% American Indian, 1% Asian, 12% Black, 3% Hispanic, 1% multiracial, 0% Pacific Islander, 70% white, 1% international; 69% from in state; 53% live on campus; 17% of students in fraternities, 21% in sororities
Most popular majors: 10% Business/Commerce, General, 10% Health Professions and Related Clinical Sciences, Other, 10% Psychology, General, 8% Criminal Justice/Safety Studies, 7% Kinesiology and Exercise Science
Expenses: 2019-2020: $27,200; room/board: $10,217
Financial aid: (270) 852-3130

Lindsey Wilson College
Columbia KY
(800) 264-0138
U.S. News ranking: Reg. U. (S), No. 89
Website: www.lindsey.edu
Admissions email: admissions@lindsey.edu
Private; founded 1903
Affiliation: United Methodist
Freshman admissions: selective; 2019-2020: N/A applied, N/A accepted. Either SAT or ACT required. ACT 25/75 percentile: 18-24. High school rank: 13% in top tenth, 35% in top quarter, 73% in top half
Early decision deadline: N/A, notification date: N/A
Early action deadline: N/A, notification date: N/A
Application deadline (fall): rolling
Undergraduate student body: 1,814 full time, 147 part time; 39% male, 61% female; 0% American Indian, 0% Asian, 9% Black, 1% Hispanic, 2% multiracial, 0% Pacific Islander, 65% white, 0% international; 82% from in state; 54% live on campus; N/A of students in fraternities, N/A in sororities
Most popular majors: 49% Social Work, 11% Business Administration and Management, General, 6% Criminal Justice/Safety Studies, 5% Speech Communication and Rhetoric, 4% Registered Nursing/Registered Nurse
Expenses: 2020-2021: $25,718; room/board: $9,495
Financial aid: (270) 384-8022; 93% of undergrads determined to have financial need; average aid package $22,815

Midway University
Midway KY
(800) 952-4122
U.S. News ranking: Reg. U. (S), No. 89
Website: www.midway.edu
Admissions email: admissions@midway.edu
Private; founded 1847
Affiliation: Christian Church (Disciples of Christ)

Freshman admissions: selective; 2019-2020: 1,162 applied, 693 accepted. Either SAT or ACT required. ACT 25/75 percentile: 19-23. High school rank: 9% in top tenth, 30% in top quarter, 71% in top half
Early decision deadline: N/A, notification date: N/A
Early action deadline: N/A, notification date: N/A
Application deadline (fall): rolling
Undergraduate student body: 887 full time, 594 part time; 32% male, 68% female; 0% American Indian, 1% Asian, 8% Black, 7% Hispanic, 3% multiracial, 0% Pacific Islander, 74% white, 0% international; 81% from in state; 33% live on campus; N/A of students in fraternities, N/A in sororities
Most popular majors: 27% Business/Commerce, General, 17% Health/Health Care Administration/Management, 16% Education, General, 12% Psychology, General, 7% Sport and Fitness Administration/Management
Expenses: 2020-2021: $24,850; room/board: $8,600
Financial aid: (859) 846-5494; 88% of undergrads determined to have financial need; average aid package $17,846

Morehead State University
Morehead KY
(800) 585-6781
U.S. News ranking: Reg. U. (S), No. 40
Website: www.moreheadstate.edu
Admissions email: admissions@moreheadstate.edu
Public; founded 1887
Freshman admissions: selective; 2019-2020: 8,032 applied, 6,233 accepted. Either SAT or ACT required. ACT 25/75 percentile: 20-26. High school rank: 22% in top tenth, 49% in top quarter, 83% in top half
Early decision deadline: N/A, notification date: N/A
Early action deadline: N/A, notification date: N/A
Application deadline (fall): rolling
Undergraduate student body: 5,393 full time, 3,571 part time; 39% male, 61% female; 0% American Indian, 0% Asian, 4% Black, 2% Hispanic, 3% multiracial, 0% Pacific Islander, 89% white, 2% international; N/A from in state; 44% live on campus; 6% of students in fraternities, 8% in sororities
Most popular majors: 14% Business, Management, Marketing, and Related Support Services, 12% Liberal Arts and Sciences, General Studies and Humanities, 11% Health Professions and Related Programs, 9% Education, 7% Biological and Biomedical Sciences
Expenses: 2020-2021: $9,290 in state, $13,876 out of state; room/board: $9,810
Financial aid: (606) 783-2011; 76% of undergrads determined to have financial need; average aid package $12,520

Murray State University

Murray KY
(270) 809-3741
U.S. News ranking: Reg. U. (S), No. 26
Website: www.murraystate.edu
Admissions email:
msu.admissions@murraystate.edu
Public; founded 1922
Freshman admissions: selective; 2019-2020: 8,304 applied, 6,861 accepted. Neither SAT nor ACT required. ACT 25/75 percentile: 21-28. High school rank: 25% in top tenth, 51% in top quarter, 82% in top half
Early decision deadline: N/A, notification date: N/A
Early action deadline: N/A, notification date: N/A
Application deadline (fall): rolling
Undergraduate student body: 6,219 full time, 1,996 part time; 39% male, 61% female; 0% American Indian, 1% Asian, 6% Black, 2% Hispanic, 3% multiracial, 0% Pacific Islander, 82% white, 3% international; 29% from in state; 34% live on campus; N/A of students in fraternities, N/A in sororities
Most popular majors: 17% Health Professions and Related Programs, 11% Business, Management, Marketing, and Related Support Services, 10% Engineering Technologies and Engineering-Related Fields, 8% Education, 7% Agriculture, Agriculture Operations, and Related Sciences
Expenses: 2020-2021: $9,168 in state, $13,920 out of state; room/board: $10,038
Financial aid: (270) 809-2546; 67% of undergrads determined to have financial need; average aid package $13,315

Northern Kentucky University

Highland Heights KY
(859) 572-5220
U.S. News ranking: Nat. U., second tier
Website: www.nku.edu/
Admissions email:
beanorse@nku.edu
Public; founded 1968
Freshman admissions: selective; 2019-2020: 6,080 applied, 5,483 accepted. Either SAT or ACT required. ACT 25/75 percentile: 20-26. High school rank: N/A
Early decision deadline: N/A, notification date: N/A
Early action deadline: N/A, notification date: N/A
Application deadline (fall): 8/21
Undergraduate student body: 8,257 full time, 3,625 part time; 41% male, 59% female; 0% American Indian, 1% Asian, 7% Black, 4% Hispanic, 3% multiracial, 0% Pacific Islander, 80% white, 3% international; 68% from in state; 22% live on campus; 9% of students in fraternities, 12% in sororities
Most popular majors: 9% Business Administration and Management, General, 8% Registered Nursing/Registered Nurse, 5% Organizational Behavior Studies,

4% Liberal Arts and Sciences/Liberal Studies, 4% Psychology, General
Expenses: 2019-2020: $10,296 in state, $20,256 out of state; room/board: $10,212
Financial aid: (859) 572-5143

Spalding University[1]

Louisville KY
(502) 585-7111
U.S. News ranking: Nat. U., second tier
Website: www.spalding.edu
Admissions email:
admissions@spalding.edu
Private; founded 1814
Application deadline (fall): rolling
Undergraduate student body: N/A full time, N/A part time
Expenses: 2019-2020: $25,200; room/board: $7,900
Financial aid: N/A

Sullivan University[1]

Louisville KY
(502) 456-6504
U.S. News ranking: Reg. U. (S), unranked
Website: www.sullivan.edu
Admissions email:
admissions@sullivan.edu
For-profit
Application deadline (fall): N/A
Undergraduate student body: N/A full time, N/A part time
Expenses: 2019-2020: $12,870; room/board: $10,485
Financial aid: N/A

Thomas More University

Crestview Hills KY
(800) 825-4557
U.S. News ranking: Reg. U. (S), No. 65
Website: www.thomasmore.edu
Admissions email: admissions@thomasmore.edu
Private; founded 1921
Affiliation: Roman Catholic
Freshman admissions: selective; 2019-2020: 2,410 applied, 2,183 accepted. Either SAT or ACT required. ACT 25/75 percentile: 19-25. High school rank: 12% in top tenth, 32% in top quarter, 65% in top half
Early decision deadline: N/A, notification date: N/A
Early action deadline: N/A, notification date: N/A
Application deadline (fall): rolling
Undergraduate student body: 1,295 full time, 735 part time; 47% male, 53% female; 0% American Indian, 1% Asian, 8% Black, 3% Hispanic, 5% multiracial, 0% Pacific Islander, 78% white, 1% international; 59% from in state; 25% live on campus; N/A of students in fraternities, N/A in sororities
Most popular majors: 28% Business Administration and Management, General, 14% Registered Nursing/Registered Nurse, 7% Biology/Biological Sciences, General, 7% Education, 7% Liberal Arts and Sciences/Liberal Studies
Expenses: 2020-2021: $33,420; room/board: $9,100

Financial aid: (859) 344-3319; 80% of undergrads determined to have financial need; average aid package $23,793

Transylvania University

Lexington KY
(859) 233-8242
U.S. News ranking: Nat. Lib. Arts, No. 84
Website: www.transy.edu
Admissions email:
admissions@transy.edu
Private; founded 1780
Affiliation: Christian Church (Disciples of Christ)
Freshman admissions: more selective; 2019-2020: 1,782 applied, 1,599 accepted. Neither SAT nor ACT required. ACT 25/75 percentile: 23-30. High school rank: 28% in top tenth, 61% in top quarter, 90% in top half
Early decision deadline: N/A, notification date: N/A
Early action deadline: 10/15, notification date: 11/1
Application deadline (fall): rolling
Undergraduate student body: 946 full time, 3 part time; 40% male, 60% female; 0% American Indian, 2% Asian, 5% Black, 4% Hispanic, 5% multiracial, 0% Pacific Islander, 79% white, 0% international; 78% from in state; 68% live on campus; 45% of students in fraternities, 41% in sororities
Most popular majors: 15% Business, Management, Marketing, and Related Support Services, 14% Biological and Biomedical Sciences, 11% Social Sciences, 9% Parks, Recreation, Leisure, and Fitness Studies, 8% Psychology
Expenses: 2020-2021: $41,610; room/board: $11,310
Financial aid: (859) 233-8239; 72% of undergrads determined to have financial need; average aid package $30,215

Union College[1]

Barbourville KY
(606) 546-4151
U.S. News ranking: Reg. U. (S), second tier
Website: www.unionky.edu
Admissions email:
enroll@unionky.edu
Private
Application deadline (fall): N/A
Undergraduate student body: N/A full time, N/A part time
Expenses: 2019-2020: $27,950; room/board: $7,575
Financial aid: (606) 546-1224

University of Kentucky

Lexington KY
(859) 257-2000
U.S. News ranking: Nat. U., No. 133
Website: www.uky.edu
Admissions email:
admissions@uky.edu
Public; founded 1865
Freshman admissions: more selective; 2019-2020: 18,759 applied, 17,981 accepted. Either SAT or ACT required. ACT 25/75

percentile: 22-29. High school rank: 33% in top tenth, 59% in top quarter, 85% in top half
Early decision deadline: N/A, notification date: N/A
Early action deadline: 12/1, notification date: N/A
Application deadline (fall): 2/15
Undergraduate student body: 20,622 full time, 1,614 part time; 44% male, 56% female; 0% American Indian, 3% Asian, 7% Black, 5% Hispanic, 4% multiracial, 0% Pacific Islander, 75% white, 2% international; 69% from in state; 33% live on campus; 22% of students in fraternities, 35% in sororities
Most popular majors: 22% Business, Management, Marketing, and Related Support Services, 10% Engineering, 10% Health Professions and Related Programs, 8% Communication, Journalism, and Related Programs, 8% Education
Expenses: 2020-2021: $12,484 in state, $31,294 out of state; room/board: $13,588
Financial aid: (859) 257-3172; 52% of undergrads determined to have financial need; average aid package $14,611

University of Louisville

Louisville KY
(502) 852-6531
U.S. News ranking: Nat. U., No. 176
Website: www.louisville.edu
Admissions email:
admitme@louisville.edu
Public; founded 1798
Affiliation: Undenominational
Freshman admissions: selective; 2019-2020: 14,447 applied, 10,075 accepted. Either SAT or ACT required. ACT 25/75 percentile: 22-29. High school rank: 27% in top tenth, 54% in top quarter, 82% in top half
Early decision deadline: N/A, notification date: N/A
Early action deadline: N/A, notification date: N/A
Application deadline (fall): 8/1
Undergraduate student body: 11,560 full time, 4,300 part time; 46% male, 54% female; 0% American Indian, 4% Asian, 12% Black, 6% Hispanic, 6% multiracial, 0% Pacific Islander, 70% white, 1% international; 82% from in state; 23% live on campus; 16% of students in fraternities, 14% in sororities
Most popular majors: 18% Business, Management, Marketing, and Related Support Services, 13% Engineering, 11% Health Professions and Related Programs, 8% Education, 8% Parks, Recreation, Leisure, and Fitness Studies
Expenses: 2019-2020: $11,928 in state, $27,954 out of state; room/board: $9,452
Financial aid: (502) 852-5511; 63% of undergrads determined to have financial need; average aid package $13,464

University of Pikeville

Pikeville KY
(606) 218-5251
U.S. News ranking: Nat. Lib. Arts, second tier
Website: www.upike.edu/
Admissions email:
wewantyou@upike.edu
Private; founded 1889
Affiliation:
Presbyterian Church (USA)
Freshman admissions: selective; 2019-2020: 1,925 applied, 1,925 accepted. Either SAT or ACT required. ACT 25/75 percentile: 18-24. High school rank: 17% in top tenth, 35% in top quarter, 66% in top half
Early decision deadline: N/A, notification date: N/A
Early action deadline: N/A, notification date: N/A
Application deadline (fall): rolling
Undergraduate student body: 1,075 full time, 329 part time; 49% male, 51% female; 1% American Indian, 1% Asian, 12% Black, 1% Hispanic, 0% multiracial, 0% Pacific Islander, 83% white, 2% international; 79% from in state; 53% live on campus; N/A of students in fraternities, N/A in sororities
Most popular majors: 25% Business, Management, Marketing, and Related Support Services, 12% Biological and Biomedical Sciences, 11% Education, 8% Psychology, 7% Health Professions and Related Programs
Expenses: 2020-2021: $22,050; room/board: $8,050
Financial aid: (606) 218-5254; 99% of undergrads determined to have financial need; average aid package $22,417

University of the Cumberlands[1]

Williamsburg KY
(800) 343-1609
U.S. News ranking: Nat. U., second tier
Website: www.ucumberlands.edu
Admissions email:
admiss@ucumberlands.edu
Private; founded 1888
Affiliation: Baptist
Application deadline (fall): 8/31
Undergraduate student body: N/A full time, N/A part time
Expenses: 2019-2020: $9,875; room/board: $9,300
Financial aid: (606) 539-4239

Western Kentucky University

Bowling Green KY
(270) 745-2551
U.S. News ranking: Nat. U., second tier
Website: www.wku.edu
Admissions email:
admission@wku.edu
Public; founded 1906
Freshman admissions: selective; 2019-2020: 8,245 applied, 8,019 accepted. Either SAT or ACT required. ACT 25/75 percentile: 19-27. High school rank: 22% in top tenth, 45% in top quarter, 74% in top half

Early decision deadline: N/A, notification date: N/A
Early action deadline: N/A, notification date: N/A
Application deadline (fall): 8/1
Undergraduate student body: 11,815 full time, 4,080 part time; 40% male, 60% female; 0% American Indian, 2% Asian, 9% Black, 4% Hispanic, 3% multiracial, 0% Pacific Islander, 79% white, 2% international; 76% from in state; 34% live on campus; 16% of students in fraternities, 18% in sororities
Most popular majors: 8% General Studies, 8% Registered Nursing/Registered Nurse, 5% Business Administration and Management, General, 4% Psychology, General, 3% Organizational Leadership
Expenses: 2020-2021: $10,802 in state, $26,496 out of state; room/board: N/A
Financial aid: (270) 745-2051; 63% of undergrads determined to have financial need; average aid package $15,177

LOUISIANA

Centenary College
Shreveport LA
(318) 869-5011
U.S. News ranking: Nat. Lib. Arts, No. 155
Website: www.centenary.edu/
Admissions email: admission@centenary.edu
Private; founded 1825
Affiliation: United Methodist
Freshman admissions: more selective; 2019-2020: 920 applied, 550 accepted. Neither SAT nor ACT required. ACT 25/75 percentile: 19-26. High school rank: 25% in top tenth, 50% in top quarter, 82% in top half
Early decision deadline: N/A, notification date: N/A
Early action deadline: 12/1, notification date: 1/15
Application deadline (fall): rolling
Undergraduate student body: 541 full time, 8 part time; 40% male, 60% female; 0% American Indian, 3% Asian, 17% Black, 11% Hispanic, 4% multiracial, 0% Pacific Islander, 64% white, 1% international
Most popular majors: 24% Biology/Biological Sciences, General, 17% Psychology, General, 11% Business Administration and Management, General, 7% Mass Communication/Media Studies, 6% Mathematics, General
Expenses: 2020-2021: $38,060; room/board: $13,940
Financial aid: (318) 869-5137; 78% of undergrads determined to have financial need; average aid package $32,543

Dillard University[1]
New Orleans LA
(800) 216-6637
U.S. News ranking: Nat. Lib. Arts, second tier
Website: www.dillard.edu
Admissions email: admissions@dillard.edu
Private; founded 1869
Affiliation: United Methodist

Application deadline (fall): 8/1
Undergraduate student body: N/A full time, N/A part time
Expenses: 2019-2020: $19,281; room/board: $10,218
Financial aid: (504) 816-4864

Grambling State University[1]
Grambling LA
(318) 274-6183
U.S. News ranking: Reg. U. (S), second tier
Website: www.gram.edu/
Admissions email: admissions@gram.edu
Public; founded 1901
Application deadline (fall): rolling
Undergraduate student body: N/A full time, N/A part time
Expenses: 2019-2020: $7,683 in state, $7,683 out of state; room/board: $10,306
Financial aid: (318) 274-6328

Louisiana College[7]
Pineville LA
(318) 487-7259
U.S. News ranking: Reg. U. (S), second tier
Website: www.lacollege.edu
Admissions email: admissions@lacollege.edu
Private; founded 1906
Affiliation: Southern Baptist
Freshman admissions: selective; 2019-2020: 1,018 applied, 606 accepted. Either SAT or ACT required. ACT 25/75 percentile: 18-23. High school rank: N/A
Early decision deadline: N/A, notification date: N/A
Early action deadline: N/A, notification date: N/A
Application deadline (fall): rolling
Undergraduate student body: 890 full time, 114 part time
Most popular majors: 45% Elementary Education and Teaching, 10% Registered Nursing/Registered Nurse, 9% Social Work, 8% Business Administration and Management, General, 7% Health and Physical Education/Fitness, General
Expenses: 2019-2020: $17,500; room/board: $5,274
Financial aid: (318) 487-7387

Louisiana State University–Alexandria
Alexandria LA
(318) 473-6417
U.S. News ranking: Nat. Lib. Arts, second tier
Website: www.lsua.edu
Admissions email: admissions@lsua.edu
Public; founded 1960
Freshman admissions: selective; 2019-2020: 2,647 applied, 1,781 accepted. Either SAT or ACT required. ACT 25/75 percentile: 17-21. High school rank: 15% in top tenth, 31% in top quarter, 56% in top half
Early decision deadline: N/A, notification date: N/A
Early action deadline: N/A, notification date: N/A
Application deadline (fall): 8/1
Undergraduate student body: 1,894 full time, 1,488 part time; 30% male, 70% female; 7% American

Indian, 1% Asian, 19% Black, 2% Hispanic, 3% multiracial, 0% Pacific Islander, 66% white, 2% international
Most popular majors: 23% Registered Nursing/Registered Nurse, 16% Business Administration and Management, General, 15% General Studies, 8% Psychology, General, 7% Criminal Justice/Safety Studies
Expenses: 2019-2020: $6,669 in state, $14,024 out of state; room/board: $7,950
Financial aid: (318) 473-6477

Louisiana State University–Baton Rouge
Baton Rouge LA
(225) 578-1175
U.S. News ranking: Nat. U., No. 153
Website: www.lsu.edu
Admissions email: admissions@lsu.edu
Public; founded 1860
Freshman admissions: more selective; 2019-2020: 24,501 applied, 18,272 accepted. Either SAT or ACT required. ACT 25/75 percentile: 23-29. High school rank: 24% in top tenth, 48% in top quarter, 76% in top half
Early decision deadline: N/A, notification date: N/A
Early action deadline: N/A, notification date: N/A
Application deadline (fall): 4/15
Undergraduate student body: 22,726 full time, 3,100 part time; 47% male, 53% female; 0% American Indian, 5% Asian, 13% Black, 7% Hispanic, 3% multiracial, 0% Pacific Islander, 69% white, 2% international; N/A from in state; 32% live on campus; 14% of students in fraternities, 26% in sororities
Most popular majors: 24% Business, Management, Marketing, and Related Support Services, 17% Engineering, 10% Education, 6% Biological and Biomedical Sciences, 6% Social Sciences
Expenses: 2020-2021: $11,962 in state, $28,639 out of state; room/board: $12,708
Financial aid: (225) 578-3103; 52% of undergrads determined to have financial need; average aid package $15,254

Louisiana State University–Shreveport
Shreveport LA
(318) 797-5061
U.S. News ranking: Reg. U. (S), second tier
Website: www.lsus.edu
Admissions email: admissions@lsus.edu
Public; founded 1967
Freshman admissions: selective; 2019-2020: 716 applied, 687 accepted. Either SAT or ACT required. ACT 25/75 percentile: 20-24. High school rank: N/A
Early decision deadline: N/A, notification date: N/A

Early action deadline: N/A, notification date: N/A
Application deadline (fall): rolling
Undergraduate student body: 1,728 full time, 849 part time; 39% male, 61% female; 0% American Indian, 2% Asian, 21% Black, 5% Hispanic, 5% multiracial, 0% Pacific Islander, 52% white, 4% international; 87% from in state; 3% live on campus; 1% of students in fraternities, 1% in sororities
Most popular majors: 29% Business, Management, Marketing, and Related Support Services, 12% Liberal Arts and Sciences, General Studies and Humanities, 11% Biological and Biomedical Sciences, 7% Psychology, 6% Education
Expenses: 2019-2020: $7,519 in state, $20,673 out of state; room/board: N/A
Financial aid: (318) 797-5363

Louisiana Tech University
Ruston LA
(318) 257-3036
U.S. News ranking: Nat. U., second tier
Website: www.latech.edu
Admissions email: bulldog@latech.edu
Public; founded 1894
Freshman admissions: more selective; 2019-2020: 7,552 applied, 4,840 accepted. Either SAT or ACT required. ACT 25/75 percentile: 22-28. High school rank: 25% in top tenth, 51% in top quarter, 80% in top half
Early decision deadline: N/A, notification date: N/A
Early action deadline: N/A, notification date: N/A
Application deadline (fall): rolling
Undergraduate student body: 8,131 full time, 2,158 part time; 52% male, 48% female; 0% American Indian, 1% Asian, 12% Black, 4% Hispanic, 3% multiracial, 0% Pacific Islander, 71% white, 2% international; 86% from in state; 23% live on campus; 11% of students in fraternities, 22% in sororities
Most popular majors: 19% Business, Management, Marketing, and Related Support Services, 17% Engineering, 6% Biological and Biomedical Sciences, 6% Education, 6% Health Professions and Related Programs
Expenses: 2020-2021: $10,635 in state, $19,588 out of state; room/board: $8,664
Financial aid: (318) 257-2641; 60% of undergrads determined to have financial need; average aid package $11,886

Loyola University New Orleans
New Orleans LA
(800) 456-9652
U.S. News ranking: Nat. U., No. 196
Website: www.loyno.edu
Admissions email: admit@loyno.edu
Private; founded 1912

Affiliation: Roman Catholic
Freshman admissions: selective; 2019-2020: 5,857 applied, 4,394 accepted. Neither SAT nor ACT required. ACT 25/75 percentile: 22-28. High school rank: 20% in top tenth, 41% in top quarter, 78% in top half
Early decision deadline: N/A, notification date: N/A
Early action deadline: 11/15, notification date: 12/1
Application deadline (fall): rolling
Undergraduate student body: 2,886 full time, 302 part time; 34% male, 66% female; 0% American Indian, 3% Asian, 17% Black, 19% Hispanic, 5% multiracial, 0% Pacific Islander, 46% white, 3% international; 43% from in state; 50% live on campus; 7% of students in fraternities, 15% in sororities
Most popular majors: 10% Music Management, 8% Psychology, General, 5% Biology/Biological Sciences, General, 5% Marketing/Marketing Management, General, 4% Public Relations, Advertising, and Applied Communication
Expenses: 2020-2021: $42,030; room/board: $13,606
Financial aid: (504) 865-3231; 74% of undergrads determined to have financial need; average aid package $33,885

McNeese State University
Lake Charles LA
(337) 475-5504
U.S. News ranking: Reg. U. (S), No. 94
Website: www.mcneese.edu
Admissions email: admissions@mcneese.edu
Public; founded 1939
Freshman admissions: selective; 2019-2020: 2,352 applied, 1,899 accepted. Either SAT or ACT required. ACT 25/75 percentile: 20-24. High school rank: 20% in top tenth, 46% in top quarter, 79% in top half
Early decision deadline: N/A, notification date: N/A
Early action deadline: N/A, notification date: N/A
Application deadline (fall): 8/1
Undergraduate student body: 5,405 full time, 1,288 part time; 41% male, 59% female; 0% American Indian, 2% Asian, 16% Black, 4% Hispanic, 3% multiracial, 0% Pacific Islander, 68% white, 7% international; N/A from in state; 14% live on campus; N/A of students in fraternities, N/A in sororities
Most popular majors: Information not available
Expenses: 2019-2020: $8,102 in state, $16,140 out of state; room/board: $8,624
Financial aid: (337) 475-5065

Nicholls State University
Thibodaux LA
(985) 448-4507
U.S. News ranking: Reg. U. (S), No. 80
Website: www.nicholls.edu
Admissions email: nicholls@nicholls.edu

Public; founded 1948
Freshman admissions: selective; 2019-2020: 2,815 applied, 2,477 accepted. Either SAT or ACT required. ACT 25/75 percentile: 20-25. High school rank: 19% in top tenth, 43% in top quarter, 74% in top half
Early decision deadline: N/A, notification date: N/A
Early action deadline: N/A, notification date: N/A
Application deadline (fall): 8/1
Undergraduate student body: 4,975 full time, 943 part time; 36% male, 64% female; 2% American Indian, 1% Asian, 19% Black, 4% Hispanic, 3% multiracial, 0% Pacific Islander, 69% white, 2% international; 95% from in state; 22% live on campus; 11% of students in fraternities, 14% in sororities
Most popular majors: 23% Business, Management, Marketing, and Related Support Services, 20% Health Professions and Related Programs, 11% Multi/Interdisciplinary Studies, 7% Education, 7% Psychology
Expenses: 2020-2021: $7,898 in state, $8,991 out of state; room/board: $7,608
Financial aid: (985) 448-4047; 67% of undergrads determined to have financial need; average aid package $8,444

Northwestern State University of Louisiana
Natchitoches LA
(800) 767-8115
U.S. News ranking: Reg. U. (S), No. 89
Website: www.nsula.edu
Admissions email: applications@nsula.edu
Public; founded 1884
Freshman admissions: selective; 2019-2020: 5,089 applied, 3,236 accepted. Either SAT or ACT required. ACT 25/75 percentile: 19-24. High school rank: 16% in top tenth, 42% in top quarter, 73% in top half
Early decision deadline: N/A, notification date: N/A
Early action deadline: N/A, notification date: N/A
Application deadline (fall): 10/15
Undergraduate student body: 6,340 full time, 3,493 part time; 29% male, 71% female; 1% American Indian, 1% Asian, 32% Black, 7% Hispanic, 5% multiracial, 0% Pacific Islander, 52% white, 1% international; 87% from in state; 16% live on campus; 18% of students in fraternities, 14% in sororities
Most popular majors: 26% Health Professions and Related Programs, 13% Business, Management, Marketing, and Related Support Services, 11% Liberal Arts and Sciences, General Studies and Humanities, 9% Psychology, 7% Biological and Biomedical Sciences
Expenses: 2020-2021: $8,670 in state, $19,458 out of state; room/board: $9,374

Financial aid: (318) 357-5961; 84% of undergrads determined to have financial need; average aid package $14,859

Southeastern Louisiana University
Hammond LA
(985) 549-5637
U.S. News ranking: Reg. U. (S), No. 99
Website: www.southeastern.edu
Admissions email: admissions@southeastern.edu
Public; founded 1925
Freshman admissions: selective; 2019-2020: 4,325 applied, 3,925 accepted. Either SAT or ACT required. ACT 25/75 percentile: 20-25. High school rank: 13% in top tenth, 36% in top quarter, 71% in top half
Early decision deadline: N/A, notification date: N/A
Early action deadline: N/A, notification date: N/A
Application deadline (fall): 8/1
Undergraduate student body: 9,248 full time, 4,048 part time; 38% male, 62% female; 0% American Indian, 1% Asian, 22% Black, 7% Hispanic, 4% multiracial, 0% Pacific Islander, 63% white, 1% international; 96% from in state; 23% live on campus; 4% of students in fraternities, 7% in sororities
Most popular majors: 21% Business, Management, Marketing, and Related Support Services, 13% Health Professions and Related Programs, 12% Liberal Arts and Sciences, General Studies and Humanities, 7% Education, 7% Parks, Recreation, Leisure, and Fitness Studies
Expenses: 2020-2021: $8,289 in state, $20,767 out of state; room/board: $8,710
Financial aid: (985) 549-2244; 65% of undergrads determined to have financial need; average aid package $12,928

Southern University and A&M College
Baton Rouge LA
(225) 771-2430
U.S. News ranking: Reg. U. (S), second tier
Website: www.subr.edu/
Admissions email: admit@subr.edu
Public; founded 1880
Freshman admissions: selective; 2019-2020: 10,514 applied, 3,684 accepted. Either SAT or ACT required. ACT 25/75 percentile: 17-20. High school rank: 4% in top tenth, 14% in top quarter, 39% in top half
Early decision deadline: N/A, notification date: N/A
Early action deadline: N/A, notification date: N/A
Application deadline (fall): 9/30
Undergraduate student body: 4,875 full time, 1,449 part time; 35% male, 65% female; 0% American Indian, 0% Asian, 93% Black, 1% Hispanic, 2% multiracial, 0% Pacific Islander, 2% white, 1% international; 65% from in state; N/A live on campus; N/A of students in fraternities, N/A in sororities

Most popular majors: 22% Health Professions and Related Programs, 12% Business, Management, Marketing, and Related Support Services, 12% Homeland Security, Law Enforcement, Firefighting and Related Protective Services, 7% Public Administration and Social Service Professions, 6% Psychology
Expenses: 2020-2021: $43,374 in state, $53,816 out of state; room/board: $11,053
Financial aid: (225) 771-4530; 90% of undergrads determined to have financial need

Southern University–New Orleans
New Orleans LA
(504) 286-5314
U.S. News ranking: Reg. U. (S), second tier
Website: www.suno.edu
Admissions email: N/A
Public; founded 1956
Freshman admissions: less selective; 2019-2020: 1,016 applied, 613 accepted. Either SAT or ACT required. ACT 25/75 percentile: 15-18. High school rank: 9% in top tenth, 27% in top quarter, 53% in top half
Early decision deadline: N/A, notification date: N/A
Early action deadline: N/A, notification date: N/A
Application deadline (fall): N/A
Undergraduate student body: 1,382 full time, 512 part time; 28% male, 72% female; N/A American Indian, N/A Asian, N/A Black, N/A Hispanic, N/A multiracial, N/A Pacific Islander, N/A white, N/A international
Most popular majors: Information not available
Expenses: 2019-2020: $7,169 in state, $16,070 out of state; room/board: $9,040
Financial aid: (504) 286-5263

Tulane University
New Orleans LA
(504) 865-5731
U.S. News ranking: Nat. U., No. 41
Website: tulane.edu
Admissions email: undergrad.admission@tulane.edu
Private; founded 1834
Freshman admissions: most selective; 2019-2020: 42,185 applied, 5,431 accepted. Either SAT or ACT required. ACT 25/75 percentile: 31-33. High school rank: 64% in top tenth, 88% in top quarter, 97% in top half
Early decision deadline: 11/1, notification date: 12/15
Early action deadline: 11/15, notification date: 1/15
Application deadline (fall): 11/15
Undergraduate student body: 6,934 full time, 34 part time; 41% male, 59% female; 0% American Indian, 6% Asian, 5% Black, 7% Hispanic, 4% multiracial, 0% Pacific Islander, 71% white, 5% international; 20% from in state; 46% live on campus; 22% of students in fraternities, 51% in sororities

Most popular majors: 26% Business, Management, Marketing, and Related Support Services, 17% Social Sciences, 11% Biological and Biomedical Sciences, 8% Health Professions and Related Programs, 6% Psychology
Expenses: 2020-2021: $58,852; room/board: $16,248
Financial aid: (504) 865-5723; 30% of undergrads determined to have financial need; average aid package $47,419

University of Holy Cross[1]
New Orleans LA
(504) 398-2175
U.S. News ranking: Reg. U. (S), No. 99
Website: www.uhcno.edu/
Admissions email: admissions@UHCNO.edu
Private; founded 1916
Affiliation: Roman Catholic
Application deadline (fall): rolling
Undergraduate student body: N/A full time, N/A part time
Expenses: 2019-2020: $14,720; room/board: $10,749
Financial aid: (504) 398-2133

University of Louisiana at Lafayette
Lafayette LA
(337) 482-6553
U.S. News ranking: Nat. U., second tier
Website: www.louisiana.edu
Admissions email: admissions@louisiana.edu
Public; founded 1898
Freshman admissions: selective; 2019-2020: 9,138 applied, 6,206 accepted. Either SAT or ACT required. ACT 25/75 percentile: 21-26. High school rank: 17% in top tenth, 38% in top quarter, 74% in top half
Early decision deadline: N/A, notification date: N/A
Early action deadline: N/A, notification date: N/A
Application deadline (fall): rolling
Undergraduate student body: 11,929 full time, 2,674 part time; 43% male, 57% female; 0% American Indian, 3% Asian, 21% Black, 6% Hispanic, 3% multiracial, 0% Pacific Islander, 64% white, 1% international; 92% from in state; 24% live on campus; 9% of students in fraternities, 12% in sororities
Most popular majors: 22% Health Professions and Related Programs, 13% Business, Management, Marketing, and Related Support Services, 11% Engineering, 11% Liberal Arts and Sciences, General Studies and Humanities, 10% Education
Expenses: 2020-2021: $5,840 in state, $19,568 out of state; room/board: N/A
Financial aid: (337) 482-6506; 65% of undergrads determined to have financial need; average aid package $10,794

University of Louisiana–Monroe
Monroe LA
(318) 342-7777
U.S. News ranking: Nat. U., second tier
Website: www.ulm.edu
Admissions email: admissions@ulm.edu
Public; founded 1931
Freshman admissions: selective; 2019-2020: 4,036 applied, 3,203 accepted. Either SAT or ACT required. ACT 25/75 percentile: 20-25. High school rank: 22% in top tenth, 45% in top quarter, 72% in top half
Early decision deadline: N/A, notification date: N/A
Early action deadline: N/A, notification date: N/A
Application deadline (fall): 8/15
Undergraduate student body: 4,760 full time, 2,116 part time; 36% male, 64% female; 0% American Indian, 2% Asian, 24% Black, 3% Hispanic, 3% multiracial, 0% Pacific Islander, 61% white, 5% international; N/A from in state; 29% live on campus; N/A of students in fraternities, N/A in sororities
Most popular majors: 11% Psychology, General, 8% General Studies, 8% Registered Nursing/Registered Nurse, 7% Business Administration and Management, General, 7% Kinesiology and Exercise Science
Expenses: 2020-2021: $8,974 in state, $21,074 out of state; room/board: $7,855
Financial aid: (318) 342-5329; 66% of undergrads determined to have financial need; average aid package $12,600

University of New Orleans
New Orleans LA
(504) 280-6595
U.S. News ranking: Nat. U., second tier
Website: www.uno.edu
Admissions email: admissions@uno.edu
Public; founded 1958
Freshman admissions: selective; 2019-2020: 5,882 applied, 3,267 accepted. Either SAT or ACT required. ACT 25/75 percentile: 20-25. High school rank: 14% in top tenth, 37% in top quarter, 67% in top half
Early decision deadline: N/A, notification date: N/A
Early action deadline: N/A, notification date: N/A
Application deadline (fall): 8/20
Undergraduate student body: 4,905 full time, 1,808 part time; 49% male, 51% female; 0% American Indian, 9% Asian, 19% Black, 14% Hispanic, 5% multiracial, 0% Pacific Islander, 48% white, 3% international; N/A from in state; 11% live on campus; 3% of students in fraternities, 4% in sororities
Most popular majors: 28% Business, Management, Marketing, and Related Support Services, 14% Engineering, 10% Biological and Biomedical Sciences,

10% Multi/Interdisciplinary Studies, 8% Visual and Performing Arts
Expenses: 2020-2021: $13,780 in state, $13,780 out of state; room/board: $11,200
Financial aid: (504) 280-6603; 71% of undergrads determined to have financial need; average aid package $10,366

Xavier University of Louisiana
New Orleans LA
(504) 520-7388
U.S. News ranking: Reg. U. (S), No. 16
Website: www.xula.edu
Admissions email: apply@xula.edu
Private; founded 1915
Affiliation: Roman Catholic
Freshman admissions: selective; 2019-2020: 9,291 applied, 5,573 accepted. Either SAT or ACT required. ACT 25/75 percentile: 20-26. High school rank: 30% in top tenth, 59% in top quarter, 85% in top half
Early decision deadline: N/A, notification date: N/A
Early action deadline: N/A, notification date: N/A
Application deadline (fall): 7/1
Undergraduate student body: 2,424 full time, 106 part time; 24% male, 76% female; 0% American Indian, 4% Asian, 82% Black, 4% Hispanic, 4% multiracial, 0% Pacific Islander, 2% white, 2% international; 36% from in state; 62% live on campus; 1% of students in fraternities, 5% in sororities
Most popular majors: 43% Biology/ Biological Sciences, General, 13% Physical Sciences, 11% Psychology, General, 8% Business Administration and Management, General, 6% Public Health, General
Expenses: 2020-2021: $25,947; room/board: $9,458
Financial aid: (504) 520-7835; 74% of undergrads determined to have financial need; average aid package $10,046

MAINE

Bates College
Lewiston ME
(855) 228-3755
U.S. News ranking: Nat. Lib. Arts, No. 22
Website: www.bates.edu
Admissions email: admission@bates.edu
Private; founded 1855
Freshman admissions: most selective; 2019-2020: 8,222 applied, 998 accepted. Neither SAT nor ACT required. SAT 25/75 percentile: 1270-1480. High school rank: 71% in top tenth, 90% in top quarter, 99% in top half
Early decision deadline: 11/15, notification date: 12/20
Early action deadline: N/A, notification date: N/A
Application deadline (fall): 1/1
Undergraduate student body: 1,820 full time, 0 part time; 50% male, 50% female; 0% American

Indian, 5% Asian, 6% Black, 8% Hispanic, 6% multiracial, 0% Pacific Islander, 67% white, 8% international
Most popular majors: 31% Social Sciences, 14% Biological and Biomedical Sciences, 11% Psychology, 10% English Language and Literature/Letters, 8% Visual and Performing Arts
Expenses: 2020-2021: $57,353; room/board: $16,177
Financial aid: (207) 786-6096; 43% of undergrads determined to have financial need; average aid package $51,099

Bowdoin College
Brunswick ME
(207) 725-3100
U.S. News ranking: Nat. Lib. Arts, No. 6
Website: www.bowdoin.edu
Admissions email: admissions@bowdoin.edu
Private; founded 1794
Affiliation: Other
Freshman admissions: most selective; 2019-2020: 9,332 applied, 845 accepted. Neither SAT nor ACT required. SAT 25/75 percentile: 1330-1520. High school rank: 85% in top tenth, 97% in top quarter, 100% in top half
Early decision deadline: 11/15, notification date: 12/15
Early action deadline: N/A, notification date: N/A
Application deadline (fall): 1/1
Undergraduate student body: 1,834 full time, 1 part time; 49% male, 51% female; 0% American Indian, 7% Asian, 8% Black, 11% Hispanic, 7% multiracial, 0% Pacific Islander, 59% white, 7% international; 11% from in state; 92% live on campus; N/A of students in fraternities, N/A in sororities
Most popular majors: 23% Political Science and Government, General, 14% Economics, General, 11% Mathematics, General, 7% History, General, 6% Computer Science
Expenses: 2020-2021: $56,350; room/board: N/A
Financial aid: (207) 725-3144; 49% of undergrads determined to have financial need; average aid package $51,107

Colby College
Waterville ME
(800) 723-3032
U.S. News ranking: Nat. Lib. Arts, No. 15
Website: www.colby.edu
Admissions email: admissions@colby.edu
Private; founded 1813
Freshman admissions: most selective; 2019-2020: 13,584 applied, 1,314 accepted. Neither SAT nor ACT required. SAT 25/75 percentile: 1380-1520. High school rank: 68% in top tenth, 90% in top quarter, 99% in top half
Early decision deadline: 11/15, notification date: 12/15
Early action deadline: N/A, notification date: N/A

Application deadline (fall): 1/1
Undergraduate student body: 2,003 full time, 0 part time; 46% male, 54% female; 0% American Indian, 8% Asian, 5% Black, 8% Hispanic, 5% multiracial, 0% Pacific Islander, 61% white, 10% international; 9% from in state; 96% live on campus; 0% of students in fraternities, 0% in sororities
Most popular majors: 29% Social Sciences, 12% Natural Resources and Conservation, 11% Multi/ Interdisciplinary Studies, 10% Psychology, 6% Biological and Biomedical Sciences
Expenses: 2020-2021: $59,430; room/board: $15,295
Financial aid: (800) 723-4033; 45% of undergrads determined to have financial need; average aid package $50,475

College of the Atlantic
Bar Harbor ME
(800) 528-0025
U.S. News ranking: Nat. Lib. Arts, No. 101
Website: www.coa.edu/
Admissions email: inquiry@coa.edu
Private; founded 1969
Freshman admissions: selective; 2019-2020: 451 applied, 325 accepted. Neither SAT nor ACT required. SAT 25/75 percentile: 1170-1340. High school rank: 22% in top tenth, 53% in top quarter, 84% in top half
Early decision deadline: 12/1, notification date: 12/15
Early action deadline: N/A, notification date: N/A
Application deadline (fall): 2/1
Undergraduate student body: 346 full time, 9 part time; 26% male, 74% female; 0% American Indian, 2% Asian, 1% Black, 6% Hispanic, 2% multiracial, 0% Pacific Islander, 61% white, 26% international; 21% from in state; 52% live on campus; 0% of students in fraternities, 0% in sororities
Most popular majors: Information not available
Expenses: 2020-2021: $43,542; room/board: $9,747
Financial aid: (207) 801-5645; 86% of undergrads determined to have financial need; average aid package $41,235

Husson University
Bangor ME
(207) 941-7100
U.S. News ranking: Nat. U., second tier
Website: www.husson.edu
Admissions email: admit@husson.edu
Private; founded 1898
Freshman admissions: selective; 2019-2020: 2,529 applied, 2,139 accepted. Either SAT or ACT required. SAT 25/75 percentile: 960-1140. High school rank: 12% in top tenth, 39% in top quarter, 75% in top half
Early decision deadline: N/A, notification date: N/A
Early action deadline: N/A, notification date: N/A
Application deadline (fall): rolling

Undergraduate student body: 2,407 full time, 459 part time; 42% male, 58% female; 0% American Indian, 1% Asian, 5% Black, 1% Hispanic, 3% multiracial, 0% Pacific Islander, 83% white, 2% international; 74% from in state; 43% live on campus; 5% of students in fraternities, 5% in sororities
Most popular majors: 31% Health Professions and Related Programs, 26% Business, Management, Marketing, and Related Support Services, 11% Homeland Security, Law Enforcement, Firefighting and Related Protective Services, 9% Communications Technologies/ Technicians and Support Services, 6% Psychology
Expenses: 2020-2021: $19,772; room/board: $10,632
Financial aid: (207) 941-7156; 81% of undergrads determined to have financial need; average aid package $16,761

Maine College of Art[1]
Portland ME
(800) 699-1509
U.S. News ranking: Arts, unranked
Website: www.meca.edu
Admissions email: admissions@meca.edu
Private; founded 1882
Application deadline (fall): rolling
Undergraduate student body: N/A full time, N/A part time
Expenses: 2019-2020: $36,424; room/board: $12,770
Financial aid: (207) 699-5073

Maine Maritime Academy
Castine ME
(207) 326-2206
U.S. News ranking: Reg. Coll. (N), No. 4
Website: www.mainemaritime.edu
Admissions email: admissions@mma.edu
Public; founded 1941
Freshman admissions: selective; 2019-2020: 1,441 applied, 653 accepted. Either SAT or ACT required. SAT 25/75 percentile: 1010-1200. High school rank: 12% in top tenth, 40% in top quarter, 75% in top half
Early decision deadline: N/A, notification date: N/A
Early action deadline: 11/30, notification date: 2/1
Application deadline (fall): 3/1
Undergraduate student body: 967 full time, 24 part time; 84% male, 16% female; 1% American Indian, 1% Asian, 2% Black, 3% Hispanic, 0% multiracial, 0% Pacific Islander, 84% white, 1% international
Most popular majors: 41% Naval Architecture and Marine Engineering, 23% Marine Science/ Merchant Marine Officer, 12% Engineering Technologies and Engineering-Related Fields, Other, 11% International Business/ Trade/Commerce, 11% Systems Engineering
Expenses: 2020-2021: $14,058 in state, $28,438 out of state; room/board: $10,720

Financial aid: (207) 326-2339; 69% of undergrads determined to have financial need; average aid package $10,877

St. Joseph's College[1]
Standish ME
(207) 893-7746
U.S. News ranking: Reg. U. (N), second tier
Website: www.sjcme.edu
Admissions email: admission@sjcme.edu
Private
Application deadline (fall): N/A
Undergraduate student body: N/A full time, N/A part time
Expenses: 2019-2020: $36,720; room/board: $14,090
Financial aid: N/A

Thomas College[1]
Waterville ME
(800) 339-7001
U.S. News ranking: Reg. U. (N), second tier
Website: www.thomas.edu
Admissions email: admiss@thomas.edu
Private; founded 1894
Application deadline (fall): rolling
Undergraduate student body: N/A full time, N/A part time
Expenses: 2020-2021: $28,430; room/board: $11,560
Financial aid: (207) 859-1105; 86% of undergrads determined to have financial need; average aid package $22,254

Unity College[1]
Unity ME
(800) 624-1024
U.S. News ranking: Reg. Coll. (N), No. 11
Website: www.unity.edu
Admissions email: admissions@unity.edu
Private; founded 1965
Application deadline (fall): rolling
Undergraduate student body: N/A full time, N/A part time
Expenses: 2019-2020: $30,000; room/board: $11,030
Financial aid: (207) 509-7235

University of Maine
Orono ME
(877) 486-2364
U.S. News ranking: Nat. U., No. 206
Website: www.umaine.edu
Admissions email: umaineadmissions@maine.edu
Public; founded 1865
Freshman admissions: selective; 2019-2020: 13,118 applied, 11,838 accepted. Either SAT or ACT required. SAT 25/75 percentile: 1050-1260. High school rank: 20% in top tenth, 46% in top quarter, 79% in top half
Early decision deadline: N/A, notification date: N/A
Early action deadline: 12/1, notification date: 1/15
Application deadline (fall): 2/1
Undergraduate student body: 8,060 full time, 1,370 part time; 53% male, 47% female; 1% American Indian, 2% Asian, 2% Black, 4% Hispanic, 4% multiracial,

0% Pacific Islander, 84% white, 2% international; 67% from in state; 38% live on campus; N/A of students in fraternities, N/A in sororities
Most popular majors: 17% Business, Management, Marketing, and Related Support Services, 14% Engineering, 8% Education, 8% Social Sciences, 6% Natural Resources and Conservation
Expenses: 2020-2021: $11,738 in state, $32,528 out of state; room/board: $11,286
Financial aid: (207) 581-1324; 64% of undergrads determined to have financial need; average aid package $14,450

University of Maine–Augusta[1]
Augusta ME
(207) 621-3465
U.S. News ranking: Reg. Coll. (N), second tier
Website: www.uma.edu
Admissions email: umaadm@maine.edu
Public; founded 1965
Application deadline (fall): 9/1
Undergraduate student body: N/A full time, N/A part time
Expenses: 2019-2020: $8,168 in state, $18,338 out of state; room/board: $8,000
Financial aid: (207) 621-3141

University of Maine–Farmington
Farmington ME
(207) 778-7050
U.S. News ranking: Reg. Coll. (N), No. 6
Website: www.farmington.edu
Admissions email: umfadmit@maine.edu
Public; founded 1864
Freshman admissions: selective; 2019-2020: 1,744 applied, 1,586 accepted. Neither SAT nor ACT required. SAT 25/75 percentile: 940-1160. High school rank: 15% in top tenth, 37% in top quarter, 72% in top half
Early decision deadline: N/A, notification date: N/A
Early action deadline: 11/15, notification date: 12/15
Application deadline (fall): rolling
Undergraduate student body: 1,505 full time, 169 part time; 34% male, 66% female; 1% American Indian, 1% Asian, 3% Black, 3% Hispanic, 3% multiracial, 0% Pacific Islander, 88% white, 0% international; 83% from in state; 53% live on campus; 0% of students in fraternities, 0% in sororities
Most popular majors: 36% Education, 13% Health Professions and Related Programs, 12% Psychology, 9% English Language and Literature/Letters, 7% Business, Management, Marketing, and Related Support Services
Expenses: 2020-2021: $9,572 in state, $20,282 out of state; room/board: $10,238

Financial aid: (207) 778-7100; 77% of undergrads determined to have financial need; average aid package $14,932

University of Maine–Fort Kent
Fort Kent ME
(207) 834-7600
U.S. News ranking: Reg. Coll. (N), No. 37
Website: www.umfk.edu
Admissions email: umfkadm@maine.edu
Public; founded 1878
Freshman admissions: least selective; 2019-2020: 742 applied, 737 accepted. Neither SAT nor ACT required. SAT 25/75 percentile: 880-1070. High school rank: 0% in top tenth, 13% in top quarter, 52% in top half
Early decision deadline: 12/1, notification date: 12/1
Early action deadline: 12/1, notification date: 12/1
Application deadline (fall): rolling
Undergraduate student body: 554 full time, 1,035 part time; 30% male, 70% female; 1% American Indian, 1% Asian, 5% Black, 3% Hispanic, 5% multiracial, 0% Pacific Islander, 76% white, 6% international
Most popular majors: 73% Health Professions and Related Programs, 8% Business, Management, Marketing, and Related Support Services, 4% Biological and Biomedical Sciences, 4% Public Administration and Social Service Professions, 3% Social Sciences
Expenses: 2020-2021: $8,504 in state, $12,914 out of state; room/board: $8,360
Financial aid: (207) 834-7607; 67% of undergrads determined to have financial need; average aid package $12,004

University of Maine–Machias
Machias ME
(888) 468-6866
U.S. News ranking: Nat. Lib. Arts, second tier
Website: machias.edu/
Admissions email: ummadmissions@maine.edu
Public; founded 1909
Freshman admissions: less selective; 2019-2020: 591 applied, 584 accepted. Neither SAT nor ACT required. SAT 25/75 percentile: 850-1080. High school rank: 4% in top tenth, 24% in top quarter, 49% in top half
Early decision deadline: N/A, notification date: N/A
Early action deadline: 12/15, notification date: N/A
Application deadline (fall): 8/15
Undergraduate student body: 325 full time, 334 part time; 30% male, 70% female; 6% American Indian, 1% Asian, 4% Black, 5% Hispanic, 4% multiracial, 0% Pacific Islander, 74% white, 3% international; 89% from in state; 25% live on campus; N/A of students in fraternities, N/A in sororities

Most popular majors: 26% Psychology, 24% Biological and Biomedical Sciences, 15% Liberal Arts and Sciences, General Studies and Humanities, 8% Business, Management, Marketing, and Related Support Services, 8% Parks, Recreation, Leisure, and Fitness Studies
Expenses: 2020-2021: $9,198 in state, $16,458 out of state; room/board: $9,456
Financial aid: (207) 255-1203; 84% of undergrads determined to have financial need; average aid package $13,042

University of Maine–Presque Isle
Presque Isle ME
(207) 768-9532
U.S. News ranking: Reg. Coll. (N), No. 28
Website: www.umpi.edu/admissions/
Admissions email: umpi-admissions@maine.edu
Public; founded 1903
Freshman admissions: least selective; 2019-2020: 736 applied, 729 accepted. Neither SAT nor ACT required. SAT 25/75 percentile: 870-1080. High school rank: 7% in top tenth, 23% in top quarter, 62% in top half
Early decision deadline: N/A, notification date: N/A
Early action deadline: N/A, notification date: N/A
Application deadline (fall): rolling
Undergraduate student body: 621 full time, 824 part time; 37% male, 63% female; 2% American Indian, 1% Asian, 3% Black, 3% Hispanic, 2% multiracial, 0% Pacific Islander, 81% white, 5% international; 84% from in state; 44% live on campus; 0% of students in fraternities, 0% in sororities
Most popular majors: 30% Business, Management, Marketing, and Related Support Services, 12% Liberal Arts and Sciences, General Studies and Humanities, 9% Psychology, 8% Homeland Security, Law Enforcement, Firefighting and Related Protective Services, 7% Public Administration and Social Service Professions
Expenses: 2020-2021: $8,574 in state, $12,984 out of state; room/board: $8,738
Financial aid: (207) 768-9510; 71% of undergrads determined to have financial need; average aid package $12,438

University of New England
Biddeford ME
(800) 477-4863
U.S. News ranking: Nat. U., No. 249
Website: www.une.edu
Admissions email: admissions@une.edu
Private; founded 1831
Freshman admissions: selective; 2019-2020: 5,175 applied, 4,367 accepted. Neither SAT nor ACT required. SAT 25/75

percentile: 1040-1220. High school rank: N/A
Early decision deadline: N/A, notification date: N/A
Early action deadline: 12/1, notification date: 12/15
Application deadline (fall): 2/15
Undergraduate student body: 2,425 full time, 1,850 part time; 26% male, 74% female; 0% American Indian, 3% Asian, 2% Black, 0% Hispanic, 2% multiracial, 0% Pacific Islander, 88% white, 0% international; 17% from in state; 35% live on campus; 0% of students in fraternities, 0% in sororities
Most popular majors: 45% Health Professions and Related Programs, 24% Biological and Biomedical Sciences, 10% Parks, Recreation, Leisure, and Fitness Studies, 5% Business, Management, Marketing, and Related Support Services, 4% Psychology
Expenses: 2020-2021: $38,750; room/board: $14,410
Financial aid: (207) 602-2342; 81% of undergrads determined to have financial need; average aid package $24,465

University of Southern Maine
Portland ME
(207) 780-5670
U.S. News ranking: Reg. U. (N), second tier
Website: www.usm.maine.edu
Admissions email: admitusm@maine.edu
Public; founded 1878
Freshman admissions: selective; 2019-2020: 4,996 applied, 4,042 accepted. Neither SAT nor ACT required. SAT 25/75 percentile: 950-1160. High school rank: 9% in top tenth, 36% in top quarter, 71% in top half
Early decision deadline: N/A, notification date: N/A
Early action deadline: N/A, notification date: N/A
Application deadline (fall): rolling
Undergraduate student body: 4,062 full time, 2,613 part time; 43% male, 57% female; 1% American Indian, 2% Asian, 7% Black, 3% Hispanic, 4% multiracial, 0% Pacific Islander, 79% white, 1% international
Most popular majors: 23% Business, Management, Marketing, and Related Support Services, 21% Health Professions and Related Programs, 12% Social Sciences, 6% Communication, Journalism, and Related Programs, 5% Biological and Biomedical Sciences
Expenses: 2019-2020: $9,850 in state, $23,590 out of state; room/board: $9,826
Financial aid: (207) 780-5118; 72% of undergrads determined to have financial need; average aid package $14,271

MARYLAND

Bowie State University
Bowie MD
(301) 860-3415
U.S. News ranking: Reg. U. (N), second tier
Website: www.bowiestate.edu
Admissions email: ugradadmissions@bowiestate.edu
Public; founded 1865
Freshman admissions: less selective; 2019-2020: 4,849 applied, 3,863 accepted. Either SAT or ACT required. SAT 25/75 percentile: 860-1030. High school rank: N/A
Early decision deadline: N/A, notification date: N/A
Early action deadline: N/A, notification date: N/A
Application deadline (fall): 5/15
Undergraduate student body: 4,329 full time, 898 part time; 39% male, 61% female; 0% American Indian, 1% Asian, 82% Black, 5% Hispanic, 4% multiracial, 0% Pacific Islander, 2% white, 2% international; 89% from in state; 27% live on campus; N/A of students in fraternities, N/A in sororities
Most popular majors: 18% Business Administration and Management, General, 14% Radio and Television Broadcasting Technology/Technician, 10% Criminal Justice/Safety Studies, 10% Psychology, General, 7% Biology/Biological Sciences, General
Expenses: 2020-2021: $8,444 in state, $19,136 out of state; room/board: $11,444
Financial aid: (301) 860-3540; 86% of undergrads determined to have financial need; average aid package $8,916

Coppin State University[1]
Baltimore MD
(410) 951-3600
U.S. News ranking: Reg. U. (N), second tier
Website: www.coppin.edu
Admissions email: admissions@coppin.edu
Public; founded 1900
Application deadline (fall): rolling
Undergraduate student body: N/A full time, N/A part time
Expenses: 2019-2020: $6,716 in state, $13,113 out of state; room/board: $10,654
Financial aid: (410) 951-3636

Frostburg State University[1]
Frostburg MD
(301) 687-4201
U.S. News ranking: Reg. U. (N), No. 113
Website: www.frostburg.edu
Admissions email: fsuadmissions@frostburg.edu
Public; founded 1898
Application deadline (fall): rolling
Undergraduate student body: N/A full time, N/A part time

Expenses: 2019-2020: $9,410 in state, $23,510 out of state; room/board: $10,788
Financial aid: (301) 687-4301

Goucher College

Baltimore MD
(410) 337-6100
U.S. News ranking: Nat. Lib. Arts, No. 120
Website: www.goucher.edu
Admissions email: admissions@goucher.edu
Private; founded 1885
Freshman admissions: selective; 2019-2020: 2,610 applied, 2,122 accepted. Neither SAT nor ACT required. SAT 25/75 percentile: 1030-1260. High school rank: 12% in top tenth, 44% in top quarter, 82% in top half
Early decision deadline: 11/15, notification date: 12/15
Early action deadline: 12/1, notification date: 2/1
Application deadline (fall): 1/15
Undergraduate student body: 1,325 full time, 124 part time; 33% male, 67% female; N/A American Indian, N/A Asian, N/A Black, N/A Hispanic, N/A multiracial, N/A Pacific Islander, N/A white, N/A international; N/A from in state; 85% live on campus; 0% of students in fraternities, 0% in sororities
Most popular majors: 17% Social Sciences, 13% Psychology, 13% Visual and Performing Arts, 8% English Language and Literature/Letters, 7% Biological and Biomedical Sciences
Expenses: 2020-2021: $47,300; room/board: $15,100
Financial aid: (410) 337-6141; 73% of undergrads determined to have financial need; average aid package $40,413

Hood College

Frederick MD
(800) 922-1599
U.S. News ranking: Reg. U. (N), No. 56
Website: www.hood.edu
Admissions email: admission@hood.edu
Private; founded 1893
Affiliation: United Church of Christ
Freshman admissions: selective; 2019-2020: 3,513 applied, 2,295 accepted. Neither SAT nor ACT required. SAT 25/75 percentile: 1000-1210. High school rank: 10% in top tenth, 37% in top quarter, 77% in top half
Early decision deadline: N/A, notification date: N/A
Early action deadline: N/A, notification date: N/A
Application deadline (fall): rolling
Undergraduate student body: 1,057 full time, 69 part time; 37% male, 63% female; 0% American Indian, 4% Asian, 18% Black, 12% Hispanic, 6% multiracial, 0% Pacific Islander, 58% white, 2% international; 74% from in state; 57% live on campus; 0% of students in fraternities, 0% in sororities

Most popular majors: 15% Business, Management, Marketing, and Related Support Services, 11% Biological and Biomedical Sciences, 9% Health Professions and Related Programs, 9% Psychology, 8% Communication, Journalism, and Related Programs
Expenses: 2020-2021: $42,300; room/board: $13,010
Financial aid: (301) 696-3411; 83% of undergrads determined to have financial need; average aid package $33,284

Johns Hopkins University

Baltimore MD
(410) 516-8171
U.S. News ranking: Nat. U., No. 9
Website: www.jhu.edu
Admissions email: gotojhu@jhu.edu
Private; founded 1876
Freshman admissions: most selective; 2019-2020: 30,164 applied, 2,937 accepted. Either SAT or ACT required. SAT 25/75 percentile: 1470-1570. High school rank: 98% in top tenth, 99% in top quarter, 100% in top half
Early decision deadline: 11/1, notification date: 12/15
Early action deadline: N/A, notification date: N/A
Application deadline (fall): 1/2
Undergraduate student body: 5,658 full time, 598 part time; 47% male, 53% female; 0% American Indian, 26% Asian, 8% Black, 15% Hispanic, 6% multiracial, 0% Pacific Islander, 28% white, 12% international; 10% from in state; 47% live on campus; 20% of students in fraternities, 32% in sororities
Most popular majors: 11% Neuroscience, 11% Public Health, General, 9% Cell/Cellular and Molecular Biology, 8% Bioengineering and Biomedical Engineering, 7% Chemical Engineering
Expenses: 2020-2021: $57,010; room/board: $16,800
Financial aid: (410) 516-8028; 52% of undergrads determined to have financial need; average aid package $49,032

Loyola University Maryland

Baltimore MD
(410) 617-5012
U.S. News ranking: Reg. U. (N), No. 4
Website: www.loyola.edu
Admissions email: admissions@loyola.edu
Private; founded 1852
Affiliation: Roman Catholic
Freshman admissions: more selective; 2019-2020: 10,077 applied, 8,082 accepted. Neither SAT nor ACT required. SAT 25/75 percentile: 1143-1320. High school rank: 30% in top tenth, 60% in top quarter, 91% in top half
Early decision deadline: N/A, notification date: N/A
Early action deadline: 11/15, notification date: 1/15

Application deadline (fall): 1/15
Undergraduate student body: 3,883 full time, 42 part time; 42% male, 58% female; 0% American Indian, 3% Asian, 5% Black, 12% Hispanic, 3% multiracial, 0% Pacific Islander, 76% white, 1% international; 20% from in state; 81% live on campus; 0% of students in fraternities, 0% in sororities
Most popular majors: 40% Business, Management, Marketing, and Related Support Services, 11% Communication, Journalism, and Related Programs, 9% Social Sciences, 7% Biological and Biomedical Sciences, 7% Psychology
Expenses: 2020-2021: $51,100; room/board: $17,160
Financial aid: (410) 617-2576; 54% of undergrads determined to have financial need; average aid package $36,672

Maryland Institute College of Art

Baltimore MD
(410) 225-2222
U.S. News ranking: Arts, unranked
Website: www.mica.edu
Admissions email: admissions@mica.edu
Private; founded 1826
Freshman admissions: selective; 2019-2020: 4,024 applied, 2,571 accepted. Either SAT or ACT required. SAT 25/75 percentile: 1080-1350. High school rank: N/A
Early decision deadline: 11/1, notification date: 12/6
Early action deadline: 12/1, notification date: 1/13
Application deadline (fall): 2/1
Undergraduate student body: 1,667 full time, 29 part time; 25% male, 75% female; 0% American Indian, 10% Asian, 8% Black, 10% Hispanic, 6% multiracial, 0% Pacific Islander, 36% white, 29% international; 74% from in state; 88% live on campus; N/A of students in fraternities, N/A in sororities
Most popular majors: 21% Illustration, 19% Graphic Design, 12% Intermedia/Multimedia, 8% Digital Arts, 8% Painting
Expenses: 2020-2021: $49,190; room/board: $15,050
Financial aid: (410) 225-2285

McDaniel College

Westminster MD
(800) 638-5005
U.S. News ranking: Reg. U. (N), No. 34
Website: www.mcdaniel.edu
Admissions email: admissions@mcdaniel.edu
Private; founded 1867
Freshman admissions: selective; 2019-2020: 3,761 applied, 3,454 accepted. Neither SAT nor ACT required. SAT 25/75 percentile: 988-1190. High school rank: 20% in top tenth, 44% in top quarter, 75% in top half
Early decision deadline: 11/1, notification date: 12/1
Early action deadline: 12/15, notification date: 1/15

Application deadline (fall): rolling
Undergraduate student body: 1,653 full time, 27 part time; 48% male, 52% female; 0% American Indian, 2% Asian, 21% Black, 6% Hispanic, 3% multiracial, 0% Pacific Islander, 57% white, 3% international; 68% from in state; 86% live on campus; 14% of students in fraternities, 15% in sororities
Most popular majors: 17% Business, Management, Marketing, and Related Support Services, 13% Social Sciences, 9% Parks, Recreation, Leisure, and Fitness Studies, 8% Psychology, 7% Biological and Biomedical Sciences
Expenses: 2020-2021: $45,876; room/board: $12,246
Financial aid: (410) 857-2233; 76% of undergrads determined to have financial need; average aid package $39,063

Morgan State University

Baltimore MD
(800) 332-6674
U.S. News ranking: Nat. U., second tier
Website: morgan.edu
Admissions email: admissions@morgan.edu
Public; founded 1867
Freshman admissions: less selective; 2019-2020: 8,156 applied, 5,532 accepted. Either SAT or ACT required. SAT 25/75 percentile: 920-1070. High school rank: 8% in top tenth, 22% in top quarter, 56% in top half
Early decision deadline: N/A, notification date: N/A
Early action deadline: 11/15, notification date: 2/15
Application deadline (fall): 2/15
Undergraduate student body: 5,759 full time, 702 part time; 43% male, 57% female; 0% American Indian, 1% Asian, 83% Black, 4% Hispanic, 3% multiracial, 0% Pacific Islander, 2% white, 6% international; 73% from in state; 40% live on campus; 3% of students in fraternities, 5% in sororities
Most popular majors: 21% Business, Management, Marketing, and Related Support Services, 16% Engineering, 8% Liberal Arts and Sciences, General Studies and Humanities, 7% Communication, Journalism, and Related Programs, 7% Education
Expenses: 2019-2020: $8,008 in state, $18,480 out of state; room/board: $10,994
Financial aid: (443) 885-3170; 78% of undergrads determined to have financial need; average aid package $10,978

Mount St. Mary's University

Emmitsburg MD
(800) 448-4347
U.S. News ranking: Reg. U. (N), No. 38
Website: msmary.edu
Admissions email: admissions@msmary.edu
Private; founded 1808

Affiliation: Roman Catholic
Freshman admissions: selective; 2019-2020: 4,716 applied, 3,527 accepted. Neither SAT nor ACT required. SAT 25/75 percentile: 990-1200. High school rank: 12% in top tenth, 35% in top quarter, 68% in top half
Early decision deadline: N/A, notification date: N/A
Early action deadline: 12/1, notification date: N/A
Application deadline (fall): 3/1
Undergraduate student body: 1,762 full time, 136 part time; 50% male, 50% female; 0% American Indian, 3% Asian, 17% Black, 13% Hispanic, 5% multiracial, 1% Pacific Islander, 58% white, 1% international; N/A from in state; 68% live on campus; 0% of students in fraternities, 0% in sororities
Most popular majors: 31% Business, Management, Marketing, and Related Support Services, 14% Social Sciences, 11% Education, 5% Health Professions and Related Programs, 5% Parks, Recreation, Leisure, and Fitness Studies
Expenses: 2020-2021: $43,650; room/board: $13,630
Financial aid: (301) 447-8364; 71% of undergrads determined to have financial need; average aid package $31,489

Notre Dame of Maryland University

Baltimore MD
(410) 532-5330
U.S. News ranking: Reg. U. (N), No. 59
Website: www.ndm.edu
Admissions email: admiss@ndm.edu
Private; founded 1895
Affiliation: Roman Catholic
Freshman admissions: selective; 2019-2020: 1,155 applied, 713 accepted. Neither SAT nor ACT required. SAT 25/75 percentile: 920-1140. High school rank: 21% in top tenth, 42% in top quarter, 75% in top half
Early decision deadline: N/A, notification date: N/A
Early action deadline: N/A, notification date: N/A
Application deadline (fall): rolling
Undergraduate student body: 533 full time, 250 part time; 4% male, 96% female; 0% American Indian, 7% Asian, 28% Black, 12% Hispanic, 5% multiracial, 0% Pacific Islander, 38% white, 2% international; 94% from in state; 28% live on campus; 0% of students in fraternities, 0% in sororities
Most popular majors: 51% Health Professions and Related Programs, 26% Liberal Arts and Sciences, General Studies and Humanities, 4% Biological and Biomedical Sciences, 3% Physical Sciences, 3% Social Sciences
Expenses: 2020-2021: $39,675; room/board: $12,566
Financial aid: (410) 532-5369; 66% of undergrads determined to have financial need; average aid package $29,157

Salisbury University
Salisbury MD
(410) 543-6161
U.S. News ranking: Reg. U. (N),
No. 67
Website: www.salisbury.edu/
Admissions email:
admissions@salisbury.edu
Public; founded 1925
Freshman admissions: selective;
2019-2020: 8,421 applied,
6,190 accepted. Neither SAT
nor ACT required. SAT 25/75
percentile: 1120-1280. High
school rank: 15% in top tenth,
45% in top quarter, 81% in
top half
Early decision deadline: 11/15,
notification date: 12/15
Early action deadline: 12/1,
notification date: 1/15
Application deadline (fall): 1/15
Undergraduate student body: 7,060
full time, 583 part time; 44%
male, 56% female; 1% American
Indian, 4% Asian, 14% Black,
5% Hispanic, 2% multiracial,
0% Pacific Islander, 70% white,
1% international; 87% from in
state; 31% live on campus; 10%
of students in fraternities, 7% in
sororities
Most popular majors: 17%
Business, Management,
Marketing, and Related Support
Services, 10% Education, 8%
Communication, Journalism, and
Related Programs, 8% Psychology,
7% Public Administration and
Social Service Professions
Expenses: 2020-2021: $10,044
in state, $20,110 out of state;
room/board: $12,260
Financial aid: (410) 543-6165;
55% of undergrads determined to
have financial need; average aid
package $8,767

Stevenson University
Stevenson MD
(877) 468-6852
U.S. News ranking: Reg. U. (N),
No. 81
Website: www.stevenson.edu/
Admissions email:
admissions@stevenson.edu
Private; founded 1947
Freshman admissions: selective;
2019-2020: 4,413 applied,
3,565 accepted. Either SAT
or ACT required. SAT 25/75
percentile: 1010-1190. High
school rank: 18% in top tenth,
44% in top quarter, 76% in
top half
Early decision deadline: N/A,
notification date: N/A
Early action deadline: N/A,
notification date: N/A
Application deadline (fall): rolling
Undergraduate student body: 2,724
full time, 383 part time; 36%
male, 64% female; 0% American
Indian, 4% Asian, 26% Black,
7% Hispanic, 5% multiracial,
0% Pacific Islander, 55% white,
1% international; 78% from in
state; 54% live on campus; 1%
of students in fraternities, 1% in
sororities
Most popular majors: 24% Health
Professions and Related Programs,
20% Business, Management,
Marketing, and Related
Support Services, 8% Biological
and Biomedical Sciences,

7% Computer and Information
Sciences and Support Services,
7% Homeland Security, Law
Enforcement, Firefighting and
Related Protective Services
Expenses: 2020-2021: $37,808;
room/board: $13,966
Financial aid: (443) 334-3200;
77% of undergrads determined to
have financial need; average aid
package $26,376

St. John's College
Annapolis MD
(410) 626-2522
U.S. News ranking: Nat. Lib. Arts,
No. 63
Website: www.sjc.edu
Admissions email:
annapolis.admissions@sjc.edu
Private; founded 1696
Freshman admissions: more
selective; 2019-2020: 909
applied, 544 accepted. Neither
SAT nor ACT required. SAT
25/75 percentile: 1200-1420.
High school rank: 29% in top
tenth, 56% in top quarter, 82%
in top half
Early decision deadline: 11/1,
notification date: 12/1
Early action deadline: 11/15,
notification date: 12/15
Application deadline (fall): rolling
Undergraduate student body:
490 full time, 4 part time; 54%
male, 46% female; 0% American
Indian, 4% Asian, 1% Black,
6% Hispanic, 5% multiracial,
0% Pacific Islander, 63% white,
20% international; 18% from in
state; 80% live on campus; 0%
of students in fraternities, 0% in
sororities
Most popular majors: 100% Liberal
Arts and Sciences/Liberal Studies
Expenses: 2020-2021: $35,935;
room/board: $13,386
Financial aid: (410) 626-2502;
69% of undergrads determined to
have financial need; average aid
package $29,906

St. Mary's College of Maryland
St. Marys City MD
(800) 492-7181
U.S. News ranking: Nat. Lib. Arts,
No. 80
Website: www.smcm.edu
Admissions email:
admissions@smcm.edu
Public; founded 1840
Freshman admissions: selective;
2019-2020: 1,621 applied,
1,366 accepted. Neither SAT
nor ACT required. SAT 25/75
percentile: 1060-1290. High
school rank: 26% in top tenth,
55% in top quarter, 83% in
top half
Early decision deadline: 11/1,
notification date: 12/1
Early action deadline: 11/1,
notification date: 1/1
Application deadline (fall): 1/15
Undergraduate student body: 1,435
full time, 56 part time; 41%
male, 59% female; 0% American
Indian, 4% Asian, 10% Black,
7% Hispanic, 6% multiracial,
0% Pacific Islander, 71% white,

0% international; 95% from in
state; 80% live on campus; 0%
of students in fraternities, 0% in
sororities
Most popular majors: 20% Social
Sciences, 14% Biological and
Biomedical Sciences, 11%
Psychology, 8% English Language
and Literature/Letters, 8% Visual
and Performing Arts
Expenses: 2020-2021: $15,124
in state, $31,200 out of state;
room/board: $13,595
Financial aid: (240) 895-3000;
52% of undergrads determined to
have financial need; average aid
package $14,914

Towson University
Towson MD
(410) 704-2113
U.S. News ranking: Nat. U.,
No. 196
Website: www.towson.edu
Admissions email:
admissions@towson.edu
Public; founded 1866
Freshman admissions: selective;
2019-2020: 12,678 applied,
9,674 accepted. Either SAT
or ACT required. SAT 25/75
percentile: 1060-1220. High
school rank: 15% in top tenth,
42% in top quarter, 79% in
top half
Early decision deadline: N/A,
notification date: N/A
Early action deadline: 12/1,
notification date: 12/31
Application deadline (fall): 1/15
Undergraduate student body:
17,209 full time, 2,410 part
time; 41% male, 59% female;
0% American Indian, 7% Asian,
24% Black, 9% Hispanic, 5%
multiracial, 0% Pacific Islander,
52% white, 2% international;
89% from in state; 30% live
on campus; 10% of students in
fraternities, 9% in sororities
Most popular majors: 15%
Business, Management,
Marketing, and Related Support
Services, 13% Health Professions
and Related Programs, 10%
Communication, Journalism, and
Related Programs, 10% Social
Sciences, 8% Psychology
Expenses: 2020-2021: $10,456
in state, $25,508 out of state;
room/board: $13,132
Financial aid: (410) 704-4236;
57% of undergrads determined to
have financial need; average aid
package $11,275

United States Naval Academy
Annapolis MD
(410) 293-1858
U.S. News ranking: Nat. Lib. Arts,
No. 6
Website: www.usna.edu
Admissions email:
inquire@usna.edu
Public; founded 1845
Freshman admissions: most
selective; 2019-2020: 16,331
applied, 1,362 accepted. Either
SAT or ACT required. SAT 25/75
percentile: 1240-1460. High
school rank: 54% in top tenth,
81% in top quarter, 95% in
top half

Early decision deadline: N/A,
notification date: N/A
Early action deadline: N/A,
notification date: N/A
Application deadline (fall): 1/31
Undergraduate student body:
4,524 full time, 0 part time; 73%
male, 27% female; 0% American
Indian, 7% Asian, 7% Black,
12% Hispanic, 10% multiracial,
1% Pacific Islander, 61% white,
1% international; N/A from in
state; 100% live on campus; N/A
of students in fraternities, N/A in
sororities
Most popular majors: 39%
Engineering, 26% Social
Sciences, 11% Physical Sciences,
5% Computer and Information
Sciences and Support Services,
5% English Language and
Literature/Letters
Expenses: 2020-2021: $0 in
state, $0 out of state; room/
board: N/A
Financial aid: N/A; 0% of
undergrads determined to have
financial need

University of Baltimore
Baltimore MD
(410) 837-4777
U.S. News ranking: Reg. U. (N),
No. 111
Website: www.ubalt.edu
Admissions email:
admissions@ubalt.edu
Public; founded 1925
Freshman admissions: selective;
2019-2020: 254 applied, 198
accepted. Either SAT or ACT
required. SAT 25/75 percentile:
970-1135. High school rank: N/A
Early decision deadline: N/A,
notification date: N/A
Early action deadline: N/A,
notification date: N/A
Application deadline (fall): rolling
Undergraduate student body: 1,146
full time, 856 part time; 41%
male, 59% female; 1% American
Indian, 5% Asian, 48% Black,
6% Hispanic, 4% multiracial,
1% Pacific Islander, 30% white,
2% international; 94% from in
state; N/A live on campus; N/A
of students in fraternities, N/A in
sororities
Most popular majors: 36%
Business/Commerce, General,
10% Criminal Justice/Police
Science, 8% Health Services
Administration, 7% Animation,
Interactive Technology, Video
Graphics and Special Effects, 5%
Digital Communication and Media/
Multimedia
Expenses: 2020-2021: $9,356 in
state, $21,964 out of state; room/
board: N/A
Financial aid: (410) 837-4772;
75% of undergrads determined to
have financial need; average aid
package $12,053

University of Maryland–Baltimore County
Baltimore MD
(410) 455-2292
U.S. News ranking: Nat. U.,
No. 160
Website: www.umbc.edu

Admissions email:
admissions@umbc.edu
Public; founded 1966
Freshman admissions: more
selective; 2019-2020: 11,842
applied, 7,227 accepted. Either
SAT or ACT required. SAT 25/75
percentile: 1180-1360. High
school rank: 21% in top tenth,
51% in top quarter, 83% in
top half
Early decision deadline: N/A,
notification date: N/A
Early action deadline: 11/1,
notification date: 12/15
Application deadline (fall): 2/1
Undergraduate student body: 9,436
full time, 1,624 part time; 55%
male, 45% female; 0% American
Indian, 22% Asian, 19% Black,
8% Hispanic, 5% multiracial,
0% Pacific Islander, 39% white,
4% international; 91% from in
state; 36% live on campus; 3%
of students in fraternities, 5% in
sororities
Most popular majors: 21%
Computer and Information
Sciences and Support Services,
15% Biological and Biomedical
Sciences, 11% Psychology, 10%
Engineering, 10% Social Sciences
Expenses: 2020-2021: $12,028
in state, $27,662 out of state;
room/board: $12,350
Financial aid: (410) 455-2538;
54% of undergrads determined to
have financial need; average aid
package $11,728

University of Maryland–College Park
College Park MD
(301) 314-8385
U.S. News ranking: Nat. U., No. 58
Website: www.umd.edu/
Admissions email:
ApplyMaryland@umd.edu
Public; founded 1856
Freshman admissions: more
selective; 2019-2020: 32,987
applied, 14,560 accepted. Either
SAT or ACT required. SAT 25/75
percentile: 1280-1480. High
school rank: 69% in top tenth,
89% in top quarter, 99% in
top half
Early decision deadline: N/A,
notification date: N/A
Early action deadline: 11/1,
notification date: 1/31
Application deadline (fall): 1/20
Undergraduate student body:
28,390 full time, 2,121 part
time; 52% male, 48% female;
0% American Indian, 18% Asian,
11% Black, 9% Hispanic, 5%
multiracial, 0% Pacific Islander,
49% white, 4% international;
77% from in state; 39% live
on campus; 14% of students in
fraternities, 19% in sororities
Most popular majors: 8%
Computer Science, 6% Biology/
Biological Sciences, General,
6% Economics, General, 4%
Computer Engineering, General,
4% Finance, General
Expenses: 2020-2021: $10,778
in state, $36,890 out of state;
room/board: $12,874
Financial aid: (301) 314-9000;
39% of undergrads determined to
have financial need; average aid
package $12,780

University of Maryland Eastern Shore

Princess Anne MD
(410) 651-6410
U.S. News ranking: Nat. U., second tier
Website: www.umes.edu
Admissions email: umesadmissions@umes.edu
Public; founded 1886
Freshman admissions: less selective; 2019-2020: 3,929 applied, 2,541 accepted. Neither SAT nor ACT required. SAT 25/75 percentile: 850-1030. High school rank: N/A
Early decision deadline: N/A, notification date: N/A
Early action deadline: N/A, notification date: N/A
Application deadline (fall): 6/30
Undergraduate student body: 2,095 full time, 239 part time; 45% male, 55% female; 0% American Indian, 2% Asian, 58% Black, 5% Hispanic, 3% multiracial, 0% Pacific Islander, 10% white, 3% international; 17% from in state; N/A live on campus; N/A of students in fraternities, N/A in sororities
Most popular majors: 15% Criminal Justice/Police Science, 9% Biology/Biological Sciences, General, 6% Kinesiology and Exercise Science, 5% Sociology, 4% Engineering, General
Expenses: 2019-2020: $8,558 in state, $18,968 out of state; room/board: $10,085
Financial aid: (410) 651-6172

University of Maryland Global Campus

Adelphi MD
(800) 888-8682
U.S. News ranking: Reg. U. (N), second tier
Website: www.umgc.edu/
Admissions email: studentsfirst@umgc.edu
Public; founded 1947
Freshman admissions: least selective; 2019-2020: 3,165 applied, 3,165 accepted. Neither SAT nor ACT required. SAT 25/75 percentile: N/A. High school rank: N/A
Early decision deadline: N/A, notification date: N/A
Early action deadline: N/A, notification date: N/A
Application deadline (fall): rolling
Undergraduate student body: 9,472 full time, 36,690 part time; 55% male, 45% female; 0% American Indian, 5% Asian, 27% Black, 15% Hispanic, 5% multiracial, 1% Pacific Islander, 38% white, 1% international
Most popular majors: 35% Computer and Information Sciences and Support Services, 30% Business, Management, Marketing, and Related Support Services, 7% Health Professions and Related Programs, 7% Homeland Security, Law Enforcement, Firefighting and Related Protective Services, 7% Psychology

Expenses: 2020-2021: $7,704 in state, $12,336 out of state; room/board: N/A
Financial aid: (301) 985-7510; 59% of undergrads determined to have financial need; average aid package $7,858

Washington Adventist University[1]

Takoma Park MD
(301) 891-4000
U.S. News ranking: Reg. U. (N), second tier
Website: www.wau.edu
Admissions email: enroll@wau.edu
Private; founded 1904
Affiliation: Seventh Day Adventist
Application deadline (fall): 8/1
Undergraduate student body: N/A full time, N/A part time
Expenses: 2020-2021: $24,300; room/board: $9,830
Financial aid: (301) 891-4005

Washington College

Chestertown MD
(410) 778-7700
U.S. News ranking: Nat. Lib. Arts, No. 96
Website: www.washcoll.edu
Admissions email: wc_admissions@washcoll.edu
Private; founded 1782
Freshman admissions: selective; 2019-2020: 2,225 applied, 2,055 accepted. Either SAT or ACT required. SAT 25/75 percentile: 1090-1300. High school rank: 28% in top tenth, 53% in top quarter, 83% in top half
Early decision deadline: 11/15, notification date: 12/15
Early action deadline: 12/1, notification date: 1/15
Application deadline (fall): 2/15
Undergraduate student body: 1,265 full time, 23 part time; 40% male, 60% female; 0% American Indian, 3% Asian, 11% Black, 6% Hispanic, 0% multiracial, 0% Pacific Islander, 69% white, 5% international; 58% from in state; 80% live on campus; 5% of students in fraternities, 12% in sororities
Most popular majors: 20% Social Sciences, 16% Business, Management, Marketing, and Related Support Services, 11% Biological and Biomedical Sciences, 9% Psychology, 7% English Language and Literature/Letters
Expenses: 2020-2021: $49,768; room/board: $13,038
Financial aid: (410) 778-7214; 69% of undergrads determined to have financial need; average aid package $36,163

MASSACHUSETTS

American International College

Springfield MA
(413) 205-3201
U.S. News ranking: Reg. U. (N), second tier
Website: www.aic.edu

Admissions email: admissions@aic.edu
Private; founded 1885
Freshman admissions: least selective; 2019-2020: N/A applied, N/A accepted. Neither SAT nor ACT required. SAT 25/75 percentile: 920-1100. High school rank: N/A
Early decision deadline: N/A, notification date: N/A
Early action deadline: N/A, notification date: N/A
Application deadline (fall): 9/7
Undergraduate student body: 1,231 full time, 102 part time; 38% male, 62% female; 1% American Indian, 1% Asian, 23% Black, 22% Hispanic, 5% multiracial, 1% Pacific Islander, 36% white, 4% international
Most popular majors: Information not available
Expenses: 2019-2020: $36,930; room/board: $14,520
Financial aid: (413) 205-3521

Amherst College

Amherst MA
(413) 542-2328
U.S. News ranking: Nat. Lib. Arts, No. 2
Website: www.amherst.edu
Admissions email: admission@amherst.edu
Private; founded 1821
Freshman admissions: most selective; 2019-2020: 10,569 applied, 1,195 accepted. Either SAT or ACT required. SAT 25/75 percentile: 1410-1550. High school rank: 88% in top tenth, 98% in top quarter, 100% in top half
Early decision deadline: 11/1, notification date: 12/15
Early action deadline: N/A, notification date: N/A
Application deadline (fall): 1/4
Undergraduate student body: 1,839 full time, 0 part time; 50% male, 50% female; 0% American Indian, 15% Asian, 10% Black, 13% Hispanic, 7% multiracial, 0% Pacific Islander, 43% white, 9% international; 14% from in state; 98% live on campus; 0% of students in fraternities, 0% in sororities
Most popular majors: 10% Econometrics and Quantitative Economics, 10% Mathematics, General, 8% Research and Experimental Psychology, Other, 7% Computer Science, 6% English Language and Literature, General
Expenses: 2020-2021: $60,890; room/board: $15,910
Financial aid: (413) 542-2296; 57% of undergrads determined to have financial need; average aid package $58,806

Anna Maria College[1]

Paxton MA
(508) 849-3360
U.S. News ranking: Reg. U. (N), second tier
Website: www.annamaria.edu
Admissions email: admissions@annamaria.edu
Private; founded 1946
Affiliation: Roman Catholic

Application deadline (fall): rolling
Undergraduate student body: 920 full time, 207 part time
Expenses: 2019-2020: $38,630; room/board: $14,580
Financial aid: (508) 849-3363

Assumption University

Worcester MA
(866) 477-7776
U.S. News ranking: Reg. U. (N), No. 43
Website: www.assumption.edu
Admissions email: admiss@assumption.edu
Private; founded 1904
Affiliation: Roman Catholic
Freshman admissions: selective; 2019-2020: 4,460 applied, 3,615 accepted. Neither SAT nor ACT required. SAT 25/75 percentile: 1090-1238. High school rank: 14% in top tenth, 41% in top quarter, 76% in top half
Early decision deadline: 11/1, notification date: 12/1
Early action deadline: 11/1, notification date: 12/15
Application deadline (fall): 2/15
Undergraduate student body: 1,946 full time, 36 part time; 44% male, 56% female; 0% American Indian, 3% Asian, 5% Black, 7% Hispanic, 3% multiracial, 0% Pacific Islander, 77% white, 1% international; N/A from in state; 85% live on campus; N/A of students in fraternities, N/A in sororities
Most popular majors: 20% Business, Management, Marketing, and Related Support Services, 14% Health Professions and Related Programs, 13% Social Sciences, 9% English Language and Literature/Letters, 8% Psychology
Expenses: 2020-2021: $43,978; room/board: N/A
Financial aid: (508) 767-7158; 75% of undergrads determined to have financial need; average aid package $30,845

Babson College

Babson Park MA
(781) 239-4006
U.S. News ranking: Business, unranked
Website: www.babson.edu
Admissions email: ugradadmission@babson.edu
Private; founded 1919
Freshman admissions: more selective; 2019-2020: 6,362 applied, 1,680 accepted. Either SAT or ACT required. SAT 25/75 percentile: 1270-1450. High school rank: N/A
Early decision deadline: 11/1, notification date: 12/15
Early action deadline: 11/1, notification date: 1/1
Application deadline (fall): 1/2
Undergraduate student body: 2,347 full time, 39 part time; 53% male, 47% female; 0% American Indian, 11% Asian, 4% Black, 12% Hispanic, 2% multiracial, 0% Pacific Islander, 34% white, 30% international; 18% from in state; 76% live on campus; 4% of students in fraternities, 8% in sororities

Most popular majors: Economics, General, Entrepreneurship/Entrepreneurial Studies, Finance, General, Management Sciences and Quantitative Methods, Marketing/Marketing Management, General
Expenses: 2020-2021: $54,144; room/board: $17,668
Financial aid: (781) 239-4015; 42% of undergrads determined to have financial need; average aid package $44,823

Bard College at Simon's Rock[7]

Great Barrington MA
(800) 235-7186
U.S. News ranking: Reg. Coll. (N), No. 15
Website: www.simons-rock.edu
Admissions email: admit@simons-rock.edu
Private; founded 1966
Freshman admissions: less selective; 2019-2020: 209 applied, 192 accepted. Neither SAT nor ACT required. SAT 25/75 percentile: N/A. High school rank: 50% in top tenth, 72% in top quarter, 97% in top half
Early decision deadline: N/A, notification date: N/A
Early action deadline: N/A, notification date: N/A
Application deadline (fall): rolling
Undergraduate student body: 391 full time, 6 part time
Most popular majors: 22% Visual and Performing Arts, 12% English Language and Literature/Letters, 10% Psychology, 7% Biological and Biomedical Sciences, 6% Physical Sciences
Expenses: 2020-2021: $60,098; room/board: $15,902
Financial aid: (413) 528-7297

Bay Path University

Longmeadow MA
(413) 565-1331
U.S. News ranking: Reg. U. (N), No. 105
Website: www.baypath.edu
Admissions email: admiss@baypath.edu
Private; founded 1897
Freshman admissions: selective; 2019-2020: 1,123 applied, 806 accepted. Neither SAT nor ACT required. SAT 25/75 percentile: 960-1170. High school rank: 18% in top tenth, 51% in top quarter, 79% in top half
Early decision deadline: N/A, notification date: N/A
Early action deadline: 12/15, notification date: 1/2
Application deadline (fall): 8/1
Undergraduate student body: 1,165 full time, 652 part time; 0% male, 100% female; 0% American Indian, 2% Asian, 14% Black, 22% Hispanic, 2% multiracial, 0% Pacific Islander, 54% white, 1% international
Most popular majors: Information not available
Expenses: 2020-2021: $35,081; room/board: $12,799
Financial aid: (413) 565-1256; 91% of undergrads determined to have financial need; average aid package $30,111

Bay State College[1]
Boston MA
(617) 217-9000
U.S. News ranking: Reg. Coll. (N), second tier
Website: www.baystate.edu/
Admissions email: admissions@baystate.edu
For-profit; founded 1946
Affiliation: Undenominational
Application deadline (fall): rolling
Undergraduate student body: N/A full time, N/A part time
Expenses: 2019-2020: $23,500; room/board: $13,300
Financial aid: (617) 217-9003

Becker College[1]
Worcester MA
(877) 523-2537
U.S. News ranking: Reg. Coll. (N), second tier
Website: www.beckercollege.edu
Admissions email: admissions@beckercollege.edu
Private; founded 1784
Application deadline (fall): rolling
Undergraduate student body: N/A full time, N/A part time
Expenses: 2019-2020: $40,150; room/board: $13,800
Financial aid: (508) 373-9430

Bentley University
Waltham MA
(781) 891-2244
U.S. News ranking: Reg. U. (N), No. 1
Website: www.bentley.edu
Admissions email: ugadmission@bentley.edu
Private; founded 1917
Freshman admissions: more selective; 2019-2020: 9,017 applied, 4,213 accepted. Either SAT or ACT required. SAT 25/75 percentile: 1230-1410. High school rank: 37% in top tenth, 73% in top quarter, 97% in top half
Early decision deadline: 11/15, notification date: 12/31
Early action deadline: N/A, notification date: N/A
Application deadline (fall): 1/7
Undergraduate student body: 4,177 full time, 51 part time; 59% male, 41% female; 0% American Indian, 9% Asian, 4% Black, 7% Hispanic, 3% multiracial, 0% Pacific Islander, 58% white, 15% international; 42% from in state; 78% live on campus; 5% of students in fraternities, 10% in sororities
Most popular majors: 24% Finance, General, 14% Business Administration and Management, General, 12% Business, Management, Marketing, and Related Support Services, Other, 11% Accounting, 11% Marketing/Marketing Management, General
Expenses: 2020-2021: $53,790; room/board: $17,620
Financial aid: (781) 891-3441; 47% of undergrads determined to have financial need; average aid package $37,731

Berklee College of Music
Boston MA
(800) 237-5533
U.S. News ranking: Arts, unranked
Website: www.berklee.edu
Admissions email: admissions@berklee.edu
Private; founded 1945
Freshman admissions: least selective; 2019-2020: 6,763 applied, 3,479 accepted. Neither SAT nor ACT required. SAT 25/75 percentile: N/A. High school rank: N/A
Early decision deadline: N/A, notification date: N/A
Early action deadline: 11/1, notification date: 1/31
Application deadline (fall): 1/15
Undergraduate student body: 5,041 full time, 1,398 part time; 59% male, 41% female; 0% American Indian, 5% Asian, 7% Black, 10% Hispanic, 5% multiracial, 0% Pacific Islander, 43% white, 28% international; N/A from in state; 30% live on campus; N/A of students in fraternities, N/A in sororities
Most popular majors: 62% Visual and Performing Arts, 24% Computer and Information Sciences and Support Services, 10% Engineering Technologies and Engineering-Related Fields, 3% Health Professions and Related Programs, 1% Education
Expenses: 2020-2021: $47,230; room/board: $18,830
Financial aid: (617) 747-2274; 41% of undergrads determined to have financial need; average aid package $24,330

Boston Architectural College[1]
Boston MA
(617) 585-0123
U.S. News ranking: Arts, unranked
Website: www.the-bac.edu
Admissions email: admissions@the-bac.edu
Private; founded 1889
Application deadline (fall): rolling
Undergraduate student body: 265 full time, 73 part time
Expenses: 2020-2021: $21,844; room/board: N/A
Financial aid: (617) 585-0183

Boston College
Chestnut Hill MA
(617) 552-3100
U.S. News ranking: Nat. U., No. 35
Website: www.bc.edu
Admissions email: admission@bc.edu
Private; founded 1863
Affiliation: Roman Catholic
Freshman admissions: most selective; 2019-2020: 35,552 applied, 9,679 accepted. Either SAT or ACT required. SAT 25/75 percentile: 1340-1500. High school rank: 82% in top tenth, 93% in top quarter, 98% in top half
Early decision deadline: 11/1, notification date: 12/15
Early action deadline: N/A, notification date: N/A

Application deadline (fall): 1/1
Undergraduate student body: 9,370 full time, 0 part time; 47% male, 53% female; 0% American Indian, 11% Asian, 4% Black, 12% Hispanic, 4% multiracial, 0% Pacific Islander, 58% white, 8% international
Most popular majors: 14% Economics, General, 12% Finance, General, 9% Biology/Biological Sciences, General, 7% Political Science and Government, General, 7% Speech Communication and Rhetoric
Expenses: 2020-2021: $60,202; room/board: $15,220
Financial aid: (617) 552-3300; 42% of undergrads determined to have financial need; average aid package $47,647

Boston University
Boston MA
(617) 353-2300
U.S. News ranking: Nat. U., No. 42
Website: www.bu.edu
Admissions email: admissions@bu.edu
Private; founded 1839
Freshman admissions: more selective; 2019-2020: 62,224 applied, 11,786 accepted. Neither SAT nor ACT required. SAT 25/75 percentile: 1340-1510. High school rank: 64% in top tenth, 92% in top quarter, 100% in top half
Early decision deadline: 11/1, notification date: 12/15
Early action deadline: N/A, notification date: N/A
Application deadline (fall): 1/1
Undergraduate student body: 16,978 full time, 1,005 part time; 41% male, 59% female; 0% American Indian, 17% Asian, 4% Black, 12% Hispanic, 4% multiracial, 0% Pacific Islander, 36% white, 22% international; 28% from in state; 70% live on campus; N/A of students in fraternities, 3% in sororities
Most popular majors: 16% Business Administration and Management, General, 9% Communication and Media Studies, 6% Economics, General, 5% Psychology, General, 4% Computer Science
Expenses: 2020-2021: $58,072; room/board: $16,640
Financial aid: (617) 353-2965; 42% of undergrads determined to have financial need; average aid package $46,252

Brandeis University
Waltham MA
(781) 736-3500
U.S. News ranking: Nat. U., No. 42
Website: www.brandeis.edu
Admissions email: admissions@brandeis.edu
Private; founded 1948
Freshman admissions: most selective; 2019-2020: 11,343 applied, 3,393 accepted. Neither SAT nor ACT required. SAT 25/75 percentile: 1350-1520. High school rank: 56% in top tenth, 83% in top quarter, 97% in top half

Early decision deadline: 11/1, notification date: 12/15
Early action deadline: N/A, notification date: N/A
Application deadline (fall): 1/1
Undergraduate student body: 3,673 full time, 15 part time; 39% male, 61% female; 0% American Indian, 14% Asian, 5% Black, 8% Hispanic, 4% multiracial, 0% Pacific Islander, 46% white, 20% international; 70% from in state; 76% live on campus; 0% of students in fraternities, 0% in sororities
Most popular majors: 10% Business/Commerce, General, 9% Econometrics and Quantitative Economics, 7% Biology/Biological Sciences, General, 6% Mathematics, General, 5% Health Policy Analysis
Expenses: 2020-2021: $57,615; room/board: $15,890
Financial aid: (781) 736-3700; 46% of undergrads determined to have financial need; average aid package $47,713

Bridgewater State University
Bridgewater MA
(508) 531-1237
U.S. News ranking: Reg. U. (N), No. 105
Website: www.bridgew.edu/admissions
Admissions email: admission@bridgew.edu
Public; founded 1840
Freshman admissions: selective; 2019-2020: 9,800 applied, 8,591 accepted. Neither SAT nor ACT required. SAT 25/75 percentile: 970-1150. High school rank: N/A
Early decision deadline: N/A, notification date: N/A
Early action deadline: 11/15, notification date: 12/15
Application deadline (fall): rolling
Undergraduate student body: 7,681 full time, 1,782 part time; 41% male, 59% female; 0% American Indian, 2% Asian, 12% Black, 8% Hispanic, 5% multiracial, 0% Pacific Islander, 71% white, 0% international; N/A from in state; 41% live on campus; N/A of students in fraternities, N/A in sororities
Most popular majors: 18% Education, 17% Business, Management, Marketing, and Related Support Services, 13% Psychology, 10% Homeland Security, Law Enforcement, Firefighting and Related Protective Services, 7% Communication, Journalism, and Related Programs
Expenses: 2020-2021: $10,732 in state, $16,872 out of state; room/board: $13,832
Financial aid: (508) 531-1341; 73% of undergrads determined to have financial need; average aid package $9,108

Cambridge College[1]
Cambridge MA
(617) 868-1000
U.S. News ranking: Reg. U. (N), second tier
Website: www.cambridgecollege.edu

Admissions email: N/A
Private; founded 1971
Application deadline (fall): N/A
Undergraduate student body: N/A full time, N/A part time
Expenses: 2019-2020: $16,164; room/board: N/A
Financial aid: (617) 873-0440

Clark University
Worcester MA
(508) 793-7431
U.S. News ranking: Nat. U., No. 103
Website: www.clarku.edu
Admissions email: admissions@clarku.edu
Private; founded 1887
Freshman admissions: more selective; 2019-2020: 7,639 applied, 4,032 accepted. Neither SAT nor ACT required. SAT 25/75 percentile: 1180-1370. High school rank: 27% in top tenth, 67% in top quarter, 94% in top half
Early decision deadline: 11/15, notification date: 12/15
Early action deadline: 11/15, notification date: 12/15
Application deadline (fall): 1/15
Undergraduate student body: 2,281 full time, 68 part time; 39% male, 61% female; 0% American Indian, 8% Asian, 4% Black, 9% Hispanic, 3% multiracial, 0% Pacific Islander, 60% white, 11% international; N/A from in state; 67% live on campus; 0% of students in fraternities, 0% in sororities
Most popular majors: 28% Social Sciences, 18% Psychology, 10% Biological and Biomedical Sciences, 8% Visual and Performing Arts, 6% Business, Management, Marketing, and Related Support Services
Expenses: 2020-2021: $48,602; room/board: $9,800
Financial aid: (508) 793-7478; 64% of undergrads determined to have financial need; average aid package $34,421

College of the Holy Cross
Worcester MA
(508) 793-2443
U.S. News ranking: Nat. Lib. Arts, No. 36
Website: www.holycross.edu
Admissions email: admissions@holycross.edu
Private; founded 1843
Affiliation: Roman Catholic
Freshman admissions: more selective; 2019-2020: 7,200 applied, 2,464 accepted. Neither SAT nor ACT required. SAT 25/75 percentile: 1260-1430. High school rank: 53% in top tenth, 86% in top quarter, 100% in top half
Early decision deadline: 11/15, notification date: 12/15
Early action deadline: N/A, notification date: N/A
Application deadline (fall): 1/15
Undergraduate student body: 3,142 full time, 32 part time; 47% male, 53% female; 0% American Indian, 4% Asian, 5% Black, 11% Hispanic, 3% multiracial, 0% Pacific Islander, 70% white,

3% international; 60% from in state; 90% live on campus; 0% of students in fraternities, 0% in sororities
Most popular majors: 14% Economics, General, 13% Psychology, General, 10% Political Science and Government, General, 8% English Language and Literature, General, 7% Biology/Biological Sciences, General
Expenses: 2020-2021: $56,520; room/board: $15,560
Financial aid: (508) 793-2265; 54% of undergrads determined to have financial need; average aid package $41,584

Curry College
Milton MA
(800) 669-0686
U.S. News ranking: Reg. U. (N), second tier
Website: www.curry.edu
Admissions email: adm@curry.edu
Private; founded 1879
Freshman admissions: less selective; 2019-2020: 6,136 applied, 5,601 accepted. Neither SAT nor ACT required. SAT 25/75 percentile: 943-1108. High school rank: 4% in top tenth, 23% in top quarter, 47% in top half
Early decision deadline: N/A, notification date: N/A
Early action deadline: 12/1, notification date: 12/15
Application deadline (fall): rolling
Undergraduate student body: 1,969 full time, 343 part time; 41% male, 59% female; 0% American Indian, 3% Asian, 12% Black, 8% Hispanic, 3% multiracial, 0% Pacific Islander, 64% white, 1% international; 74% from in state; 59% live on campus; 0% of students in fraternities, 0% in sororities
Most popular majors: 36% Health Professions and Related Programs, 15% Business, Management, Marketing, and Related Support Services, 15% Homeland Security, Law Enforcement, Firefighting and Related Protective Services, 10% Psychology, 9% Communication, Journalism, and Related Programs
Expenses: 2020-2021: $42,055; room/board: $16,830
Financial aid: (617) 333-2354

Dean College
Franklin MA
(508) 541-1508
U.S. News ranking: Reg. Coll. (N), No. 34
Website: www.dean.edu
Admissions email: admissions@dean.edu
Private; founded 1865
Freshman admissions: less selective; 2019-2020: 6,241 applied, 4,293 accepted. Neither SAT nor ACT required. SAT 25/75 percentile: 910-1105. High school rank: N/A
Early decision deadline: N/A, notification date: N/A
Early action deadline: 12/1, notification date: 1/15
Application deadline (fall): 9/7
Undergraduate student body: 1,184 full time, 136 part time; 48% male, 52% female; 0% American Indian, 2% Asian, 14% Black,

9% Hispanic, 4% multiracial, 0% Pacific Islander, 57% white, 4% international; 48% from in state; 80% live on campus; 0% of students in fraternities, 0% in sororities
Most popular majors: 33% Visual and Performing Arts, 30% Business Administration and Management, General, 12% Psychology, General, 9% Parks, Recreation, Leisure, and Fitness Studies, 5% Communication, Journalism, and Related Programs
Expenses: 2020-2021: $41,318; room/board: $17,648
Financial aid: (508) 541-1518; 78% of undergrads determined to have financial need; average aid package $31,567

Eastern Nazarene College
Quincy MA
(617) 745-3711
U.S. News ranking: Reg. Coll. (N), second tier
Website: www.enc.edu
Admissions email: admissions@enc.edu
Private; founded 1918
Affiliation: Church of the Nazarene
Freshman admissions: less selective; 2019-2020: 1,110 applied, 655 accepted. Either SAT or ACT required. SAT 25/75 percentile: 880-1110. High school rank: N/A
Early decision deadline: N/A, notification date: N/A
Early action deadline: N/A, notification date: N/A
Application deadline (fall): rolling
Undergraduate student body: 550 full time, 58 part time; 47% male, 53% female; 1% American Indian, 4% Asian, 18% Black, 16% Hispanic, 5% multiracial, 0% Pacific Islander, 46% white, 8% international
Most popular majors: Information not available
Expenses: 2020-2021: $26,952; room/board: $9,985
Financial aid: (617) 745-3865

Elms College
Chicopee MA
(413) 592-3189
U.S. News ranking: Reg. U. (N), No. 93
Website: www.elms.edu
Admissions email: admissions@elms.edu
Private; founded 1928
Affiliation: Roman Catholic
Freshman admissions: selective; 2019-2020: 875 applied, 657 accepted. Either SAT or ACT required. SAT 25/75 percentile: 970-1130. High school rank: 8% in top tenth, 38% in top quarter, 77% in top half
Early decision deadline: N/A, notification date: N/A
Early action deadline: N/A, notification date: N/A
Application deadline (fall): rolling
Undergraduate student body: 997 full time, 126 part time; 24% male, 76% female; 0% American Indian, 2% Asian, 8% Black, 14% Hispanic, 2% multiracial, 0% Pacific Islander, 51% white, 0% international; 73% from in

state; 32% live on campus; 0% of students in fraternities, 0% in sororities
Most popular majors: 43% Health Professions and Related Programs, 15% Public Administration and Social Service Professions, 10% Business, Management, Marketing, and Related Support Services, 6% Biological and Biomedical Sciences, 6% Education
Expenses: 2020-2021: $38,391; room/board: $14,010
Financial aid: (413) 265-2303; 88% of undergrads determined to have financial need; average aid package $22,908

Emerson College
Boston MA
(617) 824-8600
U.S. News ranking: Reg. U. (N), No. 9
Website: www.emerson.edu
Admissions email: admission@emerson.edu
Private; founded 1880
Freshman admissions: more selective; 2019-2020: 15,353 applied, 5,120 accepted. Neither SAT nor ACT required. SAT 25/75 percentile: 1200-1410. High school rank: 27% in top tenth, 65% in top quarter, 93% in top half
Early decision deadline: N/A, notification date: N/A
Early action deadline: 11/1, notification date: 12/15
Application deadline (fall): 1/15
Undergraduate student body: 3,827 full time, 51 part time; 39% male, 61% female; 0% American Indian, 5% Asian, 4% Black, 13% Hispanic, 4% multiracial, 0% Pacific Islander, 59% white, 13% international; 22% from in state; 70% live on campus; 2% of students in fraternities, 3% in sororities
Most popular majors: 47% Cinematography and Film/Video Production, 13% Creative Writing, 11% Marketing/Marketing Management, General, 7% Journalism, 5% Political Communication
Expenses: 2020-2021: $51,148; room/board: $18,768
Financial aid: (617) 824-8655; 54% of undergrads determined to have financial need; average aid package $25,428

Emmanuel College
Boston MA
(617) 735-9715
U.S. News ranking: Nat. Lib. Arts, second tier
Website: www.emmanuel.edu
Admissions email: enroll@emmanuel.edu
Private; founded 1919
Affiliation: Roman Catholic
Freshman admissions: selective; 2019-2020: 5,832 applied, 4,557 accepted. Neither SAT nor ACT required. SAT 25/75 percentile: 1090-1250. High school rank: 15% in top tenth, 27% in top quarter, 82% in top half

Early decision deadline: N/A, notification date: N/A
Early action deadline: 11/1, notification date: 12/15
Application deadline (fall): 2/15
Undergraduate student body: 1,953 full time, 159 part time; 24% male, 76% female; 0% American Indian, 5% Asian, 7% Black, 11% Hispanic, 3% multiracial, 0% Pacific Islander, 69% white, 1% international; 60% from in state; 74% live on campus; N/A of students in fraternities, N/A in sororities
Most popular majors: 17% Biological and Biomedical Sciences, 13% Psychology, 13% Social Sciences, 10% Business, Management, Marketing, and Related Support Services, 8% Education
Expenses: 2020-2021: $42,516; room/board: $15,846
Financial aid: (617) 735-9938; 80% of undergrads determined to have financial need; average aid package $30,737

Endicott College
Beverly MA
(978) 921-1000
U.S. News ranking: Reg. U. (N), No. 23
Website: www.endicott.edu
Admissions email: admission@endicott.edu
Private; founded 1939
Freshman admissions: selective; 2019-2020: 5,031 applied, 3,487 accepted. Neither SAT nor ACT required. SAT 25/75 percentile: 1090-1240. High school rank: 20% in top tenth, 45% in top quarter, 81% in top half
Early decision deadline: 11/1, notification date: 12/15
Early action deadline: 11/1, notification date: 1/15
Application deadline (fall): 2/15
Undergraduate student body: 3,063 full time, 259 part time; 38% male, 62% female; 0% American Indian, 2% Asian, 2% Black, 4% Hispanic, 3% multiracial, 0% Pacific Islander, 81% white, 2% international; 52% from in state; 93% live on campus; N/A of students in fraternities, N/A in sororities
Most popular majors: 12% Registered Nursing/Registered Nurse, 11% Business Administration and Management, General, 8% Sport and Fitness Administration/Management, 7% Early Childhood Education and Teaching, 7% Marketing/Marketing Management, General
Expenses: 2020-2021: $35,320; room/board: $16,130
Financial aid: (978) 232-2060; 62% of undergrads determined to have financial need; average aid package $22,560

Fisher College
Boston MA
(617) 236-8818
U.S. News ranking: Reg. Coll. (N), No. 34
Website: www.fisher.edu
Admissions email: admissions@fisher.edu

Private; founded 1903
Freshman admissions: less selective; 2019-2020: 2,068 applied, 1,433 accepted. Neither SAT nor ACT required. SAT 25/75 percentile: 830-1030. High school rank: N/A
Early decision deadline: N/A, notification date: N/A
Early action deadline: N/A, notification date: N/A
Application deadline (fall): rolling
Undergraduate student body: 648 full time, 903 part time; 28% male, 72% female; 0% American Indian, 1% Asian, 12% Black, 13% Hispanic, 3% multiracial, 0% Pacific Islander, 26% white, 11% international; N/A from in state; 52% live on campus; N/A of students in fraternities, N/A in sororities
Most popular majors: 39% Business, Management, Marketing, and Related Support Services, 17% Public Administration and Social Service Professions, 13% Homeland Security, Law Enforcement, Firefighting and Related Protective Services, 9% Health Professions and Related Programs, 8% Communication, Journalism, and Related Programs
Expenses: 2020-2021: $32,700; room/board: $16,569
Financial aid: (617) 236-8821; 73% of undergrads determined to have financial need; average aid package $27,992

Fitchburg State University
Fitchburg MA
(978) 665-3144
U.S. News ranking: Reg. U. (N), No. 96
Website: www.fitchburgstate.edu
Admissions email: admissions@fitchburgstate.edu
Public; founded 1894
Freshman admissions: less selective; 2019-2020: 2,902 applied, 2,564 accepted. Neither SAT nor ACT required. SAT 25/75 percentile: 990-1150. High school rank: N/A
Early decision deadline: N/A, notification date: N/A
Early action deadline: N/A, notification date: N/A
Application deadline (fall): rolling
Undergraduate student body: 3,164 full time, 880 part time; 47% male, 53% female; 0% American Indian, 3% Asian, 11% Black, 13% Hispanic, 4% multiracial, 0% Pacific Islander, 69% white, 1% international; 92% from in state; 36% live on campus; N/A of students in fraternities, N/A in sororities
Most popular majors: 13% Communication, Journalism, and Related Programs, 12% Business, Management, Marketing, and Related Support Services, 12% Health Professions and Related Programs, 8% Multi/Interdisciplinary Studies, 7% Homeland Security, Law Enforcement, Firefighting and Related Protective Services
Expenses: 2019-2020: $10,610 in state, $16,690 out of state; room/board: $11,250

Financial aid: (978) 665-3302; 67% of undergrads determined to have financial need; average aid package $10,055

Framingham State University

Framingham MA
(508) 626-4500
U.S. News ranking: Reg. U. (N), No. 105
Website: www.framingham.edu
Admissions email: admissions@framingham.edu
Public; founded 1839
Freshman admissions: selective; 2019-2020: 5,942 applied, 4,417 accepted. Either SAT or ACT required. SAT 25/75 percentile: 960-1130. High school rank: N/A
Early decision deadline: N/A, notification date: N/A
Early action deadline: 11/15, notification date: 12/15
Application deadline (fall): rolling
Undergraduate student body: 3,376 full time, 481 part time; 44% male, 56% female; 0% American Indian, 3% Asian, 14% Black, 17% Hispanic, 4% multiracial, 0% Pacific Islander, 61% white, 0% international; N/A from in state; 47% live on campus; N/A of students in fraternities, N/A in sororities
Most popular majors: 22% Business, Management, Marketing, and Related Support Services, 15% Social Sciences, 10% Psychology, 9% Family and Consumer Sciences/Human Sciences, 6% Health Professions and Related Programs
Expenses: 2019-2020: $17,180 in state, N/A out of state; room/board: $12,604
Financial aid: N/A

Franklin W. Olin College of Engineering

Needham MA
(781) 292-2222
U.S. News ranking: Engineering, unranked
Website: www.olin.edu/
Admissions email: info@olin.edu
Private; founded 1997
Freshman admissions: more selective; 2019-2020: 905 applied, 142 accepted. Either SAT or ACT required. SAT 25/75 percentile: 1460-1560. High school rank: N/A
Early decision deadline: N/A, notification date: N/A
Early action deadline: N/A, notification date: N/A
Application deadline (fall): 1/1
Undergraduate student body: 347 full time, 39 part time; 47% male, 53% female; 0% American Indian, 16% Asian, 3% Black, 12% Hispanic, 9% multiracial, 0% Pacific Islander, 47% white, 8% international; 12% from in state; 100% live on campus; 0% of students in fraternities, 0% in sororities
Most popular majors: 54% Engineering, General, 23% Electrical and Electronics

Engineering, 23% Mechanical Engineering
Expenses: 2020-2021: $54,700; room/board: $17,460
Financial aid: (781) 292-2215; 47% of undergrads determined to have financial need; average aid package $50,583

Gordon College

Wenham MA
(866) 464-6736
U.S. News ranking: Nat. Lib. Arts, No. 155
Website: www.gordon.edu
Admissions email: admissions@gordon.edu
Private; founded 1889
Affiliation: Other
Freshman admissions: selective; 2019-2020: 2,624 applied, 1,943 accepted. Either SAT or ACT required. SAT 25/75 percentile: 1060-1310. High school rank: 25% in top tenth, 51% in top quarter, 80% in top half
Early decision deadline: N/A, notification date: N/A
Early action deadline: 12/1, notification date: 12/15
Application deadline (fall): 8/1
Undergraduate student body: 1,440 full time, 67 part time; 38% male, 62% female; 0% American Indian, 4% Asian, 4% Black, 10% Hispanic, 3% multiracial, 0% Pacific Islander, 68% white, 10% international; 31% from in state; 88% live on campus; 0% of students in fraternities, 0% in sororities
Most popular majors: 10% Business Administration and Management, General, 10% Psychology, General, 10% Speech Communication and Rhetoric, 6% English Language and Literature, General, 5% Youth Ministry
Expenses: 2020-2021: $39,230; room/board: $11,420
Financial aid: (800) 343-1379; 67% of undergrads determined to have financial need; average aid package $27,240

Hampshire College[1]

Amherst MA
(413) 549-4600
U.S. News ranking: Nat. Lib. Arts, second tier
Website: www.hampshire.edu
Admissions email: admissions@hampshire.edu
Private; founded 1965
Application deadline (fall): N/A
Undergraduate student body: N/A full time, N/A part time
Expenses: 2019-2020: $52,068; room/board: $14,120
Financial aid: (413) 559-5739

Harvard University

Cambridge MA
(617) 495-1551
U.S. News ranking: Nat. U., No. 2
Website: www.harvard.edu/
Admissions email: college@fas.harvard.edu
Private; founded 1636
Freshman admissions: most selective; 2019-2020: 43,330 applied, 2,009 accepted. Either SAT or ACT required. SAT 25/75

percentile: 1460-1570. High school rank: 93% in top tenth, 98% in top quarter, 100% in top half
Early decision deadline: N/A, notification date: N/A
Early action deadline: 11/1, notification date: 12/15
Application deadline (fall): 1/1
Undergraduate student body: 6,740 full time, 15 part time; 51% male, 49% female; 0% American Indian, 21% Asian, 9% Black, 11% Hispanic, 8% multiracial, 0% Pacific Islander, 37% white, 12% international; 16% from in state; 98% live on campus; N/A of students in fraternities, N/A in sororities
Most popular majors: 28% Social Sciences, General, 14% Biology/Biological Sciences, General, 11% Mathematics, General, 9% Computer Science, 9% History, General
Expenses: 2020-2021: $54,002; room/board: $18,389
Financial aid: (617) 495-1581; 52% of undergrads determined to have financial need; average aid package $61,186

Lasell University

Newton MA
(617) 243-2225
U.S. News ranking: Reg. U. (N), No. 125
Website: www.lasell.edu
Admissions email: info@lasell.edu
Private; founded 1851
Freshman admissions: less selective; 2019-2020: 2,489 applied, 2,082 accepted. Neither SAT nor ACT required. SAT 25/75 percentile: 980-1170. High school rank: 10% in top tenth, 32% in top quarter, 62% in top half
Early decision deadline: N/A, notification date: N/A
Early action deadline: 11/15, notification date: 12/1
Application deadline (fall): rolling
Undergraduate student body: 1,604 full time, 35 part time; 36% male, 64% female; 0% American Indian, 3% Asian, 9% Black, 10% Hispanic, 2% multiracial, 0% Pacific Islander, 65% white, 5% international; 39% from in state; 75% live on campus; 0% of students in fraternities, 0% in sororities
Most popular majors: 11% Communication and Media Studies, 9% Fashion Merchandising, 9% Sport and Fitness Administration/Management, 7% Criminology, 6% Marketing/Marketing Management, General
Expenses: 2020-2021: $39,000; room/board: $16,000
Financial aid: (617) 243-2227; 80% of undergrads determined to have financial need; average aid package $24,710

Lesley University

Cambridge MA
(617) 349-8800
U.S. News ranking: Nat. U., No. 249
Website: www.lesley.edu
Admissions email: admissions@lesley.edu

Private; founded 1909
Freshman admissions: selective; 2019-2020: 3,049 applied, 2,277 accepted. Either SAT or ACT required. SAT 25/75 percentile: 1000-1210. High school rank: 5% in top tenth, 28% in top quarter, 67% in top half
Early decision deadline: N/A, notification date: N/A
Early action deadline: 12/1, notification date: 12/23
Application deadline (fall): 7/15
Undergraduate student body: 1,599 full time, 529 part time; 23% male, 77% female; 0% American Indian, 4% Asian, 8% Black, 14% Hispanic, 3% multiracial, 0% Pacific Islander, 50% white, 4% international; N/A from in state; 43% live on campus; N/A of students in fraternities, N/A in sororities
Most popular majors: 24% Visual and Performing Arts, 19% Psychology, 15% Liberal Arts and Sciences, General Studies and Humanities, 9% Business, Management, Marketing, and Related Support Services, 9% Health Professions and Related Programs
Expenses: 2020-2021: $29,450; room/board: $16,630
Financial aid: (617) 349-8760; 67% of undergrads determined to have financial need; average aid package $17,787

Massachusetts College of Art and Design

Boston MA
(617) 879-7222
U.S. News ranking: Arts, unranked
Website: www.massart.edu
Admissions email: admissions@massart.edu
Public; founded 1873
Freshman admissions: least selective; 2019-2020: 3,087 applied, 1,785 accepted. Neither SAT nor ACT required. SAT 25/75 percentile: N/A. High school rank: N/A
Early decision deadline: N/A, notification date: N/A
Early action deadline: 12/1, notification date: 1/5
Application deadline (fall): 2/1
Undergraduate student body: 1,682 full time, 273 part time; 27% male, 73% female; 0% American Indian, 5% Asian, 5% Black, 11% Hispanic, 3% multiracial, 0% Pacific Islander, 59% white, 5% international; 74% from in state; 44% live on campus; N/A of students in fraternities, N/A in sororities
Most popular majors: 18% Illustration, 13% Film/Video and Photographic Arts, Other, 11% Graphic Design, 8% Painting, 7% Photography
Expenses: 2020-2021: $14,200 in state, $39,800 out of state; room/board: $14,800
Financial aid: (617) 879-7849; 63% of undergrads determined to have financial need; average aid package $12,403

Massachusetts College of Liberal Arts

North Adams MA
(413) 662-5410
U.S. News ranking: Nat. Lib. Arts, No. 149
Website: www.mcla.edu
Admissions email: admissions@mcla.edu
Public; founded 1894
Freshman admissions: selective; 2019-2020: 1,754 applied, 1,432 accepted. Either SAT or ACT required. SAT 25/75 percentile: 960-1170. High school rank: 11% in top tenth, 30% in top quarter, 72% in top half
Early decision deadline: N/A, notification date: N/A
Early action deadline: 12/1, notification date: 12/1
Application deadline (fall): rolling
Undergraduate student body: 1,145 full time, 200 part time; 40% male, 60% female; 0% American Indian, 2% Asian, 10% Black, 10% Hispanic, 3% multiracial, 0% Pacific Islander, 70% white, 0% international; 70% from in state; 62% live on campus; N/A of students in fraternities, N/A in sororities
Most popular majors: 18% English Language and Literature/Letters, 17% Multi/Interdisciplinary Studies, 15% Business, Management, Marketing, and Related Support Services, 11% Visual and Performing Arts, 10% Psychology
Expenses: 2020-2021: $11,105 in state, $20,050 out of state; room/board: $11,430
Financial aid: (413) 662-5219; 76% of undergrads determined to have financial need; average aid package $16,911

Massachusetts Institute of Technology

Cambridge MA
(617) 253-3400
U.S. News ranking: Nat. U., No. 4
Website: web.mit.edu/
Admissions email: admissions@mit.edu
Private; founded 1861
Freshman admissions: most selective; 2019-2020: 21,312 applied, 1,427 accepted. Either SAT or ACT required. SAT 25/75 percentile: 1510-1570. High school rank: 95% in top tenth, 99% in top quarter, 100% in top half
Early decision deadline: N/A, notification date: N/A
Early action deadline: 11/1, notification date: 12/20
Application deadline (fall): 1/1
Undergraduate student body: 4,501 full time, 29 part time; 53% male, 47% female; 0% American Indian, 30% Asian, 6% Black, 15% Hispanic, 8% multiracial, 0% Pacific Islander, 29% white, 10% international; 9% from in state; 92% live on campus; 45% of students in fraternities, 25% in sororities

Most popular majors: 31% Computer Science, 14% Mechanical Engineering, 8% Mathematics, General, 6% Physics, General, 4% Electrical and Electronics Engineering
Expenses: 2020-2021: $53,818; room/board: $12,000
Financial aid: (617) 258-8600; 63% of undergrads determined to have financial need; average aid package $54,015

Massachusetts Maritime Academy

Buzzards Bay MA
(800) 544-3411
U.S. News ranking: Reg. Coll. (N), No. 5
Website: www.maritime.edu
Admissions email: admissions@maritime.edu
Public; founded 1891
Freshman admissions: selective; 2019-2020: 774 applied, 707 accepted. Either SAT or ACT required. SAT 25/75 percentile: 1020-1180. High school rank: N/A
Early decision deadline: N/A, notification date: N/A
Early action deadline: 11/15, notification date: 12/7
Application deadline (fall): 4/15
Undergraduate student body: 1,616 full time, 77 part time; 87% male, 13% female; 0% American Indian, 1% Asian, 1% Black, 4% Hispanic, 3% multiracial, 0% Pacific Islander, 85% white, 1% international; 80% from in state; 96% live on campus; 0% of students in fraternities, 0% in sororities
Most popular majors: 43% Engineering, 15% Business, Management, Marketing, and Related Support Services, 15% Transportation and Materials Moving, 14% Natural Resources and Conservation, 13% Homeland Security, Law Enforcement, Firefighting and Related Protective Services
Expenses: 2020-2021: $9,894 in state, $25,014 out of state; room/board: $13,352
Financial aid: (508) 830-5087; 58% of undergrads determined to have financial need; average aid package $14,285

Merrimack College

North Andover MA
(978) 837-5100
U.S. News ranking: Reg. U. (N), No. 45
Website: www.merrimack.edu
Admissions email: Admission@Merrimack.edu
Private; founded 1947
Affiliation: Roman Catholic
Freshman admissions: selective; 2019-2020: 9,747 applied, 7,983 accepted. Neither SAT nor ACT required. SAT 25/75 percentile: 1033-1200. High school rank: 9% in top tenth, 24% in top quarter, 61% in top half
Early decision deadline: 11/15, notification date: 12/15
Early action deadline: 1/15, notification date: 2/15
Application deadline (fall): 2/15

Undergraduate student body: 3,898 full time, 117 part time; 48% male, 52% female; 0% American Indian, 2% Asian, 4% Black, 7% Hispanic, 2% multiracial, 0% Pacific Islander, 77% white, 2% international; 71% from in state; 71% live on campus; 6% of students in fraternities, 8% in sororities
Most popular majors: 26% Business, Management, Marketing, and Related Support Services, 11% Family and Consumer Sciences/Human Sciences, 10% Health Professions and Related Programs, 8% Engineering, 7% Education
Expenses: 2019-2020: $43,340; room/board: $16,320
Financial aid: (978) 837-5186; 71% of undergrads determined to have financial need; average aid package $26,574

Montserrat College of Art[1]

Beverly MA
(978) 922-8222
U.S. News ranking: Arts, unranked
Website: www.montserrat.edu
Admissions email: admissions@montserrat.edu
Private; founded 1970
Application deadline (fall): N/A
Undergraduate student body: N/A full time, N/A part time
Expenses: 2019-2020: $34,350; room/board: $12,500
Financial aid: (978) 921-4242

Mount Holyoke College

South Hadley MA
(413) 538-2023
U.S. News ranking: Nat. Lib. Arts, No. 34
Website: www.mtholyoke.edu
Admissions email: admission@mtholyoke.edu
Private; founded 1837
Freshman admissions: more selective; 2019-2020: 3,908 applied, 1,491 accepted. Neither SAT nor ACT required. SAT 25/75 percentile: 1270-1490. High school rank: 52% in top tenth, 82% in top quarter, 97% in top half
Early decision deadline: 11/15, notification date: 1/1
Early action deadline: N/A, notification date: N/A
Application deadline (fall): 1/15
Undergraduate student body: 2,157 full time, 33 part time; 0% male, 100% female; 0% American Indian, 8% Asian, 5% Black, 7% Hispanic, 4% multiracial, 0% Pacific Islander, 47% white, 27% international; 19% from in state; 96% live on campus; 0% of students in fraternities, 0% in sororities
Most popular majors: 10% Computer Science, 8% Biology/Biological Sciences, General, 8% Economics, General, 8% Experimental Psychology, 8% Political Science and Government, General
Expenses: 2020-2021: $54,618; room/board: $16,020

Financial aid: (413) 538-2291; 61% of undergrads determined to have financial need; average aid package $42,565

New England Conservatory of Music[1]

Boston MA
(617) 585-1101
U.S. News ranking: Arts, unranked
Website: www.newenglandconservatory.edu
Admissions email: admission@newenglandconservatory.edu
Private; founded 1867
Application deadline (fall): 12/1
Undergraduate student body: N/A full time, N/A part time
Expenses: 2020-2021: $52,440; room/board: $17,060
Financial aid: (617) 585-1110; 42% of undergrads determined to have financial need; average aid package $28,577

Nichols College

Dudley MA
(800) 470-3379
U.S. News ranking: Business, unranked
Website: www.nichols.edu/
Admissions email: admissions@nichols.edu
Private; founded 1815
Freshman admissions: selective; 2019-2020: 2,488 applied, 1,984 accepted. Neither SAT nor ACT required. SAT 25/75 percentile: 950-1140. High school rank: N/A
Early decision deadline: N/A, notification date: N/A
Early action deadline: 12/1, notification date: N/A
Application deadline (fall): rolling
Undergraduate student body: 1,218 full time, 108 part time; 63% male, 37% female; 0% American Indian, 1% Asian, 6% Black, 9% Hispanic, 4% multiracial, 0% Pacific Islander, 77% white, 2% international; 59% from in state; 74% live on campus; 0% of students in fraternities, 0% in sororities
Most popular majors: 24% Business/Commerce, General, 14% Sport and Fitness Administration/Management, 12% Marketing/Marketing Management, General, 11% Accounting, 7% Finance, General
Expenses: 2020-2021: $36,540; room/board: $13,950
Financial aid: (508) 213-2288; 78% of undergrads determined to have financial need; average aid package $29,884

Northeastern University

Boston MA
(617) 373-2200
U.S. News ranking: Nat. U., No. 49
Website: www.northeastern.edu/
Admissions email: admissions@northeastern.edu
Private; founded 1898
Freshman admissions: most selective; 2019-2020: 62,263 applied, 11,240 accepted. Either SAT or ACT required. SAT 25/75

percentile: 1390-1540. High school rank: 75% in top tenth, 93% in top quarter, 99% in top half
Early decision deadline: 11/1, notification date: 12/15
Early action deadline: 11/1, notification date: 2/1
Application deadline (fall): 1/1
Undergraduate student body: 14,156 full time, 46 part time; 48% male, 52% female; 0% American Indian, 14% Asian, 4% Black, 9% Hispanic, 5% multiracial, 0% Pacific Islander, 44% white, 17% international; 27% from in state; 47% live on campus; 10% of students in fraternities, 17% in sororities
Most popular majors: 24% Business, Management, Marketing, and Related Support Services, 20% Engineering, 10% Health Professions and Related Programs, 10% Social Sciences, 9% Biological and Biomedical Sciences
Expenses: 2020-2021: $55,382; room/board: $17,480
Financial aid: (617) 373-3190; 28% of undergrads determined to have financial need; average aid package $33,485

Pine Manor College

Chestnut Hill MA
(617) 731-7111
U.S. News ranking: Nat. Lib. Arts, second tier
Website: www.pmc.edu
Admissions email: admission@pmc.edu
Private; founded 1911
Freshman admissions: least selective; 2019-2020: 537 applied, 244 accepted. Neither SAT nor ACT required. SAT 25/75 percentile: 740-915. High school rank: N/A
Early decision deadline: N/A, notification date: N/A
Early action deadline: N/A, notification date: N/A
Application deadline (fall): rolling
Undergraduate student body: 329 full time, 6 part time; 60% male, 40% female; 2% American Indian, 2% Asian, 33% Black, 28% Hispanic, 8% multiracial, 0% Pacific Islander, 11% white, 1% international
Most popular majors: Information not available
Expenses: 2020-2021: $31,660; room/board: $13,830
Financial aid: (617) 731-7628; 91% of undergrads determined to have financial need; average aid package $32,966

Salem State University

Salem MA
(978) 542-6200
U.S. News ranking: Reg. U. (N), No. 125
Website: www.salemstate.edu
Admissions email: admissions@salemstate.edu
Public; founded 1854
Freshman admissions: less selective; 2019-2020: 5,825 applied, 4,985 accepted. Neither

SAT nor ACT required. SAT 25/75 percentile: 970-1150. High school rank: N/A
Early decision deadline: N/A, notification date: N/A
Early action deadline: 11/15, notification date: 1/1
Application deadline (fall): rolling
Undergraduate student body: 4,997 full time, 1,276 part time; 38% male, 62% female; 0% American Indian, 3% Asian, 9% Black, 19% Hispanic, 3% multiracial, 0% Pacific Islander, 60% white, 3% international; N/A from in state; 31% live on campus; N/A of students in fraternities, N/A in sororities
Most popular majors: 23% Business, Management, Marketing, and Related Support Services, 14% Health Professions and Related Programs, 9% Education, 9% Psychology, 7% Biological and Biomedical Sciences
Expenses: 2019-2020: $11,128 in state, $17,994 out of state; room/board: $14,052
Financial aid: N/A

Simmons University

Boston MA
(617) 521-2051
U.S. News ranking: Nat. U., No. 133
Website: www.simmons.edu
Admissions email: ugadm@simmons.edu
Private; founded 1899
Freshman admissions: selective; 2019-2020: 2,933 applied, 2,145 accepted. Either SAT or ACT required. SAT 25/75 percentile: 1110-1290. High school rank: 28% in top tenth, 69% in top quarter, 72% in top half
Early decision deadline: N/A, notification date: N/A
Early action deadline: 11/1, notification date: 12/15
Application deadline (fall): 2/1
Undergraduate student body: 1,607 full time, 170 part time; 0% male, 100% female; 0% American Indian, 11% Asian, 7% Black, 8% Hispanic, 5% multiracial, 0% Pacific Islander, 62% white, 5% international; 62% from in state; 61% live on campus; 0% of students in fraternities, 0% in sororities
Most popular majors: 35% Registered Nursing/Registered Nurse, 8% Kinesiology and Exercise Science, 6% Communication and Media Studies, 6% Psychology, General, 6% Social Work
Expenses: 2020-2021: $43,316; room/board: $15,580
Financial aid: (617) 521-2001; 76% of undergrads determined to have financial need; average aid package $34,461

Smith College

Northampton MA
(413) 585-2500
U.S. News ranking: Nat. Lib. Arts, No. 15
Website: www.smith.edu
Admissions email: admission@smith.edu

Private; founded 1871
Freshman admissions: most selective; 2019-2020: 5,597 applied, 1,817 accepted. Neither SAT nor ACT required. SAT 25/75 percentile: 1330-1520. High school rank: 75% in top tenth, 96% in top quarter, 100% in top half
Early decision deadline: 11/15, notification date: 12/15
Early action deadline: N/A, notification date: N/A
Application deadline (fall): 1/15
Undergraduate student body: 2,519 full time, 12 part time; 0% male, 100% female; 0% American Indian, 10% Asian, 6% Black, 12% Hispanic, 5% multiracial, 0% Pacific Islander, 49% white, 14% international; 19% from in state; 94% live on campus; 0% of students in fraternities, 0% in sororities
Most popular majors: 8% Political Science and Government, General, 7% Economics, General, 5% Engineering, General, 5% English Language and Literature, General, 5% Research and Experimental Psychology, Other
Expenses: 2020-2021: $56,114; room/board: $18,760
Financial aid: (413) 585-2530; 60% of undergrads determined to have financial need; average aid package $56,230

Springfield College
Springfield MA
(413) 748-3136
U.S. News ranking: Reg. U. (N), No. 26
Website: springfield.edu/
Admissions email: admissions@ springfieldcollege.edu
Private; founded 1885
Freshman admissions: selective; 2019-2020: 3,616 applied, 2,461 accepted. Either SAT or ACT required. SAT 25/75 percentile: 1020-1220. High school rank: 11% in top tenth, 33% in top quarter, 71% in top half
Early decision deadline: 12/1, notification date: 2/1
Early action deadline: N/A, notification date: N/A
Application deadline (fall): 8/1
Undergraduate student body: 2,158 full time, 17 part time; 50% male, 50% female; 0% American Indian, 2% Asian, 5% Black, 8% Hispanic, 3% multiracial, 0% Pacific Islander, 73% white, 4% international; 36% from in state; 87% live on campus; N/A of students in fraternities, N/A in sororities
Most popular majors: 8% Health Professions and Related Programs, 8% Kinesiology and Exercise Science, 8% Physical Therapy/ Therapist, 7% Psychology, General, 7% Sport and Fitness Administration/Management
Expenses: 2020-2021: $39,720; room/board: $13,320
Financial aid: (413) 748-3108; 80% of undergrads determined to have financial need; average aid package $28,667

Stonehill College
Easton MA
(508) 565-1373
U.S. News ranking: Nat. Lib. Arts, No. 113
Website: www.stonehill.edu
Admissions email: admission@stonehill.edu
Private; founded 1948
Affiliation: Roman Catholic
Freshman admissions: selective; 2019-2020: 6,961 applied, 4,712 accepted. Neither SAT nor ACT required. SAT 25/75 percentile: 1120-1290. High school rank: 19% in top tenth, 51% in top quarter, 88% in top half
Early decision deadline: 12/1, notification date: 12/31
Early action deadline: 11/1, notification date: 12/31
Application deadline (fall): 1/15
Undergraduate student body: 2,481 full time, 28 part time; 41% male, 59% female; 0% American Indian, 2% Asian, 4% Black, 5% Hispanic, 2% multiracial, 0% Pacific Islander, 83% white, 1% international; 65% from in state; 86% live on campus; N/A of students in fraternities, N/A in sororities
Most popular majors: 11% Psychology, General, 9% Accounting, 8% Marketing/ Marketing Management, General, 6% Criminology, 6% Speech Communication and Rhetoric
Expenses: 2020-2021: $46,642; room/board: $16,620
Financial aid: (508) 565-1088; 62% of undergrads determined to have financial need; average aid package $31,521

Suffolk University
Boston MA
(617) 573-8460
U.S. News ranking: Reg. U. (N), No. 31
Website: www.suffolk.edu
Admissions email: admission@suffolk.edu
Private; founded 1906
Freshman admissions: selective; 2019-2020: 8,362 applied, 7,001 accepted. Either SAT or ACT required. SAT 25/75 percentile: 1020-1210. High school rank: 15% in top tenth, 43% in top quarter, 81% in top half
Early decision deadline: N/A, notification date: N/A
Early action deadline: 11/15, notification date: 12/15
Application deadline (fall): rolling
Undergraduate student body: 4,783 full time, 200 part time; 44% male, 56% female; 0% American Indian, 7% Asian, 5% Black, 13% Hispanic, 3% multiracial, 0% Pacific Islander, 48% white, 20% international; 68% from in state; 31% live on campus; 3% of students in fraternities, 2% in sororities
Most popular majors: 45% Business, Management, Marketing, and Related Support Services, 12% Social Sciences, 11% Communication, Journalism, and Related Programs, 5% Computer and Information

Sciences and Support Services, 5% Psychology
Expenses: 2020-2021: $41,648; room/board: $18,134
Financial aid: (617) 573-8470; 61% of undergrads determined to have financial need; average aid package $28,833

Tufts University
Medford MA
(617) 627-3170
U.S. News ranking: Nat. U., No. 30
Website: www.tufts.edu
Admissions email: undergratuate. admissions@tufts.edu
Private; founded 1852
Freshman admissions: most selective; 2019-2020: 22,766 applied, 3,404 accepted. Either SAT or ACT required. SAT 25/75 percentile: 1390-1540. High school rank: 80% in top tenth, 95% in top quarter, 99% in top half
Early decision deadline: 11/1, notification date: 12/15
Early action deadline: N/A, notification date: N/A
Application deadline (fall): 1/1
Undergraduate student body: 2,481 full time, 28 part time; 47% male, 53% female; 0% American Indian, 14% Asian, 4% Black, 7% Hispanic, 5% multiracial, 0% Pacific Islander, 53% white, 11% international; 25% from in state; 65% live on campus; 10% of students in fraternities, 15% in sororities
Most popular majors: 30% Social Sciences, 14% Multi/ Interdisciplinary Studies, 10% Computer and Information Sciences and Support Services, 10% Engineering, 9% Biological and Biomedical Sciences
Expenses: 2020-2021: $60,862; room/board: $15,630
Financial aid: (617) 627-2000; 37% of undergrads determined to have financial need; average aid package $49,215

University of Massachusetts– Amherst
Amherst MA
(413) 545-0222
U.S. News ranking: Nat. U., No. 66
Website: www.umass.edu
Admissions email: mail@admissions.umass.edu
Public; founded 1863
Freshman admissions: more selective; 2019-2020: 42,157 applied, 26,895 accepted. Either SAT or ACT required. SAT 25/75 percentile: 1190-1390. High school rank: 31% in top tenth, 70% in top quarter, 96% in top half
Early decision deadline: N/A, notification date: N/A
Early action deadline: 11/5, notification date: 1/15
Application deadline (fall): 1/15
Undergraduate student body: 22,491 full time, 1,718 part time; 50% male, 50% female; 0% American Indian, 11% Asian, 5% Black, 8% Hispanic, 3% multiracial, 0% Pacific Islander,

61% white, 7% international; 77% from in state; 63% live on campus; 7% of students in fraternities, 7% in sororities
Most popular majors: 15% Business, Management, Marketing, and Related Support Services, 12% Social Sciences, 10% Biological and Biomedical Sciences, 9% Health Professions and Related Programs, 8% Psychology
Expenses: 2019-2020: $16,389 in state, $35,710 out of state; room/board: $13,598
Financial aid: (413) 545-0801; 53% of undergrads determined to have financial need; average aid package $18,223

University of Massachusetts– Boston
Boston MA
(617) 287-6100
U.S. News ranking: Nat. U., No. 227
Website: www.umb.edu
Admissions email: undergrad.admissions@umb.edu
Public; founded 1964
Freshman admissions: selective; 2019-2020: 13,649 applied, 10,393 accepted. Neither SAT nor ACT required. SAT 25/75 percentile: 1010-1220. High school rank: 15% in top tenth, 41% in top quarter, 76% in top half
Early decision deadline: N/A, notification date: N/A
Early action deadline: 11/1, notification date: 12/31
Application deadline (fall): 3/1
Undergraduate student body: 9,995 full time, 2,600 part time; 45% male, 55% female; 0% American Indian, 14% Asian, 17% Black, 17% Hispanic, 3% multiracial, 0% Pacific Islander, 34% white, 10% international; N/A from in state; 9% live on campus; N/A of students in fraternities, N/A in sororities
Most popular majors: 18% Business, Management, Marketing, and Related Support Services, 12% Health Professions and Related Programs, 11% Psychology, 10% Social Sciences, 8% Biological and Biomedical Sciences
Expenses: 2020-2021: $14,677 in state, $35,139 out of state; room/board: $17,437
Financial aid: (617) 297-6300; 69% of undergrads determined to have financial need; average aid package $17,239

University of Massachusetts– Dartmouth
North Dartmouth MA
(508) 999-8605
U.S. News ranking: Nat. U., No. 217
Website: www.umassd.edu
Admissions email: admissions@umassd.edu
Public; founded 1895
Freshman admissions: selective; 2019-2020: 8,623 applied, 6,453 accepted. Neither SAT

nor ACT required. SAT 25/75 percentile: 990-1190. High school rank: 14% in top tenth, 35% in top quarter, 70% in top half
Early decision deadline: N/A, notification date: N/A
Early action deadline: 11/18, notification date: 12/15
Application deadline (fall): rolling
Undergraduate student body: 5,465 full time, 940 part time; 50% male, 50% female; 0% American Indian, 4% Asian, 17% Black, 10% Hispanic, 4% multiracial, 0% Pacific Islander, 59% white, 2% international; 87% from in state; 49% live on campus; N/A of students in fraternities, N/A in sororities
Most popular majors: 29% Business, Management, Marketing, and Related Support Services, 14% Health Professions and Related Programs, 12% Engineering, 9% Social Sciences, 9% Visual and Performing Arts
Expenses: 2020-2021: $14,408 in state, $30,153 out of state; room/board: $15,065
Financial aid: (508) 999-8643; 78% of undergrads determined to have financial need; average aid package $17,000

University of Massachusetts– Lowell
Lowell MA
(978) 934-3931
U.S. News ranking: Nat. U., No. 176
Website: www.uml.edu
Admissions email: admissions@uml.edu
Public; founded 1894
Freshman admissions: more selective; 2019-2020: 12,586 applied, 9,215 accepted. Neither SAT nor ACT required. SAT 25/75 percentile: 1150-1320. High school rank: 25% in top tenth, 56% in top quarter, 89% in top half
Early decision deadline: N/A, notification date: N/A
Early action deadline: 11/1, notification date: 12/10
Application deadline (fall): 2/1
Undergraduate student body: 10,862 full time, 3,310 part time; 60% male, 40% female; 0% American Indian, 12% Asian, 7% Black, 12% Hispanic, 3% multiracial, 0% Pacific Islander, 59% white, 3% international; N/A from in state; 39% live on campus; N/A of students in fraternities, N/A in sororities
Most popular majors: 21% Business, Management, Marketing, and Related Support Services, 20% Engineering, 11% Computer and Information Sciences and Support Services, 10% Health Professions and Related Programs, 7% Homeland Security, Law Enforcement, Firefighting and Related Protective Services
Expenses: 2019-2020: $15,180 in state, $32,827 out of state; room/board: $12,748
Financial aid: (978) 934-4220; 60% of undergrads determined to have financial need; average aid package $17,201

Wellesley College

Wellesley MA
(781) 283-2270
U.S. News ranking: Nat. Lib. Arts,
No. 4
Website: www.wellesley.edu
Admissions email:
admission@wellesley.edu
Private; founded 1870
Freshman admissions: most
selective; 2019-2020: 6,395
applied, 1,379 accepted. Either
SAT or ACT required. SAT 25/75
percentile: 1360-1530. High
school rank: 79% in top tenth,
93% in top quarter, 99% in
top half
Early decision deadline: 11/1,
notification date: 12/15
Early action deadline: N/A,
notification date: N/A
Application deadline (fall): 1/8
Undergraduate student body: 2,399
full time, 120 part time; 2%
male, 98% female; 0% American
Indian, 23% Asian, 7% Black,
13% Hispanic, 7% multiracial,
0% Pacific Islander, 37% white,
13% international; 13% from in
state; 97% live on campus; N/A
of students in fraternities, N/A in
sororities
Most popular majors: 26%
Social Sciences, 12% Biological
and Biomedical Sciences, 9%
Computer and Information
Sciences and Support Services,
8% Area, Ethnic, Cultural,
Gender, and Group Studies,
8% Psychology
Expenses: 2020-2021: $58,448;
room/board: $17,772
Financial aid: (781) 283-2360;
56% of undergrads determined to
have financial need; average aid
package $54,950

Wentworth Institute of Technology

Boston MA
(617) 989-4000
U.S. News ranking: Reg. U. (N),
No. 38
Website: www.wit.edu
Admissions email:
admissions@wit.edu
Private; founded 1904
Freshman admissions: selective;
2019-2020: 7,311 applied,
5,012 accepted. Neither SAT
nor ACT required. SAT 25/75
percentile: 1060-1270. High
school rank: 16% in top tenth,
41% in top quarter, 79% in
top half
Early decision deadline: N/A,
notification date: N/A
Early action deadline: N/A,
notification date: N/A
Application deadline (fall): rolling
Undergraduate student body: 3,904
full time, 403 part time; 78%
male, 22% female; 0% American
Indian, 9% Asian, 6% Black,
8% Hispanic, 3% multiracial,
0% Pacific Islander, 63% white,
7% international; 36% from in
state; 48% live on campus; N/A
of students in fraternities, N/A in
sororities
Most popular majors: 14%
Mechanical Engineering, 12%
Construction Management,
11% Computer Science, 10%
Architecture, 6% Bioengineering
and Biomedical Engineering

Expenses: 2020-2021: $34,970;
room/board: $14,190
Financial aid: (617) 989-4020;
69% of undergrads determined to
have financial need; average aid
package $8,370

Western New England University

Springfield MA
(413) 782-1321
U.S. News ranking: Nat. U.,
No. 227
Website: www.wne.edu
Admissions email: learn@wne.edu
Private; founded 1919
Freshman admissions: selective;
2019-2020: 6,862 applied,
5,845 accepted. Neither SAT
nor ACT required. SAT 25/75
percentile: 1080-1242. High
school rank: 22% in top tenth,
52% in top quarter, 80% in
top half
Early decision deadline: N/A,
notification date: N/A
Early action deadline: N/A,
notification date: N/A
Application deadline (fall): rolling
Undergraduate student body: 2,580
full time, 118 part time; 61%
male, 39% female; 0% American
Indian, 3% Asian, 4% Black,
9% Hispanic, 3% multiracial,
0% Pacific Islander, 75% white,
3% international; 52% from in
state; 57% live on campus; 0%
of students in fraternities, 0% in
sororities
Most popular majors: 24%
Business, Management,
Marketing, and Related Support
Services, 24% Engineering, 10%
Health Professions and Related
Programs, 8% Homeland Security,
Law Enforcement, Firefighting
and Related Protective Services,
6% Psychology
Expenses: 2020-2021: $39,216;
room/board: $14,246
Financial aid: (413) 796-2080;
78% of undergrads determined to
have financial need; average aid
package $27,353

Westfield State University

Westfield MA
(413) 572-5218
U.S. News ranking: Reg. U. (N),
No. 90
Website: www.westfield.ma.edu
Admissions email:
admissions@westfield.ma.edu
Public; founded 1839
Freshman admissions: selective;
2019-2020: 4,455 applied,
3,883 accepted. Either SAT
or ACT required. SAT 25/75
percentile: 980-1150. High
school rank: 8% in top tenth, 25%
in top quarter, 60% in top half
Early decision deadline: N/A,
notification date: N/A
Early action deadline: N/A,
notification date: N/A
Application deadline (fall): 3/1
Undergraduate student body: 4,255
full time, 800 part time; 45%
male, 55% female; 0% American
Indian, 2% Asian, 5% Black,
11% Hispanic, 3% multiracial,
0% Pacific Islander, 75% white,

0% international; 92% from in
state; 48% live on campus; 0%
of students in fraternities, 0% in
sororities
Most popular majors: 15%
Business, Management,
Marketing, and Related Support
Services, 15% Homeland Security,
Law Enforcement, Firefighting and
Related Protective Services, 12%
Liberal Arts and Sciences, General
Studies and Humanities, 8%
Education, 8% Psychology
Expenses: 2020-2021: $11,139
in state, $17,219 out of state;
room/board: $11,887
Financial aid: (413) 572-5218;
64% of undergrads determined to
have financial need; average aid
package $9,327

Wheaton College

Norton MA
(508) 286-8251
U.S. News ranking: Nat. Lib. Arts,
No. 84
Website: www.wheatoncollege.edu
Admissions email: admission@
wheatoncollege.edu
Private; founded 1834
Freshman admissions: selective;
2019-2020: 3,460 applied,
2,556 accepted. Neither SAT
nor ACT required. SAT 25/75
percentile: 1150-1340. High
school rank: 23% in top tenth,
53% in top quarter, 84% in
top half
Early decision deadline: 11/15,
notification date: 12/20
Early action deadline: 11/15,
notification date: 12/20
Application deadline (fall): 1/15
Undergraduate student body: 1,764
full time, 10 part time; 40%
male, 60% female; 0% American
Indian, 4% Asian, 6% Black,
9% Hispanic, 5% multiracial,
0% Pacific Islander, 67% white,
8% international; 37% from in
state; 96% live on campus;
0% of students in fraternities,
0% in sororities
Most popular majors: 16%
Business, Management,
Marketing, and Related Support
Services, 15% Social Sciences,
14% Biological and Biomedical
Sciences, 12% Psychology, 9%
Visual and Performing Arts
Expenses: 2020-2021: $56,366;
room/board: $14,378
Financial aid: (508) 286-8232;
70% of undergrads determined to
have financial need; average aid
package $46,154

Williams College

Williamstown MA
(413) 597-2211
U.S. News ranking: Nat. Lib. Arts,
No. 1
Website: www.williams.edu
Admissions email:
admission@williams.edu
Private; founded 1793
Freshman admissions: most
selective; 2019-2020: 9,715
applied, 1,224 accepted. Neither
SAT nor ACT required. SAT
25/75 percentile: 1410-1550.
High school rank: 85% in top
tenth, 98% in top quarter, 99%
in top half

Early decision deadline: 11/15,
notification date: 12/15
Early action deadline: N/A,
notification date: N/A
Application deadline (fall): 1/1
Undergraduate student body: 2,027
full time, 51 part time; 50%
male, 50% female; 0% American
Indian, 12% Asian, 7% Black,
13% Hispanic, 6% multiracial,
0% Pacific Islander, 49% white,
9% international; 16% from in
state; 93% live on campus; N/A
of students in fraternities, N/A in
sororities
Most popular majors: 23%
Econometrics and Quantitative
Economics, 12% English
Language and Literature,
General, 11% Political Science
and Government, General, 10%
Biology/Biological Sciences,
General, 10% History, General
Expenses: 2020-2021: $50,760;
room/board: $12,750
Financial aid: (413) 597-4181;
52% of undergrads determined to
have financial need; average aid
package $59,941

Worcester Polytechnic Institute

Worcester MA
(508) 831-5286
U.S. News ranking: Nat. U., No. 66
Website: www.wpi.edu/
admissions/undergraduate
Admissions email:
admissions@wpi.edu
Private; founded 1865
Freshman admissions: most
selective; 2019-2020: 10,645
applied, 5,255 accepted. Neither
SAT nor ACT required. SAT 25/75
percentile: 1310-1470. High
school rank: 63% in top tenth,
96% in top quarter, 100% in
top half
Early decision deadline: 11/1,
notification date: 12/15
Early action deadline: 11/1,
notification date: 1/15
Application deadline (fall): 1/15
Undergraduate student body: 4,642
full time, 119 part time; 60%
male, 40% female; 0% American
Indian, 6% Asian, 3% Black,
9% Hispanic, 3% multiracial,
0% Pacific Islander, 63% white,
9% international; 41% from in
state; 60% live on campus;
27% of students in fraternities,
37% in sororities
Most popular majors: 23%
Mechanical Engineering, 15%
Computer Science, 9% Electrical
and Electronics Engineering,
8% Chemical Engineering, 7%
Mechatronics, Robotics, and
Automation Engineering
Expenses: 2020-2021: $53,826;
room/board: $15,820
Financial aid: (508) 831-5469;
61% of undergrads determined to
have financial need; average aid
package $39,360

Worcester State University

Worcester MA
(508) 929-8040
U.S. News ranking: Reg. U. (N),
No. 96
Website: www.worcester.edu
Admissions email:
admissions@worcester.edu
Public; founded 1874
Freshman admissions: selective;
2019-2020: 3,896 applied,
3,145 accepted. Neither SAT
nor ACT required. SAT 25/75
percentile: 950-1160. High
school rank: N/A
Early decision deadline: N/A,
notification date: N/A
Early action deadline: 11/15,
notification date: 12/15
Application deadline (fall): 6/1
Undergraduate student body: 4,078
full time, 1,254 part time; 38%
male, 62% female; 0% American
Indian, 5% Asian, 9% Black,
13% Hispanic, 3% multiracial,
0% Pacific Islander, 65% white,
1% international; N/A from in
state; 31% live on campus; N/A
of students in fraternities, N/A in
sororities
Most popular majors: 19% Health
Professions and Related Programs,
16% Business, Management,
Marketing, and Related Support
Services, 12% Psychology,
10% Homeland Security, Law
Enforcement, Firefighting and
Related Protective Services, 7%
Social Sciences
Expenses: 2019-2020: $10,161
in state, $16,241 out of state;
room/board: $12,360
Financial aid: (508) 929-8056;
64% of undergrads determined to
have financial need; average aid
package $19,226

MICHIGAN

Adrian College

Adrian MI
(800) 877-2246
U.S. News ranking: Reg. Coll.
(Mid. W), No. 17
Website: www.adrian.edu
Admissions email:
admissions@adrian.edu
Private; founded 1859
Affiliation: United Methodist
Freshman admissions: selective;
2019-2020: 5,219 applied,
2,919 accepted. Either SAT
or ACT required. SAT 25/75
percentile: 960-1163. High school
rank: 14% in top tenth, 29% in
top quarter, 59% in top half
Early decision deadline: N/A,
notification date: N/A
Early action deadline: N/A,
notification date: N/A
Application deadline (fall): rolling
Undergraduate student body: 1,724
full time, 56 part time; 50%
male, 50% female; 0% American
Indian, 0% Asian, 7% Black, 4%
Hispanic, 4% multiracial, 0%
Pacific Islander, 69% white, 0%
international; 75% from in state;
95% live on campus; 13% of
students in fraternities, 15% in
sororities

Most popular majors: 29% Business, Management, Marketing, and Related Support Services, 19% Parks, Recreation, Leisure, and Fitness Studies, 8% Biological and Biomedical Sciences, 8% Visual and Performing Arts, 7% Health Professions and Related Programs
Expenses: 2020-2021: $38,730; room/board: $12,130
Financial aid: (888) 876-0194; 83% of undergrads determined to have financial need; average aid package $31,363

Albion College
Albion MI
(800) 858-6770
U.S. News ranking: Nat. Lib. Arts, No. 130
Website: www.albion.edu/
Admissions email: admission@albion.edu
Private; founded 1835
Affiliation: United Methodist
Freshman admissions: selective; 2019-2020: 4,043 applied, 2,780 accepted. Neither SAT nor ACT required. SAT 25/75 percentile: 990-1200. High school rank: N/A
Early decision deadline: N/A, notification date: N/A
Early action deadline: 12/1, notification date: N/A
Application deadline (fall): rolling
Undergraduate student body: 1,455 full time, 20 part time; 46% male, 54% female; 0% American Indian, 2% Asian, 16% Black, 12% Hispanic, 3% multiracial, 0% Pacific Islander, 59% white, 2% international; 71% from in state; 94% live on campus; 35% of students in fraternities, 31% in sororities
Most popular majors: 23% Social Sciences, 13% Biological and Biomedical Sciences, 11% Business, Management, Marketing, and Related Support Services, 10% Parks, Recreation, Leisure, and Fitness Studies, 8% Psychology
Expenses: 2020-2021: $50,590; room/board: $12,380
Financial aid: (517) 629-0440; 80% of undergrads determined to have financial need; average aid package $45,275

Alma College
Alma MI
(800) 321-2562
U.S. News ranking: Reg. Coll. (Mid. W), No. 10
Website: www.alma.edu
Admissions email: admissions@alma.edu
Private; founded 1886
Affiliation: Presbyterian Church (USA)
Freshman admissions: selective; 2019-2020: 3,041 applied, 1,848 accepted. Neither SAT nor ACT required. SAT 25/75 percentile: 1030-1230. High school rank: 20% in top tenth, 29% in top quarter, 83% in top half
Early decision deadline: N/A, notification date: N/A

Early action deadline: N/A, notification date: N/A
Application deadline (fall): rolling
Undergraduate student body: 1,390 full time, 52 part time; 42% male, 58% female; 0% American Indian, 1% Asian, 3% Black, 5% Hispanic, 4% multiracial, 0% Pacific Islander, 80% white, 2% international; 91% from in state; 92% live on campus; 11% of students in fraternities, 13% in sororities
Most popular majors: 19% Health Professions and Related Programs, 16% Business, Management, Marketing, and Related Support Services, 13% Education, 9% Communication, Journalism, and Related Programs, 9% Social Sciences
Expenses: 2020-2021: $41,622; room/board: $11,790
Financial aid: (989) 463-7347; 85% of undergrads determined to have financial need; average aid package $30,408

Alpena Community College[1]
Alpena MI
(989) 356-9021
U.S. News ranking: Reg. Coll. (Mid. W), unranked
Website: www.lakemichigancollege.edu
Admissions email: N/A
Public
Application deadline (fall): N/A
Undergraduate student body: N/A full time, N/A part time
Expenses: 2019-2020: $4,650 in state, $7,050 out of state; room/board: $6,700
Financial aid: N/A

Andrews University
Berrien Springs MI
(800) 253-2874
U.S. News ranking: Nat. U., second tier
Website: www.andrews.edu
Admissions email: enroll@andrews.edu
Private; founded 1874
Affiliation: Seventh Day Adventist
Freshman admissions: more selective; 2019-2020: 1,438 applied, 964 accepted. Either SAT or ACT required. ACT 25/75 percentile: 21-29. High school rank: 17% in top tenth, 35% in top quarter, 65% in top half
Early decision deadline: N/A, notification date: N/A
Early action deadline: N/A, notification date: N/A
Application deadline (fall): rolling
Undergraduate student body: 1,352 full time, 356 part time; 46% male, 54% female; 0% American Indian, 13% Asian, 20% Black, 16% Hispanic, 6% multiracial, 0% Pacific Islander, 26% white, 17% international; 36% from in state; 60% live on campus; 0% of students in fraternities, 0% in sororities
Most popular majors: 19% Health Professions and Related Programs, 10% Business, Management, Marketing, and Related Support Services, 8% Biological and Biomedical Sciences,

6% Psychology, 6% Visual and Performing Arts
Expenses: 2020-2021: $31,008; room/board: $9,540
Financial aid: (269) 471-3334; 55% of undergrads determined to have financial need; average aid package $32,665

Aquinas College
Grand Rapids MI
(616) 632-2900
U.S. News ranking: Nat. Lib. Arts, second tier
Website: www.aquinas.edu
Admissions email: admissions@aquinas.edu
Private; founded 1886
Affiliation: Roman Catholic
Freshman admissions: selective; 2019-2020: 1,883 applied, 1,305 accepted. Either SAT or ACT required. SAT 25/75 percentile: 1000-1200. High school rank: N/A
Early decision deadline: N/A, notification date: N/A
Early action deadline: N/A, notification date: N/A
Application deadline (fall): rolling
Undergraduate student body: 1,196 full time, 260 part time; 43% male, 57% female; 0% American Indian, 1% Asian, 5% Black, 8% Hispanic, 2% multiracial, 0% Pacific Islander, 65% white, 3% international; 91% from in state; 46% live on campus; N/A of students in fraternities, N/A in sororities
Most popular majors: 21% Business, Management, Marketing, and Related Support Services, 8% Parks, Recreation, Leisure, and Fitness Studies, 7% Biological and Biomedical Sciences, 7% Education, 7% Visual and Performing Arts
Expenses: 2020-2021: $35,086; room/board: $9,876
Financial aid: (616) 632-2893; 74% of undergrads determined to have financial need; average aid package $26,667

Baker College of Flint[1]
Flint MI
(810) 767-7600
U.S. News ranking: Reg. U. (Mid. W), second tier
Website: www.baker.edu
Admissions email: troy.crowe@baker.edu
Private
Application deadline (fall): N/A
Undergraduate student body: N/A full time, N/A part time
Expenses: 2019-2020: $9,920; room/board: $5,900
Financial aid: N/A

Calvin University
Grand Rapids MI
(800) 688-0122
U.S. News ranking: Reg. U. (Mid. W), No. 3
Website: calvin.edu
Admissions email: admissions@calvin.edu
Private; founded 1876
Affiliation: Christian Reformed Church

Freshman admissions: more selective; 2019-2020: 3,401 applied, 2,616 accepted. Neither SAT nor ACT required. SAT 25/75 percentile: 1130-1350. High school rank: 35% in top tenth, 62% in top quarter, 87% in top half
Early decision deadline: N/A, notification date: N/A
Early action deadline: N/A, notification date: N/A
Application deadline (fall): 8/15
Undergraduate student body: 3,234 full time, 233 part time; 47% male, 53% female; 0% American Indian, 5% Asian, 4% Black, 5% Hispanic, 3% multiracial, 0% Pacific Islander, 69% white, 13% international; 59% from in state; 59% live on campus; 0% of students in fraternities, 0% in sororities
Most popular majors: 12% Engineering, General, 7% Business/Commerce, General, 7% Registered Nursing/Registered Nurse, 5% Psychology, General, 4% Elementary Education and Teaching
Expenses: 2020-2021: $37,806; room/board: $10,800
Financial aid: (616) 526-6134; 57% of undergrads determined to have financial need; average aid package $25,974

Central Michigan University
Mount Pleasant MI
(989) 774-3076
U.S. News ranking: Nat. U., No. 249
Website: www.cmich.edu
Admissions email: cmuadmit@cmich.edu
Public; founded 1892
Freshman admissions: selective; 2019-2020: 16,411 applied, 11,408 accepted. Either SAT or ACT required. SAT 25/75 percentile: 990-1200. High school rank: 18% in top tenth, 39% in top quarter, 72% in top half
Early decision deadline: N/A, notification date: N/A
Early action deadline: N/A, notification date: N/A
Application deadline (fall): rolling
Undergraduate student body: 12,800 full time, 1,872 part time; 41% male, 59% female; 1% American Indian, 1% Asian, 10% Black, 5% Hispanic, 4% multiracial, 0% Pacific Islander, 76% white, 2% international; 90% from in state; 33% live on campus; 10% of students in fraternities, 9% in sororities
Most popular majors: 28% Business, Management, Marketing, and Related Support Services, 9% Communication, Journalism, and Related Programs, 8% Health Professions and Related Programs, 8% Parks, Recreation, Leisure, and Fitness Studies, 7% Education
Expenses: 2020-2021: $13,260 in state, $13,260 out of state; room/board: $10,676
Financial aid: (989) 774-3674; 67% of undergrads determined to have financial need; average aid package $14,914

Cleary University[1]
Howell MI
(800) 686-1883
U.S. News ranking: Business, unranked
Website: www.cleary.edu
Admissions email: admissions@cleary.edu
Private; founded 1883
Application deadline (fall): 8/24
Undergraduate student body: N/A full time, N/A part time
Expenses: 2019-2020: $20,550; room/board: $10,500
Financial aid: (517) 338-3015

College for Creative Studies[1]
Detroit MI
(313) 664-7425
U.S. News ranking: Arts, unranked
Website: www.collegeforcreativestudies.edu
Admissions email: admissions@collegeforcreativestudies.edu
Private; founded 1906
Application deadline (fall): N/A
Undergraduate student body: N/A full time, N/A part time
Expenses: 2019-2020: $45,815; room/board: $7,750
Financial aid: (313) 664-7495

Cornerstone University
Grand Rapids MI
(616) 222-1426
U.S. News ranking: Reg. U. (Mid. W), No. 76
Website: www.cornerstone.edu
Admissions email: admissions@cornerstone.edu
Private; founded 1941
Affiliation: Interdenominational
Freshman admissions: selective; 2019-2020: 2,519 applied, 1,954 accepted. Either SAT or ACT required. SAT 25/75 percentile: 950-1190. High school rank: 21% in top tenth, 47% in top quarter, 78% in top half
Early decision deadline: N/A, notification date: N/A
Early action deadline: N/A, notification date: N/A
Application deadline (fall): rolling
Undergraduate student body: 1,020 full time, 484 part time; 37% male, 63% female; 0% American Indian, 2% Asian, 10% Black, 5% Hispanic, 2% multiracial, 0% Pacific Islander, 76% white, 4% international; N/A from in state; 58% live on campus; 0% of students in fraternities, 0% in sororities
Most popular majors: 40% Business, Management, Marketing, and Related Support Services, 12% Psychology, 9% Theology and Religious Vocations, 7% Communication, Journalism, and Related Programs, 7% Education
Expenses: 2020-2021: $26,250; room/board: $9,960
Financial aid: (616) 222-1424; 76% of undergrads determined to have financial need; average aid package $19,549

Davenport University

Grand Rapids MI
(866) 925-3884
U.S. News ranking: Reg. U.
(Mid. W), No. 91
Website: www.davenport.edu
Admissions email: Davenport.
Admissions@davenport.edu
Private; founded 1866
Freshman admissions: selective;
2019-2020: 2,568 applied,
2,104 accepted. Neither SAT
nor ACT required. SAT 25/75
percentile: 970-1160. High
school rank: N/A
Early decision deadline: N/A,
notification date: N/A
Early action deadline: N/A,
notification date: N/A
Application deadline (fall): rolling
Undergraduate student body: 2,501
full time, 2,611 part time; 45%
male, 55% female; 1% American
Indian, 2% Asian, 12% Black,
5% Hispanic, 3% multiracial,
0% Pacific Islander, 68% white,
3% international
Most popular majors: Information
not available
Expenses: 2019-2020: $19,338;
room/board: $10,068
Financial aid: (616) 732-1132

Eastern Michigan University

Ypsilanti MI
(734) 487-3060
U.S. News ranking: Nat. U.,
second tier
Website: www.emich.edu
Admissions email:
admissions@emich.edu
Public; founded 1849
Freshman admissions: selective;
2019-2020: 14,323 applied,
10,607 accepted. Either SAT
or ACT required. SAT 25/75
percentile: 970-1190. High school
rank: 13% in top tenth, 37% in
top quarter, 70% in top half
Early decision deadline: N/A,
notification date: N/A
Early action deadline: N/A,
notification date: N/A
Application deadline (fall): rolling
Undergraduate student body:
10,572 full time, 4,300 part
time; 40% male, 60% female;
0% American Indian, 3% Asian,
17% Black, 6% Hispanic, 4%
multiracial, 0% Pacific Islander,
62% white, 2% international;
90% from in state; 21% live
on campus; N/A of students in
fraternities, N/A in sororities
Most popular majors: 20% Health
Professions and Related Programs,
19% Business, Management,
Marketing, and Related Support
Services, 7% Education, 7%
Social Sciences, 6% Psychology
Expenses: 2020-2021: $13,698
in state, $13,698 out of state;
room/board: $10,820
Financial aid: (734) 487-1048;
67% of undergrads determined to
have financial need; average aid
package $10,889

Ferris State University

Big Rapids MI
(231) 591-2100
U.S. News ranking: Nat. U.,
second tier
Website: www.ferris.edu
Admissions email:
admissions@ferris.edu
Public; founded 1884
Freshman admissions: less
selective; 2019-2020: 9,175
applied, 7,949 accepted. Neither
SAT nor ACT required. SAT 25/75
percentile: 930-1170. High
school rank: N/A
Early decision deadline: N/A,
notification date: N/A
Early action deadline: N/A,
notification date: N/A
Application deadline (fall): rolling
Undergraduate student body: 7,779
full time, 3,405 part time; 47%
male, 53% female; 0% American
Indian, 1% Asian, 8% Black,
6% Hispanic, 4% multiracial,
0% Pacific Islander, 77% white,
1% international; 94% from in
state; 30% live on campus; 2%
of students in fraternities, 2% in
sororities
Most popular majors: 8% Criminal
Justice/Law Enforcement
Administration, 6% Health
Professions and Related Clinical
Sciences, Other, 6% Pharmacy,
5% Business Administration
and Management, General,
4% Elementary Education and
Teaching
Expenses: 2020-2021: $13,098
in state, $13,098 out of state;
room/board: $10,036
Financial aid: (231) 591-2115;
69% of undergrads determined to
have financial need; average aid
package $12,300

Finlandia University[1]

Hancock MI
(906) 487-7274
U.S. News ranking: Reg. Coll.
(Mid. W), second tier
Website: www.finlandia.edu
Admissions email:
admissions@finlandia.edu
Private; founded 1896
Affiliation:
Evangelical Lutheran Church
Application deadline (fall): N/A
Undergraduate student body: N/A
full time, N/A part time
Expenses: 2019-2020: $23,308;
room/board: $8,888
Financial aid: N/A

Grand Valley State University

Allendale MI
(800) 748-0246
U.S. News ranking: Reg. U.
(Mid. W), No. 28
Website: www.gvsu.edu
Admissions email:
admissions@gvsu.edu
Public; founded 1960
Freshman admissions: selective;
2019-2020: 16,511 applied,
13,707 accepted. Either SAT
or ACT required. SAT 25/75
percentile: 1040-1250. High
school rank: 20% in top tenth,
46% in top quarter, 84% in
top half

Early decision deadline: N/A,
notification date: N/A
Early action deadline: N/A,
notification date: N/A
Application deadline (fall): 5/1
Undergraduate student body:
18,801 full time, 2,298 part
time; 40% male, 60% female;
0% American Indian, 2% Asian,
4% Black, 6% Hispanic, 4%
multiracial, 0% Pacific Islander,
82% white, 1% international;
92% from in state; 28% live
on campus; N/A of students in
fraternities, N/A in sororities
Most popular majors: 23%
Business, Management,
Marketing, and Related Support
Services, 18% Health Professions
and Related Programs, 7%
Communication, Journalism, and
Related Programs, 6% Parks,
Recreation, Leisure, and Fitness
Studies, 6% Psychology
Expenses: 2020-2021: $13,244
in state, $18,844 out of state;
room/board: $9,000
Financial aid: (616) 331-3234;
56% of undergrads determined to
have financial need; average aid
package $10,716

Henry Ford College[1]

Dearborn MI
(313) 845-9600
U.S. News ranking: Reg. Coll.
(Mid. W), unranked
Website: www.schoolcraft.edu
Admissions email: N/A
Public
Application deadline (fall): N/A
Undergraduate student body: N/A
full time, N/A part time
Expenses: 2019-2020: $5,020 in
state, $6,904 out of state; room/
board: $9,153
Financial aid: N/A

Hillsdale College

Hillsdale MI
(517) 607-2327
U.S. News ranking: Nat. Lib. Arts,
No. 54
Website: www.hillsdale.edu/
Admissions email:
admissions@hillsdale.edu
Private; founded 1844
Affiliation: Undenominational
Freshman admissions: more
selective; 2019-2020: 1,593
applied, 769 accepted. Either
SAT or ACT required. ACT 25/75
percentile: 29-33. High school
rank: N/A
Early decision deadline: 11/1,
notification date: 12/1
Early action deadline: N/A,
notification date: N/A
Application deadline (fall): 4/1
Undergraduate student body: 1,431
full time, 37 part time; 52%
male, 48% female; 0% American
Indian, 0% Asian, 0% Black, 0%
Hispanic, 0% multiracial, 0%
Pacific Islander, 0% white, 0%
international; 31% from in state;
74% live on campus; 22% of
students in fraternities, 33% in
sororities
Most popular majors: 11%
Economics, General, 9% Biology/
Biological Sciences, General, 9%
English Language and Literature,
General, 9% History, General, 8%
Finance, General

Expenses: 2020-2021: $29,482;
room/board: $11,910
Financial aid: (517) 607-2250;
51% of undergrads determined to
have financial need; average aid
package $20,665

Hope College

Holland MI
(616) 395-7850
U.S. News ranking: Nat. Lib. Arts,
No. 112
Website: www.hope.edu
Admissions email:
admissions@hope.edu
Private; founded 1866
Affiliation:
Reformed Church in America
Freshman admissions: more
selective; 2019-2020: 3,748
applied, 3,211 accepted. Either
SAT or ACT required. SAT 25/75
percentile: 1130-1330. High
school rank: 37% in top tenth,
71% in top quarter, 94% in
top half
Early decision deadline: N/A,
notification date: N/A
Early action deadline: 11/2,
notification date: 11/26
Application deadline (fall): rolling
Undergraduate student body: 2,917
full time, 139 part time; 38%
male, 62% female; 0% American
Indian, 2% Asian, 2% Black,
8% Hispanic, 3% multiracial,
0% Pacific Islander, 82% white,
2% international; 69% from in
state; 78% live on campus; N/A
of students in fraternities, N/A in
sororities
Most popular majors: 18%
Business/Managerial Economics,
10% Psychology, General, 8%
Biology/Biological Sciences,
General, 8% Education/
Teaching of Individuals with
Specific Learning Disabilities,
7% Sociology
Expenses: 2020-2021: $36,650;
room/board: $10,940
Financial aid: (616) 395-7765;
57% of undergrads determined to
have financial need; average aid
package $28,350

Jackson College[1]

Jackson MI
(517) 796-8622
U.S. News ranking: Reg. Coll.
(Mid. W), unranked
Admissions email: N/A
Public
Application deadline (fall): N/A
Undergraduate student body: N/A
full time, N/A part time
Expenses: 2019-2020: $9,164 in
state, $11,728 out of state; room/
board: $9,900
Financial aid: N/A

Kalamazoo College

Kalamazoo MI
(800) 253-3602
U.S. News ranking: Nat. Lib. Arts,
No. 67
Website: www.kzoo.edu
Admissions email:
admission@kzoo.edu
Private; founded 1833
Freshman admissions: more
selective; 2019-2020: 3,576
applied, 2,716 accepted. Neither
SAT nor ACT required. SAT

25/75 percentile: 1170-1370.
High school rank: 52% in top
tenth, 83% in top quarter, 99%
in top half
Early decision deadline: 11/1,
notification date: 12/1
Early action deadline: 11/1,
notification date: 12/20
Application deadline (fall): 1/15
Undergraduate student body: 1,275
full time, 11 part time; 44%
male, 56% female; 0% American
Indian, 7% Asian, 7% Black,
15% Hispanic, 5% multiracial,
0% Pacific Islander, 56% white,
7% international; N/A from in
state; 53% live on campus; 0%
of students in fraternities, 0% in
sororities
Most popular majors: 17%
Social Sciences, 14% Biological
and Biomedical Sciences,
12% Physical Sciences,
10% Psychology, 9% Foreign
Languages, Literatures, and
Linguistics
Expenses: 2020-2021: $52,380;
room/board: $10,530
Financial aid: (269) 337-7192;
72% of undergrads determined to
have financial need; average aid
package $44,311

Kettering University

Flint MI
(800) 955-4464
U.S. News ranking: Reg. U.
(Mid. W), No. 9
Website: www.kettering.edu
Admissions email:
admissions@kettering.edu
Private; founded 1919
Freshman admissions: more
selective; 2019-2020: 2,262
applied, 1,651 accepted. Either
SAT or ACT required. SAT 25/75
percentile: 1190-1360. High
school rank: 46% in top tenth,
76% in top quarter, 95% in
top half
Early decision deadline: N/A,
notification date: N/A
Early action deadline: 11/15,
notification date: 12/15
Application deadline (fall): rolling
Undergraduate student body: 1,720
full time, 79 part time; 79%
male, 21% female; 0% American
Indian, 6% Asian, 2% Black,
5% Hispanic, 4% multiracial,
0% Pacific Islander, 76% white,
4% international; N/A from in
state; N/A live on campus; 8%
of students in fraternities, 7% in
sororities
Most popular majors: 83%
Engineering, 6% Computer
and Information Sciences and
Support Services, 4% Biological
and Biomedical Sciences, 3%
Mathematics and Statistics, 3%
Psychology
Expenses: 2020-2021: $44,380;
room/board: $8,400
Financial aid: (810) 762-7859;
71% of undergrads determined to
have financial need; average aid
package $23,747

Kuyper College[1]

Grand Rapids MI
(800) 511-3749
U.S. News ranking: Reg. Coll.
(Mid. W), No. 56
Website: www.kuyper.edu

Admissions email:
admissions@kuyper.edu
Private
Application deadline (fall): N/A
Undergraduate student body: N/A
full time, N/A part time
Expenses: 2019-2020: $22,886;
room/board: $7,570
Financial aid: (616) 988-3656

Lake Michigan College[1]
Benton Harbor MI
(269) 927-8100
U.S. News ranking: Reg. Coll.
(Mid. W), unranked
Website:
www.theamericancollege.edu
Admissions email: N/A
Public
Application deadline (fall): N/A
Undergraduate student body: N/A
full time, N/A part time
Expenses: 2019-2020: $6,653 in
state, $6,653 out of state; room/
board: $9,980
Financial aid: N/A

Lake Superior State University
Sault Ste. Marie MI
(906) 635-2231
U.S. News ranking: Reg. Coll.
(Mid. W), No. 46
Website: www.lssu.edu
Admissions email:
admissions@lssu.edu
Public; founded 1946
Freshman admissions: selective;
2019-2020: 1,657 applied, 941
accepted. Neither SAT nor ACT
required. SAT 25/75 percentile:
970-1160. High school rank: 9%
in top tenth, 29% in top quarter,
62% in top half
Early decision deadline: N/A,
notification date: N/A
Early action deadline: N/A,
notification date: N/A
Application deadline (fall): rolling
Undergraduate student body: 1,542
full time, 442 part time; 46%
male, 54% female; 9% American
Indian, 1% Asian, 1% Black,
2% Hispanic, 0% multiracial,
0% Pacific Islander, 80% white,
4% international; 93% from in
state; 70% live on campus; N/A
of students in fraternities, N/A in
sororities
Most popular majors: 16%
Business, Management,
Marketing, and Related Support
Services, 15% Homeland Security,
Law Enforcement, Firefighting and
Related Protective Services, 12%
Health Professions and Related
Programs, 8% Natural Resources
and Conservation, 7% Parks,
Recreation, Leisure, and Fitness
Studies
Expenses: 2020-2021: $12,811
in state, $12,811 out of state;
room/board: $10,472
Financial aid: (906) 635-2678;
69% of undergrads determined to
have financial need; average aid
package $11,732

Lawrence Technological University
Southfield MI
(248) 204-3160
U.S. News ranking: Reg. U.
(Mid. W), No. 37
Website: www.ltu.edu
Admissions email:
admissions@ltu.edu
Private; founded 1932
Freshman admissions: selective;
2019-2020: 2,398 applied,
1,901 accepted. Either SAT
or ACT required. SAT 25/75
percentile: 1020-1270. High
school rank: 0% in top tenth, 40%
in top quarter, 80% in top half
Early decision deadline: N/A,
notification date: N/A
Early action deadline: N/A,
notification date: N/A
Application deadline (fall): rolling
Undergraduate student body: 1,677
full time, 459 part time; 71%
male, 29% female; 0% American
Indian, 3% Asian, 9% Black,
3% Hispanic, 2% multiracial,
0% Pacific Islander, 68% white,
11% international; 91% from in
state; 41% live on campus; 8%
of students in fraternities, 13%
in sororities
Most popular majors: 19%
Mechanical Engineering, 9%
Architectural and Building
Sciences/Technology, 8%
Computer Science, 8% Electrical
and Electronics Engineering, 7%
Bioengineering and Biomedical
Engineering
Expenses: 2020-2021: $36,630;
room/board: $10,900
Financial aid: (248) 204-2280;
66% of undergrads determined to
have financial need; average aid
package $25,648

Madonna University
Livonia MI
(734) 432-5339
U.S. News ranking: Reg. U.
(Mid. W), No. 60
Website: www.madonna.edu
Admissions email:
admissions@madonna.edu
Private; founded 1937
Affiliation: Roman Catholic
Freshman admissions: selective;
2019-2020: 1,693 applied,
1,498 accepted. Either SAT
or ACT required. SAT 25/75
percentile: 920-1140. High school
rank: 11% in top tenth, 31% in
top quarter, 65% in top half
Early decision deadline: 12/1,
notification date: 1/15
Early action deadline: N/A,
notification date: N/A
Application deadline (fall): rolling
Undergraduate student body: 1,645
full time, 796 part time; 34%
male, 66% female; 0% American
Indian, 3% Asian, 11% Black,
5% Hispanic, 3% multiracial,
0% Pacific Islander, 60% white,
14% international; 98% from in
state; 14% live on campus; 0%
of students in fraternities, 0% in
sororities
Most popular majors: 25%
Business, Management,
Marketing, and Related
Support Services, 23% Health
Professions and Related Programs,

17% Homeland Security, Law
Enforcement, Firefighting and
Related Protective Services,
5% Biological and Biomedical
Sciences, 3% Education
Expenses: 2020-2021: $24,000;
room/board: $10,450
Financial aid: (734) 432-5662;
74% of undergrads determined to
have financial need; average aid
package $14,589

Michigan State University
East Lansing MI
(517) 355-8332
U.S. News ranking: Nat. U., No. 80
Website: www.msu.edu/
Admissions email: admis@msu.edu
Public; founded 1855
Freshman admissions: more
selective; 2019-2020: 44,322
applied, 31,522 accepted. Either
SAT or ACT required. SAT 25/75
percentile: 1100-1320. High
school rank: 28% in top tenth,
65% in top quarter, 93% in
top half
Early decision deadline: N/A,
notification date: N/A
Early action deadline: 11/1,
notification date: 1/15
Application deadline (fall): rolling
Undergraduate student body:
35,722 full time, 3,454 part
time; 49% male, 51% female;
0% American Indian, 6% Asian,
7% Black, 5% Hispanic, 3%
multiracial, 0% Pacific Islander,
68% white, 9% international;
N/A from in state; 39% live on
campus; 11% of students in
fraternities, 12% in sororities
Most popular majors: 18%
Business, Management,
Marketing, and Related Support
Services, 12% Biological and
Biomedical Sciences, 12%
Communication, Journalism,
and Related Programs, 9%
Engineering, 9% Social Sciences
Expenses: 2020-2021: $14,460
in state, $39,766 out of state;
room/board: $10,472
Financial aid: (517) 353-5940;
47% of undergrads determined to
have financial need; average aid
package $16,389

Michigan Technological University
Houghton MI
(906) 487-2335
U.S. News ranking: Nat. U.,
No. 153
Website: www.mtu.edu
Admissions email: mtu4u@mtu.edu
Public; founded 1885
Freshman admissions: more
selective; 2019-2020: 5,978
applied, 4,442 accepted. Either
SAT or ACT required. SAT 25/75
percentile: 1170-1370. High
school rank: 31% in top tenth,
65% in top quarter, 91% in
top half
Early decision deadline: N/A,
notification date: N/A
Early action deadline: N/A,
notification date: N/A
Application deadline (fall): rolling

Undergraduate student body: 5,393
full time, 371 part time; 71%
male, 29% female; 0% American
Indian, 2% Asian, 1% Black,
2% Hispanic, 4% multiracial,
0% Pacific Islander, 88% white,
2% international; 78% from in
state; 46% live on campus; 9%
of students in fraternities, 11%
in sororities
Most popular majors: 64%
Engineering, 6% Computer
and Information Sciences and
Support Services, 6% Engineering
Technologies and Engineering-
Related Fields, 5% Business,
Management, Marketing, and
Related Support Services,
3% Natural Resources and
Conservation
Expenses: 2020-2021: $16,436
in state, $36,738 out of state;
room/board: $11,314
Financial aid: (906) 487-2622;
63% of undergrads determined to
have financial need; average aid
package $16,038

Northern Michigan University
Marquette MI
(906) 227-2650
U.S. News ranking: Reg. U.
(Mid. W), No. 76
Website: www.nmu.edu
Admissions email:
admissions@nmu.edu
Public; founded 1899
Freshman admissions: selective;
2019-2020: 7,677 applied,
5,035 accepted. Either SAT
or ACT required. SAT 25/75
percentile: 970-1190. High
school rank: N/A
Early decision deadline: N/A,
notification date: N/A
Early action deadline: N/A,
notification date: N/A
Application deadline (fall): rolling
Undergraduate student body: 6,191
full time, 945 part time; 44%
male, 56% female; 1% American
Indian, 1% Asian, 2% Black,
4% Hispanic, 5% multiracial,
0% Pacific Islander, 85% white,
1% international; 76% from in
state; 46% live on campus; N/A
of students in fraternities, N/A in
sororities
Most popular majors: 16%
Business, Management,
Marketing, and Related Support
Services, 16% Health Professions
and Related Programs, 11%
Biological and Biomedical
Sciences, 8% Visual and
Performing Arts, 7% Parks,
Recreation, Leisure, and Fitness
Studies
Expenses: 2020-2021: $11,256
in state, $16,752 out of state;
room/board: $11,072
Financial aid: (906) 227-2327;
67% of undergrads determined to
have financial need; average aid
package $11,281

Northwestern Michigan College[1]
Traverse City MI
(231) 995-1000
U.S. News ranking: Reg. Coll.
(Mid. W), unranked
Admissions email: N/A

Public
Application deadline (fall): N/A
Undergraduate student body: N/A
full time, N/A part time
Expenses: 2019-2020: $8,280 in
state, $10,491 out of state; room/
board: $8,275
Financial aid: N/A

Northwood University
Midland MI
(989) 837-4273
U.S. News ranking: Business,
unranked
Website: www.northwood.edu
Admissions email:
miadmit@northwood.edu
Private; founded 1959
Freshman admissions: selective;
2019-2020: 1,075 applied, 845
accepted. Either SAT or ACT
required. SAT 25/75 percentile:
1000-1190. High school rank:
10% in top tenth, 26% in top
quarter, 72% in top half
Early decision deadline: N/A,
notification date: N/A
Early action deadline: N/A,
notification date: N/A
Application deadline (fall): rolling
Undergraduate student body: 1,155
full time, 56 part time; 67%
male, 33% female; 0% American
Indian, 1% Asian, 6% Black,
4% Hispanic, 3% multiracial,
0% Pacific Islander, 72% white,
6% international; 90% from in
state; 53% live on campus; 9%
of students in fraternities, 11%
in sororities
Most popular majors: 92%
Business, Management,
Marketing, and Related Support
Services, 5% Parks, Recreation,
Leisure, and Fitness Studies, 1%
Communication, Journalism, and
Related Programs, 1% Computer
and Information Sciences and
Support Services, 1% Health
Professions and Related Programs
Expenses: 2020-2021: $29,480;
room/board: $11,110
Financial aid: (989) 837-4230;
62% of undergrads determined to
have financial need; average aid
package $22,522

Oakland University
Rochester MI
(248) 370-3360
U.S. News ranking: Nat. U.,
second tier
Website: www.oakland.edu
Admissions email:
visit@oakland.edu
Public; founded 1957
Freshman admissions: selective;
2019-2020: 12,443 applied,
10,334 accepted. Either SAT
or ACT required. SAT 25/75
percentile: 1020-1230. High
school rank: 22% in top tenth,
51% in top quarter, 83% in
top half
Early decision deadline: N/A,
notification date: N/A
Early action deadline: N/A,
notification date: N/A
Application deadline (fall): rolling
Undergraduate student body:
12,454 full time, 3,089 part
time; 43% male, 57% female;
0% American Indian, 5% Asian,
8% Black, 4% Hispanic, 3%
multiracial, 0% Pacific Islander,

72% white, 2% international; 98% from in state; 19% live on campus; 3% of students in fraternities, 4% in sororities
Most popular majors: 23% Health Professions and Related Programs, 18% Business, Management, Marketing, and Related Support Services, 10% Engineering, 5% Biological and Biomedical Sciences, 5% Communication, Journalism, and Related Programs
Expenses: 2020-2021: $13,934 in state, $24,708 out of state; room/board: $11,022
Financial aid: (248) 370-2550; 62% of undergrads determined to have financial need; average aid package $10,463

Olivet College[1]
Olivet MI
(800) 456-7189
U.S. News ranking: Reg. Coll. (Mid. W), No. 46
Website: www.olivetcollege.edu
Admissions email: admissions@olivetcollege.edu
Private; founded 1844
Affiliation: United Church of Christ
Application deadline (fall): 8/31
Undergraduate student body: N/A full time, N/A part time
Expenses: 2020-2021: $30,120; room/board: $10,508
Financial aid: (269) 749-7645; 93% of undergrads determined to have financial need; average aid package $21,125

Rochester University
Rochester Hills MI
(248) 218-2222
U.S. News ranking: Reg. Coll. (Mid. W), No. 54
Website: www.RochesterU.edu
Admissions email: admissions@rc.edu
Private; founded 1959
Affiliation: Churches of Christ
Freshman admissions: less selective; 2019-2020: 432 applied, 432 accepted. Either SAT or ACT required. SAT 25/75 percentile: 850-1070. High school rank: N/A
Early decision deadline: N/A, notification date: N/A
Early action deadline: N/A, notification date: N/A
Application deadline (fall): rolling
Undergraduate student body: 658 full time, 386 part time; 36% male, 64% female; 0% American Indian, 1% Asian, 20% Black, 2% Hispanic, 3% multiracial, 0% Pacific Islander, 70% white, 3% international; 95% from in state; 26% live on campus; N/A of students in fraternities, N/A in sororities
Most popular majors: 27% Education, 24% Business, Management, Marketing, and Related Support Services, 11% Communication, Journalism, and Related Programs, 10% Health Professions and Related Programs, 10% Psychology
Expenses: 2019-2020: $23,996; room/board: $8,580
Financial aid: (248) 218-2038

Saginaw Valley State University
University Center MI
(989) 964-4200
U.S. News ranking: Reg. U. (Mid. W), second tier
Website: www.svsu.edu
Admissions email: admissions@svsu.edu
Public; founded 1963
Freshman admissions: selective; 2019-2020: 7,149 applied, 5,227 accepted. Either SAT or ACT required. SAT 25/75 percentile: 980-1190. High school rank: 18% in top tenth, 44% in top quarter, 78% in top half
Early decision deadline: N/A, notification date: N/A
Early action deadline: N/A, notification date: N/A
Application deadline (fall): rolling
Undergraduate student body: 6,359 full time, 1,131 part time; 38% male, 62% female; 0% American Indian, 1% Asian, 8% Black, 5% Hispanic, 4% multiracial, 0% Pacific Islander, 76% white, 5% international; 94% from in state; 33% live on campus; 3% of students in fraternities, 3% in sororities
Most popular majors: 24% Health Professions and Related Programs, 18% Business, Management, Marketing, and Related Support Services, 6% Parks, Recreation, Leisure, and Fitness Studies, 6% Public Administration and Social Service Professions, 5% Education
Expenses: 2020-2021: $10,814 in state, $25,401 out of state; room/board: $10,850
Financial aid: (989) 964-4900; 69% of undergrads determined to have financial need; average aid package $10,187

Schoolcraft College[1]
Livonia MI
(734) 462-4400
U.S. News ranking: Reg. Coll. (Mid. W), unranked
Website: www.ptcollege.edu
Admissions email: N/A
Public
Application deadline (fall): N/A
Undergraduate student body: N/A full time, N/A part time
Expenses: 2019-2020: $5,384 in state, $7,490 out of state; room/board: $7,714
Financial aid: N/A

Siena Heights University[7]
Adrian MI
(517) 264-7180
U.S. News ranking: Reg. U. (Mid. W), No. 91
Website: www.sienaheights.edu
Admissions email: admissions@sienaheights.edu
Private; founded 1919
Affiliation: Roman Catholic
Freshman admissions: less selective; 2019-2020: N/A applied, N/A accepted. Neither SAT nor ACT required. SAT 25/75 percentile: 870-1090. High school rank: N/A
Early decision deadline: N/A, notification date: N/A

Early action deadline: N/A, notification date: N/A
Application deadline (fall): 8/1
Undergraduate student body: 1,257 full time, 873 part time
Most popular majors: Information not available
Expenses: 2019-2020: $27,152; room/board: $10,990
Financial aid: (517) 264-7110

Spring Arbor University
Spring Arbor MI
(800) 968-0011
U.S. News ranking: Reg. U. (Mid. W), No. 51
Website: www.arbor.edu/
Admissions email: admissions@arbor.edu
Private; founded 1873
Affiliation: Free Methodist
Freshman admissions: selective; 2019-2020: 1,459 applied, 958 accepted. Either SAT or ACT required. SAT 25/75 percentile: 980-1220. High school rank: 22% in top tenth, 50% in top quarter, 86% in top half
Early decision deadline: N/A, notification date: N/A
Early action deadline: N/A, notification date: N/A
Application deadline (fall): 8/1
Undergraduate student body: 1,134 full time, 480 part time; 33% male, 67% female; 1% American Indian, 1% Asian, 10% Black, 5% Hispanic, 3% multiracial, 0% Pacific Islander, 75% white, 1% international; 84% from in state; 69% live on campus; 0% of students in fraternities, 0% in sororities
Most popular majors: 17% Business Administration and Management, General, 13% Teacher Education and Professional Development, Specific Subject Areas, 10% Psychology, General, 10% Religion/Religious Studies, 9% Social Work
Expenses: 2020-2021: $30,472; room/board: $10,456
Financial aid: (517) 750-6463; 79% of undergrads determined to have financial need; average aid package $25,524

University of Detroit Mercy
Detroit MI
(313) 993-1245
U.S. News ranking: Nat. U., No. 187
Website: www.udmercy.edu
Admissions email: admissions@udmercy.edu
Private; founded 1877
Affiliation: Roman Catholic
Freshman admissions: selective; 2019-2020: 4,358 applied, 3,377 accepted. Either SAT or ACT required. SAT 25/75 percentile: 1060-1250. High school rank: 26% in top tenth, 53% in top quarter, 86% in top half
Early decision deadline: 11/1, notification date: 12/1
Early action deadline: N/A, notification date: N/A
Application deadline (fall): 3/1

Undergraduate student body: 2,350 full time, 395 part time; 38% male, 62% female; 0% American Indian, 6% Asian, 13% Black, 7% Hispanic, 3% multiracial, 0% Pacific Islander, 59% white, 7% international; 88% from in state; 31% live on campus; 9% of students in fraternities, 5% in sororities
Most popular majors: 38% Registered Nursing/Registered Nurse, 12% Biology/Biological Sciences, General, 7% Business Administration and Management, General, 6% Engineering, General, 5% Architecture
Expenses: 2020-2021: $29,416; room/board: $10,190
Financial aid: (313) 993-3354; 64% of undergrads determined to have financial need; average aid package $23,941

University of Michigan–Ann Arbor
Ann Arbor MI
(734) 764-7433
U.S. News ranking: Nat. U., No. 24
Website: umich.edu
Admissions email: N/A
Public; founded 1817
Freshman admissions: most selective; 2019-2020: 64,972 applied, 14,883 accepted. Neither SAT nor ACT required. SAT 25/75 percentile: 1340-1530. High school rank: 78% in top tenth, 96% in top quarter, 100% in top half
Early decision deadline: N/A, notification date: N/A
Early action deadline: 11/15, notification date: 1/31
Application deadline (fall): 2/1
Undergraduate student body: 30,204 full time, 1,062 part time; 50% male, 50% female; 0% American Indian, 16% Asian, 4% Black, 7% Hispanic, 5% multiracial, 0% Pacific Islander, 57% white, 7% international; 58% from in state; 31% live on campus; 9% of students in fraternities, 19% in sororities
Most popular majors: 9% Business Administration and Management, General, 9% Computer and Information Sciences, General, 6% Economics, General, 4% Computer Engineering, General, 4% Experimental Psychology
Expenses: 2020-2021: $15,948 in state, $52,266 out of state; room/board: $12,224
Financial aid: (734) 763-6600; 40% of undergrads determined to have financial need; average aid package $28,711

University of Michigan–Dearborn
Dearborn MI
(313) 593-5100
U.S. News ranking: Reg. U. (Mid. W), No. 31
Website: umdearborn.edu/
Admissions email: umd-admissions@umich.edu
Public; founded 1959
Freshman admissions: selective; 2019-2020: 6,470 applied, 4,009 accepted. Either SAT

or ACT required. SAT 25/75 percentile: 1070-1300. High school rank: N/A
Early decision deadline: N/A, notification date: N/A
Early action deadline: N/A, notification date: N/A
Application deadline (fall): 9/4
Undergraduate student body: 5,045 full time, 1,861 part time; 54% male, 46% female; 0% American Indian, 9% Asian, 8% Black, 6% Hispanic, 4% multiracial, 0% Pacific Islander, 68% white, 2% international
Most popular majors: 25% Business, Management, Marketing, and Related Support Services, 19% Engineering, 9% Biological and Biomedical Sciences, 8% Psychology, 6% Computer and Information Sciences and Support Services
Expenses: 2020-2021: $13,552 in state, $27,520 out of state; room/board: N/A
Financial aid: (313) 593-5300; 66% of undergrads determined to have financial need; average aid package $13,486

University of Michigan–Flint
Flint MI
(810) 762-3300
U.S. News ranking: Nat. U., second tier
Website: www.umflint.edu
Admissions email: admissions@umflint.edu
Public; founded 1956
Freshman admissions: selective; 2019-2020: 4,254 applied, 2,806 accepted. Either SAT or ACT required. SAT 25/75 percentile: 970-1220. High school rank: 19% in top tenth, 41% in top quarter, 77% in top half
Early decision deadline: N/A, notification date: N/A
Early action deadline: N/A, notification date: N/A
Application deadline (fall): 8/22
Undergraduate student body: 3,633 full time, 2,229 part time; 38% male, 62% female; 1% American Indian, 2% Asian, 13% Black, 6% Hispanic, 4% multiracial, 0% Pacific Islander, 70% white, 3% international; 98% from in state; 6% live on campus; 1% of students in fraternities, 2% in sororities
Most popular majors: 35% Health Professions and Related Programs, 18% Business, Management, Marketing, and Related Support Services, 7% Biological and Biomedical Sciences, 6% Psychology, 4% Education
Expenses: 2020-2021: $12,892 in state, $24,622 out of state; room/board: $9,092
Financial aid: (810) 762-3444

Wayne State University
Detroit MI
(313) 577-2100
U.S. News ranking: Nat. U., No. 249
Website: wayne.edu/
Admissions email: studentservice@wayne.edu
Public; founded 1868

Freshman admissions: selective; 2019-2020: 15,716 applied, 11,495 accepted. Either SAT or ACT required. SAT 25/75 percentile: 1010-1230. High school rank: N/A
Early decision deadline: N/A, notification date: N/A
Early action deadline: N/A, notification date: N/A
Application deadline (fall): 8/1
Undergraduate student body: 13,104 full time, 4,547 part time; 43% male, 57% female; 0% American Indian, 11% Asian, 15% Black, 6% Hispanic, 5% multiracial, 0% Pacific Islander, 58% white, 2% international; 96% from in state; 15% live on campus; N/A of students in fraternities, N/A in sororities
Most popular majors: 8% Psychology, General, 6% Biology/Biological Sciences, General, 5% International Business/Trade/Commerce, 4% Organizational Behavior Studies, 4% Social Work
Expenses: 2020-2021: $14,629 in state, $31,499 out of state; room/board: $11,425
Financial aid: (313) 577-2100; 71% of undergrads determined to have financial need; average aid package $12,324

Western Michigan University
Kalamazoo MI
(269) 387-2000
U.S. News ranking: Nat. U., No. 258
Website: wmich.edu/
Admissions email: ask-wmu@wmich.edu
Public; founded 1903
Freshman admissions: selective; 2019-2020: 17,698 applied, 14,133 accepted. Either SAT or ACT required. SAT 25/75 percentile: 1000-1210. High school rank: 12% in top tenth, 34% in top quarter, 69% in top half
Early decision deadline: N/A, notification date: N/A
Early action deadline: N/A, notification date: N/A
Application deadline (fall): rolling
Undergraduate student body: 14,558 full time, 2,493 part time; 51% male, 49% female; 0% American Indian, 2% Asian, 11% Black, 7% Hispanic, 4% multiracial, 0% Pacific Islander, 69% white, 6% international; 85% from in state; 27% live on campus; 8% of students in fraternities, 8% in sororities
Most popular majors: 24% Business, Management, Marketing, and Related Support Services, 10% Health Professions and Related Programs, 8% Engineering, 7% Multi/Interdisciplinary Studies, 7% Visual and Performing Arts
Expenses: 2020-2021: $13,017 in state, $16,041 out of state; room/board: $10,567
Financial aid: (269) 387-6000; 58% of undergrads determined to have financial need; average aid package $11,667

MINNESOTA

Augsburg University
Minneapolis MN
(612) 330-1001
U.S. News ranking: Reg. U. (Mid. W), No. 21
Website: www.augsburg.edu
Admissions email: admissions@augsburg.edu
Private; founded 1869
Affiliation: Evangelical Lutheran Church
Freshman admissions: selective; 2019-2020: 3,435 applied, 2,014 accepted. Neither SAT nor ACT required. ACT 25/75 percentile: 18-23. High school rank: N/A
Early decision deadline: N/A, notification date: N/A
Early action deadline: N/A, notification date: N/A
Application deadline (fall): 8/1
Undergraduate student body: 2,178 full time, 334 part time; 44% male, 56% female; 1% American Indian, 10% Asian, 19% Black, 12% Hispanic, 6% multiracial, 0% Pacific Islander, 44% white, 3% international; N/A from in state; 38% live on campus; N/A of students in fraternities, N/A in sororities
Most popular majors: 27% Business, Management, Marketing, and Related Support Services, 9% Health Professions and Related Programs, 8% Social Sciences, 7% Psychology, 7% Visual and Performing Arts
Expenses: 2020-2021: $41,086; room/board: $10,885
Financial aid: (612) 330-1046; 82% of undergrads determined to have financial need; average aid package $32,507

Bemidji State University
Bemidji MN
(218) 755-2040
U.S. News ranking: Reg. U. (Mid. W), No. 86
Website: www.bemidjistate.edu
Admissions email: admissions@bemidjistate.edu
Public; founded 1919
Freshman admissions: selective; 2019-2020: 3,312 applied, 2,177 accepted. Either SAT or ACT required. ACT 25/75 percentile: 19-24. High school rank: 9% in top tenth, 36% in top quarter, 80% in top half
Early decision deadline: N/A, notification date: N/A
Early action deadline: N/A, notification date: N/A
Application deadline (fall): rolling
Undergraduate student body: 3,053 full time, 1,434 part time; 43% male, 57% female; 3% American Indian, 1% Asian, 3% Black, 3% Hispanic, 4% multiracial, 0% Pacific Islander, 83% white, 2% international
Most popular majors: 23% Business, Management, Marketing, and Related Support Services, 16% Health Professions and Related Programs, 13% Education, 7% Psychology, 6% Homeland Security, Law

Enforcement, Firefighting and Related Protective Services
Expenses: 2020-2021: $8,940 in state, $8,940 out of state; room/board: $8,920
Financial aid: (218) 755-2034; 62% of undergrads determined to have financial need; average aid package $10,512

Bethany Lutheran College
Mankato MN
(507) 344-7331
U.S. News ranking: Nat. Lib. Arts, second tier
Website: www.blc.edu
Admissions email: admiss@blc.edu
Private; founded 1927
Affiliation: Other
Freshman admissions: selective; 2019-2020: 636 applied, 462 accepted. Either SAT or ACT required. ACT 25/75 percentile: 20-26. High school rank: 24% in top tenth, 43% in top quarter, 77% in top half
Early decision deadline: N/A, notification date: N/A
Early action deadline: N/A, notification date: N/A
Application deadline (fall): 7/1
Undergraduate student body: 592 full time, 151 part time; 45% male, 55% female; 0% American Indian, 2% Asian, 3% Black, 5% Hispanic, 3% multiracial, 0% Pacific Islander, 71% white, 14% international; 73% from in state; 71% live on campus; 0% of students in fraternities, 0% in sororities
Most popular majors: 30% Business, Management, Marketing, and Related Support Services, 19% Visual and Performing Arts, 12% Biological and Biomedical Sciences, 12% Communication, Journalism, and Related Programs, 9% Education
Expenses: 2020-2021: $28,380; room/board: $8,150
Financial aid: (507) 344-7328; 72% of undergrads determined to have financial need; average aid package $23,779

Bethel University
St. Paul MN
(800) 255-8706
U.S. News ranking: Nat. U., No. 196
Website: www.bethel.edu
Admissions email: undergrad-admissions@bethel.edu
Private; founded 1871
Affiliation: Baptist
Freshman admissions: more selective; 2019-2020: 2,435 applied, 1,912 accepted. Either SAT or ACT required. ACT 25/75 percentile: 21-27. High school rank: 24% in top tenth, 52% in top quarter, 85% in top half
Early decision deadline: N/A, notification date: N/A
Early action deadline: N/A, notification date: N/A
Application deadline (fall): rolling
Undergraduate student body: 2,327 full time, 472 part time; 37% male, 63% female; 0% American Indian, 5% Asian, 4% Black, 5% Hispanic, 4% multiracial, 0% Pacific Islander, 79% white,

1% international; 82% from in state; 63% live on campus; N/A of students in fraternities, N/A in sororities
Most popular majors: 22% Business, Management, Marketing, and Related Support Services, 18% Health Professions and Related Programs, 10% Education, 7% Communication, Journalism, and Related Programs, 6% Biological and Biomedical Sciences
Expenses: 2020-2021: $39,030; room/board: $10,960
Financial aid: (651) 638-6241; 74% of undergrads determined to have financial need; average aid package $31,730

Carleton College
Northfield MN
(507) 222-4190
U.S. News ranking: Nat. Lib. Arts, No. 9
Website: www.carleton.edu
Admissions email: admissions@carleton.edu
Private; founded 1866
Freshman admissions: most selective; 2019-2020: 7,324 applied, 1,401 accepted. Either SAT or ACT required. SAT 25/75 percentile: 1360-1540. High school rank: 71% in top tenth, 93% in top quarter, 100% in top half
Early decision deadline: 11/15, notification date: 12/15
Early action deadline: N/A, notification date: N/A
Application deadline (fall): 1/15
Undergraduate student body: 2,097 full time, 22 part time; 49% male, 51% female; 0% American Indian, 9% Asian, 5% Black, 8% Hispanic, 7% multiracial, 0% Pacific Islander, 58% white, 11% international; 17% from in state; 96% live on campus; 0% of students in fraternities, 0% in sororities
Most popular majors: 20% Social Sciences, 14% Physical Sciences, 10% Computer and Information Sciences and Support Services, 9% Biological and Biomedical Sciences, 9% Mathematics and Statistics
Expenses: 2020-2021: $59,352; room/board: $15,147
Financial aid: (507) 222-4138; 56% of undergrads determined to have financial need; average aid package $51,761

College of St. Benedict
St. Joseph MN
(320) 363-5060
U.S. News ranking: Nat. Lib. Arts, No. 96
Website: www.csbsju.edu
Admissions email: admissions@csbsju.edu
Private; founded 1913
Affiliation: Roman Catholic
Freshman admissions: more selective; 2019-2020: 2,052 applied, 1,651 accepted. Either SAT or ACT required. ACT 25/75 percentile: 22-28. High school rank: 28% in top tenth, 62% in top quarter, 92% in top half

Early decision deadline: N/A, notification date: N/A
Early action deadline: 12/15, notification date: 1/15
Application deadline (fall): rolling
Undergraduate student body: 1,731 full time, 17 part time; 0% male, 100% female; 1% American Indian, 5% Asian, 3% Black, 9% Hispanic, 0% multiracial, 0% Pacific Islander, 80% white, 3% international; 84% from in state; 93% live on campus; 0% of students in fraternities, 0% in sororities
Most popular majors: 12% Registered Nursing/Registered Nurse, 10% Biology/Biological Sciences, General, 10% Nutrition Sciences, 9% Elementary Education and Teaching, 9% Psychology, General
Expenses: 2020-2021: $48,444; room/board: $11,346
Financial aid: (320) 363-5388; 73% of undergrads determined to have financial need; average aid package $38,360

College of St. Scholastica
Duluth MN
(218) 723-6046
U.S. News ranking: Nat. U., No. 258
Website: www.css.edu
Admissions email: admissions@css.edu
Private; founded 1912
Affiliation: Roman Catholic
Freshman admissions: selective; 2019-2020: 2,046 applied, 1,536 accepted. Neither SAT nor ACT required. ACT 25/75 percentile: 22-26. High school rank: 23% in top tenth, 48% in top quarter, 77% in top half
Early decision deadline: N/A, notification date: N/A
Early action deadline: N/A, notification date: N/A
Application deadline (fall): rolling
Undergraduate student body: 2,062 full time, 419 part time; 29% male, 71% female; 1% American Indian, 3% Asian, 3% Black, 4% Hispanic, 3% multiracial, 0% Pacific Islander, 83% white, 2% international; 88% from in state; 49% live on campus; N/A of students in fraternities, N/A in sororities
Most popular majors: 52% Health Professions and Related Programs, 12% Business, Management, Marketing, and Related Support Services, 9% Biological and Biomedical Sciences, 8% Public Administration and Social Service Professions, 7% Psychology
Expenses: 2020-2021: $39,410; room/board: $10,340
Financial aid: (218) 723-7027; 79% of undergrads determined to have financial need; average aid package $27,478

Concordia College–Moorhead
Moorhead MN
(800) 699-9897
U.S. News ranking: Nat. Lib. Arts, No. 130
Website: www.concordiacollege.edu

Admissions email: admissions@cord.edu
Private; founded 1891
Affiliation:
Evangelical Lutheran Church
Freshman admissions: more selective; 2019-2020: 3,395 applied, 2,321 accepted. Either SAT or ACT required. ACT 25/75 percentile: 21-27. High school rank: 19% in top tenth, 50% in top quarter, 81% in top half
Early decision deadline: N/A, notification date: N/A
Early action deadline: N/A, notification date: N/A
Application deadline (fall): 9/10
Undergraduate student body: 1,955 full time, 54 part time; 42% male, 58% female; 1% American Indian, 2% Asian, 3% Black, 3% Hispanic, 2% multiracial, 0% Pacific Islander, 83% white, 4% international; 71% from in state; 57% live on campus; N/A of students in fraternities, N/A in sororities
Most popular majors: 16% Business, Management, Marketing, and Related Support Services, 13% Biological and Biomedical Sciences, 13% Education, 7% Multi/Interdisciplinary Studies, 7% Visual and Performing Arts
Expenses: 2020-2021: $43,266; room/board: $8,890
Financial aid: (218) 299-3010; 73% of undergrads determined to have financial need; average aid package $32,140

Concordia University–St. Paul
St. Paul MN
(651) 641-8230
U.S. News ranking: Reg. U. (Mid. W), No. 80
Website: www.csp.edu
Admissions email: admissions@csp.edu
Private; founded 1893
Affiliation: Lutheran Church–Missouri Synod
Freshman admissions: selective; 2019-2020: 1,323 applied, 1,297 accepted. Neither SAT nor ACT required. ACT 25/75 percentile: 17-24. High school rank: N/A
Early decision deadline: N/A, notification date: N/A
Early action deadline: N/A, notification date: N/A
Application deadline (fall): 8/1
Undergraduate student body: 1,786 full time, 1,341 part time; 38% male, 62% female; 0% American Indian, 10% Asian, 12% Black, 7% Hispanic, 4% multiracial, 0% Pacific Islander, 59% white, 4% international; 79% from in state; 16% live on campus; 0% of students in fraternities, 0% in sororities
Most popular majors: 19% Business Administration and Management, General, 11% Kinesiology and Exercise Science, 8% Nursing Practice, 5% Marketing/Marketing Management, General, 5% Psychology, General
Expenses: 2020-2021: $23,400; room/board: $9,600

Financial aid: (651) 603-6300; 75% of undergrads determined to have financial need; average aid package $16,836

Crown College[1]
St. Bonifacius MN
(952) 446-4142
U.S. News ranking: Reg. U. (Mid. W), second tier
Website: www.crown.edu
Admissions email: admissions@crown.edu
Private; founded 1916
Affiliation: Christ and Missionary Alliance Church
Application deadline (fall): 8/20
Undergraduate student body: N/A full time, N/A part time
Expenses: 2019-2020: $26,970; room/board: $8,930
Financial aid: (952) 446-4177

Dunwoody College of Technology
Minneapolis MN
(800) 292-4625
U.S. News ranking: Reg. Coll. (Mid. W), No. 25
Website: www.dunwoody.edu
Admissions email: info@dunwoody.edu
Private; founded 1914
Freshman admissions: less selective; 2019-2020: 672 applied, 434 accepted. Neither SAT nor ACT required. SAT 25/75 percentile: N/A. High school rank: 9% in top tenth, 30% in top quarter, 65% in top half
Early decision deadline: N/A, notification date: N/A
Early action deadline: N/A, notification date: N/A
Application deadline (fall): rolling
Undergraduate student body: 1,109 full time, 249 part time; 82% male, 18% female; 1% American Indian, 5% Asian, 4% Black, 3% Hispanic, 6% multiracial, 0% Pacific Islander, 68% white, 0% international; 3% from in state; 1% live on campus; 0% of students in fraternities, 0% in sororities
Most popular majors: 30% Business Administration and Management, General, 28% Manufacturing Engineering, 19% Interior Design, 12% Computer Systems Analysis/Analyst, 11% Architecture
Expenses: 2020-2021: $23,670; room/board: N/A
Financial aid: (612) 381-3347; 71% of undergrads determined to have financial need; average aid package $12

Gustavus Adolphus College
St. Peter MN
(507) 933-7676
U.S. News ranking: Nat. Lib. Arts, No. 84
Website: gustavus.edu
Admissions email: admission@gustavus.edu
Private; founded 1862
Affiliation:
Evangelical Lutheran Church

Freshman admissions: more selective; 2019-2020: 4,957 applied, 3,432 accepted. Neither SAT nor ACT required. ACT 25/75 percentile: 25-30. High school rank: 31% in top tenth, 62% in top quarter, 93% in top half
Early decision deadline: N/A, notification date: N/A
Early action deadline: 11/1, notification date: 11/15
Application deadline (fall): 5/1
Undergraduate student body: 2,213 full time, 22 part time; 41% male, 59% female; 0% American Indian, 5% Asian, 3% Black, 5% Hispanic, 4% multiracial, 0% Pacific Islander, 78% white, 3% international; 83% from in state; 92% live on campus; 16% of students in fraternities, 15% in sororities
Most popular majors: 12% Social Sciences, 11% Business, Management, Marketing, and Related Support Services, 10% Biological and Biomedical Sciences, 10% Psychology, 7% Physical Sciences
Expenses: 2020-2021: $48,460; room/board: $10,430
Financial aid: (507) 933-7527; 73% of undergrads determined to have financial need; average aid package $44,800

Hamline University
St. Paul MN
(651) 523-2207
U.S. News ranking: Reg. U. (Mid. W), No. 15
Website: www.hamline.edu
Admissions email: admission@hamline.edu
Private; founded 1854
Affiliation: United Methodist
Freshman admissions: selective; 2019-2020: 4,602 applied, 3,117 accepted. Either SAT or ACT required. ACT 25/75 percentile: 19-26. High school rank: 13% in top tenth, 44% in top quarter, 81% in top half
Early decision deadline: 11/1, notification date: 11/15
Early action deadline: 12/1, notification date: N/A
Application deadline (fall): rolling
Undergraduate student body: 2,008 full time, 80 part time; 37% male, 63% female; 0% American Indian, 9% Asian, 10% Black, 10% Hispanic, 6% multiracial, 0% Pacific Islander, 62% white, 1% international; 82% from in state; 34% live on campus; N/A of students in fraternities, N/A in sororities
Most popular majors: 21% Social Sciences, 15% Business, Management, Marketing, and Related Support Services, 9% Psychology, 8% Biological and Biomedical Sciences, 8% Multi/Interdisciplinary Studies
Expenses: 2020-2021: $44,230; room/board: $10,810
Financial aid: (651) 523-2933; 85% of undergrads determined to have financial need; average aid package $33,689

Macalester College
St. Paul MN
(651) 696-6357
U.S. News ranking: Nat. Lib. Arts, No. 27
Website: www.macalester.edu
Admissions email: admissions@macalester.edu
Private; founded 1874
Freshman admissions: most selective; 2019-2020: 6,598 applied, 2,129 accepted. Either SAT or ACT required. SAT 25/75 percentile: 1320-1510. High school rank: 64% in top tenth, 88% in top quarter, 99% in top half
Early decision deadline: 11/15, notification date: 12/15
Early action deadline: N/A, notification date: N/A
Application deadline (fall): 1/15
Undergraduate student body: 2,074 full time, 24 part time; 42% male, 58% female; 0% American Indian, 8% Asian, 4% Black, 9% Hispanic, 7% multiracial, 0% Pacific Islander, 57% white, 15% international; 19% from in state; 62% live on campus; 0% of students in fraternities, 0% in sororities
Most popular majors: 29% Social Sciences, 8% Biological and Biomedical Sciences, 8% Computer and Information Sciences and Support Services, 8% Mathematics and Statistics, 8% Multi/Interdisciplinary Studies
Expenses: 2020-2021: $58,478; room/board: $13,084
Financial aid: (651) 696-6214; 66% of undergrads determined to have financial need; average aid package $49,693

Metropolitan State University[1]
St. Paul MN
(651) 772-7600
U.S. News ranking: Nat. U., second tier
Website: www.metrostate.edu
Admissions email: admissions@metrostate.edu
Public
Application deadline (fall): N/A
Undergraduate student body: N/A full time, N/A part time
Expenses: 2019-2020: $8,114 in state, $15,428 out of state; room/board: $10,832
Financial aid: N/A

Minneapolis College of Art and Design
Minneapolis MN
(612) 874-3800
U.S. News ranking: Arts, unranked
Website: www.mcad.edu
Admissions email: admissions@mcad.edu
Private; founded 1886
Freshman admissions: selective; 2019-2020: 747 applied, 437 accepted. Either SAT or ACT required. ACT 25/75 percentile: 20-25. High school rank: N/A
Early decision deadline: N/A, notification date: N/A
Early action deadline: 12/1, notification date: 12/15
Application deadline (fall): 4/1

Undergraduate student body: 698 full time, 11 part time; 30% male, 70% female; 2% American Indian, 9% Asian, 5% Black, 9% Hispanic, 3% multiracial, 0% Pacific Islander, 67% white, 2% international; N/A from in state; 38% live on campus; 0% of students in fraternities, 0% in sororities
Most popular majors: 69% Visual and Performing Arts, 16% Communications Technologies/Technicians and Support Services, 6% Communication, Journalism, and Related Programs, 5% Business, Management, Marketing, and Related Support Services, 4% Precision Production
Expenses: 2020-2021: $41,794; room/board: N/A
Financial aid: (612) 874-3733; 80% of undergrads determined to have financial need; average aid package $28,900

Minnesota State University–Mankato
Mankato MN
(507) 389-1822
U.S. News ranking: Reg. U. (Mid. W), No. 80
Website: mankato.mnsu.edu/
Admissions email: admissions@mnsu.edu
Public; founded 1868
Freshman admissions: selective; 2019-2020: 10,349 applied, 6,490 accepted. ACT required. ACT 25/75 percentile: 19-24. High school rank: 7% in top tenth, 27% in top quarter, 68% in top half
Early decision deadline: N/A, notification date: N/A
Early action deadline: N/A, notification date: N/A
Application deadline (fall): rolling
Undergraduate student body: 10,413 full time, 2,037 part time; 47% male, 53% female; 0% American Indian, 4% Asian, 5% Black, 5% Hispanic, 4% multiracial, 0% Pacific Islander, 73% white, 9% international; 85% from in state; 23% live on campus; N/A of students in fraternities, N/A in sororities
Most popular majors: 20% Business, Management, Marketing, and Related Support Services, 16% Health Professions and Related Programs, 7% Education, 6% Communication, Journalism, and Related Programs, 6% Parks, Recreation, Leisure, and Fitness Studies
Expenses: 2020-2021: $17,230 in state, $17,230 out of state; room/board: $10,078
Financial aid: (507) 389-1866; 50% of undergrads determined to have financial need; average aid package $9,901

Minnesota State University–Moorhead
Moorhead MN
(800) 593-7246
U.S. News ranking: Reg. U. (Mid. W), No. 98
Website: www.mnstate.edu
Admissions email: admissions@mnstate.edu
Public; founded 1887

Freshman admissions: selective; 2019-2020: 3,963 applied, 2,591 accepted. Either SAT or ACT required. ACT 25/75 percentile: 19-24. High school rank: 10% in top tenth, 31% in top quarter, 63% in top half
Early decision deadline: N/A, notification date: N/A
Early action deadline: N/A, notification date: N/A
Application deadline (fall): rolling
Undergraduate student body: 3,788 full time, 887 part time; 39% male, 61% female; 1% American Indian, 1% Asian, 4% Black, 3% Hispanic, 4% multiracial, 0% Pacific Islander, 80% white, 5% international; 69% from in state; 28% live on campus; 3% of students in fraternities, 3% in sororities
Most popular majors: 19% Education, 17% Business, Management, Marketing, and Related Support Services, 12% Health Professions and Related Programs, 8% Visual and Performing Arts, 5% Biological and Biomedical Sciences
Expenses: 2020-2021: $8,980 in state, $16,612 out of state; room/board: $9,628
Financial aid: (218) 477-2251; 62% of undergrads determined to have financial need; average aid package $3,392

North Central University
Minneapolis MN
(800) 289-6222
U.S. News ranking: Reg. Coll. (Mid. W), No. 53
Website: www.northcentral.edu
Admissions email: admissions@northcentral.edu
Private; founded 1930
Affiliation: Assemblies of God Church
Freshman admissions: selective; 2019-2020: 653 applied, 587 accepted. Either SAT or ACT required. ACT 25/75 percentile: 18-24. High school rank: 7% in top tenth, 27% in top quarter, 65% in top half
Early decision deadline: N/A, notification date: N/A
Early action deadline: 12/1, notification date: 8/1
Application deadline (fall): rolling
Undergraduate student body: 967 full time, 118 part time; 42% male, 58% female; 1% American Indian, 4% Asian, 6% Black, 10% Hispanic, 5% multiracial, 0% Pacific Islander, 69% white, 0% international; 54% from in state; 78% live on campus; 0% of students in fraternities, 0% in sororities
Most popular majors: 11% Business Administration and Management, General, 9% Education, General, 8% Youth Ministry, 7% Entrepreneurship/ Entrepreneurial Studies, 7% Marketing/Marketing Management, General
Expenses: 2020-2021: $26,280; room/board: $8,180
Financial aid: (612) 343-4485; 77% of undergrads determined to have financial need; average aid package $20,191

Southwest Minnesota State University[1]
Marshall MN
(507) 537-6286
U.S. News ranking: Reg. U. (Mid. W), No. 117
Website: www.smsu.edu
Admissions email: smsu.admissions@smsu.edu
Public; founded 1963
Application deadline (fall): 9/1
Undergraduate student body: N/A full time, N/A part time
Expenses: 2019-2020: $8,874 in state, $8,874 out of state; room/board: $8,790
Financial aid: (507) 537-6281; 64% of undergrads determined to have financial need; average aid package $9,838

St. Catherine University
St. Paul MN
(800) 945-4599
U.S. News ranking: Nat. U., No. 249
Website: www.stkate.edu
Admissions email: admissions@stkate.edu
Private; founded 1905
Affiliation: Roman Catholic
Freshman admissions: selective; 2019-2020: 2,443 applied, 1,645 accepted. Either SAT or ACT required. ACT 25/75 percentile: 19-25. High school rank: 27% in top tenth, 59% in top quarter, 83% in top half
Early decision deadline: N/A, notification date: N/A
Early action deadline: N/A, notification date: N/A
Application deadline (fall): rolling
Undergraduate student body: 2,004 full time, 1,149 part time; 5% male, 95% female; 0% American Indian, 12% Asian, 10% Black, 11% Hispanic, 4% multiracial, 0% Pacific Islander, 60% white, 1% international; N/A from in state; 39% live on campus; N/A of students in fraternities, N/A in sororities
Most popular majors: 45% Health Professions and Related Programs, 11% Business, Management, Marketing, and Related Support Services, 6% Public Administration and Social Service Professions, 6% Social Sciences, 5% Psychology
Expenses: 2020-2021: $42,594; room/board: N/A
Financial aid: (651) 690-6061; 83% of undergrads determined to have financial need; average aid package $38,266

St. Cloud State University
St. Cloud MN
(320) 308-2244
U.S. News ranking: Reg. U. (Mid. W), No. 86
Website: www.stcloudstate.edu
Admissions email: scsu4u@stcloudstate.edu
Public; founded 1869
Freshman admissions: selective; 2019-2020: 5,171 applied, 4,656 accepted. Either SAT or ACT required. ACT 25/75 percentile: 18-24. High school

rank: 5% in top tenth, 16% in top quarter, 60% in top half
Early decision deadline: N/A, notification date: N/A
Early action deadline: N/A, notification date: N/A
Application deadline (fall): 8/11
Undergraduate student body: 6,952 full time, 3,962 part time; 47% male, 53% female; 0% American Indian, 7% Asian, 9% Black, 4% Hispanic, 4% multiracial, 0% Pacific Islander, 65% white, 11% international; 89% from in state; 19% live on campus; 2% of students in fraternities, 2% in sororities
Most popular majors: 24% Business, Management, Marketing, and Related Support Services, 10% Education, 10% Health Professions and Related Programs, 7% Communication, Journalism, and Related Programs, 6% Psychology
Expenses: 2020-2021: $8,892 in state, $17,434 out of state; room/board: $9,268
Financial aid: (320) 308-2047; 58% of undergrads determined to have financial need; average aid package $12,336

St. John's University
Collegeville MN
(320) 363-5060
U.S. News ranking: Nat. Lib. Arts, No. 102
Website: www.csbsju.edu/admission
Admissions email: admissions@csbsju.edu
Private; founded 1857
Affiliation: Roman Catholic
Freshman admissions: selective; 2019-2020: 1,746 applied, 1,367 accepted. Either SAT or ACT required. ACT 25/75 percentile: 22-27. High school rank: 15% in top tenth, 43% in top quarter, 81% in top half
Early decision deadline: N/A, notification date: N/A
Early action deadline: 12/15, notification date: 1/15
Application deadline (fall): rolling
Undergraduate student body: 1,608 full time, 17 part time; 100% male, 0% female; 1% American Indian, 4% Asian, 4% Black, 8% Hispanic, 0% multiracial, 0% Pacific Islander, 79% white, 5% international; 80% from in state; 89% live on campus; 0% of students in fraternities, 0% in sororities
Most popular majors: 17% Business Administration and Management, General, 15% Accounting, 11% Economics, General, 8% Biology/Biological Sciences, General, 5% Biochemistry
Expenses: 2020-2021: $48,166; room/board: $11,362
Financial aid: (320) 363-3664; 68% of undergrads determined to have financial need; average aid package $36,572

St. Mary's University of Minnesota
Winona MN
(507) 457-1700
U.S. News ranking: Reg. U. (Mid. W), No. 33
Website: www.smumn.edu/admission
Admissions email: admissions@smumn.edu
Private; founded 1912
Affiliation: Roman Catholic
Freshman admissions: selective; 2019-2020: 1,498 applied, 1,378 accepted. Either SAT or ACT required. ACT 25/75 percentile: 20-26. High school rank: N/A
Early decision deadline: N/A, notification date: N/A
Early action deadline: N/A, notification date: N/A
Application deadline (fall): 5/1
Undergraduate student body: 1,132 full time, 335 part time; 44% male, 56% female; 1% American Indian, 3% Asian, 9% Black, 8% Hispanic, 0% multiracial, 0% Pacific Islander, 71% white, 3% international; 54% from in state; 85% live on campus; 4% of students in fraternities, 3% in sororities
Most popular majors: 17% Business/Commerce, General, 10% Health/Health Care Administration/Management, 8% Marketing/Marketing Management, General, 6% Accounting, 5% Finance, General
Expenses: 2020-2021: $38,280; room/board: $9,630
Financial aid: (612) 238-4552; 75% of undergrads determined to have financial need; average aid package $29,369

St. Olaf College
Northfield MN
(507) 786-3025
U.S. News ranking: Nat. Lib. Arts, No. 67
Website: wp.stolaf.edu/
Admissions email: admissions@stolaf.edu
Private; founded 1874
Affiliation: Evangelical Lutheran Church
Freshman admissions: more selective; 2019-2020: 5,694 applied, 2,705 accepted. Neither SAT nor ACT required. ACT 25/75 percentile: 26-32. High school rank: 46% in top tenth, 74% in top quarter, 96% in top half
Early decision deadline: 11/15, notification date: 12/15
Early action deadline: N/A, notification date: N/A
Application deadline (fall): 1/15
Undergraduate student body: 3,050 full time, 22 part time; 42% male, 58% female; 0% American Indian, 7% Asian, 3% Black, 7% Hispanic, 4% multiracial, 0% Pacific Islander, 68% white, 10% international; N/A from in state; 95% live on campus; N/A of students in fraternities, N/A in sororities
Most popular majors: 19% Social Sciences, 11% Visual and Performing Arts, 10% Biological and Biomedical Sciences, 8% Foreign Languages, Literatures,

and Linguistics, 8% Mathematics and Statistics
Expenses: 2020-2021: $51,450; room/board: $11,660
Financial aid: (507) 786-3019; 77% of undergrads determined to have financial need; average aid package $44,181

University of Minnesota–Crookston[1]
Crookston MN
(800) 232-6466
U.S. News ranking: Reg. Coll. (Mid. W), No. 27
Website: www.crk.umn.edu
Admissions email: UMCinfo@umn.edu
Public; founded 1966
Application deadline (fall): rolling
Undergraduate student body: N/A full time, N/A part time
Expenses: 2020-2021: $12,116 in state, $12,116 out of state; room/board: $9,020
Financial aid: (218) 281-8564

University of Minnesota–Duluth
Duluth MN
(218) 726-7171
U.S. News ranking: Reg. U. (Mid. W), No. 39
Website: www.d.umn.edu
Admissions email: umdadmis@d.umn.edu
Public; founded 1947
Freshman admissions: selective; 2019-2020: 8,601 applied, 6,521 accepted. Either SAT or ACT required. ACT 25/75 percentile: 21-26. High school rank: 19% in top tenth, 48% in top quarter, 86% in top half
Early decision deadline: N/A, notification date: N/A
Early action deadline: N/A, notification date: N/A
Application deadline (fall): 8/1
Undergraduate student body: 8,535 full time, 1,312 part time; 52% male, 48% female; 1% American Indian, 4% Asian, 2% Black, 3% Hispanic, 3% multiracial, 0% Pacific Islander, 84% white, 1% international; 86% from in state; 33% live on campus; N/A of students in fraternities, N/A in sororities
Most popular majors: 20% Business, Management, Marketing, and Related Support Services, 15% Engineering, 9% Biological and Biomedical Sciences, 8% Social Sciences, 7% Psychology
Expenses: 2020-2021: $13,576 in state, $18,776 out of state; room/board: $8,470
Financial aid: (218) 726-8000; 56% of undergrads determined to have financial need; average aid package $13,136

University of Minnesota Morris
Morris MN
(888) 866-3382
U.S. News ranking: Nat. Lib. Arts, No. 140
Website: morris.umn.edu/

Admissions email:
admissions@morris.umn.edu
Public; founded 1959
Freshman admissions: more selective; 2019-2020: 3,265 applied, 1,852 accepted. Either SAT or ACT required. ACT 25/75 percentile: 21-28. High school rank: 26% in top tenth, 52% in top quarter, 81% in top half
Early decision deadline: N/A, notification date: N/A
Early action deadline: N/A, notification date: N/A
Application deadline (fall): 8/1
Undergraduate student body: 1,368 full time, 131 part time; 42% male, 58% female; 8% American Indian, 2% Asian, 3% Black, 6% Hispanic, 16% multiracial, 0% Pacific Islander, 56% white, 8% international; 82% from in state; 50% live on campus; N/A of students in fraternities, N/A in sororities
Most popular majors: 15% Biology/Biological Sciences, General, 13% Psychology, General, 8% Business Administration and Management, General, 7% Computer Science, 7% Statistics, General
Expenses: 2020-2021: $13,578 in state, $15,632 out of state; room/board: $8,632
Financial aid: (320) 589-6046; 66% of undergrads determined to have financial need; average aid package $13,247

University of Minnesota–Twin Cities

Minneapolis MN
(800) 752-1000
U.S. News ranking: Nat. U., No. 66
Website: twin-cities.umn.edu/
Admissions email: N/A
Public; founded 1851
Freshman admissions: more selective; 2019-2020: 40,673 applied, 23,076 accepted. Either SAT or ACT required. ACT 25/75 percentile: 26-31. High school rank: 50% in top tenth, 83% in top quarter, 98% in top half
Early decision deadline: N/A, notification date: N/A
Early action deadline: 11/1, notification date: 1/31
Application deadline (fall): rolling
Undergraduate student body: 29,939 full time, 5,226 part time; 46% male, 54% female; 0% American Indian, 10% Asian, 5% Black, 5% Hispanic, 4% multiracial, 0% Pacific Islander, 65% white, 8% international; 73% from in state; 23% live on campus; N/A of students in fraternities, N/A in sororities
Most popular majors: 11% Biological and Biomedical Sciences, 11% Engineering, 11% Social Sciences, 10% Business, Management, Marketing, and Related Support Services, 7% Psychology
Expenses: 2020-2021: $15,027 in state, $33,325 out of state; room/board: $10,768
Financial aid: (800) 400-8636; 46% of undergrads determined to have financial need; average aid package $14,347

University of Northwestern–St. Paul

St. Paul MN
(800) 692-4020
U.S. News ranking: Reg. U. (Mid. W), No. 65
Website: www.unwsp.edu
Admissions email: admissions@unwsp.edu
Private; founded 1902
Affiliation: Undenominational
Freshman admissions: selective; 2019-2020: 1,243 applied, 1,141 accepted. Neither SAT nor ACT required. ACT 25/75 percentile: 21-28. High school rank: 25% in top tenth, 46% in top quarter, 76% in top half
Early decision deadline: N/A, notification date: N/A
Early action deadline: 11/15, notification date: 12/1
Application deadline (fall): 8/1
Undergraduate student body: 2,073 full time, 1,303 part time; 37% male, 63% female; 0% American Indian, 3% Asian, 3% Black, 5% Hispanic, 4% multiracial, 0% Pacific Islander, 82% white, 1% international; 79% from in state; 59% live on campus; 0% of students in fraternities, 0% in sororities
Most popular majors: 12% Business Administration and Management, General, 11% Registered Nursing/Registered Nurse, 6% Psychology, General, 4% Theology/Theological Studies, 3% Elementary Education and Teaching
Expenses: 2020-2021: $33,200; room/board: $10,000
Financial aid: (651) 631-5321; 79% of undergrads determined to have financial need; average aid package $23,485

University of St. Thomas

St. Paul MN
(651) 962-6150
U.S. News ranking: Nat. U., No. 133
Website: www.stthomas.edu
Admissions email: admissions@stthomas.edu
Private; founded 1885
Affiliation: Roman Catholic
Freshman admissions: more selective; 2019-2020: 6,718 applied, 5,587 accepted. Either SAT or ACT required. ACT 25/75 percentile: 24-29. High school rank: 21% in top tenth, 49% in top quarter, 84% in top half
Early decision deadline: N/A, notification date: N/A
Early action deadline: 11/1, notification date: 12/15
Application deadline (fall): rolling
Undergraduate student body: 6,184 full time, 218 part time; 53% male, 47% female; 0% American Indian, 5% Asian, 4% Black, 6% Hispanic, 3% multiracial, 0% Pacific Islander, 76% white, 3% international; 79% from in state; 37% live on campus; N/A of students in fraternities, N/A in sororities

Most popular majors: 43% Business, Management, Marketing, and Related Support Services, 9% Engineering, 7% Biological and Biomedical Sciences, 7% Social Sciences, 5% Philosophy and Religious Studies
Expenses: 2020-2021: $45,780; room/board: $11,162
Financial aid: (651) 962-6168; 55% of undergrads determined to have financial need; average aid package $31,311

Winona State University

Winona MN
(507) 457-5100
U.S. News ranking: Reg. U. (Mid. W), No. 46
Website: www.winona.edu
Admissions email: admissions@winona.edu
Public; founded 1858
Freshman admissions: selective; 2019-2020: 7,663 applied, 5,204 accepted. Either SAT or ACT required. ACT 25/75 percentile: 19-24. High school rank: 9% in top tenth, 32% in top quarter, 69% in top half
Early decision deadline: N/A, notification date: N/A
Early action deadline: N/A, notification date: N/A
Application deadline (fall): 7/16
Undergraduate student body: 6,107 full time, 865 part time; 34% male, 66% female; 0% American Indian, 2% Asian, 3% Black, 5% Hispanic, 3% multiracial, 0% Pacific Islander, 84% white, 2% international; 71% from in state; N/A live on campus; N/A of students in fraternities, N/A in sororities
Most popular majors: 22% Business, Management, Marketing, and Related Support Services, 18% Health Professions and Related Programs, 15% Education, 7% Parks, Recreation, Leisure, and Fitness Studies, 6% Public Administration and Social Service Professions
Expenses: 2019-2020: $9,666 in state, $15,766 out of state; room/board: $9,098
Financial aid: (507) 457-2800

Alcorn State University

Lorman MS
(601) 877-6147
U.S. News ranking: Reg. U. (S), No. 84
Website: www.alcorn.edu
Admissions email: ksampson@alcorn.edu
Public; founded 1871
Freshman admissions: selective; 2019-2020: 5,236 applied, 3,049 accepted. Either SAT or ACT required. ACT 25/75 percentile: 17-24. High school rank: 16% in top tenth, 24% in top quarter, 73% in top half
Early decision deadline: N/A, notification date: N/A
Early action deadline: N/A, notification date: N/A

Application deadline (fall): rolling
Undergraduate student body: 2,729 full time, 339 part time; 36% male, 64% female; 0% American Indian, 0% Asian, 92% Black, 1% Hispanic, 0% multiracial, 0% Pacific Islander, 2% white, 5% international
Most popular majors: 21% Biological and Biomedical Sciences, 16% Liberal Arts and Sciences, General Studies and Humanities, 9% Business, Management, Marketing, and Related Support Services, 7% Health Professions and Related Programs, 6% Public Administration and Social Service Professions
Expenses: 2020-2021: $7,320 in state, $7,320 out of state; room/board: $10,788
Financial aid: (601) 877-6672; 34% of undergrads determined to have financial need; average aid package $8,015

Belhaven University

Jackson MS
(601) 968-5940
U.S. News ranking: Reg. U. (S), No. 53
Website: www.belhaven.edu
Admissions email: admission@belhaven.edu
Private; founded 1883
Affiliation: Presbyterian
Freshman admissions: selective; 2019-2020: 1,698 applied, 839 accepted. Either SAT or ACT required. ACT 25/75 percentile: 22-26. High school rank: N/A
Early decision deadline: N/A, notification date: N/A
Early action deadline: N/A, notification date: N/A
Application deadline (fall): rolling
Undergraduate student body: 1,156 full time, 1,084 part time; 35% male, 65% female; 0% American Indian, 10% Asian, 37% Black, 5% Hispanic, 2% multiracial, 0% Pacific Islander, 37% white, 1% international; 59% from in state; 22% live on campus; N/A of students in fraternities, N/A in sororities
Most popular majors: 31% Business Administration and Management, General, 6% Bible/Biblical Studies, 6% Health/Health Care Administration/Management, 5% Applied Psychology, 5% Sport and Fitness Administration/Management
Expenses: 2020-2021: $27,025; room/board: $8,800
Financial aid: (601) 968-5933; 68% of undergrads determined to have financial need; average aid package $21,720

Blue Mountain College

Blue Mountain MS
(662) 685-4161
U.S. News ranking: Reg. Coll. (S), No. 14
Website: bmc.edu/
Admissions email: admissions@bmc.edu
Private; founded 1873
Affiliation: Southern Baptist

Freshman admissions: selective; 2019-2020: 233 applied, 223 accepted. Either SAT or ACT required. ACT 25/75 percentile: 18-23. High school rank: 30% in top tenth, 38% in top quarter, 69% in top half
Early decision deadline: N/A, notification date: N/A
Early action deadline: N/A, notification date: N/A
Application deadline (fall): rolling
Undergraduate student body: 590 full time, 211 part time; 45% male, 55% female; 1% American Indian, 0% Asian, 13% Black, 3% Hispanic, 3% multiracial, 0% Pacific Islander, 76% white, 4% international; 81% from in state; 53% live on campus; 0% of students in fraternities, 0% in sororities
Most popular majors: 20% Business Administration and Management, General, 17% Elementary Education and Teaching, 16% Psychology, General, 11% Bible/Biblical Studies, 11% Kinesiology and Exercise Science
Expenses: 2020-2021: $15,800; room/board: $7,800
Financial aid: (662) 685-4771; 79% of undergrads determined to have financial need; average aid package $13,251

Delta State University

Cleveland MS
(662) 846-4020
U.S. News ranking: Reg. U. (S), No. 77
Website: deltastate.edu
Admissions email: admissions@deltastate.edu
Public; founded 1924
Freshman admissions: selective; 2019-2020: 1,072 applied, 1,008 accepted. Either SAT or ACT required. ACT 25/75 percentile: 18-24. High school rank: 19% in top tenth, 41% in top quarter, 70% in top half
Early decision deadline: N/A, notification date: N/A
Early action deadline: N/A, notification date: N/A
Application deadline (fall): rolling
Undergraduate student body: 1,981 full time, 1,128 part time; 42% male, 58% female; 0% American Indian, 1% Asian, 31% Black, 2% Hispanic, 2% multiracial, 0% Pacific Islander, 58% white, 5% international; 83% from in state; 35% live on campus; 15% of students in fraternities, 17% in sororities
Most popular majors: 13% Registered Nursing/Registered Nurse, 10% Physical Education Teaching and Coaching, 7% Biology/Biological Sciences, General, 6% Elementary Education and Teaching, 6% Family and Consumer Sciences/Human Sciences, General
Expenses: 2020-2021: $8,121 in state, $8,121 out of state; room/board: $7,985
Financial aid: (662) 846-4670

Jackson State University[1]
Jackson MS
(601) 979-2100
U.S. News ranking: Nat. U., second tier
Website: www.jsums.edu
Admissions email: admappl@jsums.edu
Public; founded 1877
Application deadline (fall): 9/19
Undergraduate student body: N/A full time, N/A part time
Expenses: 2019-2020: $8,620 in state, $19,620 out of state; room/board: N/A
Financial aid: (601) 979-2227

Millsaps College
Jackson MS
(601) 974-1050
U.S. News ranking: Nat. Lib. Arts, No. 113
Website: www.millsaps.edu
Admissions email: admissions@millsaps.edu
Private; founded 1890
Affiliation: United Methodist
Freshman admissions: selective; 2019-2020: 5,223 applied, 3,594 accepted. Either SAT or ACT required. ACT 25/75 percentile: 21-26. High school rank: N/A
Early decision deadline: N/A, notification date: N/A
Early action deadline: 11/15, notification date: 1/15
Application deadline (fall): 7/1
Undergraduate student body: 769 full time, 11 part time; 45% male, 55% female; 1% American Indian, 3% Asian, 24% Black, 5% Hispanic, 0% multiracial, 0% Pacific Islander, 60% white, 5% international; 45% from in state; 87% live on campus; 58% of students in fraternities, 49% in sororities
Most popular majors: 50% Business, Management, Marketing, and Related Support Services, 15% Biological and Biomedical Sciences, 8% Psychology, 8% Social Sciences, 5% Visual and Performing Arts
Expenses: 2020-2021: $41,314; room/board: $14,210
Financial aid: (601) 974-1220; 66% of undergrads determined to have financial need; average aid package $36,923

Mississippi College[1]
Clinton MS
(601) 925-3800
U.S. News ranking: Nat. U., second tier
Website: www.mc.edu
Admissions email: admissions@mc.edu
Private; founded 1826
Affiliation: Southern Baptist
Application deadline (fall): rolling
Undergraduate student body: N/A full time, N/A part time
Expenses: 2019-2020: $18,610; room/board: $10,610
Financial aid: (601) 925-3212

Mississippi State University
Mississippi State MS
(662) 325-2224
U.S. News ranking: Nat. U., No. 206
Website: www.msstate.edu
Admissions email: admit@admissions.msstate.edu
Public; founded 1878
Freshman admissions: more selective; 2019-2020: 18,269 applied, 12,113 accepted. Either SAT or ACT required. ACT 25/75 percentile: 22-30. High school rank: 30% in top tenth, 57% in top quarter, 85% in top half
Early decision deadline: N/A, notification date: N/A
Early action deadline: N/A, notification date: N/A
Application deadline (fall): rolling
Undergraduate student body: 17,113 full time, 1,679 part time; 51% male, 49% female; 1% American Indian, 1% Asian, 18% Black, 3% Hispanic, 2% multiracial, 0% Pacific Islander, 73% white, 1% international; 67% from in state; 28% live on campus; 14% of students in fraternities, 18% in sororities
Most popular majors: 17% Engineering, 16% Business, Management, Marketing, and Related Support Services, 7% Education, 7% Multi/Interdisciplinary Studies, 7% Parks, Recreation, Leisure, and Fitness Studies
Expenses: 2020-2021: $9,020 in state, $24,420 out of state; room/board: $10,436
Financial aid: (662) 325-2450; 67% of undergrads determined to have financial need; average aid package $14,785

Mississippi University for Women
Columbus MS
(662) 329-7106
U.S. News ranking: Reg. U. (S), No. 47
Website: www.muw.edu
Admissions email: admissions@muw.edu
Public; founded 1884
Freshman admissions: selective; 2019-2020: 535 applied, 517 accepted. Either SAT or ACT required. ACT 25/75 percentile: 18-25. High school rank: 22% in top tenth, 51% in top quarter, 83% in top half
Early decision deadline: N/A, notification date: N/A
Early action deadline: N/A, notification date: N/A
Application deadline (fall): rolling
Undergraduate student body: 2,026 full time, 568 part time; 21% male, 79% female; 1% American Indian, 1% Asian, 41% Black, 0% Hispanic, 0% multiracial, 0% Pacific Islander, 55% white, 2% international; 85% from in state; 22% live on campus; 9% of students in fraternities, 17% in sororities
Most popular majors: 48% Registered Nursing/Registered Nurse, 14% Business Administration and Management,

General, 6% Public Health Education and Promotion, 4% Health and Physical Education/Fitness, General, 4% Speech-Language Pathology/Pathologist
Expenses: 2020-2021: $7,525 in state, $7,525 out of state; room/board: $7,648
Financial aid: (662) 329-7114; 76% of undergrads determined to have financial need; average aid package $8,751

Mississippi Valley State University
Itta Bena MS
(662) 254-3344
U.S. News ranking: Reg. U. (S), second tier
Website: www.mvsu.edu
Admissions email: admsn@mvsu.edu
Public; founded 1950
Freshman admissions: less selective; 2019-2020: 2,837 applied, 1,846 accepted. Either SAT or ACT required. ACT 25/75 percentile: 16-21. High school rank: N/A
Early decision deadline: N/A, notification date: N/A
Early action deadline: N/A, notification date: N/A
Application deadline (fall): 8/17
Undergraduate student body: 1,419 full time, 414 part time; 39% male, 61% female; 0% American Indian, 0% Asian, 90% Black, 1% Hispanic, 1% multiracial, 0% Pacific Islander, 2% white, 0% international; 27% from in state; 50% live on campus; 6% of students in fraternities, 10% in sororities
Most popular majors: 13% Public Administration and Social Service Professions, 12% Business, Management, Marketing, and Related Support Services, 10% Biological and Biomedical Sciences, 10% Parks, Recreation, Leisure, and Fitness Studies, 9% Homeland Security, Law Enforcement, Firefighting and Related Protective Services
Expenses: 2020-2021: $6,746 in state, $6,746 out of state; room/board: $7,998
Financial aid: (662) 254-3335

Rust College[1]
Holly Springs MS
(662) 252-8000
U.S. News ranking: Nat. Lib. Arts, second tier
Website: www.rustcollege.edu
Admissions email: admissions@rustcollege.edu
Private; founded 1866
Affiliation: United Methodist
Application deadline (fall): rolling
Undergraduate student body: N/A full time, N/A part time
Expenses: 2019-2020: $9,900; room/board: $4,300
Financial aid: (662) 252-8000

Tougaloo College[1]
Tougaloo MS
(601) 977-7768
U.S. News ranking: Nat. Lib. Arts, second tier
Website: www.tougaloo.edu

Admissions email: admission@tougaloo.edu
Private; founded 1869
Affiliation: United Church of Christ
Application deadline (fall): 7/1
Undergraduate student body: N/A full time, N/A part time
Expenses: 2020-2021: $11,398; room/board: $6,720
Financial aid: (601) 977-7769; 95% of undergrads determined to have financial need; average aid package $12,500

University of Mississippi
University MS
(662) 915-7226
U.S. News ranking: Nat. U., No. 160
Website: www.olemiss.edu
Admissions email: admissions@olemiss.edu
Public; founded 1848
Freshman admissions: more selective; 2019-2020: 16,253 applied, 14,325 accepted. Neither SAT nor ACT required. ACT 25/75 percentile: 21-29. High school rank: 25% in top tenth, 49% in top quarter, 76% in top half
Early decision deadline: N/A, notification date: N/A
Early action deadline: N/A, notification date: N/A
Application deadline (fall): rolling
Undergraduate student body: 15,902 full time, 1,248 part time; 44% male, 56% female; 0% American Indian, 2% Asian, 12% Black, 4% Hispanic, 2% multiracial, 0% Pacific Islander, 78% white, 1% international; 56% from in state; 25% live on campus; 32% of students in fraternities, 43% in sororities
Most popular majors: 10% General Studies, 7% Accounting, 7% Digital Communication and Media/Multimedia, 6% Finance, General, 6% Psychology, General
Expenses: 2020-2021: $8,818 in state, $25,090 out of state; room/board: $10,734
Financial aid: (662) 915-5788; 50% of undergrads determined to have financial need; average aid package $12,094

University of Southern Mississippi
Hattiesburg MS
(601) 266-5000
U.S. News ranking: Nat. U., second tier
Website: www.usm.edu/admissions
Admissions email: admissions@usm.edu
Public; founded 1910
Freshman admissions: selective; 2019-2020: 9,217 applied, 8,485 accepted. Either SAT or ACT required. ACT 25/75 percentile: 19-26. High school rank: N/A
Early decision deadline: N/A, notification date: N/A
Early action deadline: N/A, notification date: N/A
Application deadline (fall): rolling
Undergraduate student body: 9,654 full time, 1,940 part time; 37% male, 63% female; 0% American Indian, 1% Asian, 27% Black, 3% Hispanic, 3% multiracial,

0% Pacific Islander, 57% white, 2% international; N/A from in state; N/A live on campus; 10% of students in fraternities, 14% in sororities
Most popular majors: 8% Business Administration and Management, General, 8% Registered Nursing/Registered Nurse, 6% Elementary Education and Teaching, 6% Liberal Arts and Sciences/Liberal Studies, 5% Psychology, General
Expenses: 2020-2021: $9,160 in state, $11,160 out of state; room/board: $11,260
Financial aid: (601) 266-4774; 73% of undergrads determined to have financial need; average aid package $10,669

William Carey University
Hattiesburg MS
(601) 318-6103
U.S. News ranking: Nat. U., No. 272
Website: www.wmcarey.edu
Admissions email: admissions@wmcarey.edu
Private; founded 1892
Affiliation: Southern Baptist
Freshman admissions: more selective; 2019-2020: 774 applied, 426 accepted. Either SAT or ACT required. ACT 25/75 percentile: 20-28. High school rank: 26% in top tenth, 53% in top quarter, 81% in top half
Early decision deadline: N/A, notification date: N/A
Early action deadline: N/A, notification date: N/A
Application deadline (fall): rolling
Undergraduate student body: 1,901 full time, 1,309 part time; 36% male, 64% female; 0% American Indian, 1% Asian, 26% Black, 2% Hispanic, 0% multiracial, 0% Pacific Islander, 63% white, 6% international; 79% from in state; 23% live on campus; 0% of students in fraternities, 2% in sororities
Most popular majors: 19% Registered Nursing/Registered Nurse, 12% Business Administration and Management, General, 10% General Studies, 9% Elementary Education and Teaching, 9% Psychology, General
Expenses: 2020-2021: $13,650; room/board: $4,485
Financial aid: (601) 318-6153; 96% of undergrads determined to have financial need; average aid package $17,100

MISSOURI

Avila University[1]
Kansas City MO
(816) 501-2400
U.S. News ranking: Reg. U. (Mid. W), second tier
Website: www.Avila.edu
Admissions email: admissions@mail.avila.edu
Private
Application deadline (fall): N/A
Undergraduate student body: N/A full time, N/A part time
Expenses: 2019-2020: $20,500; room/board: $8,764
Financial aid: N/A

Central Methodist University–College of Liberal Arts and Sciences
Fayette MO
(660) 248-6251
U.S. News ranking: Reg. Coll. (Mid. W), No. 31
Website: www.centralmethodist.edu
Admissions email: admissions@centralmethodist.edu
Private; founded 1854
Affiliation: United Methodist
Freshman admissions: selective; 2019-2020: 1,486 applied, 1,397 accepted. Either SAT or ACT required. ACT 25/75 percentile: 19-25. High school rank: 14% in top tenth, 39% in top quarter, 75% in top half
Early decision deadline: N/A, notification date: N/A
Early action deadline: N/A, notification date: N/A
Application deadline (fall): 8/15
Undergraduate student body: 1,114 full time, 31 part time; 49% male, 51% female; 0% American Indian, 1% Asian, 10% Black, 9% Hispanic, 3% multiracial, 0% Pacific Islander, 67% white, 6% international; 69% from in state; 68% live on campus; 19% of students in fraternities, 26% in sororities
Most popular majors: 22% Health Professions and Related Programs, 11% Education, 11% Parks, Recreation, Leisure, and Fitness Studies, 10% Homeland Security, Law Enforcement, Firefighting and Related Protective Services, 9% Biological and Biomedical Sciences
Expenses: 2020-2021: $25,770; room/board: $8,400
Financial aid: (660) 248-6245; 80% of undergrads determined to have financial need; average aid package $22,115

College of the Ozarks
Point Lookout MO
(800) 222-0525
U.S. News ranking: Reg. Coll. (Mid. W), No. 4
Website: www.cofo.edu
Admissions email: admissions@cofo.edu
Private; founded 1906
Affiliation: Interdenominational
Freshman admissions: more selective; 2019-2020: 3,027 applied, 273 accepted. Either SAT or ACT required. ACT 25/75 percentile: 21-26. High school rank: 31% in top tenth, 66% in top quarter, 92% in top half
Early decision deadline: N/A, notification date: N/A
Early action deadline: N/A, notification date: N/A
Application deadline (fall): 7/31
Undergraduate student body: 1,504 full time, 42 part time; 45% male, 55% female; 1% American Indian, 1% Asian, 1% Black, 3% Hispanic, 3% multiracial, 0% Pacific Islander, 86% white, 2% international; 26% from in state; 88% live on campus; N/A of students in fraternities, N/A in sororities

Most popular majors: 16% Business Administration and Management, General, 10% Adult and Continuing Education and Teaching, 10% Registered Nursing/Registered Nurse, 8% Animal Sciences, General, 7% Psychology, General
Expenses: 2020-2021: $19,960; room/board: $7,900
Financial aid: (417) 690-3292; 91% of undergrads determined to have financial need; average aid package $19,200

Columbia College[1]
Columbia MO
(573) 875-7352
U.S. News ranking: Reg. U. (Mid. W), second tier
Website: www.ccis.edu
Admissions email: admissions@ccis.edu
Private; founded 1851
Application deadline (fall): rolling
Undergraduate student body: N/A full time, N/A part time
Expenses: 2019-2020: $23,498; room/board: $8,400
Financial aid: (573) 875-7390

Cottey College
Nevada MO
(888) 526-8839
U.S. News ranking: Reg. Coll. (Mid. W), No. 1
Website: www.cottey.edu
Admissions email: admit@cottey.edu
Private; founded 1884
Freshman admissions: selective; 2019-2020: 309 applied, 263 accepted. Either SAT or ACT required. ACT 25/75 percentile: 19-24. High school rank: 21% in top tenth, 52% in top quarter, 79% in top half
Early decision deadline: N/A, notification date: N/A
Early action deadline: N/A, notification date: N/A
Application deadline (fall): rolling
Undergraduate student body: 254 full time, 2 part time; 0% male, 100% female; 1% American Indian, 0% Asian, 5% Black, 8% Hispanic, 5% multiracial, 0% Pacific Islander, 68% white, 13% international; 20% from in state; 89% live on campus; 0% of students in fraternities, 0% in sororities
Most popular majors: 44% Business, Management, Marketing, and Related Support Services, 17% Biological and Biomedical Sciences, 13% Psychology, 8% English Language and Literature/Letters, 8% Social Sciences
Expenses: 2020-2021: $22,770; room/board: $7,800
Financial aid: (417) 667-8181; 75% of undergrads determined to have financial need; average aid package $23,108

Culver-Stockton College
Canton MO
(800) 537-1883
U.S. News ranking: Reg. Coll. (Mid. W), No. 36
Website: www.culver.edu

Admissions email: admission@culver.edu
Private; founded 1853
Affiliation: Christian Church (Disciples of Christ)
Freshman admissions: selective; 2019-2020: 3,277 applied, 1,710 accepted. Either SAT or ACT required. ACT 25/75 percentile: 18-22. High school rank: 6% in top tenth, 23% in top quarter, 53% in top half
Early decision deadline: N/A, notification date: N/A
Early action deadline: N/A, notification date: N/A
Application deadline (fall): rolling
Undergraduate student body: 880 full time, 91 part time; 51% male, 49% female; 1% American Indian, 1% Asian, 13% Black, 7% Hispanic, 5% multiracial, 0% Pacific Islander, 69% white, 5% international; 49% from in state; 76% live on campus; 38% of students in fraternities, 43% in sororities
Most popular majors: 18% Criminal Justice/Law Enforcement Administration, 14% Business Administration and Management, General, 13% Psychology, General, 8% Accounting, 6% Registered Nursing/Registered Nurse
Expenses: 2020-2021: $27,740; room/board: $8,865
Financial aid: (573) 288-6307; 81% of undergrads determined to have financial need; average aid package $20,869

Drury University
Springfield MO
(417) 873-7205
U.S. News ranking: Reg. U. (Mid. W), No. 26
Website: www.drury.edu
Admissions email: druryad@drury.edu
Private; founded 1873
Affiliation: Christian Church (Disciples of Christ)
Freshman admissions: more selective; 2019-2020: 1,664 applied, 1,072 accepted. Either SAT or ACT required. ACT 25/75 percentile: 22-28. High school rank: 29% in top tenth, 60% in top quarter, 87% in top half
Early decision deadline: N/A, notification date: N/A
Early action deadline: N/A, notification date: N/A
Application deadline (fall): 8/30
Undergraduate student body: 1,443 full time, 35 part time; 42% male, 58% female; 1% American Indian, 1% Asian, 3% Black, 2% Hispanic, 3% multiracial, 0% Pacific Islander, 81% white, 6% international; 80% from in state; 63% live on campus; 21% of students in fraternities, 25% in sororities
Most popular majors: 18% Biological and Biomedical Sciences, 17% Business, Management, Marketing, and Related Support Services, 10% Architecture and Related Services, 9% Visual and Performing Arts, 7% Social Sciences
Expenses: 2020-2021: $30,915; room/board: $9,172

Financial aid: (417) 873-7312; 68% of undergrads determined to have financial need; average aid package $23,426

Evangel University[7]
Springfield MO
(800) 382-6435
U.S. News ranking: Reg. U. (Mid. W), second tier
Website: www.evangel.edu
Admissions email: admissions@evangel.edu
Private; founded 1955
Affiliation: Assemblies of God Church
Freshman admissions: less selective; 2019-2020: 1,249 applied, 920 accepted. Neither SAT nor ACT required. SAT 25/75 percentile: N/A. High school rank: N/A
Early decision deadline: N/A, notification date: N/A
Early action deadline: N/A, notification date: N/A
Application deadline (fall): rolling
Undergraduate student body: 1,539 full time, 254 part time
Most popular majors: 22% Business, Management, Marketing, and Related Support Services, 18% Theology and Religious Vocations, 9% Communication, Journalism, and Related Programs, 6% Psychology, 6% Public Administration and Social Service Professions
Expenses: 2019-2020: $24,202; room/board: $8,522
Financial aid: (417) 865-2811

Fontbonne University
St. Louis MO
(314) 889-1400
U.S. News ranking: Reg. U. (Mid. W), No. 51
Website: www.fontbonne.edu
Admissions email: admissions@fontbonne.edu
Private; founded 1923
Affiliation: Roman Catholic
Freshman admissions: selective; 2019-2020: 789 applied, 621 accepted. Either SAT or ACT required. ACT 25/75 percentile: 18-23. High school rank: N/A
Early decision deadline: N/A, notification date: N/A
Early action deadline: N/A, notification date: N/A
Application deadline (fall): rolling
Undergraduate student body: 770 full time, 98 part time; 61% male, 39% female; 0% American Indian, 2% Asian, 19% Black, 3% Hispanic, 4% multiracial, 0% Pacific Islander, 65% white, 5% international; 85% from in state; 27% live on campus; N/A of students in fraternities, N/A in sororities
Most popular majors: 12% Business Administration and Management, General, 8% Dietetics/Dietitian, 7% General Studies, 6% Social Work, 6% Special Education and Teaching, General
Expenses: 2020-2021: $27,790; room/board: $10,495
Financial aid: (314) 889-1414; 76% of undergrads determined to have financial need; average aid package $23,103

Hannibal-LaGrange University[1]
Hannibal MO
(800) 454-1119
U.S. News ranking: Reg. Coll. (Mid. W), second tier
Website: www.hlg.edu
Admissions email: admissions@hlg.edu
Private; founded 1858
Affiliation: Southern Baptist
Application deadline (fall): 8/27
Undergraduate student body: N/A full time, N/A part time
Expenses: 2019-2020: $23,590; room/board: $8,300
Financial aid: N/A

Harris-Stowe State University
St. Louis MO
(314) 340-3300
U.S. News ranking: Reg. Coll. (Mid. W), second tier
Website: www.hssu.edu
Admissions email: admissions@hssu.edu
Public; founded 1857
Freshman admissions: less selective; 2019-2020: 6,669 applied, 3,500 accepted. Either SAT or ACT required. ACT 25/75 percentile: 15-19. High school rank: N/A
Early decision deadline: N/A, notification date: N/A
Early action deadline: N/A, notification date: N/A
Application deadline (fall): rolling
Undergraduate student body: 1,370 full time, 260 part time; 31% male, 69% female; 0% American Indian, 0% Asian, 84% Black, 3% Hispanic, 3% multiracial, 0% Pacific Islander, 4% white, 2% international; N/A from in state; 37% live on campus; N/A of students in fraternities, N/A in sororities
Most popular majors: 31% Business, Management, Marketing, and Related Support Services, 23% Education, 20% Homeland Security, Law Enforcement, Firefighting and Related Protective Services, 10% Biological and Biomedical Sciences, 10% Social Sciences
Expenses: 2020-2021: $5,484 in state, $10,116 out of state; room/board: $9,491
Financial aid: (314) 340-3502

Kansas City Art Institute[1]
Kansas City MO
(816) 472-4852
U.S. News ranking: Arts, unranked
Website: www.kcai.edu
Admissions email: admiss@kcai.edu
Private; founded 1885
Application deadline (fall): N/A
Undergraduate student body: N/A full time, N/A part time
Expenses: 2019-2020: $39,200; room/board: $11,150
Financial aid: (816) 802-3448

Lincoln University

Jefferson City MO
(573) 681-5102
U.S. News ranking: Reg. Coll.
(Mid. W), second tier
Website: www.lincolnu.edu
Admissions email:
admissions@lincolnu.edu
Public; founded 1866
Freshman admissions: least
selective; 2019-2020: N/A
applied, N/A accepted. Either
SAT or ACT required. ACT 25/75
percentile: 14-19. High school
rank: 5% in top tenth, 13% in top
quarter, 43% in top half
Early decision deadline: N/A,
notification date: N/A
Early action deadline: N/A,
notification date: N/A
Application deadline (fall): rolling
Undergraduate student body: 1,593
full time, 730 part time; 41%
male, 59% female; 0% American
Indian, 1% Asian, 57% Black,
2% Hispanic, 3% multiracial,
0% Pacific Islander, 29% white,
3% international; 70% from in
state; 49% live on campus; N/A
of students in fraternities, N/A in
sororities
Most popular majors: 12%
Business Administration and
Management, General, 11%
Criminal Justice/Law Enforcement
Administration, 11% Registered
Nursing/Registered Nurse, 7%
Health-Related Knowledge and
Skills, Other, 7% Liberal Arts and
Sciences/Liberal Studies
Expenses: 2020-2021: $7,910 in
state, $14,712 out of state; room/
board: $7,282
Financial aid: (573) 681-5032;
79% of undergrads determined to
have financial need; average aid
package $2,033

Lindenwood University

St. Charles MO
(636) 949-4949
U.S. News ranking: Nat. U.,
second tier
Website: www.lindenwood.edu
Admissions email:
admissions@lindenwood.edu
Private; founded 1827
Freshman admissions: selective;
2019-2020: 3,899 applied,
3,414 accepted. Neither SAT
nor ACT required. ACT 25/75
percentile: 20-25. High school
rank: N/A
Early decision deadline: N/A,
notification date: N/A
Early action deadline: N/A,
notification date: N/A
Application deadline (fall): rolling
Undergraduate student body: 5,014
full time, 654 part time; 45%
male, 55% female; 0% American
Indian, 1% Asian, 13% Black,
5% Hispanic, 3% multiracial,
1% Pacific Islander, 58% white,
11% international; 63% from in
state; 51% live on campus; 13%
of students in fraternities, 8% in
sororities
Most popular majors: 20%
Business/Commerce, General,
6% Criminal Justice/Safety
Studies, 5% Human Resources
Management/Personnel
Administration, General,

5% Kinesiology and Exercise
Science, 4% Psychology, General
Expenses: 2020-2021: $18,100;
room/board: $9,200
Financial aid: (636) 949-4106;
63% of undergrads determined to
have financial need; average aid
package $15,803

Maryville University of St. Louis

St Louis MO
(800) 627-9855
U.S. News ranking: Nat. U.,
No. 196
Website: www.maryville.edu
Admissions email:
admissions@maryville.edu
Private; founded 1872
Freshman admissions: selective;
2019-2020: 2,901 applied,
2,405 accepted. Neither SAT
nor ACT required. ACT 25/75
percentile: 20-25. High school
rank: 25% in top tenth, 55% in
top quarter, 85% in top half
Early decision deadline: N/A,
notification date: N/A
Early action deadline: N/A,
notification date: N/A
Application deadline (fall): 8/15
Undergraduate student body: 2,990
full time, 1,464 part time; 34%
male, 66% female; 0% American
Indian, 3% Asian, 12% Black,
6% Hispanic, 4% multiracial,
0% Pacific Islander, 68% white,
4% international; 62% from in
state; 16% live on campus; 0%
of students in fraternities, 0% in
sororities
Most popular majors: 37% Health
Professions and Related Programs,
19% Business, Management,
Marketing, and Related Support
Services, 11% Psychology,
7% Military Technologies and
Applied Sciences, 5% Visual and
Performing Arts
Expenses: 2020-2021: $28,470;
room/board: $10,300
Financial aid: (314) 529-2827;
67% of undergrads determined to
have financial need; average aid
package $20,367

Missouri Baptist University[1]

St. Louis MO
(314) 434-2290
U.S. News ranking: Reg. U.
(Mid. W), second tier
Website: www.mobap.edu
Admissions email:
admissions@mobap.edu
Private; founded 1964
Application deadline (fall): rolling
Undergraduate student body: N/A
full time, N/A part time
Expenses: 2019-2020: $28,220;
room/board: $10,200
Financial aid: (314) 744-7639

Missouri Southern State University

Joplin MO
(417) 781-6778
U.S. News ranking: Reg. Coll.
(Mid. W), No. 57
Website: www.mssu.edu
Admissions email:
admissions@mssu.edu
Public; founded 1937

Freshman admissions: selective;
2019-2020: 2,296 applied,
2,159 accepted. Either SAT
or ACT required. ACT 25/75
percentile: 18-24. High school
rank: 18% in top tenth, 40% in
top quarter, 71% in top half
Early decision deadline: N/A,
notification date: N/A
Early action deadline: N/A,
notification date: N/A
Application deadline (fall): rolling
Undergraduate student body: 3,844
full time, 1,631 part time; 39%
male, 61% female; 3% American
Indian, 3% Asian, 6% Black,
8% Hispanic, 2% multiracial,
0% Pacific Islander, 73% white,
2% international; 77% from in
state; 15% live on campus; 2%
of students in fraternities, 3% in
sororities
Most popular majors: 26%
Business, Management,
Marketing, and Related Support
Services, 14% Health Professions
and Related Programs, 11%
Education, 10% Homeland
Security, Law Enforcement,
Firefighting and Related Protective
Services, 8% Liberal Arts and
Sciences, General Studies and
Humanities
Expenses: 2020-2021: $7,462 in
state, $14,924 out of state; room/
board: $7,137
Financial aid: (417) 659-5422;
76% of undergrads determined to
have financial need; average aid
package $9,838

Missouri State University[1]

Springfield MO
(800) 492-7900
U.S. News ranking: Nat. U.,
second tier
Website: www.missouristate.edu
Admissions email:
info@missouristate.edu
Public; founded 1906
Undergraduate student body: N/A
full time, N/A part time
Expenses: 2019-2020: $7,750 in
state, $15,910 out of state; room/
board: $8,808
Financial aid: (417) 836-5262

Missouri University of Science and Technology

Rolla MO
(573) 341-4165
U.S. News ranking: Nat. U.,
No. 176
Website: www.mst.edu
Admissions email:
admissions@mst.edu
Public; founded 1870
Freshman admissions: more
selective; 2019-2020: 5,107
applied, 4,046 accepted. Either
SAT or ACT required. ACT 25/75
percentile: 26-32. High school
rank: 41% in top tenth, 73% in
top quarter, 94% in top half
Early decision deadline: N/A,
notification date: N/A
Early action deadline: N/A,
notification date: N/A
Application deadline (fall): 7/1
Undergraduate student body: 5,692
full time, 770 part time; 76%
male, 24% female; 0% American

Indian, 4% Asian, 3% Black, 4%
Hispanic, 3% multiracial, 0%
Pacific Islander, 81% white, 3%
international; N/A from in state;
45% live on campus; 23% of
students in fraternities, 23% in
sororities
Most popular majors: 69%
Engineering, 11% Computer
and Information Sciences and
Support Services, 6% Engineering
Technologies and Engineering-
Related Fields, 3% Biological and
Biomedical Sciences, 3% Physical
Sciences
Expenses: 2020-2021: $10,876
in state, $30,259 out of state;
room/board: $10,722
Financial aid: (573) 341-4282;
56% of undergrads determined to
have financial need; average aid
package $14,487

Missouri Valley College

Marshall MO
(660) 831-4114
U.S. News ranking: Reg. Coll.
(Mid. W), second tier
Website: www.moval.edu
Admissions email:
admissions@moval.edu
Private; founded 1889
Affiliation: Presbyterian
Freshman admissions: selective;
2019-2020: 2,327 applied,
1,257 accepted. Neither SAT
nor ACT required. ACT 25/75
percentile: 12-27. High school
rank: 6% in top tenth, 47% in top
quarter, 51% in top half
Early decision deadline: N/A,
notification date: N/A
Early action deadline: N/A,
notification date: N/A
Application deadline (fall): rolling
Undergraduate student body: 1,348
full time, 392 part time; 53%
male, 47% female; 1% American
Indian, 1% Asian, 18% Black,
10% Hispanic, 4% multiracial,
1% Pacific Islander, 45% white,
18% international; 50% from in
state; 71% live on campus; 5%
of students in fraternities, 5% in
sororities
Most popular majors: Information
not available
Expenses: 2020-2021: $21,500;
room/board: $9,600
Financial aid: N/A

Missouri Western State University[1]

St. Joseph MO
(816) 271-4266
U.S. News ranking: Reg. U.
(Mid. W), second tier
Website: www.missouriwestern.edu
Admissions email: admission@
missouriwestern.edu
Public; founded 1969
Application deadline (fall): rolling
Undergraduate student body: N/A
full time, N/A part time
Expenses: 2019-2020: $8,225 in
state, $14,135 out of state; room/
board: $9,125
Financial aid: (816) 271-4361

Northwest Missouri State University

Maryville MO
(800) 633-1175
U.S. News ranking: Reg. U.
(Mid. W), No. 103
Website: www.nwmissouri.edu
Admissions email:
admissions@nwmissouri.edu
Public; founded 1905
Freshman admissions: selective;
2019-2020: 9,015 applied,
6,357 accepted. Either SAT
or ACT required. ACT 25/75
percentile: 19-24. High school
rank: 16% in top tenth, 38% in
top quarter, 74% in top half
Early decision deadline: N/A,
notification date: N/A
Early action deadline: N/A,
notification date: N/A
Application deadline (fall): rolling
Undergraduate student body: 4,954
full time, 756 part time; 42%
male, 58% female; 0% American
Indian, 1% Asian, 5% Black, 4%
Hispanic, 4% multiracial, 0%
Pacific Islander, 82% white, 3%
international; 66% from in state;
34% live on campus; 12% of
students in fraternities, 16% in
sororities
Most popular majors: 21%
Education, 17% Business,
Management, Marketing, and
Related Support Services,
13% Agriculture, Agriculture
Operations, and Related
Sciences, 10% Psychology, 7%
Communication, Journalism, and
Related Programs
Expenses: 2020-2021: $10,624
in state, $18,071 out of state;
room/board: $9,270
Financial aid: (660) 562-1138;
68% of undergrads determined to
have financial need; average aid
package $10,112

Park University

Parkville MO
(877) 505-1059
U.S. News ranking: Reg. U.
(Mid. W), second tier
Website: www.park.edu
Admissions email:
enrollmentservices@park.edu
Private; founded 1875
Freshman admissions: less
selective; 2019-2020: N/A
applied, N/A accepted. Neither
SAT nor ACT required. ACT 25/75
percentile: 17-23. High school
rank: N/A
Early decision deadline: N/A,
notification date: N/A
Early action deadline: N/A,
notification date: N/A
Application deadline (fall): rolling
Undergraduate student body: 4,151
full time, 5,395 part time; 56%
male, 44% female; 1% American
Indian, 2% Asian, 19% Black,
23% Hispanic, 5% multiracial,
1% Pacific Islander, 44% white,
2% international; 22% from in
state; 5% live on campus; 0%
of students in fraternities, 0% in
sororities
Most popular majors: 27%
Business Administration and
Management, General, 13%
Social Psychology, 10% Criminal
Justice/Law Enforcement
Administration, 9% Human

Resources Management/Personnel Administration, General, 8% Computer and Information Sciences, General
Expenses: 2020-2021: $12,750; room/board: $7,845
Financial aid: (816) 584-6250; 79% of undergrads determined to have financial need; average aid package $9,082

Ranken Technical College[1]

Saint Louis MO
(314) 371-0236
U.S. News ranking: Reg. Coll. (Mid. W), second tier
Website: www.ranken.edu
Admissions email: N/A
Private
Application deadline (fall): N/A
Undergraduate student body: N/A full time, N/A part time
Expenses: 2019-2020: $14,889; room/board: $5,200
Financial aid: N/A

Rockhurst University

Kansas City MO
(816) 501-4100
U.S. News ranking: Reg. U. (Mid. W), No. 13
Website: www.rockhurst.edu
Admissions email: admission@rockhurst.edu
Private; founded 1910
Affiliation: Roman Catholic
Freshman admissions: more selective; 2019-2020: 3,278 applied, 2,087 accepted. Either SAT or ACT required. ACT 25/75 percentile: 21-27. High school rank: 29% in top tenth, 59% in top quarter, 87% in top half
Early decision deadline: N/A, notification date: N/A
Early action deadline: N/A, notification date: N/A
Application deadline (fall): rolling
Undergraduate student body: 1,454 full time, 731 part time; 42% male, 58% female; 1% American Indian, 3% Asian, 6% Black, 11% Hispanic, 1% multiracial, 0% Pacific Islander, 72% white, 1% international; 69% from in state; 49% live on campus; 37% of students in fraternities, 40% in sororities
Most popular majors: 30% Health Professions and Related Programs, 21% Business, Management, Marketing, and Related Support Services, 9% Psychology, 8% Parks, Recreation, Leisure, and Fitness Studies, 6% Biological and Biomedical Sciences
Expenses: 2020-2021: $39,780; room/board: $9,800
Financial aid: (816) 501-4600; 69% of undergrads determined to have financial need; average aid package $34,987

Saint Louis University

St. Louis MO
(314) 977-2500
U.S. News ranking: Nat. U., No. 103
Website: www.slu.edu
Admissions email: admission@slu.edu
Private; founded 1818
Affiliation: Roman Catholic

Freshman admissions: more selective; 2019-2020: 15,573 applied, 9,076 accepted. Either SAT or ACT required. ACT 25/75 percentile: 25-30. High school rank: 38% in top tenth, 72% in top quarter, 92% in top half
Early decision deadline: N/A, notification date: N/A
Early action deadline: N/A, notification date: N/A
Application deadline (fall): rolling
Undergraduate student body: 6,732 full time, 485 part time; 40% male, 60% female; 0% American Indian, 11% Asian, 6% Black, 7% Hispanic, 4% multiracial, 0% Pacific Islander, 67% white, 5% international; 39% from in state; 55% live on campus; 15% of students in fraternities, 25% in sororities
Most popular majors: 25% Health Professions and Related Programs, 22% Business, Management, Marketing, and Related Support Services, 9% Biological and Biomedical Sciences, 6% Engineering, 6% Parks, Recreation, Leisure, and Fitness Studies
Expenses: 2020-2021: $47,124; room/board: $12,920
Financial aid: (314) 977-2350; 61% of undergrads determined to have financial need; average aid package $37,724

Southeast Missouri State University

Cape Girardeau MO
(573) 651-2590
U.S. News ranking: Reg. U. (Mid. W), No. 76
Website: www.semo.edu
Admissions email: admissions@semo.edu
Public; founded 1873
Freshman admissions: selective; 2019-2020: 4,785 applied, 4,124 accepted. Neither SAT nor ACT required. ACT 25/75 percentile: 19-25. High school rank: 15% in top tenth, 42% in top quarter, 78% in top half
Early decision deadline: N/A, notification date: N/A
Early action deadline: N/A, notification date: N/A
Application deadline (fall): 7/1
Undergraduate student body: 7,152 full time, 2,372 part time; 41% male, 59% female; 0% American Indian, 1% Asian, 9% Black, 2% Hispanic, 2% multiracial, 0% Pacific Islander, 80% white, 4% international; N/A from in state; 31% live on campus; 20% of students in fraternities, 19% in sororities
Most popular majors: 15% Business, Management, Marketing, and Related Support Services, 10% Education, 9% Health Professions and Related Programs, 8% Liberal Arts and Sciences, General Studies and Humanities, 7% Biological and Biomedical Sciences
Expenses: 2020-2021: $8,033 in state, $14,205 out of state; room/board: $9,834
Financial aid: (573) 651-2253; 63% of undergrads determined to have financial need; average aid package $9,873

Southwest Baptist University

Bolivar MO
(417) 328-1810
U.S. News ranking: Reg. U. (Mid. W), No. 112
Website: www.sbuniv.edu
Admissions email: admissions@sbuniv.edu
Private; founded 1878
Affiliation: Southern Baptist
Freshman admissions: selective; 2019-2020: 2,090 applied, 1,490 accepted. Either SAT or ACT required. ACT 25/75 percentile: 19-25. High school rank: 22% in top tenth, 47% in top quarter, 74% in top half
Early decision deadline: N/A, notification date: N/A
Early action deadline: N/A, notification date: N/A
Application deadline (fall): rolling
Undergraduate student body: 1,701 full time, 887 part time; 36% male, 64% female; 1% American Indian, 1% Asian, 5% Black, 3% Hispanic, 2% multiracial, 0% Pacific Islander, 79% white, 1% international; 74% from in state; 44% live on campus; 0% of students in fraternities, 0% in sororities
Most popular majors: 16% Registered Nursing/Registered Nurse, 12% Elementary Education and Teaching, 9% Business Administration and Management, General, 7% Psychology, General, 6% Kinesiology and Exercise Science
Expenses: 2020-2021: $25,440; room/board: $8,040
Financial aid: (417) 328-1823; 82% of undergrads determined to have financial need; average aid package $22,411

Stephens College[1]

Columbia MO
(800) 876-7207
U.S. News ranking: Reg. U. (Mid. W), No. 46
Website: www.stephens.edu
Admissions email: apply@stephens.edu
Private; founded 1833
Application deadline (fall): rolling
Undergraduate student body: N/A full time, N/A part time
Expenses: 2019-2020: $22,700; room/board: $10,632
Financial aid: (573) 876-7106

Truman State University

Kirksville MO
(660) 785-4114
U.S. News ranking: Reg. U. (Mid. W), No. 7
Website: www.truman.edu
Admissions email: admissions@truman.edu
Public; founded 1867
Freshman admissions: more selective; 2019-2020: 4,595 applied, 2,877 accepted. Either SAT or ACT required. ACT 25/75 percentile: 24-31. High school rank: 57% in top tenth, 82% in top quarter, 97% in top half
Early decision deadline: N/A, notification date: N/A

Early action deadline: N/A, notification date: N/A
Application deadline (fall): rolling
Undergraduate student body: 4,269 full time, 670 part time; 41% male, 59% female; 0% American Indian, 3% Asian, 4% Black, 3% Hispanic, 4% multiracial, 0% Pacific Islander, 77% white, 8% international; 78% from in state; 43% live on campus; 22% of students in fraternities, 21% in sororities
Most popular majors: 18% Business Administration and Management, General, 14% Public Health Education and Promotion, 9% Health and Physical Education/Fitness, 8% Biology/Biological Sciences, General, 8% Psychology, General
Expenses: 2019-2020: $8,120 in state, $15,314 out of state; room/board: $9,012
Financial aid: (660) 785-4130; 49% of undergrads determined to have financial need; average aid package $13,000

University of Central Missouri

Warrensburg MO
(660) 543-4290
U.S. News ranking: Reg. U. (Mid. W), No. 76
Website: www.ucmo.edu
Admissions email: admit@ucmo.edu
Public; founded 1871
Freshman admissions: selective; 2019-2020: 5,699 applied, 3,706 accepted. Neither SAT nor ACT required. ACT 25/75 percentile: 19-25. High school rank: 12% in top tenth, 34% in top quarter, 71% in top half
Early decision deadline: N/A, notification date: N/A
Early action deadline: N/A, notification date: N/A
Application deadline (fall): rolling
Undergraduate student body: 6,688 full time, 2,216 part time; 45% male, 55% female; 0% American Indian, 1% Asian, 10% Black, 5% Hispanic, 5% multiracial, 0% Pacific Islander, 77% white, 2% international; N/A from in state; 30% live on campus; 12% of students in fraternities, 11% in sororities
Most popular majors: 15% Education, 14% Business, Management, Marketing, and Related Support Services, 12% Health Professions and Related Programs, 9% Engineering Technologies and Engineering-Related Fields, 8% Homeland Security, Law Enforcement, Firefighting and Related Protective Services
Expenses: 2020-2021: $8,306 in state, $15,434 out of state; room/board: $9,196
Financial aid: (660) 543-8266; 60% of undergrads determined to have financial need; average aid package $9,164

University of Missouri

Columbia MO
(573) 882-7786
U.S. News ranking: Nat. U., No. 124
Website: www.missouri.edu
Admissions email: mu4u@missouri.edu
Public; founded 1839
Freshman admissions: more selective; 2019-2020: 20,015 applied, 16,158 accepted. Either SAT or ACT required. ACT 25/75 percentile: 23-29. High school rank: 33% in top tenth, 63% in top quarter, 91% in top half
Early decision deadline: N/A, notification date: N/A
Early action deadline: N/A, notification date: N/A
Application deadline (fall): rolling
Undergraduate student body: 20,676 full time, 1,940 part time; 47% male, 53% female; 0% American Indian, 3% Asian, 7% Black, 5% Hispanic, 4% multiracial, 0% Pacific Islander, 78% white, 2% international; 80% from in state; N/A live on campus; 24% of students in fraternities, 31% in sororities
Most popular majors: 16% Business, Management, Marketing, and Related Support Services, 16% Health Professions and Related Programs, 11% Communication, Journalism, and Related Programs, 9% Engineering, 5% Biological and Biomedical Sciences
Expenses: 2020-2021: $10,723 in state, $29,005 out of state; room/board: $11,478
Financial aid: (573) 882-7506; 51% of undergrads determined to have financial need; average aid package $13,093

University of Missouri–Kansas City

Kansas City MO
(816) 235-8652
U.S. News ranking: Nat. U., No. 272
Website: www.umkc.edu
Admissions email: admissions@umkc.edu
Public; founded 1929
Freshman admissions: more selective; 2019-2020: 5,754 applied, 3,527 accepted. Either SAT or ACT required. ACT 25/75 percentile: 21-28. High school rank: 30% in top tenth, 58% in top quarter, 86% in top half
Early decision deadline: N/A, notification date: N/A
Early action deadline: N/A, notification date: N/A
Application deadline (fall): 6/15
Undergraduate student body: 6,487 full time, 4,828 part time; 42% male, 58% female; 0% American Indian, 9% Asian, 12% Black, 10% Hispanic, 5% multiracial, 0% Pacific Islander, 56% white, 5% international; 79% from in state; 15% live on campus; 1% of students in fraternities, 4% in sororities
Most popular majors: 27% Business, Management, Marketing, and Related Support Services, 11% Health Professions and Related Programs,

8% Biological and Biomedical Sciences, 8% Psychology, 7% Computer and Information Sciences and Support Services
Expenses: 2020-2021: $10,788 in state, $26,889 out of state; room/board: $10,864
Financial aid: (816) 235-1154; 61% of undergrads determined to have financial need; average aid package $10,320

University of Missouri–St. Louis
St. Louis MO
(314) 516-5451
U.S. News ranking: Nat. U., No. 258
Website: www.umsl.edu
Admissions email: admissions@umsl.edu
Public; founded 1963
Freshman admissions: more selective; 2019-2020: 2,413 applied, 1,758 accepted. Either SAT or ACT required. ACT 25/75 percentile: 21-27. High school rank: 32% in top tenth, 64% in top quarter, 91% in top half
Early decision deadline: N/A, notification date: N/A
Early action deadline: N/A, notification date: N/A
Application deadline (fall): 8/21
Undergraduate student body: 5,098 full time, 7,947 part time; 43% male, 57% female; 0% American Indian, 5% Asian, 15% Black, 3% Hispanic, 4% multiracial, 0% Pacific Islander, 61% white, 3% international; 89% from in state; 11% live on campus; 2% of students in fraternities, 1% in sororities
Most popular majors: 28% Business, Management, Marketing, and Related Support Services, 10% Health Professions and Related Programs, 9% Psychology, 9% Social Sciences, 7% Education
Expenses: 2020-2021: $11,142 in state, $29,970 out of state; room/board: $9,632
Financial aid: (314) 516-5526; 71% of undergrads determined to have financial need; average aid package $11,676

Washington University in St. Louis
St. Louis MO
(800) 638-0700
U.S. News ranking: Nat. U., No. 16
Website: www.wustl.edu
Admissions email: admissions@wustl.edu
Private; founded 1853
Freshman admissions: most selective; 2019-2020: 25,426 applied, 3,522 accepted. Neither SAT nor ACT required. ACT 25/75 percentile: 33-35. High school rank: 84% in top tenth, 96% in top quarter, 100% in top half
Early decision deadline: 11/1, notification date: 12/15
Early action deadline: N/A, notification date: N/A
Application deadline (fall): 1/2
Undergraduate student body: 7,139 full time, 683 part time; 46% male, 54% female; 0% American

Indian, 16% Asian, 9% Black, 10% Hispanic, 5% multiracial, 0% Pacific Islander, 49% white, 8% international; 11% from in state; 72% live on campus; 26% of students in fraternities, 39% in sororities
Most popular majors: 14% Engineering, 14% Social Sciences, 12% Biological and Biomedical Sciences, 11% Business, Management, Marketing, and Related Support Services, 8% Psychology
Expenses: 2020-2021: $57,386; room/board: $17,402
Financial aid: (888) 547-6670; 42% of undergrads determined to have financial need; average aid package $53,500

Webster University
St. Louis MO
(314) 246-7800
U.S. News ranking: Reg. U. (Mid. W), No. 15
Website: www.webster.edu
Admissions email: admit@webster.edu
Private; founded 1915
Freshman admissions: selective; 2019-2020: 2,094 applied, 1,200 accepted. Either SAT or ACT required. ACT 25/75 percentile: 21-28. High school rank: N/A
Early decision deadline: N/A, notification date: N/A
Early action deadline: N/A, notification date: N/A
Application deadline (fall): 8/1
Undergraduate student body: 2,098 full time, 278 part time; 44% male, 56% female; 0% American Indian, 2% Asian, 10% Black, 6% Hispanic, 4% multiracial, 0% Pacific Islander, 68% white, 3% international
Most popular majors: 19% Business, Management, Marketing, and Related Support Services, 9% Visual and Performing Arts, 6% Computer and Information Sciences and Support Services, 3% Communication, Journalism, and Related Programs, 3% Communications Technologies/ Technicians and Support Services
Expenses: 2020-2021: $28,600; room/board: $11,380
Financial aid: (800) 983-4623; 65% of undergrads determined to have financial need; average aid package $24,921

Westminster College[1]
Fulton MO
(800) 475-3361
U.S. News ranking: Nat. Lib. Arts, No. 155
Website: www.wcmo.edu/
Admissions email: admissions@ westminster-mo.edu
Private; founded 1851
Affiliation: Presbyterian
Application deadline (fall): rolling
Undergraduate student body: N/A full time, N/A part time
Expenses: 2019-2020: $26,490; room/board: $10,478
Financial aid: (573) 592-5364

William Jewell College
Liberty MO
(888) 253-9355
U.S. News ranking: Reg. Coll. (Mid. W), No. 8
Website: www.jewell.edu
Admissions email: admission@ william.jewell.edu
Private; founded 1849
Freshman admissions: more selective; 2019-2020: 1,167 applied, 538 accepted. Neither SAT nor ACT required. ACT 25/75 percentile: 22-27. High school rank: 34% in top tenth, 61% in top quarter, 86% in top half
Early decision deadline: N/A, notification date: N/A
Early action deadline: N/A, notification date: N/A
Application deadline (fall): 8/1
Undergraduate student body: 724 full time, 10 part time; 46% male, 54% female; 0% American Indian, 1% Asian, 5% Black, 7% Hispanic, 4% multiracial, 0% Pacific Islander, 78% white, 2% international; 63% from in state; 85% live on campus; 33% of students in fraternities, 37% in sororities
Most popular majors: 31% Registered Nursing/Registered Nurse, 27% Business Administration and Management, General, 9% Psychology, General, 6% Political Science and Government, General
Expenses: 2020-2021: $34,450; room/board: $10,220
Financial aid: (816) 415-5973; 71% of undergrads determined to have financial need; average aid package $29,926

William Woods University[1]
Fulton MO
(800) 995-3159
U.S. News ranking: Nat. U., second tier
Website: www.williamwoods.edu
Admissions email: admissions@williamwoods.edu
Private; founded 1870
Affiliation: Christian Church (Disciples of Christ)
Application deadline (fall): rolling
Undergraduate student body: N/A full time, N/A part time
Expenses: 2019-2020: $24,830; room/board: $9,890
Financial aid: (573) 592-1793

MONTANA

Carroll College
Helena MT
(406) 447-4384
U.S. News ranking: Reg. Coll. (W), No. 1
Website: www.carroll.edu
Admissions email: admission@carroll.edu
Private; founded 1909
Affiliation: Roman Catholic
Freshman admissions: more selective; 2019-2020: 2,650 applied, 1,826 accepted. Neither SAT nor ACT required. ACT 25/75 percentile: 21-26. High school rank: 28% in top tenth, 72% in top quarter, 94% in top half

Early decision deadline: N/A, notification date: N/A
Early action deadline: 12/1, notification date: 1/1
Application deadline (fall): 6/15
Undergraduate student body: 1,140 full time, 75 part time; 38% male, 62% female; 0% American Indian, 1% Asian, 1% Black, 4% Hispanic, 3% multiracial, 0% Pacific Islander, 81% white, 1% international; 43% from in state; 82% live on campus; 0% of students in fraternities, 0% in sororities
Most popular majors: 29% Health Professions and Related Programs, 15% Business, Management, Marketing, and Related Support Services, 11% Biological and Biomedical Sciences, 7% Education, 6% Social Sciences
Expenses: 2020-2021: $37,262; room/board: $10,262
Financial aid: (406) 447-5425; 63% of undergrads determined to have financial need; average aid package $29,419

Montana State University
Bozeman MT
(406) 994-2452
U.S. News ranking: Nat. U., No. 249
Website: www.montana.edu
Admissions email: admissions@montana.edu
Public; founded 1893
Freshman admissions: selective; 2019-2020: 19,142 applied, 15,684 accepted. Either SAT or ACT required. ACT 25/75 percentile: 21-27. High school rank: 21% in top tenth, 46% in top quarter, 75% in top half
Early decision deadline: N/A, notification date: N/A
Early action deadline: N/A, notification date: N/A
Application deadline (fall): rolling
Undergraduate student body: 12,298 full time, 2,413 part time; 53% male, 47% female; 1% American Indian, 1% Asian, 0% Black, 5% Hispanic, 5% multiracial, 0% Pacific Islander, 85% white, 2% international
Most popular majors: Information not available
Expenses: 2020-2021: $7,472 in state, $25,708 out of state; room/board: $10,300
Financial aid: (406) 994-2845; 45% of undergrads determined to have financial need; average aid package $12,112

Montana State University–Billings
Billings MT
(406) 657-2158
U.S. News ranking: Reg. U. (W), second tier
Website: www.msubillings.edu
Admissions email: admissions@msubillings.edu
Public; founded 1927
Freshman admissions: less selective; 2019-2020: 1,539 applied, 1,538 accepted. Neither SAT nor ACT required. ACT 25/75 percentile: 17-23. High school rank: 8% in top tenth, 31% in top quarter, 62% in top half

Early decision deadline: N/A, notification date: N/A
Early action deadline: N/A, notification date: N/A
Application deadline (fall): rolling
Undergraduate student body: 2,216 full time, 1,815 part time; 35% male, 65% female; 5% American Indian, 1% Asian, 1% Black, 6% Hispanic, 4% multiracial, 0% Pacific Islander, 79% white, 2% international; N/A from in state; 9% live on campus; N/A of students in fraternities, N/A in sororities
Most popular majors: 30% Business, Management, Marketing, and Related Support Services, 16% Education, 9% Health Professions and Related Programs, 7% Multi/ Interdisciplinary Studies, 7% Psychology
Expenses: 2020-2021: $5,993 in state, $19,186 out of state; room/board: $7,420
Financial aid: (406) 657-2188; 61% of undergrads determined to have financial need; average aid package $10,523

Montana State University–Northern[1]
Havre MT
(406) 265-3704
U.S. News ranking: Reg. Coll. (W), unranked
Website: www.msun.edu
Admissions email: admissions@msun.edu
Public
Application deadline (fall): N/A
Undergraduate student body: N/A full time, N/A part time
Expenses: 2019-2020: $5,955 in state, $18,665 out of state; room/board: $6,470
Financial aid: N/A

Montana Technological University
Butte MT
(406) 496-4256
U.S. News ranking: Reg. U. (W), No. 35
Website: www.mtech.edu/
Admissions email: admissions@mtech.edu
Public; founded 1893
Freshman admissions: selective; 2019-2020: 1,307 applied, 1,199 accepted. Either SAT or ACT required. ACT 25/75 percentile: 21-26. High school rank: 21% in top tenth, 55% in top quarter, 85% in top half
Early decision deadline: N/A, notification date: N/A
Early action deadline: N/A, notification date: N/A
Application deadline (fall): rolling
Undergraduate student body: 1,697 full time, 503 part time; 59% male, 41% female; 2% American Indian, 1% Asian, 1% Black, 2% Hispanic, 0% multiracial, 0% Pacific Islander, 81% white, 6% international
Most popular majors: 17% Engineering, General, 14% Petroleum Engineering, 13% Mechanical Engineering, 10% Business/Commerce, General,

10% Registered Nursing/Registered Nurse
Expenses: 2020-2021: $7,397 in state, $22,560 out of state; room/board: $10,170
Financial aid: (406) 496-4223; 53% of undergrads determined to have financial need; average aid package $11,078

Rocky Mountain College
Billings MT
(406) 657-1026
U.S. News ranking: Reg. U. (W), No. 57
Website: www.rocky.edu
Admissions email: admissions@rocky.edu
Private; founded 1878
Affiliation: Presbyterian Church (USA)
Freshman admissions: selective; 2019-2020: 1,558 applied, 922 accepted. Either SAT or ACT required. ACT 25/75 percentile: 19-24. High school rank: 13% in top tenth, 36% in top quarter, 69% in top half
Early decision deadline: N/A, notification date: N/A
Early action deadline: N/A, notification date: N/A
Application deadline (fall): rolling
Undergraduate student body: 829 full time, 21 part time; 51% male, 49% female; 3% American Indian, 0% Asian, 2% Black, 7% Hispanic, 7% multiracial, 1% Pacific Islander, 76% white, 3% international; 58% from in state; 53% live on campus; N/A of students in fraternities, N/A in sororities
Most popular majors: 19% Business, Management, Marketing, and Related Support Services, 16% Parks, Recreation, Leisure, and Fitness Studies, 13% Biological and Biomedical Sciences, 9% Transportation and Materials Moving, 7% Education
Expenses: 2020-2021: $30,586; room/board: $8,596
Financial aid: (406) 657-1031; 75% of undergrads determined to have financial need; average aid package $25,766

University of Montana
Missoula MT
(800) 462-8636
U.S. News ranking: Nat. U., No. 258
Website: www.umt.edu
Admissions email: admiss@umontana.edu
Public; founded 1893
Freshman admissions: selective; 2019-2020: 4,910 applied, 4,614 accepted. Either SAT or ACT required. ACT 25/75 percentile: 20-26. High school rank: 16% in top tenth, 40% in top quarter, 73% in top half
Early decision deadline: N/A, notification date: N/A
Early action deadline: N/A, notification date: N/A
Application deadline (fall): 7/31
Undergraduate student body: 6,163 full time, 1,551 part time; 44% male, 56% female; 3% American Indian, 1% Asian, 1% Black, 5% Hispanic, 5% multiracial,

0% Pacific Islander, 78% white, 1% international; N/A from in state; 37% live on campus; 6% of students in fraternities, 6% in sororities
Most popular majors: 18% Business, Management, Marketing, and Related Support Services, 12% Social Sciences, 11% Biological and Biomedical Sciences, 10% Natural Resources and Conservation, 7% Psychology
Expenses: 2020-2021: $7,412 in state, $27,166 out of state; room/board: $10,154
Financial aid: (406) 243-5504; 59% of undergrads determined to have financial need; average aid package $11,977

University of Montana Western
Dillon MT
(877) 683-7331
U.S. News ranking: Reg. Coll. (W), unranked
Website: w.umwestern.edu/
Admissions email: admissions@umwestern.edu
Public; founded 1893
Freshman admissions: less selective; 2019-2020: 802 applied, 448 accepted. Either SAT or ACT required. ACT 25/75 percentile: 17-22. High school rank: 8% in top tenth, 22% in top quarter, 54% in top half
Early decision deadline: N/A, notification date: N/A
Early action deadline: N/A, notification date: N/A
Application deadline (fall): rolling
Undergraduate student body: 1,126 full time, 232 part time; 37% male, 63% female; 3% American Indian, 1% Asian, 1% Black, 5% Hispanic, 4% multiracial, 1% Pacific Islander, 84% white, 0% international
Most popular majors: 42% Education, 16% Business Administration and Management, General, 6% Agriculture, Agriculture Operations, and Related Sciences, 6% Biological and Biomedical Sciences, 6% Health and Physical Education/Fitness, General
Expenses: 2020-2021: $5,747 in state, $17,137 out of state; room/board: $7,260
Financial aid: (406) 683-7893; 71% of undergrads determined to have financial need; average aid package $3,449

University of Providence
Great Falls MT
(406) 791-5210
U.S. News ranking: Reg. Coll. (W), unranked
Website: www.uprovidence.edu
Admissions email: melanie.houge@uprovidence.edu
Private; founded 1932
Affiliation: Roman Catholic
Freshman admissions: less selective; 2019-2020: 316 applied, 308 accepted. Either SAT or ACT required. ACT 25/75 percentile: 16-23. High school rank: N/A
Early decision deadline: N/A, notification date: N/A

Early action deadline: N/A, notification date: N/A
Application deadline (fall): 9/1
Undergraduate student body: 484 full time, 301 part time; 33% male, 67% female; N/A American Indian, N/A Asian, N/A Black, N/A Hispanic, N/A multiracial, N/A Pacific Islander, N/A white, N/A international; N/A from in state; 32% live on campus; N/A of students in fraternities, N/A in sororities
Most popular majors: 66% Health Professions and Related Programs, 6% Business, Management, Marketing, and Related Support Services, 5% Biological and Biomedical Sciences, 5% Public Administration and Social Service Professions, 4% Psychology
Expenses: 2020-2021: $26,962; room/board: $10,170
Financial aid: (406) 791-5235; 76% of undergrads determined to have financial need; average aid package $20,583

NEBRASKA

Bellevue University[1]
Bellevue NE
(402) 293-2000
U.S. News ranking: Reg. U. (Mid. W), second tier
Website: www.bellevue.edu
Admissions email: info@bellevue.edu
Private
Application deadline (fall): N/A
Undergraduate student body: N/A full time, N/A part time
Expenses: 2019-2020: $7,851; room/board: $8,940
Financial aid: (402) 557-7095

Chadron State College[1]
Chadron NE
(308) 432-6000
U.S. News ranking: Reg. U. (Mid. W), second tier
Website: www.csc.edu
Admissions email: inquire@csc.edu
Public; founded 1911
Application deadline (fall): N/A
Undergraduate student body: N/A full time, N/A part time
Expenses: 2019-2020: $7,556 in state, $7,586 out of state; room/board: $7,820
Financial aid: N/A

College of Saint Mary
Omaha NE
(402) 399-2407
U.S. News ranking: Reg. U. (Mid. W), No. 74
Website: www.csm.edu
Admissions email: enroll@csm.edu
Private; founded 1923
Affiliation: Roman Catholic
Freshman admissions: selective; 2019-2020: 481 applied, 237 accepted. Either SAT or ACT required. ACT 25/75 percentile: 19-23. High school rank: 1% in top tenth, 42% in top quarter, 76% in top half
Early decision deadline: N/A, notification date: N/A
Early action deadline: N/A, notification date: N/A

Application deadline (fall): rolling
Undergraduate student body: 774 full time, 34 part time; 0% male, 100% female; 1% American Indian, 3% Asian, 8% Black, 9% Hispanic, 8% multiracial, 0% Pacific Islander, 70% white, 1% international
Most popular majors: Information not available
Expenses: 2020-2021: $21,370; room/board: $8,000
Financial aid: (402) 399-2362; 80% of undergrads determined to have financial need; average aid package $16,708

Concordia University
Seward NE
(800) 535-5494
U.S. News ranking: Reg. U. (Mid. W), No. 37
Website: www.cune.edu
Admissions email: admiss@cune.edu
Private; founded 1894
Affiliation: Lutheran Church–Missouri Synod
Freshman admissions: selective; 2019-2020: 1,681 applied, 1,318 accepted. Either SAT or ACT required. ACT 25/75 percentile: 20-26. High school rank: 16% in top tenth, 46% in top quarter, 74% in top half
Early decision deadline: N/A, notification date: N/A
Early action deadline: N/A, notification date: N/A
Application deadline (fall): 8/1
Undergraduate student body: 1,203 full time, 1,023 part time; 47% male, 53% female; 0% American Indian, 1% Asian, 3% Black, 7% Hispanic, 2% multiracial, 0% Pacific Islander, 80% white, 2% international; N/A from in state; 56% live on campus; N/A of students in fraternities, N/A in sororities
Most popular majors: 36% Education, 11% Business, Management, Marketing, and Related Support Services, 10% Theology and Religious Vocations, 9% Biological and Biomedical Sciences, 8% Psychology
Expenses: 2020-2021: $34,800; room/board: $9,240
Financial aid: (402) 643-7270; 77% of undergrads determined to have financial need; average aid package $26,591

Creighton University
Omaha NE
(800) 282-5835
U.S. News ranking: Nat. U., No. 112
Website: www.creighton.edu
Admissions email: admissions@creighton.edu
Private; founded 1878
Affiliation: Roman Catholic
Freshman admissions: more selective; 2019-2020: 9,381 applied, 6,915 accepted. Neither SAT nor ACT required. ACT 25/75 percentile: 23-29. High school rank: 35% in top tenth, 66% in top quarter, 91% in top half
Early decision deadline: N/A, notification date: N/A
Early action deadline: 11/1, notification date: N/A

Application deadline (fall): rolling
Undergraduate student body: 4,325 full time, 147 part time; 42% male, 58% female; 0% American Indian, 9% Asian, 2% Black, 8% Hispanic, 5% multiracial, 0% Pacific Islander, 72% white, 2% international; 22% from in state; 53% live on campus; 25% of students in fraternities, 50% in sororities
Most popular majors: 28% Business, Management, Marketing, and Related Support Services, 22% Health Professions and Related Programs, 15% Biological and Biomedical Sciences, 8% Social Sciences, 6% Psychology
Expenses: 2020-2021: $43,018; room/board: $11,600
Financial aid: (402) 280-2731; 50% of undergrads determined to have financial need; average aid package $29,120

Doane University
Crete NE
(402) 826-8222
U.S. News ranking: Nat. Lib. Arts, No. 166
Website: www.doane.edu
Admissions email: admissions@doane.edu
Private; founded 1872
Freshman admissions: selective; 2019-2020: 2,116 applied, 1,511 accepted. Neither SAT nor ACT required. ACT 25/75 percentile: 20-25. High school rank: 13% in top tenth, 39% in top quarter, 88% in top half
Early decision deadline: N/A, notification date: N/A
Early action deadline: N/A, notification date: N/A
Application deadline (fall): rolling
Undergraduate student body: 1,213 full time, 138 part time; 49% male, 51% female; 0% American Indian, 2% Asian, 3% Black, 10% Hispanic, 4% multiracial, 0% Pacific Islander, 78% white, 2% international; 74% from in state; 78% live on campus; 22% of students in fraternities, 35% in sororities
Most popular majors: 16% Business, Management, Marketing, and Related Support Services, 16% Education, 13% Biological and Biomedical Sciences, 9% Visual and Performing Arts, 7% Social Sciences
Expenses: 2020-2021: $37,000; room/board: $10,100
Financial aid: (402) 826-8260; 74% of undergrads determined to have financial need; average aid package $27,876

Hastings College
Hastings NE
(800) 532-7642
U.S. News ranking: Reg. Coll. (Mid. W), No. 20
Website: www.hastings.edu
Admissions email: hcadmissions@hastings.edu
Private; founded 1882
Affiliation: Presbyterian
Freshman admissions: selective; 2019-2020: 1,893 applied, 1,265 accepted. Either SAT

or ACT required. ACT 25/75 percentile: 18-24. High school rank: N/A
Early decision deadline: N/A, notification date: N/A
Early action deadline: N/A, notification date: N/A
Application deadline (fall): 8/1
Undergraduate student body: 958 full time, 9 part time; 50% male, 50% female; 0% American Indian, 1% Asian, 5% Black, 11% Hispanic, 3% multiracial, 0% Pacific Islander, 74% white, 4% international
Most popular majors: 22% Business, Management, Marketing, and Related Support Services, 17% Education, 11% Social Sciences, 9% Biological and Biomedical Sciences, 7% Parks, Recreation, Leisure, and Fitness Studies
Expenses: 2020-2021: $32,770; room/board: $10,290
Financial aid: (402) 461-7431; 77% of undergrads determined to have financial need; average aid package $26,410

Midland University[1]
Fremont NE
(402) 941-6501
U.S. News ranking: Reg. U. (Mid. W), second tier
Website: www.midlandu.edu/
Admissions email: admissions@midlandu.edu
Private; founded 1883
Application deadline (fall): rolling
Undergraduate student body: N/A full time, N/A part time
Expenses: 2019-2020: $34,040; room/board: $8,914
Financial aid: N/A

Nebraska Wesleyan University
Lincoln NE
(402) 465-2218
U.S. News ranking: Reg. U. (Mid. W), No. 15
Website: www.nebrwesleyan.edu/
Admissions email: admissions@nebrwesleyan.edu
Private; founded 1887
Affiliation: United Methodist
Freshman admissions: more selective; 2019-2020: 2,405 applied, 1,630 accepted. Neither SAT nor ACT required. ACT 25/75 percentile: 22-28. High school rank: 22% in top tenth, 53% in top quarter, 80% in top half
Early decision deadline: N/A, notification date: N/A
Early action deadline: 10/15, notification date: N/A
Application deadline (fall): 8/15
Undergraduate student body: 1,705 full time, 137 part time; 41% male, 59% female; 0% American Indian, 2% Asian, 3% Black, 7% Hispanic, 3% multiracial, 0% Pacific Islander, 81% white, 1% international; 85% from in state; 58% live on campus; 14% of students in fraternities, 22% in sororities
Most popular majors: 16% Business, Management, Marketing, and Related Support Services, 13% Biological and Biomedical Sciences, 13% Health Professions and Related Programs,

10% Parks, Recreation, Leisure, and Fitness Studies, 9% Visual and Performing Arts
Expenses: 2020-2021: $36,854; room/board: $10,529
Financial aid: (402) 465-2167; 77% of undergrads determined to have financial need; average aid package $25,729

Peru State College[1]
Peru NE
(402) 872-3815
U.S. News ranking: Reg. U. (Mid. W), second tier
Website: www.peru.edu
Admissions email: admissions@peru.edu
Public
Application deadline (fall): N/A
Undergraduate student body: N/A full time, N/A part time
Expenses: 2019-2020: $7,704 in state, $7,704 out of state; room/board: $9,088
Financial aid: N/A

Union College
Lincoln NE
(800) 228-4600
U.S. News ranking: Reg. Coll. (Mid. W), No. 38
Website: www.ucollege.edu
Admissions email: enroll@ucollege.edu
Private; founded 1891
Affiliation: Seventh Day Adventist
Freshman admissions: selective; 2019-2020: 1,322 applied, 930 accepted. Either SAT or ACT required. ACT 25/75 percentile: 18-26. High school rank: N/A
Early decision deadline: N/A, notification date: N/A
Early action deadline: N/A, notification date: N/A
Application deadline (fall): 8/26
Undergraduate student body: 633 full time, 90 part time; 41% male, 59% female; 0% American Indian, 6% Asian, 9% Black, 25% Hispanic, 4% multiracial, 1% Pacific Islander, 48% white, 7% international; N/A from in state; 73% live on campus; N/A of students in fraternities, N/A in sororities
Most popular majors: 22% Health Professions and Related Programs, 10% Business, Management, Marketing, and Related Support Services, 8% Education, 6% Biological and Biomedical Sciences, 5% Psychology
Expenses: 2020-2021: $25,340; room/board: $7,170
Financial aid: (402) 486-2505; 75% of undergrads determined to have financial need; average aid package $18,262

University of Nebraska–Kearney
Kearney NE
(800) 532-7639
U.S. News ranking: Reg. U. (Mid. W), No. 33
Website: www.unk.edu
Admissions email: admissionsug@unk.edu
Public; founded 1903
Freshman admissions: selective; 2019-2020: 5,324 applied, 4,535 accepted. Either SAT

or ACT required. ACT 25/75 percentile: 20-26. High school rank: 20% in top tenth, 45% in top quarter, 76% in top half
Early decision deadline: N/A, notification date: N/A
Early action deadline: N/A, notification date: N/A
Application deadline (fall): 8/28
Undergraduate student body: 3,827 full time, 602 part time; 40% male, 60% female; 0% American Indian, 1% Asian, 2% Black, 12% Hispanic, 2% multiracial, 0% Pacific Islander, 76% white, 5% international; 88% from in state; 35% live on campus; 16% of students in fraternities, 17% in sororities
Most popular majors: 15% Business Administration and Management, General, 15% Elementary Education and Teaching, 7% Operations Management and Supervision, 6% Family and Consumer Economics and Related Services, Other, 6% Parks, Recreation and Leisure Studies
Expenses: 2019-2020: $7,701 in state, $14,901 out of state; room/board: $10,072
Financial aid: (308) 865-8520; 68% of undergrads determined to have financial need; average aid package $11,610

University of Nebraska–Lincoln
Lincoln NE
(800) 742-8800
U.S. News ranking: Nat. U., No. 133
Website: www.unl.edu
Admissions email: Admissions@unl.edu
Public; founded 1869
Freshman admissions: more selective; 2019-2020: 16,829 applied, 13,165 accepted. Either SAT or ACT required. ACT 25/75 percentile: 22-28. High school rank: 28% in top tenth, 56% in top quarter, 87% in top half
Early decision deadline: N/A, notification date: N/A
Early action deadline: N/A, notification date: N/A
Application deadline (fall): 5/1
Undergraduate student body: 19,132 full time, 1,346 part time; 53% male, 47% female; 0% American Indian, 3% Asian, 3% Black, 7% Hispanic, 3% multiracial, 0% Pacific Islander, 75% white, 8% international; 75% from in state; 41% live on campus; 19% of students in fraternities, 27% in sororities
Most popular majors: 23% Business, Management, Marketing, and Related Support Services, 11% Engineering, 9% Agriculture, Agriculture Operations, and Related Sciences, 8% Communication, Journalism, and Related Programs, 7% Family and Consumer Sciences/Human Sciences
Expenses: 2020-2021: $9,690 in state, $26,820 out of state; room/board: $12,186
Financial aid: (402) 472-3484; 47% of undergrads determined to have financial need; average aid package $14,935

University of Nebraska–Omaha
Omaha NE
(402) 554-2393
U.S. News ranking: Nat. U., No. 284
Website: www.unomaha.edu/
Admissions email: unoadmissions@unomaha.edu
Public; founded 1908
Freshman admissions: selective; 2019-2020: 8,565 applied, 7,148 accepted. Either SAT or ACT required. ACT 25/75 percentile: 19-26. High school rank: 16% in top tenth, 39% in top quarter, 74% in top half
Early decision deadline: N/A, notification date: N/A
Early action deadline: N/A, notification date: N/A
Application deadline (fall): 8/1
Undergraduate student body: 9,921 full time, 2,324 part time; 46% male, 54% female; 0% American Indian, 4% Asian, 7% Black, 14% Hispanic, 5% multiracial, 0% Pacific Islander, 64% white, 5% international; 91% from in state; 13% live on campus; 2% of students in fraternities, 2% in sororities
Most popular majors: 11% Criminal Justice/Safety Studies, 5% Biology/Biological Sciences, General, 5% Business Administration and Management, General, 5% Marketing/Marketing Management, General, 5% Psychology, General
Expenses: 2019-2020: $7,980 in state, $21,244 out of state; room/board: $9,920
Financial aid: (402) 554-3408; 61% of undergrads determined to have financial need; average aid package $10,398

Wayne State College
Wayne NE
(800) 228-9972
U.S. News ranking: Reg. U. (Mid. W), No. 91
Website: www.wsc.edu/
Admissions email: admit1@wsc.edu
Public; founded 1909
Freshman admissions: selective; 2019-2020: 2,060 applied, 2,060 accepted. Neither SAT nor ACT required. ACT 25/75 percentile: 18-25. High school rank: 12% in top tenth, 32% in top quarter, 62% in top half
Early decision deadline: N/A, notification date: N/A
Early action deadline: N/A, notification date: N/A
Application deadline (fall): 8/24
Undergraduate student body: 2,635 full time, 513 part time; 42% male, 58% female; 1% American Indian, 1% Asian, 3% Black, 10% Hispanic, 3% multiracial, 0% Pacific Islander, 78% white, 3% international; 84% from in state; 44% live on campus; N/A of students in fraternities, N/A in sororities
Most popular majors: 27% Education, 17% Business, Management, Marketing, and Related Support Services, 10% Homeland Security, Law Enforcement, Firefighting and

Related Protective Services, 8% Psychology, 6% Parks, Recreation, Leisure, and Fitness Studies
Expenses: 2020-2021: $7,428 in state, $13,008 out of state; room/board: $8,210
Financial aid: (402) 375-7230; 68% of undergrads determined to have financial need; average aid package $9,764

York College
York NE
(800) 950-9675
U.S. News ranking: Reg. Coll. (Mid. W), No. 45
Website: www.york.edu
Admissions email: enroll@york.edu
Private; founded 1890
Affiliation: Churches of Christ
Freshman admissions: selective; 2019-2020: 523 applied, 296 accepted. Either SAT or ACT required. ACT 25/75 percentile: 17-21. High school rank: 7% in top tenth, 43% in top quarter, 70% in top half
Early decision deadline: N/A, notification date: N/A
Early action deadline: N/A, notification date: N/A
Application deadline (fall): 8/31
Undergraduate student body: 400 full time, 22 part time; 52% male, 48% female; 1% American Indian, 0% Asian, 11% Black, 18% Hispanic, 0% multiracial, 1% Pacific Islander, 53% white, 10% international; 29% from in state; 85% live on campus; 25% of students in fraternities, 25% in sororities
Most popular majors: 31% Business Administration and Management, General, 13% Psychology, General, 12% General Studies, 9% Biology/Biological Sciences, General, 7% Elementary Education and Teaching
Expenses: 2019-2020: $19,310; room/board: $8,450
Financial aid: (402) 363-5624

NEVADA

College of Southern Nevada[1]
Las Vegas NV
(702) 651-5000
U.S. News ranking: Reg. Coll. (W), unranked
Website: www.csn.edu
Admissions email: N/A
Public; founded 1971
Application deadline (fall): N/A
Undergraduate student body: N/A full time, N/A part time
Expenses: 2019-2020: $3,652 in state, $10,842 out of state; room/board: $10,287
Financial aid: N/A

Great Basin College[1]
Elko NV
(775) 738-8493
U.S. News ranking: Reg. Coll. (W), unranked
Website: www.gbcnv.edu
Admissions email: N/A
Public
Application deadline (fall): N/A
Undergraduate student body: N/A full time, N/A part time

More @ usnews.com/bestcolleges

Expenses: 2019-2020: $9,248 in state, $16,603 out of state; room/board: N/A
Financial aid: N/A

Nevada State College[1]
Henderson NV
(702) 992-2130
U.S. News ranking: Reg. Coll. (W), unranked
Website: nsc.nevada.edu
Admissions email: N/A
Public; founded 2002
Application deadline (fall): rolling
Undergraduate student body: N/A full time, N/A part time
Expenses: 2019-2020: $5,663 in state, $18,162 out of state; room/board: $9,216
Financial aid: N/A

Sierra Nevada University[1]
Incline Village NV
(866) 412-4636
U.S. News ranking: Reg. U. (W), second tier
Website: www.sierranevada.edu
Admissions email: admissions@sierranevada.edu
Private; founded 1969
Application deadline (fall): 8/26
Undergraduate student body: N/A full time, N/A part time
Expenses: 2020-2021: $52,422; room/board: $13,825
Financial aid: (775) 881-7428; 61% of undergrads determined to have financial need; average aid package $25,462

University of Nevada–Las Vegas
Las Vegas NV
(702) 774-8658
U.S. News ranking: Nat. U., No. 258
Website: www.unlv.edu
Admissions email: admissions@unlv.edu
Public; founded 1957
Freshman admissions: selective; 2019-2020: 12,720 applied, 10,264 accepted. Either SAT or ACT required. ACT 25/75 percentile: 19-25. High school rank: 23% in top tenth, 52% in top quarter, 83% in top half
Early decision deadline: N/A, notification date: N/A
Early action deadline: N/A, notification date: N/A
Application deadline (fall): 6/1
Undergraduate student body: 19,524 full time, 6,307 part time; 43% male, 57% female; 0% American Indian, 17% Asian, 8% Black, 31% Hispanic, 11% multiracial, 1% Pacific Islander, 29% white, 3% international; N/A from in state; 7% live on campus; 4% of students in fraternities, 4% in sororities
Most popular majors: 27% Business, Management, Marketing, and Related Support Services, 8% Psychology, 7% Biological and Biomedical Sciences, 7% Social Sciences, 6% Homeland Security, Law Enforcement, Firefighting and Related Protective Services

Expenses: 2020-2021: $8,704 in state, $24,356 out of state; room/board: $10,924
Financial aid: (833) 318-1228; 63% of undergrads determined to have financial need; average aid package $8,503

University of Nevada–Reno
Reno NV
(775) 784-4700
U.S. News ranking: Nat. U., No. 227
Website: www.unr.edu
Admissions email: asknevada@unr.edu
Public; founded 1874
Freshman admissions: selective; 2019-2020: 9,064 applied, 7,996 accepted. Either SAT or ACT required. ACT 25/75 percentile: 21-26. High school rank: 28% in top tenth, 57% in top quarter, 87% in top half
Early decision deadline: N/A, notification date: N/A
Early action deadline: 11/1, notification date: 11/15
Application deadline (fall): 4/7
Undergraduate student body: 14,788 full time, 2,519 part time; 47% male, 53% female; 1% American Indian, 8% Asian, 3% Black, 22% Hispanic, 7% multiracial, 1% Pacific Islander, 55% white, 1% international; 74% from in state; 18% live on campus; 5% of students in fraternities, 5% in sororities
Most popular majors: 16% Business, Management, Marketing, and Related Support Services, 15% Health Professions and Related Programs, 12% Engineering, 11% Social Sciences, 10% Biological and Biomedical Sciences
Expenses: 2020-2021: $8,366 in state, $24,020 out of state; room/board: $12,216
Financial aid: (775) 784-4666; 52% of undergrads determined to have financial need; average aid package $9,500

Western Nevada College[1]
Carson City NV
(775) 445-3000
U.S. News ranking: Reg. Coll. (W), unranked
Website: www.wnc.edu
Admissions email: N/A
Public; founded 1971
Application deadline (fall): N/A
Undergraduate student body: N/A full time, N/A part time
Expenses: 2019-2020: $3,428 in state, $10,618 out of state; room/board: $10,100
Financial aid: N/A

Colby-Sawyer College
New London NH
(800) 272-1015
U.S. News ranking: Reg. Coll. (N), No. 8
Website: colby-sawyer.edu/
Admissions email: admissions@colby-sawyer.edu

Private; founded 1837
Freshman admissions: selective; 2019-2020: 2,676 applied, 2,398 accepted. Neither SAT nor ACT required. SAT 25/75 percentile: 1030-1230. High school rank: N/A
Early decision deadline: N/A, notification date: N/A
Early action deadline: 12/1, notification date: 12/15
Application deadline (fall): rolling
Undergraduate student body: 803 full time, 34 part time; 29% male, 71% female; 1% American Indian, 3% Asian, 5% Black, 2% Hispanic, 0% multiracial, 0% Pacific Islander, 80% white, 2% international
Most popular majors: 17% Registered Nursing/Registered Nurse, 12% Business Administration and Management, General, 12% Kinesiology and Exercise Science, 8% Biology/Biological Sciences, General, 7% Sport and Fitness Administration/Management
Expenses: 2020-2021: $44,930; room/board: $15,428
Financial aid: (603) 526-3717; 81% of undergrads determined to have financial need; average aid package $36,601

Dartmouth College
Hanover NH
(603) 646-2875
U.S. News ranking: Nat. U., No. 13
Website: www.dartmouth.edu
Admissions email: apply@dartmouth.edu
Private; founded 1769
Freshman admissions: most selective; 2019-2020: 23,650 applied, 1,875 accepted. Either SAT or ACT required. SAT 25/75 percentile: 1440-1560. High school rank: 95% in top tenth, 99% in top quarter, 100% in top half
Early decision deadline: 11/1, notification date: 12/15
Early action deadline: N/A, notification date: N/A
Application deadline (fall): 1/2
Undergraduate student body: 4,401 full time, 58 part time; 51% male, 49% female; 1% American Indian, 15% Asian, 6% Black, 11% Hispanic, 6% multiracial, 0% Pacific Islander, 51% white, 10% international; 3% from in state; 85% live on campus; 27% of students in fraternities, 31% in sororities
Most popular majors: 35% Social Sciences, 9% Engineering, 8% Biological and Biomedical Sciences, 7% Computer and Information Sciences and Support Services, 6% Mathematics and Statistics
Expenses: 2020-2021: $59,458; room/board: $17,022
Financial aid: (800) 443-3605; 51% of undergrads determined to have financial need; average aid package $54,535

Franklin Pierce University[1]
Rindge NH
(800) 437-0048
U.S. News ranking: Reg. U. (N), second tier
Website: www.franklinpierce.edu/
Admissions email: admissions@franklinpierce.edu
Private; founded 1962
Application deadline (fall): rolling
Undergraduate student body: N/A full time, N/A part time
Expenses: 2019-2020: $38,200; room/board: $13,900
Financial aid: (877) 372-7347

Granite State College
Concord NH
(603) 513-1391
U.S. News ranking: Reg. U. (N), second tier
Website: www.granite.edu
Admissions email: gsc.admissions@granite.edu
Public; founded 1972
Freshman admissions: least selective; 2019-2020: 282 applied, 282 accepted. Neither SAT nor ACT required. SAT 25/75 percentile: N/A. High school rank: N/A
Early decision deadline: N/A, notification date: N/A
Early action deadline: N/A, notification date: N/A
Application deadline (fall): rolling
Undergraduate student body: 827 full time, 902 part time; 32% male, 68% female; 0% American Indian, 1% Asian, 4% Black, 5% Hispanic, 2% multiracial, 0% Pacific Islander, 82% white, 0% international; 74% from in state; 0% live on campus; 0% of students in fraternities, 0% in sororities
Most popular majors: 27% Business, Management, Marketing, and Related Support Services, 16% Multi/Interdisciplinary Studies, 15% Psychology, 13% Health Professions and Related Programs, 9% Education
Expenses: 2020-2021: $7,791 in state, $9,015 out of state; room/board: N/A
Financial aid: (603) 513-1392; 68% of undergrads determined to have financial need; average aid package $7,375

Keene State College
Keene NH
(603) 358-2276
U.S. News ranking: Reg. Coll. (N), No. 9
Website: www.keene.edu
Admissions email: admissions@keene.edu
Public; founded 1909
Freshman admissions: selective; 2019-2020: 4,978 applied, 4,400 accepted. Neither SAT nor ACT required. SAT 25/75 percentile: 960-1140. High school rank: 5% in top tenth, 20% in top quarter, 49% in top half
Early decision deadline: N/A, notification date: N/A
Early action deadline: N/A, notification date: N/A
Application deadline (fall): 4/1

Undergraduate student body: 3,305 full time, 99 part time; 46% male, 54% female; 0% American Indian, 1% Asian, 2% Black, 4% Hispanic, 2% multiracial, 0% Pacific Islander, 83% white, 0% international; 45% from in state; 55% live on campus; 6% of students in fraternities, 6% in sororities
Most popular majors: 15% Education, 12% Engineering Technologies and Engineering-Related Fields, 10% Visual and Performing Arts, 9% Health Professions and Related Programs, 8% Social Sciences
Expenses: 2020-2021: $14,638 in state, $24,350 out of state; room/board: $13,204
Financial aid: (603) 358-2280; 69% of undergrads determined to have financial need; average aid package $13,647

New England College
Henniker NH
(603) 428-2223
U.S. News ranking: Reg. U. (N), second tier
Website: www.nec.edu
Admissions email: admission@nec.edu
Private; founded 1946
Freshman admissions: less selective; 2019-2020: 10,183 applied, 10,179 accepted. Neither SAT nor ACT required. SAT 25/75 percentile: 920-940. High school rank: N/A
Early decision deadline: N/A, notification date: N/A
Early action deadline: N/A, notification date: N/A
Application deadline (fall): rolling
Undergraduate student body: 2,082 full time, 113 part time; 39% male, 61% female; 1% American Indian, 1% Asian, 18% Black, 2% Hispanic, 3% multiracial, 0% Pacific Islander, 45% white, 3% international; 27% from in state; 41% live on campus; 0% of students in fraternities, 0% in sororities
Most popular majors: 25% Business, Management, Marketing, and Related Support Services, 17% Psychology, 15% Homeland Security, Law Enforcement, Firefighting and Related Protective Services, 10% Health Professions and Related Programs, 7% Parks, Recreation, Leisure, and Fitness Studies
Expenses: 2020-2021: $39,648; room/board: $16,070
Financial aid: (603) 428-2436; 79% of undergrads determined to have financial need; average aid package $20,648

New Hampshire Institute of Art[1]
Manchester NH
(603) 623-0313
U.S. News ranking: Arts, unranked
Admissions email: N/A
Private
Application deadline (fall): N/A
Undergraduate student body: N/A full time, N/A part time
Expenses: 2019-2020: $10,950; room/board: N/A
Financial aid: N/A

Plymouth State University
Plymouth NH
(603) 535-2237
U.S. News ranking: Reg. U. (N), No. 121
Website: www.plymouth.edu
Admissions email: admissions@plymouth.edu
Public; founded 1871
Freshman admissions: less selective; 2019-2020: 8,035 applied, 6,815 accepted. Neither SAT nor ACT required. SAT 25/75 percentile: 824-1174. High school rank: 3% in top tenth, 16% in top quarter, 48% in top half
Early decision deadline: N/A, notification date: N/A
Early action deadline: N/A, notification date: N/A
Application deadline (fall): 4/1
Undergraduate student body: 3,676 full time, 153 part time; 50% male, 50% female; 0% American Indian, 2% Asian, 3% Black, 4% Hispanic, 3% multiracial, 0% Pacific Islander, 81% white, 2% international; 54% from in state; 61% live on campus; 2% of students in fraternities, 4% in sororities
Most popular majors: 27% Business, Management, Marketing, and Related Support Services, 11% Education, 8% Parks, Recreation, Leisure, and Fitness Studies, 7% Homeland Security, Law Enforcement, Firefighting and Related Protective Services, 6% Health Professions and Related Programs
Expenses: 2020-2021: $14,492 in state, $23,902 out of state; room/board: $11,580
Financial aid: (603) 535-2338; 69% of undergrads determined to have financial need; average aid package $13,026

Rivier University[1]
Nashua NH
(603) 888-1311
U.S. News ranking: Reg. U. (N), second tier
Website: rivier.edu
Admissions email: admissions@rivier.edu
Private
Application deadline (fall): rolling
Undergraduate student body: N/A full time, N/A part time
Expenses: 2019-2020: $33,540; room/board: $13,570
Financial aid: N/A

Saint Anselm College
Manchester NH
(603) 641-7500
U.S. News ranking: Nat. Lib. Arts, No. 102
Website: www.anselm.edu
Admissions email: admission@anselm.edu
Private; founded 1889
Affiliation: Roman Catholic
Freshman admissions: selective; 2019-2020: 3,742 applied, 2,813 accepted. Neither SAT nor ACT required. SAT 25/75 percentile: 1140-1300. High school rank: 28% in top tenth, 61% in top quarter, 91% in top half
Early decision deadline: 12/1, notification date: 1/1

Early action deadline: 11/15, notification date: 1/15
Application deadline (fall): 2/1
Undergraduate student body: 2,039 full time, 4 part time; 39% male, 61% female; 0% American Indian, 1% Asian, 2% Black, 5% Hispanic, 2% multiracial, 0% Pacific Islander, 86% white, 0% international; 14% from in state; 94% live on campus; N/A of students in fraternities, N/A in sororities
Most popular majors: 20% Social Sciences, 18% Health Professions and Related Programs, 15% Business, Management, Marketing, and Related Support Services, 8% Psychology, 6% Communication, Journalism, and Related Programs
Expenses: 2020-2021: $43,140; room/board: $15,120
Financial aid: (603) 641-7110; 68% of undergrads determined to have financial need; average aid package $31,666

Southern New Hampshire University
Manchester NH
(603) 645-9611
U.S. News ranking: Reg. U. (N), No. 75
Website: www.snhu.edu
Admissions email: admission@snhu.edu
Private; founded 1932
Freshman admissions: less selective; 2019-2020: 4,874 applied, 4,215 accepted. Neither SAT nor ACT required. SAT 25/75 percentile: N/A. High school rank: 8% in top tenth, 28% in top quarter, 69% in top half
Early decision deadline: N/A, notification date: N/A
Early action deadline: 11/15, notification date: 12/15
Application deadline (fall): rolling
Undergraduate student body: 2,956 full time, 87 part time; 52% male, 48% female; 0% American Indian, 2% Asian, 3% Black, 5% Hispanic, 2% multiracial, 0% Pacific Islander, 76% white, 4% international; N/A from in state; 61% live on campus; 1% of students in fraternities, 5% in sororities
Most popular majors: 41% Business, Management, Marketing, and Related Support Services, 9% Education, 9% Psychology, 8% Social Sciences, 7% Homeland Security, Law Enforcement, Firefighting and Related Protective Services
Expenses: 2020-2021: $9,980; room/board: $12,800
Financial aid: (877) 455-7648; 72% of undergrads determined to have financial need; average aid package $22,854

Thomas More College of Liberal Arts[1]
Merrimack NH
(603) 880-8308
U.S. News ranking: Nat. Lib. Arts, unranked
Website: www.thomasmorecollege.edu

Admissions email: admissions@thomasmorecollege.edu
Private; founded 1978
Affiliation: Roman Catholic
Application deadline (fall): N/A
Undergraduate student body: N/A full time, N/A part time
Expenses: 2019-2020: $21,600; room/board: $9,700
Financial aid: (603) 880-8308

University of New Hampshire
Durham NH
(603) 862-1234
U.S. News ranking: Nat. U., No. 143
Website: www.unh.edu
Admissions email: admissions@unh.edu
Public; founded 1866
Freshman admissions: selective; 2019-2020: 18,040 applied, 15,159 accepted. Neither SAT nor ACT required. SAT 25/75 percentile: 1070-1270. High school rank: 22% in top tenth, 49% in top quarter, 85% in top half
Early decision deadline: N/A, notification date: N/A
Early action deadline: 11/15, notification date: 1/1
Application deadline (fall): 2/1
Undergraduate student body: 11,931 full time, 271 part time; 44% male, 56% female; 0% American Indian, 3% Asian, 1% Black, 4% Hispanic, 2% multiracial, 0% Pacific Islander, 83% white, 3% international; 48% from in state; 55% live on campus; 13% of students in fraternities, 17% in sororities
Most popular majors: 22% Business, Management, Marketing, and Related Support Services, 11% Engineering, 9% Biological and Biomedical Sciences, 7% Social Sciences, 6% Health Professions and Related Programs
Expenses: 2020-2021: $18,938 in state, $36,278 out of state; room/board: $12,242
Financial aid: (603) 862-3600; 66% of undergrads determined to have financial need; average aid package $24,851

NEW JERSEY

Berkeley College
Woodland Park NJ
(800) 446-5400
U.S. News ranking: Reg. Coll. (N), second tier
Website: berkeleycollege.edu/
Admissions email: admissions@berkeleycollege.edu
For-profit; founded 1931
Freshman admissions: least selective; 2019-2020: 1,240 applied, 1,218 accepted. Neither SAT nor ACT required. SAT 25/75 percentile: N/A. High school rank: N/A
Early decision deadline: N/A, notification date: N/A
Early action deadline: N/A, notification date: N/A
Application deadline (fall): 9/1
Undergraduate student body: 1,972 full time, 710 part time; 28%

male, 72% female; 0% American Indian, 1% Asian, 16% Black, 42% Hispanic, 0% multiracial, 0% Pacific Islander, 10% white, 1% international; 97% from in state; 0% live on campus; N/A of students in fraternities, N/A in sororities
Most popular majors: 24% Business Administration and Management, General, 21% Criminal Justice/Law Enforcement Administration, 11% Health/Health Care Administration/Management, 8% Accounting, 8% Fashion Merchandising
Expenses: 2020-2021: $27,000; room/board: N/A
Financial aid: (973) 278-5400

Bloomfield College[1]
Bloomfield NJ
(973) 748-9000
U.S. News ranking: Nat. Lib. Arts, second tier
Website: www.bloomfield.edu
Admissions email: admission@bloomfield.edu
Private; founded 1868
Affiliation: Presbyterian Church (USA)
Application deadline (fall): 8/1
Undergraduate student body: N/A full time, N/A part time
Expenses: 2019-2020: $30,310; room/board: $12,300
Financial aid: (973) 748-9000

Caldwell University
Caldwell NJ
(973) 618-3600
U.S. News ranking: Reg. U. (N), No. 67
Website: www.caldwell.edu
Admissions email: admissions@caldwell.edu
Private; founded 1939
Affiliation: Roman Catholic
Freshman admissions: selective; 2019-2020: 3,529 applied, 3,287 accepted. Either SAT or ACT required. SAT 25/75 percentile: 940-1150. High school rank: 9% in top tenth, 27% in top quarter, 67% in top half
Early decision deadline: N/A, notification date: N/A
Early action deadline: 12/1, notification date: 12/31
Application deadline (fall): 4/1
Undergraduate student body: 1,608 full time, 96 part time; 36% male, 64% female; 0% American Indian, 3% Asian, 15% Black, 31% Hispanic, 1% multiracial, 0% Pacific Islander, 32% white, 11% international; 84% from in state; 36% live on campus; 1% of students in fraternities, 8% in sororities
Most popular majors: 25% Health Professions and Related Programs, 18% Business, Management, Marketing, and Related Support Services, 17% Psychology, 7% Social Sciences, 6% Biological and Biomedical Sciences
Expenses: 2020-2021: $36,900; room/board: $12,760
Financial aid: (973) 618-3221; 79% of undergrads determined to have financial need; average aid package $32,209

Centenary University
Hackettstown NJ
(800) 236-8679
U.S. News ranking: Reg. U. (N), No. 96
Website: www.centenaryuniversity.edu
Admissions email: CentUAdmissions@centenaryuniversity.edu
Private; founded 1867
Affiliation: United Methodist
Freshman admissions: selective; 2019-2020: 1,362 applied, 1,022 accepted. Either SAT or ACT required. SAT 25/75 percentile: 938-1148. High school rank: N/A
Early decision deadline: N/A, notification date: N/A
Early action deadline: N/A, notification date: N/A
Application deadline (fall): 8/15
Undergraduate student body: 1,038 full time, 155 part time; 34% male, 66% female; 0% American Indian, 1% Asian, 10% Black, 15% Hispanic, 2% multiracial, 0% Pacific Islander, 60% white, 1% international; N/A from in state; 46% live on campus; N/A of students in fraternities, N/A in sororities
Most popular majors: 37% Business, Management, Marketing, and Related Support Services, 9% Visual and Performing Arts, 8% Agriculture, Agriculture Operations, and Related Sciences, 8% Homeland Security, Law Enforcement, Firefighting and Related Protective Services, 6% Social Sciences
Expenses: 2020-2021: $34,498; room/board: $12,386
Financial aid: (908) 852-1400

College of New Jersey
Ewing NJ
(609) 771-2131
U.S. News ranking: Reg. U. (N), No. 5
Website: www.tcnj.edu
Admissions email: admiss@tcnj.edu
Public; founded 1855
Freshman admissions: more selective; 2019-2020: 13,824 applied, 6,812 accepted. Either SAT or ACT required. SAT 25/75 percentile: 1160-1360. High school rank: 36% in top tenth, 71% in top quarter, 97% in top half
Early decision deadline: 11/1, notification date: 12/1
Early action deadline: N/A, notification date: N/A
Application deadline (fall): 2/1
Undergraduate student body: 6,981 full time, 208 part time; 43% male, 57% female; 0% American Indian, 12% Asian, 6% Black, 14% Hispanic, 1% multiracial, 0% Pacific Islander, 62% white, 1% international; 6% from in state; 53% live on campus; 15% of students in fraternities, 13% in sororities
Most popular majors: 19% Business Administration, Management and Operations, 7% Teacher Education and Professional Development, Specific Levels and Methods, 6% Biology, General, 6% Psychology,

General, 5% Registered Nursing, Nursing Administration, Nursing Research and Clinical Nursing
Expenses: 2020-2021: $16,029 in state, $28,007 out of state; room/board: $14,216
Financial aid: (609) 771-2211; 51% of undergrads determined to have financial need; average aid package $11,920

Drew University
Madison NJ
(973) 408-3739
U.S. News ranking: Nat. Lib. Arts, No. 113
Website: www.drew.edu
Admissions email: cadm@drew.edu
Private; founded 1867
Affiliation: United Methodist
Freshman admissions: more selective; 2019-2020: 3,928 applied, 2,805 accepted. Neither SAT nor ACT required. SAT 25/75 percentile: 1105-1300. High school rank: 23% in top tenth, 49% in top quarter, 86% in top half
Early decision deadline: 11/15, notification date: 12/15
Early action deadline: 12/15, notification date: 1/25
Application deadline (fall): 2/1
Undergraduate student body: 1,688 full time, 24 part time; 42% male, 58% female; 0% American Indian, 5% Asian, 8% Black, 17% Hispanic, 3% multiracial, 0% Pacific Islander, 50% white, 12% international; N/A from in state; 81% live on campus; N/A of students in fraternities, N/A in sororities
Most popular majors: 20% Social Sciences, 16% Biological and Biomedical Sciences, 13% Business, Management, Marketing, and Related Support Services, 10% Psychology, 10% Visual and Performing Arts
Expenses: 2020-2021: $42,952; room/board: $15,258
Financial aid: (973) 408-3112; 68% of undergrads determined to have financial need; average aid package $37,235

Fairleigh Dickinson University
Teaneck NJ
(800) 338-8803
U.S. News ranking: Reg. U. (N), No. 50
Website: www.fdu.edu
Admissions email: admissions@fdu.edu
Private; founded 1942
Freshman admissions: selective; 2019-2020: 5,762 applied, 5,361 accepted. Neither SAT nor ACT required. SAT 25/75 percentile: 1000-1180. High school rank: 14% in top tenth, 42% in top quarter, 75% in top half
Early decision deadline: N/A, notification date: N/A
Early action deadline: N/A, notification date: N/A
Application deadline (fall): rolling
Undergraduate student body: 4,636 full time, 4,308 part time; 42% male, 58% female; 0% American Indian, 5% Asian, 9% Black, 32% Hispanic, 2% multiracial,

0% Pacific Islander, 38% white, 3% international; 83% from in state; 24% live on campus; N/A of students in fraternities, N/A in sororities
Most popular majors: 28% Liberal Arts and Sciences, General Studies and Humanities, 12% Business, Management, Marketing, and Related Support Services, 10% Psychology, 5% Biological and Biomedical Sciences, 5% Visual and Performing Arts
Expenses: 2020-2021: $43,490; room/board: $13,966
Financial aid: (973) 443-8700; 80% of undergrads determined to have financial need; average aid package $37,638

Felician University
Lodi NJ
(201) 355-1457
U.S. News ranking: Reg. U. (N), second tier
Website: www.felician.edu
Admissions email: admissions@felician.edu
Private; founded 1942
Affiliation: Roman Catholic
Freshman admissions: less selective; 2019-2020: 2,545 applied, 2,191 accepted. Either SAT or ACT required. SAT 25/75 percentile: 900-1080. High school rank: 12% in top tenth, 31% in top quarter, 48% in top half
Early decision deadline: N/A, notification date: N/A
Early action deadline: 11/15, notification date: 12/23
Application deadline (fall): rolling
Undergraduate student body: 1,640 full time, 212 part time; 28% male, 72% female; 0% American Indian, 4% Asian, 20% Black, 32% Hispanic, 1% multiracial, 0% Pacific Islander, 27% white, 4% international; N/A from in state; 28% live on campus; N/A of students in fraternities, N/A in sororities
Most popular majors: 41% Health Professions and Related Programs, 16% Business, Management, Marketing, and Related Support Services, 8% Biological and Biomedical Sciences, 7% Homeland Security, Law Enforcement, Firefighting and Related Protective Services, 6% Psychology
Expenses: 2020-2021: $35,000; room/board: $13,140
Financial aid: (201) 559-6040; 90% of undergrads determined to have financial need; average aid package $29,394

Georgian Court University
Lakewood NJ
(800) 458-8422
U.S. News ranking: Reg. U. (N), No. 113
Website: georgian.edu
Admissions email: admissions@georgian.edu
Private; founded 1908
Affiliation: Roman Catholic
Freshman admissions: selective; 2019-2020: 1,934 applied, 1,377 accepted. Either SAT or ACT required. SAT 25/75

percentile: 958-1160. High school rank: 15% in top tenth, 33% in top quarter, 81% in top half
Early decision deadline: N/A, notification date: N/A
Early action deadline: 12/1, notification date: N/A
Application deadline (fall): 8/1
Undergraduate student body: 1,417 full time, 376 part time; 28% male, 72% female; 1% American Indian, 3% Asian, 10% Black, 15% Hispanic, 1% multiracial, 0% Pacific Islander, 63% white, 2% international; 91% from in state; 25% live on campus; 0% of students in fraternities, 0% in sororities
Most popular majors: 14% Psychology, General, 14% Registered Nursing/Registered Nurse, 10% English Language and Literature, General, 8% Business Administration and Management, General, 8% Elementary Education and Teaching
Expenses: 2020-2021: $33,640; room/board: $11,424
Financial aid: (732) 987-2258; 82% of undergrads determined to have financial need; average aid package $29,570

Kean University
Union NJ
(908) 737-7100
U.S. News ranking: Reg. U. (N), No. 132
Website: www.kean.edu
Admissions email: admitme@kean.edu
Public; founded 1855
Freshman admissions: less selective; 2019-2020: 9,540 applied, 6,541 accepted. Either SAT or ACT required. SAT 25/75 percentile: 920-1100. High school rank: N/A
Early decision deadline: N/A, notification date: N/A
Early action deadline: 12/1, notification date: 1/1
Application deadline (fall): 8/15
Undergraduate student body: 9,817 full time, 2,303 part time; 40% male, 60% female; 0% American Indian, 6% Asian, 20% Black, 31% Hispanic, 2% multiracial, 0% Pacific Islander, 30% white, 4% international; N/A from in state; 15% live on campus; N/A of students in fraternities, N/A in sororities
Most popular majors: 15% Psychology, General, 9% Business Administration and Management, General, 7% Biology/Biological Sciences, General, 7% Criminal Justice/Law Enforcement Administration, 7% Speech Communication and Rhetoric
Expenses: 2020-2021: $12,445 in state, $19,621 out of state; room/board: N/A
Financial aid: (908) 737-3190; 72% of undergrads determined to have financial need; average aid package $11,242

Monmouth University
West Long Branch NJ
(800) 543-9671
U.S. News ranking: Reg. U. (N), No. 23
Website: www.monmouth.edu

Admissions email: admission@monmouth.edu
Private; founded 1933
Freshman admissions: selective; 2019-2020: 8,984 applied, 6,886 accepted. Either SAT or ACT required. SAT 25/75 percentile: 1030-1210. High school rank: 15% in top tenth, 42% in top quarter, 78% in top half
Early decision deadline: N/A, notification date: N/A
Early action deadline: 12/1, notification date: 1/15
Application deadline (fall): 3/1
Undergraduate student body: 4,301 full time, 149 part time; 41% male, 59% female; 0% American Indian, 3% Asian, 5% Black, 14% Hispanic, 3% multiracial, 0% Pacific Islander, 70% white, 1% international; 81% from in state; 40% live on campus; 7% of students in fraternities, 17% in sororities
Most popular majors: 29% Business, Management, Marketing, and Related Support Services, 10% Health Professions and Related Programs, 8% Communication, Journalism, and Related Programs, 6% Education, 6% Social Sciences
Expenses: 2020-2021: $40,680; room/board: $15,260
Financial aid: (732) 571-3463; 71% of undergrads determined to have financial need; average aid package $28,763

Montclair State University
Montclair NJ
(973) 655-4444
U.S. News ranking: Nat. U., No. 176
Website: www.montclair.edu
Admissions email: undergraduate. admissions@montclair.edu
Public; founded 1908
Freshman admissions: selective; 2019-2020: 12,729 applied, 9,713 accepted. Neither SAT nor ACT required. SAT 25/75 percentile: 990-1180. High school rank: 12% in top tenth, 35% in top quarter, 74% in top half
Early decision deadline: N/A, notification date: N/A
Early action deadline: 11/15, notification date: 12/15
Application deadline (fall): 3/1
Undergraduate student body: 14,859 full time, 1,828 part time; 39% male, 61% female; 0% American Indian, 6% Asian, 14% Black, 30% Hispanic, 3% multiracial, 0% Pacific Islander, 41% white, 1% international; 96% from in state; 30% live on campus; N/A of students in fraternities, N/A in sororities
Most popular majors: 21% Business, Management, Marketing, and Related Support Services, 11% Family and Consumer Sciences/Human Sciences, 11% Psychology, 11% Visual and Performing Arts, 6% Multi/Interdisciplinary Studies
Expenses: 2020-2021: $13,071 in state, $21,031 out of state; room/board: $16,193

Financial aid: (973) 655-7020; 74% of undergrads determined to have financial need; average aid package $10,658

New Jersey City University
Jersey City NJ
(888) 441-6528
U.S. News ranking: Reg. U. (N), second tier
Website: www.njcu.edu/
Admissions email: admissions@njcu.edu
Public; founded 1927
Freshman admissions: least selective; 2019-2020: 4,868 applied, 4,606 accepted. Either SAT or ACT required. SAT 25/75 percentile: 860-1080. High school rank: N/A
Early decision deadline: N/A, notification date: N/A
Early action deadline: N/A, notification date: N/A
Undergraduate student body: 4,990 full time, 1,147 part time; 42% male, 58% female; 0% American Indian, 8% Asian, 24% Black, 39% Hispanic, 3% multiracial, 0% Pacific Islander, 19% white, 1% international; 98% from in state; 12% live on campus; N/A of students in fraternities, N/A in sororities
Most popular majors: 20% Business, Management, Marketing, and Related Support Services, 20% Health Professions and Related Programs, 15% Homeland Security, Law Enforcement, Firefighting and Related Protective Services, 12% Psychology, 8% Visual and Performing Arts
Expenses: 2020-2021: $13,019 in state, $22,999 out of state; room/board: N/A
Financial aid: (201) 200-3171; 88% of undergrads determined to have financial need; average aid package $11,398

New Jersey Institute of Technology
Newark NJ
(973) 596-3300
U.S. News ranking: Nat. U., No. 118
Website: www.njit.edu
Admissions email: admissions@njit.edu
Public; founded 1881
Freshman admissions: more selective; 2019-2020: 8,201 applied, 5,971 accepted. Either SAT or ACT required. SAT 25/75 percentile: 1190-1390. High school rank: 31% in top tenth, 57% in top quarter, 85% in top half
Early decision deadline: N/A, notification date: N/A
Early action deadline: 11/11, notification date: 12/16
Application deadline (fall): 3/1
Undergraduate student body: 6,878 full time, 1,916 part time; 75% male, 25% female; 0% American Indian, 23% Asian, 9% Black, 22% Hispanic, 3% multiracial, 0% Pacific Islander, 34% white, 6% international; 96% from in

state; 23% live on campus; 5% of students in fraternities, 5% in sororities

Most popular majors: 41% Engineering, 24% Computer and Information Sciences and Support Services, 14% Engineering Technologies and Engineering-Related Fields, 6% Business, Management, Marketing, and Related Support Services, 5% Architecture and Related Services

Expenses: 2020-2021: $17,674 in state, $33,386 out of state; room/board: $13,900

Financial aid: (973) 596-3476; 71% of undergrads determined to have financial need; average aid package $14,681

Princeton University

Princeton NJ
(609) 258-3060
U.S. News ranking: Nat. U., No. 1
Website: www.princeton.edu
Admissions email: uaoffice@princeton.edu
Private; founded 1746
Freshman admissions: most selective; 2019-2020: 32,804 applied, 1,895 accepted. Either SAT or ACT required. SAT 25/75 percentile: 1460-1570. High school rank: 91% in top tenth, 98% in top quarter, 100% in top half
Early decision deadline: N/A, notification date: N/A
Early action deadline: 11/1, notification date: 12/15
Application deadline (fall): 1/1
Undergraduate student body: 5,328 full time, 94 part time; 50% male, 50% female; 0% American Indian, 22% Asian, 8% Black, 11% Hispanic, 5% multiracial, 0% Pacific Islander, 40% white, 12% international; 16% from in state; 96% live on campus; N/A of students in fraternities, N/A in sororities
Most popular majors: 21% Social Sciences, 17% Engineering, 11% Biological and Biomedical Sciences, 11% Computer and Information Sciences and Support Services, 9% Public Administration and Social Service Professions
Expenses: 2020-2021: $53,890; room/board: $17,820
Financial aid: (609) 258-3330; 62% of undergrads determined to have financial need; average aid package $59,389

Ramapo College of New Jersey

Mahwah NJ
(201) 684-7300
U.S. News ranking: Reg. U. (N), No. 34
Website: www.ramapo.edu
Admissions email: admissions@ramapo.edu
Public; founded 1969
Freshman admissions: selective; 2019-2020: 7,331 applied, 4,808 accepted. Either SAT or ACT required. SAT 25/75 percentile: 1030-1220. High school rank: 16% in top tenth, 41% in top quarter, 77% in top half

Early decision deadline: 11/1, notification date: 12/5
Early action deadline: 12/15, notification date: 2/1
Application deadline (fall): 2/1
Undergraduate student body: 4,870 full time, 704 part time; 44% male, 56% female; 1% American Indian, 8% Asian, 6% Black, 20% Hispanic, 0% multiracial, 0% Pacific Islander, 60% white, 2% international; 95% from in state; 45% live on campus; 5% of students in fraternities, 2% in sororities
Most popular majors: 17% Business, Management, Marketing, and Related Support Services, 9% Communication, Journalism, and Related Programs, 9% Health Professions and Related Programs, 9% Psychology, 7% Biological and Biomedical Sciences
Expenses: 2020-2021: $15,047 in state, $24,825 out of state; room/board: $12,792
Financial aid: (201) 684-7549; 56% of undergrads determined to have financial need; average aid package $11,069

Rider University

Lawrenceville NJ
(609) 896-9026
U.S. News ranking: Reg. U. (N), No. 38
Website: www.rider.edu
Admissions email: admissions@rider.edu
Private; founded 1865
Freshman admissions: selective; 2019-2020: 9,388 applied, 6,710 accepted. Neither SAT nor ACT required. SAT 25/75 percentile: 1020-1210. High school rank: 14% in top tenth, 35% in top quarter, 77% in top half
Early decision deadline: N/A, notification date: N/A
Early action deadline: 11/15, notification date: 12/15
Application deadline (fall): rolling
Undergraduate student body: 3,466 full time, 297 part time; 44% male, 56% female; 0% American Indian, 5% Asian, 14% Black, 17% Hispanic, 4% multiracial, 0% Pacific Islander, 56% white, 3% international; 77% from in state; 53% live on campus; 11% of students in fraternities, 12% in sororities
Most popular majors: 37% Business Administration and Management, General, 12% Education, General, 11% Psychology, General, 10% Visual and Performing Arts, General, 7% Communication, Journalism, and Related Programs
Expenses: 2020-2021: $45,860; room/board: $15,500
Financial aid: (609) 896-5188; 77% of undergrads determined to have financial need; average aid package $33,444

Rowan University

Glassboro NJ
(856) 256-4200
U.S. News ranking: Nat. U., No. 187
Website: www.rowan.edu

Admissions email: admissions@rowan.edu
Public; founded 1923
Freshman admissions: selective; 2019-2020: 14,370 applied, 10,676 accepted. Either SAT or ACT required. SAT 25/75 percentile: 990-1200. High school rank: N/A
Early decision deadline: N/A, notification date: N/A
Early action deadline: N/A, notification date: N/A
Application deadline (fall): 3/1
Undergraduate student body: 14,055 full time, 1,956 part time; 54% male, 46% female; 0% American Indian, 5% Asian, 10% Black, 11% Hispanic, 4% multiracial, 0% Pacific Islander, 67% white, 1% international
Most popular majors: 19% Business, Management, Marketing, and Related Support Services, 9% Psychology, 8% Biological and Biomedical Sciences, 8% Communication, Journalism, and Related Programs, 8% Engineering
Expenses: 2020-2021: $13,697 in state, $22,339 out of state; room/board: $14,854
Financial aid: (856) 256-4281; 68% of undergrads determined to have financial need; average aid package $10,346

Rutgers University–Camden

Camden NJ
(856) 225-6104
U.S. News ranking: Nat. U., No. 153
Website: www.camden.rutgers.edu/
Admissions email: admissions@camden.rutgers.edu
Public; founded 1926
Freshman admissions: selective; 2019-2020: 10,451 applied, 8,277 accepted. Either SAT or ACT required. SAT 25/75 percentile: 980-1170. High school rank: 19% in top tenth, 45% in top quarter, 81% in top half
Early decision deadline: N/A, notification date: N/A
Early action deadline: 11/1, notification date: 1/31
Application deadline (fall): rolling
Undergraduate student body: 4,767 full time, 972 part time; 39% male, 61% female; 0% American Indian, 11% Asian, 18% Black, 17% Hispanic, 4% multiracial, 0% Pacific Islander, 44% white, 3% international; N/A from in state; 16% live on campus; N/A of students in fraternities, N/A in sororities
Most popular majors: 18% Registered Nursing/Registered Nurse, 15% Business Administration and Management, General, 8% Health Professions and Related Programs, 8% Psychology, General, 6% Criminal Justice/Safety Studies
Expenses: 2020-2021: $14,877 in state, $31,113 out of state; room/board: $12,691
Financial aid: (856) 225-6039; 80% of undergrads determined to have financial need; average aid package $15,741

Rutgers University–Newark

Newark NJ
(973) 353-5205
U.S. News ranking: Nat. U., No. 118
Website: www.newark.rutgers.edu/
Admissions email: newark@admissions.rutgers.edu
Public; founded 1908
Freshman admissions: selective; 2019-2020: 13,732 applied, 9,873 accepted. Either SAT or ACT required. SAT 25/75 percentile: 1020-1200. High school rank: 22% in top tenth, 51% in top quarter, 84% in top half
Early decision deadline: N/A, notification date: N/A
Early action deadline: 11/1, notification date: 1/31
Application deadline (fall): rolling
Undergraduate student body: 7,975 full time, 1,344 part time; 43% male, 57% female; 0% American Indian, 17% Asian, 19% Black, 29% Hispanic, 3% multiracial, 0% Pacific Islander, 20% white, 9% international; N/A from in state; 16% live on campus; N/A of students in fraternities, N/A in sororities
Most popular majors: 11% Criminal Justice/Safety Studies, 11% Psychology, General, 10% Accounting, 9% Biology/Biological Sciences, General, 9% Finance, General
Expenses: 2020-2021: $14,502 in state, $31,284 out of state; room/board: $13,929
Financial aid: (973) 353-5151; 77% of undergrads determined to have financial need; average aid package $14,809

Rutgers University– New Brunswick

Piscataway NJ
(732) 445-4636
U.S. News ranking: Nat. U., No. 63
Website: newbrunswick.rutgers.edu
Admissions email: admissions@ugadm.rutgers.edu
Public; founded 1766
Freshman admissions: more selective; 2019-2020: 41,286 applied, 25,277 accepted. Either SAT or ACT required. SAT 25/75 percentile: 1210-1430. High school rank: 38% in top tenth, 73% in top quarter, 94% in top half
Early decision deadline: N/A, notification date: N/A
Early action deadline: 11/1, notification date: 1/31
Application deadline (fall): rolling
Undergraduate student body: 34,285 full time, 1,873 part time; 50% male, 50% female; 0% American Indian, 29% Asian, 6% Black, 13% Hispanic, 4% multiracial, 0% Pacific Islander, 36% white, 10% international; N/A from in state; 43% live on campus; N/A of students in fraternities, N/A in sororities
Most popular majors: 6% Computer and Information Sciences, General, 6% Psychology, General, 5% Biology/Biological Sciences, General, 4% Human Resources Management/Personnel

Administration, General, 4% Registered Nursing/Registered Nurse
Expenses: 2020-2021: $15,003 in state, $31,785 out of state; room/board: $13,075
Financial aid: (848) 932-2695; 50% of undergrads determined to have financial need; average aid package $14,033

Saint Elizabeth University

Morristown NJ
(973) 290-4700
U.S. News ranking: Reg. U. (N), second tier
Website: www.cse.edu
Admissions email: apply@cse.edu
Private; founded 1899
Affiliation: Roman Catholic
Freshman admissions: less selective; 2019-2020: 1,682 applied, 1,236 accepted. Neither SAT nor ACT required. SAT 25/75 percentile: 890-1096. High school rank: N/A
Early decision deadline: N/A, notification date: N/A
Early action deadline: N/A, notification date: N/A
Application deadline (fall): rolling
Undergraduate student body: 628 full time, 200 part time; 30% male, 70% female; 0% American Indian, 3% Asian, 33% Black, 27% Hispanic, 1% multiracial, 1% Pacific Islander, 23% white, 2% international; 95% from in state; 49% live on campus; 0% of students in fraternities, 0% in sororities
Most popular majors: 50% Health Professions and Related Programs, 13% Multi/Interdisciplinary Studies, 10% Psychology, 7% Business, Management, Marketing, and Related Support Services, 4% Social Sciences
Expenses: 2020-2021: $34,956; room/board: $12,744
Financial aid: (973) 290-4445

Saint Peter's University

Jersey City NJ
(201) 761-7100
U.S. News ranking: Reg. U. (N), No. 75
Website: www.saintpeters.edu
Admissions email: admissions@saintpeters.edu
Private; founded 1872
Affiliation: Roman Catholic
Freshman admissions: selective; 2019-2020: 4,323 applied, 3,500 accepted. Neither SAT nor ACT required. SAT 25/75 percentile: 930-1100. High school rank: 15% in top tenth, 38% in top quarter, 68% in top half
Early decision deadline: N/A, notification date: N/A
Early action deadline: 12/15, notification date: 1/30
Application deadline (fall): rolling
Undergraduate student body: 2,203 full time, 220 part time; 38% male, 62% female; 0% American Indian, 8% Asian, 20% Black, 49% Hispanic, 1% multiracial, 1% Pacific Islander, 13% white, 2% international; N/A from in

state; 27% live on campus; N/A of students in fraternities, N/A in sororities

Most popular majors: 21% Business, Management, Marketing, and Related Support Services, 16% Biological and Biomedical Sciences, 11% Health Professions and Related Programs, 11% Homeland Security, Law Enforcement, Firefighting and Related Protective Services, 7% Psychology

Expenses: 2020-2021: $38,700; room/board: $15,950

Financial aid: (201) 761-6060; 89% of undergrads determined to have financial need; average aid package $35,749

Seton Hall University
South Orange NJ
(800) 843-4255
U.S. News ranking: Nat. U., No. 133
Website: www.shu.edu
Admissions email: thehall@shu.edu
Private; founded 1856
Affiliation: Roman Catholic
Freshman admissions: more selective; 2019-2020: 19,757 applied, 14,548 accepted. Either SAT or ACT required. SAT 25/75 percentile: 1150-1330. High school rank: 34% in top tenth, 60% in top quarter, 87% in top half
Early decision deadline: N/A, notification date: N/A
Early action deadline: 12/15, notification date: 1/31
Application deadline (fall): rolling
Undergraduate student body: 5,782 full time, 320 part time; 48% male, 52% female; 0% American Indian, 11% Asian, 8% Black, 18% Hispanic, 4% multiracial, 0% Pacific Islander, 50% white, 4% international; 69% from in state; 40% live on campus; 13% of students in fraternities, 23% in sororities
Most popular majors: 10% Biology/Biological Sciences, General, 10% Humanities/Humanistic Studies, 9% Finance, General, 9% Registered Nursing/Registered Nurse, 5% International Relations and Affairs
Expenses: 2020-2021: $45,290; room/board: $15,368
Financial aid: (973) 761-9350

Stevens Institute of Technology
Hoboken NJ
(201) 216-5194
U.S. News ranking: Nat. U., No. 80
Website: www.stevens.edu
Admissions email: admissions@stevens.edu
Private; founded 1870
Freshman admissions: most selective; 2019-2020: 10,475 applied, 4,186 accepted. Neither SAT nor ACT required. SAT 25/75 percentile: 1340-1500. High school rank: 74% in top tenth, 94% in top quarter, 100% in top half
Early decision deadline: 11/15, notification date: 12/15
Early action deadline: N/A, notification date: N/A

Application deadline (fall): 1/15
Undergraduate student body: 3,464 full time, 20 part time; 70% male, 30% female; 0% American Indian, 17% Asian, 2% Black, 12% Hispanic, 0% multiracial, 0% Pacific Islander, 62% white, 3% international; 61% from in state; 51% live on campus; 27% of students in fraternities, 36% in sororities
Most popular majors: 24% Mechanical Engineering, 11% Business Administration and Management, General, 10% Computer Science, 8% Chemical Engineering, 8% Computer Engineering, General
Expenses: 2020-2021: $55,952; room/board: $16,244
Financial aid: (201) 216-3400; 68% of undergrads determined to have financial need; average aid package $32,200

Stockton University
Galloway NJ
(609) 652-4261
U.S. News ranking: Reg. U. (N), No. 34
Website: www.stockton.edu
Admissions email: admissions@stockton.edu
Public; founded 1969
Freshman admissions: selective; 2019-2020: 6,914 applied, 5,277 accepted. Neither SAT nor ACT required. SAT 25/75 percentile: 1020-1210. High school rank: 17% in top tenth, 41% in top quarter, 79% in top half
Early decision deadline: N/A, notification date: N/A
Early action deadline: N/A, notification date: N/A
Application deadline (fall): 8/15
Undergraduate student body: 8,459 full time, 434 part time; 41% male, 59% female; 0% American Indian, 7% Asian, 9% Black, 15% Hispanic, 3% multiracial, 0% Pacific Islander, 65% white, 1% international; 98% from in state; 37% live on campus; 6% of students in fraternities, 10% in sororities
Most popular majors: 17% Business Administration and Management, General, 15% Health Professions and Related Programs, 9% Psychology, General, 8% Criminology, 6% Biology/Biological Sciences, General
Expenses: 2020-2021: $14,327 in state, $21,761 out of state; room/board: $12,824
Financial aid: (609) 652-4203; 72% of undergrads determined to have financial need; average aid package $17,758

William Paterson University of New Jersey
Wayne NJ
(973) 720-2125
U.S. News ranking: Reg. U. (N), No. 90
Website: www.wpunj.edu/
Admissions email: admissions@wpunj.edu
Public; founded 1855

Freshman admissions: less selective; 2019-2020: 9,340 applied, 8,554 accepted. Neither SAT nor ACT required. SAT 25/75 percentile: 890-1090. High school rank: N/A
Early decision deadline: N/A, notification date: N/A
Early action deadline: N/A, notification date: N/A
Application deadline (fall): 6/1
Undergraduate student body: 7,164 full time, 1,419 part time; 44% male, 56% female; 0% American Indian, 7% Asian, 19% Black, 33% Hispanic, 3% multiracial, 0% Pacific Islander, 36% white, 1% international; 98% from in state; 24% live on campus; 1% of students in fraternities, 1% in sororities
Most popular majors: 19% Business, Management, Marketing, and Related Support Services, 10% Communication, Journalism, and Related Programs, 10% Psychology, 9% Health Professions and Related Programs, 8% Social Sciences
Expenses: 2019-2020: $13,370 in state, $21,768 out of state; room/board: $11,900
Financial aid: (973) 720-3945; 75% of undergrads determined to have financial need; average aid package $11,939

NEW MEXICO

Eastern New Mexico University[1]
Portales NM
(575) 562-2178
U.S. News ranking: Reg. U. (W), second tier
Website: www.enmu.edu
Admissions email: admissions.office@enmu.edu
Public; founded 1934
Application deadline (fall): rolling
Undergraduate student body: N/A full time, N/A part time
Expenses: 2019-2020: $6,450 in state, $8,448 out of state; room/board: $7,300
Financial aid: (575) 562-2708

New Mexico Highlands University
Las Vegas NM
(505) 454-3434
U.S. News ranking: Reg. U. (W), second tier
Website: www.nmhu.edu
Admissions email: admissions@nmhu.edu
Public; founded 1893
Freshman admissions: less selective; 2019-2020: 1,395 applied, 903 accepted. Neither SAT nor ACT required. ACT 25/75 percentile: 15-20. High school rank: 11% in top tenth, 30% in top quarter, 63% in top half
Early decision deadline: N/A, notification date: N/A
Early action deadline: N/A, notification date: N/A
Application deadline (fall): rolling
Undergraduate student body: 1,191 full time, 606 part time; 36% male, 64% female; 10% American Indian, 0% Asian, 6% Black,

58% Hispanic, 2% multiracial, 0% Pacific Islander, 19% white, 3% international; N/A from in state; 26% live on campus; N/A of students in fraternities, N/A in sororities
Most popular majors: 37% Health Professions and Related Programs, 16% Education, 14% Business, Management, Marketing, and Related Support Services, 7% Psychology, 4% Liberal Arts and Sciences, General Studies and Humanities
Expenses: 2019-2020: $6,278 in state, $10,590 out of state; room/board: $8,126
Financial aid: (505) 454-3430

New Mexico Institute of Mining and Technology
Socorro NM
(575) 835-5424
U.S. News ranking: Reg. U. (W), No. 18
Website: www.nmt.edu
Admissions email: Admission@nmt.edu
Public; founded 1889
Freshman admissions: more selective; 2019-2020: 1,143 applied, 912 accepted. Either SAT or ACT required. ACT 25/75 percentile: 23-29. High school rank: 36% in top tenth, 68% in top quarter, 92% in top half
Early decision deadline: N/A, notification date: N/A
Early action deadline: N/A, notification date: N/A
Application deadline (fall): 8/1
Undergraduate student body: 1,175 full time, 146 part time; 67% male, 33% female; 4% American Indian, 4% Asian, 1% Black, 32% Hispanic, 4% multiracial, 0% Pacific Islander, 52% white, 1% international; 90% from in state; 50% live on campus; 0% of students in fraternities, 0% in sororities
Most popular majors: 26% Mechanical Engineering, 14% Chemical Engineering, 9% Computer and Information Sciences, General, 9% Petroleum Engineering, 6% Electrical and Electronics Engineering
Expenses: 2020-2021: $8,361 in state, $24,190 out of state; room/board: $8,624
Financial aid: (575) 835-5333; 56% of undergrads determined to have financial need; average aid package $13,367

New Mexico State University
Las Cruces NM
(575) 646-3121
U.S. News ranking: Nat. U., No. 241
Website: www.nmsu.edu
Admissions email: admissions@nmsu.edu
Public; founded 1888
Freshman admissions: selective; 2019-2020: 11,809 applied, 6,468 accepted. Either SAT or ACT required. ACT 25/75 percentile: 18-23. High school rank: 22% in top tenth, 52% in top quarter, 84% in top half

Early decision deadline: N/A, notification date: N/A
Early action deadline: N/A, notification date: N/A
Application deadline (fall): rolling
Undergraduate student body: 9,741 full time, 1,934 part time; 44% male, 56% female; 2% American Indian, 1% Asian, 2% Black, 63% Hispanic, 2% multiracial, 0% Pacific Islander, 25% white, 3% international; 74% from in state; 22% live on campus; N/A of students in fraternities, N/A in sororities
Most popular majors: 15% Business, Management, Marketing, and Related Support Services, 14% Engineering, 7% Health Professions and Related Programs, 7% Liberal Arts and Sciences, General Studies and Humanities, 6% Homeland Security, Law Enforcement, Firefighting and Related Protective Services
Expenses: 2020-2021: $8,044 in state, $25,666 out of state; room/board: $10,228
Financial aid: (575) 646-4105; 68% of undergrads determined to have financial need; average aid package $15,818

Northern New Mexico College[1]
Espanola NM
(505) 747-2100
U.S. News ranking: Reg. Coll. (W), No. 24
Website: www.nnmc.edu
Admissions email: N/A
Public
Application deadline (fall): N/A
Undergraduate student body: N/A full time, N/A part time
Expenses: 2019-2020: $4,952 in state, $13,676 out of state; room/board: $8,506
Financial aid: N/A

St. John's College
Santa Fe NM
(505) 984-6060
U.S. News ranking: Nat. Lib. Arts, No. 76
Website: www.sjc.edu
Admissions email: santafe.admissions@sjc.edu
Private; founded 1696
Freshman admissions: more selective; 2019-2020: 422 applied, 280 accepted. Neither SAT nor ACT required. SAT 25/75 percentile: 1270-1460. High school rank: 42% in top tenth, 58% in top quarter, 81% in top half
Early decision deadline: 11/1, notification date: 12/1
Early action deadline: 11/15, notification date: 12/15
Application deadline (fall): rolling
Undergraduate student body: 312 full time, 5 part time; 53% male, 47% female; 0% American Indian, 2% Asian, 0% Black, 10% Hispanic, 7% multiracial, 0% Pacific Islander, 58% white, 21% international; 17% from in state; 85% live on campus; 0% of students in fraternities, 0% in sororities

Most popular majors: 100% Liberal Arts and Sciences/Liberal Studies
Expenses: 2020-2021: $36,410; room/board: $13,570
Financial aid: (505) 984-6058; 79% of undergrads determined to have financial need; average aid package $29,102

University of New Mexico

Albuquerque NM
(505) 277-8900
U.S. News ranking: Nat. U., No. 187
Website: www.unm.edu
Admissions email: apply@unm.edu
Public; founded 1889
Freshman admissions: selective; 2019-2020: 12,181 applied, 5,973 accepted. Either SAT or ACT required. ACT 25/75 percentile: 19-25. High school rank: N/A
Early decision deadline: N/A, notification date: N/A
Early action deadline: N/A, notification date: N/A
Application deadline (fall): rolling
Undergraduate student body: 12,676 full time, 3,986 part time; 44% male, 56% female; 5% American Indian, 4% Asian, 2% Black, 50% Hispanic, 4% multiracial, 0% Pacific Islander, 31% white, 3% international; N/A from in state; 11% live on campus; 5% of students in fraternities, 6% in sororities
Most popular majors: 16% Health Professions and Related Programs, 14% Business, Management, Marketing, and Related Support Services, 10% Psychology, 8% Biological and Biomedical Sciences, 6% Education
Expenses: 2020-2021: $8,863 in state, $24,924 out of state; room/board: $10,262
Financial aid: (505) 277-8900; 61% of undergrads determined to have financial need

University of the Southwest[1]

Hobbs NM
(575) 392-6563
U.S. News ranking: Reg. U. (W), second tier
Website: www.usw.edu
Admissions email: admissions@usw.edu
Private; founded 1962
Application deadline (fall): rolling
Undergraduate student body: N/A full time, N/A part time
Expenses: 2019-2020: $16,200; room/board: $8,570
Financial aid: N/A

Western New Mexico University[1]

Silver City NM
(575) 538-6011
U.S. News ranking: Reg. U. (W), second tier
Website: www.wnmu.edu
Admissions email: admissions@wnmu.edu
Public; founded 1893
Application deadline (fall): N/A

Undergraduate student body: N/A full time, N/A part time
Expenses: 2019-2020: $6,306 in state, $13,539 out of state; room/board: $10,568
Financial aid: N/A

NEW YORK

Adelphi University

Garden City NY
(800) 233-5744
U.S. News ranking: Nat. U., No. 170
Website: www.adelphi.edu
Admissions email: admissions@adelphi.edu
Private; founded 1896
Freshman admissions: selective; 2019-2020: 13,919 applied, 10,342 accepted. Neither SAT nor ACT required. SAT 25/75 percentile: 1090-1270. High school rank: 28% in top tenth, 61% in top quarter, 91% in top half
Early decision deadline: N/A, notification date: N/A
Early action deadline: 12/1, notification date: 12/31
Application deadline (fall): rolling
Undergraduate student body: 5,063 full time, 297 part time; 31% male, 69% female; 0% American Indian, 11% Asian, 9% Black, 17% Hispanic, 3% multiracial, 0% Pacific Islander, 50% white, 4% international; 94% from in state; 21% live on campus; 10% of students in fraternities, 13% in sororities
Most popular majors: 37% Registered Nursing/Registered Nurse, 6% Psychology, General, 5% Biology/Biological Sciences, General, 5% Business Administration and Management, General, 3% Kinesiology and Exercise Science
Expenses: 2020-2021: $41,435; room/board: $15,590
Financial aid: (516) 877-3080; 69% of undergrads determined to have financial need; average aid package $25,500

Alfred University

Alfred NY
(800) 541-9229
U.S. News ranking: Reg. U. (N), No. 45
Website: www.alfred.edu
Admissions email: admissions@alfred.edu
Private; founded 1836
Freshman admissions: selective; 2019-2020: 4,272 applied, 2,801 accepted. Either SAT or ACT required. SAT 25/75 percentile: 940-1180. High school rank: 14% in top tenth, 33% in top quarter, 69% in top half
Early decision deadline: 12/1, notification date: 12/15
Early action deadline: N/A, notification date: N/A
Application deadline (fall): rolling
Undergraduate student body: 1,647 full time, 68 part time; 52% male, 48% female; 0% American Indian, 2% Asian, 13% Black, 9% Hispanic, 3% multiracial, 0% Pacific Islander, 58% white,

7% international; 24% from in state; 71% live on campus; 0% of students in fraternities, 0% in sororities
Most popular majors: 21% Fine/Studio Arts, General, 10% Mechanical Engineering, 10% Psychology, General, 6% Business Administration and Management, General, 5% Biology/Biological Sciences, General
Expenses: 2020-2021: $36,276; room/board: $12,924
Financial aid: (607) 871-2150; 89% of undergrads determined to have financial need; average aid package $28,774

Bard College

Annandale on Hudson NY
(845) 758-7472
U.S. News ranking: Nat. Lib. Arts, No. 54
Website: www.bard.edu
Admissions email: admissions@bard.edu
Private; founded 1860
Freshman admissions: more selective; 2019-2020: 4,912 applied, 3,181 accepted. Neither SAT nor ACT required. SAT 25/75 percentile: 1244-1413. High school rank: 40% in top tenth, 68% in top quarter, 94% in top half
Early decision deadline: 11/1, notification date: 1/1
Early action deadline: 11/1, notification date: 1/1
Application deadline (fall): 1/1
Undergraduate student body: 1,899 full time, 55 part time; 40% male, 60% female; 0% American Indian, 4% Asian, 6% Black, 12% Hispanic, 5% multiracial, 0% Pacific Islander, 55% white, 12% international
Most popular majors: 35% Social Sciences, 30% Visual and Performing Arts, 17% English Language and Literature/Letters, 17% Multi/Interdisciplinary Studies
Expenses: 2020-2021: $56,036; room/board: $16,272
Financial aid: (845) 758-7526; 72% of undergrads determined to have financial need; average aid package $51,774

Barnard College

New York NY
(212) 854-2014
U.S. News ranking: Nat. Lib. Arts, No. 22
Website: www.barnard.edu
Admissions email: admissions@barnard.edu
Private; founded 1889
Freshman admissions: most selective; 2019-2020: 9,320 applied, 1,027 accepted. Either SAT or ACT required. SAT 25/75 percentile: 1340-1520. High school rank: 84% in top tenth, 99% in top quarter, 100% in top half
Early decision deadline: 11/1, notification date: 12/15
Early action deadline: N/A, notification date: N/A
Application deadline (fall): 1/1
Undergraduate student body: 2,584 full time, 47 part time; 0% male, 100% female; 0% American

Indian, 15% Asian, 5% Black, 11% Hispanic, 6% multiracial, 0% Pacific Islander, 50% white, 11% international; 71% from in state; 91% live on campus; N/A of students in fraternities, N/A in sororities
Most popular majors: 28% Social Sciences, 13% Biological and Biomedical Sciences, 9% English Language and Literature/Letters, 9% Visual and Performing Arts, 8% Psychology
Expenses: 2020-2021: $57,668; room/board: N/A
Financial aid: (212) 854-2154; 38% of undergrads determined to have financial need; average aid package $50,557

Berkeley College

New York NY
(800) 446-5400
U.S. News ranking: Business, unranked
Website: www.berkeleycollege.edu
Admissions email: admissions@berkeleycollege.edu
For-profit; founded 1931
Freshman admissions: least selective; 2019-2020: 1,047 applied, 998 accepted. Neither SAT nor ACT required. SAT 25/75 percentile: N/A. High school rank: N/A
Early decision deadline: N/A, notification date: N/A
Early action deadline: N/A, notification date: N/A
Application deadline (fall): 9/1
Undergraduate student body: 2,221 full time, 733 part time; 35% male, 65% female; 0% American Indian, 2% Asian, 21% Black, 23% Hispanic, 0% multiracial, 0% Pacific Islander, 5% white, 9% international; 87% from in state; 4% live on campus; N/A of students in fraternities, N/A in sororities
Most popular majors: 25% Business Administration and Management, General, 16% Criminal Justice/Law Enforcement Administration, 14% Health/Health Care Administration/Management, 11% Fashion Merchandising, 9% Marketing/Marketing Management, General
Expenses: 2020-2021: $27,000; room/board: $9,400
Financial aid: (212) 986-4343

Binghamton University–SUNY

Binghamton NY
(607) 777-2171
U.S. News ranking: Nat. U., No. 88
Website: www.binghamton.edu
Admissions email: admit@binghamton.edu
Public; founded 1946
Freshman admissions: more selective; 2019-2020: 37,516 applied, 15,206 accepted. Either SAT or ACT required. SAT 25/75 percentile: 1280-1440. High school rank: 55% in top tenth, 89% in top quarter, 98% in top half
Early decision deadline: N/A, notification date: N/A
Early action deadline: 11/1, notification date: 1/15
Application deadline (fall): rolling

Undergraduate student body: 13,845 full time, 320 part time; 50% male, 50% female; 0% American Indian, 15% Asian, 5% Black, 12% Hispanic, 3% multiracial, 0% Pacific Islander, 58% white, 6% international; 88% from in state; 50% live on campus; 16% of students in fraternities, 16% in sororities
Most popular majors: 8% Psychology, General, 7% Neuroscience, 6% Accounting, 6% Biology/Biological Sciences, General, 6% Economics, General
Expenses: 2020-2021: $10,494 in state, $27,884 out of state; room/board: $16,549
Financial aid: (607) 777-6358; 51% of undergrads determined to have financial need; average aid package $14,458

Boricua College

New York NY
(212) 694-1000
U.S. News ranking: Reg. Coll. (N), second tier
Website: www.boricuacollege.edu/
Admissions email: isanchez@boricuacollege.edu
Private; founded 1973
Freshman admissions: least selective; 2019-2020: N/A applied, N/A accepted. Neither SAT nor ACT required. SAT 25/75 percentile: N/A. High school rank: N/A
Early decision deadline: N/A, notification date: N/A
Early action deadline: N/A, notification date: N/A
Application deadline (fall): rolling
Undergraduate student body: 630 full time, 0 part time; 22% male, 78% female; N/A American Indian, N/A Asian, N/A Black, N/A Hispanic, N/A multiracial, N/A Pacific Islander, N/A white, N/A international
Most popular majors: Information not available
Expenses: 2019-2020: $11,025; room/board: N/A
Financial aid: N/A

Canisius College

Buffalo NY
(800) 843-1517
U.S. News ranking: Reg. U. (N), No. 19
Website: www.canisius.edu
Admissions email: admissions@canisius.edu
Private; founded 1870
Affiliation: Roman Catholic
Freshman admissions: selective; 2019-2020: 3,422 applied, 2,830 accepted. Either SAT or ACT required. SAT 25/75 percentile: 1030-1270. High school rank: 18% in top tenth, 45% in top quarter, 78% in top half
Early decision deadline: N/A, notification date: N/A
Early action deadline: 11/1, notification date: 12/15
Application deadline (fall): rolling
Undergraduate student body: 2,112 full time, 101 part time; 52% male, 48% female; 0% American Indian, 3% Asian, 9% Black, 7% Hispanic, 2% multiracial, 0% Pacific Islander, 71% white,

3% international; 85% from in state; 35% live on campus; 1% of students in fraternities, 1% in sororities
Most popular majors: 25% Business, Management, Marketing, and Related Support Services, 13% Biological and Biomedical Sciences, 12% Communication, Journalism, and Related Programs, 11% Social Sciences, 10% Psychology
Expenses: 2020-2021: $30,230; room/board: $11,758
Financial aid: (716) 888-2300; 70% of undergrads determined to have financial need; average aid package $24,265

Cazenovia College
Cazenovia NY
(800) 654-3210
U.S. News ranking: Reg. Coll. (N), No. 12
Website: www.cazenovia.edu
Admissions email: admission@cazenovia.edu
Private; founded 1824
Freshman admissions: less selective; 2019-2020: 2,050 applied, 1,921 accepted. Neither SAT nor ACT required. SAT 25/75 percentile: 989-1239. High school rank: 2% in top tenth, 10% in top quarter, 42% in top half
Early decision deadline: N/A, notification date: N/A
Early action deadline: N/A, notification date: N/A
Application deadline (fall): rolling
Undergraduate student body: 694 full time, 162 part time; 26% male, 74% female; 1% American Indian, 1% Asian, 11% Black, 6% Hispanic, 6% multiracial, 0% Pacific Islander, 69% white, 0% international
Most popular majors: 28% Business, Management, Marketing, and Related Support Services, 20% Visual and Performing Arts, 19% Public Administration and Social Service Professions, 10% Homeland Security, Law Enforcement, Firefighting and Related Protective Services, 7% Psychology
Expenses: 2020-2021: $36,668; room/board: $14,734
Financial aid: (315) 655-7000; 80% of undergrads determined to have financial need; average aid package $31,109

Clarkson University
Potsdam NY
(800) 527-6577
U.S. News ranking: Nat. U., No. 124
Website: www.clarkson.edu/
Admissions email: admissions@clarkson.edu
Private; founded 1896
Freshman admissions: more selective; 2019-2020: 6,673 applied, 4,978 accepted. Neither SAT nor ACT required. SAT 25/75 percentile: 1160-1350. High school rank: 37% in top tenth, 69% in top quarter, 94% in top half
Early decision deadline: 12/1, notification date: 1/1
Early action deadline: N/A, notification date: N/A

Application deadline (fall): 1/15
Undergraduate student body: 3,012 full time, 69 part time; 69% male, 31% female; 0% American Indian, 4% Asian, 3% Black, 5% Hispanic, 4% multiracial, 0% Pacific Islander, 79% white, 3% international; 69% from in state; 82% live on campus; 14% of students in fraternities, 11% in sororities
Most popular majors: 54% Engineering, General, 25% Business Administration and Management, General, 6% Biology/Biological Sciences, General, 4% Computer Science, 2% Psychology, General
Expenses: 2020-2021: $52,724; room/board: $17,118
Financial aid: (315) 268-6413; 81% of undergrads determined to have financial need; average aid package $46,636

Colgate University
Hamilton NY
(315) 228-7401
U.S. News ranking: Nat. Lib. Arts, No. 20
Website: www.colgate.edu
Admissions email: admission@colgate.edu
Private; founded 1819
Freshman admissions: most selective; 2019-2020: 9,951 applied, 2,247 accepted. Either SAT or ACT required. SAT 25/75 percentile: 1330-1500. High school rank: 69% in top tenth, 92% in top quarter, 100% in top half
Early decision deadline: 11/15, notification date: 12/15
Early action deadline: N/A, notification date: N/A
Application deadline (fall): 1/15
Undergraduate student body: 2,968 full time, 12 part time; 45% male, 55% female; 0% American Indian, 5% Asian, 4% Black, 9% Hispanic, 4% multiracial, 0% Pacific Islander, 65% white, 9% international; 23% from in state; 92% live on campus; 21% of students in fraternities, 31% in sororities
Most popular majors: 11% Political Science and Government, General, 7% Economics, General, 6% Econometrics and Quantitative Economics, 5% Computer Science, 5% Research and Experimental Psychology, Other
Expenses: 2020-2021: $60,015; room/board: $15,035
Financial aid: (315) 228-7431; 33% of undergrads determined to have financial need; average aid package $57,355

College of Mount St. Vincent
Bronx NY
(718) 405-3267
U.S. News ranking: Reg. U. (N), No. 113
Website: www.mountsaintvincent.edu
Admissions email: admissions. office@mountsaintvincent.edu
Private; founded 1847
Affiliation: Roman Catholic
Freshman admissions: less selective; 2019-2020: 2,696

applied, 2,484 accepted. Either SAT or ACT required. SAT 25/75 percentile: 910-1110. High school rank: N/A
Early decision deadline: N/A, notification date: N/A
Early action deadline: 11/15, notification date: 12/15
Application deadline (fall): rolling
Undergraduate student body: 1,788 full time, 62 part time; 28% male, 72% female; 0% American Indian, 7% Asian, 18% Black, 43% Hispanic, 4% multiracial, 0% Pacific Islander, 22% white, 1% international; 88% from in state; 46% live on campus; 0% of students in fraternities, 0% in sororities
Most popular majors: 37% Health Professions and Related Programs, 18% Business, Management, Marketing, and Related Support Services, 14% Psychology, 8% Biological and Biomedical Sciences, 8% Social Sciences
Expenses: 2020-2021: $40,980; room/board: $11,000
Financial aid: (718) 405-3289

College of Saint Rose
Albany NY
(518) 454-5150
U.S. News ranking: Reg. U. (N), No. 96
Website: www.strose.edu
Admissions email: admit@strose.edu
Private; founded 1920
Freshman admissions: less selective; 2019-2020: 6,576 applied, 5,743 accepted. Neither SAT nor ACT required. SAT 25/75 percentile: 990-1210. High school rank: 15% in top tenth, 37% in top quarter, 72% in top half
Early decision deadline: N/A, notification date: N/A
Early action deadline: 12/1, notification date: 12/15
Application deadline (fall): 5/1
Undergraduate student body: 2,363 full time, 70 part time; 34% male, 66% female; 0% American Indian, 3% Asian, 18% Black, 6% Hispanic, 12% multiracial, 0% Pacific Islander, 54% white, 3% international; N/A from in state; 52% live on campus; N/A of students in fraternities, N/A in sororities
Most popular majors: 20% Education, 18% Business, Management, Marketing, and Related Support Services, 10% Homeland Security, Law Enforcement, Firefighting and Related Protective Services, 10% Visual and Performing Arts, 9% Psychology
Expenses: 2020-2021: $34,354; room/board: $13,158
Financial aid: (518) 337-4915; 84% of undergrads determined to have financial need; average aid package $24,919

The College of Westchester[1]
White Plains NY
(914) 331-0853
U.S. News ranking: Reg. Coll. (N), second tier
Admissions email: N/A
For-profit

Application deadline (fall): N/A
Undergraduate student body: N/A full time, N/A part time
Expenses: 2019-2020: $22,410; room/board: N/A
Financial aid: N/A

Columbia University
New York NY
(212) 854-2522
U.S. News ranking: Nat. U., No. 3
Website: www.columbia.edu
Admissions email: ugrad-ask@columbia.edu
Private; founded 1754
Freshman admissions: most selective; 2019-2020: 42,569 applied, 2,245 accepted. Either SAT or ACT required. SAT 25/75 percentile: 1450-1570. High school rank: 96% in top tenth, 99% in top quarter, 100% in top half
Early decision deadline: 11/1, notification date: 12/15
Early action deadline: N/A, notification date: N/A
Application deadline (fall): 1/1
Undergraduate student body: 6,245 full time, 0 part time; 50% male, 50% female; 1% American Indian, 21% Asian, 9% Black, 13% Hispanic, 3% multiracial, 0% Pacific Islander, 33% white, 17% international; 21% from in state; 92% live on campus; 20% of students in fraternities, 14% in sororities
Most popular majors: 21% Social Sciences, 15% Engineering, 11% Computer and Information Sciences and Support Services, 6% Biological and Biomedical Sciences, 5% Visual and Performing Arts
Expenses: 2020-2021: $64,380; room/board: $14,970
Financial aid: (212) 854-3711; 50% of undergrads determined to have financial need; average aid package $63,945

Concordia College–New York[1]
Bronxville NY
(800) 937-2655
U.S. News ranking: Reg. U. (N), second tier
Website: www.concordia-ny.edu
Admissions email: admission@concordia-ny.edu
Private; founded 1881
Affiliation: Lutheran Church–Missouri Synod
Application deadline (fall): 8/15
Undergraduate student body: N/A full time, N/A part time
Expenses: 2019-2020: $34,600; room/board: $13,470
Financial aid: (914) 337-9300

Cooper Union for the Advancement of Science and Art
New York NY
(212) 353-4120
U.S. News ranking: Reg. Coll. (N), No. 2
Website: cooper.edu
Admissions email: admissions@cooper.edu
Private; founded 1859

Freshman admissions: more selective; 2019-2020: 2,326 applied, 369 accepted. Neither SAT nor ACT required. SAT 25/75 percentile: 1305-1530. High school rank: N/A
Early decision deadline: 12/1, notification date: 2/1
Early action deadline: N/A, notification date: N/A
Application deadline (fall): 1/5
Undergraduate student body: 854 full time, 3 part time; 58% male, 42% female; 0% American Indian, 24% Asian, 5% Black, 12% Hispanic, 4% multiracial, 0% Pacific Islander, 32% white, 16% international; 47% from in state; 20% live on campus; 4% of students in fraternities, 0% in sororities
Most popular majors: 26% Fine/Studio Arts, General, 22% Electrical and Electronics Engineering, 18% Mechanical Engineering, 11% Civil Engineering, General, 9% Chemical Engineering
Expenses: 2020-2021: $46,820; room/board: $17,410
Financial aid: (212) 353-4113; 57% of undergrads determined to have financial need; average aid package $46,025

Cornell University
Ithaca NY
(607) 255-5241
U.S. News ranking: Nat. U., No. 18
Website: www.cornell.edu
Admissions email: admissions@cornell.edu
Private; founded 1865
Freshman admissions: most selective; 2019-2020: 49,114 applied, 5,330 accepted. Either SAT or ACT required. SAT 25/75 percentile: 1400-1560. High school rank: 83% in top tenth, 96% in top quarter, 99% in top half
Early decision deadline: 11/1, notification date: 12/15
Early action deadline: N/A, notification date: N/A
Application deadline (fall): 1/2
Undergraduate student body: 15,043 full time, 0 part time; 46% male, 54% female; 0% American Indian, 20% Asian, 7% Black, 14% Hispanic, 5% multiracial, 0% Pacific Islander, 36% white, 10% international; 36% from in state; 52% live on campus; 27% of students in fraternities, 24% in sororities
Most popular majors: 15% Business, Management, Marketing, and Related Support Services, 15% Engineering, 14% Biological and Biomedical Sciences, 12% Agriculture, Agriculture Operations, and Related Sciences, 12% Computer and Information Sciences and Support Services
Expenses: 2020-2021: $59,316; room/board: $15,846
Financial aid: (607) 255-5145; 47% of undergrads determined to have financial need; average aid package $50,492

CUNY–Baruch College
New York NY
(646) 312-1400
U.S. News ranking: Reg. U. (N),
No. 16
Website: www.baruch.cuny.edu
Admissions email:
admissions@baruch.cuny.edu
Public; founded 1919
Freshman admissions: more
selective; 2019-2020: 20,303
applied, 8,811 accepted. Either
SAT or ACT required. SAT 25/75
percentile: 1130-1330. High
school rank: 41% in top tenth,
74% in top quarter, 92% in
top half
Early decision deadline: N/A,
notification date: N/A
Early action deadline: N/A,
notification date: N/A
Application deadline (fall): 2/1
Undergraduate student body:
12,091 full time, 3,391 part
time; 53% male, 47% female;
0% American Indian, 34% Asian,
9% Black, 26% Hispanic, 2%
multiracial, 0% Pacific Islander,
20% white, 10% international;
97% from in state; 2% live
on campus; 0% of students in
fraternities, 0% in sororities
Most popular majors: 77%
Business, Management,
Marketing, and Related Support
Services, 7% Computer and
Information Sciences and Support
Services, 4% Social Sciences, 3%
Communication, Journalism, and
Related Programs, 3% Psychology
Expenses: 2020-2021: $8,071 in
state, $19,971 out of state; room/
board: $15,795
Financial aid: (646) 312-1399;
66% of undergrads determined to
have financial need; average aid
package $10,044

CUNY–Brooklyn College
Brooklyn NY
(718) 951-5001
U.S. News ranking: Reg. U. (N),
No. 62
Website: www.brooklyn.cuny.edu
Admissions email:
adminqry@brooklyn.cuny.edu
Public; founded 1930
Freshman admissions: selective;
2019-2020: 26,973 applied,
12,136 accepted. Either SAT
or ACT required. SAT 25/75
percentile: 1040-1220. High
school rank: N/A
Early decision deadline: N/A,
notification date: N/A
Early action deadline: N/A,
notification date: N/A
Application deadline (fall): N/A
Undergraduate student body:
11,189 full time, 3,781 part
time; 43% male, 57% female;
0% American Indian, 21% Asian,
20% Black, 25% Hispanic, 2%
multiracial, 0% Pacific Islander,
28% white, 3% international;
98% from in state; 0% live
on campus; 3% of students in
fraternities, 3% in sororities
Most popular majors: 18%
Business Administration and
Management, General, 17%
Psychology, General, 9%
Accounting, 5% Computer and
Information Sciences, General,
3% Finance, General

Expenses: 2020-2021: $7,440 in
state, $19,110 out of state; room/
board: N/A
Financial aid: (718) 951-5051;
80% of undergrads determined to
have financial need; average aid
package $9,627

CUNY–City College[1]
New York NY
(212) 650-7000
U.S. News ranking: Nat. U.,
No. 176
Website:
www.cuny.edu/admissions
Admissions email:
admissions@ccny.cuny.edu
Public; founded 1847
Application deadline (fall): rolling
Undergraduate student body: N/A
full time, N/A part time
Expenses: 2019-2020: $7,205 in
state, $18,475 out of state; room/
board: N/A
Financial aid: (212) 650-5824

CUNY–College of Staten Island
Staten Island NY
(718) 982-2010
U.S. News ranking: Reg. U. (N),
No. 132
Website: www.csi.cuny.edu
Admissions email:
admissions@csi.cuny.edu
Public; founded 1976
Freshman admissions: selective;
2019-2020: 14,466 applied,
13,440 accepted. Either SAT
or ACT required. SAT 25/75
percentile: 1010-1190. High
school rank: N/A
Early decision deadline: N/A,
notification date: N/A
Early action deadline: N/A,
notification date: N/A
Application deadline (fall): rolling
Undergraduate student body: 9,124
full time, 2,576 part time; 45%
male, 55% female; 0% American
Indian, 11% Asian, 14% Black,
27% Hispanic, 2% multiracial,
0% Pacific Islander, 42% white,
3% international; 99% from in
state; 1% live on campus; 0%
of students in fraternities, 0% in
sororities
Most popular majors: 20%
Business, Management,
Marketing, and Related Support
Services, 18% Psychology, 11%
Social Sciences, 8% English
Language and Literature/Letters,
7% Health Professions and
Related Programs
Expenses: 2020-2021: $7,489 in
state, $19,159 out of state; room/
board: N/A
Financial aid: (718) 982-2030;
74% of undergrads determined to
have financial need; average aid
package $8,505

CUNY–Hunter College
New York NY
(212) 772-4490
U.S. News ranking: Reg. U. (N),
No. 17
Website: www.hunter.cuny.edu
Admissions email:
admissions@hunter.cuny.edu
Public; founded 1870

Freshman admissions: more
selective; 2019-2020: 33,750
applied, 11,871 accepted. Either
SAT or ACT required. SAT 25/75
percentile: 1150-1350. High
school rank: N/A
Early decision deadline: N/A,
notification date: N/A
Early action deadline: N/A,
notification date: N/A
Application deadline (fall): 3/15
Undergraduate student body:
12,991 full time, 4,130 part
time; 36% male, 64% female;
0% American Indian, 32% Asian,
12% Black, 24% Hispanic, 0%
multiracial, 0% Pacific Islander,
28% white, 5% international
Most popular majors: 21%
Psychology, 17% Social Sciences,
10% Biological and Biomedical
Sciences, 8% Health Professions
and Related Programs, 7% English
Language and Literature/Letters
Expenses: 2020-2021: $7,380 in
state, $19,050 out of state; room/
board: $12,123
Financial aid: (212) 772-4804;
77% of undergrads determined to
have financial need; average aid
package $8,333

CUNY–John Jay College of Criminal Justice
New York NY
(212) 237-8866
U.S. News ranking: Reg. U. (N),
No. 67
Website: www.jjay.cuny.edu/
Admissions email:
admissions@jjay.cuny.edu
Public; founded 1965
Freshman admissions: selective;
2019-2020: 20,564 applied,
8,331 accepted. Either SAT
or ACT required. SAT 25/75
percentile: 960-1130. High
school rank: N/A
Early decision deadline: N/A,
notification date: N/A
Early action deadline: N/A,
notification date: N/A
Application deadline (fall): rolling
Undergraduate student body:
11,200 full time, 2,546 part
time; 41% male, 59% female;
0% American Indian, 13% Asian,
20% Black, 44% Hispanic, 0%
multiracial, 0% Pacific Islander,
19% white, 3% international; N/A
from in state; 1% live on campus;
N/A of students in fraternities, N/A
in sororities
Most popular majors: 55%
Criminal Justice/Law Enforcement
Administration, 15% Social
Sciences, 14% Forensic
Psychology, 6% Legal Professions
and Studies, 3% Public
Administration
Expenses: 2020-2021: $3,465 in
state, $18,000 out of state; room/
board: N/A
Financial aid: (212) 237-8897;
77% of undergrads determined to
have financial need; average aid
package $8,776

CUNY–Lehman College
Bronx NY
(718) 960-8700
U.S. News ranking: Reg. U. (N),
No. 56
Website: www.lehman.cuny.edu
Admissions email: undergraduate.
admissions@lehman.cuny.edu
Public; founded 1968
Freshman admissions: less
selective; 2019-2020: 19,759
applied, 7,462 accepted. Either
SAT or ACT required. SAT 25/75
percentile: 950-1110. High
school rank: N/A
Early decision deadline: N/A,
notification date: N/A
Early action deadline: N/A,
notification date: N/A
Application deadline (fall): 2/1
Undergraduate student body: 8,066
full time, 4,936 part time; 32%
male, 68% female; 0% American
Indian, 7% Asian, 31% Black,
53% Hispanic, 0% multiracial,
0% Pacific Islander, 6% white,
3% international
Most popular majors: 37% Health
Professions and Related Programs,
25% Business, Management,
Marketing, and Related Support
Services, 7% Family and
Consumer Sciences/Human
Sciences, 6% Computer and
Information Sciences and Support
Services, 4% Education
Expenses: 2020-2021: $7,210 in
state, $18,480 out of state; room/
board: N/A
Financial aid: (718) 960-8545;
83% of undergrads determined to
have financial need; average aid
package $8,076

CUNY–Medgar Evers College
Brooklyn NY
(718) 270-6024
U.S. News ranking: Reg. Coll. (N),
second tier
Website: ares.mec.cuny.edu/
admissions/admissions/
Admissions email:
mecadmissions@mec.cuny.edu
Public; founded 1970
Freshman admissions: least
selective; 2019-2020: 13,709
applied, 12,369 accepted. Neither
SAT nor ACT required. SAT 25/75
percentile: 810-1000. High
school rank: N/A
Early decision deadline: N/A,
notification date: N/A
Early action deadline: N/A,
notification date: N/A
Application deadline (fall): rolling
Undergraduate student body: 4,118
full time, 1,680 part time; 28%
male, 72% female; 0% American
Indian, 3% Asian, 67% Black,
15% Hispanic, 0% multiracial,
0% Pacific Islander, 1% white,
1% international; 100% from in
state; 0% live on campus; 0%
of students in fraternities, 0% in
sororities
Most popular majors: 25%
Liberal Arts and Sciences,
General Studies and Humanities,
23% Business, Management,
Marketing, and Related Support
Services, 23% Psychology, 13%

Public Administration and Social
Service Professions, 4% Health
Professions and Related Programs
Expenses: 2020-2021: $7,130 in
state, $18,800 out of state; room/
board: N/A
Financial aid: (718) 270-6038;
89% of undergrads determined to
have financial need; average aid
package $9,555

CUNY–New York City College of Technology
Brooklyn NY
(718) 260-5500
U.S. News ranking: Reg. Coll. (N),
No. 39
Website: www.citytech.cuny.edu
Admissions email:
admissions@citytech.cuny.edu
Public; founded 1946
Freshman admissions: less
selective; 2019-2020: 21,546
applied, 18,896 accepted. Neither
SAT nor ACT required. SAT 25/75
percentile: N/A. High school
rank: N/A
Early decision deadline: N/A,
notification date: N/A
Early action deadline: N/A,
notification date: N/A
Application deadline (fall): 2/1
Undergraduate student body:
10,572 full time, 6,464 part
time; 55% male, 45% female;
0% American Indian, 20% Asian,
28% Black, 35% Hispanic, 2%
multiracial, 0% Pacific Islander,
10% white, 4% international
Most popular majors: 20%
Engineering Technologies and
Engineering-Related Fields,
16% Computer and Information
Sciences and Support Services,
13% Business, Management,
Marketing, and Related Support
Services, 13% Health Professions
and Related Programs, 11% Visual
and Performing Arts
Expenses: 2019-2020: $7,320 in
state, $15,270 out of state; room/
board: $15,577
Financial aid: N/A

CUNY–Queens College
Queens NY
(718) 997-5600
U.S. News ranking: Reg. U. (N),
No. 50
Website: www.qc.cuny.edu/
Admissions email:
admissions@qc.cuny.edu
Public; founded 1937
Freshman admissions: selective;
2019-2020: 24,277 applied,
11,845 accepted. Either SAT
or ACT required. SAT 25/75
percentile: 1040-1200. High
school rank: N/A
Early decision deadline: N/A,
notification date: N/A
Early action deadline: N/A,
notification date: N/A
Application deadline (fall): 2/1
Undergraduate student body:
12,532 full time, 4,334 part
time; 46% male, 54% female;
0% American Indian, 29% Asian,
9% Black, 30% Hispanic, 2%
multiracial, 0% Pacific Islander,
23% white, 5% international;
99% from in state; 2% live
on campus; 1% of students in
fraternities, 1% in sororities

NEW YORK

Most popular majors: 23% Social Sciences, 18% Psychology, 16% Business, Management, Marketing, and Related Support Services, 6% Computer and Information Sciences and Support Services, 6% Education
Expenses: 2020-2021: $7,538 in state, $19,208 out of state; room/board: $14,311
Financial aid: (718) 997-5102; 71% of undergrads determined to have financial need; average aid package $6,503

CUNY–York College
Jamaica NY
(718) 262-2165
U.S. News ranking: Reg. Coll. (N), No. 38
Website: www.york.cuny.edu
Admissions email: admissions@york.cuny.edu
Public; founded 1966
Freshman admissions: less selective; 2019-2020: 14,633 applied, 10,658 accepted. Either SAT or ACT required. SAT 25/75 percentile: 880-1040. High school rank: N/A
Early decision deadline: N/A, notification date: N/A
Early action deadline: N/A, notification date: N/A
Application deadline (fall): 6/1
Undergraduate student body: 5,113 full time, 3,003 part time; 34% male, 66% female; 1% American Indian, 21% Asian, 39% Black, 27% Hispanic, 3% multiracial, 1% Pacific Islander, 5% white, 4% international; 99% from in state; 0% live on campus; 0% of students in fraternities, 0% in sororities
Most popular majors: 23% Health Professions and Related Programs, 20% Business, Management, Marketing, and Related Support Services, 16% Psychology, 8% Public Administration and Social Service Professions, 8% Social Sciences
Expenses: 2020-2021: $7,357 in state, $19,027 out of state; room/board: N/A
Financial aid: (718) 262-2230; 85% of undergrads determined to have financial need; average aid package $7,189

Daemen College
Amherst NY
(716) 839-8225
U.S. News ranking: Nat. U., second tier
Website: www.daemen.edu/
Admissions email: admissions@daemen.edu
Private; founded 1947
Freshman admissions: selective; 2019-2020: 3,239 applied, 1,994 accepted. Neither SAT nor ACT required. SAT 25/75 percentile: 1040-1240. High school rank: 22% in top tenth, 57% in top quarter, 85% in top half
Early decision deadline: 11/1, notification date: N/A
Early action deadline: N/A, notification date: N/A
Application deadline (fall): rolling
Undergraduate student body: 1,480 full time, 229 part time;

30% male, 70% female; 0% American Indian, 3% Asian, 11% Black, 7% Hispanic, 1% multiracial, 0% Pacific Islander, 75% white, 2% international; N/A from in state; 38% live on campus; N/A of students in fraternities, N/A in sororities
Most popular majors: 47% Health Professions and Related Programs, 25% Multi/Interdisciplinary Studies, 9% Business, Management, Marketing, and Related Support Services, 5% Visual and Performing Arts, 3% Psychology
Expenses: 2020-2021: $29,430; room/board: $13,400
Financial aid: (716) 839-8254; 78% of undergrads determined to have financial need; average aid package $22,064

Dominican College
Orangeburg NY
(845) 848-7901
U.S. News ranking: Reg. U. (N), second tier
Website: www.dc.edu
Admissions email: admissions@dc.edu
Private; founded 1952
Freshman admissions: less selective; 2019-2020: 2,314 applied, 1,800 accepted. Neither SAT nor ACT required. SAT 25/75 percentile: 900-1110. High school rank: N/A
Early decision deadline: N/A, notification date: N/A
Early action deadline: N/A, notification date: N/A
Application deadline (fall): rolling
Undergraduate student body: 1,268 full time, 109 part time; 34% male, 66% female; 0% American Indian, 6% Asian, 17% Black, 34% Hispanic, 3% multiracial, 1% Pacific Islander, 30% white, 2% international; 76% from in state; 48% live on campus; N/A of students in fraternities, N/A in sororities
Most popular majors: 28% Registered Nursing/Registered Nurse, 19% Social Sciences, General, 8% Occupational Therapy/Therapist, 7% Criminal Justice/Law Enforcement Administration, 5% Communication, Journalism, and Related Programs
Expenses: 2020-2021: $30,720; room/board: $13,750
Financial aid: (845) 848-7818; 82% of undergrads determined to have financial need; average aid package $23,609

D'Youville College
Buffalo NY
(716) 829-7600
U.S. News ranking: Nat. U., No. 284
Website: www.dyc.edu
Admissions email: admissions@dyc.edu
Private; founded 1908
Freshman admissions: selective; 2019-2020: 1,439 applied, 1,268 accepted. Either SAT or ACT required. SAT 25/75 percentile: 1080-1200. High school rank: N/A

Early decision deadline: N/A, notification date: N/A
Early action deadline: N/A, notification date: N/A
Application deadline (fall): rolling
Undergraduate student body: 1,179 full time, 430 part time; 25% male, 75% female; 1% American Indian, 6% Asian, 10% Black, 5% Hispanic, 2% multiracial, 0% Pacific Islander, 69% white, 2% international; 91% from in state; 17% live on campus; 0% of students in fraternities, 0% in sororities
Most popular majors: 69% Health Professions and Related Programs, 10% Biological and Biomedical Sciences, 10% Multi/Interdisciplinary Studies, 5% Business, Management, Marketing, and Related Support Services, 3% Physical Sciences
Expenses: 2020-2021: $28,886; room/board: $9,500
Financial aid: (716) 829-7500; 68% of undergrads determined to have financial need; average aid package $19,493

Elmira College[1]
Elmira NY
(800) 935-6472
U.S. News ranking: Reg. Coll. (N), No. 6
Website: www.elmira.edu
Admissions email: admissions@elmira.edu
Private; founded 1855
Application deadline (fall): rolling
Undergraduate student body: N/A full time, N/A part time
Expenses: 2020-2021: $36,228; room/board: $13,125
Financial aid: (607) 735-1728; 82% of undergrads determined to have financial need; average aid package $27,799

Farmingdale State College–SUNY
Farmingdale NY
(934) 420-2200
U.S. News ranking: Reg. Coll. (N), No. 21
Website: www.farmingdale.edu
Admissions email: admissions@farmingdale.edu
Public; founded 1912
Freshman admissions: selective; 2019-2020: 6,952 applied, 3,816 accepted. Either SAT or ACT required. SAT 25/75 percentile: 990-1150. High school rank: 7% in top tenth, 28% in top quarter, 64% in top half
Early decision deadline: N/A, notification date: N/A
Early action deadline: N/A, notification date: N/A
Application deadline (fall): 5/1
Undergraduate student body: 7,785 full time, 2,154 part time; 58% male, 42% female; 0% American Indian, 9% Asian, 9% Black, 23% Hispanic, 3% multiracial, 0% Pacific Islander, 53% white, 2% international; 100% from in state; 6% live on campus; 3% of students in fraternities, 5% in sororities
Most popular majors: 22% Business, Management, Marketing, and Related Support Services, 14% Multi/

Interdisciplinary Studies, 12% Engineering Technologies and Engineering-Related Fields, 11% Homeland Security, Law Enforcement, Firefighting and Related Protective Services, 9% Health Professions and Related Programs
Expenses: 2019-2020: $8,538 in state, $18,448 out of state; room/board: $13,318
Financial aid: (934) 420-2578; 58% of undergrads determined to have financial need; average aid package $8,170

Fashion Institute of Technology
New York NY
(212) 217-3760
U.S. News ranking: Reg. U. (N), unranked
Website: www.fitnyc.edu
Admissions email: FITinfo@fitnyc.edu
Public; founded 1944
Freshman admissions: less selective; 2019-2020: 4,444 applied, 2,395 accepted. Neither SAT nor ACT required. SAT 25/75 percentile: N/A. High school rank: N/A
Early decision deadline: N/A, notification date: N/A
Early action deadline: N/A, notification date: N/A
Application deadline (fall): 1/1
Undergraduate student body: 7,340 full time, 1,168 part time; 18% male, 82% female; 0% American Indian, 11% Asian, 9% Black, 22% Hispanic, 4% multiracial, 0% Pacific Islander, 42% white, 12% international; N/A from in state; 20% live on campus; 0% of students in fraternities, 0% in sororities
Most popular majors: 41% Business, Management, Marketing, and Related Support Services, 37% Visual and Performing Arts, 17% Communication, Journalism, and Related Programs, 4% Family and Consumer Sciences/Human Sciences, 1% Communications Technologies/Technicians and Support Services
Expenses: 2019-2020: $6,110 in state, $16,490 out of state; room/board: $14,556
Financial aid: (212) 217-3560

Five Towns College
Dix Hills NY
(631) 424-7000
U.S. News ranking: Reg. Coll. (N), second tier
Website: www.ftc.edu
Admissions email: admissions@ftc.edu
For-profit; founded 1972
Freshman admissions: less selective; 2019-2020: 765 applied, 257 accepted. Neither SAT nor ACT required. SAT 25/75 percentile: N/A. High school rank: N/A
Early decision deadline: N/A, notification date: N/A
Early action deadline: 12/31, notification date: 1/31
Application deadline (fall): rolling
Undergraduate student body: 590 full time, 27 part time; 69%

male, 31% female; 0% American Indian, 3% Asian, 22% Black, 14% Hispanic, 7% multiracial, 0% Pacific Islander, 50% white, 3% international; 93% from in state; 30% live on campus; N/A of students in fraternities, N/A in sororities
Most popular majors: 51% Business, Management, Marketing, and Related Support Services, 38% Visual and Performing Arts, 7% Education, 4% Communication, Journalism, and Related Programs
Expenses: 2020-2021: $25,070; room/board: $10,450
Financial aid: (631) 656-2164; 81% of undergrads determined to have financial need; average aid package $14,288

Fordham University
New York NY
(718) 817-4000
U.S. News ranking: Nat. U., No. 66
Website: www.fordham.edu
Admissions email: enroll@fordham.edu
Private; founded 1841
Affiliation: Roman Catholic
Freshman admissions: more selective; 2019-2020: 47,930 applied, 21,988 accepted. Either SAT or ACT required. SAT 25/75 percentile: 1240-1450. High school rank: 46% in top tenth, 80% in top quarter, 97% in top half
Early decision deadline: 11/1, notification date: 12/20
Early action deadline: 11/1, notification date: 12/20
Application deadline (fall): 1/1
Undergraduate student body: 9,229 full time, 538 part time; 43% male, 57% female; 0% American Indian, 11% Asian, 4% Black, 16% Hispanic, 4% multiracial, 0% Pacific Islander, 56% white, 8% international; 42% from in state; 49% live on campus; N/A of students in fraternities, N/A in sororities
Most popular majors: 8% Business Administration and Management, General, 7% Economics, General, 7% Finance, General, 6% Psychology, General, 5% Political Science and Government, General
Expenses: 2020-2021: $55,788; room/board: $19,066
Financial aid: (718) 817-3800; 59% of undergrads determined to have financial need; average aid package $38,157

Hamilton College
Clinton NY
(800) 843-2655
U.S. News ranking: Nat. Lib. Arts, No. 9
Website: www.hamilton.edu
Admissions email: admission@hamilton.edu
Private; founded 1812
Freshman admissions: most selective; 2019-2020: 8,339 applied, 1,367 accepted. Either SAT or ACT required. SAT 25/75 percentile: 1370-1520. High school rank: 83% in top tenth, 96% in top quarter, 100% in top half

Early decision deadline: 11/15, notification date: 12/15
Early action deadline: N/A, notification date: N/A
Application deadline (fall): 1/1
Undergraduate student body: 1,915 full time, 9 part time; 48% male, 52% female; 0% American Indian, 7% Asian, 4% Black, 9% Hispanic, 5% multiracial, 0% Pacific Islander, 64% white, 7% international; N/A from in state; 100% live on campus; 21% of students in fraternities, 15% in sororities
Most popular majors: 13% Economics, General, 9% Mathematics, General, 7% Political Science and Government, General, 5% General Literature, 4% Hispanic and Latin American Languages, Literatures, and Linguistics, General
Expenses: 2020-2021: $58,510; room/board: $14,860
Financial aid: (800) 859-4413; 52% of undergrads determined to have financial need; average aid package $51,770

Hartwick College
Oneonta NY
(607) 431-4150
U.S. News ranking: Nat. Lib. Arts, No. 149
Website: www.hartwick.edu
Admissions email: admissions@hartwick.edu
Private; founded 1797
Freshman admissions: selective; 2019-2020: 4,449 applied, 3,566 accepted. Neither SAT nor ACT required. SAT 25/75 percentile: 1030-1210. High school rank: N/A
Early decision deadline: 11/1, notification date: 11/15
Early action deadline: N/A, notification date: N/A
Application deadline (fall): rolling
Undergraduate student body: 1,169 full time, 24 part time; 40% male, 60% female; 1% American Indian, 3% Asian, 10% Black, 7% Hispanic, 0% multiracial, 0% Pacific Islander, 62% white, 2% international; 71% from in state; N/A live on campus; N/A of students in fraternities, N/A in sororities
Most popular majors: 20% Business Administration and Management, General, 14% Registered Nursing/Registered Nurse, 9% Biology/Biological Sciences, General, 5% Sociology, 4% Public Health, General
Expenses: 2020-2021: $48,364; room/board: $13,219
Financial aid: (607) 431-4130; 82% of undergrads determined to have financial need; average aid package $41,447

Hilbert College[1]
Hamburg NY
(716) 649-7900
U.S. News ranking: Reg. Coll. (N), No. 40
Website: www.hilbert.edu/
Admissions email: admissions@hilbert.edu
Private
Application deadline (fall): N/A

Undergraduate student body: N/A full time, N/A part time
Expenses: 2019-2020: $23,450; room/board: $9,850
Financial aid: N/A

Hobart and William Smith Colleges
Geneva NY
(315) 781-3622
U.S. News ranking: Nat. Lib. Arts, No. 72
Website: www.hws.edu
Admissions email: admissions@hws.edu
Private; founded 1822
Freshman admissions: more selective; 2019-2020: 3,439 applied, 2,267 accepted. Neither SAT nor ACT required. SAT 25/75 percentile: 1180-1360. High school rank: 33% in top tenth, 63% in top quarter, 90% in top half
Early decision deadline: 11/15, notification date: 12/15
Early action deadline: N/A, notification date: N/A
Application deadline (fall): 2/1
Undergraduate student body: 2,045 full time, 16 part time; 48% male, 52% female; 0% American Indian, 3% Asian, 6% Black, 6% Hispanic, 2% multiracial, 0% Pacific Islander, 73% white, 5% international; 41% from in state; 90% live on campus; 15% of students in fraternities, 3% in sororities
Most popular majors: 12% Economics, General, 11% Mass Communication/Media Studies, 9% Biology/Biological Sciences, General, 7% Political Science and Government, General, 6% Psychology, General
Expenses: 2020-2021: $58,630; room/board: $15,090
Financial aid: (315) 781-3315; 65% of undergrads determined to have financial need; average aid package $43,044

Hofstra University
Hempstead NY
(516) 463-6700
U.S. News ranking: Nat. U., No. 160
Website: www.hofstra.edu
Admissions email: admission@hofstra.edu
Private; founded 1935
Freshman admissions: more selective; 2019-2020: 24,425 applied, 16,728 accepted. Neither SAT nor ACT required. SAT 25/75 percentile: 1160-1340. High school rank: 32% in top tenth, 60% in top quarter, 91% in top half
Early decision deadline: N/A, notification date: N/A
Early action deadline: 11/15, notification date: 12/15
Application deadline (fall): rolling
Undergraduate student body: 6,156 full time, 342 part time; 45% male, 55% female; 0% American Indian, 12% Asian, 9% Black, 13% Hispanic, 3% multiracial, 0% Pacific Islander, 55% white, 5% international; 63% from in state; 43% live on campus; 8% of students in fraternities, 12% in sororities

Most popular majors: 6% Finance, General, 6% Psychology, General, 5% Accounting, 4% Marketing/Marketing Management, General, 4% Radio, Television, and Digital Communication, Other
Expenses: 2019-2020: $47,510; room/board: $16,428
Financial aid: (516) 463-8000; 64% of undergrads determined to have financial need; average aid package $34,000

Houghton College
Houghton NY
(800) 777-2556
U.S. News ranking: Nat. Lib. Arts, No. 127
Website: www.houghton.edu
Admissions email: admission@houghton.edu
Private; founded 1883
Affiliation: Wesleyan
Freshman admissions: selective; 2019-2020: 991 applied, 922 accepted. Neither SAT nor ACT required. SAT 25/75 percentile: 1060-1320. High school rank: 24% in top tenth, 50% in top quarter, 82% in top half
Early decision deadline: N/A, notification date: N/A
Early action deadline: N/A, notification date: N/A
Application deadline (fall): rolling
Undergraduate student body: 883 full time, 63 part time; 39% male, 61% female; 1% American Indian, 2% Asian, 5% Black, 1% Hispanic, 5% multiracial, 0% Pacific Islander, 74% white, 4% international; 480% from in state; 78% live on campus; 0% of students in fraternities, 0% in sororities
Most popular majors: 10% Biology/Biological Sciences, General, 10% Business Administration and Management, General, 8% Elementary Education and Teaching, 8% Psychology, General, 6% Regional Studies (US, Canadian, Foreign)
Expenses: 2020-2021: $34,466; room/board: $9,856
Financial aid: (585) 567-9328; 82% of undergrads determined to have financial need; average aid package $21,090

Iona College
New Rochelle NY
(914) 633-2502
U.S. News ranking: Reg. U. (N), No. 50
Website: www.iona.edu
Admissions email: admissions@iona.edu
Private; founded 1940
Affiliation: Roman Catholic
Freshman admissions: selective; 2019-2020: 9,965 applied, 8,382 accepted. Neither SAT nor ACT required. SAT 25/75 percentile: 990-1170. High school rank: 11% in top tenth, 35% in top quarter, 68% in top half
Early decision deadline: N/A, notification date: N/A
Early action deadline: 12/1, notification date: 1/15
Application deadline (fall): 2/15
Undergraduate student body: 2,709 full time, 272 part time; 51% male, 49% female; 1% American

Indian, 3% Asian, 12% Black, 25% Hispanic, 2% multiracial, 0% Pacific Islander, 51% white, 3% international; 77% from in state; 45% live on campus; 8% of students in fraternities, 18% in sororities
Most popular majors: 40% Business, Management, Marketing, and Related Support Services, 11% Communication, Journalism, and Related Programs, 9% Psychology, 7% Health Professions and Related Programs, 7% Homeland Security, Law Enforcement, Firefighting and Related Protective Services
Expenses: 2020-2021: $41,580; room/board: $16,208
Financial aid: (914) 633-2497; 86% of undergrads determined to have financial need; average aid package $27,937

Ithaca College
Ithaca NY
(800) 429-4274
U.S. News ranking: Reg. U. (N), No. 9
Website: www.ithaca.edu
Admissions email: admission@ithaca.edu
Private; founded 1892
Freshman admissions: selective; 2019-2020: 14,192 applied, 10,326 accepted. Neither SAT nor ACT required. SAT 25/75 percentile: 1160-1350. High school rank: 23% in top tenth, 57% in top quarter, 88% in top half
Early decision deadline: 11/1, notification date: 12/15
Early action deadline: 12/1, notification date: 2/1
Application deadline (fall): 2/1
Undergraduate student body: 5,739 full time, 113 part time; 43% male, 57% female; 0% American Indian, 4% Asian, 6% Black, 9% Hispanic, 3% multiracial, 0% Pacific Islander, 73% white, 2% international; 45% from in state; 73% live on campus; 0% of students in fraternities, 1% in sororities
Most popular majors: 10% Business Administration and Management, General, 10% Radio and Television, 7% Public Relations, Advertising, and Applied Communication, 6% Physical Therapy/Therapist, 5% Cinematography and Film/Video Production
Expenses: 2020-2021: $46,610; room/board: $15,844
Financial aid: (607) 274-3131; 69% of undergrads determined to have financial need; average aid package $40,304

Jamestown Business College[1]
Jamestown NY
(716) 664-5100
U.S. News ranking: Business, unranked
Admissions email: N/A
For-profit
Application deadline (fall): N/A
Undergraduate student body: N/A full time, N/A part time

Expenses: 2019-2020: $12,645; room/board: N/A
Financial aid: N/A

Juilliard School[1]
New York NY
(212) 799-5000
U.S. News ranking: Arts, unranked
Website: www.juilliard.edu
Admissions email: admissions@juilliard.edu
Private; founded 1905
Application deadline (fall): 12/1
Undergraduate student body: N/A full time, N/A part time
Expenses: 2020-2021: $49,510; room/board: $18,870
Financial aid: (212) 799-5000; 73% of undergrads determined to have financial need; average aid package $38,146

Keuka College
Keuka Park NY
(315) 279-5254
U.S. News ranking: Reg. U. (N), No. 121
Website: www.keuka.edu
Admissions email: admissions@keuka.edu
Private; founded 1890
Affiliation: American Baptist
Freshman admissions: selective; 2019-2020: 2,212 applied, 1,899 accepted. Neither SAT nor ACT required. SAT 25/75 percentile: 970-1178. High school rank: N/A
Early decision deadline: N/A, notification date: N/A
Early action deadline: N/A, notification date: N/A
Application deadline (fall): rolling
Undergraduate student body: 1,285 full time, 244 part time; 27% male, 73% female; 0% American Indian, 1% Asian, 6% Black, 6% Hispanic, 3% multiracial, 0% Pacific Islander, 77% white, 1% international; N/A from in state; 59% live on campus; N/A of students in fraternities, N/A in sororities
Most popular majors: 30% Public Administration and Social Service Professions, 21% Business, Management, Marketing, and Related Support Services, 21% Health Professions and Related Programs, 6% Homeland Security, Law Enforcement, Firefighting and Related Protective Services, 5% Foreign Languages, Literatures, and Linguistics
Expenses: 2020-2021: $34,032; room/board: $12,144
Financial aid: (315) 279-5232; 90% of undergrads determined to have financial need; average aid package $33,134

The King's College
New York NY
(212) 659-3610
U.S. News ranking: Nat. Lib. Arts, second tier
Website: www.tkc.edu/
Admissions email: admissions@tkc.edu
Private; founded 1938
Affiliation: Undenominational
Freshman admissions: selective; 2019-2020: 2,798 applied, 1,166 accepted. Either SAT

or ACT required. SAT 25/75 percentile: 1100-1310. High school rank: N/A
Early decision deadline: N/A, notification date: N/A
Early action deadline: 11/15, notification date: 12/15
Application deadline (fall): rolling
Undergraduate student body: 523 full time, 21 part time; 34% male, 66% female; 2% American Indian, 4% Asian, 6% Black, 11% Hispanic, 0% multiracial, 0% Pacific Islander, 68% white, 3% international
Most popular majors: 68% Liberal Arts and Sciences, General Studies and Humanities, 25% Business, Management, Marketing, and Related Support Services, 7% Philosophy and Religious Studies
Expenses: 2020-2021: $37,690; room/board: $17,264
Financial aid: (646) 237-8902; 65% of undergrads determined to have financial need; average aid package $28,888

Le Moyne College
Syracuse NY
(315) 445-4300
U.S. News ranking: Reg. U. (N), No. 17
Website: www.lemoyne.edu
Admissions email: admission@lemoyne.edu
Private; founded 1946
Affiliation: Roman Catholic
Freshman admissions: selective; 2019-2020: 7,323 applied, 5,391 accepted. Neither SAT nor ACT required. SAT 25/75 percentile: 1073-1280. High school rank: 21% in top tenth, 53% in top quarter, 87% in top half
Early decision deadline: N/A, notification date: N/A
Early action deadline: 11/15, notification date: 12/15
Application deadline (fall): rolling
Undergraduate student body: 2,392 full time, 373 part time; 39% male, 61% female; 0% American Indian, 3% Asian, 6% Black, 7% Hispanic, 3% multiracial, 0% Pacific Islander, 76% white, 1% international; 93% from in state; 57% live on campus; 0% of students in fraternities, 0% in sororities
Most popular majors: 16% Biology/Biological Sciences, General, 13% Registered Nursing/Registered Nurse, 12% Psychology, General, 7% Marketing/Marketing Management, General, 5% Finance, General
Expenses: 2020-2021: $35,910; room/board: $14,470
Financial aid: (315) 445-4400; 80% of undergrads determined to have financial need; average aid package $28,182

LIM College
New York NY
(800) 677-1323
U.S. News ranking: Business, unranked
Website: www.limcollege.edu
Admissions email: admissions@limcollege.edu

For-profit; founded 1939
Freshman admissions: less selective; 2019-2020: 1,415 applied, 1,182 accepted. Neither SAT nor ACT required. SAT 25/75 percentile: 940-1130. High school rank: N/A
Early decision deadline: N/A, notification date: N/A
Early action deadline: 11/15, notification date: 12/15
Application deadline (fall): rolling
Undergraduate student body: 1,265 full time, 185 part time; 10% male, 90% female; 1% American Indian, 12% Asian, 20% Black, 17% Hispanic, 0% multiracial, 1% Pacific Islander, 42% white, 0% international; N/A from in state; 21% live on campus; N/A of students in fraternities, N/A in sororities
Most popular majors: 93% Business, Management, Marketing, and Related Support Services, 7% Visual and Performing Arts
Expenses: 2020-2021: $28,756; room/board: $21,346
Financial aid: (212) 310-0689; 65% of undergrads determined to have financial need; average aid package $15,547

Long Island University
Brookville NY
(516) 299-2900
U.S. News ranking: Nat. U., No. 272
Website: www.liu.edu
Admissions email: admissions@liu.edu
Private; founded 1926
Freshman admissions: selective; 2019-2020: 13,328 applied, 10,675 accepted. Either SAT or ACT required. SAT 25/75 percentile: 1080-1290. High school rank: 19% in top tenth, 47% in top quarter, 75% in top half
Early decision deadline: N/A, notification date: N/A
Early action deadline: 12/1, notification date: 12/15
Application deadline (fall): rolling
Undergraduate student body: 5,630 full time, 5,077 part time; 38% male, 62% female; 0% American Indian, 11% Asian, 14% Black, 14% Hispanic, 2% multiracial, 0% Pacific Islander, 38% white, 4% international; 88% from in state; 22% live on campus; 14% of students in fraternities, 6% in sororities
Most popular majors: 16% Registered Nursing/Registered Nurse, 8% Health Professions and Related Clinical Sciences, Other, 7% Business Administration and Management, General, 6% Psychology, General, 5% Biology/Biological Sciences, General
Expenses: 2020-2021: $39,136; room/board: $14,664
Financial aid: N/A; 78% of undergrads determined to have financial need; average aid package $26,799

Manhattan College
Riverdale NY
(718) 862-7200
U.S. News ranking: Reg. U. (N), No. 13
Website: manhattan.edu
Admissions email: admit@manhattan.edu
Private; founded 1853
Affiliation: Roman Catholic
Freshman admissions: selective; 2019-2020: 8,736 applied, 6,434 accepted. Either SAT or ACT required. SAT 25/75 percentile: 1060-1280. High school rank: 18% in top tenth, 52% in top quarter, 76% in top half
Early decision deadline: 11/15, notification date: 12/15
Early action deadline: N/A, notification date: N/A
Application deadline (fall): rolling
Undergraduate student body: 3,308 full time, 177 part time; 57% male, 43% female; 0% American Indian, 4% Asian, 5% Black, 23% Hispanic, 2% multiracial, 0% Pacific Islander, 55% white, 4% international; N/A from in state; 49% live on campus; 2% of students in fraternities, 2% in sororities
Most popular majors: 32% Engineering, 26% Business, Management, Marketing, and Related Support Services, 10% Communication, Journalism, and Related Programs, 6% Education, 5% Psychology
Expenses: 2019-2020: $44,560; room/board: $16,870
Financial aid: (718) 862-7178

Manhattan School of Music[1]
New York NY
(917) 493-4436
U.S. News ranking: Arts, unranked
Website: msmnyc.edu/
Admissions email: admission@msmnyc.edu
Private; founded 1917
Application deadline (fall): N/A
Undergraduate student body: N/A full time, N/A part time
Expenses: 2019-2020: $49,130; room/board: $16,195
Financial aid: (917) 493-4809

Manhattanville College
Purchase NY
(914) 323-5464
U.S. News ranking: Reg. U. (N), No. 81
Website: www.mville.edu
Admissions email: admissions@mville.edu
Private; founded 1841
Freshman admissions: selective; 2019-2020: 3,435 applied, 3,100 accepted. Neither SAT nor ACT required. SAT 25/75 percentile: 980-1170. High school rank: 14% in top tenth, 19% in top quarter, 75% in top half
Early decision deadline: N/A, notification date: N/A
Early action deadline: 12/1, notification date: 1/1
Application deadline (fall): rolling
Undergraduate student body: 1,474 full time, 67 part time; 42%

male, 58% female; 0% American Indian, 2% Asian, 10% Black, 29% Hispanic, 3% multiracial, 0% Pacific Islander, 48% white, 5% international; 75% from in state; 59% live on campus; 0% of students in fraternities, 0% in sororities
Most popular majors: 26% Business Administration and Management, General, 12% Speech Communication and Rhetoric, 10% Social Sciences, General, 8% Psychology, General, 8% Visual and Performing Arts, General
Expenses: 2020-2021: $40,330; room/board: $14,810
Financial aid: (914) 323-5357; 69% of undergrads determined to have financial need; average aid package $29,753

Marist College
Poughkeepsie NY
(845) 575-3226
U.S. News ranking: Reg. U. (N), No. 11
Website: www.marist.edu
Admissions email: admissions@marist.edu
Private; founded 1929
Freshman admissions: more selective; 2019-2020: 11,260 applied, 5,543 accepted. Neither SAT nor ACT required. SAT 25/75 percentile: 1150-1330. High school rank: 23% in top tenth, 57% in top quarter, 86% in top half
Early decision deadline: 11/15, notification date: 12/15
Early action deadline: 11/15, notification date: 1/15
Application deadline (fall): 2/1
Undergraduate student body: 5,199 full time, 625 part time; 42% male, 58% female; 0% American Indian, 3% Asian, 4% Black, 12% Hispanic, 3% multiracial, 0% Pacific Islander, 74% white, 3% international; 52% from in state; 64% live on campus; 3% of students in fraternities, 3% in sororities
Most popular majors: 35% Business, Management, Marketing, and Related Support Services, 16% Communication, Journalism, and Related Programs, 10% Psychology, 8% Computer and Information Sciences and Support Services, 4% Biological and Biomedical Sciences
Expenses: 2020-2021: $43,155; room/board: $18,530
Financial aid: (845) 575-3230; 57% of undergrads determined to have financial need; average aid package $25,803

Marymount Manhattan College
New York NY
(212) 517-0430
U.S. News ranking: Nat. Lib. Arts, second tier
Website: www.mmm.edu
Admissions email: admissions@mmm.edu
Private; founded 1936
Freshman admissions: selective; 2019-2020: 5,566 applied, 4,433 accepted. Either SAT or ACT required. SAT 25/75

percentile: 980-1200. High school rank: N/A
Early decision deadline: 11/1, notification date: 12/1
Early action deadline: 12/1, notification date: 12/22
Undergraduate student body: 1,660 full time, 232 part time; 21% male, 79% female; 0% American Indian, 3% Asian, 10% Black, 17% Hispanic, 5% multiracial, 0% Pacific Islander, 56% white, 3% international; 28% from in state; 34% live on campus; N/A of students in fraternities, N/A in sororities
Most popular majors: 52% Visual and Performing Arts, 15% Business, Management, Marketing, and Related Support Services, 15% Communication, Journalism, and Related Programs, 4% Multi/Interdisciplinary Studies, 3% Psychology
Expenses: 2020-2021: $37,410; room/board: $18,894
Financial aid: (212) 517-0500; 68% of undergrads determined to have financial need; average aid package $19,868

Medaille College[1]
Buffalo NY
(716) 880-2200
U.S. News ranking: Reg. U. (N), second tier
Website: www.medaille.edu
Admissions email: admissionsug@medaille.edu
Private; founded 1937
Application deadline (fall): rolling
Undergraduate student body: N/A full time, N/A part time
Expenses: 2019-2020: $30,450; room/board: $14,000
Financial aid: (716) 880-2256

Mercy College
Dobbs Ferry NY
(877) 637-2946
U.S. News ranking: Reg. U. (N), second tier
Website: www.mercy.edu
Admissions email: admissions@mercy.edu
Private; founded 1950
Freshman admissions: less selective; 2019-2020: 6,720 applied, 5,485 accepted. Neither SAT nor ACT required. SAT 25/75 percentile: 890-1080. High school rank: N/A
Early decision deadline: N/A, notification date: N/A
Early action deadline: N/A, notification date: N/A
Application deadline (fall): rolling
Undergraduate student body: 6,223 full time, 1,770 part time; 30% male, 70% female; 0% American Indian, 4% Asian, 27% Black, 40% Hispanic, 1% multiracial, 0% Pacific Islander, 17% white, 1% international; 93% from in state; 10% live on campus; N/A of students in fraternities, N/A in sororities
Most popular majors: 22% Business, Management, Marketing, and Related Support Services, 21% Health Professions and Related Programs, 19% Social Sciences, 10% Psychology, 7% Homeland Security, Law

Enforcement, Firefighting and Related Protective Services
Expenses: 2020-2021: $20,378; room/board: $13,800
Financial aid: (888) 464-6737; 91% of undergrads determined to have financial need; average aid package $14,841

Metropolitan College of New York[1]
New York NY
(212) 343-1234
U.S. News ranking: Reg. U. (N), second tier
Website: www.mcny.edu
Admissions email: admissions@mcny.edu
Private; founded 1964
Application deadline (fall): rolling
Undergraduate student body: N/A full time, N/A part time
Expenses: 2019-2020: $19,828; room/board: N/A
Financial aid: (212) 343-1234

Molloy College
Rockville Centre NY
(516) 323-4000
U.S. News ranking: Reg. U. (N), No. 26
Website: www.molloy.edu
Admissions email: admissions@molloy.edu
Private; founded 1955
Freshman admissions: selective; 2019-2020: 4,624 applied, 3,605 accepted. Either SAT or ACT required. SAT 25/75 percentile: 1020-1220. High school rank: 19% in top tenth, 56% in top quarter, 85% in top half
Early decision deadline: N/A, notification date: N/A
Early action deadline: 12/1, notification date: 12/15
Application deadline (fall): rolling
Undergraduate student body: 2,780 full time, 716 part time; 27% male, 73% female; 0% American Indian, 8% Asian, 9% Black, 19% Hispanic, 2% multiracial, 0% Pacific Islander, 60% white, 1% international; 95% from in state; 10% live on campus; N/A of students in fraternities, N/A in sororities
Most popular majors: 54% Health Professions and Related Programs, 13% Business, Management, Marketing, and Related Support Services, 8% Education, 4% Biological and Biomedical Sciences, 4% Visual and Performing Arts
Expenses: 2020-2021: $32,600; room/board: $15,560
Financial aid: (516) 323-4200; 80% of undergrads determined to have financial need; average aid package $18,062

Monroe College
Bronx NY
(800) 556-6676
U.S. News ranking: Reg. U. (N), No. 62
Website: www.monroecollege.edu
Admissions email: admissions@monroecollege.edu
For-profit; founded 1933

Freshman admissions: less selective; 2019-2020: 6,793 applied, 3,260 accepted. Neither SAT nor ACT required. SAT 25/75 percentile: 960-1100. High school rank: N/A
Early decision deadline: N/A, notification date: N/A
Early action deadline: 12/15, notification date: 1/31
Application deadline (fall): rolling
Undergraduate student body: 4,507 full time, 1,171 part time; 37% male, 63% female; 0% American Indian, 2% Asian, 42% Black, 43% Hispanic, 0% multiracial, 0% Pacific Islander, 3% white, 9% international
Most popular majors: 16% Business, Management, Marketing, and Related Support Services, 11% Health Professions and Related Programs, 9% Homeland Security, Law Enforcement, Firefighting and Related Protective Services, 5% Biological and Biomedical Sciences, 3% Public Administration and Social Service Professions
Expenses: 2020-2021: $16,536; room/board: $11,300
Financial aid: (718) 933-6700; 89% of undergrads determined to have financial need; average aid package $11,587

Mount St. Mary College
Newburgh NY
(845) 569-3488
U.S. News ranking: Reg. U. (N), No. 105
Website: www.msmc.edu
Admissions email: admissions@msmc.edu
Private; founded 1959
Freshman admissions: selective; 2019-2020: 3,249 applied, 3,048 accepted. Either SAT or ACT required. SAT 25/75 percentile: 970-1160. High school rank: 8% in top tenth, 28% in top quarter, 66% in top half
Early decision deadline: N/A, notification date: N/A
Early action deadline: N/A, notification date: N/A
Application deadline (fall): 8/15
Undergraduate student body: 1,596 full time, 285 part time; 28% male, 72% female; 0% American Indian, 2% Asian, 8% Black, 18% Hispanic, 1% multiracial, 0% Pacific Islander, 57% white, 0% international; 88% from in state; 46% live on campus; N/A of students in fraternities, N/A in sororities
Most popular majors: 36% Health Professions and Related Programs, 19% Business, Management, Marketing, and Related Support Services, 13% Psychology, 6% History, 5% Social Sciences
Expenses: 2020-2021: $34,412; room/board: $16,658
Financial aid: (845) 569-3394; 78% of undergrads determined to have financial need; average aid package $22,634

Nazareth College
Rochester NY
(585) 389-2860
U.S. News ranking: Reg. U. (N), No. 45
Website: www.naz.edu
Admissions email: admissions@naz.edu
Private; founded 1924
Freshman admissions: more selective; 2019-2020: 4,477 applied, 2,887 accepted. Neither SAT nor ACT required. SAT 25/75 percentile: 1100-1290. High school rank: 30% in top tenth, 59% in top quarter, 85% in top half
Early decision deadline: 11/15, notification date: 12/15
Early action deadline: N/A, notification date: N/A
Application deadline (fall): 2/1
Undergraduate student body: 2,180 full time, 102 part time; 27% male, 73% female; 0% American Indian, 3% Asian, 5% Black, 6% Hispanic, 3% multiracial, 0% Pacific Islander, 78% white, 1% international; 88% from in state; 54% live on campus; 0% of students in fraternities, 0% in sororities
Most popular majors: 24% Health Professions and Related Programs, 12% Education, 11% Visual and Performing Arts, 10% Business, Management, Marketing, and Related Support Services, 7% Public Administration and Social Service Professions
Expenses: 2020-2021: $36,520; room/board: $14,660
Financial aid: (585) 389-2310; 82% of undergrads determined to have financial need; average aid package $28,616

The New School
New York NY
(800) 292-3040
U.S. News ranking: Nat. U., No. 133
Website: www.newschool.edu
Admissions email: admission@newschool.edu
Private; founded 1919
Freshman admissions: selective; 2019-2020: 9,413 applied, 5,404 accepted. Neither SAT nor ACT required. SAT 25/75 percentile: 1150-1380. High school rank: 20% in top tenth, 26% in top quarter, 80% in top half
Early decision deadline: N/A, notification date: N/A
Early action deadline: 11/1, notification date: 12/20
Application deadline (fall): 8/1
Undergraduate student body: 6,737 full time, 693 part time; 25% male, 75% female; 0% American Indian, 11% Asian, 4% Black, 12% Hispanic, 4% multiracial, 0% Pacific Islander, 33% white, 31% international; 15% from in state; 20% live on campus; 0% of students in fraternities, 0% in sororities
Most popular majors: 18% Fashion/Apparel Design, 11% Web Page, Digital/Multimedia and Information Resources Design, 10% Fine and Studio Arts Management, 8% Liberal Arts

and Sciences/Liberal Studies, 5% Fine/Studio Arts, General
Expenses: 2019-2020: $50,954; room/board: $17,600
Financial aid: (212) 229-8930

New York Institute of Technology
Old Westbury NY
(800) 345-6948
U.S. News ranking: Reg. U. (N), No. 34
Website: www.nyit.edu
Admissions email: admissions@nyit.edu
Private; founded 1955
Freshman admissions: selective; 2019-2020: 11,848 applied, 8,033 accepted. Either SAT or ACT required. SAT 25/75 percentile: 1070-1295. High school rank: N/A
Early decision deadline: N/A, notification date: N/A
Early action deadline: N/A, notification date: N/A
Application deadline (fall): rolling
Undergraduate student body: 3,357 full time, 337 part time; 61% male, 39% female; 0% American Indian, 19% Asian, 10% Black, 19% Hispanic, 5% multiracial, 0% Pacific Islander, 26% white, 15% international; 86% from in state; 15% live on campus; 3% of students in fraternities, 4% in sororities
Most popular majors: 14% Architectural and Building Sciences/Technology, 12% Computer and Information Sciences, General, 11% Business Administration and Management, General, 10% Biology/Biological Sciences, General, 8% Electrical and Electronics Engineering
Expenses: 2020-2021: $39,760; room/board: $14,920
Financial aid: (516) 686-7680; 72% of undergrads determined to have financial need; average aid package $29,446

New York School of Interior Design[1]
New York NY
(212) 472-1500
U.S. News ranking: Arts, unranked
Website: www.nysid.edu
Admissions email: N/A
Private
Application deadline (fall): N/A
Undergraduate student body: N/A full time, N/A part time
Expenses: 2019-2020: $26,322; room/board: $21,600
Financial aid: N/A

New York University
New York NY
(212) 998-4500
U.S. News ranking: Nat. U., No. 30
Website: www.nyu.edu
Admissions email: admissions@nyu.edu
Private; founded 1831
Freshman admissions: most selective; 2019-2020: 79,462 applied, 12,873 accepted. Neither SAT nor ACT required. SAT 25/75 percentile: 1350-1530. High

school rank: 79% in top tenth, 100% in top quarter, 100% in top half
Early decision deadline: 11/1, notification date: 12/15
Early action deadline: N/A, notification date: N/A
Application deadline (fall): 1/1
Undergraduate student body: 25,872 full time, 1,109 part time; 42% male, 58% female; 0% American Indian, 19% Asian, 8% Black, 16% Hispanic, 4% multiracial, 0% Pacific Islander, 25% white, 22% international; 33% from in state; 44% live on campus; 3% of students in fraternities, 7% in sororities
Most popular majors: 18% Visual and Performing Arts, 14% Business, Management, Marketing, and Related Support Services, 14% Social Sciences, 9% Liberal Arts and Sciences, General Studies and Humanities, 8% Health Professions and Related Programs
Expenses: 2020-2021: $54,880; room/board: $19,244
Financial aid: (212) 998-4444; 45% of undergrads determined to have financial need; average aid package $37,841

Niagara University
Niagara University NY
(716) 286-8700
U.S. News ranking: Reg. U. (N), No. 23
Website: www.niagara.edu
Admissions email: admissions@niagara.edu
Private; founded 1856
Affiliation: Roman Catholic
Freshman admissions: selective; 2019-2020: 3,660 applied, 3,265 accepted. Neither SAT nor ACT required. SAT 25/75 percentile: 1020-1230. High school rank: 16% in top tenth, 40% in top quarter, 74% in top half
Early decision deadline: N/A, notification date: N/A
Early action deadline: 12/15, notification date: 1/3
Application deadline (fall): 8/30
Undergraduate student body: 2,692 full time, 117 part time; 36% male, 64% female; 1% American Indian, 1% Asian, 5% Black, 5% Hispanic, 3% multiracial, 0% Pacific Islander, 66% white, 17% international; 90% from in state; 42% live on campus; N/A of students in fraternities, N/A in sororities
Most popular majors: 28% Business, Management, Marketing, and Related Support Services, 24% Education, 10% Social Sciences, 8% Health Professions and Related Programs, 5% Biological and Biomedical Sciences
Expenses: 2020-2021: $35,240; room/board: $11,850
Financial aid: (716) 286-8686; 68% of undergrads determined to have financial need; average aid package $28,001

Nyack College

New York NY
(646) 378-6101
U.S. News ranking: Reg. U. (N), second tier
Website: www.nyack.edu
Admissions email: admissions@nyack.edu
Private; founded 1882
Affiliation: Christ and Missionary Alliance Church
Freshman admissions: least selective; 2019-2020: 223 applied, 218 accepted. Neither SAT nor ACT required. SAT 25/75 percentile: 820-1070. High school rank: 18% in top tenth, 24% in top quarter, 61% in top half
Early decision deadline: N/A, notification date: N/A
Early action deadline: N/A, notification date: N/A
Application deadline (fall): rolling
Undergraduate student body: 840 full time, 188 part time; 45% male, 55% female; 1% American Indian, 6% Asian, 30% Black, 33% Hispanic, 3% multiracial, 0% Pacific Islander, 15% white, 8% international; 72% from in state; 30% live on campus; 0% of students in fraternities, 0% in sororities
Most popular majors: 31% Business, Management, Marketing, and Related Support Services, 13% Theology and Religious Vocations, 9% Multi/Interdisciplinary Studies, 8% Health Professions and Related Programs, 7% Public Administration and Social Service Professions
Expenses: 2020-2021: $25,500; room/board: $15,000
Financial aid: (845) 675-4737

Pace University

New York NY
(800) 874-7223
U.S. News ranking: Nat. U., No. 217
Website: www.pace.edu
Admissions email: undergradadmission@pace.edu
Private; founded 1906
Freshman admissions: selective; 2019-2020: 22,411 applied, 17,640 accepted. Neither SAT nor ACT required. SAT 25/75 percentile: 1050-1230. High school rank: 18% in top tenth, 47% in top quarter, 80% in top half
Early decision deadline: 11/1, notification date: 12/1
Early action deadline: 11/1, notification date: 12/1
Application deadline (fall): 2/15
Undergraduate student body: 7,837 full time, 908 part time; 38% male, 62% female; 0% American Indian, 8% Asian, 10% Black, 14% Hispanic, 4% multiracial, 0% Pacific Islander, 49% white, 10% international; 54% from in state; 41% live on campus; 4% of students in fraternities, 6% in sororities
Most popular majors: 30% Business, Management, Marketing, and Related Support Services, 14% Health Professions and Related Programs, 14% Visual and Performing Arts,

12% Communication, Journalism, and Related Programs, 6% Psychology
Expenses: 2020-2021: $46,446; room/board: $19,148
Financial aid: (877) 672-1830; 67% of undergrads determined to have financial need; average aid package $34,496

Paul Smith's College

Paul Smiths NY
(888) 873-6570
U.S. News ranking: Reg. Coll. (N), No. 27
Website: www.paulsmiths.edu
Admissions email: admissions@paulsmiths.edu
Private; founded 1946
Freshman admissions: less selective; 2019-2020: 1,325 applied, 925 accepted. Neither SAT nor ACT required. SAT 25/75 percentile: N/A. High school rank: N/A
Early decision deadline: N/A, notification date: N/A
Early action deadline: N/A, notification date: N/A
Application deadline (fall): rolling
Undergraduate student body: 703 full time, 9 part time; 67% male, 33% female; 2% American Indian, 1% Asian, 5% Black, 3% Hispanic, 1% multiracial, 0% Pacific Islander, 83% white, 0% international; 68% from in state; 81% live on campus; 0% of students in fraternities, 0% in sororities
Most popular majors: 55% Natural Resources and Conservation, 11% Multi/Interdisciplinary Studies, 11% Personal and Culinary Services, 8% Biological and Biomedical Sciences, 8% Parks, Recreation, Leisure, and Fitness Studies
Expenses: 2019-2020: $29,313; room/board: $14,280
Financial aid: (518) 327-6119

Plaza College[1]

Forest Hills NY
(718) 779-1430
U.S. News ranking: Reg. Coll. (N), unranked
Website: www.plazacollege.edu
Admissions email: N/A
For-profit; founded 1916
Application deadline (fall): N/A
Undergraduate student body: N/A full time, N/A part time
Expenses: 2019-2020: $13,450; room/board: N/A
Financial aid: N/A

Pratt Institute

Brooklyn NY
(718) 636-3514
U.S. News ranking: Arts, unranked
Website: www.pratt.edu
Admissions email: admissions@pratt.edu
Private; founded 1887
Freshman admissions: more selective; 2019-2020: 7,090 applied, 3,454 accepted. Either SAT or ACT required. SAT 25/75 percentile: 1190-1410. High school rank: N/A
Early decision deadline: N/A, notification date: N/A

Early action deadline: 11/1, notification date: 12/22
Application deadline (fall): 1/5
Undergraduate student body: 3,376 full time, 107 part time; 29% male, 71% female; 0% American Indian, 13% Asian, 3% Black, 9% Hispanic, 3% multiracial, 0% Pacific Islander, 35% white, 34% international; 26% from in state; 50% live on campus; 5% of students in fraternities, 3% in sororities
Most popular majors: 77% Visual and Performing Arts, 17% Architecture and Related Services, 2% Education, 2% English Language and Literature/Letters, 2% Multi/Interdisciplinary Studies
Expenses: 2020-2021: $53,814; room/board: $13,294
Financial aid: (718) 636-3599; 40% of undergrads determined to have financial need; average aid package $34,352

Purchase College–SUNY

Purchase NY
(914) 251-6300
U.S. News ranking: Nat. Lib. Arts, No. 155
Website: www.purchase.edu
Admissions email: admissions@purchase.edu
Public; founded 1967
Freshman admissions: selective; 2019-2020: 6,486 applied, 3,341 accepted. Neither SAT nor ACT required. SAT 25/75 percentile: 1060-1260. High school rank: N/A
Early decision deadline: N/A, notification date: N/A
Early action deadline: 11/15, notification date: 1/1
Application deadline (fall): 7/1
Undergraduate student body: 3,771 full time, 310 part time; 42% male, 58% female; 0% American Indian, 4% Asian, 12% Black, 25% Hispanic, 5% multiracial, 0% Pacific Islander, 51% white, 2% international; 87% from in state; 68% live on campus; N/A of students in fraternities, N/A in sororities
Most popular majors: 12% Liberal Arts and Sciences/Liberal Studies, 5% Dance, General, 5% Drama and Dramatics/Theatre Arts, General, 5% Mass Communication/Media Studies, 5% Psychology, General
Expenses: 2020-2021: $9,163 in state, $19,073 out of state; room/board: $14,548
Financial aid: (914) 251-6354; 68% of undergrads determined to have financial need; average aid package $11,299

Rensselaer Polytechnic Institute

Troy NY
(518) 276-6216
U.S. News ranking: Nat. U., No. 53
Website: www.rpi.edu
Admissions email: admissions@rpi.edu
Private; founded 1824
Freshman admissions: most selective; 2019-2020: 18,635

applied, 8,835 accepted. Either SAT or ACT required. SAT 25/75 percentile: 1330-1510. High school rank: 63% in top tenth, 92% in top quarter, 98% in top half
Early decision deadline: 11/1, notification date: 12/15
Early action deadline: N/A, notification date: N/A
Application deadline (fall): 1/15
Undergraduate student body: 6,218 full time, 23 part time; 68% male, 32% female; 0% American Indian, 15% Asian, 4% Black, 10% Hispanic, 5% multiracial, 0% Pacific Islander, 47% white, 16% international; 34% from in state; 57% live on campus; 30% of students in fraternities, 16% in sororities
Most popular majors: 51% Engineering, 16% Computer and Information Sciences and Support Services, 6% Business, Management, Marketing, and Related Support Services, 5% Engineering Technologies and Engineering-Related Fields, 5% Physical Sciences
Expenses: 2020-2021: $57,012; room/board: $15,954
Financial aid: (518) 276-6813; 56% of undergrads determined to have financial need; average aid package $42,951

Roberts Wesleyan College

Rochester NY
(585) 594-6400
U.S. News ranking: Reg. U. (N), No. 83
Website: www.roberts.edu
Admissions email: admissions@roberts.edu
Private; founded 1866
Affiliation: Free Methodist
Freshman admissions: selective; 2019-2020: 1,888 applied, 1,257 accepted. Neither SAT nor ACT required. SAT 25/75 percentile: 1020-1270. High school rank: 18% in top tenth, 47% in top quarter, 85% in top half
Early decision deadline: N/A, notification date: N/A
Early action deadline: 11/15, notification date: 12/6
Application deadline (fall): 8/20
Undergraduate student body: 1,176 full time, 117 part time; 33% male, 67% female; 0% American Indian, 2% Asian, 9% Black, 7% Hispanic, 4% multiracial, 0% Pacific Islander, 73% white, 5% international; 90% from in state; 61% live on campus; 0% of students in fraternities, 0% in sororities
Most popular majors: 39% Health Professions and Related Programs, 19% Business, Management, Marketing, and Related Support Services, 10% Education, 7% Public Administration and Social Service Professions, 5% Homeland Security, Law Enforcement, Firefighting and Related Protective Services
Expenses: 2020-2021: $33,500; room/board: $11,110

Financial aid: (585) 594-6150; 57% of undergrads determined to have financial need; average aid package $26,985

Rochester Institute of Technology

Rochester NY
(585) 475-6631
U.S. News ranking: Nat. U., No. 112
Website: www.rit.edu
Admissions email: admissions@rit.edu
Private; founded 1829
Freshman admissions: more selective; 2019-2020: 19,494 applied, 13,732 accepted. Neither SAT nor ACT required. SAT 25/75 percentile: 1220-1410. High school rank: 39% in top tenth, 73% in top quarter, 94% in top half
Early decision deadline: 11/1, notification date: 12/15
Early action deadline: N/A, notification date: N/A
Application deadline (fall): rolling
Undergraduate student body: 12,254 full time, 1,059 part time; 67% male, 33% female; 0% American Indian, 10% Asian, 4% Black, 8% Hispanic, 4% multiracial, 0% Pacific Islander, 65% white, 6% international; N/A from in state; 49% live on campus; 4% of students in fraternities, 2% in sororities
Most popular majors: 23% Engineering, 17% Computer and Information Sciences and Support Services, 11% Engineering Technologies and Engineering-Related Fields, 10% Business, Management, Marketing, and Related Support Services, 10% Visual and Performing Arts
Expenses: 2020-2021: $51,240; room/board: $13,976
Financial aid: (585) 475-2186; 73% of undergrads determined to have financial need; average aid package $38,000

Russell Sage College

Troy NY
(518) 244-2217
U.S. News ranking: Nat. U., No. 206
Website: www.sage.edu
Admissions email: admission@sage.edu
Private; founded 1916
Freshman admissions: less selective; 2019-2020: 1,561 applied, 1,327 accepted. Neither SAT nor ACT required. SAT 25/75 percentile: 900-1100. High school rank: 15% in top tenth, 38% in top quarter, 77% in top half
Early decision deadline: N/A, notification date: N/A
Early action deadline: N/A, notification date: N/A
Application deadline (fall): N/A
Undergraduate student body: 1,234 full time, 119 part time; 22% male, 78% female; 1% American Indian, 5% Asian, 11% Black, 10% Hispanic, 4% multiracial, 0% Pacific Islander, 60% white, 1% international; 92% from in

state; 46% live on campus; N/A of students in fraternities, N/A in sororities
Most popular majors: 40% Health Professions and Related Programs, 10% Business, Management, Marketing, and Related Support Services, 10% Psychology, 10% Visual and Performing Arts, 9% Biological and Biomedical Sciences
Expenses: 2020-2021: $32,950; room/board: $13,070
Financial aid: (518) 244-4525; 89% of undergrads determined to have financial need

Sarah Lawrence College
Bronxville NY
(914) 395-2510
U.S. News ranking: Nat. Lib. Arts, No. 63
Website: www.slc.edu
Admissions email: slcadmit@sarahlawrence.edu
Private; founded 1926
Freshman admissions: more selective; 2019-2020: 4,053 applied, 2,152 accepted. Neither SAT nor ACT required. SAT 25/75 percentile: 1240-1422. High school rank: 36% in top tenth, 67% in top quarter, 93% in top half
Early decision deadline: 11/1, notification date: 12/15
Early action deadline: 11/1, notification date: 12/15
Application deadline (fall): 1/15
Undergraduate student body: 1,421 full time, 12 part time; 25% male, 75% female; 0% American Indian, 2% Asian, 4% Black, 9% Hispanic, 5% multiracial, 0% Pacific Islander, 61% white, 11% international; N/A from in state; 84% live on campus; N/A of students in fraternities, N/A in sororities
Most popular majors: 100% English Language and Literature/Letters
Expenses: 2020-2021: $57,520; room/board: $15,820
Financial aid: (914) 395-2570; 57% of undergrads determined to have financial need; average aid package $39,758

School of Visual Arts
New York NY
(212) 592-2100
U.S. News ranking: Arts, unranked
Website: www.sva.edu/admissions/undergraduate
Admissions email: admissions@sva.edu
For-profit; founded 1947
Freshman admissions: selective; 2019-2020: 4,261 applied, 3,031 accepted. Neither SAT nor ACT required. SAT 25/75 percentile: 1080-1360. High school rank: N/A
Early decision deadline: N/A, notification date: N/A
Early action deadline: N/A, notification date: N/A
Application deadline (fall): N/A
Undergraduate student body: 3,784 full time, 88 part time; 28% male, 72% female; 0% American Indian, 14% Asian, 4% Black, 10% Hispanic, 0% multiracial,

0% Pacific Islander, 20% white, 51% international
Most popular majors: 50% Visual and Performing Arts, 35% Computer and Information Sciences and Support Services, 11% Communications Technologies/Technicians and Support Services, 4% Communication, Journalism, and Related Programs
Expenses: 2020-2021: $43,400; room/board: $22,300
Financial aid: (212) 592-2043; 34% of undergrads determined to have financial need; average aid package $20,950

Siena College
Loudonville NY
(518) 783-2423
U.S. News ranking: Reg. U. (N), No. 15
Website: www.siena.edu
Admissions email: admissions@siena.edu
Private; founded 1937
Affiliation: Roman Catholic
Freshman admissions: selective; 2019-2020: 7,728 applied, 6,269 accepted. Neither SAT nor ACT required. SAT 25/75 percentile: 1070-1280. High school rank: 19% in top tenth, 51% in top quarter, 88% in top half
Early decision deadline: 12/1, notification date: 1/1
Early action deadline: 12/1, notification date: 1/7
Application deadline (fall): 3/1
Undergraduate student body: 3,028 full time, 163 part time; 43% male, 57% female; 0% American Indian, 5% Asian, 3% Black, 8% Hispanic, 3% multiracial, 0% Pacific Islander, 77% white, 3% international; 82% from in state; 75% live on campus; 0% of students in fraternities, 0% in sororities
Most popular majors: 17% Marketing/Marketing Management, General, 13% Accounting, 11% Psychology, General, 8% Finance, General, 5% Political Science and Government, General
Expenses: 2020-2021: $39,500; room/board: $15,800
Financial aid: (518) 783-2427; 76% of undergrads determined to have financial need; average aid package $32,555

Skidmore College
Saratoga Springs NY
(518) 580-5570
U.S. News ranking: Nat. Lib. Arts, No. 36
Website: www.skidmore.edu
Admissions email: admissions@skidmore.edu
Private; founded 1903
Freshman admissions: more selective; 2019-2020: 11,102 applied, 3,336 accepted. Neither SAT nor ACT required. SAT 25/75 percentile: 1220-1400. High school rank: 32% in top tenth, 62% in top quarter, 90% in top half
Early decision deadline: 11/15, notification date: 12/15
Early action deadline: N/A, notification date: N/A

Application deadline (fall): 1/15
Undergraduate student body: 2,622 full time, 40 part time; 40% male, 60% female; 0% American Indian, 6% Asian, 5% Black, 9% Hispanic, 5% multiracial, 0% Pacific Islander, 62% white, 11% international; 34% from in state; 89% live on campus; 0% of students in fraternities, 0% in sororities
Most popular majors: 21% Social Sciences, 13% Business, Management, Marketing, and Related Support Services, 13% Visual and Performing Arts, 10% Psychology, 8% Biological and Biomedical Sciences
Expenses: 2020-2021: $58,128; room/board: $15,524
Financial aid: (518) 580-5750; 46% of undergrads determined to have financial need; average aid package $53,700

St. Bonaventure University
St. Bonaventure NY
(800) 462-5050
U.S. News ranking: Reg. U. (N), No. 19
Website: www.sbu.edu
Admissions email: admissions@sbu.edu
Private; founded 1858
Affiliation: Roman Catholic
Freshman admissions: selective; 2019-2020: 3,058 applied, 2,295 accepted. Neither SAT nor ACT required. SAT 25/75 percentile: 1030-1240. High school rank: 16% in top tenth, 39% in top quarter, 73% in top half
Early decision deadline: N/A, notification date: N/A
Early action deadline: N/A, notification date: N/A
Application deadline (fall): 7/1
Undergraduate student body: 1,767 full time, 73 part time; 53% male, 47% female; 1% American Indian, 4% Asian, 6% Black, 7% Hispanic, 2% multiracial, 0% Pacific Islander, 74% white, 3% international; 75% from in state; 82% live on campus; 0% of students in fraternities, 0% in sororities
Most popular majors: 11% Finance, General, 10% Accounting, 10% Marketing/Marketing Management, General, 8% Sport and Fitness Administration/Management, 7% Digital Communication and Media/Multimedia
Expenses: 2020-2021: $36,515; room/board: $13,620
Financial aid: (716) 375-2020; 75% of undergrads determined to have financial need; average aid package $28,144

St. Francis College
Brooklyn Heights NY
(718) 489-5200
U.S. News ranking: Reg. Coll. (N), No. 13
Website: www.sfc.edu
Admissions email: admissions@sfc.edu
Private; founded 1859
Freshman admissions: less selective; 2019-2020: 3,857 applied, 3,013 accepted. Neither

SAT nor ACT required. SAT 25/75 percentile: 920-1130. High school rank: N/A
Early decision deadline: N/A, notification date: N/A
Early action deadline: N/A, notification date: N/A
Application deadline (fall): rolling
Undergraduate student body: 2,374 full time, 133 part time; 39% male, 61% female; 0% American Indian, 5% Asian, 21% Black, 27% Hispanic, 3% multiracial, 2% Pacific Islander, 30% white, 8% international; 97% from in state; 4% live on campus; 2% of students in fraternities, 2% in sororities
Most popular majors: 24% Registered Nursing, Nursing Administration, Nursing Research and Clinical Nursing, 18% Business Administration, Management and Operations, 9% Communication and Media Studies, 8% Criminal Justice and Corrections, 8% Economics
Expenses: 2020-2021: $27,798; room/board: $19,800
Financial aid: (718) 489-5259; 73% of undergrads determined to have financial need; average aid package $20,983

St. John Fisher College
Rochester NY
(585) 385-8064
U.S. News ranking: Nat. U., No. 176
Website: www.sjfc.edu
Admissions email: admissions@sjfc.edu
Private; founded 1948
Affiliation: Roman Catholic
Freshman admissions: selective; 2019-2020: 4,720 applied, 3,044 accepted. Either SAT or ACT required. SAT 25/75 percentile: 1070-1260. High school rank: 21% in top tenth, 55% in top quarter, 90% in top half
Early decision deadline: 12/1, notification date: 1/15
Early action deadline: N/A, notification date: N/A
Application deadline (fall): rolling
Undergraduate student body: 2,542 full time, 123 part time; 41% male, 59% female; 0% American Indian, 3% Asian, 4% Black, 5% Hispanic, 2% multiracial, 0% Pacific Islander, 84% white, 0% international; 96% from in state; 53% live on campus; 0% of students in fraternities, 0% in sororities
Most popular majors: 31% Health Professions and Related Programs, 26% Business, Management, Marketing, and Related Support Services, 9% Biological and Biomedical Sciences, 7% Social Sciences, 5% Education
Expenses: 2020-2021: $35,150; room/board: $12,650
Financial aid: (585) 385-8042; 78% of undergrads determined to have financial need; average aid package $23,529

St. John's University
Queens NY
(718) 990-2000
U.S. News ranking: Nat. U., No. 170
Website: www.stjohns.edu/
Admissions email: admhelp@stjohns.edu
Private; founded 1870
Affiliation: Roman Catholic
Freshman admissions: more selective; 2019-2020: 29,059 applied, 21,020 accepted. Neither SAT nor ACT required. SAT 25/75 percentile: 1080-1300. High school rank: 21% in top tenth, 48% in top quarter, 79% in top half
Early decision deadline: 11/15, notification date: 12/15
Early action deadline: 12/1, notification date: 1/1
Application deadline (fall): rolling
Undergraduate student body: 11,527 full time, 5,561 part time; 43% male, 57% female; 0% American Indian, 16% Asian, 14% Black, 15% Hispanic, 5% multiracial, 0% Pacific Islander, 42% white, 5% international; 82% from in state; 25% live on campus; 5% of students in fraternities, 9% in sororities
Most popular majors: 26% Business, Management, Marketing, and Related Support Services, 10% Biological and Biomedical Sciences, 10% Communication, Journalism, and Related Programs, 9% Health Professions and Related Programs, 8% Homeland Security, Law Enforcement, Firefighting and Related Protective Services
Expenses: 2020-2021: $44,760; room/board: $17,970
Financial aid: (718) 990-2000; 74% of undergrads determined to have financial need; average aid package $29,999

St. Joseph's College–Brooklyn
Brooklyn NY
(718) 940-5800
U.S. News ranking: Reg. U. (N), No. 50
Website: www.sjcny.edu/brooklyn
Admissions email: bkadmissions@sjcny.edu
Private; founded 1916
Freshman admissions: selective; 2019-2020: 2,427 applied, 1,729 accepted. Either SAT or ACT required. SAT 25/75 percentile: 990-1190. High school rank: N/A
Early decision deadline: N/A, notification date: N/A
Early action deadline: N/A, notification date: N/A
Application deadline (fall): rolling
Undergraduate student body: 886 full time, 75 part time; 35% male, 65% female; 0% American Indian, 5% Asian, 18% Black, 26% Hispanic, 3% multiracial, 0% Pacific Islander, 36% white, 5% international; 91% from in state; 15% live on campus; N/A of students in fraternities, N/A in sororities
Most popular majors: 19% Registered Nursing/Registered Nurse, 13% Business

Administration and Management, General, 9% Special Education and Teaching, General, 7% Criminal Justice/Law Enforcement Administration, 7% Psychology, General
Expenses: 2020-2021: $29,200; room/board: N/A
Financial aid: (631) 687-2600; 79% of undergrads determined to have financial need; average aid package $21,937

St. Joseph's College–Long Island
Patchogue NY
(631) 687-4500
U.S. News ranking: Reg. U. (N), No. 71
Website: www.sjcny.edu
Admissions email: liadmissions@sjcny.edu
Private; founded 1916
Freshman admissions: selective; 2019-2020: 1,744 applied, 1,273 accepted. Either SAT or ACT required. SAT 25/75 percentile: 1038-1200. High school rank: N/A
Early decision deadline: N/A, notification date: N/A
Early action deadline: N/A, notification date: N/A
Application deadline (fall): rolling
Undergraduate student body: 2,611 full time, 411 part time; 31% male, 69% female; 0% American Indian, 2% Asian, 5% Black, 17% Hispanic, 2% multiracial, 0% Pacific Islander, 63% white, 0% international; 99% from in state; 0% live on campus; N/A of students in fraternities, N/A in sororities
Most popular majors: 16% Special Education and Teaching, General, 15% Business Administration and Management, General, 6% Accounting, 6% Psychology, General, 6% Registered Nursing/Registered Nurse
Expenses: 2020-2021: $29,200; room/board: N/A
Financial aid: (631) 687-2611; 78% of undergrads determined to have financial need; average aid package $16,703

St. Lawrence University
Canton NY
(315) 229-5261
U.S. News ranking: Nat. Lib. Arts, No. 54
Website: www.stlawu.edu
Admissions email: admissions@stlawu.edu
Private; founded 1856
Freshman admissions: more selective; 2019-2020: 6,998 applied, 2,968 accepted. Neither SAT nor ACT required. SAT 25/75 percentile: 1160-1350. High school rank: 42% in top tenth, 77% in top quarter, 97% in top half
Early decision deadline: 11/1, notification date: N/A
Early action deadline: N/A, notification date: N/A
Application deadline (fall): 2/1
Undergraduate student body: 2,365 full time, 27 part time; 45% male, 55% female; 0% American Indian, 2% Asian, 4% Black,

5% Hispanic, 2% multiracial, 0% Pacific Islander, 77% white, 10% international; 39% from in state; 98% live on campus; 12% of students in fraternities, 17% in sororities
Most popular majors: 28% Social Sciences, 12% Business, Management, Marketing, and Related Support Services, 11% Biological and Biomedical Sciences, 11% Psychology, 6% Mathematics and Statistics
Expenses: 2020-2021: $58,750; room/board: $15,150
Financial aid: (315) 229-5265; 62% of undergrads determined to have financial need; average aid package $51,110

Stony Brook University–SUNY
Stony Brook NY
(631) 632-6868
U.S. News ranking: Nat. U., No. 88
Website: www.stonybrook.edu
Admissions email: enroll@stonybrook.edu
Public; founded 1957
Freshman admissions: more selective; 2019-2020: 37,079 applied, 16,370 accepted. Either SAT or ACT required. SAT 25/75 percentile: 1230-1440. High school rank: 51% in top tenth, 80% in top quarter, 96% in top half
Early decision deadline: N/A, notification date: N/A
Early action deadline: N/A, notification date: N/A
Application deadline (fall): 1/15
Undergraduate student body: 16,697 full time, 1,212 part time; 51% male, 49% female; 0% American Indian, 27% Asian, 7% Black, 13% Hispanic, 3% multiracial, 0% Pacific Islander, 30% white, 14% international; 80% from in state; 52% live on campus; 3% of students in fraternities, 3% in sororities
Most popular majors: 16% Health Professions and Related Programs, 13% Biological and Biomedical Sciences, 10% Business, Management, Marketing, and Related Support Services, 10% Engineering, 9% Psychology
Expenses: 2020-2021: $10,530 in state, $28,200 out of state; room/board: $14,798
Financial aid: (631) 632-6840; 56% of undergrads determined to have financial need; average aid package $14,200

St. Thomas Aquinas College
Sparkill NY
(845) 398-4100
U.S. News ranking: Reg. U. (N), No. 113
Website: www.stac.edu
Admissions email: admissions@stac.edu
Private; founded 1952
Affiliation: Roman Catholic
Freshman admissions: less selective; 2019-2020: 1,864 applied, 1,502 accepted. Either SAT or ACT required. SAT 25/75 percentile: 890-1160. High school rank: 13% in top tenth, 27% in top quarter, 53% in top half

Early decision deadline: N/A, notification date: N/A
Early action deadline: N/A, notification date: N/A
Application deadline (fall): rolling
Undergraduate student body: 1,134 full time, 663 part time; 50% male, 50% female; 0% American Indian, 3% Asian, 11% Black, 24% Hispanic, 1% multiracial, 0% Pacific Islander, 50% white, 6% international; 85% from in state; 26% live on campus; 0% of students in fraternities, 0% in sororities
Most popular majors: 25% Business Administration and Management, General, 23% Special Education and Teaching, General, 10% Criminal Justice/Law Enforcement Administration, 9% Social Sciences, General, 5% Psychology, General
Expenses: 2020-2021: $34,200; room/board: $14,200
Financial aid: (845) 398-4097; 72% of undergrads determined to have financial need; average aid package $18,500

SUNY Brockport
Brockport NY
(585) 395-2751
U.S. News ranking: Reg. U. (N), No. 83
Website: www.brockport.edu/
Admissions email: admit@brockport.edu
Public; founded 1835
Freshman admissions: selective; 2019-2020: 9,672 applied, 5,294 accepted. Neither SAT nor ACT required. SAT 25/75 percentile: 1010-1190. High school rank: 11% in top tenth, 32% in top quarter, 74% in top half
Early decision deadline: N/A, notification date: N/A
Early action deadline: N/A, notification date: N/A
Application deadline (fall): 8/1
Undergraduate student body: 5,960 full time, 713 part time; 43% male, 57% female; 0% American Indian, 2% Asian, 12% Black, 8% Hispanic, 3% multiracial, 0% Pacific Islander, 70% white, 1% international; 99% from in state; 34% live on campus; 2% of students in fraternities, 2% in sororities
Most popular majors: 23% Health Professions and Related Programs, 13% Business, Management, Marketing, and Related Support Services, 11% Parks, Recreation, Leisure, and Fitness Studies, 7% Psychology, 6% Homeland Security, Law Enforcement, Firefighting and Related Protective Services
Expenses: 2020-2021: $8,926 in state, $18,836 out of state; room/board: $14,160
Financial aid: (585) 395-2501; 75% of undergrads determined to have financial need; average aid package $11,711

SUNY Buffalo State
Buffalo NY
(716) 878-4017
U.S. News ranking: Reg. U. (N), No. 105
Website: www.buffalostate.edu
Admissions email: admissions@buffalostate.edu
Public; founded 1871
Freshman admissions: less selective; 2019-2020: 14,582 applied, 9,771 accepted. Either SAT or ACT required. SAT 25/75 percentile: 880-1070. High school rank: N/A
Early decision deadline: N/A, notification date: N/A
Early action deadline: N/A, notification date: N/A
Application deadline (fall): rolling
Undergraduate student body: 6,916 full time, 731 part time; 43% male, 57% female; 0% American Indian, 4% Asian, 32% Black, 13% Hispanic, 4% multiracial, 0% Pacific Islander, 45% white, 1% international; 2% from in state; 30% live on campus; 1% of students in fraternities, 1% in sororities
Most popular majors: 16% Business, Management, Marketing, and Related Support Services, 9% Education, 9% Homeland Security, Law Enforcement, Firefighting and Related Protective Services, 8% Liberal Arts and Sciences, General Studies and Humanities, 8% Social Sciences
Expenses: 2020-2021: $8,672 in state, $18,382 out of state; room/board: $14,506
Financial aid: (716) 878-4902; 81% of undergrads determined to have financial need; average aid package $13,582

SUNY Cobleskill
Cobleskill NY
(518) 255-5525
U.S. News ranking: Reg. Coll. (N), No. 18
Website: www.cobleskill.edu
Admissions email: admissionsoffice@cobleskill.edu
Public; founded 1911
Freshman admissions: less selective; 2019-2020: 2,984 applied, 2,765 accepted. Neither SAT nor ACT required. SAT 25/75 percentile: 890-1100. High school rank: 7% in top tenth, 18% in top quarter, 54% in top half
Early decision deadline: N/A, notification date: N/A
Early action deadline: N/A, notification date: N/A
Application deadline (fall): rolling
Undergraduate student body: 2,085 full time, 123 part time; 46% male, 54% female; 0% American Indian, 2% Asian, 11% Black, 12% Hispanic, 3% multiracial, 0% Pacific Islander, 70% white, 1% international; 92% from in state; 58% live on campus; 5% of students in fraternities, 4% in sororities
Most popular majors: 35% Agriculture, Agriculture Operations, and Related Sciences, 20% Business, Management, Marketing, and Related Support Services, 18% Natural Resources and Conservation, 10% Computer

and Information Sciences and Support Services
Expenses: 2020-2021: $8,684 in state, $18,594 out of state; room/board: $14,122
Financial aid: (518) 255-5637; 76% of undergrads determined to have financial need; average aid package $10,781

SUNY College–Cortland
Cortland NY
(607) 753-4711
U.S. News ranking: Reg. U. (N), No. 71
Website: www2.cortland.edu/home/
Admissions email: admissions@cortland.edu
Public; founded 1868
Freshman admissions: selective; 2019-2020: 12,942 applied, 5,959 accepted. Neither SAT nor ACT required. SAT 25/75 percentile: 1090-1230. High school rank: 12% in top tenth, 45% in top quarter, 82% in top half
Early decision deadline: N/A, notification date: N/A
Early action deadline: 11/15, notification date: 1/1
Application deadline (fall): rolling
Undergraduate student body: 6,170 full time, 125 part time; 44% male, 56% female; 0% American Indian, 1% Asian, 6% Black, 13% Hispanic, 2% multiracial, 0% Pacific Islander, 72% white, 1% international
Most popular majors: 24% Education, 20% Parks, Recreation, Leisure, and Fitness Studies, 10% Health Professions and Related Programs, 9% Social Sciences, 8% Business, Management, Marketing, and Related Support Services
Expenses: 2020-2021: $9,052 in state, $19,102 out of state; room/board: $12,910
Financial aid: (607) 753-4717; 65% of undergrads determined to have financial need; average aid package $15,332

SUNY College of Environmental Science and Forestry
Syracuse NY
(315) 470-6600
U.S. News ranking: Nat. U., No. 118
Website: www.esf.edu
Admissions email: esfinfo@esf.edu
Public; founded 1911
Freshman admissions: more selective; 2019-2020: 1,661 applied, 1,155 accepted. Either SAT or ACT required. SAT 25/75 percentile: 1120-1300. High school rank: 31% in top tenth, 63% in top quarter, 92% in top half
Early decision deadline: 12/1, notification date: 1/15
Early action deadline: N/A, notification date: N/A
Application deadline (fall): 2/1
Undergraduate student body: 1,747 full time, 65 part time; 52% male, 48% female; 0% American Indian, 4% Asian, 2% Black,

6% Hispanic, 3% multiracial, 0% Pacific Islander, 78% white, 3% international; 78% from in state; 35% live on campus; 2% of students in fraternities, 2% in sororities
Most popular majors: 35% Biological and Biomedical Sciences, 34% Natural Resources and Conservation, 19% Engineering, 4% Business, Management, Marketing, and Related Support Services, 3% Physical Sciences
Expenses: 2020-2021: $9,215 in state, $19,125 out of state; room/board: $16,270
Financial aid: (315) 470-6670; 57% of undergrads determined to have financial need; average aid package $10,079

SUNY College of Technology at Alfred
Alfred NY
(800) 425-3733
U.S. News ranking: Reg. Coll. (N), No. 9
Website: www.alfredstate.edu
Admissions email: admissions@alfredstate.edu
Public; founded 1908
Freshman admissions: selective; 2019-2020: 6,683 applied, 4,460 accepted. Neither SAT nor ACT required. SAT 25/75 percentile: 940-1170. High school rank: N/A
Early decision deadline: N/A, notification date: N/A
Early action deadline: N/A, notification date: N/A
Application deadline (fall): rolling
Undergraduate student body: 3,482 full time, 298 part time; 63% male, 37% female; 0% American Indian, 1% Asian, 13% Black, 9% Hispanic, 3% multiracial, 0% Pacific Islander, 72% white, 0% international; 96% from in state; 61% live on campus; 5% of students in fraternities, 9% in sororities
Most popular majors: 39% Business, Management, Marketing, and Related Support Services, 21% Engineering Technologies and Engineering-Related Fields, 16% Health Professions and Related Programs, 8% Computer and Information Sciences and Support Services, 5% Architecture and Related Services
Expenses: 2020-2021: $8,694 in state, $12,664 out of state; room/board: $13,180
Financial aid: (607) 587-4253; 83% of undergrads determined to have financial need; average aid package $11,164

SUNY College of Technology–Canton
Canton NY
(800) 388-7123
U.S. News ranking: Reg. Coll. (N), No. 19
Website: www.canton.edu/
Admissions email: admissions@canton.edu
Public; founded 1906

Freshman admissions: less selective; 2019-2020: 3,816 applied, 3,229 accepted. Neither SAT nor ACT required. SAT 25/75 percentile: 920-1110. High school rank: 5% in top tenth, 17% in top quarter, 51% in top half
Early decision deadline: N/A, notification date: N/A
Early action deadline: N/A, notification date: N/A
Application deadline (fall): rolling
Undergraduate student body: 2,784 full time, 444 part time; 44% male, 56% female; 2% American Indian, 1% Asian, 13% Black, 11% Hispanic, 3% multiracial, 0% Pacific Islander, 66% white, 2% international; 97% from in state; 39% live on campus; 2% of students in fraternities, 2% in sororities
Most popular majors: 12% Health/Health Care Administration/Management, 11% Corrections and Criminal Justice, Other, 10% Business Administration and Management, General, 8% Registered Nursing/Registered Nurse, 6% Veterinary/Animal Health Technology/Technician and Veterinary Assistant
Expenses: 2020-2021: $8,660 in state, $18,570 out of state; room/board: $13,610
Financial aid: (315) 386-7616; 83% of undergrads determined to have financial need; average aid package $11,125

SUNY College of Technology–Delhi
Delhi NY
(607) 746-4550
U.S. News ranking: Reg. Coll. (N), No. 14
Website: www.delhi.edu/
Admissions email: enroll@delhi.edu
Public; founded 1913
Freshman admissions: less selective; 2019-2020: 5,148 applied, 3,708 accepted. Neither SAT nor ACT required. SAT 25/75 percentile: 920-1120. High school rank: 6% in top tenth, 18% in top quarter, 55% in top half
Early decision deadline: N/A, notification date: N/A
Early action deadline: 12/1, notification date: 12/15
Application deadline (fall): 8/15
Undergraduate student body: 2,391 full time, 608 part time; 46% male, 54% female; 0% American Indian, 2% Asian, 17% Black, 17% Hispanic, 3% multiracial, 0% Pacific Islander, 58% white, 0% international; 97% from in state; 53% live on campus; N/A of students in fraternities, N/A in sororities
Most popular majors: 38% Health Professions and Related Programs, 34% Business, Management, Marketing, and Related Support Services, 12% Homeland Security, Law Enforcement, Firefighting and Related Protective Services, 6% Personal and Culinary Services, 5% Natural Resources and Conservation
Expenses: 2019-2020: $8,610 in state, $12,380 out of state; room/board: $12,900

Financial aid: (607) 746-4570; 80% of undergrads determined to have financial need; average aid package $11,317

SUNY College–Old Westbury
Old Westbury NY
(516) 876-3200
U.S. News ranking: Reg. U. (N), second tier
Website: www.oldwestbury.edu
Admissions email: enroll@oldwestbury.edu
Public; founded 1965
Freshman admissions: less selective; 2019-2020: 4,756 applied, 3,703 accepted. Either SAT or ACT required. SAT 25/75 percentile: 910-1090. High school rank: N/A
Early decision deadline: N/A, notification date: N/A
Early action deadline: N/A, notification date: N/A
Application deadline (fall): rolling
Undergraduate student body: 4,121 full time, 795 part time; 42% male, 58% female; N/A American Indian, N/A Asian, N/A Black, N/A Hispanic, N/A multiracial, N/A Pacific Islander, N/A white, N/A international
Most popular majors: Information not available
Expenses: 2019-2020: $8,368 in state, $18,278 out of state; room/board: $11,530
Financial aid: N/A

SUNY College–Oneonta[1]
Oneonta NY
(607) 436-2524
U.S. News ranking: Reg. U. (N), No. 75
Website: suny.oneonta.edu/
Admissions email: admissions@oneonta.edu
Public; founded 1889
Application deadline (fall): rolling
Undergraduate student body: N/A full time, N/A part time
Expenses: 2019-2020: $8,740 in state, $18,650 out of state; room/board: $13,640
Financial aid: N/A

SUNY College–Potsdam
Potsdam NY
(315) 267-2180
U.S. News ranking: Reg. U. (N), No. 71
Website: www.potsdam.edu
Admissions email: admissions@potsdam.edu
Public; founded 1816
Freshman admissions: selective; 2019-2020: 5,078 applied, 3,452 accepted. Neither SAT nor ACT required. SAT 25/75 percentile: 1030-1245. High school rank: 10% in top tenth, 30% in top quarter, 70% in top half
Early decision deadline: N/A, notification date: N/A
Early action deadline: N/A, notification date: N/A
Application deadline (fall): rolling
Undergraduate student body: 2,977 full time, 86 part time; 38%

male, 62% female; 1% American Indian, 2% Asian, 12% Black, 14% Hispanic, 3% multiracial, 0% Pacific Islander, 64% white, 0% international; 96% from in state; 55% live on campus; 2% of students in fraternities, 7% in sororities
Most popular majors: 17% Visual and Performing Arts, 15% Education, 11% Business, Management, Marketing, and Related Support Services, 10% Social Sciences, 7% Psychology
Expenses: 2020-2021: $8,711 in state, $18,621 out of state; room/board: $13,900
Financial aid: (315) 267-2162; 78% of undergrads determined to have financial need; average aid package $15,149

SUNY Empire State College
Saratoga Springs NY
(518) 587-2100
U.S. News ranking: Reg. U. (N), second tier
Website: www.esc.edu
Admissions email: admissions@esc.edu
Public; founded 1971
Freshman admissions: less selective; 2019-2020: 538 applied, 340 accepted. Neither SAT nor ACT required. SAT 25/75 percentile: N/A. High school rank: N/A
Early decision deadline: N/A, notification date: N/A
Early action deadline: N/A, notification date: N/A
Application deadline (fall): rolling
Undergraduate student body: 3,267 full time, 5,828 part time; 37% male, 63% female; 0% American Indian, 3% Asian, 16% Black, 14% Hispanic, 3% multiracial, 0% Pacific Islander, 56% white, 1% international
Most popular majors: 35% Business, Management, Marketing, and Related Support Services, 23% Public Administration and Social Service Professions, 9% Health Professions and Related Programs, 9% Psychology, 7% Physical Sciences
Expenses: 2020-2021: $7,605 in state, $17,515 out of state; room/board: N/A
Financial aid: N/A

SUNY–Fredonia
Fredonia NY
(800) 252-1212
U.S. News ranking: Reg. U. (N), No. 67
Website: www.fredonia.edu
Admissions email: admissions@fredonia.edu
Public; founded 1826
Freshman admissions: selective; 2019-2020: 6,277 applied, 4,464 accepted. Either SAT or ACT required. SAT 25/75 percentile: 990-1200. High school rank: 15% in top tenth, 41% in top quarter, 70% in top half
Early decision deadline: N/A, notification date: N/A
Early action deadline: N/A, notification date: N/A
Application deadline (fall): rolling

Undergraduate student body: 4,143 full time, 83 part time; 43% male, 57% female; 1% American Indian, 2% Asian, 9% Black, 10% Hispanic, 3% multiracial, 0% Pacific Islander, 71% white, 2% international; N/A from in state; 51% live on campus; 1% of students in fraternities, 1% in sororities
Most popular majors: 16% Visual and Performing Arts, 14% Business, Management, Marketing, and Related Support Services, 12% Education, 9% Communication, Journalism, and Related Programs, 6% Biological and Biomedical Sciences
Expenses: 2020-2021: $8,945 in state, $18,325 out of state; room/board: $13,240
Financial aid: (716) 673-3253; 73% of undergrads determined to have financial need; average aid package $12,659

SUNY–Geneseo
Geneseo NY
(585) 245-5571
U.S. News ranking: Reg. U. (N), No. 13
Website: www.geneseo.edu
Admissions email: admissions@geneseo.edu
Public; founded 1871
Freshman admissions: more selective; 2019-2020: 10,433 applied, 6,831 accepted. Either SAT or ACT required. SAT 25/75 percentile: 1120-1310. High school rank: 28% in top tenth, 63% in top quarter, 93% in top half
Early decision deadline: 11/15, notification date: 12/15
Early action deadline: N/A, notification date: N/A
Application deadline (fall): 1/1
Undergraduate student body: 5,099 full time, 141 part time; 38% male, 62% female; 0% American Indian, 5% Asian, 3% Black, 8% Hispanic, 2% multiracial, 0% Pacific Islander, 77% white, 1% international; 99% from in state; 55% live on campus; 20% of students in fraternities, 21% in sororities
Most popular majors: 18% Social Sciences, 14% Biological and Biomedical Sciences, 14% Business, Management, Marketing, and Related Support Services, 14% Psychology, 11% Education
Expenses: 2019-2020: $8,927 in state, $18,837 out of state; room/board: $14,018
Financial aid: (585) 245-5731; 53% of undergrads determined to have financial need; average aid package $10,463

SUNY Maritime College
Throggs Neck NY
(718) 409-7221
U.S. News ranking: Reg. U. (N), No. 56
Website: www.sunymaritime.edu
Admissions email: admissions@sunymaritime.edu
Public; founded 1874
Freshman admissions: selective; 2019-2020: 1,323 applied, 974

accepted. Either SAT or ACT required. SAT 25/75 percentile: 1090-1260. High school rank: 0% in top tenth, 33% in top quarter, 100% in top half
Early decision deadline: 11/1, notification date: 12/15
Early action deadline: N/A, notification date: N/A
Application deadline (fall): 1/31
Undergraduate student body: 1,474 full time, 48 part time; 86% male, 14% female; 0% American Indian, 4% Asian, 5% Black, 17% Hispanic, 2% multiracial, 0% Pacific Islander, 67% white, 1% international; N/A from in state; 83% live on campus; N/A of students in fraternities, N/A in sororities
Most popular majors: 42% Marine Science/Merchant Marine Officer, 21% Mechanical Engineering, 10% Business, Management, Marketing, and Related Support Services, Other, 10% Naval Architecture and Marine Engineering, 6% Electrical and Electronics Engineering
Expenses: 2020-2021: $8,742 in state, $18,652 out of state; room/board: $13,637
Financial aid: (718) 409-7400; 58% of undergrads determined to have financial need; average aid package $4,836

SUNY Morrisville
Morrisville NY
(315) 684-6046
U.S. News ranking: Reg. Coll. (N), No. 25
Website: www.morrisville.edu
Admissions email: admissions@morrisville.edu
Public; founded 1908
Freshman admissions: less selective; 2019-2020: 4,808 applied, 3,599 accepted. Neither SAT nor ACT required. SAT 25/75 percentile: 930-1100. High school rank: 7% in top tenth, 16% in top quarter, 54% in top half
Early decision deadline: N/A, notification date: N/A
Early action deadline: N/A, notification date: N/A
Application deadline (fall): 8/17
Undergraduate student body: 2,283 full time, 498 part time; 49% male, 51% female; 0% American Indian, 1% Asian, 24% Black, 8% Hispanic, 3% multiracial, 0% Pacific Islander, 61% white, 1% international; 96% from in state; 55% live on campus; 0% of students in fraternities, 0% in sororities
Most popular majors: 25% Agriculture, Agriculture Operations, and Related Sciences, 19% Health Professions and Related Programs, 13% Business, Management, Marketing, and Related Support Services, 12% Mechanic and Repair Technologies/Technicians, 9% Liberal Arts and Sciences, General Studies and Humanities
Expenses: 2020-2021: $8,870 in state, $12,920 out of state; room/board: $15,600
Financial aid: (315) 684-6289; 84% of undergrads determined to have financial need; average aid package $10,794

SUNY–New Paltz
New Paltz NY
(845) 257-3200
U.S. News ranking: Reg. U. (N), No. 45
Website: www.newpaltz.edu
Admissions email: admissions@newpaltz.edu
Public; founded 1828
Freshman admissions: selective; 2019-2020: 14,425 applied, 6,517 accepted. Either SAT or ACT required. SAT 25/75 percentile: 1090-1280. High school rank: 18% in top tenth, 58% in top quarter, 88% in top half
Early decision deadline: N/A, notification date: N/A
Early action deadline: 11/15, notification date: 12/15
Application deadline (fall): 4/1
Undergraduate student body: 6,291 full time, 516 part time; 37% male, 63% female; 0% American Indian, 5% Asian, 6% Black, 21% Hispanic, 3% multiracial, 0% Pacific Islander, 59% white, 2% international; 98% from in state; 45% live on campus; 5% of students in fraternities, 5% in sororities
Most popular majors: 15% Business, Management, Marketing, and Related Support Services, 13% Social Sciences, 12% Communication, Journalism, and Related Programs, 11% Visual and Performing Arts, 10% Psychology
Expenses: 2019-2020: $8,502 in state, $18,412 out of state; room/board: $13,928
Financial aid: (845) 257-3256; 63% of undergrads determined to have financial need; average aid package $12,224

SUNY–Oswego
Oswego NY
(315) 312-2250
U.S. News ranking: Reg. U. (N), No. 50
Website: www.oswego.edu
Admissions email: admiss@oswego.edu
Public; founded 1861
Freshman admissions: selective; 2019-2020: 12,669 applied, 6,848 accepted. Either SAT or ACT required. SAT 25/75 percentile: 1040-1220. High school rank: 12% in top tenth, 53% in top quarter, 86% in top half
Early decision deadline: N/A, notification date: N/A
Early action deadline: 11/30, notification date: 12/15
Application deadline (fall): rolling
Undergraduate student body: 6,561 full time, 359 part time; 49% male, 51% female; 0% American Indian, 2% Asian, 10% Black, 13% Hispanic, 3% multiracial, 0% Pacific Islander, 68% white, 3% international; 95% from in state; 54% live on campus; 7% of students in fraternities, 6% in sororities
Most popular majors: 28% Business, Management, Marketing, and Related Support Services, 13% Communication, Journalism, and Related Programs, 9% Biological and Biomedical

Sciences, 9% Psychology, 7% Education
Expenses: 2020-2021: $8,717 in state, $18,627 out of state; room/board: $14,213
Financial aid: (315) 312-2248; 70% of undergrads determined to have financial need; average aid package $11,230

SUNY–Plattsburgh
Plattsburgh NY
(888) 673-0012
U.S. News ranking: Reg. U. (N), No. 75
Website: www.plattsburgh.edu
Admissions email: admissions@plattsburgh.edu
Public; founded 1889
Freshman admissions: selective; 2019-2020: 7,968 applied, 4,535 accepted. Either SAT or ACT required. SAT 25/75 percentile: 980-1180. High school rank: 12% in top tenth, 36% in top quarter, 76% in top half
Early decision deadline: N/A, notification date: N/A
Early action deadline: N/A, notification date: N/A
Application deadline (fall): rolling
Undergraduate student body: 4,420 full time, 451 part time; 42% male, 58% female; 1% American Indian, 3% Asian, 10% Black, 12% Hispanic, 2% multiracial, 0% Pacific Islander, 63% white, 6% international
Most popular majors: 20% Business, Management, Marketing, and Related Support Services, 9% Communication, Journalism, and Related Programs, 8% Health Professions and Related Programs, 7% Psychology, 6% Homeland Security, Law Enforcement, Firefighting and Related Protective Services
Expenses: 2020-2021: $9,144 in state, $19,190 out of state; room/board: $14,225
Financial aid: (518) 564-2072; 68% of undergrads determined to have financial need; average aid package $15,088

SUNY Polytechnic Institute–Albany/Utica
Utica NY
(315) 792-7500
U.S. News ranking: Reg. U. (N), No. 12
Website: www.sunypoly.edu
Admissions email: admissions@sunypoly.edu
Public; founded 1966
Freshman admissions: selective; 2019-2020: 3,167 applied, 2,186 accepted. Either SAT or ACT required. SAT 25/75 percentile: 1000-1360. High school rank: 47% in top tenth, 70% in top quarter, 96% in top half
Early decision deadline: N/A, notification date: N/A
Early action deadline: 11/15, notification date: 12/15
Application deadline (fall): 6/1
Undergraduate student body: 1,909 full time, 299 part time; 66% male, 34% female; 0% American Indian, 8% Asian, 7% Black, 9% Hispanic, 3% multiracial, 0% Pacific Islander, 71% white,

1% international; 99% from in state; 41% live on campus; N/A of students in fraternities, N/A in sororities
Most popular majors: 11% Computer and Information Sciences, General, 9% Business Administration and Management, General, 8% Mechanical Engineering/Mechanical Technology/Technician, 8% Registered Nursing/Registered Nurse, 6% Computer and Information Systems Security/Information Assurance
Expenses: 2020-2021: $8,761 in state, $18,471 out of state; room/board: $14,305
Financial aid: (315) 792-7210; 69% of undergrads determined to have financial need; average aid package $10,971

Syracuse University
Syracuse NY
(315) 443-3611
U.S. News ranking: Nat. U., No. 58
Website: www.syracuse.edu
Admissions email: orange@syr.edu
Private; founded 1870
Freshman admissions: more selective; 2019-2020: 35,299 applied, 15,664 accepted. Neither SAT nor ACT required. SAT 25/75 percentile: 1180-1380. High school rank: 33% in top tenth, 66% in top quarter, 91% in top half
Early decision deadline: 11/15, notification date: 12/15
Early action deadline: N/A, notification date: N/A
Application deadline (fall): 1/1
Undergraduate student body: 14,727 full time, 548 part time; 47% male, 53% female; 1% American Indian, 6% Asian, 7% Black, 10% Hispanic, 3% multiracial, 0% Pacific Islander, 56% white, 15% international; 37% from in state; 53% live on campus; 24% of students in fraternities, 42% in sororities
Most popular majors: 15% Communication, Journalism, and Related Programs, 14% Social Sciences, 10% Business, Management, Marketing, and Related Support Services, 10% Visual and Performing Arts, 8% Engineering
Expenses: 2020-2021: $55,926; room/board: $16,356
Financial aid: (315) 443-1513; 41% of undergrads determined to have financial need; average aid package $42,550

Touro College
New York NY
(212) 463-0400
U.S. News ranking: Nat. U., No. 284
Website: www.touro.edu
Admissions email: admissions.nyscas@touro.edu
Private; founded 1971
Freshman admissions: selective; 2019-2020: 2,070 applied, 1,437 accepted. Neither SAT nor ACT required. ACT 25/75 percentile: 22-29. High school rank: N/A
Early decision deadline: N/A, notification date: N/A

Early action deadline: N/A, notification date: N/A
Application deadline (fall): rolling
Undergraduate student body: 3,830 full time, 1,859 part time; 29% male, 71% female; 0% American Indian, 3% Asian, 13% Black, 9% Hispanic, 1% multiracial, 0% Pacific Islander, 59% white, 4% international
Most popular majors: 22% Psychology, 21% Health Professions and Related Programs, 16% Business, Management, Marketing, and Related Support Services, 14% Multi/Interdisciplinary Studies, 9% Biological and Biomedical Sciences
Expenses: 2020-2021: $20,750; room/board: $12,486
Financial aid: (646) 565-6000; 74% of undergrads determined to have financial need; average aid package $11,288

Union College
Schenectady NY
(518) 388-6112
U.S. News ranking: Nat. Lib. Arts, No. 44
Website: www.union.edu
Admissions email: admissions@union.edu
Private; founded 1795
Freshman admissions: more selective; 2019-2020: 6,086 applied, 2,612 accepted. Neither SAT nor ACT required. SAT 25/75 percentile: 1220-1420. High school rank: 63% in top tenth, 86% in top quarter, 98% in top half
Early decision deadline: 11/15, notification date: 12/15
Early action deadline: 11/1, notification date: N/A
Application deadline (fall): 1/15
Undergraduate student body: 2,173 full time, 16 part time; 54% male, 46% female; 0% American Indian, 6% Asian, 4% Black, 9% Hispanic, 3% multiracial, 0% Pacific Islander, 68% white, 10% international; N/A from in state; 93% live on campus; 27% of students in fraternities, 35% in sororities
Most popular majors: 24% Social Sciences, 22% Engineering, 15% Biological and Biomedical Sciences, 7% Psychology, 6% Liberal Arts and Sciences, General Studies and Humanities
Expenses: 2020-2021: $59,427; room/board: $14,583
Financial aid: (518) 388-6123; 54% of undergrads determined to have financial need; average aid package $46,730

United States Merchant Marine Academy[1]
Kings Point NY
(866) 546-4778
U.S. News ranking: Reg. Coll. (N), No. 3
Website: www.usmma.edu
Admissions email: admissions@usmma.edu
Public; founded 1943
Application deadline (fall): 2/1
Undergraduate student body: N/A full time, N/A part time

Expenses: 2020-2021: $1,095 in state, $1,095 out of state; room/board: N/A
Financial aid: (516) 726-5638; 100% of undergrads determined to have financial need; average aid package $6,500

United States Military Academy
West Point NY
(845) 938-4041
U.S. News ranking: Nat. Lib. Arts, No. 15
Website: westpoint.edu
Admissions email: admissions@westpoint.edu
Public; founded 1802
Freshman admissions: more selective; 2019-2020: 11,675 applied, 1,199 accepted. Either SAT or ACT required. SAT 25/75 percentile: 1160-1380. High school rank: 48% in top tenth, 71% in top quarter, 94% in top half
Early decision deadline: N/A, notification date: N/A
Early action deadline: N/A, notification date: N/A
Application deadline (fall): 1/31
Undergraduate student body: 4,457 full time, 0 part time; 77% male, 23% female; 1% American Indian, 8% Asian, 12% Black, 10% Hispanic, 3% multiracial, 0% Pacific Islander, 63% white, 1% international; 6% from in state; 100% live on campus; N/A of students in fraternities, N/A in sororities
Most popular majors: 28% Engineering, 15% Social Sciences, 7% Business, Management, Marketing, and Related Support Services, 7% Foreign Languages, Literatures, and Linguistics, 5% Computer and Information Sciences and Support Services
Expenses: N/A
Financial aid: N/A

University at Albany–SUNY
Albany NY
(518) 442-5435
U.S. News ranking: Nat. U., No. 160
Website: www.albany.edu
Admissions email: ugadmissions@albany.edu
Public; founded 1844
Freshman admissions: selective; 2019-2020: 27,529 applied, 14,951 accepted. Either SAT or ACT required. SAT 25/75 percentile: 1090-1250. High school rank: 18% in top tenth, 46% in top quarter, 82% in top half
Early decision deadline: N/A, notification date: N/A
Early action deadline: 11/1, notification date: 1/15
Application deadline (fall): 3/1
Undergraduate student body: 12,568 full time, 718 part time; 48% male, 52% female; 0% American Indian, 9% Asian, 19% Black, 18% Hispanic, 4% multiracial, 0% Pacific Islander, 44% white, 5% international;

91% from in state; 47% live on campus; 2% of students in fraternities, 3% in sororities
Most popular majors: 31% Social Sciences, 12% Business, Management, Marketing, and Related Support Services, 9% Psychology, 7% Communication, Journalism, and Related Programs, 7% Computer and Information Sciences and Support Services
Expenses: 2020-2021: $10,236 in state, $27,826 out of state; room/board: $14,620
Financial aid: (518) 442-3202; 68% of undergrads determined to have financial need; average aid package $11,515

University at Buffalo–SUNY
Buffalo NY
(716) 645-6900
U.S. News ranking: Nat. U., No. 88
Website: www.buffalo.edu
Admissions email: ub-admissions@buffalo.edu
Public; founded 1846
Freshman admissions: more selective; 2019-2020: 29,900 applied, 18,264 accepted. Either SAT or ACT required. SAT 25/75 percentile: 1160-1340. High school rank: 30% in top tenth, 65% in top quarter, 94% in top half
Early decision deadline: N/A, notification date: N/A
Early action deadline: 11/15, notification date: N/A
Application deadline (fall): rolling
Undergraduate student body: 20,401 full time, 1,520 part time; 56% male, 44% female; 0% American Indian, 15% Asian, 8% Black, 7% Hispanic, 2% multiracial, 0% Pacific Islander, 47% white, 14% international; 98% from in state; 34% live on campus; 1% of students in fraternities, 3% in sororities
Most popular majors: 18% Business, Management, Marketing, and Related Support Services, 16% Engineering, 16% Social Sciences, 10% Psychology, 8% Biological and Biomedical Sciences
Expenses: 2020-2021: $10,724 in state, $28,194 out of state; room/board: $14,136
Financial aid: (716) 645-8232; 57% of undergrads determined to have financial need; average aid package $10,631

University of Rochester
Rochester NY
(585) 275-3221
U.S. News ranking: Nat. U., No. 34
Website: www.rochester.edu
Admissions email: admit@ admissions.rochester.edu
Private; founded 1850
Affiliation: Undenominational
Freshman admissions: more selective; 2019-2020: 21,642 applied, 6,425 accepted. Neither SAT nor ACT required. SAT 25/75 percentile: 1310-1500. High school rank: 69% in top tenth, 95% in top quarter, 100% in top half

Early decision deadline: 11/1, notification date: 12/15
Early action deadline: N/A, notification date: N/A
Application deadline (fall): 1/5
Undergraduate student body: 6,410 full time, 370 part time; 49% male, 51% female; 0% American Indian, 11% Asian, 5% Black, 7% Hispanic, 3% multiracial, 0% Pacific Islander, 42% white, 27% international; 42% from in state; 74% live on campus; 17% of students in fraternities, 17% in sororities
Most popular majors: 15% Engineering, 14% Social Sciences, 13% Health Professions and Related Programs, 10% Biological and Biomedical Sciences, 8% Psychology
Expenses: 2020-2021: $58,208; room/board: $17,144
Financial aid: (585) 275-3226; 55% of undergrads determined to have financial need; average aid package $50,665

Utica College
Utica NY
(315) 792-3006
U.S. News ranking: Reg. U. (N), No. 96
Website: www.utica.edu
Admissions email: admiss@utica.edu
Private; founded 1946
Freshman admissions: selective; 2019-2020: 3,837 applied, 3,332 accepted. Neither SAT nor ACT required. SAT 25/75 percentile: 1010-1210. High school rank: 8% in top tenth, 31% in top quarter, 66% in top half
Early decision deadline: 11/15, notification date: 12/15
Early action deadline: 11/15, notification date: 12/15
Application deadline (fall): rolling
Undergraduate student body: 2,824 full time, 664 part time; 41% male, 59% female; 0% American Indian, 4% Asian, 10% Black, 9% Hispanic, 2% multiracial, 0% Pacific Islander, 68% white, 1% international; 70% from in state; 28% live on campus; 2% of students in fraternities, 2% in sororities
Most popular majors: 48% Health Professions and Related Programs, 18% Homeland Security, Law Enforcement, Firefighting and Related Protective Services, 5% Psychology
Expenses: 2020-2021: $22,110; room/board: $11,670
Financial aid: (315) 792-3215; 82% of undergrads determined to have financial need; average aid package $14,855

Vassar College
Poughkeepsie NY
(845) 437-7300
U.S. News ranking: Nat. Lib. Arts, No. 13
Website: www.vassar.edu
Admissions email: admissions@vassar.edu
Private; founded 1861
Freshman admissions: most selective; 2019-2020: 8,961 applied, 2,127 accepted. Either SAT or ACT required. SAT 25/75

percentile: 1370-1530. High school rank: 73% in top tenth, 93% in top quarter, 98% in top half
Early decision deadline: 11/15, notification date: 12/15
Early action deadline: N/A, notification date: N/A
Application deadline (fall): 1/1
Undergraduate student body: 2,425 full time, 16 part time; 41% male, 59% female; 0% American Indian, 5% Asian, 4% Black, 11% Hispanic, 9% multiracial, 0% Pacific Islander, 55% white, 9% international; N/A from in state; 97% live on campus; N/A of students in fraternities, N/A in sororities
Most popular majors: 23% Social Sciences, 13% Biological and Biomedical Sciences, 11% Visual and Performing Arts, 9% Foreign Languages, Literatures, and Linguistics, 7% Psychology
Expenses: 2020-2021: $60,930; room/board: $14,990
Financial aid: (845) 437-5320; 61% of undergrads determined to have financial need; average aid package $56,675

Vaughn College of Aeronautics and Technology
Flushing NY
(718) 429-6600
U.S. News ranking: Reg. Coll. (N), No. 24
Website: www.vaughn.edu
Admissions email: admitme@vaughn.edu
Private; founded 1932
Freshman admissions: less selective; 2019-2020: 755 applied, 620 accepted. Either SAT or ACT required. SAT 25/75 percentile: 963-1165. High school rank: N/A
Early decision deadline: N/A, notification date: N/A
Early action deadline: N/A, notification date: N/A
Application deadline (fall): rolling
Undergraduate student body: 1,365 full time, 254 part time; 88% male, 12% female; 1% American Indian, 12% Asian, 17% Black, 34% Hispanic, 1% multiracial, 1% Pacific Islander, 12% white, 7% international; N/A from in state; 11% live on campus; 2% of students in fraternities, 0% in sororities
Most popular majors: 56% Transportation and Materials Moving, 26% Engineering Technologies and Engineering-Related Fields, 17% Engineering
Expenses: 2019-2020: $26,640; room/board: $14,725
Financial aid: (718) 429-6600

Villa Maria College[1]
Buffalo NY
(716) 896-0700
U.S. News ranking: Reg. Coll. (N), second tier
Admissions email: N/A
Private
Application deadline (fall): N/A
Undergraduate student body: N/A full time, N/A part time

Expenses: 2019-2020: $24,370; room/board: N/A
Financial aid: (716) 961-1849

Wagner College
Staten Island NY
(718) 390-3411
U.S. News ranking: Reg. U. (N), No. 26
Website: www.wagner.edu
Admissions email: admissions@wagner.edu
Private; founded 1883
Freshman admissions: selective; 2019-2020: 2,809 applied, 1,987 accepted. Neither SAT nor ACT required. SAT 25/75 percentile: 1070-1270. High school rank: 21% in top tenth, 51% in top quarter, 82% in top half
Early decision deadline: N/A, notification date: N/A
Early action deadline: 12/1, notification date: 1/5
Application deadline (fall): 2/15
Undergraduate student body: 1,677 full time, 64 part time; 33% male, 67% female; 0% American Indian, 5% Asian, 8% Black, 13% Hispanic, 3% multiracial, 0% Pacific Islander, 61% white, 4% international
Most popular majors: 36% Health Professions and Related Programs, 19% Visual and Performing Arts, 13% Business, Management, Marketing, and Related Support Services, 7% Social Sciences, 5% Biological and Biomedical Sciences
Expenses: 2020-2021: $49,010; room/board: $14,800
Financial aid: (718) 390-3122; 67% of undergrads determined to have financial need; average aid package $32,161

Webb Institute
Glen Cove NY
(516) 671-8355
U.S. News ranking: Engineering, unranked
Website: www.webb.edu
Admissions email: admissions@webb.edu
Private; founded 1889
Freshman admissions: more selective; 2019-2020: 129 applied, 31 accepted. Either SAT or ACT required. SAT 25/75 percentile: 1410-1520. High school rank: 82% in top tenth, 100% in top quarter, 100% in top half
Early decision deadline: 10/15, notification date: 12/15
Early action deadline: N/A, notification date: N/A
Application deadline (fall): 1/15
Undergraduate student body: 102 full time, 0 part time; 77% male, 23% female; 0% American Indian, 8% Asian, 0% Black, 4% Hispanic, 8% multiracial, 0% Pacific Islander, 80% white, 0% international; 30% from in state; 100% live on campus; 0% of students in fraternities, 0% in sororities
Most popular majors: 100% Naval Architecture and Marine Engineering
Expenses: 2020-2021: $52,880; room/board: $15,750

Financial aid: (516) 403-5928; 12% of undergrads determined to have financial need; average aid package $59,400

Wells College[7]
Aurora NY
(800) 952-9355
U.S. News ranking: Nat. Lib. Arts, No. 136
Website: www.wells.edu/
Admissions email: admissions@wells.edu
Private; founded 1868
Freshman admissions: less selective; 2019-2020: 1,848 applied, 1,537 accepted. Neither SAT nor ACT required. SAT 25/75 percentile: 950-1240. High school rank: 19% in top tenth, 37% in top quarter, 66% in top half
Early decision deadline: 12/15, notification date: 1/1
Early action deadline: 12/15, notification date: 1/15
Application deadline (fall): 3/1
Undergraduate student body: 414 full time, 5 part time
Most popular majors: 25% Biological and Biomedical Sciences, 17% Psychology, 16% Business, Management, Marketing, and Related Support Services, 12% Social Sciences, 7% English Language and Literature/Letters
Expenses: 2020-2021: $31,800; room/board: $14,500
Financial aid: (315) 364-3289; 91% of undergrads determined to have financial need; average aid package $27,376

Yeshiva University
New York NY
(212) 960-5277
U.S. News ranking: Nat. U., No. 76
Website: www.yu.edu
Admissions email: yuadmit@ymail.yu.edu
Private; founded 1886
Freshman admissions: more selective; 2019-2020: 1,660 applied, 919 accepted. Either SAT or ACT required. ACT 25/75 percentile: 24-30. High school rank: N/A
Early decision deadline: 11/1, notification date: 12/15
Early action deadline: N/A, notification date: N/A
Application deadline (fall): 2/1
Undergraduate student body: 1,971 full time, 67 part time; 53% male, 47% female; 0% American Indian, 0% Asian, 0% Black, 0% Hispanic, 0% multiracial, 0% Pacific Islander, 91% white, 8% international; 40% from in state; 62% live on campus; N/A of students in fraternities, N/A in sororities
Most popular majors: 19% Biology/Biological Sciences, General, 13% Accounting, 12% Psychology, General, 10% Business Administration and Management, General, 10% Finance, General
Expenses: 2020-2021: $46,475; room/board: $12,750
Financial aid: (212) 960-5399; 53% of undergrads determined to have financial need; average aid package $42,654

NORTH CAROLINA

Appalachian State University
Boone NC
(828) 262-2120
U.S. News ranking: Reg. U. (S), No. 6
Website: www.appstate.edu
Admissions email: admissions@appstate.edu
Public; founded 1899
Freshman admissions: selective; 2019-2020: 16,664 applied, 12,800 accepted. Either SAT or ACT required. ACT 25/75 percentile: 21-26. High school rank: 16% in top tenth, 52% in top quarter, 90% in top half
Early decision deadline: N/A, notification date: N/A
Early action deadline: 11/1, notification date: 1/25
Application deadline (fall): 2/1
Undergraduate student body: 16,622 full time, 896 part time; 44% male, 56% female; 0% American Indian, 2% Asian, 4% Black, 7% Hispanic, 4% multiracial, 0% Pacific Islander, 82% white, 0% international; 93% from in state; 32% live on campus; 2% of students in fraternities, 4% in sororities
Most popular majors: 21% Business, Management, Marketing, and Related Support Services, 11% Health Professions and Related Programs, 9% Education, 8% Communication, Journalism, and Related Programs, 7% Parks, Recreation, Leisure, and Fitness Studies
Expenses: 2020-2021: $7,410 in state, $22,217 out of state; room/board: $9,174
Financial aid: (828) 262-2190; 52% of undergrads determined to have financial need; average aid package $10,279

Barton College
Wilson NC
(800) 345-4973
U.S. News ranking: Reg. Coll. (S), No. 10
Website: www.barton.edu
Admissions email: enroll@barton.edu
Private; founded 1902
Affiliation: Christian Church (Disciples of Christ)
Freshman admissions: selective; 2019-2020: 4,244 applied, 1,922 accepted. Either SAT or ACT required. SAT 25/75 percentile: 940-1130. High school rank: 11% in top tenth, 37% in top quarter, 74% in top half
Early decision deadline: N/A, notification date: N/A
Early action deadline: N/A, notification date: N/A
Application deadline (fall): rolling
Undergraduate student body: 990 full time, 75 part time; 41% male, 59% female; 1% American Indian, 1% Asian, 22% Black, 8% Hispanic, 3% multiracial, 0% Pacific Islander, 57% white, 6% international; 77% from in state; 55% live on campus; N/A of students in fraternities, N/A in sororities

Bennett College[1]
Greensboro NC
(336) 370-8624
U.S. News ranking: Nat. Lib. Arts, second tier
Website: www.bennett.edu
Admissions email: admiss@bennett.edu
Private; founded 1873
Affiliation: United Methodist
Application deadline (fall): rolling
Undergraduate student body: N/A full time, N/A part time
Expenses: 2019-2020: $18,513; room/board: $8,114
Financial aid: (336) 517-2209

Most popular majors: 24% Health Professions and Related Programs, 17% Business, Management, Marketing, and Related Support Services, 11% Public Administration and Social Service Professions, 8% Parks, Recreation, Leisure, and Fitness Studies, 7% Biological and Biomedical Sciences
Expenses: 2020-2021: $32,590; room/board: $10,700
Financial aid: (252) 399-6371; 83% of undergrads determined to have financial need; average aid package $25,681

Belmont Abbey College
Belmont NC
(888) 222-0110
U.S. News ranking: Reg. Coll. (S), No. 18
Website: www.belmontabbeycollege.edu
Admissions email: admissions@bac.edu
Private; founded 1876
Affiliation: Roman Catholic
Freshman admissions: selective; 2019-2020: 2,134 applied, 1,721 accepted. Neither SAT nor ACT required. SAT 25/75 percentile: 970-1220. High school rank: 13% in top tenth, 28% in top quarter, 59% in top half
Early decision deadline: N/A, notification date: N/A
Early action deadline: 10/30, notification date: 11/5
Application deadline (fall): rolling
Undergraduate student body: 1,388 full time, 119 part time; 51% male, 49% female; 1% American Indian, 2% Asian, 13% Black, 2% Hispanic, 0% multiracial, 0% Pacific Islander, 61% white, 3% international; N/A from in state; 54% live on campus; N/A of students in fraternities, N/A in sororities
Most popular majors: 26% Business Administration and Management, General, 10% Accounting, 10% Sport and Fitness Administration/Management, 8% Education, General, 8% Multicultural Education
Expenses: 2020-2021: $18,500; room/board: $10,390
Financial aid: (704) 461-7006; 64% of undergrads determined to have financial need; average aid package $13,565

Brevard College
Brevard NC
(828) 641-0461
U.S. News ranking: Reg. Coll. (S), No. 24
Website: www.brevard.edu
Admissions email: admissions@brevard.edu
Private; founded 1853
Affiliation: United Methodist
Freshman admissions: less selective; 2019-2020: 2,068 applied, 1,215 accepted. Neither SAT nor ACT required. ACT 25/75 percentile: 18-22. High school rank: 5% in top tenth, 19% in top quarter, 50% in top half
Early decision deadline: N/A, notification date: N/A
Early action deadline: N/A, notification date: N/A
Application deadline (fall): rolling
Undergraduate student body: 728 full time, 22 part time; 55% male, 45% female; 1% American Indian, 1% Asian, 14% Black, 9% Hispanic, 5% multiracial, 0% Pacific Islander, 67% white, 1% international
Most popular majors: Information not available
Expenses: 2020-2021: $30,250; room/board: $10,400
Financial aid: (828) 641-0113; 81% of undergrads determined to have financial need; average aid package $27,400

Campbell University
Buies Creek NC
(910) 893-1200
U.S. News ranking: Nat. U., No. 258
Website: www.campbell.edu
Admissions email: admissions@campbell.edu
Private; founded 1887
Affiliation: Baptist
Freshman admissions: selective; 2019-2020: 5,422 applied, 4,213 accepted. Either SAT or ACT required. SAT 25/75 percentile: 1030-1230. High school rank: 27% in top tenth, 58% in top quarter, 87% in top half
Early decision deadline: N/A, notification date: N/A
Early action deadline: N/A, notification date: N/A
Application deadline (fall): 8/26
Undergraduate student body: 3,257 full time, 723 part time; 48% male, 52% female; 0% American Indian, 2% Asian, 15% Black, 10% Hispanic, 5% multiracial, 0% Pacific Islander, 58% white, 2% international; 82% from in state; 57% live on campus; 3% of students in fraternities, 4% in sororities
Most popular majors: 10% Business Administration and Management, General, 7% Biology/Biological Sciences, General, 7% Kinesiology and Exercise Science, 7% Psychology, General, 6% Science Technologies/Technicians, Other
Expenses: 2020-2021: $35,990; room/board: $12,624
Financial aid: (910) 893-1310; 76% of undergrads determined to have financial need; average aid package $26,472

Catawba College
Salisbury NC
(800) 228-2922
U.S. News ranking: Reg. Coll. (S), No. 7
Website: www.catawba.edu
Admissions email: admission@catawba.edu
Private; founded 1851
Affiliation: United Church of Christ
Freshman admissions: less selective; 2019-2020: 2,805 applied, 1,663 accepted. Neither SAT nor ACT required. SAT 25/75 percentile: 930-1120. High school rank: 11% in top tenth, 31% in top quarter, 67% in top half
Early decision deadline: N/A, notification date: N/A
Early action deadline: N/A, notification date: N/A
Undergraduate student body: 1,229 full time, 102 part time; 45% male, 55% female; 1% American Indian, 1% Asian, 21% Black, 9% Hispanic, 4% multiracial, 0% Pacific Islander, 59% white, 3% international; 80% from in state; 61% live on campus; 0% of students in fraternities, 0% in sororities
Most popular majors: 22% Business, Management, Marketing, and Related Support Services, 13% Education, 12% Parks, Recreation, Leisure, and Fitness Studies, 11% Visual and Performing Arts, 8% Biological and Biomedical Sciences
Expenses: 2020-2021: $31,486; room/board: $10,804
Financial aid: (704) 637-4416; 82% of undergrads determined to have financial need; average aid package $27,292

Chowan University
Murfreesboro NC
(252) 398-1236
U.S. News ranking: Nat. Lib. Arts, second tier
Website: chowan.edu/
Admissions email: admissions@chowan.edu
Private; founded 1848
Affiliation: Baptist
Freshman admissions: least selective; 2019-2020: 3,687 applied, 2,520 accepted. Either SAT or ACT required. SAT 25/75 percentile: 790-970. High school rank: 3% in top tenth, 9% in top quarter, 33% in top half
Early decision deadline: N/A, notification date: N/A
Early action deadline: N/A, notification date: N/A
Application deadline (fall): rolling
Undergraduate student body: 1,243 full time, 16 part time; 53% male, 47% female; 1% American Indian, 0% Asian, 65% Black, 3% Hispanic, 2% multiracial, 0% Pacific Islander, 17% white, 3% international
Most popular majors: 19% Homeland Security, Law Enforcement, Firefighting and Related Protective Services, 16% Multi/Interdisciplinary Studies, 14% Business, Management, Marketing, and Related Support Services, 13% Psychology, 10% Parks, Recreation, Leisure, and Fitness Studies

Expenses: 2020-2021: $25,880; room/board: $9,600
Financial aid: (252) 398-6269; 93% of undergrads determined to have financial need; average aid package $22,457

Davidson College

Davidson NC
(800) 768-0380
U.S. News ranking: Nat. Lib. Arts, No. 15
Website: davidson.edu
Admissions email: admission@davidson.edu
Private; founded 1837
Affiliation: Presbyterian Church (USA)
Freshman admissions: most selective; 2019-2020: 5,982 applied, 1,080 accepted. Neither SAT nor ACT required. SAT 25/75 percentile: 1310-1485. High school rank: 72% in top tenth, 95% in top quarter, 100% in top half
Early decision deadline: 11/15, notification date: 12/15
Early action deadline: N/A, notification date: N/A
Application deadline (fall): 1/7
Undergraduate student body: 1,837 full time, 0 part time; 51% male, 49% female; 0% American Indian, 5% Asian, 7% Black, 8% Hispanic, 5% multiracial, 0% Pacific Islander, 67% white, 7% international; 22% from in state; 95% live on campus; 30% of students in fraternities, 49% in sororities
Most popular majors: 17% Political Science and Government, General, 16% Econometrics and Quantitative Economics, 12% Biology/Biological Sciences, General, 9% English Language and Literature, General, 8% Psychology, General
Expenses: 2020-2021: $55,060; room/board: $15,225
Financial aid: (704) 894-2232; 50% of undergrads determined to have financial need; average aid package $51,275

Duke University

Durham NC
(919) 684-3214
U.S. News ranking: Nat. U., No. 12
Website: www.duke.edu/
Admissions email: undergrad-admissions@duke.edu
Private; founded 1838
Freshman admissions: most selective; 2019-2020: 41,471 applied, 3,190 accepted. Either SAT or ACT required. ACT 25/75 percentile: 33-35. High school rank: 95% in top tenth, 98% in top quarter, 100% in top half
Early decision deadline: 11/1, notification date: 12/15
Early action deadline: N/A, notification date: N/A
Application deadline (fall): 1/3
Undergraduate student body: 6,597 full time, 52 part time; 49% male, 51% female; 1% American Indian, 21% Asian, 9% Black, 7% Hispanic, 8% multiracial, 0% Pacific Islander, 41% white, 10% international
Most popular majors: Information not available

East Carolina University

Greenville NC
(252) 328-6640
U.S. News ranking: Nat. U., No. 217
Website: www.ecu.edu
Admissions email: admissions@ecu.edu
Public; founded 1907
Freshman admissions: selective; 2019-2020: 19,234 applied, 15,140 accepted. Either SAT or ACT required. SAT 25/75 percentile: 1030-1190. High school rank: 13% in top tenth, 36% in top quarter, 71% in top half
Early decision deadline: N/A, notification date: N/A
Early action deadline: N/A, notification date: N/A
Application deadline (fall): 3/1
Undergraduate student body: 19,204 full time, 3,877 part time; 43% male, 57% female; 1% American Indian, 3% Asian, 16% Black, 8% Hispanic, 4% multiracial, 0% Pacific Islander, 66% white, 1% international; 90% from in state; 25% live on campus; 8% of students in fraternities, 12% in sororities
Most popular majors: 18% Health Professions and Related Programs, 17% Business, Management, Marketing, and Related Support Services, 7% Education, 6% Biological and Biomedical Sciences, 6% Engineering Technologies and Engineering-Related Fields
Expenses: 2020-2021: $7,239 in state, $23,516 out of state; room/board: $10,136
Financial aid: (252) 328-6610; 59% of undergrads determined to have financial need; average aid package $10,758

Elizabeth City State University

Elizabeth City NC
(252) 335-3305
U.S. News ranking: Reg. Coll. (S), No. 36
Website: www.ecsu.edu
Admissions email: admissions@mail.ecsu.edu
Public; founded 1891
Freshman admissions: less selective; 2019-2020: 2,549 applied, 1,673 accepted. Either SAT or ACT required. SAT 25/75 percentile: 875-1050. High school rank: 2% in top tenth, 5% in top quarter, 33% in top half
Early decision deadline: N/A, notification date: N/A
Early action deadline: N/A, notification date: N/A
Application deadline (fall): 8/1
Undergraduate student body: 1,516 full time, 176 part time; 41% male, 59% female; 0% American Indian, 1% Asian, 71% Black,

4% Hispanic, 5% multiracial, 0% Pacific Islander, 16% white, 1% international
Most popular majors: 5% Business, Management, Marketing, and Related Support Services, 5% Education, 5% Homeland Security, Law Enforcement, Firefighting and Related Protective Services, 4% Biological and Biomedical Sciences, 4% Public Administration and Social Service Professions
Expenses: 2020-2021: $3,979 in state, $7,979 out of state; room/board: $8,782
Financial aid: (252) 335-4850

Elon University

Elon NC
(800) 334-8448
U.S. News ranking: Nat. U., No. 88
Website: www.elon.edu
Admissions email: admissions@elon.edu
Private; founded 1889
Freshman admissions: more selective; 2019-2020: 10,500 applied, 8,236 accepted. Neither SAT nor ACT required. SAT 25/75 percentile: 1160-1320. High school rank: 25% in top tenth, 56% in top quarter, 84% in top half
Early decision deadline: 11/1, notification date: 12/1
Early action deadline: 11/1, notification date: 12/20
Application deadline (fall): 1/10
Undergraduate student body: 6,079 full time, 198 part time; 40% male, 60% female; 0% American Indian, 2% Asian, 5% Black, 7% Hispanic, 3% multiracial, 0% Pacific Islander, 80% white, 2% international; 19% from in state; 64% live on campus; 20% of students in fraternities, 39% in sororities
Most popular majors: 34% Business/Commerce, General, 19% Communication and Media Studies, 8% Public Administration, 6% Health and Physical Education/Fitness, 6% Psychology, General
Expenses: 2020-2021: $37,921; room/board: $13,141
Financial aid: (336) 278-7640; 34% of undergrads determined to have financial need; average aid package $21,162

Fayetteville State University

Fayetteville NC
(910) 672-1371
U.S. News ranking: Reg. U. (S), No. 89
Website: www.uncfsu.edu/fsu-admissions/undergraduate-admissions
Admissions email: admissions@uncfsu.edu
Public; founded 1867
Freshman admissions: less selective; 2019-2020: 4,858 applied, 3,328 accepted. Either SAT or ACT required. SAT 25/75 percentile: 870-1010. High school rank: 6% in top tenth, 27% in top quarter, 64% in top half
Early decision deadline: N/A, notification date: N/A

Early action deadline: N/A, notification date: N/A
Application deadline (fall): 6/30
Undergraduate student body: 4,071 full time, 1,573 part time; 31% male, 69% female; 2% American Indian, 1% Asian, 60% Black, 9% Hispanic, 4% multiracial, 0% Pacific Islander, 20% white, 1% international; 94% from in state; 25% live on campus; 1% of students in fraternities, 1% in sororities
Most popular majors: 21% Registered Nursing/Registered Nurse, 17% Criminal Justice/Safety Studies, 15% Psychology, General, 13% Business Administration and Management, General, 6% Biology/Biological Sciences, General
Expenses: 2020-2021: $5,310 in state, $16,918 out of state; room/board: $8,615
Financial aid: (910) 672-1325; 84% of undergrads determined to have financial need; average aid package $10,659

Gardner-Webb University

Boiling Springs NC
(800) 253-6472
U.S. News ranking: Nat. U., No. 284
Website: www.gardner-webb.edu
Admissions email: admissions@gardner-webb.edu
Private; founded 1905
Affiliation: Baptist
Freshman admissions: selective; 2019-2020: 4,835 applied, 3,225 accepted. Either SAT or ACT required. SAT 25/75 percentile: 970-1180. High school rank: 13% in top tenth, 41% in top quarter, 72% in top half
Early decision deadline: N/A, notification date: N/A
Early action deadline: N/A, notification date: N/A
Application deadline (fall): rolling
Undergraduate student body: 1,633 full time, 366 part time; 35% male, 65% female; 1% American Indian, 1% Asian, 16% Black, 5% Hispanic, 2% multiracial, 0% Pacific Islander, 64% white, 0% international
Most popular majors: 22% Business, Management, Marketing, and Related Support Services, 19% Health Professions and Related Programs, 13% Psychology, 6% Biological and Biomedical Sciences, 6% Homeland Security, Law Enforcement, Firefighting and Related Protective Services
Expenses: 2020-2021: $31,460; room/board: $10,390
Financial aid: (704) 406-4247; 76% of undergrads determined to have financial need; average aid package $27,929

Greensboro College

Greensboro NC
(336) 272-7102
U.S. News ranking: Reg. Coll. (S), No. 36
Website: www.greensboro.edu
Admissions email: admissions@greensboro.edu

Private; founded 1838
Affiliation: United Methodist
Freshman admissions: less selective; 2019-2020: 1,936 applied, 878 accepted. Either SAT or ACT required. SAT 25/75 percentile: 900-1090. High school rank: 10% in top tenth, 25% in top quarter, 52% in top half
Early decision deadline: N/A, notification date: N/A
Early action deadline: N/A, notification date: N/A
Application deadline (fall): rolling
Undergraduate student body: 715 full time, 169 part time; 49% male, 51% female; 0% American Indian, 0% Asian, 27% Black, 4% Hispanic, 6% multiracial, 0% Pacific Islander, 51% white, 0% international; 76% from in state; 38% live on campus; N/A of students in fraternities, N/A in sororities
Most popular majors: 10% Business/Managerial Economics, 9% Health Professions and Related Programs, 9% Kinesiology and Exercise Science, 9% Liberal Arts and Sciences/Liberal Studies, 8% Psychology, General
Expenses: 2020-2021: $18,960; room/board: $10,950
Financial aid: (336) 272-7102; 83% of undergrads determined to have financial need; average aid package $8,286

Guilford College

Greensboro NC
(800) 992-7759
U.S. News ranking: Nat. Lib. Arts, No. 155
Website: www.guilford.edu
Admissions email: admission@guilford.edu
Private; founded 1837
Affiliation: Friends
Freshman admissions: selective; 2019-2020: 3,305 applied, 2,479 accepted. Neither SAT nor ACT required. SAT 25/75 percentile: 933-1180. High school rank: 13% in top tenth, 32% in top quarter, 63% in top half
Early decision deadline: N/A, notification date: N/A
Early action deadline: 12/1, notification date: 12/15
Application deadline (fall): 8/10
Undergraduate student body: 1,373 full time, 152 part time; 47% male, 53% female; 0% American Indian, 3% Asian, 24% Black, 12% Hispanic, 4% multiracial, 0% Pacific Islander, 53% white, 1% international
Most popular majors: 13% Business, Management, Marketing, and Related Support Services, 10% Parks, Recreation, Leisure, and Fitness Studies, 9% Psychology, 7% Homeland Security, Law Enforcement, Firefighting and Related Protective Services, 6% Social Sciences
Expenses: 2020-2021: $40,120; room/board: $12,200
Financial aid: (336) 316-2354; 44% of undergrads determined to have financial need; average aid package $30,307

High Point University
High Point NC
(800) 345-6993
U.S. News ranking: Reg. Coll. (S), No. 1
Website: www.highpoint.edu
Admissions email: admiss@highpoint.edu
Private; founded 1924
Affiliation: United Methodist
Freshman admissions: selective; 2019-2020: 11,298 applied, 8,333 accepted. Neither SAT nor ACT required. SAT 25/75 percentile: 1090-1260. High school rank: 17% in top tenth, 43% in top quarter, 73% in top half
Early decision deadline: 11/1, notification date: 11/22
Early action deadline: 11/15, notification date: 12/15
Application deadline (fall): 3/1
Undergraduate student body: 4,557 full time, 34 part time; 43% male, 57% female; 0% American Indian, 2% Asian, 5% Black, 6% Hispanic, 5% multiracial, 0% Pacific Islander, 78% white, 2% international; 26% from in state; 95% live on campus; 7% of students in fraternities, 25% in sororities
Most popular majors: 37% Business, Management, Marketing, and Related Support Services, 20% Communication, Journalism, and Related Programs, 7% Biological and Biomedical Sciences, 7% Parks, Recreation, Leisure, and Fitness Studies, 6% Visual and Performing Arts
Expenses: 2020-2021: $38,080; room/board: $15,438
Financial aid: (336) 841-9124; 42% of undergrads determined to have financial need; average aid package $19,083

Johnson C. Smith University[1]
Charlotte NC
(704) 378-1010
U.S. News ranking: Nat. Lib. Arts, second tier
Website: www.jcsu.edu
Admissions email: admissions@jcsu.edu
Private; founded 1867
Application deadline (fall): rolling
Undergraduate student body: 1,359 full time, 76 part time
Expenses: 2020-2021: $18,784; room/board: $8,014
Financial aid: (704) 378-1498; 93% of undergrads determined to have financial need; average aid package $16,260

Lees-McRae College
Banner Elk NC
(828) 898-5241
U.S. News ranking: Reg. Coll. (S), No. 26
Website: www.lmc.edu
Admissions email: admissions@lmc.edu
Private; founded 1900
Affiliation: Presbyterian Church (USA)
Freshman admissions: selective; 2019-2020: 1,399 applied, 767 accepted. Neither SAT nor ACT

required. ACT 25/75 percentile: 18-24. High school rank: N/A
Early decision deadline: N/A, notification date: N/A
Early action deadline: N/A, notification date: N/A
Application deadline (fall): rolling
Undergraduate student body: 795 full time, 53 part time; 32% male, 68% female; 1% American Indian, 0% Asian, 7% Black, 7% Hispanic, 2% multiracial, 0% Pacific Islander, 71% white, 4% international; 70% from in state; 65% live on campus; 0% of students in fraternities, 0% in sororities
Most popular majors: 20% Health Professions and Related Programs, 18% Homeland Security, Law Enforcement, Firefighting and Related Protective Services, 17% Biological and Biomedical Sciences, 14% Education, 11% Business, Management, Marketing, and Related Support Services
Expenses: 2020-2021: $27,390; room/board: $11,470
Financial aid: (828) 898-8740

Lenoir-Rhyne University
Hickory NC
(828) 328-7300
U.S. News ranking: Reg. U. (S), No. 42
Website: www.lr.edu
Admissions email: admission@lr.edu
Private; founded 1891
Affiliation: Evangelical Lutheran Church
Freshman admissions: selective; 2019-2020: 4,791 applied, 3,734 accepted. Either SAT or ACT required. ACT 25/75 percentile: 18-24. High school rank: N/A
Early decision deadline: N/A, notification date: N/A
Early action deadline: 11/13, notification date: 11/13
Application deadline (fall): rolling
Undergraduate student body: 1,589 full time, 257 part time; 41% male, 59% female; 0% American Indian, 2% Asian, 11% Black, 9% Hispanic, 5% multiracial, 0% Pacific Islander, 67% white, 4% international; 81% from in state; 52% live on campus; 10% of students in fraternities, 11% in sororities
Most popular majors: 20% Health Professions and Related Programs, 19% Parks, Recreation, Leisure, and Fitness Studies, 18% Business, Management, Marketing, and Related Support Services, 7% Education, 5% Biological and Biomedical Sciences
Expenses: 2020-2021: $39,900; room/board: $12,700
Financial aid: (828) 328-7300; 84% of undergrads determined to have financial need; average aid package $32,464

Livingstone College
Salisbury NC
(704) 216-6001
U.S. News ranking: Reg. Coll. (S), second tier
Website: www.livingstone.edu/
Admissions email: admissions@livingstone.edu
Private; founded 1879
Affiliation: African Methodist Episcopal Zion Church
Freshman admissions: least selective; 2019-2020: 6,084 applied, 3,432 accepted. Either SAT or ACT required. SAT 25/75 percentile: 710-855. High school rank: 2% in top tenth, 5% in top quarter, 30% in top half
Early decision deadline: N/A, notification date: N/A
Early action deadline: N/A, notification date: N/A
Application deadline (fall): rolling
Undergraduate student body: 1,110 full time, 12 part time; 51% male, 49% female; N/A American Indian, N/A Asian, N/A Black, N/A Hispanic, N/A multiracial, N/A Pacific Islander, N/A white, N/A international; 61% from in state; 97% live on campus; N/A of students in fraternities, N/A in sororities
Most popular majors: 18% Business Administration and Management, General, 16% Criminal Justice/Safety Studies, 16% Sport and Fitness Administration/Management, 14% Biology/Biological Sciences, General, 8% Social Work
Expenses: 2020-2021: $18,031; room/board: $6,596
Financial aid: (704) 216-6069; 96% of undergrads determined to have financial need; average aid package $14,477

Mars Hill University
Mars Hill NC
(866) 642-4968
U.S. News ranking: Reg. Coll. (S), No. 26
Website: www.mhu.edu
Admissions email: admissions@mhu.edu
Private; founded 1856
Freshman admissions: selective; 2019-2020: 1,838 applied, 1,164 accepted. Either SAT or ACT required. ACT 25/75 percentile: 18-23. High school rank: 9% in top tenth, 27% in top quarter, 63% in top half
Early decision deadline: N/A, notification date: N/A
Early action deadline: N/A, notification date: N/A
Application deadline (fall): rolling
Undergraduate student body: 987 full time, 55 part time; 46% male, 54% female; 1% American Indian, 1% Asian, 17% Black, 7% Hispanic, 4% multiracial, 0% Pacific Islander, 64% white, 4% international; 73% from in state; 69% live on campus; N/A of students in fraternities, N/A in sororities
Most popular majors: 20% Business, Management, Marketing, and Related Support Services, 15% Education, 12% Homeland Security, Law Enforcement, Firefighting and Related Protective Services,

11% Health Professions and Related Programs
Expenses: 2019-2020: $34,118; room/board: $9,878
Financial aid: (828) 689-1103

Meredith College
Raleigh NC
(919) 760-8581
U.S. News ranking: Nat. Lib. Arts, No. 136
Website: www.meredith.edu
Admissions email: admissions@meredith.edu
Private; founded 1891
Freshman admissions: selective; 2019-2020: 1,936 applied, 1,253 accepted. Either SAT or ACT required. SAT 25/75 percentile: 1020-1220. High school rank: 17% in top tenth, 45% in top quarter, 80% in top half
Early decision deadline: 10/30, notification date: 11/15
Early action deadline: 12/1, notification date: 12/15
Application deadline (fall): 2/15
Undergraduate student body: 1,464 full time, 64 part time; 0% male, 100% female; 0% American Indian, 4% Asian, 9% Black, 10% Hispanic, 4% multiracial, 0% Pacific Islander, 67% white, 1% international; N/A from in state; 53% live on campus; N/A of students in fraternities, N/A in sororities
Most popular majors: 18% Business, Management, Marketing, and Related Support Services, 11% Psychology, 10% Social Sciences, 9% Biological and Biomedical Sciences, 9% Communication, Journalism, and Related Programs
Expenses: 2020-2021: $39,952; room/board: $11,746
Financial aid: (919) 760-8565; 73% of undergrads determined to have financial need; average aid package $30,971

Methodist University[1]
Fayetteville NC
(910) 630-7027
U.S. News ranking: Reg. U. (S), No. 73
Website: www.methodist.edu
Admissions email: admissions@methodist.edu
Private; founded 1956
Affiliation: United Methodist
Application deadline (fall): rolling
Undergraduate student body: N/A full time, N/A part time
Expenses: 2020-2021: $36,076; room/board: $12,828
Financial aid: (910) 630-7000; 76% of undergrads determined to have financial need; average aid package $23,452

Montreat College
Montreat NC
(800) 622-6968
U.S. News ranking: Reg. U. (S), second tier
Website: www.montreat.edu
Admissions email: admissions@montreat.edu
Private; founded 1916
Freshman admissions: selective; 2019-2020: N/A applied, N/A

accepted. Either SAT or ACT required. SAT 25/75 percentile: 920-1140. High school rank: N/A
Early decision deadline: N/A, notification date: N/A
Early action deadline: N/A, notification date: N/A
Application deadline (fall): rolling
Undergraduate student body: 559 full time, 185 part time; 51% male, 49% female; 1% American Indian, 1% Asian, 14% Black, 6% Hispanic, 2% multiracial, 1% Pacific Islander, 65% white, 4% international
Most popular majors: Information not available
Expenses: 2020-2021: $28,750; room/board: $9,842
Financial aid: (800) 545-4656; 80% of undergrads determined to have financial need; average aid package $22,707

North Carolina Agricultural and Technical State University
Greensboro NC
(336) 334-7946
U.S. News ranking: Nat. U., No. 272
Website: www.ncat.edu
Admissions email: uadmit@ncat.edu
Public; founded 1891
Freshman admissions: selective; 2019-2020: 15,084 applied, 8,789 accepted. Either SAT or ACT required. SAT 25/75 percentile: 960-1130. High school rank: 12% in top tenth, 38% in top quarter, 78% in top half
Early decision deadline: N/A, notification date: N/A
Early action deadline: 10/15, notification date: 12/15
Application deadline (fall): 6/30
Undergraduate student body: 10,013 full time, 1,026 part time; 42% male, 58% female; 0% American Indian, 1% Asian, 83% Black, 4% Hispanic, 5% multiracial, 0% Pacific Islander, 5% white, 1% international; 74% from in state; 27% live on campus; N/A of students in fraternities, N/A in sororities
Most popular majors: 13% Engineering, 9% Business, Management, Marketing, and Related Support Services, 9% Communication, Journalism, and Related Programs, 8% Liberal Arts and Sciences, General Studies and Humanities, 7% Parks, Recreation, Leisure, and Fitness Studies
Expenses: 2020-2021: $6,657 in state, $20,167 out of state; room/board: $7,930
Financial aid: (336) 334-7973; 85% of undergrads determined to have financial need; average aid package $12,226

North Carolina Central University
Durham NC
(919) 530-6298
U.S. News ranking: Reg. U. (S), No. 47
Website: www.nccu.edu

Admissions email: admissions@nccu.edu
Public; founded 1910
Freshman admissions: less selective; 2019-2020: 8,311 applied, 5,649 accepted. Either SAT or ACT required. SAT 25/75 percentile: 890-1050. High school rank: 7% in top tenth, 24% in top quarter, 65% in top half
Early decision deadline: N/A, notification date: N/A
Early action deadline: N/A, notification date: N/A
Application deadline (fall): rolling
Undergraduate student body: 5,012 full time, 1,089 part time; 32% male, 68% female; 0% American Indian, 1% Asian, 81% Black, 6% Hispanic, 5% multiracial, 0% Pacific Islander, 5% white, 0% international; 84% from in state; 53% live on campus; N/A of students in fraternities, N/A in sororities
Most popular majors: 12% Criminal Justice/Safety Studies, 9% Business Administration and Management, General, 8% Family and Consumer Sciences/Human Sciences, General, 8% Psychology, General, 8% Social Sciences, General
Expenses: 2020-2021: $6,629 in state, $19,336 out of state; room/board: $9,545
Financial aid: (919) 530-6180; 82% of undergrads determined to have financial need; average aid package $10,077

North Carolina State University
Raleigh NC
(919) 515-2434
U.S. News ranking: Nat. U., No. 80
Website: admissions.ncsu.edu
Admissions email: undergrad-admissions@ncsu.edu
Public; founded 1887
Freshman admissions: more selective; 2019-2020: 30,995 applied, 13,902 accepted. Neither SAT nor ACT required. SAT 25/75 percentile: 1250-1420. High school rank: 50% in top tenth, 86% in top quarter, 99% in top half
Early decision deadline: N/A, notification date: N/A
Early action deadline: 11/1, notification date: 1/30
Application deadline (fall): 1/15
Undergraduate student body: 22,820 full time, 3,153 part time; 52% male, 48% female; 0% American Indian, 8% Asian, 6% Black, 6% Hispanic, 4% multiracial, 0% Pacific Islander, 68% white, 4% international; 88% from in state; 37% live on campus; 12% of students in fraternities, 16% in sororities
Most popular majors: 28% Engineering, 15% Business, Management, Marketing, and Related Support Services, 9% Biological and Biomedical Sciences, 7% Agriculture, Agriculture Operations, and Related Sciences, 4% Computer and Information Sciences and Support Services
Expenses: 2020-2021: $9,101 in state, $29,220 out of state; room/board: $11,601

Financial aid: (919) 515-2421; 46% of undergrads determined to have financial need; average aid package $13,488

North Carolina Wesleyan College
Rocky Mount NC
(800) 488-6292
U.S. News ranking: Reg. Coll. (S), No. 47
Website: www.ncwc.edu
Admissions email: adm@ncwc.edu
Private; founded 1956
Affiliation: United Methodist
Freshman admissions: less selective; 2019-2020: 3,176 applied, 1,975 accepted. Neither SAT nor ACT required. SAT 25/75 percentile: 860-1070. High school rank: 5% in top tenth, 15% in top quarter, 59% in top half
Early decision deadline: N/A, notification date: N/A
Early action deadline: N/A, notification date: N/A
Application deadline (fall): rolling
Undergraduate student body: 1,600 full time, 222 part time; 42% male, 58% female; 1% American Indian, 1% Asian, 42% Black, 4% Hispanic, 4% multiracial, 0% Pacific Islander, 28% white, 7% international; 86% from in state; 72% live on campus; 1% of students in fraternities, 2% in sororities
Most popular majors: 51% Business Administration and Management, General, 15% Criminal Justice/Law Enforcement Administration, 13% Psychology, General, 6% Computer and Information Sciences, General, 2% Sociology
Expenses: 2020-2021: $32,950; room/board: $11,476
Financial aid: (252) 985-5290; 82% of undergrads determined to have financial need; average aid package $24,347

Pfeiffer University[1]
Misenheimer NC
(800) 338-2060
U.S. News ranking: Reg. U. (S), No. 72
Website: www.pfeiffer.edu
Admissions email: admissions@pfeiffer.edu
Private; founded 1885
Affiliation: United Methodist
Application deadline (fall): rolling
Undergraduate student body: N/A full time, N/A part time
Expenses: 2019-2020: $31,050; room/board: $11,508
Financial aid: (704) 463-3060

Queens University of Charlotte
Charlotte NC
(800) 849-0202
U.S. News ranking: Reg. U. (S), No. 13
Website: www.queens.edu
Admissions email: admissions@queens.edu
Private; founded 1857
Affiliation: Presbyterian
Freshman admissions: selective; 2019-2020: 3,419 applied, 2,230 accepted. Neither SAT nor ACT required. SAT 25/75

percentile: 1040-1240. High school rank: 11% in top tenth, 41% in top quarter, 78% in top half
Early decision deadline: 11/1, notification date: 12/1
Early action deadline: 12/2, notification date: 12/31
Application deadline (fall): 9/5
Undergraduate student body: 1,570 full time, 163 part time; 33% male, 67% female; 1% American Indian, 3% Asian, 15% Black, 12% Hispanic, 1% multiracial, 0% Pacific Islander, 55% white, 9% international; 60% from in state; 54% live on campus; 5% of students in fraternities, 12% in sororities
Most popular majors: 27% Health Professions and Related Programs, 20% Business, Management, Marketing, and Related Support Services, 9% Biological and Biomedical Sciences, 9% Communication, Journalism, and Related Programs, 7% Visual and Performing Arts
Expenses: 2020-2021: $37,332; room/board: $12,257
Financial aid: (704) 337-2339; 68% of undergrads determined to have financial need; average aid package $26,200

Salem College
Winston-Salem NC
(336) 721-2621
U.S. News ranking: Nat. Lib. Arts, No. 140
Website: www.salem.edu
Admissions email: admissions@salem.edu
Private; founded 1772
Affiliation: Moravian Church
Freshman admissions: selective; 2019-2020: 833 applied, 666 accepted. Either SAT or ACT required. ACT 25/75 percentile: 17-23. High school rank: 14% in top tenth, 52% in top quarter, 85% in top half
Early decision deadline: N/A, notification date: N/A
Early action deadline: N/A, notification date: N/A
Application deadline (fall): rolling
Undergraduate student body: 475 full time, 137 part time; 3% male, 97% female; 0% American Indian, 2% Asian, 17% Black, 16% Hispanic, 6% multiracial, 0% Pacific Islander, 55% white, 0% international; 77% from in state; 57% live on campus; 0% of students in fraternities, 0% in sororities
Most popular majors: Information not available
Expenses: 2020-2021: $31,016; room/board: $12,300
Financial aid: (336) 721-2808; 84% of undergrads determined to have financial need; average aid package $34,898

Shaw University
Raleigh NC
(800) 214-6683
U.S. News ranking: Reg. Coll. (S), second tier
Website: www.shawu.edu
Admissions email: admissions@shawu.edu
Private; founded 1865

Affiliation: Baptist
Freshman admissions: least selective; 2019-2020: 4,310 applied, 2,732 accepted. Either SAT or ACT required. SAT 25/75 percentile: 737-902. High school rank: 1% in top tenth, 6% in top quarter, 26% in top half
Early decision deadline: N/A, notification date: N/A
Early action deadline: N/A, notification date: N/A
Application deadline (fall): 7/30
Undergraduate student body: 1,082 full time, 92 part time; 40% male, 60% female; 0% American Indian, 3% Asian, 56% Black, 3% Hispanic, 16% multiracial, 0% Pacific Islander, 1% white, 5% international; 61% from in state; 54% live on campus; N/A of students in fraternities, N/A in sororities
Most popular majors: 16% Social Work, 15% Business Administration and Management, General, 10% Kinesiology and Exercise Science, 9% Mass Communication/Media Studies, 8% Criminal Justice/Safety Studies
Expenses: 2019-2020: $16,480; room/board: $8,514
Financial aid: (919) 546-8565

Southeastern Baptist Theological Seminary[1]
Wake Forest NC
(919) 761-2246
U.S. News ranking: Reg. U. (S), second tier
Website: www.sebts.edu/
Admissions email: admissions@sebts.edu
Private; founded 1950
Affiliation: Southern Baptist
Application deadline (fall): 8/1
Undergraduate student body: N/A full time, N/A part time
Expenses: 2019-2020: $10,072; room/board: $6,518
Financial aid: N/A

St. Augustine's University[1]
Raleigh NC
(919) 516-4012
U.S. News ranking: Reg. Coll. (S), No. 65
Website: www.st-aug.edu
Admissions email: admissions@st-aug.edu
Private; founded 1867
Affiliation: Episcopal Church, Reformed
Application deadline (fall): rolling
Undergraduate student body: N/A full time, N/A part time
Expenses: 2020-2021: $16,884; room/board: $7,942
Financial aid: (919) 516-4309

University of Mount Olive
Mount Olive NC
(919) 658-2502
U.S. News ranking: Reg. U. (S), No. 65
Website: www.umo.edu/
Admissions email: admissions@umo.edu
Private; founded 1951

Affiliation: Original Free Will Baptist
Freshman admissions: less selective; 2019-2020: 2,158 applied, 1,262 accepted. Neither SAT nor ACT required. ACT 25/75 percentile: 16-22. High school rank: N/A
Early decision deadline: N/A, notification date: N/A
Early action deadline: N/A, notification date: N/A
Application deadline (fall): rolling
Undergraduate student body: 1,494 full time, 1,118 part time; 34% male, 66% female; 0% American Indian, 1% Asian, 27% Black, 8% Hispanic, 4% multiracial, 0% Pacific Islander, 54% white, 4% international
Most popular majors: Business Administration and Management, General, Criminal Justice/Safety Studies, Early Childhood Education and Teaching, Health/Health Care Administration/Management
Expenses: 2019-2020: $21,194; room/board: $8,800
Financial aid: (919) 658-2502

University of North Carolina Asheville
Asheville NC
(828) 251-6481
U.S. News ranking: Nat. Lib. Arts, No. 140
Website: www.unca.edu
Admissions email: admissions@unca.edu
Public; founded 1927
Freshman admissions: selective; 2019-2020: 3,750 applied, 3,150 accepted. Either SAT or ACT required. SAT 25/75 percentile: 1090-1270. High school rank: 14% in top tenth, 39% in top quarter, 78% in top half
Early decision deadline: 11/1, notification date: 12/15
Early action deadline: N/A, notification date: N/A
Application deadline (fall): 8/1
Undergraduate student body: 3,036 full time, 551 part time; 42% male, 58% female; 0% American Indian, 2% Asian, 5% Black, 9% Hispanic, 4% multiracial, 0% Pacific Islander, 74% white, 1% international; 89% from in state; 46% live on campus; 1% of students in fraternities, 2% in sororities
Most popular majors: 12% Psychology, General, 8% Environmental Studies, 7% Biology/Biological Sciences, General, 6% Business Administration and Management, General, 6% Public Health Education and Promotion
Expenses: 2020-2021: $7,244 in state, $24,592 out of state; room/board: $9,950
Financial aid: (828) 251-6535; 59% of undergrads determined to have financial need; average aid package $14,310

University of North Carolina–Chapel Hill

Chapel Hill NC
(919) 966-3621
U.S. News ranking: Nat. U., No. 28
Website: www.unc.edu
Admissions email:
unchelp@admissions.unc.edu
Public; founded 1789
Freshman admissions: most
selective; 2019-2020: 42,466
applied, 9,608 accepted. Either
SAT or ACT required. ACT 25/75
percentile: 27-33. High school
rank: 78% in top tenth, 95% in
top quarter, 99% in top half
Early decision deadline: N/A,
notification date: N/A
Early action deadline: 10/15,
notification date: 1/31
Application deadline (fall): 1/15
Undergraduate student body:
18,728 full time, 627 part time;
41% male, 59% female; 0%
American Indian, 11% Asian,
8% Black, 9% Hispanic, 5%
multiracial, 0% Pacific Islander,
59% white, 4% international;
83% from in state; 52% live
on campus; 18% of students in
fraternities, 17% in sororities
Most popular majors: 16% Social
Sciences, 10% Biological and
Biomedical Sciences, 10%
Communication, Journalism, and
Related Programs, 7% Business,
Management, Marketing, and
Related Support Services, 7%
Psychology
Expenses: 2020-2021: $9,021 in
state, $36,200 out of state; room/
board: $11,740
Financial aid: (919) 962-8396;
44% of undergrads determined to
have financial need; average aid
package $18,973

University of North Carolina–Charlotte

Charlotte NC
(704) 687-5507
U.S. News ranking: Nat. U.,
No. 227
Website: www.uncc.edu/
Admissions email:
admissions@uncc.edu
Public; founded 1946
Freshman admissions: more
selective; 2019-2020: 21,867
applied, 14,224 accepted. Either
SAT or ACT required. SAT 25/75
percentile: 1120-1290. High
school rank: 17% in top tenth,
49% in top quarter, 83% in
top half
Early decision deadline: N/A,
notification date: N/A
Early action deadline: 11/1,
notification date: 1/30
Application deadline (fall): 6/1
Undergraduate student body:
20,877 full time, 3,193 part
time; 53% male, 47% female;
0% American Indian, 8% Asian,
16% Black, 11% Hispanic, 5%
multiracial, 0% Pacific Islander,
56% white, 2% international;
92% from in state; 25% live
on campus; 7% of students in
fraternities, 10% in sororities
Most popular majors: 18%
Business, Management,
Marketing, and Related Support

Services, 9% Computer and
Information Sciences and Support
Services, 8% Engineering, 8%
Health Professions and Related
Programs, 7% Communication,
Journalism, and Related Programs
Expenses: 2020-2021: $7,300 in
state, $20,737 out of state; room/
board: $12,800
Financial aid: (704) 687-5504;
61% of undergrads determined to
have financial need; average aid
package $9,482

University of North Carolina–Greensboro

Greensboro NC
(336) 334-5243
U.S. News ranking: Nat. U.,
No. 258
Website: www.uncg.edu/
Admissions email:
admissions@uncg.edu
Public; founded 1891
Freshman admissions: selective;
2019-2020: 9,972 applied,
8,221 accepted. Either SAT
or ACT required. SAT 25/75
percentile: 1000-1160. High
school rank: 13% in top tenth,
39% in top quarter, 77% in
top half
Early decision deadline: N/A,
notification date: N/A
Early action deadline: N/A,
notification date: N/A
Application deadline (fall): rolling
Undergraduate student body:
14,007 full time, 2,574 part
time; 33% male, 67% female;
0% American Indian, 5% Asian,
30% Black, 12% Hispanic, 5%
multiracial, 0% Pacific Islander,
46% white, 1% international;
95% from in state; 34% live
on campus; 85% of students in
fraternities, 2% in sororities
Most popular majors: 19%
Business, Management,
Marketing, and Related Support
Services, 10% Health Professions
and Related Programs, 8% Parks,
Recreation, Leisure, and Fitness
Studies, 8% Visual and Performing
Arts, 7% Social Sciences
Expenses: 2020-2021: $7,404 in
state, $22,564 out of state; room/
board: $9,482
Financial aid: (336) 334-5702;
74% of undergrads determined to
have financial need; average aid
package $10,782

University of North Carolina–Pembroke

Pembroke NC
(910) 521-6262
U.S. News ranking: Reg. U. (S),
No. 73
Website: www.uncp.edu
Admissions email:
admissions@uncp.edu
Public; founded 1887
Freshman admissions: selective;
2019-2020: 5,604 applied,
4,760 accepted. Either SAT
or ACT required. ACT 25/75
percentile: 17-21. High school
rank: 12% in top tenth, 37% in
top quarter, 75% in top half
Early decision deadline: N/A,
notification date: N/A

Early action deadline: N/A,
notification date: N/A
Application deadline (fall): 5/1
Undergraduate student body: 5,109
full time, 1,244 part time; 39%
male, 61% female; 14% American
Indian, 1% Asian, 32% Black,
8% Hispanic, 6% multiracial,
0% Pacific Islander, 37% white,
1% international; 94% from in
state; 33% live on campus; 2%
of students in fraternities, 3% in
sororities
Most popular majors: 13%
Biological and Biomedical
Sciences, 13% Business,
Management, Marketing, and
Related Support Services, 12%
Social Sciences, 11% Homeland
Security, Law Enforcement,
Firefighting and Related Protective
Services, 10% Parks, Recreation,
Leisure, and Fitness Studies
Expenses: 2020-2021: $1,000 in
state, $5,000 out of state; room/
board: N/A
Financial aid: (910) 521-6255;
76% of undergrads determined to
have financial need; average aid
package $9,010

University of North Carolina School of the Arts[1]

Winston-Salem NC
(336) 770-3291
U.S. News ranking: Arts, unranked
Website: www.uncsa.edu
Admissions email:
admissions@uncsa.edu
Public; founded 1963
Application deadline (fall): 3/15
Undergraduate student body: 901
full time, 28 part time
Expenses: 2020-2021: $9,358 in
state, $26,095 out of state; room/
board: $9,456
Financial aid: (336) 770-3297;
56% of undergrads determined to
have financial need; average aid
package $14,787

University of North Carolina–Wilmington

Wilmington NC
(910) 962-3243
U.S. News ranking: Nat. U.,
No. 187
Website: uncw.edu/admissions/
Admissions email:
admissions@uncw.edu
Public; founded 1947
Freshman admissions: more
selective; 2019-2020: 13,287
applied, 8,697 accepted. Either
SAT or ACT required. ACT 25/75
percentile: 22-27. High school
rank: 24% in top tenth, 63% in
top quarter, 95% in top half
Early decision deadline: N/A,
notification date: N/A
Early action deadline: 11/1,
notification date: 1/20
Application deadline (fall): 2/1
Undergraduate student body:
12,480 full time, 2,305 part
time; 37% male, 63% female;
0% American Indian, 2% Asian,
4% Black, 7% Hispanic, 4%
multiracial, 0% Pacific Islander,
79% white, 1% international;

88% from in state; 25% live
on campus; 10% of students in
fraternities, 9% in sororities
Most popular majors: 20%
Registered Nursing/Registered
Nurse, 19% Business
Administration and Management,
General, 6% Psychology, General,
5% Speech Communication and
Rhetoric, 4% Biology/Biological
Sciences, General
Expenses: 2020-2021: $7,318 in
state, $21,871 out of state; room/
board: $11,346
Financial aid: (910) 962-3177;
56% of undergrads determined to
have financial need; average aid
package $9,430

Wake Forest University

Winston-Salem NC
(336) 758-5201
U.S. News ranking: Nat. U., No. 28
Website: www.wfu.edu
Admissions email:
admissions@wfu.edu
Private; founded 1834
Freshman admissions: most
selective; 2019-2020: 12,559
applied, 3,717 accepted. Neither
SAT nor ACT required. ACT 25/75
percentile: 30-33. High school
rank: 75% in top tenth, 92% in
top quarter, 98% in top half
Early decision deadline: 11/15,
notification date: N/A
Early action deadline: N/A,
notification date: N/A
Application deadline (fall): 1/1
Undergraduate student body: 5,240
full time, 47 part time; 47%
male, 53% female; 0% American
Indian, 3% Asian, 6% Black, 7%
Hispanic, 4% multiracial, 0%
Pacific Islander, 69% white, 10%
international; N/A from in state;
77% live on campus; 29% of
students in fraternities, 59% in
sororities
Most popular majors: 23%
Social Sciences, 18% Business,
Management, Marketing, and
Related Support Services, 9%
Communication, Journalism, and
Related Programs, 8% Biological
and Biomedical Sciences, 8%
Psychology
Expenses: 2020-2021: $57,760;
room/board: $17,334
Financial aid: (336) 758-5154;
29% of undergrads determined to
have financial need; average aid
package $53,115

Warren Wilson College

Asheville NC
(800) 934-3536
U.S. News ranking: Nat. Lib. Arts,
No. 162
Website: www.warren-wilson.edu/
Admissions email:
admit@warren-wilson.edu
Private; founded 1894
Freshman admissions: selective;
2019-2020: 1,195 applied,
1,011 accepted. Neither SAT
nor ACT required. SAT 25/75
percentile: 1040-1315. High
school rank: 8% in top tenth, 29%
in top quarter, 64% in top half
Early decision deadline: 11/1,
notification date: 12/1

Early action deadline: 11/15,
notification date: 12/1
Application deadline (fall): rolling
Undergraduate student body: 688
full time, 18 part time; 33%
male, 67% female; 1% American
Indian, 1% Asian, 6% Black,
9% Hispanic, 5% multiracial,
0% Pacific Islander, 76% white,
2% international; 39% from in
state; 90% live on campus; 0%
of students in fraternities, 0% in
sororities
Most popular majors: 26%
Environmental Studies, 12%
Psychology, General, 11%
Sociology, 11% Visual and
Performing Arts, General, 10%
Social Sciences, Other
Expenses: 2020-2021: $38,350;
room/board: $11,750
Financial aid: (828) 771-2082

Western Carolina University

Cullowhee NC
(828) 227-7317
U.S. News ranking: Reg. U. (S),
No. 25
Website: www.wcu.edu
Admissions email:
admiss@email.wcu.edu
Public; founded 1889
Freshman admissions: selective;
2019-2020: 17,766 applied,
7,614 accepted. Either SAT
or ACT required. ACT 25/75
percentile: 20-25. High school
rank: 15% in top tenth, 39% in
top quarter, 78% in top half
Early decision deadline: N/A,
notification date: N/A
Early action deadline: 11/15,
notification date: 12/15
Application deadline (fall): 3/1
Undergraduate student body: 8,934
full time, 1,535 part time; 45%
male, 55% female; 1% American
Indian, 1% Asian, 5% Black,
7% Hispanic, 4% multiracial,
0% Pacific Islander, 79% white,
1% international; 90% from in
state; N/A live on campus; N/A
of students in fraternities, N/A in
sororities
Most popular majors: 19%
Business, Management,
Marketing, and Related Support
Services, 17% Health Professions
and Related Programs, 12%
Education, 7% Homeland
Security, Law Enforcement,
Firefighting and Related
Protective Services, 6% Public
Administration and Social Service
Professions
Expenses: 2020-2021: $4,535 in
state, $8,535 out of state; room/
board: N/A
Financial aid: (828) 227-7290

William Peace University

Raleigh NC
(919) 508-2214
U.S. News ranking: Reg. Coll. (S),
No. 24
Website: www.peace.edu
Admissions email:
admissions@peace.edu
Private; founded 1857
Affiliation:
Presbyterian Church (USA)

Freshman admissions: selective; 2019-2020: 2,129 applied, 978 accepted. Either SAT or ACT required. SAT 25/75 percentile: 920-1140. High school rank: N/A
Early decision deadline: N/A, notification date: N/A
Early action deadline: N/A, notification date: N/A
Application deadline (fall): rolling
Undergraduate student body: 802 full time, 87 part time; 46% male, 54% female; 1% American Indian, 2% Asian, 24% Black, 12% Hispanic, 5% multiracial, 0% Pacific Islander, 53% white, 0% international; N/A from in state; 55% live on campus; N/A of students in fraternities, N/A in sororities
Most popular majors: 27% Business, Management, Marketing, and Related Support Services, 16% Social Sciences, 13% Visual and Performing Arts, 11% Psychology, 7% Biological and Biomedical Sciences
Expenses: 2020-2021: $32,450; room/board: $11,880
Financial aid: (919) 508-2394; 91% of undergrads determined to have financial need; average aid package $23,386

Wingate University
Wingate NC
(800) 755-5550
U.S. News ranking: Nat. U., second tier
Website: www.wingate.edu/
Admissions email: admit@wingate.edu
Private; founded 1896
Freshman admissions: selective; 2019-2020: 17,353 applied, 15,553 accepted. Either SAT or ACT required. SAT 25/75 percentile: 930-1130. High school rank: 13% in top tenth, 36% in top quarter, 73% in top half
Early decision deadline: N/A, notification date: N/A
Early action deadline: N/A, notification date: N/A
Application deadline (fall): rolling
Undergraduate student body: 2,706 full time, 58 part time; 39% male, 61% female; 0% American Indian, 2% Asian, 20% Black, 2% Hispanic, 8% multiracial, 0% Pacific Islander, 54% white, 4% international; N/A from in state; 76% live on campus; 6% of students in fraternities, 13% in sororities
Most popular majors: 19% Business, Management, Marketing, and Related Support Services, 15% Biological and Biomedical Sciences, 14% Parks, Recreation, Leisure, and Fitness Studies, 8% Education, 7% Communication, Journalism, and Related Programs
Expenses: 2020-2021: $38,896; room/board: $9,910
Financial aid: (704) 233-8010; 80% of undergrads determined to have financial need; average aid package $31,238

Winston-Salem State University[1]
Winston-Salem NC
(336) 750-2070
U.S. News ranking: Reg. U. (S), No. 59
Website: www.wssu.edu
Admissions email: admissions@wssu.edu
Public; founded 1892
Application deadline (fall): 3/15
Undergraduate student body: N/A full time, N/A part time
Expenses: 2019-2020: $5,941 in state, $16,188 out of state; room/board: $10,575
Financial aid: N/A

NORTH DAKOTA

Bismarck State College
Bismarck ND
(701) 224-2459
U.S. News ranking: Reg. Coll. (Mid. W), unranked
Website: bismarckstate.edu/
Admissions email: bsc.admissions@bismarckstate.edu
Public; founded 1939
Freshman admissions: least selective; 2019-2020: N/A applied, N/A accepted. Neither SAT nor ACT required. ACT 25/75 percentile: 17-23. High school rank: N/A
Early decision deadline: N/A, notification date: N/A
Early action deadline: N/A, notification date: N/A
Application deadline (fall): rolling
Undergraduate student body: 2,033 full time, 1,706 part time; 57% male, 43% female; 2% American Indian, 1% Asian, 3% Black, 4% Hispanic, 4% multiracial, 0% Pacific Islander, 85% white, 0% international; 84% from in state; 11% live on campus; N/A of students in fraternities, N/A in sororities
Most popular majors: Information not available
Expenses: 2020-2021: $5,694 in state, $8,102 out of state; room/board: $7,103
Financial aid: (701) 224-5441

Dickinson State University
Dickinson ND
(701) 483-2175
U.S. News ranking: Reg. Coll. (Mid. W), No. 44
Website: www.dickinsonstate.edu/
Admissions email: dsu.hawks@dsu.nodak.edu
Public; founded 1918
Freshman admissions: selective; 2019-2020: 376 applied, 375 accepted. Neither SAT nor ACT required. ACT 25/75 percentile: 18-23. High school rank: N/A
Early decision deadline: N/A, notification date: N/A
Early action deadline: N/A, notification date: N/A
Application deadline (fall): 8/15
Undergraduate student body: 922 full time, 399 part time; 38% male, 62% female; 2% American Indian, 1% Asian, 4% Black, 6% Hispanic, 3% multiracial,

0% Pacific Islander, 78% white, 4% international; 76% from in state; N/A live on campus; N/A of students in fraternities, N/A in sororities
Most popular majors: 47% Business, Management, Marketing, and Related Support Services, 10% Multi/Interdisciplinary Studies, 8% Education, 6% Computer and Information Sciences and Support Services, 6% Health Professions and Related Programs
Expenses: 2020-2021: $9,118 in state, $11,218 out of state; room/board: $7,486
Financial aid: (701) 483-2371; 58% of undergrads determined to have financial need; average aid package $10,394

Mayville State University
Mayville ND
(701) 788-4667
U.S. News ranking: Reg. Coll. (Mid. W), No. 54
Website: www.mayvillestate.edu
Admissions email: masuadmissions@mayvillestate.edu
Public; founded 1889
Freshman admissions: less selective; 2019-2020: N/A applied, N/A accepted. Either SAT or ACT required. ACT 25/75 percentile: 18-25. High school rank: N/A
Early decision deadline: N/A, notification date: N/A
Early action deadline: N/A, notification date: N/A
Application deadline (fall): rolling
Undergraduate student body: 589 full time, 598 part time; 36% male, 64% female; N/A American Indian, N/A Asian, N/A Black, N/A Hispanic, N/A multiracial, N/A Pacific Islander, N/A white, N/A international; 67% from in state; 10% live on campus; 0% of students in fraternities, 0% in sororities
Most popular majors: Information not available
Expenses: 2020-2021: $8,888 in state, $10,394 out of state; room/board: $6,945
Financial aid: (701) 788-4767; 63% of undergrads determined to have financial need; average aid package $11,685

Minot State University
Minot ND
(701) 858-3350
U.S. News ranking: Reg. U. (Mid. W), No. 110
Website: www.minotstateu.edu
Admissions email: askmsu@minotstateu.edu
Public; founded 1913
Freshman admissions: selective; 2019-2020: 787 applied, 583 accepted. Either SAT or ACT required. ACT 25/75 percentile: 18-23. High school rank: 10% in top tenth, 31% in top quarter, 68% in top half
Early decision deadline: N/A, notification date: N/A
Early action deadline: N/A, notification date: N/A

Application deadline (fall): rolling
Undergraduate student body: 1,921 full time, 911 part time; 39% male, 61% female; 2% American Indian, 1% Asian, 4% Black, 8% Hispanic, 4% multiracial, 0% Pacific Islander, 68% white, 11% international
Most popular majors: 32% Business Administration and Management, General, 16% Education, General, 15% Registered Nursing/Registered Nurse, 8% Social Work, 6% Corrections
Expenses: 2020-2021: $7,896 in state, $7,896 out of state; room/board: $7,434
Financial aid: (701) 858-3375; 48% of undergrads determined to have financial need; average aid package $10,953

North Dakota State University
Fargo ND
(701) 231-8643
U.S. News ranking: Nat. U., No. 284
Website: www.ndsu.edu
Admissions email: NDSU.Admission@ndsu.edu
Public; founded 1890
Freshman admissions: selective; 2019-2020: 6,211 applied, 5,811 accepted. Either SAT or ACT required. ACT 25/75 percentile: 21-26. High school rank: 16% in top tenth, 40% in top quarter, 74% in top half
Early decision deadline: N/A, notification date: N/A
Early action deadline: N/A, notification date: N/A
Application deadline (fall): 8/1
Undergraduate student body: 9,638 full time, 1,193 part time; 53% male, 47% female; 1% American Indian, 1% Asian, 3% Black, 3% Hispanic, 4% multiracial, 0% Pacific Islander, 87% white, 1% international; 42% from in state; 33% live on campus; 8% of students in fraternities, 9% in sororities
Most popular majors: 16% Business, Management, Marketing, and Related Support Services, 15% Engineering, 13% Health Professions and Related Programs, 11% Agriculture, Agriculture Operations, and Related Sciences, 7% Family and Consumer Sciences/Human Sciences
Expenses: 2019-2020: $10,516 in state, $13,628 out of state; room/board: $9,088
Financial aid: (701) 231-6221

University of Jamestown
Jamestown ND
(701) 252-3467
U.S. News ranking: Reg. Coll. (Mid. W), No. 38
Website: www.uj.edu
Admissions email: admissions@uj.edu
Private; founded 1883
Affiliation: Presbyterian Church (USA)
Freshman admissions: selective; 2019-2020: 1,106 applied, 766 accepted. Either SAT or ACT

required. ACT 25/75 percentile: 19-25. High school rank: 15% in top tenth, 35% in top quarter, 73% in top half
Early decision deadline: N/A, notification date: N/A
Early action deadline: N/A, notification date: N/A
Application deadline (fall): 9/10
Undergraduate student body: 887 full time, 21 part time; 54% male, 46% female; 0% American Indian, 1% Asian, 7% Black, 10% Hispanic, 3% multiracial, 0% Pacific Islander, 72% white, 7% international; 40% from in state; 75% live on campus; 0% of students in fraternities, 0% in sororities
Most popular majors: 18% Kinesiology and Exercise Science, 14% Business Administration and Management, General, 12% Registered Nursing/Registered Nurse, 8% Biology/Biological Sciences, General, 4% Accounting
Expenses: 2020-2021: $22,958; room/board: $8,316
Financial aid: (701) 252-3467; 66% of undergrads determined to have financial need; average aid package $17,733

University of Mary
Bismarck ND
(701) 355-8030
U.S. News ranking: Nat. U., second tier
Website: www.umary.edu
Admissions email: marauder@umary.edu
Private; founded 1959
Affiliation: Roman Catholic
Freshman admissions: selective; 2019-2020: 1,326 applied, 1,297 accepted. Either SAT or ACT required. ACT 25/75 percentile: 21-26. High school rank: N/A
Early decision deadline: N/A, notification date: N/A
Early action deadline: N/A, notification date: N/A
Application deadline (fall): rolling
Undergraduate student body: 1,867 full time, 660 part time; 40% male, 60% female; 2% American Indian, 1% Asian, 2% Black, 5% Hispanic, 2% multiracial, 0% Pacific Islander, 76% white, 0% international; 49% from in state; 44% live on campus; 0% of students in fraternities, 0% in sororities
Most popular majors: 23% Health Professions and Related Programs, 22% Business, Management, Marketing, and Related Support Services, 13% Education, 7% Psychology, 6% Parks, Recreation, Leisure, and Fitness Studies
Expenses: 2020-2021: $19,730; room/board: $7,840
Financial aid: (701) 355-8226

University of North Dakota
Grand Forks ND
(800) 225-5863
U.S. News ranking: Nat. U., No. 258
Website: und.edu
Admissions email: admissions@und.edu
Public; founded 1883

Freshman admissions: selective; 2019-2020: 4,964 applied, 4,027 accepted. Either SAT or ACT required. ACT 25/75 percentile: 20-26. High school rank: 19% in top tenth, 44% in top quarter, 78% in top half
Early decision deadline: N/A, notification date: N/A
Early action deadline: N/A, notification date: N/A
Application deadline (fall): rolling
Undergraduate student body: 7,628 full time, 2,535 part time; 57% male, 43% female; 1% American Indian, 2% Asian, 2% Black, 4% Hispanic, 5% multiracial, 0% Pacific Islander, 80% white, 5% international; 38% from in state; 25% live on campus; 11% of students in fraternities, 13% in sororities
Most popular majors: 7% Psychology, General, 7% Registered Nursing/Registered Nurse, 6% Aeronautics/Aviation/Aerospace Science and Technology, General, 5% General Studies, 4% Mechanical Engineering
Expenses: 2020-2021: $10,276 in state, $14,546 out of state; room/board: $9,976
Financial aid: (701) 777-3121; 49% of undergrads determined to have financial need; average aid package $15,351

Valley City State University

Valley City ND
(800) 532-8641
U.S. News ranking: Reg. Coll. (Mid. W), No. 49
Website: www.vcsu.edu
Admissions email: enrollment.services@vcsu.edu
Public; founded 1890
Freshman admissions: selective; 2019-2020: 514 applied, 394 accepted. Either SAT or ACT required. ACT 25/75 percentile: 18-23. High school rank: N/A
Early decision deadline: N/A, notification date: N/A
Early action deadline: N/A, notification date: N/A
Application deadline (fall): rolling
Undergraduate student body: 904 full time, 620 part time; 42% male, 58% female; 1% American Indian, 0% Asian, 3% Black, 6% Hispanic, 5% multiracial, 0% Pacific Islander, 80% white, 2% international; 62% from in state; 36% live on campus; 1% of students in fraternities, 1% in sororities
Most popular majors: 63% Education, 9% Business, Management, Marketing, and Related Support Services, 4% Natural Resources and Conservation, 3% English Language and Literature/Letters, 3% Parks, Recreation, Leisure, and Fitness Studies
Expenses: 2020-2021: $7,944 in state, $12,534 out of state; room/board: $6,684
Financial aid: (701) 845-7541; 56% of undergrads determined to have financial need; average aid package $12,248

Northern Marianas College[1]

Saipan MP
(670) 237-6700
U.S. News ranking: Reg. Coll. (W), unranked
Website: www.hiwassee.edu
Admissions email: N/A
Public
Application deadline (fall): N/A
Undergraduate student body: N/A full time, N/A part time
Expenses: 2019-2020: $4,038 in state, $5,520 out of state; room/board: $6,000
Financial aid: N/A

Art Academy of Cincinnati

Cincinnati OH
(513) 562-6262
U.S. News ranking: Arts, unranked
Website: www.artacademy.edu
Admissions email: admissions@artacademy.edu
Private; founded 1869
Freshman admissions: least selective; 2019-2020: 1,405 applied, 350 accepted. Neither SAT nor ACT required. SAT 25/75 percentile: N/A. High school rank: N/A
Early decision deadline: N/A, notification date: N/A
Early action deadline: N/A, notification date: N/A
Application deadline (fall): 8/1
Undergraduate student body: 206 full time, 8 part time; 27% male, 73% female; 0% American Indian, 1% Asian, 17% Black, 6% Hispanic, 4% multiracial, 0% Pacific Islander, 70% white, 0% international; 71% from in state; 37% live on campus; 0% of students in fraternities, 0% in sororities
Most popular majors: 26% Illustration, 22% Design and Visual Communications, General, 20% Painting, 10% Sculpture, 8% Photography
Expenses: 2020-2021: $34,854; room/board: $7,400
Financial aid: (513) 562-8757

Ashland University

Ashland OH
(419) 289-5052
U.S. News ranking: Reg. U. (Mid. W), No. 51
Website: www.ashland.edu/admissions
Admissions email: enrollme@ashland.edu
Private; founded 1878
Freshman admissions: selective; 2019-2020: 4,235 applied, 2,988 accepted. Either SAT or ACT required. ACT 25/75 percentile: 19-24. High school rank: 20% in top tenth, 43% in top quarter, 76% in top half
Early decision deadline: N/A, notification date: N/A
Early action deadline: N/A, notification date: N/A

Application deadline (fall): rolling
Undergraduate student body: 3,575 full time, 2,247 part time; 56% male, 44% female; 1% American Indian, 1% Asian, 18% Black, 3% Hispanic, 2% multiracial, 0% Pacific Islander, 69% white, 1% international; 90% from in state; 66% live on campus; 4% of students in fraternities, 6% in sororities
Most popular majors: 16% Health Professions and Related Programs, 15% Business, Management, Marketing, and Related Support Services, 13% Education, 6% Communication, Journalism, and Related Programs, 4% Homeland Security, Law Enforcement, Firefighting and Related Protective Services
Expenses: 2020-2021: $22,540; room/board: $10,640
Financial aid: (419) 289-5002; 81% of undergrads determined to have financial need; average aid package $14,785

Baldwin Wallace University

Berea OH
(440) 826-2222
U.S. News ranking: Reg. U. (Mid. W), No. 10
Website: www.bw.edu
Admissions email: admission@bw.edu
Private; founded 1845
Freshman admissions: selective; 2019-2020: 3,922 applied, 2,851 accepted. Neither SAT nor ACT required. ACT 25/75 percentile: 21-27. High school rank: 16% in top tenth, 48% in top quarter, 82% in top half
Early decision deadline: N/A, notification date: N/A
Early action deadline: N/A, notification date: N/A
Application deadline (fall): rolling
Undergraduate student body: 2,792 full time, 172 part time; 46% male, 54% female; 0% American Indian, 1% Asian, 8% Black, 6% Hispanic, 5% multiracial, 0% Pacific Islander, 79% white, 1% international; 74% from in state; 57% live on campus; 15% of students in fraternities, 16% in sororities
Most popular majors: 24% Business, Management, Marketing, and Related Support Services, 12% Health Professions and Related Programs, 12% Visual and Performing Arts, 8% Biological and Biomedical Sciences, 7% Psychology
Expenses: 2020-2021: $34,504; room/board: $11,946
Financial aid: (440) 826-2108; 75% of undergrads determined to have financial need; average aid package $26,293

Bluffton University

Bluffton OH
(800) 488-3257
U.S. News ranking: Reg. Coll. (Mid. W), No. 28
Website: www.bluffton.edu
Admissions email: admissions@bluffton.edu
Private; founded 1899
Affiliation: Mennonite Church

Freshman admissions: selective; 2019-2020: 1,676 applied, 958 accepted. Either SAT or ACT required. ACT 25/75 percentile: 18-23. High school rank: 4% in top tenth, 16% in top quarter, 41% in top half
Early decision deadline: N/A, notification date: N/A
Early action deadline: N/A, notification date: N/A
Application deadline (fall): rolling
Undergraduate student body: 634 full time, 76 part time; 57% male, 43% female; 1% American Indian, 0% Asian, 11% Black, 3% Hispanic, 3% multiracial, 0% Pacific Islander, 74% white, 3% international; 87% from in state; 90% live on campus; 0% of students in fraternities, 0% in sororities
Most popular majors: 31% Business, Management, Marketing, and Related Support Services, 12% Parks, Recreation, Leisure, and Fitness Studies, 11% Education, 9% Family and Consumer Sciences/Human Sciences, 5% Psychology
Expenses: 2020-2021: $34,502; room/board: $11,346
Financial aid: (419) 358-3266; 83% of undergrads determined to have financial need; average aid package $30,037

Bowling Green State University

Bowling Green OH
(419) 372-2478
U.S. News ranking: Nat. U., No. 258
Website: www.bgsu.edu
Admissions email: choosebgsu@bgsu.edu
Public; founded 1910
Freshman admissions: selective; 2019-2020: 17,179 applied, 12,338 accepted. Either SAT or ACT required. ACT 25/75 percentile: 20-25. High school rank: 16% in top tenth, 42% in top quarter, 75% in top half
Early decision deadline: N/A, notification date: N/A
Early action deadline: N/A, notification date: N/A
Application deadline (fall): 7/15
Undergraduate student body: 12,936 full time, 2,167 part time; 44% male, 56% female; 0% American Indian, 1% Asian, 8% Black, 4% Hispanic, 3% multiracial, 0% Pacific Islander, 79% white, 2% international; 88% from in state; 41% live on campus; 12% of students in fraternities, 11% in sororities
Most popular majors: 5% Education/Teaching of Individuals in Early Childhood Special Education Programs, 4% Biology/Biological Sciences, General, 4% Criminal Justice/Safety Studies, 4% Psychology, General, 3% Rhetoric and Composition
Expenses: 2020-2021: N/A in state, N/A out of state; room/board: $9,662
Financial aid: (419) 372-2651; 63% of undergrads determined to have financial need; average aid package $14,376

Capital University

Columbus OH
(866) 544-6175
U.S. News ranking: Reg. U. (Mid. W), No. 30
Website: www.capital.edu
Admissions email: admission@capital.edu
Private; founded 1830
Affiliation: Evangelical Lutheran Church
Freshman admissions: selective; 2019-2020: 4,794 applied, 3,475 accepted. Either SAT or ACT required. ACT 25/75 percentile: 20-26. High school rank: 19% in top tenth, 47% in top quarter, 82% in top half
Early decision deadline: N/A, notification date: N/A
Early action deadline: N/A, notification date: N/A
Application deadline (fall): 5/1
Undergraduate student body: 2,400 full time, 104 part time; 37% male, 63% female; 0% American Indian, 2% Asian, 9% Black, 4% Hispanic, 6% multiracial, 0% Pacific Islander, 76% white, 2% international; 93% from in state; 57% live on campus; 5% of students in fraternities, 10% in sororities
Most popular majors: 23% Health Professions and Related Programs, 13% Business, Management, Marketing, and Related Support Services, 9% Education, 9% Social Sciences, 9% Visual and Performing Arts
Expenses: 2020-2021: $38,298; room/board: $11,716
Financial aid: (614) 236-6771; 81% of undergrads determined to have financial need; average aid package $30,129

Case Western Reserve University

Cleveland OH
(216) 368-4450
U.S. News ranking: Nat. U., No. 42
Website: www.case.edu
Admissions email: admission@case.edu
Private; founded 1826
Freshman admissions: most selective; 2019-2020: 28,786 applied, 7,876 accepted. Either SAT or ACT required. SAT 25/75 percentile: 1340-1510. High school rank: 70% in top tenth, 92% in top quarter, 99% in top half
Early decision deadline: 11/1, notification date: 12/19
Early action deadline: 11/1, notification date: 12/19
Application deadline (fall): 1/15
Undergraduate student body: 5,237 full time, 146 part time; 54% male, 46% female; 0% American Indian, 21% Asian, 5% Black, 9% Hispanic, 5% multiracial, 0% Pacific Islander, 45% white, 14% international; 72% from in state; 80% live on campus; 36% of students in fraternities, 34% in sororities
Most popular majors: 10% Bioengineering and Biomedical Engineering, 7% Biology/Biological Sciences, General, 7% Mechanical Engineering, 6% Computer Science, 6% Registered Nursing/Registered Nurse

Expenses: 2020-2021: $52,948; room/board: $16,080
Financial aid: (216) 368-4530; 47% of undergrads determined to have financial need; average aid package $47,883

Cedarville University
Cedarville OH
(800) 233-2784
U.S. News ranking: Reg. U. (Mid. W), No. 21
Website: www.cedarville.edu
Admissions email: admissions@cedarville.edu
Private; founded 1887
Affiliation: Baptist
Freshman admissions: more selective; 2019-2020: 3,869 applied, 3,050 accepted. Either SAT or ACT required. ACT 25/75 percentile: 23-29. High school rank: 32% in top tenth, 62% in top quarter, 86% in top half
Early decision deadline: N/A, notification date: N/A
Early action deadline: N/A, notification date: N/A
Application deadline (fall): 8/1
Undergraduate student body: 3,438 full time, 441 part time; 46% male, 54% female; 0% American Indian, 3% Asian, 2% Black, 1% Hispanic, 3% multiracial, 0% Pacific Islander, 88% white, 2% international; 41% from in state; 71% live on campus; N/A of students in fraternities, N/A in sororities
Most popular majors: 20% Health Professions and Related Programs, 14% Business, Management, Marketing, and Related Support Services, 10% Engineering, 9% Theology and Religious Vocations, 9% Visual and Performing Arts
Expenses: 2020-2021: $32,564; room/board: $7,922
Financial aid: (937) 766-7866; 69% of undergrads determined to have financial need; average aid package $23,708

Central State University
Wilberforce OH
(937) 376-6348
U.S. News ranking: Reg. Coll. (Mid. W), second tier
Website: www.centralstate.edu
Admissions email: admissions@centralstate.edu
Public; founded 1887
Freshman admissions: least selective; 2019-2020: 13,464 applied, 7,646 accepted. Neither SAT nor ACT required. ACT 25/75 percentile: 14-17. High school rank: N/A
Early decision deadline: N/A, notification date: N/A
Early action deadline: N/A, notification date: N/A
Application deadline (fall): rolling
Undergraduate student body: 1,919 full time, 114 part time; 39% male, 61% female; 0% American Indian, 0% Asian, 88% Black, 1% Hispanic, 2% multiracial, 0% Pacific Islander, 2% white, 5% international
Most popular majors: 30% Business, Management, Marketing, and Related Support Services, 11% Communication,

Journalism, and Related Programs, 10% Homeland Security, Law Enforcement, Firefighting and Related Protective Services, 10% Psychology, 9% Public Administration and Social Service Professions
Expenses: 2019-2020: $6,726 in state, $8,726 out of state; room/board: $10,480
Financial aid: (937) 376-6574

Cleveland Institute of Art
Cleveland OH
(216) 421-7418
U.S. News ranking: Arts, unranked
Website: www.cia.edu
Admissions email: admissions@cia.edu
Private; founded 1882
Freshman admissions: selective; 2019-2020: 1,147 applied, 801 accepted. Neither SAT nor ACT required. ACT 25/75 percentile: 20-27. High school rank: 10% in top tenth, 35% in top quarter, 66% in top half
Early decision deadline: N/A, notification date: N/A
Early action deadline: 12/1, notification date: N/A
Application deadline (fall): rolling
Undergraduate student body: 620 full time, 12 part time; 29% male, 71% female; 0% American Indian, 3% Asian, 10% Black, 8% Hispanic, 6% multiracial, 0% Pacific Islander, 68% white, 5% international; 65% from in state; 50% live on campus; 1% of students in fraternities, 1% in sororities
Most popular majors: 16% Graphic Design, 12% Illustration, 11% Animation, Interactive Technology, Video Graphics and Special Effects, 10% Photography, 8% Medical Illustration/Medical Illustrator
Expenses: 2020-2021: $44,385; room/board: $11,590
Financial aid: (216) 421-7425; 84% of undergrads determined to have financial need; average aid package $27,493

Cleveland Institute of Music
Cleveland OH
(216) 795-3107
U.S. News ranking: Arts, unranked
Website: www.cim.edu/
Admissions email: admission@cim.edu
Private; founded 1920
Freshman admissions: least selective; 2019-2020: 500 applied, 183 accepted. Neither SAT nor ACT required. SAT 25/75 percentile: N/A. High school rank: N/A
Early decision deadline: N/A, notification date: N/A
Early action deadline: N/A, notification date: N/A
Application deadline (fall): 12/1
Undergraduate student body: 230 full time, 0 part time; 52% male, 48% female; 0% American Indian, 10% Asian, 3% Black, 8% Hispanic, 8% multiracial, 0% Pacific Islander, 38% white, 26% international

Most popular majors: 100% Music
Expenses: 2020-2021: $44,774; room/board: $12,500
Financial aid: (216) 795-3192; 50% of undergrads determined to have financial need; average aid package $31,615

Cleveland State University
Cleveland OH
(216) 687-5411
U.S. News ranking: Nat. U., second tier
Website: www.csuohio.edu
Admissions email: admissions@csuohio.edu
Public; founded 1964
Freshman admissions: selective; 2019-2020: 10,646 applied, 10,008 accepted. Either SAT or ACT required. ACT 25/75 percentile: 18-24. High school rank: 14% in top tenth, 40% in top quarter, 70% in top half
Early decision deadline: N/A, notification date: N/A
Early action deadline: 5/1, notification date: N/A
Application deadline (fall): 8/16
Undergraduate student body: 9,098 full time, 2,686 part time; 46% male, 54% female; 0% American Indian, 3% Asian, 15% Black, 7% Hispanic, 4% multiracial, 0% Pacific Islander, 64% white, 5% international; 92% from in state; 8% live on campus; 1% of students in fraternities, 1% in sororities
Most popular majors: 9% Psychology, General, 8% Clinical/Medical Laboratory Science and Allied Professions, Other, 5% Mechanical Engineering, 4% Accounting, 4% Registered Nursing/Registered Nurse
Expenses: 2020-2021: $11,096 in state, $16,004 out of state; room/board: $11,684
Financial aid: (216) 687-5594; 70% of undergrads determined to have financial need; average aid package $9,686

College of Wooster
Wooster OH
(330) 263-2322
U.S. News ranking: Nat. Lib. Arts, No. 69
Website: www.wooster.edu/
Admissions email: admissions@wooster.edu
Private; founded 1866
Freshman admissions: more selective; 2019-2020: 6,352 applied, 3,472 accepted. Either SAT or ACT required. SAT 25/75 percentile: 1150-1380. High school rank: 46% in top tenth, 72% in top quarter, 92% in top half
Early decision deadline: 11/1, notification date: 11/15
Early action deadline: 11/15, notification date: 12/31
Application deadline (fall): 2/15
Undergraduate student body: 1,934 full time, 13 part time; 46% male, 54% female; 0% American Indian, 4% Asian, 9% Black, 6% Hispanic, 4% multiracial, 0% Pacific Islander, 61% white,

16% international; 27% from in state; 99% live on campus; N/A of students in fraternities, N/A in sororities
Most popular majors: 9% Biology/Biological Sciences, General, 9% History, General, 8% English Language and Literature, General, 8% Psychology, General, 7% Political Science and Government, General
Expenses: 2020-2021: $54,000; room/board: $12,750
Financial aid: (330) 263-2317; 66% of undergrads determined to have financial need; average aid package $47,142

Columbus College of Art and Design[1]
Columbus OH
(614) 222-3261
U.S. News ranking: Arts, unranked
Website: www.ccad.edu
Admissions email: admissions@ccad.edu
Private; founded 1879
Application deadline (fall): 8/1
Undergraduate student body: N/A full time, N/A part time
Expenses: 2019-2020: $36,750; room/board: $9,680
Financial aid: (614) 222-3274

Defiance College
Defiance OH
(419) 783-2359
U.S. News ranking: Reg. Coll. (Mid. W), No. 49
Website: www.defiance.edu
Admissions email: admissions@defiance.edu
Private; founded 1850
Affiliation: United Church of Christ
Freshman admissions: less selective; 2019-2020: 2,000 applied, 1,002 accepted. Either SAT or ACT required. ACT 25/75 percentile: 17-21. High school rank: 6% in top tenth, 23% in top quarter, 56% in top half
Early decision deadline: N/A, notification date: N/A
Early action deadline: N/A, notification date: N/A
Application deadline (fall): rolling
Undergraduate student body: 462 full time, 44 part time; 56% male, 44% female; 1% American Indian, 1% Asian, 18% Black, 10% Hispanic, 4% multiracial, 0% Pacific Islander, 66% white, 1% international; 67% from in state; N/A live on campus; N/A of students in fraternities, N/A in sororities
Most popular majors: 10% Business/Commerce, General, 10% Early Childhood Education and Teaching, 10% Kinesiology and Exercise Science, 9% Social Work, 9% Sport and Fitness Administration/Management
Expenses: 2019-2020: $33,260; room/board: $10,540
Financial aid: (419) 783-2376

Denison University
Granville OH
(740) 587-6276
U.S. News ranking: Nat. Lib. Arts, No. 44
Website: www.denison.edu

Admissions email: admission@denison.edu
Private; founded 1831
Freshman admissions: more selective; 2019-2020: 8,812 applied, 2,590 accepted. Neither SAT nor ACT required. ACT 25/75 percentile: 27-31. High school rank: 70% in top tenth, 84% in top quarter, 100% in top half
Early decision deadline: 11/15, notification date: 12/15
Early action deadline: N/A, notification date: N/A
Application deadline (fall): 1/15
Undergraduate student body: 2,263 full time, 30 part time; 47% male, 53% female; 0% American Indian, 4% Asian, 6% Black, 8% Hispanic, 3% multiracial, 0% Pacific Islander, 62% white, 14% international; 21% from in state; 100% live on campus; 26% of students in fraternities, 42% in sororities
Most popular majors: 21% Social Sciences, 9% Biological and Biomedical Sciences, 9% Business, Management, Marketing, and Related Support Services, 9% Communication, Journalism, and Related Programs, 8% Visual and Performing Arts
Expenses: 2020-2021: $56,680; room/board: $13,720
Financial aid: (740) 587-6276; 60% of undergrads determined to have financial need; average aid package $44,087

Franciscan University of Steubenville
Steubenville OH
(740) 283-6226
U.S. News ranking: Reg. U. (Mid. W), No. 15
Website: www.franciscan.edu
Admissions email: admissions@franciscan.edu
Private; founded 1946
Affiliation: Roman Catholic
Freshman admissions: more selective; 2019-2020: 2,043 applied, 1,445 accepted. Either SAT or ACT required. SAT 25/75 percentile: 1090-1300. High school rank: 38% in top tenth, 74% in top quarter, 93% in top half
Early decision deadline: N/A, notification date: N/A
Early action deadline: N/A, notification date: N/A
Application deadline (fall): rolling
Undergraduate student body: 2,063 full time, 179 part time; 41% male, 59% female; 0% American Indian, 2% Asian, 1% Black, 13% Hispanic, 2% multiracial, 0% Pacific Islander, 79% white, 1% international; 22% from in state; 79% live on campus; 0% of students in fraternities, 0% in sororities
Most popular majors: 26% Theology/Theological Studies, 10% Business Administration and Management, General, 10% Registered Nursing/Registered Nurse, 9% Elementary Education and Teaching, 6% Psychology, General
Expenses: 2020-2021: $30,180; room/board: $8,870

Financial aid: (740) 284-5216; 65% of undergrads determined to have financial need; average aid package $19,793

Franklin University[1]
Columbus OH
(888) 341-6237
U.S. News ranking: Business, unranked
Website: www.franklin.edu
Admissions email: info@franklin.edu
Private; founded 1902
Application deadline (fall): N/A
Undergraduate student body: N/A full time, N/A part time
Expenses: 2019-2020: $9,577; room/board: $10,224
Financial aid: N/A

Heidelberg University
Tiffin OH
(419) 448-2330
U.S. News ranking: Reg. Coll. (Mid. W), No. 21
Website: www.heidelberg.edu
Admissions email: adminfo@heidelberg.edu
Private; founded 1850
Affiliation: United Church of Christ
Freshman admissions: selective; 2019-2020: 1,758 applied, 1,280 accepted. Either SAT or ACT required. ACT 25/75 percentile: 19-25. High school rank: N/A
Early decision deadline: N/A, notification date: N/A
Early action deadline: N/A, notification date: N/A
Application deadline (fall): 8/1
Undergraduate student body: 1,043 full time, 33 part time; 50% male, 50% female; 0% American Indian, 0% Asian, 9% Black, 4% Hispanic, 4% multiracial, 0% Pacific Islander, 81% white, 1% international
Most popular majors: Information not available
Expenses: 2020-2021: $32,300; room/board: $10,900
Financial aid: (419) 448-2293; 87% of undergrads determined to have financial need; average aid package $27,506

Hiram College
Hiram OH
(330) 569-5169
U.S. News ranking: Reg. Coll. (Mid. W), No. 15
Website: www.hiram.edu
Admissions email: admission@hiram.edu
Private; founded 1850
Freshman admissions: selective; 2019-2020: 2,834 applied, 1,691 accepted. Neither SAT nor ACT required. ACT 25/75 percentile: 18-25. High school rank: 12% in top tenth, 27% in top quarter, 52% in top half
Early decision deadline: N/A, notification date: N/A
Early action deadline: N/A, notification date: N/A
Application deadline (fall): rolling
Undergraduate student body: 808 full time, 459 part time; 42% male, 58% female; 0% American Indian, 2% Asian, 19% Black, 6% Hispanic, 4% multiracial,

0% Pacific Islander, 58% white, 1% international; 78% from in state; 85% live on campus; 3% of students in fraternities, 7% in sororities
Most popular majors: 31% Business, Management, Marketing, and Related Support Services, 13% Health Professions and Related Programs, 8% Biological and Biomedical Sciences, 7% Education, 6% Natural Resources and Conservation
Expenses: 2020-2021: $24,500; room/board: $10,290
Financial aid: (330) 569-5441; 91% of undergrads determined to have financial need; average aid package $29,456

John Carroll University
University Heights OH
(888) 335-6800
U.S. News ranking: Reg. U. (Mid. W), No. 2
Website: jcu.edu/
Admissions email: admission@jcu.edu
Private; founded 1886
Affiliation: Roman Catholic
Freshman admissions: more selective; 2019-2020: 3,782 applied, 3,265 accepted. Either SAT or ACT required. ACT 25/75 percentile: 22-28. High school rank: 26% in top tenth, 49% in top quarter, 81% in top half
Early decision deadline: N/A, notification date: N/A
Early action deadline: 12/1, notification date: 12/15
Application deadline (fall): rolling
Undergraduate student body: 2,925 full time, 92 part time; 54% male, 46% female; 0% American Indian, 3% Asian, 4% Black, 4% Hispanic, 2% multiracial, 0% Pacific Islander, 85% white, 1% international; 66% from in state; 52% live on campus; 9% of students in fraternities, 21% in sororities
Most popular majors: 37% Business, Management, Marketing, and Related Support Services, 9% Biological and Biomedical Sciences, 9% Parks, Recreation, Leisure, and Fitness Studies, 9% Social Sciences, 7% Communication, Journalism, and Related Programs
Expenses: 2020-2021: $44,405; room/board: $12,560
Financial aid: (888) 335-6800; 72% of undergrads determined to have financial need; average aid package $33,709

Kent State University[7]
Kent OH
(330) 672-2444
U.S. News ranking: Nat. U., No. 217
Website: www.kent.edu
Admissions email: admissions@kent.edu
Public; founded 1910
Freshman admissions: selective; 2019-2020: 16,308 applied, 13,950 accepted. Either SAT or ACT required. ACT 25/75 percentile: 20-26. High school

rank: 17% in top tenth, 43% in top quarter, 77% in top half
Early decision deadline: N/A, notification date: N/A
Early action deadline: N/A, notification date: N/A
Application deadline (fall): 5/1
Undergraduate student body: 19,716 full time, 2,546 part time
Most popular majors: 23% Business, Management, Marketing, and Related Support Services, 14% Health Professions and Related Programs, 9% Education, 8% Communication, Journalism, and Related Programs, 6% Visual and Performing Arts
Expenses: 2020-2021: $11,588 in state, $20,464 out of state; room/board: $12,084
Financial aid: (330) 672-2972; 61% of undergrads determined to have financial need; average aid package $11,224

Kenyon College
Gambier OH
(740) 427-5776
U.S. News ranking: Nat. Lib. Arts, No. 28
Website: www.kenyon.edu
Admissions email: admissions@kenyon.edu
Private; founded 1824
Freshman admissions: more selective; 2019-2020: 6,662 applied, 2,271 accepted. Either SAT or ACT required. SAT 25/75 percentile: 1270-1460. High school rank: 57% in top tenth, 79% in top quarter, 98% in top half
Early decision deadline: 11/15, notification date: 12/18
Early action deadline: N/A, notification date: N/A
Application deadline (fall): 1/15
Undergraduate student body: 1,734 full time, 13 part time; 45% male, 55% female; 0% American Indian, 4% Asian, 3% Black, 7% Hispanic, 5% multiracial, 0% Pacific Islander, 71% white, 9% international; 86% from in state; 99% live on campus; 19% of students in fraternities, 14% in sororities
Most popular majors: 11% English Language and Literature, General, 10% Economics, General, 6% History, General, 6% Political Science and Government, General, 6% Psychology, General
Expenses: 2020-2021: $61,100; room/board: $12,830
Financial aid: (740) 427-5430; 44% of undergrads determined to have financial need; average aid package $46,639

Lake Erie College[1]
Painesville OH
(855) 467-8676
U.S. News ranking: Reg. U. (Mid. W), second tier
Website: www.lec.edu
Admissions email: admissions@lec.edu
Private; founded 1856
Application deadline (fall): 8/1
Undergraduate student body: N/A full time, N/A part time
Expenses: 2020-2021: $33,172; room/board: $10,160
Financial aid: (440) 375-7100

Lourdes University[1]
Sylvania OH
(419) 885-5291
U.S. News ranking: Reg. U. (Mid. W), second tier
Website: www.lourdes.edu
Admissions email: luadmits@lourdes.edu
Private; founded 1958
Affiliation: Roman Catholic
Application deadline (fall): rolling
Undergraduate student body: N/A full time, N/A part time
Expenses: 2019-2020: $23,550; room/board: $10,590
Financial aid: (419) 824-3504

Malone University
Canton OH
(330) 471-8145
U.S. News ranking: Reg. U. (Mid. W), No. 71
Website: www.malone.edu
Admissions email: admissions@malone.edu
Private; founded 1892
Affiliation: Friends
Freshman admissions: selective; 2019-2020: 1,899 applied, 1,346 accepted. Either SAT or ACT required. ACT 25/75 percentile: 19-26. High school rank: N/A
Early decision deadline: N/A, notification date: N/A
Early action deadline: N/A, notification date: N/A
Application deadline (fall): rolling
Undergraduate student body: 923 full time, 254 part time; 39% male, 61% female; 0% American Indian, 0% Asian, 8% Black, 2% Hispanic, 4% multiracial, 0% Pacific Islander, 78% white, 2% international; 90% from in state; 60% live on campus; 0% of students in fraternities, 0% in sororities
Most popular majors: 14% Registered Nursing/Registered Nurse, 9% Business Administration and Management, General, 5% Communication, Journalism, and Related Programs, Other, 5% Marketing/Marketing Management, General, 5% Social Work
Expenses: 2020-2021: $32,416; room/board: $9,900
Financial aid: (330) 471-8161

Marietta College
Marietta OH
(800) 331-7896
U.S. News ranking: Reg. Coll. (Mid. W), No. 8
Website: www.marietta.edu
Admissions email: admit@marietta.edu
Private; founded 1835
Freshman admissions: selective; 2019-2020: 2,922 applied, 2,068 accepted. Either SAT or ACT required. ACT 25/75 percentile: 20-26. High school rank: N/A
Early decision deadline: N/A, notification date: N/A
Early action deadline: 11/1, notification date: 11/15
Application deadline (fall): rolling
Undergraduate student body: 1,062 full time, 79 part time; 55% male, 45% female; 0% American Indian, 1% Asian, 4% Black,

3% Hispanic, 4% multiracial, 0% Pacific Islander, 78% white, 7% international; 63% from in state; 81% live on campus; 4% of students in fraternities, 6% in sororities
Most popular majors: 35% Petroleum Engineering, 5% Marketing/Marketing Management, General, 4% Accounting, 4% Economics, General, 3% Early Childhood Education and Teaching
Expenses: 2020-2021: $36,764; room/board: $11,548
Financial aid: (740) 376-4712; 79% of undergrads determined to have financial need; average aid package $36,400

Miami University–Oxford
Oxford OH
(513) 529-2531
U.S. News ranking: Nat. U., No. 103
Website: www.MiamiOH.edu
Admissions email: admission@MiamiOH.edu
Public; founded 1809
Freshman admissions: more selective; 2019-2020: 28,920 applied, 23,248 accepted. Either SAT or ACT required. ACT 25/75 percentile: 26-31. High school rank: 32% in top tenth, 62% in top quarter, 91% in top half
Early decision deadline: 11/15, notification date: 12/15
Early action deadline: 12/1, notification date: 2/1
Application deadline (fall): 2/1
Undergraduate student body: 16,682 full time, 564 part time; 50% male, 50% female; 0% American Indian, 2% Asian, 4% Black, 5% Hispanic, 4% multiracial, 0% Pacific Islander, 72% white, 12% international; 64% from in state; 31% live on campus; 25% of students in fraternities, 40% in sororities
Most popular majors: 24% Business, Management, Marketing, and Related Support Services, 9% Communication, Journalism, and Related Programs, 9% Social Sciences, 8% Health Professions and Related Programs, 6% Engineering
Expenses: 2020-2021: $15,330 in state, $34,727 out of state; room/board: $13,870
Financial aid: (513) 529-8734; 34% of undergrads determined to have financial need; average aid package $15,916

Mount St. Joseph University
Cincinnati OH
(513) 244-4389
U.S. News ranking: Reg. U. (Mid. W), No. 80
Admissions email: N/A
Private
Freshman admissions: selective; 2019-2020: 1,315 applied, 808 accepted. Either SAT or ACT required. ACT 25/75 percentile: 20-25. High school rank: 9% in top tenth, 31% in top quarter, 75% in top half
Early decision deadline: N/A, notification date: N/A

Early action deadline: N/A, notification date: N/A
Application deadline (fall): 8/17
Undergraduate student body: 1,008 full time, 442 part time; 40% male, 60% female; 0% American Indian, 1% Asian, 11% Black, 3% Hispanic, 4% multiracial, 0% Pacific Islander, 80% white, 0% international; 22% from in state; N/A live on campus; N/A of students in fraternities, N/A in sororities
Most popular majors: Business, Management, Marketing, and Related Support Services, Education, Health Professions and Related Programs, Parks, Recreation, Leisure, and Fitness Studies, Social Sciences
Expenses: 2020-2021: $32,200; room/board: $9,720
Financial aid: (513) 244-4418; 79% of undergrads determined to have financial need; average aid package $23,281

Mount Vernon Nazarene University
Mount Vernon OH
(866) 462-6868
U.S. News ranking: Reg. U. (Mid. W), No. 71
Website: www.mvnu.edu/
Admissions email: admissions@mvnu.edu
Private; founded 1968
Affiliation: Church of the Nazarene
Freshman admissions: selective; 2019-2020: 1,305 applied, 953 accepted. Either SAT or ACT required. ACT 25/75 percentile: 20-25. High school rank: 22% in top tenth, 48% in top quarter, 82% in top half
Early decision deadline: N/A, notification date: N/A
Early action deadline: N/A, notification date: N/A
Application deadline (fall): 7/15
Undergraduate student body: 1,501 full time, 315 part time; 39% male, 61% female; 0% American Indian, 0% Asian, 3% Black, 3% Hispanic, 3% multiracial, 0% Pacific Islander, 86% white, 1% international; N/A from in state; 55% live on campus; N/A of students in fraternities, N/A in sororities
Most popular majors: 18% Business Administration and Management, General, 13% Social Work, 10% Registered Nursing/Registered Nurse, 5% Biology/Biological Sciences, General, 5% Early Childhood Education and Teaching
Expenses: 2020-2021: $31,610; room/board: $8,890
Financial aid: (740) 397-9000

Muskingum University
New Concord OH
(740) 826-8137
U.S. News ranking: Reg. U. (Mid. W), No. 46
Website: www.muskingum.edu
Admissions email: adminfo@muskingum.edu
Private; founded 1837
Affiliation: Presbyterian Church (USA)
Freshman admissions: selective; 2019-2020: 2,404 applied,

1,938 accepted. Either SAT or ACT required. ACT 25/75 percentile: 18-23. High school rank: 14% in top tenth, 40% in top quarter, 70% in top half
Early decision deadline: N/A, notification date: N/A
Early action deadline: N/A, notification date: N/A
Application deadline (fall): rolling
Undergraduate student body: 1,364 full time, 238 part time; 44% male, 56% female; 0% American Indian, 1% Asian, 5% Black, 3% Hispanic, 3% multiracial, 0% Pacific Islander, 82% white, 2% international; 89% from in state; 52% live on campus; 19% of students in fraternities, 23% in sororities
Most popular majors: 20% Health Professions and Related Programs, 16% Business, Management, Marketing, and Related Support Services, 9% Education, 8% Psychology, 7% Biological and Biomedical Sciences
Expenses: 2020-2021: $29,740; room/board: $11,860
Financial aid: (740) 826-8139; 83% of undergrads determined to have financial need; average aid package $23,292

Notre Dame College of Ohio[1]
Cleveland OH
(216) 373-5355
U.S. News ranking: Reg. U. (Mid. W), second tier
Website: www.notredamecollege.edu
Admissions email: admissions@ndc.edu
Private; founded 1922
Application deadline (fall): rolling
Undergraduate student body: N/A full time, N/A part time
Expenses: 2019-2020: $30,160; room/board: $10,600
Financial aid: (216) 373-5263

Oberlin College
Oberlin OH
(440) 775-8411
U.S. News ranking: Nat. Lib. Arts, No. 36
Website: www.oberlin.edu
Admissions email: college.admissions@oberlin.edu
Private; founded 1833
Freshman admissions: more selective; 2019-2020: 7,708 applied, 2,806 accepted. Either SAT or ACT required. SAT 25/75 percentile: 1280-1480. High school rank: 54% in top tenth, 84% in top quarter, 98% in top half
Early decision deadline: 12/15, notification date: 1/5
Early action deadline: N/A, notification date: N/A
Application deadline (fall): 1/15
Undergraduate student body: 2,819 full time, 27 part time; 42% male, 58% female; 0% American Indian, 4% Asian, 5% Black, 8% Hispanic, 8% multiracial, 0% Pacific Islander, 61% white, 12% international; 7% from in state; 90% live on campus; N/A of students in fraternities, N/A in sororities

Most popular majors: 12% Music, 6% Biology, General, 6% History, 5% English Language and Literature, General, 5% Environmental Studies
Expenses: 2020-2021: $58,504; room/board: $17,334
Financial aid: (440) 775-8142; 55% of undergrads determined to have financial need; average aid package $45,295

Ohio Christian University
Circleville OH
(877) 762-8669
U.S. News ranking: Reg. U. (Mid. W), second tier
Website: www.ohiochristian.edu/
Admissions email: enroll@ohiochristian.edu
Private; founded 1948
Affiliation: Churches of Christ
Freshman admissions: less selective; 2019-2020: N/A applied, N/A accepted. Neither SAT nor ACT required. SAT 25/75 percentile: N/A. High school rank: N/A
Early decision deadline: N/A, notification date: N/A
Early action deadline: N/A, notification date: N/A
Application deadline (fall): N/A
Undergraduate student body: 1,627 full time, 904 part time; 35% male, 65% female; 1% American Indian, 1% Asian, 37% Black, 4% Hispanic, 3% multiracial, 0% Pacific Islander, 49% white, 0% international
Most popular majors: 28% Business Administration and Management, General, 16% Divinity/Ministry, 9% Substance Abuse/Addiction Counseling, 7% Public Administration and Social Service Professions, 4% Teacher Education and Professional Development, Specific Levels and Methods, Other
Expenses: 2020-2021: $21,390; room/board: $8,568
Financial aid: N/A

Ohio Dominican University
Columbus OH
(614) 251-4500
U.S. News ranking: Reg. U. (Mid. W), No. 103
Website: www.ohiodominican.edu
Admissions email: admissions@ohiodominican.edu
Private; founded 1911
Affiliation: Roman Catholic
Freshman admissions: selective; 2019-2020: 1,395 applied, 1,171 accepted. Neither SAT nor ACT required. ACT 25/75 percentile: 19-25. High school rank: 17% in top tenth, 40% in top quarter, 74% in top half
Early decision deadline: N/A, notification date: N/A
Early action deadline: N/A, notification date: N/A
Application deadline (fall): rolling
Undergraduate student body: 920 full time, 161 part time; 46% male, 54% female; 1% American Indian, 2% Asian, 26% Black, 5% Hispanic, 6% multiracial, 0% Pacific Islander, 53% white, 3% international

Most popular majors: 25% Business Administration and Management, General, 12% Physician Assistant, 8% Educational Leadership and Administration, General, 7% Biology/Biological Sciences, General, 5% Multi/Interdisciplinary Studies
Expenses: 2020-2021: $32,880; room/board: $11,340
Financial aid: (614) 251-4778; 82% of undergrads determined to have financial need; average aid package $26,221

Ohio Northern University
Ada OH
(888) 408-4668
U.S. News ranking: Reg. Coll. (Mid. W), No. 3
Website: www.onu.edu
Admissions email: admissions-ug@onu.edu
Private; founded 1871
Affiliation: United Methodist
Freshman admissions: more selective; 2019-2020: 3,901 applied, 2,735 accepted. Either SAT or ACT required. ACT 25/75 percentile: 23-28. High school rank: 32% in top tenth, 57% in top quarter, 88% in top half
Early decision deadline: N/A, notification date: N/A
Early action deadline: N/A, notification date: N/A
Application deadline (fall): 8/15
Undergraduate student body: 2,095 full time, 144 part time; 54% male, 46% female; 0% American Indian, 2% Asian, 3% Black, 1% Hispanic, 3% multiracial, 0% Pacific Islander, 78% white, 1% international; 83% from in state; 73% live on campus; N/A of students in fraternities, N/A in sororities
Most popular majors: Information not available
Expenses: 2020-2021: $34,440; room/board: $12,400
Financial aid: (419) 772-2271; 82% of undergrads determined to have financial need; average aid package $28,942

Ohio State University–Columbus
Columbus OH
(614) 292-3980
U.S. News ranking: Nat. U., No. 53
Website: www.osu.edu
Admissions email: askabuckeye@osu.edu
Public; founded 1870
Freshman admissions: more selective; 2019-2020: 47,703 applied, 25,634 accepted. Neither SAT nor ACT required. ACT 25/75 percentile: 28-32. High school rank: 60% in top tenth, 93% in top quarter, 99% in top half
Early decision deadline: N/A, notification date: N/A
Early action deadline: 11/15, notification date: 1/31
Application deadline (fall): 2/1
Undergraduate student body: 42,776 full time, 4,042 part time; 51% male, 49% female; 0% American Indian, 8% Asian, 7% Black, 5% Hispanic, 4% multiracial, 0% Pacific Islander,

66% white, 8% international; 75% from in state; 33% live on campus; 7% of students in fraternities, 11% in sororities
Most popular majors: 6% Finance, General, 5% Psychology, General, 4% Biology/Biological Sciences, General, 4% Marketing/Marketing Management, General, 4% Speech Communication and Rhetoric
Expenses: 2020-2021: $11,517 in state, $33,501 out of state; room/board: $13,026
Financial aid: (614) 292-0300; 46% of undergrads determined to have financial need; average aid package $15,392

Ohio University
Athens OH
(740) 593-4100
U.S. News ranking: Nat. U., No. 176
Website: www.ohio.edu
Admissions email: admissions@ohio.edu
Public; founded 1804
Freshman admissions: selective; 2019-2020: 24,179 applied, 19,843 accepted. Either SAT or ACT required. ACT 25/75 percentile: 21-26. High school rank: 20% in top tenth, 47% in top quarter, 82% in top half
Early decision deadline: N/A, notification date: N/A
Early action deadline: 11/15, notification date: N/A
Application deadline (fall): 2/1
Undergraduate student body: 16,192 full time, 4,452 part time; 40% male, 60% female; 0% American Indian, 1% Asian, 6% Black, 3% Hispanic, 4% multiracial, 0% Pacific Islander, 82% white, 1% international; 82% from in state; 43% live on campus; 5% of students in fraternities, 8% in sororities
Most popular majors: 35% Registered Nursing/Registered Nurse, 4% Business Administration and Management, General, 4% Speech Communication and Rhetoric, 3% Liberal Arts and Sciences, General Studies and Humanities, Other, 3% Marketing/Marketing Management, General
Expenses: 2020-2021: $12,612 in state, $22,406 out of state; room/board: $12,172
Financial aid: (740) 593-4141; 56% of undergrads determined to have financial need; average aid package $9,164

Ohio Wesleyan University
Delaware OH
(740) 368-3020
U.S. News ranking: Nat. Lib. Arts, No. 93
Website: www.owu.edu
Admissions email: owuadmit@owu.edu
Private; founded 1842
Affiliation: United Methodist
Freshman admissions: more selective; 2019-2020: 4,281 applied, 2,880 accepted. Neither SAT nor ACT required. ACT 25/75 percentile: 22-28. High school rank: 32% in top tenth, 60% in top quarter, 91% in top half

Early decision deadline: 11/15,
notification date: 11/30
Early action deadline: 12/1,
notification date: 12/15
Application deadline (fall): 3/1
Undergraduate student body:
1,487 full time, 7 part time; 44%
male, 56% female; 0% American
Indian, 3% Asian, 8% Black, 6%
Hispanic, 5% multiracial, 0%
Pacific Islander, 69% white, 7%
international; N/A from in state;
83% live on campus; 26% of
students in fraternities, 27% in
sororities
Most popular majors: 16%
Biological and Biomedical
Sciences, 16% Business,
Management, Marketing, and
Related Support Services, 11%
Social Sciences, 9% Parks,
Recreation, Leisure, and Fitness
Studies, 7% Psychology
Expenses: 2020-2021: $47,130;
room/board: $12,696
Financial aid: (740) 368-3050;
73% of undergrads determined to
have financial need; average aid
package $38,958

Otterbein University
Westerville OH
(614) 823-1500
U.S. News ranking: Reg. U.
(Mid. W), No. 21
Website: www.otterbein.edu
Admissions email:
UOtterB@Otterbein.edu
Private; founded 1847
Affiliation: United Methodist
Freshman admissions: selective;
2019-2020: 2,697 applied,
2,184 accepted. Either SAT
or ACT required. ACT 25/75
percentile: 20-27. High school
rank: 25% in top tenth, 56% in
top quarter, 88% in top half
Early decision deadline: N/A,
notification date: N/A
Early action deadline: N/A,
notification date: N/A
Application deadline (fall): rolling
Undergraduate student body: 2,332
full time, 169 part time; 39%
male, 61% female; 0% American
Indian, 3% Asian, 8% Black, 5%
Hispanic, 5% multiracial, 0%
Pacific Islander, 77% white, 0%
international; N/A from in state;
60% live on campus; 27% of
students in fraternities, 26% in
sororities
Most popular majors: 17% Health
Professions and Related Programs,
12% Business, Management,
Marketing, and Related Support
Services, 9% Biological and
Biomedical Sciences, 8%
Education, 8% Visual and
Performing Arts
Expenses: 2020-2021: $33,074;
room/board: $11,468
Financial aid: (614) 823-1502;
73% of undergrads determined to
have financial need; average aid
package $21,705

Shawnee State University
Portsmouth OH
(740) 347-1749
U.S. News ranking: Reg. U.
(Mid. W), second tier
Website: www.shawnee.edu

Admissions email:
To_SSU@shawnee.edu
Public; founded 1986
Freshman admissions: selective;
2019-2020: 1,912 applied,
1,897 accepted. Neither SAT
nor ACT required. ACT 25/75
percentile: 18-24. High school
rank: 14% in top tenth, 37% in
top quarter, 71% in top half
Early decision deadline: N/A,
notification date: N/A
Early action deadline: N/A,
notification date: N/A
Application deadline (fall): rolling
Undergraduate student body: 2,717
full time, 749 part time; 45%
male, 55% female; 1% American
Indian, 1% Asian, 5% Black,
1% Hispanic, 3% multiracial,
0% Pacific Islander, 86% white,
1% international
Most popular majors: 6% Health
and Medical Administrative
Services, Other, 5% Art/Art
Studies, General, 5% Registered
Nursing/Registered Nurse, 4%
Nursing Assistant/Aide and
Patient Care Assistant/Aide, 4%
Plastics and Polymer Engineering
Technology/Technician
Expenses: 2020-2021: $8,604 in
state, $14,647 out of state; room/
board: $10,862
Financial aid: (740) 351-4243;
68% of undergrads determined to
have financial need; average aid
package $10,552

Tiffin University
Tiffin OH
(419) 448-3423
U.S. News ranking: Reg. U.
(Mid. W), second tier
Website: www.tiffin.edu
Admissions email:
admiss@tiffin.edu
Private; founded 1888
Freshman admissions: selective;
2019-2020: 4,219 applied,
2,907 accepted. Neither SAT
nor ACT required. ACT 25/75
percentile: 17-22. High school
rank: N/A
Early decision deadline: N/A,
notification date: N/A
Early action deadline: N/A,
notification date: N/A
Application deadline (fall): rolling
Undergraduate student body: 1,661
full time, 545 part time; 50%
male, 50% female; 0% American
Indian, 1% Asian, 15% Black,
3% Hispanic, 2% multiracial,
0% Pacific Islander, 54% white,
9% international; 77% from in
state; 46% live on campus; 3%
of students in fraternities, 3% in
sororities
Most popular majors: 37%
Business, Management,
Marketing, and Related Support
Services, 32% Homeland Security,
Law Enforcement, Firefighting and
Related Protective Services, 12%
Psychology, 6% Computer and
Information Sciences and Support
Services, 4% Parks, Recreation,
Leisure, and Fitness Studies
Expenses: 2020-2021: $27,610;
room/board: $11,700
Financial aid: (419) 448-3279;
79% of undergrads determined to
have financial need; average aid
package $19,763

Union Institute and University[1]
Cincinnati OH
(800) 861-6400
U.S. News ranking: Nat. U.,
second tier
Website: www.myunion.edu
Admissions email:
admissions@myunion.edu
Private; founded 1964
Affiliation: Other
Application deadline (fall): rolling
Undergraduate student body: N/A
full time, N/A part time
Expenses: 2019-2020: $13,256;
room/board: N/A
Financial aid: (513) 487-1126

University of Akron
Akron OH
(330) 972-7077
U.S. News ranking: Nat. U.,
No. 272
Website: www.uakron.edu
Admissions email:
admissions@uakron.edu
Public; founded 1870
Freshman admissions: selective;
2019-2020: 14,553 applied,
10,629 accepted. Either SAT
or ACT required. ACT 25/75
percentile: 19-25. High school
rank: 16% in top tenth, 41% in
top quarter, 77% in top half
Early decision deadline: N/A,
notification date: N/A
Early action deadline: 11/1,
notification date: 12/15
Application deadline (fall): 7/1
Undergraduate student body:
11,641 full time, 3,152 part
time; 53% male, 47% female;
0% American Indian, 3% Asian,
10% Black, 3% Hispanic, 4%
multiracial, 0% Pacific Islander,
76% white, 2% international;
94% from in state; 20% live
on campus; N/A of students in
fraternities, N/A in sororities
Most popular majors: 19%
Marketing/Marketing Management,
General, 18% Engineering,
General, 15% Chiropractic, 7%
Education, General, 4% Biology/
Biological Sciences, General
Expenses: 2020-2021: $11,636
in state, $17,784 out of state;
room/board: $12,200
Financial aid: (330) 972-5860;
68% of undergrads determined to
have financial need; average aid
package $8,781

University of Cincinnati
Cincinnati OH
(513) 556-1100
U.S. News ranking: Nat. U.,
No. 143
Website: www.uc.edu
Admissions email:
admissions@uc.edu
Public; founded 1819
Freshman admissions: more
selective; 2019-2020: 23,609
applied, 18,102 accepted. Either
SAT or ACT required. ACT 25/75
percentile: 23-29. High school
rank: 24% in top tenth, 51% in
top quarter, 83% in top half
Early decision deadline: N/A,
notification date: N/A
Early action deadline: N/A,
notification date: N/A

Application deadline (fall): 3/1
Undergraduate student body:
23,712 full time, 4,664 part
time; 50% male, 50% female;
0% American Indian, 4% Asian,
7% Black, 3% Hispanic, 4%
multiracial, 0% Pacific Islander,
75% white, 4% international;
83% from in state; 24% live
on campus; 9% of students in
fraternities, 11% in sororities
Most popular majors: 21%
Business, Management,
Marketing, and Related Support
Services, 19% Health Professions
and Related Programs, 13%
Engineering, 6% Biological and
Biomedical Sciences, 6% Visual
and Performing Arts
Expenses: 2020-2021: $24,012
in state, $39,346 out of state;
room/board: N/A
Financial aid: (513) 556-6982;
48% of undergrads determined to
have financial need; average aid
package $8,364

University of Cincinnati– UC Blue Ash College[1]
Cincinnati OH
(513) 745-5600
U.S. News ranking: Reg. Coll.
(Mid. W), unranked
Website: www.rwc.uc.edu/
Admissions email: N/A
Public
Application deadline (fall): N/A
Undergraduate student body: N/A
full time, N/A part time
Expenses: 2019-2020: $6,010 in
state, $14,808 out of state; room/
board: $11,668
Financial aid: N/A

University of Dayton
Dayton OH
(937) 229-4411
U.S. News ranking: Nat. U.,
No. 133
Website: www.udayton.edu
Admissions email:
admission@udayton.edu
Private; founded 1850
Affiliation: Roman Catholic
Freshman admissions: selective;
2019-2020: 17,462 applied,
12,578 accepted. Either SAT
or ACT required. ACT 25/75
percentile: 23-29. High school
rank: 27% in top tenth, 59% in
top quarter, 88% in top half
Early decision deadline: N/A,
notification date: N/A
Early action deadline: 11/1,
notification date: 12/15
Application deadline (fall): 3/1
Undergraduate student body: 8,046
full time, 437 part time; 52%
male, 48% female; 0% American
Indian, 1% Asian, 3% Black, 7%
Hispanic, 5% multiracial, 0%
Pacific Islander, 78% white, 5%
international; N/A from in state;
74% live on campus; 10% of
students in fraternities, 21% in
sororities
Most popular majors: 30%
Business, Management,
Marketing, and Related Support
Services, 20% Engineering, 7%
Education, 6% Biological and
Biomedical Sciences, 6% Health
Professions and Related Programs

Expenses: 2020-2021: $44,890;
room/board: $14,580
Financial aid: (800) 427-5029;
57% of undergrads determined to
have financial need; average aid
package $34,786

University of Findlay
Findlay OH
(419) 434-4732
U.S. News ranking: Nat. U.,
No. 241
Website: www.findlay.edu
Admissions email:
admissions@findlay.edu
Private; founded 1882
Affiliation: Church of God
Freshman admissions: selective;
2019-2020: 3,376 applied,
2,586 accepted. Either SAT
or ACT required. ACT 25/75
percentile: 21-26. High school
rank: 22% in top tenth, 58% in
top quarter, 84% in top half
Early decision deadline: N/A,
notification date: N/A
Early action deadline: N/A,
notification date: N/A
Application deadline (fall): rolling
Undergraduate student body: 2,189
full time, 1,335 part time; 35%
male, 65% female; 0% American
Indian, 1% Asian, 4% Black, 3%
Hispanic, 2% multiracial, 0%
Pacific Islander, 78% white, 6%
international
Most popular majors: 34% Health
Professions and Related Programs,
20% Business, Management,
Marketing, and Related Support
Services, 13% Agriculture,
Agriculture Operations, and
Related Sciences, 8% Education,
4% Parks, Recreation, Leisure,
and Fitness Studies
Expenses: 2020-2021: $36,484;
room/board: $10,200
Financial aid: (419) 434-4791;
49% of undergrads determined to
have financial need; average aid
package $28,860

University of Mount Union
Alliance OH
(330) 823-2590
U.S. News ranking: Reg. Coll.
(Mid. W), No. 10
Website: www.mountunion.edu/
Admissions email:
admission@mountunion.edu
Private; founded 1846
Freshman admissions: selective;
2019-2020: 3,007 applied,
2,333 accepted. Either SAT
or ACT required. ACT 25/75
percentile: 20-25. High school
rank: 34% in top tenth, 61% in
top quarter, 86% in top half
Early decision deadline: N/A,
notification date: N/A
Early action deadline: N/A,
notification date: N/A
Application deadline (fall): rolling
Undergraduate student body: 1,994
full time, 41 part time; 51%
male, 49% female; 0% American
Indian, 1% Asian, 7% Black, 4%
Hispanic, 4% multiracial, 0%
Pacific Islander, 79% white, 2%
international; 79% from in state;
69% live on campus; 17% of
students in fraternities, 26% in
sororities

Most popular majors: 24% Business, Management, Marketing, and Related Support Services, 14% Parks, Recreation, Leisure, and Fitness Studies, 9% Education, 7% Biological and Biomedical Sciences, 7% Health Professions and Related Programs
Expenses: 2020-2021: $32,600; room/board: $10,700
Financial aid: (330) 823-2674; 79% of undergrads determined to have financial need; average aid package $23,968

University of Northwestern Ohio[1]
Lima OH
(419) 998-3120
U.S. News ranking: Reg. Coll. (Mid. W), second tier
Website: www.unoh.edu/
Admissions email: info@unoh.edu
Private
Application deadline (fall): N/A
Undergraduate student body: N/A full time, N/A part time
Expenses: 2019-2020: $11,500; room/board: $6,900
Financial aid: N/A

University of Rio Grande[1]
Rio Grande OH
(740) 245-7208
U.S. News ranking: Reg. Coll. (Mid. W), second tier
Website: www.rio.edu
Admissions email: admissions@rio.edu
Private; founded 1876
Application deadline (fall): rolling
Undergraduate student body: N/A full time, N/A part time
Expenses: 2020-2021: $21,186; room/board: $8,342
Financial aid: (740) 245-7285

University of Toledo
Toledo OH
(419) 530-8888
U.S. News ranking: Nat. U., second tier
Website: www.utoledo.edu
Admissions email: enroll@utoledo.edu
Public; founded 1872
Freshman admissions: selective; 2019-2020: 10,228 applied, 9,722 accepted. Either SAT or ACT required. ACT 25/75 percentile: 20-26. High school rank: 21% in top tenth, 45% in top quarter, 76% in top half
Early decision deadline: N/A, notification date: N/A
Early action deadline: N/A, notification date: N/A
Application deadline (fall): rolling
Undergraduate student body: 12,548 full time, 3,020 part time; 50% male, 50% female; 0% American Indian, 2% Asian, 10% Black, 5% Hispanic, 4% multiracial, 0% Pacific Islander, 69% white, 6% international; N/A from in state; 24% live on campus; N/A of students in fraternities, N/A in sororities
Most popular majors: 25% Business, Management, Marketing, and Related Support Services, 18% Health Professions and Related Programs, 14%

Engineering, 5% Multi/Interdisciplinary Studies, 4% Education
Expenses: 2020-2021: $11,244 in state, $20,604 out of state; room/board: $12,590
Financial aid: (419) 530-8700; 62% of undergrads determined to have financial need; average aid package $11,699

Ursuline College
Pepper Pike OH
(440) 449-4203
U.S. News ranking: Reg. U. (Mid. W), No. 46
Website: www.ursuline.edu
Admissions email: admission@ursuline.edu
Private; founded 1871
Affiliation: Roman Catholic
Freshman admissions: selective; 2019-2020: 543 applied, 463 accepted. Either SAT or ACT required. ACT 25/75 percentile: 17-23. High school rank: 12% in top tenth, 51% in top quarter, 80% in top half
Early decision deadline: N/A, notification date: N/A
Early action deadline: N/A, notification date: N/A
Application deadline (fall): rolling
Undergraduate student body: 491 full time, 160 part time; 7% male, 93% female; 0% American Indian, 3% Asian, 23% Black, 2% Hispanic, 5% multiracial, 0% Pacific Islander, 60% white, 3% international; 88% from in state; 30% live on campus; N/A of students in fraternities, N/A in sororities
Most popular majors: 60% Health Professions and Related Programs, 10% Business, Management, Marketing, and Related Support Services, 7% Biological and Biomedical Sciences, 5% Psychology, 4% Visual and Performing Arts
Expenses: 2020-2021: $34,620; room/board: $11,232
Financial aid: (440) 646-8309; 84% of undergrads determined to have financial need; average aid package $24,961

Walsh University
North Canton OH
(800) 362-9846
U.S. News ranking: Reg. U. (Mid. W), No. 39
Website: www.walsh.edu
Admissions email: admissions@walsh.edu
Private; founded 1958
Affiliation: Roman Catholic
Freshman admissions: selective; 2019-2020: 2,001 applied, 1,525 accepted. Neither SAT nor ACT required. ACT 25/75 percentile: 19-26. High school rank: N/A
Early decision deadline: N/A, notification date: N/A
Early action deadline: N/A, notification date: N/A
Application deadline (fall): rolling
Undergraduate student body: 1,628 full time, 309 part time; 42% male, 58% female; 0% American Indian, 1% Asian, 7% Black, 4% Hispanic, 3% multiracial, 0% Pacific Islander, 54% white,

6% international; N/A from in state; 46% live on campus; N/A of students in fraternities, N/A in sororities
Most popular majors: 21% Business, Management, Marketing, and Related Support Services, 15% Health Professions and Related Programs, 14% Education, 11% Biological and Biomedical Sciences, 9% Psychology
Expenses: 2020-2021: $31,609; room/board: $11,140
Financial aid: (330) 490-7146; 79% of undergrads determined to have financial need; average aid package $25,232

Wilberforce University[1]
Wilberforce OH
(800) 367-8568
U.S. News ranking: Reg. Coll. (Mid. W), second tier
Website: www.wilberforce.edu
Admissions email: admissions@wilberforce.edu
Private
Application deadline (fall): N/A
Undergraduate student body: N/A full time, N/A part time
Expenses: 2019-2020: $13,250; room/board: $7,000
Financial aid: N/A

Wilmington College
Wilmington OH
(937) 481-2260
U.S. News ranking: Reg. Coll. (Mid. W), No. 38
Website: www.wilmington.edu/
Admissions email: admission@wilmington.edu
Private; founded 1870
Affiliation: Friends
Freshman admissions: selective; 2019-2020: 1,650 applied, 1,290 accepted. Either SAT or ACT required. ACT 25/75 percentile: 18-23. High school rank: 13% in top tenth, 42% in top quarter, 78% in top half
Early decision deadline: N/A, notification date: N/A
Early action deadline: N/A, notification date: N/A
Application deadline (fall): 8/1
Undergraduate student body: 1,167 full time, 64 part time; 47% male, 53% female; 0% American Indian, 1% Asian, 10% Black, 2% Hispanic, 4% multiracial, 0% Pacific Islander, 75% white, 2% international; 90% from in state; 62% live on campus; 20% of students in fraternities, 22% in sororities
Most popular majors: 21% Agricultural Business and Management, General, 20% Business Administration and Management, General, 10% Education, General, 6% Accounting, 6% Sport and Fitness Administration/Management
Expenses: 2020-2021: $27,400; room/board: $10,100
Financial aid: (937) 481-2337

Wittenberg University
Springfield OH
(937) 327-6314
U.S. News ranking: Nat. Lib. Arts, No. 153
Website: www.wittenberg.edu/
Admissions email: admission@wittenberg.edu
Private; founded 1845
Affiliation: Evangelical Lutheran Church
Freshman admissions: selective; 2019-2020: 2,392 applied, 2,184 accepted. Neither SAT nor ACT required. ACT 25/75 percentile: 20-27. High school rank: 14% in top tenth, 39% in top quarter, 76% in top half
Early decision deadline: 11/15, notification date: 12/1
Early action deadline: 12/1, notification date: 1/1
Application deadline (fall): rolling
Undergraduate student body: 1,504 full time, 73 part time; 45% male, 55% female; 0% American Indian, 1% Asian, 9% Black, 4% Hispanic, 6% multiracial, 0% Pacific Islander, 78% white, 1% international; N/A from in state; 87% live on campus; 27% of students in fraternities, 30% in sororities
Most popular majors: 21% Business, Management, Marketing, and Related Support Services, 11% Parks, Recreation, Leisure, and Fitness Studies, 10% Biological and Biomedical Sciences, 10% Social Sciences, 6% Education
Expenses: 2020-2021: $41,476; room/board: $10,830
Financial aid: (937) 327-7318; 78% of undergrads determined to have financial need; average aid package $34,552

Wright State University
Dayton OH
(937) 775-5700
U.S. News ranking: Nat. U., second tier
Website: www.wright.edu
Admissions email: admissions@wright.edu
Public; founded 1967
Freshman admissions: selective; 2019-2020: 5,849 applied, 5,583 accepted. Either SAT or ACT required. ACT 25/75 percentile: 18-25. High school rank: 19% in top tenth, 41% in top quarter, 71% in top half
Early decision deadline: N/A, notification date: N/A
Early action deadline: N/A, notification date: N/A
Application deadline (fall): 8/20
Undergraduate student body: 7,226 full time, 2,145 part time; 47% male, 53% female; 0% American Indian, 3% Asian, 12% Black, 4% Hispanic, 5% multiracial, 0% Pacific Islander, 73% white, 2% international; N/A from in state; 19% live on campus; N/A of students in fraternities, N/A in sororities
Most popular majors: 26% Business, Management, Marketing, and Related Support Services, 14% Engineering, 10% Health Professions and

Related Programs, 8% Psychology, 6% Education
Expenses: 2020-2021: $9,962 in state, $19,380 out of state; room/board: $12,414
Financial aid: (937) 775-4000; 63% of undergrads determined to have financial need; average aid package $11,457

Xavier University
Cincinnati OH
(877) 982-3648
U.S. News ranking: Reg. U. (Mid. W), No. 5
Website: www.xavier.edu
Admissions email: xuadmit@xavier.edu
Private; founded 1831
Affiliation: Roman Catholic
Freshman admissions: selective; 2019-2020: 14,758 applied, 11,271 accepted. Neither SAT nor ACT required. ACT 25/75 percentile: 22-28. High school rank: 23% in top tenth, 52% in top quarter, 82% in top half
Early decision deadline: N/A, notification date: N/A
Early action deadline: N/A, notification date: N/A
Application deadline (fall): rolling
Undergraduate student body: 4,834 full time, 213 part time; 46% male, 54% female; 0% American Indian, 3% Asian, 9% Black, 6% Hispanic, 4% multiracial, 0% Pacific Islander, 75% white, 1% international; 43% from in state; 46% live on campus; N/A of students in fraternities, N/A in sororities
Most popular majors: 25% Business, Management, Marketing, and Related Support Services, 22% Health Professions and Related Programs, 7% Liberal Arts and Sciences, General Studies and Humanities, 6% Social Sciences, 5% Psychology
Expenses: 2020-2021: $42,460; room/board: $13,310
Financial aid: (513) 745-3142; 57% of undergrads determined to have financial need; average aid package $26,257

Youngstown State University
Youngstown OH
(877) 468-6978
U.S. News ranking: Reg. U. (Mid. W), No. 112
Website: www.ysu.edu
Admissions email: enroll@ysu.edu
Public; founded 1908
Freshman admissions: selective; 2019-2020: 9,243 applied, 6,246 accepted. Either SAT or ACT required. ACT 25/75 percentile: 18-24. High school rank: 14% in top tenth, 35% in top quarter, 68% in top half
Early decision deadline: N/A, notification date: N/A
Early action deadline: N/A, notification date: N/A
Application deadline (fall): 8/1
Undergraduate student body: 8,756 full time, 2,245 part time; 46% male, 54% female; 0% American Indian, 1% Asian, 8% Black, 4% Hispanic, 4% multiracial, 0% Pacific Islander, 75% white, 3% international; 84% from in

state; 13% live on campus; 2% of students in fraternities, 2% in sororities

Most popular majors: 7% Criminal Justice/Safety Studies, 7% Registered Nursing/Registered Nurse, 6% Biomedical Sciences, General, 6% General Studies, 5% Social Work

Expenses: 2020-2021: $10,016 in state, $15,656 out of state; room/board: N/A

Financial aid: (330) 941-2031; 68% of undergrads determined to have financial need; average aid package $10,157

OKLAHOMA

Bacone College[1]

Muskogee OK
(888) 682-5514
U.S. News ranking: Reg. Coll. (W), second tier
Website: www.bacone.edu/
Admissions email: admissions@bacone.edu
Private
Application deadline (fall): rolling
Undergraduate student body: N/A full time, N/A part time
Expenses: 2019-2020: $14,700; room/board: $8,600
Financial aid: N/A

Cameron University

Lawton OK
(580) 581-2289
U.S. News ranking: Reg. U. (W), second tier
Website: www.cameron.edu/
Admissions email: admissions@cameron.edu
Public; founded 1908
Freshman admissions: less selective; 2019-2020: 993 applied, 992 accepted. Neither SAT nor ACT required. ACT 25/75 percentile: 16-21. High school rank: 3% in top tenth, 13% in top quarter, 42% in top half
Early decision deadline: N/A, notification date: N/A
Early action deadline: N/A, notification date: N/A
Application deadline (fall): rolling
Undergraduate student body: 2,563 full time, 1,253 part time; 37% male, 63% female; 6% American Indian, 2% Asian, 12% Black, 15% Hispanic, 10% multiracial, 0% Pacific Islander, 48% white, 3% international; 87% from in state; 9% live on campus; 3% of students in fraternities, 1% in sororities
Most popular majors: 11% Business Administration and Management, General, 10% Corrections and Criminal Justice, Other, 8% Psychology, General, 6% Accounting, 6% Information Technology
Expenses: 2020-2021: N/A in state, N/A out of state; room/board: $5,670
Financial aid: (580) 581-2293; 68% of undergrads determined to have financial need; average aid package $9,994

East Central University

Ada OK
(580) 559-5628
U.S. News ranking: Reg. U. (W), second tier
Website: www.ecok.edu
Admissions email: admissions@ecok.edu
Public; founded 1909
Freshman admissions: selective; 2019-2020: 1,178 applied, 699 accepted. ACT required. ACT 25/75 percentile: 17-23. High school rank: N/A
Early decision deadline: N/A, notification date: N/A
Early action deadline: N/A, notification date: N/A
Application deadline (fall): rolling
Undergraduate student body: 2,471 full time, 510 part time; 42% male, 58% female; 5% American Indian, 0% Asian, 15% Black, 5% Hispanic, 4% multiracial, 1% Pacific Islander, 56% white, 10% international; 91% from in state; 35% live on campus; 3% of students in fraternities, 3% in sororities
Most popular majors: 14% Business, Management, Marketing, and Related Support Services, 14% Health Professions and Related Programs, 10% Parks, Recreation, Leisure, and Fitness Studies, 9% Public Administration and Social Service Professions, 8% Biological and Biomedical Sciences
Expenses: 2019-2020: $7,052 in state, $16,412 out of state; room/board: $6,848
Financial aid: (580) 559-5243; 68% of undergrads determined to have financial need; average aid package $6,222

Langston University[1]

Langston OK
(405) 466-3231
U.S. News ranking: Reg. U. (W), second tier
Website: www.langston.edu/
Admissions email: admissions@langston.edu
Public; founded 1897
Application deadline (fall): rolling
Undergraduate student body: N/A full time, N/A part time
Expenses: 2019-2020: $6,421 in state, $13,840 out of state; room/board: $10,446
Financial aid: (405) 466-3357

Mid-America Christian University[1]

Oklahoma City OK
(405) 691-3800
U.S. News ranking: Reg. U. (W), second tier
Website: www.macu.edu
Admissions email: info@macu.edu
Private
Application deadline (fall): N/A
Undergraduate student body: N/A full time, N/A part time
Expenses: 2019-2020: $18,838; room/board: $8,166
Financial aid: N/A

Northeastern State University

Tahlequah OK
(918) 444-2200
U.S. News ranking: Reg. U. (W), No. 93
Website: www.nsuok.edu
Admissions email: nsuinfo@nsuok.edu
Public; founded 1846
Freshman admissions: selective; 2019-2020: 1,073 applied, 1,067 accepted. ACT required. ACT 25/75 percentile: 18-24. High school rank: 27% in top tenth, 52% in top quarter, 82% in top half
Early decision deadline: N/A, notification date: N/A
Early action deadline: N/A, notification date: N/A
Application deadline (fall): rolling
Undergraduate student body: 4,352 full time, 1,936 part time; 38% male, 62% female; 19% American Indian, 2% Asian, 4% Black, 6% Hispanic, 18% multiracial, 0% Pacific Islander, 47% white, 2% international; 95% from in state; 19% live on campus; N/A of students in fraternities, N/A in sororities
Most popular majors: 10% Research and Experimental Psychology, Other, 6% Accounting, 6% Criminal Justice/Law Enforcement Administration, 6% General Studies, 6% Registered Nursing/Registered Nurse
Expenses: 2020-2021: $6,915 in state, $15,315 out of state; room/board: $8,074
Financial aid: (918) 444-3410; 67% of undergrads determined to have financial need; average aid package $13,932

Northwestern Oklahoma State University

Alva OK
(580) 327-8545
U.S. News ranking: Reg. U. (W), second tier
Website: www.nwosu.edu
Admissions email: recruit@nwosu.edu
Public; founded 1897
Freshman admissions: selective; 2019-2020: 1,145 applied, 774 accepted. Either SAT or ACT required. ACT 25/75 percentile: 17-22. High school rank: 5% in top tenth, 9% in top quarter, 13% in top half
Early decision deadline: N/A, notification date: N/A
Early action deadline: N/A, notification date: N/A
Application deadline (fall): rolling
Undergraduate student body: 1,377 full time, 391 part time; 40% male, 60% female; 8% American Indian, 1% Asian, 7% Black, 11% Hispanic, 2% multiracial, 0% Pacific Islander, 59% white, 1% international
Most popular majors: 12% Parks, Recreation, Leisure, and Fitness Studies, Other, 11% Registered Nursing/Registered Nurse, 9% Business Administration and

Management, General, 8% Psychology, General, 7% General Studies
Expenses: 2019-2020: $8,018 in state, $15,136 out of state; room/board: $5,000
Financial aid: N/A

Oklahoma Baptist University

Shawnee OK
(405) 585-5000
U.S. News ranking: Reg. Coll. (W), No. 8
Website: www.okbu.edu
Admissions email: admissions@okbu.edu
Private; founded 1910
Affiliation: Southern Baptist
Freshman admissions: selective; 2019-2020: 4,292 applied, 2,466 accepted. Either SAT or ACT required. ACT 25/75 percentile: 20-26. High school rank: 12% in top tenth, 21% in top quarter, 82% in top half
Early decision deadline: N/A, notification date: N/A
Early action deadline: N/A, notification date: N/A
Application deadline (fall): 8/1
Undergraduate student body: 1,703 full time, 49 part time; 40% male, 60% female; 4% American Indian, 1% Asian, 5% Black, 2% Hispanic, 13% multiracial, 0% Pacific Islander, 71% white, 4% international
Most popular majors: Information not available
Expenses: 2020-2021: $31,352; room/board: $7,720
Financial aid: (405) 585-5020; 74% of undergrads determined to have financial need; average aid package $21,528

Oklahoma Christian University

Oklahoma City OK
(405) 425-5050
U.S. News ranking: Reg. U. (W), No. 47
Website: www.oc.edu/
Admissions email: admissions@oc.edu
Private; founded 1950
Affiliation: Churches of Christ
Freshman admissions: selective; 2019-2020: 2,206 applied, 1,468 accepted. Either SAT or ACT required. ACT 25/75 percentile: 21-27. High school rank: 26% in top tenth, 51% in top quarter, 80% in top half
Early decision deadline: N/A, notification date: N/A
Early action deadline: N/A, notification date: N/A
Application deadline (fall): rolling
Undergraduate student body: 1,654 full time, 97 part time; 49% male, 51% female; 2% American Indian, 1% Asian, 5% Black, 7% Hispanic, 8% multiracial, 0% Pacific Islander, 72% white, 5% international; 48% from in state; 76% live on campus; 30% of students in fraternities, 37% in sororities
Most popular majors: 18% Business, Management, Marketing, and Related Support Services, 11% Engineering, 11% Health Professions and Related

Programs, 8% Communication, Journalism, and Related Programs, 8% Education
Expenses: 2020-2021: $25,040; room/board: $7,900
Financial aid: (405) 425-5190; 68% of undergrads determined to have financial need; average aid package $25,006

Oklahoma City University[1]

Oklahoma City OK
(405) 208-5050
U.S. News ranking: Nat. U., No. 241
Website: www.okcu.edu
Admissions email: uadmissions@okcu.edu
Private; founded 1904
Affiliation: United Methodist
Application deadline (fall): rolling
Undergraduate student body: 1,514 full time, 72 part time
Expenses: 2020-2021: $32,744; room/board: $12,700
Financial aid: (405) 208-5211; 61% of undergrads determined to have financial need; average aid package $22,070

Oklahoma Panhandle State University

Goodwell OK
(580) 349-1373
U.S. News ranking: Reg. Coll. (W), No. 23
Website: www.opsu.edu
Admissions email: academicrecords@opsu.edu
Public; founded 1909
Freshman admissions: less selective; 2019-2020: 1,394 applied, 1,258 accepted. Neither SAT nor ACT required. ACT 25/75 percentile: 7-22. High school rank: 8% in top tenth, 21% in top quarter, 55% in top half
Early decision deadline: N/A, notification date: N/A
Early action deadline: N/A, notification date: N/A
Application deadline (fall): rolling
Undergraduate student body: 956 full time, 286 part time; 48% male, 52% female; 6% American Indian, 1% Asian, 9% Black, 29% Hispanic, 1% multiracial, 0% Pacific Islander, 51% white, 3% international
Most popular majors: 40% Registered Nursing/Registered Nurse, 9% Business Administration and Management, General, 7% Biology/Biological Sciences, General, 7% Computer and Information Sciences, General, 5% Animal Sciences, General
Expenses: 2020-2021: $7,665 in state, $7,665 out of state; room/board: $5,972
Financial aid: (580) 349-1580; 61% of undergrads determined to have financial need

Oklahoma State University

Stillwater OK
(405) 744-5358
U.S. News ranking: Nat. U., No. 187
Website: go.okstate.edu

Admissions email: admissions@okstate.edu
Public; founded 1890
Freshman admissions: more selective; 2019-2020: 15,277 applied, 10,691 accepted. Either SAT or ACT required. ACT 25/75 percentile: 21-28. High school rank: 27% in top tenth, 54% in top quarter, 84% in top half
Early decision deadline: N/A, notification date: N/A
Early action deadline: N/A, notification date: N/A
Application deadline (fall): rolling
Undergraduate student body: 17,213 full time, 2,811 part time; 50% male, 50% female; 4% American Indian, 2% Asian, 4% Black, 8% Hispanic, 10% multiracial, 0% Pacific Islander, 68% white, 3% international; N/A from in state; 42% live on campus; 20% of students in fraternities, 25% in sororities
Most popular majors: 25% Business, Management, Marketing, and Related Support Services, 13% Engineering, 10% Agriculture, Agriculture Operations, and Related Sciences, 7% Biological and Biomedical Sciences, 5% Liberal Arts and Sciences, General Studies and Humanities
Expenses: 2020-2021: $9,019 in state, $24,539 out of state; room/board: $9,106
Financial aid: (405) 744-6604; 54% of undergrads determined to have financial need; average aid package $15,840

Oklahoma State University Institute of Technology–Okmulgee
Okmulgee OK
(918) 293-4680
U.S. News ranking: Reg. Coll. (W), No. 20
Website: osuit.edu/admissions
Admissions email: osuit.admissions@okstate.edu
Public; founded 1946
Freshman admissions: less selective; 2019-2020: 2,518 applied, 734 accepted. Either SAT or ACT required. ACT 25/75 percentile: 15-20. High school rank: 10% in top tenth, 24% in top quarter, 57% in top half
Early decision deadline: N/A, notification date: N/A
Early action deadline: N/A, notification date: N/A
Application deadline (fall): rolling
Undergraduate student body: 1,464 full time, 845 part time; 65% male, 35% female; 12% American Indian, 1% Asian, 3% Black, 7% Hispanic, 15% multiracial, 0% Pacific Islander, 55% white, 1% international; 91% from in state; 26% live on campus; 0% of students in fraternities, 0% in sororities
Most popular majors: 48% Information Technology, 44% Instrumentation Technology/Technician, 6% Civil Engineering Technology/Technician

Expenses: 2020-2021: $5,774 in state, $11,384 out of state; room/board: $6,988
Financial aid: (918) 293-5222; 71% of undergrads determined to have financial need; average aid package $11,363

Oklahoma State University–Oklahoma City[1]
Oklahoma City OK
(405) 945-3224
U.S. News ranking: Reg. Coll. (W), second tier
Website: www.osuokc.edu/
Admissions email: admissions@osuokc.edu
Public; founded 1961
Application deadline (fall): rolling
Undergraduate student body: N/A full time, N/A part time
Expenses: 2019-2020: $5,034 in state, $10,872 out of state; room/board: $5,534
Financial aid: (405) 945-3211

Oklahoma Wesleyan University[1]
Bartlesville OK
(866) 222-8226
U.S. News ranking: Reg. U. (W), second tier
Website: www.okwu.edu
Admissions email: admissions@okwu.edu
Private; founded 1972
Affiliation: Wesleyan
Application deadline (fall): rolling
Undergraduate student body: N/A full time, N/A part time
Expenses: 2019-2020: $27,996; room/board: $8,470
Financial aid: (918) 335-6282

Oral Roberts University
Tulsa OK
(800) 678-8876
U.S. News ranking: Reg. Coll. (W), No. 5
Website: www.oru.edu
Admissions email: admissions@oru.edu
Private; founded 1963
Affiliation: Interdenominational
Freshman admissions: selective; 2019-2020: 3,437 applied, 2,348 accepted. Either SAT or ACT required. ACT 25/75 percentile: 18-25. High school rank: 18% in top tenth, 43% in top quarter, 74% in top half
Early decision deadline: N/A, notification date: N/A
Early action deadline: N/A, notification date: N/A
Application deadline (fall): rolling
Undergraduate student body: 2,563 full time, 897 part time; 41% male, 59% female; 3% American Indian, 2% Asian, 15% Black, 13% Hispanic, 5% multiracial, 0% Pacific Islander, 42% white, 15% international; N/A from in state; 57% live on campus; N/A of students in fraternities, N/A in sororities
Most popular majors: 19% Business, Management, Marketing, and Related Support Services, 16% Theology and Religious Vocations,

8% Communication, Journalism, and Related Programs, 8% Psychology, 7% Visual and Performing Arts
Expenses: 2020-2021: $30,930; room/board: $8,650
Financial aid: (918) 495-6510; 69% of undergrads determined to have financial need; average aid package $30,260

Rogers State University
Claremore OK
(918) 343-7545
U.S. News ranking: Reg. Coll. (W), second tier
Website: www.rsu.edu/
Admissions email: admissions@rsu.edu
Public; founded 1909
Freshman admissions: less selective; 2019-2020: 1,263 applied, 1,127 accepted. Either SAT or ACT required. ACT 25/75 percentile: 16-20. High school rank: 15% in top tenth, 18% in top quarter, 65% in top half
Early decision deadline: N/A, notification date: N/A
Early action deadline: N/A, notification date: N/A
Application deadline (fall): rolling
Undergraduate student body: 2,280 full time, 1,303 part time; 38% male, 62% female; 13% American Indian, 3% Asian, 4% Black, 7% Hispanic, 16% multiracial, 0% Pacific Islander, 56% white, 0% international
Most popular majors: 30% Business Administration and Management, General, 10% Biology/Biological Sciences, General, 9% Registered Nursing/Registered Nurse, 9% Social Sciences, General, 8% Multi-/Interdisciplinary Studies, Other
Expenses: 2020-2021: $7,200 in state, $15,540 out of state; room/board: $9,814
Financial aid: (918) 343-7553; 88% of undergrads determined to have financial need; average aid package $9,693

Southeastern Oklahoma State University[1]
Durant OK
(580) 745-2060
U.S. News ranking: Reg. U. (W), second tier
Website: www.se.edu
Admissions email: admissions@se.edu
Public; founded 1909
Affiliation: Other
Application deadline (fall): rolling
Undergraduate student body: N/A full time, N/A part time
Expenses: 2019-2020: $6,750 in state, $15,390 out of state; room/board: $6,958
Financial aid: (580) 745-2186

Southern Nazarene University
Bethany OK
(405) 491-6324
U.S. News ranking: Reg. U. (W), No. 68
Website: www.snu.edu

Admissions email: admissions@snu.edu
Private; founded 1899
Affiliation: Church of the Nazarene
Freshman admissions: selective; 2019-2020: 678 applied, 559 accepted. Either SAT or ACT required. ACT 25/75 percentile: 18-24. High school rank: N/A
Early decision deadline: N/A, notification date: N/A
Early action deadline: N/A, notification date: N/A
Application deadline (fall): 8/6
Undergraduate student body: 1,328 full time, 287 part time; 48% male, 52% female; 4% American Indian, 1% Asian, 13% Black, 15% Hispanic, 8% multiracial, 0% Pacific Islander, 56% white, 2% international; 70% from in state; 51% live on campus; 0% of students in fraternities, 0% in sororities
Most popular majors: 27% Business Administration and Management, General, 18% Organizational Behavior Studies, 7% Human Development and Family Studies, General, 7% Registered Nursing/Registered Nurse, 6% General Studies
Expenses: 2020-2021: $26,000; room/board: $8,800
Financial aid: (405) 491-6310; 76% of undergrads determined to have financial need; average aid package $19,270

Southwestern Christian University
Bethany OK
(405) 789-7661
U.S. News ranking: Reg. Coll. (W), second tier
Website: www.swcu.edu/
Admissions email: admissions@swcu.edu
Private; founded 1946
Affiliation: Pentecostal Holiness Church
Freshman admissions: less selective; 2019-2020: 340 applied, 211 accepted. Either SAT or ACT required. ACT 25/75 percentile: 16-20. High school rank: N/A
Early decision deadline: N/A, notification date: N/A
Early action deadline: N/A, notification date: N/A
Application deadline (fall): rolling
Undergraduate student body: 438 full time, 54 part time; 55% male, 45% female; 5% American Indian, 1% Asian, 24% Black, 11% Hispanic, 3% multiracial, 1% Pacific Islander, 39% white, 14% international
Most popular majors: 26% Business Administration and Management, General, 23% Sport and Fitness Administration/Management, 20% Organizational Leadership, 8% Theology and Religious Vocations, Other, 7% Public Administration and Social Service Professions
Expenses: 2020-2021: $19,114; room/board: $8,600
Financial aid: (405) 789-7661

Southwestern Oklahoma State University
Weatherford OK
(580) 774-3782
U.S. News ranking: Reg. U. (W), No. 84
Website: www.swosu.edu
Admissions email: admissions@swosu.edu
Public; founded 1901
Freshman admissions: selective; 2019-2020: 2,225 applied, 2,017 accepted. Neither SAT nor ACT required. ACT 25/75 percentile: 18-24. High school rank: 25% in top tenth, 49% in top quarter, 79% in top half
Early decision deadline: N/A, notification date: N/A
Early action deadline: N/A, notification date: N/A
Application deadline (fall): rolling
Undergraduate student body: 3,233 full time, 857 part time; 39% male, 61% female; 4% American Indian, 2% Asian, 4% Black, 12% Hispanic, 9% multiracial, 0% Pacific Islander, 62% white, 4% international; 92% from in state; 26% live on campus; 1% of students in fraternities, 3% in sororities
Most popular majors: 28% Registered Nursing/Registered Nurse, 15% Business Administration and Management, General, 8% Elementary Education and Teaching, 6% Parks, Recreation and Leisure Facilities Management, General, 5% Health Professions and Related Clinical Sciences, Other
Expenses: 2019-2020: $7,695 in state, $14,235 out of state; room/board: $6,030
Financial aid: (580) 774-3786

University of Central Oklahoma
Edmond OK
(405) 974-2727
U.S. News ranking: Reg. U. (W), No. 68
Website: www.uco.edu/
Admissions email: onestop@uco.edu
Public; founded 1890
Freshman admissions: selective; 2019-2020: 5,447 applied, 4,190 accepted. Either SAT or ACT required. ACT 25/75 percentile: 19-24. High school rank: 16% in top tenth, 40% in top quarter, 72% in top half
Early decision deadline: N/A, notification date: N/A
Early action deadline: N/A, notification date: N/A
Application deadline (fall): rolling
Undergraduate student body: 9,726 full time, 3,605 part time; 40% male, 60% female; 3% American Indian, 4% Asian, 8% Black, 12% Hispanic, 10% multiracial, 0% Pacific Islander, 54% white, 4% international
Most popular majors: Information not available
Expenses: 2020-2021: $7,753 in state, $18,640 out of state; room/board: $7,750

Financial aid: (405) 974-2727; 63% of undergrads determined to have financial need; average aid package $10,864

University of Oklahoma

Norman OK
(405) 325-2252
U.S. News ranking: Nat. U., No. 133
Website: www.ou.edu
Admissions email: admissions@ou.edu
Public; founded 1890
Freshman admissions: more selective; 2019-2020: 15,672 applied, 12,602 accepted. Either SAT or ACT required. ACT 25/75 percentile: 23-29. High school rank: 33% in top tenth, 61% in top quarter, 89% in top half
Early decision deadline: N/A, notification date: N/A
Early action deadline: N/A, notification date: N/A
Application deadline (fall): 2/1
Undergraduate student body: 18,982 full time, 2,786 part time; 49% male, 51% female; 4% American Indian, 7% Asian, 5% Black, 11% Hispanic, 9% multiracial, 0% Pacific Islander, 60% white, 3% international; 49% from in state; 34% live on campus; 25% of students in fraternities, 32% in sororities
Most popular majors: 22% Business, Management, Marketing, and Related Support Services, 15% Engineering, 8% Communication, Journalism, and Related Programs, 7% Liberal Arts and Sciences, General Studies and Humanities, 7% Social Sciences
Expenses: 2020-2021: $11,687 in state, $27,068 out of state; room/board: $11,324
Financial aid: (405) 325-9000; 47% of undergrads determined to have financial need; average aid package $14,464

University of Science and Arts of Oklahoma

Chickasha OK
(405) 574-1357
U.S. News ranking: Nat. Lib. Arts, second tier
Website: www.usao.edu
Admissions email: usao-admissions@usao.edu
Public; founded 1908
Freshman admissions: selective; 2019-2020: 470 applied, 303 accepted. Neither SAT nor ACT required. ACT 25/75 percentile: 19-24. High school rank: N/A
Early decision deadline: N/A, notification date: N/A
Early action deadline: N/A, notification date: N/A
Application deadline (fall): 8/30
Undergraduate student body: 726 full time, 74 part time; 36% male, 64% female; 5% American Indian, 1% Asian, 5% Black, 12% Hispanic, 12% multiracial, 0% Pacific Islander, 54% white, 9% international
Most popular majors: Information not available

Expenses: 2020-2021: $8,040 in state, $18,900 out of state; room/board: $6,180
Financial aid: (405) 574-1350; 68% of undergrads determined to have financial need; average aid package $13,415

University of Tulsa

Tulsa OK
(918) 631-2307
U.S. News ranking: Nat. U., No. 143
Website: utulsa.edu
Admissions email: admission@utulsa.edu
Private; founded 1894
Affiliation: Presbyterian Church (USA)
Freshman admissions: more selective; 2019-2020: 9,793 applied, 3,510 accepted. Either SAT or ACT required. ACT 25/75 percentile: 24-31. High school rank: 56% in top tenth, 72% in top quarter, 93% in top half
Early decision deadline: N/A, notification date: N/A
Early action deadline: 11/1, notification date: 12/15
Application deadline (fall): rolling
Undergraduate student body: 3,172 full time, 104 part time; 54% male, 46% female; 3% American Indian, 6% Asian, 7% Black, 9% Hispanic, 8% multiracial, 0% Pacific Islander, 54% white, 12% international; 57% from in state; 72% live on campus; 23% of students in fraternities, 23% in sororities
Most popular majors: 24% Engineering, 22% Business, Management, Marketing, and Related Support Services, 8% Visual and Performing Arts, 6% Biological and Biomedical Sciences, 6% Computer and Information Sciences and Support Services
Expenses: 2020-2021: $43,490; room/board: $12,062
Financial aid: (918) 631-2624; 55% of undergrads determined to have financial need; average aid package $35,615

OREGON

Bushnell University[7]

Eugene OR
(541) 684-7201
U.S. News ranking: Reg. U. (W), No. 82
Website: www.bushnell.edu/
Admissions email: admissions@nwcu.edu
Private; founded 1895
Affiliation: Christian Church (Disciples of Christ)
Freshman admissions: selective; 2019-2020: N/A applied, N/A accepted. Either SAT or ACT required. SAT 25/75 percentile: 935-1170. High school rank: N/A
Early decision deadline: N/A, notification date: N/A
Early action deadline: N/A, notification date: N/A
Application deadline (fall): rolling
Undergraduate student body: 450 full time, 142 part time
Most popular majors: Information not available

Expenses: 2020-2021: $32,320; room/board: $10,050
Financial aid: (541) 684-7201; 80% of undergrads determined to have financial need; average aid package $22,913

Corban University[1]

Salem OR
(800) 845-3005
U.S. News ranking: Reg. Coll. (W), No. 11
Website: www.corban.edu
Admissions email: admissions@corban.edu
Private; founded 1935
Affiliation: Evangelical Christian
Application deadline (fall): 8/1
Undergraduate student body: N/A full time, N/A part time
Expenses: 2019-2020: $33,378; room/board: $10,316
Financial aid: (503) 375-7106

Eastern Oregon University

La Grande OR
(541) 962-3393
U.S. News ranking: Reg. U. (W), No. 88
Website: www.eou.edu
Admissions email: admissions@eou.edu
Public; founded 1929
Freshman admissions: selective; 2019-2020: 890 applied, 872 accepted. Either SAT or ACT required. SAT 25/75 percentile: 930-1145. High school rank: 19% in top tenth, 40% in top quarter, 76% in top half
Early decision deadline: N/A, notification date: N/A
Early action deadline: 2/1, notification date: N/A
Application deadline (fall): 9/1
Undergraduate student body: 1,639 full time, 1,228 part time; 40% male, 60% female; 2% American Indian, 2% Asian, 2% Black, 12% Hispanic, 6% multiracial, 4% Pacific Islander, 69% white, 2% international; N/A from in state; 6% live on campus; N/A of students in fraternities, N/A in sororities
Most popular majors: 27% Business, Management, Marketing, and Related Support Services, 15% Education, 10% Multi/Interdisciplinary Studies, 9% Parks, Recreation, Leisure, and Fitness Studies, 5% Psychology
Expenses: 2020-2021: $9,405 in state, $22,509 out of state; room/board: $10,150
Financial aid: (541) 962-3550; 73% of undergrads determined to have financial need; average aid package $10,596

George Fox University

Newberg OR
(800) 765-4369
U.S. News ranking: Nat. U., No. 227
Website: www.georgefox.edu
Admissions email: admissions@georgefox.edu
Private; founded 1891
Affiliation: Friends
Freshman admissions: selective; 2019-2020: 3,010 applied, 2,480 accepted. Either SAT

or ACT required. SAT 25/75 percentile: 1030-1270. High school rank: 32% in top tenth, 60% in top quarter, 88% in top half
Early decision deadline: N/A, notification date: N/A
Early action deadline: 11/1, notification date: 12/9
Application deadline (fall): rolling
Undergraduate student body: 2,424 full time, 204 part time; 42% male, 58% female; 1% American Indian, 4% Asian, 1% Black, 14% Hispanic, 8% multiracial, 1% Pacific Islander, 69% white, 1% international; 58% from in state; 53% live on campus; 0% of students in fraternities, 0% in sororities
Most popular majors: 16% Business Administration, Management and Operations, 7% Engineering, General, 7% Registered Nursing, Nursing Administration, Nursing Research and Clinical Nursing, 7% Teacher Education and Professional Development, Specific Levels and Methods, 5% Psychology, General
Expenses: 2020-2021: $38,370; room/board: $12,090
Financial aid: (503) 554-2302; 73% of undergrads determined to have financial need; average aid package $24,325

Lewis & Clark College

Portland OR
(800) 444-4111
U.S. News ranking: Nat. Lib. Arts, No. 76
Website: www.lclark.edu
Admissions email: admissions@lclark.edu
Private; founded 1867
Freshman admissions: more selective; 2019-2020: 5,863 applied, 4,231 accepted. Neither SAT nor ACT required. SAT 25/75 percentile: 1210-1400. High school rank: 37% in top tenth, 73% in top quarter, 95% in top half
Early decision deadline: 11/1, notification date: 12/15
Early action deadline: 11/1, notification date: 12/31
Application deadline (fall): 1/15
Undergraduate student body: 1,934 full time, 31 part time; 39% male, 61% female; 0% American Indian, 4% Asian, 3% Black, 13% Hispanic, 7% multiracial, 1% Pacific Islander, 65% white, 4% international; N/A from in state; 69% live on campus; N/A of students in fraternities, N/A in sororities
Most popular majors: 22% Social Sciences, 14% Biological and Biomedical Sciences, 14% Psychology, 9% English Language and Literature/Letters, 8% Visual and Performing Arts
Expenses: 2020-2021: $55,266; room/board: $13,324
Financial aid: (503) 768-7090; 58% of undergrads determined to have financial need; average aid package $44,874

Linfield University

McMinnville OR
(800) 640-2287
U.S. News ranking: Nat. Lib. Arts, No. 120
Website: www.linfield.edu
Admissions email: admission@linfield.edu
Private; founded 1858
Affiliation: American Baptist
Freshman admissions: selective; 2019-2020: 2,390 applied, 1,953 accepted. Neither SAT nor ACT required. SAT 25/75 percentile: 1020-1220. High school rank: N/A
Early decision deadline: N/A, notification date: N/A
Early action deadline: 11/1, notification date: 1/15
Application deadline (fall): rolling
Undergraduate student body: 1,383 full time, 31 part time; 38% male, 62% female; 1% American Indian, 5% Asian, 1% Black, 19% Hispanic, 7% multiracial, 1% Pacific Islander, 62% white, 2% international; 60% from in state; 77% live on campus; 29% of students in fraternities, 30% in sororities
Most popular majors: 22% Business, Management, Marketing, and Related Support Services, 12% Education, 10% Social Sciences, 9% Biological and Biomedical Sciences, 9% Parks, Recreation, Leisure, and Fitness Studies
Expenses: 2020-2021: $45,062; room/board: $12,930
Financial aid: (503) 883-2225; 76% of undergrads determined to have financial need; average aid package $38,507

Oregon State University

Corvallis OR
(541) 737-4411
U.S. News ranking: Nat. U., No. 153
Website: oregonstate.edu
Admissions email: osuadmit@oregonstate.edu
Public; founded 1868
Freshman admissions: more selective; 2019-2020: 15,786 applied, 13,196 accepted. Either SAT or ACT required. SAT 25/75 percentile: 1080-1320. High school rank: 27% in top tenth, 55% in top quarter, 87% in top half
Early decision deadline: N/A, notification date: N/A
Early action deadline: 11/1, notification date: 12/15
Application deadline (fall): 9/1
Undergraduate student body: 18,554 full time, 7,693 part time; 53% male, 47% female; 1% American Indian, 8% Asian, 1% Black, 11% Hispanic, 7% multiracial, 0% Pacific Islander, 63% white, 6% international; 60% from in state; 17% live on campus; 11% of students in fraternities, 15% in sororities
Most popular majors: 11% Computer Science, 9% Business Administration, Management and Operations, 5% Human Development, Family Studies, and Related Services, 4% Health

and Physical Education/Fitness, 4% Mechanical Engineering
Expenses: 2020-2021: $12,167 in state, $32,357 out of state; room/board: $13,485
Financial aid: (541) 737-2241; 50% of undergrads determined to have financial need; average aid package $11,613

Oregon Tech
Klamath Falls OR
(541) 885-1150
U.S. News ranking: Reg. Coll. (W), No. 5
Website: www.oit.edu
Admissions email: oit@oit.edu
Public; founded 1947
Freshman admissions: selective; 2019-2020: 1,206 applied, 1,171 accepted. Either SAT or ACT required. SAT 25/75 percentile: 1000-1200. High school rank: 17% in top tenth, 50% in top quarter, 82% in top half
Early decision deadline: N/A, notification date: N/A
Early action deadline: N/A, notification date: N/A
Application deadline (fall): 9/4
Undergraduate student body: 2,371 full time, 2,807 part time; 51% male, 49% female; 1% American Indian, 6% Asian, 2% Black, 11% Hispanic, 6% multiracial, 1% Pacific Islander, 69% white, 2% international; 29% from in state; 16% live on campus; 0% of students in fraternities, 0% in sororities
Most popular majors: 43% Health Professions and Related Programs, 20% Engineering, 14% Engineering Technologies and Engineering-Related Fields, 7% Business, Management, Marketing, and Related Support Services, 5% Psychology
Expenses: 2020-2021: $11,265 in state, $31,377 out of state; room/board: $9,936
Financial aid: (541) 885-1280; 66% of undergrads determined to have financial need; average aid package $11,082

Pacific Northwest College of Art[1]
Portland OR
(503) 226-4391
U.S. News ranking: Arts, unranked
Website: www.pnca.edu
Admissions email: admissions@pnca.edu
Private
Application deadline (fall): N/A
Undergraduate student body: N/A full time, N/A part time
Expenses: 2019-2020: $40,375; room/board: $13,363
Financial aid: N/A

Pacific University
Forest Grove OR
(503) 352-2218
U.S. News ranking: Nat. U., No. 187
Website: www.pacificu.edu
Admissions email: admissions@pacificu.edu
Private; founded 1849
Freshman admissions: selective; 2019-2020: 2,524 applied,

2,186 accepted. Either SAT or ACT required. SAT 25/75 percentile: 1060-1260. High school rank: N/A
Early decision deadline: N/A, notification date: N/A
Early action deadline: N/A, notification date: N/A
Application deadline (fall): 8/15
Undergraduate student body: 1,759 full time, 105 part time; 36% male, 64% female; 1% American Indian, 12% Asian, 2% Black, 16% Hispanic, 13% multiracial, 2% Pacific Islander, 49% white, 1% international; N/A from in state; 56% live on campus; 2% of students in fraternities, 8% in sororities
Most popular majors: 17% Health Professions and Related Programs, 13% Business, Management, Marketing, and Related Support Services, 9% Parks, Recreation, Leisure, and Fitness Studies, 9% Social Sciences, 7% Biological and Biomedical Sciences
Expenses: 2020-2021: $48,260; room/board: $13,420
Financial aid: (503) 352-2871; 81% of undergrads determined to have financial need; average aid package $35,931

Portland State University
Portland OR
(800) 547-8887
U.S. News ranking: Nat. U., No. 284
Website: www.pdx.edu
Admissions email: admissions@pdx.edu
Public; founded 1946
Freshman admissions: selective; 2019-2020: 6,861 applied, 6,573 accepted. Neither SAT nor ACT required. SAT 25/75 percentile: 1000-1220. High school rank: 15% in top tenth, 43% in top quarter, 83% in top half
Early decision deadline: N/A, notification date: N/A
Early action deadline: N/A, notification date: N/A
Application deadline (fall): rolling
Undergraduate student body: 13,951 full time, 7,015 part time; 46% male, 54% female; 1% American Indian, 10% Asian, 4% Black, 17% Hispanic, 7% multiracial, 1% Pacific Islander, 52% white, 5% international; N/A from in state; 9% live on campus; 1% of students in fraternities, 1% in sororities
Most popular majors: 24% Business, Management, Marketing, and Related Support Services, 12% Social Sciences, 7% Health Professions and Related Programs, 7% Psychology, 6% Multi/Interdisciplinary Studies
Expenses: 2020-2021: $10,112 in state, $29,001 out of state; room/board: $11,523
Financial aid: (503) 725-3461; 68% of undergrads determined to have financial need; average aid package $10,884

Reed College[1]
Portland OR
(503) 777-7511
U.S. News ranking: Nat. Lib. Arts, No. 63
Website: www.reed.edu/
Admissions email: admission@reed.edu
Private
Application deadline (fall): N/A
Undergraduate student body: N/A full time, N/A part time
Expenses: 2019-2020: $58,440; room/board: $14,620
Financial aid: N/A

Southern Oregon University
Ashland OR
(541) 552-6411
U.S. News ranking: Reg. U. (W), No. 75
Website: www.sou.edu
Admissions email: admissions@sou.edu
Public; founded 1926
Freshman admissions: less selective; 2019-2020: 2,514 applied, 1,966 accepted. Either SAT or ACT required. SAT 25/75 percentile: 980-1200. High school rank: N/A
Early decision deadline: N/A, notification date: N/A
Early action deadline: N/A, notification date: N/A
Application deadline (fall): rolling
Undergraduate student body: 3,187 full time, 1,824 part time; 40% male, 60% female; 1% American Indian, 2% Asian, 2% Black, 13% Hispanic, 10% multiracial, 1% Pacific Islander, 59% white, 2% international; 61% from in state; 17% live on campus; N/A of students in fraternities, N/A in sororities
Most popular majors: 15% Business, Management, Marketing, and Related Support Services, 12% Visual and Performing Arts, 11% Psychology, 10% Education, 8% Parks, Recreation, Leisure, and Fitness Studies
Expenses: 2019-2020: $10,479 in state, $26,814 out of state; room/board: $14,589
Financial aid: N/A

University of Oregon
Eugene OR
(800) 232-3825
U.S. News ranking: Nat. U., No. 103
Website: www.uoregon.edu
Admissions email: uoadmit@uoregon.edu
Public; founded 1876
Freshman admissions: selective; 2019-2020: 27,358 applied, 22,329 accepted. Neither SAT nor ACT required. SAT 25/75 percentile: 1100-1310. High school rank: 26% in top tenth, 57% in top quarter, 86% in top half
Early decision deadline: N/A, notification date: N/A
Early action deadline: 11/1, notification date: 12/15
Application deadline (fall): 1/15

Undergraduate student body: 17,419 full time, 1,469 part time; 46% male, 54% female; 1% American Indian, 6% Asian, 2% Black, 14% Hispanic, 8% multiracial, 0% Pacific Islander, 59% white, 7% international; 55% from in state; 26% live on campus; 16% of students in fraternities, 18% in sororities
Most popular majors: 11% Business/Commerce, General, 8% Social Sciences, General, 7% Economics, General, 6% Advertising, 6% Psychology, General
Expenses: 2020-2021: $13,136 in state, $37,728 out of state; room/board: $12,783
Financial aid: (541) 346-3221; 46% of undergrads determined to have financial need; average aid package $11,936

University of Portland[1]
Portland OR
(888) 627-5601
U.S. News ranking: Reg. U. (W), No. 2
Website: www.up.edu
Admissions email: admissions@up.edu
Private; founded 1901
Affiliation: Roman Catholic
Application deadline (fall): 1/15
Undergraduate student body: 3,739 full time, 57 part time
Expenses: 2020-2021: $49,864; room/board: $14,196
Financial aid: (503) 943-7311; 56% of undergrads determined to have financial need; average aid package $34,119

Warner Pacific University
Portland OR
(503) 517-1020
U.S. News ranking: Reg. Coll. (W), No. 9
Website: www.warnerpacific.edu
Admissions email: admissions@warnerpacific.edu
Private; founded 1937
Affiliation: Church of God
Freshman admissions: less selective; 2019-2020: 508 applied, 495 accepted. Either SAT or ACT required. ACT 25/75 percentile: 15-20. High school rank: 19% in top tenth, 45% in top quarter, 81% in top half
Early decision deadline: N/A, notification date: N/A
Early action deadline: N/A, notification date: N/A
Application deadline (fall): rolling
Undergraduate student body: 381 full time, 20 part time; 45% male, 55% female; 1% American Indian, 6% Asian, 12% Black, 35% Hispanic, 9% multiracial, 1% Pacific Islander, 35% white, 1% international; N/A from in state; N/A live on campus; 0% of students in fraternities, 0% in sororities
Most popular majors: 16% Human Development and Family Studies, General, 9% Accounting, 8% Business Administration and Management, General, 8% Elementary Education and Teaching, 7% Sport and Fitness Administration/Management

Expenses: 2020-2021: $19,670; room/board: $9,306
Financial aid: (503) 517-1091; 85% of undergrads determined to have financial need; average aid package $16,839

Western Oregon University
Monmouth OR
(503) 838-8211
U.S. News ranking: Reg. U. (W), No. 68
Website: www.wou.edu
Admissions email: wolfgram@wou.edu
Public; founded 1856
Freshman admissions: less selective; 2019-2020: 3,069 applied, 2,596 accepted. Neither SAT nor ACT required. SAT 25/75 percentile: 960-1170. High school rank: 9% in top tenth, 20% in top quarter, 38% in top half
Early decision deadline: N/A, notification date: N/A
Early action deadline: N/A, notification date: N/A
Application deadline (fall): rolling
Undergraduate student body: 3,703 full time, 723 part time; 36% male, 64% female; 1% American Indian, 4% Asian, 3% Black, 20% Hispanic, 4% multiracial, 2% Pacific Islander, 59% white, 4% international; N/A from in state; 25% live on campus; 1% of students in fraternities, 1% in sororities
Most popular majors: 13% Education, 12% Business, Management, Marketing, and Related Support Services, 10% Multi/Interdisciplinary Studies, 10% Psychology, 9% Homeland Security, Law Enforcement, Firefighting and Related Protective Services
Expenses: 2020-2021: $10,194 in state, $29,004 out of state; room/board: $10,802
Financial aid: (503) 838-8475

Willamette University
Salem OR
(877) 542-2787
U.S. News ranking: Nat. Lib. Arts, No. 72
Website: www.willamette.edu
Admissions email: bearcat@willamette.edu
Private; founded 1842
Affiliation: United Methodist
Freshman admissions: more selective; 2019-2020: 3,972 applied, 3,095 accepted. Neither SAT nor ACT required. SAT 25/75 percentile: 1140-1340. High school rank: 48% in top tenth, 78% in top quarter, 97% in top half
Early decision deadline: 11/15, notification date: 12/30
Early action deadline: 11/15, notification date: 12/30
Application deadline (fall): 1/15
Undergraduate student body: 1,473 full time, 42 part time; 41% male, 59% female; 1% American Indian, 6% Asian, 2% Black, 15% Hispanic, 8% multiracial, 0% Pacific Islander, 65% white, 1% international; N/A from in state; 60% live on campus;

26% of students in fraternities, 16% in sororities
Most popular majors: 25% Social Sciences, 9% Visual and Performing Arts, 8% Biological and Biomedical Sciences, 8% Physical Sciences, 6% Natural Resources and Conservation
Expenses: 2020-2021: $53,624; room/board: $13,328
Financial aid: (503) 370-6273; 65% of undergrads determined to have financial need; average aid package $32,918

PENNSYLVANIA

Albright College[1]
Reading PA
(800) 252-1856
U.S. News ranking: Nat. Lib. Arts, second tier
Website: www.albright.edu/
Admissions email: admission@albright.edu
Private; founded 1856
Affiliation: United Methodist
Application deadline (fall): rolling
Undergraduate student body: N/A full time, N/A part time
Expenses: 2019-2020: $25,642; room/board: $12,480
Financial aid: (610) 921-7515

Allegheny College
Meadville PA
(800) 521-5293
U.S. News ranking: Nat. Lib. Arts, No. 80
Website: allegheny.edu
Admissions email: admissions@allegheny.edu
Private; founded 1815
Affiliation: United Methodist
Freshman admissions: more selective; 2019-2020: 5,208 applied, 3,237 accepted. Neither SAT nor ACT required. SAT 25/75 percentile: 1170-1360. High school rank: 40% in top tenth, 63% in top quarter, 85% in top half
Early decision deadline: 11/1, notification date: 11/15
Early action deadline: 12/1, notification date: 1/1
Application deadline (fall): 2/15
Undergraduate student body: 1,710 full time, 57 part time; 44% male, 56% female; 0% American Indian, 4% Asian, 8% Black, 9% Hispanic, 4% multiracial, 0% Pacific Islander, 68% white, 3% international; 52% from in state; 95% live on campus; 21% of students in fraternities, 22% in sororities
Most popular majors: 16% Psychology, General, 11% Biology/Biological Sciences, General, 11% Economics, General, 8% Neuroscience, 8% Speech Communication and Rhetoric
Expenses: 2020-2021: $50,980; room/board: $13,080
Financial aid: (800) 835-7780; 77% of undergrads determined to have financial need; average aid package $45,117

Alvernia University
Reading PA
(610) 796-8220
U.S. News ranking: Reg. U. (N), No. 96
Website: www.alvernia.edu/
Admissions email: admissions@alvernia.edu
Private; founded 1958
Affiliation: Roman Catholic
Freshman admissions: selective; 2019-2020: 3,767 applied, 2,419 accepted. Either SAT or ACT required. SAT 25/75 percentile: 943-1130. High school rank: N/A
Early decision deadline: N/A, notification date: N/A
Early action deadline: N/A, notification date: N/A
Application deadline (fall): rolling
Undergraduate student body: 1,656 full time, 467 part time; 30% male, 70% female; 0% American Indian, 2% Asian, 12% Black, 12% Hispanic, 3% multiracial, 0% Pacific Islander, 68% white, 1% international; 72% from in state; 64% live on campus; 0% of students in fraternities, 0% in sororities
Most popular majors: 51% Health Professions and Related Programs, 17% Business, Management, Marketing, and Related Support Services, 9% Homeland Security, Law Enforcement, Firefighting and Related Protective Services, 4% Biological and Biomedical Sciences, 4% Public Administration and Social Service Professions
Expenses: 2019-2020: $36,350; room/board: $12,800
Financial aid: (610) 796-8356

Arcadia University
Glenside PA
(215) 572-2910
U.S. News ranking: Reg. U. (N), No. 45
Website: www.arcadia.edu
Admissions email: admiss@arcadia.edu
Private; founded 1853
Freshman admissions: selective; 2019-2020: 10,216 applied, 6,709 accepted. Neither SAT nor ACT required. SAT 25/75 percentile: 1030-1260. High school rank: 22% in top tenth, 47% in top quarter, 82% in top half
Early decision deadline: N/A, notification date: N/A
Early action deadline: N/A, notification date: N/A
Application deadline (fall): rolling
Undergraduate student body: 1,929 full time, 220 part time; 33% male, 67% female; 0% American Indian, 5% Asian, 10% Black, 10% Hispanic, 5% multiracial, 0% Pacific Islander, 63% white, 3% international; 63% from in state; 51% live on campus; 0% of students in fraternities, 0% in sororities
Most popular majors: 14% Biology/Biological Sciences, General, 10% Psychology, General, 6% International/Global Studies, 5% Criminology, 4% Health/Health Care Administration/Management

Expenses: 2019-2020: $44,440; room/board: $13,900
Financial aid: (215) 572-2980

Bloomsburg University of Pennsylvania
Bloomsburg PA
(570) 389-4316
U.S. News ranking: Reg. U. (N), No. 121
Website: www.bloomu.edu
Admissions email: buadmiss@bloomu.edu
Public; founded 1839
Freshman admissions: selective; 2019-2020: 8,164 applied, 6,875 accepted. Either SAT or ACT required. SAT 25/75 percentile: 950-1150. High school rank: 10% in top tenth, 27% in top quarter, 60% in top half
Early decision deadline: N/A, notification date: N/A
Early action deadline: N/A, notification date: 5/1
Application deadline (fall): rolling
Undergraduate student body: 7,263 full time, 723 part time; 42% male, 58% female; 0% American Indian, 1% Asian, 7% Black, 8% Hispanic, 2% multiracial, 0% Pacific Islander, 77% white, 0% international; 92% from in state; 43% live on campus; 9% of students in fraternities, 11% in sororities
Most popular majors: 24% Business, Management, Marketing, and Related Support Services, 14% Health Professions and Related Programs, 10% Communication, Journalism, and Related Programs, 8% Homeland Security, Law Enforcement, Firefighting and Related Protective Services, 7% Education
Expenses: 2020-2021: $10,958 in state, $22,532 out of state; room/board: $10,528
Financial aid: (570) 389-4297; 65% of undergrads determined to have financial need; average aid package $10,181

Bryn Athyn College of the New Church
Bryn Athyn PA
(267) 502-6000
U.S. News ranking: Nat. Lib. Arts, No. 162
Website: www.brynathyn.edu
Admissions email: admissions@brynathyn.edu
Private; founded 1877
Affiliation: Other
Freshman admissions: selective; 2019-2020: N/A applied, N/A accepted. Either SAT or ACT required. SAT 25/75 percentile: 996-1203. High school rank: N/A
Early decision deadline: N/A, notification date: N/A
Early action deadline: N/A, notification date: N/A
Application deadline (fall): rolling
Undergraduate student body: N/A full time, N/A part time; N/A% male; N/A% female; N/A American Indian, N/A Asian, N/A Black, N/A Hispanic, N/A multiracial, N/A Pacific Islander, N/A white, N/A international; N/A from in state; 49% live on campus;

N/A of students in fraternities, N/A in sororities
Most popular majors: 31% Biological and Biomedical Sciences, 20% Business, Management, Marketing, and Related Support Services, 11% Education, 11% Psychology, 9% Philosophy and Religious Studies
Expenses: 2020-2021: $25,449; room/board: $12,606
Financial aid: (267) 502-6000

Bryn Mawr College
Bryn Mawr PA
(610) 526-5152
U.S. News ranking: Nat. Lib. Arts, No. 28
Website: www.brynmawr.edu
Admissions email: admissions@brynmawr.edu
Private; founded 1885
Freshman admissions: most selective; 2019-2020: 3,332 applied, 1,102 accepted. Neither SAT nor ACT required. SAT 25/75 percentile: 1290-1510. High school rank: 67% in top tenth, 95% in top quarter, 99% in top half
Early decision deadline: 11/15, notification date: 12/20
Early action deadline: N/A, notification date: N/A
Application deadline (fall): 1/15
Undergraduate student body: 1,372 full time, 12 part time; 0% male, 100% female; 0% American Indian, 11% Asian, 5% Black, 10% Hispanic, 5% multiracial, 0% Pacific Islander, 43% white, 21% international; 15% from in state; 92% live on campus; N/A of students in fraternities, N/A in sororities
Most popular majors: 23% Social Sciences, 11% Psychology, 9% Foreign Languages, Literatures, and Linguistics, 9% Mathematics and Statistics, 9% Multi/Interdisciplinary Studies
Expenses: 2020-2021: $56,610; room/board: $17,720
Financial aid: (610) 526-5245; 52% of undergrads determined to have financial need; average aid package $53,763

Bucknell University
Lewisburg PA
(570) 577-3000
U.S. News ranking: Nat. Lib. Arts, No. 34
Website: www.bucknell.edu
Admissions email: admissions@bucknell.edu
Private; founded 1846
Freshman admissions: more selective; 2019-2020: 9,845 applied, 3,370 accepted. Neither SAT nor ACT required. SAT 25/75 percentile: 1255-1430. High school rank: 58% in top tenth, 83% in top quarter, 98% in top half
Early decision deadline: 11/15, notification date: 12/15
Early action deadline: N/A, notification date: N/A
Application deadline (fall): 1/15
Undergraduate student body: 3,606 full time, 21 part time; 49% male, 51% female; 0% American Indian, 5% Asian, 3% Black, 7% Hispanic, 4% multiracial,

0% Pacific Islander, 74% white, 6% international; 21% from in state; 91% live on campus; 35% of students in fraternities, 42% in sororities
Most popular majors: 9% Accounting and Finance, 9% Economics, General, 7% Psychology, General, 6% Biology/Biological Sciences, General, 6% Political Science and Government, General
Expenses: 2020-2021: $58,202; room/board: $14,670
Financial aid: (570) 577-1331; 38% of undergrads determined to have financial need; average aid package $37,000

Cabrini University[1]
Radnor PA
(610) 902-8552
U.S. News ranking: Reg. U. (N), second tier
Website: www.cabrini.edu
Admissions email: admit@cabrini.edu
Private; founded 1957
Affiliation: Roman Catholic
Application deadline (fall): 9/5
Undergraduate student body: N/A full time, N/A part time
Expenses: 2019-2020: $32,775; room/board: $12,590
Financial aid: (610) 902-8424

Cairn University[1]
Langhorne PA
(215) 702-4235
U.S. News ranking: Reg. U. (N), second tier
Website: cairn.edu/
Admissions email: admissions@cairn.edu
Private; founded 1913
Affiliation: Undenominational
Application deadline (fall): rolling
Undergraduate student body: N/A full time, N/A part time
Expenses: 2019-2020: $28,918; room/board: $10,706
Financial aid: (215) 702-4243

California University of Pennsylvania
California PA
(724) 938-4404
U.S. News ranking: Reg. U. (N), second tier
Website: www.calu.edu/
Admissions email: admissions@calu.edu
Public; founded 1852
Affiliation: Episcopal Church, Reformed
Freshman admissions: less selective; 2019-2020: 3,083 applied, 2,994 accepted. Neither SAT nor ACT required. SAT 25/75 percentile: 910-1100. High school rank: 7% in top tenth, 25% in top quarter, 61% in top half
Early decision deadline: N/A, notification date: N/A
Early action deadline: N/A, notification date: N/A
Application deadline (fall): 8/21
Undergraduate student body: 3,979 full time, 877 part time; 45% male, 55% female; 0% American Indian, 1% Asian, 12% Black, 4% Hispanic, 4% multiracial, 0% Pacific Islander, 76% white, 1% international; 89% from in

state; 37% live on campus; 5% of students in fraternities, 6% in sororities
Most popular majors: 21% Health Professions and Related Programs, 11% Business, Management, Marketing, and Related Support Services, 9% Parks, Recreation, Leisure, and Fitness Studies, 8% Homeland Security, Law Enforcement, Firefighting and Related Protective Services, 7% Social Sciences
Expenses: 2020-2021: $11,108 in state, $14,966 out of state; room/board: $10,416
Financial aid: (724) 938-4415; 80% of undergrads determined to have financial need; average aid package $10,525

Carlow University
Pittsburgh PA
(412) 578-6059
U.S. News ranking: Reg. U. (N), No. 71
Website: www.carlow.edu
Admissions email: admissions@carlow.edu
Private; founded 1929
Affiliation: Roman Catholic
Freshman admissions: selective; 2019-2020: 722 applied, 663 accepted. Either SAT or ACT required. SAT 25/75 percentile: 980-1153. High school rank: N/A
Early decision deadline: N/A, notification date: N/A
Early action deadline: N/A, notification date: N/A
Application deadline (fall): rolling
Undergraduate student body: 1,037 full time, 261 part time; 17% male, 83% female; 0% American Indian, 3% Asian, 18% Black, 2% Hispanic, 4% multiracial, 0% Pacific Islander, 69% white, 0% international; 5% from in state; 28% live on campus; 0% of students in fraternities, 5% in sororities
Most popular majors: 35% Registered Nursing/Registered Nurse, 13% Biology/Biological Sciences, General, 7% Psychology, General, 5% Business Administration and Management, General, 5% Respiratory Care Therapy/Therapist
Expenses: 2020-2021: $31,446; room/board: $12,260
Financial aid: (412) 578-6171

Carnegie Mellon University
Pittsburgh PA
(412) 268-2082
U.S. News ranking: Nat. U., No. 26
Website: www.cmu.edu
Admissions email: admission@andrew.cmu.edu
Private; founded 1900
Freshman admissions: most selective; 2019-2020: 27,634 applied, 4,267 accepted. Either SAT or ACT required. SAT 25/75 percentile: 1460-1560. High school rank: 88% in top tenth, 96% in top quarter, 99% in top half
Early decision deadline: 11/1, notification date: 12/15
Early action deadline: N/A, notification date: N/A
Application deadline (fall): 1/1

Undergraduate student body: 6,805 full time, 217 part time; 50% male, 50% female; 0% American Indian, 31% Asian, 4% Black, 9% Hispanic, 4% multiracial, 0% Pacific Islander, 25% white, 22% international; 14% from in state; 56% live on campus; 7% of students in fraternities, 5% in sororities
Most popular majors: 27% Engineering, 12% Computer and Information Sciences and Support Services, 10% Business, Management, Marketing, and Related Support Services, 10% Mathematics and Statistics, 10% Multi/Interdisciplinary Studies
Expenses: 2020-2021: $58,924; room/board: $15,550
Financial aid: (412) 268-8981; 39% of undergrads determined to have financial need; average aid package $48,843

Cedar Crest College
Allentown PA
(800) 360-1222
U.S. News ranking: Reg. U. (N), No. 96
Website: www.cedarcrest.edu
Admissions email: admissions@cedarcrest.edu
Private; founded 1867
Freshman admissions: selective; 2019-2020: 1,375 applied, 837 accepted. Either SAT or ACT required. SAT 25/75 percentile: 963-1180. High school rank: 19% in top tenth, 42% in top quarter, 83% in top half
Early decision deadline: N/A, notification date: N/A
Early action deadline: N/A, notification date: N/A
Application deadline (fall): rolling
Undergraduate student body: 872 full time, 344 part time; 8% male, 92% female; 0% American Indian, 3% Asian, 9% Black, 14% Hispanic, 2% multiracial, 0% Pacific Islander, 60% white, 7% international; 81% from in state; 37% live on campus; N/A of students in fraternities, N/A in sororities
Most popular majors: 26% Health Professions and Related Programs, 18% Business, Management, Marketing, and Related Support Services, 9% Biological and Biomedical Sciences, 9% Psychology, 7% Public Administration and Social Service Professions
Expenses: 2020-2021: $41,567; room/board: $12,322
Financial aid: (610) 606-4666; 90% of undergrads determined to have financial need; average aid package $30,972

Central Penn College[1]
Summerdale PA
(717) 728-2401
U.S. News ranking: Reg. Coll. (N), second tier
Website: www.centralpenn.edu
Admissions email: admissions@centralpenn.edu
For-profit; founded 1881
Application deadline (fall): rolling
Undergraduate student body: N/A full time, N/A part time

Expenses: 2019-2020: $18,714; room/board: $8,094
Financial aid: (717) 728-2261

Chatham University
Pittsburgh PA
(800) 837-1290
U.S. News ranking: Nat. U., No. 187
Website: www.chatham.edu
Admissions email: admissions@chatham.edu
Private; founded 1869
Freshman admissions: more selective; 2019-2020: 2,531 applied, 1,574 accepted. Neither SAT nor ACT required. SAT 25/75 percentile: 1050-1270. High school rank: 24% in top tenth, 52% in top quarter, 84% in top half
Early decision deadline: N/A, notification date: N/A
Early action deadline: N/A, notification date: N/A
Application deadline (fall): 8/1
Undergraduate student body: 1,142 full time, 266 part time; 27% male, 73% female; 0% American Indian, 3% Asian, 5% Black, 5% Hispanic, 3% multiracial, 0% Pacific Islander, 78% white, 2% international; 77% from in state; 62% live on campus; N/A of students in fraternities, N/A in sororities
Most popular majors: 16% Biological and Biomedical Sciences, 14% Health Professions and Related Programs, 12% Psychology, 9% Business, Management, Marketing, and Related Support Services, 9% Parks, Recreation, Leisure, and Fitness Studies
Expenses: 2020-2021: $39,902; room/board: $13,245
Financial aid: (412) 365-1849; 78% of undergrads determined to have financial need; average aid package $31,286

Chestnut Hill College
Philadelphia PA
(215) 248-7001
U.S. News ranking: Reg. U. (N), No. 113
Website: www.chc.edu
Admissions email: admissions@chc.edu
Private; founded 1924
Affiliation: Roman Catholic
Freshman admissions: less selective; 2019-2020: 1,440 applied, 935 accepted. Either SAT or ACT required. SAT 25/75 percentile: 918-1100. High school rank: 4% in top tenth, 22% in top quarter, 50% in top half
Early decision deadline: N/A, notification date: N/A
Early action deadline: N/A, notification date: N/A
Application deadline (fall): rolling
Undergraduate student body: 1,001 full time, 196 part time; 41% male, 59% female; 0% American Indian, 1% Asian, 32% Black, 12% Hispanic, 4% multiracial, 0% Pacific Islander, 40% white, 3% international; 78% from in state; 36% live on campus; 0% of students in fraternities, 0% in sororities

Most popular majors: 24% Business, Management, Marketing, and Related Support Services, 18% Public Administration and Social Service Professions, 16% Homeland Security, Law Enforcement, Firefighting and Related Protective Services, 9% Education, 8% Psychology
Expenses: 2020-2021: $38,270; room/board: $11,200
Financial aid: (215) 248-7182; 84% of undergrads determined to have financial need; average aid package $28,602

Cheyney University of Pennsylvania[1]
Cheyney PA
(610) 399-2275
U.S. News ranking: Nat. Lib. Arts, second tier
Website: www.cheyney.edu
Admissions email: admissions@cheyney.edu
Public; founded 1837
Application deadline (fall): N/A
Undergraduate student body: N/A full time, N/A part time
Expenses: 2019-2020: $10,904 in state, $16,170 out of state; room/board: $11,506
Financial aid: N/A

Clarion University of Pennsylvania
Clarion PA
(814) 393-2306
U.S. News ranking: Reg. U. (N), No. 113
Website: www.clarion.edu
Admissions email: admissions@clarion.edu
Public; founded 1867
Freshman admissions: selective; 2019-2020: 2,622 applied, 2,491 accepted. Either SAT or ACT required. SAT 25/75 percentile: 940-1130. High school rank: 13% in top tenth, 36% in top quarter, 71% in top half
Early decision deadline: N/A, notification date: N/A
Early action deadline: N/A, notification date: N/A
Application deadline (fall): rolling
Undergraduate student body: 2,995 full time, 781 part time; 32% male, 68% female; 0% American Indian, 1% Asian, 8% Black, 3% Hispanic, 2% multiracial, 0% Pacific Islander, 82% white, 0% international; 93% from in state; 37% live on campus; 6% of students in fraternities, 11% in sororities
Most popular majors: 25% Health Professions and Related Programs, 19% Business, Management, Marketing, and Related Support Services, 13% Liberal Arts and Sciences, General Studies and Humanities, 7% Education, 4% Biological and Biomedical Sciences
Expenses: 2020-2021: $11,149 in state, $15,007 out of state; room/board: $12,660
Financial aid: (814) 393-2315; 80% of undergrads determined to have financial need; average aid package $11,687

Curtis Institute of Music[1]
Philadelphia PA
(215) 893-5252
U.S. News ranking: Arts, unranked
Website: www.curtis.edu
Admissions email: admissions@curtis.edu
Private; founded 1924
Application deadline (fall): N/A
Undergraduate student body: N/A full time, N/A part time
Expenses: 2019-2020: $2,900; room/board: $14,560
Financial aid: (215) 717-3188

Delaware Valley University
Doylestown PA
(215) 489-2211
U.S. News ranking: Reg. U. (N), No. 125
Website: www.delval.edu
Admissions email: admitme@delval.edu
Private; founded 1896
Freshman admissions: selective; 2019-2020: 1,676 applied, 1,554 accepted. Neither SAT nor ACT required. SAT 25/75 percentile: 970-1170. High school rank: 15% in top tenth, 35% in top quarter, 66% in top half
Early decision deadline: N/A, notification date: N/A
Early action deadline: N/A, notification date: N/A
Application deadline (fall): rolling
Undergraduate student body: 1,649 full time, 275 part time; 41% male, 59% female; 0% American Indian, 1% Asian, 9% Black, 8% Hispanic, 2% multiracial, 0% Pacific Islander, 68% white, 0% international; 62% from in state; 55% live on campus; 2% of students in fraternities, 1% in sororities
Most popular majors: 40% Agriculture, Agriculture Operations, and Related Sciences, 19% Business, Management, Marketing, and Related Support Services, 11% Biological and Biomedical Sciences, 11% Natural Resources and Conservation, 6% Psychology
Expenses: 2020-2021: $40,620; room/board: $14,850
Financial aid: (215) 489-2975; 81% of undergrads determined to have financial need; average aid package $31,252

DeSales University
Center Valley PA
(610) 282-4443
U.S. News ranking: Reg. U. (N), No. 75
Website: www.desales.edu
Admissions email: admiss@desales.edu
Private; founded 1964
Affiliation: Roman Catholic
Freshman admissions: selective; 2019-2020: 3,272 applied, 2,579 accepted. Neither SAT nor ACT required. SAT 25/75 percentile: 1030-1260. High school rank: N/A
Early decision deadline: N/A, notification date: N/A
Early action deadline: N/A, notification date: N/A

Application deadline (fall): 8/1
Undergraduate student body: 1,963 full time, 529 part time; 36% male, 64% female; 0% American Indian, 3% Asian, 5% Black, 12% Hispanic, 3% multiracial, 0% Pacific Islander, 70% white, 0% international; 74% from in state; 41% live on campus; N/A of students in fraternities, N/A in sororities
Most popular majors: 19% Registered Nursing/Registered Nurse, 9% Business Administration and Management, General, 9% Health Professions and Related Clinical Sciences, Other, 7% Criminal Justice/Safety Studies, 7% Psychology, General
Expenses: 2020-2021: $39,500; room/board: $13,300
Financial aid: (610) 282-1100; 78% of undergrads determined to have financial need; average aid package $26,908

Dickinson College
Carlisle PA
(800) 644-1773
U.S. News ranking: Nat. Lib. Arts, No. 47
Website: www.dickinson.edu
Admissions email: admissions@dickinson.edu
Private; founded 1783
Freshman admissions: more selective; 2019-2020: 6,426 applied, 2,574 accepted. Neither SAT nor ACT required. SAT 25/75 percentile: 1240-1410. High school rank: 42% in top tenth, 72% in top quarter, 96% in top half
Early decision deadline: 11/15, notification date: 12/15
Early action deadline: N/A, notification date: N/A
Application deadline (fall): 1/15
Undergraduate student body: 2,107 full time, 26 part time; 43% male, 57% female; 0% American Indian, 4% Asian, 5% Black, 9% Hispanic, 4% multiracial, 0% Pacific Islander, 64% white, 13% international; 22% from in state; 100% live on campus; 5% of students in fraternities, 25% in sororities
Most popular majors: 11% International Business/Trade/ Commerce, 7% Psychology, General, 6% Econometrics and Quantitative Economics, 6% Economics, General, 6% International Relations and Affairs
Expenses: 2020-2021: $56,498; room/board: $14,672
Financial aid: (717) 245-1308; 64% of undergrads determined to have financial need; average aid package $49,622

Drexel University
Philadelphia PA
(800) 237-3935
U.S. News ranking: Nat. U., No. 133
Website: www.drexel.edu
Admissions email: enroll@drexel.edu
Private; founded 1891
Freshman admissions: more selective; 2019-2020: 31,824 applied, 23,771 accepted. Either SAT or ACT required. SAT 25/75

percentile: 1190-1390. High school rank: 35% in top tenth, 67% in top quarter, 92% in top half
Early decision deadline: 11/1, notification date: 12/15
Early action deadline: 11/1, notification date: 12/15
Application deadline (fall): 1/15
Undergraduate student body: 13,878 full time, 1,468 part time; 52% male, 48% female; 0% American Indian, 20% Asian, 6% Black, 7% Hispanic, 4% multiracial, 0% Pacific Islander, 50% white, 10% international; 49% from in state; 22% live on campus; 11% of students in fraternities, 10% in sororities
Most popular majors: 22% Business, Management, Marketing, and Related Support Services, 22% Health Professions and Related Programs, 20% Engineering, 10% Visual and Performing Arts, 5% Computer and Information Sciences and Support Services
Expenses: 2020-2021: $56,238; room/board: $16,008
Financial aid: (215) 895-1600; 64% of undergrads determined to have financial need; average aid package $38,995

Duquesne University
Pittsburgh PA
(412) 396-6222
U.S. News ranking: Nat. U., No. 143
Website: www.duq.edu
Admissions email: admissions@duq.edu
Private; founded 1878
Affiliation: Roman Catholic
Freshman admissions: more selective; 2019-2020: 7,231 applied, 5,375 accepted. Neither SAT nor ACT required. SAT 25/75 percentile: 1130-1300. High school rank: 25% in top tenth, 55% in top quarter, 85% in top half
Early decision deadline: N/A, notification date: N/A
Early action deadline: N/A, notification date: N/A
Application deadline (fall): 7/1
Undergraduate student body: 5,732 full time, 107 part time; 36% male, 64% female; 0% American Indian, 3% Asian, 5% Black, 4% Hispanic, 3% multiracial, 0% Pacific Islander, 81% white, 2% international; 72% from in state; 61% live on campus; 18% of students in fraternities, 24% in sororities
Most popular majors: 20% Nursing Science, 7% Biology/ Biological Sciences, General, 4% Accounting, 4% Logistics, Materials, and Supply Chain Management, 4% Psychology, General
Expenses: 2020-2021: $41,892; room/board: $13,612
Financial aid: (412) 396-6607; 66% of undergrads determined to have financial need; average aid package $27,960

Eastern University
St. Davids PA
(800) 452-0996
U.S. News ranking: Reg. U. (N), No. 83
Website: www.eastern.edu
Admissions email: admissions@eastern.edu
Private; founded 1952
Affiliation: American Baptist
Freshman admissions: selective; 2019-2020: 2,207 applied, 1,349 accepted. Neither SAT nor ACT required. SAT 25/75 percentile: 1030-1230. High school rank: 30% in top tenth, 58% in top quarter, 89% in top half
Early decision deadline: N/A, notification date: N/A
Early action deadline: N/A, notification date: N/A
Application deadline (fall): rolling
Undergraduate student body: 1,328 full time, 424 part time; 31% male, 69% female; 0% American Indian, 2% Asian, 21% Black, 18% Hispanic, 2% multiracial, 0% Pacific Islander, 49% white, 2% international; 71% from in state; 78% live on campus; N/A of students in fraternities, N/A in sororities
Most popular majors: 17% Early Childhood Education and Teaching, 10% Registered Nursing/Registered Nurse, 7% Social Work, 6% Psychology, General, 4% Business Administration and Management, General
Expenses: 2020-2021: $34,706; room/board: $11,824
Financial aid: (610) 225-5102; 83% of undergrads determined to have financial need; average aid package $28,184

East Stroudsburg University
East Stroudsburg PA
(570) 422-3542
U.S. News ranking: Reg. U. (N), second tier
Website: www.esu.edu/ admissions/index.cfm
Admissions email: admission@esu.edu
Public; founded 1893
Freshman admissions: less selective; 2019-2020: 7,479 applied, 5,697 accepted. Neither SAT nor ACT required. SAT 25/75 percentile: 910-1100. High school rank: 5% in top tenth, 20% in top quarter, 55% in top half
Early decision deadline: N/A, notification date: N/A
Early action deadline: N/A, notification date: N/A
Application deadline (fall): 5/1
Undergraduate student body: 4,954 full time, 463 part time; 44% male, 56% female; 0% American Indian, 2% Asian, 20% Black, 14% Hispanic, 4% multiracial, 0% Pacific Islander, 56% white, 0% international; 81% from in state; 47% live on campus; N/A of students in fraternities, N/A in sororities
Most popular majors: 15% Business, Management, Marketing, and Related Support

Services, 14% Health Professions and Related Programs, 11% Parks, Recreation, Leisure, and Fitness Studies, 9% Education, 8% Homeland Security, Law Enforcement, Firefighting and Related Protective Services
Expenses: 2020-2021: $11,975 in state, $24,875 out of state; room/board: $12,120
Financial aid: (570) 422-2800; 82% of undergrads determined to have financial need; average aid package $8,091

Edinboro University of Pennsylvania
Edinboro PA
(888) 846-2676
U.S. News ranking: Reg. U. (N), No. 131
Website: www.edinboro.edu
Admissions email: admissions@edinboro.edu
Public; founded 1857
Freshman admissions: selective; 2019-2020: 2,872 applied, 2,393 accepted. Either SAT or ACT required. SAT 25/75 percentile: 970-1160. High school rank: 10% in top tenth, 30% in top quarter, 67% in top half
Early decision deadline: N/A, notification date: N/A
Early action deadline: N/A, notification date: N/A
Application deadline (fall): rolling
Undergraduate student body: 2,998 full time, 401 part time; 42% male, 58% female; 0% American Indian, 1% Asian, 6% Black, 4% Hispanic, 4% multiracial, 0% Pacific Islander, 82% white, 1% international; N/A from in state; 30% live on campus; 5% of students in fraternities, 7% in sororities
Most popular majors: 13% Business, Management, Marketing, and Related Support Services, 12% Health Professions and Related Programs, 12% Visual and Performing Arts, 8% Education, 8% Liberal Arts and Sciences, General Studies and Humanities
Expenses: 2020-2021: $10,543 in state, $14,401 out of state; room/board: N/A
Financial aid: (814) 732-3500; 77% of undergrads determined to have financial need; average aid package $12,388

Elizabethtown College
Elizabethtown PA
(717) 361-1400
U.S. News ranking: Nat. Lib. Arts, No. 113
Website: www.etown.edu
Admissions email: admissions@etown.edu
Private; founded 1899
Freshman admissions: more selective; 2019-2020: 1,893 applied, 1,530 accepted. Either SAT or ACT required. SAT 25/75 percentile: 1080-1290. High school rank: 29% in top tenth, 61% in top quarter, 86% in top half
Early decision deadline: N/A, notification date: N/A

Early action deadline: N/A, notification date: N/A
Application deadline (fall): rolling
Undergraduate student body: 1,502 full time, 226 part time; 39% male, 61% female; 0% American Indian, 3% Asian, 4% Black, 4% Hispanic, 2% multiracial, 0% Pacific Islander, 86% white, 1% international; 72% from in state; 74% live on campus; 0% of students in fraternities, 0% in sororities
Most popular majors: 24% Business, Management, Marketing, and Related Support Services, 13% Health Professions and Related Programs, 10% Education, 7% Biological and Biomedical Sciences, 6% Communication, Journalism, and Related Programs
Expenses: 2020-2021: $32,960; room/board: $12,060
Financial aid: (717) 361-1404; 71% of undergrads determined to have financial need; average aid package $22,695

Franklin & Marshall College
Lancaster PA
(717) 358-3953
U.S. News ranking: Nat. Lib. Arts, No. 43
Website: www.fandm.edu
Admissions email: admission@fandm.edu
Private; founded 1787
Freshman admissions: more selective; 2019-2020: 9,502 applied, 2,888 accepted. Neither SAT nor ACT required. SAT 25/75 percentile: 1250-1460. High school rank: 71% in top tenth, 88% in top quarter, 99% in top half
Early decision deadline: 11/15, notification date: 12/15
Early action deadline: N/A, notification date: N/A
Application deadline (fall): 1/15
Undergraduate student body: 2,306 full time, 9 part time; 45% male, 55% female; 0% American Indian, 5% Asian, 6% Black, 11% Hispanic, 3% multiracial, 0% Pacific Islander, 55% white, 19% international; 30% from in state; 98% live on campus; 13% of students in fraternities, 13% in sororities
Most popular majors: 13% Political Science and Government, General, 12% Multi-/Interdisciplinary Studies, Other, 9% Business Administration and Management, General, 7% Economics, General, 6% Behavioral Sciences
Expenses: 2020-2021: $61,062; room/board: $14,739
Financial aid: (717) 358-3991; 55% of undergrads determined to have financial need; average aid package $54,166

Gannon University
Erie PA
(814) 871-7240
U.S. News ranking: Nat. U., No. 227
Website: www.gannon.edu
Admissions email: admissions@gannon.edu
Private; founded 1925

Affiliation: Roman Catholic
Freshman admissions: selective; 2019-2020: 4,727 applied, 3,570 accepted. Either SAT or ACT required. SAT 25/75 percentile: 1030-1240. High school rank: 31% in top tenth, 63% in top quarter, 93% in top half
Early decision deadline: N/A, notification date: N/A
Early action deadline: N/A, notification date: N/A
Application deadline (fall): rolling
Undergraduate student body: 2,775 full time, 657 part time; 39% male, 61% female; 0% American Indian, 2% Asian, 5% Black, 4% Hispanic, 3% multiracial, 0% Pacific Islander, 70% white, 9% international; 72% from in state; 45% live on campus; 13% of students in fraternities, 10% in sororities
Most popular majors: 32% Health Professions and Related Programs, 15% Business, Management, Marketing, and Related Support Services, 13% Engineering, 7% Biological and Biomedical Sciences, 7% Parks, Recreation, Leisure, and Fitness Studies
Expenses: 2020-2021: $34,526; room/board: $14,090
Financial aid: (814) 871-7337; 76% of undergrads determined to have financial need; average aid package $27,213

Geneva College
Beaver Falls PA
(724) 847-6500
U.S. News ranking: Reg. U. (N), No. 93
Website: www.geneva.edu
Admissions email: admissions@geneva.edu
Private; founded 1848
Affiliation: Reformed Presbyterian Church
Freshman admissions: selective; 2019-2020: 2,801 applied, 1,491 accepted. Either SAT or ACT required. SAT 25/75 percentile: 1020-1240. High school rank: 21% in top tenth, 51% in top quarter, 75% in top half
Early decision deadline: N/A, notification date: N/A
Early action deadline: N/A, notification date: N/A
Application deadline (fall): rolling
Undergraduate student body: 1,116 full time, 174 part time; 53% male, 47% female; 0% American Indian, 2% Asian, 8% Black, 2% Hispanic, 3% multiracial, 0% Pacific Islander, 80% white, 2% international; 72% from in state; 67% live on campus; N/A of students in fraternities, N/A in sororities
Most popular majors: 17% Engineering, General, 8% Human Resources Management/Personnel Administration, General, 7% Computer and Information Sciences, General, 7% Teacher Education, Multiple Levels, 5% International Business/Trade/Commerce
Expenses: 2020-2021: $29,040; room/board: $10,850

Financial aid: (724) 847-6532; 84% of undergrads determined to have financial need; average aid package $22,821

Gettysburg College
Gettysburg PA
(800) 431-0803
U.S. News ranking: Nat. Lib. Arts, No. 54
Website: www.gettysburg.edu/
Admissions email: admiss@gettysburg.edu
Private; founded 1832
Freshman admissions: more selective; 2019-2020: 5,916 applied, 2,842 accepted. Either SAT or ACT required. SAT 25/75 percentile: 1280-1410. High school rank: 60% in top tenth, 85% in top quarter, 99% in top half
Early decision deadline: 11/15, notification date: 12/15
Early action deadline: N/A, notification date: N/A
Application deadline (fall): 1/15
Undergraduate student body: 2,368 full time, 3 part time; 48% male, 52% female; 0% American Indian, 2% Asian, 4% Black, 9% Hispanic, 3% multiracial, 0% Pacific Islander, 74% white, 6% international; 73% from in state; 95% live on campus; 31% of students in fraternities, 33% in sororities
Most popular majors: 25% Social Sciences, 12% Biological and Biomedical Sciences, 11% Business, Management, Marketing, and Related Support Services, 7% Psychology, 6% English Language and Literature/Letters
Expenses: 2020-2021: $58,505; room/board: $13,965
Financial aid: (717) 337-6611; 61% of undergrads determined to have financial need; average aid package $44,448

Grove City College[1]
Grove City PA
(724) 458-2100
U.S. News ranking: Nat. Lib. Arts, No. 113
Website: www.gcc.edu
Admissions email: admissions@gcc.edu
Private; founded 1876
Affiliation: Undenominational
Application deadline (fall): 3/20
Undergraduate student body: N/A full time, N/A part time
Expenses: 2020-2021: $18,930; room/board: $10,310
Financial aid: (724) 458-3300; 48% of undergrads determined to have financial need; average aid package $8,022

Gwynedd Mercy University
Gwynedd Valley PA
(215) 641-5510
U.S. News ranking: Reg. U. (N), No. 113
Website: www.gmercyu.edu/
Admissions email: admissions@gmercyu.edu
Private; founded 1948
Affiliation: Roman Catholic

Freshman admissions: less selective; 2019-2020: 1,030 applied, 980 accepted. Either SAT or ACT required. SAT 25/75 percentile: 930-1100. High school rank: 8% in top tenth, 22% in top quarter, 60% in top half
Early decision deadline: N/A, notification date: N/A
Early action deadline: N/A, notification date: N/A
Application deadline (fall): 8/20
Undergraduate student body: 1,699 full time, 458 part time; 28% male, 72% female; 1% American Indian, 6% Asian, 21% Black, 6% Hispanic, 1% multiracial, 0% Pacific Islander, 62% white, 0% international; 87% from in state; 20% live on campus; N/A of students in fraternities, N/A in sororities
Most popular majors: 71% Health Professions and Related Programs, 12% Business, Management, Marketing, and Related Support Services, 6% Education, 4% Psychology, 3% Homeland Security, Law Enforcement, Firefighting and Related Protective Services
Expenses: 2020-2021: $35,600; room/board: $12,680
Financial aid: (215) 646-7300; 83% of undergrads determined to have financial need; average aid package $22,614

Harrisburg University of Science and Technology
Harrisburg PA
(717) 901-5150
U.S. News ranking: Reg. U. (N), second tier
Website: www.harrisburgu.edu
Admissions email: admissions@harrisburgu.edu
Private; founded 2001
Freshman admissions: less selective; 2019-2020: 1,420 applied, 1,196 accepted. Neither SAT nor ACT required. SAT 25/75 percentile: N/A. High school rank: 16% in top tenth, 39% in top quarter, 74% in top half
Early decision deadline: N/A, notification date: N/A
Early action deadline: N/A, notification date: N/A
Application deadline (fall): rolling
Undergraduate student body: 639 full time, 62 part time; 61% male, 39% female; 1% American Indian, 4% Asian, 35% Black, 14% Hispanic, 4% multiracial, 0% Pacific Islander, 39% white, 1% international
Most popular majors: 39% Natural Sciences, 37% Computer and Information Sciences, General, 12% Game and Interactive Media Design, 8% Biotechnology, 4% Geological and Earth Sciences/Geosciences, Other
Expenses: 2020-2021: $23,900; room/board: N/A
Financial aid: (717) 901-5115; 91% of undergrads determined to have financial need; average aid package $22,980

Haverford College
Haverford PA
(610) 896-1350
U.S. News ranking: Nat. Lib. Arts, No. 15
Website: www.haverford.edu
Admissions email: admission@haverford.edu
Private; founded 1833
Freshman admissions: most selective; 2019-2020: 4,963 applied, 810 accepted. Either SAT or ACT required. SAT 25/75 percentile: 1380-1540. High school rank: 92% in top tenth, 99% in top quarter, 100% in top half
Early decision deadline: 11/15, notification date: 12/15
Early action deadline: N/A, notification date: N/A
Application deadline (fall): 1/15
Undergraduate student body: 1,314 full time, 3 part time; 47% male, 53% female; 0% American Indian, 12% Asian, 6% Black, 9% Hispanic, 7% multiracial, 0% Pacific Islander, 53% white, 11% international; 14% from in state; 98% live on campus; 0% of students in fraternities, 0% in sororities
Most popular majors: 28% Social Sciences, General, 15% Physical Sciences, 9% Biology/Biological Sciences, General, 9% Foreign Languages and Literatures, General, 7% Psychology, General
Expenses: 2020-2021: $58,900; room/board: $17,066
Financial aid: (610) 896-1350; 45% of undergrads determined to have financial need; average aid package $54,803

Holy Family University[1]
Philadelphia PA
(215) 637-3050
U.S. News ranking: Reg. U. (N), second tier
Website: www.holyfamily.edu
Admissions email: admissions@holyfamily.edu
Private; founded 1954
Affiliation: Roman Catholic
Application deadline (fall): rolling
Undergraduate student body: N/A full time, N/A part time
Expenses: 2019-2020: $31,040; room/board: $14,140
Financial aid: (267) 341-3233

Immaculata University
Immaculata PA
(610) 647-4400
U.S. News ranking: Nat. U., No. 241
Website: www.immaculata.edu
Admissions email: admiss@immaculata.edu
Private; founded 1920
Affiliation: Roman Catholic
Freshman admissions: less selective; 2019-2020: 1,969 applied, 1,602 accepted. Neither SAT nor ACT required. SAT 25/75 percentile: 980-1198. High school rank: 7% in top tenth, 19% in top quarter, 57% in top half
Early decision deadline: N/A, notification date: N/A
Early action deadline: N/A, notification date: N/A

Application deadline (fall): rolling
Undergraduate student body: 904 full time, 599 part time; 29% male, 71% female; 0% American Indian, 2% Asian, 15% Black, 9% Hispanic, 2% multiracial, 0% Pacific Islander, 69% white, 2% international; 77% from in state; 35% live on campus; 2% of students in fraternities, 7% in sororities
Most popular majors: 47% Health Professions and Related Programs, 21% Business, Management, Marketing, and Related Support Services, 7% Parks, Recreation, Leisure, and Fitness Studies, 5% Psychology, 4% Education
Expenses: 2020-2021: $27,750; room/board: $12,620
Financial aid: (610) 647-4400

Indiana University of Pennsylvania
Indiana PA
(724) 357-2230
U.S. News ranking: Nat. U., No. 284
Website: www.iup.edu
Admissions email: admissions-inquiry@iup.edu
Public; founded 1875
Freshman admissions: less selective; 2019-2020: 10,061 applied, 9,398 accepted. Either SAT or ACT required. SAT 25/75 percentile: 910-1120. High school rank: 9% in top tenth, 27% in top quarter, 59% in top half
Early decision deadline: N/A, notification date: N/A
Early action deadline: N/A, notification date: N/A
Application deadline (fall): rolling
Undergraduate student body: 7,489 full time, 745 part time; 42% male, 58% female; 0% American Indian, 1% Asian, 12% Black, 5% Hispanic, 5% multiracial, 0% Pacific Islander, 74% white, 2% international; 93% from in state; 32% live on campus; 9% of students in fraternities, 9% in sororities
Most popular majors: 27% Business, Management, Marketing, and Related Support Services, 14% Social Sciences, 11% Health Professions and Related Programs, 6% Communication, Journalism, and Related Programs, 5% Visual and Performing Arts
Expenses: 2020-2021: $13,144 in state, $17,464 out of state; room/board: $12,744
Financial aid: (724) 357-2218; 72% of undergrads determined to have financial need; average aid package $10,896

Juniata College
Huntingdon PA
(877) 586-4282
U.S. News ranking: Nat. Lib. Arts, No. 84
Website: www.juniata.edu
Admissions email: admissions@juniata.edu
Private; founded 1876
Freshman admissions: more selective; 2019-2020: 2,344 applied, 1,659 accepted. Neither SAT nor ACT required. SAT 25/75 percentile: 1118-1320.

High school rank: 30% in top tenth, 62% in top quarter, 91% in top half
Early decision deadline: 11/15, notification date: 12/1
Early action deadline: 1/5, notification date: 2/15
Application deadline (fall): 3/15
Undergraduate student body: 1,306 full time, 83 part time; 44% male, 56% female; 0% American Indian, 2% Asian, 4% Black, 6% Hispanic, 3% multiracial, 0% Pacific Islander, 76% white, 7% international; 65% from in state; 91% live on campus; 0% of students in fraternities, 0% in sororities
Most popular majors: 22% Biological and Biomedical Sciences, 20% Business, Management, Marketing, and Related Support Services, 10% Natural Resources and Conservation, 7% Education, 5% Communication, Journalism, and Related Programs
Expenses: 2020-2021: $49,175; room/board: $13,050
Financial aid: (814) 641-3144; 72% of undergrads determined to have financial need; average aid package $38,628

Keystone College
La Plume PA
(570) 945-8111
U.S. News ranking: Reg. Coll. (N), No. 31
Website: www.keystone.edu
Admissions email: admissions@keystone.edu
Private; founded 1868
Freshman admissions: less selective; 2019-2020: 2,051 applied, 1,615 accepted. Neither SAT nor ACT required. SAT 25/75 percentile: 880-1070. High school rank: N/A
Early decision deadline: N/A, notification date: N/A
Early action deadline: N/A, notification date: N/A
Application deadline (fall): rolling
Undergraduate student body: 1,067 full time, 221 part time; 42% male, 58% female; 1% American Indian, 1% Asian, 13% Black, 8% Hispanic, 3% multiracial, 0% Pacific Islander, 67% white, 0% international; 80% from in state; 37% live on campus; 0% of students in fraternities, 0% in sororities
Most popular majors: 25% Business, Management, Marketing, and Related Support Services, 11% Biological and Biomedical Sciences, 9% Education, 9% Homeland Security, Law Enforcement, Firefighting and Related Protective Services, 9% Parks, Recreation, Leisure, and Fitness Studies
Expenses: 2020-2021: $17,000; room/board: $11,900
Financial aid: N/A

King's College
Wilkes-Barre PA
(888) 546-4772
U.S. News ranking: Reg. U. (N), No. 62
Website: www.kings.edu

Admissions email: admissions@kings.edu
Private; founded 1946
Affiliation: Roman Catholic
Freshman admissions: selective; 2019-2020: 4,176 applied, 3,380 accepted. Neither SAT nor ACT required. SAT 25/75 percentile: 990-1220. High school rank: 15% in top tenth, 35% in top quarter, 67% in top half
Early decision deadline: 12/1, notification date: 12/15
Early action deadline: 12/1, notification date: 12/15
Application deadline (fall): rolling
Undergraduate student body: 2,042 full time, 189 part time; 53% male, 47% female; 0% American Indian, 2% Asian, 4% Black, 9% Hispanic, 3% multiracial, 0% Pacific Islander, 69% white, 9% international; 72% from in state; 51% live on campus; 0% of students in fraternities, 0% in sororities
Most popular majors: 15% Health Professions and Related Clinical Sciences, Other, 7% Accounting, 7% Business Administration and Management, General, 7% Criminal Justice/Safety Studies, 7% Early Childhood Education and Teaching
Expenses: 2020-2021: $40,080; room/board: $14,008
Financial aid: (570) 208-5900; 77% of undergrads determined to have financial need; average aid package $28,268

Kutztown University of Pennsylvania
Kutztown PA
(610) 683-4060
U.S. News ranking: Reg. U. (N), No. 125
Website: www.kutztown.edu
Admissions email: admissions@kutztown.edu
Public; founded 1866
Freshman admissions: selective; 2019-2020: 6,893 applied, 6,117 accepted. Either SAT or ACT required. SAT 25/75 percentile: 970-1140. High school rank: 8% in top tenth, 27% in top quarter, 60% in top half
Early decision deadline: N/A, notification date: N/A
Early action deadline: N/A, notification date: N/A
Application deadline (fall): rolling
Undergraduate student body: 6,462 full time, 742 part time; 45% male, 55% female; 0% American Indian, 2% Asian, 8% Black, 9% Hispanic, 3% multiracial, 0% Pacific Islander, 74% white, 1% international; 88% from in state; 49% live on campus; 6% of students in fraternities, 8% in sororities
Most popular majors: 19% Business Administration and Management, General, 6% Communication and Media Studies, 6% Psychology, General, 6% Social Work, 5% Criminal Justice/Safety Studies
Expenses: 2020-2021: $11,048 in state, $14,906 out of state; room/board: $10,660

Financial aid: (610) 683-4077; 74% of undergrads determined to have financial need; average aid package $9,403

Lackawanna College
Scranton PA
(570) 961-7898
U.S. News ranking: Reg. Coll. (N), unranked
Website: www.lackawanna.edu
Admissions email: admissions@lackawanna.edu
Private
Freshman admissions: least selective; 2019-2020: 1,627 applied, 570 accepted. Neither SAT nor ACT required. SAT 25/75 percentile: N/A. High school rank: N/A
Early decision deadline: N/A, notification date: N/A
Early action deadline: N/A, notification date: N/A
Application deadline (fall): rolling
Undergraduate student body: 1,335 full time, 656 part time; 44% male, 56% female; N/A American Indian, N/A Asian, N/A Black, N/A Hispanic, N/A multiracial, N/A Pacific Islander, N/A white, N/A international; N/A from in state; 17% live on campus; N/A of students in fraternities, N/A in sororities
Most popular majors: 5% Business, Management, Marketing, and Related Support Services, 3% Health Professions and Related Programs, 3% Homeland Security, Law Enforcement, Firefighting and Related Protective Services, 0% Liberal Arts and Sciences, General Studies and Humanities
Expenses: 2020-2021: $16,130; room/board: $10,300
Financial aid: N/A

Lafayette College
Easton PA
(610) 330-5100
U.S. News ranking: Nat. Lib. Arts, No. 40
Website: www.lafayette.edu/
Admissions email: admissions@lafayette.edu
Private; founded 1826
Freshman admissions: more selective; 2019-2020: 8,521 applied, 2,682 accepted. Either SAT or ACT required. SAT 25/75 percentile: 1250-1440. High school rank: 54% in top tenth, 81% in top quarter, 97% in top half
Early decision deadline: 11/15, notification date: 12/15
Early action deadline: N/A, notification date: N/A
Application deadline (fall): 1/15
Undergraduate student body: 2,633 full time, 29 part time; 49% male, 51% female; 0% American Indian, 4% Asian, 5% Black, 7% Hispanic, 3% multiracial, 0% Pacific Islander, 65% white, 10% international; 19% from in state; 93% live on campus; 26% of students in fraternities, 33% in sororities
Most popular majors: 34% Social Sciences, 18% Engineering, 9% Biological and Biomedical

Sciences, 8% Psychology, 8% Visual and Performing Arts
Expenses: 2020-2021: $57,052; room/board: $16,874
Financial aid: (610) 330-5055; 35% of undergrads determined to have financial need; average aid package $51,240

Lancaster Bible College
Lancaster PA
(717) 569-7071
U.S. News ranking: Reg. U. (N), second tier
Website: www.lbc.edu/
Admissions email: admissions@lbc.edu
Private; founded 1933
Affiliation: Other
Freshman admissions: selective; 2019-2020: 276 applied, 265 accepted. Either SAT or ACT required. SAT 25/75 percentile: 1000-1200. High school rank: N/A
Early decision deadline: N/A, notification date: N/A
Early action deadline: N/A, notification date: N/A
Application deadline (fall): N/A
Undergraduate student body: 994 full time, 746 part time; 46% male, 54% female; 0% American Indian, 1% Asian, 17% Black, 4% Hispanic, 17% multiracial, 0% Pacific Islander, 50% white, 0% international
Most popular majors: Information not available
Expenses: 2020-2021: $27,390; room/board: $9,500
Financial aid: (717) 560-8254; 80% of undergrads determined to have financial need; average aid package $21,306

La Roche University
Pittsburgh PA
(800) 838-4572
U.S. News ranking: Reg. U. (N), No. 132
Website: www.laroche.edu
Admissions email: admissions@laroche.edu
Private; founded 1963
Affiliation: Roman Catholic
Freshman admissions: less selective; 2019-2020: 1,220 applied, 1,213 accepted. Either SAT or ACT required. SAT 25/75 percentile: 870-1140. High school rank: 8% in top tenth, 26% in top quarter, 63% in top half
Early decision deadline: N/A, notification date: N/A
Early action deadline: N/A, notification date: N/A
Application deadline (fall): rolling
Undergraduate student body: 1,070 full time, 171 part time; 43% male, 57% female; 0% American Indian, 1% Asian, 10% Black, 5% Hispanic, 3% multiracial, 0% Pacific Islander, 61% white, 15% international; 89% from in state; 40% live on campus; N/A of students in fraternities, N/A in sororities
Most popular majors: 9% Marketing/Marketing Management, General, 8% Information Technology, 7% Health Professions and Related Clinical Sciences, Other, 7% Psychology,

General, 7% Registered Nursing/Registered Nurse
Expenses: 2020-2021: $30,320; room/board: $12,270
Financial aid: (412) 536-1125; 71% of undergrads determined to have financial need; average aid package $31,428

La Salle University
Philadelphia PA
(215) 951-1500
U.S. News ranking: Reg. U. (N), No. 26
Website: www.lasalle.edu
Admissions email: admiss@lasalle.edu
Private; founded 1863
Affiliation: Roman Catholic
Freshman admissions: selective; 2019-2020: 6,442 applied, 5,009 accepted. Neither SAT nor ACT required. SAT 25/75 percentile: 990-1190. High school rank: 15% in top tenth, 34% in top quarter, 63% in top half
Early decision deadline: N/A, notification date: N/A
Early action deadline: 11/1, notification date: 12/15
Application deadline (fall): rolling
Undergraduate student body: 3,186 full time, 471 part time; 37% male, 63% female; 0% American Indian, 5% Asian, 18% Black, 19% Hispanic, 3% multiracial, 0% Pacific Islander, 50% white, 3% international
Most popular majors: 13% Registered Nursing/Registered Nurse, 8% Communication and Media Studies, Other, 7% Marketing/Marketing Management, General, 6% Accounting, 6% Finance, General
Expenses: 2020-2021: $32,450; room/board: $15,222
Financial aid: (215) 951-1070; 68% of undergrads determined to have financial need; average aid package $25,162

Lebanon Valley College[1]
Annville PA
(717) 867-6181
U.S. News ranking: Reg. U. (N), No. 38
Website: www.lvc.edu
Admissions email: admission@lvc.edu
Private; founded 1866
Affiliation: United Methodist
Application deadline (fall): rolling
Undergraduate student body: N/A full time, N/A part time
Expenses: 2019-2020: $44,910; room/board: $12,200
Financial aid: (717) 867-6126

Lehigh University
Bethlehem PA
(610) 758-3100
U.S. News ranking: Nat. U., No. 49
Website: www1.lehigh.edu
Admissions email: admissions@lehigh.edu
Private; founded 1865
Freshman admissions: more selective; 2019-2020: 15,649 applied, 5,023 accepted. Either SAT or ACT required. SAT 25/75 percentile: 1280-1450. High

school rank: 58% in top tenth, 85% in top quarter, 97% in top half
Early decision deadline: 11/1, notification date: 12/15
Early action deadline: N/A, notification date: N/A
Application deadline (fall): 1/1
Undergraduate student body: 5,107 full time, 71 part time; 54% male, 46% female; 0% American Indian, 8% Asian, 4% Black, 9% Hispanic, 4% multiracial, 0% Pacific Islander, 62% white, 9% international; 24% from in state; 61% live on campus; 26% of students in fraternities, 37% in sororities
Most popular majors: 15% Finance, General, 9% Mechanical Engineering, 5% Accounting, 5% Industrial Engineering, 4% Marketing/Marketing Management, General
Expenses: 2020-2021: $55,260; room/board: $14,740
Financial aid: (610) 758-3181; 41% of undergrads determined to have financial need; average aid package $53,951

Lincoln University

Lincoln University PA
(800) 790-0191
U.S. News ranking: Reg. U. (N), second tier
Website: www.lincoln.edu
Admissions email: admissions@lincoln.edu
Public; founded 1854
Freshman admissions: least selective; 2019-2020: 4,429 applied, 3,666 accepted. Either SAT or ACT required. SAT 25/75 percentile: 870-1010. High school rank: 7% in top tenth, 16% in top quarter, 53% in top half
Early decision deadline: N/A, notification date: N/A
Early action deadline: N/A, notification date: N/A
Application deadline (fall): 5/1
Undergraduate student body: 1,901 full time, 139 part time; 34% male, 66% female; 0% American Indian, 0% Asian, 85% Black, 5% Hispanic, 3% multiracial, 0% Pacific Islander, 1% white, 3% international; 50% from in state; 88% live on campus; 4% of students in fraternities, 3% in sororities
Most popular majors: 17% Health Professions and Related Programs, 14% Public Administration and Social Service Professions, 13% Communication, Journalism, and Related Programs, 10% Business, Management, Marketing, and Related Support Services, 10% Homeland Security, Law Enforcement, Firefighting and Related Protective Services
Expenses: 2020-2021: $11,266 in state, $16,636 out of state; room/board: $9,828
Financial aid: (800) 561-2606; 90% of undergrads determined to have financial need; average aid package $12,747

Lock Haven University of Pennsylvania

Lock Haven PA
(570) 484-2011
U.S. News ranking: Reg. U. (N), No. 111
Website: www.lockhaven.edu
Admissions email: admissions@lockhaven.edu
Public; founded 1870
Freshman admissions: less selective; 2019-2020: 2,203 applied, 2,089 accepted. Either SAT or ACT required. SAT 25/75 percentile: 920-1130. High school rank: 10% in top tenth, 29% in top quarter, 64% in top half
Early decision deadline: N/A, notification date: N/A
Early action deadline: N/A, notification date: N/A
Application deadline (fall): rolling
Undergraduate student body: 2,480 full time, 268 part time; 40% male, 60% female; 0% American Indian, 1% Asian, 7% Black, 3% Hispanic, 2% multiracial, 0% Pacific Islander, 84% white, 0% international; 95% from in state; 31% live on campus; 3% of students in fraternities, 4% in sororities
Most popular majors: 11% Criminal Justice/Law Enforcement Administration, 11% Health Professions and Related Clinical Sciences, Other, 8% Business Administration and Management, General, 6% Sport and Fitness Administration/Management, 5% Social Work
Expenses: 2020-2021: $10,878 in state, $20,452 out of state; room/board: $10,368
Financial aid: (570) 484-2452; 78% of undergrads determined to have financial need; average aid package $9,379

Lycoming College

Williamsport PA
(800) 345-3920
U.S. News ranking: Nat. Lib. Arts, No. 120
Website: www.lycoming.edu/
Admissions email: admissions@lycoming.edu
Private; founded 1812
Affiliation: United Methodist
Freshman admissions: selective; 2019-2020: 3,204 applied, 1,996 accepted. Neither SAT nor ACT required. SAT 25/75 percentile: 1040-1220. High school rank: 25% in top tenth, 43% in top quarter, 76% in top half
Early decision deadline: 11/15, notification date: 12/1
Early action deadline: 12/1, notification date: 12/15
Application deadline (fall): rolling
Undergraduate student body: 1,130 full time, 10 part time; 48% male, 52% female; 0% American Indian, 1% Asian, 14% Black, 13% Hispanic, 4% multiracial, 0% Pacific Islander, 59% white, 5% international; 43% from in state; 87% live on campus; 11% of students in fraternities, 18% in sororities
Most popular majors: 23% Social Sciences, 20% Business, Management, Marketing, and

Related Support Services, 17% Psychology, 12% Visual and Performing Arts, 6% Biological and Biomedical Sciences
Expenses: 2020-2021: $42,714; room/board: $13,384
Financial aid: (570) 321-4140; 86% of undergrads determined to have financial need; average aid package $43,039

Mansfield University of Pennsylvania

Mansfield PA
(800) 577-6826
U.S. News ranking: Nat. Lib. Arts, second tier
Website: www.mansfield.edu
Admissions email: admissns@mansfield.edu
Public; founded 1857
Freshman admissions: less selective; 2019-2020: 1,892 applied, 1,777 accepted. Neither SAT nor ACT required. SAT 25/75 percentile: 920-1120. High school rank: 9% in top tenth, 29% in top quarter, 69% in top half
Early decision deadline: N/A, notification date: N/A
Early action deadline: N/A, notification date: N/A
Application deadline (fall): rolling
Undergraduate student body: 1,484 full time, 156 part time; 37% male, 63% female; 0% American Indian, 1% Asian, 11% Black, 5% Hispanic, 2% multiracial, 0% Pacific Islander, 77% white, 1% international; 81% from in state; 57% live on campus; N/A of students in fraternities, N/A in sororities
Most popular majors: 16% Health Professions and Related Programs, 11% Psychology, 10% Visual and Performing Arts, 7% Homeland Security, Law Enforcement, Firefighting and Related Protective Services, 6% Natural Resources and Conservation
Expenses: 2020-2021: $10,846 in state, $13,162 out of state; room/board: N/A
Financial aid: N/A; 86% of undergrads determined to have financial need; average aid package $1,858

Marywood University

Scranton PA
(866) 279-9663
U.S. News ranking: Reg. U. (N), No. 59
Website: www.marywood.edu
Admissions email: YourFuture@marywood.edu
Private; founded 1915
Affiliation: Roman Catholic
Freshman admissions: selective; 2019-2020: 2,005 applied, 1,559 accepted. Either SAT or ACT required. SAT 25/75 percentile: 1000-1190. High school rank: 15% in top tenth, 49% in top quarter, 82% in top half
Early decision deadline: N/A, notification date: N/A
Early action deadline: N/A, notification date: N/A
Application deadline (fall): rolling
Undergraduate student body: 1,649 full time, 154 part time; 33% male, 67% female; 0% American

Indian, 2% Asian, 2% Black, 8% Hispanic, 2% multiracial, 0% Pacific Islander, 74% white, 1% international; 72% from in state; 34% live on campus; 6% of students in fraternities, 8% in sororities
Most popular majors: 31% Health Professions and Related Programs, 15% Business, Management, Marketing, and Related Support Services, 9% Architecture and Related Services, 9% Biological and Biomedical Sciences, 7% Education
Expenses: 2020-2021: $36,928; room/board: $14,338
Financial aid: (570) 348-6225; 81% of undergrads determined to have financial need; average aid package $28,358

Mercyhurst University

Erie PA
(814) 824-2202
U.S. News ranking: Reg. U. (N), No. 38
Website: www.mercyhurst.edu
Admissions email: admug@mercyhurst.edu
Private; founded 1926
Affiliation: Roman Catholic
Freshman admissions: selective; 2019-2020: 2,922 applied, 2,542 accepted. Neither SAT nor ACT required. SAT 25/75 percentile: 1030-1220. High school rank: N/A
Early decision deadline: N/A, notification date: N/A
Early action deadline: N/A, notification date: N/A
Application deadline (fall): rolling
Undergraduate student body: 2,305 full time, 99 part time; 41% male, 59% female; 1% American Indian, 2% Asian, 4% Black, 4% Hispanic, 0% multiracial, 0% Pacific Islander, 81% white, 5% international; 34% from in state; 74% live on campus; 0% of students in fraternities, 0% in sororities
Most popular majors: 22% Business, Management, Marketing, and Related Support Services, 14% Health Professions and Related Programs, 13% Military Technologies and Applied Sciences, 9% Homeland Security, Law Enforcement, Firefighting and Related Protective Services, 6% Biological and Biomedical Sciences
Expenses: 2020-2021: $41,340; room/board: $13,260
Financial aid: (814) 824-2288; 78% of undergrads determined to have financial need; average aid package $31,146

Messiah University

Mechanicsburg PA
(717) 691-6000
U.S. News ranking: Reg. U. (N), No. 19
Website: www.messiah.edu
Admissions email: admissions@messiah.edu
Private; founded 1909
Affiliation: Interdenominational
Freshman admissions: more selective; 2019-2020: 2,640 applied, 2,003 accepted. Neither SAT nor ACT required. SAT

25/75 percentile: 1090-1310. High school rank: 34% in top tenth, 64% in top quarter, 91% in top half
Early decision deadline: N/A, notification date: N/A
Early action deadline: N/A, notification date: N/A
Application deadline (fall): rolling
Undergraduate student body: 2,545 full time, 164 part time; 39% male, 61% female; 0% American Indian, 2% Asian, 3% Black, 6% Hispanic, 4% multiracial, 0% Pacific Islander, 81% white, 4% international; 65% from in state; 87% live on campus; N/A of students in fraternities, N/A in sororities
Most popular majors: 8% Engineering, General, 6% Business Administration and Management, General, 6% Registered Nursing/Registered Nurse, 4% Health Professions and Related Programs, 4% Psychology, General
Expenses: 2020-2021: $37,180; room/board: $10,900
Financial aid: (717) 691-6007; 74% of undergrads determined to have financial need; average aid package $26,020

Millersville University of Pennsylvania

Millersville PA
(717) 871-4625
U.S. News ranking: Reg. U. (N), No. 96
Website: www.millersville.edu
Admissions email: Admissions@millersville.edu
Public; founded 1855
Freshman admissions: selective; 2019-2020: 6,560 applied, 4,979 accepted. Either SAT or ACT required. SAT 25/75 percentile: 980-1170. High school rank: 8% in top tenth, 29% in top quarter, 66% in top half
Early decision deadline: N/A, notification date: N/A
Early action deadline: N/A, notification date: N/A
Application deadline (fall): rolling
Undergraduate student body: 5,499 full time, 1,280 part time; 42% male, 58% female; 0% American Indian, 3% Asian, 9% Black, 11% Hispanic, 1% multiracial, 0% Pacific Islander, 73% white, 1% international; 92% from in state; 32% live on campus; 4% of students in fraternities, 4% in sororities
Most popular majors: 13% Business, Management, Marketing, and Related Support Services, 10% Education, 10% Health Professions and Related Programs, 10% Social Sciences, 8% Communication, Journalism, and Related Programs
Expenses: 2020-2021: $12,250 in state, $21,970 out of state; room/board: N/A
Financial aid: (717) 871-5100; 66% of undergrads determined to have financial need; average aid package $8,877

Misericordia University
Dallas PA
(570) 674-6264
U.S. News ranking: Nat. U., No. 206
Website: www.misericordia.edu/
Admissions email: admiss@misericordia.edu
Private; founded 1924
Affiliation: Roman Catholic
Freshman admissions: selective; 2019-2020: 1,547 applied, 1,327 accepted. Either SAT or ACT required. SAT 25/75 percentile: 1050-1220. High school rank: 18% in top tenth, 49% in top quarter, 80% in top half
Early decision deadline: N/A, notification date: N/A
Early action deadline: N/A, notification date: N/A
Application deadline (fall): rolling
Undergraduate student body: 1,584 full time, 380 part time; 32% male, 68% female; 0% American Indian, 1% Asian, 3% Black, 3% Hispanic, 4% multiracial, 0% Pacific Islander, 85% white, 0% international; 72% from in state; 44% live on campus; N/A of students in fraternities, N/A in sororities
Most popular majors: 51% Health Professions and Related Programs, 18% Business, Management, Marketing, and Related Support Services, 5% Education, 4% Biological and Biomedical Sciences, 4% Social Sciences
Expenses: 2020-2021: $35,940; room/board: $14,520
Financial aid: (570) 674-6222; 82% of undergrads determined to have financial need; average aid package $25,422

Moore College of Art & Design[1]
Philadelphia PA
(215) 965-4015
U.S. News ranking: Arts, unranked
Website: www.moore.edu
Admissions email: admiss@moore.edu
Private; founded 1848
Application deadline (fall): rolling
Undergraduate student body: N/A full time, N/A part time
Expenses: 2019-2020: $43,082; room/board: $16,188
Financial aid: N/A

Moravian College
Bethlehem PA
(610) 861-1320
U.S. News ranking: Nat. Lib. Arts, No. 140
Website: www.moravian.edu
Admissions email: admission@moravian.edu
Private; founded 1742
Affiliation: Moravian Church
Freshman admissions: selective; 2019-2020: 2,136 applied, 1,600 accepted. Either SAT or ACT required. SAT 25/75 percentile: 1040-1210. High school rank: 15% in top tenth, 51% in top quarter, 83% in top half
Early decision deadline: N/A, notification date: N/A

Early action deadline: N/A, notification date: N/A
Application deadline (fall): 3/1
Undergraduate student body: 1,916 full time, 157 part time; 39% male, 61% female; 0% American Indian, 2% Asian, 3% Black, 12% Hispanic, 2% multiracial, 0% Pacific Islander, 70% white, 5% international; 75% from in state; 52% live on campus; 13% of students in fraternities, 17% in sororities
Most popular majors: 28% Health Professions and Related Programs, 19% Business, Management, Marketing, and Related Support Services, 16% Social Sciences, 6% Visual and Performing Arts, 5% Psychology
Expenses: 2020-2021: $47,367; room/board: $14,471
Financial aid: (610) 861-1330; 80% of undergrads determined to have financial need; average aid package $31,338

Mount Aloysius College
Cresson PA
(814) 886-6383
U.S. News ranking: Reg. Coll. (N), No. 34
Website: www.mtaloy.edu
Admissions email: admissions@mtaloy.edu
Private; founded 1853
Freshman admissions: less selective; 2019-2020: 1,407 applied, 1,335 accepted. Neither SAT nor ACT required. SAT 25/75 percentile: 943-1120. High school rank: N/A
Early decision deadline: N/A, notification date: N/A
Early action deadline: N/A, notification date: N/A
Application deadline (fall): rolling
Undergraduate student body: 959 full time, 832 part time; 33% male, 67% female; 0% American Indian, 1% Asian, 3% Black, 1% Hispanic, 0% multiracial, 0% Pacific Islander, 80% white, 5% international; N/A from in state; 33% live on campus; N/A of students in fraternities, N/A in sororities
Most popular majors: 42% Health Professions and Related Programs, 21% Business, Management, Marketing, and Related Support Services, 10% Biological and Biomedical Sciences, 5% Computer and Information Sciences and Support Services, 4% Psychology
Expenses: 2020-2021: $24,370; room/board: $11,296
Financial aid: (814) 886-6357

Muhlenberg College
Allentown PA
(484) 664-3200
U.S. News ranking: Nat. Lib. Arts, No. 72
Website: www.muhlenberg.edu
Admissions email: admissions@muhlenberg.edu
Private; founded 1848
Affiliation: Lutheran Church in America
Freshman admissions: more selective; 2019-2020: 4,224 applied, 2,798 accepted. Neither

SAT nor ACT required. SAT 25/75 percentile: 1150-1340. High school rank: 35% in top tenth, 72% in top quarter, 95% in top half
Early decision deadline: 11/15, notification date: 12/15
Early action deadline: N/A, notification date: N/A
Application deadline (fall): 2/1
Undergraduate student body: 2,193 full time, 58 part time; 39% male, 61% female; 0% American Indian, 3% Asian, 4% Black, 9% Hispanic, 2% multiracial, 0% Pacific Islander, 74% white, 3% international; 27% from in state; 91% live on campus; 15% of students in fraternities, 18% in sororities
Most popular majors: 12% Drama and Dramatics/Theatre Arts, General, 11% Mass Communication/Media Studies, 8% Business Administration and Management, General, 8% Finance, General, 8% Psychology, General
Expenses: 2020-2021: $56,665; room/board: $12,560
Financial aid: (484) 664-3175; 64% of undergrads determined to have financial need; average aid package $40,533

Neumann University
Aston PA
(610) 558-5616
U.S. News ranking: Reg. U. (N), No. 132
Website: www.neumann.edu
Admissions email: neumann@neumann.edu
Private; founded 1965
Affiliation: Roman Catholic
Freshman admissions: less selective; 2019-2020: 3,641 applied, 2,269 accepted. Either SAT or ACT required. SAT 25/75 percentile: 920-1090. High school rank: N/A
Early decision deadline: N/A, notification date: N/A
Early action deadline: 12/1, notification date: 12/24
Application deadline (fall): rolling
Undergraduate student body: 1,384 full time, 517 part time; 32% male, 68% female; 0% American Indian, 2% Asian, 28% Black, 6% Hispanic, 3% multiracial, 0% Pacific Islander, 56% white, 1% international; 32% from in state; 55% live on campus; N/A of students in fraternities, N/A in sororities
Most popular majors: 26% Registered Nursing, Nursing Administration, Nursing Research and Clinical Nursing, Other, 21% Liberal Arts and Sciences/Liberal Studies, 9% Homeland Security, Law Enforcement, Firefighting and Related Protective Services, Other, 7% Business Administration and Management, General, 7% Communication and Media Studies, Other
Expenses: 2020-2021: $32,960; room/board: $13,680
Financial aid: (610) 558-5521; 85% of undergrads determined to have financial need; average aid package $28,406

Peirce College
Philadelphia PA
(888) 467-3472
U.S. News ranking: Reg. Coll. (N), No. 28
Website: www.peirce.edu
Admissions email: info@peirce.edu
Private; founded 1865
Freshman admissions: least selective; 2019-2020: N/A applied, N/A accepted. Neither SAT nor ACT required. SAT 25/75 percentile: N/A. High school rank: N/A
Early decision deadline: N/A, notification date: N/A
Early action deadline: N/A, notification date: N/A
Application deadline (fall): rolling
Undergraduate student body: 297 full time, 792 part time; 30% male, 70% female; 0% American Indian, 3% Asian, 56% Black, 8% Hispanic, 2% multiracial, 0% Pacific Islander, 20% white, 1% international
Most popular majors: 29% Business, Management, Marketing, and Related Support Services, 28% Health Professions and Related Programs, 24% Homeland Security, Law Enforcement, Firefighting and Related Protective Services, 12% Legal Professions and Studies, 6% Computer and Information Sciences and Support Services
Expenses: 2019-2020: $15,060; room/board: N/A
Financial aid: N/A

Pennsylvania Academy of the Fine Arts[1]
Philadelphia PA
(215) 972-7625
U.S. News ranking: Arts, unranked
Website: www.pafa.edu
Admissions email: admissions@pafa.edu
Private; founded 1805
Application deadline (fall): 8/29
Undergraduate student body: N/A full time, N/A part time
Expenses: 2020-2021: $42,000; room/board: $13,420
Financial aid: N/A

Pennsylvania College of Art & Design
Lancaster PA
(800) 689-0379
U.S. News ranking: Arts, unranked
Website: pcad.edu
Admissions email: admissions@pcad.edu
Private; founded 1982
Freshman admissions: selective; 2019-2020: 392 applied, 172 accepted. Neither SAT nor ACT required. SAT 25/75 percentile: 856-1166. High school rank: 3% in top tenth, 18% in top quarter, 55% in top half
Early decision deadline: N/A, notification date: N/A
Early action deadline: N/A, notification date: N/A
Application deadline (fall): rolling
Undergraduate student body: 232 full time, 13 part time; 30% male, 70% female; 1% American Indian, 4% Asian, 8% Black, 3% Hispanic, 6% multiracial,

0% Pacific Islander, 76% white, 0% international; 75% from in state; N/A live on campus; 0% of students in fraternities, 0% in sororities
Most popular majors: 42% Illustration, 17% Fine/Studio Arts, General, 17% Graphic Design, 12% Game and Interactive Media Design, 12% Photography
Expenses: 2019-2020: $26,600; room/board: $10,754
Financial aid: N/A

Pennsylvania College of Technology
Williamsport PA
(570) 327-4761
U.S. News ranking: Reg. Coll. (N), No. 15
Website: www.pct.edu
Admissions email: admissions@pct.edu
Public; founded 1914
Freshman admissions: less selective; 2019-2020: 3,704 applied, 2,902 accepted. Neither SAT nor ACT required. SAT 25/75 percentile: 970-1170. High school rank: 7% in top tenth, 22% in top quarter, 56% in top half
Early decision deadline: N/A, notification date: N/A
Early action deadline: N/A, notification date: N/A
Application deadline (fall): 7/1
Undergraduate student body: 4,110 full time, 873 part time; 63% male, 37% female; 0% American Indian, 1% Asian, 3% Black, 4% Hispanic, 2% multiracial, 0% Pacific Islander, 88% white, 0% international; 90% from in state; 32% live on campus; N/A of students in fraternities, N/A in sororities
Most popular majors: 31% Engineering Technologies and Engineering-Related Fields, 28% Health Professions and Related Programs, 9% Computer and Information Sciences and Support Services, 5% Construction Trades, 2% Visual and Performing Arts
Expenses: 2020-2021: $17,610 in state, $25,170 out of state; room/board: $11,060
Financial aid: (570) 327-4766; 77% of undergrads determined to have financial need

Pennsylvania State University–Erie, The Behrend College
Erie PA
(814) 898-6100
U.S. News ranking: Unranked
Website: behrend.psu.edu/
Admissions email: behrend.admissions@psu.edu
Public; founded 1948
Freshman admissions: N/A; 2019-2020: 4,765 applied, 3,997 accepted. Either SAT or ACT required. SAT 25/75 percentile: 1050-1280. High school rank: N/A
Early decision deadline: N/A, notification date: N/A
Early action deadline: N/A, notification date: N/A
Application deadline (fall): rolling
Undergraduate student body: 3,763 full time, 201 part time; 66%

male, 34% female; 0% American Indian, 3% Asian, 3% Black, 4% Hispanic, 3% multiracial, 0% Pacific Islander, 78% white, 8% international; 84% from in state; 41% live on campus; 4% of students in fraternities, 4% in sororities
Most popular majors: 36% Business, Management, Marketing, and Related Support Services, 27% Engineering, 7% Engineering Technologies and Engineering-Related Fields, 5% Biological and Biomedical Sciences, 5% Psychology
Expenses: 2019-2020: $15,206 in state, $24,916 out of state; room/board: $11,884
Financial aid: (814) 865-6301

Pennsylvania State University– Harrisburg[1]
Middletown PA
(717) 948-6250
U.S. News ranking: Unranked
Website: www.hbg.psu.edu/
Admissions email: hbgadmit@psu.edu
Public
Application deadline (fall): N/A
Undergraduate student body: 3,914 full time, 332 part time
Expenses: 2019-2020: $15,206 in state, $15,206 out of state; room/board: $11,884
Financial aid: N/A

Pennsylvania State University– University Park
University Park PA
(814) 865-5471
U.S. News ranking: Nat. U., No. 63
Website: www.psu.edu
Admissions email: admissions@psu.edu
Public; founded 1855
Freshman admissions: more selective; 2019-2020: 71,903 applied, 35,302 accepted. Either SAT or ACT required. SAT 25/75 percentile: 1160-1370. High school rank: N/A
Early decision deadline: N/A, notification date: N/A
Early action deadline: 11/1, notification date: 12/24
Application deadline (fall): rolling
Undergraduate student body: 39,529 full time, 1,110 part time; 53% male, 47% female; 0% American Indian, 6% Asian, 4% Black, 7% Hispanic, 3% multiracial, 0% Pacific Islander, 65% white, 12% international; N/A from in state; 36% live on campus; 17% of students in fraternities, 20% in sororities
Most popular majors: 17% Engineering, 15% Business, Management, Marketing, and Related Support Services, 10% Computer and Information Sciences and Support Services, 8% Communication, Journalism, and Related Programs, 8% Social Sciences
Expenses: 2020-2021: $18,450 in state, $35,514 out of state; room/board: $10,592

Financial aid: (814) 865-6301; 47% of undergrads determined to have financial need; average aid package $11,076

Pittsburgh Technical College
Oakdale PA
(412) 809-5100
U.S. News ranking: Reg. Coll. (N), No. 25
Website: www.ptcollege.edu
Admissions email: james@ptcollege.edu
Private; founded 1946
Affiliation: Undenominational
Freshman admissions: less selective; 2019-2020: 1,540 applied, 1,188 accepted. Neither SAT nor ACT required. SAT 25/75 percentile: N/A. High school rank: N/A
Early decision deadline: N/A, notification date: N/A
Early action deadline: N/A, notification date: N/A
Application deadline (fall): rolling
Undergraduate student body: 1,598 full time, 146 part time; 56% male, 44% female; 0% American Indian, 1% Asian, 7% Black, 1% Hispanic, 2% multiracial, 0% Pacific Islander, 54% white, 0% international; 85% from in state; 48% live on campus; N/A of students in fraternities, N/A in sororities
Most popular majors: 4% Computer Technology/Computer Systems Technology, 2% Business Administration and Management, General
Expenses: 2020-2021: $16,485; room/board: $10,602
Financial aid: (412) 809-5100; 96% of undergrads determined to have financial need

Point Park University[1]
Pittsburgh PA
(800) 321-0129
U.S. News ranking: Reg. U. (N), No. 83
Website: www.pointpark.edu
Admissions email: enroll@pointpark.edu
Private; founded 1960
Application deadline (fall): rolling
Undergraduate student body: 2,626 full time, 474 part time
Expenses: 2020-2021: $34,200; room/board: $12,680
Financial aid: (412) 392-3930; 92% of undergrads determined to have financial need; average aid package $26,683

Robert Morris University
Moon Township PA
(412) 397-5200
U.S. News ranking: Nat. U., No. 196
Website: www.rmu.edu
Admissions email: admissions@rmu.edu
Private; founded 1921
Freshman admissions: selective; 2019-2020: 5,956 applied, 5,030 accepted. Either SAT or ACT required. SAT 25/75 percentile: 1020-1210. High

school rank: 16% in top tenth, 42% in top quarter, 79% in top half
Early decision deadline: N/A, notification date: N/A
Early action deadline: N/A, notification date: N/A
Application deadline (fall): rolling
Undergraduate student body: 3,500 full time, 270 part time; 56% male, 44% female; 0% American Indian, 1% Asian, 7% Black, 3% Hispanic, 3% multiracial, 0% Pacific Islander, 75% white, 9% international; 86% from in state; 49% live on campus; 14% of students in fraternities, 17% in sororities
Most popular majors: 11% Engineering, Other, 10% Registered Nursing/Registered Nurse, 9% Accounting, 7% Marketing/Marketing Management, General, 6% Business Administration and Management, General
Expenses: 2020-2021: $32,130; room/board: $12,070
Financial aid: (412) 397-6250; 73% of undergrads determined to have financial need; average aid package $25,555

Rosemont College
Rosemont PA
(610) 526-2966
U.S. News ranking: Reg. U. (N), second tier
Website: www.rosemont.edu
Admissions email: admissions@rosemont.edu
Private; founded 1921
Affiliation: Roman Catholic
Freshman admissions: selective; 2019-2020: 1,039 applied, 684 accepted. Neither SAT nor ACT required. SAT 25/75 percentile: 920-1130. High school rank: N/A
Early decision deadline: N/A, notification date: N/A
Early action deadline: N/A, notification date: N/A
Application deadline (fall): rolling
Undergraduate student body: 390 full time, 128 part time; 34% male, 66% female; 0% American Indian, 2% Asian, 42% Black, 10% Hispanic, 3% multiracial, 1% Pacific Islander, 35% white, 1% international
Most popular majors: 40% Business, Management, Marketing, and Related Support Services, 24% Psychology, 15% English Language and Literature/Letters, 15% Homeland Security, Law Enforcement, Firefighting and Related Protective Services, 6% Visual and Performing Arts
Expenses: 2019-2020: $20,785; room/board: $12,820
Financial aid: (610) 527-0200

Saint Joseph's University
Philadelphia PA
(610) 660-1300
U.S. News ranking: Reg. U. (N), No. 8
Website: www.sju.edu
Admissions email: admit@sju.edu
Private; founded 1851
Affiliation: Roman Catholic
Freshman admissions: more selective; 2019-2020: 8,692

applied, 6,513 accepted. Neither SAT nor ACT required. SAT 25/75 percentile: 1120-1300. High school rank: 22% in top tenth, 52% in top quarter, 82% in top half
Early decision deadline: 11/1, notification date: 12/20
Early action deadline: 11/1, notification date: 12/20
Application deadline (fall): rolling
Undergraduate student body: 4,221 full time, 562 part time; 46% male, 54% female; 0% American Indian, 3% Asian, 6% Black, 8% Hispanic, 3% multiracial, 0% Pacific Islander, 78% white, 2% international; 46% from in state; 49% live on campus; 5% of students in fraternities, 26% in sororities
Most popular majors: 54% Business, Management, Marketing, and Related Support Services, 7% Social Sciences, 6% Biological and Biomedical Sciences, 6% Education, 6% Health Professions and Related Programs
Expenses: 2020-2021: $47,940; room/board: $14,840
Financial aid: (610) 660-1346; 62% of undergrads determined to have financial need; average aid package $32,276

Saint Vincent College
Latrobe PA
(800) 782-5549
U.S. News ranking: Nat. Lib. Arts, No. 140
Website: www.stvincent.edu
Admissions email: admission@stvincent.edu
Private; founded 1846
Affiliation: Roman Catholic
Freshman admissions: selective; 2019-2020: 2,025 applied, 1,371 accepted. Either SAT or ACT required. SAT 25/75 percentile: 1030-1240. High school rank: 20% in top tenth, 46% in top quarter, 74% in top half
Early decision deadline: N/A, notification date: N/A
Early action deadline: N/A, notification date: N/A
Application deadline (fall): 5/1
Undergraduate student body: 1,491 full time, 69 part time; 53% male, 47% female; 0% American Indian, 1% Asian, 6% Black, 5% Hispanic, 2% multiracial, 0% Pacific Islander, 83% white, 1% international; N/A from in state; 69% live on campus; N/A of students in fraternities, N/A in sororities
Most popular majors: 25% Business, Management, Marketing, and Related Support Services, 12% Social Sciences, 10% Biological and Biomedical Sciences, 7% Education, 6% Engineering
Expenses: 2020-2021: $38,020; room/board: $12,156
Financial aid: (724) 805-2555; 79% of undergrads determined to have financial need; average aid package $32,749

Seton Hill University
Greensburg PA
(724) 838-4281
U.S. News ranking: Reg. U. (N), No. 43
Website: www.setonhill.edu
Admissions email: admit@setonhill.edu
Private; founded 1883
Affiliation: Roman Catholic
Freshman admissions: selective; 2019-2020: 2,509 applied, 1,927 accepted. Neither SAT nor ACT required. SAT 25/75 percentile: 1000-1220. High school rank: 17% in top tenth, 44% in top quarter, 78% in top half
Early decision deadline: N/A, notification date: N/A
Early action deadline: N/A, notification date: N/A
Application deadline (fall): 8/15
Undergraduate student body: 1,584 full time, 142 part time; 35% male, 65% female; 0% American Indian, 2% Asian, 8% Black, 4% Hispanic, 3% multiracial, 0% Pacific Islander, 80% white, 1% international; 77% from in state; 51% live on campus; 0% of students in fraternities, 0% in sororities
Most popular majors: 21% Business, Management, Marketing, and Related Support Services, 12% Health Professions and Related Programs, 11% Visual and Performing Arts, 8% Biological and Biomedical Sciences, 8% Parks, Recreation, Leisure, and Fitness Studies
Expenses: 2020-2021: $37,946; room/board: $12,516
Financial aid: (724) 830-1010; 82% of undergrads determined to have financial need; average aid package $27,783

Shippensburg University of Pennsylvania
Shippensburg PA
(717) 477-1231
U.S. News ranking: Reg. U. (N), No. 88
Website: www.ship.edu
Admissions email: admiss@ship.edu
Public; founded 1871
Freshman admissions: selective; 2019-2020: 5,927 applied, 5,399 accepted. Either SAT or ACT required. SAT 25/75 percentile: 930-1150. High school rank: 10% in top tenth, 26% in top quarter, 59% in top half
Early decision deadline: N/A, notification date: N/A
Early action deadline: N/A, notification date: N/A
Application deadline (fall): rolling
Undergraduate student body: 4,861 full time, 413 part time; 48% male, 52% female; 0% American Indian, 1% Asian, 13% Black, 6% Hispanic, 5% multiracial, 0% Pacific Islander, 74% white, 1% international; 93% from in state; 34% live on campus; 11% of students in fraternities, 11% in sororities
Most popular majors: 9% Psychology, General, 8% Business Administration and Management,

General, 7% Biology/Biological Sciences, General, 7% Criminal Justice/Safety Studies, 7% Marketing/Marketing Management, General
Expenses: 2020-2021: $13,394 in state, $13,872 out of state; room/board: $12,006
Financial aid: (717) 477-1131; 72% of undergrads determined to have financial need; average aid package $10,154

Slippery Rock University of Pennsylvania
Slippery Rock PA
(800) 929-4778
U.S. News ranking: Reg. U. (N), No. 83
Website: www.sru.edu/admissions
Admissions email: asktherock@sru.edu
Public; founded 1889
Freshman admissions: selective; 2019-2020: 5,807 applied, 4,084 accepted. Either SAT or ACT required. SAT 25/75 percentile: 1000-1170. High school rank: 13% in top tenth, 36% in top quarter, 74% in top half
Early decision deadline: N/A, notification date: N/A
Early action deadline: N/A, notification date: N/A
Application deadline (fall): rolling
Undergraduate student body: 6,968 full time, 500 part time; 44% male, 56% female; 0% American Indian, 1% Asian, 5% Black, 3% Hispanic, 4% multiracial, 0% Pacific Islander, 86% white, 1% international; 92% from in state; 37% live on campus; 6% of students in fraternities, 7% in sororities
Most popular majors: 24% Health Professions and Related Programs, 11% Engineering Technologies and Engineering-Related Fields, 10% Business, Management, Marketing, and Related Support Services, 8% Parks, Recreation, Leisure, and Fitness Studies, 7% Education
Expenses: 2020-2021: $10,482 in state, $18,198 out of state; room/board: $10,968
Financial aid: (724) 738-2044; 68% of undergrads determined to have financial need; average aid package $9,560

St. Francis University
Loretto PA
(814) 472-3100
U.S. News ranking: Reg. U. (N), No. 26
Website: www.francis.edu/undergraduate_admissions
Admissions email: admissions@francis.edu
Private; founded 1847
Affiliation: Roman Catholic
Freshman admissions: selective; 2019-2020: 1,748 applied, 1,303 accepted. Either SAT or ACT required. SAT 25/75 percentile: 1030-1250. High school rank: 30% in top tenth, 52% in top quarter, 88% in top half
Early decision deadline: N/A, notification date: N/A

Early action deadline: N/A, notification date: N/A
Application deadline (fall): rolling
Undergraduate student body: 1,449 full time, 200 part time; 35% male, 65% female; 0% American Indian, 3% Asian, 7% Black, 2% Hispanic, 2% multiracial, 0% Pacific Islander, 82% white, 2% international; 72% from in state; 86% live on campus; 3% of students in fraternities, 9% in sororities
Most popular majors: 11% Physician Assistant, 8% Occupational Therapy/Therapist, 6% Physical Therapy/Therapist, 5% Business Administration and Management, General, 5% Registered Nursing/Registered Nurse
Expenses: 2019-2020: $38,170; room/board: $12,948
Financial aid: (814) 472-3010

Susquehanna University
Selinsgrove PA
(800) 326-9672
U.S. News ranking: Nat. Lib. Arts, No. 113
Website: www.susqu.edu
Admissions email: suadmiss@susqu.edu
Private; founded 1858
Affiliation: Evangelical Lutheran Church
Freshman admissions: more selective; 2019-2020: 4,865 applied, 4,123 accepted. Neither SAT nor ACT required. SAT 25/75 percentile: 1100-1290. High school rank: 25% in top tenth, 63% in top quarter, 88% in top half
Early decision deadline: 11/15, notification date: 12/1
Early action deadline: 11/1, notification date: 12/1
Application deadline (fall): rolling
Undergraduate student body: 2,200 full time, 112 part time; 44% male, 56% female; 0% American Indian, 2% Asian, 6% Black, 7% Hispanic, 3% multiracial, 0% Pacific Islander, 79% white, 2% international; N/A from in state; 89% live on campus; 19% of students in fraternities, 17% in sororities
Most popular majors: 22% Business, Management, Marketing, and Related Support Services, 14% Communication, Journalism, and Related Programs, 11% Biological and Biomedical Sciences, 9% Social Sciences, 9% Visual and Performing Arts
Expenses: 2020-2021: $51,140; room/board: $13,680
Financial aid: (570) 372-4450; 80% of undergrads determined to have financial need; average aid package $39,750

Swarthmore College
Swarthmore PA
(610) 328-8300
U.S. News ranking: Nat. Lib. Arts, No. 3
Website: www.swarthmore.edu
Admissions email: admissions@swarthmore.edu
Private; founded 1864

Freshman admissions: most selective; 2019-2020: 11,442 applied, 1,022 accepted. Neither SAT nor ACT required. SAT 25/75 percentile: 1380-1540. High school rank: 87% in top tenth, 100% in top quarter, 100% in top half
Early decision deadline: 11/15, notification date: 12/15
Early action deadline: N/A, notification date: N/A
Application deadline (fall): 1/1
Undergraduate student body: 1,591 full time, 3 part time; 49% male, 51% female; 0% American Indian, 16% Asian, 8% Black, 13% Hispanic, 7% multiracial, 0% Pacific Islander, 37% white, 14% international; N/A from in state; 95% live on campus; N/A of students in fraternities, N/A in sororities
Most popular majors: 26% Social Sciences, 11% Biological and Biomedical Sciences, 10% Mathematics and Statistics, 9% Computer and Information Sciences and Support Services, 6% Psychology
Expenses: 2020-2021: $54,656; room/board: $16,653
Financial aid: (610) 328-8358; 54% of undergrads determined to have financial need; average aid package $56,048

Temple University
Philadelphia PA
(215) 204-7200
U.S. News ranking: Nat. U., No. 103
Website: www.temple.edu
Admissions email: askanowl@temple.edu
Public; founded 1884
Freshman admissions: more selective; 2019-2020: 35,599 applied, 21,375 accepted. Neither SAT nor ACT required. SAT 25/75 percentile: 1120-1320. High school rank: 36% in top tenth, 76% in top quarter, 92% in top half
Early decision deadline: N/A, notification date: N/A
Early action deadline: 11/1, notification date: 1/10
Application deadline (fall): 2/1
Undergraduate student body: 26,210 full time, 2,464 part time; 46% male, 54% female; 0% American Indian, 12% Asian, 13% Black, 8% Hispanic, 4% multiracial, 0% Pacific Islander, 55% white, 5% international; 79% from in state; 18% live on campus; 4% of students in fraternities, 7% in sororities
Most popular majors: 26% Business, Management, Marketing, and Related Support Services, 12% Communication, Journalism, and Related Programs, 7% Visual and Performing Arts, 6% Biological and Biomedical Sciences, 6% Health Professions and Related Programs
Expenses: 2020-2021: $19,749 in state, $34,049 out of state; room/board: $10,817
Financial aid: (215) 204-2244; 67% of undergrads determined to have financial need; average aid package $13,237

Thiel College
Greenville PA
(800) 248-4435
U.S. News ranking: Reg. Coll. (N), No. 30
Website: www.thiel.edu
Admissions email: admission@thiel.edu
Private; founded 1866
Affiliation: Evangelical Lutheran Church
Freshman admissions: less selective; 2019-2020: 1,826 applied, 1,450 accepted. Either SAT or ACT required. SAT 25/75 percentile: 890-1150. High school rank: 13% in top tenth, 29% in top quarter, 63% in top half
Early decision deadline: N/A, notification date: N/A
Early action deadline: N/A, notification date: N/A
Application deadline (fall): rolling
Undergraduate student body: 701 full time, 4 part time; 53% male, 47% female; N/A American Indian, N/A Asian, N/A Black, N/A Hispanic, N/A multiracial, N/A Pacific Islander, N/A white, N/A international
Most popular majors: Information not available
Expenses: 2020-2021: $41,440; room/board: $13,496
Financial aid: (724) 589-2178

Thomas Jefferson University
Philadelphia PA
(800) 951-7287
U.S. News ranking: Nat. U., No. 176
Website: www.jefferson.edu/
Admissions email: enroll@jefferson.edu
Private; founded 1824
Freshman admissions: selective; 2019-2020: 4,317 applied, 2,844 accepted. Either SAT or ACT required. SAT 25/75 percentile: 1070-1270. High school rank: 23% in top tenth, 55% in top quarter, 84% in top half
Early decision deadline: N/A, notification date: N/A
Early action deadline: N/A, notification date: 11/15
Application deadline (fall): rolling
Undergraduate student body: 3,124 full time, 610 part time; 26% male, 74% female; 0% American Indian, 6% Asian, 14% Black, 11% Hispanic, 7% multiracial, 0% Pacific Islander, 56% white, 2% international; 63% from in state; 34% live on campus; 1% of students in fraternities, 1% in sororities
Most popular majors: Architecture, Business Administration and Management, General, Diagnostic Medical Sonography/Sonographer and Ultrasound Technician, Family Practice Nurse/Nursing, Fashion Merchandising
Expenses: 2020-2021: $41,715; room/board: $13,881
Financial aid: (215) 951-2940

University of Pennsylvania
Philadelphia PA
(215) 898-7507
U.S. News ranking: Nat. U., No. 8
Website: www.upenn.edu
Admissions email: info@admissions.upenn.edu
Private; founded 1740
Freshman admissions: most selective; 2019-2020: 44,961 applied, 3,446 accepted. Either SAT or ACT required. SAT 25/75 percentile: 1450-1560. High school rank: 94% in top tenth, 98% in top quarter, 100% in top half
Early decision deadline: 11/1, notification date: 12/15
Early action deadline: N/A, notification date: N/A
Application deadline (fall): 1/5
Undergraduate student body: 9,774 full time, 245 part time; 48% male, 52% female; 0% American Indian, 22% Asian, 8% Black, 10% Hispanic, 5% multiracial, 0% Pacific Islander, 39% white, 13% international
Most popular majors: 21% Business, Management, Marketing, and Related Support Services, 14% Social Sciences, 10% Biological and Biomedical Sciences, 10% Engineering, 10% Health Professions and Related Programs
Expenses: 2020-2021: $60,042; room/board: $16,784
Financial aid: (215) 898-1988; 46% of undergrads determined to have financial need; average aid package $54,314

University of Pittsburgh at Bradford
Bradford PA
(800) 872-1787
U.S. News ranking: Reg. Coll. (N), No. 19
Website: www.upb.pitt.edu
Admissions email: admissions@pitt.edu
Public; founded 1963
Freshman admissions: selective; 2019-2020: 2,852 applied, 1,642 accepted. Either SAT or ACT required. SAT 25/75 percentile: 970-1160. High school rank: 10% in top tenth, 39% in top quarter, 66% in top half
Early decision deadline: N/A, notification date: N/A
Early action deadline: N/A, notification date: N/A
Application deadline (fall): rolling
Undergraduate student body: 1,259 full time, 67 part time; 43% male, 57% female; 0% American Indian, 3% Asian, 14% Black, 7% Hispanic, 4% multiracial, 0% Pacific Islander, 67% white, 2% international; 74% from in state; 76% live on campus; 2% of students in fraternities, 3% in sororities
Most popular majors: 11% Biology/Biological Sciences, General, 10% Information Technology, 9% Business/Commerce, General, 9% Kinesiology and Exercise Science, 8% Criminal Justice/Law Enforcement Administration

Expenses: 2020-2021: $14,158 in state, $25,626 out of state; room/board: $9,612
Financial aid: (814) 362-7550; 84% of undergrads determined to have financial need; average aid package $15,266

University of Pittsburgh–Johnstown[1]

Johnstown PA
(814) 269-7000
U.S. News ranking: Reg. Coll. (N), No. 31
Admissions email: N/A
Public
Application deadline (fall): N/A
Undergraduate student body: N/A full time, N/A part time
Expenses: 2019-2020: $14,156 in state, $25,624 out of state; room/board: $10,060
Financial aid: N/A

University of Pittsburgh–Pittsburgh Campus

Pittsburgh PA
(412) 624-7488
U.S. News ranking: Nat. U., No. 58
Website: www.oafa.pitt.edu/
Admissions email: oafa@pitt.edu
Public; founded 1787
Freshman admissions: more selective; 2019-2020: 32,091 applied, 18,180 accepted. Either SAT or ACT required. SAT 25/75 percentile: 1260-1440. High school rank: 53% in top tenth, 86% in top quarter, 98% in top half
Early decision deadline: N/A, notification date: N/A
Early action deadline: N/A, notification date: N/A
Application deadline (fall): rolling
Undergraduate student body: 18,343 full time, 857 part time; 47% male, 53% female; 0% American Indian, 11% Asian, 5% Black, 5% Hispanic, 4% multiracial, 0% Pacific Islander, 68% white, 5% international; 66% from in state; 42% live on campus; 10% of students in fraternities, 12% in sororities
Most popular majors: 15% Business, Management, Marketing, and Related Support Services, 13% Engineering, 11% Health Professions and Related Programs, 10% Social Sciences, 9% Biological and Biomedical Sciences
Expenses: 2020-2021: $19,678 in state, $33,706 out of state; room/board: $11,250
Financial aid: (412) 624-7180; 49% of undergrads determined to have financial need; average aid package $13,834

University of Scranton

Scranton PA
(570) 941-7540
U.S. News ranking: Reg. U. (N), No. 6
Website: www.scranton.edu
Admissions email: admissions@scranton.edu
Private; founded 1888
Affiliation: Roman Catholic

Freshman admissions: more selective; 2019-2020: 9,545 applied, 7,285 accepted. Either SAT or ACT required. SAT 25/75 percentile: 1120-1310. High school rank: 34% in top tenth, 68% in top quarter, 92% in top half
Early decision deadline: N/A, notification date: N/A
Early action deadline: 11/15, notification date: 12/15
Application deadline (fall): 3/1
Undergraduate student body: 3,626 full time, 166 part time; 42% male, 58% female; 0% American Indian, 3% Asian, 2% Black, 10% Hispanic, 2% multiracial, 0% Pacific Islander, 78% white, 1% international; N/A from in state; 64% live on campus; N/A of students in fraternities, N/A in sororities
Most popular majors: 25% Business, Management, Marketing, and Related Support Services, 18% Health Professions and Related Programs, 13% Biological and Biomedical Sciences, 6% Parks, Recreation, Leisure, and Fitness Studies, 4% Communication, Journalism, and Related Programs
Expenses: 2020-2021: $47,084; room/board: $15,646
Financial aid: (570) 941-7701; 72% of undergrads determined to have financial need; average aid package $31,832

University of the Arts[1]

Philadelphia PA
(215) 717-6049
U.S. News ranking: Arts, unranked
Website: www.uarts.edu
Admissions email: admissions@uarts.edu
Private; founded 1876
Application deadline (fall): rolling
Undergraduate student body: N/A full time, N/A part time
Expenses: 2019-2020: $46,680; room/board: $16,958
Financial aid: (215) 717-6170

University of Valley Forge

Phoenixville PA
(800) 432-8322
U.S. News ranking: Reg. Coll. (N), No. 33
Website: www.valleyforge.edu/
Admissions email: admissions@valleyforge.edu
Private; founded 1939
Affiliation: Assemblies of God Church
Freshman admissions: less selective; 2019-2020: 394 applied, 247 accepted. Neither SAT nor ACT required. SAT 25/75 percentile: 950-1180. High school rank: 8% in top tenth, 19% in top quarter, 67% in top half
Early decision deadline: N/A, notification date: N/A
Early action deadline: N/A, notification date: N/A
Application deadline (fall): 8/1
Undergraduate student body: 423 full time, 127 part time; 47% male, 53% female; 0% American Indian, 2% Asian, 13% Black, 19% Hispanic, 6% multiracial, 0% Pacific Islander, 54% white,

2% international; 42% from in state; 89% live on campus; 0% of students in fraternities, 0% in sororities
Most popular majors: 34% Theology and Religious Vocations, 16% Communication, Journalism, and Related Programs, 12% Psychology, 9% Business, Management, Marketing, and Related Support Services, 8% Public Administration and Social Service Professions
Expenses: 2020-2021: $22,616; room/board: $9,360
Financial aid: (610) 917-1475; 85% of undergrads determined to have financial need; average aid package $17,241

Ursinus College

Collegeville PA
(610) 409-3200
U.S. News ranking: Nat. Lib. Arts, No. 84
Website: www.ursinus.edu
Admissions email: admission@ursinus.edu
Private; founded 1869
Freshman admissions: more selective; 2019-2020: 3,530 applied, 2,792 accepted. Neither SAT nor ACT required. SAT 25/75 percentile: 1150-1350. High school rank: 21% in top tenth, 50% in top quarter, 83% in top half
Early decision deadline: 12/1, notification date: 12/15
Early action deadline: 11/1, notification date: 12/15
Application deadline (fall): 2/1
Undergraduate student body: 1,457 full time, 15 part time; 50% male, 50% female; 0% American Indian, 4% Asian, 8% Black, 8% Hispanic, 3% multiracial, 0% Pacific Islander, 73% white, 1% international; 62% from in state; 93% live on campus; 13% of students in fraternities, 21% in sororities
Most popular majors: 31% Biological and Biomedical Sciences, 17% Social Sciences, 10% Psychology, 5% English Language and Literature/Letters, 4% Computer and Information Sciences and Support Services
Expenses: 2020-2021: $55,210; room/board: $13,530
Financial aid: (610) 409-3600; 75% of undergrads determined to have financial need; average aid package $42,703

Villanova University

Villanova PA
(610) 519-4500
U.S. News ranking: Nat. U., No. 53
Website: www.villanova.edu
Admissions email: gotovu@villanova.edu
Private; founded 1842
Affiliation: Roman Catholic
Freshman admissions: most selective; 2019-2020: 22,909 applied, 6,470 accepted. Either SAT or ACT required. SAT 25/75 percentile: 1320-1470. High school rank: 72% in top tenth, 93% in top quarter, 99% in top half
Early decision deadline: 11/1, notification date: 12/20

Early action deadline: 11/1, notification date: 1/15
Application deadline (fall): 1/15
Undergraduate student body: 6,528 full time, 337 part time; 47% male, 53% female; 0% American Indian, 6% Asian, 5% Black, 8% Hispanic, 3% multiracial, 0% Pacific Islander, 73% white, 3% international; 22% from in state; 76% live on campus; 21% of students in fraternities, 26% in sororities
Most popular majors: 26% Business, Management, Marketing, and Related Support Services, 14% Health Professions and Related Programs, 13% Engineering, 12% Social Sciences, 9% Communication, Journalism, and Related Programs
Expenses: 2020-2021: $57,710; room/board: $14,975
Financial aid: (610) 519-4010; 47% of undergrads determined to have financial need; average aid package $42,523

Washington and Jefferson College

Washington PA
(724) 223-6025
U.S. News ranking: Nat. Lib. Arts, No. 96
Website: www.washjeff.edu
Admissions email: admission@washjeff.edu
Private; founded 1781
Freshman admissions: selective; 2019-2020: 2,722 applied, 2,320 accepted. Neither SAT nor ACT required. SAT 25/75 percentile: 1090-1280. High school rank: 24% in top tenth, 48% in top quarter, 85% in top half
Early decision deadline: 12/1, notification date: 12/15
Early action deadline: 1/15, notification date: 2/15
Application deadline (fall): 3/1
Undergraduate student body: 1,259 full time, 3 part time; 49% male, 51% female; 0% American Indian, 2% Asian, 7% Black, 6% Hispanic, 3% multiracial, 0% Pacific Islander, 74% white, 3% international; 73% from in state; 92% live on campus; 31% of students in fraternities, 29% in sororities
Most popular majors: 21% Business/Commerce, General, 13% Psychology, General, 13% Social Sciences, General, 11% Biology/Biological Sciences, General, 6% English Language and Literature, General
Expenses: 2020-2021: $50,192; room/board: $13,272
Financial aid: (724) 223-6019; 79% of undergrads determined to have financial need; average aid package $40,457

Waynesburg University

Waynesburg PA
(800) 225-7393
U.S. News ranking: Reg. U. (N), No. 62
Website: www.waynesburg.edu/
Admissions email: admissions@waynesburg.edu
Private; founded 1849

Affiliation: Presbyterian Church (USA)
Freshman admissions: selective; 2019-2020: 1,589 applied, 1,470 accepted. Either SAT or ACT required. SAT 25/75 percentile: 950-1150. High school rank: 12% in top tenth, 38% in top quarter, 74% in top half
Early decision deadline: N/A, notification date: N/A
Early action deadline: N/A, notification date: N/A
Application deadline (fall): rolling
Undergraduate student body: 1,239 full time, 38 part time; 41% male, 59% female; 0% American Indian, 1% Asian, 3% Black, 3% Hispanic, 3% multiracial, 0% Pacific Islander, 85% white, 0% international; 77% from in state; 80% live on campus; N/A of students in fraternities, N/A in sororities
Most popular majors: 29% Registered Nursing/Registered Nurse, 12% Criminal Justice/Law Enforcement Administration, 11% Business Administration and Management, General, 8% Speech Communication and Rhetoric
Expenses: 2020-2021: $26,500; room/board: $11,030
Financial aid: (724) 852-3208; 81% of undergrads determined to have financial need; average aid package $21,679

West Chester University of Pennsylvania

West Chester PA
(610) 436-3414
U.S. News ranking: Reg. U. (N), No. 50
Website: www.wcupa.edu/
Admissions email: ugadmiss@wcupa.edu
Public; founded 1871
Freshman admissions: selective; 2019-2020: 15,085 applied, 11,354 accepted. Either SAT or ACT required. SAT 25/75 percentile: 1040-1210. High school rank: 10% in top tenth, 34% in top quarter, 69% in top half
Early decision deadline: N/A, notification date: N/A
Early action deadline: N/A, notification date: N/A
Application deadline (fall): rolling
Undergraduate student body: 13,044 full time, 1,571 part time; 41% male, 59% female; 0% American Indian, 2% Asian, 11% Black, 6% Hispanic, 4% multiracial, 0% Pacific Islander, 74% white, 0% international; 90% from in state; 36% live on campus; 11% of students in fraternities, 15% in sororities
Most popular majors: 25% Business, Management, Marketing, and Related Support Services, 16% Health Professions and Related Programs, 10% Education, 7% English Language and Literature/Letters, 6% Parks, Recreation, Leisure, and Fitness Studies
Expenses: 2020-2021: $9,993 in state, $21,567 out of state; room/board: $9,494

Financial aid: (610) 436-2627; 58% of undergrads determined to have financial need; average aid package $8,647

Westminster College

New Wilmington PA
(724) 946-7100
U.S. News ranking: Nat. Lib. Arts, No. 120
Website: www.westminster.edu
Admissions email: admis@westminster.edu
Private; founded 1852
Affiliation: Presbyterian Church (USA)
Freshman admissions: selective; 2019-2020: 2,459 applied, 1,636 accepted. Neither SAT nor ACT required. SAT 25/75 percentile: 970-1180. High school rank: 16% in top tenth, 48% in top quarter, 73% in top half
Early decision deadline: N/A, notification date: N/A
Early action deadline: 11/15, notification date: 12/1
Application deadline (fall): 5/1
Undergraduate student body: 1,110 full time, 55 part time; 47% male, 53% female; 1% American Indian, 0% Asian, 6% Black, 2% Hispanic, 1% multiracial, 0% Pacific Islander, 74% white, 0% international
Most popular majors: 11% Business Administration and Management, General, 10% Biology/Biological Sciences, General, 8% Education, Other, 7% Psychology, General, 5% Music Teacher Education
Expenses: 2020-2021: $37,675; room/board: $11,550
Financial aid: (724) 946-7102; 86% of undergrads determined to have financial need; average aid package $31,472

Widener University

Chester PA
(610) 499-4126
U.S. News ranking: Nat. U., No. 206
Website: www.widener.edu
Admissions email: admissions.office@widener.edu
Private; founded 1821
Freshman admissions: selective; 2019-2020: 6,245 applied, 4,490 accepted. Either SAT or ACT required. SAT 25/75 percentile: 1040-1210. High school rank: N/A
Early decision deadline: N/A, notification date: N/A
Early action deadline: N/A, notification date: N/A
Application deadline (fall): rolling
Undergraduate student body: 2,784 full time, 431 part time; 43% male, 57% female; 0% American Indian, 3% Asian, 12% Black, 5% Hispanic, 3% multiracial, 0% Pacific Islander, 73% white, 1% international; 59% from in state; 43% live on campus; 14% of students in fraternities, 19% in sororities
Most popular majors: 29% Health Professions and Related Programs, 18% Business, Management, Marketing, and Related Support Services, 17% Engineering,

7% Psychology, 5% Biological and Biomedical Sciences
Expenses: 2020-2021: $48,740; room/board: $14,812
Financial aid: (610) 499-4161; 78% of undergrads determined to have financial need; average aid package $35,270

Wilkes University

Wilkes-Barre PA
(570) 408-4400
U.S. News ranking: Nat. U., No. 217
Website: www.wilkes.edu
Admissions email: admissions@wilkes.edu
Private; founded 1933
Freshman admissions: selective; 2019-2020: 3,756 applied, 2,953 accepted. Either SAT or ACT required. SAT 25/75 percentile: 1020-1218. High school rank: 20% in top tenth, 47% in top quarter, 83% in top half
Early decision deadline: N/A, notification date: N/A
Early action deadline: N/A, notification date: N/A
Application deadline (fall): rolling
Undergraduate student body: 2,110 full time, 241 part time; 50% male, 50% female; 0% American Indian, 3% Asian, 4% Black, 7% Hispanic, 3% multiracial, 0% Pacific Islander, 74% white, 6% international; 77% from in state; 43% live on campus; N/A of students in fraternities, N/A in sororities
Most popular majors: 21% Business, Management, Marketing, and Related Support Services, 18% Health Professions and Related Programs, 17% Engineering, 7% Biological and Biomedical Sciences, 6% Social Sciences
Expenses: 2020-2021: $38,752; room/board: $15,400
Financial aid: (570) 408-4512; 81% of undergrads determined to have financial need; average aid package $28,253

Wilson College

Chambersburg PA
(800) 421-8402
U.S. News ranking: Reg. U. (N), No. 125
Website: www.wilson.edu
Admissions email: admissions@wilson.edu
Private; founded 1869
Affiliation: Presbyterian Church (USA)
Freshman admissions: selective; 2019-2020: 805 applied, 747 accepted. Neither SAT nor ACT required. SAT 25/75 percentile: 910-1190. High school rank: 10% in top tenth, 41% in top quarter, 83% in top half
Early decision deadline: N/A, notification date: N/A
Early action deadline: N/A, notification date: N/A
Application deadline (fall): rolling
Undergraduate student body: 689 full time, 383 part time; 21% male, 79% female; 0% American Indian, 1% Asian, 7% Black, 6% Hispanic, 2% multiracial, 0% Pacific Islander, 74% white, 3% international; 72% from in

state; 47% live on campus; 0% of students in fraternities, 0% in sororities
Most popular majors: 31% Registered Nursing/Registered Nurse, 23% Veterinary/Animal Health Technology/Technician and Veterinary Assistant, 5% Animal-Assisted Therapy, 4% Agriculture, Agriculture Operations, and Related Sciences, Other, 4% Biology/Biological Sciences, General
Expenses: 2020-2021: $26,090; room/board: $11,716
Financial aid: (717) 264-3787; 87% of undergrads determined to have financial need; average aid package $20,139

York College of Pennsylvania

York PA
(717) 849-1600
U.S. News ranking: Reg. U. (N), No. 93
Website: www.ycp.edu
Admissions email: admissions@ycp.edu
Private; founded 1787
Freshman admissions: selective; 2019-2020: 5,991 applied, 4,126 accepted. Either SAT or ACT required. SAT 25/75 percentile: 1000-1210. High school rank: 10% in top tenth, 33% in top quarter, 72% in top half
Early decision deadline: 12/15, notification date: 10/1
Early action deadline: N/A, notification date: N/A
Application deadline (fall): 9/5
Undergraduate student body: 3,685 full time, 351 part time; 44% male, 56% female; 0% American Indian, 2% Asian, 6% Black, 7% Hispanic, 3% multiracial, 0% Pacific Islander, 78% white, 1% international; N/A from in state; 55% live on campus; 6% of students in fraternities, 7% in sororities
Most popular majors: 23% Business, Management, Marketing, and Related Support Services, 16% Health Professions and Related Programs, 11% Education, 7% Engineering, 6% Homeland Security, Law Enforcement, Firefighting and Related Protective Services
Expenses: 2020-2021: $21,700; room/board: $11,890
Financial aid: (717) 815-6539; 68% of undergrads determined to have financial need; average aid package $14,171

PUERTO RICO

American University of Puerto Rico–Bayamon[1]

Bayamon PR
(787) 620-2040
U.S. News ranking: Reg. Coll. (S), second tier
Website: www.clark.edu
Admissions email: N/A
Private
Application deadline (fall): N/A

Undergraduate student body: N/A full time, N/A part time
Expenses: 2019-2020: N/A; room/board: N/A
Financial aid: N/A

American University of Puerto Rico–Manati[1]

Bayamon PR
(787) 620-2040
U.S. News ranking: Reg. Coll. (S), second tier
Website: www.aupr.edu/
Admissions email: N/A
Private
Application deadline (fall): N/A
Undergraduate student body: N/A full time, N/A part time
Expenses: 2019-2020: $6,365; room/board: N/A
Financial aid: N/A

Bayamon Central University[1]

Bayamon PR
(787) 786-3030
U.S. News ranking: Reg. U. (S), second tier
Website: www.ucb.edu.pr/
Admissions email: N/A
Private
Application deadline (fall): N/A
Undergraduate student body: N/A full time, N/A part time
Expenses: 2019-2020: $6,260; room/board: $5,724
Financial aid: N/A

Caribbean University[1]

Bayamon PR
(787) 780-0070
U.S. News ranking: Reg. U. (S), second tier
Website: www.caribbean.edu/
Admissions email: N/A
Private
Application deadline (fall): N/A
Undergraduate student body: N/A full time, N/A part time
Expenses: 2019-2020: $5,542; room/board: N/A
Financial aid: N/A

Colegio Universitario de San Juan[1]

San Juan PR
(787) 480-2400
U.S. News ranking: Reg. Coll. (S), second tier
Website: www.pierce.ctc.edu
Admissions email: N/A
Public
Application deadline (fall): N/A
Undergraduate student body: N/A full time, N/A part time
Expenses: 2019-2020: $2,370 in state, $2,370 out of state; room/board: $7,350
Financial aid: N/A

EDP University of Puerto Rico Inc–San Juan[1]

San Juan PR
(787) 765-3560
U.S. News ranking: Reg. U. (S), No. 77
Website: www.greenriver.edu/

Admissions email: N/A
Private
Application deadline (fall): N/A
Undergraduate student body: N/A full time, N/A part time
Expenses: 2019-2020: $6,200; room/board: N/A
Financial aid: N/A

Escuela de Artes Plasticas de Puerto Rico[1]

San Juan PR
(787) 725-8120
U.S. News ranking: Arts, unranked
Website: www.eap.edu
Admissions email: N/A
Public
Application deadline (fall): N/A
Undergraduate student body: N/A full time, N/A part time
Expenses: 2019-2020: $3,462 in state, $5,622 out of state; room/board: $8,144
Financial aid: N/A

Pontifical Catholic University of Puerto Rico–Arecibo[1]

Arecibo PR
(787) 841-2000
U.S. News ranking: Reg. U. (S), second tier
Website: www.edcc.edu
Admissions email: N/A
Private
Undergraduate student body: N/A full time, N/A part time
Expenses: 2019-2020: $5,478; room/board: N/A
Financial aid: N/A

Pontifical Catholic University of Puerto Rico–Ponce[1]

Ponce PR
(787) 841-2000
U.S. News ranking: Nat. U., second tier
Website: www.pucpr.edu
Admissions email: admisiones@pucpr.edu
Private; founded 1948
Affiliation: Roman Catholic
Application deadline (fall): 8/19
Undergraduate student body: N/A full time, N/A part time
Expenses: 2019-2020: $5,580; room/board: $5,091
Financial aid: (787) 841-2000

Puerto Rico Conservatory of Music[1]

San Juan PR
(787) 751-0160
U.S. News ranking: Arts, unranked
Website: www.cmpr.edu
Admissions email: admisiones@cmpr.edu
Public
Application deadline (fall): N/A
Undergraduate student body: N/A full time, N/A part time
Expenses: 2019-2020: $3,370 in state, $3,850 out of state; room/board: $10,000
Financial aid: N/A

Universidad Adventista de las Antillas[1]
Mayaguez PR
(787) 834-9595
U.S. News ranking: Reg. Coll. (S), second tier
Website: www.uaa.edu/esp/
Admissions email: N/A
Private
Application deadline (fall): N/A
Undergraduate student body: N/A full time, N/A part time
Expenses: 2019-2020: $7,250; room/board: $6,200
Financial aid: N/A

Universidad Ana G. Mendez– Carolina Campus[1]
Carolina PR
(787) 705-1403
U.S. News ranking: Reg. U. (S), second tier
Website: www.suagm.edu/une/
Admissions email: N/A
Private; founded 1949
Application deadline (fall): rolling
Undergraduate student body: N/A full time, N/A part time
Expenses: 2019-2020: $5,820; room/board: N/A
Financial aid: N/A

Universidad Ana G. Mendez– Cupey Campus[1]
Rio Piedras PR
(787) 766-1717
U.S. News ranking: Reg. U. (S), second tier
Website: www.suagm.edu/
Admissions email: N/A
Private
Application deadline (fall): rolling
Undergraduate student body: N/A full time, N/A part time
Expenses: 2019-2020: $5,820; room/board: N/A
Financial aid: N/A

Universidad Ana G. Mendez– Gurabo Campus[1]
Gurabo PR
(787) 743-7979
U.S. News ranking: Nat. U., second tier
Website: www.ut.suagm.edu
Admissions email: admisiones-ut@suagm.edu
Private; founded 1972
Application deadline (fall): rolling
Undergraduate student body: N/A full time, N/A part time
Expenses: 2019-2020: $5,820; room/board: N/A
Financial aid: N/A

Universidad Politecnica de Puerto Rico
Hato Rey PR
(787) 622-8000
U.S. News ranking: Engineering, unranked
Website: www.pupr.edu
Admissions email: admisiones@pupr.edu
Private; founded 1966

Freshman admissions: least selective; 2019-2020: 862 applied, 739 accepted. Neither SAT nor ACT required. SAT 25/75 percentile: N/A. High school rank: N/A
Early decision deadline: N/A, notification date: N/A
Early action deadline: N/A, notification date: N/A
Application deadline (fall): rolling
Undergraduate student body: 1,788 full time, 1,901 part time; 76% male, 24% female; 0% American Indian, 0% Asian, 0% Black, 100% Hispanic, 0% multiracial, 0% Pacific Islander, 0% white, 0% international; N/A from in state; 1% live on campus; N/A of students in fraternities, N/A in sororities
Most popular majors: 18% Engineering Mechanics, 14% Computer Engineering, General, 13% Electrical and Electronics Engineering, 10% Industrial Engineering, 8% Architecture
Expenses: 2019-2020: $8,640; room/board: $11,928
Financial aid: N/A

University of Puerto Rico– Aguadilla[1]
Aguadilla PR
(787) 890-2681
U.S. News ranking: Reg. Coll. (S), No. 31
Website: www.uprag.edu/
Admissions email: melba.serrano@upr.edu
Public; founded 1972
Application deadline (fall): 5/31
Undergraduate student body: N/A full time, N/A part time
Expenses: 2019-2020: $4,684 in state, $6,639 out of state; room/board: $11,161
Financial aid: (787) 890-2681

University of Puerto Rico–Arecibo
Arecibo PR
(787) 815-0000
U.S. News ranking: Reg. Coll. (S), No. 43
Website: www.upra.edu/
Admissions email: admisiones.arecibo@upr.edu
Public; founded 1967
Freshman admissions: less selective; 2019-2020: 1,658 applied, 918 accepted. Neither SAT nor ACT required. SAT 25/75 percentile: N/A. High school rank: N/A
Early decision deadline: N/A, notification date: N/A
Early action deadline: N/A, notification date: N/A
Application deadline (fall): 1/31
Undergraduate student body: 3,301 full time, 244 part time; 40% male, 60% female; 0% American Indian, 0% Asian, 0% Black, 100% Hispanic, 0% multiracial, 0% Pacific Islander, 0% white, 0% international
Most popular majors: 15% Microbiology, General, 14% Radio and Television Broadcasting Technology/Technician, 12% Registered Nursing/Registered Nurse, 11% Industrial and

Organizational Psychology, 8% Office Management and Supervision
Expenses: 2019-2020: $4,178 in state, $6,162 out of state; room/board: $11,161
Financial aid: (787) 815-0000

University of Puerto Rico– Bayamon[1]
Bayamon PR
(787) 993-8952
U.S. News ranking: Reg. Coll. (S), No. 43
Website: www.uprb.edu/
Admissions email: N/A
Public; founded 1971
Application deadline (fall): 2/15
Undergraduate student body: N/A full time, N/A part time
Expenses: 2019-2020: $4,089 in state, $7,999 out of state; room/board: N/A
Financial aid: (787) 993-8953

University of Puerto Rico–Cayey[1]
Cayey PR
(787) 738-2161
U.S. News ranking: Nat. Lib. Arts, No. 166
Website: cayey.upr.edu/oficina-de-admisiones/
Admissions email: admisiones.cayey@upr.edu
Public; founded 1967
Application deadline (fall): N/A
Undergraduate student body: N/A full time, N/A part time
Expenses: 2019-2020: $4,208 in state, $6,192 out of state; room/board: $11,161
Financial aid: (787) 738-2161

University of Puerto Rico– Humacao[1]
Humacao PR
(787) 850-9301
U.S. News ranking: Reg. Coll. (S), No. 18
Website: www.uprh.edu/~admision/
Admissions email: carmen.rivera19@upr.edu
Public; founded 1962
Application deadline (fall): 1/31
Undergraduate student body: N/A full time, N/A part time
Expenses: 2019-2020: $4,208 in state, $6,192 out of state; room/board: $11,161
Financial aid: N/A

University of Puerto Rico– Mayaguez[1]
Mayaguez PR
(787) 832-4040
U.S. News ranking: Reg. U. (S), No. 45
Website: www.uprm.edu
Admissions email: admisiones@uprm.edu
Public; founded 1911
Affiliation: Undenominational
Application deadline (fall): 6/11
Undergraduate student body: N/A full time, N/A part time

Expenses: 2019-2020: $4,168 in state, $6,152 out of state; room/board: $11,161
Financial aid: (787) 265-3863

University of Puerto Rico–Ponce[1]
Ponce PR
(787) 844-8181
U.S. News ranking: Nat. Lib. Arts, second tier
Website: www.uprp.edu
Admissions email: admi.ponce@upr.edu
Public; founded 1970
Application deadline (fall): 1/31
Undergraduate student body: N/A full time, N/A part time
Expenses: 2019-2020: $4,394 in state, $6,536 out of state; room/board: N/A
Financial aid: (787) 844-8181

University of Puerto Rico– Rio Piedras[1]
Rio Piedras PR
(787) 764-3680
U.S. News ranking: Nat. U., No. 196
Website: www.uprrp.edu/
Admissions email: N/A
Public; founded 1903
Application deadline (fall): 1/31
Undergraduate student body: N/A full time, N/A part time
Expenses: 2019-2020: $4,178 in state, $6,162 out of state; room/board: $11,161
Financial aid: (787) 552-1324

University of Puerto Rico–Utuado[1]
Utuado PR
(787) 894-2316
U.S. News ranking: Reg. Coll. (S), second tier
Website: www.uprutuado.edu
Admissions email: admisiones.utuado@upr.edu
Public; founded 1978
Application deadline (fall): 1/31
Undergraduate student body: N/A full time, N/A part time
Expenses: 2019-2020: $4,198 in state, $6,182 out of state; room/board: $6,146
Financial aid: (787) 894-3810

University of the Sacred Heart[1]
Santurce PR
(787) 728-1515
U.S. News ranking: Reg. U. (S), second tier
Website: www.sagrado.edu/
Admissions email: admision@sagrado.edu
Private; founded 1935
Affiliation: Roman Catholic
Application deadline (fall): N/A
Undergraduate student body: N/A full time, N/A part time
Expenses: 2019-2020: $6,000; room/board: $9,400
Financial aid: (787) 728-1515

Brown University
Providence RI
(401) 863-2378
U.S. News ranking: Nat. U., No. 14
Website: www.brown.edu/admission/undergraduate/
Admissions email: admission@brown.edu
Private; founded 1764
Freshman admissions: most selective; 2019-2020: 38,674 applied, 2,733 accepted. Either SAT or ACT required. SAT 25/75 percentile: 1440-1570. High school rank: 91% in top tenth, 98% in top quarter, 100% in top half
Early decision deadline: 11/1, notification date: 12/15
Early action deadline: N/A, notification date: N/A
Application deadline (fall): 1/1
Undergraduate student body: 6,826 full time, 334 part time; 47% male, 53% female; 0% American Indian, 17% Asian, 7% Black, 11% Hispanic, 6% multiracial, 0% Pacific Islander, 43% white, 11% international; 5% from in state; 72% live on campus; 11% of students in fraternities, 12% in sororities
Most popular majors: 11% Computer Science, 8% Econometrics and Quantitative Economics, 7% Biology/Biological Sciences, General, 5% Entrepreneurship/Entrepreneurial Studies, 5% History, General
Expenses: 2020-2021: $60,696; room/board: $15,908
Financial aid: (401) 863-2721; 42% of undergrads determined to have financial need; average aid package $55,513

Bryant University
Smithfield RI
(800) 622-7001
U.S. News ranking: Reg. U. (N), No. 7
Website: www.bryant.edu
Admissions email: admission@bryant.edu
Private; founded 1863
Freshman admissions: more selective; 2019-2020: 7,633 applied, 5,419 accepted. Neither SAT nor ACT required. SAT 25/75 percentile: 1130-1300. High school rank: 20% in top tenth, 48% in top quarter, 88% in top half
Early decision deadline: 11/1, notification date: 12/1
Early action deadline: 11/15, notification date: 1/15
Application deadline (fall): 2/1
Undergraduate student body: 3,205 full time, 54 part time; 63% male, 37% female; 0% American Indian, 3% Asian, 3% Black, 6% Hispanic, 2% multiracial, 0% Pacific Islander, 75% white, 8% international; N/A from in state; 81% live on campus; 7% of students in fraternities, 13% in sororities
Most popular majors: 79% Business, Management, Marketing, and Related Support Services, 5% Mathematics and Statistics, 4% Communication,

Journalism, and Related Programs, 4% Social Sciences, 3% Biological and Biomedical Sciences
Expenses: 2020-2021: $46,863; room/board: $15,893
Financial aid: (401) 232-6020; 58% of undergrads determined to have financial need; average aid package $25,940

Johnson & Wales University
Providence RI
(800) 342-5598
U.S. News ranking: Reg. U. (N), No. 96
Website: www.jwu.edu/
Admissions email: pvd@admissions.jwu.edu
Private; founded 1914
Freshman admissions: selective; 2019-2020: 11,668 applied, 10,819 accepted. Neither SAT nor ACT required. SAT 25/75 percentile: 1000-1190. High school rank: 5% in top tenth, 30% in top quarter, 78% in top half
Early decision deadline: N/A, notification date: N/A
Early action deadline: 11/1, notification date: 11/15
Application deadline (fall): rolling
Undergraduate student body: 5,767 full time, 356 part time; 40% male, 60% female; 0% American Indian, 3% Asian, 13% Black, 13% Hispanic, 2% multiracial, 0% Pacific Islander, 56% white, 6% international
Most popular majors: 37% Business, Management, Marketing, and Related Support Services, 17% Family and Consumer Sciences/Human Sciences, 10% Parks, Recreation, Leisure, and Fitness Studies, 10% Personal and Culinary Services, 8% Homeland Security, Law Enforcement, Firefighting and Related Protective Services
Expenses: 2020-2021: $34,736; room/board: $12,950
Financial aid: (401) 598-1857; 76% of undergrads determined to have financial need; average aid package $26,281

New England Institute of Technology
East Greenwich RI
(800) 736-7744
U.S. News ranking: Reg. Coll. (N), No. 15
Website: www.neit.edu/
Admissions email: NEITAdmissions@neit.edu
Private; founded 1940
Freshman admissions: selective; 2019-2020: 1,969 applied, 1,254 accepted. Neither SAT nor ACT required. SAT 25/75 percentile: 970-1147. High school rank: N/A
Early decision deadline: N/A, notification date: N/A
Early action deadline: N/A, notification date: N/A
Application deadline (fall): rolling
Undergraduate student body: 2,020 full time, 294 part time; 65% male, 35% female; 0% American Indian, 0% Asian, 1% Black,

10% Hispanic, 3% multiracial, 0% Pacific Islander, 13% white, 1% international; 48% from in state; 10% live on campus; 0% of students in fraternities, 0% in sororities
Most popular majors: Computer Programming/Programmer, General, Computer and Information Systems Security/Information Assurance, Game and Interactive Media Design, Mechanical Engineering, Registered Nursing/Registered Nurse
Expenses: 2020-2021: $31,545; room/board: $13,425
Financial aid: (401) 780-4108

Providence College
Providence RI
(401) 865-2535
U.S. News ranking: Reg. U. (N), No. 1
Website: www.providence.edu
Admissions email: pcadmiss@providence.edu
Private; founded 1917
Affiliation: Roman Catholic
Freshman admissions: more selective; 2019-2020: 11,478 applied, 5,447 accepted. Neither SAT nor ACT required. SAT 25/75 percentile: 1210-1350. High school rank: 41% in top tenth, 75% in top quarter, 96% in top half
Early decision deadline: 11/15, notification date: 1/1
Early action deadline: 11/1, notification date: 1/1
Application deadline (fall): 1/15
Undergraduate student body: 4,158 full time, 209 part time; 46% male, 54% female; 0% American Indian, 1% Asian, 4% Black, 10% Hispanic, 2% multiracial, 0% Pacific Islander, 77% white, 2% international; 9% from in state; 80% live on campus; 0% of students in fraternities, 0% in sororities
Most popular majors: 42% Business, Management, Marketing, and Related Support Services, 11% Social Sciences, 10% Biological and Biomedical Sciences, 7% Psychology, 5% Education
Expenses: 2020-2021: $54,388; room/board: $15,590
Financial aid: (401) 865-2286; 48% of undergrads determined to have financial need; average aid package $36,988

Rhode Island College
Providence RI
(800) 669-5760
U.S. News ranking: Reg. U. (N), No. 113
Website: www.ric.edu
Admissions email: admissions@ric.edu
Public; founded 1854
Freshman admissions: less selective; 2019-2020: 4,753 applied, 3,726 accepted. Either SAT or ACT required. SAT 25/75 percentile: 880-1080. High school rank: 16% in top tenth, 37% in top quarter, 75% in top half
Early decision deadline: N/A, notification date: N/A

Early action deadline: N/A, notification date: N/A
Application deadline (fall): 3/15
Undergraduate student body: 4,942 full time, 1,490 part time; 31% male, 69% female; 0% American Indian, 3% Asian, 11% Black, 23% Hispanic, 2% multiracial, 0% Pacific Islander, 55% white, 0% international; N/A from in state; 14% live on campus; N/A of students in fraternities, N/A in sororities
Most popular majors: 21% Business, Management, Marketing, and Related Support Services, 20% Health Professions and Related Programs, 11% Psychology, 9% Education, 8% Public Administration and Social Service Professions
Expenses: 2020-2021: $10,195 in state, $14,612 out of state; room/board: $12,660
Financial aid: (401) 456-8033; 72% of undergrads determined to have financial need; average aid package $9,843

Rhode Island School of Design
Providence RI
(401) 454-6300
U.S. News ranking: Arts, unranked
Website: www.risd.edu
Admissions email: admissions@risd.edu
Private; founded 1877
Freshman admissions: more selective; 2019-2020: 3,832 applied, 987 accepted. Neither SAT nor ACT required. SAT 25/75 percentile: 1230-1470. High school rank: N/A
Early decision deadline: 11/1, notification date: 12/12
Early action deadline: N/A, notification date: N/A
Application deadline (fall): 2/1
Undergraduate student body: 2,009 full time, 0 part time; 32% male, 68% female; 0% American Indian, 19% Asian, 4% Black, 9% Hispanic, 6% multiracial, 0% Pacific Islander, 27% white, 32% international; 4% from in state; 60% live on campus; N/A of students in fraternities, N/A in sororities
Most popular majors: 17% Illustration, 17% Systems Science and Theory, 12% Graphic Design, 8% Film/Video and Photographic Arts, Other, 8% Painting
Expenses: 2020-2021: $54,890; room/board: $14,430
Financial aid: (401) 454-6661; 36% of undergrads determined to have financial need; average aid package $33,321

Roger Williams University
Bristol RI
(800) 458-7144
U.S. News ranking: Reg. U. (N), No. 31
Website: www.rwu.edu
Admissions email: admit@rwu.edu
Private; founded 1956
Freshman admissions: selective; 2019-2020: 8,906 applied, 7,601 accepted. Neither SAT nor ACT required. SAT 25/75 percentile: 1065-1240. High

school rank: 12% in top tenth, 37% in top quarter, 69% in top half
Early decision deadline: N/A, notification date: N/A
Early action deadline: 11/15, notification date: 12/1
Application deadline (fall): 2/1
Undergraduate student body: 4,022 full time, 501 part time; 49% male, 51% female; 0% American Indian, 2% Asian, 2% Black, 8% Hispanic, 2% multiracial, 0% Pacific Islander, 77% white, 1% international; 22% from in state; 73% live on campus; N/A of students in fraternities, N/A in sororities
Most popular majors: 29% Business, Management, Marketing, and Related Support Services, 10% Homeland Security, Law Enforcement, Firefighting and Related Protective Services, 8% Architecture and Related Services, 7% Biological and Biomedical Sciences, 7% Psychology
Expenses: 2020-2021: $38,274; room/board: $15,698
Financial aid: (401) 254-3100; 67% of undergrads determined to have financial need; average aid package $24,895

Salve Regina University
Newport RI
(888) 467-2583
U.S. News ranking: Reg. U. (N), No. 31
Website: www.salve.edu
Admissions email: admissions@salve.edu
Private; founded 1934
Affiliation: Roman Catholic
Freshman admissions: selective; 2019-2020: 4,889 applied, 3,607 accepted. Neither SAT nor ACT required. SAT 25/75 percentile: 1100-1260. High school rank: 18% in top tenth, 43% in top quarter, 81% in top half
Early decision deadline: N/A, notification date: N/A
Early action deadline: 11/1, notification date: 12/25
Application deadline (fall): rolling
Undergraduate student body: 2,091 full time, 76 part time; 35% male, 65% female; 0% American Indian, 1% Asian, 2% Black, 7% Hispanic, 3% multiracial, 0% Pacific Islander, 82% white, 2% international; 16% from in state; 59% live on campus; 0% of students in fraternities, 0% in sororities
Most popular majors: 23% Business Administration and Management, General, 18% Registered Nursing/Registered Nurse, 11% Education, 8% Criminal Justice/Law Enforcement Administration, 7% Biology/Biological Sciences, General
Expenses: 2020-2021: $42,920; room/board: $15,400
Financial aid: (401) 341-2901; 76% of undergrads determined to have financial need; average aid package $28,725

University of Rhode Island
Kingston RI
(401) 874-7100
U.S. News ranking: Nat. U., No. 170
Website: www.uri.edu
Admissions email: admission@uri.edu
Public; founded 1892
Freshman admissions: selective; 2019-2020: 22,687 applied, 16,908 accepted. Either SAT or ACT required. SAT 25/75 percentile: 1080-1260. High school rank: 18% in top tenth, 49% in top quarter, 85% in top half
Early decision deadline: N/A, notification date: N/A
Early action deadline: 12/1, notification date: 1/31
Application deadline (fall): 2/1
Undergraduate student body: 12,591 full time, 1,199 part time; 44% male, 56% female; 0% American Indian, 3% Asian, 5% Black, 11% Hispanic, 3% multiracial, 0% Pacific Islander, 73% white, 1% international; 51% from in state; 43% live on campus; 17% of students in fraternities, 28% in sororities
Most popular majors: 11% Registered Nursing/Registered Nurse, 7% Psychology, General, 6% Speech Communication and Rhetoric, 4% Kinesiology and Exercise Science, 3% Health-Related Knowledge and Skills, Other
Expenses: 2020-2021: $15,004 in state, $32,578 out of state; room/board: $12,977
Financial aid: (401) 874-9500; 82% of undergrads determined to have financial need; average aid package $17,680

SOUTH CAROLINA

Allen University[1]
Columbia SC
(803) 376-5735
U.S. News ranking: Nat. Lib. Arts, second tier
Website: www.allenuniversity.edu
Admissions email: admissions@allenuniversity.edu
Private; founded 1870
Application deadline (fall): rolling
Undergraduate student body: N/A full time, N/A part time
Expenses: 2019-2020: $13,340; room/board: $7,592
Financial aid: (803) 376-5930

Anderson University
Anderson SC
(864) 231-5607
U.S. News ranking: Reg. U. (S), No. 42
Website: www.andersonuniversity.edu
Admissions email: admission@andersonuniversity.edu
Private; founded 1911
Affiliation: Southern Baptist
Freshman admissions: more selective; 2019-2020: 2,276 applied, 1,564 accepted. Either SAT or ACT required. SAT 25/75 percentile: 1060-1250. High school rank: 41% in top tenth,

62% in top quarter, 85% in top half
Early decision deadline: N/A, notification date: N/A
Early action deadline: N/A, notification date: N/A
Application deadline (fall): rolling
Undergraduate student body: 2,544 full time, 349 part time; 31% male, 69% female; 0% American Indian, 1% Asian, 5% Black, 4% Hispanic, 2% multiracial, 0% Pacific Islander, 84% white, 1% international; 80% from in state; 49% live on campus; N/A of students in fraternities, N/A in sororities
Most popular majors: 26% Business, Management, Marketing, and Related Support Services, 19% Health Professions and Related Programs, 18% Education, 9% Visual and Performing Arts, 5% Homeland Security, Law Enforcement, Firefighting and Related Protective Services
Expenses: 2020-2021: $29,980; room/board: $10,640
Financial aid: (864) 231-2181; 76% of undergrads determined to have financial need; average aid package $21,124

Benedict College[1]
Columbia SC
(803) 253-5143
U.S. News ranking: Reg. Coll. (S), second tier
Website: www.benedict.edu
Admissions email: admissions@benedict.edu
Private; founded 1870
Application deadline (fall): rolling
Undergraduate student body: N/A full time, N/A part time
Expenses: 2019-2020: $16,600; room/board: $6,200
Financial aid: N/A

Bob Jones University
Greenville SC
(800) 252-6363
U.S. News ranking: Reg. U. (S), No. 33
Website: www.bju.edu/admission
Admissions email: admission@bju.edu
Private; founded 1927
Affiliation: Evangelical Christian
Freshman admissions: selective; 2019-2020: 1,275 applied, 1,045 accepted. Either SAT or ACT required. ACT 25/75 percentile: 20-28. High school rank: 13% in top tenth, 35% in top quarter, 62% in top half
Early decision deadline: N/A, notification date: N/A
Early action deadline: N/A, notification date: N/A
Application deadline (fall): rolling
Undergraduate student body: 2,313 full time, 338 part time; 45% male, 55% female; 0% American Indian, 2% Asian, 2% Black, 5% Hispanic, 2% multiracial, 0% Pacific Islander, 58% white, 7% international; 35% from in state; 74% live on campus; N/A of students in fraternities, N/A in sororities
Most popular majors: 8% Business Administration and Management,

General, 6% Health Professions and Related Programs, 5% Accounting, 5% Registered Nursing/Registered Nurse, 4% Biology/Biological Sciences, General
Expenses: 2020-2021: $20,700; room/board: $7,900
Financial aid: (864) 242-5100; 71% of undergrads determined to have financial need; average aid package $14,368

Charleston Southern University
Charleston SC
(843) 863-7050
U.S. News ranking: Reg. U. (S), No. 62
Website: www.charlestonsouthern.edu/
Admissions email: N/A
Private; founded 1964
Affiliation: Baptist
Freshman admissions: selective; 2019-2020: 5,398 applied, 2,680 accepted. Either SAT or ACT required. SAT 25/75 percentile: 1020-1200. High school rank: 21% in top tenth, 50% in top quarter, 80% in top half
Early decision deadline: N/A, notification date: N/A
Early action deadline: N/A, notification date: N/A
Application deadline (fall): rolling
Undergraduate student body: 2,558 full time, 326 part time; 36% male, 64% female; 0% American Indian, 2% Asian, 19% Black, 5% Hispanic, 4% multiracial, 0% Pacific Islander, 61% white, 1% international; 84% from in state; N/A live on campus; 0% of students in fraternities, 0% in sororities
Most popular majors: 12% Registered Nursing/Registered Nurse, 6% Biology/Biological Sciences, General, 6% Kinesiology and Exercise Science, 6% Psychology, General, 5% Criminal Justice/Law Enforcement Administration
Expenses: 2020-2021: $27,800; room/board: $10,400
Financial aid: (843) 863-7050

The Citadel, The Military College of South Carolina
Charleston SC
(843) 953-5230
U.S. News ranking: Reg. U. (S), No. 2
Website: www.citadel.edu
Admissions email: admissions@citadel.edu
Public; founded 1842
Affiliation: Undenominational
Freshman admissions: selective; 2019-2020: 2,740 applied, 2,049 accepted. Either SAT or ACT required. SAT 25/75 percentile: 1050-1230. High school rank: 11% in top tenth, 31% in top quarter, 71% in top half
Early decision deadline: N/A, notification date: N/A
Early action deadline: N/A, notification date: N/A

Application deadline (fall): rolling
Undergraduate student body: 2,688 full time, 235 part time; 87% male, 13% female; 0% American Indian, 2% Asian, 7% Black, 7% Hispanic, 5% multiracial, 0% Pacific Islander, 76% white, 1% international; 67% from in state; 100% live on campus; 0% of students in fraternities, 0% in sororities
Most popular majors: 28% Business Administration and Management, General, 25% Engineering, General, 10% Criminal Justice/Law Enforcement Administration, 8% Social Sciences, General, 7% Kinesiology and Exercise Science
Expenses: 2020-2021: $14,643 in state, $38,528 out of state; room/board: $7,957
Financial aid: (843) 953-5187; 56% of undergrads determined to have financial need; average aid package $19,584

Claflin University
Orangeburg SC
(800) 922-1276
U.S. News ranking: Reg. Coll. (S), No. 9
Website: www.claflin.edu
Admissions email: admissions@claflin.edu
Private; founded 1869
Affiliation: United Methodist
Freshman admissions: less selective; 2019-2020: 9,081 applied, 5,013 accepted. Either SAT or ACT required. SAT 25/75 percentile: 880-1040. High school rank: 12% in top tenth, 33% in top quarter, 78% in top half
Early decision deadline: N/A, notification date: N/A
Early action deadline: N/A, notification date: N/A
Application deadline (fall): 8/1
Undergraduate student body: 1,889 full time, 97 part time; 32% male, 68% female; 1% American Indian, 1% Asian, 91% Black, 1% Hispanic, 0% multiracial, 0% Pacific Islander, 1% white, 3% international; 76% from in state; 76% live on campus; 10% of students in fraternities, 10% in sororities
Most popular majors: 13% Psychology, General, 10% Criminal Justice/Safety Studies, 10% Mass Communication/Media Studies, 9% Biology/Biological Sciences, General, 9% Business Administration and Management, General
Expenses: 2019-2020: $17,192; room/board: $9,480
Financial aid: (803) 535-5720

Clemson University
Clemson SC
(864) 656-2287
U.S. News ranking: Nat. U., No. 74
Website: www.clemson.edu
Admissions email: cuadmissions@clemson.edu
Public; founded 1889
Freshman admissions: more selective; 2019-2020: 29,070 applied, 14,900 accepted. Either SAT or ACT required. SAT 25/75 percentile: 1230-1400. High

school rank: 56% in top tenth, 87% in top quarter, 98% in top half
Early decision deadline: N/A, notification date: N/A
Early action deadline: N/A, notification date: N/A
Application deadline (fall): 5/1
Undergraduate student body: 19,486 full time, 709 part time; 50% male, 50% female; 0% American Indian, 3% Asian, 6% Black, 6% Hispanic, 4% multiracial, 0% Pacific Islander, 81% white, 1% international; 67% from in state; 33% live on campus; 16% of students in fraternities, 31% in sororities
Most popular majors: 21% Engineering, 19% Business, Management, Marketing, and Related Support Services, 10% Biological and Biomedical Sciences, 7% Health Professions and Related Programs, 6% Social Sciences
Expenses: 2019-2020: $15,120 in state, $38,112 out of state; room/board: $11,414
Financial aid: (864) 656-2280; 46% of undergrads determined to have financial need; average aid package $11,679

Coastal Carolina University
Conway SC
(843) 349-2170
U.S. News ranking: Reg. U. (S), No. 45
Website: www.coastal.edu
Admissions email: admissions@coastal.edu
Public; founded 1954
Freshman admissions: selective; 2019-2020: 15,061 applied, 10,373 accepted. Either SAT or ACT required. SAT 25/75 percentile: 1010-1170. High school rank: 12% in top tenth, 35% in top quarter, 69% in top half
Early decision deadline: N/A, notification date: N/A
Early action deadline: N/A, notification date: N/A
Application deadline (fall): rolling
Undergraduate student body: 8,810 full time, 950 part time; 45% male, 55% female; 0% American Indian, 1% Asian, 18% Black, 5% Hispanic, 5% multiracial, 0% Pacific Islander, 67% white, 1% international; 50% from in state; 45% live on campus; 2% of students in fraternities, 6% in sororities
Most popular majors: 9% Speech Communication and Rhetoric, 8% Business Administration and Management, General, 7% Kinesiology and Exercise Science, 7% Marine Biology and Biological Oceanography, 7% Marketing/Marketing Management, General
Expenses: 2020-2021: $11,640 in state, $27,394 out of state; room/board: $9,290
Financial aid: (843) 349-2313; 68% of undergrads determined to have financial need; average aid package $11,712

Coker College[1]
Hartsville SC
(843) 383-8050
U.S. News ranking: Reg. U. (S), No. 59
Website: www.coker.edu
Admissions email: admissions@coker.edu
Private; founded 1908
Undergraduate student body: N/A full time, N/A part time
Expenses: 2020-2021: $31,524; room/board: $9,892
Financial aid: (843) 383-8050

College of Charleston
Charleston SC
(843) 953-5670
U.S. News ranking: Reg. U. (S), No. 8
Website: www.cofc.edu
Admissions email: admissions@cofc.edu
Public; founded 1770
Freshman admissions: selective; 2019-2020: 11,783 applied, 9,230 accepted. Either SAT or ACT required. SAT 25/75 percentile: 1080-1260. High school rank: 22% in top tenth, 52% in top quarter, 86% in top half
Early decision deadline: 11/1, notification date: 12/1
Early action deadline: 12/1, notification date: 1/15
Application deadline (fall): 2/15
Undergraduate student body: 8,762 full time, 838 part time; 36% male, 64% female; 0% American Indian, 2% Asian, 7% Black, 6% Hispanic, 4% multiracial, 0% Pacific Islander, 78% white, 1% international; 65% from in state; 33% live on campus; 15% of students in fraternities, 24% in sororities
Most popular majors: 25% Business, Management, Marketing, and Related Support Services, 12% Biological and Biomedical Sciences, 10% Social Sciences, 9% Visual and Performing Arts, 6% Psychology
Expenses: 2020-2021: $12,978 in state, $33,308 out of state; room/board: N/A
Financial aid: (843) 953-5540; 49% of undergrads determined to have financial need; average aid package $14,372

Columbia College
Columbia SC
(800) 277-1301
U.S. News ranking: Reg. U. (S), No. 47
Website: www.columbiasc.edu
Admissions email: admissions@columbiasc.edu
Private; founded 1854
Affiliation: United Methodist
Freshman admissions: least selective; 2019-2020: 820 applied, 792 accepted. Neither SAT nor ACT required. SAT 25/75 percentile: 840-1040. High school rank: 8% in top tenth, 15% in top quarter, 63% in top half
Early decision deadline: N/A, notification date: N/A
Early action deadline: N/A, notification date: N/A
Application deadline (fall): rolling

Undergraduate student body: 763 full time, 339 part time; 16% male, 84% female; 0% American Indian, 1% Asian, 37% Black, 6% Hispanic, 4% multiracial, 0% Pacific Islander, 34% white, 1% international; 87% from in state; 37% live on campus; 0% of students in fraternities, 4% in sororities
Most popular majors: 25% Criminal Justice/Safety Studies, 9% Crisis/Emergency/Disaster Management, 7% Business Administration and Management, General, 5% Biology/Biological Sciences, General, 5% Psychology, General
Expenses: 2020-2021: $19,890; room/board: $8,300
Financial aid: (803) 786-3612; 87% of undergrads determined to have financial need; average aid package $14,022

Columbia International University
Columbia SC
(800) 777-2227
U.S. News ranking: Reg. U. (S), No. 42
Website: www.ciu.edu
Admissions email: yesciu@ciu.edu
Private; founded 1923
Affiliation: Multiple Protestant Denominations
Freshman admissions: selective; 2019-2020: 336 applied, 161 accepted. Either SAT or ACT required. SAT 25/75 percentile: 930-1140. High school rank: 10% in top tenth, 26% in top quarter, 65% in top half
Early decision deadline: N/A, notification date: N/A
Early action deadline: N/A, notification date: N/A
Application deadline (fall): 8/1
Undergraduate student body: 531 full time, 90 part time; 50% male, 50% female; 0% American Indian, 1% Asian, 19% Black, 6% Hispanic, 1% multiracial, 0% Pacific Islander, 63% white, 5% international; N/A from in state; 72% live on campus; N/A of students in fraternities, N/A in sororities
Most popular majors: 57% Theology and Religious Vocations, 12% Liberal Arts and Sciences, General Studies and Humanities, 6% Psychology, 5% Business, Management, Marketing, and Related Support Services, 4% Education
Expenses: 2020-2021: $24,650; room/board: $8,950
Financial aid: (803) 807-5037; 84% of undergrads determined to have financial need; average aid package $19,354

Converse College[1]
Spartanburg SC
(864) 596-9040
U.S. News ranking: Reg. U. (S), No. 22
Website: www.converse.edu
Admissions email: admissions@converse.edu
Private; founded 1889
Application deadline (fall): 8/1
Undergraduate student body: N/A full time, N/A part time

Expenses: 2020-2021: $19,860; room/board: $11,600
Financial aid: (864) 596-9019

Erskine College
Due West SC
(864) 379-8838
U.S. News ranking: Reg. Coll. (S), No. 7
Website: www.erskine.edu
Admissions email: admissions@erskine.edu
Private; founded 1839
Affiliation: Presbyterian
Freshman admissions: selective; 2019-2020: 1,074 applied, 748 accepted. Either SAT or ACT required. SAT 25/75 percentile: 920-1140. High school rank: 14% in top tenth, 28% in top quarter, 71% in top half
Early decision deadline: N/A, notification date: N/A
Early action deadline: N/A, notification date: N/A
Application deadline (fall): rolling
Undergraduate student body: 771 full time, 13 part time; 64% male, 36% female; 1% American Indian, 2% Asian, 21% Black, 4% Hispanic, 0% multiracial, 1% Pacific Islander, 58% white, 0% international
Most popular majors: 26% Business Administration, Management and Operations, 17% Biology, General, 13% Parks, Recreation, Leisure, and Fitness Studies, 12% Psychology, 9% Parks, Recreation, Leisure, and Fitness Studies
Expenses: 2020-2021: $36,510; room/board: $11,465
Financial aid: (864) 379-8886

Francis Marion University
Florence SC
(843) 661-1231
U.S. News ranking: Reg. U. (S), No. 68
Website: www.fmarion.edu
Admissions email: admissions@fmarion.edu
Public; founded 1970
Freshman admissions: less selective; 2019-2020: 4,162 applied, 2,860 accepted. Either SAT or ACT required. ACT 25/75 percentile: 16-21. High school rank: 13% in top tenth, 36% in top quarter, 77% in top half
Early decision deadline: N/A, notification date: N/A
Early action deadline: N/A, notification date: N/A
Application deadline (fall): rolling
Undergraduate student body: 2,900 full time, 900 part time; 32% male, 68% female; 0% American Indian, 1% Asian, 40% Black, 3% Hispanic, 4% multiracial, 0% Pacific Islander, 49% white, 1% international; 94% from in state; 41% live on campus; 5% of students in fraternities, 7% in sororities
Most popular majors: 25% Health Professions and Related Programs, 17% Business, Management, Marketing, and Related Support Services, 15% Biological and Biomedical Sciences, 9% Psychology, 7% Social Sciences

Expenses: 2020-2021: $11,160 in state, $21,544 out of state; room/board: $8,230
Financial aid: (843) 661-1190; 82% of undergrads determined to have financial need; average aid package $11,180

Furman University
Greenville SC
(864) 294-2034
U.S. News ranking: Nat. Lib. Arts, No. 52
Website: www.furman.edu/
Admissions email: admissions@furman.edu
Private; founded 1826
Freshman admissions: more selective; 2019-2020: 5,258 applied, 2,987 accepted. Neither SAT nor ACT required. ACT 25/75 percentile: 28-32. High school rank: 55% in top tenth, 75% in top quarter, 96% in top half
Early decision deadline: 11/15, notification date: 12/1
Early action deadline: 11/1, notification date: 12/20
Application deadline (fall): 1/15
Undergraduate student body: 2,614 full time, 73 part time; 39% male, 61% female; 0% American Indian, 3% Asian, 6% Black, 5% Hispanic, 3% multiracial, 0% Pacific Islander, 79% white, 3% international; 30% from in state; 96% live on campus; 30% of students in fraternities, 57% in sororities
Most popular majors: 11% Business Administration and Management, General, 10% Speech Communication and Rhetoric, 8% Health Professions and Related Clinical Sciences, Other, 7% Political Science and Government, General, 7% Psychology, General
Expenses: 2020-2021: $52,092; room/board: $13,362
Financial aid: (864) 294-2351; 47% of undergrads determined to have financial need; average aid package $42,039

Lander University
Greenwood SC
(864) 388-8307
U.S. News ranking: Reg. Coll. (S), No. 41
Website: www.lander.edu
Admissions email: admissions@lander.edu
Public; founded 1872
Freshman admissions: selective; 2019-2020: 5,774 applied, 2,492 accepted. Either SAT or ACT required. SAT 25/75 percentile: 940-1130. High school rank: 12% in top tenth, 38% in top quarter, 72% in top half
Early decision deadline: N/A, notification date: N/A
Early action deadline: N/A, notification date: N/A
Application deadline (fall): rolling
Undergraduate student body: 2,941 full time, 203 part time; 32% male, 68% female; 1% American Indian, 1% Asian, 27% Black, 4% Hispanic, 0% multiracial, 0% Pacific Islander, 62% white, 3% international

Most popular majors: 24% Business Administration and Management, General, 10% Registered Nursing/Registered Nurse, 7% Kinesiology and Exercise Science, 6% Psychology, General, 5% Art/Art Studies, General
Expenses: 2020-2021: $11,700 in state, $21,300 out of state; room/board: $9,970
Financial aid: (864) 388-8340; 67% of undergrads determined to have financial need; average aid package $12,785

Limestone University
Gaffney SC
(864) 488-4554
U.S. News ranking: Reg. Coll. (S), No. 55
Website: www.limestone.edu
Admissions email: admiss@limestone.edu
Private; founded 1845
Affiliation: Undenominational
Freshman admissions: selective; 2019-2020: 2,446 applied, 353 accepted. Neither SAT nor ACT required. SAT 25/75 percentile: 880-1060. High school rank: 10% in top tenth, 23% in top quarter, 60% in top half
Early decision deadline: N/A, notification date: N/A
Early action deadline: N/A, notification date: N/A
Application deadline (fall): 8/22
Undergraduate student body: 1,707 full time, 469 part time; 46% male, 54% female; 1% American Indian, 0% Asian, 45% Black, 4% Hispanic, 0% multiracial, 0% Pacific Islander, 44% white, 3% international; 79% from in state; 90% live on campus; 2% of students in fraternities, 2% in sororities
Most popular majors: 27% Business, Management, Marketing, and Related Support Services, 20% Public Administration and Social Service Professions, 5% Liberal Arts and Sciences, General Studies and Humanities, 4% Health Professions and Related Programs, 4% Parks, Recreation, Leisure, and Fitness Studies
Expenses: 2020-2021: $26,300; room/board: $10,262
Financial aid: (864) 488-8251; 90% of undergrads determined to have financial need; average aid package $12,821

Morris College[1]
Sumter SC
(803) 934-3225
U.S. News ranking: Reg. Coll. (S), second tier
Website: www.morris.edu
Admissions email: admissions@morris.edu
Private; founded 1908
Affiliation: Baptist
Application deadline (fall): rolling
Undergraduate student body: N/A full time, N/A part time
Expenses: 2019-2020: $14,326; room/board: $6,344
Financial aid: N/A

Newberry College
Newberry SC
(800) 845-4955
U.S. News ranking: Reg. Coll. (S), No. 11
Website: www.newberry.edu/
Admissions email: admission@newberry.edu
Private; founded 1856
Affiliation: Lutheran Church in America
Freshman admissions: less selective; 2019-2020: 1,968 applied, 1,235 accepted. Either SAT or ACT required. SAT 25/75 percentile: 870-1100. High school rank: 5% in top tenth, 26% in top quarter, 50% in top half
Early decision deadline: N/A, notification date: N/A
Early action deadline: N/A, notification date: N/A
Application deadline (fall): rolling
Undergraduate student body: 1,225 full time, 46 part time; 56% male, 44% female; 0% American Indian, 1% Asian, 31% Black, 2% Hispanic, 3% multiracial, 0% Pacific Islander, 51% white, 6% international; 82% from in state; 83% live on campus; 11% of students in fraternities, 21% in sororities
Most popular majors: 20% Business Administration and Management, General, 14% Registered Nursing/Registered Nurse, 13% Parks, Recreation and Leisure Studies, 10% Education, General, 8% Psychology, General
Expenses: 2020-2021: $28,150; room/board: $11,300
Financial aid: (803) 321-5127; 86% of undergrads determined to have financial need; average aid package $24,660

North Greenville University
Tigerville SC
(864) 977-7001
U.S. News ranking: Reg. U. (S), No. 53
Website: www.ngu.edu
Admissions email: admissions@ngu.edu
Private; founded 1892
Affiliation: Southern Baptist
Freshman admissions: selective; 2019-2020: 1,695 applied, 1,040 accepted. Either SAT or ACT required. ACT 25/75 percentile: 19-28. High school rank: 17% in top tenth, 35% in top quarter, 73% in top half
Early decision deadline: N/A, notification date: N/A
Early action deadline: N/A, notification date: N/A
Application deadline (fall): 8/22
Undergraduate student body: 1,736 full time, 431 part time; 45% male, 55% female; 0% American Indian, 1% Asian, 7% Black, 4% Hispanic, 3% multiracial, 0% Pacific Islander, 77% white, 1% international; 78% from in state; 63% live on campus; N/A of students in fraternities, N/A in sororities
Most popular majors: 21% Business, Management, Marketing, and Related Support Services, 16% Education, 13% Liberal Arts and Sciences,

General Studies and Humanities, 10% Theology and Religious Vocations, 9% Parks, Recreation, Leisure, and Fitness Studies
Expenses: 2020-2021: $22,050; room/board: $10,450
Financial aid: (864) 977-7057; 96% of undergrads determined to have financial need; average aid package $16,987

Presbyterian College
Clinton SC
(800) 960-7583
U.S. News ranking: Nat. Lib. Arts, No. 127
Website: www.presby.edu
Admissions email: mfox@presby.edu
Private; founded 1880
Affiliation: Presbyterian Church (USA)
Freshman admissions: selective; 2019-2020: 2,141 applied, 1,616 accepted. Neither SAT nor ACT required. SAT 25/75 percentile: 1000-1230. High school rank: 24% in top tenth, 53% in top quarter, 81% in top half
Early decision deadline: N/A, notification date: N/A
Early action deadline: 11/15, notification date: 12/15
Application deadline (fall): 6/30
Undergraduate student body: 1,041 full time, 61 part time; 48% male, 52% female; 0% American Indian, 1% Asian, 16% Black, 5% Hispanic, 4% multiracial, 0% Pacific Islander, 69% white, 3% international; 69% from in state; 94% live on campus; 33% of students in fraternities, 44% in sororities
Most popular majors: 30% Business, Management, Marketing, and Related Support Services, 12% Biological and Biomedical Sciences, 12% Social Sciences, 11% Psychology, 7% History
Expenses: 2020-2021: $40,260; room/board: $10,900
Financial aid: (864) 833-8287; 79% of undergrads determined to have financial need; average aid package $36,727

South Carolina State University
Orangeburg SC
(803) 536-7185
U.S. News ranking: Reg. U. (S), No. 84
Website: www.scsu.edu
Admissions email: admissions@scsu.edu
Public; founded 1896
Freshman admissions: least selective; 2019-2020: 2,631 applied, 1,748 accepted. Either SAT or ACT required. ACT 25/75 percentile: 15-17. High school rank: 13% in top tenth, 25% in top quarter, 49% in top half
Early decision deadline: N/A, notification date: N/A
Early action deadline: N/A, notification date: N/A
Application deadline (fall): 7/31
Undergraduate student body: 1,958 full time, 197 part time; 47% male, 53% female; 0% American Indian, 0% Asian, 95% Black,

0% Hispanic, 1% multiracial, 0% Pacific Islander, 2% white, 0% international; 89% from in state; 71% live on campus; 2% of students in fraternities, 3% in sororities
Most popular majors: 15% Business, Management, Marketing, and Related Support Services, 14% Family and Consumer Sciences/Human Sciences, 13% Education, 8% Engineering Technologies and Engineering-Related Fields, 8% Homeland Security, Law Enforcement, Firefighting and Related Protective Services
Expenses: 2019-2020: $11,060 in state, $21,750 out of state; room/board: $9,890
Financial aid: (803) 536-7067

Southern Wesleyan University[1]
Central SC
(864) 644-5550
U.S. News ranking: Reg. U. (S), No. 77
Website: www.swu.edu
Admissions email: admissions@swu.edu
Private
Application deadline (fall): N/A
Undergraduate student body: N/A full time, N/A part time
Expenses: 2019-2020: $25,516; room/board: $9,190
Financial aid: N/A

University of South Carolina
Columbia SC
(803) 777-7700
U.S. News ranking: Nat. U., No. 118
Website: www.sc.edu
Admissions email: admissions-ugrad@sc.edu
Public; founded 1801
Freshman admissions: more selective; 2019-2020: 31,268 applied, 21,464 accepted. Either SAT or ACT required. SAT 25/75 percentile: 1180-1370. High school rank: 28% in top tenth, 59% in top quarter, 90% in top half
Early decision deadline: N/A, notification date: N/A
Early action deadline: 10/15, notification date: 12/20
Application deadline (fall): 12/1
Undergraduate student body: 26,400 full time, 1,102 part time; 46% male, 54% female; 0% American Indian, 3% Asian, 8% Black, 5% Hispanic, 4% multiracial, 0% Pacific Islander, 76% white, 3% international; 61% from in state; 27% live on campus; 22% of students in fraternities, 33% in sororities
Most popular majors: 7% Finance and Financial Management Services, 5% Biology, General, 5% Public Health, 4% Marketing, 4% Research and Experimental Psychology
Expenses: 2020-2021: $12,688 in state, $33,928 out of state; room/board: $10,962
Financial aid: (803) 777-8134; 49% of undergrads determined to have financial need; average aid package $9,887

University of South Carolina–Aiken
Aiken SC
(803) 641-3366
U.S. News ranking: Reg. Coll. (S), No. 12
Website: www.usca.edu/
Admissions email: admit@usca.edu
Public; founded 1961
Freshman admissions: selective; 2019-2020: 2,775 applied, 1,547 accepted. Either SAT or ACT required. SAT 25/75 percentile: 960-1140. High school rank: 16% in top tenth, 44% in top quarter, 78% in top half
Early decision deadline: N/A, notification date: N/A
Early action deadline: N/A, notification date: N/A
Application deadline (fall): 7/1
Undergraduate student body: 2,585 full time, 667 part time; 35% male, 65% female; 0% American Indian, 1% Asian, 26% Black, 5% Hispanic, 5% multiracial, 0% Pacific Islander, 58% white, 2% international; 88% from in state; 27% live on campus; 10% of students in fraternities, 8% in sororities
Most popular majors: 22% Business, Management, Marketing, and Related Support Services, 15% Health Professions and Related Programs, 12% Education, 9% Biological and Biomedical Sciences, 9% Parks, Recreation, Leisure, and Fitness Studies
Expenses: 2020-2021: $10,760 in state, $21,218 out of state; room/board: $8,010
Financial aid: (803) 641-3476; 67% of undergrads determined to have financial need; average aid package $12,097

University of South Carolina–Beaufort
Bluffton SC
(843) 208-8000
U.S. News ranking: Nat. Lib. Arts, second tier
Website: www.uscb.edu
Admissions email: admissions@uscb.edu
Public; founded 1959
Freshman admissions: selective; 2019-2020: 2,167 applied, 1,360 accepted. Either SAT or ACT required. SAT 25/75 percentile: 930-1100. High school rank: 11% in top tenth, 33% in top quarter, 68% in top half
Early decision deadline: N/A, notification date: N/A
Early action deadline: N/A, notification date: N/A
Application deadline (fall): 7/1
Undergraduate student body: 1,726 full time, 386 part time; 32% male, 68% female; 0% American Indian, 1% Asian, 22% Black, 8% Hispanic, 5% multiracial, 0% Pacific Islander, 60% white, 1% international; 84% from in state; 44% live on campus; 0% of students in fraternities, 6% in sororities
Most popular majors: 22% Business Administration and Management, General, 13% Biology/Biological Sciences,

General, 13% Sociology, 12% Registered Nursing/Registered Nurse, 11% Hospitality Administration/Management, General
Expenses: 2019-2020: $10,730 in state, $21,776 out of state; room/board: $9,186
Financial aid: (843) 521-4117

University of South Carolina–Upstate
Spartanburg SC
(864) 503-5246
U.S. News ranking: Reg. Coll. (S), No. 12
Website: www.uscupstate.edu/
Admissions email: admissions@uscupstate.edu
Public; founded 1967
Freshman admissions: selective; 2019-2020: 4,033 applied, 1,907 accepted. Either SAT or ACT required. SAT 25/75 percentile: 920-1110. High school rank: 12% in top tenth, 35% in top quarter, 73% in top half
Early decision deadline: N/A, notification date: N/A
Early action deadline: N/A, notification date: N/A
Application deadline (fall): rolling
Undergraduate student body: 4,637 full time, 1,216 part time; 34% male, 66% female; 0% American Indian, 3% Asian, 33% Black, 7% Hispanic, 4% multiracial, 0% Pacific Islander, 50% white, 2% international; N/A from in state; 18% live on campus; N/A of students in fraternities, N/A in sororities
Most popular majors: 26% Health Professions and Related Programs, 14% Business, Management, Marketing, and Related Support Services, 12% Education, 7% Biological and Biomedical Sciences, 7% Homeland Security, Law Enforcement, Firefighting and Related Protective Services
Expenses: 2020-2021: $11,925 in state, $23,427 out of state; room/board: $8,598
Financial aid: (864) 503-5340

Voorhees College
Denmark SC
(803) 780-1030
U.S. News ranking: Reg. Coll. (S), No. 55
Website: www.voorhees.edu
Admissions email: admissions@voorhees.edu
Private; founded 1897
Affiliation: Protestant Episcopal
Freshman admissions: least selective; 2019-2020: 7,036 applied, 4,538 accepted. Neither SAT nor ACT required. Average composite ACT score: 17. High school rank: N/A
Early decision deadline: N/A, notification date: N/A
Early action deadline: N/A, notification date: N/A
Application deadline (fall): N/A
Undergraduate student body: 492 full time, 18 part time; 42% male, 58% female; 0% American Indian, 0% Asian, 98% Black, 0% Hispanic, 0% multiracial, 0% Pacific Islander, 1% white, 1% international

Most popular majors: 13% Child Development, 12% Organizational Behavior Studies, 12% Sport and Fitness Administration/Management, 11% Business Administration and Management, General, 11% Criminal Justice/Law Enforcement Administration
Expenses: 2020-2021: $12,630; room/board: $7,346
Financial aid: (803) 780-1151; 96% of undergrads determined to have financial need; average aid package $14,319

Winthrop University
Rock Hill SC
(803) 323-2191
U.S. News ranking: Reg. U. (S), No. 13
Website: www.winthrop.edu
Admissions email: admissions@winthrop.edu
Public; founded 1886
Affiliation: Other
Freshman admissions: selective; 2019-2020: 6,101 applied, 4,196 accepted. Either SAT or ACT required. SAT 25/75 percentile: 950-1160. High school rank: 14% in top tenth, 41% in top quarter, 76% in top half
Early decision deadline: N/A, notification date: N/A
Early action deadline: N/A, notification date: N/A
Application deadline (fall): rolling
Undergraduate student body: 4,236 full time, 528 part time; 31% male, 69% female; 0% American Indian, 1% Asian, 31% Black, 6% Hispanic, 4% multiracial, 0% Pacific Islander, 55% white, 1% international; 90% from in state; 47% live on campus; 1% of students in fraternities, 2% in sororities
Most popular majors: 20% Business, Management, Marketing, and Related Support Services, 13% Education, 9% Visual and Performing Arts, 8% Parks, Recreation, Leisure, and Fitness Studies, 7% Social Sciences
Expenses: 2020-2021: $15,836 in state, $30,166 out of state; room/board: $8,876
Financial aid: (803) 323-2189; 74% of undergrads determined to have financial need; average aid package $13,866

Wofford College
Spartanburg SC
(864) 597-4130
U.S. News ranking: Nat. Lib. Arts, No. 69
Website: www.wofford.edu
Admissions email: admissions@wofford.edu
Private; founded 1854
Affiliation: United Methodist
Freshman admissions: more selective; 2019-2020: 3,787 applied, 2,265 accepted. Neither SAT nor ACT required. SAT 25/75 percentile: 1190-1350. High school rank: 39% in top tenth, 70% in top quarter, 94% in top half
Early decision deadline: 11/1, notification date: 12/1
Early action deadline: 11/15, notification date: 2/1

Application deadline (fall): 1/15
Undergraduate student body: 1,648 full time, 19 part time; 48% male, 52% female; 0% American Indian, 2% Asian, 8% Black, 5% Hispanic, 3% multiracial, 0% Pacific Islander, 80% white, 2% international; N/A from in state; 91% live on campus; 46% of students in fraternities, 57% in sororities
Most popular majors: 22% Business, Management, Marketing, and Related Support Services, 16% Social Sciences, 13% Biological and Biomedical Sciences, 11% Foreign Languages, Literatures, and Linguistics, 7% English Language and Literature/Letters
Expenses: 2020-2021: $47,650; room/board: $13,790
Financial aid: (864) 597-4160; 60% of undergrads determined to have financial need; average aid package $39,677

SOUTH DAKOTA

Augustana University
Sioux Falls SD
(605) 274-5516
U.S. News ranking: Reg. U. (Mid. W), No. 13
Website: www.augie.edu
Admissions email: admission@augie.edu
Private; founded 1860
Affiliation: Evangelical Lutheran Church
Freshman admissions: more selective; 2019-2020: 2,224 applied, 1,488 accepted. Neither SAT nor ACT required. ACT 25/75 percentile: 23-29. High school rank: 32% in top tenth, 64% in top quarter, 90% in top half
Early decision deadline: N/A, notification date: N/A
Early action deadline: N/A, notification date: N/A
Application deadline (fall): rolling
Undergraduate student body: 1,727 full time, 91 part time; 37% male, 63% female; 1% American Indian, 2% Asian, 2% Black, 3% Hispanic, 2% multiracial, 0% Pacific Islander, 85% white, 6% international; 51% from in state; 65% live on campus; 0% of students in fraternities, 0% in sororities
Most popular majors: 16% Education, 16% Health Professions and Related Programs, 15% Business, Management, Marketing, and Related Support Services, 10% Biological and Biomedical Sciences, 9% Social Sciences
Expenses: 2020-2021: $35,884; room/board: $8,616
Financial aid: (605) 274-5216; 61% of undergrads determined to have financial need; average aid package $27,245

Black Hills State University
Spearfish SD
(605) 642-6131
U.S. News ranking: Reg. U. (Mid. W), second tier
Website: www.bhsu.edu/

Admissions email: Admissions@bhsu.edu
Public; founded 1887
Freshman admissions: selective; 2019-2020: 1,808 applied, 1,787 accepted. Either SAT or ACT required. ACT 25/75 percentile: 18-24. High school rank: N/A
Early decision deadline: N/A, notification date: N/A
Early action deadline: N/A, notification date: N/A
Application deadline (fall): rolling
Undergraduate student body: 1,944 full time, 1,738 part time; 37% male, 63% female; 4% American Indian, 1% Asian, 1% Black, 6% Hispanic, 5% multiracial, 0% Pacific Islander, 81% white, 1% international
Most popular majors: Information not available
Expenses: 2020-2021: $9,009 in state, $12,155 out of state; room/board: $7,142
Financial aid: (605) 642-6145

Dakota State University
Madison SD
(888) 378-9988
U.S. News ranking: Reg. U. (Mid. W), No. 91
Website: www.dsu.edu
Admissions email: admissions@dsu.edu
Public; founded 1881
Freshman admissions: selective; 2019-2020: 978 applied, 757 accepted. Either SAT or ACT required. ACT 25/75 percentile: 19-25. High school rank: 8% in top tenth, 23% in top quarter, 56% in top half
Early decision deadline: N/A, notification date: N/A
Early action deadline: N/A, notification date: N/A
Application deadline (fall): rolling
Undergraduate student body: 1,503 full time, 1,315 part time; 62% male, 38% female; 1% American Indian, 2% Asian, 3% Black, 4% Hispanic, 4% multiracial, 0% Pacific Islander, 82% white, 2% international; N/A from in state; 38% live on campus; 0% of students in fraternities, 0% in sororities
Most popular majors: 52% Computer and Information Sciences and Support Services, 17% Education, 11% Business, Management, Marketing, and Related Support Services, 6% Liberal Arts and Sciences, General Studies and Humanities, 4% Health Professions and Related Programs
Expenses: 2020-2021: $9,535 in state, $12,606 out of state; room/board: $7,148
Financial aid: (605) 256-5152; 64% of undergrads determined to have financial need; average aid package $8,233

Dakota Wesleyan University
Mitchell SD
(800) 333-8506
U.S. News ranking: Reg. Coll. (Mid. W), No. 23
Website: www.dwu.edu

Admissions email: admissions@dwu.edu
Private; founded 1885
Affiliation: United Methodist
Freshman admissions: selective; 2019-2020: 916 applied, 611 accepted. Either SAT or ACT required. ACT 25/75 percentile: 19-24. High school rank: 11% in top tenth, 38% in top quarter, 67% in top half
Early decision deadline: N/A, notification date: N/A
Early action deadline: N/A, notification date: N/A
Application deadline (fall): rolling
Undergraduate student body: 630 full time, 117 part time; 43% male, 57% female; 2% American Indian, 1% Asian, 1% Black, 7% Hispanic, 3% multiracial, 0% Pacific Islander, 84% white, 2% international; 74% from in state; 89% live on campus; 0% of students in fraternities, 0% in sororities
Most popular majors: 38% Registered Nursing/Registered Nurse, 6% Elementary Education and Teaching, 5% Accounting, 5% Athletic Training/Trainer, 3% Biology/Biological Sciences, General
Expenses: 2020-2021: $29,770; room/board: $7,100
Financial aid: (605) 995-2663; 76% of undergrads determined to have financial need; average aid package $18,937

Mount Marty University
Yankton SD
(855) 686-2789
U.S. News ranking: Reg. U. (Mid. W), No. 108
Website: www.mountmarty.edu
Admissions email: mmcadmit@mtmc.edu
Private; founded 1936
Freshman admissions: selective; 2019-2020: 479 applied, 343 accepted. Either SAT or ACT required. ACT 25/75 percentile: 18-24. High school rank: N/A
Early decision deadline: N/A, notification date: N/A
Early action deadline: N/A, notification date: N/A
Application deadline (fall): 8/30
Undergraduate student body: 526 full time, 343 part time; 43% male, 57% female; 3% American Indian, 1% Asian, 5% Black, 7% Hispanic, 1% multiracial, 0% Pacific Islander, 78% white, 3% international; 48% from in state; 65% live on campus; 0% of students in fraternities, 0% in sororities
Most popular majors: 20% Registered Nursing/Registered Nurse, 17% Education, General, 10% Business Administration and Management, General, 8% Criminal Justice/Safety Studies, 7% Social Sciences, General
Expenses: 2020-2021: $29,136; room/board: $8,346
Financial aid: (605) 668-1589; 85% of undergrads determined to have financial need; average aid package $31,753

National American University[1]
Rapid City SD
(605) 394-4827
U.S. News ranking: Reg. Coll. (Mid. W), unranked
Website: www.national.edu/rc
Admissions email: N/A
For-profit
Application deadline (fall): N/A
Undergraduate student body: N/A full time, N/A part time
Expenses: 2019-2020: $15,000; room/board: N/A
Financial aid: N/A

Northern State University
Aberdeen SD
(800) 678-5330
U.S. News ranking: Reg. U. (Mid. W), No. 80
Website: www.northern.edu
Admissions email: admissions@northern.edu
Public; founded 1901
Freshman admissions: selective; 2019-2020: 1,409 applied, 1,191 accepted. Either SAT or ACT required. ACT 25/75 percentile: 19-25. High school rank: 12% in top tenth, 30% in top quarter, 61% in top half
Early decision deadline: N/A, notification date: N/A
Early action deadline: N/A, notification date: N/A
Application deadline (fall): rolling
Undergraduate student body: 1,265 full time, 1,743 part time; 42% male, 58% female; 2% American Indian, 2% Asian, 2% Black, 3% Hispanic, 4% multiracial, 0% Pacific Islander, 81% white, 4% international; 69% from in state; 41% live on campus; 0% of students in fraternities, 0% in sororities
Most popular majors: 34% Business, Management, Marketing, and Related Support Services, 23% Education, 10% Biological and Biomedical Sciences, 8% Parks, Recreation, Leisure, and Fitness Studies, 7% Social Sciences
Expenses: 2020-2021: $8,750 in state, $11,821 out of state; room/board: $8,925
Financial aid: (605) 626-2640; 63% of undergrads determined to have financial need; average aid package $12,135

South Dakota School of Mines and Technology
Rapid City SD
(605) 394-5209
U.S. News ranking: Engineering, unranked
Website: www.sdsmt.edu
Admissions email: admissions@sdsmt.edu
Public; founded 1885
Freshman admissions: more selective; 2019-2020: 1,504 applied, 1,152 accepted. Either SAT or ACT required. ACT 25/75 percentile: 24-29. High school rank: 25% in top tenth, 55% in top quarter, 86% in top half

Early decision deadline: N/A, notification date: N/A
Early action deadline: N/A, notification date: N/A
Application deadline (fall): rolling
Undergraduate student body: 1,870 full time, 336 part time; 76% male, 24% female; 1% American Indian, 1% Asian, 2% Black, 5% Hispanic, 4% multiracial, 0% Pacific Islander, 83% white, 3% international; 47% from in state; 40% live on campus; 12% of students in fraternities, 22% in sororities
Most popular majors: 21% Mechanical Engineering, 14% Civil Engineering, General, 10% Chemical Engineering, 9% Computer and Information Sciences, General, 9% Industrial Engineering
Expenses: 2020-2021: $11,020 in state, $15,400 out of state; room/board: $9,240
Financial aid: (605) 394-2274

South Dakota State University
Brookings SD
(800) 952-3541
U.S. News ranking: Nat. U., No. 284
Website: www.sdstate.edu/
Admissions email: SDSU.Admissions@sdstate.edu
Public; founded 1881
Freshman admissions: selective; 2019-2020: 5,861 applied, 5,277 accepted. Either SAT or ACT required. ACT 25/75 percentile: 19-26. High school rank: 16% in top tenth, 39% in top quarter, 73% in top half
Early decision deadline: N/A, notification date: N/A
Early action deadline: N/A, notification date: N/A
Application deadline (fall): 9/1
Undergraduate student body: 7,971 full time, 2,102 part time; 47% male, 53% female; 1% American Indian, 1% Asian, 2% Black, 3% Hispanic, 2% multiracial, 0% Pacific Islander, 87% white, 4% international; N/A from in state; N/A live on campus; 3% of students in fraternities, 3% in sororities
Most popular majors: 21% Health Professions and Related Programs, 18% Agriculture, Agriculture Operations, and Related Sciences, 8% Social Sciences, 7% Engineering, 6% Education
Expenses: 2020-2021: $9,200 in state, $12,675 out of state; room/board: $8,069
Financial aid: (605) 688-4695; 52% of undergrads determined to have financial need; average aid package $8,344

University of Sioux Falls
Sioux Falls SD
(605) 331-6600
U.S. News ranking: Reg. U. (Mid. W), No. 86
Website: www.usiouxfalls.edu
Admissions email: admissions@usiouxfalls.edu
Private; founded 1883
Affiliation: American Baptist

Freshman admissions: selective; 2019-2020: 1,929 applied, 1,764 accepted. Either SAT or ACT required. ACT 25/75 percentile: 20-25. High school rank: 12% in top tenth, 39% in top quarter, 77% in top half
Early decision deadline: N/A, notification date: N/A
Early action deadline: N/A, notification date: N/A
Application deadline (fall): rolling
Undergraduate student body: 1,206 full time, 184 part time; 37% male, 63% female; 1% American Indian, 1% Asian, 5% Black, 2% Hispanic, 6% multiracial, 0% Pacific Islander, 84% white, 1% international; 56% from in state; 43% live on campus; N/A of students in fraternities, N/A in sororities
Most popular majors: 20% Business, Management, Marketing, and Related Support Services, 19% Health Professions and Related Programs, 9% Education, 9% Parks, Recreation, Leisure, and Fitness Studies, 8% Psychology
Expenses: 2020-2021: $19,520; room/board: $7,770
Financial aid: (605) 331-6623; 66% of undergrads determined to have financial need; average aid package $13,160

University of South Dakota
Vermillion SD
(877) 269-6837
U.S. News ranking: Nat. U., No. 249
Website: www.usd.edu
Admissions email: admissions@usd.edu
Public; founded 1862
Freshman admissions: selective; 2019-2020: 4,434 applied, 3,830 accepted. Either SAT or ACT required. ACT 25/75 percentile: 19-25. High school rank: 12% in top tenth, 32% in top quarter, 67% in top half
Early decision deadline: N/A, notification date: N/A
Early action deadline: N/A, notification date: N/A
Application deadline (fall): N/A
Undergraduate student body: 4,899 full time, 2,576 part time; 37% male, 63% female; N/A American Indian, N/A Asian, N/A Black, N/A Hispanic, N/A multiracial, N/A Pacific Islander, N/A white, N/A international
Most popular majors: Information not available
Expenses: 2020-2021: $9,332 in state, $12,807 out of state; room/board: $8,598
Financial aid: (605) 658-6250

TENNESSEE

Austin Peay State University
Clarksville TN
(931) 221-7661
U.S. News ranking: Reg. U. (S), No. 53
Website: www.apsu.edu
Admissions email: admissions@apsu.edu

Public; founded 1927
Freshman admissions: selective; 2019-2020: 7,416 applied, 7,044 accepted. Neither SAT nor ACT required. ACT 25/75 percentile: 19-24. High school rank: 12% in top tenth, 34% in top quarter, 68% in top half
Early decision deadline: N/A, notification date: N/A
Early action deadline: N/A, notification date: N/A
Application deadline (fall): 8/21
Undergraduate student body: 6,773 full time, 3,198 part time; 42% male, 58% female; 0% American Indian, 2% Asian, 23% Black, 9% Hispanic, 7% multiracial, 0% Pacific Islander, 57% white, 1% international; N/A from in state; 14% live on campus; 5% of students in fraternities, 7% in sororities
Most popular majors: 13% Health Professions and Related Programs, 12% Parks, Recreation, Leisure, and Fitness Studies, 10% Business, Management, Marketing, and Related Support Services, 7% Liberal Arts and Sciences, General Studies and Humanities, 6% Psychology
Expenses: 2020-2021: $8,627 in state, $14,171 out of state; room/board: N/A
Financial aid: (931) 221-7907; 83% of undergrads determined to have financial need; average aid package $5,776

Belmont University
Nashville TN
(615) 460-6785
U.S. News ranking: Nat. U., No. 160
Website: www.Belmont.edu
Admissions email: buadmission@belmont.edu
Private; founded 1890
Affiliation: Interdenominational
Freshman admissions: more selective; 2019-2020: 7,965 applied, 6,675 accepted. Either SAT or ACT required. ACT 25/75 percentile: 24-29. High school rank: 32% in top tenth, 61% in top quarter, 91% in top half
Early decision deadline: N/A, notification date: N/A
Early action deadline: N/A, notification date: N/A
Application deadline (fall): 8/1
Undergraduate student body: 6,563 full time, 245 part time; 35% male, 65% female; 0% American Indian, 2% Asian, 5% Black, 6% Hispanic, 4% multiracial, 0% Pacific Islander, 80% white, 1% international; 29% from in state; 56% live on campus; N/A of students in fraternities, N/A in sororities
Most popular majors: 42% Visual and Performing Arts, 14% Business, Management, Marketing, and Related Support Services, 11% Health Professions and Related Programs, 6% Communication, Journalism, and Related Programs, 6% Communications Technologies/Technicians and Support Services
Expenses: 2020-2021: $37,030; room/board: $12,890

Financial aid: (615) 460-6403; 53% of undergrads determined to have financial need; average aid package $22,526

Bethel University
McKenzie TN
(731) 352-4030
U.S. News ranking: Reg. U. (S), second tier
Website: www.bethelu.edu
Admissions email: admissions@bethelu.edu
Private; founded 1842
Affiliation: Cumberland Presbyterian
Freshman admissions: less selective; 2019-2020: 1,541 applied, 1,391 accepted. Neither SAT nor ACT required. ACT 25/75 percentile: 16-20. High school rank: 5% in top tenth, 18% in top quarter, 48% in top half
Early decision deadline: N/A, notification date: N/A
Early action deadline: N/A, notification date: N/A
Application deadline (fall): 8/16
Undergraduate student body: 1,638 full time, 717 part time; 51% male, 49% female; 0% American Indian, 0% Asian, 32% Black, 2% Hispanic, 9% multiracial, 0% Pacific Islander, 52% white, 4% international; 76% from in state; 83% live on campus; 5% of students in fraternities, 4% in sororities
Most popular majors: 41% Organizational Leadership, 28% Criminal Justice/Safety Studies, 5% Business Administration and Management, General, 4% Crisis/Emergency/Disaster Management, 4% Registered Nursing/Registered Nurse
Expenses: 2019-2020: $17,010; room/board: $9,198
Financial aid: (731) 352-8412

Bryan College
Dayton TN
(800) 277-9522
U.S. News ranking: Reg. U. (S), No. 65
Website: www.bryan.edu
Admissions email: admissions@bryan.edu
Private; founded 1930
Affiliation: Evangelical Christian
Freshman admissions: more selective; 2019-2020: 990 applied, 505 accepted. Neither SAT nor ACT required. ACT 25/75 percentile: 21-26. High school rank: 23% in top tenth, 55% in top quarter, 83% in top half
Early decision deadline: N/A, notification date: N/A
Early action deadline: N/A, notification date: N/A
Application deadline (fall): rolling
Undergraduate student body: 687 full time, 579 part time; 46% male, 54% female; 0% American Indian, 1% Asian, 5% Black, 3% Hispanic, 2% multiracial, 0% Pacific Islander, 84% white, 3% international; N/A from in state; 75% live on campus; N/A of students in fraternities, N/A in sororities
Most popular majors: 48% Business, Management, Marketing, and Related Support

Services, 12% Psychology, 8% Education, 8% Parks, Recreation, Leisure, and Fitness Studies, 6% Communication, Journalism, and Related Programs
Expenses: 2020-2021: $17,100; room/board: $7,800
Financial aid: (423) 775-7339; 80% of undergrads determined to have financial need; average aid package $24,717

Carson-Newman University
Jefferson City TN
(800) 678-9061
U.S. News ranking: Nat. U., second tier
Website: www.cn.edu
Admissions email: admitme@cn.edu
Private; founded 1851
Affiliation: Baptist
Freshman admissions: selective; 2019-2020: 3,862 applied, 2,674 accepted. Either SAT or ACT required. ACT 25/75 percentile: 19-29. High school rank: N/A
Early decision deadline: N/A, notification date: N/A
Early action deadline: N/A, notification date: N/A
Application deadline (fall): rolling
Undergraduate student body: 1,716 full time, 124 part time; 40% male, 60% female; 1% American Indian, 1% Asian, 9% Black, 4% Hispanic, 2% multiracial, 0% Pacific Islander, 78% white, 3% international; N/A from in state; 50% live on campus; N/A of students in fraternities, N/A in sororities
Most popular majors: 17% Business, Management, Marketing, and Related Support Services, 15% Education, 15% Health Professions and Related Programs, 10% Parks, Recreation, Leisure, and Fitness Studies, 9% Biological and Biomedical Sciences
Expenses: 2020-2021: $29,500; room/board: $8,894
Financial aid: (865) 471-3247; 83% of undergrads determined to have financial need; average aid package $25,899

Christian Brothers University
Memphis TN
(901) 321-3205
U.S. News ranking: Reg. U. (S), No. 22
Website: www.cbu.edu
Admissions email: admissions@cbu.edu
Private; founded 1871
Affiliation: Roman Catholic
Freshman admissions: more selective; 2019-2020: 3,291 applied, 1,656 accepted. Either SAT or ACT required. ACT 25/75 percentile: 22-27. High school rank: 28% in top tenth, 59% in top quarter, 86% in top half
Early decision deadline: N/A, notification date: N/A
Early action deadline: N/A, notification date: N/A
Application deadline (fall): rolling
Undergraduate student body: 1,384 full time, 258 part time;

50% male, 50% female; 1% American Indian, 5% Asian, 22% Black, 8% Hispanic, 5% multiracial, 0% Pacific Islander, 35% white, 4% international; 72% from in state; 43% live on campus; N/A of students in fraternities, N/A in sororities
Most popular majors: 17% Business Administration and Management, General, 11% Psychology, General, 10% Natural Sciences, 7% Business/Commerce, General, 7% Mechanical Engineering
Expenses: 2020-2021: $34,820; room/board: $7,950
Financial aid: (901) 321-3305; 67% of undergrads determined to have financial need; average aid package $27,361

Cumberland University
Lebanon TN
(615) 444-2562
U.S. News ranking: Reg. U. (S), No. 86
Website: www.cumberland.edu
Admissions email: admissions@cumberland.edu
Private; founded 1842
Freshman admissions: selective; 2019-2020: 2,833 applied, 1,729 accepted. Either SAT or ACT required. ACT 25/75 percentile: 19-23. High school rank: N/A
Early decision deadline: N/A, notification date: N/A
Early action deadline: N/A, notification date: N/A
Application deadline (fall): rolling
Undergraduate student body: 1,827 full time, 452 part time; 44% male, 56% female; 1% American Indian, 1% Asian, 10% Black, 5% Hispanic, 0% multiracial, 0% Pacific Islander, 59% white, 3% international
Most popular majors: 17% Registered Nursing/Registered Nurse, 14% Liberal Arts and Sciences, General Studies and Humanities, Other, 10% Business Administration, Management and Operations, Other, 7% Business/Commerce, General, 6% Telecommunications Technology/Technician
Expenses: 2020-2021: $25,386; room/board: $8,850
Financial aid: (615) 547-1399; 84% of undergrads determined to have financial need; average aid package $14,920

East Tennessee State University
Johnson City TN
(423) 439-4213
U.S. News ranking: Nat. U., second tier
Website: www.etsu.edu
Admissions email: go2etsu@etsu.edu
Public; founded 1911
Freshman admissions: selective; 2019-2020: 7,731 applied, 6,620 accepted. Either SAT or ACT required. ACT 25/75 percentile: 20-27. High school rank: 32% in top tenth, 38% in top quarter, 51% in top half

Early decision deadline: N/A, notification date: N/A
Early action deadline: N/A, notification date: N/A
Application deadline (fall): 8/15
Undergraduate student body: 9,228 full time, 1,923 part time; 41% male, 59% female; 0% American Indian, 1% Asian, 7% Black, 3% Hispanic, 4% multiracial, 0% Pacific Islander, 81% white, 2% international
Most popular majors: Information not available
Expenses: 2019-2020: $9,259 in state, $27,406 out of state; room/board: $8,242
Financial aid: (423) 439-4300

Fisk University
Nashville TN
(888) 702-0022
U.S. News ranking: Nat. Lib. Arts, second tier
Website: www.fisk.edu
Admissions email: admissions@fisk.edu
Private; founded 1866
Freshman admissions: selective; 2019-2020: 3,034 applied, 2,834 accepted. Either SAT or ACT required. ACT 25/75 percentile: 18-24. High school rank: 20% in top tenth, 45% in top quarter, 73% in top half
Early decision deadline: N/A, notification date: N/A
Early action deadline: 11/1, notification date: 12/31
Application deadline (fall): rolling
Undergraduate student body: 822 full time, 18 part time; 31% male, 69% female; 0% American Indian, 0% Asian, 84% Black, 1% Hispanic, 2% multiracial, 0% Pacific Islander, 0% white, 6% international
Most popular majors: 19% Business Administration and Management, General, 19% Psychology, General, 17% Biology/Biological Sciences, General, 9% Political Science and Government, General, 6% English Language and Literature, General
Expenses: 2019-2020: $22,132; room/board: $11,022
Financial aid: (615) 329-8585

Freed-Hardeman University
Henderson TN
(731) 348-3481
U.S. News ranking: Reg. U. (S), No. 36
Website: www.fhu.edu
Admissions email: admissions@fhu.edu
Private; founded 1869
Affiliation: Churches of Christ
Freshman admissions: more selective; 2019-2020: 944 applied, 835 accepted. Either SAT or ACT required. ACT 25/75 percentile: 21-28. High school rank: 28% in top tenth, 56% in top quarter, 81% in top half
Early decision deadline: N/A, notification date: N/A
Early action deadline: N/A, notification date: N/A
Application deadline (fall): rolling
Undergraduate student body: 1,306 full time, 342 part time; 43% male, 57% female; 1% American

Indian, 1% Asian, 4% Black, 0% Hispanic, 1% multiracial, 0% Pacific Islander, 87% white, 1% international; N/A from in state; 83% live on campus; N/A of students in fraternities, N/A in sororities
Most popular majors: 15% Business, Management, Marketing, and Related Support Services, 15% Health Professions and Related Programs, 10% Education, 10% Theology and Religious Vocations, 7% Visual and Performing Arts
Expenses: 2020-2021: $22,950; room/board: $7,950
Financial aid: (731) 989-6662; 74% of undergrads determined to have financial need; average aid package $19,696

King University
Bristol TN
(423) 652-4861
U.S. News ranking: Reg. U. (S), No. 47
Website: www.king.edu
Admissions email: admissions@king.edu
Private; founded 1867
Affiliation: Presbyterian
Freshman admissions: selective; 2019-2020: 949 applied, 589 accepted. Neither SAT nor ACT required. ACT 25/75 percentile: 20-25. High school rank: 19% in top tenth, 41% in top quarter, 75% in top half
Early decision deadline: N/A, notification date: N/A
Early action deadline: N/A, notification date: N/A
Application deadline (fall): rolling
Undergraduate student body: 1,487 full time, 130 part time; 35% male, 65% female; 1% American Indian, 1% Asian, 6% Black, 2% Hispanic, 1% multiracial, 0% Pacific Islander, 82% white, 3% international; 58% from in state; 15% live on campus; N/A of students in fraternities, N/A in sororities
Most popular majors: 33% Business, Management, Marketing, and Related Support Services, 28% Health Professions and Related Programs, 8% Psychology, 6% Computer and Information Sciences and Support Services, 5% Homeland Security, Law Enforcement, Firefighting and Related Protective Services
Expenses: 2019-2020: $16,117; room/board: $9,024
Financial aid: (423) 652-4725; 84% of undergrads determined to have financial need; average aid package $16,246

Lane College
Jackson TN
(731) 426-7533
U.S. News ranking: Nat. Lib. Arts, second tier
Website: www.lanecollege.edu
Admissions email: admissions@lanecollege.edu
Private; founded 1882
Affiliation: Christian Methodist Episcopal
Freshman admissions: least selective; 2019-2020: 6,557 applied, 4,003 accepted. Neither

SAT nor ACT required. ACT 25/75 percentile: 14-17. High school rank: N/A
Early decision deadline: N/A, notification date: N/A
Early action deadline: N/A, notification date: N/A
Application deadline (fall): 7/1
Undergraduate student body: 1,239 full time, 28 part time; 50% male, 50% female; 0% American Indian, 0% Asian, 87% Black, 1% Hispanic, 1% multiracial, 0% Pacific Islander, 0% white, 0% international; 61% from in state; 79% live on campus; N/A of students in fraternities, N/A in sororities
Most popular majors: 25% Business Administration and Management, General, 15% Biology/Biological Sciences, General, 13% Sociology, 11% Mass Communication/Media Studies, 10% Criminal Justice/Safety Studies
Expenses: 2019-2020: $11,790; room/board: $7,610
Financial aid: N/A

Lee University
Cleveland TN
(423) 614-8500
U.S. News ranking: Reg. U. (S), No. 33
Website: www.leeuniversity.edu
Admissions email: admissions@leeuniversity.edu
Private; founded 1918
Affiliation: Church of God
Freshman admissions: more selective; 2019-2020: 2,416 applied, 1,975 accepted. Either SAT or ACT required. ACT 25/75 percentile: 21-28. High school rank: 28% in top tenth, 49% in top quarter, 74% in top half
Early decision deadline: N/A, notification date: N/A
Early action deadline: N/A, notification date: N/A
Application deadline (fall): rolling
Undergraduate student body: 3,677 full time, 1,009 part time; 39% male, 61% female; 0% American Indian, 1% Asian, 5% Black, 2% Hispanic, 4% multiracial, 0% Pacific Islander, 83% white, 3% international; 48% from in state; 47% live on campus; 8% of students in fraternities, 8% in sororities
Most popular majors: 16% Theology and Religious Vocations, 15% Education, 11% Communication, Journalism, and Related Programs, 10% Business, Management, Marketing, and Related Support Services, 10% Health Professions and Related Programs
Expenses: 2020-2021: $19,540; room/board: $8,260
Financial aid: (423) 614-8300; 71% of undergrads determined to have financial need; average aid package $13,991

LeMoyne-Owen College
Memphis TN
(901) 435-1500
U.S. News ranking: Reg. Coll. (S), second tier
Website: www.loc.edu/

Admissions email: admission@loc.edu
Private; founded 1862
Affiliation: United Church of Christ
Freshman admissions: less selective; 2019-2020: 368 applied, 150 accepted. ACT required. ACT 25/75 percentile: 15-17. High school rank: N/A
Early decision deadline: N/A, notification date: N/A
Early action deadline: N/A, notification date: N/A
Application deadline (fall): N/A
Undergraduate student body: 749 full time, 86 part time; 34% male, 66% female; 0% American Indian, 0% Asian, 97% Black, 1% Hispanic, 0% multiracial, 0% Pacific Islander, 0% white, 1% international; 80% from in state; 32% live on campus; 5% of students in fraternities, 6% in sororities
Most popular majors: 33% Business Administration and Management, General, 16% General Studies, 15% Criminal Justice/Safety Studies, 8% Biology/Biological Sciences, General, 4% Social Work
Expenses: 2019-2020: $11,216; room/board: $6,100
Financial aid: (901) 435-1550

Lincoln Memorial University
Harrogate TN
(423) 869-6280
U.S. News ranking: Nat. U., No. 227
Website: www.lmunet.edu
Admissions email: admissions@lmunet.edu
Private; founded 1897
Freshman admissions: selective; 2019-2020: 1,549 applied, 766 accepted. Neither SAT nor ACT required. ACT 25/75 percentile: 19-25. High school rank: 22% in top tenth, 47% in top quarter, 77% in top half
Early decision deadline: N/A, notification date: N/A
Early action deadline: N/A, notification date: N/A
Application deadline (fall): 9/30
Undergraduate student body: 1,427 full time, 548 part time; 29% male, 71% female; 1% American Indian, 1% Asian, 6% Black, 0% Hispanic, 0% multiracial, 0% Pacific Islander, 85% white, 4% international; 61% from in state; 38% live on campus; 1% of students in fraternities, 2% in sororities
Most popular majors: 55% Health Professions and Related Programs, 10% Business, Management, Marketing, and Related Support Services, 8% Biological and Biomedical Sciences, 8% Parks, Recreation, Leisure, and Fitness Studies, 4% Education
Expenses: 2020-2021: $23,560; room/board: $8,500
Financial aid: (423) 869-6336; 85% of undergrads determined to have financial need; average aid package $23,472

Lipscomb University
Nashville TN
(615) 966-1776
U.S. News ranking: Nat. U., No. 206
Website: www.lipscomb.edu
Admissions email: admissions@lipscomb.edu
Private; founded 1891
Affiliation: Churches of Christ
Freshman admissions: more selective; 2019-2020: 3,481 applied, 2,197 accepted. Either SAT or ACT required. ACT 25/75 percentile: 23-29. High school rank: 27% in top tenth, 60% in top quarter, 85% in top half
Early decision deadline: N/A, notification date: N/A
Early action deadline: N/A, notification date: N/A
Application deadline (fall): rolling
Undergraduate student body: 2,680 full time, 179 part time; 40% male, 60% female; 0% American Indian, 3% Asian, 7% Black, 7% Hispanic, 3% multiracial, 0% Pacific Islander, 74% white, 4% international; 64% from in state; 55% live on campus; 23% of students in fraternities, 24% in sororities
Most popular majors: 24% Business, Management, Marketing, and Related Support Services, 9% Health Professions and Related Programs, 8% Psychology, 7% Visual and Performing Arts, 6% Education
Expenses: 2020-2021: $34,744; room/board: $13,804
Financial aid: (615) 966-6205; 63% of undergrads determined to have financial need; average aid package $30,420

Martin Methodist College
Pulaski TN
(931) 363-9800
U.S. News ranking: Reg. Coll. (S), No. 36
Website: www.martinmethodist.edu
Admissions email: info@martinmethodist.edu
Private; founded 1870
Affiliation: United Methodist
Freshman admissions: selective; 2019-2020: 674 applied, 665 accepted. Either SAT or ACT required. ACT 25/75 percentile: 17-22. High school rank: N/A
Early decision deadline: N/A, notification date: N/A
Early action deadline: N/A, notification date: N/A
Application deadline (fall): rolling
Undergraduate student body: 755 full time, 135 part time; 40% male, 60% female; 0% American Indian, 1% Asian, 12% Black, 3% Hispanic, 3% multiracial, 0% Pacific Islander, 72% white, 5% international; 77% from in state; 40% live on campus; 0% of students in fraternities, 0% in sororities
Most popular majors: 21% Business Administration and Management, General, 14% Health and Physical Education/Fitness, General, 13% Behavioral Sciences, 11% Registered Nursing/Registered Nurse,

9% Criminal Justice/Law Enforcement Administration
Expenses: 2019-2020: $24,900; room/board: $8,400
Financial aid: (931) 424-7366

Maryville College

Maryville TN
(865) 981-8092
U.S. News ranking: Reg. Coll. (S), No. 3
Website: www.maryvillecollege.edu
Admissions email: admissions@maryvillecollege.edu
Private; founded 1819
Affiliation: Presbyterian Church (USA)
Freshman admissions: more selective; 2019-2020: 2,436 applied, 1,367 accepted. Either SAT or ACT required. ACT 25/75 percentile: 21-27. High school rank: 29% in top tenth, 52% in top quarter, 81% in top half
Early decision deadline: N/A, notification date: N/A
Early action deadline: N/A, notification date: N/A
Application deadline (fall): rolling
Undergraduate student body: 1,071 full time, 72 part time; 43% male, 57% female; 0% American Indian, 1% Asian, 10% Black, 6% Hispanic, 3% multiracial, 0% Pacific Islander, 76% white, 2% international; 75% from in state; 66% live on campus; 0% of students in fraternities, 0% in sororities
Most popular majors: Biological and Biomedical Sciences, Business, Management, Marketing, and Related Support Services, Health Professions and Related Programs, Parks, Recreation, Leisure, and Fitness Studies, Social Sciences
Expenses: 2020-2021: $36,292; room/board: $12,004
Financial aid: (865) 981-8100; 83% of undergrads determined to have financial need; average aid package $31,151

Middle Tennessee State University

Murfreesboro TN
(615) 898-2233
U.S. News ranking: Nat. U., second tier
Website: www.mtsu.edu
Admissions email: admissions@mtsu.edu
Public; founded 1911
Freshman admissions: selective; 2019-2020: 8,973 applied, 8,409 accepted. Either SAT or ACT required. ACT 25/75 percentile: 20-26. High school rank: N/A
Early decision deadline: N/A, notification date: N/A
Early action deadline: N/A, notification date: N/A
Application deadline (fall): rolling
Undergraduate student body: 15,721 full time, 3,740 part time; 47% male, 53% female; 0% American Indian, 4% Asian, 19% Black, 7% Hispanic, 4% multiracial, 0% Pacific Islander, 63% white, 3% international; 90% from in state; 17% live on campus; 5% of students in fraternities, 9% in sororities

Most popular majors: 16% Business, Management, Marketing, and Related Support Services, 10% Visual and Performing Arts, 9% Liberal Arts and Sciences, General Studies and Humanities, 8% Communication, Journalism, and Related Programs, 5% Biological and Biomedical Sciences
Expenses: 2020-2021: $9,424 in state, $29,038 out of state; room/board: $10,214
Financial aid: (615) 898-5454; 67% of undergrads determined to have financial need; average aid package $10,547

Milligan University

Milligan College TN
(423) 461-8730
U.S. News ranking: Reg. U. (S), No. 18
Website: www.milligan.edu
Admissions email: admissions@milligan.edu
Private; founded 1866
Affiliation: Christian Churches and Churches of Christ
Freshman admissions: selective; 2019-2020: 548 applied, 542 accepted. Either SAT or ACT required. ACT 25/75 percentile: 22-28. High school rank: N/A
Early decision deadline: N/A, notification date: N/A
Early action deadline: N/A, notification date: N/A
Application deadline (fall): 8/28
Undergraduate student body: 767 full time, 115 part time; 47% male, 53% female; 0% American Indian, 1% Asian, 4% Black, 4% Hispanic, 2% multiracial, 0% Pacific Islander, 82% white, 7% international; 66% from in state; 77% live on campus; 0% of students in fraternities, 0% in sororities
Most popular majors: 23% Business, Management, Marketing, and Related Support Services, 15% Parks, Recreation, Leisure, and Fitness Studies, 14% Health Professions and Related Programs, 10% Education, 8% Psychology
Expenses: 2020-2021: $35,600; room/board: $7,400
Financial aid: (423) 461-8968; 77% of undergrads determined to have financial need; average aid package $25,811

Rhodes College

Memphis TN
(901) 843-3700
U.S. News ranking: Nat. Lib. Arts, No. 54
Website: www.rhodes.edu
Admissions email: adminfo@rhodes.edu
Private; founded 1848
Affiliation: Presbyterian
Freshman admissions: more selective; 2019-2020: 5,207 applied, 2,328 accepted. Either SAT or ACT required. ACT 25/75 percentile: 27-32. High school rank: 52% in top tenth, 83% in top quarter, 99% in top half
Early decision deadline: 11/1, notification date: 12/1
Early action deadline: 11/15, notification date: 1/15

Application deadline (fall): 1/15
Undergraduate student body: 1,945 full time, 28 part time; 42% male, 58% female; 0% American Indian, 6% Asian, 10% Black, 7% Hispanic, 5% multiracial, 0% Pacific Islander, 66% white, 5% international; 29% from in state; 67% live on campus; 32% of students in fraternities, 38% in sororities
Most popular majors: 23% Social Sciences, 16% Business, Management, Marketing, and Related Support Services, 15% Biological and Biomedical Sciences, 7% Computer and Information Sciences and Support Services, 7% Physical Sciences
Expenses: 2020-2021: $50,910; room/board: $11,816
Financial aid: (800) 844-5969; 52% of undergrads determined to have financial need; average aid package $42,180

Southern Adventist University[1]

Collegedale TN
(423) 236-2835
U.S. News ranking: Reg. U. (S), No. 68
Website: www.southern.edu
Admissions email: admissions@southern.edu
Private; founded 1892
Affiliation: Seventh Day Adventist
Application deadline (fall): rolling
Undergraduate student body: N/A full time, N/A part time
Expenses: 2020-2021: $22,930; room/board: $7,370
Financial aid: (423) 236-2535; 67% of undergrads determined to have financial need; average aid package $17,880

Tennessee State University[7]

Nashville TN
(615) 963-5101
U.S. News ranking: Nat. U., second tier
Website: www.tnstate.edu
Admissions email: jcade@tnstate.edu
Public; founded 1912
Freshman admissions: less selective; 2019-2020: 8,664 applied, 5,697 accepted. Either SAT or ACT required. ACT 25/75 percentile: 17-21. High school rank: N/A
Early decision deadline: N/A, notification date: N/A
Early action deadline: N/A, notification date: N/A
Application deadline (fall): 7/1
Undergraduate student body: 4,807 full time, 1,068 part time
Most popular majors: Information not available
Expenses: 2020-2021: $7,251 in state, $20,607 out of state; room/board: $7,500
Financial aid: (615) 963-5701; 80% of undergrads determined to have financial need; average aid package $11,678

Tennessee Technological University

Cookeville TN
(800) 255-8881
U.S. News ranking: Nat. U., No. 272
Website: www.tntech.edu
Admissions email: admissions@tntech.edu
Public; founded 1915
Freshman admissions: more selective; 2019-2020: 6,621 applied, 5,232 accepted. Neither SAT nor ACT required. ACT 25/75 percentile: 21-27. High school rank: 28% in top tenth, 57% in top quarter, 84% in top half
Early decision deadline: N/A, notification date: N/A
Early action deadline: N/A, notification date: N/A
Application deadline (fall): rolling
Undergraduate student body: 8,004 full time, 953 part time; 55% male, 45% female; 0% American Indian, 2% Asian, 4% Black, 4% Hispanic, 4% multiracial, 0% Pacific Islander, 84% white, 2% international; 95% from in state; 25% live on campus; 13% of students in fraternities, 13% in sororities
Most popular majors: 8% Mechanical Engineering, 7% Elementary Education and Teaching, 7% Liberal Arts and Sciences/Liberal Studies, 7% Registered Nursing/Registered Nurse, 6% Business Administration and Management, General
Expenses: 2020-2021: $10,338 in state, $15,816 out of state; room/board: $8,850
Financial aid: (931) 372-3503; 71% of undergrads determined to have financial need; average aid package $13,990

Tennessee Wesleyan University

Athens TN
(423) 746-5286
U.S. News ranking: Reg. Coll. (S), No. 23
Website: www.tnwesleyan.edu
Admissions email: admissions@tnwesleyan.edu
Private; founded 1857
Affiliation: United Methodist
Freshman admissions: selective; 2019-2020: 865 applied, 543 accepted. Either SAT or ACT required. ACT 25/75 percentile: 19-25. High school rank: N/A
Early decision deadline: N/A, notification date: N/A
Early action deadline: N/A, notification date: N/A
Application deadline (fall): rolling
Undergraduate student body: 969 full time, 98 part time; 38% male, 62% female; 0% American Indian, 1% Asian, 11% Black, 5% Hispanic, 3% multiracial, 0% Pacific Islander, 72% white, 6% international; 86% from in state; 36% live on campus; 2% of students in fraternities, 4% in sororities
Most popular majors: 33% Business, Management, Marketing, and Related Support

Services, 27% Health Professions and Related Programs, 8% Education, 8% Parks, Recreation, Leisure, and Fitness Studies, 5% Psychology
Expenses: 2020-2021: $25,850; room/board: $8,210
Financial aid: (423) 746-5209; 80% of undergrads determined to have financial need; average aid package $21,445

Trevecca Nazarene University

Nashville TN
(615) 248-1320
U.S. News ranking: Nat. U., second tier
Website: www.trevecca.edu
Admissions email: admissions_und@trevecca.edu
Private; founded 1901
Affiliation: Church of the Nazarene
Freshman admissions: selective; 2019-2020: 1,662 applied, 1,036 accepted. Either SAT or ACT required. ACT 25/75 percentile: 20-26. High school rank: N/A
Early decision deadline: N/A, notification date: N/A
Early action deadline: N/A, notification date: N/A
Application deadline (fall): 8/1
Undergraduate student body: 1,768 full time, 622 part time; 39% male, 61% female; 0% American Indian, 1% Asian, 12% Black, 10% Hispanic, 3% multiracial, 0% Pacific Islander, 59% white, 10% international
Most popular majors: 37% Business, Management, Marketing, and Related Support Services, 13% Health Professions and Related Programs, 7% Theology and Religious Vocations, 5% Communication, Journalism, and Related Programs, 5% Psychology
Expenses: 2020-2021: $26,898; room/board: $9,100
Financial aid: (615) 248-1253

Tusculum University

Greeneville TN
(800) 729-0256
U.S. News ranking: Reg. U. (S), No. 86
Website: home.tusculum.edu/
Admissions email: admission@tusculum.edu
Private; founded 1794
Affiliation: Presbyterian
Freshman admissions: selective; 2019-2020: 1,965 applied, 1,422 accepted. Either SAT or ACT required. ACT 25/75 percentile: 18-23. High school rank: N/A
Early decision deadline: N/A, notification date: N/A
Early action deadline: N/A, notification date: N/A
Application deadline (fall): rolling
Undergraduate student body: 1,142 full time, 246 part time; 55% male, 45% female; 1% American Indian, 0% Asian, 14% Black, 4% Hispanic, 1% multiracial, 0% Pacific Islander, 67% white, 5% international
Most popular majors: Information not available

Expenses: 2020-2021: $25,500; room/board: $9,450
Financial aid: (423) 636-5377; 81% of undergrads determined to have financial need; average aid package $20,646

Union University

Jackson TN
(800) 338-6466
U.S. News ranking: Nat. U., No. 206
Website: www.uu.edu
Admissions email: admissions@uu.edu
Private; founded 1823
Affiliation: Southern Baptist
Freshman admissions: more selective; 2019-2020: 2,866 applied, 1,511 accepted. Either SAT or ACT required. ACT 25/75 percentile: 22-30. High school rank: 36% in top tenth, 61% in top quarter, 87% in top half
Early decision deadline: N/A, notification date: N/A
Early action deadline: N/A, notification date: N/A
Application deadline (fall): rolling
Undergraduate student body: 1,796 full time, 368 part time; 34% male, 66% female; 1% American Indian, 2% Asian, 17% Black, 2% Hispanic, 0% multiracial, 0% Pacific Islander, 73% white, 2% international; 68% from in state; 77% live on campus; 13% of students in fraternities, 21% in sororities
Most popular majors: 35% Health Professions and Related Programs, 22% Business, Management, Marketing, and Related Support Services, 6% Biological and Biomedical Sciences, 6% Public Administration and Social Service Professions, 5% English Language and Literature/Letters
Expenses: 2020-2021: $34,780; room/board: $10,880
Financial aid: (731) 661-5015; 87% of undergrads determined to have financial need; average aid package $24,879

University of Memphis

Memphis TN
(901) 678-2111
U.S. News ranking: Nat. U., No. 258
Website: www.memphis.edu
Admissions email: recruitment@memphis.edu
Public; founded 1912
Freshman admissions: selective; 2019-2020: 14,778 applied, 12,525 accepted. Either SAT or ACT required. ACT 25/75 percentile: 19-26. High school rank: 16% in top tenth, 40% in top quarter, 71% in top half
Early decision deadline: N/A, notification date: N/A
Early action deadline: N/A, notification date: N/A
Application deadline (fall): 7/1
Undergraduate student body: 12,066 full time, 5,312 part time; 41% male, 59% female; 0% American Indian, 4% Asian, 36% Black, 6% Hispanic, 4% multiracial, 0% Pacific Islander, 47% white, 1% international;

N/A from in state; 17% live on campus; N/A of students in fraternities, N/A in sororities
Most popular majors: 19% Business, Management, Marketing, and Related Support Services, 11% Parks, Recreation, Leisure, and Fitness Studies, 10% Health Professions and Related Programs, 8% Multi/Interdisciplinary Studies, 6% Psychology
Expenses: 2020-2021: $9,912 in state, $16,764 out of state; room/board: $9,732
Financial aid: (901) 678-4995; 75% of undergrads determined to have financial need; average aid package $10,718

University of Tennessee

Knoxville TN
(865) 974-1111
U.S. News ranking: Nat. U., No. 112
Website: utk.edu
Admissions email: admissions@utk.edu
Public; founded 1794
Freshman admissions: more selective; 2019-2020: 21,764 applied, 17,160 accepted. Either SAT or ACT required. ACT 25/75 percentile: 24-30. High school rank: 35% in top tenth, 63% in top quarter, 88% in top half
Early decision deadline: N/A, notification date: N/A
Early action deadline: 11/1, notification date: 12/15
Application deadline (fall): 8/20
Undergraduate student body: 22,018 full time, 1,272 part time; 49% male, 51% female; 0% American Indian, 4% Asian, 6% Black, 5% Hispanic, 4% multiracial, 0% Pacific Islander, 78% white, 1% international; 82% from in state; 34% live on campus; 17% of students in fraternities, 28% in sororities
Most popular majors: 25% Business, Management, Marketing, and Related Support Services, 11% Engineering, 8% Social Sciences, 7% Communication, Journalism, and Related Programs, 7% Parks, Recreation, Leisure, and Fitness Studies
Expenses: 2020-2021: $13,264 in state, $31,454 out of state; room/board: $11,856
Financial aid: (865) 974-1111; 55% of undergrads determined to have financial need; average aid package $13,977

University of Tennessee–Chattanooga

Chattanooga TN
(423) 425-4662
U.S. News ranking: Nat. U., second tier
Website: www.utc.edu
Admissions email: utcmocs@utc.edu
Public; founded 1886
Freshman admissions: selective; 2019-2020: 8,189 applied, 6,719 accepted. Either SAT

or ACT required. ACT 25/75 percentile: 21-26. High school rank: N/A
Early decision deadline: N/A, notification date: N/A
Early action deadline: N/A, notification date: N/A
Application deadline (fall): 5/1
Undergraduate student body: 9,224 full time, 1,072 part time; 44% male, 56% female; 0% American Indian, 2% Asian, 10% Black, 6% Hispanic, 3% multiracial, 0% Pacific Islander, 75% white, 1% international; 93% from in state; 35% live on campus; 12% of students in fraternities, 15% in sororities
Most popular majors: 20% Business, Management, Marketing, and Related Support Services, 10% Parks, Recreation, Leisure, and Fitness Studies, 9% Engineering, 8% Education, 7% Psychology
Expenses: 2020-2021: $9,656 in state, $25,774 out of state; room/board: $10,159
Financial aid: (423) 425-4677; 61% of undergrads determined to have financial need; average aid package $10,919

University of Tennessee–Martin

Martin TN
(800) 829-8861
U.S. News ranking: Reg. U. (S), No. 30
Website: www.utm.edu
Admissions email: admitme@utm.edu
Public; founded 1900
Freshman admissions: selective; 2019-2020: 9,158 applied, 5,906 accepted. ACT required. ACT 25/75 percentile: 21-26. High school rank: 15% in top tenth, 43% in top quarter, 80% in top half
Early decision deadline: N/A, notification date: N/A
Early action deadline: N/A, notification date: N/A
Application deadline (fall): rolling
Undergraduate student body: 4,757 full time, 2,022 part time; 39% male, 61% female; 0% American Indian, 1% Asian, 13% Black, 3% Hispanic, 3% multiracial, 0% Pacific Islander, 79% white, 1% international; 90% from in state; 33% live on campus; 13% of students in fraternities, 14% in sororities
Most popular majors: 20% Business, Management, Marketing, and Related Support Services, 16% Agriculture, Agriculture Operations, and Related Sciences, 13% Multi/Interdisciplinary Studies, 10% Education, 7% Parks, Recreation, Leisure, and Fitness Studies
Expenses: 2020-2021: $9,748 in state, $15,788 out of state; room/board: $6,398
Financial aid: (731) 881-7040; 75% of undergrads determined to have financial need; average aid package $11,898

The University of the South

Sewanee TN
(800) 522-2234
U.S. News ranking: Nat. Lib. Arts, No. 47
Website: www.sewanee.edu
Admissions email: admiss@sewanee.edu
Private; founded 1857
Affiliation: Protestant Episcopal
Freshman admissions: more selective; 2019-2020: 3,545 applied, 2,365 accepted. Neither SAT nor ACT required. ACT 25/75 percentile: 25-30. High school rank: 32% in top tenth, 60% in top quarter, 86% in top half
Early decision deadline: 11/15, notification date: 12/15
Early action deadline: 12/1, notification date: 2/15
Application deadline (fall): 2/1
Undergraduate student body: 1,671 full time, 24 part time; 49% male, 51% female; 0% American Indian, 1% Asian, 4% Black, 5% Hispanic, 3% multiracial, 0% Pacific Islander, 82% white, 4% international; 21% from in state; 98% live on campus; 61% of students in fraternities, 74% in sororities
Most popular majors: 16% Economics, General, 13% Psychology, General, 11% Political Science and Government, General, 10% English Language and Literature, General, 9% Biology/Biological Sciences, General
Expenses: 2020-2021: $47,980; room/board: $13,700
Financial aid: (931) 598-1312; 44% of undergrads determined to have financial need; average aid package $37,115

Vanderbilt University

Nashville TN
(800) 288-0432
U.S. News ranking: Nat. U., No. 14
Website: www.vanderbilt.edu
Admissions email: admissions@vanderbilt.edu
Private; founded 1873
Freshman admissions: most selective; 2019-2020: 37,310 applied, 3,402 accepted. Either SAT or ACT required. ACT 25/75 percentile: 33-35. High school rank: 90% in top tenth, 98% in top quarter, 99% in top half
Early decision deadline: 11/1, notification date: 12/15
Early action deadline: N/A, notification date: N/A
Application deadline (fall): 1/1
Undergraduate student body: 6,833 full time, 53 part time; 48% male, 52% female; 0% American Indian, 14% Asian, 11% Black, 10% Hispanic, 6% multiracial, 0% Pacific Islander, 44% white, 10% international; 11% from in state; 85% live on campus; 27% of students in fraternities, 43% in sororities
Most popular majors: 29% Social Sciences, 12% Engineering, 11% Multi/Interdisciplinary Studies, 8% Biological and Biomedical Sciences, 6% Mathematics and Statistics

Expenses: 2020-2021: $54,158; room/board: $17,670
Financial aid: (615) 322-3591; 49% of undergrads determined to have financial need; average aid package $54,138

Watkins College of Art, Design & Film[1]

Nashville TN
(615) 383-4848
U.S. News ranking: Arts, unranked
Website: www.watkins.edu
Admissions email: admission@watkins.edu
Private
Application deadline (fall): N/A
Undergraduate student body: N/A full time, N/A part time
Expenses: 2019-2020: $24,750; room/board: $11,000
Financial aid: N/A

Welch College

Gallatin TN
(615) 675-5359
U.S. News ranking: Reg. Coll. (S), No. 18
Website: www.welch.edu
Admissions email: recruit@welch.edu
Private; founded 1942
Affiliation: Free Will Baptist Church
Freshman admissions: selective; 2019-2020: 167 applied, 111 accepted. Either SAT or ACT required. ACT 25/75 percentile: 20-26. High school rank: 24% in top tenth, 55% in top quarter, 79% in top half
Early decision deadline: N/A, notification date: N/A
Early action deadline: N/A, notification date: N/A
Application deadline (fall): rolling
Undergraduate student body: 236 full time, 157 part time; 44% male, 56% female; 0% American Indian, 1% Asian, 7% Black, 5% Hispanic, 4% multiracial, 0% Pacific Islander, 84% white, 0% international; 62% from in state; 64% live on campus; 79% of students in fraternities, 88% in sororities
Most popular majors: 23% Theology and Religious Vocations, 15% Education, 15% Liberal Arts and Sciences, General Studies and Humanities, 13% Biological and Biomedical Sciences, 13% Psychology
Expenses: 2020-2021: $19,582; room/board: $7,932
Financial aid: (615) 675-5278; 77% of undergrads determined to have financial need; average aid package $13,718

TEXAS

Abilene Christian University

Abilene TX
(800) 460-6228
U.S. News ranking: Reg. U. (W), No. 15
Website: www.acu.edu
Admissions email: info@admissions.acu.edu
Private; founded 1906
Affiliation: Churches of Christ

Freshman admissions: selective; 2019-2020: 11,379 applied, 6,996 accepted. Neither SAT nor ACT required. ACT 25/75 percentile: 21-28. High school rank: 24% in top tenth, 56% in top quarter, 85% in top half
Early decision deadline: N/A, notification date: N/A
Early action deadline: 11/1, notification date: 11/15
Application deadline (fall): 2/15
Undergraduate student body: 3,352 full time, 173 part time; 40% male, 60% female; 0% American Indian, 1% Asian, 9% Black, 19% Hispanic, 5% multiracial, 0% Pacific Islander, 63% white, 3% international; 84% from in state; 45% live on campus; 24% of students in fraternities, 32% in sororities
Most popular majors: 8% Business Administration and Management, General, 7% Accounting, 7% Registered Nursing/Registered Nurse, 5% Psychology, General, 5% Sport and Fitness Administration/Management
Expenses: 2020-2021: $37,800; room/board: $11,350
Financial aid: (325) 674-2300; 67% of undergrads determined to have financial need; average aid package $25,017

Angelo State University
San Angelo TX
(325) 942-2041
U.S. News ranking: Reg. U. (W), No. 91
Website: www.angelo.edu
Admissions email: admissions@angelo.edu
Public; founded 1928
Freshman admissions: selective; 2019-2020: 3,913 applied, 2,997 accepted. Either SAT or ACT required. ACT 25/75 percentile: 17-23. High school rank: 13% in top tenth, 38% in top quarter, 72% in top half
Early decision deadline: N/A, notification date: N/A
Early action deadline: N/A, notification date: N/A
Application deadline (fall): rolling
Undergraduate student body: 5,503 full time, 3,543 part time; 41% male, 59% female; 0% American Indian, 1% Asian, 7% Black, 38% Hispanic, 3% multiracial, 0% Pacific Islander, 46% white, 4% international; 97% from in state; 22% live on campus; 4% of students in fraternities, 3% in sororities
Most popular majors: 19% Business, Management, Marketing, and Related Support Services, 12% Multi/Interdisciplinary Studies, 8% Parks, Recreation, Leisure, and Fitness Studies, 7% Health Professions and Related Programs, 7% Psychology
Expenses: 2020-2021: $9,011 in state, $21,281 out of state; room/board: $9,360
Financial aid: (325) 942-2246; 68% of undergrads determined to have financial need; average aid package $8,324

Art Institute of Houston[1]
Houston TX
(713) 623-2040
U.S. News ranking: Arts, unranked
Website: www.artinstitute.edu/houston/
Admissions email: N/A
For-profit
Application deadline (fall): N/A
Undergraduate student body: N/A full time, N/A part time
Expenses: 2019-2020: $19,354; room/board: N/A
Financial aid: N/A

Austin College
Sherman TX
(800) 526-4276
U.S. News ranking: Nat. Lib. Arts, No. 102
Website: www.austincollege.edu
Admissions email: admission@austincollege.edu
Private; founded 1849
Affiliation: Presbyterian
Freshman admissions: more selective; 2019-2020: 4,360 applied, 2,236 accepted. Neither SAT nor ACT required. SAT 25/75 percentile: 1110-1310. High school rank: 29% in top tenth, 59% in top quarter, 90% in top half
Early decision deadline: 12/1, notification date: 1/15
Early action deadline: 12/1, notification date: 1/15
Application deadline (fall): 3/1
Undergraduate student body: 1,290 full time, 4 part time; 48% male, 52% female; 0% American Indian, 13% Asian, 10% Black, 24% Hispanic, 3% multiracial, 0% Pacific Islander, 47% white, 1% international; 93% from in state; 74% live on campus; 13% of students in fraternities, 17% in sororities
Most popular majors: 20% Business, Management, Marketing, and Related Support Services, 16% Biological and Biomedical Sciences, 9% Psychology, 9% Social Sciences, 7% English Language and Literature/Letters
Expenses: 2020-2021: $42,590; room/board: $12,752
Financial aid: (903) 813-2900; 67% of undergrads determined to have financial need; average aid package $39,081

Baylor University
Waco TX
(800) 229-5678
U.S. News ranking: Nat. U., No. 76
Website: www.baylor.edu
Admissions email: Admissions@Baylor.edu
Private; founded 1845
Affiliation: Baptist
Freshman admissions: more selective; 2019-2020: 34,582 applied, 15,676 accepted. Either SAT or ACT required. ACT 25/75 percentile: 26-32. High school rank: 44% in top tenth, 76% in top quarter, 96% in top half
Early decision deadline: 11/1, notification date: 12/15
Early action deadline: 11/1, notification date: 1/15

Application deadline (fall): 2/1
Undergraduate student body: 13,906 full time, 202 part time; 40% male, 60% female; 0% American Indian, 7% Asian, 6% Black, 16% Hispanic, 5% multiracial, 0% Pacific Islander, 62% white, 4% international; N/A from in state; 34% live on campus; 33% of students in fraternities, 34% in sororities
Most popular majors: 8% Registered Nursing/Registered Nurse, 7% Biology/Biological Sciences, General, 6% Accounting, 5% Marketing/Marketing Management, General, 4% Finance, General
Expenses: 2019-2020: $47,364; room/board: $13,842
Financial aid: (254) 710-2611

Brazosport College[1]
Lake Jackson TX
(979) 230-3000
U.S. News ranking: Reg. Coll. (W), unranked
Website: www.brazosport.edu
Admissions email: N/A
Public
Application deadline (fall): N/A
Undergraduate student body: N/A full time, N/A part time
Expenses: 2019-2020: $2,397 in state, $3,297 out of state; room/board: $8,700
Financial aid: N/A

Concordia University Texas[1]
Austin TX
(800) 865-4282
U.S. News ranking: Reg. U. (W), second tier
Website: www.concordia.edu
Admissions email: admissions@concordia.edu
Private; founded 1926
Application deadline (fall): 8/1
Undergraduate student body: N/A full time, N/A part time
Expenses: 2019-2020: $32,860; room/board: $11,360
Financial aid: (512) 313-4672

Dallas Baptist University
Dallas TX
(214) 333-5360
U.S. News ranking: Nat. U., No. 272
Website: www.dbu.edu
Admissions email: admiss@dbu.edu
Private; founded 1898
Affiliation: Baptist
Freshman admissions: selective; 2019-2020: 3,241 applied, 2,912 accepted. Either SAT or ACT required. ACT 25/75 percentile: 21-26. High school rank: 24% in top tenth, 55% in top quarter, 83% in top half
Early decision deadline: N/A, notification date: N/A
Early action deadline: N/A, notification date: N/A
Application deadline (fall): rolling
Undergraduate student body: 2,332 full time, 551 part time; 41% male, 59% female; 0% American Indian, 2% Asian, 10% Black, 19% Hispanic, 2% multiracial, 0% Pacific Islander, 61% white,

7% international; 92% from in state; 72% live on campus; 22% of students in fraternities, 31% in sororities
Most popular majors: 13% Multi-/Interdisciplinary Studies, Other, 12% Business Administration and Management, General, 9% Psychology, General, 5% Biology/Biological Sciences, General, 5% Elementary Education and Teaching
Expenses: 2020-2021: $31,940; room/board: $8,568
Financial aid: (214) 333-5363; 64% of undergrads determined to have financial need; average aid package $19,713

East Texas Baptist University
Marshall TX
(800) 804-3828
U.S. News ranking: Reg. Coll. (W), No. 15
Website: www.etbu.edu
Admissions email: admissions@etbu.edu
Private; founded 1912
Affiliation: Baptist
Freshman admissions: selective; 2019-2020: 1,777 applied, 1,056 accepted. Either SAT or ACT required. ACT 25/75 percentile: 17-22. High school rank: 15% in top tenth, 41% in top quarter, 71% in top half
Early decision deadline: N/A, notification date: N/A
Early action deadline: N/A, notification date: N/A
Application deadline (fall): 8/25
Undergraduate student body: 1,230 full time, 241 part time; 44% male, 56% female; 1% American Indian, 1% Asian, 17% Black, 13% Hispanic, 4% multiracial, 0% Pacific Islander, 64% white, 1% international; 88% from in state; 80% live on campus; 0% of students in fraternities, 0% in sororities
Most popular majors: 18% Multi/Interdisciplinary Studies, 17% Business, Management, Marketing, and Related Support Services, 10% Education, 10% Health Professions and Related Programs, 8% Parks, Recreation, Leisure, and Fitness Studies
Expenses: 2020-2021: $27,640; room/board: $9,894
Financial aid: (903) 923-2137; 83% of undergrads determined to have financial need; average aid package $20,137

Hardin-Simmons University
Abilene TX
(325) 670-1206
U.S. News ranking: Reg. U. (W), No. 37
Website: www.hsutx.edu/
Admissions email: enroll@hsutx.edu
Private; founded 1891
Affiliation: Baptist
Freshman admissions: selective; 2019-2020: 2,189 applied, 1,834 accepted. Neither SAT nor ACT required. ACT 25/75 percentile: 18-23. High school

rank: 12% in top tenth, 39% in top quarter, 71% in top half
Early decision deadline: N/A, notification date: N/A
Early action deadline: N/A, notification date: N/A
Application deadline (fall): rolling
Undergraduate student body: 1,610 full time, 132 part time; 47% male, 53% female; 1% American Indian, 2% Asian, 11% Black, 20% Hispanic, 3% multiracial, 0% Pacific Islander, 59% white, 3% international; 95% from in state; 57% live on campus; 6% of students in fraternities, 10% in sororities
Most popular majors: 22% Business, Management, Marketing, and Related Support Services, 14% Education, 8% Parks, Recreation, Leisure, and Fitness Studies, 7% Biological and Biomedical Sciences, 7% Visual and Performing Arts
Expenses: 2020-2021: $31,366; room/board: $9,740
Financial aid: (325) 670-1010; 78% of undergrads determined to have financial need; average aid package $31,417

Houston Baptist University
Houston TX
(281) 649-3211
U.S. News ranking: Reg. U. (W), No. 64
Website: www.hbu.edu
Admissions email: admissions@hbu.edu
Private; founded 1960
Affiliation: Baptist
Freshman admissions: selective; 2019-2020: 8,441 applied, 5,943 accepted. Either SAT or ACT required. SAT 25/75 percentile: 1020-1180. High school rank: 24% in top tenth, 57% in top quarter, 83% in top half
Early decision deadline: N/A, notification date: N/A
Early action deadline: N/A, notification date: N/A
Application deadline (fall): rolling
Undergraduate student body: 2,067 full time, 565 part time; 34% male, 66% female; 0% American Indian, 8% Asian, 20% Black, 37% Hispanic, 3% multiracial, 0% Pacific Islander, 23% white, 4% international; 95% from in state; 34% live on campus; 3% of students in fraternities, 8% in sororities
Most popular majors: 23% Health Professions and Related Programs, 15% Business, Management, Marketing, and Related Support Services, 9% Biological and Biomedical Sciences, 8% Parks, Recreation, Leisure, and Fitness Studies, 8% Psychology
Expenses: 2020-2021: $34,500; room/board: $9,130
Financial aid: (281) 649-3749; 77% of undergrads determined to have financial need; average aid package $29,796

Howard Payne University

Brownwood TX
(325) 649-8020
U.S. News ranking: Reg. Coll. (W), No. 21
Website: www.hputx.edu
Admissions email: enroll@hputx.edu
Private; founded 1889
Affiliation: Baptist
Freshman admissions: selective; 2019-2020: 1,896 applied, 1,021 accepted. Either SAT or ACT required. SAT 25/75 percentile: 940-1110. High school rank: 11% in top tenth, 29% in top quarter, 63% in top half
Early decision deadline: N/A, notification date: N/A
Early action deadline: N/A, notification date: N/A
Application deadline (fall): rolling
Undergraduate student body: 738 full time, 231 part time; 53% male, 47% female; 1% American Indian, 0% Asian, 14% Black, 26% Hispanic, 4% multiracial, 0% Pacific Islander, 51% white, 0% international
Most popular majors: Information not available
Expenses: 2020-2021: $29,378; room/board: $8,980
Financial aid: (325) 649-8015; 92% of undergrads determined to have financial need; average aid package $21,954

Huston-Tillotson University

Austin TX
(512) 505-3029
U.S. News ranking: Reg. Coll. (W), second tier
Website: htu.edu/
Admissions email: admission@htu.edu
Private
Freshman admissions: least selective; 2019-2020: 2,766 applied, 1,729 accepted. Either SAT or ACT required. SAT 25/75 percentile: 800-980. High school rank: 11% in top tenth, 16% in top quarter, 53% in top half
Early decision deadline: N/A, notification date: N/A
Early action deadline: N/A, notification date: N/A
Application deadline (fall): 5/1
Undergraduate student body: 1,026 full time, 86 part time; 37% male, 63% female; 1% American Indian, 0% Asian, 64% Black, 27% Hispanic, 1% multiracial, 0% Pacific Islander, 5% white, 2% international; 95% from in state; 39% live on campus; 4% of students in fraternities, 3% in sororities
Most popular majors: 26% Business, Management, Marketing, and Related Support Services, 15% Psychology, 13% Education, 12% Parks, Recreation, Leisure, and Fitness Studies, 8% Homeland Security, Law Enforcement, Firefighting and Related Protective Services
Expenses: 2019-2020: $14,346; room/board: $7,568
Financial aid: N/A

Jarvis Christian College[1]

Hawkins TX
(903) 730-4890
U.S. News ranking: Reg. Coll. (W), second tier
Website: www.jarvis.edu
Admissions email: Recruitment@jarvis.edu
Private; founded 1912
Affiliation: Christian Church (Disciples of Christ)
Application deadline (fall): 8/1
Undergraduate student body: N/A full time, N/A part time
Expenses: 2019-2020: $11,720; room/board: $8,574
Financial aid: (903) 730-4890

Lamar University

Beaumont TX
(409) 880-8888
U.S. News ranking: Nat. U., second tier
Website: www.lamar.edu
Admissions email: admissions@lamar.edu
Public; founded 1923
Freshman admissions: selective; 2019-2020: 6,460 applied, 5,427 accepted. Either SAT or ACT required. SAT 25/75 percentile: 960-1140. High school rank: 15% in top tenth, 45% in top quarter, 79% in top half
Early decision deadline: N/A, notification date: N/A
Early action deadline: N/A, notification date: N/A
Undergraduate student body: 5,243 full time, 3,454 part time; 42% male, 58% female; 0% American Indian, 5% Asian, 24% Black, 21% Hispanic, 3% multiracial, 0% Pacific Islander, 42% white, 1% international; 97% from in state; 25% live on campus; N/A of students in fraternities, N/A in sororities
Most popular majors: 16% Health Professions and Related Programs, 14% Engineering, 13% Business, Management, Marketing, and Related Support Services, 12% Multi/Interdisciplinary Studies, 9% Liberal Arts and Sciences, General Studies and Humanities
Expenses: 2020-2021: $10,462 in state, $22,732 out of state; room/board: $9,340
Financial aid: (409) 880-7011; 80% of undergrads determined to have financial need

LeTourneau University

Longview TX
(903) 233-4300
U.S. News ranking: Reg. U. (W), No. 26
Website: www.letu.edu
Admissions email: admissions@letu.edu
Private; founded 1946
Freshman admissions: more selective; 2019-2020: 2,314 applied, 1,030 accepted. Neither SAT nor ACT required. SAT 25/75 percentile: 1090-1310. High school rank: 26% in top tenth, 53% in top quarter, 83% in top half
Early decision deadline: N/A, notification date: N/A

Early action deadline: N/A, notification date: N/A
Application deadline (fall): rolling
Undergraduate student body: 1,347 full time, 1,515 part time; 55% male, 45% female; 1% American Indian, 1% Asian, 10% Black, 6% Hispanic, 6% multiracial, 0% Pacific Islander, 64% white, 5% international; 70% from in state; 72% live on campus; N/A of students in fraternities, N/A in sororities
Most popular majors: 24% Engineering, 18% Business, Management, Marketing, and Related Support Services, 9% Education, 9% Transportation and Materials Moving, 7% Engineering Technologies and Engineering-Related Fields
Expenses: 2020-2021: $32,490; room/board: $10,070
Financial aid: (903) 233-4350; 68% of undergrads determined to have financial need; average aid package $23,645

Lubbock Christian University

Lubbock TX
(806) 720-7151
U.S. News ranking: Reg. U. (W), No. 68
Website: lcu.edu
Admissions email: admissions@lcu.edu
Private; founded 1957
Affiliation: Churches of Christ
Freshman admissions: selective; 2019-2020: 782 applied, 709 accepted. Either SAT or ACT required. SAT 25/75 percentile: 960-1170. High school rank: 19% in top tenth, 42% in top quarter, 79% in top half
Early decision deadline: 10/31, notification date: 12/15
Early action deadline: 6/15, notification date: 7/15
Application deadline (fall): 6/1
Undergraduate student body: 1,201 full time, 272 part time; 40% male, 60% female; 1% American Indian, 1% Asian, 3% Black, 21% Hispanic, 0% multiracial, 0% Pacific Islander, 67% white, 2% international; 87% from in state; 36% live on campus; 16% of students in fraternities, 19% in sororities
Most popular majors: 24% Health Professions and Related Programs, 17% Business, Management, Marketing, and Related Support Services, 12% Education, 5% Parks, Recreation, Leisure, and Fitness Studies, 5% Theology and Religious Vocations
Expenses: 2019-2020: $23,330; room/board: $6,790
Financial aid: (806) 720-7176

McMurry University

Abilene TX
(325) 793-4700
U.S. News ranking: Reg. Coll. (W), No. 13
Website: mcm.edu/
Admissions email: admissions@mcm.edu
Private; founded 1923
Affiliation: United Methodist
Freshman admissions: selective; 2019-2020: 2,116 applied, 962

accepted. Either SAT or ACT required. SAT 25/75 percentile: 940-1100. High school rank: 14% in top tenth, 39% in top quarter, 77% in top half
Early decision deadline: N/A, notification date: N/A
Early action deadline: N/A, notification date: N/A
Application deadline (fall): 8/15
Undergraduate student body: 1,020 full time, 146 part time; 49% male, 51% female; 1% American Indian, 1% Asian, 14% Black, 28% Hispanic, 3% multiracial, 0% Pacific Islander, 48% white, 4% international; 97% from in state; 47% live on campus; 15% of students in fraternities, 16% in sororities
Most popular majors: 25% Business, Management, Marketing, and Related Support Services, 17% Education, 13% Social Sciences, 10% Psychology, 8% Multi/Interdisciplinary Studies
Expenses: 2020-2021: $28,620; room/board: $8,878
Financial aid: (325) 793-4978; 81% of undergrads determined to have financial need; average aid package $21,934

Midland College[1]

Midland TX
(432) 685-4500
U.S. News ranking: Reg. Coll. (W), unranked
Website: www.midland.edu/
Admissions email: pebensberger@midland.edu
Public
Application deadline (fall): N/A
Undergraduate student body: N/A full time, N/A part time
Expenses: 2019-2020: $2,670 in state, $4,290 out of state; room/board: $5,000
Financial aid: N/A

Midwestern State University

Wichita Falls TX
(800) 842-1922
U.S. News ranking: Reg. U. (W), No. 75
Website: www.mwsu.edu
Admissions email: admissions@mwsu.edu
Public; founded 1922
Freshman admissions: selective; 2019-2020: 3,767 applied, 2,984 accepted. Neither SAT nor ACT required. ACT 25/75 percentile: 17-22. High school rank: 12% in top tenth, 39% in top quarter, 71% in top half
Early decision deadline: N/A, notification date: N/A
Early action deadline: N/A, notification date: N/A
Application deadline (fall): 8/1
Undergraduate student body: 4,084 full time, 1,142 part time; 38% male, 62% female; 1% American Indian, 3% Asian, 15% Black, 20% Hispanic, 4% multiracial, 0% Pacific Islander, 47% white, 10% international; N/A from in state; 31% live on campus; 7% of students in fraternities, 7% in sororities
Most popular majors: 38% Health Professions and Related Programs, 18% Business,

Management, Marketing, and Related Support Services, 13% Multi/Interdisciplinary Studies, 5% Biological and Biomedical Sciences, 4% Psychology
Expenses: 2020-2021: $9,581 in state, $11,531 out of state; room/board: $9,504
Financial aid: (940) 397-4214

Our Lady of the Lake University

San Antonio TX
(210) 431-3961
U.S. News ranking: Nat. U., second tier
Website: www.ollusa.edu
Admissions email: admission@ollusa.edu
Private; founded 1895
Affiliation: Roman Catholic
Freshman admissions: less selective; 2019-2020: 6,645 applied, 4,515 accepted. Neither SAT nor ACT required. SAT 25/75 percentile: 910-1070. High school rank: 14% in top tenth, 38% in top quarter, 74% in top half
Early decision deadline: N/A, notification date: N/A
Early action deadline: N/A, notification date: N/A
Application deadline (fall): 8/20
Undergraduate student body: 1,244 full time, 124 part time; 32% male, 68% female; 0% American Indian, 0% Asian, 7% Black, 78% Hispanic, 0% multiracial, 0% Pacific Islander, 9% white, 2% international
Most popular majors: 25% Social Work, 12% Business Administration and Management, General, 11% Psychology, General, 10% Criminal Justice/Safety Studies, 9% Communication Sciences and Disorders, General
Expenses: 2020-2021: $30,196; room/board: $7,990
Financial aid: (210) 434-6711; 87% of undergrads determined to have financial need; average aid package $25,162

Paul Quinn College[1]

Dallas TX
(214) 379-5546
U.S. News ranking: Reg. Coll. (W), second tier
Admissions email: N/A
Private
Application deadline (fall): N/A
Undergraduate student body: N/A full time, N/A part time
Expenses: 2019-2020: $9,125; room/board: $6,500
Financial aid: N/A

Prairie View A&M University

Prairie View TX
(936) 261-1000
U.S. News ranking: Reg. U. (W), second tier
Website: www.pvamu.edu
Admissions email: admission@pvamu.edu
Public; founded 1876
Freshman admissions: less selective; 2019-2020: 6,196 applied, 4,963 accepted. Either

SAT or ACT required. SAT 25/75 percentile: 870-1040. High school rank: 6% in top tenth, 25% in top quarter, 65% in top half
Early decision deadline: N/A, notification date: N/A
Early action deadline: N/A, notification date: N/A
Application deadline (fall): 6/1
Undergraduate student body: 7,501 full time, 608 part time; 35% male, 65% female; 0% American Indian, 2% Asian, 84% Black, 9% Hispanic, 2% multiracial, 0% Pacific Islander, 1% white, 1% international; 54% from in state; 52% live on campus; N/A of students in fraternities, N/A in sororities
Most popular majors: 18% Health Professions and Related Programs, 15% Engineering, 11% Business, Management, Marketing, and Related Support Services, 7% Parks, Recreation, Leisure, and Fitness Studies, 6% Biological and Biomedical Sciences
Expenses: 2020-2021: $11,099 in state, $26,127 out of state; room/board: $8,979
Financial aid: (936) 261-1000; 86% of undergrads determined to have financial need; average aid package $15,404

Rice University
Houston TX
(713) 348-7423
U.S. News ranking: Nat. U., No. 16
Website: www.rice.edu
Admissions email: admission@rice.edu
Private; founded 1912
Freshman admissions: most selective; 2019-2020: 27,087 applied, 2,361 accepted. Either SAT or ACT required. SAT 25/75 percentile: 1470-1570. High school rank: 93% in top tenth, 99% in top quarter, 100% in top half
Early decision deadline: 11/1, notification date: 12/15
Early action deadline: N/A, notification date: N/A
Application deadline (fall): 1/1
Undergraduate student body: 3,942 full time, 47 part time; 52% male, 48% female; 0% American Indian, 26% Asian, 7% Black, 16% Hispanic, 5% multiracial, 0% Pacific Islander, 32% white, 12% international; 41% from in state; 70% live on campus; 0% of students in fraternities, 0% in sororities
Most popular majors: 10% Computer and Information Sciences, General, 6% Mechanical Engineering, 5% Biochemistry, 5% Cognitive Science, 5% Economics, General
Expenses: 2020-2021: $51,107; room/board: $14,500
Financial aid: (713) 348-4958; 43% of undergrads determined to have financial need; average aid package $52,943

Sam Houston State University
Huntsville TX
(936) 294-1828
U.S. News ranking: Nat. U., No. 272
Website: www.shsu.edu
Admissions email: admissions@shsu.edu
Public; founded 1879
Freshman admissions: selective; 2019-2020: 11,569 applied, 9,649 accepted. Either SAT or ACT required. SAT 25/75 percentile: 990-1140. High school rank: N/A
Early decision deadline: N/A, notification date: N/A
Early action deadline: N/A, notification date: N/A
Application deadline (fall): 8/1
Undergraduate student body: 15,296 full time, 3,487 part time; 38% male, 62% female; 1% American Indian, 2% Asian, 18% Black, 25% Hispanic, 3% multiracial, 0% Pacific Islander, 49% white, 1% international; 98% from in state; 20% live on campus; N/A of students in fraternities, N/A in sororities
Most popular majors: 21% Business, Management, Marketing, and Related Support Services, 20% Homeland Security, Law Enforcement, Firefighting and Related Protective Services, 9% Health Professions and Related Programs, 9% Multi/Interdisciplinary Studies, 5% Psychology
Expenses: 2020-2021: $10,756 in state, $23,026 out of state; room/board: $9,670
Financial aid: (936) 294-1774; 67% of undergrads determined to have financial need; average aid package $12,038

Schreiner University
Kerrville TX
(830) 792-7217
U.S. News ranking: Reg. Coll. (W), No. 7
Website: www.schreiner.edu
Admissions email: admissions@schreiner.edu
Private; founded 1923
Affiliation: Presbyterian Church (USA)
Freshman admissions: less selective; 2019-2020: 1,191 applied, 1,113 accepted. Either SAT or ACT required. SAT 25/75 percentile: 920-1110. High school rank: 6% in top tenth, 32% in top quarter, 63% in top half
Early decision deadline: N/A, notification date: N/A
Early action deadline: N/A, notification date: N/A
Application deadline (fall): 8/1
Undergraduate student body: 1,087 full time, 170 part time; 44% male, 56% female; 0% American Indian, 1% Asian, 4% Black, 43% Hispanic, 2% multiracial, 0% Pacific Islander, 48% white, 1% international; N/A from in state; 64% live on campus; 5% of students in fraternities, 13% in sororities
Most popular majors: 33% Health Professions and Related Programs, 19% Business, Management, Marketing, and Related Support

Services, 9% Biological and Biomedical Sciences, 8% Psychology, 7% Visual and Performing Arts
Expenses: 2020-2021: $31,938; room/board: $10,578
Financial aid: (830) 792-7229; 78% of undergrads determined to have financial need; average aid package $24,526

Southern Methodist University
Dallas TX
(800) 323-0672
U.S. News ranking: Nat. U., No. 66
Website: www.smu.edu
Admissions email: ugadmission@smu.edu
Private; founded 1911
Affiliation: United Methodist
Freshman admissions: more selective; 2019-2020: 13,959 applied, 6,601 accepted. Either SAT or ACT required. SAT 25/75 percentile: 29-33. High school rank: 49% in top tenth, 79% in top quarter, 97% in top half
Early decision deadline: 11/1, notification date: 12/31
Early action deadline: 11/1, notification date: 12/31
Application deadline (fall): 1/15
Undergraduate student body: 6,519 full time, 191 part time; 51% male, 49% female; 0% American Indian, 7% Asian, 4% Black, 12% Hispanic, 4% multiracial, 0% Pacific Islander, 64% white, 7% international; N/A from in state; 54% live on campus; 27% of students in fraternities, 36% in sororities
Most popular majors: 27% Business, Management, Marketing, and Related Support Services, 13% Social Sciences, 9% Communication, Journalism, and Related Programs, 9% Engineering, 6% Mathematics and Statistics
Expenses: 2020-2021: $58,540; room/board: $17,110
Financial aid: (214) 768-3417; 31% of undergrads determined to have financial need; average aid package $44,634

South Texas College[1]
McAllen TX
(956) 872-8311
U.S. News ranking: Reg. Coll. (W), unranked
Website: www.southtexascollege.edu/
Admissions email: N/A
Public
Application deadline (fall): N/A
Undergraduate student body: N/A full time, N/A part time
Expenses: 2019-2020: $4,140 in state, $4,440 out of state; room/board: $6,123
Financial aid: N/A

Southwestern Adventist University[1]
Keene TX
(817) 202-6749
U.S. News ranking: Reg. Coll. (W), No. 11
Website: www.swau.edu
Admissions email: admissions@swau.edu

Private; founded 1893
Affiliation: Seventh Day Adventist
Application deadline (fall): 8/1
Undergraduate student body: N/A full time, N/A part time
Expenses: 2019-2020: $22,188; room/board: $7,800
Financial aid: (817) 202-6262

Southwestern Assemblies of God University[1]
Waxahachie TX
(888) 937-7248
U.S. News ranking: Reg. U. (W), second tier
Website: www.sagu.edu/
Admissions email: admissions@sagu.edu
Private; founded 1927
Application deadline (fall): rolling
Undergraduate student body: N/A full time, N/A part time
Expenses: 2019-2020: $19,834; room/board: $7,500
Financial aid: (972) 825-4730

Southwestern Christian College[1]
Terrell TX
(972) 524-3341
U.S. News ranking: Reg. Coll. (W), unranked
Website: www.swcc.edu
Admissions email: N/A
Private
Application deadline (fall): N/A
Undergraduate student body: N/A full time, N/A part time
Expenses: 2019-2020: $8,131; room/board: $6,270
Financial aid: N/A

Southwestern University
Georgetown TX
(512) 863-1200
U.S. News ranking: Nat. Lib. Arts, No. 102
Website: www.southwestern.edu
Admissions email: admission@southwestern.edu
Private; founded 1840
Affiliation: United Methodist
Freshman admissions: more selective; 2019-2020: 4,766 applied, 2,337 accepted. Neither SAT nor ACT required. SAT 25/75 percentile: 1140-1320. High school rank: 35% in top tenth, 67% in top quarter, 94% in top half
Early decision deadline: 11/1, notification date: 12/1
Early action deadline: 12/1, notification date: 3/1
Application deadline (fall): 2/1
Undergraduate student body: 1,495 full time, 12 part time; 45% male, 55% female; 0% American Indian, 4% Asian, 6% Black, 23% Hispanic, 4% multiracial, 0% Pacific Islander, 61% white, 1% international; 89% from in state; 78% live on campus; 22% of students in fraternities, 22% in sororities
Most popular majors: 15% Business, Management, Marketing, and Related Support Services, 14% Social Sciences, 10% Biological and

Biomedical Sciences, 9% Visual and Performing Arts, 8% Communication, Journalism, and Related Programs
Expenses: 2020-2021: $45,120; room/board: $12,450
Financial aid: (512) 863-1259; 61% of undergrads determined to have financial need; average aid package $37,072

St. Edward's University
Austin TX
(512) 448-8500
U.S. News ranking: Reg. U. (W), No. 8
Website: www.stedwards.edu
Admissions email: seu.admit@stedwards.edu
Private; founded 1885
Affiliation: Roman Catholic
Freshman admissions: selective; 2019-2020: 5,672 applied, 5,003 accepted. Either SAT or ACT required. SAT 25/75 percentile: 1060-1245. High school rank: 20% in top tenth, 51% in top quarter, 81% in top half
Early decision deadline: N/A, notification date: N/A
Early action deadline: N/A, notification date: N/A
Application deadline (fall): 5/1
Undergraduate student body: 3,199 full time, 244 part time; 38% male, 62% female; 1% American Indian, 3% Asian, 4% Black, 46% Hispanic, 3% multiracial, 0% Pacific Islander, 36% white, 7% international; 79% from in state; 43% live on campus; N/A of students in fraternities, N/A in sororities
Most popular majors: 24% Business, Management, Marketing, and Related Support Services, 10% Communication, Journalism, and Related Programs, 9% Biological and Biomedical Sciences, 9% Psychology, 8% Social Sciences
Expenses: 2020-2021: $49,076; room/board: $13,912
Financial aid: (512) 448-8516; 70% of undergrads determined to have financial need; average aid package $37,746

Stephen F. Austin State University[1]
Nacogdoches TX
(936) 468-2504
U.S. News ranking: Nat. U., second tier
Website: www.sfasu.edu
Admissions email: admissions@sfasu.edu
Public; founded 1923
Application deadline (fall): rolling
Undergraduate student body: N/A full time, N/A part time
Expenses: 2019-2020: $8,844 in state, $18,972 out of state; room/board: $9,012
Financial aid: (936) 468-2230

St. Mary's University of San Antonio

San Antonio TX
(210) 436-3126
U.S. News ranking: Reg. U. (W), No. 8
Website: www.stmarytx.edu
Admissions email: uadm@stmarytx.edu
Private; founded 1852
Affiliation: Roman Catholic
Freshman admissions: selective; 2019-2020: 4,861 applied, 3,822 accepted. Either SAT or ACT required. SAT 25/75 percentile: 1040-1220. High school rank: 30% in top tenth, 61% in top quarter, 87% in top half
Early decision deadline: N/A, notification date: N/A
Early action deadline: N/A, notification date: N/A
Application deadline (fall): 1/15
Undergraduate student body: 2,162 full time, 108 part time; 44% male, 56% female; 0% American Indian, 2% Asian, 3% Black, 68% Hispanic, 1% multiracial, 0% Pacific Islander, 15% white, 6% international; 88% from in state; 51% live on campus; 11% of students in fraternities, 10% in sororities
Most popular majors: 21% Business, Management, Marketing, and Related Support Services, 17% Social Sciences, 9% Biological and Biomedical Sciences, 8% Engineering, 8% Parks, Recreation, Leisure, and Fitness Studies
Expenses: 2020-2021: $33,720; room/board: $10,980
Financial aid: (210) 436-3141; 75% of undergrads determined to have financial need; average aid package $27,480

Sul Ross State University

Alpine TX
(432) 837-8050
U.S. News ranking: Reg. U. (W), second tier
Website: www.sulross.edu
Admissions email: admissions@sulross.edu
Public; founded 1917
Freshman admissions: least selective; 2019-2020: 1,088 applied, 881 accepted. Neither SAT nor ACT required. ACT 25/75 percentile: 15-19. High school rank: 6% in top tenth, 18% in top quarter, 60% in top half
Early decision deadline: N/A, notification date: N/A
Early action deadline: N/A, notification date: N/A
Application deadline (fall): rolling
Undergraduate student body: 1,179 full time, 670 part time; 40% male, 60% female; 1% American Indian, 0% Asian, 6% Black, 67% Hispanic, 3% multiracial, 0% Pacific Islander, 23% white, 0% international; 99% from in state; 50% live on campus; N/A of students in fraternities, N/A in sororities
Most popular majors: 19% Multi-/Interdisciplinary Studies, Other, 16% Business/Commerce, General, 14% Criminal Justice/

Safety Studies, 9% Psychology, General, 8% Kinesiology and Exercise Science
Expenses: 2020-2021: $8,441 in state, $20,058 out of state; room/board: $9,326
Financial aid: (432) 837-8059

Tarleton State University

Stephenville TX
(800) 687-8236
U.S. News ranking: Reg. U. (W), No. 64
Website: www.tarleton.edu
Admissions email: uadm@tarleton.edu
Public; founded 1899
Freshman admissions: selective; 2019-2020: 9,943 applied, 5,557 accepted. Either SAT or ACT required. ACT 25/75 percentile: 18-23. High school rank: 10% in top tenth, 35% in top quarter, 75% in top half
Early decision deadline: N/A, notification date: N/A
Early action deadline: 12/1, notification date: N/A
Application deadline (fall): 8/1
Undergraduate student body: 8,211 full time, 3,139 part time; 38% male, 62% female; 0% American Indian, 1% Asian, 8% Black, 21% Hispanic, 4% multiracial, 0% Pacific Islander, 64% white, 1% international; N/A from in state; 32% live on campus; N/A of students in fraternities, N/A in sororities
Most popular majors: 19% Business, Management, Marketing, and Related Support Services, 11% Agriculture, Agriculture Operations, and Related Sciences, 11% Multi/Interdisciplinary Studies, 10% Health Professions and Related Programs, 8% Parks, Recreation, Leisure, and Fitness Studies
Expenses: 2020-2021: $10,334 in state, $21,717 out of state; room/board: $10,712
Financial aid: (254) 968-9070; 62% of undergrads determined to have financial need; average aid package $9,700

Texas A&M International University

Laredo TX
(956) 326-2200
U.S. News ranking: Reg. U. (W), No. 58
Website: www.tamiu.edu
Admissions email: enroll@tamiu.edu
Public; founded 1970
Freshman admissions: selective; 2019-2020: 7,884 applied, 4,906 accepted. Either SAT or ACT required. SAT 25/75 percentile: 910-1090. High school rank: 21% in top tenth, 55% in top quarter, 87% in top half
Early decision deadline: N/A, notification date: N/A
Early action deadline: N/A, notification date: N/A
Application deadline (fall): 8/1
Undergraduate student body: 5,574 full time, 1,646 part time; 39% male, 61% female; 0% American

Indian, 0% Asian, 0% Black, 96% Hispanic, 0% multiracial, 0% Pacific Islander, 2% white, 1% international; 96% from in state; 9% live on campus; 1% of students in fraternities, 1% in sororities
Most popular majors: 14% Business Administration and Management, General, 12% Criminal Justice/Law Enforcement Administration, 12% Psychology, General, 6% Accounting, 6% Biology/Biological Sciences, General
Expenses: 2020-2021: $9,254 in state, $21,524 out of state; room/board: $8,809
Financial aid: (956) 326-2225; 93% of undergrads determined to have financial need; average aid package $4,837

Texas A&M University

College Station TX
(979) 845-1060
U.S. News ranking: Nat. U., No. 66
Website: www.tamu.edu
Admissions email: admissions@tamu.edu
Public; founded 1876
Freshman admissions: more selective; 2019-2020: 42,899 applied, 24,676 accepted. Either SAT or ACT required. SAT 25/75 percentile: 1160-1390. High school rank: 70% in top tenth, 93% in top quarter, 99% in top half
Early decision deadline: N/A, notification date: N/A
Early action deadline: 10/15, notification date: N/A
Application deadline (fall): 12/1
Undergraduate student body: 47,667 full time, 6,124 part time; 53% male, 47% female; 0% American Indian, 9% Asian, 3% Black, 25% Hispanic, 3% multiracial, 0% Pacific Islander, 59% white, 1% international; 95% from in state; 23% live on campus; 6% of students in fraternities, 15% in sororities
Most popular majors: 16% Business, Management, Marketing, and Related Support Services, 16% Engineering, 11% Multi/Interdisciplinary Studies, 8% Agriculture, Agriculture Operations, and Related Sciences, 7% Biological and Biomedical Sciences
Expenses: 2020-2021: $12,445 in state, $39,394 out of state; room/board: $11,400
Financial aid: (979) 845-3236; 45% of undergrads determined to have financial need; average aid package $18,068

Texas A&M University–Commerce

Commerce TX
(903) 886-5000
U.S. News ranking: Nat. U., second tier
Website: www.tamuc.edu/
Admissions email: admissions@tamuc.edu
Public; founded 1889
Freshman admissions: selective; 2019-2020: 10,593 applied, 3,816 accepted. Either SAT

or ACT required. SAT 25/75 percentile: 950-1150. High school rank: 16% in top tenth, 44% in top quarter, 80% in top half
Early decision deadline: N/A, notification date: N/A
Early action deadline: N/A, notification date: N/A
Application deadline (fall): 8/15
Undergraduate student body: 5,609 full time, 2,715 part time; 40% male, 60% female; 1% American Indian, 2% Asian, 22% Black, 22% Hispanic, 7% multiracial, 0% Pacific Islander, 41% white, 4% international; 94% from in state; 30% live on campus; 3% of students in fraternities, 2% in sororities
Most popular majors: 26% Business, Management, Marketing, and Related Support Services, 17% Multi/Interdisciplinary Studies, 12% Education, 5% Computer and Information Sciences and Support Services, 5% Liberal Arts and Sciences, General Studies and Humanities
Expenses: 2020-2021: $9,820 in state, $22,090 out of state; room/board: $9,068
Financial aid: (903) 886-5096; 71% of undergrads determined to have financial need; average aid package $10,008

Texas A&M University–Corpus Christi

Corpus Christi TX
(361) 825-2624
U.S. News ranking: Nat. U., second tier
Website: www.tamucc.edu/
Admissions email: admiss@tamucc.edu
Public; founded 1947
Freshman admissions: selective; 2019-2020: 9,839 applied, 8,206 accepted. Either SAT or ACT required. SAT 25/75 percentile: 1010-1200. High school rank: 17% in top tenth, 52% in top quarter, 85% in top half
Early decision deadline: N/A, notification date: N/A
Early action deadline: N/A, notification date: N/A
Application deadline (fall): 7/1
Undergraduate student body: 7,201 full time, 2,122 part time; 40% male, 60% female; 0% American Indian, 3% Asian, 5% Black, 51% Hispanic, 2% multiracial, 0% Pacific Islander, 36% white, 2% international; 96% from in state; 24% live on campus; 1% of students in fraternities, 1% in sororities
Most popular majors: 20% Health Professions and Related Programs, 16% Business, Management, Marketing, and Related Support Services, 10% Biological and Biomedical Sciences, 9% Multi/Interdisciplinary Studies, 7% Psychology
Expenses: 2020-2021: $10,317 in state, $22,949 out of state; room/board: $11,247
Financial aid: (361) 825-2332; 65% of undergrads determined to have financial need; average aid package $11,533

Texas A&M University–Kingsville

Kingsville TX
(361) 593-2315
U.S. News ranking: Nat. U., second tier
Website: www.tamuk.edu
Admissions email: admissions@tamuk.edu
Public; founded 1925
Freshman admissions: selective; 2019-2020: 6,330 applied, 4,892 accepted. Either SAT or ACT required. SAT 25/75 percentile: 940-1120. High school rank: 16% in top tenth, 43% in top quarter, 80% in top half
Early decision deadline: N/A, notification date: N/A
Early action deadline: N/A, notification date: N/A
Application deadline (fall): 8/1
Undergraduate student body: 4,670 full time, 1,504 part time; 50% male, 50% female; 0% American Indian, 1% Asian, 5% Black, 73% Hispanic, 1% multiracial, 0% Pacific Islander, 16% white, 4% international; 99% from in state; 26% live on campus; 2% of students in fraternities, 2% in sororities
Most popular majors: 24% Engineering, 10% Business, Management, Marketing, and Related Support Services, 8% Multi/Interdisciplinary Studies, 7% Agriculture, Agriculture Operations, and Related Sciences, 7% Parks, Recreation, Leisure, and Fitness Studies
Expenses: 2020-2021: $9,688 in state, $23,106 out of state; room/board: $8,848
Financial aid: (361) 593-3911; 75% of undergrads determined to have financial need; average aid package $11,044

Texas A&M University–San Antonio[1]

San Antonio TX
(210) 784-1000
San Antonio TX
U.S. News ranking: Reg. U. (W), unranked
Admissions email: N/A
Public
Application deadline (fall): N/A
Undergraduate student body: N/A full time, N/A part time
Expenses: 2019-2020: $8,864 in state, $21,877 out of state; room/board: $10,420
Financial aid: N/A

Texas A&M University–Texarkana

Texarkana TX
(903) 223-3069
U.S. News ranking: Reg. U. (W), No. 80
Website: www.tamut.edu
Admissions email: admissions@tamut.edu
Public; founded 1971
Freshman admissions: selective; 2019-2020: 2,393 applied, 2,239 accepted. Neither SAT nor ACT required. ACT 25/75

percentile: 19-23. High school rank: 8% in top tenth, 36% in top quarter, 75% in top half
Early decision deadline: N/A, notification date: N/A
Early action deadline: N/A, notification date: N/A
Application deadline (fall): rolling
Undergraduate student body: 1,242 full time, 481 part time; 38% male, 62% female; 1% American Indian, 1% Asian, 17% Black, 18% Hispanic, 5% multiracial, 0% Pacific Islander, 52% white, 2% international; N/A from in state; 16% live on campus; N/A of students in fraternities, N/A in sororities
Most popular majors: 28% Multi/Interdisciplinary Studies, 20% Business, Management, Marketing, and Related Support Services, 9% Liberal Arts and Sciences, General Studies and Humanities, 7% Homeland Security, Law Enforcement, Firefighting and Related Protective Services, 7% Psychology
Expenses: 2020-2021: $7,458 in state, $8,358 out of state; room/board: $8,621
Financial aid: (903) 334-6601; 73% of undergrads determined to have financial need; average aid package $11,012

Texas Christian University
Fort Worth TX
(800) 828-3764
U.S. News ranking: Nat. U., No. 80
Website: www.tcu.edu
Admissions email: frogmail@tcu.edu
Private; founded 1873
Affiliation: Christian Church (Disciples of Christ)
Freshman admissions: more selective; 2019-2020: 19,028 applied, 8,966 accepted. Neither SAT nor ACT required. ACT 25/75 percentile: 25-31. High school rank: 47% in top tenth, 75% in top quarter, 95% in top half
Early decision deadline: 11/1, notification date: 12/1
Early action deadline: 11/1, notification date: 12/15
Application deadline (fall): 2/1
Undergraduate student body: 9,219 full time, 255 part time; 42% male, 58% female; 1% American Indian, 3% Asian, 5% Black, 15% Hispanic, 2% multiracial, 0% Pacific Islander, 68% white, 5% international; 51% from in state; 52% live on campus; 18% of students in fraternities, 32% in sororities
Most popular majors: 23% Business, Management, Marketing, and Related Support Services, 17% Communication, Journalism, and Related Programs, 13% Health Professions and Related Programs, 10% Social Sciences, 5% Psychology
Expenses: 2020-2021: $51,660; room/board: $14,040
Financial aid: (817) 257-7858; 39% of undergrads determined to have financial need; average aid package $33,516

Texas College[1]
Tyler TX
(903) 593-8311
U.S. News ranking: Reg. Coll. (W), unranked
Website: www.texascollege.edu
Admissions email: cmarshall-biggins@texascollege.edu
Private
Application deadline (fall): N/A
Undergraduate student body: N/A full time, N/A part time
Expenses: 2019-2020: $10,000; room/board: $8,000
Financial aid: N/A

Texas Lutheran University
Seguin TX
(800) 771-8521
U.S. News ranking: Reg. Coll. (W), No. 4
Website: www.tlu.edu
Admissions email: admissions@tlu.edu
Private; founded 1891
Affiliation: Evangelical Lutheran Church
Freshman admissions: selective; 2019-2020: 3,000 applied, 1,672 accepted. Either SAT or ACT required. SAT 25/75 percentile: 990-1160. High school rank: 20% in top tenth, 48% in top quarter, 81% in top half
Early decision deadline: N/A, notification date: N/A
Early action deadline: 12/15, notification date: 2/15
Application deadline (fall): 2/1
Undergraduate student body: 1,380 full time, 65 part time; 49% male, 51% female; 0% American Indian, 1% Asian, 9% Black, 40% Hispanic, 2% multiracial, 0% Pacific Islander, 46% white, 1% international; 98% from in state; 53% live on campus; 7% of students in fraternities, 11% in sororities
Most popular majors: 25% Business, Management, Marketing, and Related Support Services, 17% Parks, Recreation, Leisure, and Fitness Studies, 13% Education, 11% Health Professions and Related Programs, 5% Social Sciences
Expenses: 2020-2021: $31,850; room/board: $10,690
Financial aid: (830) 372-8010; 79% of undergrads determined to have financial need; average aid package $26,094

Texas Southern University
Houston TX
(713) 313-7071
U.S. News ranking: Nat. U., second tier
Website: www.tsu.edu
Admissions email: admissions@tsu.edu
Public; founded 1927
Freshman admissions: least selective; 2019-2020: 8,554 applied, 7,772 accepted. Either SAT or ACT required. SAT 25/75 percentile: 840-1000. High school rank: 5% in top tenth, 19% in top quarter, 53% in top half

Early decision deadline: 12/1, notification date: N/A
Early action deadline: N/A, notification date: N/A
Application deadline (fall): 8/1
Undergraduate student body: 6,032 full time, 1,060 part time; 41% male, 59% female; 0% American Indian, 1% Asian, 82% Black, 8% Hispanic, 3% multiracial, 0% Pacific Islander, 1% white, 5% international; 85% from in state; 25% live on campus; N/A of students in fraternities, N/A in sororities
Most popular majors: 8% Banking and Financial Support Services, 7% Biology/Biological Sciences, General, 6% Business Administration and Management, General, 6% Criminal Justice/Law Enforcement Administration, 6% General Studies
Expenses: 2019-2020: $9,173 in state, $21,833 out of state; room/board: $9,664
Financial aid: (713) 313-7071

Texas State University
San Marcos TX
(512) 245-2364
U.S. News ranking: Nat. U., second tier
Website: www.txstate.edu
Admissions email: admissions@txstate.edu
Public; founded 1899
Freshman admissions: selective; 2019-2020: 23,583 applied, 19,134 accepted. Either SAT or ACT required. SAT 25/75 percentile: 1010-1180. High school rank: 12% in top tenth, 46% in top quarter, 90% in top half
Early decision deadline: N/A, notification date: N/A
Early action deadline: N/A, notification date: N/A
Undergraduate student body: 27,923 full time, 5,994 part time; 42% male, 58% female; 0% American Indian, 3% Asian, 9% Black, 40% Hispanic, 4% multiracial, 0% Pacific Islander, 43% white, 0% international; 98% from in state; 20% live on campus; 5% of students in fraternities, 5% in sororities
Most popular majors: 8% Multi-/Interdisciplinary Studies, Other, 6% Business Administration and Management, General, 6% Psychology, General, 5% Kinesiology and Exercise Science, 4% Marketing/Marketing Management, General
Expenses: 2020-2021: $11,550 in state, $23,820 out of state; room/board: $11,336
Financial aid: (512) 245-2315; 59% of undergrads determined to have financial need; average aid package $11,730

Texas Tech University
Lubbock TX
(806) 742-1480
U.S. News ranking: Nat. U., No. 217
Website: www.ttu.edu
Admissions email: admissions@ttu.edu
Public; founded 1923

Freshman admissions: more selective; 2019-2020: 25,384 applied, 17,493 accepted. Either SAT or ACT required. SAT 25/75 percentile: 1070-1260. High school rank: 19% in top tenth, 53% in top quarter, 88% in top half
Early decision deadline: N/A, notification date: N/A
Early action deadline: N/A, notification date: N/A
Application deadline (fall): 8/1
Undergraduate student body: 28,062 full time, 4,063 part time; 52% male, 48% female; 0% American Indian, 3% Asian, 6% Black, 29% Hispanic, 3% multiracial, 0% Pacific Islander, 55% white, 3% international; 92% from in state; 26% live on campus; 13% of students in fraternities, 20% in sororities
Most popular majors: 18% Business, Management, Marketing, and Related Support Services, 13% Engineering, 9% Multi/Interdisciplinary Studies, 7% Communication, Journalism, and Related Programs, 7% Family and Consumer Sciences/Human Sciences
Expenses: 2020-2021: $11,319 in state, $23,979 out of state; room/board: $9,956
Financial aid: (806) 834-1780; 48% of undergrads determined to have financial need; average aid package $10,477

Texas Wesleyan University
Fort Worth TX
(817) 531-4422
U.S. News ranking: Nat. U., second tier
Website: www.txwes.edu
Admissions email: admission@txwes.edu
Private; founded 1890
Affiliation: United Methodist
Freshman admissions: selective; 2019-2020: 4,521 applied, 853 accepted. Either SAT or ACT required. SAT 25/75 percentile: 975-1090. High school rank: N/A
Early decision deadline: N/A, notification date: N/A
Early action deadline: N/A, notification date: N/A
Application deadline (fall): rolling
Undergraduate student body: 1,327 full time, 160 part time; 46% male, 54% female; 1% American Indian, 1% Asian, 15% Black, 34% Hispanic, 8% multiracial, 0% Pacific Islander, 27% white, 13% international
Most popular majors: 10% Criminal Justice/Safety Studies, 8% Multi-/Interdisciplinary Studies, Other, 8% Psychology, General, 7% Bilingual and Multilingual Education, 7% Management Science
Expenses: 2020-2021: $33,408; room/board: $9,730
Financial aid: (817) 531-4420; 98% of undergrads determined to have financial need; average aid package $14,288

Texas Woman's University
Denton TX
(940) 898-3188
U.S. News ranking: Nat. U., second tier
Website: www.twu.edu
Admissions email: admissions@twu.edu
Public; founded 1901
Freshman admissions: selective; 2019-2020: 5,650 applied, 5,277 accepted. Neither SAT nor ACT required. SAT 25/75 percentile: 930-1150. High school rank: 18% in top tenth, 46% in top quarter, 77% in top half
Early decision deadline: N/A, notification date: N/A
Early action deadline: N/A, notification date: N/A
Application deadline (fall): 8/25
Undergraduate student body: 7,032 full time, 3,559 part time; 13% male, 87% female; 0% American Indian, 9% Asian, 18% Black, 33% Hispanic, 3% multiracial, 0% Pacific Islander, 33% white, 2% international; 98% from in state; 25% live on campus; 2% of students in fraternities, 3% in sororities
Most popular majors: 33% Health Professions and Related Programs, 11% Liberal Arts and Sciences, General Studies and Humanities, 10% Business, Management, Marketing, and Related Support Services, 8% Multi/Interdisciplinary Studies, 7% Parks, Recreation, Leisure, and Fitness Studies
Expenses: 2020-2021: $10,060 in state, $22,330 out of state; room/board: $9,730
Financial aid: (940) 898-3064; 67% of undergrads determined to have financial need; average aid package $14,143

Trinity University
San Antonio TX
(800) 874-6489
U.S. News ranking: Reg. U. (W), No. 1
Website: www.trinity.edu
Admissions email: admissions@trinity.edu
Private; founded 1869
Affiliation: Presbyterian
Freshman admissions: more selective; 2019-2020: 9,864 applied, 2,837 accepted. Either SAT or ACT required. SAT 25/75 percentile: 1290-1450. High school rank: 50% in top tenth, 82% in top quarter, 98% in top half
Early decision deadline: 11/1, notification date: 12/15
Early action deadline: 11/1, notification date: 12/15
Application deadline (fall): 1/15
Undergraduate student body: 2,476 full time, 52 part time; 47% male, 53% female; 0% American Indian, 8% Asian, 4% Black, 21% Hispanic, 5% multiracial, 0% Pacific Islander, 56% white, 4% international; N/A from in state; 81% live on campus; N/A of students in fraternities, N/A in sororities
Most popular majors: 21% Business, Management, Marketing, and Related Support

Services, 13% Biological and Biomedical Sciences, 13% Social Sciences, 7% Engineering, 7% Foreign Languages, Literatures, and Linguistics
Expenses: 2020-2021: $46,456; room/board: $13,740
Financial aid: (210) 999-8005; 44% of undergrads determined to have financial need; average aid package $41,170

Tyler Junior College[1]
Tyler TX
(903) 510-2200
U.S. News ranking: Reg. Coll. (W), unranked
Admissions email: N/A
Public
Application deadline (fall): rolling
Undergraduate student body: N/A full time, N/A part time
Expenses: 2019-2020: $2,962 in state, $4,762 out of state; room/board: $8,640
Financial aid: N/A

University of Dallas
Irving TX
(800) 628-6999
U.S. News ranking: Reg. U. (W), No. 6
Website: www.udallas.edu
Admissions email: ugadmis@udallas.edu
Private; founded 1956
Affiliation: Roman Catholic
Freshman admissions: more selective; 2019-2020: 4,676 applied, 2,120 accepted. Neither SAT nor ACT required. SAT 25/75 percentile: 1130-1360. High school rank: 32% in top tenth, 66% in top quarter, 91% in top half
Early decision deadline: N/A, notification date: N/A
Early action deadline: 12/1, notification date: 1/15
Application deadline (fall): 8/1
Undergraduate student body: 1,443 full time, 32 part time; 47% male, 53% female; 0% American Indian, 7% Asian, 2% Black, 25% Hispanic, 3% multiracial, 0% Pacific Islander, 59% white, 3% international; 52% from in state; 55% live on campus; 0% of students in fraternities, 0% in sororities
Most popular majors: 17% Biological and Biomedical Sciences, 17% Social Sciences, 15% Business, Management, Marketing, and Related Support Services, 12% English Language and Literature/Letters, 6% Theology and Religious Vocations
Expenses: 2020-2021: $44,810; room/board: $13,080
Financial aid: (972) 721-5266; 63% of undergrads determined to have financial need; average aid package $36,788

University of Houston
Houston TX
(713) 743-1010
U.S. News ranking: Nat. U., No. 176
Website: www.uh.edu
Admissions email: admissions@uh.edu
Public; founded 1927

Freshman admissions: more selective; 2019-2020: 25,393 applied, 16,500 accepted. Either SAT or ACT required. SAT 25/75 percentile: 1140-1310. High school rank: 32% in top tenth, 64% in top quarter, 88% in top half
Early decision deadline: N/A, notification date: N/A
Early action deadline: N/A, notification date: N/A
Application deadline (fall): 6/1
Undergraduate student body: 28,368 full time, 10,229 part time; 50% male, 50% female; 0% American Indian, 23% Asian, 10% Black, 36% Hispanic, 3% multiracial, 0% Pacific Islander, 22% white, 4% international; 98% from in state; 17% live on campus; 3% of students in fraternities, 4% in sororities
Most popular majors: 28% Business, Management, Marketing, and Related Support Services, 9% Engineering, 8% Psychology, 6% Biological and Biomedical Sciences, 6% Computer and Information Sciences and Support Services
Expenses: 2020-2021: $11,569 in state, $26,839 out of state; room/board: $9,750
Financial aid: (713) 743-1010; 63% of undergrads determined to have financial need; average aid package $12,716

University of Houston–Clear Lake
Houston TX
(281) 283-2500
U.S. News ranking: Reg. U. (W), unranked
Website: www.uhcl.edu
Admissions email: admissions@uhcl.edu
Public; founded 1974
Freshman admissions: selective; 2019-2020: 1,311 applied, 1,024 accepted. Either SAT or ACT required. SAT 25/75 percentile: 1020-1190. High school rank: 16% in top tenth, 44% in top quarter, 78% in top half
Early decision deadline: N/A, notification date: N/A
Early action deadline: N/A, notification date: N/A
Application deadline (fall): 8/1
Undergraduate student body: 3,356 full time, 3,069 part time; 38% male, 62% female; 0% American Indian, 7% Asian, 7% Black, 43% Hispanic, 3% multiracial, 0% Pacific Islander, 37% white, 1% international; N/A from in state; 3% live on campus; N/A of students in fraternities, N/A in sororities
Most popular majors: 24% Business, Management, Marketing, and Related Support Services, 22% Multi/Interdisciplinary Studies, 8% Psychology, 6% Health Professions and Related Programs, 5% Biological and Biomedical Sciences
Expenses: 2020-2021: $7,961 in state, $24,755 out of state; room/board: $5,109

Financial aid: (281) 283-2482; 68% of undergrads determined to have financial need; average aid package $9,757

University of Houston–Downtown
Houston TX
(713) 221-8522
U.S. News ranking: Reg. U. (W), second tier
Website: www.uhd.edu
Admissions email: uhdadmit@uhd.edu
Public; founded 1974
Freshman admissions: less selective; 2019-2020: 5,617 applied, 4,981 accepted. Either SAT or ACT required. SAT 25/75 percentile: 920-1080. High school rank: 6% in top tenth, 30% in top quarter, 68% in top half
Early decision deadline: N/A, notification date: N/A
Early action deadline: N/A, notification date: N/A
Application deadline (fall): 6/1
Undergraduate student body: 6,629 full time, 6,507 part time; 40% male, 60% female; 0% American Indian, 9% Asian, 18% Black, 54% Hispanic, 1% multiracial, 0% Pacific Islander, 14% white, 2% international; N/A from in state; 0% live on campus; 1% of students in fraternities, 1% in sororities
Most popular majors: 30% Multi/Interdisciplinary Studies, 29% Business, Management, Marketing, and Related Support Services, 9% Homeland Security, Law Enforcement, Firefighting and Related Protective Services, 7% Psychology, 4% Communication, Journalism, and Related Programs
Expenses: 2020-2021: $8,664 in state, $21,024 out of state; room/board: N/A
Financial aid: (713) 221-8041; 77% of undergrads determined to have financial need; average aid package $8,452

University of Houston–Victoria[1]
Victoria TX
(877) 970-4848
U.S. News ranking: Reg. U. (W), second tier
Website: www.uhv.edu/
Admissions email: admissions@uhv.edu
Public; founded 1973
Application deadline (fall): 8/1
Undergraduate student body: N/A full time, N/A part time
Expenses: 2019-2020: $6,781 in state, $16,909 out of state; room/board: $8,407
Financial aid: N/A

University of Mary Hardin-Baylor
Belton TX
(254) 295-4520
U.S. News ranking: Reg. U. (W), No. 46
Website: www.umhb.edu
Admissions email: admission@umhb.edu
Private; founded 1845
Affiliation: Baptist

Freshman admissions: selective; 2019-2020: 15,355 applied, 13,417 accepted. Either SAT or ACT required. SAT 25/75 percentile: 1000-1190. High school rank: 19% in top tenth, 47% in top quarter, 77% in top half
Early decision deadline: N/A, notification date: N/A
Early action deadline: N/A, notification date: N/A
Application deadline (fall): rolling
Undergraduate student body: 3,113 full time, 248 part time; 35% male, 65% female; 1% American Indian, 2% Asian, 14% Black, 23% Hispanic, 3% multiracial, 0% Pacific Islander, 53% white, 1% international; 97% from in state; 58% live on campus; N/A of students in fraternities, N/A in sororities
Most popular majors: 29% Health Professions and Related Programs, 15% Business, Management, Marketing, and Related Support Services, 12% Education, 7% Psychology, 6% Biological and Biomedical Sciences
Expenses: 2020-2021: $30,850; room/board: $9,134
Financial aid: (254) 295-4517; 81% of undergrads determined to have financial need; average aid package $18,818

University of North Texas
Denton TX
(940) 565-2681
U.S. News ranking: Nat. U., No. 249
Website: www.unt.edu
Admissions email: unt.freshmen@unt.edu
Public; founded 1890
Freshman admissions: selective; 2019-2020: 21,546 applied, 15,883 accepted. Either SAT or ACT required. SAT 25/75 percentile: 1060-1260. High school rank: 23% in top tenth, 53% in top quarter, 92% in top half
Early decision deadline: N/A, notification date: N/A
Early action deadline: N/A, notification date: N/A
Application deadline (fall): 8/1
Undergraduate student body: 26,090 full time, 6,036 part time; 47% male, 53% female; 0% American Indian, 7% Asian, 14% Black, 27% Hispanic, 4% multiracial, 0% Pacific Islander, 42% white, 4% international; 93% from in state; 21% live on campus; 5% of students in fraternities, 6% in sororities
Most popular majors: 19% Business, Management, Marketing, and Related Support Services, 11% Multi/Interdisciplinary Studies, 9% Liberal Arts and Sciences, General Studies and Humanities, 8% Visual and Performing Arts, 7% Communication, Journalism, and Related Programs
Expenses: 2020-2021: $11,281 in state, $23,941 out of state; room/board: $9,888

Financial aid: (940) 565-3901; 61% of undergrads determined to have financial need; average aid package $13,063

University of North Texas–Dallas[1]
Dallas TX
(972) 780-3600
U.S. News ranking: Reg. U. (W), No. 60
Admissions email: N/A
Public; founded 2010
Application deadline (fall): 8/10
Undergraduate student body: N/A full time, N/A part time
Expenses: 2019-2020: $9,140 in state, $21,811 out of state; room/board: $8,948
Financial aid: N/A

University of St. Thomas
Houston TX
(713) 525-3500
U.S. News ranking: Reg. U. (W), No. 18
Website: www.stthom.edu
Admissions email: admissions@stthom.edu
Private; founded 1947
Affiliation: Roman Catholic
Freshman admissions: selective; 2019-2020: 1,101 applied, 961 accepted. Either SAT or ACT required. SAT 25/75 percentile: 1057-1242. High school rank: 19% in top tenth, 48% in top quarter, 82% in top half
Early decision deadline: N/A, notification date: N/A
Early action deadline: N/A, notification date: N/A
Application deadline (fall): 8/15
Undergraduate student body: 1,693 full time, 481 part time; 38% male, 62% female; 0% American Indian, 12% Asian, 7% Black, 47% Hispanic, 2% multiracial, 0% Pacific Islander, 21% white, 7% international; 97% from in state; 21% live on campus; N/A of students in fraternities, N/A in sororities
Most popular majors: 25% Business, Management, Marketing, and Related Support Services, 12% Biological and Biomedical Sciences, 12% Social Sciences, 11% Liberal Arts and Sciences, General Studies and Humanities, 10% Health Professions and Related Programs
Expenses: 2020-2021: $31,560; room/board: $9,470
Financial aid: (713) 525-2170; 70% of undergrads determined to have financial need; average aid package $25,335

University of Texas at Arlington
Arlington TX
(817) 272-6287
U.S. News ranking: Nat. U., second tier
Website: www.uta.edu
Admissions email: admissions@uta.edu
Public; founded 1895
Freshman admissions: selective; 2019-2020: 12,650 applied, 10,485 accepted. Either SAT

or ACT required. SAT 25/75 percentile: 1040-1250. High school rank: 25% in top tenth, 60% in top quarter, 87% in top half
Early decision deadline: N/A, notification date: N/A
Early action deadline: N/A, notification date: N/A
Application deadline (fall): N/A
Undergraduate student body: 19,441 full time, 15,379 part time; 39% male, 61% female; 0% American Indian, 12% Asian, 14% Black, 30% Hispanic, 4% multiracial, 0% Pacific Islander, 33% white, 5% international; 86% from in state; 10% live on campus; 1% of students in fraternities, 1% in sororities
Most popular majors: 43% Health Professions and Related Programs, 15% Business, Management, Marketing, and Related Support Services, 6% Engineering, 4% Biological and Biomedical Sciences, 4% Liberal Arts and Sciences, General Studies and Humanities
Expenses: 2020-2021: $11,378 in state, $28,524 out of state; room/board: $10,370
Financial aid: (817) 272-3568; 67% of undergrads determined to have financial need; average aid package $11,052

University of Texas at Austin

Austin TX
(512) 475-7399
U.S. News ranking: Nat. U., No. 42
Website: www.utexas.edu
Admissions email: admissions@austin.utexas.edu
Public; founded 1883
Freshman admissions: most selective; 2019-2020: 53,525 applied, 17,029 accepted. Either SAT or ACT required. SAT 25/75 percentile: 1230-1480. High school rank: 87% in top tenth, 96% in top quarter, 99% in top half
Early decision deadline: N/A, notification date: N/A
Early action deadline: N/A, notification date: N/A
Application deadline (fall): 12/1
Undergraduate student body: 37,515 full time, 2,648 part time; 46% male, 54% female; 0% American Indian, 23% Asian, 4% Black, 24% Hispanic, 4% multiracial, 0% Pacific Islander, 39% white, 5% international; 5% from in state; 18% live on campus; 13% of students in fraternities, 17% in sororities
Most popular majors: 13% Engineering, 12% Business, Management, Marketing, and Related Support Services, 12% Social Sciences, 11% Biological and Biomedical Sciences, 11% Communication, Journalism, and Related Programs
Expenses: 2020-2021: $11,106 in state, $39,322 out of state; room/board: $12,286
Financial aid: (512) 475-6282; 40% of undergrads determined to have financial need; average aid package $12,189

University of Texas at Dallas

Richardson TX
(972) 883-2270
U.S. News ranking: Nat. U., No. 143
Website: www.utdallas.edu
Admissions email: interest@utdallas.edu
Public; founded 1969
Freshman admissions: more selective; 2019-2020: 14,327 applied, 11,260 accepted. Either SAT or ACT required. SAT 25/75 percentile: 1240-1460. High school rank: 39% in top tenth, 71% in top quarter, 95% in top half
Early decision deadline: N/A, notification date: N/A
Early action deadline: N/A, notification date: N/A
Application deadline (fall): 5/1
Undergraduate student body: 17,941 full time, 3,053 part time; 57% male, 43% female; 0% American Indian, 35% Asian, 5% Black, 18% Hispanic, 4% multiracial, 0% Pacific Islander, 30% white, 4% international; 93% from in state; 24% live on campus; 5% of students in fraternities, 7% in sororities
Most popular majors: 23% Business, Management, Marketing, and Related Support Services, 14% Computer and Information Sciences and Support Services, 14% Engineering, 12% Biological and Biomedical Sciences, 8% Health Professions and Related Programs
Expenses: 2020-2021: $13,992 in state, $38,970 out of state; room/board: $11,762
Financial aid: (972) 883-4020; 51% of undergrads determined to have financial need; average aid package $14,492

University of Texas at San Antonio

San Antonio TX
(210) 458-8000
U.S. News ranking: Nat. U., second tier
Website: www.utsa.edu
Admissions email: prospects@utsa.edu
Public; founded 1969
Freshman admissions: selective; 2019-2020: 17,122 applied, 13,113 accepted. Either SAT or ACT required. SAT 25/75 percentile: 1030-1220. High school rank: 19% in top tenth, 60% in top quarter, 91% in top half
Early decision deadline: N/A, notification date: N/A
Early action deadline: N/A, notification date: N/A
Application deadline (fall): 6/1
Undergraduate student body: 22,414 full time, 5,861 part time; 50% male, 50% female; 0% American Indian, 6% Asian, 9% Black, 58% Hispanic, 4% multiracial, 0% Pacific Islander, 22% white, 2% international; 2% from in state; 8% live on campus; 3% of students in fraternities, 4% in sororities
Most popular majors: 20% Business, Management,

Marketing, and Related Support Services, 8% Engineering, 8% Psychology, 7% Computer and Information Sciences and Support Services, 7% Parks, Recreation, Leisure, and Fitness Studies
Expenses: 2020-2021: $10,168 in state, $25,174 out of state; room/board: $7,626
Financial aid: (210) 458-8000; 68% of undergrads determined to have financial need; average aid package $9,745

University of Texas at Tyler

Tyler TX
(903) 566-7203
U.S. News ranking: Nat. U., second tier
Website: www.uttyler.edu
Admissions email: admissions@uttyler.edu
Public; founded 1971
Freshman admissions: selective; 2019-2020: 2,742 applied, 2,281 accepted. Either SAT or ACT required. SAT 25/75 percentile: 1070-1240. High school rank: 14% in top tenth, 42% in top quarter, 75% in top half
Early decision deadline: N/A, notification date: N/A
Early action deadline: N/A, notification date: N/A
Application deadline (fall): 8/24
Undergraduate student body: 4,764 full time, 2,231 part time; 43% male, 57% female; 0% American Indian, 4% Asian, 10% Black, 22% Hispanic, 3% multiracial, 0% Pacific Islander, 57% white, 3% international; 97% from in state; 23% live on campus; 5% of students in fraternities, 8% in sororities
Most popular majors: 24% Registered Nursing/Registered Nurse, 11% Mechanical Engineering, 11% Multi-/Interdisciplinary Studies, Other, 5% Kinesiology and Exercise Science, 5% Psychology, General
Expenses: 2020-2021: $9,146 in state, $23,736 out of state; room/board: $9,618
Financial aid: (903) 566-7180; 79% of undergrads determined to have financial need; average aid package $8,736

University of Texas–El Paso

El Paso TX
(915) 747-5890
U.S. News ranking: Nat. U., second tier
Website: www.utep.edu
Admissions email: futureminer@utep.edu
Public; founded 1914
Freshman admissions: less selective; 2019-2020: 10,972 applied, 10,971 accepted. Neither SAT nor ACT required. SAT 25/75 percentile: 900-1110. High school rank: 19% in top tenth, 40% in top quarter, 68% in top half
Early decision deadline: N/A, notification date: N/A
Early action deadline: N/A, notification date: N/A
Application deadline (fall): 9/5

Undergraduate student body: 13,858 full time, 7,569 part time; 46% male, 54% female; 0% American Indian, 1% Asian, 2% Black, 85% Hispanic, 1% multiracial, 0% Pacific Islander, 5% white, 5% international; 96% from in state; N/A live on campus; N/A of students in fraternities, N/A in sororities
Most popular majors: 17% Business, Management, Marketing, and Related Support Services, 12% Engineering, 12% Health Professions and Related Programs, 12% Multi/Interdisciplinary Studies, 9% Biological and Biomedical Sciences
Expenses: 2019-2020: $8,961 in state, $24,324 out of state; room/board: $9,496
Financial aid: (915) 747-5204; 77% of undergrads determined to have financial need; average aid package $13,871

University of Texas of the Permian Basin

Odessa TX
(432) 552-2605
U.S. News ranking: Reg. U. (W), No. 68
Website: www.utpb.edu
Admissions email: admissions@utpb.edu
Public; founded 1973
Freshman admissions: selective; 2019-2020: 1,137 applied, 891 accepted. Either SAT or ACT required. SAT 25/75 percentile: 940-1132. High school rank: 20% in top tenth, 48% in top quarter, 84% in top half
Early decision deadline: N/A, notification date: N/A
Early action deadline: N/A, notification date: N/A
Application deadline (fall): 8/26
Undergraduate student body: 1,862 full time, 2,485 part time; 42% male, 58% female; 0% American Indian, 2% Asian, 6% Black, 53% Hispanic, 2% multiracial, 0% Pacific Islander, 32% white, 3% international
Most popular majors: Business Administration and Management, General, Multi-/Interdisciplinary Studies, Other, Petroleum Engineering, Psychology, General, Registered Nursing/Registered Nurse
Expenses: 2020-2021: $10,044 in state, $11,094 out of state; room/board: $11,099
Financial aid: (432) 552-2620

University of Texas–Rio Grande Valley

Edinburg TX
(888) 882-4026
U.S. News ranking: Nat. U., No. 284
Website: www.utrgv.edu/en-us/index.htm
Admissions email: admissions@utrgv.edu
Public; founded 2013
Freshman admissions: selective; 2019-2020: 10,680 applied, 8,523 accepted. Either SAT or ACT required. ACT 25/75

percentile: 17-22. High school rank: 23% in top tenth, 54% in top quarter, 84% in top half
Early decision deadline: N/A, notification date: N/A
Early action deadline: N/A, notification date: N/A
Application deadline (fall): 7/1
Undergraduate student body: 19,922 full time, 5,043 part time; 43% male, 57% female; 0% American Indian, 1% Asian, 0% Black, 92% Hispanic, 0% multiracial, 0% Pacific Islander, 2% white, 2% international; N/A from in state; 3% live on campus; N/A of students in fraternities, N/A in sororities
Most popular majors: 13% Biological and Biomedical Sciences, 13% Business, Management, Marketing, and Related Support Services, 10% Health Professions and Related Programs, 10% Homeland Security, Law Enforcement, Firefighting and Related Protective Services, 8% Psychology
Expenses: 2019-2020: $8,132 in state, $18,260 out of state; room/board: $8,252
Financial aid: N/A

University of the Incarnate Word

San Antonio TX
(210) 829-6005
U.S. News ranking: Nat. U., No. 272
Website: www.uiw.edu
Admissions email: admis@uiwtx.edu
Private; founded 1881
Affiliation: Roman Catholic
Freshman admissions: selective; 2019-2020: 6,296 applied, 5,912 accepted. Either SAT or ACT required. SAT 25/75 percentile: 950-1160. High school rank: 18% in top tenth, 45% in top quarter, 75% in top half
Early decision deadline: N/A, notification date: N/A
Early action deadline: N/A, notification date: N/A
Application deadline (fall): rolling
Undergraduate student body: 4,093 full time, 1,275 part time; 39% male, 61% female; 0% American Indian, 2% Asian, 7% Black, 59% Hispanic, 2% multiracial, 0% Pacific Islander, 18% white, 4% international; 94% from in state; 20% live on campus; N/A of students in fraternities, N/A in sororities
Most popular majors: 12% Business Administration and Management, General, 8% Registered Nursing/Registered Nurse, 7% Biology/Biological Sciences, General, 7% Psychology, General, 5% Rehabilitation Science
Expenses: 2020-2021: $32,286; room/board: $13,014
Financial aid: (210) 829-6008; 78% of undergrads determined to have financial need; average aid package $22,348

Wade College[1]
Dallas TX
(214) 637-3530
U.S. News ranking: Reg. Coll. (W), unranked
Admissions email: N/A
For-profit
Application deadline (fall): N/A
Undergraduate student body: N/A full time, N/A part time
Expenses: 2019-2020: $14,515; room/board: N/A
Financial aid: N/A

Wayland Baptist University
Plainview TX
(806) 291-3500
U.S. News ranking: Reg. U. (W), second tier
Website: www.wbu.edu
Admissions email: admitme@wbu.edu
Private; founded 1908
Affiliation: Baptist
Freshman admissions: less selective; 2019-2020: 635 applied, 619 accepted. Either SAT or ACT required. ACT 25/75 percentile: 16-22. High school rank: 8% in top tenth, 22% in top quarter, 50% in top half
Early decision deadline: N/A, notification date: N/A
Early action deadline: N/A, notification date: N/A
Application deadline (fall): rolling
Undergraduate student body: 869 full time, 2,143 part time; 49% male, 51% female; 1% American Indian, 2% Asian, 17% Black, 33% Hispanic, 5% multiracial, 3% Pacific Islander, 35% white, 2% international; 70% from in state; 17% live on campus; N/A of students in fraternities, N/A in sororities
Most popular majors: 37% Business, Management, Marketing, and Related Support Services, 25% Liberal Arts and Sciences, General Studies and Humanities, 8% Education, 8% Homeland Security, Law Enforcement, Firefighting and Related Protective Services, 4% Philosophy and Religious Studies
Expenses: 2020-2021: $21,304; room/board: $7,722
Financial aid: (806) 291-3520; 74% of undergrads determined to have financial need; average aid package $14,139

West Texas A&M University
Canyon TX
(806) 651-2020
U.S. News ranking: Reg. U. (W), No. 83
Website: www.wtamu.edu
Admissions email: admissions@wtamu.edu
Public; founded 1910
Freshman admissions: selective; 2019-2020: 5,587 applied, 3,842 accepted. Either SAT or ACT required. ACT 25/75 percentile: 18-23. High school rank: 15% in top tenth, 42% in top quarter, 75% in top half
Early decision deadline: N/A, notification date: N/A

Early action deadline: N/A, notification date: N/A
Application deadline (fall): 8/1
Undergraduate student body: 5,582 full time, 1,773 part time; 42% male, 58% female; 0% American Indian, 2% Asian, 5% Black, 31% Hispanic, 3% multiracial, 0% Pacific Islander, 55% white, 2% international; N/A from in state; 28% live on campus; 4% of students in fraternities, 5% in sororities
Most popular majors: 18% Business, Management, Marketing, and Related Support Services, 13% Health Professions and Related Programs, 10% Education, 9% Agriculture, Agriculture Operations, and Related Sciences, 5% Liberal Arts and Sciences, General Studies and Humanities
Expenses: 2020-2021: $9,040 in state, $10,672 out of state; room/board: $8,515
Financial aid: (806) 651-2055; 63% of undergrads determined to have financial need; average aid package $9,628

Wiley College[1]
Marshall TX
(800) 658-6889
U.S. News ranking: Reg. Coll. (W), second tier
Website: www.wileyc.edu
Admissions email: admissions@wileyc.edu
Private; founded 1873
Application deadline (fall): rolling
Undergraduate student body: N/A full time, N/A part time
Expenses: 2019-2020: $12,522; room/board: $7,084
Financial aid: (903) 927-3216

UTAH

Brigham Young University–Provo
Provo UT
(801) 422-4104
U.S. News ranking: Nat. U., No. 80
Website: www.byu.edu
Admissions email: admissions@byu.edu
Private; founded 1875
Affiliation: Latter Day Saints (Mormon Church)
Freshman admissions: more selective; 2019-2020: 10,500 applied, 7,086 accepted. Either SAT or ACT required. ACT 25/75 percentile: 26-31. High school rank: 56% in top tenth, 86% in top quarter, 98% in top half
Early decision deadline: N/A, notification date: N/A
Early action deadline: N/A, notification date: N/A
Application deadline (fall): 12/15
Undergraduate student body: 28,288 full time, 3,004 part time; 50% male, 50% female; 0% American Indian, 2% Asian, 0% Black, 7% Hispanic, 4% multiracial, 1% Pacific Islander, 81% white, 3% international; 68% from in state; 16% live on campus; N/A of students in fraternities, N/A in sororities
Most popular majors: 13% Business, Management,

Marketing, and Related Support Services, 12% Biological and Biomedical Sciences, 8% Health Professions and Related Programs, 8% Social Sciences, 7% Engineering
Expenses: 2020-2021: $5,970; room/board: $7,808
Financial aid: (801) 422-4104; 49% of undergrads determined to have financial need; average aid package $8,257

Dixie State University[1]
Saint George UT
(435) 652-7702
U.S. News ranking: Reg. Coll. (W), No. 24
Website: www.dixie.edu
Admissions email: admissions@dixie.edu
Public; founded 1911
Application deadline (fall): 8/15
Undergraduate student body: N/A full time, N/A part time
Expenses: 2019-2020: $5,516 in state, $15,798 out of state; room/board: $6,974
Financial aid: (435) 652-7575

Snow College[1]
Ephraim UT
(435) 283-7159
U.S. News ranking: Reg. Coll. (W), unranked
Website: www.snow.edu/admissions/
Admissions email: admissions@snow.edu
Public; founded 1888
Application deadline (fall): rolling
Undergraduate student body: N/A full time, N/A part time
Expenses: 2019-2020: $3,836 in state, $12,876 out of state; room/board: $3,900
Financial aid: N/A

Southern Utah University
Cedar City UT
(435) 586-7740
U.S. News ranking: Reg. U. (W), No. 62
Website: www.suu.edu
Admissions email: adminfo@suu.edu
Public; founded 1897
Freshman admissions: selective; 2019-2020: 12,248 applied, 9,596 accepted. Either SAT or ACT required. ACT 25/75 percentile: 20-27. High school rank: 17% in top tenth, 45% in top quarter, 75% in top half
Early decision deadline: N/A, notification date: N/A
Early action deadline: N/A, notification date: N/A
Undergraduate student body: 7,097 full time, 3,177 part time; 41% male, 59% female; 1% American Indian, 1% Asian, 2% Black, 8% Hispanic, 2% multiracial, 1% Pacific Islander, 74% white, 6% international
Most popular majors: 13% Business, Management, Marketing, and Related Support Services, 9% Education, 8% Family and Consumer Sciences/Human Sciences, 7% Biological and Biomedical Sciences,

7% Parks, Recreation, Leisure, and Fitness Studies
Expenses: 2020-2021: $6,770 in state, $20,586 out of state; room/board: $7,520
Financial aid: (435) 586-7735; 62% of undergrads determined to have financial need; average aid package $9,841

University of Utah
Salt Lake City UT
(801) 581-8761
U.S. News ranking: Nat. U., No. 97
Website: www.utah.edu/
Admissions email: admissions@utah.edu
Public; founded 1850
Freshman admissions: more selective; 2019-2020: 24,404 applied, 15,159 accepted. Either SAT or ACT required. ACT 25/75 percentile: 22-29. High school rank: N/A
Early decision deadline: N/A, notification date: N/A
Early action deadline: N/A, notification date: N/A
Application deadline (fall): 4/1
Undergraduate student body: 18,628 full time, 5,857 part time; 53% male, 47% female; 0% American Indian, 6% Asian, 1% Black, 13% Hispanic, 6% multiracial, 0% Pacific Islander, 67% white, 5% international; 78% from in state; 13% live on campus; 6% of students in fraternities, 7% in sororities
Most popular majors: 7% Research and Experimental Psychology, Other, 7% Speech Communication and Rhetoric, 4% Biology/Biological Sciences, General, 4% Kinesiology and Exercise Science, 4% Registered Nursing/Registered Nurse
Expenses: 2020-2021: $9,498 in state, $30,132 out of state; room/board: $10,201
Financial aid: (801) 581-6211; 45% of undergrads determined to have financial need; average aid package $23,875

Utah State University
Logan UT
(435) 797-1079
U.S. News ranking: Nat. U., No. 241
Website: www.usu.edu
Admissions email: admit@usu.edu
Public; founded 1888
Freshman admissions: selective; 2019-2020: 15,276 applied, 13,894 accepted. Either SAT or ACT required. ACT 25/75 percentile: 21-28. High school rank: 23% in top tenth, 49% in top quarter, 79% in top half
Early decision deadline: N/A, notification date: N/A
Early action deadline: N/A, notification date: N/A
Application deadline (fall): rolling
Undergraduate student body: 17,063 full time, 7,606 part time; 45% male, 55% female; 2% American Indian, 1% Asian, 1% Black, 6% Hispanic, 2% multiracial, 0% Pacific Islander, 83% white, 1% international; N/A from in state; N/A live on campus; 4% of students in fraternities, 3% in sororities

Most popular majors: 8% Communication Sciences and Disorders, General, 8% Economics, General, 4% Business Administration and Management, General, 4% Physical Education Teaching and Coaching, 4% Special Education and Teaching, General
Expenses: 2020-2021: $7,860 in state, $22,806 out of state; room/board: $5,960
Financial aid: (435) 797-0173; 54% of undergrads determined to have financial need; average aid package $11,738

Utah Valley University[7]
Orem UT
(801) 863-8706
U.S. News ranking: Reg. U. (W), second tier
Website: www.uvu.edu/
Admissions email: admissions@uvu.edu
Public; founded 1941
Freshman admissions: selective; 2019-2020: 11,190 applied, 11,190 accepted. Neither SAT nor ACT required. ACT 25/75 percentile: 18-25. High school rank: 9% in top tenth, 27% in top quarter, 59% in top half
Early decision deadline: N/A, notification date: N/A
Early action deadline: N/A, notification date: N/A
Application deadline (fall): 8/1
Undergraduate student body: 19,799 full time, 21,387 part time
Most popular majors: 21% Business, Management, Marketing, and Related Support Services, 12% Psychology, 7% Education, 7% Visual and Performing Arts, 6% Computer and Information Sciences and Support Services
Expenses: 2020-2021: $5,906 in state, $16,806 out of state; room/board: N/A
Financial aid: (801) 863-6746; 58% of undergrads determined to have financial need; average aid package $8,019

Weber State University
Ogden UT
(801) 626-6743
U.S. News ranking: Reg. U. (W), No. 84
Website: weber.edu
Admissions email: admissions@weber.edu
Public; founded 1889
Freshman admissions: selective; 2019-2020: 6,853 applied, 6,103 accepted. Neither SAT nor ACT required. ACT 25/75 percentile: 18-24. High school rank: 11% in top tenth, 30% in top quarter, 62% in top half
Early decision deadline: N/A, notification date: N/A
Early action deadline: N/A, notification date: N/A
Application deadline (fall): 8/31
Undergraduate student body: 11,854 full time, 16,989 part time; 44% male, 56% female; 1% American Indian, 2% Asian,

2% Black, 12% Hispanic, 4% multiracial, 1% Pacific Islander, 74% white, 1% international
Most popular majors: Information not available
Expenses: 2020-2021: $7,103 in state, $17,286 out of state; room/board: $8,400
Financial aid: (801) 626-7569; 52% of undergrads determined to have financial need; average aid package $6,663

Westminster College
Salt Lake City UT
(801) 832-2200
U.S. News ranking: Reg. U. (W), No. 18
Website: www.westminstercollege.edu
Admissions email: admission@westminstercollege.edu
Private; founded 1875
Affiliation: Undenominational
Freshman admissions: selective; 2019-2020: 1,666 applied, 1,530 accepted. Either SAT or ACT required. ACT 25/75 percentile: 19-29. High school rank: 23% in top tenth, 51% in top quarter, 81% in top half
Early decision deadline: N/A, notification date: N/A
Early action deadline: N/A, notification date: N/A
Application deadline (fall): rolling
Undergraduate student body: 1,649 full time, 91 part time; 39% male, 61% female; 0% American Indian, 3% Asian, 2% Black, 12% Hispanic, 5% multiracial, 0% Pacific Islander, 70% white, 4% international; 61% from in state; 35% live on campus; 0% of students in fraternities, 0% in sororities
Most popular majors: 25% Health Professions and Related Programs, 23% Business, Management, Marketing, and Related Support Services, 8% Biological and Biomedical Sciences, 5% Psychology, 5% Social Sciences
Expenses: 2020-2021: $37,960; room/board: $11,097
Financial aid: (801) 832-2500; 63% of undergrads determined to have financial need; average aid package $29,823

VERMONT

Bennington College
Bennington VT
(800) 833-6845
U.S. News ranking: Nat. Lib. Arts, No. 76
Website: www.bennington.edu
Admissions email: admissions@bennington.edu
Private; founded 1932
Freshman admissions: more selective; 2019-2020: 1,344 applied, 817 accepted. Neither SAT nor ACT required. SAT 25/75 percentile: 1250-1440. High school rank: 29% in top tenth, 69% in top quarter, 91% in top half
Early decision deadline: 11/15, notification date: 12/13
Early action deadline: 12/1, notification date: 1/31

Application deadline (fall): 1/15
Undergraduate student body: 687 full time, 46 part time; 35% male, 65% female; 0% American Indian, 1% Asian, 4% Black, 10% Hispanic, 4% multiracial, 0% Pacific Islander, 58% white, 20% international; 4% from in state; 98% live on campus; 0% of students in fraternities, 0% in sororities
Most popular majors: 48% Visual and Performing Arts, 9% English Language and Literature/Letters, 7% Social Sciences, 6% Foreign Languages, Literatures, and Linguistics, 5% Public Administration and Social Service Professions
Expenses: 2020-2021: $58,124; room/board: $16,840
Financial aid: (802) 440-4325; 77% of undergrads determined to have financial need; average aid package $45,867

Castleton University[1]
Castleton VT
(800) 639-8521
U.S. News ranking: Reg. Coll. (N), No. 23
Website: www.castleton.edu
Admissions email: info@castleton.edu
Public; founded 1787
Application deadline (fall): rolling
Undergraduate student body: N/A full time, N/A part time
Expenses: 2019-2020: $12,470 in state, $29,150 out of state; room/board: $11,020
Financial aid: N/A

Champlain College
Burlington VT
(800) 570-5858
U.S. News ranking: Reg. U. (N), No. 75
Website: www.champlain.edu
Admissions email: admission@champlain.edu
Private; founded 1878
Freshman admissions: selective; 2019-2020: 3,629 applied, 3,090 accepted. Neither SAT nor ACT required. SAT 25/75 percentile: 1110-1320. High school rank: 14% in top tenth, 39% in top quarter, 74% in top half
Early decision deadline: 11/15, notification date: 12/15
Early action deadline: N/A, notification date: N/A
Application deadline (fall): 1/15
Undergraduate student body: 2,024 full time, 54 part time; 64% male, 36% female; 0% American Indian, 3% Asian, 3% Black, 7% Hispanic, 4% multiracial, 0% Pacific Islander, 75% white, 1% international; 22% from in state; 72% live on campus; 0% of students in fraternities, 0% in sororities
Most popular majors: 8% Cyber/Computer Forensics and Counterterrorism, 8% Writing, General, 6% Accounting, 6% Computer Science, 6% Graphic Design
Expenses: 2020-2021: $42,784; room/board: $15,854

Financial aid: (802) 865-5435; 67% of undergrads determined to have financial need; average aid package $31,913

Goddard College[1]
Plainfield VT
(800) 906-8312
U.S. News ranking: Reg. U. (N), second tier
Website: www.goddard.edu
Admissions email: admissions@goddard.edu
Private; founded 1863
Application deadline (fall): N/A
Undergraduate student body: N/A full time, N/A part time
Expenses: 2019-2020: $17,084; room/board: N/A
Financial aid: (800) 468-4888

Landmark College
Putney VT
(802) 387-6718
U.S. News ranking: Reg. Coll. (N), unranked
Website: www.landmark.edu
Admissions email: admissions@landmark.edu
Private; founded 1985
Freshman admissions: least selective; 2019-2020: 419 applied, 197 accepted. Neither SAT nor ACT required. SAT 25/75 percentile: N/A. High school rank: N/A
Early decision deadline: N/A, notification date: N/A
Early action deadline: N/A, notification date: N/A
Application deadline (fall): N/A
Undergraduate student body: 345 full time, 157 part time; 66% male, 34% female; 1% American Indian, 3% Asian, 4% Black, 6% Hispanic, 4% multiracial, 0% Pacific Islander, 66% white, 1% international; 98% from in state; 95% live on campus; 0% of students in fraternities, 0% in sororities
Most popular majors: 59% Liberal Arts and Sciences, General Studies and Humanities, 22% Computer and Information Sciences and Support Services, 19% Visual and Performing Arts
Expenses: 2020-2021: $60,280; room/board: $13,420
Financial aid: (802) 781-6178; 61% of undergrads determined to have financial need; average aid package $31,074

Marlboro College[1]
Marlboro VT
(800) 343-0049
U.S. News ranking: Nat. Lib. Arts, No. 155
Website: www.marlboro.edu
Admissions email: admissions@marlboro.edu
Private; founded 1946
Application deadline (fall): rolling
Undergraduate student body: N/A full time, N/A part time
Expenses: 2019-2020: $27,485; room/board: $12,595
Financial aid: (802) 258-9237

Middlebury College
Middlebury VT
(802) 443-3000
U.S. News ranking: Nat. Lib. Arts, No. 9
Website: www.middlebury.edu
Admissions email: admissions@middlebury.edu
Private; founded 1800
Freshman admissions: most selective; 2019-2020: 9,754 applied, 1,498 accepted. Either SAT or ACT required. SAT 25/75 percentile: 1360-1530. High school rank: 79% in top tenth, 96% in top quarter, 99% in top half
Early decision deadline: 11/1, notification date: 12/15
Early action deadline: N/A, notification date: N/A
Application deadline (fall): 1/1
Undergraduate student body: 2,555 full time, 24 part time; 47% male, 53% female; 0% American Indian, 7% Asian, 4% Black, 10% Hispanic, 5% multiracial, 0% Pacific Islander, 62% white, 10% international; 5% from in state; 95% live on campus; 0% of students in fraternities, 0% in sororities
Most popular majors: 14% Economics, General, 7% Computer Science, 6% Neuroscience, 6% Political Science and Government, General, 5% Environmental Studies
Expenses: 2020-2021: $58,316; room/board: $16,630
Financial aid: (802) 443-5228; 46% of undergrads determined to have financial need; average aid package $53,261

Northern Vermont University[1]
Johnson VT
(800) 635-2356
U.S. News ranking: Reg. U. (N), second tier
Website: www.jsc.edu
Admissions email: JSCAdmissions@jsc.edu
Public; founded 1828
Application deadline (fall): rolling
Undergraduate student body: N/A full time, N/A part time
Expenses: 2019-2020: $12,422 in state, $26,126 out of state; room/board: $11,020
Financial aid: N/A

Norwich University
Northfield VT
(800) 468-6679
U.S. News ranking: Reg. U. (N), No. 62
Website: www.norwich.edu
Admissions email: nuadm@norwich.edu
Private; founded 1819
Freshman admissions: selective; 2019-2020: 3,831 applied, 2,877 accepted. Neither SAT nor ACT required. SAT 25/75 percentile: 1040-1230. High school rank: 7% in top tenth, 34% in top quarter, 64% in top half
Early decision deadline: N/A, notification date: N/A
Early action deadline: N/A, notification date: N/A
Application deadline (fall): rolling

Undergraduate student body: 2,643 full time, 623 part time; 75% male, 25% female; 1% American Indian, 3% Asian, 6% Black, 10% Hispanic, 4% multiracial, 0% Pacific Islander, 69% white, 3% international; 15% from in state; 70% live on campus; N/A of students in fraternities, N/A in sororities
Most popular majors: 25% Military Technologies and Applied Sciences, 16% Homeland Security, Law Enforcement, Firefighting and Related Protective Services, 11% Business, Management, Marketing, and Related Support Services, 8% Engineering, 7% Computer and Information Sciences and Support Services
Expenses: 2020-2021: $42,950; room/board: $14,854
Financial aid: (802) 485-3015; 53% of undergrads determined to have financial need; average aid package $39,584

Saint Michael's College
Colchester VT
(800) 762-8000
U.S. News ranking: Nat. Lib. Arts, No. 120
Website: www.smcvt.edu
Admissions email: admission@smcvt.edu
Private; founded 1904
Affiliation: Roman Catholic
Freshman admissions: selective; 2019-2020: 3,967 applied, 3,297 accepted. Neither SAT nor ACT required. SAT 25/75 percentile: 1155-1310. High school rank: 21% in top tenth, 49% in top quarter, 79% in top half
Early decision deadline: N/A, notification date: N/A
Early action deadline: 11/1, notification date: 12/21
Application deadline (fall): 2/1
Undergraduate student body: 1,558 full time, 27 part time; 46% male, 54% female; 0% American Indian, 1% Asian, 3% Black, 6% Hispanic, 3% multiracial, 0% Pacific Islander, 82% white, 3% international
Most popular majors: 22% Business, Management, Marketing, and Related Support Services, 15% Social Sciences, 13% Biological and Biomedical Sciences, 10% Psychology, 6% Natural Resources and Conservation
Expenses: 2020-2021: $48,175; room/board: $13,600
Financial aid: (802) 654-3243; 65% of undergrads determined to have financial need; average aid package $36,683

Sterling College[1]
Craftsbury Common VT
(802) 586-7711
U.S. News ranking: Nat. Lib. Arts, second tier
Website: www.sterlingcollege.edu
Admissions email: admissions@sterlingcollege.edu
Private; founded 1958
Application deadline (fall): N/A

Undergraduate student body: N/A full time, N/A part time
Expenses: 2019-2020: $39,020; room/board: $9,900
Financial aid: N/A

University of Vermont
Burlington VT
(802) 656-3370
U.S. News ranking: Nat. U., No. 118
Website: www.uvm.edu
Admissions email: admissions@uvm.edu
Public; founded 1791
Freshman admissions: more selective; 2019-2020: 19,233 applied, 12,943 accepted. Either SAT or ACT required. SAT 25/75 percentile: 1180-1360. High school rank: 34% in top tenth, 75% in top quarter, 98% in top half
Early decision deadline: N/A, notification date: N/A
Early action deadline: 11/1, notification date: 12/15
Application deadline (fall): 1/15
Undergraduate student body: 10,501 full time, 942 part time; 41% male, 59% female; 0% American Indian, 3% Asian, 1% Black, 4% Hispanic, 3% multiracial, 0% Pacific Islander, 82% white, 4% international; 28% from in state; 51% live on campus; 8% of students in fraternities, 7% in sororities
Most popular majors: 10% Business Administration and Management, General, 5% Psychology, General, 4% Environmental Studies, 3% Computer Science, 3% Registered Nursing/Registered Nurse
Expenses: 2020-2021: $19,062 in state, $43,950 out of state; room/board: $13,324
Financial aid: (802) 656-5700; 55% of undergrads determined to have financial need; average aid package $27,935

Vermont Technical College
Randolph Center VT
(802) 728-1244
U.S. News ranking: Reg. Coll. (N), No. 21
Website: www.vtc.edu
Admissions email: admissions@vtc.edu
Public; founded 1866
Freshman admissions: less selective; 2019-2020: 1,087 applied, 740 accepted. Neither SAT nor ACT required. SAT 25/75 percentile: 980-1170. High school rank: N/A
Early decision deadline: N/A, notification date: N/A
Early action deadline: N/A, notification date: N/A
Application deadline (fall): rolling
Undergraduate student body: 1,089 full time, 582 part time; 54% male, 46% female; 0% American Indian, 1% Asian, 1% Black, 2% Hispanic, 30% multiracial, 0% Pacific Islander, 63% white, 1% international; N/A from in state; 34% live on campus; N/A of students in fraternities, N/A in sororities

Most popular majors: 35% Engineering Technologies and Engineering-Related Fields, 22% Health Professions and Related Programs, 15% Business, Management, Marketing, and Related Support Services, 10% Construction Trades, 6% Transportation and Materials Moving
Expenses: 2020-2021: $16,471 in state, $29,887 out of state; room/board: $11,694
Financial aid: (802) 728-1248; 81% of undergrads determined to have financial need; average aid package $14,270

VIRGIN ISLANDS

University of the Virgin Islands
St. Thomas VI
(340) 693-1150
U.S. News ranking: Reg. Coll. (S), No. 36
Website: www.uvi.edu
Admissions email: admit@uvi.edu
Public; founded 1962
Freshman admissions: least selective; 2019-2020: 914 applied, 899 accepted. Neither SAT nor ACT required. SAT 25/75 percentile: 792-1027. High school rank: 11% in top tenth, 32% in top quarter, 64% in top half
Early decision deadline: N/A, notification date: N/A
Early action deadline: N/A, notification date: N/A
Application deadline (fall): 4/30
Undergraduate student body: 1,251 full time, 599 part time; 31% male, 69% female; 0% American Indian, 1% Asian, 71% Black, 11% Hispanic, 1% multiracial, 0% Pacific Islander, 4% white, 6% international
Most popular majors: 17% Registered Nursing/Registered Nurse, 13% Business Administration and Management, General, 10% Biology/Biological Sciences, General, 9% Criminal Justice/Police Science, 8% Accounting
Expenses: 2019-2020: $5,235 in state, $14,496 out of state; room/board: $9,900
Financial aid: (340) 692-4192

VIRGINIA

Averett University
Danville VA
(434) 791-5600
U.S. News ranking: Reg. Coll. (S), No. 18
Website: www.averett.edu
Admissions email: admit@averett.edu
Private; founded 1859
Affiliation: Other
Freshman admissions: less selective; 2019-2020: 2,745 applied, 1,785 accepted. Either SAT or ACT required. SAT 25/75 percentile: 860-1060. High school rank: 4% in top tenth, 19% in top quarter, 58% in top half
Early decision deadline: N/A, notification date: N/A
Early action deadline: N/A, notification date: N/A

Application deadline (fall): rolling
Undergraduate student body: 876 full time, 27 part time; 56% male, 44% female; 1% American Indian, 1% Asian, 28% Black, 4% Hispanic, 4% multiracial, 1% Pacific Islander, 55% white, 7% international; 40% from in state; 56% live on campus; 5% of students in fraternities, 4% in sororities
Most popular majors: 21% Business, Management, Marketing, and Related Support Services, 15% Health Professions and Related Programs, 13% Parks, Recreation, Leisure, and Fitness Studies, 6% Computer and Information Sciences and Support Services, 6% Homeland Security, Law Enforcement, Firefighting and Related Protective Services
Expenses: 2019-2020: $35,600; room/board: $10,560
Financial aid: (434) 791-5646

Bluefield College[1]
Bluefield VA
(276) 326-4231
U.S. News ranking: Reg. Coll. (S), No. 59
Website: www.bluefield.edu
Admissions email: admissions@bluefield.edu
Private; founded 1922
Affiliation: Baptist
Application deadline (fall): rolling
Undergraduate student body: N/A full time, N/A part time
Expenses: 2020-2021: $27,570; room/board: $9,598
Financial aid: (276) 326-4280; 91% of undergrads determined to have financial need; average aid package $17,722

Bridgewater College
Bridgewater VA
(800) 759-8328
U.S. News ranking: Nat. Lib. Arts, second tier
Website: www.bridgewater.edu
Admissions email: admissions@bridgewater.edu
Private; founded 1880
Affiliation: Church of Brethren
Freshman admissions: selective; 2019-2020: 6,279 applied, 4,225 accepted. Either SAT or ACT required. SAT 25/75 percentile: 960-1180. High school rank: 14% in top tenth, 40% in top quarter, 74% in top half
Early decision deadline: N/A, notification date: N/A
Early action deadline: N/A, notification date: N/A
Application deadline (fall): 5/1
Undergraduate student body: 1,707 full time, 6 part time; 45% male, 55% female; 0% American Indian, 1% Asian, 15% Black, 7% Hispanic, 6% multiracial, 0% Pacific Islander, 65% white, 2% international; 77% from in state; 81% live on campus; 0% of students in fraternities, 0% in sororities
Most popular majors: 27% Business, Management, Marketing, and Related Support Services, 12% Parks, Recreation, Leisure, and Fitness Studies, 9% Biological and Biomedical

Sciences, 8% Psychology, 8% Social Sciences
Expenses: 2020-2021: $37,720; room/board: $13,360
Financial aid: (540) 828-5376; 84% of undergrads determined to have financial need; average aid package $36,959

Christopher Newport University
Newport News VA
(757) 594-7015
U.S. News ranking: Reg. U. (S), No. 7
Website: www.cnu.edu
Admissions email: admit@cnu.edu
Public; founded 1960
Freshman admissions: selective; 2019-2020: 7,204 applied, 5,179 accepted. Neither SAT nor ACT required. SAT 25/75 percentile: 1110-1280. High school rank: 16% in top tenth, 48% in top quarter, 87% in top half
Early decision deadline: 11/15, notification date: 12/15
Early action deadline: 12/1, notification date: 1/15
Application deadline (fall): 2/1
Undergraduate student body: 4,742 full time, 95 part time; 45% male, 55% female; 0% American Indian, 3% Asian, 6% Black, 6% Hispanic, 5% multiracial, 0% Pacific Islander, 77% white, 0% international; 92% from in state; 79% live on campus; 26% of students in fraternities, 32% in sororities
Most popular majors: 16% Business Administration and Management, General, 15% Biology/Biological Sciences, General, 11% Psychology, General, 9% Speech Communication and Rhetoric, 7% Political Science and Government, General
Expenses: 2020-2021: $14,924 in state, $27,390 out of state; room/board: $11,760
Financial aid: (757) 594-7170; 43% of undergrads determined to have financial need; average aid package $11,007

Eastern Mennonite University
Harrisonburg VA
(800) 368-2665
U.S. News ranking: Reg. U. (S), No. 31
Website: www.emu.edu
Admissions email: admiss@emu.edu
Private; founded 1917
Affiliation: Mennonite Church
Freshman admissions: selective; 2019-2020: 1,435 applied, 927 accepted. Either SAT or ACT required. SAT 25/75 percentile: 980-1210. High school rank: N/A
Early decision deadline: N/A, notification date: N/A
Early action deadline: N/A, notification date: N/A
Application deadline (fall): rolling
Undergraduate student body: 830 full time, 150 part time; 39% male, 61% female; 0% American Indian, 2% Asian, 9% Black, 8% Hispanic, 5% multiracial, 0% Pacific Islander, 69% white,

3% international; 63% from in state; 44% live on campus; 0% of students in fraternities, 0% in sororities
Most popular majors: 39% Health Professions and Related Programs, 15% Business, Management, Marketing, and Related Support Services, 8% Liberal Arts and Sciences, General Studies and Humanities, 6% Biological and Biomedical Sciences, 5% Public Administration and Social Service Professions
Expenses: 2020-2021: $39,220; room/board: $11,730
Financial aid: (540) 432-4137; 76% of undergrads determined to have financial need; average aid package $33,326

ECPI University
Virginia Beach VA
(866) 499-0336
U.S. News ranking: Reg. U. (S), second tier
Website: www.ecpi.edu/
Admissions email: request@ecpi.edu
For-profit; founded 1966
Freshman admissions: less selective; 2019-2020: 5,701 applied, 4,208 accepted. Neither SAT nor ACT required. SAT 25/75 percentile: N/A. High school rank: N/A
Early decision deadline: N/A, notification date: N/A
Early action deadline: N/A, notification date: N/A
Application deadline (fall): rolling
Undergraduate student body: 13,005 full time, 137 part time; 41% male, 59% female; 1% American Indian, 3% Asian, 33% Black, 9% Hispanic, 3% multiracial, 0% Pacific Islander, 34% white, 0% international
Most popular majors: 42% Health Professions and Related Programs, 34% Computer and Information Sciences and Support Services, 17% Engineering Technologies and Engineering-Related Fields, 7% Homeland Security, Law Enforcement, Firefighting and Related Protective Services
Expenses: 2020-2021: $16,639; room/board: N/A
Financial aid: N/A

Emory and Henry College
Emory VA
(800) 848-5493
U.S. News ranking: Nat. Lib. Arts, No. 154
Website: www.ehc.edu
Admissions email: ehadmiss@ehc.edu
Private; founded 1836
Affiliation: United Methodist
Freshman admissions: selective; 2019-2020: 1,646 applied, 1,203 accepted. Either SAT or ACT required. SAT 25/75 percentile: 960-1170. High school rank: 22% in top tenth, 31% in top quarter, 82% in top half
Early decision deadline: 11/15, notification date: 12/15
Early action deadline: N/A, notification date: N/A
Application deadline (fall): rolling

Undergraduate student body: 988 full time, 31 part time; 49% male, 51% female; 0% American Indian, 1% Asian, 9% Black, 3% Hispanic, 4% multiracial, 0% Pacific Islander, 81% white, 0% international; 66% from in state; 77% live on campus; N/A of students in fraternities, N/A in sororities
Most popular majors: 19% Social Sciences, 12% Business, Management, Marketing, and Related Support Services, 10% Psychology, 9% Education, 7% Parks, Recreation, Leisure, and Fitness Studies
Expenses: 2020-2021: $35,100; room/board: $13,125
Financial aid: (276) 944-6105; 88% of undergrads determined to have financial need; average aid package $37,101

Ferrum College
Ferrum VA
(800) 868-9797
U.S. News ranking: Reg. Coll. (S), No. 50
Website: www.ferrum.edu
Admissions email: admissions@ferrum.edu
Private; founded 1913
Freshman admissions: least selective; 2019-2020: 3,770 applied, 2,758 accepted. Neither SAT nor ACT required. SAT 25/75 percentile: 860-1060. High school rank: N/A
Early decision deadline: N/A, notification date: N/A
Early action deadline: N/A, notification date: N/A
Application deadline (fall): rolling
Undergraduate student body: 1,034 full time, 16 part time; 57% male, 43% female; 1% American Indian, 0% Asian, 30% Black, 5% Hispanic, 7% multiracial, 0% Pacific Islander, 53% white, 2% international; N/A from in state; 90% live on campus; 5% of students in fraternities, 11% in sororities
Most popular majors: 14% Education, 12% Business, Management, Marketing, and Related Support Services, 10% Health Professions and Related Programs, 8% Parks, Recreation, Leisure, and Fitness Studies, 7% Natural Resources and Conservation
Expenses: 2019-2020: $35,365; room/board: $11,980
Financial aid: N/A

George Mason University
Fairfax VA
(703) 993-2400
U.S. News ranking: Nat. U., No. 143
Website: www2.gmu.edu
Admissions email: admissions@gmu.edu
Public; founded 1972
Freshman admissions: selective; 2019-2020: 19,554 applied, 16,962 accepted. Neither SAT nor ACT required. SAT 25/75 percentile: 1110-1320. High school rank: 15% in top tenth, 44% in top quarter, 81% in top half

Early decision deadline: N/A, notification date: N/A
Early action deadline: 11/1, notification date: 12/15
Application deadline (fall): 1/15
Undergraduate student body: 21,672 full time, 4,990 part time; 51% male, 49% female; 0% American Indian, 21% Asian, 11% Black, 16% Hispanic, 5% multiracial, 0% Pacific Islander, 38% white, 6% international; 87% from in state; 21% live on campus; 5% of students in fraternities, 6% in sororities
Most popular majors: 6% Criminal Justice/Police Science, 6% Information Technology, 6% Psychology, General, 5% Biology/Biological Sciences, General, 4% Management Sciences and Quantitative Methods, Other
Expenses: 2020-2021: $13,014 in state, $36,474 out of state; room/board: $12,090
Financial aid: (703) 993-2353; 56% of undergrads determined to have financial need; average aid package $13,956

Hampden-Sydney College
Hampden-Sydney VA
(800) 755-0733
U.S. News ranking: Nat. Lib. Arts, No. 102
Website: www.hsc.edu
Admissions email: hsapp@hsc.edu
Private; founded 1775
Affiliation: Presbyterian
Freshman admissions: selective; 2019-2020: 3,056 applied, 1,755 accepted. Either SAT or ACT required. SAT 25/75 percentile: 1060-1320. High school rank: 7% in top tenth, 24% in top quarter, 53% in top half
Early decision deadline: 11/1, notification date: 12/1
Early action deadline: 1/15, notification date: 2/15
Application deadline (fall): 3/1
Undergraduate student body: 993 full time, 0 part time; 99% male, 1% female; 0% American Indian, 1% Asian, 5% Black, 5% Hispanic, 3% multiracial, 0% Pacific Islander, 85% white, 0% international; 70% from in state; 95% live on campus; 33% of students in fraternities, 0% in sororities
Most popular majors: 27% Business/Managerial Economics, 13% Economics, General, 12% History, General, 11% Biology/Biological Sciences, General, 10% Political Science and Government, General
Expenses: 2020-2021: $48,110; room/board: $13,876
Financial aid: (434) 223-6265; 67% of undergrads determined to have financial need; average aid package $34,703

Hampton University
Hampton VA
(757) 727-5328
U.S. News ranking: Nat. U., No. 217
Website: www.hamptonu.edu
Admissions email: admissions@hamptonu.edu
Private; founded 1868

Freshman admissions: selective; 2019-2020: 9,551 applied, 3,438 accepted. Neither SAT nor ACT required. ACT 25/75 percentile: 20-25. High school rank: 12% in top tenth, 25% in top quarter, 74% in top half
Early decision deadline: N/A, notification date: N/A
Early action deadline: 11/1, notification date: 12/31
Application deadline (fall): 3/1
Undergraduate student body: 3,491 full time, 223 part time; 34% male, 66% female; 0% American Indian, 0% Asian, 95% Black, 1% Hispanic, 0% multiracial, 0% Pacific Islander, 1% white, 2% international; 27% from in state; 57% live on campus; 5% of students in fraternities, 4% in sororities
Most popular majors: 10% Psychology, General, 8% Biology/Biological Sciences, General, 8% Organizational Communication, General, 7% Business Administration and Management, General, 6% Liberal Arts and Sciences/Liberal Studies
Expenses: 2020-2021: $29,287; room/board: $12,986
Financial aid: (757) 727-5635; 58% of undergrads determined to have financial need; average aid package $6,490

Hollins University
Roanoke VA
(800) 456-9595
U.S. News ranking: Nat. Lib. Arts, No. 102
Website: www.hollins.edu
Admissions email: huadm@hollins.edu
Private; founded 1842
Freshman admissions: selective; 2019-2020: 3,204 applied, 2,282 accepted. Either SAT or ACT required. SAT 25/75 percentile: 1070-1300. High school rank: 29% in top tenth, 56% in top quarter, 86% in top half
Early decision deadline: 11/1, notification date: 11/15
Early action deadline: 11/15, notification date: 12/1
Application deadline (fall): rolling
Undergraduate student body: 659 full time, 9 part time; 0% male, 100% female; 0% American Indian, 2% Asian, 9% Black, 8% Hispanic, 7% multiracial, 0% Pacific Islander, 62% white, 10% international; N/A from in state; 83% live on campus; N/A of students in fraternities, N/A in sororities
Most popular majors: 18% Visual and Performing Arts, 11% Social Sciences, 10% Biological and Biomedical Sciences, 8% Business, Management, Marketing, and Related Support Services, 8% Psychology
Expenses: 2020-2021: $40,110; room/board: $14,300
Financial aid: (540) 362-6332; 75% of undergrads determined to have financial need; average aid package $38,450

James Madison University
Harrisonburg VA
(540) 568-5681
U.S. News ranking: Reg. U. (S), No. 3
Website: www.jmu.edu
Admissions email: admissions@jmu.edu
Public; founded 1908
Freshman admissions: selective; 2019-2020: 23,578 applied, 18,097 accepted. Neither SAT nor ACT required. SAT 25/75 percentile: 1120-1290. High school rank: 17% in top tenth, 33% in top quarter, 90% in top half
Early decision deadline: N/A, notification date: N/A
Early action deadline: 11/1, notification date: 1/15
Application deadline (fall): 1/15
Undergraduate student body: 18,798 full time, 1,097 part time; 42% male, 58% female; 0% American Indian, 5% Asian, 5% Black, 7% Hispanic, 5% multiracial, 0% Pacific Islander, 75% white, 2% international; 78% from in state; 32% live on campus; 4% of students in fraternities, 7% in sororities
Most popular majors: 20% Health Professions and Related Programs, 16% Business, Management, Marketing, and Related Support Services, 9% Communication, Journalism, and Related Programs, 8% Social Sciences, 5% Liberal Arts and Sciences, General Studies and Humanities
Expenses: 2020-2021: $12,330 in state, $29,230 out of state; room/board: $11,348
Financial aid: (540) 568-7820; 41% of undergrads determined to have financial need; average aid package $9,333

Liberty University
Lynchburg VA
(800) 543-5317
U.S. News ranking: Nat. U., second tier
Website: www.liberty.edu
Admissions email: admissions@liberty.edu
Private; founded 1971
Affiliation: Evangelical Christian
Freshman admissions: selective; 2019-2020: 42,358 applied, 21,657 accepted. Either SAT or ACT required. SAT 25/75 percentile: 1040-1260. High school rank: N/A
Early decision deadline: N/A, notification date: N/A
Early action deadline: N/A, notification date: N/A
Application deadline (fall): rolling
Undergraduate student body: 28,487 full time, 18,538 part time; 42% male, 58% female; 0% American Indian, 1% Asian, 10% Black, 6% Hispanic, 3% multiracial, 0% Pacific Islander, 55% white, 1% international; 40% from in state; 59% live on campus; N/A of students in fraternities, N/A in sororities
Most popular majors: 21% Business, Management, Marketing, and Related Support Services, 15% Multi/

Interdisciplinary Studies, 12% Psychology, 9% Philosophy and Religious Studies, 7% Education
Expenses: 2020-2021: $24,910; room/board: $10,540
Financial aid: (434) 582-2270; 71% of undergrads determined to have financial need; average aid package $15,336

Longwood University
Farmville VA
(434) 395-2060
U.S. News ranking: Reg. U. (S), No. 16
Website: www.longwood.edu/
Admissions email: admissions@longwood.edu
Public; founded 1839
Freshman admissions: selective; 2019-2020: 4,431 applied, 3,983 accepted. Either SAT or ACT required. SAT 25/75 percentile: 960-1150. High school rank: 17% in top tenth, 33% in top quarter, 65% in top half
Early decision deadline: N/A, notification date: N/A
Early action deadline: 12/1, notification date: 1/15
Application deadline (fall): rolling
Undergraduate student body: 3,439 full time, 420 part time; 32% male, 68% female; 0% American Indian, 1% Asian, 10% Black, 6% Hispanic, 5% multiracial, 0% Pacific Islander, 75% white, 1% international; 99% from in state; 59% live on campus; 14% of students in fraternities, 18% in sororities
Most popular majors: 14% Business, Management, Marketing, and Related Support Services, 14% Liberal Arts and Sciences, General Studies and Humanities, 12% Health Professions and Related Programs, 12% Social Sciences, 10% Biological and Biomedical Sciences
Expenses: 2020-2021: $13,520 in state, $29,480 out of state; room/board: $12,020
Financial aid: (434) 395-2077; 61% of undergrads determined to have financial need; average aid package $12,427

Mary Baldwin University
Staunton VA
(800) 468-2262
U.S. News ranking: Nat. U., second tier
Website: www.marybaldwin.edu
Admissions email: admit@marybaldwin.edu
Private; founded 1842
Freshman admissions: selective; 2019-2020: 6,461 applied, 6,451 accepted. Either SAT or ACT required. SAT 25/75 percentile: 950-1130. High school rank: 10% in top tenth, 34% in top quarter, 62% in top half
Early decision deadline: N/A, notification date: N/A
Early action deadline: N/A, notification date: N/A
Application deadline (fall): rolling
Undergraduate student body: 1,190 full time, 143 part time; 18% male, 82% female; 0% American Indian, 1% Asian, 35% Black,

8% Hispanic, 4% multiracial, 0% Pacific Islander, 46% white, 2% international

Most popular majors: 15% Business Administration and Management, General, 12% Liberal Arts and Sciences/Liberal Studies, 11% Social Work, 10% Psychology, General, 10% Registered Nursing/Registered Nurse

Expenses: 2020-2021: $31,085; room/board: $9,730

Financial aid: (540) 887-7022; 89% of undergrads determined to have financial need; average aid package $26,439

Marymount University

Arlington VA
(703) 284-1500
U.S. News ranking: Reg. U. (S), No. 31
Website: www.marymount.edu
Admissions email: admissions@marymount.edu
Private; founded 1950
Affiliation: Roman Catholic
Freshman admissions: less selective; 2019-2020: 3,315 applied, 2,684 accepted. Neither SAT nor ACT required. SAT 25/75 percentile: 940-1190. High school rank: 11% in top tenth, 30% in top quarter, 66% in top half
Early decision deadline: N/A, notification date: N/A
Early action deadline: 11/15, notification date: 12/14
Application deadline (fall): rolling
Undergraduate student body: 1,951 full time, 207 part time; 35% male, 65% female; 0% American Indian, 8% Asian, 16% Black, 22% Hispanic, 3% multiracial, 0% Pacific Islander, 31% white, 16% international; 62% from in state; 31% live on campus; N/A of students in fraternities, N/A in sororities
Most popular majors: 25% Registered Nursing/Registered Nurse, 15% Business Administration and Management, General, 10% Health Professions and Related Programs, 9% Information Technology, 5% Biology/Biological Sciences, General
Expenses: 2020-2021: $33,950; room/board: $14,400
Financial aid: (703) 284-1530; 63% of undergrads determined to have financial need; average aid package $25,938

Norfolk State University

Norfolk VA
(757) 823-8396
U.S. News ranking: Reg. U. (S), No. 80
Website: www.nsu.edu
Admissions email: admissions@nsu.edu
Public; founded 1935
Freshman admissions: least selective; 2019-2020: 7,164 applied, 6,476 accepted. SAT or ACT required. SAT 25/75 percentile: 860-1040. High school rank: 6% in top tenth, 20% in top quarter, 56% in top half
Early decision deadline: N/A, notification date: N/A

Early action deadline: N/A, notification date: N/A
Undergraduate student body: 4,583 full time, 529 part time; 33% male, 67% female; 0% American Indian, 0% Asian, 85% Black, 4% Hispanic, 6% multiracial, 0% Pacific Islander, 3% white, 0% international
Most popular majors: Business/Commerce, General, Electrical/Electronics Equipment Installation and Repair, General, Health/Health Care Administration/Management, Psychology, General, Sociology
Expenses: 2020-2021: $9,622 in state, $20,790 out of state; room/board: N/A
Financial aid: (757) 823-8381

Old Dominion University

Norfolk VA
(757) 683-3685
U.S. News ranking: Nat. U., No. 258
Website: www.odu.edu
Admissions email: admissions@odu.edu
Public; founded 1930
Freshman admissions: selective; 2019-2020: 13,761 applied, 12,293 accepted. Neither SAT nor ACT required. SAT 25/75 percentile: 980-1180. High school rank: 10% in top tenth, 28% in top quarter, 67% in top half
Early decision deadline: N/A, notification date: N/A
Early action deadline: 12/1, notification date: 1/15
Application deadline (fall): 2/1
Undergraduate student body: 14,702 full time, 4,474 part time; 45% male, 55% female; 0% American Indian, 5% Asian, 32% Black, 9% Hispanic, 7% multiracial, 0% Pacific Islander, 44% white, 1% international; 92% from in state; 25% live on campus; 7% of students in fraternities, 4% in sororities
Most popular majors: 17% Business, Management, Marketing, and Related Support Services, 17% Health Professions and Related Programs, 11% Social Sciences, 7% Engineering, 7% Psychology
Expenses: 2020-2021: $11,520 in state, $31,680 out of state; room/board: $12,988
Financial aid: (757) 683-3683; 68% of undergrads determined to have financial need; average aid package $11,108

Radford University

Radford VA
(540) 831-5371
U.S. News ranking: Reg. U. (S), No. 33
Website: www.radford.edu
Admissions email: admissions@radford.edu
Public; founded 1910
Freshman admissions: less selective; 2019-2020: 16,001 applied, 12,059 accepted. Neither SAT nor ACT required. SAT 25/75 percentile: 940-1110. High school rank: 7% in top tenth, 21% in top quarter, 59% in top half

Early decision deadline: N/A, notification date: N/A
Early action deadline: 12/1, notification date: 1/15
Application deadline (fall): rolling
Undergraduate student body: 7,494 full time, 473 part time; 39% male, 61% female; 0% American Indian, 2% Asian, 17% Black, 7% Hispanic, 6% multiracial, 0% Pacific Islander, 64% white, 1% international; 93% from in state; 45% live on campus; N/A of students in fraternities, N/A in sororities
Most popular majors: 8% Criminal Justice/Safety Studies, 8% Multi-/Interdisciplinary Studies, Other, 8% Physical Education Teaching and Coaching, 8% Psychology, General, 7% Business Administration and Management, General
Expenses: 2020-2021: $11,416 in state, $23,051 out of state; room/board: $9,743
Financial aid: (540) 831-5408; 69% of undergrads determined to have financial need; average aid package $11,147

Randolph College

Lynchburg VA
(800) 745-7692
U.S. News ranking: Nat. Lib. Arts, No. 140
Website: www.randolphcollege.edu/
Admissions email: admissions@randolphcollege.edu
Private; founded 1891
Freshman admissions: selective; 2019-2020: 1,177 applied, 1,054 accepted. Neither SAT nor ACT required. SAT 25/75 percentile: 970-1180. High school rank: 15% in top tenth, 49% in top quarter, 81% in top half
Early decision deadline: N/A, notification date: N/A
Early action deadline: 11/15, notification date: N/A
Application deadline (fall): rolling
Undergraduate student body: 545 full time, 20 part time; 39% male, 61% female; 1% American Indian, 3% Asian, 16% Black, 8% Hispanic, 7% multiracial, 1% Pacific Islander, 60% white, 3% international; N/A from in state; 77% live on campus; N/A of students in fraternities, N/A in sororities
Most popular majors: 12% Biological and Biomedical Sciences, 11% Social Sciences, 10% Education, 9% Parks, Recreation, Leisure, and Fitness Studies, 8% Visual and Performing Arts
Expenses: 2020-2021: $25,610; room/board: $11,000
Financial aid: (434) 947-8128; 83% of undergrads determined to have financial need; average aid package $35,737

Randolph-Macon College

Ashland VA
(800) 888-1762
U.S. News ranking: Nat. Lib. Arts, No. 102
Website: www.rmc.edu

Admissions email: admissions@rmc.edu
Private; founded 1830
Affiliation: United Methodist
Freshman admissions: selective; 2019-2020: 2,460 applied, 1,744 accepted. Either SAT or ACT required. SAT 25/75 percentile: 1050-1240. High school rank: 22% in top tenth, 50% in top quarter, 79% in top half
Early decision deadline: N/A, notification date: N/A
Early action deadline: 11/15, notification date: 1/1
Application deadline (fall): 3/1
Undergraduate student body: 1,520 full time, 23 part time; 47% male, 53% female; 0% American Indian, 1% Asian, 10% Black, 4% Hispanic, 5% multiracial, 0% Pacific Islander, 77% white, 2% international; 78% from in state; 80% live on campus; 29% of students in fraternities, 25% in sororities
Most popular majors: 14% Business/Commerce, General, 11% Biology/Biological Sciences, General, 10% Communication and Media Studies, 7% Political Science and Government, General, 6% Psychology, General
Expenses: 2020-2021: $43,940; room/board: $12,680
Financial aid: (804) 752-7259; 70% of undergrads determined to have financial need; average aid package $31,700

Regent University

Virginia Beach VA
(888) 718-1222
U.S. News ranking: Nat. U., second tier
Website: www.regent.edu/
Admissions email: admissions@regent.edu
Private; founded 1978
Affiliation: Undenominational
Freshman admissions: selective; 2019-2020: 2,344 applied, 2,005 accepted. Either SAT or ACT required. SAT 25/75 percentile: 990-1220. High school rank: 10% in top tenth, 34% in top quarter, 65% in top half
Early decision deadline: N/A, notification date: N/A
Early action deadline: N/A, notification date: N/A
Application deadline (fall): 8/1
Undergraduate student body: 2,380 full time, 2,033 part time; 39% male, 61% female; 0% American Indian, 2% Asian, 27% Black, 9% Hispanic, 5% multiracial, 0% Pacific Islander, 54% white, 0% international; 41% from in state; 16% live on campus; 0% of students in fraternities, 0% in sororities
Most popular majors: 22% Business Administration, Management and Operations, 14% Communication and Media Studies, 14% Psychology, General, 13% Theological and Ministerial Studies, 7% English Language and Literature, General
Expenses: 2020-2021: $20,120; room/board: $7,220

Financial aid: (757) 352-4125; 81% of undergrads determined to have financial need; average aid package $8,704

Roanoke College

Salem VA
(540) 375-2270
U.S. News ranking: Nat. Lib. Arts, No. 130
Website: www.roanoke.edu
Admissions email: admissions@roanoke.edu
Private; founded 1842
Affiliation: Evangelical Lutheran Church
Freshman admissions: selective; 2019-2020: 5,453 applied, 4,079 accepted. Neither SAT nor ACT required. SAT 25/75 percentile: 1050-1260. High school rank: 17% in top tenth, 46% in top quarter, 82% in top half
Early decision deadline: 11/15, notification date: 12/15
Early action deadline: N/A, notification date: N/A
Application deadline (fall): 3/15
Undergraduate student body: 1,942 full time, 63 part time; 42% male, 58% female; 0% American Indian, 1% Asian, 5% Black, 5% Hispanic, 4% multiracial, 0% Pacific Islander, 81% white, 2% international; 55% from in state; 79% live on campus; 20% of students in fraternities, 20% in sororities
Most popular majors: 18% Business Administration and Management, General, 11% Psychology, General, 6% Biology/Biological Sciences, General, 6% Communication and Media Studies, 6% Kinesiology and Exercise Science
Expenses: 2020-2021: $46,600; room/board: $14,580
Financial aid: (540) 375-2235; 76% of undergrads determined to have financial need; average aid package $38,476

Shenandoah University

Winchester VA
(540) 665-4581
U.S. News ranking: Nat. U., No. 241
Website: www.su.edu
Admissions email: admit@su.edu
Private; founded 1875
Affiliation: United Methodist
Freshman admissions: selective; 2019-2020: 2,203 applied, 1,670 accepted. Either SAT or ACT required. SAT 25/75 percentile: 1000-1200. High school rank: 11% in top tenth, 37% in top quarter, 67% in top half
Early decision deadline: N/A, notification date: N/A
Early action deadline: N/A, notification date: N/A
Application deadline (fall): rolling
Undergraduate student body: 1,989 full time, 51 part time; 40% male, 60% female; 1% American Indian, 3% Asian, 12% Black, 7% Hispanic, 1% multiracial, 0% Pacific Islander, 60% white, 2% international; 61% from in

state; 52% live on campus; N/A of students in fraternities, N/A in sororities

Most popular majors: 31% Nurse Midwife/Nursing Midwifery, 15% Biology/Biological Sciences, General, 13% Music Performance, General, 12% Business Administration and Management, General, 7% Psychology, General **Expenses:** 2020-2021: $33,830; room/board: $10,810 **Financial aid:** (540) 665-4538; 76% of undergrads determined to have financial need; average aid package $21,001

Southern Virginia University[1]

Buena Vista VA
(540) 261-8400
U.S. News ranking: Nat. Lib. Arts, second tier
Admissions email: N/A
Private
Application deadline (fall): N/A
Undergraduate student body: N/A full time, N/A part time
Expenses: 2019-2020: $17,290; room/board: $8,040
Financial aid: (540) 261-8463

Sweet Briar College[7]

Sweet Briar VA
(800) 381-6142
U.S. News ranking: Nat. Lib. Arts, No. 162
Website: www.sbc.edu
Admissions email: admissions@sbc.edu
Private; founded 1901
Freshman admissions: selective; 2019-2020: 627 applied, 601 accepted. Neither SAT nor ACT required. SAT 25/75 percentile: 1010-1210. High school rank: N/A
Early decision deadline: N/A, notification date: N/A
Early action deadline: 11/1, notification date: 11/16
Application deadline (fall): rolling
Undergraduate student body: 350 full time, 1 part time
Most popular majors: 6% Business/Commerce, General, 3% General Studies, 2% Creative Writing, 2% Engineering Science, 2% Liberal Arts and Sciences/Liberal Studies
Expenses: 2020-2021: $22,700; room/board: $13,500
Financial aid: (434) 381-6156; 70% of undergrads determined to have financial need; average aid package $21,791

University of Lynchburg

Lynchburg VA
(434) 544-8300
U.S. News ranking: Reg. U. (S), No. 22
Website: www.lynchburg.edu
Admissions email: admissions@lynchburg.edu
Private; founded 1903
Affiliation: Christian Church (Disciples of Christ)
Freshman admissions: selective; 2019-2020: 4,477 applied, 4,076 accepted. Either SAT or ACT required. SAT 25/75 percentile: 970-1170. High

school rank: 13% in top tenth, 22% in top quarter, 67% in top half
Early decision deadline: 11/15, notification date: 12/15
Early action deadline: N/A, notification date: N/A
Application deadline (fall): rolling
Undergraduate student body: 1,820 full time, 115 part time; 39% male, 61% female; 0% American Indian, 1% Asian, 11% Black, 6% Hispanic, 3% multiracial, 0% Pacific Islander, 75% white, 1% international; 73% from in state; 74% live on campus; 12% of students in fraternities, 12% in sororities
Most popular majors: 18% Health Professions and Related Programs, 15% Biological and Biomedical Sciences, 13% Social Sciences, 11% Business, Management, Marketing, and Related Support Services, 9% Education
Expenses: 2020-2021: $41,880; room/board: $12,138
Financial aid: (800) 426-8101; 78% of undergrads determined to have financial need; average aid package $30,535

University of Mary Washington

Fredericksburg VA
(540) 654-2000
U.S. News ranking: Reg. U. (S), No. 18
Website: www.umw.edu
Admissions email: admit@umw.edu
Public; founded 1908
Freshman admissions: selective; 2019-2020: 5,939 applied, 4,438 accepted. Neither SAT nor ACT required. SAT 25/75 percentile: 1080-1280. High school rank: 16% in top tenth, 41% in top quarter, 76% in top half
Early decision deadline: 11/1, notification date: 12/10
Early action deadline: 11/15, notification date: 1/31
Undergraduate student body: 3,694 full time, 488 part time; 36% male, 64% female; 0% American Indian, 4% Asian, 7% Black, 10% Hispanic, 6% multiracial, 0% Pacific Islander, 69% white, 1% international; 4% from in state; 57% live on campus; 0% of students in fraternities, 0% in sororities
Most popular majors: 16% Business, Management, Marketing, and Related Support Services, 16% Social Sciences, 11% Liberal Arts and Sciences, General Studies and Humanities, 10% Psychology, 8% English Language and Literature/Letters
Expenses: 2019-2020: $13,845 in state, $30,522 out of state; room/board: $11,938
Financial aid: (540) 654-2468

University of Richmond

Univ. of Richmond VA
(804) 289-8640
U.S. News ranking: Nat. Lib. Arts, No. 22
Website: www.richmond.edu
Admissions email: admission@richmond.edu

Private; founded 1830
Freshman admissions: most selective; 2019-2020: 12,356 applied, 3,500 accepted. Either SAT or ACT required. SAT 25/75 percentile: 1290-1460. High school rank: 59% in top tenth, 86% in top quarter, 96% in top half
Early decision deadline: 11/1, notification date: 12/15
Early action deadline: 11/1, notification date: 1/20
Application deadline (fall): 1/15
Undergraduate student body: 2,979 full time, 182 part time; 48% male, 52% female; 0% American Indian, 7% Asian, 7% Black, 9% Hispanic, 5% multiracial, 0% Pacific Islander, 58% white, 9% international; 24% from in state; 91% live on campus; 18% of students in fraternities, 27% in sororities
Most popular majors: 36% Business, Management, Marketing, and Related Support Services, 16% Social Sciences, 9% Biological and Biomedical Sciences, 6% Multi/Interdisciplinary Studies, 5% Psychology
Expenses: 2020-2021: $56,860; room/board: $13,430
Financial aid: (804) 289-8438; 39% of undergrads determined to have financial need; average aid package $52,064

University of Virginia

Charlottesville VA
(434) 982-3200
U.S. News ranking: Nat. U., No. 26
Website: www.virginia.edu
Admissions email: undergradadmission@virginia.edu
Public; founded 1819
Freshman admissions: most selective; 2019-2020: 40,839 applied, 9,778 accepted. Either SAT or ACT required. SAT 25/75 percentile: 1340-1520. High school rank: 90% in top tenth, 98% in top quarter, 99% in top half
Early decision deadline: N/A, notification date: N/A
Early action deadline: 11/1, notification date: 1/31
Application deadline (fall): 1/1
Undergraduate student body: 16,280 full time, 730 part time; 45% male, 55% female; 0% American Indian, 15% Asian, 7% Black, 7% Hispanic, 5% multiracial, 0% Pacific Islander, 56% white, 4% international
Most popular majors: 9% Economics, General, 6% Biology/Biological Sciences, General, 6% Business/Commerce, General, 4% International Relations and Affairs, 4% Psychology, General
Expenses: 2020-2021: $18,878 in state, $52,957 out of state; room/board: $12,350
Financial aid: (434) 982-6000; 36% of undergrads determined to have financial need; average aid package $30,591

University of Virginia–Wise

Wise VA
(888) 282-9324
U.S. News ranking: Nat. Lib. Arts, No. 166
Website: www.uvawise.edu
Admissions email: admissions@uvawise.edu
Public; founded 1954
Freshman admissions: selective; 2019-2020: 951 applied, 733 accepted. Either SAT or ACT required. SAT 25/75 percentile: 970-1160. High school rank: 14% in top tenth, 42% in top quarter, 73% in top half
Early decision deadline: N/A, notification date: N/A
Early action deadline: 12/1, notification date: 12/15
Application deadline (fall): 8/15
Undergraduate student body: 1,106 full time, 872 part time; 40% male, 60% female; 0% American Indian, 1% Asian, 9% Black, 1% Hispanic, 0% multiracial, 0% Pacific Islander, 79% white, 0% international; 7% from in state; 37% live on campus; N/A of students in fraternities, N/A in sororities
Most popular majors: 19% Business, Management, Marketing, and Related Support Services, 15% Social Sciences, 14% Education, 10% Psychology
Expenses: 2020-2021: $10,842 in state, $29,346 out of state; room/board: $11,288
Financial aid: (276) 328-0139; 81% of undergrads determined to have financial need; average aid package $6,833

Virginia Commonwealth University

Richmond VA
(800) 841-3638
U.S. News ranking: Nat. U., No. 160
Website: www.vcu.edu
Admissions email: ugrad@vcu.edu
Public; founded 1838
Freshman admissions: selective; 2019-2020: 17,244 applied, 14,973 accepted. Neither SAT nor ACT required. SAT 25/75 percentile: 1070-1260. High school rank: 18% in top tenth, 45% in top quarter, 79% in top half
Early decision deadline: N/A, notification date: N/A
Early action deadline: N/A, notification date: N/A
Application deadline (fall): 1/15
Undergraduate student body: 19,825 full time, 3,012 part time; 39% male, 61% female; 0% American Indian, 14% Asian, 20% Black, 11% Hispanic, 7% multiracial, 0% Pacific Islander, 43% white, 3% international; 93% from in state; 27% live on campus; 7% of students in fraternities, 6% in sororities
Most popular majors: 13% Visual and Performing Arts, 12% Business, Management, Marketing, and Related Support Services, 10% Psychology, 7% Biological and Biomedical Sciences, 7% Education

Expenses: 2020-2021: $14,710 in state, $35,358 out of state; room/board: $11,035
Financial aid: (804) 827-1329; 60% of undergrads determined to have financial need; average aid package $13,367

Virginia Military Institute

Lexington VA
(800) 767-4207
U.S. News ranking: Nat. Lib. Arts, No. 69
Website: www.vmi.edu
Admissions email: admissions@vmi.edu
Public; founded 1839
Freshman admissions: selective; 2019-2020: 1,515 applied, 902 accepted. Either SAT or ACT required. SAT 25/75 percentile: 1090-1270. High school rank: 10% in top tenth, 39% in top quarter, 78% in top half
Early decision deadline: 11/15, notification date: 12/15
Early action deadline: N/A, notification date: N/A
Application deadline (fall): 2/1
Undergraduate student body: 1,698 full time, 0 part time; 86% male, 14% female; 1% American Indian, 4% Asian, 6% Black, 8% Hispanic, 2% multiracial, 0% Pacific Islander, 77% white, 2% international; 64% from in state; 100% live on campus; 0% of students in fraternities, 0% in sororities
Most popular majors: 15% Civil Engineering, General, 15% International Relations and Affairs, 14% Economics, General, 10% Biology/Biological Sciences, General, 8% Computer Science
Expenses: 2019-2020: $19,118 in state, $45,962 out of state; room/board: $9,766
Financial aid: (540) 464-7208

Virginia State University[1]

Petersburg VA
(804) 524-5902
U.S. News ranking: Reg. U. (S), No. 80
Website: www.vsu.edu
Admissions email: admiss@vsu.edu
Public; founded 1882
Application deadline (fall): 5/1
Undergraduate student body: N/A full time, N/A part time
Expenses: 2020-2021: $9,056 in state, $19,576 out of state; room/board: $11,208
Financial aid: (800) 823-7214; 92% of undergrads determined to have financial need; average aid package $12,695

Virginia Tech

Blacksburg VA
(540) 231-6267
U.S. News ranking: Nat. U., No. 74
Website: www.vt.edu
Admissions email: admissions@vt.edu
Public; founded 1872
Freshman admissions: more selective; 2019-2020: 31,974 applied, 22,393 accepted. Neither SAT nor ACT required. SAT 25/75 percentile: 1180-1390.

High school rank: 29% in top tenth, 68% in top quarter, 88% in top half
Early decision deadline: 11/1, notification date: 12/15
Early action deadline: 12/1, notification date: 2/22
Application deadline (fall): 1/15
Undergraduate student body: 28,584 full time, 716 part time; 57% male, 43% female; 0% American Indian, 10% Asian, 4% Black, 7% Hispanic, 5% multiracial, 0% Pacific Islander, 65% white, 7% international; N/A from in state; 35% live on campus; 13% of students in fraternities, 19% in sororities
Most popular majors: 24% Engineering, 20% Business, Management, Marketing, and Related Support Services, 9% Family and Consumer Sciences/Human Sciences, 8% Social Sciences, 7% Biological and Biomedical Sciences
Expenses: 2020-2021: $13,749 in state, $32,893 out of state; room/board: $9,556
Financial aid: (540) 231-5179; 41% of undergrads determined to have financial need; average aid package $11,219

Virginia Union University
Richmond VA
(804) 257-5600
U.S. News ranking: Nat. Lib. Arts, second tier
Website: www.vuu.edu/
Admissions email: admissions@vuu.edu
Private; founded 1865
Affiliation: Baptist
Freshman admissions: least selective; 2019-2020: 4,182 applied, 2,639 accepted. Neither SAT nor ACT required. SAT 25/75 percentile: 770-929. High school rank: 3% in top tenth, 11% in top quarter, 38% in top half
Early decision deadline: N/A, notification date: N/A
Early action deadline: N/A, notification date: N/A
Application deadline (fall): 6/30
Undergraduate student body: 1,015 full time, 117 part time; 48% male, 52% female; 0% American Indian, 0% Asian, 94% Black, 2% Hispanic, 1% multiracial, 0% Pacific Islander, 1% white, 2% international
Most popular majors: 16% Criminology, 12% Business Administration and Management, General, 9% Biology/Biological Sciences, General, 9% Psychology, General, 8% Computer and Information Sciences, General
Expenses: 2020-2021: $13,530; room/board: $8,834
Financial aid: (804) 257-5882; 75% of undergrads determined to have financial need; average aid package $15,808

Virginia Wesleyan University
Virginia Beach VA
(757) 455-3208
U.S. News ranking: Nat. Lib. Arts, second tier
Website: www.vwu.edu
Admissions email: enrollment@vwu.edu
Private; founded 1961
Affiliation: United Methodist
Freshman admissions: selective; 2019-2020: 2,323 applied, 1,785 accepted. Either SAT or ACT required. SAT 25/75 percentile: 950-1180. High school rank: 20% in top tenth, 41% in top quarter, 68% in top half
Early decision deadline: N/A, notification date: N/A
Early action deadline: N/A, notification date: N/A
Application deadline (fall): rolling
Undergraduate student body: 1,245 full time, 142 part time; 41% male, 59% female; 1% American Indian, 2% Asian, 24% Black, 8% Hispanic, 7% multiracial, 0% Pacific Islander, 54% white, 1% international; 77% from in state; 68% live on campus; N/A of students in fraternities, N/A in sororities
Most popular majors: 15% Business, Management, Marketing, and Related Support Services, 10% Homeland Security, Law Enforcement, Firefighting and Related Protective Services, 10% Psychology, 9% Social Sciences, 6% Biological and Biomedical Sciences
Expenses: 2020-2021: $36,910; room/board: $10,338
Financial aid: (757) 455-3345; 84% of undergrads determined to have financial need; average aid package $25,553

Washington and Lee University
Lexington VA
(540) 458-8710
U.S. News ranking: Nat. Lib. Arts, No. 9
Website: www.wlu.edu
Admissions email: admissions@wlu.edu
Private; founded 1749
Freshman admissions: most selective; 2019-2020: 6,178 applied, 1,147 accepted. Either SAT or ACT required. SAT 25/75 percentile: 1360-1500. High school rank: 82% in top tenth, 96% in top quarter, 99% in top half
Early decision deadline: 11/1, notification date: 12/15
Early action deadline: N/A, notification date: N/A
Application deadline (fall): 1/1
Undergraduate student body: 1,845 full time, 15 part time; 50% male, 50% female; 0% American Indian, 4% Asian, 3% Black, 6% Hispanic, 4% multiracial, 0% Pacific Islander, 79% white, 4% international; 18% from in state; 74% live on campus; 77% of students in fraternities, 71% in sororities
Most popular majors: 15% Economics, General, 12% Business Administration and

Management, General, 10% Political Science and Government, General, 7% Accounting and Business/Management, 6% History, General
Expenses: 2020-2021: $57,285; room/board: $15,810
Financial aid: (540) 458-8717; 45% of undergrads determined to have financial need; average aid package $57,291

William & Mary
Williamsburg VA
(757) 221-4223
U.S. News ranking: Nat. U., No. 39
Website: www.wm.edu
Admissions email: admission@wm.edu
Public; founded 1693
Freshman admissions: most selective; 2019-2020: 14,680 applied, 5,532 accepted. Either SAT or ACT required. SAT 25/75 percentile: 1320-1510. High school rank: 75% in top tenth, 97% in top quarter, 99% in top half
Early decision deadline: 11/1, notification date: 12/1
Early action deadline: N/A, notification date: N/A
Application deadline (fall): 1/1
Undergraduate student body: 6,190 full time, 66 part time; 42% male, 58% female; 0% American Indian, 8% Asian, 7% Black, 10% Hispanic, 6% multiracial, 0% Pacific Islander, 58% white, 6% international; 69% from in state; 70% live on campus; 31% of students in fraternities, 29% in sororities
Most popular majors: 23% Social Sciences, 11% Business, Management, Marketing, and Related Support Services, 9% Biological and Biomedical Sciences, 8% Multi/Interdisciplinary Studies, 7% Psychology
Expenses: 2020-2021: $23,362 in state, $46,283 out of state; room/board: $13,356
Financial aid: (757) 221-2420; 37% of undergrads determined to have financial need; average aid package $25,454

WASHINGTON

Bellevue College[1]
Bellevue WA
(425) 564-1000
U.S. News ranking: Reg. Coll. (W), unranked
Website: www.bellevuecollege.edu
Admissions email: N/A
Public
Application deadline (fall): N/A
Undergraduate student body: N/A full time, N/A part time
Expenses: 2019-2020: $3,866 in state, $9,246 out of state; room/board: $12,390
Financial aid: N/A

Bellingham Technical College[1]
Bellingham WA
(360) 752-7000
U.S. News ranking: Reg. Coll. (W), unranked
Website: www.spokanefalls.edu
Admissions email: N/A
Public
Application deadline (fall): N/A
Undergraduate student body: N/A full time, N/A part time
Expenses: 2019-2020: $3,834 in state, $4,807 out of state; room/board: $10,200
Financial aid: N/A

Cascadia College[1]
Bothell WA
(425) 352-8000
U.S. News ranking: Reg. Coll. (W), unranked
Admissions email: admissions@cascadia.edu
Public; founded 2000
Application deadline (fall): rolling
Undergraduate student body: N/A full time, N/A part time
Expenses: 2019-2020: $4,055 in state, $9,435 out of state; room/board: $10,140
Financial aid: N/A

Centralia College[1]
Centralia WA
(360) 736-9391
U.S. News ranking: Reg. Coll. (W), unranked
Admissions email: N/A
Public
Application deadline (fall): N/A
Undergraduate student body: N/A full time, N/A part time
Expenses: 2019-2020: $4,542 in state, $4,991 out of state; room/board: $10,770
Financial aid: N/A

Central Washington University
Ellensburg WA
(509) 963-1211
U.S. News ranking: Reg. U. (W), No. 47
Website: www.cwu.edu
Admissions email: admissions@cwu.edu
Public; founded 1891
Freshman admissions: less selective; 2019-2020: 9,940 applied, 8,689 accepted. Neither SAT nor ACT required. SAT 25/75 percentile: 940-1130. High school rank: N/A
Early decision deadline: N/A, notification date: N/A
Early action deadline: N/A, notification date: N/A
Application deadline (fall): rolling
Undergraduate student body: 9,913 full time, 971 part time; 48% male, 52% female; 1% American Indian, 4% Asian, 4% Black, 17% Hispanic, 8% multiracial, 1% Pacific Islander, 50% white, 3% international; N/A from in state; 26% live on campus; N/A of students in fraternities, N/A in sororities

Most popular majors: 22% Education, 18% Business, Management, Marketing, and Related Support Services, 9% Computer and Information Sciences and Support Services, 8% Social Sciences, 6% Psychology
Expenses: 2020-2021: $7,701 in state, $23,727 out of state; room/board: $13,269
Financial aid: (509) 963-1611; 67% of undergrads determined to have financial need; average aid package $10,893

City University of Seattle[1]
Seattle WA
(888) 422-4898
U.S. News ranking: Reg. U. (W), second tier
Website: www.cityu.edu
Admissions email: info@cityu.edu
Private; founded 1973
Application deadline (fall): N/A
Undergraduate student body: N/A full time, N/A part time
Expenses: 2019-2020: $13,120; room/board: N/A
Financial aid: N/A

Clark College[1]
Vancouver WA
(360) 992-2000
U.S. News ranking: Reg. Coll. (W), unranked
Admissions email: N/A
Public
Application deadline (fall): N/A
Undergraduate student body: N/A full time, N/A part time
Expenses: 2019-2020: $3,879 in state, $9,258 out of state; room/board: $10,770
Financial aid: N/A

Clover Park Technical College[1]
Lakewood WA
(253) 589-5800
U.S. News ranking: Reg. Coll. (W), unranked
Website: www.cptc.edu
Admissions email: admissions@cptc.edu
Public
Application deadline (fall): N/A
Undergraduate student body: N/A full time, N/A part time
Expenses: 2019-2020: $5,740 in state, $5,740 out of state; room/board: $9,690
Financial aid: N/A

Columbia Basin College[1]
Pasco WA
(509) 547-0511
U.S. News ranking: Reg. Coll. (W), unranked
Admissions email: N/A
Public
Application deadline (fall): N/A
Undergraduate student body: N/A full time, N/A part time
Expenses: 2019-2020: $5,613 in state, $7,294 out of state; room/board: $9,875
Financial aid: N/A

Cornish College of the Arts[1]

Seattle WA
(800) 726-2787
U.S. News ranking: Arts, unranked
Website: www.cornish.edu
Admissions email: admission@cornish.edu
Private; founded 1914
Application deadline (fall): N/A
Undergraduate student body: 563 full time, 23 part time
Expenses: 2020-2021: $34,398; room/board: $13,036
Financial aid: (206) 726-5063; 69% of undergrads determined to have financial need; average aid package $19,052

DigiPen Institute of Technology

Redmond WA
(425) 629-5001
U.S. News ranking: Reg. Coll. (W), unranked
Website: www.digipen.edu
Admissions email: admissions@digipen.edu
For-profit; founded 1988
Freshman admissions: more selective; 2019-2020: 997 applied, 334 accepted. Either SAT or ACT required. SAT 25/75 percentile: 1128-1400. High school rank: N/A
Early decision deadline: N/A, notification date: N/A
Early action deadline: N/A, notification date: N/A
Application deadline (fall): rolling
Undergraduate student body: 1,027 full time, 57 part time; 74% male, 26% female; 0% American Indian, 8% Asian, 1% Black, 7% Hispanic, 7% multiracial, 0% Pacific Islander, 53% white, 11% international; 58% from in state; 20% live on campus; 0% of students in fraternities, 0% in sororities
Most popular majors: 34% Animation, Interactive Technology, Video Graphics and Special Effects, 28% Computer Programming, Specific Applications, 11% Human Computer Interaction, 11% Modeling, Virtual Environments and Simulation, 5% Music Theory and Composition
Expenses: 2020-2021: $33,900; room/board: $10,304
Financial aid: (425) 629-5002; 56% of undergrads determined to have financial need; average aid package $12,617

Eastern Washington University

Cheney WA
(509) 359-2397
U.S. News ranking: Reg. U. (W), No. 52
Website: www.ewu.edu
Admissions email: admissions@ewu.edu
Public; founded 1882
Freshman admissions: less selective; 2019-2020: 5,299 applied, 5,069 accepted. Either SAT or ACT required. SAT 25/75 percentile: 880-1100. High school rank: N/A

Early decision deadline: N/A, notification date: N/A
Early action deadline: N/A, notification date: N/A
Application deadline (fall): 5/15
Undergraduate student body: 9,458 full time, 1,213 part time; 45% male, 55% female; 1% American Indian, 3% Asian, 4% Black, 17% Hispanic, 8% multiracial, 1% Pacific Islander, 59% white, 3% international; N/A from in state; 46% live on campus; 7% of students in fraternities, 6% in sororities
Most popular majors: 20% Business, Management, Marketing, and Related Support Services, 10% Biological and Biomedical Sciences, 8% Health Professions and Related Programs, 8% Psychology, 8% Social Sciences
Expenses: 2020-2021: $7,525 in state, $25,056 out of state; room/board: $12,406
Financial aid: (509) 359-2314

Edmonds Community College[1]

Lynnwood WA
(425) 640-1459
U.S. News ranking: Reg. Coll. (W), unranked
Admissions email: N/A
Public
Application deadline (fall): N/A
Undergraduate student body: N/A full time, N/A part time
Expenses: 2019-2020: $4,017 in state, $9,369 out of state; room/board: $10,770
Financial aid: N/A

Evergreen State College

Olympia WA
(360) 867-6170
U.S. News ranking: Reg. U. (W), No. 43
Website: www.evergreen.edu
Admissions email: admissions@evergreen.edu
Public; founded 1967
Freshman admissions: selective; 2019-2020: 1,303 applied, 1,275 accepted. Neither SAT nor ACT required. SAT 25/75 percentile: 960-1210. High school rank: 0% in top tenth, 26% in top quarter, 53% in top half
Early decision deadline: N/A, notification date: N/A
Early action deadline: N/A, notification date: N/A
Application deadline (fall): rolling
Undergraduate student body: 2,366 full time, 210 part time; 41% male, 59% female; 4% American Indian, 3% Asian, 5% Black, 13% Hispanic, 6% multiracial, 0% Pacific Islander, 63% white, 0% international; 16% from in state; 23% live on campus; N/A of students in fraternities, N/A in sororities
Most popular majors: 82% Liberal Arts and Sciences/Liberal Studies, 18% Biological and Physical Sciences

Expenses: 2019-2020: $8,217 in state, $27,537 out of state; room/board: $12,363
Financial aid: (360) 867-6205

Gonzaga University

Spokane WA
(800) 322-2584
U.S. News ranking: Nat. U., No. 80
Website: www.gonzaga.edu
Admissions email: admissions@gonzaga.edu
Private; founded 1887
Affiliation: Roman Catholic
Freshman admissions: more selective; 2019-2020: 9,279 applied, 5,744 accepted. Either SAT or ACT required. SAT 25/75 percentile: 1200-1360. High school rank: 40% in top tenth, 75% in top quarter, 95% in top half
Early decision deadline: N/A, notification date: N/A
Early action deadline: N/A, notification date: N/A
Application deadline (fall): 2/1
Undergraduate student body: 5,138 full time, 100 part time; 47% male, 53% female; 0% American Indian, 6% Asian, 1% Black, 11% Hispanic, 7% multiracial, 0% Pacific Islander, 71% white, 1% international; 48% from in state; 51% live on campus; 0% of students in fraternities, 0% in sororities
Most popular majors: 28% Business, Management, Marketing, and Related Support Services, 12% Engineering, 12% Social Sciences, 10% Biological and Biomedical Sciences, 7% Psychology
Expenses: 2020-2021: $44,920; room/board: $12,951
Financial aid: (509) 313-6562; 49% of undergrads determined to have financial need; average aid package $26,000

Grays Harbor College[1]

Aberdeen WA
(360) 532-9020
U.S. News ranking: Reg. Coll. (W), unranked
Admissions email: N/A
Public
Application deadline (fall): N/A
Undergraduate student body: N/A full time, N/A part time
Expenses: 2019-2020: $4,204 in state, $9,576 out of state; room/board: $10,770
Financial aid: N/A

Green River College[1]

Auburn WA
(253) 833-9111
U.S. News ranking: Reg. Coll. (W), unranked
Admissions email: N/A
Public
Application deadline (fall): N/A
Undergraduate student body: N/A full time, N/A part time
Expenses: 2019-2020: $4,141 in state, $4,584 out of state; room/board: $10,770
Financial aid: N/A

Heritage University[1]

Toppenish WA
(509) 865-8500
U.S. News ranking: Reg. U. (W), second tier
Website: www.heritage.edu
Admissions email: admissions@heritage.edu
Private
Application deadline (fall): N/A
Undergraduate student body: N/A full time, N/A part time
Expenses: 2019-2020: $18,029; room/board: N/A
Financial aid: N/A

Highline College[1]

Des Moines WA
(206) 878-3710
U.S. News ranking: Reg. Coll. (W), unranked
Admissions email: N/A
Public
Application deadline (fall): N/A
Undergraduate student body: N/A full time, N/A part time
Expenses: 2019-2020: $4,127 in state, $4,576 out of state; room/board: $9,864
Financial aid: N/A

Lake Washington Institute of Technology[1]

Kirkland WA
(425) 739-8104
U.S. News ranking: Reg. Coll. (W), unranked
Website: www.lwtech.edu/
Admissions email: admissions@lwtech.edu
Public; founded 1949
Application deadline (fall): rolling
Undergraduate student body: N/A full time, N/A part time
Expenses: 2019-2020: $7,743 in state, $19,288 out of state; room/board: N/A
Financial aid: (425) 739-8106

North Seattle College[1]

Seattle WA
(206) 934-3600
U.S. News ranking: Reg. Coll. (W), unranked
Admissions email: N/A
Public
Application deadline (fall): N/A
Undergraduate student body: N/A full time, N/A part time
Expenses: 2019-2020: $4,625 in state, $4,625 out of state; room/board: $10,770
Financial aid: N/A

Northwest University

Kirkland WA
(425) 889-5231
U.S. News ranking: Reg. U. (W), No. 52
Website: www.northwestu.edu
Admissions email: admissions@northwestu.edu
Private; founded 1934
Affiliation: Assemblies of God Church
Freshman admissions: selective; 2019-2020: 587 applied, 544 accepted. Either SAT or ACT

required. SAT 25/75 percentile: 1010-1215. High school rank: N/A
Early decision deadline: N/A, notification date: N/A
Early action deadline: N/A, notification date: N/A
Application deadline (fall): 8/1
Undergraduate student body: 923 full time, 24 part time; 32% male, 68% female; 1% American Indian, 5% Asian, 4% Black, 10% Hispanic, 7% multiracial, 2% Pacific Islander, 63% white, 5% international
Most popular majors: 19% Health Professions and Related Programs, 15% Business, Management, Marketing, and Related Support Services, 13% Theology and Religious Vocations, 9% Communication, Journalism, and Related Programs, 9% Psychology
Expenses: 2020-2021: $33,980; room/board: $9,420
Financial aid: (425) 889-5336; 78% of undergrads determined to have financial need; average aid package $26,258

Olympic College[1]

Bremerton WA
(360) 792-6050
U.S. News ranking: Reg. Coll. (W), unranked
Website: www.olympic.edu
Admissions email: N/A
Public
Application deadline (fall): N/A
Undergraduate student body: N/A full time, N/A part time
Expenses: 2019-2020: $3,880 in state, $4,361 out of state; room/board: $10,355
Financial aid: N/A

Pacific Lutheran University

Tacoma WA
(800) 274-6758
U.S. News ranking: Reg. U. (W), No. 22
Website: www.plu.edu
Admissions email: admission@plu.edu
Private; founded 1890
Affiliation: Lutheran Church in America
Freshman admissions: selective; 2019-2020: 3,679 applied, 3,165 accepted. Neither SAT nor ACT required. SAT 25/75 percentile: 1080-1290. High school rank: N/A
Early decision deadline: N/A, notification date: N/A
Early action deadline: N/A, notification date: N/A
Application deadline (fall): 8/15
Undergraduate student body: 2,618 full time, 66 part time; 36% male, 64% female; 0% American Indian, 10% Asian, 4% Black, 13% Hispanic, 11% multiracial, 1% Pacific Islander, 57% white, 2% international; 76% from in state; 48% live on campus; N/A of students in fraternities, N/A in sororities
Most popular majors: 14% Business, Management, Marketing, and Related Support Services, 10% Health Professions and Related Programs, 9% Biological and Biomedical

Sciences, 9% Social Sciences, 7% Physical Sciences
Expenses: 2020-2021: $46,200; room/board: $11,150
Financial aid: (253) 535-7161; 75% of undergrads determined to have financial need; average aid package $41,085

Peninsula College[1]
Port Angeles WA
(360) 452-9277
U.S. News ranking: Reg. Coll. (W), unranked
Website: www.pencol.edu
Admissions email: N/A
Public
Application deadline (fall): N/A
Undergraduate student body: N/A full time, N/A part time
Expenses: 2019-2020: $4,126 in state, $4,550 out of state; room/board: $10,170
Financial aid: N/A

Renton Technical College[1]
Renton WA
(425) 235-2352
U.S. News ranking: Reg. Coll. (W), unranked
Admissions email: N/A
Public
Application deadline (fall): N/A
Undergraduate student body: N/A full time, N/A part time
Expenses: 2019-2020: $5,567 in state, $6,016 out of state; room/board: $10,770
Financial aid: N/A

Saint Martin's University
Lacey WA
(800) 368-8803
U.S. News ranking: Reg. U. (W), No. 33
Website: www.stmartin.edu
Admissions email: admissions@stmartin.edu
Private; founded 1895
Affiliation: Roman Catholic
Freshman admissions: selective; 2019-2020: 1,614 applied, 1,548 accepted. Neither SAT nor ACT required. SAT 25/75 percentile: 970-1170. High school rank: 27% in top tenth, 57% in top quarter, 88% in top half
Early decision deadline: N/A, notification date: N/A
Early action deadline: N/A, notification date: N/A
Application deadline (fall): 7/31
Undergraduate student body: 1,256 full time, 132 part time; 48% male, 52% female; 1% American Indian, 9% Asian, 6% Black, 15% Hispanic, 10% multiracial, 5% Pacific Islander, 46% white, 4% international; 73% from in state; 44% live on campus; 0% of students in fraternities, 0% in sororities
Most popular majors: 22% Business, Management, Marketing, and Related Support Services, 15% Engineering, 12% Psychology, 10% Biological and Biomedical Sciences, 8% Education

Expenses: 2020-2021: $39,940; room/board: $12,410
Financial aid: (360) 486-8868; 75% of undergrads determined to have financial need; average aid package $32,445

Seattle Central College[1]
Seattle WA
(206) 934-5450
U.S. News ranking: Reg. Coll. (W), unranked
Website: www.seattlecentral.edu/
Admissions email: Admissions. Central@seattlecolleges.edu
Public; founded 1966
Application deadline (fall): rolling
Undergraduate student body: N/A full time, N/A part time
Expenses: 2019-2020: $3,779 in state, $3,779 out of state; room/board: $10,568
Financial aid: N/A

Seattle Pacific University
Seattle WA
(800) 366-3344
U.S. News ranking: Nat. U., No. 196
Website: www.spu.edu
Admissions email: admissions@spu.edu
Private; founded 1891
Affiliation: Free Methodist
Freshman admissions: selective; 2019-2020: 4,387 applied, 3,975 accepted. Either SAT or ACT required. SAT 25/75 percentile: 1020-1250. High school rank: N/A
Early decision deadline: N/A, notification date: N/A
Early action deadline: 11/15, notification date: 1/5
Application deadline (fall): 2/1
Undergraduate student body: 2,636 full time, 81 part time; 34% male, 66% female; 0% American Indian, 13% Asian, 5% Black, 14% Hispanic, 9% multiracial, 1% Pacific Islander, 48% white, 6% international; N/A from in state; 55% live on campus; N/A of students in fraternities, N/A in sororities
Most popular majors: 11% Business, Management, Marketing, and Related Support Services, 11% Health Professions and Related Programs, 9% Engineering, 9% Social Sciences, 8% Biological and Biomedical Sciences
Expenses: 2020-2021: $47,244; room/board: $12,687
Financial aid: (206) 281-2061; 70% of undergrads determined to have financial need; average aid package $40,803

Seattle University
Seattle WA
(206) 296-2000
U.S. News ranking: Nat. U., No. 124
Website: www.seattleu.edu
Admissions email: admissions@seattleu.edu
Private; founded 1891
Affiliation: Roman Catholic
Freshman admissions: more selective; 2019-2020: 7,968

applied, 6,253 accepted. Either SAT or ACT required. SAT 25/75 percentile: 1150-1330. High school rank: 28% in top tenth, 64% in top quarter, 92% in top half
Early decision deadline: N/A, notification date: N/A
Early action deadline: 11/15, notification date: 12/23
Application deadline (fall): rolling
Undergraduate student body: 4,455 full time, 245 part time; 39% male, 61% female; 0% American Indian, 18% Asian, 3% Black, 12% Hispanic, 9% multiracial, 1% Pacific Islander, 40% white, 11% international; N/A from in state; 51% live on campus; N/A of students in fraternities, N/A in sororities
Most popular majors: 26% Business, Management, Marketing, and Related Support Services, 11% Health Professions and Related Programs, 7% Engineering, 6% Biological and Biomedical Sciences, 6% Psychology
Expenses: 2020-2021: $48,390; room/board: $12,780
Financial aid: (206) 296-5852; 56% of undergrads determined to have financial need; average aid package $39,057

Skagit Valley College[1]
Mount Vernon WA
(360) 416-7600
U.S. News ranking: Reg. Coll. (W), unranked
Admissions email: N/A
Public
Application deadline (fall): N/A
Undergraduate student body: N/A full time, N/A part time
Expenses: 2019-2020: $4,000 in state, $6,884 out of state; room/board: $9,600
Financial aid: N/A

South Seattle College[1]
Seattle WA
(206) 764-5300
U.S. News ranking: Reg. Coll. (W), unranked
Website: www.southseattle.edu
Admissions email: N/A
Public
Application deadline (fall): N/A
Undergraduate student body: N/A full time, N/A part time
Expenses: 2019-2020: $4,717 in state, $4,717 out of state; room/board: $10,383
Financial aid: N/A

Spokane Community College[1]
Spokane WA
(509) 533-7000
U.S. News ranking: Reg. Coll. (W), unranked
Admissions email: N/A
Public
Application deadline (fall): N/A
Undergraduate student body: N/A full time, N/A part time

Expenses: 2019-2020: $3,634 in state, $4,881 out of state; room/board: $9,780
Financial aid: N/A

Spokane Falls Community College[1]
Spokane WA
(509) 533-3500
U.S. News ranking: Reg. Coll. (W), unranked
Admissions email: N/A
Public
Application deadline (fall): N/A
Undergraduate student body: N/A full time, N/A part time
Expenses: 2019-2020: $3,634 in state, $4,881 out of state; room/board: $9,780
Financial aid: N/A

Tacoma Community College[1]
Tacoma WA
(253) 566-5000
U.S. News ranking: Reg. Coll. (W), unranked
Admissions email: N/A
Public
Application deadline (fall): N/A
Undergraduate student body: N/A full time, N/A part time
Expenses: 2019-2020: $4,419 in state, $9,862 out of state; room/board: $10,170
Financial aid: N/A

University of Puget Sound
Tacoma WA
(253) 879-3211
U.S. News ranking: Nat. Lib. Arts, No. 84
Website: www.pugetsound.edu
Admissions email: admission@pugetsound.edu
Private; founded 1888
Freshman admissions: more selective; 2019-2020: 5,182 applied, 4,343 accepted. Neither SAT nor ACT required. SAT 25/75 percentile: 1150-1370. High school rank: 30% in top tenth, 64% in top quarter, 91% in top half
Early decision deadline: 11/15, notification date: 12/15
Early action deadline: 11/15, notification date: 1/15
Application deadline (fall): 1/15
Undergraduate student body: 2,271 full time, 28 part time; 41% male, 59% female; 0% American Indian, 7% Asian, 2% Black, 10% Hispanic, 10% multiracial, 0% Pacific Islander, 67% white, 0% international; 25% from in state; 67% live on campus; 25% of students in fraternities, 25% in sororities
Most popular majors: 20% Social Sciences, 12% Business, Management, Marketing, and Related Support Services, 11% Biological and Biomedical Sciences, 10% Psychology, 7% Visual and Performing Arts
Expenses: 2020-2021: $53,800; room/board: $13,480
Financial aid: (253) 879-3214; 56% of undergrads determined to

have financial need; average aid package $38,542

University of Washington
Seattle WA
(206) 543-9686
U.S. News ranking: Nat. U., No. 58
Website: www.washington.edu
Admissions email: pseegert@uw.edu
Public; founded 1861
Freshman admissions: more selective; 2019-2020: 45,579 applied, 23,592 accepted. Either SAT or ACT required. SAT 25/75 percentile: 1220-1470. High school rank: 59% in top tenth, 89% in top quarter, 99% in top half
Early decision deadline: N/A, notification date: N/A
Early action deadline: N/A, notification date: N/A
Application deadline (fall): 11/15
Undergraduate student body: 29,332 full time, 2,714 part time; 46% male, 54% female; 0% American Indian, 26% Asian, 3% Black, 9% Hispanic, 8% multiracial, 0% Pacific Islander, 37% white, 16% international; N/A from in state; 29% live on campus; 14% of students in fraternities, 15% in sororities
Most popular majors: 12% Social Sciences, 10% Biological and Biomedical Sciences, 10% Computer and Information Sciences and Support Services, 10% Engineering, 8% Business, Management, Marketing, and Related Support Services
Expenses: 2020-2021: $12,092 in state, $39,461 out of state; room/board: $13,887
Financial aid: (206) 543-6101; 41% of undergrads determined to have financial need; average aid package $17,487

University of Washington–Bothell[1]
Bothell WA
(425) 352-5000
U.S. News ranking: Reg. U. (W), No. 29
Admissions email: N/A
Public
Application deadline (fall): N/A
Undergraduate student body: N/A full time, N/A part time
Expenses: 2019-2020: $11,390 in state, $38,091 out of state; room/board: $12,636
Financial aid: N/A

University of Washington–Tacoma[1]
Tacoma WA
(253) 692-4000
U.S. News ranking: Reg. U. (W), No. 35
Admissions email: N/A
Public
Application deadline (fall): N/A
Undergraduate student body: N/A full time, N/A part time
Expenses: 2019-2020: $11,639 in state, $38,340 out of state; room/board: $11,748
Financial aid: N/A

Walla Walla University[1]

College Place WA
(509) 527-2327
U.S. News ranking: Reg. U. (W), No. 75
Website: www.wallawalla.edu
Admissions email: info@wallawalla.edu
Private; founded 1892
Affiliation: Seventh Day Adventist
Application deadline (fall): rolling
Undergraduate student body: N/A full time, N/A part time
Expenses: 2019-2020: $28,881; room/board: $7,680
Financial aid: (509) 527-2815

Washington State University

Pullman WA
(888) 468-6978
U.S. News ranking: Nat. U., No. 176
Website: www.wsu.edu
Admissions email: admissions@wsu.edu
Public; founded 1890
Freshman admissions: selective; 2019-2020: 21,434 applied, 16,247 accepted. Either SAT or ACT required. SAT 25/75 percentile: 1020-1240. High school rank: N/A
Early decision deadline: N/A, notification date: N/A
Early action deadline: N/A, notification date: N/A
Application deadline (fall): rolling
Undergraduate student body: 23,092 full time, 2,970 part time; 47% male, 53% female; 1% American Indian, 6% Asian, 3% Black, 16% Hispanic, 7% multiracial, 0% Pacific Islander, 61% white, 4% international; 81% from in state; 25% live on campus; 18% of students in fraternities, 21% in sororities
Most popular majors: 20% Business, Management, Marketing, and Related Support Services, 11% Engineering, 10% Social Sciences, 8% Psychology, 7% Health Professions and Related Programs
Expenses: 2020-2021: $12,170 in state, $27,113 out of state; room/board: $11,750
Financial aid: (509) 335-9711; 56% of undergrads determined to have financial need; average aid package $13,604

Washington State University–Vancouver[1]

Vancouver, WA
(360) 546-9788
U.S. News ranking: Unranked
Admissions email: N/A
Public
Application deadline (fall): N/A
Undergraduate student body: N/A full time, N/A part time
Expenses: 2019-2020: $10,552 in state, $25,130 out of state; room/board: $11,648
Financial aid: N/A

Wenatchee Valley College[1]

Wenatchee WA
(509) 682-6800
U.S. News ranking: Reg. Coll. (W), unranked
Admissions email: N/A
Public
Application deadline (fall): N/A
Undergraduate student body: N/A full time, N/A part time
Expenses: 2019-2020: $4,188 in state, $4,208 out of state; room/board: $6,750
Financial aid: N/A

Western Washington University

Bellingham WA
(360) 650-3440
U.S. News ranking: Reg. U. (W), No. 18
Website: www.wwu.edu
Admissions email: admit@wwu.edu
Public; founded 1893
Freshman admissions: selective; 2019-2020: 10,513 applied, 9,502 accepted. Either SAT or ACT required. SAT 25/75 percentile: 1060-1280. High school rank: 21% in top tenth, 51% in top quarter, 85% in top half
Early decision deadline: N/A, notification date: N/A
Early action deadline: 11/1, notification date: 12/31
Application deadline (fall): 1/31
Undergraduate student body: 13,887 full time, 1,353 part time; 43% male, 57% female; 0% American Indian, 6% Asian, 2% Black, 10% Hispanic, 9% multiracial, 0% Pacific Islander, 70% white, 1% international; 88% from in state; 26% live on campus; N/A of students in fraternities, N/A in sororities
Most popular majors: 13% Business, Management, Marketing, and Related Support Services, 12% Social Sciences, 8% Multi/Interdisciplinary Studies, 7% Natural Resources and Conservation, 6% Psychology
Expenses: 2020-2021: $8,508 in state, $25,266 out of state; room/board: $12,518
Financial aid: (360) 650-2422; 47% of undergrads determined to have financial need; average aid package $18,108

Whatcom Community College[1]

Bellingham WA
(360) 383-3000
U.S. News ranking: Reg. Coll. (W), unranked
Admissions email: N/A
Public
Application deadline (fall): N/A
Undergraduate student body: N/A full time, N/A part time
Expenses: 2019-2020: $4,650 in state, $10,095 out of state; room/board: $8,100
Financial aid: N/A

Whitman College[1]

Walla Walla WA
(509) 527-5176
U.S. News ranking: Nat. Lib. Arts, No. 47
Website: www.whitman.edu
Admissions email: admission@whitman.edu
Private; founded 1883
Application deadline (fall): 1/15
Undergraduate student body: N/A full time, N/A part time
Expenses: 2019-2020: $53,820; room/board: $13,512
Financial aid: (509) 527-5178

Whitworth University

Spokane WA
(800) 533-4668
U.S. News ranking: Reg. U. (W), No. 4
Website: www.whitworth.edu
Admissions email: admissions@whitworth.edu
Private; founded 1890
Affiliation: Presbyterian Church (USA)
Freshman admissions: selective; 2019-2020: 3,817 applied, 3,488 accepted. Neither SAT nor ACT required. SAT 25/75 percentile: 1050-1290. High school rank: 33% in top tenth, 64% in top quarter, 92% in top half
Early decision deadline: N/A, notification date: N/A
Early action deadline: 1/15, notification date: 2/15
Application deadline (fall): 8/1
Undergraduate student body: 2,360 full time, 41 part time; 41% male, 59% female; 1% American Indian, 5% Asian, 2% Black, 12% Hispanic, 10% multiracial, 1% Pacific Islander, 65% white, 4% international; 68% from in state; 54% live on campus; N/A of students in fraternities, N/A in sororities
Most popular majors: 12% Business, Management, Marketing, and Related Support Services, 12% Social Sciences, 10% Multi/Interdisciplinary Studies, 8% Health Professions and Related Programs, 8% Psychology
Expenses: 2020-2021: $46,250; room/board: $12,150
Financial aid: (509) 777-3215; 72% of undergrads determined to have financial need; average aid package $41,387

Yakima Valley College[1]

Yakima WA
(509) 574-4600
U.S. News ranking: Reg. Coll. (W), unranked
Admissions email: N/A
Public
Application deadline (fall): N/A
Undergraduate student body: N/A full time, N/A part time
Expenses: 2019-2020: $4,285 in state, $4,729 out of state; room/board: $8,100
Financial aid: N/A

WEST VIRGINIA

Alderson Broaddus University

Philippi WV
(800) 263-1549
U.S. News ranking: Reg. Coll. (S), No. 55
Website: www.ab.edu
Admissions email: admissions@ab.edu
Private; founded 1871
Affiliation: American Baptist
Freshman admissions: less selective; 2019-2020: 3,915 applied, 1,846 accepted. Either SAT or ACT required. SAT 25/75 percentile: 860-1060. High school rank: 7% in top tenth, 22% in top quarter, 52% in top half
Early decision deadline: N/A, notification date: N/A
Early action deadline: N/A, notification date: N/A
Application deadline (fall): 8/25
Undergraduate student body: 790 full time, 46 part time; 57% male, 43% female; 1% American Indian, 0% Asian, 30% Black, 7% Hispanic, 1% multiracial, 0% Pacific Islander, 56% white, 4% international; 39% from in state; 82% live on campus; 4% of students in fraternities, 5% in sororities
Most popular majors: 16% Business Administration and Management, General, 15% Physician Assistant, 13% Registered Nursing/Registered Nurse, 10% English Language and Literature/Letters, 8% Biology/Biological Sciences, General
Expenses: 2020-2021: $29,220; room/board: $9,400
Financial aid: (304) 457-6354; 89% of undergrads determined to have financial need; average aid package $26,875

Bethany College

Bethany WV
(304) 829-7611
U.S. News ranking: Nat. Lib. Arts, second tier
Website: www.bethanywv.edu
Admissions email: enrollment@bethanywv.edu
Private; founded 1840
Affiliation: Christian Church (Disciples of Christ)
Freshman admissions: less selective; 2019-2020: 1,150 applied, 1,096 accepted. Either SAT or ACT required. SAT 25/75 percentile: 890-1120. High school rank: 5% in top tenth, 20% in top quarter, 60% in top half
Early decision deadline: N/A, notification date: N/A
Early action deadline: N/A, notification date: N/A
Application deadline (fall): rolling
Undergraduate student body: 511 full time, 5 part time; 54% male, 46% female; 0% American Indian, 0% Asian, 20% Black, 5% Hispanic, 6% multiracial, 0% Pacific Islander, 57% white, 2% international
Most popular majors: Information not available
Expenses: 2020-2021: $30,700; room/board: $11,540

Financial aid (Alderson Broaddus, cont.)

Financial aid: (304) 829-7601; 87% of undergrads determined to have financial need; average aid package $37,840

Bluefield State College

Bluefield WV
(304) 327-4065
U.S. News ranking: Reg. Coll. (S), No. 50
Website: bluefieldstate.edu/
Admissions email: bscadmit@bluefieldstate.edu
Public; founded 1895
Freshman admissions: less selective; 2019-2020: 475 applied, 446 accepted. Either SAT or ACT required. ACT 25/75 percentile: 16-21. High school rank: 20% in top tenth, 48% in top quarter, 84% in top half
Early decision deadline: N/A, notification date: N/A
Early action deadline: N/A, notification date: N/A
Application deadline (fall): rolling
Undergraduate student body: 950 full time, 291 part time; 36% male, 64% female; 0% American Indian, 0% Asian, 10% Black, 1% Hispanic, 3% multiracial, 0% Pacific Islander, 83% white, 2% international
Most popular majors: 26% Health Professions and Related Programs, 21% Liberal Arts and Sciences, General Studies and Humanities, 16% Engineering Technologies and Engineering-Related Fields, 12% Business, Management, Marketing, and Related Support Services, 7% Homeland Security, Law Enforcement, Firefighting and Related Protective Services
Expenses: 2020-2021: $7,584 in state, $10,680 out of state; room/board: N/A
Financial aid: (304) 327-4020; 87% of undergrads determined to have financial need; average aid package $3,018

Concord University

Athens WV
(888) 384-5249
U.S. News ranking: Reg. U. (S), No. 94
Website: www.concord.edu
Admissions email: admissions@concord.edu
Public; founded 1872
Freshman admissions: selective; 2019-2020: 1,886 applied, 1,543 accepted. Either SAT or ACT required. SAT 25/75 percentile: 900-1110. High school rank: 13% in top tenth, 36% in top quarter, 72% in top half
Early decision deadline: N/A, notification date: N/A
Early action deadline: N/A, notification date: N/A
Application deadline (fall): rolling
Undergraduate student body: 1,436 full time, 134 part time; 41% male, 59% female; 0% American Indian, 1% Asian, 6% Black, 1% Hispanic, 3% multiracial, 0% Pacific Islander, 81% white, 5% international; 83% from in state; 44% live on campus; N/A of students in fraternities, N/A in sororities

Most popular majors: 19% Liberal Arts and Sciences, General Studies and Humanities, 17% Business, Management, Marketing, and Related Support Services, 14% Education, 11% Public Administration and Social Service Professions, 7% Biological and Biomedical Sciences
Expenses: 2020-2021: $8,385 in state, $18,037 out of state; room/board: $9,304
Financial aid: (304) 384-5358; 75% of undergrads determined to have financial need; average aid package $8,849

Davis and Elkins College

Elkins WV
(304) 637-1230
U.S. News ranking: Reg. Coll. (S), No. 43
Website: www.dewv.edu/
Admissions email: admission@dewv.edu
Private; founded 1904
Freshman admissions: selective; 2019-2020: 1,927 applied, 827 accepted. Either SAT or ACT required. SAT 25/75 percentile: 930-1110. High school rank: N/A
Early decision deadline: N/A, notification date: N/A
Early action deadline: N/A, notification date: N/A
Application deadline (fall): rolling
Undergraduate student body: 751 full time, 25 part time; 41% male, 59% female; 0% American Indian, 1% Asian, 4% Black, 3% Hispanic, 1% multiracial, 0% Pacific Islander, 36% white, 6% international; 59% from in state; 63% live on campus; 2% of students in fraternities, 3% in sororities
Most popular majors: Business Administration and Management, General, Criminology, Kinesiology and Exercise Science, Psychology, General, Registered Nursing/Registered Nurse
Expenses: 2020-2021: $29,960; room/board: $9,800
Financial aid: (304) 637-1366; 79% of undergrads determined to have financial need; average aid package $28,359

Fairmont State University

Fairmont WV
(304) 367-4010
U.S. News ranking: Reg. U. (S), No. 99
Website: www.fairmontstate.edu
Admissions email: admit@fairmontstate.edu
Public; founded 1865
Freshman admissions: selective; 2019-2020: 2,713 applied, 2,316 accepted. Either SAT or ACT required. SAT 25/75 percentile: 910-1110. High school rank: 14% in top tenth, 36% in top quarter, 72% in top half
Early decision deadline: N/A, notification date: N/A
Early action deadline: N/A, notification date: N/A
Application deadline (fall): 8/1
Undergraduate student body: 2,955 full time, 607 part time; 42% male, 58% female; 0% American

Indian, 0% Asian, 4% Black, 2% Hispanic, 3% multiracial, 0% Pacific Islander, 87% white, 2% international; 90% from in state; 26% live on campus; 1% of students in fraternities, 2% in sororities
Most popular majors: 17% Business, Management, Marketing, and Related Support Services, 13% Engineering Technologies and Engineering-Related Fields, 13% Health Professions and Related Programs, 10% Homeland Security, Law Enforcement, Firefighting and Related Protective Services, 8% Psychology
Expenses: 2020-2021: $7,890 in state, $17,140 out of state; room/board: $10,064
Financial aid: (304) 367-4826; 69% of undergrads determined to have financial need; average aid package $9,607

Glenville State College

Glenville WV
(304) 462-4128
U.S. News ranking: Reg. Coll. (S), No. 55
Website: www.glenville.edu
Admissions email: admissions@glenville.edu
Public; founded 1872
Freshman admissions: less selective; 2019-2020: 2,382 applied, 2,381 accepted. Either SAT or ACT required. SAT 25/75 percentile: 840-1040. High school rank: 8% in top tenth, 24% in top quarter, 58% in top half
Early decision deadline: N/A, notification date: N/A
Early action deadline: N/A, notification date: N/A
Application deadline (fall): rolling
Undergraduate student body: 999 full time, 576 part time; 51% male, 49% female; 0% American Indian, 0% Asian, 14% Black, 3% Hispanic, 3% multiracial, 0% Pacific Islander, 75% white, 1% international; N/A from in state; 51% live on campus; N/A of students in fraternities, N/A in sororities
Most popular majors: 30% Education, 14% Homeland Security, Law Enforcement, Firefighting and Related Protective Services, 12% Natural Resources and Conservation, 10% Liberal Arts and Sciences, General Studies and Humanities, 9% Visual and Performing Arts
Expenses: 2020-2021: $7,886 in state, $9,514 out of state; room/board: $10,382
Financial aid: (304) 462-6171; 84% of undergrads determined to have financial need; average aid package $13,225

Marshall University

Huntington WV
(800) 642-3499
U.S. News ranking: Nat. U., No. 284
Website: www.marshall.edu
Admissions email: admissions@marshall.edu
Public; founded 1837

Freshman admissions: selective; 2019-2020: 6,299 applied, 5,482 accepted. Either SAT or ACT required. ACT 25/75 percentile: 19-25. High school rank: N/A
Early decision deadline: N/A, notification date: N/A
Early action deadline: N/A, notification date: N/A
Undergraduate student body: 7,123 full time, 2,292 part time; 42% male, 58% female; 0% American Indian, 1% Asian, 6% Black, 2% Hispanic, 3% multiracial, 0% Pacific Islander, 85% white, 2% international; 82% from in state; N/A live on campus; N/A of students in fraternities, N/A in sororities
Most popular majors: 19% Health Professions and Related Programs, 17% Business, Management, Marketing, and Related Support Services, 13% Liberal Arts and Sciences, General Studies and Humanities, 7% Education, 7% Psychology
Expenses: 2020-2021: $8,612 in state, $19,466 out of state; room/board: $9,974
Financial aid: (304) 696-3162; 72% of undergrads determined to have financial need; average aid package $11,618

Ohio Valley University

Vienna WV
(877) 446-8668
U.S. News ranking: Reg. Coll. (S), second tier
Website: www.ovu.edu
Admissions email: admissions@ovu.edu
Private; founded 1958
Affiliation: Churches of Christ
Freshman admissions: less selective; 2019-2020: 740 applied, 318 accepted. Neither SAT nor ACT required. ACT 25/75 percentile: 17-23. High school rank: N/A
Early decision deadline: N/A, notification date: N/A
Early action deadline: N/A, notification date: N/A
Application deadline (fall): 8/14
Undergraduate student body: 272 full time, 32 part time; 57% male, 43% female; 1% American Indian, 0% Asian, 5% Black, 4% Hispanic, 2% multiracial, 0% Pacific Islander, 61% white, 19% international; 29% from in state; 44% live on campus; 20% of students in fraternities, 15% in sororities
Most popular majors: 54% Business, Management, Marketing, and Related Support Services, 12% Education, 10% Liberal Arts and Sciences, General Studies and Humanities, 6% Psychology, 6% Theology and Religious Vocations
Expenses: 2020-2021: $22,550; room/board: $8,090
Financial aid: (304) 865-6077; 99% of undergrads determined to have financial need; average aid package $15,400

Salem University[1]

Salem WV
(304) 326-1109
U.S. News ranking: Reg. U. (S), second tier
Website: www.salemu.edu
Admissions email: admissions@salemu.edu
For-profit
Application deadline (fall): N/A
Undergraduate student body: N/A full time, N/A part time
Expenses: 2019-2020: $16,700; room/board: $8,400
Financial aid: N/A

Shepherd University

Shepherdstown WV
(304) 876-5212
U.S. News ranking: Nat. Lib. Arts, second tier
Website: www.shepherd.edu
Admissions email: admission@shepherd.edu
Public; founded 1871
Freshman admissions: selective; 2019-2020: 1,370 applied, 1,319 accepted. Either SAT or ACT required. SAT 25/75 percentile: 970-1170. High school rank: N/A
Early decision deadline: N/A, notification date: N/A
Early action deadline: 11/15, notification date: 12/1
Application deadline (fall): rolling
Undergraduate student body: 2,354 full time, 846 part time; 42% male, 58% female; 0% American Indian, 1% Asian, 8% Black, 7% Hispanic, 4% multiracial, 0% Pacific Islander, 75% white, 1% international; 68% from in state; 32% live on campus; 3% of students in fraternities, 4% in sororities
Most popular majors: 11% General Studies, 11% Registered Nursing/Registered Nurse, 10% Business Administration and Management, General, 6% Biology/Biological Sciences, General, 5% Parks, Recreation and Leisure Studies
Expenses: 2020-2021: $7,784 in state, $18,224 out of state; room/board: $10,654
Financial aid: (304) 876-5470; 63% of undergrads determined to have financial need; average aid package $11,267

University of Charleston

Charleston WV
(800) 995-4682
U.S. News ranking: Nat. U., second tier
Website: www.ucwv.edu
Admissions email: admissions@ucwv.edu
Private; founded 1888
Freshman admissions: selective; 2019-2020: 2,454 applied, 1,228 accepted. Neither SAT nor ACT required. ACT 25/75 percentile: 19-24. High school rank: N/A
Early decision deadline: N/A, notification date: N/A
Early action deadline: N/A, notification date: N/A
Application deadline (fall): rolling
Undergraduate student body: 1,172 full time, 735 part time; 56% male, 44% female; 1% American

Indian, 1% Asian, 9% Black, 3% Hispanic, 0% multiracial, 0% Pacific Islander, 51% white, 7% international
Most popular majors: Information not available
Expenses: 2020-2021: $31,400; room/board: $9,510
Financial aid: (304) 357-4944

West Liberty University

West Liberty WV
(304) 336-8076
U.S. News ranking: Reg. U. (S), No. 68
Website: www.westliberty.edu
Admissions email: admissions@westliberty.edu
Public; founded 1837
Freshman admissions: selective; 2019-2020: 1,829 applied, 1,292 accepted. Either SAT or ACT required. ACT 25/75 percentile: 17-24. High school rank: 18% in top tenth, 38% in top quarter, 72% in top half
Early decision deadline: N/A, notification date: N/A
Early action deadline: N/A, notification date: N/A
Application deadline (fall): rolling
Undergraduate student body: 1,837 full time, 346 part time; 36% male, 64% female; 0% American Indian, 1% Asian, 3% Black, 1% Hispanic, 2% multiracial, 0% Pacific Islander, 76% white, 2% international; N/A from in state; 39% live on campus; 3% of students in fraternities, 4% in sororities
Most popular majors: 13% Business Administration and Management, General, 11% General Studies, 9% Dental Hygiene/Hygienist, 8% Biology/Biological Sciences, General, 8% Registered Nursing/Registered Nurse
Expenses: 2019-2020: $7,990 in state, $15,930 out of state; room/board: $9,614
Financial aid: (304) 336-8016

West Virginia State University[1]

Institute WV
(304) 766-4345
U.S. News ranking: Reg. Coll. (S), No. 59
Website: www.wvstateu.edu
Admissions email: admissions@wvstateu.edu
Public; founded 1891
Application deadline (fall): 8/17
Undergraduate student body: N/A full time, N/A part time
Expenses: 2019-2020: $8,237 in state, $17,691 out of state; room/board: $12,538
Financial aid: (304) 204-4361

West Virginia University[1]

Morgantown WV
(304) 442-3146
U.S. News ranking: Nat. U., No. 241
Website: www.wvu.edu
Admissions email: go2wvu@mail.wvu.edu
Public; founded 1867

Application deadline (fall): 8/1
Undergraduate student body: N/A
full time, N/A part time
Expenses: 2019-2020: $8,976 in
state, $25,320 out of state; room/
board: $11,062
Financial aid: (304) 293-8571

West Virginia University Institute of Technology[1]

Beckley WV
(304) 442-3146
U.S. News ranking: Unranked
Website: www.wvutech.edu
Admissions email:
tech-admissions@mail.wvu.edu
Public; founded 1895
Application deadline (fall): rolling
Undergraduate student body: N/A
full time, N/A part time
Expenses: 2019-2020: $7,560 in
state, $18,912 out of state; room/
board: $11,628
Financial aid: (304) 293-8571

West Virginia University–Parkersburg[1]

Parkersburg WV
(304) 424-8000
U.S. News ranking: Reg. Coll. (S),
second tier
Website: www.wvup.edu
Admissions email:
info@mail.wvup.edu
Public
Application deadline (fall): N/A
Undergraduate student body: N/A
full time, N/A part time
Expenses: 2019-2020: $3,890 in
state, $8,642 out of state; room/
board: $7,200
Financial aid: N/A

West Virginia Wesleyan College

Buckhannon WV
(800) 722-9933
U.S. News ranking: Reg. U. (S),
No. 62
Website: www.wvwc.edu
Admissions email:
admissions@wvwc.edu
Private; founded 1890
Affiliation: United Methodist
Freshman admissions: selective;
2019-2020: 2,287 applied,
1,467 accepted. Either SAT
or ACT required. SAT 25/75
percentile: 940-1120. High school
rank: 18% in top tenth, 43% in
top quarter, 77% in top half
Early decision deadline: N/A,
notification date: N/A
Early action deadline: N/A,
notification date: N/A
Application deadline (fall): 8/15
Undergraduate student body: 1,118
full time, 13 part time; 45%
male, 55% female; 0% American
Indian, 0% Asian, 10% Black,
4% Hispanic, 4% multiracial,
0% Pacific Islander, 75% white,
6% international; 61% from in
state; 74% live on campus; 25%
of students in fraternities, 25%
in sororities
Most popular majors: 15%
Business, Management,
Marketing, and Related Support
Services, 13% Parks, Recreation,
Leisure, and Fitness Studies,

11% Physical Sciences, 9%
Health Professions and Related
Programs, 8% Social Sciences
Expenses: 2020-2021: $32,252;
room/board: $9,576
Financial aid: (304) 473-8080;
79% of undergrads determined to
have financial need; average aid
package $29,422

Wheeling University

Wheeling WV
(304) 243-2359
U.S. News ranking: Reg. U. (S),
No. 59
Website: www.wju.edu/admissions/
Admissions email: admiss@wju.edu
Private; founded 1954
Affiliation: Roman Catholic
Freshman admissions: selective;
2019-2020: 2,034 applied,
1,403 accepted. Either SAT
or ACT required. ACT 25/75
percentile: 19-24. High school
rank: N/A
Early decision deadline: N/A,
notification date: N/A
Early action deadline: N/A,
notification date: N/A
Application deadline (fall): rolling
Undergraduate student body: 484
full time, 139 part time; 42%
male, 58% female; N/A American
Indian, N/A Asian, N/A Black, N/A
Hispanic, N/A multiracial, N/A
Pacific Islander, N/A white, N/A
international
Most popular majors: 19%
Business/Commerce, General,
14% Criminal Justice and
Corrections, 13% Registered
Nursing, Nursing Administration,
Nursing Research and Clinical
Nursing, 11% Allied Health
Diagnostic, Intervention, and
Treatment Professions, 10%
Health and Physical Education/
Fitness
Expenses: 2020-2021: $29,290;
room/board: $10,620
Financial aid: (304) 243-2304;
77% of undergrads determined to
have financial need; average aid
package $28,683

WISCONSIN

Alverno College

Milwaukee WI
(414) 382-6100
U.S. News ranking: Reg. U.
(Mid. W), No. 65
Website: www.alverno.edu
Admissions email:
admissions@alverno.edu
Private; founded 1887
Affiliation: Roman Catholic
Freshman admissions: selective;
2019-2020: 777 applied, 539
accepted. Either SAT or ACT
required. ACT 25/75 percentile:
18-21. High school rank: N/A
Early decision deadline: N/A,
notification date: N/A
Early action deadline: N/A,
notification date: N/A
Application deadline (fall): rolling
Undergraduate student body: 906
full time, 198 part time; 1%
male, 99% female; 1% American
Indian, 5% Asian, 14% Black,
33% Hispanic, 5% multiracial,
0% Pacific Islander, 43% white,
0% international; N/A from in
state; 16% live on campus; N/A

of students in fraternities, 0% in
sororities
Most popular majors: 32% Health
Professions and Related Programs,
17% Business, Management,
Marketing, and Related Support
Services, 16% Liberal Arts and
Sciences, General Studies and
Humanities, 13% Education, 7%
Psychology
Expenses: 2020-2021: $30,658;
room/board: $8,620
Financial aid: (414) 382-6040;
90% of undergrads determined to
have financial need; average aid
package $21,594

Beloit College

Beloit WI
(608) 363-2500
U.S. News ranking: Nat. Lib. Arts,
No. 80
Website: www.beloit.edu
Admissions email:
admiss@beloit.edu
Private; founded 1846
Freshman admissions: more
selective; 2019-2020: 3,657
applied, 2,269 accepted. Neither
SAT nor ACT required. SAT
25/75 percentile: 1080-1380.
High school rank: 29% in top
tenth, 67% in top quarter, 92%
in top half
Early decision deadline: 11/1,
notification date: 12/1
Early action deadline: 12/1,
notification date: 1/1
Application deadline (fall): 7/1
Undergraduate student body: 1,082
full time, 61 part time; 45%
male, 55% female; 0% American
Indian, 4% Asian, 7% Black,
13% Hispanic, 4% multiracial,
0% Pacific Islander, 50% white,
18% international; N/A from in
state; 87% live on campus; 13%
of students in fraternities, 16%
in sororities
Most popular majors: 23%
Social Sciences, 10% Physical
Sciences, 8% Foreign Languages,
Literatures, and Linguistics, 8%
Visual and Performing Arts, 6%
Psychology
Expenses: 2020-2021: $53,348;
room/board: $9,688
Financial aid: (608) 363-2696;
63% of undergrads determined to
have financial need; average aid
package $48,229

Cardinal Stritch University

Milwaukee WI
(414) 410-4040
U.S. News ranking: Nat. U.,
second tier
Website: www.stritch.edu
Admissions email:
admissions@stritch.edu
Private; founded 1937
Affiliation: Roman Catholic
Freshman admissions: selective;
2019-2020: 1,140 applied, 929
accepted. Neither SAT nor ACT
required. ACT 25/75 percentile:
18-23. High school rank: 22%
in top tenth, 45% in top quarter,
74% in top half
Early decision deadline: N/A,
notification date: N/A
Early action deadline: N/A,
notification date: N/A

Application deadline (fall): rolling
Undergraduate student body: 721
full time, 527 part time; 31%
male, 69% female; 0% American
Indian, 3% Asian, 20% Black,
19% Hispanic, 3% multiracial,
1% Pacific Islander, 36% white,
18% international; 64% from in
state; 28% live on campus; 0%
of students in fraternities, 0% in
sororities
Most popular majors: Information
not available
Expenses: 2020-2021: $33,770;
room/board: $9,488
Financial aid: (414) 410-4016;
66% of undergrads determined to
have financial need; average aid
package $24,454

Carroll University[1]

Waukesha WI
(262) 524-7220
U.S. News ranking: Reg. U.
(Mid. W), No. 39
Website: www.carrollu.edu/
Admissions email:
info@carrollu.edu
Private; founded 1846
Affiliation: Presbyterian
Application deadline (fall): rolling
Undergraduate student body: N/A
full time, N/A part time
Expenses: 2020-2021: $33,990;
room/board: $10,120
Financial aid: (262) 524-7296;
76% of undergrads determined to
have financial need; average aid
package $26,245

Carthage College

Kenosha WI
(262) 551-6000
U.S. News ranking: Reg. Coll.
(Mid. W), No. 12
Website: www.carthage.edu
Admissions email:
admissions@carthage.edu
Private; founded 1847
Freshman admissions: selective;
2019-2020: 7,018 applied,
4,772 accepted. Neither SAT
nor ACT required. ACT 25/75
percentile: 20-27. High school
rank: 22% in top tenth, 50% in
top quarter, 81% in top half
Early decision deadline: N/A,
notification date: N/A
Early action deadline: 11/15,
notification date: 11/22
Application deadline (fall): rolling
Undergraduate student body: 2,548
full time, 106 part time; 42%
male, 58% female; 1% American
Indian, 2% Asian, 5% Black,
14% Hispanic, 3% multiracial,
0% Pacific Islander, 68% white,
1% international; 38% from in
state; 65% live on campus; 9%
of students in fraternities, 6% in
sororities
Most popular majors: 26%
Business, Management,
Marketing, and Related Support
Services, 8% Biological and
Biomedical Sciences, 7%
Communication, Journalism, and
Related Programs, 7% Social
Sciences, 6% Education
Expenses: 2020-2021: $31,500;
room/board: $12,400
Financial aid: (262) 551-6001;
79% of undergrads determined to
have financial need; average aid
package $35,126

Concordia University Wisconsin

Mequon WI
(262) 243-4300
U.S. News ranking: Nat. U.,
No. 258
Website: www.cuw.edu
Admissions email:
admissions@cuw.edu
Private; founded 1881
Affiliation: Lutheran Church–
Missouri Synod
Freshman admissions: more
selective; 2019-2020: 3,772
applied, 2,419 accepted. Either
SAT or ACT required. ACT 25/75
percentile: 21-26. High school
rank: 32% in top tenth, 61% in
top quarter, 89% in top half
Early decision deadline: N/A,
notification date: N/A
Early action deadline: N/A,
notification date: N/A
Application deadline (fall): N/A
Undergraduate student body: 2,317
full time, 991 part time; 37%
male, 63% female; 1% American
Indian, 2% Asian, 10% Black,
0% Hispanic, 3% multiracial,
0% Pacific Islander, 73% white,
6% international; N/A from in
state; 43% live on campus; N/A
of students in fraternities, N/A in
sororities
Most popular majors: 32%
Business, Management,
Marketing, and Related Support
Services, 28% Health Professions
and Related Programs, 7%
Education, 6% Homeland
Security, Law Enforcement,
Firefighting and Related Protective
Services, 5% Biological and
Biomedical Sciences
Expenses: 2020-2021: $31,182;
room/board: $11,470
Financial aid: (262) 243-2025;
78% of undergrads determined to
have financial need; average aid
package $25,017

Edgewood College

Madison WI
(608) 663-2294
U.S. News ranking: Nat. U.,
No. 227
Website: www.edgewood.edu
Admissions email:
admissions@edgewood.edu
Private; founded 1927
Affiliation: Roman Catholic
Freshman admissions: selective;
2019-2020: 1,397 applied,
1,011 accepted. Either SAT
or ACT required. ACT 25/75
percentile: 20-25. High school
rank: 16% in top tenth, 50% in
top quarter, 83% in top half
Early decision deadline: N/A,
notification date: N/A
Early action deadline: N/A,
notification date: N/A
Application deadline (fall): 8/1
Undergraduate student body: 1,191
full time, 216 part time; 27%
male, 73% female; 0% American
Indian, 2% Asian, 4% Black,
9% Hispanic, 4% multiracial,
0% Pacific Islander, 76% white,
3% international; 88% from in
state; 33% live on campus; N/A
of students in fraternities, N/A in
sororities
Most popular majors: 28%
Registered Nursing/Registered
Nurse, 9% Business/Commerce,

General, 7% Psychology, General, 5% Communication and Media Studies, 4% Biology/Biological Sciences, General
Expenses: 2020-2021: $31,700; room/board: $11,700
Financial aid: (608) 663-4300; 71% of undergrads determined to have financial need; average aid package $23,653

Herzing University[1]
Madison WI
(800) 596-0724
U.S. News ranking: Reg. U. (Mid. W), second tier
Website: www.herzing.edu/
Admissions email: info@msn.herzing.edu
Private; founded 1965
Affiliation: Other
Application deadline (fall): N/A
Undergraduate student body: N/A full time, N/A part time
Expenses: 2019-2020: $14,200; room/board: N/A
Financial aid: N/A

Lakeland University[1]
Plymouth WI
(920) 565-1226
U.S. News ranking: Reg. U. (Mid. W), second tier
Website: www.lakeland.edu
Admissions email: admissions@lakeland.edu
Private; founded 1862
Application deadline (fall): rolling
Undergraduate student body: N/A full time, N/A part time
Expenses: 2019-2020: $29,880; room/board: $9,624
Financial aid: N/A

Lawrence University
Appleton WI
(800) 227-0982
U.S. News ranking: Nat. Lib. Arts, No. 63
Website: www.lawrence.edu
Admissions email: admissions@lawrence.edu
Private; founded 1847
Freshman admissions: more selective; 2019-2020: 3,463 applied, 2,150 accepted. Neither SAT nor ACT required. ACT 25/75 percentile: 25-32. High school rank: 39% in top tenth, 77% in top quarter, 98% in top half
Early decision deadline: 11/1, notification date: 12/1
Early action deadline: 11/1, notification date: 12/15
Application deadline (fall): 1/15
Undergraduate student body: 1,402 full time, 43 part time; 46% male, 54% female; 0% American Indian, 6% Asian, 6% Black, 10% Hispanic, 4% multiracial, 0% Pacific Islander, 61% white, 12% international; 25% from in state; 95% live on campus; 9% of students in fraternities, 13% in sororities
Most popular majors: 23% Visual and Performing Arts, 15% Social Sciences, 14% Biological and Biomedical Sciences, 7% English Language and Literature/Letters, 7% Psychology
Expenses: 2020-2021: $50,958; room/board: $10,977

Financial aid: (920) 832-6584; 62% of undergrads determined to have financial need; average aid package $43,652

Maranatha Baptist University
Watertown WI
(920) 206-2327
U.S. News ranking: Reg. Coll. (Mid. W), No. 36
Website: www.mbu.edu
Admissions email: admissions@mbu.edu
Private; founded 1968
Affiliation: Baptist
Freshman admissions: selective; 2019-2020: 213 applied, 157 accepted. Either SAT or ACT required. ACT 25/75 percentile: 19-26. High school rank: 17% in top tenth, 52% in top quarter, 63% in top half
Early decision deadline: N/A, notification date: N/A
Early action deadline: N/A, notification date: N/A
Application deadline (fall): rolling
Undergraduate student body: 508 full time, 104 part time; 44% male, 56% female; 0% American Indian, 2% Asian, 1% Black, 4% Hispanic, 4% multiracial, 0% Pacific Islander, 85% white, 1% international
Most popular majors: 20% Business, Management, Marketing, and Related Support Services, 19% Education, 13% Multi/Interdisciplinary Studies, 12% Theology and Religious Vocations, 10% Health Professions and Related Programs
Expenses: 2019-2020: $16,660; room/board: $7,300
Financial aid: (920) 206-2318

Marian University
Fond du Lac WI
(920) 923-7650
U.S. News ranking: Reg. U. (Mid. W), No. 110
Website: www.marianuniversity.edu/
Admissions email: admissions@marianuniversity.edu
Private; founded 1936
Affiliation: Roman Catholic
Freshman admissions: less selective; 2019-2020: 1,868 applied, 1,207 accepted. Either SAT or ACT required. ACT 25/75 percentile: 17-21. High school rank: 1% in top tenth, 24% in top quarter, 60% in top half
Early decision deadline: N/A, notification date: N/A
Early action deadline: N/A, notification date: N/A
Application deadline (fall): rolling
Undergraduate student body: 1,171 full time, 174 part time; 31% male, 69% female; 1% American Indian, 2% Asian, 6% Black, 9% Hispanic, 3% multiracial, 0% Pacific Islander, 72% white, 3% international
Most popular majors: 37% Registered Nursing/Registered Nurse, 8% Business Administration and Management, General, 8% Radiologic Technology/Science-Radiographer, 7% Psychology,

General, 5% Criminal Justice/Safety Studies
Expenses: 2020-2021: $28,560; room/board: $7,810
Financial aid: (920) 923-8737; 79% of undergrads determined to have financial need; average aid package $21,537

Marquette University
Milwaukee WI
(800) 222-6544
U.S. News ranking: Nat. U., No. 88
Website: www.marquette.edu
Admissions email: admissions@marquette.edu
Private; founded 1881
Affiliation: Roman Catholic
Freshman admissions: more selective; 2019-2020: 15,078 applied, 12,509 accepted. Either SAT or ACT required. ACT 25/75 percentile: 24-29. High school rank: 33% in top tenth, 63% in top quarter, 94% in top half
Early decision deadline: N/A, notification date: N/A
Early action deadline: N/A, notification date: N/A
Application deadline (fall): 12/1
Undergraduate student body: 8,175 full time, 340 part time; 46% male, 54% female; 0% American Indian, 7% Asian, 4% Black, 14% Hispanic, 3% multiracial, 0% Pacific Islander, 69% white, 2% international; 30% from in state; 46% live on campus; N/A of students in fraternities, N/A in sororities
Most popular majors: 23% Business, Management, Marketing, and Related Support Services, 13% Biological and Biomedical Sciences, 12% Social Sciences, 11% Engineering, 10% Communication, Journalism, and Related Programs
Expenses: 2020-2021: $45,666; room/board: $13,656
Financial aid: (414) 288-4000; 59% of undergrads determined to have financial need; average aid package $32,164

Milwaukee Institute of Art and Design[1]
Milwaukee WI
(414) 291-8070
U.S. News ranking: Arts, unranked
Website: www.miad.edu
Admissions email: admissions@miad.edu
Private; founded 1974
Application deadline (fall): 8/15
Undergraduate student body: N/A full time, N/A part time
Expenses: 2019-2020: $38,550; room/board: $9,300
Financial aid: (414) 847-3270

Milwaukee School of Engineering
Milwaukee WI
(800) 332-6763
U.S. News ranking: Reg. U. (Mid. W), No. 8
Website: www.msoe.edu
Admissions email: explore@msoe.edu
Private; founded 1903
Freshman admissions: more selective; 2019-2020: 3,552 applied, 2,192 accepted. Either

SAT or ACT required. ACT 25/75 percentile: 25-30. High school rank: N/A
Early decision deadline: N/A, notification date: N/A
Early action deadline: N/A, notification date: N/A
Application deadline (fall): rolling
Undergraduate student body: 2,478 full time, 88 part time; 74% male, 26% female; 0% American Indian, 5% Asian, 2% Black, 8% Hispanic, 3% multiracial, 0% Pacific Islander, 69% white, 6% international; 65% from in state; 43% live on campus; N/A of students in fraternities, N/A in sororities
Most popular majors: 79% Engineering, 12% Health Professions and Related Programs, 9% Business, Management, Marketing, and Related Support Services
Expenses: 2020-2021: $43,575; room/board: $10,125
Financial aid: (414) 277-7224; 80% of undergrads determined to have financial need; average aid package $30,355

Mount Mary University
Milwaukee WI
(414) 930-3024
U.S. News ranking: Reg. U. (Mid. W), No. 58
Website: www.mtmary.edu
Admissions email: mmu-admiss@mtmary.edu
Private; founded 1913
Affiliation: Roman Catholic
Freshman admissions: selective; 2019-2020: 724 applied, 419 accepted. Either SAT or ACT required. ACT 25/75 percentile: 16-20. High school rank: 25% in top tenth, 46% in top quarter, 90% in top half
Early decision deadline: N/A, notification date: N/A
Early action deadline: N/A, notification date: N/A
Application deadline (fall): rolling
Undergraduate student body: 585 full time, 74 part time; 0% male, 100% female; 0% American Indian, 7% Asian, 19% Black, 27% Hispanic, 4% multiracial, 0% Pacific Islander, 40% white, 1% international; 9% from in state; 24% live on campus; 0% of students in fraternities, 0% in sororities
Most popular majors: 17% Health Professions and Related Programs, 15% Business, Management, Marketing, and Related Support Services, 12% Visual and Performing Arts, 11% Psychology, 7% Public Administration and Social Service Professions
Expenses: 2020-2021: $32,120; room/board: $9,180
Financial aid: (414) 930-3431; 95% of undergrads determined to have financial need; average aid package $25,017

Northland College
Ashland WI
(715) 682-1224
U.S. News ranking: Reg. Coll. (Mid. W), No. 18
Website: www.northland.edu

Admissions email: admit@northland.edu
Private; founded 1892
Affiliation: United Church of Christ
Freshman admissions: selective; 2019-2020: 1,442 applied, 959 accepted. Neither SAT nor ACT required. ACT 25/75 percentile: 18-27. High school rank: 13% in top tenth, 43% in top quarter, 72% in top half
Early decision deadline: N/A, notification date: N/A
Early action deadline: N/A, notification date: N/A
Application deadline (fall): rolling
Undergraduate student body: 577 full time, 32 part time; 47% male, 53% female; 2% American Indian, 2% Asian, 4% Black, 5% Hispanic, 5% multiracial, 0% Pacific Islander, 75% white, 5% international; 48% from in state; 61% live on campus; N/A of students in fraternities, N/A in sororities
Most popular majors: 26% Natural Resources and Conservation, 13% Biological and Biomedical Sciences, 12% Business, Management, Marketing, and Related Support Services, 11% Physical Sciences, 8% Parks, Recreation, Leisure, and Fitness Studies
Expenses: 2020-2021: $38,596; room/board: $9,688
Financial aid: (715) 682-1255; 85% of undergrads determined to have financial need; average aid package $32,197

Ripon College
Ripon WI
(920) 748-8115
U.S. News ranking: Nat. Lib. Arts, No. 120
Website: www.ripon.edu
Admissions email: adminfo@ripon.edu
Private; founded 1851
Freshman admissions: selective; 2019-2020: 2,900 applied, 2,016 accepted. Neither SAT nor ACT required. ACT 25/75 percentile: 19-25. High school rank: 14% in top tenth, 49% in top quarter, 78% in top half
Early decision deadline: N/A, notification date: N/A
Early action deadline: N/A, notification date: N/A
Application deadline (fall): rolling
Undergraduate student body: 772 full time, 15 part time; 46% male, 54% female; 0% American Indian, 2% Asian, 4% Black, 10% Hispanic, 3% multiracial, 0% Pacific Islander, 78% white, 2% international; 70% from in state; N/A live on campus; 38% of students in fraternities, 37% in sororities
Most popular majors: 15% Business/Commerce, General, 14% History, General, 11% Biology/Biological Sciences, General, 10% Psychology, General, 9% Economics, General
Expenses: 2020-2021: $47,123; room/board: $8,653
Financial aid: (920) 748-8101; 88% of undergrads determined to have financial need; average aid package $38,388

Silver Lake College[1]

Manitowoc WI
(920) 686-6175
U.S. News ranking: Reg. U. (Mid. W), second tier
Website: www.sl.edu
Admissions email: admissions@sl.edu
Private; founded 1935
Affiliation: Roman Catholic
Application deadline (fall): rolling
Undergraduate student body: N/A full time, N/A part time
Expenses: 2019-2020: $29,600; room/board: $11,510
Financial aid: (920) 686-6175

St. Norbert College

De Pere WI
(800) 236-4878
U.S. News ranking: Nat. Lib. Arts, No. 130
Website: www.snc.edu
Admissions email: admit@snc.edu
Private; founded 1898
Affiliation: Roman Catholic
Freshman admissions: more selective; 2019-2020: 3,355 applied, 2,677 accepted. Either SAT or ACT required. ACT 25/75 percentile: 21-27. High school rank: 23% in top tenth, 47% in top quarter, 84% in top half
Early decision deadline: N/A, notification date: N/A
Early action deadline: N/A, notification date: N/A
Application deadline (fall): rolling
Undergraduate student body: 1,962 full time, 38 part time; 42% male, 58% female; 1% American Indian, 1% Asian, 2% Black, 5% Hispanic, 1% multiracial, 0% Pacific Islander, 87% white, 1% international; 77% from in state; 86% live on campus; 10% of students in fraternities, 10% in sororities
Most popular majors: 25% Business/Commerce, General, 11% Biology/Biological Sciences, General, 11% Elementary Education and Teaching, 11% Psychology, General, 7% Speech Communication and Rhetoric
Expenses: 2020-2021: $40,885; room/board: $10,885
Financial aid: (920) 403-3071; 70% of undergrads determined to have financial need; average aid package $27,795

University of Wisconsin–Eau Claire

Eau Claire WI
(715) 836-5415
U.S. News ranking: Reg. U. (Mid. W), No. 39
Website: www.uwec.edu
Admissions email: admissions@uwec.edu
Public; founded 1916
Freshman admissions: selective; 2019-2020: 5,568 applied, 4,972 accepted. Either SAT or ACT required. ACT 25/75 percentile: 21-26. High school rank: 17% in top tenth, 48% in top quarter, 88% in top half
Early decision deadline: N/A, notification date: N/A
Early action deadline: N/A, notification date: N/A
Application deadline (fall): 8/20

Undergraduate student body: 9,461 full time, 607 part time; 38% male, 62% female; 0% American Indian, 3% Asian, 1% Black, 4% Hispanic, 3% multiracial, 0% Pacific Islander, 86% white, 2% international; 69% from in state; 21% live on campus; N/A of students in fraternities, N/A in sororities
Most popular majors: 25% Business, Management, Marketing, and Related Support Services, 14% Health Professions and Related Programs, 9% Education, 6% Biological and Biomedical Sciences, 5% Communication, Journalism, and Related Programs
Expenses: 2020-2021: $8,870 in state, $17,146 out of state; room/board: $8,475
Financial aid: (715) 836-3000; 48% of undergrads determined to have financial need; average aid package $9,822

University of Wisconsin–Green Bay[1]

Green Bay WI
(920) 465-2111
U.S. News ranking: Reg. U. (Mid. W), No. 103
Website: www.uwgb.edu
Admissions email: uwgb@uwgb.edu
Public; founded 1965
Application deadline (fall): rolling
Undergraduate student body: N/A full time, N/A part time
Expenses: 2019-2020: $7,873 in state, $16,091 out of state; room/board: $7,170
Financial aid: (920) 465-2111

University of Wisconsin–La Crosse

La Crosse WI
(608) 785-8939
U.S. News ranking: Reg. U. (Mid. W), No. 33
Website: www.uwlax.edu
Admissions email: admissions@uwlax.edu
Public; founded 1909
Freshman admissions: more selective; 2019-2020: 5,843 applied, 4,670 accepted. Either SAT or ACT required. ACT 25/75 percentile: 23-27. High school rank: 22% in top tenth, 57% in top quarter, 96% in top half
Early decision deadline: N/A, notification date: N/A
Early action deadline: N/A, notification date: N/A
Application deadline (fall): N/A
Undergraduate student body: 9,051 full time, 544 part time; 44% male, 56% female; 0% American Indian, 2% Asian, 1% Black, 4% Hispanic, 3% multiracial, 0% Pacific Islander, 89% white, 0% international; 35% live on campus; N/A of students in fraternities, N/A in sororities
Most popular majors: 22% Business, Management, Marketing, and Related Support Services, 13% Biological and Biomedical Sciences, 10% Health Professions and Related Programs,

9% Psychology, 8% Parks, Recreation, Leisure, and Fitness Studies
Expenses: 2019-2020: $8,953 in state, $17,772 out of state; room/board: $6,331
Financial aid: (608) 785-8604; 46% of undergrads determined to have financial need; average aid package $7,947

University of Wisconsin–Madison

Madison WI
(608) 262-3961
U.S. News ranking: Nat. U., No. 42
Website: www.wisc.edu
Admissions email: onwisconsin@admissions.wisc.edu
Public; founded 1848
Freshman admissions: more selective; 2019-2020: 43,921 applied, 23,887 accepted. Either SAT or ACT required. ACT 25/75 percentile: 27-32. High school rank: 57% in top tenth, 90% in top quarter, 100% in top half
Early decision deadline: N/A, notification date: N/A
Early action deadline: 11/1, notification date: 12/31
Application deadline (fall): 2/1
Undergraduate student body: 30,198 full time, 3,258 part time; 48% male, 52% female; 0% American Indian, 7% Asian, 2% Black, 5% Hispanic, 4% multiracial, 0% Pacific Islander, 69% white, 10% international; 62% from in state; 26% live on campus; 9% of students in fraternities, 8% in sororities
Most popular majors: 9% Economics, General, 8% Computer and Information Sciences, General, 6% Biology/Biological Sciences, General, 6% Psychology, General, 4% Finance, General
Expenses: 2020-2021: $10,741 in state, $38,629 out of state; room/board: $12,220
Financial aid: (608) 262-3060; 35% of undergrads determined to have financial need; average aid package $17,473

University of Wisconsin–Milwaukee

Milwaukee WI
(414) 229-2222
U.S. News ranking: Nat. U., second tier
Website: www.uwm.edu
Admissions email: undergraduateadmissions@uwm.edu
Public; founded 1956
Freshman admissions: selective; 2019-2020: 8,946 applied, 8,481 accepted. Neither SAT nor ACT required. ACT 25/75 percentile: 19-24. High school rank: 9% in top tenth, 21% in top quarter, 66% in top half
Early decision deadline: N/A, notification date: N/A
Early action deadline: N/A, notification date: N/A
Application deadline (fall): 8/1
Undergraduate student body: 17,442 full time, 4,067 part time; 47% male, 53% female;

0% American Indian, 7% Asian, 7% Black, 12% Hispanic, 4% multiracial, 0% Pacific Islander, 67% white, 3% international; 88% from in state; 17% live on campus; N/A of students in fraternities, N/A in sororities
Most popular majors: 28% Business, Management, Marketing, and Related Support Services, 14% Health Professions and Related Programs, 8% Computer and Information Sciences and Support Services, 8% Engineering, 7% Visual and Performing Arts
Expenses: 2019-2020: $9,526 in state, $21,168 out of state; room/board: $10,792
Financial aid: N/A

University of Wisconsin–Oshkosh[1]

Oshkosh WI
(920) 424-3164
U.S. News ranking: Reg. U. (Mid. W), No. 108
Website: www.uwosh.edu
Admissions email: admissions@uwosh.edu
Public; founded 1871
Application deadline (fall): rolling
Undergraduate student body: N/A full time, N/A part time
Expenses: 2019-2020: $7,656 in state, $15,229 out of state; room/board: $8,260
Financial aid: (920) 424-3377

University of Wisconsin–Parkside

Kenosha WI
(262) 595-2355
U.S. News ranking: Nat. Lib. Arts, second tier
Website: www.uwp.edu/
Admissions email: admissions@uwp.edu
Public; founded 1968
Freshman admissions: selective; 2019-2020: 1,676 applied, 1,485 accepted. Neither SAT nor ACT required. ACT 25/75 percentile: 17-23. High school rank: 11% in top tenth, 38% in top quarter, 72% in top half
Early decision deadline: N/A, notification date: N/A
Early action deadline: N/A, notification date: N/A
Application deadline (fall): rolling
Undergraduate student body: 3,143 full time, 795 part time; 45% male, 55% female; 0% American Indian, 4% Asian, 8% Black, 19% Hispanic, 4% multiracial, 0% Pacific Islander, 63% white, 1% international; 84% from in state; 21% live on campus; N/A of students in fraternities, N/A in sororities
Most popular majors: 28% Business, Management, Marketing, and Related Support Services, 10% Psychology, 8% Homeland Security, Law Enforcement, Firefighting and Related Protective Services, 7% Biological and Biomedical Sciences, 6% Visual and Performing Arts

Expenses: 2019-2020: $7,421 in state, $15,691 out of state; room/board: $8,200
Financial aid: (262) 595-2574; 65% of undergrads determined to have financial need; average aid package $9,133

University of Wisconsin–Platteville[1]

Platteville WI
(608) 342-1125
U.S. News ranking: Reg. U. (Mid. W), No. 98
Website: www.uwplatt.edu
Admissions email: admit@uwplatt.edu
Public; founded 1866
Application deadline (fall): rolling
Undergraduate student body: N/A full time, N/A part time
Expenses: 2019-2020: $7,353 in state, $15,473 out of state; room/board: $7,700
Financial aid: (608) 342-6188

University of Wisconsin–River Falls

River Falls WI
(715) 425-3500
U.S. News ranking: Reg. U. (Mid. W), No. 86
Website: www.uwrf.edu
Admissions email: admissions@uwrf.edu
Public; founded 1874
Freshman admissions: selective; 2019-2020: 2,969 applied, 2,342 accepted. Either SAT or ACT required. ACT 25/75 percentile: 20-25. High school rank: 9% in top tenth, 31% in top quarter, 73% in top half
Early decision deadline: N/A, notification date: N/A
Early action deadline: N/A, notification date: N/A
Application deadline (fall): rolling
Undergraduate student body: 5,061 full time, 555 part time; 36% male, 64% female; 0% American Indian, 3% Asian, 1% Black, 4% Hispanic, 3% multiracial, 0% Pacific Islander, 88% white, 1% international; 50% from in state; 47% live on campus; 7% of students in fraternities, 3% in sororities
Most popular majors: 19% Business, Management, Marketing, and Related Support Services, 18% Agriculture, Agriculture Operations, and Related Sciences, 14% Education, 9% Social Sciences, 7% Biological and Biomedical Sciences
Expenses: 2020-2021: $8,063 in state, $15,636 out of state; room/board: $6,600
Financial aid: (715) 425-3141; 56% of undergrads determined to have financial need; average aid package $6,896

University of Wisconsin–Stevens Point

Stevens Point WI
(715) 346-2441
U.S. News ranking: Reg. U. (Mid. W), No. 65
Website: www.uwsp.edu
Admissions email: admiss@uwsp.edu
Public; founded 1894
Freshman admissions: selective; 2019-2020: 4,217 applied, 3,557 accepted. Neither SAT nor ACT required. ACT 25/75 percentile: 19-25. High school rank: 10% in top tenth, 33% in top quarter, 68% in top half
Early decision deadline: N/A, notification date: N/A
Early action deadline: N/A, notification date: N/A
Application deadline (fall): rolling
Undergraduate student body: 6,639 full time, 1,102 part time; 45% male, 55% female; 0% American Indian, 4% Asian, 2% Black, 4% Hispanic, 3% multiracial, 0% Pacific Islander, 86% white, 1% international; 88% from in state; 35% live on campus; 5% of students in fraternities, 5% in sororities
Most popular majors: 9% Business Administration and Management, General, 6% Biology/Biological Sciences, General, 5% Natural Resources Management and Policy, 5% Psychology, General, 5% Speech Communication and Rhetoric
Expenses: 2020-2021: $8,379 in state, $17,083 out of state; room/board: $7,630
Financial aid: (715) 346-4771; 57% of undergrads determined to have financial need; average aid package $9,896

University of Wisconsin–Stout

Menomonie WI
(715) 232-1232
U.S. News ranking: Reg. U. (Mid. W), No. 71
Website: www.uwstout.edu
Admissions email: admissions@uwstout.edu
Public; founded 1891
Freshman admissions: selective; 2019-2020: 3,227 applied, 2,874 accepted. Either SAT or ACT required. ACT 25/75 percentile: 20-25. High school rank: 9% in top tenth, 28% in top quarter, 64% in top half
Early decision deadline: N/A, notification date: N/A

Early action deadline: N/A, notification date: N/A
Application deadline (fall): rolling
Undergraduate student body: 5,995 full time, 1,294 part time; 57% male, 43% female; 0% American Indian, 4% Asian, 2% Black, 3% Hispanic, 3% multiracial, 0% Pacific Islander, 86% white, 2% international; N/A from in state; 39% live on campus; 2% of students in fraternities, 3% in sororities
Most popular majors: 35% Business, Management, Marketing, and Related Support Services, 11% Visual and Performing Arts, 8% Family and Consumer Sciences/Human Sciences, 7% Computer and Information Sciences and Support Services, 7% Engineering Technologies and Engineering-Related Fields
Expenses: 2019-2020: $9,463 in state, $17,430 out of state; room/board: $6,947
Financial aid: (715) 232-1363; 52% of undergrads determined to have financial need; average aid package $11,079

University of Wisconsin–Superior

Superior WI
(715) 394-8230
U.S. News ranking: Nat. Lib. Arts, second tier
Website: www.uwsuper.edu
Admissions email: admissions@uwsuper.edu
Public; founded 1893
Freshman admissions: selective; 2019-2020: 897 applied, 696 accepted. Either SAT or ACT required. ACT 25/75 percentile: 18-23. High school rank: 8% in top tenth, 24% in top quarter, 55% in top half
Early decision deadline: N/A, notification date: N/A
Early action deadline: N/A, notification date: N/A
Application deadline (fall): 8/1
Undergraduate student body: 1,715 full time, 542 part time; 37% male, 63% female; 2% American Indian, 1% Asian, 2% Black, 3% Hispanic, 4% multiracial, 0% Pacific Islander, 80% white, 9% international; 46% from in state; 31% live on campus; N/A of students in fraternities, N/A in sororities
Most popular majors: 20% Business, Management, Marketing, and Related Support Services, 14% Education, 10% Multi/Interdisciplinary Studies,

6% Biological and Biomedical Sciences, 6% Psychology
Expenses: 2020-2021: $8,142 in state, $15,712 out of state; room/board: $7,200
Financial aid: (715) 394-8200; 61% of undergrads determined to have financial need; average aid package $11,230

University of Wisconsin–Whitewater

Whitewater WI
(262) 472-1440
U.S. News ranking: Reg. U. (Mid. W), No. 58
Website: www.uww.edu
Admissions email: uwwadmit@uww.edu
Public; founded 1868
Freshman admissions: selective; 2019-2020: 5,125 applied, 4,772 accepted. Either SAT or ACT required. ACT 25/75 percentile: 19-24. High school rank: 9% in top tenth, 31% in top quarter, 70% in top half
Early decision deadline: N/A, notification date: N/A
Early action deadline: N/A, notification date: N/A
Application deadline (fall): 5/1
Undergraduate student body: 9,546 full time, 1,474 part time; 51% male, 49% female; 0% American Indian, 2% Asian, 4% Black, 8% Hispanic, 4% multiracial, 0% Pacific Islander, 82% white, 1% international; 84% from in state; 41% live on campus; 5% of students in fraternities, 6% in sororities
Most popular majors: 35% Business, Management, Marketing, and Related Support Services, 14% Education, 7% Communication, Journalism, and Related Programs, 7% Public Administration and Social Service Professions, 7% Social Sciences
Expenses: 2020-2021: $7,695 in state, $16,416 out of state; room/board: $6,877
Financial aid: (262) 472-1130; 56% of undergrads determined to have financial need; average aid package $8,430

Viterbo University

La Crosse WI
(608) 796-3010
U.S. News ranking: Reg. U. (Mid. W), No. 65
Website: www.viterbo.edu
Admissions email: admission@viterbo.edu
Private; founded 1890

Affiliation: Roman Catholic
Freshman admissions: selective; 2019-2020: 1,276 applied, 981 accepted. Neither SAT nor ACT required. ACT 25/75 percentile: 21-25. High school rank: 17% in top tenth, 47% in top quarter, 87% in top half
Early decision deadline: N/A, notification date: N/A
Early action deadline: N/A, notification date: N/A
Application deadline (fall): rolling
Undergraduate student body: 1,433 full time, 318 part time; 27% male, 73% female; 0% American Indian, 2% Asian, 4% Black, 4% Hispanic, 2% multiracial, 0% Pacific Islander, 84% white, 2% international; 73% from in state; 38% live on campus; 0% of students in fraternities, 0% in sororities
Most popular majors: 52% Health Professions and Related Programs, 21% Business, Management, Marketing, and Related Support Services, 7% Visual and Performing Arts, 4% Biological and Biomedical Sciences, 3% Psychology
Expenses: 2020-2021: $29,350; room/board: $9,670
Financial aid: (608) 796-3900

Wisconsin Lutheran College

Milwaukee WI
(414) 443-8811
U.S. News ranking: Reg. Coll. (Mid. W), No. 18
Website: www.wlc.edu/
Admissions email: admissions@wlc.edu
Private; founded 1973
Affiliation: Wisconsin Evangelical Lutheran Synod
Freshman admissions: selective; 2019-2020: 751 applied, 670 accepted. Either SAT or ACT required. ACT 25/75 percentile: 21-27. High school rank: 25% in top tenth, 46% in top quarter, 76% in top half
Early decision deadline: N/A, notification date: N/A
Early action deadline: N/A, notification date: N/A
Application deadline (fall): rolling
Undergraduate student body: 915 full time, 88 part time; 45% male, 55% female; 0% American Indian, 1% Asian, 5% Black, 7% Hispanic, 3% multiracial, 0% Pacific Islander, 82% white, 1% international; 76% from in state; 63% live on campus; 0% of students in fraternities, 0% in sororities

Most popular majors: 34% Business, Management, Marketing, and Related Support Services, 11% Biological and Biomedical Sciences, 9% Health Professions and Related Programs, 8% Communication, Journalism, and Related Programs, 8% Education
Expenses: 2020-2021: $31,754; room/board: $10,730
Financial aid: (414) 443-8856

WYOMING

University of Wyoming

Laramie WY
(307) 766-5160
U.S. News ranking: Nat. U., No. 196
Website: www.uwyo.edu
Admissions email: admissions@uwyo.edu
Public; founded 1886
Freshman admissions: selective; 2019-2020: 5,348 applied, 5,132 accepted. Either SAT or ACT required. ACT 25/75 percentile: 22-28. High school rank: 24% in top tenth, 51% in top quarter, 83% in top half
Early decision deadline: N/A, notification date: N/A
Early action deadline: N/A, notification date: N/A
Application deadline (fall): 8/10
Undergraduate student body: 8,332 full time, 1,475 part time; 49% male, 51% female; 1% American Indian, 1% Asian, 1% Black, 7% Hispanic, 4% multiracial, 0% Pacific Islander, 74% white, 3% international; 65% from in state; 25% live on campus; 6% of students in fraternities, 7% in sororities
Most popular majors: 15% Business, Management, Marketing, and Related Support Services, 14% Engineering, 8% Education, 8% Health Professions and Related Programs, 7% Biological and Biomedical Sciences
Expenses: 2020-2021: $5,791 in state, $19,531 out of state; room/board: $10,615
Financial aid: (307) 766-2116; 48% of undergrads determined to have financial need; average aid package $10,431

A

Abilene Christian University, TX
32, 33, 88, 131, 147, D-137
Abraham Baldwin Agricultural
College, GA 94, D-30
Academy of Art University, CA
90, 148, D-8
Adams State University, CO
90, D-19
Adelphi University, NY
67, 110, 128, D-88
Adrian College, MI 32, 95, D-67
Agnes Scott College, GA 32, 33
74, 111, 129, 146, D-30
Alabama Agricultural and
Mechanical University
84, 99, 148, D-3
Alabama State University
84, 99, 148, D-3
Alaska Pacific University
90, 113, D-5
Albany State University, GA
84, 99, D-30
Albertus Magnus
College, CT 79, 112, D-21
Albion College, MI 76, D-68
Albright
College, PA 77, 111, D-117
Alcorn State University, MS
82, 98, 112, D-75
Alderson Broaddus
University, WV 94, D-154
Alfred University, NY
79, 112, 147, D-88
Alice Lloyd College, KY
93, 113, 147, D-52
Allegheny College, PA 74, D-117
Allen University, SC
77, 99, 148, D-129
Alliant International
University, CA 70, 149, D-8
Alma College, MI 95, 147, D-68
Alpena Community
College, MI D-68
Alvernia
University, PA 79, D-117
Alverno College, WI
32, 86, 148, D-156
American Academy of Art, IL D-36
American International
College, MA 80, D-61
American Jewish
University, CA D-8
American Samoa
Community College, AS D-5
American University, DC
33, 64, 100, D-23
American University of
Puerto Rico–Bayamon 94, D-127
American University of
Puerto Rico–Manati 94, D-127
Amherst College, MA 32, 33, 72
104, 111, 146, 149, D-61
Anderson University, IN 86, D-42
Anderson University, SC
82, 107, 130, D-129
Andrew College, GA D-30
Andrews University, MI 70, D-68
Angelo State
University, TX 90, D-138
Anna Maria
College, MA 80, 111, D-61
Antelope Valley College, CA D-8
Appalachian State
University, NC 32, 33, 81, 91
101, 107, 130, D-101
Aquinas College, MI 77, D-68
Arcadia University, PA
33, 79, 129, D-117
Arizona Christian University, AZ
97, 113, 147, D-5
Arizona State University–Tempe
32, 64, 100, 101, 103
104, 106, 109, 128, D-5
Arizona State University–West D-6
Arkansas Baptist
College 94, 99, D-6

Arkansas State University
70, 109, D-6
Arkansas Tech University 82, D-6
Art Academy of Cincinnati D-107
ArtCenter College
of Design, CA D-8
Art Institute of Atlanta D-30
Art Institute of Houston D-138
Asbury University, KY
81, 112, 130, 147, D-52
Ashland University, OH
86, 108, 112, D-107
Assumption
University, MA 79, 129, D-61
Atlanta Metropolitan
State College D-30
Auburn University, AL
64, 100, 103, 104, D-3
Auburn University at
Montgomery, AL 82, 108, D-3
Augsburg University, MN
86, 112, 147, D-72
Augustana College, IL
74, 129, D-36
Augustana University, SD
86, 131, 147, D-133
Augusta University, GA 70, D-30
Aurora University, IL 70, D-36
Austin College, TX
74, 111, 129, D-138
Austin Peay State
University, TN 82, D-134
Ave Maria University, FL 77, D-24
Averett
University, VA 93, 113, D-147
Avila
University, MO 88, 112, D-76
Azusa Pacific
University, CA 68, 110, D-8

B

Babson
College, MA 100, 101, D-61
Bacone
College, OK 97, 148, D-113
Baker College of
Flint, MI 88, D-68
Bakersfield College, CA D-9
Baker
University, KS 69, 128, D-49
Baldwin Wallace University, OH
86, 112, 131, D-107
Ball State University, IN
69, 101, 106, 109, D-42
Bard
College, NY 32, 74, 146, D-88
Bard College at
Simon's Rock, MA 92, D-61
Barnard
College, NY 72, 149, D-88
Barry University, FL
70, 111, 148, D-24
Barton College, NC
93, 113, 147, D-101
Bates College, ME
32, 72, 146, 149, D-57
Bayamon Central
University, PR 84, D-127
Baylor University, TX
32, 64, 100, 104, D-138
Bay Path University, MA 80, D-61
Bay State College, MA 93, D-62
Beacon College, FL 94, D-24
Becker College, MA 93, D-62
Belhaven University, MS 82, D-75
Bellarmine
University, KY 68, D-52
Bellevue College, WA D-151
Bellevue University, NE 88, D-81
Bellingham Technical
College, WA D-151
Belmont Abbey
College, NC 93, D-101
Belmont University, TN
32, 66, 101, 128, D-134
Beloit College, WI 74, 111, D-156

Bemidji State
University, MN 87, 112, D-72
Benedict College, SC
94, 99, 148, D-130
Benedictine
College, KS 95, 131, D-49
Benedictine
University, IL 70, 110, D-36
Bennett College, NC
77, 99, 111, 148, D-101
Bennington College, VT 74, D-146
Bentley University, MA
78, 100, 147, D-62
Berea
College, KY 32, 33, 72, 111
129, 149, D-52
Berkeley
College, NJ 93, 109, D-84
Berkeley
College, NY 107, D-88
Berklee College
of Music, MA D-62
Berry College, GA
81, 130, 147, D-30
Bethany College, KS 96, D-50
Bethany College, WV 77, D-154
Bethany Lutheran
College, MN 77, D-72
Bethel College, KS 96, D-50
Bethel
University, IN 86, 112, D-42
Bethel
University MN 68, 128, D-72
Bethel University, TN 84, D-134
Bethune-Cookman University, FL
77, 99, 111, 148, D-24
Binghamton University–SUNY
64, 100, 104, 111, D-88
Biola University, CA
67, 111, 128, D-9
Birmingham-Southern College
76, 129, D-3
Bismarck State College, ND D-106
Blackburn
College, IL 77, 111, D-37
Black Hills State
University, SD 88, D-133
Bloomfield College, NJ
77, 111, 148, D-84
Bloomsburg University
of Pennsylvania 80, D-117
Bluefield
College, VA 94, 108, D-147
Bluefield State
College, WV 94, 99, D-154
Blue Mountain
College, MS 93, 147, D-75
Bluffton
University, OH 96, 113, D-107
Bob Jones University, SC
82, 112, 147, D-130
Boise State University, ID
70, 101, 105, D-36
Boricua College, NY 93, 149, D-88
Boston Architectural College D-62
Boston College
33, 62, 100, 104, 146, D-62
Boston University
62, 100, 103, 104, 146, D-62
Bowdoin College, ME
72, 105, 146, 149, D-57
Bowie State
University, MD 80, 98, D-58
Bowling Green State
University, OH 69, 101, 105
107, 109, 128, D-107
Bradley University, IL
84, 101, 102, 131, 147, D-37
Brandeis University, MA
62, 100, 104, 146, D-62
Brandman University, CA 107
Brazosport College, TX D-138
Brenau
University, GA 82, 112, D-31
Brescia University, KY 94, D-52
Brevard College, NC 93, D-101
Brewton-Parker
College, GA 77, 148, D-31

Briar Cliff University, IA 96, D-46
Bridgewater College, VA 77, D-147
Bridgewater State
University, MA 80, D-62
Brigham Young University–Hawaii
97, 149, D-35
Brigham Young University–Idaho
97, 102, 149, D-36
Brigham Young University–
Provo, UT 64, 100, 101
104, 146, 149, D-145
Broward College, FL D-25
Brown University, RI 32, 33, 62
103, 104, 146, D-128
Bryan College, TN 82, D-134
Bryant University, RI
78, 101, 129, D-128
Bryn Athyn College of the
New Church, PA 76, 111, D-117
Bryn Mawr
College, PA 72, 146, D-117
Bucknell University, PA
72, 100, 102, 104, D-117
Buena Vista University, IA
86, 112, 147, D-47
Bushnell University, OR 90, D-115
Butler University, IN
32, 33, 84, 100, 131, D-42

C

Cabrini University, PA 80, D-117
Cairn University, PA 80, D-117
Caldwell University, NJ
79, 111, 147, D-84
California Baptist University
89, 107, 109, 131, D-9
California College
of the Arts D-9
California Institute of
Technology 33, 62, 103
104, 146, 149, D-9
California Institute of the Arts D-9
California Lutheran
University 88, 131, 147, D-9
California Polytechnic State
University–San Luis Obispo
88, 91, 100, 102, 104, D-9
California State Polytechnic
University–Pomona 88, 91
101, 102, 104, 113, D-9
California State University–
Bakersfield 89, 113, D-9
California State University–
Channel Islands 89, 113, D-9
California State University–
Chico 89, 91, 108, D-10
California State University–
Dominguez Hills
89, 107, 113, D-10
California State University–
East Bay 90, 113, D-10
California State University–
Fresno 68, 110, 149, D-10
California State University–
Fullerton 88, 91, 101, 102
105, 113, 131, D-10
California State University–
Long Beach
88, 91, 105, 112, D-10
California State University–
Los Angeles 89, 91, 100, 102
104, 113, 147, 149, D-10
California State University–
Maritime Academy
97, 102, D-10
California State University–
Monterey Bay
89, 91, 113, 149, D-10
California State University–
Northridge 89, 102, 113, D-11
California State University–
Sacramento
89, 102, 113, D-11
California State University–
San Bernardino 89, 113, D-11
California State University–
San Marcos 89, 113, D-11

California State University–
Stanislaus 89, 91, 113, D-11
California University of
Pennsylvania 80, D-117
Calumet College of
St. Joseph, IN 88, 112, D-42
Calvin University, MI
84, 102, 131, 147, D-68
Cambridge College, MA 80, D-62
Cameron University, OK 90, D-113
Campbellsville
University, KY 84, 108, D-52
Campbell
University, NC 69, 108, D-101
Canisius
College, NY 78, 129, 147, D-88
Capital
University, OH 86, 131, D-107
Cardinal Stritch
University, WI 70, 148, D-156
Caribbean
University, PR 84, D-127
Carleton College, MN 32, 33, 72
104, 146, 149, D-72
Carlow University, PA
79, 111, D-118
Carnegie Mellon University, PA
32, 33, 62, 100, 101
103, 104, 105, 146, D-118
Carroll College, MT
97, 131, 147, D-80
Carroll University, WI 86, D-156
Carson-Newman
University, TN 70, 110, D-134
Carthage
College, WI 95, 131, D-156
Cascadia College, WA D-151
Case Western Reserve
University, OH 62, 100, 103
104, 146, D-107
Castleton University, VT 92, D-146
Catawba College, NC
93, 113, D-101
The Catholic University
of America, DC 66, D-23
Cazenovia College, NY
92, 113, 147, D-89
Cedar Crest
College, PA 79, 111, D-118
Cedarville University, OH
86, 102, 131, D-108
Centenary College, LA 76, D-55
Centenary
University, NJ 79, 112, D-84
Central Baptist
College, AR 94, 113, D-6
Central Christian
College, KS 96, 113, D-50
Central College, IA 76, D-47
Central Connecticut State
University 80, D-21
Centralia College, WA D-151
Central Methodist University–
College of Liberal Arts
and Sciences, MO 96, D-77
Central Michigan
University 69, 108, 148, D-68
Central Penn College 93, D-118
Central State University, OH
96, 99, 148, D-108
Central Washington
University 89, 107, D-151
Centre College, KY 74, 146, D-53
Chadron State
College, NE 88, D-81
Chaminade University of
Honolulu 89, 131, D-35
Champlain College, VT
79, 109, D-146
Chapman
University, CA 66, 101, D-11
Charleston Southern University, SC
82, 106, 109, D-130
Chatham University, PA
68, 110, 128, D-118
Chestnut Hill
College, PA 80, 111, D-118
Cheyney University of Pennsylvania
77, 99, 111, D-118

Chicago State
University   88, 148, D-37
Chipola College, FL   D-25
Chowan
University, NC   77, 148, D-101
Christian Brothers University, TN
81, 112, 130, 147, D-134
Christopher Newport University, VA
81, 91, 130, D-147
The Citadel, SC   81, 91, 101
102, 105, 108, 147, D-130
City University of
Seattle   90, 106, 109, D-151
Claflin University, SC
93, 98, 113, D-130
Claremont McKenna College, CA
32, 72, 146, 149, D-11
Clarion University of Pennsylvania
80, 106, D-118
Clark Atlanta University
70, 98, 110, 148, D-31
Clark College, WA   D-151
Clarke University, IA
68, 110, 148, D-47
Clarkson University, NY   66, 101
105, 111, 128, 146, D-89
Clark University, MA
64, 101, 146, D-62
Clayton State
University, GA   84, 112, D-31
Cleary University, MI   D-68
Clemson University, SC   32, 33
64, 71, 100, 103, 104, D-130
Cleveland Institute of Art   D-108
Cleveland Institute of Music D-108
Cleveland State
University   70, D-108
Clover Park Technical
College, WA   D-151
Coastal Carolina
University, SC   82, 147, D-130
Coe College, IA
76, 111, 129, D-47
Cogswell University of
Silicon Valley, CA   D-11
Coker College, SC   82, D-130
Colby College, ME   72, 146, D-57
Colby-Sawyer College, NH
92, 113, 147, D-83
Colegio Universitario
de San Juan, PR   94, D-127
Colgate University, NY
72, 105, 146, 149, D-89
College for
Creative Studies, MI   D-68
College of Central Florida   D-25
College of Charleston, SC
81, 91, 131, D-130
College of Coastal
Georgia   94, 109, D-31
College of Idaho   76, 111, D-36
College of Mount St. Vincent, NY
80, 111, D-89
College of
New Jersey   78, 91, D-84
College of
Saint Mary, NE   87, D-81
College of
Saint Rose, NY   80, D-89
College of Southern Nevada   D-82
College of
St. Benedict, MN 74, 129, D-72
College of St. Scholastica, MN
69, 128, D-72
College of the Atlantic, ME
74, 111, 129, 146, D-57
College of the
Holy Cross, MA   72, D-62
College of the Ozarks, MO
33, 95, 113, 131, 147, D-77
The College of
Westchester, NY   93, D-89
College of
Wooster, OH 32, 33, 74, D-108
Colorado Christian
University   89, 148, D-19
Colorado College   72, 149, D-19
Colorado Mesa University 90, D-19

Colorado Mountain College   D-19
Colorado School
of Mines   64, 103, 104, D-19
Colorado State University   66, 100
104, 106, 109, 128, D-19
Colorado State
University–Pueblo   90, D-19
Colorado Technical
University   70, 109, 148, D-19
Columbia Basin
College, WA   D-151
Columbia College, MO   88, D-77
Columbia
College, SC   82, 112, D-130
Columbia College
Chicago   87, D-37
Columbia College
Hollywood, CA   D-11
Columbia International
University, SC   82, 112
147, D-131
Columbia University, NY
33, 62, 103, 104, 146, D-89
Columbus College of
Art and Design, OH   D-108
Columbus State
University, GA   82, D-31
Community College of Denver D-19
Concordia College–Moorhead, MN
76, 111, 129, D-72
Concordia College–
New York, NY   80, D-89
Concordia
University, CA   89, 131, D-12
Concordia
University, NE   86, 131, D-81
Concordia University Chicago
87, 107, 109, 112, D-37
Concordia University–
St. Paul, MN   87, 108, D-73
Concordia University
Texas   90, D-138
Concordia University
Wisconsin 69, 106, 128, D-156
Concord University, WV 84, D-154
Connecticut College   74, D-21
Converse College, SC   81, D-131
Cooper Union for the Advancement
of Science and Art, NY
92, 102, 147, D-89
Coppin State
University, MD   80, 99, D-58
Corban
University, OR   97, 113, D-115
Cornell
College, IA 74, 111, 129, D-47
Cornell University, NY   32, 33, 62
100, 103, 104, 146, 149, D-89
Cornerstone University, MI
87, 107, 112, D-68
Cornish College
of the Arts, WA   D-152
Cottey College, MO
95, 113, 147, 149, D-77
Covenant
College, GA 76, 111, 129, D-31
Creighton University, NE
33, 66, 100, 107, 128, D-81
Crowley's Ridge
College, AR   94, 113, D-7
Crown College, MN   88, 112, D-73
Culver-Stockton
College, MO   96, D-77
Cumberland
University, TN   82, D-134
CUNY–Baruch College   78, 91
100, 111, 129, 149, D-90
CUNY–Brooklyn College   79, 91
111, 149, D-90
CUNY–City College
67, 104, 110, 149, D-90
CUNY–College of
Staten Island   80, D-90
CUNY–Hunter College
78, 91, 105, 111, D-90
CUNY–John Jay College of
Criminal Justice
79, 111, 149, D-90

CUNY–Lehman College
79, 91, 111, 149, D-90
CUNY–Medgar Evers College
93, 149, D-90
CUNY–New York City College of
Technology 93, 113, 148, D-90
CUNY–Queens College
79, 91, 111, 149, D-90
CUNY School of Professionals
Studies   106, 109
CUNY–York College 93, 149, D-91
Curry College, MA   80, D-63
Curtis Institute
of Music, PA   D-118
Cypress College, CA   D-12

D

Daemen College, NY   70, D-91
Dakota State
University, SD   87, 105, D-133
Dakota Wesleyan
University, SD   96, 106, D-133
Dallas Baptist
University   69, D-138
Dalton State
College, GA   94, D-31
Dartmouth College, NH   33, 62
103, 104, 146, 149, D-83
Davenport
University, MI   87, D-69
Davidson College, NC
33, 72, 146, D-102
Davis and Elkins
College, WV   94, D-155
Daytona State
College, FL 106, 109, D-25
Dean College, MA   92, D-63
Defiance College, OH   96, D-108
Delaware State University
69, 98, 110, 148, D-23
Delaware Technical
Community College–Terry D-23
Delaware Valley
University, PA   80, D-118
Delta State
University, MS   82, D-75
Denison University, OH 72, D-108
DePaul University, IL
66, 100, 105, D-37
DePauw University, IN   72, D-42
DeSales University, PA 79, D-118
Design Institute of
San Diego   D-12
DeVry University, IL 88, 148, D-37
Dickinson
College, PA   33, 72, D-119
Dickinson State
University, ND   96, 97, D-106
DigiPen Institute
of Technology, WA   D-152
Dillard University, LA
77, 98, 111, 148, D-55
Dixie State
University, UT   97, D-145
Doane University, NE   76, D-81
Dominican
College, NY   80, 112, D-91
Dominican University, IL
86, 112, 131, 147, D-37
Dominican University of
California   89, 131, D-12
Donnelly
College, KS   96, 149, D-50
Dordt University, IA
95, 113, 131, D-47
Drake University, IA   66, D-47
Drew University, NJ
76, 111, 129, D-85
Drexel University, PA 32, 66, 100
103, 104, 107, D-119
Drury University, MO
86, 112, 131, 147, D-77
Duke University, NC   32, 33, 62
103, 104, 146, 149, D-102
Dunwoody College of
Technology, MN   96, D-73

Duquesne University, PA
66, 101, 108, 128, 148, D-119
D'Youville College, NY
69, 110, D-91

E

Earlham
College, IN   74, 146, D-43
East Carolina University, NC
68, 110, D-102
East Central
University, OK   90, D-113
Eastern Connecticut
State University   79, D-21
Eastern Florida
State College   D-25
Eastern Illinois
University   86, 91, D-37
Eastern Kentucky
University 82, 107, 109, D-53
Eastern Mennonite
University, VA   82, D-147
Eastern Michigan
University   70, D-69
Eastern Nazarene
College, MA   93, D-63
Eastern New Mexico
University   90, D-87
Eastern Oregon
University   90, 108, D-115
Eastern
University, PA   79, 129, D-119
Eastern Washington
University   89, D-152
East Georgia State College   D-31
East Stroudsburg
University, PA   80, D-119
East Tennessee State
University   70, D-134
East Texas Baptist
University   97, 147, D-138
East-West University, IL   77, D-37
Eckerd College, FL   76, D-25
ECPI University, VA   84, D-147
Edgewood College, WI
68, 110, 128, D-156
Edinboro University
of Pennsylvania   80, D-119
Edmonds Community
College, WA   D-152
EDP University of Puerto Rico Inc–
San Juan, PR   82, 112, D-127
Edward Waters
College, FL 94, 99, 113, D-25
Elizabeth City State University, NC
94, 98, 113, D-102
Elizabethtown
College, PA   76, 129, D-119
Elmhurst University, IL
86, 112, 131, D-37
Elmira
College, NY 92, 113, 147, D-91
Elms College, MA   79, 111, D-63
Elon University, NC   32, 33, 64
100, 128, D-102
Embry-Riddle Aeronautical
University, FL
81, 105, 106, 109, D-25
Embry-Riddle Aeronautical
University–Prescott, AZ 102, D-6
Emerson College, MA   78, D-63
Emmanuel
College, GA   94, 147, D-31
Emmanuel College, MA   77, D-63
Emory and Henry
College, VA   76, D-147
Emory University, GA
62, 100, 104, 146, D-32
Emporia State
University, KS   87, D-50
Endicott College, MA
32, 78, 129, D-63
Erskine
College, SC   93, 113, D-131
Escuela de Artes
Plasticas de Puerto Rico   D-127

Eureka College, IL   96, D-38
Evangel
University, MO   88, 112, D-77
Everglades University, FL
84, 112, 148, D-25
Evergreen State
College, WA   32, 89, D-152

F

Fairfield University, CT
33, 78, 101, 129, D-21
Fairleigh Dickinson University, NJ
79, 112, 129, D-85
Fairmont State
University, WV   84, D-155
Farmingdale State
College–SUNY   92, D-91
Fashion Institute of Design &
Merchandising, CA   D-12
Fashion Institute of
Technology, NY   D-91
Faulkner University, AL   84, D-3
Fayetteville State University, NC
82, 98, 112, D-102
Feather River Community
College District, CA   D-12
Felician
University, NJ   80, 111, D-85
Ferris State
University, MI   70, 108, D-69
Ferrum College, VA   94, D-148
Finlandia
University, MI   96, 113, D-69
Fisher College, MA 92, 113, D-63
Fisk
University, TN   77, 98, D-135
Fitchburg State
University, MA   80, D-63
Five Towns College, NY   93, D-91
Flagler College, FL   93, D-25
Florida A&M University
68, 98, 105, 110, D-25
Florida Atlantic
University   69, 101, 105
107, 110, 128, D-25
Florida College   94, 149, D-25
Florida Gateway College   D-26
Florida Gulf Coast
University   82, 131, D-26
Florida Institute of Technology
68, 105, 108, 148, D-26
Florida International
University   68, 100, 101, 105
107, 109, 110, 128, D-26
Florida Keys
Community College   D-26
Florida Memorial
University   94, 99, D-26
Florida National University–
Main Campus   93, 113, D-26
Florida Polytechnic
University   D-26
Florida Southern
College   81, 131, D-26
Florida SouthWestern
State College   D-26
Florida State College–
Jacksonville   D-26
Florida State
University   64, 71, 100, 101
104, 109, 110, 128, D-27
Fontbonne
University, MO   86, D-77
Foothill College, CA   D-12
Fordham
University, NY   64, 100, D-91
Fort Hays State University, KS
87, 107, 109, D-50
Fort Lewis College, CO   77, D-19
Fort Valley State University, GA
84, 99, 112, 148, D-32
Framingham State
University, MA   80, D-64
Franciscan University of
Steubenville, OH
86, 131, 147, D-108

Francis Marion
    University, SC   82, D-131
Franklin
    College, IN   76, 111, D-43
Franklin & Marshall
    College, PA   72, 146, D-119
Franklin Pierce
    University, NH   80, D-83
Franklin University, OH   D-109
Franklin W. Olin College
    of Engineering, MA   102, D-64
Freed-Hardeman University, TN
                82, 131, 147, D-135
Fresno Pacific
    University, CA   89, 112, D-12
Friends University, KS   87, D-50
Frostburg State
    University, MD   80, 112, D-58
Furman University, SC   74, D-131

G

Gallaudet University, DC
            66, 110, 146, D-24
Gannon University, PA
            68, 128, 148, D-119
Gardner-Webb
    University, NC   69, D-102
Geneva
    College, PA   79, 129, D-120
George Fox
    University, OR   68, 128, D-115
George Mason University, VA
        66, 100, 104, 128, D-148
Georgetown College, KY   77, D-53
Georgetown
    University, DC   33, 62, 100
            101, 104, 146, D-24
George Washington
    University, DC   32, 64, 100
            104, 106, 109, D-24
Georgia College & State
    University   81, 91, 101, D-32
Georgia Gwinnett College   94, D-32
Georgia Highlands College   D-32
Georgia Institute of
    Technology   32, 33, 62, 71
    100, 101, 103, 104, 105, D-32
Georgia Military College   D-32
Georgian Court
    University, NJ   80, D-85
Georgia Southern
    University   70, 109, D-32
Georgia Southwestern State
    University   84, D-32
Georgia State University   32, 68
    100, 101, 105, 110, D-32
Gettysburg College, PA   74, D-120
Glenville State
    College, WV   94, D-155
Goddard College, VT   80, D-146
Goldey-Beacom College, DE   D-23
Gonzaga University, WA
        64, 100, 102, 105, D-152
Gordon College, MA   76, 129, D-64
Gordon State College, GA   94, D-33
Goshen College, IN
        95, 113, 131, 147, D-43
Goucher College, MD
            33, 76, 129, D-59
Governors State
    University, IL   D-38
Grace College and
    Seminary, IN   87, 112, D-43
Graceland
    University, IA   88, 109, D-47
Grambling State University, LA
        84, 99, 112, 148, D-55
Grand Canyon
    University, AZ   70, 110, D-6
Grand Valley State University, MI
        86, 91, 131, D-69
Grand View University, IA 96, D-47
Granite State
    College, NH   80, 108, D-83
Grays Harbor College, WA   D-152
Great Basin College, NV   D-82

Green River College, WA   D-152
Greensboro College, NC 94, D-102
Greenville
    University, IL   87, 112, D-38
Grinnell College, IA
    72, 104, 111, 146, 149, D-48
Grove City College, PA   76, D-120
Guilford
    College, NC   76, 111, D-102
Gulf Coast State
    College, FL   D-27
Gustavus Adolphus College, MN
        74, 111, 129, D-73
Gwynedd Mercy
    University, PA   80, D-120

H

Hamilton College, NY
        33, 72, 146, 149, D-91
Hamline University, MN
        86, 112, 147, D-73
Hampden-Sydney
    College, VA   74, D-148
Hampshire College, MA   77, D-64
Hampton University, VA
        68, 98, 110, D-148
Hannibal-LaGrange
    University, MO   96, D-77
Hanover College, IN
        74, 111, 129, 146, D-43
Harding University, AR
            69, 128, D-7
Hardin-Simmons
    University, TX   89, D-138
Harrisburg University of Science
    and Technology, PA   80, D-120
Harris-Stowe State University, MO
        96, 99, 148, D-77
Hartwick
    College, NY   76, 111, D-92
Harvard
    University, MA   32, 33, 62
    103, 104, 146, 149, D-64
Harvey Mudd College, CA
        33, 72, 102, 104, D-12
Hastings College, NE   96, D-81
Haverford College, PA
        72, 146, 149, D-120
Hawaii Pacific University 89, D-35
Heidelberg University, OH
        96, 113, 147, D-109
Henderson State
    University, AR   82, D-7
Hendrix College, AR 74, 146, D-7
Henry Ford College, MI   D-69
Heritage
    University, WA   90, D-152
Herzing University, WI
        88, 107, 112, D-157
Hesston College, KS   D-50
Highline College, WA   D-152
High Point University, NC
        93, 131, D-103
Hilbert College, NY 93, 113, D-92
Hillsdale College, MI   74, D-69
Hiram
    College, OH   95, 113, D-109
Hobart and William Smith
    Colleges, NY   74, D-92
Hodges University, FL   84, D-27
Hofstra University, NY
        66, 100, 102, 128, D-92
Hollins University, VA
        74, 111, 129, D-148
Holy Cross College at
    Notre Dame, IN   96, D-43
Holy Family
    University, PA   81, D-120
Holy Names
    University, CA   89, D-12
Hood College, MD   79, D-59
Hope College, MI   76, 129, D-69
Hope International
    University, CA   90, 113, D-12
Houghton College, NY
        76, 111, 129, D-92

Houston Baptist
    University   89, 108, D-138
Howard Payne
    University, TX   97, D-139
Howard University, DC   64, 98
    100, 104, 110, 128, D-24
Hult International
    Business School, CA   D-12
Humboldt State
    University, CA   89, 113, D-13
Humphreys College, CA   D-13
Huntingdon
    College, AL   93, 147, D-3
Huntington
    University, IN   86, 112, D-43
Husson University, ME
        70, 110, 148, D-57
Huston-Tillotson
    University, TX   97, 99, D-139

I

Idaho State
    University   70, 101, 105, D-36
Illinois College   76, 111, D-38
Illinois Institute of Technology
        66, 104, 110, 146, D-38
Illinois State
    University   68, 101, 106, D-38
Illinois Wesleyan
    University   74, 129, D-38
Immaculata
    University, PA   68, 148, D-120
Indiana State University   70, D-43
Indiana Tech   87, D-43
Indiana University–
    Bloomington   64, 100, 101
        104, 106, 109, D-44
Indiana University
    East   88, 112, D-44
Indiana University–
    Kokomo   96, D-44
Indiana University
    Northwest   88, D-44
Indiana University of
    Pennsylvania   69, 148, D-120
Indiana University-
    Purdue University–Indianapolis
        68, 105, D-44
Indiana University–
    South Bend   88, D-44
Indiana University
    Southeast   88, D-44
Indiana Wesleyan University–
    Marion   86, 131, D-44
Indian River
    State College, FL   D-27
Iona College, NY   79, D-92
Iowa State University
    66, 100, 103, 104, 128, D-48
Iowa Wesleyan
    University   96, 109, D-48
Ithaca College, NY
        78, 101, 129, 147, D-92

J

Jackson College, MI   D-69
Jackson State University, MS
        70, 98, 110, 148, D-76
Jacksonville State
    University, AL   82, D-3
Jacksonville
    University, FL   81, 112, D-27
James Madison University, VA
        81, 91, 100, 102, D-148
Jamestown Business
    College, NY   D-92
Jarvis Christian College, TX
        97, 99, 148, D-139
John Brown
    University, AR   81, 131, D-7
John Carroll University, OH
        84, 101, 131, D-109
John Paul the Great
    Catholic University, CA   D-13

Johns Hopkins
    University, MD   33, 62, 100
        103, 104, 146, D-59
Johnson C. Smith University, NC
        77, 99, 148, D-103
Johnson & Wales
    University, RI   80, 108, D-129
Judson College, AL   77, D-3
Judson University, IL   87, D-38
Juilliard School, NY   D-92
Juniata
    College, PA   74, 129, D-120

K

Kalamazoo
    College, MI   33, 74, 146, D-69
Kansas City
    Art Institute, MO   D-77
Kansas State University   67, 100
    104, 107, 109, 128, D-50
Kansas Wesleyan
    University   96, D-51
Kean
    University, NJ   80, 112, D-85
Keene State
    College, NH   92, 147, D-83
Keiser
    University, FL   69, 110, D-27
Kennesaw State University, GA
    70, 100, 105, 110, D-33
Kent State University, OH
    68, 101, 105, 128, D-109
Kentucky Christian
    University   94, D-53
Kentucky State
    University   94, 98, 147, D-53
Kentucky Wesleyan College
        93, 107, D-53
Kenyon College, OH
        72, 149, D-109
Kettering University, MI
        86, 102, 148, D-69
Keuka College, NY   80, D-92
Keystone
    College, PA   92, 113, D-121
The King's College, NY   77, D-92
King's College, PA   79, D-121
King University, TN
        82, 112, 147, D-135
Knox College, IL
    74, 111, 129, 146, D-38
Kutztown University
    of Pennsylvania   80, D-121
Kuyper College, MI   96, D-69

L

Lackawanna College, PA   D-121
Lafayette College, PA
    72, 102, 105, D-121
LaGrange College, GA   93, D-33
Laguna College
    of Art and Design, CA   D-13
Lake Erie College, OH   88, D-109
Lake Forest College, IL
    74, 111, 129, 146, D-39
Lakeland University, WI
        88, 112, D-157
Lake Michigan College   D-70
Lake-Sumter State
    College, FL   D-27
Lake Superior State
    University, MI   96, 97, D-70
Lake Washington Institute
    of Technology, WA   D-152
Lamar
    University, TX   70, 109, D-139
Lancaster Bible
    College, PA   81, D-121
Lander University, SC   94, D-131
Landmark College, VT   D-146
Lane College, TN
        77, 99, 148, D-135
Langston University, OK
        90, 99, D-113

La Roche University, PA
        80, 112, D-121
La Salle University, PA
        78, 108, 112, D-121
Lasell University, MA   80, D-64
La Sierra University, CA
        89, 113, 148, D-13
Lawrence Technological
    University, MI
        86, 105, 131, D-70
Lawrence
    University, WI   74, 146, D-157
Lebanon Valley
    College, PA   78, D-121
Lees-McRae
    College, NC   93, D-103
Lee University, TN
    82, 107, 109, 131, 147, D-135
Lehigh University, PA
    62, 100, 103, 104, 146, D-121
Le Moyne College, NY
        78, 129, 147, D-93
LeMoyne-Owen College, TN
        94, 99, D-135
Lenoir-Rhyne
    University, NC   82, D-103
Lesley University, MA   69, D-64
LeTourneau University, TX
    89, 102, 131, 147, D-139
Lewis & Clark
    College, OR   74, D-115
Lewis-Clark State
    College, ID   97, D-36
Lewis University, IL
    86, 112, 131, D-39
Liberty University, VA   70, D-148
Life Pacific
    College, CA   97, 113, D-13
LIM College, NY   D-93
Limestone
    University, SC   94, 109, D-131
Lincoln College, IL   96, D-39
Lincoln Memorial University, TN
        68, 110, D-135
Lincoln University, MO
        96, 99, D-78
Lincoln University, PA
    81, 98, 112, 148, D-122
Lindenwood University, MO
    70, 108, 148, D-78
Lindsey Wilson
    College, KY   82, D-53
Linfield University, OR
        76, 107, D-115
Lipscomb University, TN
        68, 128, D-135
Livingstone College, NC
        94, 99, 148, D-103
Lock Haven University of
    Pennsylvania   80, D-122
Long Island University, NY
        69, 110, 128, D-93
Longwood
    University, VA   81, 91, D-148
Loras College, IA   95, 147, D-48
Louisiana College   84, D-55
Louisiana State
    University–Alexandria 77, D-55
Louisiana State University–
    Baton Rouge   66, 100, 103
        104, 128, D-55
Louisiana State
    University–Shreveport 84, D-55
Louisiana Tech
    University   70, 105, D-55
Lourdes
    University, OH   88, D-109
Loyola Marymount University, CA
        64, 100, 102, D-13
Loyola University Chicago
    66, 100, 106, 128, D-39
Loyola University Maryland
    78, 100, 105, 129, D-59
Loyola University New Orleans
    68, 101, 109, 128, D-55
Lubbock Christian
    University, TX   89, D-139
Luther College, IA   74, 129, D-48

Lycoming College, PA
76, 111, 129, D-122
Lynn University, FL
82, 108, 149, D-27
Lyon College, AR   76, 111, D-7

M

Macalester
College, MN   72, 146, D-73
Madonna University, MI   86, D-70
Maharishi International
University, IA
88, 112, 148, D-48
Maine College of Art   D-57
Maine Maritime Academy
92, 97, 131, 147, D-57
Malone
University, OH   87, D-109
Manchester
University, IN   96, D-44
Manhattan College, NY
78, 102, 129, D-93
Manhattan School
of Music, NY   D-93
Manhattanville
College, NY   79, 111, D-93
Mansfield University of
Pennsylvania   77, 111, D-122
Maranatha Baptist University, WI
96, 106, 113, D-157
Marian University, IN
86, 108, 147, D-44
Marian University, WI   87, D-157
Marietta College, OH
95, 113, 147, D-109
Marist College, NY
78, 107, 129, D-93
Marlboro College, VT   76, D-146
Marquette University, WI
64, 100, 105, 128, D-157
Marshall
University, WV   69, D-155
Mars Hill
University, NC   93, D-103
Martin Methodist
College, TN   94, D-135
Martin
University, IN   96, 148, D-45
Mary Baldwin University, VA
70, 110, 148, D-148
Maryland Institute
College of Art   D-59
Marymount California
University   77, 111, D-13
Marymount Manhattan
College, NY   77, D-93
Marymount
University, VA   82, D-149
Maryville College, TN
93, 113, 147, D-136
Maryville University of St. Louis
68, 109, 128, D-78
Marywood
University, PA   79, 129, D-122
Massachusetts College
of Art and Design   D-64
Massachusetts College of
Liberal Arts   73, 76, 111, D-64
Massachusetts Institute
of Technology   32, 33, 62
100, 101, 103, 104
105, 146, 149, D-64
Massachusetts Maritime Academy
92, 97, 102, 147, D-65
The Master's University and
Seminary , CA   89, 131, D-13
Mayville State
University, ND   96, 97, D-106
McDaniel College, MD
78, 129, 147, D-59
McKendree University, IL
86, 107, 109, D-39
McMurry University, TX
97, 113, 147, 148, D-139
McNeese State
University, LA   84, D-55

McPherson
College, KS   96, 113, D-51
Medaille College, NY   81, D-93
Menlo College, CA   D-13
Mercer University, GA
66, 128, 146, D-33
Mercy College, NY   81, 111, D-93
Mercyhurst
University, PA   79, D-122
Meredith College, NC
76, 111, 129, D-103
Merrimack College, MA   79, D-65
Messiah
University, PA   78, 129, D-122
Methodist
University, NC   82, D-103
Metropolitan College of
New York   81, 148, D-94
Metropolitan State
University, MN   70, 110, D-73
Metropolitan State University
of Denver   90, D-20
Miami Dade College, FL   D-27
Miami International
University of Art & Design   D-27
Miami University–Oxford, OH
64, 100, 102, 105, D-109
Michigan State
University   32, 33, 64, 100
101, 103, 104, 128, D-70
Michigan Technological
University   66, 104, D-70
Mid-America Christian
University, OK   90, D-113
MidAmerica Nazarene
University, KS
87, 112, 149, D-51
Middlebury College, VT
33, 72, 105, 146, 149, D-146
Middle Georgia State
University   94, D-33
Middle Tennessee State
University   70, 110, D-136
Midland College, TX   D-139
Midland University, NE   88, D-82
Midway
University, KY   82, 112, D-53
Midwestern Baptist Theological
Seminary, MO   109
Midwestern State
University, TX   89, 113, D-139
Miles College, AL   94, 99, D-3
Millersville University of
Pennsylvania   80, 109, D-122
Milligan University, TN
81, 112, 147, D-136
Millikin University, IL   95, D-39
Millsaps College, MS   76, D-76
Mills College, CA
88, 113, 147, D-13
Milwaukee Institute of
Art and Design   D-157
Milwaukee School of Engineering
86, 102, 147, D-157
Minneapolis College of
Art and Design   D-73
Minnesota State
University–Mankato   87, D-73
Minnesota State
University–Moorhead   87, D-73
Minot State
University, ND   87, D-106
MiraCosta College, CA   D-14
Misericordia
University, PA   68, 128, D-123
Mississippi College   70, D-76
Mississippi State University
68, 100, 104, 128, D-76
Mississippi University
for Women   82, 149, D-76
Mississippi Valley State
University   84, 99, 112, D-76
Missouri Baptist
University   88, D-78
Missouri Southern State
University   96, D-78
Missouri State
University   70, 110, D-78

Missouri University of Science
and Technology   67, 104, D-78
Missouri Valley College   96, D-78
Missouri Western
State University   88, D-78
Mitchell College, CT 93, 113, D-21
Modesto Junior College, CA   D-14
Molloy College, NY   78, 129, D-94
Monmouth
College, IL   76, 111, D-39
Monmouth
University, NJ   78, 129, D-85
Monroe College, NY 79, 111, D-94
Montana State University
69, 101, 104, 128, D-80
Montana State
University–Billings   90, D-80
Montana State
University–Northern   D-80
Montana Technological
University   89, 91, 131, D-80
Montclair State
University, NJ   67, 110, D-85
Montreat
College, NC   84, D-103
Montserrat College
of Art, MA   D-65
Moody Bible Institute, IL   107
Moore College of
Art & Design, PA   D-123
Moravian College, PA
76, 111, 129, D-123
Morehead State
University, KY   82, D-53
Morehouse College, GA
76, 98, 101, 111, D-33
Morgan State University, MD
70, 98, 110, 148, D-59
Morningside
College, IA   86, 112, D-48
Morris
College, SC 94, 99, 113, D-131
Mount Aloysius
College, PA   92, D-123
Mount Holyoke
College, MA   72, 105, D-65
Mount Marty
University, SD   87, D-133
Mount Mary
University, WI   86, 112, D-157
Mount Mercy University, IA
86, 108, 112, D-48
Mount Saint Mary's
University, CA   89, 112, D-14
Mount St. Joseph
University, OH   87, D-109
Mount St. Mary
College, NY   80, D-94
Mount St. Mary's
University, MD   79, D-59
Mount Vernon Nazarene
University, OH
87, 112, 131, D-110
Muhlenberg
College, PA   74, 129, D-123
Murray State University, KY
81, 91, 131, D-54
Muskingum
University, OH 86, 112, D-110

N

Naropa University, CO   90, D-20
National American
University, SD   D-133
National Louis
University, IL   70, D-39
National University, CA   90, D-14
Nazareth
College, NY   79, 129, D-94
Nebraska Wesleyan
University   86, 131, D-82
Neumann
University, PA   80, 108, D-123
Nevada State College   D-83
Newberry College, SC
93, 113, 147, D-131

New College of
Florida   73, 74, 149, D-27
New England
College, NH   81, D-83
New England College of
Business and Finance, MA   107
New England
Conservatory of Music, MA D-65
New England Institute of
Technology, RI   92, 113, D-129
New Hampshire Institute
of Art   D-83
New Jersey
City University   81, 111, D-85
New Jersey Institute of Technology
66, 101, 104, 110, D-85
Newman
University, KS   87, D-51
New Mexico Highlands
University   90, 149, D-87
New Mexico Institute of
Mining and Technology
89, 91, 105, 131, D-87
New Mexico State
University   69, 101, 105, D-87
The New School, NY   66, D-94
NewSchool of Architecture
and Design, CA   D-14
New York Institute of
Technology 78, 102, 105, D-94
New York School of
Interior Design   D-94
New York University
33, 62, 100, 101, 104, D-94
Niagara University, NY
78, 129, 147, D-94
Nicholls State
University, LA   82, 109, D-55
Nichols College, MA   D-65
Norfolk State University, VA
82, 98, 112, D-149
North Carolina Agricultural and
Technical State University
69, 98, 105, 110, 148, D-103
North Carolina Central University
82, 98, 112, D-103
North Carolina State University
64, 100, 103, 104, 106, D-104
North Carolina
Wesleyan College   94, D-104
North Central
College, IL   86, 131, D-39
North Central
University, MN   96, 113, D-74
North Dakota State University
69, 105, 128, D-106
Northeastern Illinois
University   88, 112, 149, D-40
Northeastern State
University, OK 90, 108, D-113
Northeastern
University, MA   32, 33, 62
100, 103, 104, D-65
Northern Arizona
University   69, 101, 102
105, 107, 109, D-6
Northern Illinois
University   70, 101, 102, D-40
Northern Kentucky
University   70, D-54
Northern Marianas
College, MP   D-107
Northern Michigan
University   87, D-70
Northern New Mexico
College   97, 149, D-87
Northern State
University, SD   87, D-133
Northern Vermont
University, VT   81, D-146
North Florida
Community College   D-27
North Greenville
University, SC 82, 112, D-131
Northland
College, WI   95, 147, D-157
North Park
University, IL   86, 112, D-40
North Seattle College, WA   D-152

Northwestern
College, IA 95, 108, 131, D-48
Northwestern
Michigan College   D-70
Northwestern Oklahoma
State University   90, D-113
Northwestern State University
of Louisiana   84, D-56
Northwestern
University, IL   32, 62, 103
104, 146, 149, D-40
Northwest Florida
State College   D-27
Northwest Missouri
State University   87, D-78
Northwest Nazarene
University, ID   89, D-36
Northwest University, WA
89, 109, 147, D-152
Northwood University, MI   D-70
Norwich
University, VT   79, D-146
Notre Dame College
of Ohio   88, D-110
Notre Dame de Namur
University, CA   89, D-14
Notre Dame of Maryland
University   79, 111, D-59
Nova Southeastern
University, FL   68, 128, D-27
Nyack College, NY   81, D-95

O

Oakland City
University, IN   96, 113, D-45
Oakland University, MI
70, 105, 108, D-70
Oakwood
University, AL   94, 98, D-3
Oberlin College, OH   72, D-110
Occidental College, CA   72, D-14
Oglethorpe University, GA
76, 111, 129, D-33
Ohio Christian
University   88, 112, D-110
Ohio Dominican
University   87, D-110
Ohio Northern University
95, 102, 131, 147, D-110
Ohio State University–
Columbus   64, 71, 100, 101
103, 104, 106, D-110
Ohio University   67, 100, 105
107, 128, D-110
Ohio Valley
University, WV   95, D-155
Ohio Wesleyan University
74, 111, 129, D-110
Oklahoma Baptist
University   97, 147, D-113
Oklahoma Christian
University   89, 131, D-113
Oklahoma City
University   69, D-113
Oklahoma Panhandle State
University   97, 113, D-113
Oklahoma State University
68, 100, 104, 128, D-113
Oklahoma State University Institute
of Technology–Okmulgee
97, 113, 149, D-114
Oklahoma State University–
Oklahoma City 97, 149, D-114
Oklahoma Wesleyan
University   90, D-114
Old Dominion
University, VA   69, 101, 105
107, 109, D-149
Olivet College, MI 96, 113, D-71
Olivet Nazarene
University, IL   86, 147, D-40
Olympic College, WA   D-152
Oral Roberts University, OK
97, 147, D-114
Oregon Health and
Science University   108

Oregon State University 66, 100 104, 106, 109, 128, D-115
Oregon Tech 97, 102, 131, D-116
Otis College of Art and Design, CA D-14
Ottawa University, KS 96, D-51
Otterbein University, OH 86, 131, D-111
Ouachita Baptist University, AR 93, 131, 147, D-7
Our Lady of the Lake University, TX 70, 110, D-139

P

Pace University, NY 68, 101, 106, 110, 128, D-95
Pacific Lutheran University, WA 89, 147, D-152
Pacific Northwest College of Art, OR D-116
Pacific Union College, CA D-14
Pacific University, OR 68, D-116
Paine College, GA 95, 99, 148, D-33
Palm Beach Atlantic University, FL 70, D-28
Palm Beach State College, FL D-28
Park University, MO 88, D-78
Pasco-Hernando State College, FL D-28
Paul Quinn College, TX 97, D-139
Paul Smith's College, NY 92, D-95
Peirce College, PA 92, 148, D-123
Peninsula College, WA D-153
Pennsylvania Academy of the Fine Arts D-123
Pennsylvania College of Art & Design D-123
Pennsylvania College of Technology 92, D-123
Pennsylvania State University– Erie, The Behrend College 102, D-123
Pennsylvania State University–Harrisburg D-124
Pennsylvania State University– University Park 64, 71, 100, 101, 103 104, 106, 109, D-124
Pensacola State College, FL 94, 97, 107, 113, 149, D-28
Pepperdine University, CA 33, 62, 100, 146, D-14
Peru State College, NE 88, D-82
Pfeiffer University, NC 82, 112, D-104
Philander Smith College, AR 94, 99, D-7
Piedmont College, GA 82, 112, D-33
Pine Manor College, MA 77, 111, 148, D-65
Pittsburgh Technical College 92, D-124
Pittsburg State University, KS 87, D-51
Pitzer College, CA 72, 149, D-14
Plaza College, NY D-95
Plymouth State University, NH 80, D-84
Point Loma Nazarene University, CA 88, 131, D-14
Point Park University, PA 79, D-124
Point University, GA 94, 113, D-33
Polk State College, FL D-28
Pomona College, CA 72, 104, 146, 149, D-15
Pontifical Catholic University of Puerto Rico–Arecibo 84, D-127
Pontifical Catholic University of Puerto Rico–Ponce 70, 110, D-127

Portland State University, OR 33, 69, 101 105, 109, 110, D-116
Post University, CT 81, 148, D-21
Prairie View A&M University, TX 90, 98, 148, D-139
Pratt Institute, NY D-95
Presbyterian College, SC 76, 111, 129, D-132
Prescott College, AZ 90, 113, D-6
Princeton University, NJ 32, 33, 62, 103, 104 105, 146, 149, D-86
Principia College, IL 74, 129, 146, D-40
Providence Christian College, CA 77, D-15
Providence College, RI 78, 101, 129, 147, D-129
Pueblo Community College, CO D-20
Puerto Rico Conservatory of Music D-127
Purchase College–SUNY 73, 76, 111, D-95
Purdue University–Fort Wayne 87, 101, 102, 105, 109, D-45
Purdue University– Northwest, IN 88, 106, D-45
Purdue University– West Lafayette, IN 32, 64, 71 100, 103, 104, D-45

Q

Queens University of Charlotte, NC 81, 131, D-104
Quincy University, IL 96, 113, D-40
Quinnipiac University, CT 66, 101, D-22

R

Radford University, VA 82, 91, D-149
Ramapo College of New Jersey 78, 91, 129, D-86
Randolph College, VA 76, D-149
Randolph-Macon College, VA 74, 129, D-149
Ranken Technical College, MO 96, 149, D-79
Red Rocks Community College, CO D-20
Reed College, OR 74, 149, D-116
Regent University, VA 70, 107, 109, D-149
Regis University, CO 68, 110, 128, D-20
Reinhardt University, GA 84, 112, D-33
Rensselaer Polytechnic Institute, NY 64, 100, 103 104, 146, D-95
Renton Technical College, WA D-153
Rhode Island College 80, 112, D-129
Rhode Island School of Design D-129
Rhodes College, TN 74, D-136
Rice University, TX 33, 62, 103 104, 146, 149, D-140
Rider University, NJ 79, D-86
Ringling College of Art and Design, FL D-28
Rio Hondo College, CA D-15
Ripon College, WI 76, 111, D-157
Rivier University, NH 81, D-84
Roanoke College, VA 76, 129, D-149
Robert Morris University, PA 68, 108, 128, 148, D-124
Roberts Wesleyan College, NY 79, 112, 129, D-95

Rochester Institute of Technology, NY 32, 66, 100 103, 104, 111, 146, 148, D-95
Rochester University, MI 96, D-71
Rockford University, IL 88, D-40
Rockhurst University, MO 86, 131, D-79
Rocky Mountain College, MT 89, 147, D-81
Rocky Mountain College of Art and Design, CO D-20
Rogers State University, OK 97, D-114
Roger Williams University, RI 78, D-129
Rollins College, FL 81, 101, 131, 147, D-28
Roosevelt University, IL 70, 111, D-40
Rose-Hulman Institute of Technology, IN 102, 104, D-45
Rosemont College, PA 81, 111, D-124
Rowan University, NJ 68, 102, D-86
Russell Sage College, NY 68, 110, D-95
Rust College, MS 77, 99, 148, D-76
Rutgers University–Camden, NJ 66, 100, 107, 110, 128, D-86
Rutgers University–Newark, NJ 66, 100, 110, 128, D-86
Rutgers University– New Brunswick, NJ 64, 71 100, 103, 104, 110, D-86

S

Sacred Heart University, CT 68, 107, D-22
Saginaw Valley State University, MI 88, D-71
Saint Anselm College, NH 74, 129, D-84
Saint Elizabeth University, NJ 81, 111, D-86
Saint Johns River State College, FL D-28
Saint Joseph's University, PA 78, 100, 108, 129, D-124
Saint Leo University, FL 81, 107, 109, 112, 147, D-28
Saint Louis University 64, 100, 105, 128, 146, D-79
Saint Martin's University, WA 89, 147, D-153
Saint Mary-of-the-Woods College, IN 86, 112, D-45
Saint Mary's College, IN 74, 129, D-45
Saint Michael's College, VT 76, 129, D-146
Saint Peter's University, NJ 79, 111, 147, D-86
Saint Vincent College, PA 76, 111, 129, D-124
Saint Xavier University, IL 86, 112, D-40
Salem College, NC 76, 111, D-104
Salem State University, MA 80, 112, D-65
Salem University, WV 84, 149, D-155
Salisbury University, MD 79, 129, D-60
Salve Regina University, RI 78, 130, D-129
Samford University, AL 66, 128, D-3
Sam Houston State University, TX 69, 107, 109, 110, D-140
San Diego Christian College 97, 113, D-15
San Diego Mesa College D-15

San Diego State University 66, 100, 104 110, 128, 149, D-15
San Francisco Conservatory of Music D-15
San Francisco State University 89, 91, 101 102, 105, 113, D-15
San Joaquin Valley College–Visalia, CA D-15
San Jose State University, CA 89, 91, 101 102, 104, 113, D-15
Santa Ana College, CA D-15
Santa Clara University, CA 64, 100, 104, D-15
Santa Fe College, FL D-28
Santa Monica College, CA D-15
Sarah Lawrence College, NY 74, 149, D-96
Savannah College of Art and Design, GA 107, D-34
Savannah State University, GA 84, 99, D-34
Schoolcraft College, MI D-71
School of the Art Institute of Chicago D-41
School of Visual Arts, NY D-96
Schreiner University, TX 97, 147, D-140
Scripps College, CA 72, 149, D-15
Seattle Central College, WA D-153
Seattle Pacific University 68, D-153
Seattle University 33, 66, 100 102, 105, 128, D-153
Seminole State College of Florida 95, 149, D-28
Seton Hall University, NJ 66, 100, 128, D-87
Seton Hill University, PA 79, 130, D-124
Shasta College, CA D-16
Shawnee State University, OH 88, D-111
Shaw University, NC 95, 99, 148, D-104
Shenandoah University, VA 69, D-149
Shepherd University, WV 77, D-155
Shippensburg University of Pennsylvania 79, D-124
Shorter University, GA 82, 112, D-34
Siena College, NY 78, 130, 147, D-96
Siena Heights University, MI 87, 106, 109, 149, D-71
Sierra Nevada University, NV 90, 113, D-83
Silver Lake College, WI 88, 112, D-158
Simmons University, MA 66, 110, 128, 146, D-65
Simpson College, IA 76, 111, D-49
Simpson University, CA 90, D-16
Skagit Valley College, WA D-153
Skidmore College, NY 72, D-96
Skyline College, CA D-16
Slippery Rock University of Pennsylvania 79, 109, D-125
Smith College, MA 72, 102, 104, 146, D-65
Snow College, UT D-145
Soka University of America, CA 72, 111, 146, D-16
Solano Community College, CA D-16
Sonoma State University, CA 89, 91, D-16
South Carolina State University 82, 99, D-132
South Dakota School of Mines and Technology 105, D-133
South Dakota State University 69, D-133

Southeastern Baptist Theological Seminary, NC 84, D-104
Southeastern Louisiana University 84, D-56
Southeastern Oklahoma State University 90, D-114
Southeastern University, FL 84, D-28
Southeast Missouri State University 87, 108, 112, D-79
Southern Adventist University, TN 82, 112, D-136
Southern Arkansas University 84, D-7
Southern California Institute of Architecture D-16
Southern Connecticut State University 80, D-22
Southern Illinois University– Carbondale 69, 101, 105, D-41
Southern Illinois University Edwardsville 70, D-41
Southern Methodist University, TX 64, 100, 105, D-140
Southern Nazarene University, OK 89, D-114
Southern New Hampshire University 79, 112, D-84
Southern Oregon University 89, D-116
Southern University and A&M College, LA 84, 99, D-56
Southern University– New Orleans 84, 99, D-56
Southern Utah University 89, 149, D-145
Southern Virginia University 77, 111, D-150
Southern Wesleyan University, SC 82, 112, D-132
South Florida State College 94, 149, D-29
South Georgia State College D-34
South Seattle College D-153
South Texas College D-140
Southwest Baptist University, MO 87, D-79
Southwestern Adventist University, TX 97, 113, D-140
Southwestern Assemblies of God University, TX 90, D-140
Southwestern Christian College, TX D-140
Southwestern Christian University, OK 97, D-114
Southwestern College, KS 88, 108, D-51
Southwestern Oklahoma State University 90, 109, D-114
Southwestern University, TX 74, 129, D-140
Southwest Minnesota State University 87, D-74
Southwest University of Visual Arts, AZ D-6
Spalding University, KY 70, D-54
Spelman College, GA 74, 98, 111, 129, D-34
Spokane Community College, WA D-153
Spokane Falls Community College, WA D-153
Spring Arbor University, MI 86, 112, 131, D-71
Springfield College, MA 78, D-66
Spring Hill College, AL 77, D-4
St. Ambrose University, IA 86, 131, D-49
Stanford University, CA 32, 33, 62 103, 104, 105, 146, 149, D-16
State College of Florida– Manatee-Sarasota D-29
St. Augustine College, IL 96, 113, 149, D-41
St. Augustine's University, NC 94, 99, 148, D-104
St. Bonaventure University, NY 78, 147, D-96

More @ usnews.com/bestcolleges

St. Catherine
University, MN   69, 110, D-74
St. Cloud State
University, MN   87, D-74
St. Edward's
University, TX   88, 131, D-140
Stephen F. Austin State
University, TX   70, 110, D-140
Stephens
College, MO   86, 112, D-79
Sterling College, KS 96, 113, D-51
Sterling College, VT   77, D-146
Stetson University, FL
    81, 131, 147, D-29
Stevens Institute of Technology, NJ
    64, 101, 104, D-87
Stevenson
University, MD   79, 130, D-60
St. Francis College, NY
    92, 113, 147, D-96
St. Francis
University, PA 78, 130, D-125
Stillman College, AL
    77, 99, 111, 148, D-4
St. John Fisher College, NY
    67, 110, 128, 146, D-96
St. John's
College, MD   74, 146, D-60
St. John's College, NM   74, D-87
St. John's
University, MN   74, 129, D-74
St. John's University, NY
    67, 101, 110, 128, D-96
St. Joseph's College, ME 81, D-57
St. Joseph's College–Brooklyn
    79, 108, 111, D-96
St. Joseph's College–
Long Island, NY   79, D-97
St. Lawrence
University, NY   74, 129, D-97
St. Mary's College
of California   88, D-16
St. Mary's College
of Maryland 73, 74, 129, D-60
St. Mary's University
of Minnesota   86, D-74
St. Mary's University
of San Antonio
    88, 113, 147, D-141
St. Norbert
College, WI   76, 129, D-158
Stockton University, NJ
    78, 91, 130, D-87
St. Olaf
College, MN 33, 74, 146, D-74
Stonehill
College, MA   76, 129, D-66
Stony Brook University–SUNY
    64, 104, 110, D-97
St. Petersburg College, FL
    94, 107, 109, D-29
Strayer
University, DC   81, 148, D-24
St. Thomas Aquinas
College, NY   80, 112, D-97
St. Thomas
University, FL   84, D-29
Suffolk University, MA
    78, 112, 130, D-66
Sullivan University, KY   D-54
Sul Ross State
University, TX   90, D-141
SUNY Brockport   79, 111, D-97
SUNY Buffalo
State   80, 111, D-97
SUNY Cobleskill   92, 113, D-97
SUNY College–
Cortland   79, 130, D-97
SUNY College of Environmental
Science and Forestry
    66, 128, D-97
SUNY College of Technology
at Alfred   92, 147, D-98
SUNY College of Technology–
Canton   92, 108, D-98
SUNY College of Technology–
Delhi   92, 107, D-98
SUNY College–
Old Westbury   81, 111, D-98

SUNY College–Oneonta   79, D-98
SUNY College–
Potsdam   79, 112, D-98
SUNY Empire
State College   81, 112, D-98
SUNY–
Fredonia   79, 112, 130, D-98
SUNY–Geneseo 78, 91, 130, D-98
SUNY
Maritime College   79, 91, D-98
SUNY
Morrisville, NY   92, 113, D-99
SUNY–
New Paltz   79, 91, 130, D-99
SUNY–Oswego
    79, 91, 112, 130, 147, D-99
SUNY–Plattsburgh 79, 112, D-99
SUNY Polytechnic Institute–
Albany/Utica   78, 91, 109
    111, 147, D-99
Susquehanna University, PA
    76, 111, 129, D-125
Swarthmore College, PA
    72, 102, 146, D-125
Sweet Briar
College, VA   76, D-150
Syracuse University, NY   33, 64
100, 104, 108, 111, 148, D-99

T

Tabor College, KS   96, D-51
Tacoma Community
College, WA   D-153
Talladega College, AL
    77, 99, 111, 148, D-4
Tallahassee
Community College, FL   D-29
Tarleton State
University, TX   89, D-141
Taylor
University, IN   95, 131, D-45
Temple University, PA   64, 100
    101, 104, 128, D-125
Tennessee State
University 70, 99, 148, D-136
Tennessee Technological University
    69, 105, 128, D-136
Tennessee Wesleyan
University   93, D-136
Texas A&M International
University   89, 113, D-141
Texas A&M University   64, 71
100, 103, 104, 110, D-141
Texas A&M University–Commerce
    70, 107, 111, D-141
Texas A&M University–
Corpus Christi   70, D-141
Texas A&M University–
Kingsville   70, D-141
Texas A&M University–
San Antonio   D-141
Texas A&M University–
Texarkana   90, D-141
Texas Christian
University 64, 100, 102, D-142
Texas College   D-142
Texas Lutheran
University   97, 147, D-142
Texas Southern
University 70, 99, 148, D-142
Texas State University   70, D-142
Texas Tech University   68, 100
103, 104, 108, 128, D-142
Texas Wesleyan
University   70, D-142
Texas Woman's
University   70, D-142
Thiel College, PA   92, D-125
Thomas Aquinas College, CA
    72, 111, 149, D-16
Thomas
College, ME   81, 111, D-57
Thomas Jefferson
University, PA 67, 128, D-125
Thomas More College
of Liberal Arts, NH   D-84

Thomas More
University, KY   82, D-54
Thomas University, GA   84, D-34
Tiffin University, OH   88, D-111
Toccoa Falls College, GA
    93, 109, 113, D-34
Tougaloo College, MS
    77, 98, 111, 148, D-76
Touro College, NY   69, 149, D-99
Towson University, MD
    68, 105, 128, D-60
Transylvania
University, KY   74, 129, D-54
Trevecca Nazarene
University, TN   71, D-136
Trine University, IN   86, D-46
Trinity Christian
College, IL   96, D-41
Trinity College, CT   72, D-22
Trinity International
University, IL   71, 110, D-41
Trinity University, TX
    88, 101, 102, 147, D-142
Trinity Washington University, DC
    81, 112, 148, D-24
Troy University, AL
    82, 107, 109, D-4
Truett McConnell
University, GA   94, D-34
Truman State University, MO
    86, 91, 147, D-79
Tufts University, MA
    62, 103, 104, 146, D-66
Tulane University, LA
    33, 62, 100, 104, D-56
Tusculum
University, TN   82, D-136
Tuskegee University, AL
    81, 98, 112, D-4
Tyler Junior College, TX   D-143

U

Union College, KY   84, D-54
Union College, NE   96, 113, D-82
Union College, NY   72, 102, D-99
Union Institute and
University, OH 71, 109, D-111
Union
University, TN   68, 128, D-137
United States Air Force
Academy, CO
    72, 73, 100, 102, 104, D-20
United States Coast Guard
Academy, CT
    92, 97, 100, 102, D-22
United States Merchant Marine
Academy, NY
    92, 97, 102, 149, D-99
United States Military
Academy, NY
    72, 73, 102, 104, D-100
United States Naval Academy, MD
    72, 73, 102, 104, D-60
United States University, CA   D-16
Unity College, ME   92, 113, D-57
Universidad Adventista de las
Antillas, PR   95, 113, D-128
Universidad Ana G. Mendez–
Carolina Campus, PR
    84, 112, D-128
Universidad Ana G. Mendez–
Cupey Campus, PR
    84, 112, D-128
Universidad Ana G. Mendez–
Gurabo Campus, PR 71, D-128
Universidad Politecnica
de Puerto Rico   D-128
University at Albany–SUNY
    66, 100, 104, 110, 128, D-100
University at Buffalo–SUNY
    64, 100, 104, 106
    110, 128, D-100
University of
Akron, OH   69, 105, D-111
University of
Alabama   66, 100, 104, D-4

University of Alabama–
Birmingham   66, 100, 104
    106, 109, 128, D-4
University of Alabama–Huntsville
    69, 101, 105, D-4
University of Alaska–
Anchorage   89, D-5
University of Alaska–
Fairbanks   71, 105, 107, D-5
University of Alaska–
Southeast   90, 113, D-5
University of
Antelope Valley, CA   D-16
University of Arizona 64, 100, 101
103, 104, 106, 109, 110, D-6
University of Arkansas   66, 100
    105, 106, 109, 128, D-7
University of Arkansas at
Little Rock 71, 101, 105, D-8
University of Arkansas–
Fort Smith   94, D-8
University of Arkansas–
Monticello   84, 149, D-8
University of Arkansas–
Pine Bluff   94, 99, D-8
University of Baltimore   80, D-60
University of
Bridgeport, CT   71, D-22
University of California–
Berkeley   62, 71, 100, 101
103, 104, 105, 110, 149, D-16
University of California–
Davis   62, 71, 103
    104, 110, 149, D-16
University of California–
Irvine   62, 71, 100
    103, 104, 110, D-17
University of California–
Los Angeles   62, 71, 103
    104, 110, 149, D-17
University of California–
Merced   64, 110, D-17
University of California–Riverside
    64, 100, 104, 110, D-17
University of California–
San Diego   62, 71, 100, 103
    104, 105, 110, D-17
University of California–
Santa Barbara 62, 71, 103, 104
    110, 149, D-17
University of California–
Santa Cruz 64, 104, 110, D-17
University of
Central Arkansas   71, D-8
University of Central Florida
    67, 100, 104, 106
    109, 110, 128, D-29
University of
Central Missouri   87, D-79
University of
Central Oklahoma   89, D-114
University of
Charleston, WV   71, D-155
University of
Chicago   62, 104, 146, D-41
University of Cincinnati   32, 66
    100, 105, 107, 128, D-111
University of Cincinnati–
UC Blue Ash College   D-111
University of Colorado Boulder
    64, 100, 103, 104, D-20
University of Colorado–
Colorado Springs   71, 101
    105, 109, D-20
University of Colorado Denver
    68, 100, 105, 111, D-20
University of Connecticut
    64, 71, 100, 104, D-22
University of
Dallas   88, 101, 147, D-143
University of Dayton, OH
    66, 101, 105, 128, 146, D-111
University of Delaware
    64, 100, 103, 104, D-23
University of Denver
    64, 100, 105, 107, D-20
University of Detroit Mercy
    68, 128, 146, D-71
University of Dubuque, IA 87, D-49

University of Evansville, IN
    33, 84, 131, 147, D-46
University of Findlay, OH
    69, 110, 128, D-111
University of Florida 62, 71, 100
103, 104, 106, 109, 110, D-29
University of Georgia 62, 71, 100
    101, 104, 106, D-34
University of Guam   90, D-35
University of Hartford, CT
    68, 101, 148, D-22
University of Hawaii–
Hilo   71, 110, D-35
University of Hawaii–Manoa
    67, 100, 105, 128, D-35
University of Hawaii–
Maui College   D-36
University of Hawaii–
West Oahu   97, D-36
University of
Holy Cross, LA   84, D-56
University of Houston
67, 100, 104, 110, 128, D-143
University of Houston–
Clear Lake   D-143
University of Houston–Downtown
    90, 107, D-143
University of Houston–Victoria
    90, D-143
University of Idaho 67, 101, 105
    111, 128, 146, D-36
University of Illinois–
Chicago   66, 100, 104
    106, 110, 128, D-41
University of Illinois–
Springfield   86, 91, 106, 109
    112, 131, 149, D-41
University of Illinois–
Urbana-Champaign 62, 71, 100
    101, 103, 104, 105, D-42
University of Indianapolis 68, D-46
University of Iowa
    33, 64, 100, 104, 128, D-49
University of
Jamestown, ND   96, D-106
University of Kansas
    66, 100, 104, 128, D-51
University of Kentucky
    66, 100, 104, 128, D-54
University of La Verne, CA
    66, 108, 110, 128, D-17
University of Louisiana at
Lafayette 71, 105, 108, D-56
University of Louisiana–
Monroe   71, D-56
University of Louisville, KY
    67, 100, 107, 109, 128, D-54
University of
Lynchburg, VA   81, D-150
University of Maine
    68, 101, 105, 128, D-57
University of Maine–
Augusta   93, 107, D-58
University of Maine–Farmington
    92, 97, 113, 147, D-58
University of Maine–
Fort Kent   92, D-58
University of Maine–
Machias   77, 111, D-58
University of Maine–
Presque Isle   92, D-58
University of
Mary, ND   71, D-106
University of
Mary Hardin-Baylor, TX
    89, 113, D-143
University of Maryland–
Baltimore County 67, 104, D-60
University of Maryland–
College Park   33, 64, 71, 100
    103, 104, D-60
University of Maryland
Eastern Shore
    71, 98, 110, 148, D-61
University of Maryland
Global Campus   81, D-61
University of
Mary Washington, VA
    81, 91, 131, D-150

University of Massachusetts–
Amherst   64, 71, 100
104, 106, 109, D-66
University of Massachusetts–
Boston   68, 101, 102
105, 107, 110, 128, D-66
University of Massachusetts–
Dartmouth   68, 101, 105
108, 110, D-66
University of Massachusetts–
Lowell   67, 101, 105
106, 109, 128, D-66
University of Memphis   69, 100
105, 107, 109, 111, D-137
University of Miami, FL
62, 100, 105, D-29
University of Michigan–
Ann Arbor   32, 33, 62, 71, 100
101, 103, 104, 105, 146, D-71
University of Michigan–Dearborn
86, 91, 101, 105, 112, D-71
University of Michigan–
Flint   71, 148, D-71
University of Minnesota–
Crookston   96, 97, 113, D-74
University of Minnesota–
Duluth   86, 91, 101, 102
105, 112, 131, D-74
University of Minnesota Morris
73, 76, 129, D-74
University of Minnesota–Twin Cities
64, 71, 100, 103, 104, D-75
University of Mississippi
67, 100, 105, 128, D-76
University of Missouri
66, 100, 104, 107, 128, D-79
University of Missouri–
Kansas City 69, 101, 105, D-79
University of Missouri–
St. Louis   69, 101, 105
107, 111, 128, D-80
University of
Mobile, AL   93, D-4
University of
Montana   69, 101, D-81
University of
Montana Western   D-81
University of
Montevallo, AL   81, 91, D-5
University of Mount Olive, NC
82, 112, D-104
University of Mount Union, OH
95, 131, D-111
University of Nebraska–Kearney
86, 91, 112, 131, 147, D-82
University of Nebraska–Lincoln
66, 100, 104, 128, D-82
University of Nebraska–Omaha
69, 101, 105, 107, 109, D-82
University of Nevada–Las Vegas
69, 100, 105, D-83
University of Nevada–Reno
68, 101, 105, 128, D-83
University of
New England, ME   69, D-58
University of New Hampshire
66, 101, 105, 128, 148, D-84
University of New Haven, CT
79, 105, 130, D-22
University of New Mexico
68, 100, 104, 110, D-88
University of New Orleans
71, 105, 110, D-56
University of
North Alabama   82, 131, D-5
University of North Carolina–
Asheville   73, 76, 111, D-104
University of North Carolina–
Chapel Hill   62, 71, 100
103, 104, 146, D-105
University of North Carolina–
Charlotte   68, 100, 104
106, 110, 129, D-105
University of North Carolina–
Greensboro
69, 100, 105, 109, 110, D-105
University of North Carolina–
Pembroke
82, 107, 109, 112, D-105

University of North Carolina
School of the Arts   D-105
University of North Carolina–
Wilmington
68, 106, 109, 129, D-105
University of
North Dakota   69, 101, 105
107, 109, 129, D-106
University of Northern
Colorado   71, 107, 109, D-21
University of Northern
Iowa   86, 91, 131, D-49
University of North Florida
69, 107, 129, D-29
University of North Georgia
82, 91, 131, 149, D-34
University of North Texas 69, 101
105, 107, 110, 129, D-143
University of North Texas–
Dallas   89, 149, D-143
University of Northwestern
Ohio   96, D-112
University of Northwestern–
St. Paul, MN
87, 112, 131, D-75
University of
Notre Dame, IN   33, 62, 100
103, 104, 146, D-46
University of Oklahoma   66, 100
104, 106, 109, 129, D-115
University of Oregon
66, 100, 104, 129, D-116
University of Pennsylvania 62, 100
101, 103, 104, 146, D-125
University of Phoenix, AZ   71, D-6
University of Pikeville, KY 77, D-54
University of Pittsburgh
at Bradford   92, 113, D-125
University of Pittsburgh–
Johnstown   92, D-126
University of Pittsburgh–
Pittsburgh Campus
64, 71, 100, 103, 104, D-126
University of Portland, OR
88, 101, 102, D-116
University of
Providence, MT   D-81
University of Puerto Rico–
Aguadilla   94, 97, 113, D-128
University of Puerto Rico–
Arecibo   94, 113, D-128
University of Puerto Rico–
Bayamon   94, D-128
University of Puerto Rico–
Cayey   76, 111, D-128
University of Puerto Rico–
Humacao   93, 97, 113, D-128
University of Puerto Rico–
Mayaguez 82, 105, 112, D-128
University of Puerto Rico–
Ponce   77, 111, D-128
University of Puerto Rico–
Rio Piedras   68, 110, D-128
University of Puerto Rico–
Utuado   95, D-128
University of
Puget Sound, WA   74, D-153
University of
Redlands, CA   88, 131, D-17
University of Rhode Island
67, 101, 105, 129, D-129
University of Richmond, VA
72, 100, 146, D-150
University of
Rio Grande, OH   96, D-112
University of Rochester, NY
62, 104, 146, D-100
University of
Saint Francis, IN 87, 112, D-46
University of
Saint Mary, KS   87, D-52
University of San Diego
64, 100, 102, 104, D-18
University of San Francisco
66, 100, 105, 110, 129, D-18
University of Science and
Arts of Oklahoma   77, D-115
University of Scranton, PA
78, 101, 130, D-126

University of
Sioux Falls, SD   87, D-133
University of
South Alabama   71, 107, D-5
University of South Carolina
32, 66, 100, 101, 104, D-132
University of South Carolina–
Aiken   93, 97, 107, D-132
University of South Carolina–
Beaufort   77, D-132
University of South Carolina–
Upstate   93, 97, 113, D-132
University of South Dakota
69, 101, 105, D-134
University of Southern California
62, 100, 101, 103, 104, D-18
University of
Southern Indiana   87, D-46
University of
Southern Maine   81, D-58
University of Southern
Mississippi   71, 107, D-76
University of South Florida
66, 100, 104, 110, 129, D-29
University of St. Francis, IL
68, 107, 111, D-42
University of St. Joseph, CT
67, 129, 146, 148, D-22
University of St. Thomas, MN
66, 101, 102, 129, D-75
University of St. Thomas, TX
89, 113, 131, 147, D-143
University of Tampa, FL
81, 101, 131, D-30
University of Tennessee
66, 100, 101, 104, 129, D-137
University of Tennessee–
Chattanooga   71, 101, D-137
University of Tennessee–
Martin   81, 91, 109, D-137
University of Texas at Arlington
71, 100, 104, 110, D-143
University of Texas
at Austin   32, 33, 62, 71, 100
101, 103, 104, 105, D-144
University of Texas at Dallas
66, 100, 104, 110, D-144
University of Texas at San Antonio
71, 101, 104, 110, D-144
University of Texas
at Tyler   71, D-144
University of Texas–El Paso
71, 105, 111, D-144
University of Texas of the
Permian Basin   89, D-144
University of Texas–
Rio Grande Valley
69, 110, 149, D-144
University of
the Arts, PA   D-126
University of the
Cumberlands, KY   71, D-54
University of the District
of Columbia   81, 98, D-24
University of the
Incarnate Word, TX
69, 107, 109, 110, 148, D-144
University of the
Ozarks, AR   93, 147, D-8
University of the
Pacific, CA   66, 110, D-18
University of the
Potomac, DC   D-24
University of the Sacred Heart, PR
84, 112, D-128
The University of
the South, TN   72, 129, D-137
University of
the Southwest, NM   90, D-88
University of
the Virgin Islands   94, D-147
University of
the West, CA   77, 111, D-18
University of
Toledo, OH   71, 109, D-112
University of
Tulsa, OK   66, 105, D-115
University
of Utah   64, 100, 104, D-145

University of
Valley Forge, PA   92, D-126
University of
Vermont   66, 100, 105, D-147
University of Virginia   62, 71, 100
101, 103, 104, 146, D-150
University of Virginia–
Wise   76, 111, D-150
University of
Washington   64, 71, 100, 103
104, 105, 149, D-153
University of Washington–
Bothell   89, 91, 113, D-153
University of Washington–Tacoma
89, 91, 101, 113, D-153
University of
West Alabama   84, D-5
University of West Florida   82, 91
107, 109, 112, 131, D-30
University of
West Georgia   71, 110, D-35
University of Wisconsin–Eau Claire
86, 91, 112, 131, D-158
University of Wisconsin–
Green Bay   87, D-158
University of Wisconsin–
La Crosse   86, 91, 131, D-158
University of Wisconsin–
Madison   62, 71, 100
101, 103, 104, D-158
University of Wisconsin–Milwaukee
71, 100, 105, 107, 109, D-158
University of Wisconsin–
Oshkosh   87, D-158
University of Wisconsin–
Parkside   77, D-158
University of Wisconsin–
Platteville   87, 102, D-158
University of Wisconsin–
River Falls   87, D-158
University of Wisconsin–
Stevens Point
87, 91, 112, D-159
University of Wisconsin–
Stout   87, 91, D-159
University of Wisconsin–
Superior   77, D-159
University of Wisconsin–Whitewater
86, 91, 107, 109, D-159
University of Wyoming
68, 101, 105, 129, D-159
Upper Iowa
University   88, 109, D-49
Ursinus
College, PA   74, 129, D-126
Ursuline
College, OH   86, 112, D-112
Utah State University   69, 101
105, 106, 109, 149, D-145
Utah Valley University   90, D-145
Utica College, NY
80, 107, 109, 112, D-100

V

Valdosta State
University, GA   71, 109, D-35
Valencia College, FL   D-30
Valley City State
University, ND   96, 97, D-107
Valparaiso University, IN   67, 101
102, 129, 146, 148, D-46
Vanderbilt University, TN   33, 62
103, 104, 146, 149, D-137
Vanguard University of Southern
California   89, 113, D-18
Vassar College, NY
72, 111, 146, 149, D-100
Vaughn College of Aeronautics and
Technology, NY   92, D-100
Vermont Technical
College   92, D-147
Villa Maria College, NY 93, D-100
Villanova University, PA
64, 100, 105, D-126
Vincennes
University, IN   97, 149, D-46

Virginia Commonwealth University
67, 100, 105, 110, 129, D-150
Virginia Military Institute
73, 74, 102, 105, D-150
Virginia State University
82, 98, D-150
Virginia Tech
64, 71, 100, 103, 104, D-150
Virginia Union University
77, 99, 111, 148, D-151
Virginia Wesleyan
University   77, 111, D-151
Viterbo
University, WI   87, 131, D-159
Voorhees
College, SC   94, 99, 113, D-132

W

Wabash College, IN
74, 111, 129, 146, D-46
Wade College, TX   D-145
Wagner
College, NY   78, 130, D-100
Wake Forest University, NC
62, 100, 104, 146, D-105
Waldorf
University, IA   88, 149, D-49
Walla Walla
University, WA   90, D-154
Walsh University, OH   86, D-112
Warner Pacific University, OR
97, 113, 147, 148, D-116
Warner University, FL   94, D-30
Warren Wilson
College, NC 33, 76, 111, D-105
Wartburg College, IA 76, 129, D-49
Washburn University, KS   71, D-52
Washington Adventist
University, MD   81, 111, D-61
Washington and Jefferson
College, PA   74, 129, D-126
Washington and Lee University, VA
72, 100, 146, D-151
Washington
College, MD   74, 129, D-61
Washington State University
67, 100, 104, 106, 109, D-154
Washington State
University–Vancouver   D-154
Washington University in St. Louis
62, 100, 103, 104, 146, D-80
Watkins College of Art,
Design & Film, TN   D-137
Wayland Baptist
University, TX   90, D-145
Waynesburg
University, PA   79, 147, D-126
Wayne State
College, NE   87, D-82
Wayne State University, MI
69, 101, 105, 111, D-71
Webber International
University, FL   95, D-30
Webb Institute, NY   D-100
Weber State
University, UT   90, D-145
Webster University, MO   86, D-80
Welch College, TN
93, 113, 131, D-137
Wellesley College, MA
72, 111, 146, 149, D-67
Wells College, NY   76, 111, D-101
Wenatchee Valley
College, WA   D-154
Wentworth Institute of
Technology, MA
79, 102, 130, D-67
Wesleyan College, GA   76, D-35
Wesleyan University, CT
72, 105, 146, 149, D-22
Wesley College, DE   93, 148, D-23
West Chester University
of Pennsylvania   79, 91, D-126
Westcliff University, CA   D-18
Western Carolina University, NC
81, 91, 108, 112, 147, D-105

Western Colorado
University 90, D-21
Western Connecticut State
University 80, D-23
Western Illinois
University 86, 91, 108, D-42
Western Kentucky
University 71, 106, 109, D-54
Western Michigan University
69, 101, 105, 111, D-72
Western Nevada College D-83
Western New England
University, MA 68, 129, D-67
Western New Mexico
University 90, D-88
Western Oregon
University 89, D-116
Western Washington University
89, 91, 131, D-154
Westfield State University, MA
79, 107, 109, D-67
West Liberty
University, WV 82, 112, D-155
West Los Angeles College D-18
Westminster
College, MO 76, D-80
Westminster
College, PA 76, 111, D-127

Westminster
College, UT 89, 147, D-146
Westmont
College, CA 76, 129, D-18
West Texas A&M University
90, 106, 109, D-145
West Virginia State
University 94, 99, D-155
West Virginia
University 69, 101, 105, D-155
West Virginia University
Institute of Technology D-156
West Virginia University–
Parkersburg 95, 149, D-156
West Virginia
Wesleyan College 82, D-156
Whatcom
Community College, WA D-154
Wheaton College, IL 74, D-42
Wheaton
College, MA 74, 129, D-67
Wheeling
University, WV 82, D-156
Whitman
College, WA 72, 149, D-154
Whittier College, CA 76, 111, D-18
Whitworth University, WA
88, 131, 147, D-154

Wichita State University, KS
71, 101, 105, D-52
Widener
University, PA 68, 148, D-127
Wilberforce
University, OH 97, 99, D-112
Wiley
College, TX 97, 99, 148, D-145
Wilkes
University, PA 68, 129, D-127
Willamette
University, OR 74, 129, D-116
William Carey University, MS
69, 110, 129, D-76
William Jessup University, CA
97, 113, 147, D-18
William Jewell College, MO
95, 131, 147, D-80
William & Mary, VA 32, 33, 62
71, 100, 104, D-151
William Paterson University
of New Jersey 79, 112, D-87
William Peace
University, NC 93, 113, D-105
William Penn
University, IA 97, D-49
Williams Baptist
University, AR 77, D-8

Williams College, MA
33, 72, 104, 146, 149, D-67
William Woods
University, MO 71, 110, D-80
Wilmington
College, OH 96, 113, D-112
Wilmington
University, DE 71, D-23
Wilson College, PA 80, D-127
Wingate University, NC 71, D-106
Winona State University, MN
86, 91, 112, D-75
Winston-Salem State
University, NC
82, 98, 112, D-106
Winthrop University, SC
81, 91, 112, D-132
Wisconsin Lutheran
College 96, 131, D-159
Wittenberg
University, OH 76, D-112
Wofford
College, SC 74, 129, D-132
Woodbury University, CA
89, 113, 148, D-19
Worcester Polytechnic
Institute, MA 32, 64, 101
104, 148, D-67

Worcester State
University, MA 80, D-67
Wright State
University, OH 71, 105, D-112

X, Y

Xavier University, OH
84, 101, 131, D-112
Xavier University
of Louisiana 81, 98, D-57
Yakima Valley College, WA D-154
Yale University, CT 32, 33, 62
103, 104, 146, 149, D-23
Yeshiva University, NY 64, D-101
York College, NE 96, 113, D-82
York College of
Pennsylvania 79, D-127
Young Harris College, GA 77, D-35
Youngstown State
University, OH 87, D-112